השמים לטוהר

ספר הזוהר

על התורה מאיש אלהים קדוש הוא נורא מאד התנא ר׳ שמעון בן יוחאי ז״ל עם חדושים רבים· והמה· סתרי תורה· ומדרש הנעלם· ותוספתא על קצת פרשיות· והוספנו חדושים על זולתינו גם על ספר בראשית כל חבור הרעיא מהימנא· וחדושי הבהיר· ומדרש רות מדרש חזית· ומאמר תא חזי· והיכלו׳ ומורה מקום מהפסוקי׳· ובסוף הספר תמצא לוח מפסוקי הפתיחות· ושאר כל הפסוקים הנדרשים והנכפלים בהזוהר· נדפס עם רב העיון·

בקרימונה

קרית מלך רב· אדוננו המלך פיליפו יר״ה אמן· שנת כי לא יט״ש
י״י את עמו· ונסתיים
שנת הש״ך·

ברשיון סוויקא״ריאו ואינקוויזי״טור
ייכראלו כנראה בסוף הספר

ספר הזהר

The ספר הזהר

ZOHAR

Pritzker Edition

VOLUME THREE

Translation and Commentary by

Daniel C. Matt

STANFORD UNIVERSITY PRESS
STANFORD, CALIFORNIA
2006

The translation and publication of the Zohar *is made possible through the thoughtful and generous support of the Pritzker Family Philanthropic Fund.*

Stanford University Press
Stanford, California

For further information, including the Aramaic text of the *Zohar*, please visit www.sup.org/zohar

Library of Congress Cataloging-in-Publication Data

Zohar. English.
The Zohar/translation and commentary by Daniel C. Matt.–
Pritzker ed.
v. cm.
Text includes some words in Hebrew and Aramaic.
Includes bibliographical references.
ISBN 0-8047-4747-4 (vol. 1)
ISBN 0-8047-4868-3 (vol. 2)
ISBN 0-8047-5210-9 (vol. 3)
1. Bible. O.T. Pentateuch–Commentaries–Early works to 1800.
2. Cabala–Early works to 1800. 3. Zohar. I. Matt, Daniel Chanan.
II. Title.
BM525.A52 M37 2003
296.1′62–dc22 2003014884

Original Printing 2006

Last figure below indicates year of this printing:
15 14 13 12 11 10 09 08 07 06

Printed in the United States of America
on acid-free, archival-quality paper.

Designed by Rob Ehle
Typeset by El Ot Pre Press & Computing Ltd., Tel Aviv,
in 10.5/14 Minion.

Academic Committee for the Translation of the Zohar

Contents

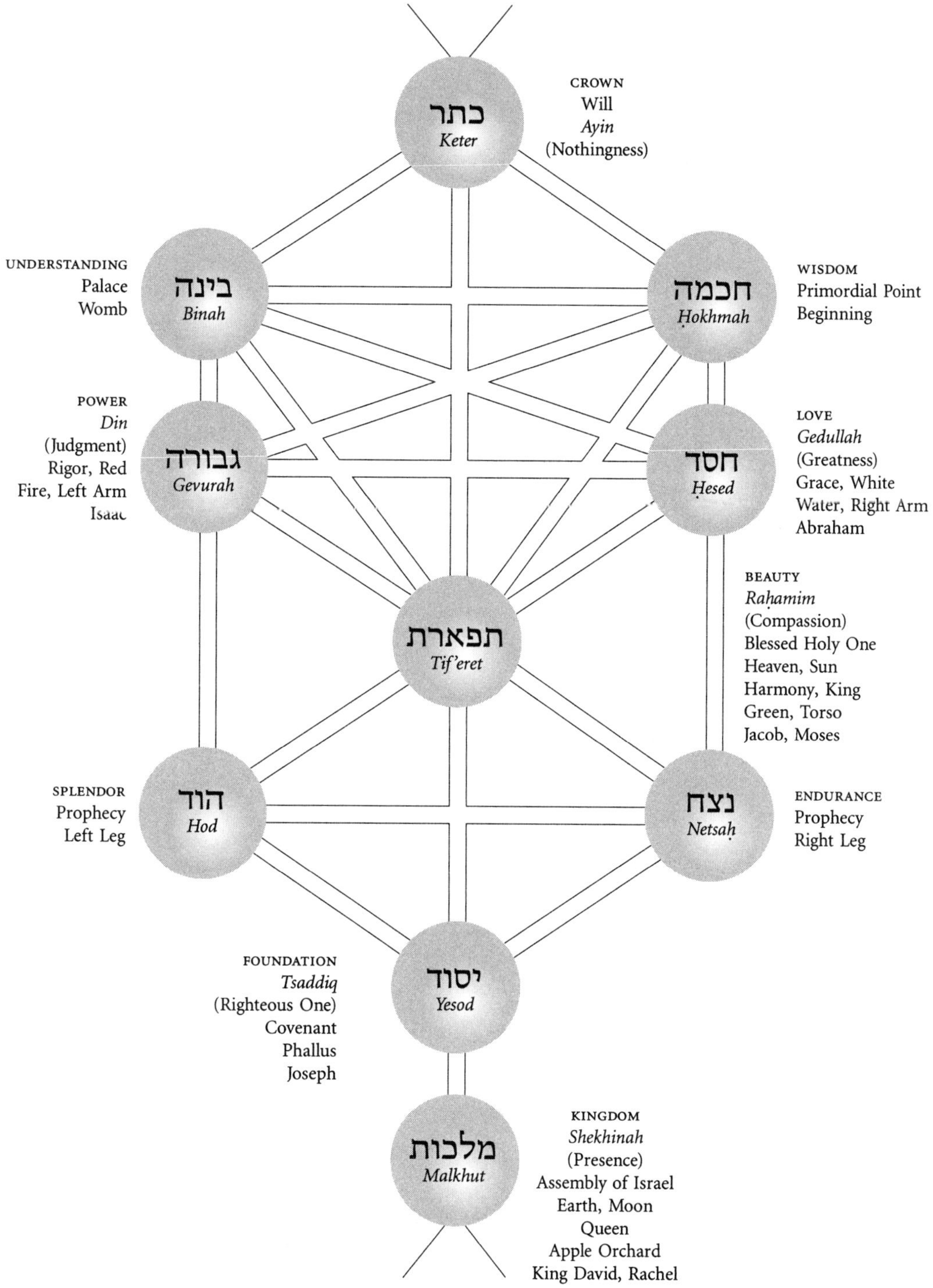

The Ten Sefirot

Preface

With joy and gratitude, I celebrate the completion of the translation of the *Zohar* on the book of Genesis. I feel blessed to have come this far; at the same time, I am anticipating farther reaches of the *Zohar*'s terrain. In the words traditionally recited at the public conclusion of each of the Five Books of Moses: חזק חזק ונתחזק (*Ḥazaq ḥazaq ve-nitḥazzeq*), "Be strong, be strong, and let us be strengthened!"

I remain deeply grateful to the people I thanked initially in the Acknowledgments of the first volume. Here, I wish to express my appreciation to several individuals for their ongoing support.

Margot Pritzker has generously sustained my work throughout this adventure, and she continues to inspire me by her passionate devotion to learning and spreading the Torah of the *Zohar*. Thank you, Margot, for providing me with the unique opportunity to delve into one of the most amazing books ever written and to convey its radiant wisdom.

I am grateful to Rabbi Yehiel Poupko for treasuring the sacred nature of this bold project and for stimulating me to complete it 'speedily in our days.'

Merav Carmeli has combed meticulously through numerous Aramaic manuscripts of the *Zohar*, preparing lists of variant readings. Without her mining this precious raw material, I could not fashion a critical Aramaic text of the *Zohar*, upon which I have based this translation.

The critical Aramaic text corresponding to the first three volumes of *The Zohar: Pritzker Edition* is available at the website of Stanford University Press: www.sup.org/zohar. I want to thank my brother, Rabbi Jonathan Matt, for editing a user-friendly version of this text.[1]

Professor Ronit Meroz, of Tel Aviv University, has generously shared with me the data that she has collected relating to hundreds of manuscripts of the

1. For a description of the various online versions of the critical text, see the website. For my methodology in constructing this text, see the website and Volume 1, Translator's Introduction, xv–xviii.

Zohar, along with her analysis of this data. Her research, funded by the Israel Science Foundation, has provided me with a panoramic picture of the manuscripts, helping me to determine which ones seem most promising. This has benefited all three volumes of the current translation.

My wife, Ḥana, continues to nourish my being and to reveal depths of meaning in the *Zohar*. Thank you for your joy and wisdom.

Finally, to the One beyond all names: Blessed are You for enlivening and sustaining us, and for bringing us to this moment.

D.C.M.

THE ZOHAR

פרשת וישלח

Parashat Va-Yishlaḥ

"HE SENT" (GENESIS 32:4–36:43)

Jacob sent מלאכים (*mal'akhim*), *messengers, ahead of him*... (Genesis 32:4).

Rabbi Yehudah opened, "*For He will command* מלאכיו (*mal'akhav*), *His angels, to guard you in all your ways* (Psalms 91:11).[1] This verse has been established: The moment a human being comes into the world, the evil impulse appears along with him, inciting him constantly, as is said: *At the opening sin crouches* (Genesis 4:7)—evil impulse.[2] David too called it 'sin,' since it causes one to sin in the presence of his Lord, as is written: *My sin confronts me constantly* (Psalms 51:5). This never leaves a person from the day he is born, forever, whereas the good impulse accompanies a person from the day he begins to purify himself. When is that? When he becomes thirteen years old.[3] Then he joins with both of them, one on the right and one on the left: good impulse on the right, evil impulse on the left. These are two real angels, empowered, accompanying a person constantly.[4]

"If one comes to purify himself, that evil impulse is overturned, and right prevails over left—both joining to guard him in all the paths he takes, as is said: *For He will command His angels to guard you in all your ways*."[5]

1. **מלאכיו (*mal'akhav*), *His angels*...** The word מלאך (*mal'akh*) means both "messenger" and "divine messenger, angel," an ambiguity exploited by both the Midrash and the *Zohar* in interpreting the verse: *Jacob sent* מלאכים (*mal'akhim*).

2. ***At the opening*...** Of the womb. The evil impulse appears from the moment of birth.

See BT *Sanhedrin* 91b; *Berakhot* 61a; *Avot de-Rabbi Natan* A, 16; B, 16, 30; *Qohelet Rabbah* on 4:13; *Midrash Tehillim* 9:5; *Zohar* 1:78b (*ST*), 179a.

3. **When he becomes thirteen years old** Mature enough to make moral decisions and legally *bar mitsvah*, obligated to fulfill the commandments of Torah.

See *Avot de-Rabbi Natan* A, 16; *Qohelet Rabbah* on 4:13; *Midrash Tehillim* 9:5; *Zohar* 1:78b (*ST*), 179a; 2:97b–98a, 101a.

4. **good impulse on the right, evil impulse on the left... two real angels...** On the two accompanying angels, see BT *Shabbat* 119b; *Ta'anit* 11a; *Zohar* 1:12b; 2:106b, 239a; ZḤ 47a; ZḤ 84d (*MhN, Rut*).

Here the angelic pair is identified with the good and evil impulses. See *Zohar* 1:49b, 144b, 155b, 174b; 3:263b; cf. BT *Berakhot* 61a.

5. **evil impulse is overturned... both joining to guard him...** On the transfor-

Rabbi El'azar applies this verse to Jacob, for the blessed Holy One designated camps of angels for him because he came completed by supernal tribes, all fittingly complete,[6] as is said: *Jacob went on his way, and angels of God encountered him* (Genesis 32:2), as has been explained. Here, since he was saved from Laban and separated from him, *Shekhinah* coupled with him and sacred camps came to encircle him;[7] so [166a] *when he saw them, Jacob said,* [*"This is the camp of* אלהים (*Elohim*), *God!"*] (ibid., 3).[8] Some of those angels he sent to Esau, as is written: *Jacob sent* מלאכים (*mal'akhim*)—*angels*, literally![9]

Rabbi Yitsḥak said, "*The angel of YHVH encamps around those in awe of Him and delivers them* (Psalms 34:8). This has been established,[10] but in one place is written *For He will command His angels*—many angels—whereas here one: *the angel of YHVH.* Because *His angels* are the other angels, whereas *angel of YHVH* is *Shekhinah*, as is said: *The angel of YHVH appeared to him in a flame of fire...* (Exodus 3:2).[11] So *the angel of YHVH encamps around those in awe of Him*, completely encompassing him to save him.[12] And when *Shekhinah* abides within
2 a person, countless holy camps manifest there.

"Come and see: King David proclaimed this[13] when he was saved from Achish king of Gath, because *Shekhinah* encircled him, delivering him from Achish and his people, all those attacking him. What is written? ויתהולל (*Va-yitholel*), *He played the lunatic, while in their hands* (1 Samuel 21:14). Why *va-yitholel*? The verse should read: וישתגע (*va-yishtagge'a*), *He played the madman*, as is said: *that you should bring this one* להשתגע (*le-hishtagge'a*), *to*

mation of evil, see BT *Shabbat* 119b, where the evil angel, against his will, joins in blessing a righteous person.

6. **he came completed by supernal tribes...** Jacob was now accompanied by eleven sons, with soon-to-be-born Benjamin gestating in Rachel's womb. See *Zohar* 1:158a–b.

7. **since he was saved from Laban and separated from him...** *Shekhinah*, along with Her angels, manifested only after Jacob separated from the wicked Laban.

See *Tanḥuma, Vayetse* 10; *Zohar* 1:85a.

8. ***This is the camp of* אלהים (*Elohim*), *God*** Referring to *Shekhinah*, known by this divine name.

9. **מלאכים (*mal'akhim*)—*angels*, literally!** Playing on the double meaning of מלאך (*mal'akh*): "messenger" and "divine messenger, angel." See above, note 1.

See *Bereshit Rabbah* 74:17; 75:4; *Tanḥuma* (Buber), *Vayishlaḥ* 3.

10. **This has been established** See *Shemot Rabbah* 32:6.

11. ***angel of YHVH* is *Shekhinah*... *in a flame of fire...*** The verse continues: *from within a bush.* At the Burning Bush, *Shekhinah*—identified as *the angel of YHVH*—manifested to Moses.

On *the angel of YHVH* as a name of *Shekhinah*, see *Zohar* 1:61a, 113a, 120b, 159b, 230a; 3:187a. Cf. *Mekhilta, Shirta* 3; *Pirqei de-Rabbi Eli'ezer* 40; *Shemot Rabbah* 2:5; Naḥmanides on Exodus 3:2.

12. **encompassing him...** Encompassing one of *those in awe of Him.*

13. **proclaimed this** The verse under discussion (Psalms 34:8): *The angel of YHVH encamps around those in awe of Him and delivers them.*

play the madman, in my presence? (ibid., 16).[14] However, it reverts to the word David uttered previously: *For I envied* הוללים (*holelim*), *lunatics* (Psalms 73:3).

"The blessed Holy One said to him, 'By your life! You will yet need this.'[15]

"When he entered the abode of Achish and was attacked, what is written? *Va-yitholel, He played the lunatic,* like those *holelim, lunatics,* he had previously envied. Then *Shekhinah* came and encircled David.

"Now, you might say '*Shekhinah* abides only in Her heritage: the Holy Land.'[16] Well, certainly She does not abide so as to be imbibed, but to protect—that is different![17] So here, when Jacob came from Laban's abode,[18] all those holy camps accompanied him."

Rabbi Ḥizkiyah said, "If all those holy camps accompanied him, why is it written *Jacob was left alone* (Genesis 32:25)?[19] For if *Shekhinah* or those holy camps were with him, he was not left alone! So why *Jacob was left alone*?"

Rabbi Yehudah replied, "Because he exposed himself to danger—after seeing
the danger with his own eyes[20]—they separated from him. Then he said, *I am*
shorn of all the kindness and faithfulness (ibid., 11)—those holy camps separating 3
from him."[21]

14. **The verse should read:** וישתגע **(*va-yishtagge'a*), *He played the madman...*** The normal term, employed by King Achish: *Do I lack madmen that you should bring this one to play the madman in my presence?*

15. **By your life! You will yet need this** You will need lunacy. See *Midrash Tehillim* 34:1.

16. ***Shekhinah* abides only in Her heritage: the Holy Land** See *Mekhilta, Pisḥa* 1: "Rabbi El'azar son of Tsadok said, '... *Shekhinah* is not revealed outside the land [of Israel].'"

See *Zohar* 1:85a, 121a, 141a; 2:5a (*MhN*), 170b. Technically, Gath and the surrounding land of the Philistines is included in the borders of Israel (see Genesis 15:18), but since this land was not conclusively conquered until the reign of King David, its status is somewhat lower. See Rashi on Genesis 26:12; *Zohar* 1:141a.

17. **certainly She does not abide to be imbibed, but to protect...** Outside Her domain, the land of Israel, *Shekhinah* does not provide the nourishing flow of emanation, but She still can protect those who are worthy.

18. **when Jacob came from Laban's abode** Although he had not yet reentered the land of Israel.

19. ***Jacob was left alone*** The verse continues: *and a man wrestled with him until the rising of dawn.*

20. **he exposed himself to danger...** Having transferred his entire camp across the Jabbok River (Genesis 32:23–24), Jacob left himself entirely alone and vulnerable in the middle of the night. See below; and on seeing the danger, *Zohar* 3:45a.

21. ***I am shorn of all the kindness and faithfulness...*** The verse continues: *that You have shown Your servant.* The first verb, קטנתי (*qatonti*), is usually rendered *I am unworthy*, but Rabbi Yehudah understands it hyperliterally: *I am shorn.*

See another hyperliteral reading in BT *Shabbat* 32a: "Rabbi Yannai ... said, 'A person should never stand in a place of danger, saying that a miracle will be performed for him; perhaps it will not. And if a miracle

Rabbi Yitsḥak said, "In order to leave him with the Prince of Esau, who arrived with permission;[22] meanwhile they went off to utter song, since at that moment the time had come for them to praise the blessed Holy One.[23] Later they returned, as is written: *I am shorn of all the kindness and faithfulness*... and now I have become two camps (ibid.)—camp of *Shekhinah* and his entire household.[24]

"*Two camps,* for he was complete on all sides, with two shares: white and red."[25]

Rabbi El'azar said, "As has been said, that night, that hour, the dominion of the side of Esau prevailed,[26] for look at what is written: *Let there be* מארת (*me'orot*), *lights* (ibid. 1:14), spelled deficiently![27] So *Jacob was left alone*—left

is performed for him, it is deducted from his merits.' Rabbi Ḥanin said, 'Which verse
4 demonstrates this? *I am diminished by all the kindness and faithfulness* [*that You have shown Your servant*].'" See *Zohar* 1:111b.

22. **to leave him with the Prince of Esau...** According to Rabbi Yitsḥak, the angels left Jacob not because he had exposed himself to danger, but rather in order to leave him alone to wrestle with Samael, Esau's heavenly Prince, so that the latter would confirm the blessings that Isaac had bestowed upon Jacob.

See *Midrash Aggadah* and Rashi on Genesis 32:27; Rashi on Hosea 12:5; Naḥmanides on Genesis 32:30; *Zohar* 1:144a; 3:45a.

On Samael as Jacob's wrestling partner, see *Tanḥuma, Vayishlaḥ* 8; *Bereshit Rabbah* 77:3; *Zohar* 1:146a, 170a, 179b.

23. **they went off to utter song...** Precisely then, those angels were scheduled to take their turn in the heavenly choir.

Cf. *Bereshit Rabbah* 78:1–2; BT *Ḥullin* 91b.

24. ***I am shorn of all the kindness and faithfulness...*** The verse reads: *I am shorn* [or: *unworthy*] *of all the kindness and faithfulness that You have shown Your servant, for with my staff I crossed this Jordan, and now I have become two camps.* See Naḥmanides, ad loc.; Ibn Ezra on Genesis 32:3.

25. **complete on all sides, with two shares: white and red** Alternatively, the phrase *two camps* refers to the double share of Jacob, who embodies *Tif'eret*: balancing right and left, *Hesed* and *Gevurah*, symbolized respectively by white and red.

26. **that night, that hour, the dominion of the side of Esau prevailed** It was the eve of Wednesday, dominated by harsh judgment, as explained below.

27. ***Let there be* מארת (*me'orot*), *lights,* spelled deficiently** On the fourth day in the account of Creation, the word מארת (*me'orot*) is written without *vavs*, the vowel letters. This deficient spelling is interpreted to mean that something was missing on the fourth day: the light of *Shekhinah* (symbolized by the moon) diminished, and Her union with *Tif'eret* (symbolized by *vav*) was disrupted. This lack creates the potential for evil or "curse": מארה (*me'erah*).

See BT *Pesaḥim* 112b: "One should not go out alone at night, neither on the eve of Wednesday [fourth day of the week] nor on the eve of Sabbath, because Agrat daughter of Maḥalat [Queen of Demons] goes out together with 180,000 angels of destruction, each empowered to wreak destruction independently."

See Proverbs 3:33; JT *Ta'anit* 4:4, 68b; *Pesiqta de-Rav Kahana* 5:1; *Soferim* 17:4; Rashi on Genesis 1:14; *Zohar* 1:1a, 12a, 19b, 33b, 146a, 169a–b; 2:167b, 205a; 3:45a, 234a; *Minḥat Shai* on Genesis 1:14.

alone because the moon was concealed from the sun.[28] However, *Shekhinah* did not withdraw from him completely, so he could not prevail against him,[29] as is written: *He saw that he could not prevail against him* (ibid. 32:26).[30] He looked to the right and saw Abraham; he looked to the left and saw Isaac.[31] He looked at the body and saw it comprising this side and that.[32] So, *when he saw that he could not prevail against him, he touched the socket of his thigh*—one pillar supporting the torso, outside the torso.[33]

"Therefore, *The angel of YHVH encamps around those in awe of Him and delivers them.* He encompassed him on all sides to save him. When *Shekhinah* dwelled within him, countless forces and camps accompanied him, and some of those angels he sent to Esau."

Jacob sent messengers.

Rabbi Abba said, "Now, why did he arouse Esau? He should have kept quiet.[34]
But Jacob thought, 'I know how deeply Esau cares about honoring Father and
has never irritated him;[35] so I know that as long as Father is alive, I don't have 5
to fear him.[36] Rather, now that Father is alive, let me reconcile with him.'
Immediately, *Jacob sent messengers ahead of him.*"

28. **left alone because the moon was concealed from the sun** Jacob's isolation reflects that of *Tif'eret,* who is symbolized by the sun and was separated from *Shekhinah,* symbolized by the moon.

On Jacob as the sun, see *Bereshit Rabbah* 68:10; *Zohar* 1:135a, 136a, 146b, 148a, 203a; *ZḤ* 14c, 27c (*MhN*); Moses de León, *Sheqel ha-Qodesh,* 50 (61); idem, *Sod Eser Sefirot,* 381.

29. **so he could not prevail against him** Therefore the Prince of Esau could not prevail against Jacob.

30. ***He saw that he could not prevail against him*** The passage reads: *A man wrestled with him until the rising of dawn, and he saw that he could not prevail against him.*

31. **He looked to the right and saw Abraham...to the left and saw Isaac** Jacob's adversary looked to the right and saw the power of *Ḥesed,* symbolized by Abraham. Then he looked to the left and saw the power of *Gevurah,* symbolized by Isaac.

32. **He looked at the body...** Jacob himself symbolizes *Tif'eret,* torso of the divine body, incorporating both right and left.

33. ***socket of his thigh*—one pillar supporting the torso...** The thigh symbolizes the *sefirah* of *Netsaḥ,* one of the two pillars supporting *Tif'eret,* the torso.

See *Zohar* 1:21b, 146a; 2:227a; Moses de León, *Sheqel ha-Qodesh,* 10–12 (13–14).

34. **Now, why did he arouse Esau?...** And thus risk reminding Esau of who had stolen his blessing. See *Bereshit Rabbah* 75:3.

35. **how deeply Esau cares about honoring Father...** On Esau's devotion to his father, Isaac, see *Shemot Rabbah* 46:4: "*A son honors his father* (Malachi 1:6)—Esau, who honored his father greatly, going out to the fields, hunting game, bringing it back, cooking it, bringing it to his father, and feeding him every day."

See *Sifrei,* Deuteronomy 336; *Bereshit Rabbah* 65:16; 76:2; *Devarim Rabbah* 1:15; *Pesiqta Rabbati* 23; *Targum Yerushalmi* and *Ba'al ha-Turim,* Deuteronomy 2:5; *Zohar* 1:146b.

36. **as long as Father is alive, I don't have**

Rabbi Shim'on opened, "*Better to be lightly esteemed and have a servant than to be self-important and lack food* (Proverbs 12:9). This verse was uttered concerning the evil impulse,[37] [166b] for he constantly incites a person, inflating his heart and desire with conceit, so that he follows him, curling his hair, until he overwhelms him and drags him to Hell.[38] Rather, *better to be lightly esteemed:* one who doesn't follow the evil impulse and is not conceited at all—humbling his spirit, heart, and desire before the blessed Holy One. Then that evil impulse is transformed into his *servant,* incapable of dominating him—rather, dominated by him, as is said: *You will rule over him* (Genesis 4:7).[39]

"*Than to be self-important,* as we have said, for he adores himself, curling his hair, inflating his spirit, while *lacking food*—lacking faith, as is said: *food of his God, food of their God* (Leviticus 21:22, 6).[40]

"Alternatively, *Better to be lightly esteemed and have a servant*—Jacob, who humbled his spirit before Esau so that eventually he would become his *servant,* ruled by him,[41] fulfilling the verse: *May peoples serve you and nations bow down*
6 *to you*... (Genesis 27:29).[42] So far, *it was not his time* at all, for Jacob had deferred it to the End of Days,[43] so right now he was *lightly esteemed,* while later that *self-important* one will become his *servant;* that one *lacking food* will serve the one endowed with *abundance of grain and new wine* (ibid., 28).[44]

"Come and see: Therefore, since Jacob knew it was necessary, he changed into *lightly esteemed,* displaying more tortuous cunning than in all his other

to fear him See Genesis 27:41: *Esau despised Jacob because of the blessing with which his father had blessed him, and Esau said in his heart, "Let the days of mourning for my father draw near, and then I will kill Jacob my brother!"*

37. **This verse was uttered concerning the evil impulse** See *Zohar* 1:144b, 174b.

38. **so that he follows him, curling his hair...** So that person follows the evil impulse, primping until the latter overwhelms him. See *Bereshit Rabbah* 22:6.

39. **transformed into his *servant*... *You will rule over him*** The verse reads: *Sin crouches at the opening, his desire toward you, but you will rule over him.* On the transformation of the evil impulse, see *Zohar* 1:144b.

40. ***lacking food*—lacking faith... *food of his God*...** Both *food* and faith symbolize *Shekhinah*, who is joined to the masculine divinity through the mystery of sacrifices. She avoids anyone who is proud.

See BT *Sotah* 5a; and on the association of *food* and the feminine, *Bereshit Rabbah* 86:5; *Zohar* 1:246a.

41. **he would become his *servant,* ruled by him** Esau would become Jacob's servant.

42. ***May peoples serve you and nations bow down to you*...** The verse continues: *Be master over your brothers, and may your mother's sons bow down to you.*

43. **for Jacob had deferred it to the End of Days** Jacob deferred his domination over Esau until the next world.

See *Zohar* 1:143b, 145a–146a, 172a. Cf. JT *Sanhedrin* 10:1, 27d.

44. **the one endowed with *abundance of grain and new wine*** Jacob, for whom Isaac's blessing stated: *May God give you of the dew of heaven and the fat of the earth, abundance of grain and new wine.*

dealings with Esau.[45] For if Esau had discovered this cunning, he would have killed himself rather than undergo this.[46] But Jacob acted totally in wisdom, and concerning him Hannah exclaimed: *The foes of YHVH will be shattered.... He will grant power to His king and raise the horn of His anointed* (1 Samuel 2:10).[47]

"*He instructed them, saying, 'So shall you say: "To my lord Esau, so says your servant Jacob..."'* (Genesis 32:5).[48] He immediately opened by turning himself into a servant, so that he wouldn't consider those blessings bestowed upon him by his father,[49] which—as we have said—Jacob had deferred until later."

Rabbi Yehudah said, "What did Jacob have in mind in sending this message to Esau: *With Laban I have sojourned* (ibid.)? What did he accomplish by transmitting this word to Esau? The answer is that Laban the Aramean's fame had spread throughout the world: no one was safe from him because he was a master magician, preeminent sorcerer, father of Beor who was father of Balaam—as is written: *Balaam son of Beor, the augur* (Joshua 13:22).[50] Laban was more skilled than all of them in magic and sorcery, but even so, he could not prevail against Jacob,[51] whom he sought to destroy with various devices, as 7
is written: *An Aramean was about to destroy my father!* (Deuteronomy 26:5)."[52]

Rabbi Abba said, "The entire world knew that Laban was the master wizard, magician, and sorcerer, and that whomever he wished to magically eliminate could not be saved. Everything Balaam knew derived from him, and of Balaam

45. **than in all his other dealings with Esau** When Jacob deprived him of the birthright and stole his blessings. See Genesis 25:29–34; 27:1–41.

46. **rather than undergo this** Being dominated by Jacob in the end of days.

47. ***The foes of YHVH will be shattered...*** The full verse reads: *The foes of YHVH will be shattered; He will thunder against them in heaven. YHVH will judge the ends of the earth. He will grant power to His king and raise the horn of His anointed.*

48. ***so says your servant Jacob...*** The verse continues with Jacob's message: *With Laban I have sojourned and I tarried till now.*

49. **so that he wouldn't consider those blessings...** So that Esau wouldn't consider the blessings bestowed upon Jacob by their father Isaac, as recounted in Genesis 27.

See *Tanḥuma* (Buber), *Vayishlaḥ* 5; *Targum Yerushalmi*, Genesis 32:5; Rashi on Genesis 32:5–6.

50. **preeminent sorcerer, father of Beor...** On Laban's powers of witchcraft, see Genesis 30:27; *Targum Yerushalmi*, Rashi, Ibn Ezra, and *Sekhel Tov*, ad loc.; *Zohar* 1:133b, 139b, 158b, 161a, 164b.

According to one view, Laban was the father of Beor and the grandfather of Balaam. See *Tanḥuma, Balaq* 12; *Sefer ha-Yashar, Va-yetse*, 142; *Zohar* 1:133b; *ZḤ* 54c; Ginzberg, *Legends*, 5:303, n. 229; 6:123, n. 722.

51. **but even so, he could not prevail against Jacob** This was Jacob's point in conveying to Esau the message that *with Laban I have sojourned.*

52. ***An Aramean was about to destroy my father*** The verse is usually understood to mean *My father was a wandering* [or: *fugitive, straying, perishing*] *Aramean.* The creative reading here appears in the Passover Haggadah, and in Septuagint, *Targum Onqelos, Targum Yerushalmi*, ad loc.

is written *For I know that whomever you bless is blessed, and whomever you curse is cursed* (Numbers 22:6). The whole world feared Laban and his sorcery, and the very first word Jacob sent to Esau was '*With Laban I have sojourned.* Now, if you think this was brief—a month or a year—not so! *I tarried till now*—for twenty years I tarried with him. And if you think I achieved nothing, *I have acquired ox and donkey* (Genesis, ibid., 6)'[53]—two decrees of judgment that join together only to torment the world. Therefore it is written: *Do not plow with an ox and a donkey together* (Deuteronomy 22:10).[54]

"*Sheep and male and female slaves* (Genesis, ibid.)—nethermost crowns slain by the blessed Holy One in Egypt: *firstborn of the livestock, firstborn of the captive* (Exodus 12:29), *firstborn of the female slave* (ibid. 11:5),[55] as is written: *sheep and male and female slaves.* He was immediately frightened[56] and went out toward him—as frightened of Jacob as Jacob was of him.

"This can be compared to a person walking on the road. While he was walking, he heard about a certain robber lying in ambush. He encountered
8 someone else and asked him, 'Who do you belong to?'

"He replied, 'I am from so-and-so's gang.'

"He exclaimed, 'Get out of my way! If anyone comes near me, I bring out a snake and kill him.'

"That person returned to the gang leader and said, 'Someone is coming—and anyone who approaches him gets bitten by a snake he brings out [167a], and dies!'

"When the gang leader heard, he became frightened, and said, 'I better go out to him and appease him.'

"As soon as the person saw him coming, he said, 'Woe is me! Now that gang leader is going to kill me!' He began bowing and prostrating himself before him.

"That gang leader said to himself, 'If he really had a deadly snake, he wouldn't bow so much before me.' He started feeling proud, and said, 'Since he bowed so low before me, I won't kill him.'

53. ***I have acquired ox and donkey*** The verse continues with Jacob's list of acquisitions: *sheep, and male and female slaves.*

54. **two decrees of judgment that join together...** Two harsh powers. The command against plowing with these two species is understood as a warning not to stimulate the union of the two dangerous forces.

See *Zohar* 1:172b; 2:6a, 64b; 3:86b, 207a.

55. **nethermost crowns slain by the blessed Holy One in Egypt...** Demonic powers beneath and corresponding to the ten holy golden crowns, or *sefirot*. See *Zohar* 2:30b; 3:41b, 70a.

56. **He was immediately frightened** Esau was frightened that Jacob had learned sorcery from Laban.

"Similarly, Jacob said, '*With Laban I have sojourned and I tarried till now*—for twenty years I tarried with him, and I am carrying a deadly snake.'

"When Esau heard,[57] he said, 'Woe is me! Who can withstand him? Now Jacob will kill me with his mouth!'[58] He began going out toward him to appease him. As soon as he saw him,[59] what is written? *Jacob was very frightened and distressed* (Genesis, ibid., 8). Approaching him, he began bowing and prostrating himself before him,[60] as is written: *He bowed to the ground seven times until he drew near his brother* (ibid. 33:3). Esau said to himself, 'If he really had so much, he wouldn't bow down to me.' He started feeling proud.

"Come and see what is written concerning Balaam: *God came to Balaam at night* (Numbers 22:20). Concerning Laban is written *God came to Laban the Aramean in a night-dream and said to him, 'Be careful* פן תדבר (*pen tedabber*), *not to speak, to Jacob either good or evil* (Genesis 31:24). *Pen tedabber, Not to speak*—The verse should read: פן תעשה (*pen ta'aseh*), *not to do, evil to Jacob.* But Laban didn't pursue Jacob with manly power to wage war against him, since Jacob and his sons would have overwhelmed him; rather, to kill him by mouth, 9
annihilating him entirely, as is written: *An Aramean was about to destroy my father!* (Deuteronomy 26:5).[61] So, *not to speak,* rather than *not to do.*

"Then it is written: *It is in my power to do you harm* (Genesis, ibid., 29). *It is in my power*—how did he know he was capable? As is said: *But the God of your father said to me last night, 'Be careful not to speak . . .'* (ibid.).[62]

"This is the testimony the blessed Holy One commanded to declare,[63] as is written: וענית (*Ve-anita*), *You shall testify,*[64] *and say before YHVH your God: An Aramean was about to destroy my father . . .* (Deuteronomy, ibid.). *Ve-anita, You shall testify,* as is said: לא תענה (*lo ta'aneh*), *you shall not testify, against your neighbor* (Exodus 20:13);[65] ענה (*anah*), *he testified, against his brother* (Deuteronomy 19:18).[66]

57. **When Esau heard** From Jacob's messengers or Esau's own forces or his own heavenly prince who wrestled with Jacob. See *OY*, Galante, *MM*.

58. **with his mouth** Through magical incantations learned from Laban.

59. **As soon as he saw him** As soon as Jacob saw Esau.

60. **Approaching him, he began bowing . . .** Approaching Esau, Jacob began bowing.

61. ***An Aramean was about to destroy my father*** See above, p. 7 and n. 52.

62. ***Be careful not to speak . . .*** The verse continues: *to Jacob either good or evil.*

63. **testimony the blessed Holy One commanded to declare** The declaration recited upon bringing first fruits to the Temple.

64. **וענית (*Ve-anita*), *You shall testify*** Usually understood as *you shall answer* [or: *respond, speak, declare, recite*], but Rabbi Abba interprets the verb according to its forensic sense "to testify," as in the two verses he cites.

65. **לא תענה (*Lo ta'aneh*), *You shall not testify, against your neighbor*** The verse continues: *as a false witness.*

66. ***he testified, against his brother*** The verse continues: *falsely.*

"Of Balaam is written *He did not go, as time after time, in search of auguries* (Numbers 24:1), for this was his habit, since he was an augur.

"Of Laban is written *I have augured* (ibid. 30:27),[67] for he examined Jacob's affairs by means of divination and sorcery, and when he sought to annihilate Jacob, he did so by those same means. But the blessed Holy One did not allow him, as alluded to by his grandson Balaam:[68] '*For there is no augury against Jacob, no divination against Israel* (Numbers 23:23). Who can prevail against them? For look, my grandfather sought to annihilate their ancestor with his augury and divination, but these failed him, since He did not allow him to curse,' as is written: *For there is no augury against Jacob, no divination against Israel.*

"Laban wielded against Jacob all ten types of sorcery and divination from dazzling dross of nethermost crowns,[69] yet he could not prevail, as is written: *You switched my wages ten* מונים (*monim*), *times* (ibid. 31:41), for Laban employed all those against him but they failed to harm him, as is written: *He switched my*
10 *wages ten monim, times, yet God has not let him harm me* (ibid., 7). What is *monim*? As translated: זינין (*zinin*), types,[70] and it is written: *to the demons after whom they* זונים (*zonim*), *go whoring* (Leviticus 17:7).[71] *Monim*—מינים (*minim*), types, literally! For there are ten types of sorcery and divination in the nethermost crowns, all of which he wielded against him—ten types, as is written: *a diviner of divinations, a soothsayer, an augur, a sorcerer, one who casts a spell, or*

67. ***I have augured*** The verse continues: *that YHVH has blessed me because of you.*

68. **his grandson Balaam** On Laban as Balaam's grandfather, see above, note 50.

69. **ten types of sorcery ... from dazzling dross of nethermost crowns** From demonic powers. See above, note 55. Dross symbolizes forces of evil left over after the refining process of emanation.

"Dazzling dross" renders the Aramaic neologism קזטיפי (*qaztiphei*), which apparently implies both projection and impurity. See the expression קסטיפא דשמשא (*qastipha de-shimsha*), "ray of the sun" (*Zohar* 3:283b); the Arabic root *qdf*, "to throw"; and the neologism קוספיתא (*quspita*), "hollow of a sling," discussed by Liebes, *Peraqim*, 345–48.

Qaztiphei may derive as well from Aramaic כוספא (*kuspa*), "pomace, husk, residue." Cf. קסטופא (*qastopha*) (*Zohar* 1:153a; below, pp. 235–36, n. 345); קספתא (*qaspeta*) (3:50b); and the related neologism סוספיתא (*suspita*) in *Zohar* 1:30a, 71b, 118b, 228a; 2:24b, 203a, 224b, 236b; Moses de León, *Sod Eser Sefirot*, 384; Scholem, *Major Trends*, 389, n. 54.

See the similar forms קוזפי (*quzpei*) (*Zohar* 1:53b) and קיזפא (*qizpa*) (below; 2:175b); *Bei'ur ha-Millim ha-Zarot*, 186, 189.

70. ***ten*** **מונים (*monim*),** ***times*** **... As translated: זינין (*zinin*), types** In both verses in Genesis, מנים (*monim*) is spelled defectively, without the ו (*vav*), and can thus be read: מינים (*minim*), "types." Although Rabbi Abba cites the Targum, *Targum Onqelos* on this verse reads: זמנין (*zimnin*), "times," not זינין (*zinin*), "types." See *Zohar* 1:161a.

71. ***to the demons after whom they*** **זונים (*zonim*),** ***go whoring*** Playing on the invented Targumic citation of זינין (*zinin*), "types."

consults a ghost or a familiar spirit, or inquires of the dead (Deuteronomy 18:10–11), totaling ten."[72]

Rabbi Yose said, "Augury and divination are two types,[73] attaining a single rung. When Balaam came, he wielded divination against Israel, as is written: *with divinations in their hand* (Numbers 22:7). Against Jacob, Laban came with augury, but both of these failed them, as is written: *For there is no augury against Jacob, no divination against Israel. For there is no augury against Jacob*—at first, in the days of Laban; *no divination against Israel*—later, in the days of Balaam.

"Balaam said to Balak, 'Come and see: Who can prevail against them, since all sorcery, divination, and augury in our crowns is filigreed from dross of supernal Kingdom, whereas She is linked with them, as is written: *YHVH their God is with them, shout of the King in their midst* (ibid. 23:21).'"[74]

Rabbi Yehudah said, "Heaven forbid that Balaam knew anything at all of supernal sanctity![75] [167b] For the blessed Holy One wants no other nation or
tongue to wield His glory—only His holy children, to whom He said: *Sanctify* 11
yourselves and be holy (Leviticus 11:44). Those who are holy will wield holiness; Israel are holy, as is written: *For you are a holy people* (Deuteronomy 14:2)—you are holy, no other people. Those who are impure encounter impurity, becoming defiled; of such is written *Impure is he; alone shall he dwell; outside the camp is his dwelling* (Leviticus 13:46). Impure calls to impure, as is said: *Impure, impure will call* (ibid., 45)—whoever is impure will call to impure.[76] Everything follows its own kind."[77]

Rabbi Yitsḥak said, "Was it seemly for Holy Jacob to say he had been defiled by Laban and his sorcery? Was this praiseworthy?"[78]

72. **ten types, as is written: *a diviner of divinations*... totaling ten** Commentators suggest various ways to identify ten distinct types in this list. See *OY*, Vital, Galante, *KP*. *Bereshit Rabbah* 65:11 includes the beginning of the first verse (*There is not to be found among you anyone who passes his son or his daughter through fire*), thereby eliciting the decade more easily. See *Zohar* 2:30b; 3:70a.

73. **Augury and divination are two types** See *Zohar* 1:164b; 3:112b, 207a, 211a, 299b.

74. **filigreed from dross of supernal Kingdom...** 'All our powers of sorcery derive from the dross of *Shekhinah*, who is known as *Malkhut* ("Kingdom"). Since She is intimately linked with Israel, we are powerless against them.'

"Dross" renders the Aramaic neologism קיזפא (*qizpa*); see above, note 69.

75. **anything at all of supernal sanctity** Of how his sorcery derived from *Shekhinah*.

76. ***Impure, impure will call*...** The clause means literally: "*Impure! Impure!*," *he shall call out.* Rabbi Yehudah reads it differently.

77. **Everything follows its own kind** See *Bereshit Rabbah* 65:3; BT *Bava Qamma* 92b; *Zohar* 1:20b, 126b, 137b.

78. **Was it seemly for Holy Jacob to say he had been defiled by Laban...** Rabbi

Rabbi Yose replied, "Even though Rabbi Yehudah has already spoken,[79] I support you. For look at what is written: *I am Esau, your firstborn* (Genesis 27:19)![80] Now, was it seemly for a righteous man like Jacob to exchange his name for an impure one? But really: *I am*—interrupted by an accent sign—that is to say: '*I am* who I am, but *Esau is your firstborn,*' as has been established.[81]

"Similarly here, *I have acquired ox and donkey* (Genesis 32:6),[82] implying: 'Do not even imagine that Father's blessing to me has been fulfilled.[83] He blessed me: *Be master over your brothers, may your mother's sons bow down to you* (ibid. 27:29); so, *your servant Jacob, to my lord Esau* (ibid. 32:5).[84]

"'He blessed me with *abundance of grain and new wine* (ibid. 27:28), but look, this hasn't been fulfilled: I haven't accumulated these, but rather, *I have acquired ox and donkey, sheep and male and female slaves*—a shepherd in the field!

"'He blessed me with *the dew of heaven and the fat of the earth* (ibid.), but look, this hasn't been fulfilled; rather, *With Laban I have sojourned* (ibid. 32:5)—like a sojourner without a single home, let alone *the fat of the earth!*'

"All this so he would not consider Jacob's blessings and accuse him."[85]

Rabbi Abba said, "Of Jacob is written *a simple man, dwelling in tents* (Genesis 25:27)—a consummate man, for he dwells in two supernal dwellings, consummating this side and that.[86] He was not saying he had been defiled

Yitsḥak is objecting to Rabbi Abba's view (above, pages 7–9), that when Jacob said *With Laban I have sojourned... I have acquired ox and donkey...*, he was implying that he had learned sorcery from a master.

79. **Even though Rabbi Yehudah has already spoken** See above, page 7, where Rabbi Yehudah interprets Jacob's statement *With Laban I have sojourned* as implying Jacob's invulnerability to Laban's sorcery. Alternatively, Rabbi Yose is referring to what Rabbi Yehudah just said: "Everything follows its own kind," implying that Jacob would never resort to sorcery.

80. ***I am Esau, your firstborn*** Jacob's declaration to his father, Isaac, when he sought the firstborn's blessing.

81. ***I am*—interrupted by an accent sign...** The accent sign over the word אנכי (*anokhi*), *I am,* indicates a slight pause, justifying an elliptical reading: "*I am* who I am, but *Esau is your firstborn.*"

See *Bereshit Rabbah* 68:18; *Tanḥuma* (Buber), *Toledot* 10; *Midrash Aggadah, Leqaḥ Tov, Sekhel Tov,* Rashi, Ibn Ezra (whose wording reappears here precisely), and *Minḥat Shai* on Genesis 27:19; *Zohar* 1:120a–b; 2:85a; 3:138a (*IR*), 187b.

82. **Similarly here, *I have acquired ox and donkey*** As in Jacob's declaration to Isaac, so too here the meaning is not what it appears to be; nor does it imply that Jacob had mastered sorcery.

83. **Do not even imagine that Father's blessing to me has been fulfilled** See *Tanḥuma* (Buber), *Vayishlaḥ* 5; *Targum Yerushalmi,* Genesis 32:5; Rashi on Genesis 32:5–6; above, page 6.

84. **so, *your servant Jacob, to my lord Esau*** Indicating that Esau is the master, and Jacob the servant.

85. **accuse him** Of having stolen them.

86. ***a simple man*... a consummate man...** The verse reads: *The boys grew up. Esau became a skilled hunter, a man of the field, while Jacob was* איש תם (*ish tam*), *a*

by his[87] sorcery; rather, in response to Rabbi Yehudah's statement,[88] his heart was completely grateful for the genuine kindness shown to him by the blessed Holy One: 'For the whole world knows how Laban acts. Who can escape him? Yet I stayed with him twenty years, and though he sought to annihilate me, the blessed Holy One delivered me.'

"All so Esau would not consider that those blessings had been fulfilled and would not bear a grudge against him.[89] Concerning this is written *For the ways of YHVH are right* (Hosea 14:10),[90] and similarly: *Be wholehearted with YHVH your God* (Deuteronomy 18:13).[91]

"*The messengers returned to Jacob, saying, 'We came to your brother, to Esau...'* (Genesis 32:7).[92] Since Scripture says: *We came to your brother,* don't we know that it's Esau? Did Jacob have any other brothers? Rather, '*We came to your brother,* and if you think he has repented and is following the correct path, not so: *Esau,* wicked as ever![93]

"'*He himself is coming to meet you* (ibid.). Now, if you think he is coming 13
alone: *and four hundred men with him!* (ibid.).'

"Why all this?[94] Because the blessed Holy One constantly desires the prayers of the righteous[95] and crowns Himself with their prayers, as they have said:

simple man, dwelling in tents. The word *tam* means "simple, innocent, plain, mild, quiet, sound, wholesome." *Targum Onqelos,* ad loc., renders it as שלים (*shelim*), "complete, perfect, consummate."

Here Rabbi Abba indicates that Jacob is complete because he spans the sefirotic realm from *Binah* to *Shekhinah,* who are symbolized respectively by his wives Leah and Rachel (see below, note 413). He also completes the sefirotic triad by harmonizing *Ḥesed* and *Gevurah,* the right and left sides, symbolized respectively by his grandfather and father, Abraham and Isaac.

87. **his** Laban's.

88. **in response to Rabbi Yehudah's statement** As to why Jacob said *With Laban I have sojourned.* See above, page 7.

89. **not bear a grudge against him** For having stolen the blessings of the firstborn. See Genesis 27:41, and *Targum Onqelos,* ad loc.

90. ***For the ways of YHVH are right*** The verse continues: *the righteous walk in them, while the rebellious stumble in them.* For Rabbi Abba, the conclusion of the verse may imply that Esau stumbled, believing that Jacob had mastered sorcery while living with Laban. Consequently, Esau feared his brother.

91. ***Be wholehearted with YHVH your God*** Jacob, who walked in the ways of God and was תמים (*tamim*), *wholehearted,* would never have resorted to sorcery. See BT *Pesaḥim* 113b.

92. ***We came to your brother, to Esau...*** In the verse the messengers continue: *and he himself is coming to meet you, and four hundred men with him!*

93. **if you think he has repented..., not so: *Esau,* wicked as ever** See *Bereshit Rabbah* 75:11; *Tanḥuma* (Buber), *Vayishlaḥ* 6; *Midrash ha-Be'ur,* cited by Kasher, *Torah Shelemah,* ad loc.

94. **Why all this?** Why did the messengers report all this, thereby frightening Jacob?

95. **the blessed Holy One constantly desires the prayers of the righteous** See *Bereshit Rabbah* 45:4; *Shemot Rabbah* 21:5; *Qohe-*

That angel appointed over the prayers of Israel takes all those prayers, fashions them into a crown, and places it on the head of Vitality of the Worlds, as they have established.[96] All the more so with prayers of the righteous, desired by the blessed Holy One, fashioned into a crown with which He is crowned.

"Now, you might say 'Since holy camps accompanied him, why was he frightened?'[97] Because the righteous do not rely on this, but rather on their prayers and supplications to their Lord.[98]

"Come and see what Rabbi Shim'on said: 'The prayer of a congregation ascends before the blessed Holy One, who crowns Himself with that prayer because it ascends in many colors, encompassing many facets. Interweaving many colors, it is made into a crown and placed upon the head of Righteous One, Vitality of the Worlds; whereas the prayer of an individual is not interwoven but monochromatic and so not as readily received as the prayer of a congregation.'[99]

"Come and see: Jacob was encompassing,[100] so the blessed Holy One yearned

let Rabbah on 9:7; BT *Yevamot* 64a; *Ḥullin* 60b; *Zohar* 1:169a.

96. **That angel... takes all those prayers, fashions them into a crown...** See *Shemot Rabbah* 21:4: "Rabbi Pinḥas said in the name of Rabbi Me'ir, and Rabbi Yirmeyah said in the name of Rabbi Abba, 'When Israel prays, you do not find them all praying as one, but rather each assembly prays on its own, one after the other. When they have all finished, the angel appointed over prayers gathers all the prayers offered in all the synagogues and fashions them into crowns, which he places on the head of the blessed Holy One.'"

In BT *Ḥagigah* 13b, it is reported that the angel Sandalfon "stands behind the Chariot, binding crowns for his Lord." See *Tosafot,* ad loc., s.v. *ve-qosher; Pesiqta Rabbati* 20; *Midrash Tehillim* 88:2; Ezra of Gerona, *Peirush Shir ha-Shirim,* 495; *Zohar* 1:37b, 132a, 162a, 168b–169a; 2:58a, 146b, 202b, 209a, 245b–246a (*Heikh*); Recanati on Genesis 19:27, 26a; Green, *Keter,* 37–38.

The title Vitality of the Worlds designates *Yesod,* who channels the vivifying flow of emanation below. On the various senses of this title, see Daniel 4:31; 12:7; Ben Sira 18:1; *Mekhilta, Pisḥa* 16; *Bereshit Rabbah* 1:5; Schäfer, *Synopse zur Hekhalot-Literatur,* §275; *Bahir* 123 (180) (and Scholem's note, ad loc.); *Zohar* 1:4b, 18a, 132a, 135b, 164a, 193b; 2:245b (*Heikh*); Moses de León, *Sheqel ha-Qodesh,* 55–56 (68).

97. **why was he frightened?** As stated in Genesis 32:8: *Jacob was very frightened and distressed.*

98. **righteous do not rely on this...** On unsolicited divine assistance. See *Devarim Rabbah* 2:1.

99. **The prayer of a congregation ascends ... in many colors...** Reflecting the unique personalities and needs of each member of the congregation. "Colors" renders the Aramaic גוונין (*gavnin*), "colors, ways, manners."

On the preferability of communal prayer, see BT *Berakhot* 7b–8a, *Ta'anit* 8b; *Zohar* 1:160b, 234a; 2:245b; Gikatilla, *Sha'arei Orah,* 30b–31b.

The title Righteous One designates *Yesod,* based on Proverbs 10:25: וצדיק יסוד עולם (*Ve-tsaddiq yesod olam*). The verse literally means *The righteous one is an everlasting foundation,* but it is understood as *The righteous one is the foundation of the world.*

See BT *Ḥagigah* 12b; *Bahir* 71 (102); Azriel of Gerona, *Peirush ha-Aggadot,* 34.

100. **Jacob was encompassing** Embodying *Tif'eret,* he combined the qualities and

for his prayer. What is written? *Jacob was very frightened and distressed* (Genesis 32:8)."[101]

Rabbi Yehudah opened, "*Happy is one who always fears, but one who hardens his heart will fall into calamity* (Proverbs 28:14). [168a] Happy are Israel, in whom the blessed Holy One delights, to whom He has given Torah of truth, to attain eternal life! For the blessed Holy One channels supernal life to anyone engaged in Torah, initiating him into life of the world that is coming, as is written: *She is your life and the length of your days* (Deuteronomy 30:20),[102] and similarly: *Through this word you will prolong your days...* (ibid. 32:47)—life in this world and life in the world that is coming."[103]

Rabbi El'azar said, "Whoever engages in Torah for her own sake does not die by means of the evil impulse,[104] since he grasps the Tree of Life,[105] never letting go. Therefore bodies of the righteous who engage in Torah do not defile, since no impurity settles upon them.[106]

colors of *Ḥesed* and *Gevurah*. See *Zohar* 1:234a.

101. ***Jacob was very frightened and distressed*** God frightened him because He yearned to hear his fervent prayer.

102. ***She is your life and the length of your days*** Rabbi Yehudah understands *she* as referring to Torah. The verse reads: *He* [or: *that*] *is your life...*, referring either to God or to loving, heeding, and cleaving to Him (mentioned immediately before). The substitution of היא (*hi*), *She*, for הוא (*hu*), *He* (or *that*), in this verse appears elsewhere, e.g., in *Tanḥuma, Yitro* 15, *Ki Tissa* 15, *Shemini* 11; *Avot de-Rabbi Natan* A, 2; *Zohar* 1:92a, 244b.

103. **life in this world and life in the world that is coming** See *Sifrei*, Deuteronomy 336.

104. **does not die by means of the evil impulse** Understood as identical with the Angel of Death. See BT *Bava Batra* 16a: "Resh Lakish said, 'Satan, the evil impulse, and the Angel of Death are one and the same.'"

On the notion that the Angel of Death is powerless against one engaged in Torah, see *Vayiqra Rabbah* 18:3; BT *Shabbat* 30b; *Eruvin* 54a; *Bava Metsi'a* 86a; *Makkot* 10a; *Zohar* 1:131b, 152b; 2:45b.

According to BT *Bava Batra* 17a, "Over six the Angel of Death had no dominion: Abraham, Isaac, and Jacob; Moses, Aaron, and Miriam," all of whom died by the kiss of God. Here, apparently, Rabbi El'azar extends this rare blissful death to all who "engage in Torah for her own sake." See the gloss interpolated here in the printed editions of the *Zohar*, which describes this type of ecstatic death.

105. **Tree of Life** Torah is identified with the Tree of Life, based on the description of wisdom in Proverbs 3:18: *She is a tree of life to those who grasp her*. See BT *Berakhot* 32b, 61b. In Kabbalah both Torah and Tree of Life symbolize *Tif'eret*.

106. **bodies of the righteous who engage in Torah do not defile...** After death. This view contradicts normative Jewish law. See Numbers 19:14; BT *Sukkah* 25b; *Bava Batra* 58a; *Sanhedrin* 39a. However, according to a statement attributed to the prophet Elijah in *Midrash Mishlei* 9:2, "No impurity contaminates the righteous [who have died]." The *Zohar*'s immediate source is apparently Naḥmanides on Numbers 19:2: "Logically, those who die by a [divine] kiss do not defile, as they have said, 'The righteous do not defile.'"

See *Tosafot, Yevamot* 61a, s.v. *mi-magga;*

"Now, Jacob was the Tree of Life;[107] so why was he frightened? After all, he couldn't prevail against him.[108] Furthermore, look at what is written: *Here, I am with you...* (Genesis 28:15),[109] and also: *Angels of God encountered him* (ibid. 32:2)! If supernal camps accompanied him, why was he frightened?

"But all was fitting.[110] Jacob didn't want to rely on a miracle of the blessed Holy One, since he considered himself unworthy. Why? Because he hadn't served his father and mother properly, he hadn't engaged in Torah,[111] and he had married two sisters.[112] Even though all has been explained,[113] still one should fear constantly and offer prayer before the blessed Holy One, as is written: *Happy is one who always fears,* as has been established.[114]

"Come and see: Prayer of the patriarchs has sustained the world. All inhabitants of the world endure through them, rely upon them. Never, ever will the merit of the patriarchs be forgotten,[115] for their merit sustains above and below. Sustenance of Jacob is most perfect of them all;[116] so when the children of Jacob

idem, *Bava Metsi'a* 114a–b, s.v. *mahu;* BT *Bava Metsi'a* 86a; *Zohar* 1:125a; 2:141a; the gloss interpolated here in the printed editions of the *Zohar* (1:168a); Ta-Shma, *Ha-Nigleh she-ba-Nistar,* 35–36.

107. **Jacob was the Tree of Life** He symbolizes *Tif'eret,* known as Tree of Life.

108. **he couldn't prevail against him** Esau, symbolizing the demonic powers, couldn't prevail against Jacob.

109. ***Here, I am with you...*** The verse continues: *I will protect you wherever you go.*

110. **But all was fitting** Jacob's fear was appropriate.

111. **he hadn't served...** During his long stay with Laban, Jacob had neglected both his parents and his study of Torah.

See *Seder Olam Rabbah* 2; BT *Megillah* 16b–17a; Rashi, *Megillah* 17a, s.v. *nimtsa;* idem on Genesis 37:34.

112. **he had married two sisters** Leah and Rachel. Such an act is explicitly forbidden in Leviticus 18:18. See BT *Pesaḥim* 119b; *Zohar* 1:76a.

113. **Even though all has been explained** In leaving home, Jacob was obeying his parents, who wanted him to marry one of Laban's daughters (Genesis 27:46–28:2). Although he neglected the study of Torah, he was engaged in the worthy task of raising children.

Rabbinic and medieval exegesis has offered various explanations for Jacob's marrying two sisters, including the fact that the Torah's prohibition had not yet been given. See *Sekhel Tov,* Genesis 29:28; Ibn Ezra on Leviticus 18:26; idem, *Yesod Mora* 5; Naḥmanides on Genesis 26:5; idem on BT *Yevamot* 97b–98a; *Ḥizzequni* on Genesis 29:28; Todros Abulafia, *Otsar ha-Kavod, Ḥagigah* 11b; Solomon ibn Adret, *Responsa,* 1:94; Yom Tov ben Abraham Ishbili on BT *Yevamot* 97b; Baḥya ben Asher on Leviticus 20:21; David ibn Zimra, *Responsa,* 2:696; Galante on this passage.

From a kabbalistic perspective, Jacob's marrying two sisters symbolizes the union of his *sefirah, Tif'eret,* with both *Binah* and *Shekhinah* (symbolized by Leah and Rachel; see below, note 413). See *Zohar* 1:153b; 2:126b; Moses de León, *Sefer ha-Rimmon,* 351–55; idem, *She'elot u-Tshuvot,* 40–41.

114. **still one should fear constantly... as has been established** See *Tanḥuma* (Buber), *Ḥuqqat* 55.

115. **Never, ever will the merit of the patriarchs be forgotten** On the question of the duration of this merit, see *Vayiqra Rabbah* 36:6; JT *Sanhedrin* 10:1, 27d; BT *Shabbat* 55a; *Tosafot,* ad loc., s.v. *ushmu'el; Aggadat Bereshit* 10:2.

116. **Sustenance of Jacob is most per-**

suffer distress, the blessed Holy One gazes upon the image of Jacob and feels compassion for the world,[117] as is said: *I will remember My covenant with* יעקוב (*Ya'aqov*), *Jacob* (Leviticus 26:42)—spelled with a ו (*vav*). Why? Because that is the genuine image of Jacob.[118]

"Come and see: Gazing upon Jacob was like gazing into the resplendent speculum.[119] As has been said: 'The beauty of Jacob resembled the beauty of Adam.'"[120]

Rabbi Yeisa said, "I have heard that whoever sees Jacob in a dream, scintillating in silver, will be granted prolonged life."[121]

fect... His *sefirah, Tif'eret,* harmonizes and completes the polar opposites *Ḥesed* and *Gevurah* (symbolized by Abraham and Isaac), so his sustaining power and merit are supreme.

See *Bereshit Rabbah* 76:1: "Rabbi Pinḥas said in the name of Rabbi Re'uven, '... The chosen of the patriarchs is Jacob, as is said: *For Yah has chosen Jacob for Himself* (Psalms 135:4).'" Cf. BT *Pesaḥim* 56a.

117. **the blessed Holy One gazes upon the image of Jacob...** Which is engraved on the divine throne.

See *Bereshit Rabbah* 68:12; 82:2; *Eikhah Rabbah* 2:2; *Targum Yerushalmi* and *Targum Yerushalmi* (frag.), Genesis 28:12; BT *Ḥullin* 91b (and Rashi, ad loc., s.v. *bidyoqno*); *Pirqei de-Rabbi Eli'ezer* 35; *Zohar* 1:72a; Moses de León, commentary on the ten *sefirot,* 338b; Wolfson, *Along the Path,* 1–62. On the link between gazing at Jacob's image and feeling compassion, see Scholem, "Parashah Ḥadashah," 431.

118. **יעקוב (*Ya'aqov*), *Jacob*—spelled with a ו (*vav*)... genuine image of Jacob** In the entire Torah, only here is the name יעקוב (*Ya'aqov*), *Jacob,* spelled with a ו (*vav*). According to Rabbi El'azar, this extra letter alludes to Jacob's sefirotic archetype, *Tif'eret,* who is symbolized by the ו (*vav*) in the divine name יהוה (*YHVH*) and who includes within Himself all six *sefirot* from *Ḥesed* through *Yesod,* corresponding to the numerical value of *vav*.

See Rashi, ad loc.; *Zohar* 1:117b, 119a; 3:66b; *Minḥat Shai,* ad loc.

119. **resplendent speculum** אספקלריא דנהרא (*Ispaqlarya de-nahara*), "A speculum that shines." See BT *Yevamot* 49b: "All the prophets gazed through an opaque glass ["an *ispaqlarya* that does not shine"], while Moses our teacher gazed through a translucent glass ["an *ispaqlarya* that shines"]." Cf. 1 Corinthians 13:12: "For now we see through a glass darkly, but then face-to-face."

In the *Zohar, Shekhinah* is the *ispaqlarya* that does not shine on its own but rather reflects the other *sefirot,* while *Tif'eret,* symbolized by Jacob, is the *ispaqlarya* that shines.

120. **The beauty of Jacob resembled the beauty of Adam** See BT *Bava Batra* 58a: "The beauty of our father Jacob resembled the beauty of Adam."

See *Bava Metsi'a* 84a; *Zohar* 1:35b, 142b, 222a; *ZḤ* 65a (*ShS*).

121. **Whoever sees Jacob in a dream, scintillating in silver...** The formula "Whoever sees... in a dream..." derives from BT *Berakhot* 56b–57b.

"Scintillating in silver" renders מקסטר בקוספוי (*meqaster be-quspoi*), a neologistic phrase incorporating the *Zohar*'s favorite letters: ר, ק, פ, ס, ט. The first word may derive from Aramaic קסיטרא (*qasitra*) and Greek *kassiteros,* "tin."

See *Targum Yerushalmi* and *Targum Yerushalmi* (frag.), Numbers 31:22; *Zohar* 1:125a, 151a, 232a (*Tos*); 2:24b; *Bei'ur ha-Millim ha-Zarot,* 186, 188.

The second word is perhaps an intentional misspelling of Aramaic כספא (*kaspa*), "silver." For other suggested meanings based on the context, see *OY* ("his countenance"), and Vital (*Derekh Emet*) and *MM* ("his garments"). See Liebes, *Peraqim,* 348. On Jacob

Rabbi Shim'on said, "As already noted, before King David existed, he had no life at all, but Adam gave him 70 years of his own; so David's existence totaled 70 years, while Adam's came to 1000 minus 70. Thus Adam and King David shared these first 1000 years."[122]

He opened, saying, "*He asked You for life; You granted it—length of days forever and ever* (Psalms 21:5). *He asked You for life*—King David, for when the blessed Holy One created the Garden of Eden, He cast King David's soul there[123] and, gazing upon it, saw that it possessed no life of its own. It stood before Him all day long.[124] Once He created Adam, He said, 'Here, indeed, is his existence!' So from Adam derived the 70 years for which King David endured in the world.

"Further, the patriarchs bequeathed some of their life to him, each and every one.[125] Abraham bequeathed to him, as did Jacob and Joseph; Isaac didn't bequeath anything to him because King David derived from his side.[126]

"Abraham bequeathed 5 years to him, since he should have endured for 180 years[127] and he endured for 175, lacking 5. Jacob should have endured for the
18 same number of days as Abraham, but he endured for only [168b] 147 years, lacking 28. Consequently, Abraham and Jacob bequeathed 33 years of life. Joseph endured for 110 years and should have endured for 147 years, the same as Jacob, so 37 years were missing. Look! Seventy years, bequeathed by them to King David, who endured for all those years bequeathed by the patriarchs.[128]

wearing Adam's garments, see *Pirqei de-Rabbi Eli'ezer* 24; *Bereshit Rabbah* 63:13; 65:16; Rashi on BT *Pesaḥim* 54b, s.v. *bigdo shel adam ha-rishon; Midrash Aggadah,* Genesis 27:15; *Zohar* 1:142b; 2:39a–b, 208b; *ZḤ* 65a (*ShS*).

122. **before King David existed, he had no life at all...** According to a midrashic tradition, King David was destined to die at childbirth, but Adam offered him 70 of his own 1000 allotted years, so David lived for 70 years and Adam for 930. Thus the two them shared the first 1000 years of human life.

See Genesis 5:5; Jubilees 4:30; *Pirqei de-Rabbi Eli'ezer* 19, and David Luria, ad loc., n. 31; *Midrash Tehillim* 92:10; *Bemidbar Rabbah* 14:12; *Bereshit Rabbati* 5:5; *Yalqut Shim'oni,* Genesis 41; *Zohar* 1:55a–b, 91b, 140a, 233b, 248b; 2:103b, 235a; *ZḤ* 67d (*ShS*), 81a (*MhN, Rut*); Moses de León, *Sheqel ha-Qodesh,* 68 (85); idem, *Sod Eser Sefirot Belimah,* 383.

123. **He cast King David's soul there** Along with the souls of future generations, which were shown to Adam.

See *Seder Olam Rabbah* 30; *Avot de-Rabbi Natan* A, 31; *Bereshit Rabbah* 24:2; BT *Sanhedrin* 38b; Moses de León, *Sheqel ha-Qodesh,* 68 (85); idem, *Sod Eser Sefirot Belimah,* 383.

124. **It stood before Him all day long** On the preexistent soul standing in God's presence, see *Zohar* 1:233b; 3:68a–b.

125. **Further, the patriarchs bequeathed some of their life to him...** See Moses de León, *Sheqel ha-Qodesh,* 68 (85). As evident from the following sentence, the phrase "each and every one" is hyperbolic.

126. **because King David derived from his side** David (symbolizing *Shekhinah*) derived from Isaac's *sefirah* (*Gevurah*), which is characterized by judgment, darkness, and limitation.

127. **he should have endured for 180 years** As did his son, Isaac.

128. **Look! Seventy years...** The sum of 5, 28, and 37.

"Now, you might ask 'Why didn't Isaac bequeath anything to him, as did these others?' Because he is darkness, and David derives from the side of darkness.[129] Whoever inhabits darkness has no light at all, no life, so David had no life at all. But these, containing light, illumined King David, who had to be illuminated and animated by them,[130] since from the side of darkness he has no life at all. Therefore Isaac did not contribute to the sum.

"Now, you might ask 'Why Joseph?' Because surely, Joseph alone equals them all, since he is called Righteous, illumining the moon more than them all.[131] So this one bequeathed to King David more life than all of them, as is written: *God placed them in the expanse of heaven to shine upon the earth* (Genesis 1:17).[132]

"Come and see: Jacob's prayer protected him from Esau, since he preferred to reserve his merit for his children after him, not to exhaust it now confronting Esau. So he offered his prayer to the blessed Holy One instead of relying on his merit in order to be saved.[133]

"*He thought, 'If Esau comes to the one camp and strikes it, the remaining camp*
will escape' (ibid. 32:9). 19

"Come and see what is written: *He divided the people who were with him, and the sheep and cattle and camels, into two camps* (ibid., 8). Why *into two camps*? Because he thought, *If Esau comes to the one camp and strikes it, the remaining camp will escape.*

129. **Because he is darkness, and David derives from the side of darkness** See above, note 126; *Zohar* 1:112b, 133a, 136a, 142a.

130. **But these, containing light, illumined King David...** Abraham, Jacob, and Joseph symbolize respectively *Hesed, Tif'eret,* and *Yesod,* which transmit emanation to David's *sefirah, Shekhinah.*

131. **Joseph alone equals them all, since he is called Righteous...** In rabbinic literature Joseph is granted the title Righteous in recognition of resisting the sexual advances of Potiphar's wife. See Genesis 39; BT *Yoma* 35b; *Bereshit Rabbah* 93:7; *Pesiqta de-Rav Kahana, nispaḥim,* 460. Cf. *Tanḥuma, Bereshit* 5 and *Pirqei de-Rabbi Eli'ezer* 38, which cite Amos 2:6.

According to Kabbalah, because of his sexual purity Joseph attained the level of *Yesod,* the divine phallus and site of the covenant. *Yesod* is known as Righteous One, based on Proverbs 10:25: וצדיק יסוד עולם (*Ve-tsaddiq yesod olam*). The verse literally means *The righteous one is an everlasting foundation,* but it is understood as *The righteous one is the foundation of the world.* See BT *Ḥagigah* 12b; *Bahir* 71 (102); Azriel of Gerona, *Peirush ha-Aggadot,* 34.

Here Rabbi Shim'on teaches that Joseph the Righteous, symbolizing *Yesod,* gathers within himself the entire sefirotic brilliance and conveys it to *Shekhinah,* symbolized by both David and the moon.

132. ***God placed them in the expanse of heaven to shine upon the earth*** In Genesis the context is the creation of the sun, moon, and stars; here *expanse of heaven* symbolizes *Yesod* (and Joseph), who illumines *Shekhinah,* symbolized by *earth* (and David).

See *Zohar* 1:20a, 34a, 162b; *ZḤ* 14a (*MhN*).

133. **Jacob's prayer protected him from Esau...** Rather than relying on his merit in order to be saved from Esau, Jacob preferred instead to pray for protection so that he could bequeath the full measure of his merit to his descendants. See *Shemot Rabbah* 44:3.

"Come and see: *Shekhinah* did not depart from the tent of Leah or the tent of Rachel. Jacob thought, 'I know that these are protected by the blessed Holy One.' What did he do? *He placed the maids and their children first* (ibid. 33:2),[134] thinking: 'If Esau kills, he will kill me and these, but as for those, I'm not afraid, since *Shekhinah* is with them.' So, *the remaining camp will escape.* Having done this, he prepared his prayer for them.[135] What is written? *Jacob said, 'God of my father Abraham and God of my father Isaac!...'* (ibid. 32:10)."[136]

Rabbi Yose opened, "*A prayer of a poor person when he is faint and pours out his complaint before YHVH* (Psalms 102:1). This verse has been established in many places, but King David uttered this when he saw and contemplated the plight of the poor, as he fled from his father-in-law,[137] exclaiming: '*A prayer of a poor person*—a prayer offered by a poor person before the blessed Holy One, a prayer preceding all prayers of the world!'[138]

"Here is written תפלה (*Tefillah*), *A prayer, of a poor person,* and it is written:
20 *Tefillah, A prayer, of Moses, the man of God* (ibid. 90:1). What is the difference between them? One is *tefillah,* phylactery, of the hand; the other, *tefillah* of the head[139]—and one should not separate *tefillah of a poor person* from *tefillah of Moses, the man of God,* which are equivalent.[140]

134. ***He placed the maids and their children first*** The verse continues: *Leah and her children behind them, and Rachel and Joseph behind them.* The term *the maids* refers to Bilhah and Zilpah, Rachel and Leah's maids.

135. **he prepared his prayer for them** For the maids and their children.

136. ***God of my father Abraham and God of my father Isaac!...*** The passage continues: *YHVH, who said to me, "Return to your land, to your birthplace, and I will deal well with you"!... O save me from the hand of my brother, from the hand of Esau! For I fear him, lest he come and strike me, mother with children* (ibid., 10, 12).

137. **King David uttered this... as he fled from his father-in-law** As David fled from King Saul in desperation (1 Samuel 19–24). The Midrash cites this verse to indicate David's self-perception as a poor man. See *Vayiqra Rabbah* 30:3; *Pesiqta de-Rav Kahana* 27:3; *Midrash Tehillim* 102:1.

138. **a prayer preceding all prayers of the world** See *Vayiqra Rabbah* 3:2; *Zohar* 1:23b (*TZ*); 3:195a.

139. ***tefillah*, phylactery, of the hand... *tefillah* of the head** The word תפלה (*tefillah*) means both "prayer" and "phylactery." The *tefillin* ("phylacteries") consist of two black leather boxes containing passages from the Torah (Exodus 13:1–10, 11–16; Deuteronomy 6:4–9; 11:13–21) written on parchment. They are bound by black leather straps on the left arm and on the head, and are worn during weekday morning services. Each of the biblical passages indicates that the Israelites should place a sign upon their hand and a frontlet (or reminder) between their eyes.

In the *Zohar* the *tefillin* of the hand and the head symbolize respectively two sefirotic rungs: *Shekhinah* and *Tif'eret*. See *Zohar* 1:14a, 132b; 2:43a. Here *poor* alludes to *Shekhinah,* who has nothing at all of Her own, but rather receives and reflects the light of the other *sefirot; Moses* alludes to his *sefirah, Tif'eret*.

140. **one should not separate...** One

"So the prayer of a poor person reaches the blessed Holy One before all prayers of the world, since it is written: *For He has not despised or disdained the suffering of the poor; He has not hidden His face from him; when he cried out to Him, He listened* (ibid. 22:25).

"Come and see: *Tefillah of the poor* is *tefillah* of the hand, for a poor person is bound to his poverty like one who has nothing at all of his own.[141]

"Alternatively, *Tefillah*—Moses; *of the poor*—David;[142] *when* יעטוף (*ya'atof*), *he covers himself*—when the moon conceals Herself and the sun conceals Himself from Her.[143] *And pours out his complaint before YHVH*—to unite with the sun.[144]

"Come and see: The prayer of all human beings is prayer, but the prayer of a poor person is a prayer that rises before the blessed Holy One,[145] breaking through gates and doors, penetrating to be received in His presence, as is written: *When he cries out to Me, I will listen, for I am compassionate* (Exodus 22:26), and similarly: *I will surely hear his cry* (ibid., 22). *And pours out his complaint before YHVH*—like one protesting the judgments of the blessed Holy One."[146]

Rabbi El'azar said, "Prayers of the righteous delight Assembly of Israel,[147] [169a] 21

should not pause or speak between putting on the two phylacteries, since doing so interrupts the union between *Shekhinah* and *Tif'eret*.

See BT *Menaḥot* 36a; *Zohar* 1:205b; Ta-Shma, *Ha-Nigleh she-ba-Nistar*, 73–79. According to *Shemot Rabbah* 21:4, the similarity in phrasing between *a prayer of the poor* and *a prayer of Moses* implies "that all are equal in prayer before the Omnipresent."

141. **like one who has nothing at all of his own** Like *Shekhinah*, who has nothing of Her own, only what She receives from above.

The expression derives from a medieval astronomic description of the moon. See Radak on Genesis 1:16; Moses de León, *Shushan Edut*, 338; idem, *Sod Eser Sefirot Belimah*, 381; *Zohar* 1:20a, 31a, 132b, 170a, 181a, 238a; 2:43a, 142a, 218b.

142. ***Tefillah*—Moses; *of the poor*—David** Moses symbolizes *Tif'eret*; David, *Shekhinah*.

143. ***when* יעטוף (*ya'atof*), *he covers himself*...** This is the continuation of Psalms 102:1, rendered earlier as "when he is faint." The root עטף (*atf*) means "cover" as well as "be faint." Here the "covering" refers to a cosmic crisis triggered by human immorality, which causes *Shekhinah* (symbolized by the moon) to conceal Herself from the world. Unadorned with human righteousness, She cannot approach *Tif'eret* (symbolized by the sun), and He, in turn, hides from Her; thus their union is disrupted.

144. ***And pours out his complaint before YHVH*—to unite with the sun** *Shekhinah* yearns for reunion.

145. **prayer of a poor person...** See *Zohar* 2:61a, 86b.

146. **like one protesting the judgments of the blessed Holy One** See *Vayiqra Rabbah* 34:16: "Rabbi Yehudah son of Rabbi Simon said, 'A poor person sits and protests: "How am I any different from so-and-so? Yet he sits at home, while I sit here! He sleeps in his bed, while I sleep on the ground!"'"

147. **Assembly of Israel** כנסת ישראל (*Keneset yisra'el*). In rabbinic literature this phrase denotes the people of Israel. The midrash on the Song of Songs describes the love affair between the maiden (the earthly community of Israel) and her lover (the Holy One, blessed be He). In the *Zohar*, *keneset*

crowning Her in the presence of the blessed Holy One.[148] So He yearns for their prayers when they are in need, since they know how to propitiate their Lord.[149] What is written concerning Jacob? *God of my father Abraham and God of my father Isaac!*... (Genesis 32:10). He interwove a crowning, clustered wreath fittingly: *God of my father Abraham*—on the right; *God of my father Isaac*—on the left. *YHVH, who said to me* (ibid.)—here he made coronation dependent on his site, between them. *'Return to your land, to your birthplace, and I will deal well with you'* (ibid.).[150]

"*I am unworthy of all the kindness* (ibid., 11).[151] What does this have to do with that?[152] Jacob was really saying, 'You promised to deal well with me, but I know that all Your actions are conditional.[153] Now look, I possess no merit: *I am unworthy of all the kindness and faithfulness You have shown.* Everything You have done for me until today wasn't because of my own virtue, but rather because of You: All that kindness and faithfulness derived from You! For look, when I first crossed, fleeing from Esau, I crossed this river all alone; yet You showed me kindness and faithfulness, and now I am crossing with two camps!'—the two camps he divided.[154]

"Up to here, arraying the praise of his Lord; from here on, he sought what he needed—demonstrating to all inhabitants of the world that one should first array the praise of his Lord and then present his request.[155] For this is how

yisra'el can refer to the earthly community but also (often primarily) to *Shekhinah*, the divine feminine counterpart of the people, the aspect of God most intimately connected with them. The lovers in the Song of Songs are pictured as the divine couple, *Tif'eret* and *Shekhinah*.

148. **crowning Her in the presence of the blessed Holy One** Crowning *Shekhinah* in the presence of *Tif'eret*. On coronation by prayer, see above, pp. 13–14 and n. 96.

149. **He yearns for their prayers when they are in need...** See *Bereshit Rabbah* 45:4; *Shir ha-Shirim Rabbah* on 2:14; *Qohelet Rabbah* on 9:7; *Shemot Rabbah* 21:5; BT *Yevamot* 64a; *Ḥullin* 60b; *Zohar* 1:137a, 167b.

On the phrase "to propitiate their Lord," see *Midrash Tanna'im*, Deuteronomy 33:6; *Vayiqra Rabbah* 5:8; 29:4; *Pesiqta de-Rav Kahana* 23:4; *Devarim Rabbah* 9:2; *Midrash Tehillim* 19:17; 81:4; *Zohar* 1:41a.

150. **He interwove... right... left... between them...** Jacob crowned *Shekhinah* with the triad of *Ḥesed*, *Gevurah*, and *Tif'eret*, symbolized respectively by Abraham, Isaac, and Jacob himself. *Shekhinah* is often referred to as *land*.

151. ***I am unworthy of all the kindness*** The verse continues: *and faithfulness that You have shown Your servant, for with my staff I crossed this Jordan, and now I have become two camps.*

152. **What does this have to do with that?** After recalling God's promise, *I will deal well with you*, why would Jacob emphasize his lack of merit by saying, *I am unworthy of all the kindness*?

153. **all Your actions are conditional** Depending on human worthiness. See *Mekhilta, Amaleq (Beshallaḥ)* 2; BT *Berakhot* 4a.

154. **the two camps he divided** See Genesis 32:8.

155. **one should first array the praise of his Lord...** See BT *Berakhot* 32a: "R. Simlai

Jacob acted: first arraying the praise of his Lord, then asking for what he needed, as is written: *O save me from the hand of my brother*... (ibid., 12).[156]

"From here we learn that one who prays should clarify his words fittingly. '*O save me.* Now, if You say that You've already saved me from Laban, *from the hand of my brother.* And if You say that other, unidentified relatives are also called "brothers,"[157] *from the hand of Esau.*' Why? To clarify the word fittingly. 'And if You ask why am I in need, *for I fear him, lest he come and strike me*...'[158] So that the word will be known above; clarified, not concealed.

"*And You Yourself said, 'I will surely deal well with you*...' (ibid., 13).[159] *And You Yourself said.* What is ואתה (*ve-Attah*), *and You*? As is said: *Ve-Attah, And You, enliven them all* (Nehemiah 9:6).[160] Here too, *ve-Attah, and You.*

"Come and see: King David said, *May the words of my mouth be acceptable*—words stated explicitly; *and the meditation of my heart* (Psalms 19:15)[161]—concealed words, inexpressible, *meditation* within the heart. So there must be a word expressed by the mouth and a word dependent on the heart, all a mystery: one corresponding to one rung, one corresponding to a supernal rung. The expressed word corresponds to the rung that must be expressed; the one dependent on the heart corresponds to a more inward rung, though all is as one.[162] So, *May the words of my mouth and the meditation of my heart be acceptable to You.* 23

expounded, 'One should always array the praise of the blessed Holy One and then pray.'"

Elsewhere the precedence of praise or petitionary prayer is debated, both sides citing the opening verse of Psalm 102, quoted above (page 20) by Rabbi Yose: *A prayer of the poor when he is faint and pours out his complaint before YHVH.* See JT *Berakhot* 4:4, 8b; BT *Avodah Zarah* 7b; *Midrash Tehillim* 102:2.

156. ***O save me from the hand of my brother*** The verse continues: *from the hand of Esau! For I fear him, lest he come and strike me, mother with children.*

157. **other, unidentified relatives are also called "brothers"** See, for example, Genesis 13:8; 14:14; and concerning Jacob himself, 29:12, 15.

158. ***for I fear him, lest he come and strike me*...** The verse continues: *mother with children.*

159. ***And You Yourself said, 'I will surely deal well with you*...** The quotation continues: *and will make your seed like the sand of the sea, too numerous to count.'*

160. ***Ve-Attah, And You, enliven them all*** Referring to *Shekhinah* (the Divine Presence, addressed directly as *You*), or to *Shekhinah* united with Her partner, *Tif'eret* (who is symbolized by the prefixed letter ו (*vav*), *and.*

See *Zohar* 1:15b, 37a; 2:70a (*RR*), 138b, 154b, 158b, 179b.

161. ***May the words of my mouth*...** The verse reads: *May the words of my mouth and the meditation of my heart be acceptable to You, YHVH, my rock and my redeemer.*

162. **corresponding to one rung... corresponding to a supernal rung...** Words that can be expressed correspond to *Shekhinah*, who is more revealed, whereas inexpressible thoughts correspond to *Tif'eret*, more inward and concealed.

"Jacob spoke similarly, first stating a word explicitly, fittingly;[163] then concealing a word dependent on meditation of the heart, as is written: *I will make your seed like the sand of the sea, too numerous to count* (Genesis, ibid.)—here a word dependent on the heart, which should not be expressed.[164] So it must be, as we have said, to consummate union perfectly, fittingly.[165]

"Happy are Israel, who know how to array the praise of their Lord fittingly and convey their requests! Therefore it is written: *He said to me, 'You are My servant, Israel, in whom I glory'* (Isaiah 49:3)."[166]

Jacob was left alone (Genesis 32:25).[167]

Rabbi Ḥiyya opened, "*No evil will befall you, no plague come near your tent* (Psalms 91:10). Come and see: When the blessed Holy One created the world, He made on every single day [169b] its own befitting work, as has been established. On the fourth day He made lights, and the moon was created defectively, a light that diminished itself. Since She is מארת (*me'orot*), *lights* (ibid. 1:14), lacking ו (*vav*), space was pro-
24 vided for all spirits, demons, and whirlwinds to prevail—all spirits of defilement ruling, roaming the world seductively.[168] They were assigned to ruins,

163. **first stating a word explicitly, fittingly** Jacob said: *O save me from the hand of my brother, from the hand of Esau! For I fear him, lest he come and strike me, mother with children.* The next verse opens: *And You Yourself said*, referring to *Shekhinah*, more revealed.

164. ***too numerous to count*... which should not be expressed** The innumerable, inexpressible nature of the blessing corresponds to the concealed rung, *Tif'eret*.

165. **to consummate union perfectly, fittingly** So that human prayer may succeed in uniting the divine female and male intimately.

166. ***You are My servant, Israel, in whom I glory*** According to Rabbi El'azar, the verse is apparently spoken by *Shekhinah*, and Her closing word, אתפאר (*etpa'ar*), *I glory*, alludes to *Tif'eret*, with whom She is united by human contemplative prayer.

167. ***Jacob was left alone*** The verse continues: *and a man wrestled with him until the rising of dawn.*

168. **On the fourth day... the moon was created defectively...** On the fourth day of Creation, God created the sun, moon, and stars. See BT *Ḥullin* 60b: "Rabbi Shim'on son of Pazzi pointed out a contradiction. 'It is written: *God made the two great lights* (Genesis 1:16), and it is written: *the greater light... and the lesser light* (ibid.). The moon said before the blessed Holy One, "Master of the Universe! Can two kings possibly wear one crown?" He answered, "Go, diminish yourself!"...'"

The diminishment of the moon is here linked with the defective spelling of the word מארת (*me'orot*), *lights* (ibid., 14), written without *vavs*, the vowel letters. This deficient spelling signifies a lack in *Shekhinah* (symbolized by the moon) and the disruption of Her union with *Tif'eret* (symbolized by *vav*). This lack creates the potential for evil or "curse": מארה (*me'erah*).

See BT *Pesaḥim* 112b: "One should not go out alone at night, neither on the eve of Wednesday [fourth day of the week] nor on the eve of Sabbath, because Agrat daughter of Maḥalat [Queen of Demons] goes out

unyielding fields, desolate wilderness—all from the side of impure spirit, as has been said.[169] For this impure spirit deriving from the tortuous serpent is really impure, empowered in the world to seduce human beings.[170] So the evil impulse prevails in the world, assigned to human beings, shadowing them, approaching them deceitfully with ploys to seduce them from the ways of the blessed Holy One. Just as he seduced Adam, inflicting death upon the entire world, so he seduces human beings, causing them to defile themselves.

"Whoever comes to defile himself attracts that impure spirit, which abides within him, clings to him. How many lie waiting to defile him! He becomes defiled both in this world and in that world, as has been said.[171] But when a person comes to purify himself, that impure spirit is overturned before him, unable to dominate him.[172] Then is written: *No evil will befall you, no plague come near your tent.*"

Rabbi Yose said, "*No evil will befall you*—Lilith;[173] *no plague come near your tent*—other demons, as has been established and explained."

Rabbi El'azar said, "We have already said that one should not go out alone at 25
night, especially at the time when the moon was created defectively, as has been established, for then the impure spirit prevails,[174] namely *evil*. Who is *evil*? The evil serpent, while *plague* is he who rides the serpent.[175] *Evil* and *plague* are as

together with 180,000 angels of destruction, each empowered to wreak destruction independently."

See Proverbs 3:33; JT *Ta'anit* 4:4, 68b; *Pesiqta de-Rav Kahana* 5:1; *Soferim* 17:4; Rashi on Genesis 1:14; *Zohar* 1:1a, 12a, 19b, 33b, 146a, 166a; 2:167b, 205a; 3:45a, 234a; *ZH* 69b–c (*ShS*); *Minḥat Shai* on Genesis 1:14.

169. **ruins, unyielding fields, desolate wilderness...** On ruins as an abode of demons, see BT *Berakhot* 3a. On their abode in the wilderness, see *Zohar* 1:14b, 126a, 178b; 2:157a, 184a, 236b–237a; 3:63b. Cf. BT *Pesaḥim* 112b.

170. **empowered in the world to seduce human beings** Testing them.

171. **Whoever comes to defile himself...** See BT *Shabbat* 104a: "Resh Lakish said, '...If one comes to defile himself, he is provided an opening; if one comes to purify himself, he is assisted.'"

Cf. *Yoma* 39a: "Our Rabbis taught: '*Do not defile yourselves with them, and thus become defiled* (Leviticus 11:43). If one defiles himself slightly, he is defiled greatly; below, he is defiled from above; in this world, he is defiled in the world to come.'"

See *Zohar* 1:53b–54a, 125b, 129b, 198b; 2:50a; 3:47a; and BT *Makkot* 10b: "Rabbah son of Bar Ḥana said in the name of Rabbi Huna (some say, Rabbi Huna said in the name of Rabbi El'azar), 'From the Torah, the Prophets, and the Writings, it can be demonstrated that one is led on the path one wishes to take.'"

172. **that impure spirit is overturned...** See above, page 1.

173. **Lilith** The demonic feminine.

174. **one should not go out alone at night...** Especially on the eve of Wednesday. See BT *Pesaḥim* 112b, quoted above, note 168. Cf. BT *Ḥullin* 91a.

175. **The evil serpent...he who rides the serpent** The serpent, Lilith, is ridden by Samael. See *Pirqei de-Rabbi Eli'ezer* 13: "Samael...took his band and descended and saw all the creatures created by the blessed Holy One. He determined that the most

one, although we have learned that *plague* refers to *plagues of* בני אדם (benei adam)—those issuing from Adam. For during all those years that Adam didn't approach his wife, impure spirits came and were inflamed by him, engendering from him, and these are called *plagues of the children of Adam.*[176]

"It has been said that when a man is dreaming—not in control of his body, his body lulled—an impure spirit comes and settles upon him.[177] Sometimes impure female spirits approach him, drawing him toward them, becoming inflamed by him, later bearing spirits and demons, *plagues of* benei adam, *the children of man,*[178] who sometimes resemble human beings, though without hair on their heads.[179]

"One must thoroughly protect himself from them, following paths of Torah, not defiling himself with them. For everyone who sleeps in bed at night tastes a taste of death, his soul departing from him.[180] Since body is left without holy

cunningly evil was the serpent, as is said: *Now, the serpent was slier than any creature of the field that* YHVH Elohim *had made.* He [the serpent] looked like a camel, and he [Samael] mounted and rode him."

See *Zohar* 1:35b, 64a, 137b, 146a, 148a (*ST*), 153a, 160b; 2:236b.

176. ***plagues of* בני אדם (*benei adam*)—those issuing from Adam...** See 2 Samuel 7:14: *I will chastise him with a human rod, with blows of* בני אדם (benei adam). In this verse, benei adam means "human beings," but Rabbi El'azar follows the Midrash in reading the phrase hyperliterally: *children of Adam*—his direct offspring.

See *Tanḥuma* (Buber), *Bereshit* 26: "Rabbi Simon said, 'For 130 years Adam separated from his wife, Eve, for after Cain was killed, Adam said, "Why should I engender children if they become cursed?" What did he do?... Female spirits approached him and heated themselves from him. As the blessed Holy One said to David, "... *When he* [Solomon] *does wrong, I will chastise him with a human rod, with blows of* בני אדם (benei adam)" (2 Samuel 7:14)..., namely, the demons.'"

See *Bereshit Rabbah* 20:11: "Rabbi Simon said, 'Throughout all 130 years that Adam separated himself from Eve, male spirits heated themselves from her and she gave birth, while female spirits heated themselves from Adam and gave birth, as is written: *When he does wrong, I will chastise him with a human rod, with blows of* בני אדם (benei adam), namely, children of Adam.'"

See BT *Eruvin* 18b; *Zohar* 1:19b, 34b, 54a–55a; 2:231b, 3:76b; Trachtenberg, *Jewish Magic and Superstition,* 51.

177. **an impure spirit comes and settles upon him** During sleep, the soul ascends and an impure spirit fills the vacuum.

See below; BT *Shabbat* 109a; *Ḥullin* 107b; *Zohar* 1:10b, 53b, 184b; 3:67a; Moses de León, *Orḥot Ḥayyim,* par. 10.

178. **impure female spirits approach him...** Succubae desiring to be impregnated by human semen. See *Zohar* 1:9b, 19b, 47b, 54b; 2:130a; Trachtenberg, *Jewish Magic and Superstition,* 51–54.

179. **without hair on their heads** According to *Tanḥuma* (Buber), *Bo* 16, "Demons have no hair."

See *Rut Rabbah* 6:1; *Zohar* 1:54b; Trachtenberg, *Jewish Magic and Superstition* 275–76, n. 18; Ginzberg, *Legends,* 6:192, n. 58. Cf. *Zohar* 3:48b: "Holiness depends on the hair," based on the description of the Nazirite in Numbers 6:5: *He shall be holy, letting the locks of the hair on his head grow untrimmed.*

180. **everyone who sleeps in bed at night**

soul, impure spirit, who is poised, spreads upon him and he is defiled. We have established that one should not pass his hands over his eyes in the morning, since impure spirit has settled upon them . . . , as has been explained.[181]

"Come and see: Even though Jacob was beloved by the blessed Holy One, because he remained alone an alien spirit poised to couple with him."[182]

Rabbi Shim'on said, "Come and see what is written concerning Balaam the wicked: *He went* שפי (*shefi*) (Numbers 23:3). What is *shefi*? Alone, as is said: שפיפון (*shefifon*), *a horned viper, on the path* (Genesis 49:17)—like a serpent moving alone, lurking on paths and trails.[183] So Balaam went alone. Why? To draw upon himself impure spirit. For whoever walks alone—even in town at certain times, and in certain places all the time[184]—is vulnerable. So one should not walk alone on the road, and in town one should not either, rather in a place where people are moving back and forth—even at night, since people are not around.[185] This is why *You must not leave his corpse on the tree overnight* (Deuteronomy 21:23), [170a] so as not to keep a spiritless body above ground at night.[186] Therefore that wicked Balaam went alone like a serpent, as they have established."

tastes a taste of death . . . Based on BT *Berakhot* 57b: "Sleep is one-sixtieth of death."

See *Zohar* 1:36a–b, 53b, 184b; 2:173a; 3:119a; Moses de León, *Sefer ha-Rimmon*, 52–53.

181. **one should not pass his hands over his eyes in the morning . . .** Before ritually washing the hands to remove the impure spirit. Otherwise the impure spirit infects the eyes and contaminates anything or any person that one sees.

See BT *Shabbat* 108b; Rashi, ad loc., s.v. *yad la-ayin; tiqqatsets; Kallah* 1:19; *Kallah Rabbati* 2:5; *Zohar* 1:184b; Moses de León, *Orḥot Ḥayyim*, par. 10.

182. **because he remained alone an alien spirit poised to couple . . .** See BT *Ḥullin* 91a: "[*Jacob was left alone,*] *and a man wrestled with him until the rising of dawn.* Rabbi Yitshak said, 'From here we learn that a disciple of the wise should not venture out alone at night.'"

"To couple" renders לאזדווגא (*le-izdavvaga*), which means primarily "to couple, join," but also "to join battle, attack."

183. **What is *shefi*? Alone . . . שפיפון (*shefifon*), *a horned viper* . . .** The rare biblical word שפי (*shefi*) is usually understood to mean either "alone" (see *Targum Onqelos*, Rashi, *Leqaḥ Tov, Midrash Aggadah*, ad loc.) or "bare height." It is linked with שפיפון (*shefifon*), "horned viper," in BT *Sotah* 10a; *Leqaḥ Tov* and *Midrash Aggadah*, Numbers 23:3; *Zohar* 1:243b; 3:194b.

On the serpent's solitary movement, see *Bereshit Rabbah* 99:11.

184. **even in town at certain times, and in certain places all the time** At night even in town, and at all times in places frequented by demonic spirits, such as those mentioned above: "ruins, unyielding fields, desolate wilderness."

185. **even at night . . .** When it's difficult not to walk alone and to remain safely near other people.

186. ***You must not leave his corpse . . . overnight . . .*** The verse continues: *rather, be sure to bury him that same day, for a hanged body is an offense to God. You must not defile the land that YHVH your God is giving you as an inheritance.* If a criminal is executed and then hung and exposed on a tree, the Torah prohibits extending the exposure past sunset;

ויאבק איש (*Va-ye'aveq ish*), *And a man wrestled, with him* (Genesis 32:25).[187] What does this mean: *va-ye'aveq*, *and he wrestled*?

Rabbi Shim'on said, "From אבק (*avaq*), ash powder, incidental to עפר (*afar*), dust.[188] What is the difference between them? Ash, residue of fire, never generating fruit; dust, yielding all fruit, totality of above and below."[189]

Rabbi Yehudah said, "If so, what is the meaning of: *He raises the poor from the dust* (1 Samuel 2:8)?"

He replied, "According to its literal sense, but in this manner:[190] *He raises the poor from the dust,* since it possesses nothing at all of its own,[191] and from that dust issues *the poor,* who possesses nothing. Yet from that dust issue all fruit and goodness of the world; through it are enacted all acts of the world,[192] as is written: *All comes from the dust* (Ecclesiastes 3:20).[193] And we have learned: '*All comes from the dust,* even the globe of the sun.'[194]

"But ash never generates fruit or vegetation, so *va-ye'aveq, and he wrestled,* arriving with that *avaq*, ash, riding upon it, to contest against Jacob.[195]

the body must be buried the same day. Based on this verse, the Mishnah teaches that all corpses should normally be buried on the day of death. See M *Sanhedrin* 6:5; BT *Sanhedrin* 46a–b.

Here, Rabbi Shim'on's point is that a spiritless corpse must be immediately buried because it is vulnerable to the impure spirit, which would not only contaminate the corpse but also *defile the land.* See *Zohar* 3:88b, 143b–144a (*IR*).

187. ***a man wrestled with him*** The verse reads: *Jacob was left alone, and a man wrestled with him until the rising of dawn.*

188. **From אבק (*avaq*), ash powder, incidental to עפר (*afar*), dust** The word *avaq* means "dust, powder," but here Rabbi Shim'on understands it as "ash, ash powder," in contrast to *afar*, "dust" of the earth.

For other links between *avaq* ("dust") and *va-ye'aveq* (*and he wrestled,* perhaps meaning "got dusty, kicked up dust"), see *Bereshit Rabbah* 77:3; *Midrash Aggadah,* Rashi, Ibn Ezra, Radak, and Naḥmanides on Genesis 32:25; cf. BT *Ḥullin* 91a.

189. **Ash... never generating fruit; dust, yielding all fruit...** Ash symbolizes Lilith, the demonic feminine, who is barren (fruitless), while dust symbolizes *Shekhinah,* who receives all emanation above and engenders all life below. See *Zohar* 2:266b.

On *Shekhinah* as dust, see *Zohar* 1:49a, 249b–250a; 2:23b–24b; 3:34b; Moses de León, *Shushan Edut,* 344–45; idem, *Sefer ha-Rimmon,* 171; idem, *Sheqel ha-Qodesh,* 57–58, 62 (70–71, 77–78).

190. **According to its literal sense, but in this manner** The verse can be read literally, but simultaneously it conveys a deeper meaning.

191. **it possesses nothing at all of its own** *Shekhinah,* the cosmic dust, possesses only what She receives from the higher *sefirot.* See above, note 141.

192. **through it are enacted all acts of the world** By conveying the flow of emanation, *Shekhinah* conducts and animates the world.

193. ***All comes from the dust*** The verse continues: *and all returns to the dust.*

194. ***All comes from the dust,* even the globe of the sun** See *Bereshit Rabbah* 12:11 and *Qohelet Rabbah* on 3:20 (both in the name of Rabbi Naḥman); *Zohar* 3:34b, 125a, 181a.

195. **arriving with that *avaq*, ash, riding upon it...** Jacob's wrestling opponent was

"*Until the rising of dawn* (Genesis, ibid.),[196] when his dominion passed away and he weakened,[197] as will be in the time to come. For now exile resembles night—it is night![198]—and that ash rules over Israel, who lie in alien dust,[199] until morning rises and day brightens. Then Israel will prevail; to them will be granted the kingdom, since they are holy ones of the Most High, as is said: *Kingdom, dominion, and grandeur of the kingdoms under the whole Heaven will be given to the people of the holy ones of the Most High*... (Daniel 7:27).[200]

He said, "Let me go, for dawn has risen!" (Genesis 32:27).[201]

Rabbi Yehudah opened, "*Who is this looking forth like the dawn, fair as the moon, bright as the sun*...? (Song of Songs 6:10).[202] This verse has been established and explained,[203] but *Who is this looking forth?*—Israel, when the blessed Holy One will raise them, bringing them out of exile. He will then open for them a tiny crack of light, then another opening, wider, until the blessed Holy One opens for them supernal gates facing the four directions of the world.[204]

"So with all the blessed Holy One does for Israel and for the righteous among them—always so, never all at once. This can be compared to a person thrown into darkness, dwelling in darkness constantly. When they want to illumine him, they must open the light to him like the eye of a needle, then wider, always gradually, until he is illumined with all the light fittingly.[205]

"Similarly with Israel, as is said: *Little by little I will drive them out before you* (Exodus 23:30).[206] And so with one who is being cured: not all at once, but little by little, until he is fortified.

the demonic Samael, Esau's heavenly prince, who came riding on Lilith.

See *Tanḥuma, Vayishlaḥ* 8; *Bereshit Rabbah* 77:3; *Zohar* 1:146a; and *Pirqei de-Rabbi Eli'ezer* 13, quoted above, note 175.

196. ***until the rising of dawn*** The verse reads: *Jacob was left alone, and a man wrestled with him until the rising of dawn.*

197. **when his dominion passed away and he weakened** As day broke, the dominion of Samael, associated with night, vanished.

198. **exile resembles night—it is night** See *Shir ha-Shirim Rabbah* on 3:1.

199. **alien dust** In foreign exile, under the sway of the demonic powers. See *Zohar* 1:80a (*ST*); 2:266b.

200. ***Kingdom, dominion, and grandeur...*** The verse concludes: *Their kingdom will be an everlasting kingdom, and all dominions will serve and obey them.*

201. ***He said, "Let me go, for dawn has risen!"*** The verse continues: *He replied, "I will not let you go unless you bless me."*

202. ***fair as the moon, bright as the sun...*** The verse continues: *awesome as bannered hosts?*

203. **This verse has been established and explained** See *Shir ha-Shirim Rabbah* on 6:10; *Shemot Rabbah* 15:6; *Zohar* 2:126b.

204. **He will then open for them a tiny crack of light...** On the gradual manifestation of the light of redemption, see JT *Berakhot* 1:1, 2c; *Shir ha-Shirim Rabbah* on 6:10; *Tanḥuma, Devarim* 1; *Midrash Tehillim* 18:36.

205. **a person...dwelling in darkness constantly...** See Moses de León, *Shushan Edut*, 351; idem, *Mishkan ha-Edut*, 59b.

206. ***Little by little I will drive them out before you*** The verse continues: *until you become fruitful and possess the land.*

"But with Esau, not so![207] Rather, he is illumined all at once and deprived little by little, until Israel are fortified and eliminate him entirely from this world and from the world that is coming. Since he blazed all at once, he is annihilated completely, whereas Israel's light increases little by little until they are invigorated and the blessed Holy One illumines them forever. Everyone asks, *Who is this looking forth like the dawn?*—at first a subtle glow; then *fair as the moon,* then *bright as the sun,* then *awesome as bannered hosts* (Song of Songs, ibid.)—beaming powerfully, intensely, fittingly.

"Come and see: When day is still dark and concealed, light advances little by little until spreading fittingly. For when the blessed Holy One will arouse to illumine Assembly of Israel, He will glow at first *like the dawn,* which is black;[208] then *fair as the moon,* then *bright as the sun,* then *awesome as bannered hosts,* as has been said. [170b]

"Come and see: When morning rises—because it is not written *for dawn has come,* but rather *has risen* (Genesis 32:27),[209] since when *dawn has come,* that prince[210] is empowered and strikes Jacob, because that hour is black, its potency empowering Esau. Once that blackness of dawn rises, light appears and Jacob is empowered, for then is his time to shine.

"What is written? *The sun rose upon him as he passed Penuel, and he was limping on his hip* (ibid., 32). *The sun rose upon him,* for that was the time to shine. *And he was limping on his hip:* intimating that although Israel remain in exile—suffering pain, trouble, and countless evils—daylight will yet shine upon them, bringing them relief. Then they will reflect on the pain in their bones from the countless evils and troubles they have suffered, and they will be amazed! So, *The sun rose upon him*—of that time of relief; then, *and he was limping on his hip*—feeling the pain and suffering of what had passed. Once the blackness of dawn had risen, he was empowered and gripped him, for his strength had faded,[211] since his dominion prevails only at night, while Jacob's prevails by day. So he said, '*Let me go, for dawn has risen!* Now I am in your power!' This has been said and established."[212]

207. **But with Esau, not so** In medieval rabbinic literature, Esau often symbolizes Christianity.

208. ***like the dawn,* which is black** The darkness preceding dawn. Rabbi Yehudah is playing on שחר (*shaḥar*), "dawn," and שחור (*shaḥor*), "black."

209. ***has risen*** The full clause reads: *Let me go, for dawn has risen!*

210. **that prince** Samael, Esau's heavenly prince, who wrestled with Jacob. See *Tanḥuma, Vayishlaḥ* 8; *Bereshit Rabbah* 77:3; *Zohar* 1:146a, 166a, 170a.

211. **he was empowered and gripped him, for his strength had faded** Jacob was empowered and gripped Samael, his wrestling partner, whose strength had faded.

212. **Now I am in your power...** See *Shir ha-Shirim Rabbah* on 3:6.

Therefore [to this day] the Children of Israel do not eat the sinew of the thigh (Genesis 32:33).[213]

Rabbi Ḥiyya said, "If this power point of Jacob had not been weakened, he would have withstood him; Esau's power would have been broken above and below."[214]

Rabbi Shim'on opened, "*I fell upon my face, and I heard the one speaking to me* (Ezekiel 1:28).[215] This verse has been discussed, but come and see! For look at what is written: *Never again did there arise in Israel a prophet like Moses* (Deuteronomy 34:10)![216] What distinguishes Moses from other prophets? Moses gazed into a speculum that shines, while other prophets gazed only into a speculum [171a] that does not shine.[217] Moses heard while standing on his feet,[218] his potency vitalized, so he knew the word clearly,[219] as is written: *in vision, not in riddles* (Numbers 12:8). Other prophets fell upon their faces, their potency weakened, so they could not comprehend the clarity of the word. Who

213. ***Therefore [to this day]...*** The full verse reads: *Therefore to this day the Children of Israel do not eat the sinew of the thigh that is by the hip socket, for he touched Jacob's hip socket at the sinew of the thigh.* This is the sciatic nerve.

I have omitted the passage that follows in the printed editions of the *Zohar* (170b, lines 14–34, in Margaliot's edition), which does not appear in the manuscripts and is essentially an Aramaic paraphrase of a passage from Joseph of Hamadan's *Sefer Ta'amei ha-Mitsvot.* See Galante; *OL;* Altmann, "Li-Sh'elat Ba'aluto," 275; Idel, "Peirush Eser Sefirot," 80–82; idem, "Olam ha-Mal'akhim," 51–52; Liebes, *Studies in the Zohar,* 194–95, n. 11.

214. **Esau's power would have been broken...** Demonic forces would have been powerless both in the supernal realm and against Israel on earth.

215. ***I fell upon my face...*** The complete verse reads: *Like the appearance of the bow in the cloud on a rainy day, so was the appearance of the radiance all around—the appearance of the semblance of the glory of YHVH. When I saw, I fell upon my face, and I heard the voice of someone speaking.* Rabbi Shim'on concludes his citation with the wording of a nearby verse (2:2): *and I heard the one speaking to me.*

216. ***Never again did there arise in Israel a prophet like Moses*** The verse continues: *whom YHVH knew face-to-face.*

217. **speculum...** אספקלריא (*Ispaqlarya*), deriving from Greek, *speklon,* "mirror, window-pane," and Latin, *speculum,* "mirror."

See BT *Yevamot* 49b: "All the prophets gazed through an opaque glass ["an *ispaqlarya* that does not shine"], while Moses our teacher gazed through a translucent glass ["an *ispaqlarya* that shines"]." See *Vayiqra Rabbah* 1:14; and cf. 1 Corinthians 13:12: "For now we see through a glass darkly, but then face-to-face."

In the *Zohar, Tif'eret* is the *ispaqlarya* that shines, while *Shekhinah* is the *ispaqlarya* that does not shine on its own but rather reflects the other *sefirot.*

218. **while standing on his feet** See *Sifrei,* Deuteronomy 357; Maimonides, *Mishneh Torah, Hilkhot Yesodei ha-Torah* 7:6; idem, *Commentary on the Mishnah, Sanhedrin* 10:1; *Zohar* 3:268b.

219. **he knew the word clearly** See *Midrash Tehillim* 90:4.

caused this? As is written: *for he touched Jacob's hip socket... and he was limping on his hip* (Genesis, ibid., 33, 32).[220]

"None of those prophets could comprehend what the blessed Holy One intends to do to Esau except for Obadiah, who was a convert, deriving from the side of Esau.[221] He comprehended Esau firmly, his potency unweakened, whereas the power of all those other prophets faded and they could not endure, receiving the word clearly, fittingly. Why? Because *he touched Jacob's hip socket at the sinew of the thigh,* drawing all the power of the thigh; so its power was broken and he was left *limping on his hip.* Therefore it must not be consumed at all.[222] For all prophets of the world could only grasp until the arrival of King Messiah; from here on they could neither grasp nor comprehend.[223]

"Come and see: The prophets did not maintain their potency fittingly, and now, one who studies Torah is unsupported, no one casting profits into his bag, fortifying him.[224] So Torah is forgotten in every generation, her power weak-

220. ***for he touched Jacob's hip socket... and he was limping on his hip*** The two verses read: *The sun rose upon him as he passed Penuel, and he was limping on his hip. Therefore to this day the Children of Israel do not eat the sinew of the thigh that is by the hip socket, for he touched Jacob's hip socket at the sinew of the thigh.*

Here, Rabbi Shim'on's point is that by injuring Jacob's thigh, Samael weakened the *sefirot* of *Netsaḥ* and *Hod,* which correspond to the right and left legs, respectively; since these two *sefirot* are the source of prophecy, nearly all future prophets could not comprehend clearly and fell. Since Moses was linked directly with the higher *sefirah* of *Tif'eret,* his prophetic potency was unaffected.

See *Zohar* 1:21b; 2:111b; Moses de León, *Sheqel ha-Qodesh,* 11 (13–14).

221. **except for Obadiah, who was a convert...** The book of Obadiah consists of only one chapter, which describes the guilt of Edom in connection with the fall of Jerusalem in 586 B.C.E. and foretells Edom's future downfall in *the day of YHVH* (Obadiah 1:15). According to a tradition in the name of Rabbi Me'ir (BT *Sanhedrin* 39b), Obadiah was an Edomite convert. According to Genesis 36:1, Edom is descended from Esau.

222. **it must not be consumed at all** This portion of the thigh of any animal must not be eaten.

223. **could only grasp until the arrival of King Messiah...** Since Samael had injured Jacob's thigh, which symbolizes the source of prophecy, prophetic vision was limited. Obadiah's vision of Edom's ultimate punishment was an exception.

Cf. BT *Berakhot* 34b: "Rabbi Ḥiyya son of Abba said in the name of Rabbi Yoḥanan, 'All the prophets prophesied only concerning the days of the Messiah, but as for the world that is coming, *No eye has seen, O God, but You,* [*what You will do for one who awaits You*] (Isaiah 64:3).'"

224. **now, one who studies Torah is unsupported...** The weakening of *Netsaḥ* and *Hod* (the two sefirotic legs and pillars) also impairs Torah (symbolizing *Tif'eret,* the torso of the sefirotic body). Consequently, those devoted to Torah suffer from a lack of support.

See BT *Pesaḥim* 53b; *Zohar* 1:8a. On the Zoharic critique of the wealthy and their lack of support for those engaged in the study of Torah, see Baer, *History,* 1:261–77; Tishby, *Wisdom of the Zohar,* 3:1438–47.

ened every day, since those engaged in her have nothing to rely on, while the wicked kingdom grows stronger every day.[225]

"Come and see the consequence of sin: Since no one supports Torah fittingly, the one with no legs or feet to stand upon is supported, fortified!"[226]

He opened, saying, "*YHVH Elohim said to the serpent, 'Because you have done this, cursed are you among all animals and among all beasts of the field. Upon your belly shall you go* (ibid. 3:14).[227] What is the meaning of *upon your belly shall you go*? His supports were broken and cut off, so he had nothing to stand on[228]—but Israel, unwilling to support Torah, provides him with supports and legs to stand fortified.

"Come and see how tortuously and cunningly the serpent-rider[229] schemed against Jacob that night! For he knew what is written: *The voice is the voice of Jacob*—and if Jacob's voice is interrupted, then *the hands are the hands of Esau* (ibid. 27:22).[230] So he looked in every direction, trying to harm Jacob and interrupt his voice, but he found him totally invulnerable: arms powerful on
this side and that, torso fortified between them, Torah completely fortified.[231] 33
When *he saw that he could not prevail against him* (ibid. 32:26), what did he do? Immediately, *he touched the socket of his thigh* (ibid.), cunningly—thinking 'Once the supports of Torah are broken, Torah will be powerless;[232] then their

225. **wicked kingdom...** The demonic power and its earthly embodiment: the Gentile oppressors of Israel.

In rabbinic literature the "wicked kingdom" refers to the Roman empire. See *Bereshit Rabbah* 2:4; BT *Berakhot* 61b; *Zohar* 2:8a, 134a–b, 184a, 204b, 240a; Moses de León, *Sod Eser Sefirot Belimah*, 384.

226. **the one with no legs or feet to stand upon...** The demonic serpent, as explained below. Falsehood is described as "having no legs" in *Alfa Beita de-Rabbi Aqiva* (*Battei Midrashot*, 2:397).

227. ***Upon your belly shall you go*** The verse continues: *and dust shall you eat all the days of your life.*

228. **His supports were broken and cut off...** According to rabbinic tradition, the serpent originally walked on legs, which were cut off as punishment for his tempting Eve to eat from the Tree of Knowledge.

See *Baraita of Thirty-Two Rules* 1:12; *Targum Yerushalmi*, Genesis 3:14; *Bereshit Rabbah* 20:5; *Qohelet Rabbah* on 10:11; *Avot de-Rabbi Natan* B, 42; *Pirqei de-Rabbi Eli'ezer* 14.

229. **serpent-rider** Samael, who wrestled with Jacob. See above, note 175.

230. **if Jacob's voice is interrupted...** According to a midrashic reading, as long as *the voice of Jacob* is engaged in prayer and the study of Torah, *the hands of Esau* are powerless against him, but if *the voice of Jacob* falls silent or complains against God, *the hands of Esau* dominate him.

See *Bereshit Rabbah* 65:20; *Eikhah Rabbah, Petiḥta* 2; *Pesiqta de-Rav Kahana* 15:5; *Zohar* 1:151a.

231. **arms powerful... torso fortified... Torah completely fortified** Jacob symbolizes the sefirotic torso, *Tif'eret*, who is flanked and fortified by the two sefirotic arms, *Ḥesed* and *Gevurah*, symbolized by Abraham and Isaac. *Tif'eret* is also known as Written Torah.

232. **Once the supports of Torah are broken, Torah will be powerless** Once *Netsaḥ* and *Hod* are impaired, *Tif'eret* (Written Torah) will be weakened.

father's words will be fulfilled: *The voice is the voice of Jacob, and the hands are the hands of Esau.* And similarly: *When you grow restive, you will tear his yoke from your neck* (ibid. 27:40).'[233]

"Thereby he contended shrewdly against Jacob, for once the power of Torah is broken, Esau becomes stronger and stronger. When he sees that he cannot prevail against Torah, he weakens the power of those supporting her, since if supporters of Torah are not to be found, then *the voice* will not be *the voice of Jacob,* and *the hands* will be *the hands of Esau.*

"When Jacob saw this, as morning rose,[234] he gripped him and overpowered him, until he blessed him and confirmed those blessings.[235] What did he say? '*Your name will no longer be* יעקב (*Ya'aqov*), *Jacob, but* ישראל (*Yisra'el*), *Israel* (ibid. 32:29)—not *Ya'aqov, Jacob,* deceitful, but rather, majestic and powerful, for no one can prevail against you.'[236]

"Come and see: From this serpent[237] countless forces diffuse in every direction, appearing in the world, confronting human beings. So we must sustain the
34 existence of that *sinew of the thigh;* for although that serpent-rider approached it, it endures vitally among us, unbroken, and Jacob's potency increases in the world.[238] We must show *that you have striven with divine and human beings, and have prevailed* (ibid.). When he sees that place unbroken, uneaten, his potent power is broken [171b] and he cannot harm the children of Jacob.[239] So we must not let any creature of the world eat it; it must not be eaten at all!"[240]

233. ***When you grow restive, you will tear his yoke from your neck*** Part of Isaac's blessing to Esau.

234. **as morning rose** Terminating the nighttime dominion of demonic power.

235. **he gripped him and overpowered him, until he blessed him...** Jacob gripped Samael and overpowered him, until Samael blessed Jacob and confirmed the earlier blessings bestowed by Isaac.

On the confirmation of the blessings, see *Midrash Aggadah* and Rashi on Genesis 32:27; Rashi on Hosea 12:5; Naḥmanides on Genesis 32:30; *Zohar* 1:144a; 3:45a.

236. ***no longer...*** **יעקב (*Ya'aqov*), *Jacob, but* ישראל (*Yisra'el*), *Israel*...** The verse continues: *for* שרית (*sarita*), *you have striven, with divine and human beings, and have prevailed.* The name יעקב (*Ya'aqov*) is taken to mean "He grips the heel" or "He deceived (or usurped)." See Genesis 25:26; 27:36. Here, Rabbi Shim'on links the name ישראל (*Yisra'el*), *Israel,* with שררה (*serarah*), "princeliness, authority."

237. **this serpent** The demonic power, ridden by Samael.

238. **we must sustain the existence of that *sinew of the thigh*...** We must preserve the sinew completely in any slaughtered animal and not cut it or eat it, so as not to weaken holiness and strengthen the demonic powers.

239. **When he sees...** The subject is Samael the serpent-rider, who wrestled with Jacob.

240. **So we must not let any creature of the world eat it...** For example, it cannot even be thrown to the dogs, in accordance with the Talmudic view of Rabbi Shim'on (BT *Pesaḥim* 22a), who forbids deriving any benefit at all from the sciatic nerve.

See Jonah Gerondi, *Sha'arei Teshuvah*

Rabbi Yeisa expounded, "*For he touched Jacob's hip socket* (Genesis 32:33). Here is written *for he touched,* and there is written *Whoever touches a corpse, the body of a human being* (Numbers 19:13).[241] Just as there impure, so here impure, for he defiled that site[242]—and from an impure site we must not benefit at all, especially a site approached by that impure side.[243] Torah says simply, *for he touched,* as is said: *Whatever the impure one touches becomes impure* (ibid., 22).[244] Blessed be the Compassionate One who gave Torah to Israel, enabling them to merit this world and the world that is coming, as is written: *Length of days in her right hand; in her left, riches and honor* (Proverbs 3:16).[245]

He went on ahead of them and he bowed to the ground seven times until he drew near his brother (Genesis 33:3).

Rabbi El'azar opened, "*You must not bow to another god*... (Exodus 34:14). Now, Jacob was consummation of the patriarchs, perfected above and below, selected as the full share of the blessed Holy One, intimately close to Him.[246] So how could he bow to that wicked Esau, who derives from the side of *another god*?[247] Whoever bows to him bows *to another god*! 35

"Now, you might say, 'Because "In the fox's season, bow to him."'[248] Not so! For Esau resembled *another god,* and Jacob would never bow to that side, to that portion. Rather, it is written: *Peace be to you, peace be to your house, peace be to all that is yours!* (1 Samuel 25:6),[249] and it has been said that it is forbidden to

3:84; *Zohar* 1:170b (in the printed editions), and *NZ,* n. 1; Margaliot, *Sha'arei Zohar, Pesaḥim* 22a; Huss, *Al Adnei Faz,* 45; Ta-Shma, *Ha-Nigleh she-ba-Nistar,* 44.

241. ***Whoever touches a corpse, the body of a human being*** The verse continues: *who has died, and does not purify himself, has defiled the Dwelling of YHVH; that person will be cut off from Israel. Since water of cleansing was not dashed on him, he shall be impure, his impurity still within him.*

242. **he defiled that site** Samael defiled the site of the sciatic nerve.

243. **that impure side** Samael.

244. **Torah says simply, *for he touched*...** Implying impurity by analogy with the verses in Numbers.

245. ***Length of days in her right hand; in her left, riches and honor*** See *Avot* 6:7; *Bereshit Rabbah* 59:2; BT *Shabbat* 63a.

246. **Jacob was consummation of the patriarchs...** See *Bereshit Rabbah* 76:1: "Rabbi Pinḥas said in the name of Rabbi Re'uven, '... The chosen of the patriarchs is Jacob, as is said: *For Yah has chosen Jacob for Himself* (Psalms 135:4).'" Cf. BT *Pesaḥim* 56a.

Jacob symbolizes *Tif'eret,* who harmonizes and completes the polar opposites *Ḥesed* and *Gevurah,* symbolized by Abraham and Isaac.

See *Zohar* 1:119b, 133a, 144b, 149b–150a, 152a (*ST*), 163b, 172b, 173b, 180a, 207a; 2:23a.

247. **from the side of *another god*** From the demonic realm.

248. **In the fox's season, bow to him** Submit to an inferior person when he is in a superior position. In BT *Megillah* 16b, this proverb is transmitted in the name of Rabbi El'azar son of Pedat to explain why (according to Genesis 47:31) Jacob bowed to his son Joseph.

249. ***Peace be to you, peace be to your***

greet the wicked first.[250] But they have established that he was really speaking to the blessed Holy One, while assuming that Nabal would think he was speaking to him.[251]

"Similarly, *Israel bowed at the head of the bed* (Genesis 47:31). Now, would he bow toward his son?[252] Rather, he bowed to the site of *Shekhinah*.[253] Here too, *He went on ahead of them*. Who is *He*? *Shekhinah*, who was going ahead of him; *He*—supernal protection.[254] As soon as Jacob saw, he said, 'Now is the time to bow!' Toward the blessed Holy One, who was going ahead of him, he bowed down seven times *until he drew near his brother*. It is not written *He bowed to Esau;* rather, as soon as he saw the blessed Holy One going ahead of him, he bowed toward Him, so as not to render honor or bow to anyone else—all fittingly.[255] Happy are the righteous, all of whose actions are for the glory of their Lord, deviating neither right nor left!"

Esau ran toward him and embraced him,
36 *flung himself upon his neck*—spelled
צוארו (*tsavvaro*), deficiently[256]—*and*
kissed him, and they wept (Genesis 33:4).

Rabbi Yitsḥak opened, "*The wicked are like the troubled sea that cannot be still, whose waters toss up mire and mud* (Isaiah 57:20). This verse has been discussed,[257] but words of Torah contain countless secrets, differing from one another, all of them one.

***house*...** King David's greeting to Nabal, who is described as an evildoer (1 Samuel 25:3).

250. **it is forbidden to greet the wicked first** Before being greeted by them. See *Kallah Rabbati* 3:1; *Sefer Ḥasidim*, ed. Margaliot, par. 51; *Zohar* 1:205a; 2:23b.

251. **he was really speaking to the blessed Holy One...** See *Zohar* 2:23b. Cf. BT *Shevu'ot* 35b.

252. **would he bow toward his son?** Would Jacob (Israel) bow to his son Joseph?

253. **he bowed to the site of *Shekhinah*** Who appeared to him.

See *Bereshit Rabbah* 96 (ed. Theodor, 1241); *Tanḥuma, Vayḥi* 3; *Targum Yerushalmi, Leqaḥ Tov, Midrash Aggadah*, Rashi, and Radak on Genesis 47:31; *Zohar* 1:99b (*ST*), 225b. According to BT *Shabbat* 12b, *Shekhinah* appears above the head of one who is sick.

254. **Who is *He*? *Shekhinah*... supernal protection** Although the pronoun apparently refers to Jacob, it really refers to the Divine Presence, who preceded him.

255. **It is not written *He bowed to Esau;* rather... he bowed toward Him...** The verse does not read *He bowed to Esau* but rather *He bowed to the ground*, implying that Jacob really bowed to God—though Esau imagined that his brother was bowing to him.

256. ***his neck*—spelled צוארו (*tsavvaro*), deficiently** The biblical word צואר (*tsavvar*), "neck," is sometimes declined in the plural, e.g., Genesis 27:16 and 45:14: צואריו (*tsavvarav*), *his neck*. In the verse discussed here (Genesis 33:4), this plural form, *tsavvarav*, is spelled deficiently, without a י (*yod*): צוארו, as if it were the simple singular form *tsavvaro*.

See below; *Sekhel Tov*, Genesis 33:4; Ibn Ezra on Genesis 45:14; *Ḥizzequni* and *Minḥat Shai* on Genesis 33:4; 45:14.

257. **This verse has been discussed** See *Shir ha-Shirim Rabbah* on 2:16; *Tanḥuma, Vayiqra* 7; *Midrash Tehillim* 2:2; *Zohar* 1:74b.

"*The wicked are like the troubled sea that cannot be still*—Esau, all of whose actions were steeped in wickedness and sin. For when he approached Jacob, he acted defectively, hostilely: *He flung himself upon* צוארו (*tsavvaro*), *his neck*—singular,[258] namely, Jerusalem, neck of the world.[259] *Tsavvaro, his neck*—not צואריו (*tsavvarav*), *his necks,* because the Temple was destroyed twice, once by Babylonia and once by the seed of Esau, who threw himself upon it once, destroying it; so *he flung himself upon tsavvaro, his neck,* singular.[260]

"וישקהו (*Va-yishshaqehu*), *And he kissed him*—dotted above, for he kissed him reluctantly.[261] We have learned that it is written: *Excessive are kisses of an enemy* (Proverbs 27:6)—Balaam, blessing Israel, for he didn't bless them wholeheartedly.[262] Similarly here, *Excessive are kisses of an enemy*—Esau."

Rabbi Yose said, "It is written: *Arise, O YHVH! Deliver me, O my God! For You strike all my enemies on the jaw; You break the teeth of the wicked* (Psalms 3:8), and we have learned: 'Do not read שברת (*shibbarta*), *You break,* but rather שרבבת (*shirbavta*), *You elongate,* for his teeth extended because he intended to bite him . . .'[263]

258. **defectively, hostilely . . .** לא . . . בשלם (*La . . . bishlam*), "Not in *shelam*." The word *shelam* means "peace," but here may imply שלימו (*shelimu*), "completeness," the lack of which is apparent both in the defective, singular spelling of צוארו (*tsavvarav, tsavvaro;* see note before last), and in Esau's conduct, which was faulty and disingenuous.

259. **Jerusalem, neck of the world** Elevated, beautiful, and vital. See *Targum Yonatan* and Radak on Isaiah 8:8; *Aggadat Bereshit* 80:1; *Zohar* 1:209b.

260. ***Tsavvaro, his neck*—not צואריו (*tsavvarav*), *his necks* . . .** See above, note 256. The Temple in Jerusalem was destroyed twice: once by the Babylonians in 586 B.C.E. and once by Rome, identified with the descendants of Esau, in 70 C.E. The full plural spelling, צואריו (*tsavvarav*), *his necks,* would allude to both these acts of destruction, but the apparently singular form, צוארו (*tsavvaro*), *his neck,* alludes to just the second, perpetrated by "the seed of Esau."

See *Bereshit Rabbah* 93:12; BT *Megillah* 16b. According to Obadiah 1:10–15 and Psalms 137:7, Edom (supposedly descended from Esau) encouraged or helped the Babylonians in the attack on Jerusalem.

261. **וישקהו (*Va-yishshaqehu*), *And he kissed him*—dotted above . . .** Certain letters in the Torah are dotted, inviting various midrashic interpretations. In this verse all the letters of וישקהו (*va-yishshaqehu*), *and he kissed him,* are dotted.

See *Sifrei,* Numbers 69; *Bereshit Rabbah* 78:9; *Shir ha-Shirim Rabbah* on 7:5; BT *Bava Metsi'a* 87a; *Soferim* 6:3; *Avot de-Rabbi Natan* A, 34; B, 37; *Tanḥuma, Vayishlaḥ* 4; *Pirqei de-Rabbi Eli'ezer* (ed. Friedlander), 37; *Midrash Mishlei* 26:24; *Bemidbar Rabbah* 3:13; *Sekhel Tov,* Genesis 33:4; *Zohar* 2:124b. Cf. Ibn Ezra on Genesis 33:4.

262. ***Excessive are kisses of an enemy* . . . Balaam . . .** See *Devarim Rabbah* (ed. Lieberman), 1.

263. **Do not read . . . because he intended to bite him** According to one midrashic tradition, the dots over the word וישקהו (*va-yishshaqehu*), *and he kissed him,* imply a slightly different spelling with a radically different meaning: וישכהו (*va-yishshakhehu*), *and he bit him.*

See *Shir ha-Shirim Rabbah* on 7:5: "וישקהו (*Va-yishshaqehu*), *And he kissed him*—entirely dotted. Rabbi Shim'on son of El'azar said, '. . . This teaches us that he didn't come to

"So, *they wept* (Genesis, ibid.)—this one wept, and that one wept, as the Companions have established.[264]

"Come and see how [172a] fervidly Esau felt toward Jacob! Even at that very moment he was scheming far into the future to harass and accuse him. So *they wept*—this one wept because he didn't think he could escape him, and that one wept because his father was still alive, so he couldn't attack him."[265]

Rabbi Abba said, "Surely at the moment he saw Jacob, Esau's wrath abated.[266] Why? Because Esau's prince had concurred with him,[267] so Esau couldn't prevail with his rage. For just so, all matters of this world depend upon above: Once they have concurred above, they concur below; dominion cannot prevail below until dominion is granted above. All is interdependent."[268]

Let my lord pass on ahead of his servant... (Genesis 33:14).[269]

Rabbi El'azar said, "This corresponds to what we said previously, that now Jacob didn't want those initial blessings bestowed upon him by his father.[270] Not even one of them had yet been fulfilled, because he reserved them for the end of days—when they would be needed by his descendants, confronting all

kiss him but rather to bite him. However, the neck of Jacob our father turned into marble and the teeth of that wicked one were blunted and melted like wax. Why then does Scripture say *and they wept* (Genesis 33:4)? This one was weeping for his neck, and that one was weeping for his teeth.'"

The midrashic emendation of שברת (*shibbarta*), *You break*, to שרבבת (*shirbavta*), *You elongate*, appears in BT *Berakhot* 54b, concerning the teeth of Og, king of Bashan. Here, Rabbi Yose's point is that Esau's teeth grew so long that he could not bite with them. See *Sekhel Tov*, Genesis 33:4: "Our rabbis expounded: שרבבת (*Shirbavta*), *You elongate*, indicating that his teeth projected sixty cubits in each direction."

See *Bereshit Rabbah* 78:9; *Targum Yerushalmi*, Genesis 33:4; *Tanḥuma*, *Vayishlaḥ* 4; *Pirqei de-Rabbi Eli'ezer* (ed. Friedlander), 37.

264. **as the Companions have established** See the preceding note.

265. **that one wept because his father was still alive...** Esau wept because his father, Isaac, was still alive, so he couldn't attack Jacob.

266. **Esau's wrath abated** See *Sefer ha-Yashar*, *Vayishlaḥ*, 153.

267. **Because Esau's prince had concurred with him** Jacob did not let go of Esau's heavenly prince, Samael, until the latter confirmed the blessings Jacob had received from his father, Isaac. See Genesis 27:27–29; above, note 235.

268. **all matters of this world depend upon above...** On the correspondence of above and below, see *Zohar* 1:38a, 57b–58a, 129a, 145b, 156b, 158b, 205b; 2:15b (*MhN*), 20a (*MhN*), 48b, 82b, 144a, 251a (*Heikh*); 3:45b, 65b; Tishby, *Wisdom of the Zohar*, 1:273.

Cf. *Mekhilta*, *Beshallaḥ* 2; *Bereshit Rabbah* 10:6; *Shir ha-Shirim Rabbah* on 8:14; *Zohar* 1:113a (*MhN*); 2:6a, 7a.

269. ***Let my lord pass on ahead of his servant*** The verse continues: *while I proceed slowly, at the pace of the livestock before me and at the pace of the children, till I come to my lord in Seir.*

270. **now Jacob didn't want those initial blessings...** See Genesis 27:27–29; *Zohar* 1:143b, 145a–146a, 166b. Cf. JT *Sanhedrin* 10:1, 27d.

nations of the world. So when Esau said *'Let us travel on* (ibid., 12):[271] we'll divide this world equally and rule together,' what did Jacob say? *Let my lord pass on ahead of his servant*—let him now rule first in this world.[272] *Let [him] pass,* as is said: *Their king will pass before them . . .* (Micah 2:13).[273] 'You rule first, *while I proceed slowly*—I reserve myself for that world that is coming, for the end of days, for those days that proceed slowly.[274]

"*At the pace of* המלאכה (*ha-melakhah*), *the livestock* (Genesis, ibid., 14). Who is *melakhah*, work?[275] The speculum that does not shine, through whom workings of the world are actualized.[276]

"*Before me* (ibid.)—She is constantly 'before YHVH.'[277]

"*And at the pace of the children* (ibid.)—mystery of the cherubim, manifesting mystery of faith, to whom he cleaves.[278]

"*Till I come to my lord in Seir* (ibid.)—'till my time comes to rule over the mount of Esau,' as is said: *Saviors will climb Mount Zion to execute judgment on Mount Esau, and then dominion will be* YHVH's (Obadiah 1:21)."[279]

39

271. ***Let us travel on*** The verse continues: *and I will go alongside you.*

272. **we'll divide this world equally . . .** See *Bereshit Rabbah* 78:14; *Devarim Rabbah* 1:20; *Tanḥuma, Terumah* 9; *Pirqei de-Rabbi Eli'ezer* (ed. Friedlander), 37; *Seder Eliyyahu Zuta* 19; *Leqaḥ Tov, Midrash Aggadah, Sekhel Tov,* and Baḥya ben Asher on Genesis 33:12.

273. **Let [*him*] *pass,* as is said: *Their king will pass . . .*** By analogy, the verb *pass* implies ruling.

274. **those days that proceed slowly** According to a commentary on *Sefer ha-Temunah* (3:58a–b), in the time to come the heavenly spheres will revolve more gradually, slowing down the process of time.

275. ***melakhah*, work** The normal meaning of the word.

276. **speculum that does not shine . . .** *Shekhinah,* who has no light of Her own but reflects the light of the other *sefirot.* See above, note 217. By conveying emanation, She animates the world.

277. ***Before me*—She is constantly 'before YHVH'** When translating the divine names *YHVH* or *Elohim, Targum Onqelos* often employs the phrase "before [or, "in the presence of"] YHVH." Here the phrase alludes to the position of *Shekhinah* before, or in the presence of, *Tif'eret,* who is known as *YHVH* and symbolized by Jacob. So when Jacob says *before me,* he is alluding to *Shekhinah,* who stands "before YHVH."

278. **mystery of the cherubim . . .** Who *guard the way to the Tree of Life* (Genesis 3:24) and support the divine throne (Ezekiel 10; Psalms 80:2). In BT *Sukkah* 5b, Rabbi Abbahu interprets the word כרוב (*keruv*), "cherub," as כרביא (*ke-ravya*), "like a child." (The plump childlike angels of Christian art conceivably derive from this tradition but more likely from the Greco-Roman *Erotes,* "loves," winged boys in the company of Aphrodite.)

Here the childlike cherubim accompany *Shekhinah,* "mystery of faith," to whom Jacob (symbolizing *Tif'eret*) cleaves and at whose pace he proceeds.

279. ***Till I come to my lord in Seir . . .*** Inhabited by Esau and his descendants (see Genesis 32:4; 36:8–9). In the time to come, Jacob will arrive there.

See JT *Avodah Zarah* 2:1, 40c; *Bereshit Rabbah* 78:14; *Tanḥuma, Terumah* 9.

Jacob journeyed to Succoth, and built himself a house, and for his cattle he made סכות (*sukkot*), *sheds;*[280] *therefore the place is called Succoth* (Genesis 33:17).

Rabbi Ḥiyya opened, "*A song of ascents. Of Solomon. Unless YHVH builds the house, its builders labor in vain. Unless YHVH watches over the city, the watchman guards in vain* (Psalms 127:1). Come and see: When it arose in the will of the blessed Holy One to create the world, He issued from the spark of impenetrable darkness[281] a single vaporous cluster,[282] flashing from the dark, lingering in ascension. The darkness descended, gleaming—flaring in a hundred paths, ways, narrow, broad,[283] constructing the house of the world.[284]

"This house stands in the center of all, countless doors and chambers round and round—supernal sacred sites, where birds of heaven nest, each according to its species.[285] Within emerges an immense, mighty tree, its branches and fruit nourishing all.[286] That tree climbs to the clouds of heaven, is

280. **סכות (*sukkot*), *sheds*** The word means "booths, sheds, shelters, huts."

281. **spark of impenetrable darkness** בוצינא דקרדינותא (*Botsina de-qardinuta*). See Vol. 1, pp. 107–8, and n. 4 there, and the wealth of material collected and analyzed by Liebes, *Peraqim*, 145–51, 161–64. קרדינותא (*Qardinuta*) recalls a phrase in BT *Pesaḥim* 7a: חיטי קורדניתא (*ḥittei qurdanaita*), "wheat from Kurdistan," which, according to Rashi, is very hard. In *Zohar* 1:15a, several witnesses record the variants קדרינותא (*qadrinuta*) or קדרוניתא (*qadrunita*), "darkness." See *ZḤ* 2a, where קדרנותא דסיהרא (*qardenuta de-sihara*) means "eclipse of the moon," corresponding to Hebrew קדרות הירח (*qadrut ha-yareaḥ*), "darkening of the moon."

The spark is so potently brilliant that it overwhelms comprehension. Many mystics convey similar paradoxical images: "a ray of divine darkness" (Dionysius, *Mystical Theology* 1:1); "the luminous darkness" (Gregory of Nyssa, *Life of Moses* 2:163); "the black light" (Iranian Sufism; see Corbin, *The Man of Light in Iranian Sufism*, 99–120). Prior to the *Zohar*, Azriel of Gerona and the author of *Ma'yan ha-Ḥokhmah* mention "the light darkened from shining." See Verman, *The Books of Contemplation*, 59–60, 158–59; Scholem, *Origins of the Kabbalah*, 336. Cf. Maimonides, *Guide of the Perplexed* 1:59: "We are dazzled by His beauty, and He is hidden from us because of the intensity with which He becomes manifest, just as the sun is hidden to eyes too weak to apprehend it."

Here the blinding light is the impulse of emanation flashing from *Ein Sof* and proceeding to delineate the various *sefirot*. See *ZḤ* 57d–58a (*QhM*); *Zohar* 1:15a, 18b, 86b; 2:133b, 177a, 233a, 254b, 260a; 3:48b–49a, 135b (*IR*), 139a (*IR*), 292b (*IZ*), 295a–b (*IZ*).

282. **vaporous cluster** קטורא (*Qetora*), meaning both "knot" and "smoke" in the *Zohar*. See 1:15a, 30a, 33b, 94b, 161b; 2:80a, 124a; 3:45b, 51a–b, 107a, 289b, 295b (*IZ*).

283. **hundred paths, ways, narrow, broad** The decade of *sefirot* in which each comprises ten aspects. They begin as subtle paths and expand into ways.

284. **house of the world** *Shekhinah*, who contains the entire flow of emanation and sustains the world. See *Zohar* 1:29b, 30b, 33a.

285. **birds of heaven...** Angels. The wording here and in the following lines derives from Daniel 4:9.

286. **immense, mighty tree...** *Tif'eret*, identified with the Tree of Life.

hidden amid three mountains,[287] emerges beneath these mountains, ascending, descending.

"This house is saturated by it; within, it secretes numerous supernal hidden treasures, unknown. Thereby this house is constructed and decorated. That tree is revealed by day, concealed by night; this house rules by night, is concealed by day.[288]

"As soon as darkness enters, enveloping, it rules; all doors close on every side.[289] Then countless spirits soar through the air, desirous to know, to enter.[290] Entering among those birds—who collect testimony[291]—they roam and see what they see, until that enveloping darkness arouses, radiating a flame, pounding all mighty hammers, opening doors, splitting boulders. That flame ascends and descends, striking the world, arousing voices above and below. Then one [172b] herald ascends, bound to the air, and proclaims. That air issues from the pillar of cloud of the inner altar;[292] issuing, it spreads in the four directions of the world. A thousand thousands stand on this side,[293] a myriad of myriads on that side—the right—and the herald stands erect, proclaiming potently. How many there are then who intone songs and render worship! Two doors open, one on the south and one on the north.[294]

"The house ascends and is placed between two sides,[295] while hymns are chanted and praises rise. Then the one who enters, enters silently,[296] and the house glows with six lights lustering in every direction.[297] Rivers of spices flow forth, watering all beasts of the field, as is said: *watering all beasts of the field... Above them dwell the birds of heaven, singing among the branches* (Psalms 104:11–12).[298] They chant till morning rises, when stars and constellations, the heavens and their hosts all sing praises, as is said: *When the morning stars sang together, and all the sons of Elohim shouted for joy* (Job 38:7).

"Come and see: *Unless YHVH builds the house, its builders labor in vain. Unless YHVH watches over the city, the watchman guards in vain. Unless YHVH*—

287. **three mountains** The towering triad of *sefirot: Keter, Ḥokhmah,* and *Binah.*

288. **That tree... this house...** *Tif'eret* manifests (and is symbolized) by day, *Shekhinah* by night.

289. **darkness enters...** Symbolizing harsh judgment.

290. **countless spirits soar through the air...** Human souls ascend from sleeping bodies, seeking knowledge.

291. **birds—who collect testimony** The angels record the testimony of the souls concerning human activity on earth.

292. **inner altar** *Binah.* See *Zohar* 2:138b; 3:30b.

293. **thousand thousands...** Of angels.

294. **south... north** Symbolizing *Ḥesed* and *Gevurah.*

295. **two sides** *Ḥesed* and *Gevurah.*

296. **one who enters...** The male partner of *Shekhinah.*

297. **six lights lustering...** The *sefirot* from *Ḥesed* through *Yesod.*

298. **beasts of the field...** The angels, nourished by *Shekhinah.* See *Zohar* 1:152a. 161b.

Supernal King,[299] constantly building this house, enhancing her. When? As ritual aspirations ascend from below fittingly.[300] *Unless YHVH watches over the city.* When? As night darkens and armed flanks hover, roaming the world,[301] and doors close shut; then she is guarded on all sides lest the uncircumcised and impure approach her, as is said: *For the uncircumcised and the impure will enter you no more* (Isaiah 52:1), since the blessed Holy One intends to eliminate him from the world. Who is *uncircumcised* and who is *impure*? All is one: *uncircumcised and impure,* the one by whom Adam and his wife were seduced, inflicting death upon the world.[302] He is the one who defiles this house, until the time when the blessed Holy One eliminates him from the world. So, *Unless YHVH watches over the city,* indeed![303]

"*Jacob journeyed to Succoth,* journeying toward the share of faith.[304] What is written above? *Esau returned that day on his way to Seir* (Genesis, ibid., 16). And it is written: *Jacob journeyed to Succoth.* But each one diverged to his own side. Esau, to the side of Seir. Who is Seir? Strange woman, alien god.[305] Whereas *Jacob journeyed to Succoth*—supernal faith.

"*He built himself a house,* as is written: *house of Jacob* (Isaiah 2:5)."

Rabbi El'azar said, "He instituted evening prayer fittingly.[306]

"*And for his cattle he made sukkot, sheds*—other *sukkot* to protect them; this one is secular.[307]

299. ***YHVH*—Supernal King** *Tif'eret.*

300. **ritual aspirations...** The pure intentions accompanying human prayer and holy deeds on earth.

301. **armed flanks...** Harsh, demonic powers.

302. **one by whom Adam and his wife were seduced...** The primordial demonic serpent.

303. **So, *Unless YHVH watches over*...** Without His protection, the angelic defense of *Shekhinah* would be inadequate.

304. ***Succoth*... share of faith** *Shekhinah,* "house of the world" and focus of faith.

305. **Who is Seir? Strange woman, alien god** Esau and his descendants inhabited שעיר (*se'ir*), *Seir* (see Genesis 32:4; 36:8–9), but the word שעיר (*sa'ir*) also means "goat, demon, satyr." See *Bereshit Rabbah* 65:15; *Zohar* 1:65a, 138b, 145b; 3:64a. "Strange woman" refers to the demonic female.

306. **He instituted evening prayer fittingly** According to rabbinic tradition, the patriarchs instituted daily prayer. See BT *Berakhot* 26b: "Rabbi Yose son of Rabbi Ḥanina said, 'The patriarchs instituted the prayers.'... Abraham instituted the morning prayer,... Isaac, the afternoon prayer,... Jacob, the evening prayer." See *Bereshit Rabbah* 68:9.

Here "evening prayer" symbolizes *Shekhinah,* identified with the night and the moon. Jacob symbolizes *Tif'eret,* the sun, who illumines *Shekhinah* and conveys to Her the sefirotic blessing. See *Zohar* 1:163a, 173b.

307. **this one is secular** Earlier in the verse, *Succoth* alludes to Jacob's sefirotic destination: *Shekhinah,* the divine "booth"; but here the same word implies simply mundane *sheds* for Jacob's cattle. For similar, rabbinic distinctions between sacred and secular meanings of a word, see BT *Shevu'ot* 35b.

"Then, *Jacob arrived* שלם (*shalem*), *in peace* (Genesis, ibid., 18)—totally *shalem*, complete, as they have established.[308] And it is written: ויהי בשלם סכו (*Vayhi ve-shalem sukko*), *In shalem was His abode* (Psalms 76:3)—all one mystery.[309] Then faith united with him, when he was complete, crowned in his appropriate site;[310] this *sukkah* was adorned along with him, for he was שלים (*shelim*), consummated, by patriarchs; consummated by his sons.[311] This is *shalem*—complete above, complete below; complete in heaven, complete on earth. Complete above, for he is consummation of the patriarchs; complete below, through his holy sons. Complete in heaven, complete on earth, so: *In shalem was His abode.*

"What is written immediately? *Dinah, Leah's daughter, went out* (Genesis 34:1), and the Companions have established this.[312] Come and see: Countless rungs and aspects diverge above, each distinguished from the other, creatures differing from one another, these contending to dominate those, to tear prey, each according to its species.[313] From the side of impure spirit, countless rungs diverge, all lying in wait to attack, these opposite those. Look at what is written: 13
Do not plow with an ox and a donkey together (Deuteronomy 22:10), for when they join, they attack the world!"[314]

308. **שלם (*shalem*), *in peace*—totally *shalem*, complete...** See BT *Shabbat* 33b: "*Jacob arrived* שלם (*shalem*), *in peace.* Rav said, '*Shalem*, complete, in his body, complete in his wealth, complete in his Torah.'"

Cf. *Bereshit Rabbah* 79:5; *Tanḥuma* (Buber), *Vayishlaḥ* 10–12; *Zohar* 1:203b.

309. **ויהי בשלם סכו (*Vayhi ve-shalem sukko*), *In shalem was His abode*...** Here *sukko* (*His abode*) apparently refers to *Shekhinah*, who Herself became *shalem* (complete) by uniting with Jacob. See *Bereshit Rabbah* 56:3; *Midrash Tehillim* 76:3; *Zohar* 1:86b; 3:90b.

310. **faith united with him...** *Shekhinah*, realm of mystical faith, united with Jacob once he had attained the rung of *Tif'eret*.

311. **שלים (*shelim*), consummated, by patriarchs...** See *Bereshit Rabbah* 76:1: "Rabbi Pinḥas said in the name of Rabbi Re'uven, '...The chosen of the patriarchs is Jacob, as is said: *For Yah has chosen Jacob for Himself* (Psalms 135:4).'"

Jacob symbolizes *Tif'eret*, who harmonizes and completes the polar opposites *Ḥesed* and *Gevurah*, symbolized by Abraham and Isaac. See *Zohar* 1:119b, 133a, 144b, 149b, 150a, 152a (*ST*), 163b, 171b, 173b, 180a, 207a; 2:23a.

According to Shim'on son of Lakish (BT *Pesaḥim* 56a), Abraham and Isaac were tainted by their sons Ishmael and Esau, whereas Jacob was fulfilled by the perfect faith of his twelve sons.

312. **Companions have established this** By "going out," Dinah exposed and endangered herself. See JT *Sanhedrin* 2:6, 20d; *Bereshit Rabbah* 80:1; *Tanḥuma, Vayishlaḥ* 5–7; *Tanḥuma* (Buber), *Vayishlaḥ* 12–19.

Here, apparently, Dinah symbolizes *Shekhinah*, who derives from *Din* (Judgment). When exposed, She becomes vulnerable to demonic forces.

313. **Countless rungs and aspects diverge above...** Holy powers on the right and the left seeking the rich flow of blessing.

314. ***Do not plow with an ox and a donkey together*...** The command against plowing with these two species is understood as a warning not to stimulate the union of two dangerous demonic forces.

See *Zohar* 1:166b; 2:6a, 64b; 3:86b, 207a.

"Come and see: The sole craving of impure rungs is to attack holy sides. Since Jacob is holy, they all lie in wait for him and attack. First the serpent bit him, as is said: *He touched the socket of his thigh* (Genesis 32:26);[315] now a donkey bit him. There he himself stood up to the serpent; now Simeon and Levi—deriving [173a] from severe Judgment—stood up to the חמור (*ḥamor*), donkey, prevailing against him on all sides, so he was overwhelmed, as is said: *Hamor and Shechem his son they slew by the edge of the sword* (ibid. 34:26).[316] Simeon, who was an ox—his zodiacal sign, Taurus—struck Hamor, so that they would not join as one, becoming his attacker.[317]

"All of them came to contend with Jacob, but he was delivered and afterward dominated them. Later came the ox, completed by donkeys, all of them from the side of the donkey. Joseph, who is an ox;[318] Egyptians, who are donkeys, of whom is written *whose flesh is the flesh of donkeys* (Ezekiel 23:20). So later the sons of Jacob fell among those donkeys—since they had coupled as one—and they all bit them, flesh and bone,[319] until Levi aroused as before and scattered those donkeys, utterly breaking their strength. He removed the ox from there, as is written: *Moses took the bones of Joseph with him* (Exodus 13:19).[320]

315. **serpent bit him . . . *touched the socket of his thigh*** The context (Genesis 32:25–26) reads: *Jacob was left alone, and a man wrestled with him until the rising of dawn. When he saw that he could not prevail against him, he touched the socket of his thigh, and the socket of Jacob's thigh was wrenched as he wrestled with him.*

According to one rabbinic tradition, Jacob's wrestling partner was Samael, identified here with the primordial serpent. See *Tanḥuma, Vayishlaḥ* 8; *Bereshit Rabbah* 77:3; *Zohar* 1:146a, 166a, 170a, 179b.

316. **Simeon and Levi—deriving from severe Judgment . . .** When Dinah was raped by Shechem son of Hamor, her brothers Simeon and Levi avenged the outrage by killing Shechem, Hamor, and all the males of the town. Here, Rabbi El'azar indicates that Dinah's brothers derived from the *sefirah* of *Din* (Judgment) and could therefore execute judgment against Shechem and Hamor (associated with the demonic power *ḥamor*, "donkey.")

See *Zohar* 1:184a, 236a, 244a; 2:6a, 11a.

317. **Simeon, who was an ox . . .** Each of the twelve tribes corresponds to one of the twelve signs of the zodiac. Simeon (associated with Taurus the bull) attacked Hamor (associated with the demonic *ḥamor*, "donkey") to prevent the union of the demonic pair, ox and donkey, who threatened to attack Jacob.

On Simeon and Taurus, see *Midrash Tehillim* 90:3 (and Buber's note 16); *Zohar* 1:200b, 236a. Cf. *Massekhet Soferim*, add. 1, 1:3; *Yalqut Shim'oni*, Exodus 418.

318. **Joseph, who is an ox** See Jacob's blessing to Joseph (Deuteronomy 33:17): *His firstling bull—majesty is his!*

319. **flesh and bone** On the power of the donkey's bite, see *Bereshit Rabbah* 97:14 (p. 1222); BT *Pesaḥim* 49b.

320. **later the sons of Jacob fell among those donkeys . . .** The successful assimilation of Joseph (identified with the ox) in Egypt (identified with donkeys) empowered the Egyptians, who thereby enslaved the Israelites. Moses the Levite severed the connection between ox and donkey by removing the bones of Joseph during the Exodus.

"Come and see: When Simeon attacked that Hamor at first, he aroused blood upon them, for they were circumcised;[321] afterward, *they killed every male* (Genesis, ibid., 25). The blessed Holy One acted similarly by the hand of the Levite against those *ḥamorim*, donkeys: first, blood;[322] then, *YHVH killed every firstborn*... (Exodus 13:15).[323] Here, concerning this Hamor: *all their wealth, all their little ones, and all their animals* (Genesis, ibid., 29).[324] There, concerning those *ḥamorim*: *objects of silver and objects of gold... And a mixed multitude also went up with them, [and sheep and cattle]*... (Exodus 12:35, 38). Simeon and Levi—one stood up to this Hamor, and one stood up to all those *ḥamorim*.[325]

"All of them sought to conspire against Holy Jacob and were poised to bite him, but together with his sons he stood up against them and subdued them.[326] Now that Esau is biting him and his sons, who will stand up to him?[327] Jacob and Joseph—one on this side, one on that side, as is written: *The house of Jacob will be fire, the house of Joseph flame, and the house of Esau stubble...* (Obadiah 1:18)."[328]

They journeyed onward, and the terror of God fell upon the towns around them 45
(Genesis 35:5). Rabbi Yose said, "They all assembled, but as they girded their weapons they began trembling and abandoned them. So, *they did not pursue the sons of Jacob* (ibid.).[329]

"*Get rid of the foreign gods* (Genesis 35:2),[330] which they had taken from

321. **for they were circumcised** As stipulated by Jacob's sons, all the male inhabitants of the town were recently circumcised. See Genesis 34:13–24.

322. **by the hand of the Levite... first, blood** By Moses, who conveyed the divine command to Aaron to inflict the first of the ten plagues: blood. See Exodus 7:19–21.

323. ***YHVH killed every firstborn...*** The verse continues: *in the land of Egypt.*

324. ***all their wealth, all their little ones, and all their animals*** The verse reads: *All their wealth, all their little ones, and their wives they captured and plundered, as well as all that was in the houses.* The preceding verse mentions *sheep, cattle, and donkeys.*

325. **Simeon and Levi—one stood up...** Simeon led the attack against Hamor, Shechem, and their townsmen; Moses the Levite led the assault on the Egyptians.

326. **together with his sons he stood up against them...** See *Bereshit Rabbah* 80:10; 97:6; *Beit ha-Midrash,* 5:159; *Sefer ha-Yashar, Vayishlaḥ,* 158–66.

327. **Now that Esau is biting him and his sons...** In the current state of exile under the oppression of medieval Christianity (symbolized by Esau).

328. ***house of Jacob will be fire... house of Esau stubble...*** The verse continues: *and they will set them on fire and consume them.*

329. **They all assembled...** The forces attacking Jacob and his sons. See *Midrash Va-Yissa'u* (ed. Lauterbach), 205–22; *Beit ha-Midrash,* 3:1–5; *Sefer ha-Yashar, Vayishlaḥ,* 168–86; Naḥmanides, Genesis 35:13; *Bereshit Rabbah* 81:4; Kasher, *Torah Shelemah,* Genesis 35:5, nn. 25–27.

330. ***Get rid of the foreign gods*** The context reads: *Get rid of the foreign gods in your midst, purify yourselves, and change your garments. Let us rise and go up to Bethel, and*

Shechem[331]—silver and gold vessels engraved with images of their gods."[332]

Rabbi Yehudah said, "These were idols made of silver and gold, and Jacob hid them there so that he wouldn't derive benefit from the aspect of idolatry, for one must never derive any benefit from it."[333]

Rabbi Yehudah and Rabbi Ḥizkiyah were walking on the way. Rabbi Ḥizkiyah said to Rabbi Yehudah, "Why is it written *He took the crown of* מלכם (*malkam*) *from his head—its weight was a talent of gold, with precious stones—and it was set on David's head* (2 Samuel 12:30)? Now, we have learned that the abomination of the Ammonites is called Milcom, and this is *the crown of malkam*.[334] Why was it *set on David's head*?[335] And why is it described as 'abomination'? Look, other false gods of the nations are described as *gods of the nations, foreign god*, whereas this one is called 'abomination'!"

He replied, "But the blessed Holy One calls all the false gods of the nations by this name, as is written: *You have seen their abominations and their filthy idols* (Deuteronomy 29:16). As to what you said concerning *He took the crown of malkam*—that this is Milcom—certainly so! But Ittai the Gittite, before converting, broke the image engraved on that crown, rendering it defective and thus permissible for use. So it was set on his head.[336]

"Come and see: Abomination of the Ammonites was a serpent engraved by incision on that crown; thus it is called 'abomination'—filth."[337]

I will build an altar there to the God who answered me on the day of my distress and was with me on the way that I went (Genesis 35:2–3)

331. **which they had taken from Shechem** As specified in *Targum Yerushalmi* and Rashi, ad loc.; *Midrash ha-Ḥefets* (cited by Kasher, *Torah Shelemah*, ad loc., 10). Cf. Genesis 34:27–29.

332. **silver and gold vessels engraved with images of their gods** Jacob considered these vessels idolatrous. See M *Avodah Zarah* 3:3; *Bereshit Rabbah* 81:3 (and Theodor, ad loc.); Radak on Genesis 32:2; Kasher, *Torah Shelemah*, Genesis 32:2, nn. 10, 16.

333. **one must never derive any benefit from it** See the sources cited in the preceding note.

334. **crown of מלכם (*malkam*)... Milcom...** The word *malkam* in this verse means either "their king" or, as Rabbi Ḥizkiyah suggests here, "Milcom," god of the Ammonites—described in 1 Kings 11:5 by the dysphemism "abomination of the Ammonites." See 1 Kings 11:33; BT *Avodah Zarah* 44a; *Zohar* 1:110a–b (*ST*).

335. **Why was it *set on David's head*?** How could King David allow himself to benefit from an idolatrous object?

336. **Ittai the Gittite, before converting, broke the image...** Ittai was a leader of a mercenary troop from the Philistine city of Gath who was loyally devoted to King David. See 2 Samuel 15:17–22. Being an idolator, he could render the idol null and void.

See M *Avodah Zarah* 4:4; and BT *Avodah Zarah* 44a: "*He took the crown of malkam from his head—its weight was a talent of gold.* But is that permitted? It entails forbidden benefit [from idolatry]! Rav Naḥman said, 'Ittai the Gittite came and annulled it.'" On the question of Ittai's conversion, see Radak on 2 Samuel 12:30.

337. **serpent... thus it is called 'abomination'—filth** Describing the impurity of the demonic serpent. See M *Avodah Zarah* 3:3;

Rabbi Yitshak said, "*Get rid of the foreign gods*—other women whom they had brought with them along with all their jewelry.[338] So it is written: *They gave Jacob all the foreign gods* (Genesis, ibid., 4), referring to the women and all that idolatrous jewelry of silver and gold. *Jacob buried them* (ibid.),[339] so that they wouldn't [173b] derive any benefit at all from the aspect of idolatry.

"Come and see that Jacob was an entirely consummate man,[340] cleaving to the blessed Holy One. What is written? *Let us rise and go up to Bethel, and I will build an altar there to the God who answered me on the day of my distress and was with me on the way that I went* (Genesis 35:3). Immediately, *They gave Jacob*.[341] From here we learn that one should praise the blessed Holy One and thank Him for the miracles and goodness He has performed for him, as is written: *and was with me on the way that I went.*

"Come and see! First is written *Let us rise and go up to Bethel*—he included his sons with him. Then is written *and I will build an altar*—not 'we will build an altar' but *I will build an altar,* excluding them from this. Why? Because the matter devolved upon him. Jacob surely arrayed evening prayer—it was he who built the altar;[342] the matter rested with him because he endured all those misfortunes from the day he fled from his brother, as is written: *and was with me on the way that I went.* Whereas they arrived later in the world, so he did not include them."

Rabbi El'azar said, "From here we learn that the one for whom a miracle has been performed should himself offer thanks.[343] Whoever eats bread at

Zohar 2:107a. Cf. BT *Shabbat* 145b–146a: "Rav Yosef taught: '. . . When the serpent copulated with Eve, he injected her with זוהמא (*zohama*), filth [or: slime, lewdness].'"

338. ***foreign gods*—other women whom they had brought . . .** Foreign women and their idolatrous jewelry. In the *Zohar,* the command *Do not bow down to another god* (Exodus 34:14) is understood to mean "Do not lie down with a foreign woman."

See *Zohar* 1:131b; 2:3b, 61a, 87b, 90a, 243a; *ZḤ* 21a (*MhN*), 78c (*MhN, Rut*); Moses de León, *Sefer ha-Rimmon,* 212; idem, *Sheqel ha-Qodesh,* 51 (63).

339. ***Jacob buried them*** The verse continues: *under the terebinth that is near Shechem.* According to Galante, Jacob buried the jewelry and sent the women away.

340. **consummate man** גבר שלים (*Gevar shelim*), borrowed from *Targum Onqelos* on Genesis 25:27, where Jacob—in contrast to Esau the hunter—is described as איש תם (*ish tam*), "a simple [or: innocent, plain, mild, quiet, sound, wholesome] man." See above, note 311.

341. ***They gave Jacob*** The verse continues: *all the foreign gods that were in their hands.*

342. **Jacob surely arrayed evening prayer . . . built the altar** Both "evening prayer" and "altar" symbolize *Shekhinah.* See above, note 306.

343. **one for whom a miracle has been performed . . .** On the question of whether others should also offer thanks, see JT *Berakhot* 9:1, 12d; BT *Berakhot* 54a; *OY;* Galante; *NO,* n. 1; *Nefesh David; NZ,* n. 2; *MmD; Entsiqlopedyah Talmudit,* 4:353; Ta-Shma, *Ha-Nigleh she-ba-Nistar,* 110, n. 20.

the table should himself offer blessing—not someone else who has eaten nothing."[344]

There he built an altar and called the place El-bethel, for there elohim *were revealed to him when he fled from his brother* (ibid., 7).[345] Come and see: *There he built an altar to YHVH;*[346] concerning these altars[347] it is not written that ascent-offerings and sacrifices were offered, since the rung worthy of arrayal was arrayed. *An altar to YHVH*—arraying the lower rung, joining it to the upper rung; so, *There he built an altar*—lower rung; *to YHVH*—upper rung.[348] *He called the place El-bethel*—this name corresponding to an upper name; for when it shines, then like mother, like daughter, and all is one.[349]

For there elohim *were revealed to him,* since they appear only with *Shekhinah.* Look! There are seventy, appearing constantly together with *Shekhinah*—thrones surrounding *Shekhinah.*[350] So, *for there* elohim *were revealed to him,* for look at what is written: *Behold! YHVH was standing upon it* (ibid. 28:13)![351]

344. **not someone else who has eaten nothing** See BT *Berakhot* 44a, 48a.

345. ***elohim were revealed to him...*** The passive verb נגלו (*niglu*) is in the plural, matching the plural form of the word *elohim.* Although all biblical translations render this verb in the singular, the *Zohar* (below) exploits the plural form.

346. ***to YHVH*** Actually, the verse does not include this phrase. Cf. Genesis 12:7, 8; 13:18.

347. **these altars** The plural apparently includes the altar built previously by Jacob, mentioned in Genesis 33:20.

348. ***an altar*—lower rung; *to YHVH*—upper rung** Alluding respectively to the two rungs *Shekhinah* and *Tif'eret.*

349. **corresponding to an upper name... like mother, like daughter...** The name בית-אל (*Beit-El*) refers to *Shekhinah,* who is the בית (*bayit*), "house" of *Hesed,* known as *El.* Similarly, *Binah,* mother of *Shekhinah,* houses and nourishes all the lower *sefirot,* including *El.* When *Shekhinah* is illumined by uniting above, She resembles Her mother. For another interpretation, see *OY.*

The phrase "like mother, like daughter" derives from Ezekiel 16:44, where it appears in a negative context. The same verse is applied negatively to Leah and Dinah. See JT *Sanhedrin* 2:6, 20d; *Bereshit Rabbah* 80:1; *Tanḥuma, Vayishlaḥ* 7; *Tanḥuma* (Buber), *Vayishlaḥ* 14; above, p. 43 and n. 312.

350. **seventy, appearing... with *Shekhinah*—thrones...** The plural formulation, *elohim were revealed,* refers to seventy angels on their thrones surrounding *Shekhinah.*

Seventy angelic names are recorded in *Zohar* 1:108a–b (*ST*). The image of seventy thrones, corresponding to the seventy nations and languages of the world or the seventy thrones of the Sanhedrin, appears in various early sources. See *Massekhet Heikhalot,* in *Beit ha-Midrash,* 2:41; *Beit ha-Midrash,* 2:84; *Battei Midrashot,* 2:284; El'azar of Worms, *Hilkhot ha-Kisse,* 24a; Azriel of Gerona, *Peirush ha-Aggadot,* 61; *Zohar* 3:20a (*RM*), 162b, 231a, 236b.

351. ***for there elohim were revealed... Behold! YHVH...*** When Jacob fled from his brother, the angels (*elohim*) surrounding *Shekhinah were revealed to him,* ascending and descending the ladder, while *Shekhinah* Herself (here indicated by the name *YHVH*) *was standing upon* the ladder.

God ascended from him at the place where He had spoken with him (Genesis 35:13).

Rabbi Shim'on said, "From here we learn that he became a holy chariot together with the patriarchs.[352] Come and see: Jacob is a supernal, holy chariot, poised to illumine the moon—a chariot by himself, as is written: *God ascended from him.*"[353]

He opened, saying, "*Who is a great nation that has gods so close to it as YHVH our God, in all our calling upon Him?* (Deuteronomy 4:7). Come and see how beloved are Israel in the presence of the blessed Holy One! Among all nations of the world, no other nation or tongue has a god who hearkens to them as the blessed Holy One is ready to receive the prayers and pleas of Israel in their hour of need, hearing them pray on account of their rung.[354]

"Come and see: The blessed Holy One named Jacob 'Israel,' as is written: *No longer will your name be called Jacob, but Israel will be your name. And He called his name Israel* (Genesis 35:10). Who *called*? *Shekhinah*, as is said: *He called to Moses* (Leviticus 1:1).[355] *Elohim said to him* (Genesis, ibid.)—they have established this: above.[356] *Israel*—totally consummated, fittingly; so he ascended his rung, perfected in this name.[357] Therefore, *He called his name Israel*, as has been said." 49

352. **he became a holy chariot together with the patriarchs** See *Bereshit Rabbah* 82:6: "*God ascended from him* [*at the place where He had spoken with him*]. Rabbi Shim'on son of Lakish said, 'The patriarchs themselves constitute the [divine] Chariot.'"

By living righteously, each of the patriarchs became a throne and vehicle for the divine. Here, the three patriarchs (Abraham on the right, Isaac on the left, and Jacob between them) symbolize the sefirotic triad of *Ḥesed, Gevurah,* and *Tif'eret,* which serves as a chariot for the higher *sefirot.*

Cf. *Bereshit Rabbah* 47:6; 69:3; Naḥmanides on Genesis 17:22; 35:13; Azriel of Gerona, *Peirush ha-Aggadot,* 57; *Zohar* 1:60b, 99a, 150a, 154b, 248b; 2:144a; 3:38a, 99a.

353. **poised to illumine the moon—a chariot by himself...** Jacob, consummation of the patriarchs, illumines *Shekhinah,* symbolized by the moon, and unites with Her by himself. See above, note 311; *Zohar* 1:97a–b (*MhN*).

354. **hearing them pray on account of their rung** On account of *Shekhinah,* who conveys their prayers above.

355. ***And He called his name Israel.* Who *called*? *Shekhinah*...** The anonymous subject *He* refers to *Shekhinah,* as does the anonymous subject of the opening verse of Leviticus. See *Zohar* 1:102b, 115a, 138a, 142b; 2:60b, 125b, 131a, 138a; 3:4b, 53b, 285a.

356. ***Elohim said to him*—they have established this: above** Whereas the anonymous wording at the end of the verse (*He called*) refers to *Shekhinah,* the opening phrase (*Elohim said to him*) refers to a higher rung ("above"), namely, *Binah.*

357. ***Israel*—totally consummated...** Jacob's new name symbolizes his attainment of the rung of *Tif'eret Yisra'el* (Beauty of Israel), which balances and integrates the polar opposites *Ḥesed* and *Gevurah.*

Rabbi El'azar and Rabbi Yose were walking on the way. Rabbi Yose said to Rabbi El'azar, "Surely, as you have said, Jacob is consummation of the patriarchs, embracing all sides.[358] He called his name Israel, as is written: *No longer will your name be called Jacob, but Israel,* and: *He called his name Israel* (Genesis, ibid.). Why, then, does the blessed Holy One revert to calling him Jacob numerous times? Everyone calls him Jacob just as before! If so, why *No longer will your name be called Jacob*?"[359]

He replied, "Well spoken!" He opened, saying, "*YHVH will go forth like a mighty one; like a warrior He will stir up His zeal...* (Isaiah 42:13). This verse has been established, but come and see! *Like a mighty one*—the verse should read: *a mighty one.* Similarly, *like a warrior*—it should read: *a warrior.*[360] However, as has already been said, *YHVH* always conveys compassion, certainly![361] [174a] The blessed Holy One is named *YHVH,* as is written: *I am YHVH, that is My name* (ibid., 8).[362] Yet we see that sometimes He is called *Elohim,* which always conveys judgment. Really, when righteous abound in the world, His name is

YHVH, called by the name of compassion; when wicked abound in the world, His name is *Elohim,* called by the name *Elohim.*[363]

"Similarly, when Jacob was not in the midst of enemies or in a foreign land, he was called Israel; when he was among enemies or in a foreign land, he was called Jacob."

He said, "The wording is still unsettling, for it is written: *No longer will your name be called,* yet we do call him so! And as for what you said—'When he was among enemies or in a foreign land, he was called Jacob'—come and see what is written: *Jacob dwelled in the land of his father's sojournings, in the land of Canaan* (Genesis 37:1). Look, he wasn't in a foreign land!"

He replied, "As I've already said, just as the blessed Holy One is called *YHVH,* yet is sometimes called *Elohim,* so too he is sometimes called Israel and some-

358. **consummation of the patriarchs...** See above, notes 311, 340.

359. **Why, then, does the blessed Holy One revert to calling him Jacob...** Why is he subsequently addressed and referred to by his old name?

360. **the verse should read: *a mighty one* ... *a warrior*** As in Psalms 24:8; Exodus 15:3. See *Zohar* 2:47b, 137a.

361. ***YHVH* always conveys compassion...** According to rabbinic tradition, the name *YHVH* conveys compassion, while *Elohim* conveys judgment. See *Sifrei,* Deuteronomy 26; *Bereshit Rabbah* 12:15; 33:3; *Shemot Rabbah* 3:6.

362. **The blessed Holy One is named *YHVH*...** "Blessed Holy One" often signifies *Tif'eret,* also known by the name *YHVH.*

363. **when righteous abound... when wicked abound...** Human behavior arouses the compassionate or judgmental qualities of God and determines which divine name will apply. However, even when wickedness arouses divine judgment, God is still inherently compassionate; He is only acting *like a mighty one, like a warrior.*

times Jacob, all on well-known rungs.[364] And as for what is said: *No longer will your name be called Jacob*—settling into this name."[365]

He said, "If so, look at what is written: *No longer will your name be called Abram; your name will be Abraham* (ibid. 17:5)!"[366]

He replied, "There it is written והיה (*ve-hayah*), *will be*, so he abided in that name; whereas here is not written *ve-hayah*, rather *but Israel* יהיה (*yihyeh*), *will be, your name*—not *ve-hayah*. Even once would have sufficed; all the more so, sometimes this, sometimes that.[367] Once his sons were adorned with priests and Levites and ascended supernal rungs, he was crowned with this name permanently."[368]

While they were walking, Rabbi Yose said to Rabbi El'azar, "It has already been said that when Rachel died, the house was possessed by one who needed to be fittingly arrayed in twelve tribes.[369] Why did Rachel die immediately?"[370]

He replied, "So that *Shekhinah* would be crowned properly, becoming *mother of children* (Psalms 113:9). Through him She began to possess the house, to be arrayed; so Benjamin always inhabits the west, no other direction. Through him

364. **sometimes called Israel... Jacob, all on well-known rungs** The patriarch is called by different names corresponding to two different sefirotic rungs. The name *Israel* corresponds to *Tif'eret Yisra'el* (Beauty of Israel). The name יעקב (*Ya'aqov*), *Jacob*, alludes to *Shekhinah*, perhaps because She is the עקב (*aqev*), *heel*, i.e., the end of the flow of emanation. When Jacob settled in Canaan, the land was still inhabited by enemies; thus his new name, Israel, was inappropriate.

See *Zohar* 1:145b, 147b–148b (*ST*), 176a, 177b, 210b; 3:210b.

365. **settling into this name** Your name will no longer be solely Jacob.

366. ***No longer will your name be called Abram...*** Following this announcement, the first patriarch is never again called by his old name, Abram.

On the difference between Abraham and Jacob in this regard, see *Bereshit Rabbah* 46:8; JT *Berakhot* 1:6, 3d; BT *Berakhot* 13a; Kasher, *Torah Shelemah*, Genesis 17:5, n. 36; 35:10, nn. 50–51.

367. **here is not written *ve-hayah*, rather ...יהיה (*yihyeh*), *will be*...** With Abraham, the perfect form of the verb, *ve-hayah* ("will be"), implies the permanence of his new name. With Jacob, the imperfect form, *yihyeh*, though still meaning "will be," implies a less permanent identity; from then on, he is sometimes called Jacob, sometimes Israel.

368. **Once his sons were adorned...** After Jacob's descendants became a nation that was modeled on the divine qualities (such as *Hesed*, symbolized by priests; *Gevurah*, symbolized by Levites), they were known permanently as *benei Yisra'el*, literally, "Children of Israel."

369. **when Rachel died...** Rachel died while giving birth to Benjamin, Jacob's twelfth son. At this point, *Shekhinah* was fittingly arrayed by the twelve (future) tribes, so She replaced Rachel as mistress of Jacob's household. See *Zohar* 1:158a, 160b, 165b, 175b.

On *Shekhinah* as Jacob's wife, see *Zohar* 1:21b, 133a, 138b, 236b; 3:187b.

370. **Why did Rachel die immediately?** As soon as Benjamin was born, rather than when he matured.

She began to be arrayed in twelve tribes; through him Kingdom of Heaven began to manifest on earth.[371]

"This mystery: Any beginning about to manifest is strained, so it entails a sentence of death, thereby settling. Here, as She was about to be arrayed, to possess the house, judgment was executed upon Rachel; then She settled, arrayed.[372] When kingdom was about to manifest on earth, it began in judgment and did not settle fittingly in its site until judgment aroused against Saul, according to his deeds; then kingdom settled, arrayed.[373]

"Come and see: Every beginning is harsh;[374] later, gentleness. On Rosh Hashanah, a harsh beginning, because the entire world is judged, each and every one according to his deeds; later: gentleness, forgiveness, atonement.[375] For beginning issues from the left, so its judgments are harsh. Later, right arouses; so, gentleness.[376]

"In time to come, the blessed Holy One intends to arouse gently against the other nations; later He will attack with harsh judgment, as is written: *YHVH will go forth like a mighty one; like a warrior He will stir up His zeal...* (Isaiah 42:13). At first, *YHVH*, compassion;[377] then, *like a mighty one*—not *a mighty one;* then, *like a warrior*—not *a warrior*. Then potency will manifest against them, empowered to destroy them, as is written: *He will shout—yes, roar—overpowering His enemies* (ibid.). And it is written: *Then YHVH will go forth and battle those*

371. **Through him She began to possess the house...** Through the birth of Benjamin, *Shekhinah* was fully arrayed and could now manifest as *mother of children*, mistress of the house, and *Malkhut* (Kingdom).

According to Rabbi Abbahu (BT *Bava Batra* 25a), "*Shekhinah* is in the west." Benjamin's connection with Her is indicated by the fact that his tribe camped to the west of the wilderness Tabernacle. See Numbers 2:18–22; *Pesiqta Rabbati* 46; *Bemidbar Rabbah* 2:10.

372. **as She was about to be arrayed... judgment was executed...** Since *Shekhinah* derives from *Din* (Judgment), as She begins to manifest, judgment is executed. Here, Her manifestation entailed a sentence of death against Rachel.

373. **When kingdom was about to manifest on earth...** Similarly, when *malkhut* (kingdom) was initiated in Israel, it could not become firmly established until Saul, descended from Benjamin, was killed (1 Samuel 31) and David was enthroned. Even so, Saul's death transpired "according to his deeds," as punishment for his various sins, including killing the inhabitants of the priestly city of Nob and failing to kill Agag king of Amalek. See ibid. 15; 22:17–19; 1 Chronicles 10:13–14; *Vayiqra Rabbah* 26:7.

374. **Every beginning is harsh** See *Mekhilta, Baḥodesh* 2: "All beginnings are difficult." Cf. *Zohar* 2:187a.

375. **later: gentleness, forgiveness, atonement** By the end of Yom Kippur, the conclusion of the Ten Days of Repentance.

376. **from the left... Later, right arouses...** From *Din* (Judgment); later *Ḥesed* (Lovingkindness) arouses.

377. ***YHVH*, compassion** See above, note 361.

nations, as when He battles on a day of war (Zechariah 14:3), and similarly: *Who is this coming from Edom, in crimsoned garments from Bozrah?...* (Isaiah 63:1)."

As her soul was departing—for she was dying—she named him Ben-oni, but his father called him Benjamin (Genesis 35:18).[378]

Rabbi Yehudah opened, "*YHVH is good, a stronghold in a day of trouble; He cares for those who seek refuge in Him* (Nahum 1:7). Happy is the share of the human being who is strengthened by the blessed Holy One, for the strength of the blessed Holy One is potent! They have established: *YHVH is good,* as is said: *YHVH is good to all* (Psalms 145:9). *A stronghold*—strength of salvation, as is written: *He is a stronghold of* [174b] *salvation for His anointed* (ibid. 28:8). *In a day of trouble*—in a day when other nations trouble Israel.

"Come and see what is written: *If you slacken in a day of trouble, how narrow is your strength!* (Proverbs 24:10). What does *if you slacken* mean? One who loses his grip on the blessed Holy One, not grasping Him. How does one grasp the blessed Holy One firmly? By grasping Torah. For whoever grasps Torah grasps the Tree of Life,[379] strengthening—as it were—Assembly of Israel, invigorating Her.[380] But if one lets go of Torah, what is written? *If you slacken*—if one lets go of Torah, *in a day of trouble, how narrow is your strength!*[381] On a day when trouble assails him, it is as if he constricts *Shekhinah*, strength of the world.[382]

"Alternatively, *how* צר (*tsar*), *narrow, is your strength!* Come and see: When a person slackens in Torah and follows an improper path, countless foes lie in wait to accuse him on a day of trouble. Even his soul—his strength and power—becomes his adversary, as is written: *tsar, an adversary, is your strength,* for she confronts him as an adversary."[383]

378. ***Ben-oni... Benjamin*** בן-אוני (*Ben-oni*) means "son of my sorrow, suffering, trouble (or vigor)," while בנימין (*Binyamin*), Benjamin, means "son of the right hand (or son of the south)."

379. **Tree of Life** Torah is identified with the Tree of Life, based on the description of wisdom in Proverbs 3:18: *She is a tree of life to those who grasp her.* See BT *Berakhot* 32b, 61b; *Zohar* 1:152b, 193a.

In the *Zohar,* Torah often symbolizes *Tif'eret,* known as the Tree of Life and the blessed Holy One, partner of *Shekhinah*.

380. **Assembly of Israel...** Referring to *Shekhinah* (see above, note 147). By studying Torah, one energizes Her.

381. **if one lets go of Torah...** See BT *Berakhot* 63a: "Rabbi Tavi said in the name of Rabbi Yoshiyah, 'Whoever relinquishes words of Torah has no strength to stand in a day of trouble, as is said: *If you slacken, in a day of trouble how narrow is your strength!*'" See *Zohar* 1:152b.

382. **as if he constricts *Shekhinah*...** See BT *Ḥagigah* 16a: "Rabbi Yitsḥak said, 'Whoever sins secretly, it is as if he squeezes [or: thrusts away] the feet of *Shekhinah*.'" See *Zohar* 1:152b.

383. **she confronts him as an adversary** Sinful action turns one's own soul into an adversary. See BT *Ta'anit* 11a: "Rabbi Ḥidka said, 'A person's soul testifies against him.'"

Rabbi Abba said, "When a person follows the paths of Torah and all his ways are properly aligned, countless advocates stand over him to speak well of him."[384]

He opened, saying, "*If he has an angel over him, an advocate, one among a thousand, to vouch for his uprightness, then He is gracious to him and says, 'Spare him from going down to the pit; I have found a ransom'* (Job 33:23–24). These verses call for contemplation. Isn't everything revealed before the blessed Holy One? Does He need an angel to announce good and evil? Well, He certainly does! For when a person has advocates to recall his merits in His presence—and no accusers—then *He is gracious to him and says, 'Spare him from going down to the pit; I have found a ransom.'*[385]

"Come and see: In this verse you will discover the lucidity of the word. It is written: *If he has an angel over him.* If nothing further had been written, it would have been fine. But it is written: *an advocate, one among a thousand.* Who is that? The angel appointed to accompany a person on the left side, as is written: *A thousand may fall at your side* (Psalms 91:7)—namely, the left side, for it is written: *ten thousand at your right* (ibid.).[386] However, *one among a thousand* is the evil impulse, who is one of those on the left, since he ascends and obtains authorization.[387] So if a person walks the way of truth, that evil impulse becomes his servant, as has been said—for it is written: *Better to be lightly esteemed and have a servant* (Proverbs 12:9). Then he ascends and is transformed into an advocate, declaring that person's merit in the presence of the blessed Holy One.[388] Then the blessed Holy One proclaims, *Spare him from going down to the pit.*

In Hebrew and Aramaic, "soul" is grammatically feminine; thus when hypostasized, the soul appears as female.

384. **to speak well of him** In the heavenly court.

385. **when a person has advocates...** The angelic advocates stimulate God's compassion. Cf. BT *Shabbat* 32a.

386. **for it is written: *ten thousand at your right*** The verse reads: *A thousand may fall at your side, ten thousand at your right, but it will not come near you.* Since the number *ten thousand* is explicitly linked with the right side, *a thousand* refers to the left. According to Rabbi Abba, apparently, angels on the right topple *ten thousand* enemies, while *a thousand* harsh forces on the left are themselves toppled.

387. **he ascends and obtains authorization** See the description of Satan's itinerary in BT *Bava Batra* 16a: "He descends and seduces, ascends and arouses wrath, obtains authorization and seizes the soul."

Satan is identified with the evil impulse on the same Talmudic page: "Resh Lakish said, 'Satan, the evil impulse, and the Angel of Death are one and the same.'" On the good and evil impulses as a pair of angels on the right and the left, respectively, see *Zohar* 1:49b, 144b, 155b, 165b; 3:263b; cf. BT *Berakhot* 61a.

388. **evil impulse becomes his servant...** On this transformation, see *Zohar* 1:114b, 144b; above, page 6.

"Nevertheless, he does not return empty-handed, since another is delivered to him—to overpower, to pluck his soul—since that person's sins precede and he becomes ransom for this one, as is written: *I have found a ransom.*[389]

"Alternatively, *I have found a ransom*—the merit that you mentioned is his ransom, redeeming him from dying and descending to Hell.[390] Therefore one should walk the way of truth, so that the accuser becomes an advocate.

"Similarly, on Yom Kippur, Israel gives him something, preoccupying him until he turns into their servant, ascending and testifying before the blessed Holy One, becoming their advocate.[391] Concerning this, Solomon said, *If your enemy is hungry, give him bread to eat; if he is thirsty, give him water to drink* (Proverbs 25:21)—referring to the evil impulse.[392]

"So, *in a day of trouble,*[393] when one slackens in Torah, he thrusts the blessed Holy One, as it were, toward that evil impulse, who becomes his accuser.[394] *How narrow is* כחכה (*koḥekha*), *your strength*—'how constricted is כח כה (*koaḥ koh*), the strength of *koh*,' for he approaches His presence to accuse and His power weakens.[395]

"Come and see: *YHVH is good, a stronghold in a day of trouble* (Nahum 1:7). What is *a day of trouble*? When Esau came to attack Jacob.[396] *He cares for those who seek refuge in Him* (ibid.)—when Dinah's misfortune befell him.[397]

389. **he does not return empty-handed...** Instead of his originally intended victim, the evil impulse plucks the soul of another sinner. On this theme, see Isaiah 43:3; *Zohar* 1:114a; 3:205a; *Zohar Ḥadash* 54a–b. Cf. BT *Ḥagigah* 4b–5a.

390. **the merit that you mentioned is his ransom...** God is speaking to the evil impulse.

391. **Similarly, on Yom Kippur...** According to Leviticus 16, a scapegoat bearing the sins of Israel is offered on Yom Kippur to the wilderness demon Azazel. (Similarly in the Babylonian Akitu ritual, a goat is substituted for a human being and offered to Ereshkigal, goddess of the Abyss.) See *Pirqei de-Rabbi Eli'ezer* 46: "They gave him [Satan] a bribe on Yom Kippur [i.e., the scapegoat] so that he would not nullify Israel's sacrifice."

The theme of assuaging demonic powers by granting them their share appears frequently in the *Zohar*. See Naḥmanides on Leviticus 16:8; *Zohar* 1:11a, 64a, 65a, 114a–b, 138b, 190a, 210b; 2:33a, 154b, 237b, 266b; 3:63a (*Piq*), 101b–102a, 202b–203a, 258b; *ZḤ* 87b–c (*MhN, Rut*); Moses de León, *She'elot u-Tshuvot,* 49; Tishby, *Wisdom of the Zohar,* 3:890–95. Cf. *Bereshit Rabbah* 57:4; *Shemot Rabbah* 21:7.

392. ***If your enemy is hungry...*** See *Sifrei,* Deuteronomy 45; *Bereshit Rabbah* 54:1; *Pesiqta de-Rav Kahana* 11:1; *Zohar* 2:262b (*Heikh*); 3:259a.

393. ***in a day of trouble*** The verse, quoted above, reads: *If you slacken in a day of trouble, how narrow is your strength!*

394. **he thrusts the blessed Holy One...** See BT *Ḥagigah* 16a: "Rabbi Yitsḥak said, 'Whoever sins secretly, it is as if he thrusts away [or: squeezes] the feet of *Shekhinah*.'" Cf. above, at note 382.

395. **כח כה (*koaḥ koh*), the strength of *koh*...** The strength of *Shekhinah* is weakened by the accusation of sin. The word כה (*koh*), "here, thus," designates the Divine Presence, which is always right here. See *Zohar* 1:152b.

396. **When Esau came to attack Jacob** See Genesis 32:4–33:11.

397. **Dinah's misfortune...** The rape of

"Come and see: The Accuser confronts a person only in time of danger.[398] Come and see: Because Jacob delayed fulfilling the vow he had made before the blessed Holy One, judgment was empowered by the Accuser—who denounced Jacob, [175a] demanding justice when Rachel was in danger.[399] He said before Him, 'Look! Jacob made his vow and did not fulfill it. Even though he dominates all in wealth, children, and everything one needs, he still did not fulfill the vow he made before You; yet You have not punished him!' Immediately, *Rachel gave birth, and she had hard labor* (Genesis 35:16). What does this mean: *she had hard*? Judgment was hardened above with the Angel of Death.

"Thereby Jacob was punished. Why? Because it is written: *If you have nothing with which to pay, why should he take your bed from under you?* (Proverbs 22:27). Therefore Rachel died; judgment was rendered by the Angel of Death.[400]

"Come and see: What did he do when Esau came? *He placed the maids and their children first, Leah and her children behind them, and Rachel and Joseph behind them* (Genesis 33:2). Why? Because he feared for Rachel—lest that wicked one gaze upon her beauty and attack him because of her.[401]

"What else is written? *The maids drew near, they and their children, and bowed. Leah too and her children drew near and bowed*—females preceding males. But of Rachel, what is written? *Afterward Joseph and Rachel drew near* (ibid., 6–7)—Joseph preceding his mother, covering her. So it is written: *A fruitful bough is Joseph, a fruitful bough* עלי עין (*alei ayin*), *by a spring* (ibid. 49:22), for he expanded his body and covered his mother. *Alei ayin*, on account of an eye, on account of the eye of that wicked one.[402]

Dinah (Genesis 34). Instead of דינה (*dinah*), several *Zohar* manuscripts read דינא (*dina*), "judgment," alluding to the following passage.

398. **The Accuser confronts a person only in time of danger** See *Midrash Tanna'im*, Deuteronomy 23:10: "Satan accuses only in time of danger."

Cf. JT *Shabbat* 2:6, 5b; *Bereshit Rabbah* 91:9; *Zohar* 1:73b, 113a.

399. **Because Jacob delayed fulfilling the vow...** When Jacob fled from Esau, he vowed that if God protected him, cared for him, and guided him safely back home, he would offer God a tithe of everything (Genesis 28:20–22). Because Jacob delayed fulfilling this vow, Satan sought to attack his wife Rachel in her vulnerable state of childbirth.

See *Vayiqra Rabbah* 37:1; *Qohelet Rabbah* on 5:4; *Tanḥuma, Vayishlaḥ* 8; cf. BT *Shabbat* 32a–b; *Sekhel Tov*, Genesis 35:16.

400. ***If you have nothing with which to pay...*** It is dangerous to make a vow, because if you cannot fulfill what you promised, your wife (*your bed*) may be seized by the Angel of Death.

See *Midrash Tanna'im*, Deuteronomy 23:22; BT *Shabbat* 32b; *Tanḥuma, Vayishlaḥ* 8; *Qohelet Zuta* on 5:4.

401. **that wicked one...** Esau.

402. **Joseph preceding his mother, covering her...** Protecting her from Esau's evil eye and evil designs.

See *Targum Yerushalmi*, Genesis 33:7; *Bereshit Rabbah* 78:10; *Pesiqta Rabbati* 12; *Sekhel Tov*, Genesis 33:7; *Zohar* 3:202b; *Zohar Ḥadash* 66c.

"Here she was punished by the evil impulse, who denounced in time of danger, and Jacob was punished for not fulfilling the vow. This was more severe for Jacob than all the troubles that befell him.[403] How do we know that it was due to him? For it is written: *Rachel died* עלי (*alai*), *upon me* (ibid. 48:7)—*alai*, on account of me—precisely: because I delayed the vow!"[404]

Rabbi Yose said, "It is written: *A causeless curse* לא תבוא (*lo tavo*), *goes nowhere* (Proverbs 26:2), and they have established: לו (*lo*), *to him*, with a ו (*vav*). Once the curse of a righteous man issues from his mouth—even unintentionally—that evil impulse snatches it and accuses with it in time of danger.[405]

"Jacob said, *With whomever you find your gods—he shall not live!* (Genesis 31:32), and even though he didn't know, that Satan—constantly present among humans—snatched that word.[406] Therefore we have learned: 'A person should never open his mouth for Satan,'[407] because he seizes that word and accuses with it above and below, especially a word of the wise or righteous. For both of these, Rachel was punished."[408]

403. **more severe for Jacob than all the troubles...** See *Bereshit Rabbah* 97 (on Genesis 48:7); *Rut Rabbah* 2:7.

404. ***Rachel died* עלי (*alai*), *upon me*... on account of me...** The word עלי (*alai*) means literally "upon me, on me," though it apparently connotes "alas, to my sorrow" (see Psalms 42:6–7). Here, drawing on midrashic tradition, Rabbi Yehudah reads it in one of its idiomatic senses: "on account of me." Furthermore, because the word *alai* is also rabbinic votive terminology (in still another sense: "it is incumbent upon me"), this connotation as well may allude to Jacob's earlier, unfulfilled vow.

See *Vayiqra Rabbah* 37:1; *Qohelet Rabbah* on 5:4; *Aggadat Bereshit* 52:1; *Leqaḥ Tov* and *Sekhel Tov*, Genesis 31:32; *Bereshit Rabbah* 74:9; *Zohar* 1:160b, 223a; above, note 399. On the formulaic use of *alai* in vows, see M *Qinnim* 1:1.

405. ***A causeless curse* לא תבוא (*lo tavo*), *goes nowhere*... לו (*lo*), *to him*...** The Masoretic spelling is לא (*lo*), "no, not," meaning that the curse does "not" reach its intended victim. However, the word is traditionally read לו (*lo*), "to him"—with a ו (*vav*) instead of an א (*alef*)—meaning that the curse backfires and "goes to him," i.e., falls upon the curser himself. See Ibn Ezra and *Minḥat Shai*, ad loc.

Here Rabbi Yose adopts the spelling לו (*lo*), "to him," and apparently understands it to mean that the unintentional curse of a righteous man goes to the evil impulse, who enacts it at an opportune moment.

Cf. BT *Makkot* 11a, in the name of Rav: "The curse of a wise man, even without cause, takes effect."

406. **even though he didn't know...** That Rachel had stolen Laban's idols, as indicated at the end of the verse. According to rabbinic tradition, Jacob's rash statement doomed Rachel to a premature death.

See *Bereshit Rabbah* 74:9; *Eikhah Rabbah* (Buber) 5:16; *Qohelet Rabbah* on 10:5; *Tanḥuma, Vayetse* 12; *Pirqei de-Rabbi Eli'ezer* 36.

407. **'A person should never open his mouth for Satan'** One should never utter ominous words, thereby providing an opening for Satan to wreak havoc. The statement is attributed to Rabbi Yose in BT *Berakhot* 19a.

See *Zohar* 1:195b; 2:266a; 3:155b.

408. **For both of these, Rachel was punished** Because Jacob unintentionally cursed her and because he delayed fulfilling his vow.

As her soul was departing—for she was dying (Genesis 35:18).[409]

Rabbi Abba said, "Since Scripture states *as her soul was departing,* don't we know that *she was dying*? But this is necessary, because it returned no more to the body and she died a bodily death. For there are humans whose souls depart yet return to their sites, as is said: *His soul returned to him* (1 Samuel 30:12); *Their heart departed* (Genesis 42:28); *My soul departed as he spoke* (Song of Songs 5:6); *There was no soul left in him* (1 Kings 17:17).[410] But as for this one, the soul departed and did not return to her site.

"*She named him Ben-oni* (Genesis 35, ibid.),[411] for the harshness of judgment decreed against her. But Jacob restored and bound him to the right, since west must be bound to the right.[412] Although he is בן אוני (*Ben oni*), son of my sorrow, side of harsh judgment, yet he is בן ימין (*Ben yamin*), *Benjamin,* son of the right, for he was bound to the right.

"She was buried by the road, as has been explained. This one's death and burial are revealed, while Leah's death and burial are not,[413] although these four matriarchs share a mystery, as has been established."[414]

409. ***As her soul was departing—for she was dying*** The verse continues: *—she named him Ben-oni, but his father called him Benjamin.*

410. **humans whose souls depart yet return to their sites...** Their souls leave only momentarily and they revive. Cf. *Mekhilta, Beshallaḥ* 6.

The verse in Samuel actually reads רוחו (*ruḥo*), *his spirit,* not נפשו (*nafsho*), *his soul.* On Song of Songs 5:6, see BT *Shabbat* 88b; *Shir ha-Shirim Rabbah,* ad loc. On 1 Kings 17:17 (concerning the son of the widow of Zarephath revived by Elijah), cf. Maimonides, *Guide of the Perplexed* 1:42.

411. ***She named him Ben-oni*** The verse continues: *but his father called him Benjamin.* The name בן-אוני (*Ben-oni*) means "son of my sorrow, suffering, trouble (or vigor)," while בנימין (*Binyamin*), Benjamin, means "son of the right hand (or son of the south)."

412. **Jacob restored and bound him to the right...** Benjamin was born in suffering and harsh judgment (characteristic of the left side), which had been decreed against Rachel. She was linked with *Shekhinah,* who is influenced by the left and symbolized by the west. However, Jacob restored Benjamin to the right side (or the south), characterized by loving-kindness; he thereby sweetened the harshness within *Shekhinah* (west), drawing Her to the right as well.

413. **She was buried by the road... revealed...** Rachel symbolizes *Shekhinah,* who is more revealed, so this matriarch's death is recorded explicitly in the Torah and her burial place is by the road (Genesis 35:19; 48:7). Leah, on the other hand, symbolizes the concealed realm of *Binah,* so her death is not recorded in the Torah and she was buried within the cave of Machpelah (ibid. 49:31; Naḥmanides, ibid. 35:8). See *Zohar* 1:152a (*ST*), 158a.

414. **these four matriarchs share a mystery...** Referring to Rachel, Leah, and their two maids (Bilhah and Zilpah), all of whose offspring symbolize various aspects of the sefirotic realm. See *Zohar* 1:154a, 155a, 158a. Cf. 1:133a–b.

Jacob set up a pillar upon her grave (Genesis 35:20).[415] Rabbi Yose said, "Why? So her site would never be concealed until the day that the blessed Holy One intends to revive the dead, as is said: *until the day* (ibid.)—until that very day!"[416]

Rabbi Yehudah said, "Until the day that *Shekhinah* returns to that site together with the exiles of Israel, as is said: *There is hope for your future, declares YHVH: children will return to their land* (Jeremiah 31:17). The blessed Holy One swore this oath to her, and as they return from exile, Israel are destined to stand by Rachel's grave and weep there, just as she wept over Israel's exile. So it is written: *With weeping they will come* (ibid., 9), and: *There is reward for your labor* (ibid., 16). At that [175b] moment, Rachel—who is by the road—is destined to rejoice along with Israel and *Shekhinah*, as the Companions have established."[417]

59 *While Israel was dwelling in that land, Reuben went and lay with Bilhah, his father's concubine* (Genesis 35:22). Rabbi El'azar said, "*While Israel was dwelling in that land*—for Leah and Rachel had died, and the house was possessed by the possessor.[418]

"Now, would you ever imagine that Reuben went and lay with Bilhah? Rather, as long as Leah and Rachel were alive, *Shekhinah* hovered over them; now that they had died, *Shekhinah* did not depart from the house, but dwelled there with Bilhah, although *Shekhinah*

415. ***Jacob set up a pillar upon her grave*** The verse concludes: *it is the pillar of Rachel's grave to this day.*

416. ***until the day*—until that very day** In this verse the word היום (*ha-yom*) is an idiom meaning "today," but Rabbi Yose insists on its literal meaning: "the day," implying the great day of resurrection.

417. **just as she wept over Israel's exile...** See the context in Jeremiah (31:15–17): *Thus says YHVH: A voice is heard in Ramah—wailing, bitter weeping—Rachel weeping for her children, refusing to be comforted for her children, because they are no more. Thus says YHVH: Restrain your voice from weeping, your eyes from tears; for there is reward for your labor, declares YHVH: they will return from the land of the enemy. There is hope for your future, declares YHVH: children will return to their land.*

See *Bereshit Rabbah* 82:10: "*Rachel died, and she was buried on the road to Ephrath* ... (Genesis 35:19). What prompted Jacob to bury Rachel on the road to Ephrath? He foresaw that the exiles [carried off by the Babylonians] would pass through there; therefore he buried her there so that she would pray for mercy for them, as is written: *Rachel weeping for her children... Thus says YHVH: Restrain your voice from weeping.... There is hope for your future...*"

See *Zohar* 1:203a; 2:12b. Rachel symbolizes *Shekhinah*, who participates in Israel's exile. See *Mekhilta, Pisḥa* 14; BT *Megillah* 29a.

418. ***in that land*... house was possessed by the possessor** Jacob (Israel) dwelled with *Shekhinah*, symbolized by *land*, because She now possessed the house. See above, note 369.

should have possessed the house fittingly.[419] Yet unless Jacob appeared in a coupling of male and female, *Shekhinah* would not have dwelled openly in the house; therefore *Shekhinah* stayed with Bilhah.[420]

"Then Reuben came and, seeing Bilhah inheriting his mother's place, he disheveled the bed. Because *Shekhinah* was present there, it is written of him: *He lay with Bilhah*."[421]

Rabbi Yeisa said that he slept on that bed, showing disrespect for *Shekhinah*.[422]

"So he was not disqualified from the count of the tribes, as immediately enumerated by the verse.[423] Therefore it is written: *Jacob's firstborn, Reuben* (ibid., 23), appointing him head of all the tribes."

Rabbi Yehudah opened, "*The ways of YHVH are right; the righteous walk in them, while transgressors stumble in them* (Hosea 14:10). All the ways of the blessed Holy One are entirely right, His paths true, but inhabitants of the world neither

419. ***Shekhinah* should have possessed the house fittingly** By Herself.

420. **Yet unless Jacob appeared in a coupling...** *Shekhinah* dwells only in a place where male and female are united, so Jacob had to join Bilhah to ensure Her presence.

421. **seeing Bilhah inheriting his mother's place...** Seeing Bilhah taking the place of Leah his mother and sleeping with Jacob, Reuben disheveled Bilhah's bed, unaware that *Shekhinah* was present there. Scripture condemns this act by exaggerating it as sexual intercourse.

See BT *Shabbat* 55b: "Rabbi Shemu'el son of Naḥmani said in the name of Rabbi Yonatan, 'Whoever says that Reuben sinned is surely mistaken, for it is said: *And the sons of Jacob were twelve* (Genesis 35:22), teaching that they were all equivalent. But then how do I establish *He lay with Bilhah, his father's concubine*? This teaches that he disheveled his father's bed, and Scripture charges him as if he lay with her.'

"It was taught: Rabbi Shim'on son of El'azar said, 'That righteous one [Reuben] was saved from that sin, and this deed never came his way. Is it possible that his seed was destined to stand on Mount Ebal and proclaim: *Cursed be he who lies with his father's wife* (Deuteronomy 27:13, 20), yet sin should come his way? But then how do I establish *He lay with Bilhah, his father's concubine*? He avenged his mother's humiliation. He said, "If my mother's sister [Rachel] was a rival to my mother [Leah], will the maid of my mother's sister [Bilhah] be a rival to my mother?" He immediately disheveled her bed.' Others say: 'He disheveled two beds: one of *Shekhinah* and one of his father.'"

Rashi (ad loc., s.v. *aḥat shel shekhinah*) explains that Jacob arranged a bed for *Shekhinah* in the tent of each of his wives, and in whichever tent he saw *Shekhinah*, he would sleep that night.

See Genesis 49:4; *Sifrei*, Deuteronomy 347; *Targum Yerushalmi*, Genesis 35:22; *Bereshit Rabbah* 97 (on Genesis 49:4) and Theodor, ad loc.; ibid. 98:4; *Tanḥuma* (Buber), *Vayḥi* 11; *Midrash Aggadah*, Genesis 35:22; *Zohar* 1:176a.

422. **he slept on that bed...** See *Tanḥuma* (Buber), *Vayḥi* 11.

423. **So he was not disqualified from the count of the tribes...** Since Reuben's act was not as reprehensible as it appears in Scripture (above, note 421), the same verse concludes: *and the sons of Jacob were twelve*, implying that Reuben was still fully one of them. See *Sifrei*, Deuteronomy 31.

know nor consider the foundation of their existence.[424] So, *the righteous walk in them,* since they know the ways of the blessed Holy One and engage in Torah. For whoever engages in Torah knows and contemplates the ways of the blessed Holy One, following them without straying right or left. *While transgressors stumble in them*—those wicked ones who neither engage in Torah nor contemplate His ways nor know which way they are going! Since they fail to contemplate and engage in Torah, they stumble on those ways in this world and in the world that is coming.

"Come and see: When any person who engages in Torah leaves this world, his soul ascends by those ways and paths of Torah—ways and paths well-known![425] Those who know ways of Torah in this world follow them in that world when they leave this world. But if they haven't engaged in Torah in this world and don't know the ways and paths, then when they leave this world they don't know how to walk those ways and paths; they stumble in them. Such a person follows other ways—not ways of Torah—and countless punishments are aroused against him, inflicted upon him. 61

"Of one who engages in Torah, what is written? *When you lie down, she will protect you; you will awake, and she will speak for you* (Proverbs 6:22).[426] *When you lie down* in the grave, Torah will protect you from the judgment of that world. *You will awake*—when the blessed Holy One awakens spirits and souls, reviving the dead, *she will speak for you,* becoming an advocate for the body, so that those bodies who engaged fully in Torah will rise fittingly.[427] These will be the first to rise for eternal life, as is said: *Many of those who sleep in the dust will awake: these to everlasting life* (Daniel 12:2)[428]—these are destined for *everlasting life* because they absorbed themselves in *everlasting life:* Torah.[429]

424. **neither know nor consider the foundation of their existence** See BT *Ḥagigah* 12b: "Rabbi Yose said, 'Woe to creatures, for they see but do not know what they see; they stand but do not know on what they stand!'"

See *Zohar* 1:99a, 195b, 203b, 224a, 226b; 2:23b, 142a; 3:77a.

425. **ways and paths well-known** To devotees of Torah.

426. ***When you lie down, she will protect you...*** The full verse reads: *When you walk, she will guide you; when you lie down, she will protect you; you will awake, and she will speak for you.* The plain sense of the final clause היא תשיחך (*hi tesiḥekha*) is *she will talk with you,* but Rabbi Yehudah, drawing on rabbinic sources (see the next note), understands it as *she will speak for you.* In Hebrew, "Torah" is grammatically feminine and therefore, when hypostasized, appears as female.

427. ***When you lie down* in the grave...** See *Avot* 6:9; *Sifra, Aḥarei Mot* 13:11, 86b; BT *Sotah* 21a; Rashi, ad loc., s.v. *hi tesiḥekha*; *Devarim Rabbah* (Lieberman), 6:9; *Aggadat Bereshit* 46; *Zohar* 1:185a.

428. **first to rise...*Many of those who sleep...*** The full verse reads: *Many of those who sleep in the dust will awake: these to everlasting life, those to shame and everlasting contempt.* See *Zohar* 1:127b (*MhN*), 140a (*MhN*), 182a.

429. ***everlasting life:* Torah** On Torah as

"Come and see: The bodies of all those who engaged in Torah endure, protected by Torah. How so? At that time the blessed Holy One will arouse a single wind comprising four winds,[430] and that wind comprising four winds is intended for all those who engaged in Torah, to revive them for eternal existence.

"Now, you might say 'Look at what is written: *Come from the four winds, O wind* (Ezekiel 37:9)![431] Why didn't they survive? They all died as before!'[432]

"Come and see: At the time that the blessed Holy One raised the dead
through Ezekiel, that wind—though composed of four winds—did not descend
in order to sustain them enduringly. Rather, it was to demonstrate that the
blessed Holy One will one day revive the dead in that manner, sustaining them
by the wind [176a] comprised in this manner. Even though the bones returned
then to their former state, the blessed Holy One wanted to show the whole
world that He will one day revive the dead. So what is written of that wind
destined to descend into the righteous? *Come from the four winds, O wind*—a
wind comprising four—since the blessed Holy One intends to sustain them en-
62 duringly, fittingly in the world. Whoever has engaged in Torah in this world—
she stands over him as his advocate in the presence of the blessed Holy One."

Rabbi Shim'on said, "All those words of Torah—all that Torah in which a person engaged in this world—those very words of Torah stand in the presence of the blessed Holy One, reciting themselves before Him. She calls out, unwaningly. At that time she *will speak*, conveying what the person attained, how he strived in this world.[433] So they will rise enduringly for eternal life, as we have said. Therefore, *The ways of YHVH are right; the righteous walk in them, while transgressors stumble in them.*"

Rabbi Ḥiyya opened, "*Now Eli was very old. He heard of all that his sons did to all Israel, and how they lay with the women who assembled at the entrance to the Tent of Meeting* (1 Samuel 2:22). Could you ever imagine that priests of YHVH would do such a thing? Look! Their sin is already stated explicitly in Scripture, as is written: *for the men treated YHVH's offering with contempt*, and: *This was the priests' practice with the people: when each man would offer a sacrifice... Even before the fat was burned, the priest's lad would come and say to the man who was*

the source of eternal life, see BT *Berakhot* 21a, 48b; *Shabbat* 10a; *Soferim* 13:6.

430. **single wind comprising four winds** See *Zohar* 1:139a (*MhN*), 235a; 2:13a–b; 3:130b (*IR*).

431. ***Come from the four winds, O wind*** The word רוח (*ruaḥ*) means "wind, spirit, breath."

432. **Why didn't they survive?...** Why didn't the dead who were resurrected through Ezekiel's prophecy remain alive? See BT *Sanhedrin* 92b: "Rabbi Eli'ezer said, 'The dead who were revived by Ezekiel stood up, uttered song, and died.'"

433. **she *will speak*...** See above, note 426.

sacrificing, 'Hand over meat to roast for the priest...'... He would say, 'No! Hand it over now; and if not, I'll take it by force.' Therefore, *the sin of the young men was very great* (1 Samuel 2:13, 15–17).[434]

"Now, everything that they took was only from those portions intended for the priests to eat; but because they treated the offering lightly, they were punished.[435] Yet here Scripture states: *how they lay with the women who assembled*!

"Perish the thought that they committed this sin—especially in that sacred place! All of Israel would have risen up and killed them. Rather, they delayed their entrance into the sanctuary, prohibiting them from entering to pray until the sacrifices had been offered, because they didn't bring sacrifices that included a priestly portion. So they delayed them, and those women would plead with them to enter. Therefore it is written: *how they lay with the women*—delaying them, as we have said.[436]

434. **Their sin is already stated explicitly...** The full passage (1 Samuel 2:12–17) reads: *The sons of Eli were scoundrels; they did not know YHVH. This was the priests' practice with the people: when each man would offer a sacrifice, the priest's lad would come while the meat was boiling, a three-pronged fork in his hand. And he would thrust into the cauldron or the pot or the vat or the kettle, and whatever the fork would bring up, the priest would take away with it. Thus they would do to all the Israelites who came there to Shiloh. Even before the fat was burned, the priest's lad would come and say to the man who was sacrificing, "Hand over meat to roast for the priest, for he won't take boiled meat from you, only raw." And if the man said, "Let the fat be burned up now, and then take whatever you want," he would say, "No! Hand it over now; and if not, I'll take it by force." The sin of the young men was very great before YHVH, for the men treated YHVH's offering with contempt.*

435. **those portions intended for the priests to eat...** According to Leviticus 7:31–36, after God's share of *zevaḥ ha-shelamim* ("the sacrifice of well-being") had been burned on the altar, the priests were then entitled to eat the breast and the right thigh of the sacrificial animal. The sons of Eli "treated the offering lightly" by seizing their portions of the sacrifice right from the cooking pots even before the altar sacrifice. See BT *Yoma* 9a–b. Cf. Rashi and Radak on 1 Samuel 2:13, and Ralbag on ibid., 14, who contend that the priests took more than their share.

436. **they delayed their entrance into the sanctuary...** Their sin consisted in the fact that they delayed the women from entering until the *shelamim* of others had been offered. These women wanted to bring their own offerings (after childbirth or abnormal discharges of blood), but since the priestly portion of such offerings consisted only of a small bird, Eli's sons delayed them, preferring to feast on more substantial meat.

See BT *Shabbat* 55b: "Rabbi Shemu'el son of Naḥmani said in the name of Rabbi Yonatan, 'Whoever says that the sons of Eli sinned is surely mistaken.... But then how do I establish *how they lay with the women*? Because they delayed their bird-offerings, preventing them from returning to their husbands, Scripture charges them as if they lay with them.'"

See Leviticus 6:19, 22; 12:6–8; 15:29–30; JT *Sotah* 1:4, 16d; *Ketubbot* 13:1, 35c–d; *Bereshit Rabbah* 85:12; *Midrash Shemu'el* 7:4; *Aggadat Bereshit* 41.

"Similarly, *He lay with Bilhah* (Genesis 35:22). Perish the thought that he lay with her! Rather, he prevented her from performing conjugal enjoinment with his father—by disheveling the bed.[437] He committed this act in the presence of *Shekhinah*, for wherever conjugal enjoinment is fulfilled, *Shekhinah* hovers over that place, manifesting there; and whoever prevents conjugal relations causes *Shekhinah* to depart from the world. So it is written: *For when you mounted your father's bed, you defiled the one who mounted my couch* (Genesis 49:4).[438] Therefore it is written: *He lay with Bilhah, his father's concubine; and Israel heard. And the sons of Jacob were twelve* (ibid. 35:22)—all included in the count, their virtue undiminished."

Rabbi El'azar said, "Why at first *Israel* and then *Jacob*, as is written: *And Israel heard. And the sons of Jacob were twelve*?[439] Because when Reuben came and
disheveled that bed, he said, 'Father was supposed to raise twelve tribes in the
world, no more; yet now he wants to engender sons. Are we defective, so that he
wants to engender others all over again?' Immediately he disheveled the bed and
64 intercourse was foiled—disgracing *Shekhinah*, as it were, who hovered over that
bed. So it is written: *And Israel heard*, since by this name he ascended into
twelve concealed ones, twelve rivers of pure balsam.[440]

"*And the sons of Jacob were twelve*—twelve tribes in which *Shekhinah* is arrayed.[441] Who are they? The ones enumerated again by Torah, [176b] as before[442]—all of them holy, all of them deemed worthy by *Shekhinah* to attain the holiness of their Lord. For if he had committed that act, Reuben would not have entered into the count.[443]

437. **Similarly, *He lay with Bilhah*...** On this reinterpretation of Reuben's action, see above, pages 59–60.

438. **whoever prevents conjugal relations...** See BT *Yevamot* 64a; *Midrash Aggadah*, Numbers 10:36. The phrase *the one who mounted my couch* is understood here as referring to *Shekhinah*.

439. **Why at first *Israel* and then *Jacob*...** Why, in one and the same verse, is the patriarch called by two different names?

440. **by this name he ascended...** By wrestling with the angel and receiving the name Israel, the patriarch attained the *sefirah* of *Tif'eret Yisra'el* (Beauty of Israel), who is filled with the fragrant flow of emanation from *Binah*. According to rabbinic tradition, thirteen rivers of balsam await the righteous in the world that is coming.

See BT *Ta'anit* 25a; *Bereshit Rabbah* 62:2; *Zohar* 1:4b, 7a, 88a (*ST*); 2:127a; 3:181a.

441. ***sons of Jacob were twelve*... in which *Shekhinah*...** The name יעקב (*Ya'aqov*), *Jacob*, alludes to *Shekhinah*, perhaps because She is the עקב (*aqev*), *heel*, i.e., the end of the flow of emanation. See *Zohar* 1:145b, 174a, 210b.

On the image of the twelve tribes arraying *Shekhinah*, see *Zohar* 1:155a, 157b–158b, 159b, 174a, 240b–241a.

442. **enumerated again by Torah...** See Genesis 35:23–26.

443. **if he had committed that act...** If Reuben had actually had intercourse with Bilhah, he would no longer have been counted among the twelve.

"Nevertheless, he was punished by being deprived of his birthright, which was given to Joseph, as is said: *The sons of Reuben, firstborn of Israel—he was the firstborn; but when he defiled his father's bed, his birthright was given to Joseph* (1 Chronicles 5:1).[444]

"Come and see: Blessed be the name of the blessed Holy One forever and ever,[445] for all His acts are true, His way just, and everything He does accords with supernal wisdom.

"Come and see how decisive human action is! For everything a person does is inscribed enduringly before the blessed Holy One. Look! When Jacob entered into Leah, all that night his heart's desire focused on Rachel, since he thought she was Rachel. From that conjugal union, from that first drop, from that desire, Leah conceived, as they have established.[446] For if Jacob had not been unaware, Reuben would not have attained the count.[447] So he didn't attain a recognized name, but rather an unspecified name: ראובן (*Re'uven*), 'See, a son!'[448]

"Nevertheless, the action returned to its site. Just as the original desire was enacted for Rachel, that desire reverted to her, for the birthright reverted to Joseph, Rachel's firstborn. The site of desire was Rachel, and all ascends to its site, since all acts of the blessed Holy One are entirely true and just."

444. **deprived of his birthright, which was given to Joseph...** Rachel's firstborn. See *Targum Yerushalmi,* Genesis 49:3; *Bereshit Rabbah* 82:11; 98:4; *Tanḥuma* (Buber), *Toledot* 23. The verse in Chronicles reads *to the sons of Joseph.* See Theodor's note in *Bereshit Rabbah* 82:11.

445. **Blessed be the name of the blessed Holy One forever and ever** A paraphrase of Daniel 2:20: *Blessed be the name of God forever and ever.*

446. **When Jacob entered into Leah...** Jacob had arranged with Laban to marry his younger daughter, Rachel; but Laban deceived him, substituting for her his older daughter, Leah. Jacob did not discover the deception and the true identity of his new bride until the morning after their first night together, so in their act of intercourse his mind focused on Rachel. See Genesis 29:15–30; *Zohar* 1:17b, 155a–b (*ST*), 222b, 235a, 236a.

According to rabbinic tradition, Jacob never experienced a nocturnal emission, so Reuben was actually conceived from his father's first drop of semen. See *Targum Yerushalmi,* Genesis 49:3; *Bereshit Rabbah* 97 (on Genesis 49:3); 99:6; *Tanḥuma, Vayḥi* 9; *Tanḥuma* (Buber), *Vayḥi* 11; BT *Yevamot* 76a; Rashi on Genesis 49:3.

447. **if Jacob had not been unaware...** If Jacob had realized that he was having intercourse with Leah and had fantasized about Rachel, then the child who was conceived (Reuben) would have been tainted and could never have been considered one of the holy tribes. See BT *Nedarim* 20b; *Zohar* 1:155a (*ST*), 222b.

448. **he didn't attain a recognized name...** Leah named her son ראובן (*Re'uven*), understood here as meaning simply ראו בן (*Re'u ven*), *See, a son!* His lack of a normal name reflects the fact that his father never intended to engender him from Leah but rather from Rachel.

See Genesis 29:32; *Bereshit Rabbah* 71:3; *Midrash ha-Gadol,* Genesis 29:32; *Zohar* 1:154b, 155a (*ST*), 222b.

One day Rabbi Ḥizkiyah found Rabbi Yose sizzling a dribbling bronchus[449] in smoldering fire, and a cloud of smoke ascended. He said to him, "If the cloud of smoke from the sacrifice offered upon the altar had risen continuously like this, wrath would not have prevailed in the world, and Israel would not have been exiled from the land."[450]

Rabbi Yose opened, saying, "*Who is this rising from the wilderness like columns of smoke, perfumed with myrrh and frankincense, with all powders of the merchant?* (Song of Songs 3:6). *Who is this rising?* Come and see: When they were walking in the wilderness, *Shekhinah* walked in front of them and they followed Her,[451] as is written: *YHVH was going before them by day in a pillar of cloud, to guide them on the way* (Exodus 13:21).[452] So it is written: *Thus says YHVH: I remember the devotion of your youth, your love as a bride, how you followed Me in the wilderness* (Jeremiah 2:2).

"*Shekhinah* walked on, accompanied by all those clouds of glory. When *Shekhinah* journeyed, they would journey, as is written: *When the cloud lifted*

449. **sizzling a dribbling bronchus** מסטמיט ססנפיא (*Mistemit saspanya*), a neologistic phrase. *Mistemit* may derive from משטמיט (*mishtemit*), "to slip," understood here as "to drip." Cordovero (*OY*) renders it contextually as "roasting," while Lavi (*KP*) combines this with the sense of נמס (*nms*), "to melt," referring to melting fat dripping from the meat.

Saspanya is apparently a corruption of (or a play on) סמפונא (*sampona*), a rabbinic term derived from Greek *siphon* ("tube, siphon") and meaning "bronchus, bronchial tube." Several witnesses (O16, V6, *OY*, *KP*) preserve (or support) the reading סמפונא (*sampona*), while a greater number (M7, N23, P4, Pr6, R1, Cremona edition) preserve (or support) the reading ססנפיא (*saspanya*).

This pungent phrase stimulates a discussion of clouds and smoke, while also alluding back to the story of Eli's sons, which involves roasting meat and burning fat. See above, note 434. Cf. *Bei'ur ha-Millim ha-Zarot*, 181; Galante; *OL*; *DE*; *Ma'arikh*; Scholem.

450. **If the cloud of smoke from the sacrifice... had risen...** Direct ascent of the smoke assuages wrath and evokes compassion.

See *Avot de-Rabbi Natan* A, 35: "Ten miracles were performed for our ancestors in the Temple:... The wind never prevailed over the pillar of smoke. When the pillar of smoke went forth from the altar of the ascent-offering, it rose straight up like a staff until it reached the sky. When the pillar of incense went forth from the golden altar, it entered straight into the chamber of the Holy of Holies."

See Genesis 8:20–22; M *Avot* 5:5; *Avot de-Rabbi Natan* B, 39; BT *Yoma* 21a–b; *Zohar* 1:35a, 45b, 70a–b, 244a, 247b–248a; 2:122b, 130a, 141a, 242b, 259b (*Heikh*); 3:32b, 35b, 224a (*RM*), 294a (*IZ*); *ZḤ* 43b, 46c; *Sefer ha-Atsamim*, 20; El'azar of Worms, *Ḥokhmat ha-Nefesh*, 15c.

451. ***Who is this rising?* Come and see:... *Shekhinah*...** *Shekhinah*, the Divine Presence, is known as זאת (*zot*), *this*.

On the verse from Song of Songs, see *Shir ha-Shirim Rabbah*, ad loc.; *Zohar* 1:10b; 2:84a, 117a (*RM*).

452. ***YHVH* was going before them...** The full verse reads: *YHVH was going before them by day in a pillar of cloud, to guide them on the way, and by night in a pillar of fire, to give them light, so as to go by day and by night.* See *Zohar* 3:283b.

from over the tent, then the Children of Israel would journey (Numbers 9:17).[453] As She ascended, that cloud ascended on high, and all inhabitants of the world saw and asked, *Who is this rising from the wilderness like columns of smoke?*

"That cloud of *Shekhinah* appeared as smoke. Why? Because the fire kindled by Abraham for his son Isaac clung to Her, never leaving, merging with Her—so smoke arose.[454]

"Nevertheless, מקוטרת (*mequtteret*), *perfumed, with myrrh and frankincense.* What does *mequtteret* mean? מתקטרא (*Mitqattera*), Linked, with two other sides: cloud of Abraham on the right, cloud of Isaac on the left.[455]

"*With all powders of the merchant*—Jacob.[456]

"Alternatively: Joseph the Righteous, for Joseph's coffin accompanied Her.[457] Why רוכל (*rokhel*), *merchant*? Because he used to רכיל (*rakheil*), peddle slander, against his brothers to his father.[458]

"Alternatively, why *rokhel*? Because just as the hands of a merchant are filled

453. **When *Shekhinah* journeyed, they would journey...** When *Shekhinah*, symbolized by the cloud, journeyed, Israel would journey. The verse quoted is a conflation of Numbers 9:17 and Exodus 40:36.

454. **fire kindled by Abraham for his son Isaac clung to Her...** As Abraham was about to bind Isaac on the altar, he prepared wood, a knife, and fire (Genesis 22:6). This fire symbolizes *Gevurah*, as does Isaac, whereas Abraham symbolizes *Ḥesed*. The fire of *Gevurah* clings to *Shekhinah*, generating smoke.

On the mystical interpretation of the binding of Isaac, see *Zohar* 1:103b–104a, 118b, 119b, 133b, 164b.

455. **cloud of Abraham on the right, cloud of Isaac on the left** Symbolizing *Ḥesed* and *Gevurah*, which both emanate to *Shekhinah*. According to *Shir ha-Shirim Rabbah* on 3:6, Abraham and Isaac are symbolized respectively by myrrh and frankincense. Cf. *Shir ha-Shirim Zuta*, ad loc.

456. ***With all powders of the merchant*—Jacob** See *Shir ha-Shirim Zuta* on 3:6: "*With all* אבקת (*avqat*), *powders of, the merchant*—this is Jacob, as is said: ויאבק איש (*Va-ye'aveq ish*), *And a man wrestled, with him* (Genesis 32:25)."

See *Shir ha-Shirim Rabbah* on 3:6; *Battei Midrashot*, 1:351; *Yalqut Shim'oni*, Song of Songs 986; *Zohar* 3:243a (*RM*).

According to another interpretation, attributed to Rabbi Tanḥuma (*Shir ha-Shirim Rabbah*, loc. cit.): "Just as a peddler's basket contains all kinds of spices, so priesthood from Jacob, Levites from Jacob, and kingship from Jacob." (The priests were descended from Aaron, the Levites from Levi, and the Davidic kings from Judah, all of whom trace back to Jacob.)

Here Jacob symbolizes *Tif'eret*, who blends the ingredients of *Ḥesed* and *Gevurah*.

457. **for Joseph's coffin accompanied Her** Joseph's dying request to his brothers was that they take his bones with them when they eventually leave Egypt. During the Exodus, Moses fulfills this request, and Joseph's coffin then accompanies *Shekhinah* through the wilderness. In the *Zohar*, Joseph symbolizes *Yesod*, who unites with *Shekhinah*, so She is "linked" with him.

See Genesis 50:25; Exodus 13:19; Joshua 24:32; *Tosefta Sotah* 4:7; *Mekhilta, Beshallaḥ, Petiḥta* (and parallels); *ZḤ* 26d.

458. **he used to רכיל (*rakheil*), peddle slander, against his brothers...** See Genesis 37:2.

with bundles of costus and powdered clay,[459] so Joseph is fulfillment of Torah, fulfilling her because all commandments of Torah are linked with preserving the holy covenant.[460]

"So *Shekhinah* is linked with Abraham and Isaac. Jacob and Joseph are as one, sharing a single image, as is written: *These are the generations of Jacob: Joseph* (Genesis 37:2).[461] So, *with all powders of the merchant,* for all is watered from the site of the flowing, gushing river, and all faces glow.[462]

"Come and see: When Israel dwelled in the land and brought offerings, they all drew near to the blessed Holy One fittingly.[463] When the offering was performed and the smoke ascended in a straight column, they knew that the smoke of the altar kindled [177a] the lamp intended to be kindled—all faces glowing, lamps ablaze.[464]

"Ever since the Temple was destroyed, not a single day passes without wrath and rage, as is said: *God rages every day* (Psalms 7:12).[465] Joy has dissipated above

459. **just as the hands of a merchant are filled...** Based on the image in *Shir ha-Shirim Rabbah* on 3:6 (quoted above, note 456): "Just as a peddler's basket contains all kinds of spices..."

"Costus" renders קיסתי (*qistei*), apparently derived from Hebrew קשט (*qosht*), the spice "costus" (Latin *costus*, Greek *kostos*), which is one of the ingredients of the incense offered in the Temple. See M *Uqtsin* 3:5; *Sifrei*, Deuteronomy 107; BT *Karetot* 6a.

"Clay" renders פולמי (*pulmei*), apparently derived from פילומא (*piloma*), "mud, clay ground" (Greek *peloma*, "mud, clay"). See M *Shabbat* 22:6 (Kaufmann MS); JT *Shabbat* 22:6, 17d; BT *Shabbat* 147a (Munich MS); Ḥanan'el and Alfasi, ad loc.; *Sekhel Tov* on Exodus 16, p. 312; Galante; *Arukh* and *Arukh ha-Shalem*, s.v. *plm*.

460. **Joseph is fulfillment of Torah...** By resisting the sexual advances of Potiphar's wife, Joseph preserved the covenant of circumcision and attained the *sefirah* of *Yesod*, the divine phallus. His sexual purity was equivalent to fulfilling the entire Torah.

See Genesis 39; *Zohar* 1:197a; 2:61a; 3:13b.

461. ***These are the generations of Jacob: Joseph*** The verse in Genesis begins: *These are the generations of Jacob: Joseph, seventeen years old, was tending the flock with his brothers.* But Rabbi Yose, borrowing the playful reading of the Midrash, conveniently breaks off his citation with the phrase *Jacob: Joseph*, implying that father and son were nearly identical. The kabbalistic twist is that their two respective *sefirot*, *Tif'eret* and *Yesod*, constitute a single male entity uniting with *Shekhinah*.

See *Tanḥuma* (Buber), *Vayeshev* 5; *Bereshit Rabbah* 84:6, 8; *Zohar* 1:21b, 85a, 180a, 182b, 222a; 2:145a, 242a.

462. **site of the flowing, gushing river...** *Yesod*, who conveys the flow of emanation to *Shekhinah* and, through Her, to all worlds.

463. **they all drew near...** Through the sacrifices, Israel drew near to God. Alternatively, "they [the sacrifices] were all offered to the blessed Holy One fittingly." See *OY*; Galante.

464. **smoke ascended in a straight column...** Direct ascent of the smoke signified that the lamp of *Shekhinah* had been kindled above, along with the other *sefirot*, spreading universal light and joy. See above, note 450.

465. **Ever since the Temple was destroyed...** See M *Sotah* 9:12: "Rabban Shim'on son of Gamli'el says in the name

and below; Israel wanders in exile, under the dominion of alien gods. Thus the verse is fulfilled: *There you will serve other gods* (Deuteronomy 28:64).[466]

"Why all this? On account of what is written: *Because you did not serve YHVH your God in joy and in gladness of heart for the abundance of everything* (ibid., 47). What does this mean: *for the abundance of everything*? Here, *for the abundance of everything*; there, *in lack of everything* (ibid., 48).[467] Until the blessed Holy One arouses and redeems them from among the nations, as is said: *YHVH your God will return your captivity and have compassion on you.... If your banished lie at the ends of heaven, from there YHVH your God will gather you, from there He will take you* (ibid. 30:3–4).[468]

"*These are the offspring of Esau, that is, Edom* (Genesis 36:1). Come and see: During Isaac's lifetime the sons of Esau were not enumerated, as were the sons of Jacob, who were enumerated before Isaac died. But as for Esau, what is written? *Isaac expired and died and was gathered to his kin, old and sated with days* (ibid. 35:29). Following this, what is written? *These are the offspring of Esau, that is, Edom*.[469] Why? Because only Jacob and his sons partake of his share, his allotted portion.[470] So Jacob and his sons are the share of the blessed Holy One and enter the count, whereas Esau—who does not share the side of faith—is counted after Isaac died, his share deviating to another site.[471] 69

of Rabbi Yehoshu'a: 'Ever since the day the Temple was destroyed, not a single day passes without a curse, dew has never descended as blessing, and flavor has been eliminated from fruit.'" Cf. *Zohar* 1:61b, 70b, 181a–b, 203a; 3:15b, 74b.

The verse from Psalms is understood as referring to *Shekhinah*, who manifests divine sternness and wrath. See *Zohar* 1:8a, 91a; 3:119b, 176b.

466. **in exile, under the dominion of alien gods...** Living outside the land of Israel is tantamount to worshiping false gods. See *Sifra, Behar* 5:4, 109c: "Every Israelite who dwells in the land of Israel accepts upon himself the yoke of the Kingdom of Heaven, and everyone who leaves the land is like an idol worshiper."

See *Tosefta Avodah Zarah* 4:5; BT *Ketubbot* 110b; *Avodah Zarah* 8a; *Avot de-Rabbi Natan* A, 26; *Zohar* 1:95b, 153a; 3:266b.

467. ***in lack of everything*** The verse reads: *So you will serve your enemies whom YHVH will send against you, in hunger and in thirst, in nakedness and in lack of everything.* The word *everything* may allude to *Yesod*, who ideally conveys the entire flow of emanation but in time of exile dries up.

468. ***YHVH your God will return your captivity...*** The first verse reads: *YHVH your God will return your captivity and have compassion on you. He will return and gather you from all the nations where YHVH your God has scattered you.*

469. **sons of Esau were not enumerated, as were the sons of Jacob...** Jacob's sons are listed in Genesis 35:22–26, before the account of Isaac's death, whereas Esau's sons are listed only afterward.

470. **his share, his allotted portion** The share of Isaac. Cf. JT *Nedarim* 3:8, 38a; BT *Nedarim* 31a.

471. **Esau—who does not share the side of faith...** In medieval rabbinic literature,

"Come and see: After Isaac died and Esau separated to his side, what is written? *Esau took his wives... and he went to a land away from his brother, Jacob* (ibid. 36:6),[472] relinquishing to Jacob both principal and profit: bondage of Egypt and the land.[473] He sold him his share of the cave of Machpelah[474] and left the land, the faith, and his share—abandoning all.

"Come and see how completely fine was Jacob's share—since Esau no longer remained with him, but parted from him, going off to his own allotted share, leaving Jacob in possession of the heritage of his father and his ancestors. So, *he went to a land away from his brother, Jacob.* What does this mean: *away from his brother, Jacob*? That he did not want his inherited portion or his share of faith.

"Happy is the share of Jacob! Of him is written *For YHVH's share is His people, Jacob His allotted inheritance* (Deuteronomy 32:9)."

These are the kings who reigned in the land of Edom before any king reigned over the Children of Israel (Genesis 36:31).

Rabbi Yeisa opened, "*Behold, I make you least among the nations; you are utterly despised* (Obadiah 1:2).[475] Come and see: When the blessed Holy One fashioned the world, He divided earth into seven regions, subdivided according to seventy appointed princes, distributing them among seventy nations, each and every one fittingly,[476] as is said: *When the Most*

Esau often symbolizes Christianity. Here Esau and, implicitly, his religion are seen as estranged from the realm of mystical faith and linked with the demonic ("another site"). For parallel medieval Christian views of the demonic nature of the Jews, see Trachtenberg, *The Devil and the Jews.*

472. ***Esau took his wives...*** The full verse reads: *Esau took his wives, his sons, his daughters, and all the members of his household, his cattle, all his animals, and all the possessions he had acquired in the land of Canaan, and he went to a land away from his brother, Jacob.*

473. **principal and profit: bondage of Egypt and the land** Israel's enslavement in Egypt was repaid and rewarded by their inheriting the Promised Land. See Genesis 15:13–16; *Zohar* 1:198a.

474. **He sold him his share of the cave of Machpelah** Abraham had purchased the cave of Machpelah as a family burial plot, but according to rabbinic tradition, Esau sold his share of the cave (in addition to his birthright) to Jacob.

See Genesis 23; *Bereshit Rabbah* 100:5; *Tanḥuma, Vayḥi* 6; *Tanḥuma* (Buber), *Vayishlaḥ* 11; BT *Sotah* 13a; *Pirqei de-Rabbi Eli'ezer* 38.

475. ***Behold, I make you least among the nations...*** A prophecy addressed to Edom.

476. **seven regions, subdivided according to seventy appointed princes...** The seven regions of earth are the "seven climates," the seven inhabitable regions recognized in Ptolemaic and medieval geography. See *Zohar* 2:30b; 3:10a.

Here these seven regions are further divided into a total of seventy parts, each of which is allocated to one of the seventy nations. Each nation is ruled over by an angel or heavenly prince appointed by God.

Seventy nations are listed in Genesis 10. On the seventy princes, see Daniel 10:13,

High allotted the nations, when He dispersed humankind... (Deuteronomy 32:8).[477]

"Of all those princes rendered to other nations, none is as despised before Him as the Archon of Esau.[478] Why? Because the side of Esau is a defiled side, and the side of defilement is despicable before the blessed Holy One. He issues from those inferior rungs behind the millstones,[479] a void of rubicund quaestors.[480] So, *Behold, I make you least among the nations; you are utterly despised,* corresponding to what is written: *On your belly shall you go and dust shall you eat all the days of your life* (Genesis 3:14).[481] *Utterly,* as is said: *Cursed are you among all animals and among all beasts of the field* (ibid.).[482]

"Come and see: Within lower rungs lie rungs upon rungs, all differing from one another, all concatenated, linked with one another.[483] Each kingdom sepa-

20–21; Septuagint, Deuteronomy 32:8–9; Jubilees 15:31–32; *Targum Yerushalmi,* Genesis 11:8, Deuteronomy 32:8–9; *Tanḥuma, Re'eh* 8; *Leqaḥ Tov,* Genesis 9:19; *Pirqei de-Rabbi Eli'ezer* 24; *Zohar* 1:46b, 61a, 84b, 108b, 149b; 2:33a, 151b, 209a–b; 3:298b; Ginzberg, *Legends,* 5:204–5, n. 91.

477. **When the Most High...** The full verse reads: *When the Most High allotted the nations, when He dispersed humankind, He set the boundaries of peoples according to the number of the Children of Israel.*

Instead of the Masoretic text's reading at the end of the verse (בני ישראל [*benei yisra'el*], *the Children of Israel*), one Qumran scroll reads בני אלהים (*benei elohim*), "sons (or children) of God (or the gods)," while the Septuagint reads "angels of God." Similarly, Rabbi Yeisa understands the verse to mean that the seventy nations were arranged according to the seventy angels.

See *Targum Yerushalmi,* ad loc.; Tigay, *Deuteronomy,* ad loc., and 513–18; Friedman, *Commentary,* ad loc.

478. **Archon of Esau** Samael, the chief demon.

479. **behind the millstones** The phrase derives from Exodus 11:5: *the slave girl who is behind the millstones.* In the *Zohar,* it refers to the realm of demons. See 1:48a, 118a, 223b; 2:28a, 37b, 80a, 191b.

480. **void of rubicund quaestors** An empty, demonic realm that is populated only by ghostly red potencies. Esau's nation is Edom, and he is associated with the color אדום (*adom*), "red," in Genesis 25:25. See *Zohar* 1:153a.

"Quaestor" renders קוסטרי (*qusterei*); the rabbinic term קוסטור (*qustor*) derives from Latin *quaestor,* a Roman official or prosecutor. See JT *Eruvin* 6:2, 23b; *Zohar* 1:20a, 53b; 2:58b, 208b; 3:13a.

481. **On your belly shall you go...** The curse pronounced upon the serpent in the Garden of Eden. The serpent symbolizes the demonic powers and is linked with Esau in *Zohar* 1:143a.

482. **Utterly...** From the verse in Obadiah just quoted: *you are utterly despised.* Just as the serpent is the most cursed among animals, so Edom is the most despised among nations.

483. **Within lower rungs lie rungs upon rungs...** Beneath the sefirotic realm extend lower rungs—a chain of interlinked potencies supervising the stars and earthly kingdoms. Commentators differ as to whether these powers are holy or demonic. See *OY*; Galante; Tishby, *Wisdom of the Zohar,* 2:450; 471, n. 16.

"Concatenated" renders קפטירין (*qaftirin*), a Zoharic neologism that connotes "tying, linking." See *Zohar* 1:211a, 217a, 218a; 2:209a; 3:6b, 62b; *Bei'ur ha-Millim ha-Zarot,* 188,

rate from the other, kingdom interlinked with kingdom; one entering, one ascending, embraced by a single nexus.

"That nexus has a single measure, three triple nexuses to that measure.[484] Within each nexus, a single crown; within each crown, a single suzerain,[485] empowered by coronation above, empowered and descending below until stars and constellations are linked with it—one star, one constellation distributed among each and every one.[486] [177b] All stars are destined in those rungs above, every rung crowned in certain suitable sites.

"As rungs diverge, you discover a pistachio cluster,[487] until they link to their suitable sides. Sides of rungs of defilement on the left all diverge into countless ways and paths—flanks of red potencies.[488] So potencies dangle below, millions and billions. Therefore, *Behold, I make you least among the nations; you are utterly despised,* as we have said.[489]

"Come and see: *These are the kings who reigned in the land of Edom*—on the side of his rung, rung of Esau, as is said: *Esau, that is, Edom* (Genesis 36:1)—all issuing from the side of impure spirit.

72

"*Before any king reigned over the Children of Israel,* for they are rungs standing at the gatehouse below, first of all.[490] So Jacob said, *Let my lord pass on ahead of his servant* (ibid. 33:14),[491] since his rungs enter first. So, *before any king reigned*

n. 185; Luria, *Va-Ye'esof David,* s.v. *qftr, qaftera*; Liebes, *Peraqim,* 349–54. On *quftera* as "rope," see *Vayiqra Rabbah* 4:2 (and Margulies's n. 3, pp. 81–82; Lieberman's note, p. 871); *Qohelet Rabbah* on 6:6; *Tanḥuma, Miqqets* 10; *Tanḥuma* (Buber), *Miqqets* 15 (and Buber's n. 116); *Arukh* and *Arukh ha-Shalem,* s.v. *pi turei*; Rashi on *Berakhot* 8a, s.v. *ke-fiturei.*

484. **three triple nexuses...** A triadic structure, characteristic of the *sefirot,* appears in the lower realms. Elsewhere the *Zohar* describes a decade of demonic potencies, grouped in three קשרין (*qishrin*), "knots, bands, nexuses," just as the decade of *sefirot* is arranged according to the triad of *Ḥesed, Gevurah,* and *Tif'eret.* See *Zohar* 2:38a, 40b.

485. **suzerain** קפסורא (*Qafsora*), a Zoharic neologism apparently meaning "ruler." See *Zohar* 3:152b; *Bei'ur ha-Millim ha-Zarot,* 191.

486. **one star, one constellation distributed...** Each star or constellation is linked with a ruling power (or an extension of that power).

487. **you discover a pistachio cluster** Rather than bearing fruit individually like some trees, the pistachio produces its nuts in heavy clusters somewhat like grapes. In the same manner, says Rabbi Yeisa, the rungs below increase and subdivide extensively.

On the term פוסתקא (*pusteqa*), "pistachio," and its variants, see JT *Kil'ayim* 1:4, 27a; *Ma'aserot* 1:2, 48d; BT *Gittin* 59a, 69a; *Zohar* 2:15b; *Bei'ur ha-Millim ha-Zarot,* 184.

488. **rungs of defilement on the left...** Deriving from the side of harsh judgment, colored red.

489. **Therefore, *Behold, I make you least...*** Esau, his prince (Samael), and his nation (Edom) lie farthest from the supernal realm of holiness.

490. **rungs standing at the gatehouse below, first of all** Since the demonic rungs of Edom are closest to earth, they gain dominion first.

491. ***Let my lord pass on ahead of his servant*** The verse continues: *while I proceed slowly, at the pace of the livestock before me*

over the Children of Israel, for the time had not yet come for Kingdom of Heaven to reign, embracing the Children of Israel. Therefore he said, *Let my lord pass on ahead of his servant.*

"Once these rungs terminated, Kingdom of Heaven aroused to reign over those below. Beginning, it began with the youngest of all the tribes, Benjamin, as is said: *There is young Benjamin, ruling them...* (Psalms 68:28). Through him kingdom began to arouse, later arriving at its site, firmly established, never to depart."[492]

Rabbi Ḥiyya opened, "*Now hear, O Jacob My servant, Israel whom I have chosen! Thus says YHVH who makes you, who forms you in the womb and will help you: Fear not, My servant Jacob, Jeshurun whom I have chosen* (Isaiah 44:1–2).[493]

"Come and see how often the blessed Holy One has promised to entitle Israel to the world that is coming! For He desired no nation or people for His share other than Israel alone; so He gave them the Torah of truth, enabling them to prove themselves worthy and know the ways of the blessed Holy One, so that they could inherit the Holy Land. For whoever attains this Holy Land has a share in the world that is coming, as is said: *Your people, all of them righteous, will inherit the land forever* (Isaiah 60:21), as already noted.[494]

"Three rungs here: first Jacob, then Israel, then Jeshurun.[495] Come and see: Jacob, as already established; Israel, similarly, although the rungs are as one.[496] Jeshurun—why is Israel called by this name? But Israel and Jeshurun are entirely one. ישורון (*Yeshurun*), Jeshurun, as is said: ישור (*Yashor*), *He lines up, men* (Job 33:27),[497] for he obtains שורא (*shura*), a row, on this side and on that

and at the pace of the children, till I come to my lord in Seir.

492. **youngest of all the tribes, Benjamin...** The first Israelite king was Saul from the tribe of Benjamin, who died in battle with the Philistines and built no lasting dynasty. Subsequently the kingdom was firmly established by David from the tribe of Judah. Eventually, according to tradition, King Messiah will be descended from him. The verse from Psalms reads: *There is young Benjamin, ruling them; the princes of Judah, commanding them.* See above, page 52.

493. ***Jeshurun...*** A poetic name for Israel meaning "the upright one." See Deuteronomy 32:15; 33:5, 26.

494. **whoever attains this Holy Land...** See BT *Ketubbot* 111a; Ibn Ezra on Genesis 33:19. The Holy Land symbolizes *Shekhinah*, while "the world that is coming" symbolizes *Binah*, constantly coming and flowing. The verse from Isaiah is cited in M *Sanhedrin* 10:1 to demonstrate that "all of Israel have a share in the world that is coming."

495. **Three rungs here...** The verse from Isaiah mentions all three names.

496. **Jacob... Israel... although the rungs are as one** As indicated above (note 364), the name *Jacob* alludes to the patriarch's initial status in the realm of *Shekhinah*, whereas *Israel* refers to his ascent to *Tif'eret*. Yet the two are united.

497. **ישור (*Yashor*), *He lines up, men*** The clause's plain sense apparently is *He sings out*

side, and because of these two שורין (*shurin*), rows, he is called *Yeshurun*; and this is Israel.[498] Israel, because he acquires grandeur and power from all;[499] Jeshurun, because of those portions: two sides, two rows that we have mentioned. All is one; those names all amount to one.

"*Jacob My servant*—sometimes he resembles a servant commanded by his master, carrying out his will. Similarly, ישראל (*Yisra'el*), *Israel, whom I have chosen*—לאשראה (*le-ashra'ah*), to hover, over him. All in supernal mystery.

"It is written: *He who creates you, O Jacob; He who forms you, O Israel* (Isaiah 43:1), and it is written: *Thus says YHVH who makes you.* All these rungs mount up to one, as they have established: creates, forms, makes—all of them rungs one above the other, and all are one.[500]

"Happy is the share of Israel, in whom the blessed Holy One delights above all other nations! For concerning all of them is written *They are vanity, objects of mockery; in the time of their punishment they will perish* (Jeremiah 10:15)[501]—when one day the blessed Holy One will eliminate them from the world and He alone will remain, as is said: *YHVH alone will be exalted on that day* (Isaiah 2:17)."[502]

Rabbi Yehudah opened, "'*Do not fear, O worm Jacob, O men of Israel! I myself will help you,' declares YHVH. 'Your Redeemer is the Holy One of Israel'* (Isaiah 41:14).

to men. However, the unusual form ישור (*yashor*) was linked midrashically with שורה (*shurah*), "line."

See JT *Yoma* 8:9, 45c; *Bava Qamma* 8:7, 6c; BT *Yoma* 87a; Rashi on Job 33:27; *Sha'arei Teshuvah*, 69.

498. **because of these two שורין (*shurin*), rows, he is called *Yeshurun*...** The name suggests the plural *shurin* ("rows"), alluding to the right and left sefirotic columns, which are harmonized by the patriarch's *sefirah*, *Tif'eret*. See above, page 50.

499. **Israel, because he acquires grandeur and power...** Alluding to the two *sefirot* on the right and the left: *Gedullah* (Greatness; referred to more often as *Ḥesed,* Lovingkindness) and *Gevurah* (Power). The name ישראל (*Yisra'el*) may also be linked here with שררה (*serarah*), "authority, power."

500. **creates, forms, makes...** The three verbs correspond respectively to three rungs: *Shekhinah*, *Tif'eret*, and *Binah*. This sequence contrasts with the later kabbalistic theory of the four worlds, in which the order of Creation, Formation, and Making is reversed.

See Abraham bar Hiyya, *Megillat ha-Megalleh*, 15–16; *Bahir* 10 (13); *Zohar* 2:155a, 192b; Moses de León, *Sefer ha-Rimmon*, 38 (and Wolfson's n. 12), 46–47, 407–8; idem, *Sefer ha-Mishqal*, 39–40; idem, *Sheqel ha-Qodesh*, 8 (11); Scholem, *Le-Ḥeqer Qabbalat R. Yitsḥaq ben Ya'aqov ha-Kohen*, 72–81; Tishby, *Wisdom of the Zohar*, 2:555–58, 687–88.

501. ***They are vanity, objects of mockery...*** In the biblical verse, the subject is idols.

502. ***YHVH alone will be exalted on that day*** The following verse reads: *Idols will utterly vanish.*

"Come and see: All nations of the world have been rendered to certain ruling archons, as has been said,[503] and they all follow their false gods, as is written: [*For all the nations*] *will walk each in the name of its god* (Micah 4:5)[504]—all shedding blood, waging war, stealing, robbing, fornicating, mingling [178a] with numerous evildoings. They intensify their power to harass, while Israel has no power to overcome them except through its mouth—like a worm whose only power and strength lies in its mouth, by its mouth penetrating all. So Israel is called *worm*.[505]

"Further, *Do not fear, O worm Jacob*—no creature in the world resembles a tusser silkworm, from which all garments of glory exude: royal tusser.[506] After-

503. **certain ruling archons...** Angels or heavenly princes empowered over the seventy nations. See above, note 476.

504. **[*All the nations*] *will walk each in the name of its god*** The verse reads: *For all the nations will walk each in the name of its god, and we will walk in the name of* YHVH *our God forever and ever.*

505. **through its mouth...** Through words of prayer and study. See *Tanḥuma, Beshallaḥ* 9: "*Do not fear, O worm Jacob!* Why is Israel compared to a worm? Just as a worm strikes the cedars only with its mouth—though soft, it strikes the hard—so Israel possesses only prayer, for the idolatrous nations are compared to cedars."

See *Mekhilta, Beshallaḥ* 2; *Zohar* 2:139a.

506. **tusser...** טיסטרא (*Tistera*), a Zoharic neologism apparently derived from the name of the wild silkworm of India and China, known in Sanskrit as *tasara*, "shuttle," from the shape of the cocoon. (Various English forms of the word include: tusser, tussore, tussah.)

The breeding of silkworms originated in ancient China, which was known to the Greeks as *Seres*, Land of Silk. This precious craft was perhaps the most zealously guarded secret in history. The technique and process of sericulture were tightly controlled by Chinese authorities: anyone caught revealing the secrets or smuggling silkworm eggs or cocoons outside the country was executed as a traitor. Along the Silk Route linking China with the Mediterranean, silk thread and fabric were prized commodities, and silk became a currency of international trade.

Supposedly in the sixth century C.E., two Nestorian monks risked their lives to smuggle silkworm eggs to the court of Emperor Justinian in Byzantium, appearing there with the eggs hidden in their bamboo walking staffs. In the eighth century, the Moors carried the art across the northern coast of Africa and into Spain, where sericulture flourished, reaching its peak in the thirteenth century, the age of the *Zohar*.

Generations of Muslim weavers supplied silk fabrics for wealthy and royal clients. Alfonso X el Sabio (1252–84) made silk a sign of royalty, legislating that a monarch must dress in silk with gold, silver, and precious stones, so that all who see him will recognize his regal identity. In one of the miracle stories included in Alfonso's *Cantigas de Santa María*, silkworms figure prominently.

Actually, the widely cultivated silkworm was the mulberry silkworm *(Bombyx mori)*, which feeds on mulberry leaves, whereas the wild tusser silkworm *(Antheraea mylitta)* feeds on oak leaves and produces a coarser, stronger silk.

See Asher ben Yeḥiel, *She'elot u-Tshuvot* 88:6; Alfonso X, *Las siete partidas* 2:5:5; idem, *Cantigas de Santa María*, cantiga 18. For an image of Alfonso X robed in heraldic silk garb, see Florence L. May, *Silk Textiles of Spain: Eighth to Fifteenth Century*, 100 and fig. 7.

ward it sows seed and dies, afterward—from that surviving seed—coming into being as before, existing enduringly.[507]

"So Israel is like this worm: though dying, it will reexist in the world as before, as has been said, since it is written: *For as clay in the hand of the potter, so are you in My hand, O house of Israel* (Jeremiah 18:6).[508] What does כחמר (*ka-ḥomer*), *as clay*, mean? The *ḥomer*, material, of glass—which even if broken can be recast, mended as before.[509]

"מתי ישראל (*Metei Yisra'el*), *O mortal men of Israel!*—Tree of Life, for since Israel cleave to the Tree of Life, they will possess life:[510] rising from the dust, abiding in the world, becoming a single people to serve the blessed Holy One, as is said: *so they may all call upon the name of YHVH and serve Him shoulder to shoulder* (Zephaniah 3:9)."

Rabbi El'azar and Rabbi Yitsḥak were walking on the way when the time arrived for reciting *Shema*.[511] Rabbi El'azar stood, recited *Shema*, and prayed.[512]

507. **Afterward it sows seed and dies...** The metamorphosis proceeds as follows: A female moth mates with a male and lays some five hundred eggs (referred to here as "seed") in four to six days, dying soon after. From the eggs emerge larvae, yellowish-white caterpillars, each of whom feeds on leaves for several weeks and then begins to exude a fine fluid. On issuing into the air, this stream hardens into a continuous thread of silk fiber, which the caterpillar spins into a mile-long cocoon. Enwrapped in the cocoon, the caterpillar is transformed into a chrysalis, which several weeks later emerges as an adult moth—and the process continues.

See Rumi, *Mathnawi* 1:5: "What God taught the silkworm of the cocoon—does any elephant know such a device?"

The image of the silkworm wrapping itself within a cocoon appears in the *Zohar*'s description of emanation. See 1:15a.

508. ***For as clay in the hand of the potter...*** The verse reads: *O house of Israel, can I not do with you as this potter?—declares YHVH. Behold, like clay in the hand of the potter, so are you in My hand, O house of Israel.*

509. **recast, mended as before** Melted into liquid and then reblown or recast. (Incidentally, the art of glassmaking passed along the Silk Route in the opposite direction, from west to east.)

In rabbinic literature, as here, the melting and reblowing of broken glass symbolizes death and resurrection. See *Bereshit Rabbah* 14:7; *Midrash Tehillim* 2:11; BT *Sanhedrin* 91a. Cf. *Avot de-Rabbi Natan* A, 24; BT *Avodah Zarah* 75b, and Rashi, ad loc., s.v. *zekhukhit*; *Rut Rabbah* 6:4.

510. **מתי ישראל (*Metei Yisra'el*), *O mortal men of Israel!*—Tree of Life...** Rabbi Yehudah seems to be playing with two near homophones: מְתֵי (*metei*), "men of" (the literal meaning in this verse) and מֵתֵי (*metei*), "dead ones of."

By studying Torah, the people of Israel cleave to the Tree of Life, which is Torah's symbol, based on the description of wisdom in Proverbs 3:18: *She is a tree of life to those who grasp her.* See BT *Berakhot* 32b, 61b; above, page 53.

In Kabbalah, Tree of Life symbolizes *Tif'eret*, whose full name is *Tif'eret Yisra'el*, "Beauty of Israel," and who is also known as Written Torah.

511. **time arrived for reciting *Shema*** Early in the morning, as clarified below. The *Shema* is recited morning and evening.

512. **prayed** He prayed the *Amidah* ("Standing"), the central prayer that is re-

Afterward, Rabbi Yitsḥaq said to him, "But we have learned that before a person sets out on the way, he should obtain permission from his Lord and pray his prayer."[513]

He replied, "Because when I set out, it wasn't time for prayer and the time for reciting *Shema* had not arrived.[514] Now that the sun is shining I've prayed;[515] but before I set out on the way, I made my request from Him and consulted Him.[516] But I didn't pray this prayer,[517] because I was engaged in Torah from midnight;[518] and from the time morning arrived up till now, it wasn't time to

cited three times daily. In the morning and evening liturgy, the *Amidah* follows the recitation of the *Shema*.

513. **before a person sets out on the way...** Before setting out on a journey, one should pray, including (or specifically) *Tefillat ha-Derekh* ("The Prayer for the Way").

See BT *Berakhot* 29b: "Elijah said to Rav Yehudah the brother of Rabbi Sala the Ḥasid, 'Do not let your anger boil and you will not sin; do not get drunk and you will not sin; and when you set out on the way, consult your Creator and then set out.' What is meant by 'consult your Creator and then set out'? Rabbi Ya'akov said in the name of Rav Ḥisda, 'This is *Tefillat ha-Derekh*.'"

See *Berakhot* 14a, 30a; *Zohar* 1:49b, 58b, 121a (*MhN*), 230a–b, 240b; 2:130b.

514. **it wasn't time for prayer...** For the *Amidah* (see above, note 512). The morning *Amidah* is ideally recited as soon as the first ray of sunlight appears. Although the *Shema* may be recited earlier (at dawn), devotees sought to complete the *Shema* (together with its blessings) immediately before the sun actually appeared, so that they could join it to the *Amidah* at precisely the first ray. One who rises early to set out on a journey is permitted to pray both *Shema* and *Amidah* at dawn, but Rabbi El'azar chose to wait for sunrise.

See BT *Berakhot* 9b: "Devotees used to complete it [the recitation of the *Shema*] with the first ray of the sun, in order to join *ge'ullah* ["redemption," the name of the blessing following the *Shema*] to *tefillah* ["prayer," the *Amidah*], and consequently pray [the *Amidah*] in the daytime. Rabbi Zeira said, 'What is its verse [its Scriptural support]? *May they revere You with the sun* (Psalms 72:5).'"

In Kabbalah the union of these two prayers symbolizes the union of the divine couple, *Tif'eret* and *Shekhinah*.

See M *Berakhot* 1:2; *Tosefta, Berakhot* 1:2 (and Lieberman, ad loc.); JT *Berakhot* 1:2, 3a–b; BT *Berakhot* 9b, 26a; *Tur, Oraḥ Ḥayyim* 58, 89; *Beit Yosef* and *Shulḥan Arukh, Oraḥ Ḥayyim* 58:1; 89:1, 3, 8.

515. **I've prayed** The morning prayer, including both the *Shema* and the *Amidah*.

516. **I made my request from Him and consulted Him** Praying the prayer for the way.

517. **this prayer** See above, note 515.

518. **engaged in Torah from midnight** See Psalms 119:62; and BT *Berakhot* 3b, in the name of Rabbi Eli'ezer: "Rabbi Shim'on the Ḥasid said, 'There was a harp suspended above [King] David's bed. As soon as midnight arrived, a north wind came and blew upon it, and it played by itself. He immediately arose and engaged in Torah until the break of dawn.'"

In the *Zohar* this legendary custom is expanded into a ritual. At midnight, God delights in the souls of the righteous in the Garden of Eden, and those who study Torah here below partake of the celestial joy. Kabbalists are expected to rise at midnight and adorn *Shekhinah* with words of Torah in preparation for Her union with *Tif'eret*.

See Scholem, *On the Kabbalah*, 146–50. This parallels the midnight vigil, common among Christian monks from early medieval times. In *Zohar* 3:119a, Rabbi Yehudah al-

pray the prayer because as darkness of dawn appears, a wife converses with her husband, in mystery as one,[519] since she has to retire to the dwelling along with her maidens who sit with her.[520] So one should not interrupt their words, uniting as one, and interpose another word between.[521]

"Now that the sun is shining, it's time to pray, as they have established, for it is written: ייראוך (*Yira'ukha*), *May they revere You, with the sun* (Psalms 72:5).[522] What does *with the sun* mean? Carrying the light of the sun with us to illumine her.[523] For יראה (*yir'ah*), reverence, must accompany sun—not dividing them. As long as day doesn't shine, reverence is not with sun, and they must be joined as one. This is: *with the sun.*"[524]

They walked on. When they reached a field, they sat down. Raising their eyes, they saw a mountain, whose peak was being scaled by strange creatures. Rabbi Yitsḥak became frightened. Rabbi El'azar asked him, "Why are you afraid?"

He replied, "I see that this mountain is fierce, and I see these creatures who are strange, and I'm scared they'll attack us."

He said, "If someone is frightened, it is the sins he possesses of which he should be frightened.[525] Come and see: These aren't those fierce creatures who used to haunt the mountains."

He opened, saying, "*These are the sons of Zibeon: Aiah and Anah—that is the Anah who in the wilderness discovered the Yemim*... (Genesis 36:24).[526] This verse

ludes to the Christian practice: "I have seen something similar among the nations of the world."

See *Sifra, Beḥuqqotai* 3:3, 111b; *Aggadat Bereshit* 23:5; BT *Sanhedrin* 102a; 2 Enoch 8:3; *Seder Gan Eden* (*Beit ha-Midrash*, 3:138); *Zohar* 1:10b, 72a, 77a, 82b, 92a–b, 136b, 231b; 2:46a, 130a–b, 136a, 173b, 195b–196a, 206b–207b; 3:21b–22b, 52b, 193a; *ZḤ* 13c (*MhN*). Cf. Matthew 25:6.

519. **wife converses with her husband...** See BT *Berakhot* 3a: "In the first watch [of the night], a donkey brays; in the second, dogs bark; in the third, a child sucks from its mother's breast, and a woman converses with her husband."

On the erotic connotation of "converses," see BT *Nedarim* 20b, and pseudo-Rashi, ad loc. Here the phrase hints at the intimacy between the divine couple, *Shekhinah* and *Tif'eret*. See *Zohar* 2:46a.

520. **she has to retire to the dwelling...** *Shekhinah* is about to retire to Her dwelling beneath the sefirotic realm, where She is accompanied by angels.

521. **interpose another word between** Any word, even a word of prayer, disturbs the union of the divine couple. Therefore Rabbi El'azar had not prayed earlier.

522. **Now that the sun is shining, it's time to pray...** See BT *Berakhot* 9b, quoted above, note 514.

523. **Carrying the light of the sun with us to illumine her** Conveying, through our prayers, the flow of emanation from *Tif'eret* (symbolized by the sun) to *Shekhinah*.

524. **יראה (*yir'ah*), reverence, must accompany sun...** *Shekhinah*, known as "reverence," must accompany Her partner, *Tif'eret*. Their union is consummated only at sunrise.

525. **If someone is frightened...** On the link between fear and sin, see BT *Berakhot* 60b; *Sotah* 43a–44a; *Zohar* 1:198a–b, 202a–b, 230b.

526. ***Anah who in the wilderness discovered the Yemim...*** The verse concludes:

has been established,[527] but come and see: not those of whom is written *The Emim formerly dwelt there...* (Deuteronomy 2:10),[528] but rather those of whom Scripture states *who in the wilderness discovered the* ימים (*yemim*)—spelled ימם (*yemim*).[529] These were strange creatures, for when Cain was banished from the face of the earth—as is said: *Here, You have driven me today from the face of the earth* (Genesis 4:14), and similarly: *He dwelled in the land of Nod* (ibid., 16), as they have established—among his descendants were those inhabiting the side of spirits, whirlwinds, and demons.[530] These existed because as the day was about to be sanctified, enduring spirits were created from that side—bodiless specters.[531] These derive neither from the Sabbath day nor the sixth day, both of whom remain uncertain about them, so they are sustained by [178b] neither one.[532]

"Spreading through the side of Cain, they materialized on that side, though not enduringly.[533] They are called ימם (*yemim*)—defective—for they were not

while tending the donkeys of his father Zibeon. The word ימים (*yemim*) is unique and its meaning uncertain. It has been rendered variously as "mules" and "hot springs."

527. **This verse has been established** See *Bereshit Rabbah* 82:14; JT *Berakhot* 8:5, 12b; BT *Pesaḥim* 54a; *Ḥullin* 7b; *Targum Onqelos, Targum Yerushalmi*, Rashi, Ibn Ezra, and Naḥmanides on this verse.

528. ***The Emim formerly dwelt there...*** This verse, describing the earlier inhabitants of Moab, reads: *The Emim formerly dwelt there, a people great and numerous, and as tall as the Anakim.*

The name אימים (*eimim*) may be related to the root אים (*aym*), "terror, dread," as suggested by *Bereshit Rabbah* 26:7, and *Targum Onqelos, Targum Yerushalmi*, and Rashi on Deuteronomy 2:10.

529. **ימים (*yemim*)—spelled ימם (*yemim*)** The defective spelling, without the second י (*yod*), alludes to their incomplete origin, as Rabbi El'azar goes on to explain.

530. ***land of Nod*... those inhabiting the side of spirits...** The name *Nod* derives from a root meaning "to wander." According to the *Zohar*, Cain wandered to a subterranean realm, where he copulated with female demons and engendered bizarre creatures.

See El'azar of Worms, *Ḥokhmat ha-Nefesh*, 26c; *Zohar* 1:9b, 54a–b; 3:76b, 122a.

531. **as the day was about to be sanctified... bodiless specters** As the primordial week of Creation was drawing to a close and Sabbath was about to be sanctified at sunset, bodiless spirits were created.

See *Tanḥuma* (Buber), *Bereshit* 17: "Here it is not written [*He ceased from all His work*] *that* [*God*] *created and made*, but rather [*that God created*] *to make* (Genesis 2:3), for Sabbath arrived first and their work was not completed. Rabbi Benaya said, 'This refers to the demons, for He created their souls, and as He was creating their bodies, the Sabbath day was hallowed. He left them, and they remained soul without body.'"

See M *Avot* 5:6: "Ten things were created on Friday eve at twilight:... Some say, 'Also the demons.'" Cf. *Bereshit Rabbah* 7:5; 11:9; Naḥmanides on Leviticus 17:7; *Zohar* 1:14a, 47b–48a; 2:155b; 3:142b (*IR*).

"Specter" renders טסירין (*tesirin*), a neologism appearing several times in the *Zohar*, perhaps derived playfully from the root טוס (*tus*), "to fly." See 1:17b, 20b, 195b; 2:29a.

532. **uncertain about them...** Uncertain about their precise origin.

533. **materialized on that side...** Through Cain's progeny.

fulfilled on either day.[534] They appear to human beings,[535] and he found them; they taught him how to bring bastards into the world.[536] Roaming the mountains, they assume a body once a day, then strip themselves.

"Come and see: This Anah was a bastard, for Zibeon copulated with his mother and engendered a bastard.[537] This one issued from the side of impure spirit that clung to him, so he found them, and they taught him all species of the side of defilement.[538]

"Come and see: These and countless others, branching out, all derive from that side—roaming the wilderness, visible there, since desolate wilderness is their habitation.[539] So whoever walks in the ways of the blessed Holy One, and fears Him, has no fear of them."

They walked on and entered the mountains. Rabbi Yitsḥak said, "Are all desolate mountains likewise the site of their habitation?"

He replied, "So it is! And of all those engaging in Torah is written *YHVH will guard you from all evil; He will guard your life. YHVH will guard your going and your coming, now and forever* (Psalms 121:7–8)."

Rabbi El'azar opened, "*Hallelujah! I praise YHVH with all my heart, in the council of the upright, in the assembly* (Psalms 111:1). This verse has been established, but come and see! All his days, King David would engage in the worship of the blessed Holy One, rising at midnight, praising and offering thanks in hymns of praise, to array his site in kingdom above. For when a north wind aroused at midnight, he knew that at the same moment the blessed Holy One aroused in

534. **ימם (*yemim*)—defective...** See above, note 529. The word's consonants can also be vocalized *yamim,* "days," alluding to their undetermined birthday.

535. **They appear to human beings** As they appeared here to Rabbi El'azar and Rabbi Yitsḥak.

536. **he found them...** Anah found these spirits, who—misbegotten themselves—taught him how to engender bastards.

According to one rabbinic tradition, the word הימים (*ha-yemim*) means "mules," and the verse in Genesis is referring to Anah's discovery of how to produce a mule by crossbreeding a horse and a donkey.

See *Bereshit Rabbah* 82:14; JT *Berakhot* 8:5, 12b; BT *Pesaḥim* 54a; *Ḥullin* 7b; Rashi on Genesis 36:24. Cf. *Sefer ha-Yashar, Vayishlaḥ,* 167–68; Ginzberg, *Legends,* 5:322–23, n. 322.

537. **Anah was a bastard...** In Genesis 36:20, Anah appears as Zibeon's brother; in verse 24, he is described as Zibeon's son. This contradiction is resolved by the notion that Zibeon copulated with his mother, engendering the bastard Anah.

See BT *Pesaḥim* 54a; *Tanḥuma, Vayeshev* 1; Rashi on Genesis 36:24.

538. **This one issued...so he found them...** Having been born of an incestuous union, Anah was drawn to the defective spirits of defilement.

539. **desolate wilderness is their habitation** On the wilderness as the abode of demons, see *Zohar* 1:14b, 126a, 169b; 2:157a, 184a, 236b–237a; 3:63b. Cf. BT *Pesaḥim* 112b.

the Garden of Eden to delight with the righteous. So he rose at that moment and invigorated himself with songs and praise until morning arose.[540]

"For we have established that when the blessed Holy One appears in the Garden of Eden, He and all the righteous in the garden together listen to his voice, as is written: *Companions listen for your voice; let me hear!* (Song of Songs 8:13).[541] Moreover, a thread of love is drawn upon him by day, as is said: *By day YHVH directs His love, in the night His song is with me* (Psalms 42:9).[542] Moreover, those words of Torah that he utters all ascend to be adorned before the blessed Holy One.[543] Therefore King David would engage at night in the worship of his Lord.

"Come and see: הללויה (*Haleluyah*), *Hallelujah!* Of all those songs and praises chanted by David, we have learned that the highest is *Haleluyah*, as has been established. Why? Because it embraces name and praise as one.[544] What does 'name and praise' mean? Name is יה (*Yah*). Who is praise? Assembly of Israel, who arranges praise constantly for the blessed Holy One, never subsiding, as is said: *O God, do not be silent; do not be quiet or still, O God!* (Psalms 83:2), for She is constantly arranging and praising arranged praise for Him. So, name and praise as one.[545]

540. **King David... rising at midnight...** See above, note 518. David's "site in kingdom above" is his link with *Shekhinah*, who is known as *Malkhut* (Kingdom).

541. **listen to his voice...** To the voice of the one engaged in midnight worship through study or song.

The full verse reads: *You who dwell in the gardens, companions listen for your voice; let me hear!* It is applied to the study of Torah in BT *Shabbat* 63a: "Rabbi Abba said in the name of Rabbi Shim'on son of Lakish, 'When two disciples of the wise listen to one another in *halakhah*, the blessed Holy One listens to their voice, as is said: *You who dwell in the gardens, companions listen for your voice; let me hear!*'"

See *Zohar* 1:77b, 92a, 207b, 231b; 2:46a; 3:13a, 22a, 213a.

542. **thread of love is drawn upon him...** See BT *Ḥagigah* 12b: "Resh Lakish said, 'To one who engages in Torah by night, the blessed Holy One extends a thread of love by day, as is said: *By day YHVH directs His love.* Why? Because *in the night His song is with me.*'" *His song* is the song of Torah.

See Maimonides, *Mishneh Torah, Hilkhot Talmud Torah* 3:13; *Zohar* 1:82b, 92a, 194b, 207b; 2:18b, 46a, 149a; 3:65a; Moses de León, *Sefer ha-Rimmon*, 54.

543. **words of Torah... ascend to be adorned...** See *Zohar* 1:4b–5a.

544. **highest is *Haleluyah*...** See BT *Pesaḥim* 117a: "Rabbi Yehoshu'a son of Levi said, 'The book of Psalms was uttered with ten expressions of praise.... The greatest of them all is הללויה (*Haleluyah*), for it embraces name and praise simultaneously.'" The word הללויה (*Haleluyah*) comprises two elements: the divine name יה (*Yah*) and the plural imperative הללו (*halelu*), "praise!"

See *Zohar* 1:232b; 2:173b; 3:101a; *Minḥat Shai* on the verse.

545. **Assembly of Israel, who arranges praise constantly...** In rabbinic literature, כנסת ישראל (*keneset yisra'el*), "Assembly of Israel," denotes the people of Israel. The midrash on the Song of Songs describes the

"*I praise YHVH with all my* לבב (*levav*), *heart*, as they have established: with the good impulse and the evil impulse; for they constantly accompany a person, as is said: *with all* לבבך (*levavekha*), *your heart* (Deuteronomy 6:5). This has been affirmed.[546]

"*In the council of the upright, in the assembly*—this is Israel, by whom all rungs are adorned: priests and Levites, righteous and devout; *the upright, in the assembly*—as is said: *in the assembly of God* (Psalms 82:1). These are the mystery by which the blessed Holy One is adorned.[547]

"Therefore a person should praise his Lord constantly, since He delights in songs of praise. If one knows how to praise the blessed Holy One fittingly, He receives his prayer and saves him, as is written: *I will set him on high, for he knows My name. When he calls on Me, I will answer him; I am with him in distress; I will rescue him and honor him. With length of days will I satisfy him, and show him My salvation* (Psalms 91:14–16)."[548]

Rabbi Yose opened, saying,[549] "*You are my hiding place; You protect me from*

love affair between the maiden (the earthly community of Israel) and her lover (the Holy One, blessed be He). In the *Zohar, keneset yisra'el* can refer to the earthly community but also (often primarily) to *Shekhinah,* the divine feminine counterpart of the people, the aspect of God most intimately connected with them. The lovers in the Song of Songs are pictured as the divine couple, *Tif'eret* and *Shekhinah*.

Here *Shekhinah* sings praise to Her divine partner. Their union is expressed by the word הללויה (*Haleluyah*): She is symbolized by *halelu* (praise!), and He is indicated by the name *Yah* (often applied to *Ḥokhmah* and *Binah*). See *Zohar* 1:77b, 86a–b; 2:256b (*Heikh*).

546. **לבב (*levav*), *heart*... with the good impulse and the evil impulse...** The normal spelling of the biblical word for "heart" is לב (*lev*), with one ב (*vet*); the double ב (*vet*) symbolizes the two impulses. See M *Berakhot* 9:5: "*With all* לבבך (*levavekha*), *your heart* (Deuteronomy 6:5)—with both your impulses: your good impulse and your evil impulse."

According to a rabbinic tradition, two angels accompany a person. Here the angelic pair is identified with the good and evil impulses.

See BT *Berakhot* 61a; *Shabbat* 119b; *Ta'anit* 11a; *Ḥagigah* 16a; *Zohar* 1:49b, 144b, 155b, 165b, 174b; 3:263b.

547. **by whom all rungs are adorned...** The various members of the community are linked with specific sefirotic rungs. Priests and Levites symbolize respectively *Ḥesed* and *Gevurah*. "Righteous and devout" symbolize respectively *Yesod* and the pair *Netsaḥ* and *Hod*. *The upright* refers to *Tif'eret* (the central column), and *assembly* alludes to *Shekhinah*, who is known as אל (*El*), "God," as in the phrase *assembly of God*. Cf. *Zohar* 1:155b. Thus, through their varied acts of worship, study, and righteous living, the people of Israel adorn God.

548. ***I will set him on high, for he knows My name...*** The verses open: *Because he desires Me, I will deliver him.*

549. **Rabbi Yose...** As a number of commentators point out, "Rabbi Yitshak" fits better here, since he is the one accompanying Rabbi El'azar on the way. But note how yet another rabbi (Rabbi Yehudah) appears at the end of this section. See *KP*; *Nefesh David*; *NZ*.

the adversary; You surround me with shouts of deliverance. Selah! (ibid. 32:7).[550] *You are my hiding place*—blessed Holy One, who is a hiding place and shield for one who walks the ways of Torah, so he is hidden in the shadow of His wings and cannot be harmed.

"*You protect me from the adversary*—from above and below. Above, a human has an archenemy; below too. Who is that? The evil impulse: [179a] *adversary* above, *adversary* below.[551] Were it not for the evil impulse, a person wouldn't find a foe in the world. So, *You protect me from the adversary.*

"תסובבני (*Tesoveveni*), *You surround me,* [*with*] *shouts of deliverance. Selah!* The verse should read: יסובבוני (*Yesovevuni*), *They surround me.*[552] Why *tesoveveni*, *You surround me*? Because these are the songs encompassing rungs of salvation: *You surround me* with them to save me on the way. This verse is orderly and backward, in either direction.[553]

"Come and see: Within these songs of praise—uttered by David—lie mysteries, supernal words of mysterious wisdom,[554] since they all were uttered through the Holy Spirit, for Holy Spirit alighted upon David and he sang.[555] So all of them were uttered as mysteries of wisdom."

Rabbi El'azar opened, saying, "*You pushed me hard, so that I would fall; but YHVH helped me* (Psalms 118:13). *You pushed me hard.* The verse should read: *They pushed me hard.*[556] Why *You pushed me hard*? This is the Other Side,[557] who constantly pushes a person, seeking to push him away and lead him astray from the blessed Holy One; this is the evil impulse, constantly accompanying a person. To him David retorted, *You pushed me hard, so that I would fall*—

550. *Selah!* A term of uncertain etymology and meaning that appears often in Psalms.

551. **evil impulse: *adversary* above, *adversary* below** According to Resh Lakish (BT *Bava Batra* 16a), the evil impulse is identical with Satan: "Satan, the evil impulse, and the Angel of Death are one and the same." On the same page of the Talmud, we find a description of Satan's itinerary below and above: "He descends and seduces, ascends and arouses wrath, obtains authorization and seizes the soul."

552. **verse should read: יסובבוני (*Yesovevuni*), *They surround me*** The verse would then read: *Shouts of deliverance surround me.*

553. **verse is orderly and backward** The verse can be read forward and backward as a formula of protection. Shim'on Lavi (*KP*, ad loc.) cites a tradition of Judah he-Ḥasid that recommends the forward spelling of two verses (including this one) and the backward spelling of a third as a technique for invoking protection. See *OY*; Galante.

554. **Within these songs...lie mysteries...** The Psalms contain mysteries of wisdom and divine names, as described in the magical text *Shimmushei Tehillim*. See Scholem, *Kabbalah*, 20–21, 359.

555. **Holy Spirit alighted upon David and he sang** See BT *Pesaḥim* 117a; *Midrash Tehillim* 24:1, 3; Rashi on Psalms 23:1; *Zohar* 1:39b, 67a; 2:50a, 140a, 170a.

556. **verse should read: *They pushed me hard*** Referring to the psalmist's enemies, who are described in the third person in the preceding verses.

557. **Other Side** The demonic realm.

because he strove against him with all those afflictions to turn him from the blessed Holy One.[558] Of him, David said, '*You pushed me hard, so that I would fall*—into Hell. *But YHVH helped me*—for I was not delivered into your hand.'

"So a person should beware of him, lest he dominate. Then the blessed Holy One guards him on all his ways, as is written: *Then you will walk your way safely and not injure your foot. When you walk, your stride will be unconstricted; if you run, you will not stumble* (Proverbs 3:23; 4:12). Similarly, *The path of the righteous is like gleaming light, shining ever brighter until full day* (ibid. 4:18)."

Rabbi Yehudah said, "Happy are Israel, for the blessed Holy One protects them in this world and in the world that is coming, as is written: *Your people, all of them righteous, will inherit the land forever* (Isaiah 60:21)!"

558. **all those afflictions...** Various temptations that assailed David, especially his attraction to Bathsheba (2 Samuel 11–12).

פרשת וישב

Parashat Va-Yeshev

"HE DWELLED" (GENESIS 37:1–40:23)

Rabbi Ḥiyya opened, "*Many are the afflictions of the righteous, but YHVH delivers him from them all* (Psalms 34:20). Come and see how intensely a person is attacked, from the day that the blessed Holy One endows him with a soul to exist in this world! For as soon as a human emerges into the atmosphere, the evil impulse lies ready to conspire with him, as has been said; for it is written: *At the opening crouches sin* (Genesis 4:7)—right then the evil impulse partners him.[1]

"Come and see that it is so! For animals all protect themselves from the day they are born, fleeing from fire and all menacing sites; yet a human being is ready at once to fling himself into fire, because the evil impulse dwells within him, instantly luring him into evil ways.[2]

"We have established what is written: *Better a poor and wise child than an old and foolish king who no longer knows how to heed warning* (Ecclesiastes 4:13). *Better a child*—the good impulse, who is a child, just recently with a person, accompanying him only from the age of thirteen, as has been said.[3]

"*Than a king*—the evil impulse, who is called king, ruling over humanity in the world. *Old and foolish*, for he is surely old, as already established, since as

1. ***At the opening...*** From the moment of birth, *at the opening* of the womb, the evil impulse joins the infant.

See BT *Berakhot* 61a; *Qiddushin* 30b; *Sanhedrin* 91b; *Avot de-Rabbi Natan* A, 16; B, 16, 30; *Qohelet Rabbah* on 4:13; *Midrash Tehillim* 9:5; *Zohar* 1:78b (*ST*), 165b; 2:219b, 267b; and Mopsik, here.

2. **animals all protect themselves... yet a human being...** The infant's failure to shun danger stems from the evil impulse.

See *Avot de-Rabbi Natan* A, 16; B, 30; *KP*; and the story of Moses and the burning coal in *Shemot Rabbah* 1:26.

3. **We have established... from the age of thirteen...** The good impulse enters only at this age, so it is a newly arrived *child*, compared with the aged evil impulse.

See *Avot de-Rabbi Natan* B, 16; *Qohelet Rabbah* on 4:13; *Midrash Tehillim* 9:5; *Zohar* 1:78a–b (*ST*), 110b (*MhN*).

soon as a person is born, emerging into the atmosphere, he [179b] accompanies that person.[4] So he is *an old and foolish king.*[5]

"*Who no longer knows how* להזהר (*le-hizzaher*), *to heed warning.* It is not written להזהיר (*le-hazhir*), *to give warning,* but rather *le-hizzaher, to heed warning*—because he is a fool, of whom Solomon said *The fool walks in darkness* (ibid. 2:14),[6] for he issues from dregs of darkness, deprived of light forever."[7]

Rabbi Shim'on said, "Come and see: *Better a poor and wise child.* Who is a child? This has been established and explained. However, *Better a child,* as is written: *I was a youth, and now I am old* (Psalms 37:25).[8] This is the youth who is *a poor child,* possessing nothing at all of his own.[9] Why is he called *youth*?

4. **he accompanies that person** The evil impulse attaches himself to the newborn.

5. **he is . . . *foolish king*** On the link between foolishness and sin, see Numbers 12:11; BT *Sotah* 3a.

6. **It is not written להזהיר (*le-hazhir*) . . . but rather *le-hizzaher* . . .** Obviously the evil impulse, who tempts humans, does not know how to warn them of the consequences of sin. But neither does he know how to heed warning, how to guard himself from being vanquished by the good impulse.

Rabbi Ḥiyya is apparently playing with the homonymous root זהר (*zhr*), "to shine." The evil impulse can illumine neither others nor himself; he *walks in darkness.*

For a range of interpretations, see *OY*; Vital; Galante; *MM*; *Nefesh David*; Tishby, *Wisdom of the Zohar,* 2:796; Mopsik; *MmD.*

7. **dregs of darkness . . .** Evil derives from the dregs of the *sefirah* of *Din* (Judgment), which is symbolized by darkness. The word סוסיתא (*susita*) is a variant of the Zoharic neologism סוספיתא (*suspita*), "dregs, scoria, slag," apparently based on Aramaic כוספא (*kuspa*), "pomace, husk, residue."

See *Zohar* 1:30a, 71b, 118b, 193a, 228a; 2:24b, 203a, 224b, 236b; *Bei'ur ha-Millim ha-Zarot,* 182; Scholem, *Major Trends,* 166, 389, n. 54 (and on its alchemical associations, idem, *Alchemie und Kabbala,* 40–43); Liebes, *Peraqim,* 336–38; Mopsik. Cf. the similar-sounding word in the converse Talmudic expression (BT *Ta'anit* 25a, *Bava Batra* 73a): צוציתא דנורא (*tsutsita de-nura*), "flash of fire."

8. ***I was a youth, and now I am old*** The verse continues: *and I have never seen a righteous man forsaken or his seed begging bread.* According to rabbinic tradition, this verse is uttered by Metatron, chief angel and prince of the world. He is also known as נער (*na'ar*), "youth, lad, heavenly servant."

See BT *Yevamot* 16b: "Rabbi Shemu'el son of Naḥmani said in the name of Rabbi Yoḥanan, 'This verse was uttered by the Prince of the World: *I was a youth, and now I am old.* Who said it? If you suggest it was the blessed Holy One, does old age pertain to Him? So David must have said it. But was he so old? Rather you must conclude that the Prince of the World uttered it.'"

See *Alfa Beita de-Rabbi Aqiva* A (*Battei Midrashot,* 2:354); *Zohar* 1:95b, 124b–125a, 126a–b (*MhN*), 143a, 162a, 181b; *ZḤ* 85c (*MhN, Rut*). On Metatron, see *Tosafot, Yevamot* 16b, s.v. *pasuq zeh;* Scholem, *Kabbalah,* 377–81; Margaliot, *Mal'akhei Elyon,* 73–108.

9. **possessing nothing at all of his own . . .** Metatron shares this designation of *Shekhinah*; both are empty or poor until filled from above. Metatron depends entirely upon *Shekhinah,* while She too has nothing of Her own but absorbs and reflects the light of *Tif'eret* and the entire array of higher *sefirot,* as the moon reflects the sun. But Metatron

Because he is renewed, for the moon renews herself constantly, and he is constantly youthful.[10] *Poor*—as we have said. *And wise*—because wisdom dwells within him.[11]

"*Than an old king*—the evil impulse, as has been said, for since the first day he existed, he has never escaped his defilement.[12] And he is *foolish*—all his ways evil, leading humans astray, not knowing how to heed warning. He sidles up to people with ploys, luring them from the good way to the evil.

"Come and see: This is why he hastens to be with a person from the day he is born, so that he will trust him.[13] For look, when the good impulse arrives, the person cannot believe him—and considers him a burden! Similarly we have learned: Who is cunningly wicked? One who pleads his case in front of the judge before the other party arrives, as is said: *The first to plead his case seems right*... (Proverbs 18:17).[14] Similarly this cunning wicked one,[15] as is said: *The serpent was cunning* (Genesis 3:1)—he arrives first, dwelling with a person before his counterpart comes to rest upon him.[16] Since he appears first, pleading his case with him, when his counterpart—the good impulse—arrives, the person finds him obnoxious and cannot raise his head, as if he loaded on his shoulders all the burdens of the world, because of that cunning wicked one who

and *Shekhinah* are not simply parallel; *Shekhinah* manifests as Metatron.

On the identification of Metatron with *Shekhinah*, see Scholem, *Origins of the Kabbalah*, 187; Wolfson, *Through a Speculum That Shines*, 256; Mopsik, 3:38–39, n. 10; *Zohar* 1:51a, 181b; 2:38b, 238a; 3:156b; Moses de León, *Sefer ha-Rimmon*, 115; idem, *Sheqel ha-Qodesh*, 42–43 (51).

The expression לית ליה מגרמיה כלום (*leit leih mi-garmeih kelum*), literally, "he has nothing at all of his own," is a masculine version of the description of *Shekhinah*: לית לה מגרמה כלום (*leit lah mi-garmah kelum*), "She has nothing at all of her own," a phrase appearing frequently in the *Zohar* and derived from a description of the moon by medieval astronomers.

See Radak on Genesis 1:16; *Zohar* 1:20a, 31a, 124b–125a, 132b, 181a, 238a, 249b; 2:43a, 142a, 145b, 215a, 218b; 3:113b; Moses de León, *Shushan Edut*, 338; idem, *Sefer ha-Rimmon*, 113; idem, *Sod Eser Sefirot Belimah*, 381. Cf. BT *Shabbat* 156a.

10. **moon renews herself constantly, and he is constantly youthful** The moon symbolizes *Shekhinah*, who clothes Herself in Metatron, renewing both Herself and him.

11. **wisdom dwells within him** *Shekhinah*, known as Lower Wisdom, dwells within Metatron.

12. **he has never escaped his defilement** The evil impulse is *an old king*, eternally impure. See Mopsik.

13. **so that he will trust him** So that the human will trust this impulse.

14. **Who is cunningly wicked? One who pleads...** A paraphrase of a rabbinic teaching found in BT *Sotah* 21b; *Tanḥuma*, *Mishpatim* 6.

The full verse in Proverbs reads: *The first to plead his case seems right, till the other comes and examines him.*

15. **this cunning wicked one** The evil impulse.

16. **before his counterpart comes to rest upon him** Before the good impulse enters the person at age thirteen.

reached him first.[17] Concerning this, Solomon said, *The poor man's wisdom is despised, and his words are not heeded* (Ecclesiastes 9:16), because the other anticipated him.[18]

"So whoever accepts a person's words before his counterpart arrives,[19] acts as if he accepts belief in another, false god.[20] Rather, *till the other comes and examines him* (Proverbs, ibid.). This is the way of the righteous, for a righteous person does not believe that cunningly wicked evil impulse before his counterpart, the good impulse, arrives. Because of this, people stumble in the world to come.[21]

"However, one who is righteous, in awe of his Lord, endures many afflictions in this world so as not to trust and consort with that evil impulse,[22] and the blessed Holy One delivers him from them all, as is written: *Many are the afflictions of the righteous, but YHVH delivers him from them all.*[23] It is not written *Many are* רעות לצדיק (*ra'ot la-tsaddiq*), *the afflictions for the righteous*, but rather צדיק (*tsaddiq*), [*of*] *the righteous*, because the blessed Holy One אתרעי (*itre'ei*), delights, in that human being and delivers him from everything in this world and in the world that is coming.[24] Happy is his share!

"Come and see how many afflictions befell Jacob in his effort not to cling to that evil impulse, to keep it away from his portion! Because of that he suffered numerous ills and had no peace."

He opened, saying, "*I had no ease, no quiet, no rest, and turmoil came* (Job 3:26). Come and see how many afflictions the righteous endure in this world—affliction after affliction, pain upon pain—to render them worthy of the world

17. **Since he appears first, pleading...** The prior advice of the evil impulse makes the subsequent advice of the good impulse seem burdensome and repulsive.

18. ***The poor man's wisdom...*** The advice of the good inclination.

19. **before his counterpart arrives** Before the other party appears.

20. **as if he accepts belief in another, false god** Listening to only one side of a dispute resembles listening to the advice of the evil impulse, identified with idolatry and the demonic "other." See BT *Shabbat* 105b; *Zohar* 3:106b; Mopsik.

21. **stumble in the world to come** They fail to merit entry into the world of bliss, or they stumble into Hell.

See *Nefesh David*; *Sullam*; Tishby, *Wisdom of the Zohar*, 2:797; Mopsik. Cf. *Zohar* 1:148a–b (*ST*).

22. **endures many afflictions...** In withstanding temptation.

23. ***Many are the afflictions...*** See above, page 85.

24. **It is not written...*for the righteous*...** This alternative reading would imply that suffering is or will be inflicted from outside, intended *for the righteous*. The point of the verse, however, according to Rabbi Shim'on, is that the suffering is intrinsically *of the righteous*, who withstands the temptations of the evil impulse. By enduring its afflictions and avoiding its traps, he merits God's delight and deliverance.

For a range of interpretations, see *OY*; Vital; Galante; *NO*; *MM*; *Nefesh David*; *Sullam*; Tishby, *Wisdom of the Zohar*, 798; Mopsik; *MmD*. Cf. Moses de León, *Sefer ha-Mishqal*, 82.

that is coming. How Jacob suffered![25] Affliction upon affliction constantly, as is said: *I had no ease*—in the house of Laban, from whom I could not be rescued;[26] *no quiet*—from Esau: that suffering inflicted on me by his prince,[27] and later the fear of Esau himself.[28] *No rest*—on account of Dinah and Shechem;[29] *and turmoil came*—the turmoil and confusion of Joseph, most severe of them all.[30] Out of Jacob's love for Joseph—mystery of covenant—he entered Egypt, for later it is written: *I have remembered My covenant* (Exodus 9:15), so that *Shekhinah* would be present there with him."[31]

Jacob dwelled in the land of his father's sojournings, in the land of Canaan (Genesis 37:1).

[180a] Rabbi Yose opened, "*The righteous one perishes, and no one takes it to heart*... (Isaiah 57:1).[32] *The righteous one perishes.* When the blessed Holy One gazes upon the world and finds it unfit, and judgment is poised to prevail in the world, the blessed Holy One removes the righteous one from among them, so that judgment will befall all the others

25. **How Jacob suffered!** The following interpretation of the verse from Job derives (with variation) from *Bereshit Rabbah* 84:3. See *Zohar* 1:216b.

26. **in the house of Laban, from whom I could not be rescued** Finally, Jacob fled from Laban. See Genesis 29:1–32:3.

27. **suffering inflicted on me by his prince** By Samael, chief demon and heavenly prince of Esau. According to Midrash and *Zohar*, he is identified with the nameless being who wrestled with Jacob.

See Genesis 32:23–33; *Tanḥuma, Vayishlaḥ* 8; *Bereshit Rabbah* 77:3; *Zohar* 1:146a, 66a, 170a–171b.

28. **fear of Esau himself** See Genesis 32:4–24; 33:1–3.

29. **Dinah and Shechem** Shechem's rape of Dinah; see Genesis 34.

30. **turmoil and confusion of Joseph...** Joseph's being sold into slavery by his brothers.

31. **Out of Jacob's love for Joseph...** Jacob, who symbolizes *Tif'eret*, went down to Egypt to join Joseph, who symbolizes the covenant of circumcision and the divine phallus, *Yesod* (above, p. 68, n. 460). Together, these two *sefirot* unite with *Shekhinah*. The hidden purpose behind Jacob's descent was to consummate the union with *Shekhinah*, ensuring that She would be there "with him," i.e., with Joseph (embodiment of the covenant) and then with all the Israelites.

On the divine purpose behind Joseph's descent to Egypt, see Genesis 50:20. On the role of *Shekhinah* in exile, see BT *Megillah* 29a: "Rabbi Shim'on son of Yoḥai says, 'Come and see how beloved are Israel in the sight of the blessed Holy One! Wherever they went in exile, *Shekhinah* accompanied them. When they were exiled to Egypt, *Shekhinah* was with them.... When they were exiled to Babylon, *Shekhinah* was with them.... And even when they are destined to be redeemed, *Shekhinah* will be with them.'" See *Mekhilta, Pisḥa* 14.

32. ***The righteous one perishes, and no one takes it to heart...*** The verse continues: *devout people are taken away, while no one understands that because of evil the righteous one was taken away.*

The simple sense of the phrase *because of evil* is apparently "as a result of evil," though it was later explained to mean "so that he not experience the impending evil." See Rashi and Radak, ad loc. Cf. BT *Bava Qamma*

and no one will be found to shield them. For as long as a righteous person dwells in the world, judgment cannot dominate the generation.[33]

"How do we know? From Moses, as is written: *He said that He would annihilate them—had not Moses, His chosen one, stood in the breach before Him*... (Psalms 103:23).[34] So the blessed Holy One takes the righteous one from among them, plucking him from the world, and then exacts retribution, collecting His due.

"The conclusion of the verse: *that* מפני (*mi-penei*), *because of, evil the righteous one was taken away* (Isaiah, ibid.)[35]—'before' evil comes to prevail in the world, the righteous one is taken away.[36]

"Alternatively, *that because of evil*—the evil impulse.[37]

"Come and see: Jacob was consummation of the patriarchs[38]—prepared to endure exile—but because he was righteous, judgment was postponed, not dominating the world. For through all Jacob's days, judgment did not befall the world, and famine was nullified.[39]

60a; *Kallah Rabbati* 3:23; 6:4; *Pirqei de-Rabbi Eli'ezer* 17, and David Luria, ad loc., n. 62; ibid. (Friedlander) 17.

33. **removes the righteous one... no one will be found to shield them...** According to a rabbinic tradition, the righteous are removed to protect their generation. See BT *Shabbat* 33a: "Rabbi Gorion (according to others, Rabbi Yosef son of Rabbi Shema'yah) said, 'When there are righteous ones in the generation, the righteous are seized [killed] for the generation. When there are no righteous in the generation, schoolchildren are seized for the generation.'"

Here Rabbi Yose contends that God intentionally removes the righteous individual in order to expose his generation to harsh judgment; without his protective virtue, they are completely vulnerable.

See *Bereshit Rabbah* 33:1; *Vayiqra Rabbah* 2:6; *Kallah Rabbati* 6:4; Rashi on BT *Ta'anit* 11a, s.v. *ha-tsaddiq avad*; *Zohar* 1:67b. Cf. *Mekhilta, Neziqin* 18.

34. ***had not Moses... stood in the breach before Him...*** The verse concludes: *to turn away His wrath from destroying them.*

35. ***that* מפני (*mi-penei*), *because of, evil the righteous one was taken away*** See above, notes 32–33.

36. **'before' evil...** Understanding מפני (*mi-penei*) in the sense of לפני (*liphnei*), "before."

37. ***because of evil*—the evil impulse** God removes the righteous one from the world while he is still pure, uncorrupted by the evil impulse.

See Wisdom of Solomon 4:10–11; *Bereshit Rabbah* 25:1; *Qohelet Rabbah* on 7:23; *Shir ha-Shirim Rabbah* on 6:2; *Zohar* 1:56b; 2:10b, 96a; *ZḤ* 20a–b (*MhN*), 36b (*ST*). Cf. M *Sanhedrin* 8:5; *Sifrei*, Deuteronomy 218.

For other interpretations, see *OY*; Galante; *MM*; *Adderet Eliyyahu*; *Sullam*; *MmD*.

38. **consummation of the patriarchs** See *Bereshit Rabbah* 76:1: "Rabbi Pinḥas said in the name of Rabbi Re'uven, '... The chosen of the patriarchs is Jacob, as is said: *For Yah has chosen Jacob for Himself* (Psalms 135:4).'"

Jacob symbolizes *Tif'eret*, who harmonizes and completes the polar opposites *Ḥesed* and *Gevurah*, symbolized by Abraham and Isaac. See above, p. 43, n. 311; *Sifra, Beḥuqqotai* 8:7, 112c; *Vayiqra Rabbah* 36:5; BT *Pesaḥim* 56a.

39. **famine was nullified** As soon as Jacob came to Egypt.

See Genesis 45:6; 47:23; *Tosefta, Sotah* 10:9;

"Through all the days of Joseph—image of his father[40]—judgment did not befall the world, since he protected them all his days. As soon as he died, exile immediately befell them, as is said: *Joseph died,*[41] followed by: *Come, let us deal shrewdly with them,* and: *They embittered their lives with harsh labor* (Exodus 1:6, 10, 14).[42] Similarly, wherever a righteous person exists and dwells upon earth, judgment does not prevail, as has been said.

"Come and see: *Jacob dwelled in the land of* מגורי אביו (megurei aviv), *his father's sojournings.* What does megurei aviv mean? As is said: מגור (magor), *terror, all around* (Jeremiah 6:25), because all his days he was terribly frightened."[43]

Jacob dwelled in the land of megurei aviv, *his father's sojournings.* Rabbi El'azar said, "Dwelling in, linked with that site gripped by darkness—*land of* megurei aviv, *his father's terror,* precisely![44] *In the land of Canaan*—site linked to its site.[45] Megurei aviv—harsh judgment.[46] *In the land of* megurei aviv—as has been said, that lenient judgment joined to harsh judgment.[47] There Jacob dwelled, embracing it.

Sifrei, Deuteronomy 38; *Bereshit Rabbah* 84:6; 89:9.

40. **Joseph—image of his father** They were nearly identical.

See *Tanḥuma* (Buber), *Vayeshev* 5; *Bereshit Rabbah* 84:6, 8; *Zohar* 1:21b, 85a, 176b, 182b, 222a; 2:145a, 242a; above, p. 68, n. 461.

41. ***Joseph died*** The verse continues: *and all his brothers, and all that generation.*

42. ***They embittered their lives with harsh labor*** The verse continues: *in mortar and bricks.* Rabbi Yose's point is that Joseph's protection of his brothers delayed any manifestation of harsh judgment. After Joseph's death, his brothers' descendants (and his) became vulnerable to judgment and were enslaved. See *Shemot Rabbah* 1:8.

43. **all his days he was terribly frightened** Of the harsh quality of the sefirah of *Din* (Judgment), symbolized by his father, Isaac. For Rabbi Yose, the verse implies: *Jacob dwelled in the land of his father's terror.*

44. **Dwelling in... that site gripped by darkness...** Jacob's act of dwelling in his father's *land* symbolizes the union of his sefirah (Tif'eret) with Shekhinah, who is symbolized by land and gripped by Isaac's sefirah (Gevurah), to whom She has an affinity. Gevurah, symbolized here by darkness, is also known as Din (Judgment) and Paḥad (Fear).

Paḥad derives from Isaac's unique name for God: פחד יצחק (Paḥad Yitsḥaq), *Fear* [or: *Terror*] *of Isaac.* This striking name appears only twice in the Bible (Genesis 31:42, 53). According to *Sekhel Tov,* Exodus 15:16, it expresses the terror felt by Isaac as he was bound upon the altar by his father, Abraham.

45. ***land of Canaan*—site linked to its site** The *land of Canaan* (the earlier name of the land of Israel) symbolizes Shekhinah, with whom it is linked. For other interpretations, see *OY*; *Sullam.*

46. **Megurei aviv—harsh judgment** The *terror* inspired by Gevurah, the sefirah of Jacob's father, Isaac. As noted above, this sefirah is also called Din (Judgment) and Paḥad (Fear).

47. **lenient judgment joined to harsh judgment** Shekhinah, lenient judgment, derives from the sefirah of Din (harsh judgment), and remains linked with it. See Mopsik.

"*These are the generations of Jacob: Joseph* (Genesis 37:2). After Jacob settled, sun coupling with moon, he began to generate offspring.[48] Who is it that generated offspring? Scripture resumes, saying: *Joseph.* For that flowing, gushing river generates offspring since its waters never cease, generating offspring in this *land*, from which generations issue to the world.[49] For although the sun draws near the moon, only that rung called Righteous One bears fruit;[50] Joseph is the rung of Jacob bearing fruit, issuing offspring to the world.[51] So, *These are the generations of Jacob: Joseph.*[52]

"*These are the generations of Jacob: Joseph.* Anyone gazing at the image of Joseph would say, 'This is the image of Jacob!'[53] Come and see that of all Jacob's sons, it is not written *These are the generations of Jacob*—except for Joseph, whose image matched his father's."[54]

Seventeen years old (ibid.). Rabbi Abba said, "The blessed Holy One hinted to him: Joseph was seventeen years old when he lost him, and for the rest of his

48. **After Jacob settled, sun coupling with moon...** Jacob (symbolizing the sun, *Tif'eret*) settles in Canaan (symbolizing the moon, *Shekhinah*).

49. ***Joseph*... that flowing, gushing river...** Joseph symbolizes the river of *Yesod*, which conveys the ceaseless flow of emanation to the *land* (*Shekhinah*), from whom souls issue to the world. The phrase "flowing, gushing river" derives from Daniel 7:10. See Mopsik.

50. **that rung called Righteous One...** *Yesod* is known as Righteous One, based on Proverbs 10:25: וצדיק יסוד עולם (*Ve-tsaddiq yesod olam*). The verse literally means *The righteous one is an everlasting foundation*, but is understood as *The righteous one is the foundation of the world.* See BT *Ḥagigah* 12b; *Bahir* 71 (102); Azriel of Gerona, *Peirush ha-Aggadot*, 34.

In rabbinic literature Joseph is granted the title Righteous in recognition of resisting the sexual advances of Potiphar's wife. See Genesis 39; BT *Yoma* 35b; *Bereshit Rabbah* 93:7; *Pesiqta de-Rav Kahana, nispaḥim*, 460. Cf. *Tanḥuma, Bereshit* 5, and *Pirqei de-Rabbi Eli'ezer* 38, which cite Amos 2:6.

According to the *Zohar*, Joseph's sexual purity enabled him to scale the sefirotic ladder and attain the rung of *Yesod*, the divine phallus and site of the covenant.

51. **Joseph is the rung of Jacob bearing fruit...** *Yesod* (symbolized by Joseph) is an extension of *Tif'eret* (symbolized by Jacob). He conveys new souls to *Shekhinah*.

52. ***These are the generations of Jacob: Joseph*** The verse in Genesis reads: *These are the generations of Jacob: Joseph, seventeen years old, was tending the flock with his brothers*... But Rabbi El'azar, borrowing a playful reading from the Midrash, conveniently breaks off his citation with the phrase *Jacob: Joseph.* This implies here that Jacob and Joseph together engendered; their respective *sefirot*, *Tif'eret* and *Yesod*, constitute a single male entity uniting with *Shekhinah*.

See *Tanḥuma* (Buber), *Vayeshev* 5; *Bereshit Rabbah* 84:6, 8; Moses de León, *Sheqel ha-Qodesh*, 10 (12–13); and *Zohar* parallels cited above, note 40.

53. **Anyone gazing at the image of Joseph...** According to the Midrash, the wording *These are the generations of Jacob: Joseph* implies that father and son were nearly identical. See the preceding note.

54. **of all Jacob's sons, it is not written...** With none of them do we find the expression *These are the generations of Jacob* (followed by one of these sons' names).

days, not seeing Joseph, he wept over those seventeen years. And just as he wept over them, the blessed Holy One granted him another seventeen years of living in the land of Egypt in joy, honor, and fulfillment, with Joseph his son as king and surrounded by all his children. For him, those seventeen years were true life. Therefore, he was *seventeen years old* when he lost him."[55]

Rabbi Ḥiyya opened, "*So listen to me, men of understanding: Far be it from God to do evil, from Shaddai to do wrong! For according to a human's deeds* [180b] *He repays him, and provides for him according to his ways* (Job 34:10–11). Come and see: When the blessed Holy One created the world, He based it on justice, and through justice it endures.[56] All doings of the world hinge on justice. However, in order to preserve the world, that it not perish, He spread compassion over it—and this compassion restrains justice, so that the world will not be destroyed. By compassion the world is conducted and thereby endures.[57]

"Now, you might say that the blessed Holy One executes judgment upon a person unjustly.[58] But as already explained, when judgment befalls someone who is innocent, this is because of His love for him.[59] For the blessed Holy One loves him passionately, drawing him near. He crushes the body to empower the

55. **hinted to him: Joseph was seventeen years old...** Joseph was sold into slavery by his brothers at age seventeen. This plunged his father, Jacob, into mourning that lasted until many years later, when Jacob was reunited with his son in Egypt. According to Rabbi Abba, Joseph's age at his disappearance was a divine hint to Jacob, alluding to the end of mourning and a corresponding seventeen years of joy: the eventual duration of Jacob's fulfilled life in Egypt following his reunion with Joseph. This was "true life."

See Genesis 47:28; *Midrash Aggadah* and *Midrash ha-Gadol*, ad loc.; Kasher, *Torah Shelemah*, ad loc., nn. 79, 82; *Zohar* 1:216b. On the phrase "true life," cf. *Zohar* 1:123a.

56. **He based it on justice...** Without justice, the moral order would disintegrate. The Aramaic word דינא (*dina*), corresponding to Hebrew דין (*din*), means "justice" and "judgment."

See M *Avot* 1:18; *Avot de-Rabbi Natan* B, 43; *Bereshit Rabbah* 14:1; *Shemot Rabbah* 30:13; *Zohar* 2:122a; 3:30b, 32a; Moses de León, *Sefer ha-Rimmon*, 291, 345; Mopsik.

57. **in order to preserve the world...He spread compassion...** If human wickedness were judged strictly, the world would be condemned to destruction, so justice must be tempered by compassion. See *Bereshit Rabbah* 12:15: "The blessed Holy One said, 'If I create the world by the quality of compassion, its sins will abound; by the quality of justice, the world will not endure. Rather, I will create it by both the quality of justice and the quality of compassion. Oh that it may endure!'"

See *Bereshit Rabbah* 8:4; *Zohar* 1:58b, 230b; 2:113b; 3:38a.

58. **executes judgment upon a person unjustly** Upon someone who is innocent. The phrase derives from BT *Berakhot* 5b.

59. **because of His love for him** Such sufferings are called "chastenings of love," which test or refine the righteous individual and increase his merit.

See below, and BT *Berakhot* 5a. Cf. *Sifrei*, Deuteronomy 32; BT *Qiddushin* 40b; and Proverbs 3:12: *For the one whom YHVH loves, He reproves.*

soul; then the person is drawn to Him in love fittingly, the soul dominant, the body weakened.[60] One needs a weak body and a strong soul, invigorated vitally; then he becomes the beloved of the blessed Holy One. When the soul is weak and the body strong, he is the enemy of the blessed Holy One, who takes no pleasure in him. So the righteous one who is constantly crushed is the beloved of the blessed Holy One—though this applies only when he has examined himself and discovered no sin deserving of punishment.[61]

"Here one should contemplate several aspects. First, we see that *Shekhinah* does not dwell in a place of sorrow, in a place without joy. If there is no joy, *Shekhinah* does not abide there, as is said: *'Now bring me a minstrel.' And then, as the minstrel was playing, the spirit of God came upon him* (2 Kings 3:15).[62] For surely *Shekhinah* does not dwell in a place of sadness. How do we know? From Jacob. Because he grieved over Joseph, *Shekhinah* departed from him. As soon as the joyful news about Joseph reached him, immediately *the spirit of Jacob their father revived* (Genesis 45:27).[63] But here with this righteous one who is crushed, weakened by pain, where is joy? He is in sorrow, with no joy at all![64]

"Further, we see that many of the beloved were righteous in the presence of the blessed Holy One yet were not crushed by sickness or pain, nor were their bodies ever weakened. Why aren't these like those? Those were broken, while these endured physically fit.[65]

60. **crushes the body to empower the soul...** The soul rules at the expense of the body.

On this dichotomy, see Maimonides, *Guide of the Perplexed* 3:51; Isaac the Blind, *Peirush Sefer Yetsirah*, 6; *Zohar* 1:140a–b; 3:168a; Moses de León, *Sefer ha-Rimmon*, 249–50; Mopsik.

61. **only when he has examined himself...** If he is really blameless, then the suffering is a sign of God's love. See BT *Berakhot* 5a.

62. ***Shekhinah* does not dwell in a place of sorrow...** As shown by the experience of the prophet Elisha, who was divinely inspired while in a state of musical joy.

See 1 Chronicles 25:1, and Rashi, ad loc.; JT *Sukkah* 5:1, 55a; BT *Shabbat* 30b, *Pesaḥim* 117a; *Midrash Tehillim* 24:3; *Zohar* 1:216b. The Masoretic text of the verse in Kings reads: *the hand of YHVH came upon him.* See *Biblia Hebraica*, ad loc.

63. **Because he grieved over Joseph, *Shekhinah* departed...** Jacob's sadness over the disappearance of Joseph repelled *Shekhinah*, thereby depriving him of prophetic vision. Years later, when Jacob realized that Joseph was still alive, She returned, and Her power of inspiration reanimated the aged patriarch.

See *Avot de-Rabbi Natan* A, 30; *Targum Yerushalmi* and *Targum Onqelos*, Genesis 45:27; *Pirqei de-Rabbi Eli'ezer* 38; *Midrash Tehillim* 24:3; Rashi on Genesis 45:27; Maimonides, *Shemonah Peraqim* 7; idem, *Guide of the Perplexed* 2:36; *Zohar* 1:197a–b, 216b.

64. **in sorrow, with no joy at all** So *Shekhinah* cannot be present, and his sufferings are no sign of divine love.

65. **Why aren't these like those?...** Why do some of the righteous suffer physically, while others maintain vigorous health?

"Now, you might say that these exist enduringly, fittingly, because they are righteous born of righteous, as has been established, whereas those others are righteous but not born of righteous.[66] But we see righteous born of righteous, even one whose father is righteous born of righteous and he himself is righteous—why is his body broken by pain, all his days in anguish?[67]

"But here lies a mystery, since all actions of the blessed Holy One are true and just, *for according to a human's deeds He repays him, and according to his ways He provides for him* (Job 34:11).[68] I have discovered in books of the ancients[69] a certain mystery, along with another mystery, one that is two.[70] For there are times when the moon is defective, abiding in judgment, unaccompanied by the sun.[71] Yet constantly, every moment, She has to issue souls into human beings, as She gathered them previously.[72] Now She releases them, while subsisting on judgment;[73] whoever obtains her at such a time will always be diminished, accompanied by poverty, continually broken by judgment through-

66. **righteous born of righteous...** See BT *Berakhot* 7a: "Rabbi Yoḥanan said in the name of Rabbi Yose, '...He [Moses] said before Him, "Master of the Universe, why do some of the righteous prosper, while others suffer? And why do some of the wicked prosper, while others suffer?" He replied to him, "Moses, a righteous one who prospers is righteous born of righteous; a righteous one who suffers is righteous born of wicked. A wicked one who prospers is wicked born of righteous; a wicked one who suffers is wicked born of wicked."'"

See *Avot de-Rabbi Natan* B, 22; *Zohar* 3:168a.

67. **But we see righteous born of righteous...** Even some of these purely righteous suffer. Why?

68. ***according to a human's deeds He repays him...*** Several commentators detect an allusion here to the doctrine of reincarnation: the suffering righteous one is atoning for misdeeds in a previous lifetime. The teaching that follows, however, presents a different cosmic scenario.

See Naḥmanides on Job 33:19, 30; Moses de León, *Shushan Edut*, 357–59; idem, *Sefer ha-Rimmon*, 248 (and Wolfson's note 14); *KP*, 2:350a–351a; Galante, 176b; *MM*; Tishby, *Mishnat ha-Zohar*, 2:727; idem, *Wisdom of the Zohar*, 3:1491; Mopsik. Cf. *Zohar* 3:177a; *Sullam* on *Zohar* 1:181a (12a, n. 35); *MmD*, 16.

69. **books of the ancients** One of the many sources housed in the fantastic library of the author(s) of the *Zohar*. These particular volumes are cited frequently.

See 1:10a, 34b, 41a (*Heikh*), 184a, 220a, 234b; 2:35a, 95b, 239a; 3:10a, 19a, 26b, 249b, 258b, 288a (*IZ*).

70. **one that is two** The double nature of the mystery involves two states of the moon (defective and full) and two corresponding types of the righteous (those who suffer and those who prosper).

71. **when the moon is defective...** When *Shekhinah* lacks the light of *Tif'eret* and is colored by harsh judgment. This dismal situation is caused by human wickedness, which interferes with the union of the divine couple.

72. **She has to issue souls...** *Shekhinah* first unites with Her partner, receiving His flow, and later—even if separated from Her partner—gives birth to new souls, transmitting them to new embryos.

73. **while subsisting on judgment** While under the influence of harsh judgment.

out his life[74]—except that prayer annuls all decrees, so through prayer he can ascend.[75]

"When that rung is complete and the flowing, gushing river performs with Her,[76] then through the soul issuing, poured into a person, he becomes totally complete: in wealth, in children, in bodily soundness—all because of [181a] that flowing, gushing flux of destiny, uniting with that rung, now fulfilled and blessed. So all depends upon מזלא (*mazzala*), flux of destiny, concerning which we have learned: 'Children, life, and sustenance do not depend on merit, but on *mazzala*.' For merit does not pertain until She is filled and illumined by the flux.[77]

"So all those crushed in this world—yet truly righteous—are all crushed and sentenced justly. How so? Because that soul is decisive.[78] Consequently, the blessed Holy One has compassion on them in the world that is coming."[79]

74. **whoever obtains her at such a time...** Any embryo receiving a soul from *Shekhinah* while She is tainted by judgment will suffer throughout life. This explains why even some righteous suffer.

See *Zohar* 2:95b, 113a; 3:168a, 281b (*RM*); *ZḤ* 36c–d; *TZ* 69, 101b–102a; Tishby, *Wisdom of the Zohar*, 2:754–57; Liebes, *Peraqim*, 335, 393.

On the joining of soul to embryo, see *Bereshit Rabbah* 34:10; BT *Sanhedrin* 91b, *Niddah* 31a.

75. **prayer annuls all decrees...** As noted in *Bereshit Rabbah* 44:13 and parallels.

76. **When that rung is complete...** When *Shekhinah* is filled by *Yesod*'s river of emanation.

"Performs" renders the Aramaic, אשתמש (*ishtammash*), which in the *Zohar* means "to have sexual relations," based on the rabbinic idiomatic extension of the root שמש (*shmsh*) —literally "to minister, serve, perform, use."

77. **flux of destiny...** The word מזלא (*mazzala*) means "constellation, planet, planetary influence, zodiacal sign, destiny, fortune, guardian angel." See BT *Mo'ed Qatan* 28a: "Rava said, 'Life, children, and sustenance do not depend on merit but on *mazzala*, destiny.'"

In the *Zohar*, *mazzala* is associated with the root נזל (*nzl*), "to flow," and often refers to the flow of emanation from *Binah* through *Yesod*, the divine phallus. *Yesod* conveys this flow to *Shekhinah*, who generates new souls. The fate of each soul depends upon the flow: if the divine couple is united as the soul enters the world, then she will live a fulfilled life; if the flow between the couple is impeded and *Shekhinah* is blemished by harsh judgment, then the emerging soul will suffer.

See *Targum*, Ecclesiastes 9:2; Ibn Ezra on Job 28:1; *Zohar* 1:43b (*Heikh*), 115a, 137a, 156b, 159b, 160b, 198a, 207b; 2:6a, 252b (*Heikh*); 3:25b, 77b, 134a (*IR*), 289a (*IZ*), 292b (*IZ*), 295b (*IZ*); Moses de León, *Sefer ha-Rimmon*, 193; idem, *Sheqel ha-Qodesh*, 65 (82); Gikatilla, *Sha'arei Orah*, 12a, 37a–b, 74a, 95a; Mopsik.

78. **Because that soul is decisive** Each person is predestined to prosper or to suffer in life depending on the dynamics of the *sefirot* at the moment that his or her soul enters the womb's embryo. See the preceding note. Cf. Galante; Mopsik; above, note 68.

79. **Consequently, the blessed Holy One has compassion on them...** Because based on their righteous behavior, their suffering was undeserved. By enduring their "chastenings of love" in this world, the righteous earn a reward in the hereafter.

Rabbi El'azar said, "Everything done by the blessed Holy One is just, in order to purify that soul and bring her to the world that is coming.[80] Thus all His deeds are just and true, to remove from her the filth she received in this world; so that body is broken and the soul purified. That is why the blessed Holy One makes the righteous one suffer affliction and pain in this world: to be totally cleansed and attain eternal life. Of this is written *YHVH refines the righteous* (Psalms 11:5)—literally, as has been said."[81]

Rabbi Shim'on opened, "*But he shall not enter before the veil, and he shall not approach the altar, for he has a defect* (Leviticus 21:23).[82] Come and see: When that flowing, gushing river issues all those souls, and the female is impregnated,[83] they all abide within, in a treasure-house within, in the portico of a treasure-house.[84] And when the moon is tainted by the aspect of that evil serpent, all souls then issuing—although all pure, all holy—issue defectively; so

80. **Everything... is just, in order to purify that soul...** Through chastening. Rabbi El'azar differs with Rabbi Ḥiyya, insisting that the soul's suffering is purposeful, not predestined.

81. ***YHVH refines the righteous*—literally...** The biblical verb יבחן (*yivḥan*), which means "tests, tries, examines," is understood here by Rabbi El'azar as "refines." See Zechariah 13:9; Proverbs 17:3; Job 23:10; *Zohar* 1:139b–140b.

82. ***But he shall not enter before the veil...*** The verse concludes: *He shall not desecrate My sanctuaries, for I am YHVH, who sanctifies them.*

In the Bible this verse is addressed to a blemished high priest; see Milgrom, *Leviticus*, 3:1830–31. On its meaning here, see below.

83. **When that flowing, gushing river issues...** When *Yesod* transmits the flow to *Shekhinah*.

84. **in a treasure-house within...** The Aramaic phrase reads: בקורטא דלגו בסיטו קורטא (*Be-qurta dilgo be-situ qurta*). *Qurta* apparently derives from Greek *kouratoreia*, "treasury." See *Targum Yerushalmi*, Numbers 22:18; 24:13; Job 3:14; 38:22; *Arukh ha-Shalem* and *Tosefot he-Arukh ha-Shalem*, s.v. *qrt*.

Situ is apparently based on the Aramaic סטו (*setav*), which derives from the Greek *stoia*, "colonnade, portico." The Temple Mount was surrounded by a double colonnade, consisting of two rows of columns, סטיו לפנים מסטיו (*setav lifnim mi-setav*), "a colonnade within a colonnade." See JT *Ta'anit* 3:11, 66d; BT *Berakhot* 33b; *Pesaḥim* 13b, 52b; *Sukkah* 45a; below, p. 207, n. 173; *Encyclopaedia Judaica*, 15:964–65. Cf. *Tosefta*, *Sukkah* 4:6.

Here the souls abide in the womb of *Shekhinah*, who is the "treasury of souls." The image of a treasury derives from Rashi's commentary on a Talmudic passage (BT *Yevamot* 62a) in which Rabbi Assi mentions a heavenly "body" containing all souls; Rashi refers to this body as אוצר (*otsar*), "a treasury." In the *Zohar* the treasure house of unborn souls is sometimes identified with *Shekhinah*.

See 3 Enoch 43:3; *Bahir* 126 (184); *Zohar* 1:28b (*TZ*), 119a; 2:142a, 157a, 161b, 174a, 253 (*Heikh*); 3:152a; *ZḤ* 10b–c (*MhN*), 60b, 69b (*ShS*); Moses de León, *Sefer ha-Mishqal*, 93; Tishby, *Mishnat ha-Zohar*, 2:728–29; idem, *Wisdom of the Zohar*, 3:1493; Liebes, *Peraqim*, 179–80, 226.

For other interpretations of this phrase, see *OY*; *KP*; Galante; *Sullam*; Liebes, *Peraqim*, 134, 393.

all the sites those souls reach are crushed and damaged by much distress and pain.[85] Yet after they are broken, these sites become the delight of the blessed Holy One, even though the souls dwell in sorrow, not in joy.[86]

"Mystery of the matter, abiding by the supernal pattern: body blemished, soul within—corresponding, corresponding precisely![87] So these must be renewed with the renewal of the moon.[88] Of them is written *From new moon to new moon and from Sabbath to Sabbath, all flesh shall come to bow down before Me* (Isaiah 66:23)—*all flesh,* literally, for these will be totally renewed and must be renewed with the renewal of the moon.[89]

"They share a single partnership with the moon, blemished by Her defect; so She dwells amid them constantly, never abandoning them,[90] as is said: *and with the crushed and lowly in spirit* (ibid. 57:15),[91] and similarly: *YHVH is near to the brokenhearted* (Psalms 34:19)[92]—those who suffer that defect together with Her: they are always near Her. So, *reviving the heart of the crushed* (Isaiah, ibid.)[93]—

85. **when the moon is tainted . . . all souls then issuing . . .** When *Shekhinah* is separated from Her partner and under the influence of demonic forces or harsh judgment, any souls issuing from Her and entering embryos are doomed to suffering. See above, pages 95–96; Mopsik.

86. **these sites become the delight of the blessed Holy One . . .** These suffering bodies are beloved of God, even though usually the Divine Presence flees from sadness. This answers Rabbi Ḥiyya's first question (above, page 94): If the Divine Presence dwells only in a place of joy, how can it dwell among the afflicted righteous?

87. **supernal pattern: body blemished, soul within . . .** In the sefirotic realm *Shekhinah* is the body of *Tif'eret*, the soul. Unlike *Tif'eret*, She can be blemished by harsh judgment or demonic forces. Similarly, on earth the righteous one who suffers has a blemished body, while his soul remains undamaged.

Apparently, Rabbi Shim'on understands Leviticus 21:23 to mean that the demonic power cannot penetrate the inner sanctum of *Shekhinah* or the soul.

See above, note 82; *OY*; Tishby, *Wisdom of the Zohar*, 3:1493, n. 226; Mopsik; *MmD*. Cf. *KP*, 2:351b. On *Shekhinah* as body, see above, note 84.

88. **these must be renewed with the renewal of the moon** The righteous who suffered will be rejuvenated along with *Shekhinah* in the time to come.

See Isaiah 30:26; BT *Sanhderin* 42a; *Pirqei de-Rabbi Eli'ezer* 51; *Zohar* 1:182a; Moses de León, *Sefer ha-Rimmon,* 188–91; Mopsik.

89. ***all flesh,* literally . . .** Their tormented bodies will be resurrected.

90. **They share a single partnership with the moon . . .** The afflicted righteous share the destiny of *Shekhinah*, which is why She never leaves them, sharing their suffering. See above, notes 31 and 86.

91. ***and with the crushed and lowly in spirit*** The verse reads: *I dwell on high, in holiness, and with the crushed and lowly in spirit—reviving the spirit of the lowly, reviving the heart of the crushed.*

92. ***YHVH is near to the brokenhearted*** The verse continues: *those crushed in spirit He delivers.*

93. ***reviving the heart of the crushed*** See above, note 91.

they will share in that vitality flowing to Her as She is renewed; those who suffered with Her will be renewed with Her.

"These are called 'chastenings of love'[94]—of love, not of that person.[95] Of love, for the light of lesser love was tainted when repelled from greater love.[96] So these are companions partnered with Her. Happy is their share in this world and in the world that is coming, for they have become worthy of being Her companions! Of them is written *For the sake of my brothers and friends, I say, 'Peace be within you'* (Psalms 122:8)."[97]

He opened, saying, "*See, My servant* ישכיל (*yaskil*), *shall prosper; he shall be exalted and raised, and be very high* (Isaiah 52:13).[98] Happy is the share of the righteous, to whom the blessed Holy One reveals ways of Torah, so that they may walk in them!

"Come and see: This verse constitutes a supernal mystery. *See, My servant shall prosper*—they have established this, but come and see:[99] When the blessed Holy One created the world, He fashioned the moon and diminished her light, for she has nothing at all of her own. Because she diminished herself, she has to be illumined by virtue of the sun, by potency of supernal lights.[100] When the

94. **chastenings of love** See above, note 59.

95. **not of that person** Not caused by that person's sins.

96. **light of lesser love was tainted...** The light of *Shekhinah* (known as "lesser love") was tinged with judgment when She was separated from *Tif'eret* and thrust away by the divine right arm, *Ḥesed*, known as "greater love." A soul issuing at that dismal time will suffer.

See *Zohar* 1:11b; 2:202b, 254b (*Heikh*), 256b (*Heikh*); *ZḤ* 42a, 52b; Galante.

97. ***'Peace be within you'*** The words are addressed to Jerusalem, which symbolizes *Shekhinah*. Cf. BT *Bava Metsi'a* 84b.

98. ***See, My servant* ישכיל (*yaskil*), *shall prosper...*** The verb ישכיל (*yaskil*) means "he will prosper, be attentive, discern, consider, be wise or enlightened." In the *Zohar* the kabbalists are referred to as משכילים (*maskilim*), "enlightened." See 1:15a–16a; 2:2a, 203a; *ZḤ* 58c (*QhM*).

This verse in Isaiah marks the beginning of the section devoted to the "suffering servant" (52:13–53:12). The identity of this servant was fiercely disputed in medieval Jewish-Christian polemics, Jews insisting that he symbolized the people of Israel (see Isaiah 41:8; 44:2), Christians maintainting that he was a prefigurment of Jesus Christ. Rabbi Shim'on here offers a cryptic messianic interpretation.

99. **they have established this...** A midrashic tradition identifies the servant as the Messiah.

See *Targum Yonatan*, ad loc.; *Tanḥuma* (Buber), *Toledot* 20 (and Buber's notes); *Tanḥuma, Toledot* 14; *Aggadat Bereshit* 45:1. Cf. Naḥmanides, *Kitvei Ramban*, 1:307, 322–26; *Zohar* 3:153b (*RM*), 280a (*RM*); *KP*; Mopsik.

100. **diminished her light...** See BT *Ḥullin* 60b: "Rabbi Shim'on son of Pazzi pointed out a contradiction. 'It is written: *God made the two great lights* (Genesis 1:16), and it is written [in the same verse]: *the greater light... and the lesser light.* The moon said before the blessed Holy One, "Master of the Universe! Can two kings possibly wear one crown?" He answered, "Go, diminish

Temple was still standing, Israel engaged in sacrifices, ascent-offerings, and rituals, performed by priests, Levites, and Israel, to join links and kindle lights.[101] Once the Temple was destroyed, light darkened: the moon is not illumined by the sun; the sun [181b] withdraws from her, so she is unillumined.[102] As has been said, not a single day passes undominated by curses, sorrow, and pain.[103]

"But of that time when the time arrives for the moon to shine, what is written?[104] *See, My servant yaskil, shall shine*—spoken of the moon.[105] *See, My servant yaskil, shall be enlightened*—mystery of faith.[106] *See,* ישכיל (*yaskil*), *he*

yourself!" She said before Him, "Master of the Universe! Because I have suggested something proper I should make myself smaller?" He replied, "Go and rule by day and night." She said, "But what is the value of this? What good is a lamp at noon?".... Seeing that her mind was uneasy [that she could not be consoled], the blessed Holy One said, "Bring an atonement for Me for making the moon smaller."' As was said by Rabbi Shim'on son of Lakish: 'Why is the goat offered on the new moon distinguished by the phrase *to* [or: *for*] *YHVH* (Numbers 28:15)? The blessed Holy One said, "Let this goat be an atonement for My having made the moon smaller."'"

In the *Zohar* the moon symbolizes *Shekhinah*, who emanates from the higher *sefirot* (here, is "fashioned" by the divine male). Once She appears, *Shekhinah* is illumined by *Tif'eret* (the sun) and the other *sefirot* but "has nothing at all of Her own." See above, note 9.

See BT *Rosh ha-Shanah* 23b; *Zohar* 1:19b–20a; 2:219b; *ZḤ* 70d–71a (*ShS*); Moses de León, *Sefer ha-Rimmon*, 189; idem, *Mishkan ha-Edut*, 35b.

101. **sacrifices...to join links and kindle lights** The sacrificial rites perform a cosmic function, stimulating sefirotic union and thereby ensuring blessing for the world. This kabbalistic view contrasts sharply with that of Maimonides, who relativized the importance of the sacrifices and tried to explain them away as a concession to the formerly primitive nature of ancient Israel.

See Rashi on BT *Ketubbot* 10b, s.v. *mezin;* Maimonides, *Guide of the Perplexed* 3:32; *Bahir* 78 (109); *Zohar* 1:164a–b; Tishby, *Wisdom of the Zohar*, 3:878–90.

102. **moon is not illumined by the sun...** Without the sacrificial ritual, the divine union is interrupted, and as *Tif'eret* withdraws, *Shekhinah* is darkened.

103. **not a single day passes...** See M *Sotah* 9:12: "Rabban Shim'on son of Gamli'el says in the name of Rabbi Yehoshu'a: 'Ever since the day the Temple was destroyed, not a single day passes without a curse, dew has never descended as blessing, and flavor has been eliminated from fruit.'"

Cf. *Zohar* 1:61b, 70b, 177a, 203a; 3:15b, 74b.

104. **when the time arrives for the moon to shine...** With the appearance of the Messiah, who in the *Zohar* is so closely linked with *Shekhinah* (the moon) that She is called King Messiah.

See Psalms 89:38; BT *Rosh ha-Shanah* 25a; *Zohar* 1:238a; Moses de León, *Shushan Edut*, 343; idem, *Sheqel ha-Qodesh*, 23 (27–28); 71–72 (90–91); Mopsik, 80.

105. ***My servant yaskil, shall shine*—spoken of the moon** The *servant* is identified with *Shekhinah* (the moon). The verb ישכיל (*yaskil*) is often rendered *will prosper*, but as indicated above (note 98), it can also mean "to discern, be wise or enlightened." Here the reference to the moon suggests an extended meaning: "to shine, illuminate."

106. ***yaskil, shall be enlightened*—mystery of faith** On *yaskil*, see the preceding note. "Mystery of faith" is another name for *She-*

shall be attentive, for an arousal is aroused above, like one who inhales a scent and is aroused לאסתכלא (*le-istakkala*), 'to investigate, contemplate.'[107]

"*He shall be exalted*, from a facet of light transcending all lights. ירום (*Yarum*), *He shall be exalted*, as is said: *Therefore* ירום (*yarum*) *He will arise, to show you compassion* (Isaiah 30:18).[108]

"*And raised*—from the aspect of Abraham. *And be high*—from the aspect of Isaac. *Very*—from the aspect of Jacob. Although they have already established it, all is one in the mystery of wisdom.[109]

"At that time the blessed Holy One will arouse supernal arousal to illumine the moon fittingly, as is said: *The light of the moon shall be as the light of the sun*,[110] *and the light of the sun shall be sevenfold, as the light of the seven days* (Isaiah 30:26).[111] So supernal spirit will be increased in her, and consequently all those dead in the dust will rouse.[112] This is: *My servant*, in whose hands lies the mystery of the keys of his Lord,[113] as is written: *his servant, elder of his household* (Genesis 24:2),[114] as is said: *Abraham said to his servant, elder of his*

khinah, culmination of the *sefirot*, which constitute the focus of faith.

107. **ישכיל (*yaskil*) ... לאסתכלא (*le-istakkala*) ...** *Shekhinah* suddenly senses the aroma of emanation from above. See *Zohar* 2:239a; 3:26b.

Here Rabbi Shim'on understands *yaskil* in the sense of "will be attentive to, detect, discern, understand." See Daniel 12:10; Naḥmanides, *Kitvei Ramban*, 1:322–23; *OY*; Mopsik.

The cognate infinitive לאסתכלא (*le-istakkala*) spans a wide range of meaning in the *Zohar*: "to see, look, gaze, reflect, consider, investigate, contemplate."

108. **from a facet of light transcending all lights ...** Receiving illumination from the highest sefirotic realm, characterized by pure compassion.

109. **from ... Abraham ... Isaac ... Jacob ... Although ... all is one ...** Receiving emanation from the patriarchal triad of *sefirot*: *Ḥesed*, *Gevurah*, and *Tif'eret*.

The closing sentence apparently means that although earlier midrashic exegesis had identified the *servant* with the Messiah (see above, note 99), this does not contradict the interpretation offered here—that the servant is *Shekhinah*—since the Messiah is linked with *Shekhinah*. An alternative meaning is: Although earlier exegesis had applied the expression *he shall be exalted and raised, and be very high* to the earthly patriarchs, the intepretation offered here alludes to their triad above; yet all is one.

See *OY*; *KP*; Galante; *MmD*.

110. ***The light of the moon shall be as the light of the sun*** As originally. See above, note 100.

111. ***as the light of the seven days*** Of Creation. See *Zohar* 1:34a, 70b, 131a.

112. **dead in the dust will rouse** Revived by the influx of spirit issuing from *Shekhinah*.

113. ***My servant*, in whose hands ...** Previously Rabbi Shim'on had identified the *servant* of Isaiah 52:13 as *Shekhinah*. Now he focuses on a particular manifestation of *Shekhinah*: Metatron, the chief angel and prince of the world, also known as נער (*na'ar*), "youth, lad, heavenly servant." See above, notes 8–9.

On the keys of Metatron, see Schäfer, *Synopse zur Hekhalot-Literatur*, §72; *Zohar* 1:37b, 223b; 3:60a, 171b; *ZḤ* 39d–40a; Mopsik.

114. **as is written: *his servant, elder of his household*** Here begins a lengthy allegorical reading of Genesis 24:2–4: *Abraham said to*

household—the moon, as has been said; Metatron, messenger servant of his Lord.

"*Elder of his household*, as is said: *I was a youth, and now I am old* (Psalms 37:25).[115] *Who ruled over all that was his* (Genesis, ibid.), for all colors appear in him: green, white, red.[116]

"*Place your hand under my thigh* (ibid.)—Righteous One, mystery of circumcision, sustaining pillar of worlds;[117] for then this servant is appointed through mystery above to revive dwellers of the dust, becoming a messenger through spirit above, to restore spirits and souls to their sites—to those bodies that wore away and decayed beneath the dust.[118]

"ואשביעך (*Ve-ashbi'akha*), *And I will have you swear, by YHVH, God of heaven* (ibid., 3). What does ואשביעך (*ve-ashbi'akha*) mean? To be garbed in mysteries of שבע (*sheva*), seven, lights—mystery of supernal consummation.[119]

his servant, elder of his household, who ruled over all that was his, "Place your hand under my thigh, and I will have you swear by YHVH, God of heaven and God of earth, that you will not take a wife for my son from the daughters of the Canaanite in whose midst I dwell. Rather, to my land and to my kindred you will go, and will take a wife for my son, for Isaac." A similar reading appears in *Zohar* 1:126a–129a (*MhN*).

115. **Metatron . . . *I was a youth, and now I am old*** According to rabbinic tradition, this verse is uttered by Metatron. Being the first of God's creations, he is the oldest yet also the primordial youth.

See *Zohar* 1:126b (*MhN*); *TZ* 67, 98a; Mopsik; above, notes 8 and 113.

116. **all colors appear in him: green, white, red** Metatron displays the colors of the sefirotic triad *Ḥesed*, *Gevurah*, and *Tif'eret*.

117. **Righteous One, mystery of circumcision, sustaining pillar . . .** *Yesod*, the divine phallus, symbolized by the covenant of circumcision. He is known as Righteous One, based on Proverbs 10:25: וצדיק יסוד עולם (*Ve-tsaddiq yesod olam*). The verse literally means *The righteous one is an everlasting foundation*, but is understood as *The righteous one is the foundation of the world.* See BT *Ḥagigah* 12b; *Bahir* 71 (102); Azriel of Gerona, *Peirush ha-Aggadot*, 34.

"Mystery of circumcision" renders רזא דמילה (*raza de-milah*), following the reading of Joseph Angelet, *Livnat ha-Sappir*, 30d, and Mopsik. The printed editions and other witnesses read רזא דמלה (*raza de-millah*), "mystery of the word [or: of the matter]," a phrase that appears often in the *Zohar* but does not fit as well here. One manuscript (Ms4) apparently betrays an attempt to insert a י (*yod*) into the original spelling—מלה (*millah*), "word"—thereby transforming it into מילה (*milah*), "circumcision."

The phrase "sustaining pillar" renders the single word קיומא (*qiyyuma*), whose wide semantic range in the *Zohar* includes both of these senses as well as "erecting, raising" (here, erecting the pillar and resurrecting the dead). See Liebes, *Peraqim*, 371–75.

118. **appointed through mystery above to revive . . .** Metatron is empowered to revive the dead through spirit issuing from *Yesod*. Each soul will then be united with a resurrected body, a restored version of the original.

See *Bereshit Rabbah* 95:1; BT *Pesaḥim* 68a, *Sanhedrin* 91b; *Qohelet Rabbah* on 1:4; *Tanḥuma, Vayiggash* 8; *Zohar* 1:115a (*MhN*), 126a (*MhN*), 130b; 2:100a; Moses de León, *Sefer ha-Mishqal*, 87–88.

119. **seven, lights—mystery of supernal consummation** The seven lower *sefirot*, from *Ḥesed* through *Shekhinah*.

"*That you will not take a wife* (ibid.)—the body beneath the dust, possessing endurance to rise from the dust.[120] For all those who attained burial in the land of Israel will rouse first, as has been established, for it is written: *Your dead will live*—first, the dead of the land of Israel; *my corpses will arise!*—the dead of other lands (Isaiah 26:19).[121] All this for those bodies of Israel buried there, not for the bodies of other nations, by which the land is defiled.[122] So, *that you will not take a wife for my son* (Genesis, ibid.). What does *for my son* mean? All souls of the world issuing from that flowing, gushing river are sons of the blessed Holy One.[123] So, *that you will not take a wife*—the body. *For my son*—the soul.[124]

"*From the daughters of the Canaanite* (ibid.)—bodies of other nations, which the blessed Holy One will one day shake out of the Holy Land, as is said: *so the wicked will be shaken out of it* (Job 38:13)—like someone shaking out a garment to eliminate its filth.[125]

"*Rather, to my land and to my kindred you will go* (Genesis, ibid., 4)—the Holy Land, preceding all other lands, as has been said. So, *Rather, to my land*—the Holy Land, which is His, whereas other lands belong to those other archons.[126]

120. ***a wife*—the body . . . possessing endurance to rise . . .** Soul and body are symbolized respectively as male and female, a distinction common in Western thought. See Aristotle, *Generation of Animals* 2:4: "While the body is from the female, it is the soul that is from the male, for the soul is the substance of a particular body." See *Zohar* 1:127a (*MhN*).

The "endurance to rise" may allude to the לוז (*luz*), "almond," a bone supposed to be at the base of the spine, shaped like an almond, and indestructible—and from which God will one day resurrect decomposed bodies.

On this miraculous bone, see *Bereshit Rabbah* 28:3 (and Theodor, n. 4); *Vayiqra Rabbah* 18:1; *Pirqei de-Rabbi Eli'ezer* 34 (and Luria, n. 58); *Zohar* 1:69a, 113a (*MhN*), 116a (*MhN*), 126a (*MhN*), 137a (*MhN*); 2:28b; 3:222a, 270b; Moses de León, *Sefer ha-Rimmon*, 271; idem, *Sefer ha-Mishqal*, 87–88.

121. **those who attained burial in the land of Israel will rouse first . . .** See *Midrash Tanna'im*, 58; *Bereshit Rabbah* 74:1; JT *Kil'ayim* 9:4, 32c; BT *Ketubbot* 111a; *Tanḥuma, Vayḥi* 3; *Zohar* 113a–b (*MhN*), 131a; 2:151b; Moses de León, *Sefer ha-Mishqal*, 89–90.

122. **for those bodies of Israel buried there . . .** The early resurrection applies only to them. On the other nations' defilement of the land, see *Zohar* 1:69a; Moses de León, *Sefer ha-Mishqal*, 89–90. On the defilement of the land by human sin, see Leviticus 18:24–27; Milgrom, *Leviticus*, 2:1571–84.

123. **souls . . . issuing . . . are sons . . .** The river of *Yesod* pours into *Shekhinah*, and their union engenders souls. See above, note 49.

124. ***you will not take a wife . . . For my son . . .*** Understood to mean: Metatron should not revive a body for this soul from among other peoples.

125. **will one day shake out of the Holy Land . . .** See *Pirqei de-Rabbi Eli'ezer* 34; *Zohar* 2:17a; 3:72b; Moses de León, *Sefer ha-Mishqal*, 89; Mopsik.

The citation from Job is from God's speech out of the whirlwind (38:12–13): *Since your days began, have you commanded morning, assigned dawn his place, to grasp the corners of the earth, so the wicked be shaken out of it?*

126. **Holy Land, preceding . . . Holy Land, which is His . . .** See BT *Ta'anit* 10a: "Our Rabbis have taught: The land of Israel was created first and all the rest of the world subsequently. . . . The land of Israel is watered by

So, *Rather, to my land and to my kindred.* Since it says *to my land*, why *to my kindred*? Because *to my land* accords with what has been said, while *my kindred* is Israel.[127]

"Come and see what is written: *The servant took* (ibid., 10), as has been said.[128] *Ten camels*—ten rungs ruled by this servant, corresponding to the pattern above.[129] *From his lord's camels*—matching that pattern precisely, as has been said. This servant rules and is arrayed in them.

"*With all the bounty of his lord in his hand* (ibid.)—all that bounty and the supernal spirits issuing from those lights and supernal lamps.[130] *With all the bounty of his lord*—performance performed by the sun with the moon.[131]

"*And he rose and went to Aram-naharaim* (ibid.)—the site in the Holy Land where Rachel wept when the Temple was destroyed.[132]

the blessed Holy One Himself, while the rest of the world is watered by a messenger.... The land of Israel drinks water directly from the rain, while the rest of the world drinks of the drippings."

See *Zohar* 1:84b, 108b; 2:152b; 3:209b; Naḥmanides on Deuteronomy 11:10. According to rabbinic tradition, Israel is ruled directly by God, while the other seventy nations of the world are governed by His appointed angels or heavenly princes. Seventy nations are listed in Genesis 10; on the seventy princes, see above, pp. 70–71, n. 476.

127. ***to my land*** **...what has been said...** ***my kindred*** **is Israel** *My land* implies that the body intended for this soul must be buried in the Holy Land; *my kindred* implies that it must be Israelite. For a different interpretation, see Galante.

128. ***The servant took,*** **as has been said** The allegorical reading of the passage in Genesis 24 continues. The full verse reads: *The servant took ten camels from his lord's camels and went, with all the bounty of his lord in his hand, and he rose and went to Aram-naharaim, to the city of Nahor.*

As indicated above (note 113), *the servant* is Metatron. See *Zohar* 1:127b (*MhN*).

129. **ten rungs ruled by this servant...** A decade of angelic potencies corresponding to the ten *sefirot*. Elsewhere they are identified with the separate intelligences, which, according to Aristotelian philosophy, move the celestial spheres. Metatron himself plays the role of the Active Intellect, directing the intelligences.

See Maimonides, *Guide of the Perplexed* 2:4; *Zohar* 1:127b (*MhN*); Moses de León, *Or Zaru'a*, 257–61; idem, *Sheqel ha-Qodesh*, 55 (70–71); Mopsik.

130. **lights and supernal lamps** The *sefirot* above Metatron and *Shekhinah*.

131. **performance performed by the sun with the moon** The conjugal union of the divine couple, engendering souls.

"Performance performed" renders the Aramaic, שמושא...דאשתמש (*shimmusha... de-ishtammash*), which in the *Zohar* means "sexual union that is consummated," based on the rabbinic idiomatic extension of the root שמש (*shmsh*)—literally "to minister, serve, perform, use." See above, note 76.

132. ***Aram-naharaim*****—the site in the Holy Land where Rachel wept...** Aram-Naharaim was Abraham's ancestral home. The name means "the Aramean state within (or along) the river," referring to the area in central Mesopotamia within the great bend of the Euphrates.

Here this Aram is confused with (or intentionally substituted for) a similar-sounding site: Ramah, north of Jersualem, which apparently served as a staging point for Jews leaving for exile to Babylon (see

"*He had the camels kneel outside the city by the well of water* (ibid., 11)[133]—so that Her powers and potencies would be invigorated fittingly before She enters to raise those bodies.[134]

"*At evening time* (ibid.). What does this mean? Sabbath eve, [182a] a time in the sixth millennium.[135] *At evening time*—as is said: *and to his labor until evening* (Psalms 104:23),[136] and similarly: *for shadows of evening are stretched* (Jeremiah 6:4).[137]

Jeremiah 40:1). The prophet links the exiles' laments with those of Rachel, whose tomb existed nearby: *Thus says YHVH: A voice is heard in Ramah—wailing, bitter weeping—Rachel weeping for her children, refusing to be comforted for her children, for they are no more. Thus says YHVH: Restrain your voice from weeping, your eyes from tears; for there is reward for your labor, declares YHVH: they will return from the land of the enemy. There is hope for your future, declares YHVH: children will return to their land* (ibid. 31:15–17).

See *Bereshit Rabbah* 82:10: "*Rachel died, and she was buried on the road to Ephrath* ... (Genesis 35:19). What prompted Jacob to bury Rachel on the road to Ephrath? He foresaw that the exiles [carried off by the Babylonians] would pass through there; therefore he buried her there so that she would pray for mercy for them, as is written: *Rachel weeping for her children ... Thus says YHVH: Restrain your voice from weeping ... There is hope for your future ...*"

A further link between Ramah and Aram lies in the fact that Rachel died near Ramah (on the road to Ephrath) as she was journeying with Jacob's clan from Paddan-aram (another name for Aram-naharaim). See Genesis 35:9, 16–20; 48:7; 1 Samuel 10:2–3; Mopsik.

Here Rabbi Shim'on associates נהרים (*naharayim*), "rivers (or: along the river)" with Rachel's river of tears. Cf. Genesis 35:8. The matriarch's mourning symbolizes that of *Shekhinah*, who participates in Israel's exile. See *Mekhilta, Pisḥa* 14; BT *Megillah* 29a; *Zohar* 1:175b, 203a; 2:12b.

133. ***He had the camels kneel...*** The full verse reads: *He had the camels kneel outside the city by the well of water at evening time, at the time when the water drawers come out.*

134. **so that Her powers and potencies would be invigorated...** So that the angelic powers (the camels) accompanying *Shekhinah* (the well) will be energized by Her flow before the process of resurrection begins.

135. ***At evening time*... Sabbath eve, a time in the sixth millennium** As the six days of Creation were followed by Sabbath, so the world will exist for 6000 years, followed by a millennial Sabbath. The sixth millennium itself began shortly before the appearance of the *Zohar* (in the year 1240/41 C.E.) and is pictured as the eve of the cosmic Sabbath.

See BT *Sanhedrin* 97a: "Rabbi Katina said, 'The world will exist for six thousand years and for one thousand lie desolate.'" See *Zohar* 1:116b–117a, 119a, 127b–128a (*MhN*); 2:9b–10a; *ZḤ* 56b–c. On the world to come as Sabbath, see BT *Berakhot* 57b; *Avodah Zarah* 3a; *Rut Rabbah* 3:3.

136. ***and to his labor until evening*** The verse describes the daily routine: *Man goes out to his work, and to his labor until evening.* Here the *labor until evening* is Metatron's work of resurrection, which will occupy him toward the end of the sixth millennial day, the eve of the Messiah.

137. ***for shadows of evening are stretched*** From a lament put in the mouths of the besieged residents of Jerusalem, under attack by the Babylonian army: *Woe to us, for the day is fading, for shadows of evening are stretched!*

Here the image signifies the closing hours

"*At the time when the water drawers come out* (ibid.), for then they are destined to rise and revive ahead of all other inhabitants of the world—those drawing waters of Torah—because they exerted themselves drawing from waters of Torah and embraced the Tree of Life.[138] They will emerge first, since the Tree of Life causes them to rise first, as has been said.

"*And the daughters of the townsmen are coming out* (Genesis 24:13).[139] What does *coming out* mean? As is said: *And earth will bring forth shades* (Isaiah 26:19), for earth is destined to disgorge all bodies within her. So it is written: *coming out.*[140]

"*To draw water*—to absorb the soul, receiving her fittingly, arrayed suitably in her realm.[141]

"*May it be that the maiden to whom I say, 'Please tip your jug so I may drink'* (Genesis, ibid., 14)[142]—because, as has been said, every soul of the world, existing in this world, who strove to know her Lord through the mystery of supernal wisdom, ascends and endures on a high rung, above all those who did not grasp or know. These are resurrected first, and this is the question that servant is poised to ask, to discover: how did that soul occupy herself in this world?[143]

of the sixth millennial day, when resurrection begins—or when judgment, symbolized by *evening*, dominates the world.

See BT *Ta'anit* 29a; *Zohar* 1:132b, 230a; 2:21b; 3:75a, 270a; *ZḤ* 7c.

138. **those drawing waters of Torah... embraced the Tree of Life** Devoted students of Torah rediscover the Tree of Life and will taste resurrection first. See *Zohar* 1:127b–128a (*MhN*), 140a (*MhN*), 175b.

According to the praise of wisdom in Proverbs 3:18, *She is a tree of life to those who grasp her.* See BT *Berakhot* 32b, 61b. In Kabbalah both Torah and Tree of Life symbolize *Tif'eret*, trunk of the sefirotic tree. See Moses de León, *Sefer ha-Rimmon,* 108.

139. ***And the daughters of the townsmen are coming out*** Part of what Abraham's servant said to God as he stood by the well: *Here I am standing by the spring of water, and the daughters of the townsmen are coming out to draw water. May it be that the maiden to whom I say, "Please tip your jug so I may drink," and she says, "Drink, and your camels too I will water"—she is the one You have appointed for your servant, for Isaac. By this I will know that You have done kindness with my lord.*

140. ***coming out... And earth will bring forth shades...*** The daughters coming out symbolize bodies emerging from the earth.

I have adopted the reading of *OY*: "to disgorge all גופין (*gufin*), bodies," instead of the version reflected in the other witnesses: "... all רוחין (*ruḥin*), spirits." See JT *Berakhot* 5:2, 9b; *Pirqei de-Rabbi Eli'ezer* 34, and David Luria, ad loc., n. 83; *Zohar* 1:113a (*MhN*), 128b (*MhN*); 2:199b; Moses de León, *Sefer ha-Mishqal,* 90; *OL*; *Adderet Eliyyahu*; *MM*; Mopsik. Galante offers an explanation for the reading *ruḥin*.

141. **her realm** The celestial Garden of Eden, residence of disembodied souls.

142. ***May it be that the maiden...*** See above, note 139.

143. **question that servant is poised to ask...** See BT *Shabbat* 31a: "Rava said, 'When a human is led in for judgment, he is asked, "Were you honest in your business dealings, did you set aside time for Torah,

"*And she says to me, 'Drink, yourself'*—you should drink and be watered first; then after you: *'and your camels too I will water.'*[144] For all those other chariots, though watered by this rung, are all watered by the worship of the righteous who know how to serve their Lord properly, since the righteous know how to supply each and every rung fittingly.[145] So, *and your camels too I will water.* Surely, *she is the woman whom YHVH has appointed for my lord's son*; surely that is the body destined for this supernal soul.[146]

"Come and see what has been said: Desire of male for female generates soul; desire of female for male ascends and blends with the one above, one and the other intermingling, generating soul.[147] So, *she is the woman*—this is surely the body destined for that desire of soul issuing from the male.[148]

"Those bodies are destined to rouse first, as we have said, and after these rise, all the rest in other lands will rise—be resurrected in full existence, renewed with the renewal of the moon.[149] The world will be renewed, as originally, and of that time is written *YHVH will rejoice in His works* (Psalms 104:31).[150]

did you generate new life, did you await salvation, did you engage in the dialectics of wisdom, did you understand one thing from another?"'"

Here the servant Metatron poses a similar question to see if this soul is worthy of early resurrection. Cf. *Zohar* 1:128a (*MhN*).

144. ***'Drink, yourself'*... *'and your camels too I will water'*** The soul responds to Metatron: "You should drink and be nourished first; then I will water the angels beneath you." The nourishment derives from the soul's righteousness and study of Torah, which stimulate emanation from above. On the angelic *camels*, see above, note 129.

The first citation is from Genesis 24:44; the second is a conflation of Genesis 24:14 and 24:44.

145. **all those other chariots... watered by... the righteous...** The angelic powers are nourished by Metatron, but both his flow and theirs depend on human devotion. The righteous know how to direct this sustenance through the intricate channels and pathways of heaven.

146. **So, *and your camels too*... Surely, *she is the woman*...** According to the biblical context, "If she says, '... and your camels too I will water,' then she is the wife-to-be." Allegorically, the woman represents the body destined for the sublime soul.

The first citation is a conflation of Genesis 24:14 and 24:44; the second is from the latter verse.

147. **Desire of male for female generates soul...** The soul is engendered by a mingling of the divine couple's overflowing desires, which yields both male and female aspects of the soul.

See *Zohar* 1:208a, 209a; 3:296a–b (*IZ*); and 1:85b: "Come and see: Desire of female for male generates soul; desire of male for female generates soul; passionate desire of male for female and his cleaving to her pours forth soul. He encompasses desire of female, absorbing it, so lower desire is comprised within desire above, becoming one passion, undivided. Then female absorbs all, is impregnated by male, both desires cleaving as one. So all comprises one another."

148. **that desire of soul...** The soul engendered by desire.

149. **Those bodies are destined to rouse first...** Those who have delved into wisdom will rise first, followed by all others.

See above, page 106. On the phrase "renewal of the moon," see above, note 88.

150. ***YHVH will rejoice in His works*** Only

"Therefore, *See, My servant yaskil, shall discern* (Isaiah 52:13)—restoring souls, every single one to its site.[151] *He shall be exalted and raised, and be very high* (ibid.)—from the aspect of all those supernal rungs, as we have said.[152]

"*Just as many were appalled at you—his appearance marred beyond that of man* (ibid., 14).[153] Come and see what has been said: When the Temple was destroyed and *Shekhinah* was exiled in alien lands among them,[154] what is written? *Behold, the Erelim cried outside; angels of peace weep bitterly* (Isaiah 33:7).[155] They all wept over this, linking weeping with mourning—all for *Shekhinah*, exiled from Her domain.[156] Just as She changes from what She was, so too Her Husband no longer beams His radiance and is changed from what He was, as is written: *The sun darkens as it rises* (ibid. 13:10). So it is written: *his appearance marred beyond that of man.*[157]

"Alternatively, *his appearance marred beyond that of man*—spoken of this servant, whose form changed its hue.[158]

then will joy be appropriate. See *Vayiqra Rabbah* 20:2.

151. ***yaskil, shall discern*—restoring souls...** Having completed his lengthy allegorical reading of Genesis 24, Rabbi Shim'on resumes his discussion of Isaiah 52:13–14. Now he understands the verb ישכיל (*yaskil*) as "shall discern," referring to Metatron's ability to identify each soul's site: its earthly body, now resurrected and renewed.

On the various senses of the verb *yaskil*, see above, notes 98, 105–7.

152. **from the aspect of all those supernal rungs...** See above, page 101.

153. ***Just as many were appalled at you...*** The full verse reads: *Just as many were appalled at you—his appearance marred beyond that of man, his form beyond that of humans.* For the context in Isaiah, see above, note 98.

154. ***Shekhinah* was exiled in alien lands among them** Sharing and assuaging their torment. See BT *Megillah* 29a: "Rabbi Shim'on son of Yoḥai says, 'Come and see how beloved are Israel in the sight of the blessed Holy One! Wherever they went in exile, *Shekhinah* accompanied them. When they were exiled to Egypt, *Shekhinah* was with them.... When they were exiled to Babylon, *Shekhinah* was with them.... And even when they are destined to be redeemed, *Shekhinah* will be with them.'" See *Mekhilta, Pisḥa* 14.

155. ***Erelim...*** Hebrew אראלם (*er'ellam*), a word whose form and meaning are dubious. In the verse in Isaiah, it has sometimes been translated: "their valiant ones, their brave men," referring to the Judeans withstanding Sennacherib's onslaught. See Isaiah 29:1–2; *ABD*, s.v. "Ariel."

In rabbinic tradition the word אראלם (*er'ellam*) is transformed into אראלים (*er'ellim*), meaning "angels" or a group of angels, while in medieval angelology they constitute one of ten such classes. Here the Erelim and the other angels are appalled at the condition of *Shekhinah*.

See *Bereshit Rabbah* 56:5; *Eikhah Rabbah* 1:23; BT *Ḥagigah* 5b, *Ketubbot* 104a; *Midrash Aggadah*, Exodus 33:22; Maimonides, *Mishneh Torah, Hilkhot Yesodei ha-Torah* 2:7; *Zohar* 1:210a; 2:43b, 250b; *Orḥot Tsaddiqim*, 26; Ginzberg, *Legends*, 5:23, n. 64; 5:417, n. 117.

156. **Her domain** The Temple and the land of Israel.

157. **Her Husband no longer beams His radiance...** *Tif'eret*, symbolized by the sun, no longer shines; He has lost His former radiance, that of the divine *man.*

158. **this servant, whose form changed its hue** Metatron is also dimmed by the destruction of the Temple.

On his colors, see above, p. 102 and n. 116.

"Alternatively, *his appearance marred beyond that of man*—as is written: *I clothe the heavens in blackness, and make sackcloth their covering* (ibid. 50:3), for ever since the day that the Temple was destroyed, *the heavens* have not sustained their radiance.[159]

"Mystery of the matter: Blessings abide solely in a place where male and female are found. This has been established, as is written: *Male and female He created them, and He blessed them* (Genesis 5:2).[160] Therefore, *his appearance marred beyond that of man.*[161]

"This corresponds to what is written: *The righteous one* אבד (*avad*), *loses* (Isaiah 57:1). It is not written אבוד (*avud*), *is lost*, or נאבד (*ne'evad*), *is destroyed*, but rather אבד (*avad*), *loses*,[162] since blessings abide only in a place where male and female appear as one, as has been said. For look, at that time,[163] male is not found [182b] with Her! So all those souls issuing are transformed from how they were when sun joined with moon, as has been said.[164] So, *These are the generations of Jacob: Joseph* (Genesis 37:2), as already explained.[165]

On his designation as servant, see above, notes 8, 113.

159. ***his appearance marred... I clothe the heavens in blackness...*** According to this interpretation, *his appearance* refers to the appearance of the heavens, which—ever since the destruction of the Temple—have lost their luster.

See BT *Berakhot* 59a: "Rafram son of Papa said in the name of Rav Ḥisda: 'Ever since the day that the Temple was destroyed, the sky has not appeared in all its purity, as is said: *I clothe the heavens in blackness, and make sackcloth their covering.*'"

160. **Blessings abide solely... where male and female are found...** When the divine couple is united. Otherwise both male and female lack blessing.

See *Zohar* 1:55b, 165a; 3:17a, 74b; 296a (*IZ*); and BT *Yevamot* 62b: "Rabbi Tanḥum said in the name of Rabbi Ḥanilai, 'Any man without a wife is without joy, without blessing, without goodness.'"

161. **Therefore, *his appearance marred beyond that of man*** The appearance of the divine male no longer resembles His original nature, *that of man*. See above, note 157.

162. ***The righteous one* אבד (*avad*), *loses*...** The phrase is usually translated: *The righteous one perishes* (see above, page 89). Rabbi Shim'on understands it to mean that *Yesod* (Foundation), known as Righteous One, loses the flow of emanation from above.

See *Zohar* 1:55b, 196b; 2:57a–b; 3:16b, 266b. *Yesod*'s title, Righteous One, is based on Proverbs 10:25: וצדיק יסוד עולם (*Ve-tsaddiq yesod olam*). The expression literally means *The righteous one is an everlasting foundation*, but is understood as *The righteous one is the foundation of the world.*

See BT *Ḥagigah* 12b; *Bahir* 71 (102); Azriel of Gerona, *Peirush ha-Aggadot*, 34.

163. **at that time** During exile.

164. **souls issuing are transformed...** Souls are originally engendered by the union of the divine couple, but those that issue at a time when the couple is separated, suffer change. See above, pages 95–99.

165. ***These are the generations of Jacob: Joseph...*** The verse in Genesis reads: *These are the generations of Jacob: Joseph, seventeen years old, was tending the flock with his brothers...* But Rabbi Shim'on, borrowing a playful reading from the Midrash, conveniently breaks off his citation with the phrase *Jacob: Joseph.* The implication here is that the *sefirot* of Jacob and Joseph (*Tif'eret* and *Yesod*) must together constitute a single male

"*And he was a lad* (ibid.)[166]—for they never part: Righteous One and Righteousness are as one. Just as She is called by the name of the male, so He too is called by Her name, as is written: *and he was a lad.*[167]

"*With the sons of Bilhah and the sons of Zilpah* (ibid.)—present among all of them, renewing them fittingly, delighting them, for all those branches and leaves are blessed by His joy.[168]

"*These are the generations of Jacob: Joseph*, as has been said, for Jacob's entire image inhered in Joseph, and whatever happened to the one happened to the other, the two of them proceeding as one.[169] This is the mystery of the letter ו"ו (*vav*), both of whom proceed as one, for they constitute a single mystery, a single image.[170]

"*Joseph brought a bad report of them.* They have explained that he used to tell his father that they were eating the limb of a living creature while it was still alive.[171]

entity in order to unite with *Shekhinah* and generate souls. If that union is maintained at the moment these souls issue, then the emerging souls will be complete and fulfilled.

See above, note 52; page 96. On Joseph as *Yesod*, see above, p. 68, n. 460.

166. ***And he was a lad*** The verse reads: *Joseph, seventeen years old, was tending the sheep with his brothers, and he was a lad with the sons of Bilhah and the sons of Zilpah, his father's wives. And Joseph brought a bad report of them to their father.* That Joseph *was a lad with* his half-brothers means that he assisted them.

167. **they never part...** Ideally, *Yesod* (symbolized by the lad Joseph and known as Righteous One) never parts from *Shekhinah*. The couple's intimate relationship is marked by their names: *Yesod* is called צדיק (*tsaddiq*), "righteous one," and *Shekhinah* is named צדק (*tsedeq*), "righteousness"; She is called נערה (*na'arah*), "maiden," but sometimes the spelling of this name is truncated, with the final ה (*he*) missing: נַעֲרָ (*na'ara*)—the same letters as the masculine נער (*na'ar*), "lad, youth," which is applied here to the divine male, *Yesod*.

On the title Righteous One, see above, note 162. On *Shekhinah* as *na'ara* and *na'arah*, see Deuteronomy 22:15–29; *Zohar* 1:51a; 2:38b, 261a; 3:156b; Moses de León, *Sefer ha-Rimmon*, 115; *Minḥat Shai* on Deuteronomy 22:19; Mopsik. On Metatron as *na'ar*, see above, note 8.

168. **present among all of them...** The flow of emanation from the youthful *Yesod* rejuvenates the powers beneath *Shekhinah* symbolized by the twelve tribes. Among these tribes, the sons of Leah and Rachel symbolize further branchings of the sefirotic tree, while the sons of Bilhah and Zilpah (Rachel and Leah's maids) symbolize the leaves. See *Zohar* 1:154a.

169. ***Jacob: Joseph*... Jacob's entire image inhered in Joseph...** According to the Midrash, the wording *These are the generations of Jacob: Joseph* implies that father and son were nearly identical and that their lives mirrored one another. See above, notes 53, 165.

170. **mystery of the letter ו"ו (*vav*), both of whom proceed as one...** Both the pronunciation of the letter ו (*vav*) and the Hebrew spelling of its name, ו"ו, demand two *vavs*: one symbolizing *Tif'eret*, and the other its extension, *Yesod*.

See *Zohar* 1:18a, 119a; 2:9b; 3:11a, 53b, 66b, 74b; *ZḤ* 2c (*SO*); Moses de León, *Sefer ha-Rimmon*, 335; Mopsik.

171. **eating the limb of a living creature...** This act is considered a basic vio-

"*Joseph brought a bad report of them.* But those sons of the maids were included in the count! How could Leah's sons have belittled them?[172] And how could they have eaten a limb from a living creature, thereby violating the command of their Lord, who commanded the sons of Noah about this: *But flesh with its life, its blood, you shall not eat* (Genesis 9:4)?[173] Would they have really eaten it, violating the command of their Lord? Rather, Joseph said so, and was therefore punished."[174]

Rabbi Yehudah said, "*A bad report of them*, as they have established: that they were eyeing the daughters of the land.[175] This was the *bad report of them:* suckling all those unholy rungs, even though they derive from the impure side."[176]

Israel loved Joseph more than all his sons (Genesis 37:3).[177]

Rabbi El'azar opened, "*Go, my people, enter your rooms and shut your doors behind you. Hide yourself for the slightness of a moment, until wrath passes* (Isaiah 26:20). Come and see how greatly the blessed Holy One loves Israel! Because of His love for them above all other nations, He warns them and seeks to protect them in whatever they do.

lation of universal morality; see below. What exactly Joseph reported to his father is discussed in *Bereshit Rabbah* 84:7: "*Joseph brought a* [*bad*] *report of them* [*to their father*] ... Rabbi Me'ir said, '[Joseph told Jacob]: "Your sons are suspected of [eating] a limb [torn] from a living animal."' Rabbi Yehudah said, 'They are belittling the sons of the maids and calling them slaves.' Rabbi Shim'on said, 'They are casting their eyes upon the daughters of the land.'"

172. **sons of the maids were included in the count...** Their sons too would each engender one of the twelve tribes. How could Leah's sons have insulted them by calling them slaves? See the passage from *Bereshit Rabbah* cited in the preceding note.

173. **violating the command of their Lord...** According to rabbinic interpretation, this verse—which forbids the eating of the flesh of a living animal—constitutes one of the seven Noahide commandments, basic moral principles intended for Noah's descendants, that is, all of humanity. See BT *Sanhedrin* 56a–57a.

174. **Joseph said so...** He made up the accusation.

On the question of whether Joseph's report was invented or not, see *Leqaḥ Tov*, Genesis 37:2; Ibn Ezra on Numbers 13:32; Naḥmanides on Genesis 37:2; Numbers 13:32; 14:37; *KP*; Kasher, *Torah Shelemah*, Genesis 37:2, n. 35.

175. **eyeing the daughters of the land** See the passage in *Bereshit Rabbah* quoted above, note 171, where this view is attributed to Rabbi Shim'on, not Rabbi Yehudah (as here). Conversely, Rabbi Yehudah's view there is alluded to above by Rabbi Shim'on.

176. **suckling all those unholy rungs...** The phrase "daughters of the land" derives from Genesis 27:46. Here, for Rabbi Yehudah it symbolizes demonic forces, who are nourished and invigorated by the lustful stares of Jacob's sons.

177. ***Israel loved Joseph more than all his sons*** The verse continues: *for he was the child of his old age, and he made him an ornamented tunic.*

"Come and see: There are times during the day when judgment looms over the world,[178] and when such a time arrives, one must protect himself from being attacked by judgment. Those times are well known and have been established.[179] For when morning rises, Abraham rouses in the world and grasps judgment, binding it to himself.[180] At the beginning of the first three hours, judgment journeys from its site to station itself in Jacob,[181] until the prayer of *minḥah* rouses, when judgment returns to its site, and lower judgment rouses to be bound with higher judgment; for then judgment links with judgment, and one must beware.[182]

"Moreover, when judgment arouses in the world and death prevails in the city, one should not walk alone in the streets, as we have established; rather, he should shut himself in so that he does not venture out—as they have established concerning Noah, who shut himself within the ark so as not to be found in the presence of the Destroyer.[183]

178. **when judgment looms over the world** When harsh powers of judgment threaten to punish humanity.

179. **Those times are well known...** See *Zohar* 1:132b; 2:21a (*MhN*); Moses de León, *Sefer ha-Rimmon,* 66–67.

180. **Abraham rouses in the world and grasps judgment...** As *Ḥesed* (the *sefirah* of Abraham) begins to manifest at dawn, its polar opposite appears too: *Din* (Judgment), symbolized by Isaac. *Ḥesed* then embraces *Din*, temporarily assuaging its harshness.

181. **judgment journeys from its site...** During the first hours of the day, *Din* appears within the *sefirah* of Jacob (*Tif'eret*), symbolized by the sun. Here too, its severity is allayed, since *Tif'eret* manifests the quality of mercy, as attested by its other name: *Raḥamim* (Compassion).

See BT *Berakhot* 7a: "How long does His wrath last? רגע (*Rega*), A moment. And how long is a *rega*? Rabbi Avin said (or according to some, Rabbi Avina), 'As long as it takes to say *rega*.' And how do we know that He seethes for a moment? For it is said: *For a moment in His anger, a lifetime in His favor* (Psalms 30:6). Or if you wish, say: *Hide yourself for the slightness of a moment, until wrath passes.* And when does He seethe? Abbaye said, 'Within those first three hours, when the comb of the rooster is white and it stands on one foot.'"

182. **prayer of *minḥah* rouses... lower judgment rouses...** As the afternoon sun declines during the time of the prayer known as *minḥah* (offering), the power of *Din* returns to its site on the left side of the sefirotic tree and then joins with *Shekhinah*, who represents a lower manifestation of judgment. Now the world turns dangerous.

See BT *Berakhot* 6b, in the name of Rav Huna: "One should always be זהיר (*zahir*), conscientious, about the prayer of *minḥah*, since Elijah was answered only during this prayer." Here Rabbi El'azar is apparently alluding to this formulation by saying that "one must לאזדהרא (*le-izdahara*), beware."

See *Zohar* 1:132b, 230a; 2:36b; 3:64b; Moses de León, *Sefer ha-Rimmon,* 87.

183. **one should not walk alone in the streets...** See BT *Bava Qamma* 60a–b: "Rabbi Yosef taught: 'What is the meaning of the verse *None of you shall go out the door of his house until morning* (Exodus 12:22)? Once permission has been granted to the Destroyer, he does not distinguish between righteous and wicked.'... Our Rabbis taught:

"So, *Go, my people, enter your rooms*—shut yourself in; *and shut your doors behind you,* so as not to be exposed in the presence of the Destroyer.

"*Hide yourself for the slightness of a moment, until wrath passes,* for once judgment has passed, the Destroyer has no power to destroy.

"Come and see: Because of the love the blessed Holy One feels for Israel, drawing them near, all other nations hate Israel, since they are distant and Israel are near.[184]

"Come and see: Because of the love Jacob felt for Joseph—more than for his brothers—even though they were all his own brothers, what is written? *They conspired against him to kill him* (Genesis 37:18). [185] All the more so, other nations toward Israel!

"Come and see the consequences of that excessive love! It caused him to be exiled from his father, and his father to be exiled along with him; it inflicted exile upon them all [183a] as well as upon *Shekhinah*, who was exiled among them.[186] Although a decree was issued,[187] they have established that because of the ornamented tunic that he made for him extravagantly, what is written? *His brothers saw that it was he their father loved...* (Genesis 37:4)."[188]

'A plague in town? Keep your feet indoors.' ...Our Rabbis taught: 'A plague in town? One should not walk in the middle of the road because the Angel of Death walks there, for as soon as permission has been granted him, he strides brazenly.'"

See *Mekhilta, Pisḥa* 11; *Devarim Rabbah* 4:4; *Zohar* 1:63a, 68a–b, 69a, 101b–102a, 107b, 108b, 113a, 197b, 204b; 2:36a (*MhN*), 196a, 227a; 3:38b, 54a–b; *ZḤ* 77a (*MhN, Rut*), 81c (*MhN, Rut*).

184. **Because of the love the blessed Holy One feels...** Anti-Semitism derives from jealousy of Israel's intimacy with God.

See the various interpretations of the wordplay on סיני (*sinai*), "Sinai," and שנאה (*sin'ah*), "hatred," in BT *Shabbat* 89a–b; *Tanḥuma, Bemidbar* 7; *Shemot Rabbah* 2:4 (and Shinan, ad loc.); *Leqaḥ Tov*, Exodus 19:18. Cf. *Yalqut Shim'oni*, Numbers 773; *Zohar* 3:221a.

185. **Because of the love Jacob felt for Joseph...** See above, note 177; *Shir ha-Shirim Rabbah* on 8:6; *Tanḥuma* (Buber), *Vayeshev* 19.

186. **caused him to be exiled from his father...** Jacob's excessive love for Joseph provoked Joseph's brothers to sell him into slavery, and he was transported to Egypt. Later Jacob and his entire clan joined Joseph there in exile, where they were accompanied by *Shekhinah*. See above, note 154.

187. **decree was issued** To Abraham, announcing the eventual enslavement of his descendants in Egypt. See Genesis 15:13–14.

188. **ornamented tunic...** The so-called coat of many colors. See above, note 177. The closing verse reads in full: *His brothers saw that it was he their father loved more than all of them, and they hated him and could not speak to him peaceably.*

See BT *Shabbat* 10b, in the name of Rav: "A man should never single out one son among his others sons. For on account of two *selas* [about thirty grams] of silk, which Jacob gave Joseph in excess of his other sons, his brothers grew jealous of him, and as the matter unfolded, our forefathers descended into Egypt."

"*Joseph dreamed a dream* (Genesis 37:5). Rabbi Ḥiyya opened, "*He said, 'Hear My words: If there be among you a prophet of YHVH, in a vision I make Myself known to him, in a dream I speak with him'* (Numbers 12:6).

"Come and see how many rungs upon rungs the blessed Holy One has made, all standing one atop the other: rung upon rung, this above that, all absorbing suitably, these on the right, those on the left—each appointed over another, all fittingly.[189]

"Come and see: All prophets of the world absorb from a single facet, through two known rungs.[190] Those rungs appeared through a dim glass,[191] as is written: במראה (*ba-mar'ah*), *in a vision, I make Myself known to him.* Who is *mar'ah*? As has been said: a mirror in which all colors appear; this is the dim glass.[192]

"*In a dream I speak with him*—one-sixtieth of prophecy, as has been established.[193] It is the sixth rung from that rung of prophecy, rung of Gabriel, appointed over dreams, as already explained.[194]

189. **rungs upon rungs...** Within the network of *sefirot* and throughout the entire chain of being, lower rungs absorb (literally, "suck") the flow of emanation from the higher. Right and left allude to *Ḥesed* and *Din*, the two poles of divine being whose opposite qualities color the world.

190. **All prophets of the world absorb from a single facet...** Prophecy derives from the divine flow, channeled through the sefirotic pair *Netsaḥ* and *Hod*, which are considered a single field of prophetic vision.

See *Zohar* 1:203a; 2:251b (*Heikh*); 3:35a, 58a; Moses de León, *Shushan Edut*, 337, 369, 378–79; idem, *Sheqel ha-Qodesh*, 47 (57–58).

191. **dim glass** אספקלריא דלא נהרא (*Ispaqlarya de-la nahara*), "Speculum [or: glass, mirror, lens] that does not shine." *Ispaqlarya* derives from Greek *speklon*, "mirror, window-pane," and Latin *speculum*, "mirror." See BT *Yevamot* 49b: "All the prophets gazed through a dim glass [literally: an *ispaqlarya* that does not shine], whereas Moses our teacher gazed through a clear glass [literally: an *ispaqlarya* that shines]." Cf. 1 Corinthians 13:12: "For now we see through a glass darkly, but then face-to-face."

In the *Zohar, Shekhinah* is the dim glass, the speculum that does not shine on its own but rather reflects and transmits the other *sefirot*. Here, She is the medium through which the prophet perceives his sefirotic vision.

See *Vayiqra Rabbah* 1:14; Azriel of Gerona, *Peirush ha-Aggadot*, 33–34; *Zohar* 1:33b, 120a; 2:23b, 221a; Ginzberg, *Legends*, 6:44–45, n. 242; Mopsik; Wolfson, *Through a Speculum That Shines*, index, s.v. "speculum"; Huss, "Ḥakham Adif mi-Navi," *Kabbalah* 4 (1999): 109–14.

192. **במראה (*ba-mar'ah*), *in a vision*... a mirror...** The Hebrew word מראה (*mar'ah*) means both "vision" and "mirror." *Shekhinah* reflects (or refracts) all the colors of the *sefirot* to the gaze of the prophet, but not with full clarity.

See *Zohar* 1:71b, 88b, 91a, 149b, 203a, 211a; 2:23a.

193. **one-sixtieth of prophecy...** According to BT *Berakhot* 57b, "A dream is one-sixtieth of prophecy." See Maimonides, *Guide of the Perplexed* 2:36.

194. **sixth rung from that rung of prophecy...** Six stages span the phenomena of prophecy and dream: the *sefirot Netsaḥ, Hod, Yesod*, and *Shekhinah*, and the first two archangels: Michael and Gabriel.

In the book of Daniel (8:16; 9:22), Gabriel

"Come and see: Every seemly dream proceeds from this rung, so you cannot have a dream without false material intermingling, as they have established.[195] Consequently, some of them are true and some are false, and you cannot have a dream that does not contain both this side and that.

"Since a dream includes all, as we have said, all dreams of the world follow oral interpretation. This has been established, for it is written: *As he interpreted to us, so it was* (Genesis 41:13).[196] Why? Because a dream contains falsehood and truth, and the word controls all, so a dream needs favorable interpretation."[197]

Rabbi Yehudah said, "Because every dream is of the rung below, controlled by Speech, so every dream follows speech."[198]

He opened, saying, "*In a dream, a vision of night, when deep sleep falls upon humans in slumber upon the bed, He then uncovers human ears, and with a warning, terrifies them* (Job 33:15–16). Come and see: When a person climbs into bed, he should first enthrone and acknowledge the Kingdom of Heaven,[199] then recite a verse of compassion, as established by the Companions.[200] For

interprets revelations. Here, he appears as prince of dreams.

See *Zohar* 149a (*ST*), 149a–b, 191b, 196a, 238a; 2:247b; Moses de León, *Shushan Edut,* 369; idem, *Sefer ha-Rimmon,* 126.

195. **you cannot have a dream without false material intermingling...** Gabriel, appointed over dreams, stands beneath *Shekhinah* and thus outside the purely divine realm; therefore demonic forces in the vicinity can smuggle false images into the dream material.

See BT *Berakhot* 55a: "Rabbi Yoḥanan said in the name of Rabbi Shim'on son of Yoḥai, 'Just as there cannot be wheat without straw, so there cannot be a dream without nonsense.'"

Cf. ibid. 55b; *Zohar* 1:83a, 130a–b, 150b, 199b–200a, 238a; 2:130a, 264a (*Heikh*); 3:25a, 156b.

196. **all dreams of the world follow oral interpretation...** The true meaning of a dream depends on its interpretation.

See BT *Berakhot* 55b: "Rabbi El'azar said: 'How do we know that all dreams follow the mouth [of the interpreter]? Because it is said: *As he interpreted to us, so it was.*'" The verse in Genesis is spoken by Pharaoh's chief cupbearer, describing how accurately Joseph interpreted his dream and that of the chief baker.

See JT *Ma'aser Sheni* 4:6, 55c; *Bereshit Rabbah* 89:8; *Eikhah Rabbah* 1:18; *Zohar* 1:191b, 194b.

197. **word controls all...** The word of the interpreter possesses the power to actualize one of the possible meanings of the dream, for better or for worse. For another view, see Tishby, *Wisdom of the Zohar,* 2:825, n. 90.

198. **rung below, controlled by Speech...** Gabriel, the rung below, is controlled by *Shekhinah*, who conveys the divine word and is known as Speech. According to Rabbi Yehudah, human interpretation is effective because it activates divine Speech (*Shekhinah*), who then translates the dream into reality.

199. **enthrone and acknowledge the Kingdom of Heaven** By reciting the *Shema*, whose opening line reads: *Hear O Israel! YHVH our God, YHVH is one!* (Deuteronomy 6:4).

See M *Berakhot* 2:2; BT *Berakhot* 4b; *Zohar* 3:211a, 260a.

200. **verse of compassion...** From

when a human sleeps upon his bed, his soul leaves him and goes wandering above, each in its own way, ascending so, as has been said.[201]

"What is written? *In a dream, a vision of night*—when people lie asleep in bed, and the soul leaves them, as is written: *in slumber upon the bed, He then uncovers human ears.* Then the blessed Holy One informs the soul—through the rung presiding over dreams[202]—of things destined to befall the world, or of things corresponding to the mind's imaginings, so that one will follow a path of admonishment in the world.[203] For one is not informed while in a state of bodily vigor, as we have said.[204] Rather, an angel informs the soul, and the soul, the person, and that dream derives from above, when souls leave the body and ascend, each in its own way.

"How many rungs upon rungs in the mystery of a dream, all in the mystery of wisdom! Come and see: Dream, one rung; vision, one rung; prophecy, one rung—all rungs upon rungs, one above another.[205]

116 "*Joseph dreamed a dream and told it to his brothers, and they hated him even more* (Genesis 37:5). From here we learn that a person should tell his dream only to one who loves him.[206] Otherwise, he may prove decisive, for if that dream changes tone, he is the cause.[207]

Psalms 31:6: *Into Your hand I entrust my spirit; You redeem me,* YHVH, *God of truth.*

See BT *Berakhot* 5a; *Zohar* 1:11a, 36b, 92a, 183a; 3:119a, 120b; *ZḤ* 18b–c (*MhN*), 89a (*MhN, Rut*); Moses de León, *Sefer ha-Rimmon,* 53–54.

201. **when a human sleeps . . . his soul leaves him . . . each in its own way . . .** Each soul ascends according to its conduct on earth.

See *Midrash Tehillim* 11; *Pirqei de-Rabbi Eli'ezer* 34; *Bereshit Rabbah* 14:9; *Zohar* 1:92a, 121b, 200a; 3:67a, 121b; Ginzberg, *Legends,* 5:74–75, n. 18; Tishby, *Wisdom of the Zohar,* 2:809–12.

202. **rung presiding over dreams** The angel Gabriel. See above, note 194.

203. **corresponding to the mind's imaginings . . .** Corresponding to the dreamer's mental images. See BT *Berakhot* 55b: "Rabbi Shemu'el son of Naḥmani said in the name of Rabbi Yoḥanan, 'A person is shown [in his dreams] only his mind's imaginings.'"

The prefiguring of the future within dreams serves as admonishment to the dreamer to return to the straight path, as suggested by the verse from Job: *He then uncovers human ears, and with a warning, terrifies them.* See Moses de León, *Sefer ha-Rimmon,* 126; Mopsik.

204. **state of bodily vigor . . .** While awake and physically active, a person cannot receive messages from beyond; for this, the body must lie quiescent, the soul roaming above.

205. **Dream . . . vision . . . prophecy . . .** Corresponding, in ascending order, to Gabriel, *Shekhinah*, and the pair *Netsaḥ* and *Hod*.

206. **a person should tell his dream only to one who loves him** See *Sefer Ḥasidim,* ed. Margaliot, par. 447; *Midrash ha-Gadol,* Genesis 37:5; *Zohar* 1:200a.

207. **Otherwise, he may prove decisive . . .** If the dreamer tells his dream to someone who hates him, this enemy can harm him by the spiteful tone of his interpretation, which affects the fulfillment of the dream. This notion is now illustrated by the brothers' interpretation of Joseph's dream.

"Come and see: Since Joseph told his dream to his brothers, they caused it to be postponed, delaying it for twenty-two years!"[208]

Rabbi Yose said, "How do we know this? Because it is written: *They hated him even more.* What does *hated him* mean? They provoked accusers against him.[209]

"What is written? *He said to them, 'Listen, please, to this dream* [183b] *that I dreamed'* (ibid., 6)—begging them to listen; then he revealed that dream to them.[210] If they had transformed its tone, so it would have been fulfilled. But they responded by saying, '*Will you really reign over us? Will you really rule us?*' (ibid., 8). Suddenly they had told him the interpretation of the dream, enacting a decree. That is why *they hated him even more.*"[211]

Rabbi Ḥiyya and Rabbi Yose were in the presence of Rabbi Shim'on. Rabbi Ḥiyya said, "We have learned: 'A dream uninterpreted is like a letter unread.' Is this because it will be fulfilled without his knowing, or because it won't be fulfilled at all?"[212]

He replied, "It will be fulfilled and unknown, for that dream depends upon it, while being unknown, and unknown as to whether it will be fulfilled or not.[213] Nothing in the world, before arriving in the world, is independent of a dream—or by means of a herald, for as has been said: Every single thing, before

208. **delaying it for twenty-two years** The first dream recounted by Joseph to his brothers is related in Genesis 37:7: *Look, we were binding sheaves in the field, and look, my sheaf arose and actually stood up, and look, your sheaves gathered around and bowed down to my sheaf!* As indicated by Rabbi Levi (BT *Berakhot* 55b), it took twenty-two years for this dream to be fulfilled, i.e., for Joseph's brothers to bow down to him in Egypt (see Genesis 42:6).

209. **They provoked accusers against him** Their hatred stimulated demonic forces to delay the fulfillment of the dream.

210. **he revealed that dream to them** See above, note 208.

211. **If they had transformed its tone...** If the brothers had interpreted the dream unfavorably for Joseph, it would have been fulfilled accordingly. However, their spontaneous, hateful response (*Will you really reign over us?*) guaranteed that the dream would be actualized precisely that way: by Joseph's dominance. By verbally expressing this interpretation, they had sealed both their fate and his. Realizing what they had done to themselves, they hated Joseph all the more.

212. **A dream uninterpreted is like a letter unread...** In BT *Berakhot* 55a, this saying is cited in the name of Rav Ḥisda. Here, Rabbi Ḥiyya wonders what the simile of an unread letter implies: that although the contents of the letter are unknown, an event foretold in the letter will still happen; or, that unless the letter is read, the event will not happen (for example, if a person writes a letter to his friend, inviting him to go somewhere). Correspondingly, for an uninterpreted dream: will it still come true without the dreamer's awareness, or will it remain unfulfilled, since without interpretation the dream cannot be actualized?

Cf. Rashi, ad loc., s.v. *ke-iggarta de-la miqqarya;* BT *Berakhot* 55b; *Zohar* 1:199b.

213. **that dream depends upon it...** The dream depends upon its interpretation and

arriving in the world, is heralded in heaven, whence it spreads throughout the world, transmitted by a herald.[214] All because it is written: *Surely YHVH Elohim does nothing without revealing His secret to His servants the prophets* (Amos 3:7)—when prophets existed in the world; if they do not, even though prophecy no longer prevails, the wise are preferable to prophets.[215] And if not, it is transmitted in a dream; and if not, words manifest through birds of the sky, as has been established."[216]

His brothers went לרעות את צאן אביהם (*lir'ot et tson avihem*), *to graze their father's flock, at Shechem* (Genesis 37:12).

Rabbi Shim'on said, "The verse should read: לרעות צאן אביהם (*lir'ot tson avihem*), *to graze their father's flock.* Why את (*et*)—dotted above? To amplify the meaning, including *Shekhinah* along with them;[217] for She dwelled among them because they were ten—since Joseph wasn't with them and Benjamin was a

will be fulfilled accordingly, although in this case the interpretation remains unknown. See Mopsik.

214. **Nothing . . . is independent of a dream . . .** Everything that happens in the world is either prefigured in a dream or announced by a heavenly herald.

See BT *Mo'ed Qatan* 18b, in the name of Shemu'el: "Every single day a heavenly echo issues, proclaiming: 'The daughter of so-and-so for so-and-so!'"

215. **the wise are preferable to prophets** Once prophecy ceased, the wise received a type of revelation, and in a sense, they surpass the prophets.

See BT *Bava Batra* 12a: "Rabbi Avdimi from Haifa said, 'Since the day when the Temple was destroyed, prophecy has been taken from the prophets and given to the wise.' . . . Amemar said, 'A wise person is preferable to a prophet.'"

See *Zohar* 1:7b, 194b; 2:6b; 3:35a; Huss, "Ḥakham Adif mi-Navi," *Kabbalah* 4 (1999): 103–39.

216. **And if not . . .** If the wise also disappear, then a type of revelation is conveyed through dreams. If dreams do not convey the message, then birds do, through their chirping and motion in flight.

On bird divination, see *Vayiqra Rabbah* 32:2 (citing Ecclesiastes 10:20); *Pesiqta de-Rav Kahana* 4:3; *Tanḥuma, Ḥuqqat* 6; *Tanḥuma* (Buber), *Ḥuqqat* 11 (and Buber's note); BT *Gittin* 45a; Rashi on 2 Chronicles 9:4; Radak on 1 Kings 5:10; Naḥmanides on Deuteronomy 18:9; *Zohar* 1:126b–127a, 194b, 217b; 2:6b; 3:204b.

217. **Why את (*et*)—dotted above? . . .** Rabbi Shim'on's question is actually a double question. First, what is the significance of the word את (*et*)? Second, why are both its letters dotted according to the Masoretic text?

As for the first query, את (*et*) is technically an accusative particle with no ascertainable independent sense. Yet already in rabbinic times, Naḥum of Gimzo and his disciple Rabbi Akiva taught that the presence of *et* in a biblical verse amplifies the apparent meaning. Here, as often in the *Zohar*, the amplification of את (*et*) connotes *Shekhinah*, who comprises the entire alphabet of divine speech, from א (*alef*) to ת (*tav*).

See BT *Pesaḥim* 22b; *Ḥagigah* 12a; *Zohar* 1:247a; 2:90a, 135b. Cf. the Christian parallel in Revelation 1:8: "I am *alpha* and *omega*."

The second half of Rabbi Shim'on's question pertains to the Masoretic tradition of dotting certain letters in the Torah, a calligraphic phenomenon that invites midrashic

little one at home, so they were ten—and when they walked, *Shekhinah* accompanied them, so it is dotted above.[218]

'Therefore when they sold Joseph, they all collaborated with *Shekhinah* and made Her a partner to the oath they swore; and until the matter of Joseph was revealed, *Shekhinah* did not rest upon Jacob.[219]

"Now, if you say that *Shekhinah* was not present among them,[220] come and see what is written: *There tribes ascend, tribes of Yah—a testimony to Israel—to praise the name of YHVH* (Psalms 122:4)—all righteous and devout, sustenance of all worlds, sustenance above and below."[221]

He opened, saying, "*I rejoiced when they said to me, 'Let us go to the house of YHVH'* (ibid., 1). This verse has been established: David had set his heart on building the House, as is said: *My father David had it in his heart to build a house for the name of YHVH*. What is written next? *Nevertheless, you yourself will not build the house, but your son, who issues from your loins—he will build the house for My name* (1 Kings 8:17, 19).[222] All of Israel knew this, and they used to say, 'When will David die so that his son Solomon will arise and build the House!

treatment. Here the Rabbi explains that the dots over the word את (*et*) highlight and reinforce the kabbalistic amplification of that same word, namely, *Shekhinah*.

On dotted letters in the Torah, see *Sifrei*, Numbers 69; BT *Bava Metsi'a* 87a; *Soferim* 6:3; *Avot de-Rabbi Natan* A, 34; B, 37; and *Bereshit Rabbah* 84:13, which offers a different explanation for these particular dots.

218. **She dwelled among them because they were ten...** According to rabbinic tradition, *Shekhinah* dwells among any group of ten who are engaged in study or prayer. Here, She accompanies Joseph's ten brothers, who—despite all appearances to the contrary—are considered righteous.

See M *Avot* 3:6; *Mekhilta, Baḥodesh* 11; BT *Berakhot* 6a. On the notion that ten constitute an *edah* (assembly), see M *Sanhedrin* 1:6; JT *Berakhot* 7:3, 11c; BT *Berakhot* 21b; *Bereshit Rabbah* 91:3.

219. **collaborated with *Shekhinah*... made Her a partner to the oath...** The brothers' apparently wicked deed actually served a divine purpose and therefore had divine sanction, as explained shortly. After selling Joseph into slavery, they included *Shekhinah* in the oath they swore not to reveal his true fate to their father, Jacob, so She withdrew Her revelatory and prophetic powers from the aging patriarch. Only many years later, when Jacob learned that Joseph was still alive, did he regain Her presence and inspiration.

See Genesis 50:20; *Targum Yerushalmi*, Genesis 45:27; *Tanḥuma, Vayeshev* 2; *Pirqei de-Rabbi Eli'ezer* (Friedlander) 38; (Higger) 37; *Zohar* 1:185b, 188b, 197b, 210b; above, note 63.

220. **if you say that *Shekhinah* was not present among them** How could She witness, sanction, or participate in such a cruel deed?

221. ***There tribes ascend*... all righteous and devout...** The verse proves that the tribes (and their progenitors, Joseph's brothers) were worthy, sustaining both upper and lower worlds. This reading is explained more fully below.

"Sustenance" renders קיומא (*qiyyuma*), whose semantic range in the *Zohar* also includes "pillar." See above, note 117.

222. **David had set his heart on building the House...** King David wanted to build a Temple for God, but he was told that only his son would fulfill this desire.

Then, *our feet are standing within your gates, O Jerusalem* (Psalms 122:2): then we will go up and bring offerings there!'

"Nevertheless—even though they said 'When will this old man die!'—right then *I rejoiced*, 'I was delighted for the sake of my son, who they said would rise in my place to complete the command of building the House.'[223] Then he began praising her: *Jerusalem—built as a city that is bound together* (ibid., 3).

"We have learned: The blessed Holy One formed Jerusalem below corresponding to the pattern above, this one arrayed facing the other, as is written: מכון (*makhon*), *dais, of Your throne, that You made, O YHVH* (Exodus 15:17).[224]

"*Built* (Psalms, ibid.)—for the blessed Holy One will one day cause Jerusalem to descend from above fittingly. Therefore, *built.*[225]

"*That is bound together* (ibid.). This they have already established: שחברה (*she-ḥubberah*), *that is bound.* The verse should read: שחברו (*she-ḥubberu*), *that are bound.* However, mother is bound to daughter, becoming as one. This has been established, as has been said.[226]

"*There tribes ascend* (ibid., 4)—sustenance of the world, adornment of the world. Do not think just the lower world, but even the higher world, as is written: *tribes of Yah, a testimony to Israel* (ibid.)—*to Israel*, precisely! Since they

223. **right then *I rejoiced*...** David rejoiced for his son. Since David intended to build the Temple and prepared materials for its construction, he inititated the project, which Solomon then completed.

See 1 Chronicles 22; 29:1–5; BT *Makkot* 10a; JT *Berakhot* 2:1, 4b; *Midrash Tehillim* 122:1–2.

224. **Jerusalem below corresponding to the pattern above...** On the image of heavenly Jerusalem, see *Tanḥuma, Pequdei* 1: "There is a Jerusalem above aligned with Jerusalem below. Out of His love for the one below, He fashioned another above.... He has sworn that His presence will not enter the heavenly Jerusalem until the earthly Jerusalem is rebuilt."

See Revelation 21:2; *Targum Yonatan*, Psalms 122:3; BT *Ta'anit* 5a; *Midrash Tehillim* 122:4; *Leqaḥ Tov* , Exodus 23:20; *Zohar* 1:1b, 80b (*ST*), 128b, 231a; 3:15b, 68b, 147b.

Here, as in rabbinic literature, this notion is linked with a play on words: מכון (*makhon*), "dais," and מכוון (*mekhuvvan*), "corresponding to, aligned with, directly opposite." Seen in that light, the verse from Exodus implies that God fashioned an earthly throne perfectly aligned with the throne on high: *mekhuvvan, that which is aligned with, Your throne, You made, O YHVH.*

See *Mekhilta, Shirta* 10; JT *Berakhot* 4:5, 8c; *Shir ha-Shirim Rabbah* on 3:9; *Tanḥuma, Vayaqhel* 7, *Pequdei* 1–3; Mopsik.

225. ***Built*...** Heavenly Jerusalem has been built by God in preparation for its eventual descent to earth.

See 1 Enoch 90:28–29; *Targum Yonatan*, Psalms 122:3; *Tanḥuma, Pequdei* 1; *Nistarot Rabbi Shim'on ben Yoḥai* (*Beit ha-Midrash*, 3:80); *ZḤ* 26b (*MhN*).

226. **שחברה (*she-ḥubberah*), *that is bound*...** If the two Jerusalems are bound together, then the verb should be in the plural: שחברו (*she-ḥubberu*), *that are bound.* However, according to Rabbi Shim'on, the singular form is correct because it emphasizes the eschatological unity of the divine mother and daughter, *Binah* and *Shekhinah*, who are symbolized respectively by heavenly and earthly Jerusalem.

See *Zohar* 1:2a, 173b; 3:78a; Moses de León, *Shushan Edut*, 346.

provide sustenance below, they bear testimony above.[227] All this, *to praise the name of YHVH*, to praise the name of the blessed Holy One in all directions, as is written: *to praise the name of YHVH*.[228]

"A man found him and, look, he was wandering in the field. The man asked him, 'What are you seeking' (Genesis 37:15).[229]

[184a] "What is written above? *Israel said to Joseph, 'Aren't your brothers pasturing at Shechem? Come, I will send you to them'* (ibid., 13). Now, why would Jacob the perfect—who loved Joseph more than all his sons and knew that all his brothers hated him—send him to them? The truth is that he did not suspect them, knowing them all to be virtuous, beyond suspicion. Rather, the blessed Holy One brought all this about in order to fulfill the decree enacted between the halves.[230]

"I have discovered in books of the ancients[231] that these sons of Jacob had to gain mastery over him before he descended to Egypt. For if he had descended without their first having dominated him, the Egyptians would have been able to dominate Israel forever, based on the fact that Joseph was sold into slavery and they dominated him. And even though later Joseph became king and the Egyptians served him, Israel came to rule them all.[232]

227. **sustenance of the world... Do not think just the lower world...** The twelve tribes adorn *Shekhinah* (known as "lower world"), fulfilling Her and thereby helping to nourish the world below. They also symbolize (or attest to) twelve higher aspects of the sefirotic realm that enthrone *Binah* ("higher world").

The divine name *Yah* symbolizes *Ḥokhmah* and *Binah*, whose union engenders the seven lower *sefirot*. *Israel* signifies *Tif'eret*, whose full name is *Tif'eret Yisra'el* (Beauty of Israel) and who constitutes the core of these *sefirot* below *Binah*.

See *Zohar* 1:155a, 157b–158a, 240b–241b; 2:229b; 3:78a, 118b; *ZḤ* 26b (*MhN*); Moses de León, *Sheqel ha-Qodesh*, 34 (41); idem, untitled fragment, 366b; Mopsik. On קיומא (*qiyyuma*), "sustenance," see above, note 221.

228. ***name of YHVH*** *Shekhinah*, who conveys divine being. See *Targum Onqelos*, Deuteronomy 12:11; Mopsik.

229. ***A man found him...*** A man found Joseph, who was seeking his brothers.

230. **decree enacted between the halves** The covenant enacted between God and Abraham, marked by a ritual in which several animals were cut in half. Toward sunset, God spoke to Abraham: *Know well that your seed will be strangers in a land not theirs, and they will be enslaved and afflicted four hundred years. But upon the nation that they serve I will bring judgment, and afterward they will go forth with great substance* (Genesis 15:13–14).

Rabbi Shim'on's point is that God intended for Joseph to be sold into slavery by his brothers as part of the cosmic plan. See Genesis 50:20; Radak on Genesis 37:13; *Zohar* 1:188b, 196a–b.

231. **books of the ancients** One of the many sources housed in the fantastic library of the author(s) of the *Zohar*. These particular volumes are cited frequently.

See 1:10a, 34b, 41a (*Heikh*), 180b, 220a, 234b; 2:35a, 95b, 239a; 3:10a, 19a, 26b, 249b, 258b, 288a (*IZ*); Mopsik.

232. **sons of Jacob had to gain mastery over him...** By seizing and selling Joseph, the brothers demonstrated their mastery over him, thereby ensuring that their descendants (the Children of Israel) would eventually dominate the Egyptians, who

"Come and see: Joseph is supernal covenant.[233] As long as covenant endured, *Shekhinah* endured with Israel in peace, fittingly. As soon as Joseph—supernal covenant—vanished from the world, then covenant, *Shekhinah*, and Israel all plunged into exile. This has been established, as is written: *A new king arose over Egypt, who did not know Joseph* (Exodus 1:8). All issued from the blessed Holy One fittingly.[234]

"Come and see: *A man found him*—this is Gabriel. As has been established, here is written *a man*, and there is written *The man Gabriel, whom I had seen before in a vision, was flown in flight* (Daniel 9:21).[235]

"*And, look, he was wandering*—wandering in every way: wandering by trusting his brothers, for he was seeking their friendship and didn't find it, he sought them and didn't find them. So, *wandering* in every way."

The man asked him, "What are you seeking?" He said, "I am seeking my brothers." The man said, "They moved on from here" (Genesis 37:15–17).[236]

Rabbi Yehudah opened, "*If only you were like a brother to me, nursing at my mother's breasts! If I found you outside, I would kiss you, yet no one would scorn me* (Song of Songs 8:1). This verse has been established by the Companions, but this verse was spoken by Assembly of Israel, to the King to whom peace belongs.[237]

served Joseph when he became Pharaoh's vizier. Because the brothers dominated Joseph, they also dominated his Egyptian subjects. If they had not initially dominated him, then the Egyptian power of enslavement would have been unchallenged and the Children of Israel would never have escaped bondage.

233. **Joseph is supernal covenant** By resisting the sexual advances of Potiphar's wife, Joseph preserved the covenant of circumcision and attained the *sefirah* of *Yesod*, the divine phallus.

See Genesis 39; *Zohar* 1:176b, 197a.

234. **As long as covenant endured...** As long as Joseph's life and influence endured, *Yesod* flowed into *Shekhinah* and harmony reigned below. Once Joseph was forgotten, the union above was ruined, plunging both Israel and divinity into exile. See above, note 154.

235. ***A man found him*—this is Gabriel...** For the full verse, see above, page 121. Based simply on verbal analogy, the anonymous *man* in this verse is identified with *the man Gabriel* in Daniel (mentioned also earlier in Daniel 8:16).

See *Targum Yerushalmi*, Genesis 37:15; *Tanḥuma, Vayeshev* 2; *Pirqei de-Rabbi Eli'ezer* 38; Rashi on Genesis 37:15; *Zohar* 2:11a, 19a (*MhN*).

236. ***The man asked him...*** The verses read: *The man asked him, "What are you seeking?" He said, "I am seeking my brothers. Tell me, please, where are they pasturing?" The man said, "They moved on from here..."* (15–17).

Rashi comments: "*They moved on from here:* They removed themselves from brotherhood." See *Bereshit Rabbah* 84:14, p. 1017, variants, line 3.

237. **established by the Companions, but...** In midrashic literature, the Song of Songs is understood as describing the love

"*If only you were like a brother to me!*—like Joseph toward his brothers when he said, '*Now, do not fear! I will sustain you and your little ones.' He comforted them and spoke to their hearts* (Genesis 50:21). He provided them with food, nourishing them in time of famine. So, *If only you were like a brother to me!*

"Alternatively, *If only you were like a brother to me!*—Joseph in relation to *Shekhinah*, with whom he united, to whom he cleaved.[238]

"*Nursing at my mother's breasts*—for then, perfect affection between them.[239]

"*If I found you outside*—in exile, in a foreign land.

"*I would kiss you*—so that spirit would cling to spirit.[240]

"*Yet no one would scorn me*—although I am in a foreign land.[241]

"Come and see: Even though Joseph's brothers did not act toward him as brothers when he fell into their hands, he was a brother to them when they fell into his hands. This has been established, as is written: *He comforted them and spoke to their hearts* (ibid.), speaking to their hearts entirely.[242]

"Come and see what is written: *They said, a man to his brother* (Genesis 37:19)[243]—Simeon and Levi, who were truly brothers in every respect, for they issued from the side of harsh judgment, so their wrath was murderous, as is written: *Cursed be their anger, so fierce* (ibid. 49:7).[244] 123

affair between the maiden (the earthly Assembly of Israel) and her lover (the Holy One, blessed be He). This particular verse is intepreted as being spoken by the people to God, asking Him to love them like a sibling. See *Pesiqta de-Rav Kahana* 16:5; *Shir ha-Shirim Rabbah* on 8:1.

In the *Zohar*, כנסת ישראל (*keneset yisra'el*), "Assembly of Israel," can refer to the earthly community but also (often primarily) to *Shekhinah*, the divine feminine counterpart of the people, the aspect of God most intimately connected with them. The lovers in the Song of Songs are pictured as the divine couple, *Shekhinah* and *Tif'eret*, and this particular verse is spoken by Her to Him.

"The King to whom peace belongs" is a designation of God in *Shir ha-Shirim Rabbah* on 1:1. Here it refers specifically to *Tif'eret*, who encompasses *Yesod* (known as "peace").

238. **Joseph in relation to *Shekhinah*...** As *Yesod* unites with *Shekhinah*. For a different interpretation, see Mopsik.

239. ***Nursing at my mother's breasts*...** At the breasts of the Divine Mother, *Binah*, who suckles both *Shekhinah* and Her partner. See Ezra of Gerona, *Peirush Shir ha-Shirim*, 513.

240. **so that spirit would cling to spirit** The outcome of a true kiss.

See *Zohar* 2:124b, 146a–b, 254a, 256b; *ZḤ* 60 (*MhN*), 63a; Moses de León, *Sefer ha-Rimmon*, 396.

241. **although I am in a foreign land** Under the influence of demonic powers.

242. **Even though Joseph's brothers did not act toward him...** See *Pesiqta de-Rav Kahana* 16:5.

243. ***They said, a man to his brother*** The context (37:19–20) reads: *They said, a man to his brother, "Here comes that dream-master! Come now, let's kill him and throw him into one of the pits, and we'll say, 'A vicious beast devoured him.' We'll see what comes of his dreams."*

244. **Simeon and Levi... from the side of harsh judgment...** The verse in Genesis does not specify which brothers hatched the plan, but midrashic tradition assigns

"Come and see the mystery of the matter: There is wrath, and then there is wrath! There is wrath blessed from above and below, called *blessed*, as has been said, for it is written: *Blessed be Abram by God the Highest* (ibid. 14:19), as they have established.[245] And there is wrath cursed above and below, as has been said, called *cursed* as is written: *Cursed are you among all animals and among all beasts of the field* (ibid. 3:14).[246] *Cursed be their anger, so fierce.*

"Upon this mystery stand two mountains, as is written: *You will give the blessing on Mount Gerizim and the curse on Mount Ebal* (Deuteronomy 11:29), corresponding to these two rungs,[247] so this is called *cursed* and that is called *blessed.* Simeon and Levi issue from the side of harsh judgment, and from the side of harsh, fierce judgment issues accursed wrath.[248]

"Come and see: From the aspect of harsh judgment issue two aspects, one that has been blessed and one that has been cursed, [184b] one *blessed* and one *cursed.* Similarly, from the side of Isaac issued two sons: one blessed and the other cursed, above and below, one branching inward and the other to his side, one dwelling in the Holy Land and the other on Mount Seir, as is written: *a skilled hunter, a man of the field*—this one's domain in wilderness, ruin, and desolation; this one *dwelling in tents* (Genesis 25:27), all as it should be.[249]

the role to Simeon and Levi. Their violent temper is evident in an earlier episode, described in Genesis 34: when their sister Dinah was raped, these two brothers avenged the outrage by killing the rapist and all the men of his town. Here Rabbi Yehudah explains that both brothers derived from the *sefirah* of *Din* (harsh Judgment).

See *Bereshit Rabbah* 97:8 (on Genesis 49:8), 99:7; *Targum Yerushalmi*, Genesis 37:19; *Tanḥuma, Vayḥi* 9; *Tanḥuma* (Buber), *Vayeshev* 13; *Zohar* 1:172b–173a, 185b, 198b, 200b, 236a, 244a; 2:6a, 11a.

245. **wrath blessed from above and below...** Righteous anger, as when Abram routed a confederacy of four kings to rescue his nephew Lot. See Genesis 14; cf. *Zohar* 2:243a; Tishby, *Wisdom of the Zohar*, 3:1333–34.

246. **wrath cursed above and below... *Cursed are you...*** Demonic wrath, linked with the serpent from the Garden of Eden, who was cursed by God. The verse reads in full: *Because you have done this, cursed are you among all animals and among all beasts of the field. Upon your belly shall you go and dust shall you eat all the days of your life.*

See *Zohar* 2:243b, 263b.

247. **two mountains... *Mount Gerizim ... Mount Ebal...*** According to Deuteronomy, when the people of Israel cross into Canaan, blessing and curse are to be proclaimed on these two mountains, which face each other north and south of Shechem.

248. **harsh judgment... harsh, fierce judgment...** The two brothers issue from the *sefirah* of *Din* (harsh Judgment); from the dregs of this *sefirah* issues demonic wrath.

249. **from the side of Isaac issued two sons...** Isaac, who symbolizes *Din*, engendered two sons, Jacob and Esau, who embody the opposite aspects of their father's *sefirah*. In the *Zohar*, Jacob and Esau often represent medieval Judaism and Christianity.

The verse reads in full: *The boys grew up. Esau became a skilled hunter, a man of the field, while Jacob was a mild man, dwelling in tents.* See *Bereshit Rabbah* 63:9; *Zohar* 1:138b–139a.

"So there are two rungs: *blessed* and *cursed*, each on its own side. From this one issue all blessings of the world above and below, all joy and goodness, all radiance, all deliverance and redemption. From that one issue all curses, all war, all bloodshed, all desolation, all evils, and all defilement."

Rabbi Shim'on opened, "*I wash my hands in purity, and circle Your altar, O YHVH* (Psalms 26:6). This verse has been established,[250] but come and see mystery of the matter here: No human being in the world avoids tasting a taste of death at night,[251] and an impure spirit settles upon his body. Why? Because the holy soul withdraws from a person and departs, and because she does so, an impure spirit settles upon that body, defiling it.[252]

"When soul returns to body, that filth disappears, yet as has been explained, filth of defilement remains on a person's hands.[253] So one should not pass his hands over his eyes, on account of that impure spirit, until he washes them.[254] Once he washes his hands, he is sanctified and called 'holy.'

"How should one sanctify himself? He needs one vessel below and one vessel above—so that he may be sanctified from the one above, while within the one below sits filth of defilement; this vessel receiving defilement, that one the source of sanctification; this one blessed, that one cursed.[255] That water should not be poured out in the house, so that no one comes near it, for within it swarm their flanks, and one can be harmed by that impure water.[256]

"Until the filth is removed from his hands, one should not offer a blessing, as

250. **This verse has been established** See BT *Berakhot* 15a, in the context of washing one's hands in the morning.

251. **tasting a taste of death at night** Based on BT *Berakhot* 57b: "Sleep is one-sixtieth of death."

See *Zohar* 1:36a–b, 53b, 169b; 2:173a; 3:119a; Moses de León, *Sefer ha-Rimmon*, 52–53.

252. **impure spirit settles...** At night, the soul withdraws and roams above, and an impure spirit reaches the body, similar to the impurity touching a corpse.

On the soul's nightly ascent, see above, p. 116 and n. 201. On the spirit of impurity and the sleeping body, see BT *Shabbat* 109a; *Ḥullin* 107b; *Zohar* 1:10b, 53b, 83a, 130a, 169b; Moses de León, *Orḥot Ḥayyim*, par. 10.

253. **filth of defilement remains on a person's hands** See the preceding note.

254. **one should not pass his hands over his eyes...** Before ritually washing the hands to remove the impure spirit. Otherwise the impure spirit infects the eyes and contaminates anything or any person that one sees.

See BT *Shabbat* 108b; Rashi, ad loc., s.v. *yad la-ayin; tiqqatsets; Kallah* 1:19; *Kallah Rabbati* 2:5; *Zohar* 1:169b; Moses de León, *Orḥot Ḥayyim*, par. 10.

255. **one vessel below and one vessel above...** One should pour the water over his hands from one vessel into another, not onto the ground.

See *Beit Yosef* and *Shulḥan Arukh, Oraḥ Ḥayyim* 4:8. Cf. BT *Ḥullin* 105a–b; *Zohar* 1:10b, 198b.

256. **within it swarm their flanks...** The used water is contaminated by impure spirits.

we have established.[257] Therefore, until a person sanctifies his hands in the morning, he is called 'impure'; once sanctified, he is called 'pure.' So, one should be washed only by a hand already purified, as is written: *The pure will sprinkle upon the impure* (Numbers 19:19)—one called *pure*, the other *impure*.[258]

"Therefore, one vessel above and one below, this one holy, that one defiled. That water must not be used in any way, but rather poured out in a place no one passes.[259] Nor should it be kept in the house overnight, for once it is spilled on the ground, an impure spirit appears, able to inflict harm. If there is a slope leading underground, so that it cannot be seen, this is better. One must not give it to witches, who can thereby afflict people because that water is cursed.[260] The blessed Holy One desires to purify Israel, so that they may be holy, as is written: *I will sprinkle pure water upon you, and you will be pure; from all you impurities and from all your idols will I purify you* (Ezekiel 36:25)."

They took him and threw him
126 *into the pit*... (Genesis 37:24).[261]

Rabbi Yehudah opened, "*The Torah of YHVH is perfect, restoring the soul* (Psalms 19:8). How vigorously people should engage in Torah! For whoever engages in Torah will have life in this world and life in the world that is coming, attaining two worlds! Even if he strives in Torah but not for her own sake, befittingly, he still gains a good reward in this world and is spared judgment in that world.[262]

257. **one should not offer a blessing...** See BT *Berakhot* 53b: "R. Zuhamai said, 'Just as a filthy [person or animal] is unfit for the Temple service, so filthy hands render one unfit for reciting a blessing [after eating].'"

Cf. *Zohar* 1:10b; 3:186a; Moses de León, *Orḥot Ḥayyim*, par. 12.

258. **one should be washed only by a hand already purified...** Ideally, one's hands should be washed by another person who has already washed.

See BT *Berakhot* 51a: "Rabbi Yishma'el son of Elisha said, 'Three things were told to me by Suriel, Prince of the [Divine] Countenance: Do not take your shirt from the hand of the attendant when dressing in the morning, do not let your hands be washed by anyone who has not washed his hands, and do not return a cup of asparagus to anyone other than the one who has handed it to you. For a band of demons (some say: a cluster of angels of destruction) lies in wait, saying: When will a human do one of these things, so that we can capture him!'"

See *Zohar* 1:53b, 198b; Moses de León, *Orḥot Ḥayyim*, par. 12; Scholem; Lieberman, *Tosefet Rishonim*, 4:147; Ta-Shma, *Ha-Nigleh she-ba-Nistar*, 31; 121, n. 59. The procedure described in Numbers 19 is a purification ritual for one who has experienced contact with a human corpse: water is mixed with the ashes of a red heifer and then sprinkled on the impure person by one who is pure.

259. **not be used in any way, but rather poured out...** See *Shulḥan Arukh, Oraḥ Ḥayyim* 4:9. Cf. *Zohar* 3:264a, 265b.

260. **witches, who can thereby afflict people...** See *ZḤ* 81b–c (*MhN, Rut*).

261. ***They took him and threw him into the pit...*** The full verse reads: *They took him and threw him into the pit, and the pit was empty, there was no water in it.*

262. **not for her own sake...** Not for the sake of Torah herself, but rather for an

"Come and see what is written: *Length of days in her right hand; in her left, riches and honor* (Proverbs 3:16). *Length of days*—referring to one who engages in Torah for her own sake, since he has *length of days* in the world filled with long days, days that are real. There lies trust in supernal holiness, for a person in this world trustingly engages in Torah in order to be vitalized in that world. [185a] *In her left, riches and honor*—he receives good reward and tranquility in this world.[263]

"If someone engages in Torah for her own sake, when he departs from this world Torah precedes him, proclaiming before him, protecting him from accosting masters of judgment.[264] When the body lies in the grave, she guards it. As the soul begins to ascend, returning to her realm, she precedes that soul, and countless gates are smashed before Torah until she enters her place.[265] She stands over the person until he awakes at the time when the dead of the world will arise, and she advocates for him, as is written: *When you walk, she will guide you . . .* (Proverbs 6:22).[266]

"*When you walk, she will guide you*, as has been said.[267]

"*When you lie down, she will protect you*—when the body lies in the grave, for right then the body is judged in the grave and Torah defends him.[268]

"*You will awake*, as has been said: when the dead of the world will awake from the dust.[269]

ulterior motive. See the following note, and *Beit ha-Midrash*, 3:196–97.

263. ***Length of days in her right hand; in her left . . .*** One who studies Torah for her own sake gains true life in the eternal world that is coming, but even one who studies for an ulterior motive finds reward in this world.

See *Avot* 6:7; *Bereshit Rabbah* 59:2; BT *Shabbat* 63a; *Zohar* 1:190a.

264. **accosting masters of judgment** Hostile powers trying to block the soul's ascent. See *ZH* 75b–c (*MhN, Rut*).

265. **countless gates are smashed before Torah . . .** The Torah that one has studied breaks through all barriers and leads the soul to her heavenly abode.

266. **she advocates for him . . .** In the final judgment, Torah testifies that this person devoted himself to studying and fulfilling the word of God.

The full verse in Proverbs reads: *When you walk, she will guide you; when you lie down, she will protect you; you will awake, and she will speak with you.* See *Avot* 6:9; *Sifra, Aḥarei Mot* 13:11, 86b; BT *Sotah* 21a; Rashi, ad loc., s.v. *hi tesiḥekha; Devarim Rabbah* (Lieberman) 6:9; *Aggadat Bereshit* 46; *Zohar* 1:175b.

267. ***When you walk, she will guide you,* as has been said** When you depart from this world. Alternatively (as in the rabbinic sources cited in the preceding note), when you walk in this world.

268. **body is judged in the grave . . .** This judgment, known as *ḥibbut ha-qever* (beating in the grave), is administered by the Angel of Death or other demonic beings.

See 3 Enoch 28:10; *Beit ha-Midrash*, 1:150–52; 5:49; *Sefer Ḥasidim*, ed. Margaliot, par. 30; *Zohar* 2:151a, 199b; 3:126b–127a.

269. **dead of the world will awake from the dust** Then the soul will be restored, as alluded to by Rabbi Yehudah's opening verse: *The Torah of YHVH is perfect, restoring the soul.* See above, note 266.

"היא תשיחך (*Hi tesiḥekha*), *She will speak for you*—serving as an advocate."[270]

Rabbi El'azar said, "*She will speak for you.* What does this mean? Even though they have arisen just now from the dust, their Torah will not be forgotten, for they will know all the Torah they left behind when they departed this world.[271] This Torah is preserved from that moment and will penetrate their inner being as before, and she will speak deep within them, with all words more refined than at first, since all those things that one could not fully grasp—striving yet not apprehending—now enter him deeply, enhanced, and Torah speaks within him, as is written: *You will awake, and she will speak for you.*"[272]

Rabbi Yehudah said, "Similarly, whoever engages in Torah in this world is entitled to engage in her in the world that is coming, as has been said.

"Come and see: As for the person who never succeeded in engaging in Torah in this world and walked in darkness: when he leaves this world he is seized and thrown into Hell—a region below where no one pities him, called *pit of desolation, slimy mud*, as is written: *He lifted me out of a pit of desolation, out of the slimy mud* (Psalms 40:3).[273]

"So, what is written concerning someone who did not engage in Torah in this world and besmirched himself with worldly filth? *They took him and threw him into the pit*—Hell, the region where they punish those who did not engage in Torah.

"*And the pit was empty*—just as he was empty. Why? Because there was no water in him.[274]

"Come and see how severe is the punishment for Torah! For Israel was exiled from the Holy Land solely because they deserted Torah, abandoning her, as is written: *What man is wise enough to understand this?... Why is the land ruined? YHVH said, 'Because they have forsaken My Torah'* (Jeremiah 9:11–12)."[275]

270. ***She will speak for you*—serving as an advocate** This final clause of the verse, היא תשיחך (*hi tesiḥekha*), means *she will talk with you*, but drawing on rabbinic sources, Rabbi Yehudah understands it as *she will speak for you*. See above, note 266.

271. **their Torah will not be forgotten...** See *Midrash Mishlei* 10:3; *Yalqut Shim'oni*, Proverbs 945.

272. **penetrate their inner being...** Literally, "enter their entrails, intestines." See Psalms 40:9: *Your Torah is within my inmost parts.*

Cf. Radak, ad loc.; *Pesiqta de-Rav Kahana* 10:6; *Seder Eliyyahu Rabbah* 24; *Sefer Ḥasidim*, ed. Margaliot, par. 1164.

273. ***pit of desolation...*** One of the regions of Hell. See BT *Eruvin* 19a; *Zohar* 1:238b; 2:263a.

274. ***And the pit was empty*...no water in him** The full verse reads: *They took him and threw him into the pit, and the pit was empty, there was no water in it.* Just as the pit was empty of water, so is this sinner empty of Torah.

On Torah as water, see *Mekhilta, Vayassa* 1; *Bereshit Rabbah* 84:16.

275. **Israel was exiled...solely because they deserted Torah...** See JT *Ḥagigah* 1:7, 76c; BT *Nedarim* 81a; *ZḤ* 8d (*MhN*).

Rabbi Yose said, "From here: *Therefore My people go into exile: for lack of knowledge* (Isaiah 5:13).[276] So all depends upon Torah, and the world is sustained only through Torah—sustaining pillar of worlds above and below, as is written: *Were it not for My covenant day and night, I would not have established the laws of heaven and earth* (Jeremiah 33:25)."[277]

They took him and threw him into the pit—alluding to the fact that they cast him into Egypt, a place totally lacking the mystery of faith.[278]

Rabbi Yitsḥak said, "Why is this attributed to Reuben: *Throw him into this pit in the wilderness*... (Genesis 37:22)?[279] Didn't he care about the fact that those snakes and scorpions would harm him?[280] How can Scripture say *to bring him back to his father*, and *in order to rescue him from their hands* (ibid.)? But actually Reuben saw the harm lurking in their hands, since he knew how much they hated him and their desire to kill him. Reuben thought, 'Better that he fall into a pit of snakes and scorpions than be delivered into the hands of his enemies who have no compassion for him!' Based upon this, they have said: 'Let a person throw himself into fire or a pit of snakes and scorpions rather than being delivered into the hands of his enemies.'[281] [185b] For here,[282] if he is righteous, the blessed Holy One will bring about a miracle for him—or sometimes ancestral merit helps a person and he is saved. But once he has been handed over to his enemies, few are able to escape.

"Therefore it says *in order to rescue him from their hands*—*from their hands*, precisely; not merely *in order to rescue him*. Rather, Reuben thought, 'Let him be

276. **From here...** Rabbi Yose offers a different proof-text. See *Avot de-Rabbi Natan* B, 5.

277. **world is sustained only through Torah, sustaining pillar...** The daily and nightly study of Torah (*My covenant*) sustains the world.

See BT *Pesaḥim* 68b (in the name of Rabbi El'azar); *Zohar* 2:46a, 94a, 200a; 3:11b, 73b; Moses de León, *Sefer ha-Rimmon*, 111. Cf. M *Avot* 1:2; BT *Shabbat* 88a. On the phrase "sustaining pillar," see above, note 117.

278. **Egypt... totally lacking the mystery of faith** Lacking belief in the oneness of God and therefore morally corrupt. In the *Zohar* "mystery of faith" is often a name for *Shekhinah*, culmination of the *sefirot*, which constitute the focus of faith.

See *Vayiqra Rabbah* 23:7; *Tanḥuma, Lekh Lekha* 5; *Zohar* 1:81b; 2:161a, 183b.

279. **attributed to Reuben...** The full verse reads: *Reuben said to them, "Don't spill any blood! Throw him into this pit in the wilderness, and don't lay a hand on him"—in order to rescue him from their hands, to bring him back to his father.*

280. **snakes and scorpions...** Infesting the pit. See *Bereshit Rabbah* 84:16: "*They took him and threw him into the pit, and the pit was empty, there was no water in it.* Water was not in it; snakes and scorpions were."

Cf. *Targum Yerushalmi*, Genesis 37:24; BT *Shabbat* 22a; *Tanḥuma, Vayeshev* 2.

281. **Based upon this, they have said...** The saying is cited as if from a traditional source, but it may be invented.

282. **For here** In a snake-infested pit or in a fire.

delivered from their hands, and if he dies, he will die in the pit.' So it is written: *Reuben heard, and he rescued him from their hands* (ibid., 21).

"Come and see Reuben's devotion! He knew that Simeon and Levi's collaboration and partnership were ruthless, for when they joined forces in Shechem they killed every male—and as if this were not enough, they seized the women and children, the silver and gold, all the cattle and precious vessels, and everything that could be found in the city. And as if this were not enough, they even took everything in the field, as is written: *and they took what was in the city and in the field* (ibid. 34:28).[283] So he thought, 'If a great city such as this was not safe from them, then if this boy falls into their hands, they won't leave a shred of his flesh! Better that he be rescued from them—since they won't leave a trace of him and Father will never see anything of him. Whereas here, if he dies, they will not eat him; his entire body will remain intact, and I can return him whole to Father.'[284] So, *in order to rescue him from their hands, to bring him back to his father*—even though he will die there. Because of this he said, *The boy is not* (ibid. 37:30); he did not say *is not alive*, but rather *is not*—not even dead![285]

"Come and see what he did, how wisely he joined himself with them, for it is written: *Let us not take his life* (ibid., 21), and not: *Do not take his life.*[286] He himself was not there when Joseph was sold, for all of them attended their father—each on one day—and that day was Reuben's.[287] So on that day of his, he did not want Joseph to disappear. Therefore it is written: *Reuben returned to the pit and, look, Joseph was not in the pit* (ibid., 29)—precisely: not alive and not even dead![288] Immediately, *he returned to his brothers and said, 'The boy is not!'*

283. **Simeon and Levi's collaboration . . . ruthless . . .** See the story of the rape of Dinah in Genesis 34; and above, p. 123 and n. 244.

284. **they will not eat him . . .** The snakes and scorpions will only kill him, not consume his body.

285. **So, *in order to rescue him . . . The boy is not* . . .** Reuben had advised his brothers to put Joseph in the pit so that even if the dreamer died, at least his body would remain intact and could be returned to Jacob, his grieving father. When Reuben discovered that the pit was totally empty—without even Joseph's corpse—he was shocked. The context (37:29–30) reads: *Reuben returned to the pit and, look, Joseph was not in the pit, and he tore his clothes. He returned to his brothers and said, "The boy is not! And I, where can I go?"*

286. **how wisely he joined himself with them . . .** By including himself with his brothers (*Let us . . .*), Reuben conveyed the impression that he shared their desire to eliminate Joseph—not by murdering him with their own hands but by throwing him into the pit, where snakes and scorpions would finish him off.

Cf. Naḥmanides on Genesis 37:22, 26.

287. **all of them attended their father . . .** They took turns going back home to help Jacob. See *Bereshit Rabbah* 84:15.

288. **he did not want Joseph to disappear . . .** Reuben was anxious about his brother's fate—especially on the day he was caring for their father—so he rushed back to the pit, where he found no trace of Joseph.

Even Reuben did not know that Joseph had been sold. As already established, they made *Shekhinah* their partner, so Reuben did not know of Joseph's being sold, and it remained unrevealed to him until the moment Joseph revealed himself to his brothers.[289]

"Come and see how much Reuben effectuated by striving to keep Joseph alive. What is written? *May Reuben live, and not die*... (Deuteronomy 33:6). Look, it was because of this: even though his birthright had been taken from him,[290] he endeavored to keep him alive! So Moses prayed, saying: *May Reuben live, and not die.* He was sustained in this world and sustained in the world that is coming.[291] Why? Because of this, and because he returned to God, repenting for that deed.[292] For whoever returns is sustained by the blessed Holy One in this world and in the world that is coming.

"Come and see what is written: *They took Joseph's tunic and slaughtered a goat*... (Genesis 37:31).[293] They have established that this is because a goat's blood resembles human blood.[294] But come and see that the blessed Holy One deals strictly with the righteous—although an incident may proceed fittingly, the blessed Holy One deals with them strictly even to a hairbreadth.[295]

"Jacob acted appropriately. How? By offering his father a goat, which derives from the side of harsh judgment.[296] But even so, since in offering it he deceived

289. **they made *Shekhinah* their partner...** The brothers included *Shekhinah* in the oath they swore not to reveal Joseph's true fate, so no one else (including Jacob and Reuben) knew what really happened to him. See above, p. 119 and n. 219.

290. **his birthright had been taken from him** Because Reuben slept with his father's concubine Bilhah, his birthright was taken from him and transferred to Joseph, Rachel's firstborn.

See Genesis 35:22; 1 Chronicles 5:1; above, p. 65 and n. 444.

291. ***May Reuben live, and not die...*** See *Sifrei,* Deuteronomy 347; BT *Sanhedrin* 92a; *Targum Onqelos, Targum Yerushalmi,* and Rashi on Deuteronomy 33:6.

292. **he returned to God, repenting for that deed** For the sin of sleeping with Bilhah.

See above, note 290; *Sifrei,* Deuteronomy 31; *Bereshit Rabbah* 84:19; *Pesiqta de-Rav Kahana* 24:9; *Targum Yerushalmi,* Genesis 37:29.

293. ***They took Joseph's tunic and slaughtered a goat...*** The context (37:31–32) reads: *They took Joseph's tunic and slaughtered a goat and dipped the tunic in the blood. They sent the ornamented tunic and had it brought to their father, and they said, "We found this. Recognize, please: is it your son's tunic or not?"*

294. **goat's blood resembles human blood** See *Bereshit Rabbah* 84:19; *Targum Yerushalmi,* Genesis 37:31.

295. **blessed Holy One deals strictly with the righteous...** See BT *Yevamot* 121b: "Rabbi Abba said, '... The blessed Holy One deals strictly with those around Him even to a hairbreadth.'"

See *Zohar* 1:140a; 2:247b.

296. **offering his father a goat...** When Jacob approached his father, Isaac, seeking the blessing of the firstborn, as related in Genesis 27. The goat symbolizes Isaac's *sefirah, Din* (Judgment). See *Zohar* 1:142a–b.

his father, who was of that side, he was punished by this—by another goat whose blood was brought to him by his sons.[297]

"Of him is written *The skins of the kids she put on his hands*... (ibid. 27:16).[298] Therefore, *they dipped the tunic in the blood* (ibid. 37:31)—they brought him the tunic to deceive him, all correspondingly. He caused to be written *Isaac trembled* (ibid. 27:33); therefore they caused him to tremble when it is written *Recognize, please: is it your son's tunic or not?* (ibid. 37:32)."[299] [186a]

Rabbi Ḥiyya said, "Of him is written *Are you really my son Esau or not?* (ibid. 27:21). To him, what is written? *Is it your son's tunic or not?* Thus, the blessed Holy One deals strictly with the righteous in whatever they do."[300]

Rabbi Abba said, "When all the tribes saw their father's suffering, they felt remorse—and would surely have surrendered themselves for Joseph, if only they could have found him! Once they saw that they could not, they confronted Judah and deposed him—for he had been king over them, so they deposed him. What is written? *It happened at that time that Judah went down from his brothers*... (ibid. 38:1).[301]

297. **punished by this—by another goat...** Since Jacob deceived his father by means of a goat, he was punished by his sons' similar act of deception.

See the Yemenite manuscript cited by Theodor, *Bereshit Rabbah* 84:19, p. 1024, n. 5; *Sekhel Tov*, Genesis 37:32; *Zohar* 1:144b; and below.

298. ***The skins of the kids she put on his hands...*** Jacob's mother, Rebekah, disguised him to look like his hairy brother, Esau, in order to fool old, blind Isaac. The context (27:15–16) reads: *Rebekah took the precious garments of Esau, her elder son, which were with her in the house, and clothed Jacob, her younger son. The skins of the kids she put on his hands and on the smooth part of his neck.*

299. **He caused to be written *Isaac trembled...*** Jacob caused his father Isaac to tremble upon realizing the deception, so years later the brothers caused Jacob to tremble at the thought of Joseph's death.

The first verse (27:33) reads: *Isaac trembled very violently and said, "Who was it then that hunted game and brought it to me, and I ate of it all before you came and I blessed him? Now blessed he will remain!"* For the second verse, see above, note 293.

300. ***Are you really my son Esau or not?...*** Isaac's question to Jacob, who is disguised as Esau. The verse reads: *Come near, so I can feel you, my son. Are you really my son Esau or not?* The appearance of the identical phrase *or not* in both stories in Genesis indicates that Jacob's act of deception was punished measure for measure by his sons' ploy.

301. **confronted Judah and deposed him *...Judah went down...*** The brothers rejected Judah because he had suggested selling Joseph.

See Genesis 37:26–27; *Tanḥuma* (Buber), *Vayeshev* 12; *Shemot Rabbah* 42:3; *Leqaḥ Tov* and *Sekhel Tov*, Genesis 38:1; *Zohar* 1:188b.

The context in Genesis (38:1–3) reads: *It happened at that time that Judah went down from his brothers and camped near an Adullamite man named Hirah. There Judah saw the daughter of a Canaanite man named Shua, and he took her and came to her. She conceived and bore a son, and he named him Er.*

Rabbi Yehudah opened, "*YHVH thundered in heaven, the Most High gave forth His voice—hail and coals of fire* (Psalms 18:14). Come and see: When the blessed Holy One created the world, He arranged for it seven pillars upon which to stand, and all those pillars stand upon one single pillar. This has already been established, as is written: *Wisdom has built her house, she has hewn her seven pillars* (Proverbs 9:1). All of these stand upon one rung among them called Righteous, as is written: *The righteous one is the foundation of the world* (ibid. 10:25).[302]

"When the world was created, it was from that place—foundation of the world and its perfection, single point of the world, center of all. Who is that? Zion, as is written: *A psalm of Asaph. God, Elohim YHVH, spoke and called forth the earth*... (Psalms 50:1). From which place? As is written: *From Zion, perfection of beauty* (ibid., 2)—from that aspect of consummation of complete faith, fittingly.[303] Zion, potency and point of the entire world. From that place, the whole world was founded and fashioned; from within it, the whole world is nourished.

"Come and see: *YHVH thundered in heaven, the Most High gave forth His voice.* Since it says *YHVH thundered in heaven,* why: *the Most High gave forth His voice?*[304] Look, here is a mystery of faith concerning what I said—that Zion is foundation and beauty of the world, source of her nourishment! For there are two rungs and they are one: Zion and Jerusalem—one, compassion; one, judgment; both are one. From here, judgment; from here, compassion.[305]

"From beyond, beyond, issues a voice that is heard.[306] Afterward issue judgments; paths of judgment and compassion radiate and diverge.[307] *YHVH*

302. **seven pillars... one single pillar...** The world is based on the structure of the seven lower *sefirot*, from *Ḥesed* through *Shekhinah*. Their power is concentrated in *Yesod*, the cosmic pillar, who is known as Righteous One, based on Proverbs 10:25: וצדיק יסוד עולם (*Ve-tsaddiq yesod olam*). The verse literally means *The righteous one is an everlasting foundation,* but is understood as *The righteous one is the foundation of the world.*

See BT *Ḥagigah* 12b; *Bahir* 71 (102); Azriel of Gerona, *Peirush ha-Aggadot*, 34; *Zohar* 1:82a–b; *ZḤ* 76b (*MhN, Rut*); Moses de León, *Sefer ha-Rimmon*, 199.

303. **from that place... Zion...** From *Yesod*, culmination and focal point of the *sefirot*, symbolized also by Zion, the center of the world.

See BT *Yoma* 54b; *Tanḥuma, Qedoshim* 10; *Zohar* 1:231a; 2:184b; 3:65b–66a; *ZḤ* 76a–b (*MhN, Rut*); Mopsik.

304. **why: *the Most High gave forth His voice?*** Why the apparent redundancy?

305. **Zion and Jerusalem...** *Yesod* and *Shekhinah*, the divine couple influenced respectively by *Tif'eret*, also known as *Raḥamim* (Compassion), and by *Din* (Judgment).

See *Zohar* 3:31a, 296b (*IZ*); Moses de León, *Shushan Edut*, 368.

306. **From beyond, beyond, issues a voice that is heard** From the upper reaches of the *sefirot*, themselves inaudible, emerges the audible voice of *Tif'eret*.

See *Zohar* 1:16b, 50b, 141b; Moses de León, *Shushan Edut*, 331, 370; idem, *Sheqel ha-Qodesh*, 6–7 (9), 42 (50).

307. **paths of judgment and compassion radiate...** To the left and the right sides.

thundered in heaven—compassionate house of judgment.[308] *The Most High*—although it cannot be found or known,[309] As soon as that voice issues, all is found: judgment and compassion, as is written: *The Most High gave forth His voice.* As soon as He *gave forth His voice*, immediately: *hail and coals of fire*, water and fire.[310]

"Come and see: When Judah was born, what is written? *She ceased bearing* (Genesis 29:35). For this is the fourth of those four foundations constituting the supernal chariot, one of those four supports.[311] What is written of him? *It happened at that time that Judah went down from his brothers* (ibid. 38:1), for he had reigned over them. Why? Because Joseph had been brought down to Egypt, as we have said.[312]

"*There Judah saw the daughter of a Canaanite man* (ibid., 2).[313] Now, was he really a Canaanite? Rather, as the Companions have established.[314]

308. ***YHVH* thundered in heaven—compassionate house of judgment** *Tif'eret* (named *YHVH* and symbolized by *heaven*) conveys the thunderous power of judgment softened by His compassion.

309. ***The Most High*...** *Binah*, inaudible and concealed.

310. **water and fire** Symbolizing *Ḥesed* and *Gevurah*, both included within the voice of *Tif'eret*.

311. ***She ceased bearing*... fourth of those four foundations...** Once Leah gave birth to her fourth son, Judah, she temporarily bore no more children. From a kabbalistic perspective, Leah symbolizes the divine mother, *Binah*, who is enthroned on a chariot supported by the quartet of *Ḥesed*, *Gevurah*, *Tif'eret*, and *Malkhut*. Here this quartet is symbolized by Leah's first four children: Reuben, Simeon, Levi, and Judah. (Elsewhere the four symbolic supports of the chariot-throne are the patriarchs: Abraham, Isaac, and Jacob, joined by King David, who is descended from Judah.) According to Rabbi Yehudah, Leah (symbolizing *Binah*) *ceased bearing* because with the birth of Judah, the divine mother's throne was now complete, standing firm on all four supports.

See *Bereshit Rabbah* 47:6: "Resh Lakish said, 'The patriarchs themselves constitute the [divine] Chariot.'" Cf. Azriel of Gerona, *Peirush ha-Aggadot,* 57; *Zohar* 1:60b, 99a, 150a, 173b, 248b; 2:144a; 3:38a, 99a, 146a, 182a, 262b; Moses de León, *Sefer ha-Rimmon,* 239–40. The expression *She ceased bearing* is interpreted similarly by Jacob ben Sheshet, *Ha-Emunah ve-ha-Bittaḥon,* 384, 440. See *Zohar* 1:155a.

On the fourth leg of the divine throne, see *Zohar* 1:5b, 20a, 82a, 89b (*ST*), 154b. On the relation between David and the patriarchs, see Acts 2:29; *Mekhilta, Pisḥa* 1; BT *Berakhot* 16b; *Pesaḥim* 117b; *Mo'ed Qatan* 16b; *Sanhedrin* 107a; *Midrash Tehillim* 18:8, 25; Moses de León, *Sheqel ha-Qodesh,* 45 (54); Jacob ben Sheshet, *Ha-Emunah ve-ha-Bittaḥon,* 384, 396, 440; Baḥya ben Asher on Genesis 32:10; Ginzberg, *Legends,* 6:265, n. 94. Cf. Vol. 2, p. 23, n. 164.

312. ***Judah went down*... Because Joseph had been brought down...** Judah's descent from royalty symbolizes the descent of *Malkhut* (Kingdom) once She is deprived of the nourishing flow from *Yesod*—a lack symbolized by Joseph's disappearance. See above, p. 132 and n. 301.

313. ***There Judah saw the daughter of a Canaanite man*** See the context above, note 301.

314. **was he really a Canaanite? Rather...** Would Judah have intermarried with a Canaanite? Rather, as explained by Rabbi

"*She conceived and bore a son, and he named him Er* (ibid., 3). Judah had three sons, only one of whom survived, namely, Shelah."[315]

Rabbi El'azar, Rabbi Yose, and Rabbi Ḥiyya were walking on the way. Rabbi Yose said to Rabbi El'azar, "Why is it written of Judah's sons, of the first one: *He named him Er* (Genesis 38:3), and of the other two: *She named him Onan, she named him Shelah* (ibid., 4–5)?"[316]

He replied, "Come and see: This portion is a mystery, and all is fitting. *Judah went down from his brothers* (ibid., 1), for the moon was concealed and descended from a perfect rung to another rung, conjoined by a serpent,[317] as is said: *and he camped near an Adullamite man.... She conceived and bore a son, and he named him* ער (*er*), *Er* (ibid., 1, 3)—which is רע (*ra*), evil, and all is one, for he came from the side of evil impulse.[318] Therefore it is written ויקרא את שמו (*va-yiqra et shemo*), *He named him*—not ויקרא שמו (*va-yiqra shemo*), but ויקרא את שמו (*va-yiqra et shemo*).[319] [186b] Of Jacob is written ויקרא שמו יעקב (*va-yiqra shemo ya'aqov*), *He named him Jacob* (ibid. 25:26), since the blessed Holy One named him Jacob.[320] Here, encompassing another rung, for he was born in filth of defilement, and this is ער (*er*), *Er*; רע (*ra*), evil; all is one.[321]

Shim'on son of Lakish (BT *Pesaḥim* 50a), *Canaanite* here means "merchant."

See Genesis 24:3; 28:1; *Targum Onqelos, Targum Yerushalmi*, Rashi, Ibn Ezra, and Naḥmanides on Genesis 38:2; *Bereshit Rabbah* 85:4. Cf. Hosea 12:8; Proverbs 31:24.

315. **three sons, only one of whom survived...** See the following verses in Genesis 38:4–11. To Rabbi Yehudah, this tragedy indicates Judah's decline.

316. **Why is it written...** ***He named him*** **...** ***She named him...*** Why the change from *he* (referring to Judah, the father) to *she* (referring to Shua's daughter, the mother)?

317. **moon was concealed... conjoined by a serpent** Judah's descent symbolizes the concealment of *Shekhinah*, the moon, whose diminished state makes Her vulnerable to the demonic serpent. See above, note 312.

318. **ער (*er*), *Er*—which is רע (*ra*), evil...** The reverse spelling of ער (*er*)—the name of Judah's firstborn son—is רע (*ra*), "evil," which indicates Er's derivation from the demonic realm, source of the evil impulse.

See *Kallah Rabbati* 2:7; *Leqaḥ Tov*, Genesis 38:7; *Zohar* 1:58b.

319. **not ויקרא שמו (*va-yiqra shemo*), but ויקרא את שמו (*va-yiqra et shemo*)** Rabbi El'azar emphasizes the tiny word את (*et*), which is technically an accusative particle with no ascertainable independent meaning. In early rabbinic times, Naḥum of Gimzo and his disciple Rabbi Akiva taught that the presence of *et* in a biblical verse amplifies the apparent meaning.

See BT *Pesaḥim* 22b; *Ḥagigah* 12a; *Zohar* 1:247a; 2:90a, 135b. In the *Zohar* (see above, note 217), the word את (*et*) often symbolizes *Shekhinah*.

320. **Of Jacob is written...** The subject *He* refers to the blessed Holy One, namely *Tif'eret*. No further amplification of meaning is intended, so the word את (*et*) does not appear.

See *Bereshit Rabbah* 63:8; *Tanḥuma, Shemot* 4; *Leqaḥ Tov* and *Midrash Aggadah*, Genesis 25:26; Rashi on this verse; *Zohar* 1:60a, 138a, 234b; Vol. 1, p. 344, n. 36.

321. **Here, encompassing another rung...**

Afterward, the site was not sweetened until Shelah appeared, essence of them all.[322] What is written? ער (*Er*), *Er, Judah's firstborn, was* רע (*ra*), *evil* (ibid. 38:7).[323] Here is written *ra*, evil, and there is written *For the devisings of the human heart are* רע (*ra*), *evil, from youth* (ibid. 8:21). *Ra*, evil, for he spilled blood, spilled seed upon the earth. Therefore, *YHVH put him to death* (ibid. 38:7).[324] What is written next? *Judah said to Onan, 'Come in to your brother's wife and fulfill your duty as brother-in-law to her...'* (ibid., 8)."[325]

Judah said... (Genesis 38:8).[326]

Rabbi Shim'on opened, "*I roused one from the north, and he comes...* (Isaiah 41:25).[327] Come and see how foolish people are! For they neither know nor reflect upon the ways of the blessed Holy One! They are all asleep, unawakened, slumber in their sockets.

This verse includes the word את (*et*): ויקרא את שמו ער (*va-yiqra et shemo er*), *He named him Er.* That tiny, potent word amplifies the subject *He* to include another rung: the impure realm of the demonic, from where Er sprang and by whom he was named.

On the identical letters of ער (*er*), *Er*, and רע (*ra*), evil, see above, note 318.

322. **until Shelah appeared...** Judah's second son, Onan, also sinned (see Genesis 38:8–10, and below, note 324). Finally the virtuous Shelah was born, banishing the demonic powers and restoring purity.

323. **ער (*Er*), *Er, Judah's firstborn, was* רע (*ra*), *evil*** The full verse reads: ער (*Er*), *Er, Judah's firstborn, was* רע (*ra*), *evil, in the eyes of YHVH, and YHVH put him to death.*

324. **Here is written *ra*, evil...for he spilled blood, spilled seed...** The word *ra* (evil) implies the evil impulse, referred to earlier in Genesis in the aftermath of the Flood (8:21). According to rabbinic tradition, the generation of the Flood indulged in spilling semen (masturbation), a sin tantamount to murder since it wastes potential life. Although Genesis does not specify the nature of Er's sin, tradition maintains that it was identical with that of his younger brother, Onan, who *wasted* [his seed] *on the ground* (Genesis 38:9).

See BT *Niddah* 13a: "Rabbi Yitsḥak and Rabbi Ammi said, '[Whoever emits semen fruitlessly] is as though he sheds blood.'" Cf. *Zohar* 1:56b–57a, 188a, 219b; Moses de León, *Shushan Edut,* 353; Tishby, *Wisdom of the Zohar,* 3:1365–66.

On the sexual sin of the generation of the Flood, see *Kallah Rabbati* 2; *Pirqei de-Rabbi Eli'ezer* 22; *Bereshit Rabbah* 26:4; Rashi on BT *Shabbat* 41a, s.v. *ke-illu mevi mabbul la-olam; Zohar* 1:62a, 69a. On the nature of Er's sin, see *Bereshit Rabbah* 85:4 (and Theodor, ad loc.); BT *Yevamot* 34b; *Targum Yerushalmi,* Genesis 38:7; Moses de León, *Sefer ha-Rimmon,* 230.

325. ***Judah said to Onan...*** The full verse reads: *Judah said to Onan, "Come in to your brother's wife and fulfill your duty as brother-in-law to her and raise up seed for your brother."* Onan is commanded to marry his deceased brother's widow and consummate their new union, thereby maintaining his brother's line. This custom of levirate marriage is legally codified in Deuteronomy 25:5–6. In Kabbalah it is understood in terms of reincarnation, as in the following passage.

326. ***Judah said...*** The full verse is cited in the preceding note.

327. ***I roused one from the north...*** The full verse reads: *I roused one from the north, and he comes; from the rising of the sun, one who invokes My name. He comes upon rulers like mortar, as a potter treading clay.*

"Come and see: The blessed Holy One formed the human being corresponding to the pattern above, all according to wisdom, for you cannot find a single human limb not founded upon supernal wisdom.[328] Look! When the whole body is arrayed in its limbs fittingly, the blessed Holy One joins with it, inserting a holy soul—to teach the human how to walk in ways of Torah and observe His commandments, so that he will perfect himself.

"As long as the holy soul is within him, a person should expand the image of the supernal King in the world.[329] This mystery is that the flowing, gushing river never ceases; therefore, a human should never cease his river and source in this world, so that he grasp it in the world that is coming.[330] Whenever a person is unsuccessful in this world, the blessed Holy One uproots him and replants him several times as before.[331]

"Come and see what is written: *I roused one from the north.* This is arousal of human coupling in this world, an arousal from the side of the north.[332]

"*And he comes*—a holy soul coming from above. *And he comes*—coming into this world and entering human beings, as we have said.

328. **corresponding to the pattern above...** Modeled on the divine archetype, the ten *sefirot*, which are imagined and depicted in the form of a divine body.

See Genesis 1:26–27; Moses de León, *Sefer ha-Rimmon,* 268. Cf. *Zohar* 1:134b; and Vol. 2, p. 258, n. 7.

329. **expand the image of the supernal King...** By engendering new life in the world, a human being expands the divine image in which he is created. The expression "expand the image" derives from rabbinic usage. See *Bereshit Rabbah* 34:14: "Ben Azzai expounded: 'Whoever abstains from procreation is as though he spilled blood and diminished the [divine] image.'"

See *Tosefta, Yevamot* 8:7; BT *Yevamot* 63b; *Mekhilta, Baḥodesh* 8; *Bereshit Rabbah* 17:2; *Devarim Rabbah* 12; *Zohar* 3:7a; Moses de León, *Sefer ha-Mishqal,* 140; David ben Judah he-Ḥasid, *The Book of Mirrors,* 28, and intro, p. 34, n. 238; Heschel, *Torah min ha-Shamayim,* 1:220–23.

330. **flowing, gushing river never ceases...** Just as the river of *Yesod*, the divine phallus, flows continually, so a man should not abstain from procreation. If he follows the sefirotic model in this world, he will grasp *Yesod* in the world that is coming.

The phrase "flowing, gushing river" derives from Daniel 7:10. See above, note 49; *Zohar* 1:12b–13a; Moses de León, *Shushan Edut,* 353–54; idem, *Sefer ha-Rimmon,* 243; idem, *Sefer ha-Mishqal,* 137.

331. **blessed Holy One uproots him and replants him...** Through a process of reincarnation, so that he can try again to engender new life.

On reincarnation in Kabbalah, see the parable in *Bahir* 135 (195) and in *ZḤ* 89b (*MhN, Rut*); *Zohar* 1:131a; 2:94b–114a passim; 3:7a; *ZḤ* 59a–c; Scholem, *Major Trends,* 242–43; idem, *Kabbalah,* 344–50.

This passage (until page 145) exhibits numerous parallels with Moses de León's Hebrew writings. See *Shushan Edut,* 353–60; *Sefer ha-Rimmon,* 240–52; *Sefer ha-Mishqal,* 136–45; and *She'elot u-Tshuvot,* 58–60.

332. ***from the north*... arousal of human coupling...** Human desire and passion stem from *Gevurah*, located on the left side of the sefirotic tree and associated with the direction north. See *Zohar* 1:133a.

"*From the rising of the sun* (ibid.)—site of the flowing, gushing river, whence the soul issues, flooded with light.[333]

"*Officials come like matter* (ibid.)—forces of the world, coming because of the arousal of souls, as a human is bodily aroused.[334]

"This is why the blessed Holy One creates coupling, casting souls into the world, so companionship prevails above and below, and the source of all is blessed.[335] This is why the blessed Holy One made the human being: to strive in His ways, to never cease his source and spring.[336] If he ceases this, when he departs this world, that person does not enter the curtain nor obtain his share in that world.[337] [187a]

"Come and see: *He did not create it a waste, He formed it for habitation* (ibid. 45:18). This is why the blessed Holy One made the human being, as we have said, and the blessed Holy One deals kindly with the world.[338]

333. ***rising of the sun*** **... flowing, gushing river...** *Yesod*, whose river of emanation conveys souls to the world.

The intermingling of water and light imageries includes a double appearance of the root נהר (*nhr*): first as נהר (*nehar*), "river," then as אתנהירת (*itnehirat*), "is illumined," rendered above as "flooded with light."

334. ***Officials come like matter*****—forces of the world...** Angels, the cosmic forces, prepare to accompany the emerging souls. See *Zohar* 1:12b–13a.

The verse in Isaiah reads literally: *He comes upon rulers like mortar* (see above, note 327), but Rabbi Shim'on turns the object (*rulers*) into the subject (*officials*), and understands the word חומר (*ḥomer*), *mortar*, according to its medieval philosophical sense: matter. Now the verse means *Officials come like matter*, i.e., Angels respond to the stirring of souls as humans are stimulated physically.

335. **companionship prevails above and below...** Masculine and feminine souls join on earth, regaining their original androgynous unity and harmonizing with the male and female powers above. By uniting on earth, the souls stimulate the union of *Yesod* and *Shekhinah*, which generates a new influx of souls. See *Zohar* 1:85b.

336. **never cease his source and spring** One should not abstain from sexual union, thereby ensuring that *Yesod* will generate new souls ceaselessly.

337. **that person does not enter the curtain...** He is not admitted into the inner realms of heaven. Cf. BT *Bava Batra* 116a: "Rabbi Yoḥanan said in the name of Rabbi Shim'on son of Yoḥai, 'Whoever does not leave a son to succeed him incurs the full wrath of the blessed Holy One.'"

See *Zohar* 1:13a, 48a, 66a, 90a, 115a, 228b; *ZḤ* 89b–c (*MhN, Rut*); Scholem, "Le-Ḥeqer Torat ha-Gilgul," 146–47.

The printed editions (186b–187a) and *OY* include here an Aramaic paraphrase of a passage in Moses de León's *Sefer ha-Mishqal*, 137–38. This material does not appear in the manuscripts. See *DE*; Galante; Scholem; above, note 331.

338. **blessed Holy One deals kindly with the world** If someone fails to engender new life on earth, God does not condemn him to eternal punishment, but rather reincarnates his soul, providing him another opportunity to perform this essential *mitsvah* and fulfill his destiny.

See Moses de León, *Sefer ha-Rimmon*, 244–45; idem, *Sefer ha-Mishqal*, 144.

"Come and see what is written: *Once again Abraham took a wife, and her name was Keturah* (Genesis 25:1)—mystery of a soul coming to be perfected as before.[339]

"Come and see what is written of that body:[340] *YHVH delights* דכאו (*dakke'o*), *in crushing him*... (Isaiah 53:10).[341] This verse calls for contemplation. Why *delights*? So that יתדכי (*yitdakkei*), he will be purified.[342]

"*If* תשים (*tasim*), *you make,* [*his soul*] *a guilt offering* (ibid.). The verse should read: *If* ישים (*yasim*), *he makes.* Why *if tasim, you make*?[343] Because the word pertains to the soul: if that soul desires to fully perfect herself, *he will see seed*—for that soul goes wandering, and she is destined to enter the seed that a man engages in, being fruitful and multiplying. Then, *he will prolong his days* (ibid.).[344]

"*And the delight of YHVH will prosper in his hand* (ibid.)—this is Torah.[345]

"Come and see: Even though a person engages in Torah day and night, if his source and spring abides in him in vain, he has no point of entry through the curtain, as has been said.[346] A well of water, if not fed by a certain source and

339. ***Abraham took a wife*... mystery of a soul...** Abraham symbolizes the soul who is reincarnated (*once again*) in a new body (*a wife*... *Keturah*). Cf. *Zohar* 1:130a (*MhN*).

340. **that body** That failed to engender new life.

341. ***YHVH delights* דכאו (*dakke'o*), *in crushing him*...** The full verse reads: *YHVH delights in crushing him by disease. If you make his soul a guilt offering, he will see seed and prolong his days, and the delight of YHVH will prosper in his hand.*

See Moses de León, *Shushan Edut,* 358–59.

342. **Why *delights*? So that יתדכי (*yitdakkei*), he will be purified** Rabbi Shim'on transforms the meaning of the verse by reinterpreting the Hebrew word דכאו (*dakke'o*), *in crushing him,* according to the similar-sounding Aramaic word יתדכי (*yitdakkei*), "he will be purified." God delights in purifying a person who has failed to be fruitful, so He crushes him with disease, removes him from the world, and reincarnates his soul.

See above, note 338; and page 97.

343. **The verse should read...** The person should be referred to as in the rest of the verse, in the third person: ישים (*yasim*), *he makes*—not in the second person: תשים (*tasim*), *you make.*

344. **word pertains to the soul... goes wandering...** The form תשים (*tasim*) means here not *you make* but *she makes,* referring to the soul who takes upon herself the guilt of not having engendered new life in the world. In order to perfect herself, she wanders in search of a human couple engaged in the *mitsvah* of procreation, so that she can enter human seed and be reincarnated. In her new body, she will have another chance to be fruitful and multiply, expanding the divine image.

345. ***delight of YHVH*... this is Torah** The newly reincarnated soul will delve deeply into Torah. Cf. above, page 128.

346. **if his source and spring abides in him in vain...** If he fails to fulfill the command of procreation on earth, he will not be admitted upon death to the innermost realms. See above, page 138.

spring, is no well, since well and source are as one, a single mystery, as we have established.[347]

"It is written: *In vain you rise early...* (Psalms 127:2).[348] Come and see how precious are the words of Torah, for every single word contains supernal, holy mysteries.[349] As has been said, when the blessed Holy One gave the Torah to Israel, He placed within it all the supernal, holy treasures—all within Torah, all transmitted to Israel when they received the Torah on Mount Sinai.

"Come and see: *In vain you rise early*—those who are single, not fittingly male and female;[350] they hasten in the morning to their work, as is written: *There is one and not a second... there is no end to all his toil* (Ecclesiastes 4:8).[351]

"מאחרי שבת (*Me'aḥarei shevet*), *sit up late* (Psalms, ibid.)[352]—postponing rest, as is said: *for on it* שבת (*shavat*), *He rested* (Genesis 2:3), because for a man, a woman constitutes true repose.[353]

"*Eating the bread of sorrow* (Psalms, ibid.). What is *the bread of sorrow*? When a person has children, the bread that he eats, he eats in joy and in heart's delight. Whereas one who has no children, the bread he eats is bread of sorrow. These are ones *eating the bread of sorrow*—precisely!

"*For surely to His beloved He grants sleep* (Psalms, ibid.). What does this mean: *to His beloved He grants*? To one whose source is blessed,[354] the blessed Holy One grants sleep in that world, as is said: *You will lie down and your sleep*

347. **well of water, if not fed...** The well of *Shekhinah* must be fed by the spring of *Yesod*. One who unites with his spouse stimulates the union of the divine couple, thereby ensuring the continued flow of emanation and souls as well as earning his own eventual entry through the curtain. See *Zohar* 1:141b.

348. ***In vain you rise early...*** The full verse reads: *In vain you rise early and sit up late, eating the bread of sorrow; for surely upon His beloved He bestows sleep.*

349. **every single word contains supernal, holy mysteries** A fundamental principle of the *Zohar*, here introducing a radical interpretation of the verse from Psalms.

See 1:54a, 135a, 145b, 163a; 2:12a, 55b–56a, 59b, 65b, 98b–99b; 3:79b, 149a, 152a, 174b, 265a; *ZḤ* 6d (*MhN*). Cf. *Sifrei*, Deuteronomy 336; *Midrash Tanna'im*, Deuteronomy 32:47; BT *Menaḥot* 29b; Maimonides, *Guide of the Perplexed* 3:50.

350. **single, not fittingly male and female** Unmarried and thus failing to imitate the divine couple. See above, note 160.

351. ***There is one and not a second...*** The verse reads: *There is one and not a second; he has neither son nor brother. There is no end to all his toil; his eye is not sated with riches. "For whom am I toiling and depriving myself of bliss?"*

352. **מאחרי שבת (*Me'aḥarei shevet*), *sit up late*** See the full verse, above, note 348.

353. ***for on it* שבת (*shavat*), *He rested...*** The full verse reads: *God blessed the seventh day and hallowed it, for on it He rested from all His work that by creating, God had made.* Rabbi Shim'on cites the clause *for on it* שבת (*shavat*), *He rested*, to justify his reading of the word שבת (*shevet*) in the verse from Psalms, which he takes to mean "rest." Those who postpone marrying fail to find true rest.

354. **one whose source is blessed** One who has engendered new life.

will be sweet (Proverbs 3:24). For he has a share in that world that is coming, for this person lies down and delights in the world that is coming, fittingly.

"*There is one and not a second; he has neither son nor brother*... (Ecclesiastes, ibid.).[355] *There is one*—a man who is single in the world; not single fittingly but rather, uncoupled.[356]

"*And not a second*—for he has no support.[357]

"*Neither son*—having not left one to establish his name in Israel.

"*Nor brother*—to bring him to perfection.[358]

"*There is no end to all his toil* (ibid.)—for he toils constantly, anticipating day and night.

"*His eye is never sated with riches* (ibid.), and he does not have the sense to consider and ask, '*For whom am I toiling and depriving my soul* [187b] *of bliss?*' You may say, so that he can eat and drink more and prepare banquets every day. Not so! For the soul does not enjoy this; rather, he is surely depriving his soul of the blissful radiance of the world that is coming, since this soul is defective, not completed fittingly.[359]

"Come and see how the blessed Holy One cares for His creatures! For He wants a person to perfect himself and not be eliminated from that world that is coming, as we have said."[360]

Rabbi Ḥiyya asked, "What about someone who is completely virtuous—who engages in Torah day and night, and all of whose actions are devoted to the name of the blessed Holy One—yet he never attained children in this world, either because he endeavored and failed or because he had some and they died? What is his status in the world that is coming?"

355. *There is one and not a second*... For the full verse, see above, note 351.

356. **not single fittingly but rather, uncoupled** Not outstanding and singular in his reputation (or, not temporarily alone for contemplation or study), but rather, unmarried.

357. **he has no support** No mate. See Genesis 2:18: *It is not good for the human to be alone. I will make him a fitting helper.* See *Targum Onqelos*, ad loc.; *Zohar* 1:34b; 3:44b.

358. *Nor brother*—**to bring him to perfection** If he had married and then died without children, his brother could have married his widow and engendered new life with her, thereby ensuring that the soul of the deceased brother would reincarnate in the new embryo.

As mentioned above (note 325), the biblical command of levirate marriage is understood in Kabbalah in terms of reincarnation. See Deuteronomy 25:5–6; Genesis 38:8 and Naḥmanides, ad loc.; above, note 331; Tishby, *Wisdom of the Zohar*, 3:1362–63. Genesis 38 provides the background for Rabbi Shim'on's exposition; see above, page 136.

359. **defective, not completed fittingly** Unmarried and therefore depriving himself of bliss both here and in the afterlife.

360. **blessed Holy One cares for His creatures...** And therefore provides reincarnation as an opportunity to mend oneself.

Rabbi Yose replied, "His deeds and that Torah shield him in that world."[361]

Rabbi Yitsḥak said, "Concerning those truly virtuous ones—such as Rabbi Yoḥanan who had children who died, or Rabbi Ḥizkiyah who was impotent[362]—of them is written *Thus says YHVH: As for the eunuchs*... What is written next? *I will give them, in My house and within My walls, a monument and a name better than sons and daughters*... (Isaiah 56:4–5).[363] For these have a share in the world that is coming."

Rabbi Yose said, "That is correct and fine!

"Come and see: A completely virtuous person, embracing all of these, fittingly consummate, yet who dies childless—seeing that he inherits his place in that world, does his wife have to marry his brother or not? Now, if you say that she has to, it is void of meaning, for he has already inherited his site in that world.[364] But indeed, she does have to, really! Because we do not know whether he acted perfectly or not.[365] And the fact that she marries his brother is not void, since the blessed Holy One has a certain place—for look, there was a man in the world who died childless and had no redeemer in the world. Once this completely virtuous one dies and his wife marries his brother, since he has already inherited his place, [the other one] can come and be perfected here. In the meantime, the blessed Holy One prepares a place in the world until this completely virtuous one dies."[366]

361. **His deeds and that Torah shield him...** Protecting him from hostile powers who try to block the soul's ascent. See above, note 264.

362. **such as Rabbi Yoḥanan... or Rabbi Ḥizkiyah...** See BT *Berakhot* 5a–b; *ZḤ* 89c (*MhN, Rut*); Moses de León, *Sefer ha-Rimmon*, 250–51; idem, *Sefer ha-Mishqal*, 141–42; Scholem.

363. ***As for the eunuchs...*** The two verses read: *Thus says YHVH: As for the eunuchs who keep My Sabbaths, who have chosen what I desire and grasp My covenant —I will give them, in My house and within My walls, a monument and a name better than sons and daughters. An everlasting name I will give them, that will not be cut off.*

364. **does his wife have to marry his brother or not?...** Being virtuous, he will inherit his place in heaven, so why should his wife have to marry his brother? How will this help him?

On levirate marriage, see above, notes 325, 358. See Moses de León, *Sefer ha-Rimmon*, 251–52; idem, *Sefer ha-Mishqal*, 142–44.

365. **whether he acted perfectly or not** Whether his apparent virtue on earth was genuine and sincere. If it was not, his soul may need reincarnation, so the levirate marriage is essential. If his life was truly virtuous, the levirate act is still purposeful, as immediately explained.

366. **man in the world who died childless and had no redeemer...** A certain unremarkable, childless man died, and no one came forward to redeem his soul by marrying his widow (see above, note 358). Now that this completely virtuous man has died and his soul abides in heaven, the other man's soul can find her redemption by reincarnating in the embryo formed from the union of the virtuous man's widow and his brother. After birth and maturation, the newly reincarnated soul will have another opportunity to engender new life and thereby perfect herself. From the time that

He opened, saying, "*For he must remain in his city of refuge until the death of the high priest*... (Numbers 35:28).[367] This accords with what we have learned: Children are destined for the righteous in their death. In their lifetime, they did not attain; in death, they attained.[368] Thus, all actions of the blessed Holy One are entirely true and just; He is compassionate to all.[369]

"*Two are better than one, for they have a good reward for their labor* (Ecclesiastes 4:9)—those engaged in engendering children in this world, since for the sake of the children they leave after them, they receive a good reward in that world. For their sake, their parents inherit a share in that world, as has been established.[370]

"Come and see: The blessed Holy One plants trees in this world. If they prosper, fine; if they do not prosper, He uproots them and replants them once again. If they prosper, fine; if not, He uproots them and replants them even many times. Thus, all the ways of the blessed Holy One are directed entirely to the good, to perfecting the world.[371]

"*Come in to your brother's wife and fulfill your duty as brother-in-law to her* (Genesis 38:8).[372] For look, Judah and all the other tribes already knew

the first childless man dies until the death of the virtuous man, God preserves the unredeemed soul in a refuge, where she awaits her deliverance. See immediately below, and *Zohar* 2:100a, 106a.

367. ***For he must remain in his city of refuge***... The verse continues: *after the death of the high priest, the slayer may return to the land of his holding.*

In the biblical context, if a man has killed another involuntarily, he can seek asylum in a city of refuge, where he will be safe from the victim's vengeful relatives and where he must remain until the death of the high priest. For Rabbi Yose, the first childless man is a *slayer* because he failed to engender new life. See *Bereshit Rabbah* 34:14: "Ben Azzai expounded: 'Whoever abstains from procreation is as though he spilled blood and diminished the [divine] image.'" (See above, note 329.) The slayer's soul requires asylum in order to escape harsh powers of judgment seeking to punish sin, to avenge the "death" of the man's potential children. The high priest symbolizes the completely virtuous man, upon whose death the soul of the slayer may be redeemed through the process described in the preceding note.

368. **Children are destined for the righteous in their death**... As here, the completely virtuous man finally attains a child—the reincarnated soul of the first childless man, born to the virtuous man's widow and his brother, and considered as his own child.

See above, note 366; Moses de León, *Sefer ha-Rimmon*, 252; idem, *Sefer ha-Mishqal*, 144.

369. **compassionate to all** Enabling those who have died childless to be reincarnated in order to have a second opportunity to engender new life.

370. **for the sake of the children they leave after them**... On the theme of children benefiting their parents in the afterlife, see *Kallah Rabbati* 2. Cf. *ZḤ* 89c (*MhN*, *Rut*).

371. **blessed Holy One plants trees in this world**... If a soul does not prosper, she can be replanted in a new body to attain fulfillment.

The parable derives from *Bahir* 135 (195). See above, note 331.

372. ***Come in to your brother's wife***...

this![373] The essence of the word is: *raise up seed for your brother* (ibid.), because that seed must mend the matter and mold an embryo for restoration, so that the stock not be separated from its root, fittingly.[374] When they are later fittingly mended, they are praised in that world, since the blessed Holy One delights in them.[375] Therefore it is written: *I praise the dead, who have already died—who have already died*, precisely!—*more than the living, who are* עדנה (*adenah*), *still, alive* (Ecclesiastes 4:2).[376] What is *adenah*? As is said: *After I have withered, am I to have* עדנה (*ednah*), *rejuvenation?* (Genesis 18:12).[377] And similarly: *He will return to the days of his youth* (Job 33:25).[378]

"*But better than both is one who has not yet been, who has not seen the evil*

The full verse reads: *Judah said to Onan, "Come in to your brother's wife and fulfill your duty as brother-in-law to her and raise up seed for your brother."* Since Er, Judah's firstborn son, died childless, Judah commands Er's brother, Onan, to marry Er's widow and maintain the line of his deceased brother.

373. **Judah and all the other tribes already knew this** They knew the secret significance of levirate marriage: how it enables the soul of the deceased brother to be reincarnated.

See above, notes 325, 358; Naḥmanides on Genesis 38:8; Abulafia, *Otsar ha-Kavod*, 25a; Moses de León, *Shushan Edut*, 355; idem, *Sefer ha-Rimmon*, 246.

374. **seed must mend the matter and mold an embryo...** The seed implanted in the womb by the brother of the deceased must heal the damaged, childless soul by generating for her a new embryo and another opportunity to engender life in this world. Once the reincarnated soul has fulfilled her mission of "expanding the image," she can return to her divine root. See above, note 329.

375. **When they are later fittingly mended...** Having succeeded in generating children.

376. ***I praise the dead, who have already died...*** The context (Ecclesiastes 4:2–3) reads: *I praise the dead, who have already died, more than the living, who are still alive. But better than both is one who has not yet been, who has not seen the evil deeds that are being done under the sun.*

For Rabbi Yose, the phrase *the dead, who have already died* refers "precisely" to those who died in a previous lifetime and were then reincarnated and enabled to fulfill their souls before dying again.

See *Zohar* 3:182b; Moses de León, *Sefer ha-Mishqal*, 144–45. For various readings of Rabbi Yose's explication, see *OY*; Galante; *KP*; *MM*; Mopsik; *MmD*.

377. **עדנה (*adenah*), *still*... עדנה (*ednah*), *rejuvenation*** The word עדנה (*adenah*), *still*, is equated with its homograph: (*ednah*), *delight*, or according to a rabbinic interpretation, *rejuvenation*. The verse from Genesis records Sarah's reaction to the divine prediction that she will bear a son at age ninety: *After I have withered, am I to have* ednah, *delight—with my husband so old?*

Rabbi Yose's point is that *the dead, who have already died*—and been reincarnated and attained fulfillment—are more praiseworthy than *the living, who are still alive*. This latter category refers apparently to those who have been reincarnated and rejuvenated but have not yet engendered new life.

See BT *Bava Metsi'a* 87a, which turns Sarah's rhetorical question into a declarative statement: "*After I have withered, I have had* ednah! Rav Ḥisda said, 'After the flesh had withered and wrinkles multiplied, the flesh נתעדן (*nitadden*), "rejuvenated, became tender," the wrinkles were smoothed out, and beauty returned to its site.'"

378. ***He will return to the days of his youth*** The soul will be reborn and begin a new life. See *Zohar* 2:101a.

deeds that are being done under the sun (Ecclesiastes 4:3). *But better than both is one who has not yet been*—who has not returned to the days of his youth and does not need to be mended and is not burdened by former sins;[379] for the blessed Holy One [188a] grants him a place in that world fittingly arrayed.

"Come and see what is written: *So I saw the wicked buried and coming, going from the holy site*... (Ecclesiastes 8:10).[380] *So I saw the wicked buried* [*and coming*], as has been said, for the blessed Holy One acts kindly and does not want the world to be destroyed, but rather, as has been said.[381] All His ways are entirely true and just. Happy is the share of the righteous, who walk in the path of truth in this world, benefiting in the world that is coming! Of them is written *The righteous will inherit the land* (Psalms 37:29)."[382]

What he did was evil in the eyes of YHVH... (Genesis 38:10).[383]

Rabbi Ḥiyya opened, "*In the morning sow your seed*... (Ecclesiastes 11:6).[384] Come and see how greatly a person should beware his sins and be heedful in his actions before the blessed Holy One! For numerous messengers and officials populate the world, roaming around, observing human actions and testifying about them, all recorded in a book.[385]

379. **who has not returned to the days of his youth...** Who succeeded in having children and thus did not have to undergo reincarnation, which would involve requital of sins from a previous lifetime.

380. ***So I saw the wicked buried and coming...*** The full verse reads: *So I saw the wicked buried and coming, going from the holy site, while those who had acted righteously were forgotten in the city.*

381. ***So I saw the wicked buried* [*and coming*], as has been said...** Those who have sinned and been buried are enabled to come again through the divine gift of reincarnation. By taking this second opportunity to mend their ways, they ensure that God will not condemn them or condemn the world because of them.

On this verse, see *Zohar* 1:130a (*MhN*); 3:216a (*RM*); *ZḤ* 59a–b; *TZ* 69, 99b–100a, 111a; Moses de León, *Shushan Edut*, 358; idem, *Sefer ha-Rimmon*, 246 (and Wolfson's note).

382. ***The righteous will inherit the land*** Their souls will return to the source, *Shekhinah*.

See M *Sanhedrin* 10:1: "All of Israel have a share in the world that is coming, as is said: *Your people, all of them righteous, will inherit the land forever—sprout of My planting, work of My hands, that I may be glorified* (Isaiah 60:21)." See *Zohar* 1:93a, 153b, 227a, 245b.

383. ***What he did was evil in the eyes of* YHVH...** The full verse reads: *What he did was evil in the eyes of* YHVH, *and He put him to death as well.* When Er, Judah's firstborn son, died childless, Judah commanded Er's brother, Onan to marry Er's widow and maintain the line of his deceased brother. See Genesis 38:8; above, page 136. Onan, however, failed to consummate the marriage and *wasted* [his seed] *on the ground* (Genesis 38:9), incurring divine punishment.

384. ***In the morning sow your seed...*** The full verse reads: *In the morning sow your seed, and at evening do not hold back your hand; for you do not know which will prosper, this or that, or whether both are equally good.*

385. **messengers... roaming around...** Angels who witness everything done by humans.

See M *Avot* 2:1: "Rabbi [Judah the Prince] says, '...Contemplate three things and you

"Come and see: Of all the sins by which a person is defiled in this world, this is the sin by which he is defiled both in this world and the world that is coming: spilling one's seed fruitlessly—emitting seed in vain by hand or foot, and becoming defiled, as is written: *For You are not a God who delights in wickedness; evil cannot abide with You* (Psalms 5:5).[386] He does not enter the curtain nor gaze upon the Countenance of Days, as we have learned, for it is written: *Evil cannot abide with You*, and similarly: *Er, Judah's firstborn, was evil* (Genesis 38:7).[387] Therefore, *Your hands are full of blood* (Isaiah 1:15).[388] Happy is the share of a person in awe of his Lord, guarded from the evil path, purifying himself to persevere in the awe of his Lord!

"Come and see: *In the morning sow your seed.* This verse has been established: *in the morning*—when a man is in his prime, in his youth; then he should strive to engender children, as is written: *sow your seed.*[389] Then is the time, as is

will not come into the grip of sin: Know what is above you: an eye that sees, an ear that hears, and all your actions recorded in a book.'"

386. **spilling one's seed fruitlessly...** In the world of the *Zohar,* masturbation is a heinous sin. See above, note 324; 1:56b–57a, 62a, 219b; Moses de León, *Shushan Edut,* 353; Tishby, *Wisdom of the Zohar,* 3:1365–66.

Cf. BT *Niddah* 13a: "Rabbi Yoḥanan said, 'Whoever emits semen fruitlessly deserves death, as is written: *What he did was evil in the eyes of YHVH, and He put him to death as well* (Genesis 38:10).' Rabbi Yitsḥak and Rabbi Ammi said, 'It is as though he sheds blood....' Rav Assi said, 'It is as though he worships idols.'"

On emitting seed by foot, see BT *Niddah* 13b.

387. **He does not enter the curtain...** He is not admitted into the inner realms of heaven. See above, pages 138–39; *Zohar* 1:57a, 69a; 3:90a, 158a; Moses de León, *Sefer ha-Mishqal,* 75–76.

See BT *Niddah* 13b: "Rabbi Ammi said, 'Whoever brings himself into the grip of lustful fantasy is barred from the domain of the blessed Holy One. Here is written [*What he did*] *was evil in the eyes of YHVH* (Genesis 38:10), and there is written *You are not a God who delights in wickedness; evil cannot abide with You* (Psalms 5:5).'"

In the Talmud, Rabbi Ammi bases his teaching on an analogy between the word *evil* in Genesis 38:10 (referring to Onan's sin of wasting seed) and the same word in Psalms 5. Here in the *Zohar,* Rabbi Ḥiyya offers a similar analogy between the word *evil* in Genesis 38:7 (describing Er) and Psalms 5. On Er's sexual sin, see above, note 324.

The expression "Countenance of Days" refers to the face of God, Ancient of Days, a title deriving from Daniel 7:9: *As I watched, thrones were placed, and the Ancient of Days sat—His garment like white snow, the hair of His head like clean fleece, His throne flames of fire, its wheels blazing fire.*

See *Bereshit Rabbah* 35:2; *Zohar* 1:83a, 89b (*ST*), 130a; 3:132b (*IR*), 201a; *ZḤ* 19a (*MhN*).

388. ***Your hands are full of blood*** Spilling seed fruitlessly by hand is tantamount to murder since it wastes potential life.

See BT *Niddah* 13a (quoted above, note 386) and 13b (where Rabbi El'azar cites this same verse from Isaiah); Moses de León, *Sefer ha-Rimmon,* 242.

389. ***In the morning*...This verse has been established...** See *Qohelet Rabbah* on this verse (11:6); BT *Yevamot* 62b; *ZḤ* 89c (*MhN, Rut*); Moses de León, *Sefer ha-Mishqal,* 141.

written: *Like arrows in the hand of a warrior, so are the children of one's youth* (Psalms 127:4),[390] since he can teach them the ways of the blessed Holy One and obtain a fine reward in the world that is coming, as is written: *Happy is the man who fills his quiver with them; they will not be put to shame*... (ibid., 5)—in that world, when masters of judgment come to accuse him; for you cannot find a better reward in that world than of one who has taught his child the awe of his Lord and the ways of Torah.[391]

"Come and see from Abraham, of whom is written *For I have known him, so that he will instruct his children*... (Genesis 18:19).[392] So the merit stands him well in that world against all masters of judgment; therefore, *In the morning sow your seed.*

"*And at evening*—even in old age, a time when a person wanes, what is written? *Do not hold back your hand*—one should not forsake engendering in this world. Why? *For you do not know which will prosper*... (Ecclesiastes, ibid.),[393] so that they can stand up for him in that world.

"Therefore, *Children are the heritage of YHVH* (Psalms 127:3).[394] Who is *heritage of YHVH*? Bundle of the soul, aspect of the world that is coming.[395] As for this heritage, who entitles one to enter *the heritage of YHVH*? *Children*—those children entitle him to *the heritage of YHVH*. So, happy is the person who attains them and teaches them the ways of Torah, as has been said.[396]

390. ***Like arrows in the hand of a warrior...*** See BT *Ḥagigah* 15a: "Shemu'el said, 'Any emission of semen that does not shoot forth like an arrow does not fructify.'"

See *Zohar* 1:6a.

391. **obtain a fine reward in the world that is coming...** Children's good deeds and merit protect their parent from harsh judgment in the hereafter.

See *Zohar* 1:115b; Moses de León, *Sefer ha-Rimmon*, 110. Cf. above, page 143. The full verse from Psalms reads: *Happy is the man who fills his quiver with them; they will not be put to shame when they contend with enemies in the gate.*

392. ***For I have known him, so that he will instruct his children...*** The verse reads: *For I have known him, so that he will instruct his children and his household after him: they will keep the way of YHVH, to do righteousness and justice.* The verse indicates that teaching one's children is vital to an intimate relationship with God.

393. ***And at evening...*** The full verse reads: *In the morning sow your seed, and at evening do not hold back your hand; for you do not know which will prosper, this or that, or whether both are equally good.*

394. ***Children are the heritage of YHVH*** The verse reads: *Children are the heritage of YHVH, the fruit of the womb a reward.*

395. **Bundle of the soul...** *Shekhinah*, source and destination of all souls. The phrase derives from 1 Samuel 25:29: *The soul of my lord will be bound in the bundle of life.* *Shekhinah* is an aspect and offspring of the divine mother, *Binah*, who is often identified with the world that is coming.

See *Zohar* 1:66a, 224b; Moses de León, *Sefer ha-Mishqal*, 77; idem, *Sheqel ha-Qodesh*, 60–61 (75–76).

396. **who entitles one to enter *the heritage of YHVH*?...** Rabbi Ḥiyya reads the verse: *Children are* [the gateway to] *the heri-*

"*She took off her widow's garments*... (Genesis 38:14).[397]

"Come and see: Tamar was the daughter of a priest.[398] Now, would you ever imagine that she set out to whore with her father-in-law, given that she was inherently modest?[399] Rather, she was righteous and did this out of wisdom. She offered herself to him only because she possessed knowledge and contemplated wisdom. So she approached him to act kindly and faithfully; that is why she came to him and engaged in this affair.[400]

"Come and see: Because she possessed knowledge and exerted herself in this affair, the blessed Holy One offered assistance in that very act and she immediately conceived. All issued [188b] from Him.[401]

"Now, you might ask: 'Why didn't the blessed Holy One bring those sons through some other woman? Why through this one?' But precisely she, and no other woman, was needed for this act.[402]

tage of YHVH, namely, to *Shekhinah*. The soul's reunion with *Shekhinah* is dependent on engendering children in this world.

See *Zohar* 1:115a–b; Moses de León, *Sefer ha-Rimmon*, 242.

397. ***She took off her widow's garments...*** The full verse reads: *She took off her widow's garments, covered herself with a veil and wrapped herself, and sat by the entrance to Enaim, which is on the road to Timnah, for she saw that Shelah had grown up and she had not been given to him as wife.*

Tamar had been married to Er, Judah's firstborn. When Er died, his brother Onan should have married her, according to custom (see above, notes 325, 358), but Onan failed to consummate the act and *wasted* [his seed] *on the ground* (Genesis 38:9). When the youngest brother, Shelah, grew up, and Tamar saw that *she had not been given to him as wife*, she took matters into her own hand.

398. **Tamar was the daughter of a priest** According to rabbinic tradition, Tamar was the daughter of Noah's son Shem, who is identified with Melchizedek, *priest of God Most High* (Genesis 14:18).

See *Bereshit Rabbah* 85:10 (and Theodor, ad loc., n. 2); *Targum Yerushalmi*, Rashi, and Naḥmanides on Genesis 38:24; Moses de León, *Sefer ha-Rimmon*, 350.

399. **set out to whore with her father-in-law...** With Judah. See above, note 397; Genesis 38:12–30. On Tamar's modesty, see BT *Megillah* 10b.

400. **she approached him to act kindly and faithfully...** Tamar seduced her father-in-law, Judah, because she wanted to ensure the reincarnation of the souls of his childless sons Er and Onan, who were respectively her husband and brother-in-law. Such reincarnation is the kabbalistic purpose of levirate marriage. Since first Onan and now Shelah had failed to consummate the marital act with Tamar, she enticed Judah to fulfill this sacred task in order "to act kindly and faithfully" with the souls of Er and Onan.

See above, notes 325, 358, 383, 397. On acting "kindly and faithfully" toward the dead, see Genesis 47:29, and *Targum Onqelos*, ad loc.; Ruth 2:20.

401. **All issued from Him** Tamar's seduction of Judah was part of the divine plan.

See *Bereshit Rabbah* 85:12; BT *Makkot* 23b; *Aggadat Bereshit* 64:3.

402. **precisely she...was needed for this act** Since she had been married to both Er and Onan, she was the most appropriate vehicle for their souls to be reincarnated.

See *OY*; Galante. Cf. *Zohar* 3:71b–72a.

"There were two women through whom the seed of Judah was established, from whom issued King David, King Solomon, and King Messiah. These two women correspond to one another: Tamar and Ruth, whose husbands died first, who exerted themselves in this action.[403]

"Tamar enticed her father-in-law, who was next of kin to his sons who had died. Why did she entice him? As is written: *for she saw that Shelah had grown up and she had not been given to him as wife*. That is why she engaged in this act with her father-in-law.[404]

"As for Ruth, her husband died and then she engaged in this act with Boaz, as is written: *She uncovered his feet and lay down* (Ruth 3:7).[405] Engaging with him, she later gave birth to Obed.[406] Now, you might ask 'Why didn't Obed issue from another woman?' But precisely she was needed, no one else.[407]

"From these two, the seed of Judah was established and consummated. Both of them acted properly, acting kindly toward the dead so that the world would later be enhanced.[408] This corresponds to what is said: *I praise the dead, who have already died* (Ecclesiastes 4:2), because when they were first alive, they were not praiseworthy, but later they were.[409] Both of them exerted themselves

403. **two women... Tamar and Ruth...** Tamar gave birth to Perez and Zerah (the reincarnations of Er and Onan). Perez was the ancestor of Boaz, who together with Ruth engendered Obed, the grandfather of King David. See Ruth 4:18–21.

404. **Tamar enticed her father-in-law...** Several generations later, the Torah explicitly forbade marriage between a man and his daughter-in-law. See Leviticus 18:15. Here, however, Tamar wanted to ensure that the souls of Judah's two sons, Er and Onan, would be reincarnated. Since their younger brother, Shelah, had not married her, she felt compelled to mate with Judah, who was next-of-kin.

See above, note 400; Moses de León, *Sefer ha-Rimmon*, 350–55. "Enticed" renders אשתדלת (*ishtaddalat*), which spans a wide spectrum of meaning: "engage, devote oneself, exert oneself, strive, wrestle, entice." For this last sense, see *Pesiqta de-Rav Kahana* 13:14; *Qohelet Rabbah* on 1:16.

405. **As for Ruth, her husband died...** After Ruth's husband (Mahlon) died, she approached his relative, Boaz, who later consummated the act of levirate marriage with her, thereby ensuring that the soul of Mahlon would be reincarnated in their offspring.

The full verse reads: *Boaz ate and drank, and his heart was content, and he went to lie down beside the pile of grain. Then she came stealthily and uncovered his feet and lay down.*

406. **Obed** Grandfather of King David.

407. **precisely she was needed...** Since she had been Mahlon's wife. See above, note 402.

408. **world would later be enhanced** By the Davidic royal line and ultimately by the Messiah. For a similar justification of the action of Lot's elder daughter, see Vol. 2, p. 160, and n. 339.

409. ***I praise the dead, who have already died...*** The context (Ecclesiastes 4:2–3) reads: *I praise the dead, who have already died, more than the living, who are still alive. But better than both is one who has not yet been, who has not seen the evil deeds that are being done under the sun.*

For Rabbi Ḥiyya, the phrase *the dead, who have already died* refers to Er, Onan, and

to act kindly and faithfully toward the dead, and the blessed Holy One assisted in that act. All was fitting![410]

"Happy is one who engages in Torah day and night, as is written: *Meditate on it day and night* (Joshua 1:8).[411]

"*Joseph was brought down to Egypt, and Potiphar bought him*... (Genesis 39:1).[412] What is written above? *Judah recognized, and said, 'She is in the right...'* (ibid. 38:26).[413] He had said to his father, *Recognize, please*... (ibid. 37:32); therefore, *Judah recognized.*[414]

"It is written: *Look, there were twins in her womb!* (ibid. 38:27)—they were twins; previously they were brothers."[415]

Mahlon. In their previous lifetimes, all three had failed to engender new life and were thus unworthy, but later Er and Onan were reincarnated as the sons of Tamar and Judah (Perez and Zerah), while Mahlon was reincarnated as the son of Ruth and Boaz (Obed). In their new bodies, thse souls were now enabled to fulfill themselves before dying again. See above, note 376.

410. **blessed Holy One assisted in that act...** See above, page 148; *Rut Rabbah* 7:7.

411. ***Meditate on it day and night*** The full verse reads: *Let not this book of Torah depart from your mouth; meditate on it day and night, so that you may be careful to act according to all that is written in it. For then you will make your way prosperous and then you will succeed.* Here the citation emphasizes the profound depths of Torah, such as the secret of reincarnation hidden within the narrative of Judah and Tamar.

412. ***Joseph was brought down to Egypt...*** The full verse reads: *Joseph was brought down to Egypt, and Potiphar, courtier of Pharaoh, captain of the guard, an Egyptian man, bought him from the hands of the Ishmaelites who had brought him down there.*

413. ***Judah recognized, and said, 'She is in the right...'*** The full verse reads: *Judah recognized, and said, "She is more in the right than I! For after all, I did not give her to Shelah, my son." And he knew her again no more.* The verse describes Judah's reaction when Tamar displays his personal belongings, which he had left with her as collateral for payment. See Genesis 38:16–18.

414. ***Recognize, please...*** The verse reads: *Recognize, please: is it your son's tunic or not?* When Joseph's brothers sent his blood-stained garment to their father, Jacob, they posed this disingenuous question. Here, through verbal analogy, Rabbi Ḥiyya links Judah's acknowledgment of guilt in the story of Tamar (*Judah recognized...*) with his immoral act of deceiving Jacob in the previous chapter (*Recognize, please...*).

See *Bereshit Rabbah* 84:19; 85:2, 11; BT *Sotah* 10b.

415. ***Look, there were twins in her womb!...*** The context (Genesis 38:27–30) describes Tamar's giving birth: *It happened at the time she gave birth that, look, there were twins in her womb! And as she was giving birth, one put out a hand, and the midwife took and bound on his hand a crimson thread, saying, "This one came out first." As he was drawing back his hand, look, out came his brother, and she said, "What a breach you have breached for yourself!" And he named him Perez. Afterward out came his brother, on whose hand was the crimson thread, and he named him Zerah.*

Rabbi Ḥiyya understands the verse: "*Look, there are* [now] *twins in her womb!* But in their previous lifetimes they were already brothers [Er and Onan]." See above, note 409.

Rabbi Ḥizkiyah said, "That's not the implication! Rather, other sons were born."[416]

Rabbi Abba said, "This is why she exerted herself: to recover what had been lost.[417]

"Come and see what is written: *As he was drawing back his hand, look, out came his brother, and she said, 'What a breach you have breached for yourself!'*[418]—alluding here to the original, licentious breach that he breached, because of which he died. This is implied by the phrase *you have breached for yourself*—for yourself you have breached a breach, since you had to trouble your Lord; consequently, you will make a breach in other nations. So, *he named him* פרץ (*Perets*), Breach.[419]

"After the entire incident of Judah has been told—how he sold Joseph and brought all of this about:[420] for if Judah had said, 'Let's return him to our father,' his brothers would have done so; consequently, his brothers demoted him from dominion over them.[421] After he was banished from his brothers and all this came upon him,[422] Scripture speaks of Joseph: *Joseph was brought down to Egypt*. Why *was brought down*? Because the blessed Holy One approved that act, to fulfill the decree that He had issued: *Know well that your seed will be strangers*... (Genesis 15:13).[423]

416. **not the implication...** The verse should be understood not in terms of reincarnation but simply according to its simple sense: Tamar conceived twins.

417. **why she exerted herself...** Rabbi Abba agrees with Rabbi Ḥiyya that by seducing Judah, Tamar intended to bring about the reincarnation of the unfulfilled, "lost" souls of Er and Onan.

On recovering the lost soul, see *ZḤ* 89d (*MhN, Rut*); Moses de León, *Sefer ha-Mishqal*, 138.

418. ***As he was drawing back his hand...*** See above, note 415.

419. **original, licentious breach...** The name of Judah and Tamar's firstborn son, פרץ (*Perets*), means "breach," which according to Rabbi Abba, alludes to the violation he committed in a previous lifetime as Er, wasting his seed and failing to engender new life with Tamar. This breach compelled God to initiate the complex process of reincarnation through Tamar's holy seduction of Judah. From their union, King David eventually issued, and he compensated for Er's licentious breach with his own bold act of breaching—piercing the defenses of Israel's enemies.

On Er's sin, see above, note 324.

420. **how he sold Joseph...** See Genesis 37:26–28.

421. **demoted him from dominion...** See above, note 301.

422. **all this came upon him** The incident of Tamar.

423. **Why *was brought down*?...** The passive conjugation of the verb implies that a higher power was responsible. Divine providence intended Joseph's descent to Egypt, in order to fulfill the covenantal promise made to Abraham: *Know well that your seed will be strangers in a land not theirs, and they will be enslaved and afflicted four hundred years. But upon the nation that they serve I will bring judgment, and afterward they will go forth with great substance.*

See above, pages 119, 121. Cf. Genesis 50:20; Radak on Genesis 37:13.

"*Potiphar bought him*—with sinful intentions he bought him."[424]

He opened, saying, "*Who commands the sun, and it does not shine; who seals up the stars* (Job 9:7). Come and see: The blessed Holy One made seven stars in the heavens, and each and every heaven contains numerous attendants appointed to serve the blessed Holy One.[425] For there is no attendant or appointee without his own service to his Lord; every single one attends to the service assigned to him, and each one knows his task to perform.

"Some of them serve as messengers of their Lord, appointed in the world over all human actions.[426] Some of them praise Him and are appointed over song. Yet although they are appointed over this, no power in heaven or among stars and constellations fails to praise the blessed Holy One.[427] For when night falls, three encamped flanks diverge in three directions, each and every direction containing thousands and myriads, all appointed over [189a] song.[428]

"There are three camps, and one holy living being appointed over them, standing over them,[429] and they all praise the blessed Holy One until morning arrives. As morning arrives, all those in the southern flank—along with all radiant stars—praise the blessed Holy One in song, as is said: *When the morning stars sang together, and all the sons of Elohim shouted for joy* (Job 38:7). *When the morning stars sang together*—stars of the south, as is said: *Abraham arose early in the morning* (Genesis 22:3).[430]

424. ***Potiphar bought him*...** The verse reads: *Joseph was brought down to Egypt, and Potiphar, courtier of Pharaoh, captain of the guard, an Egyptian man, bought him from the hands of the Ishmaelites who had brought him down there.*

According to midrashic sources, Potiphar purchased Joseph with sexual intentions. See *Bereshit Rabbah* 86:3; *Targum Yerushalmi*, Genesis 39:1; BT *Sotah* 13b.

425. **seven stars in the heavens... numerous attendants...** The seven planets of medieval astronomy, based on the Ptolemaic system, include the moon, Mercury, Venus, the sun, Mars, Jupiter, and Saturn. Each planet occupies one sphere or heaven; each heaven is populated by numerous attending angels.

See Maimonides, *Mishneh Torah, Hilkhot Yesodei ha-Torah* 3:1; Moses de León, *Sheqel ha-Qodesh*, 68–69 (86).

426. **messengers... appointed... over all human actions** Observing human behavior and occasionally intervening in the world.

427. **no power... fails to praise...** All stars, planets, and angels contribute to the symphony of praise.

See Maimonides, *Mishneh Torah, Hilkhot Yesodei ha-Torah* 3:9; idem, *Guide of the Perplexed* 2:5.

428. **three encamped flanks...** These three camps of angels correspond to the three watches of the night.

See BT *Berakhot* 3a, and Rashi, ad loc., s.v. *i kasavar; Zohar* 1:231a; 2:195b–196a; Moses de León, *Sefer ha-Rimmon*, 403; idem, *Sheqel ha-Qodesh*, 70–71 (88–89).

429. **one holy living being...** *Shekhinah*, presiding over all the angels.

See Schäfer, *Synopse zur Hekhalot-Literatur*, §406; Ezra of Gerona, *Peirush Shir ha-Shirim*, 509; *Zohar* 1:12b–13a, 46b–47a, 211a, 242a; 2:48b, 126a; 3:46b.

430. ***When the morning stars sang*... south...*Abraham*...** The morning is filled with the song of angels and stars of the

"*And all the sons of Elohim shouted for joy*—those on the left flank, merged in the right.[431]

"Then morning glows and Israel takes up song, praising the blessed Holy One by day, three times a day, corresponding to the three times of night. These stand parallel to those, so that the glory of the blessed Holy One is exalted fittingly day and night. Those six times of day and night are befitting; the blessed Holy One Himself is exalted through these six.[432]

"Concerning that holy living being who stands over them above and stands over Israel below, so that all will be fittingly arranged, what is written? *She rises while it is still night and provides food for her household* (Proverbs 31:15)—those camps above. *And a portion for her maidens* (ibid.)—camps of Israel below.[433] So the glory of the blessed Holy One is exalted from every direction, from above and below. All abides within His control, all according to His will."

Who commands the sun... (Job 9:7).[434] Rabbi Shim'on said, "This is Joseph.[435]

"ובעד כוכבים יחתם (*Uv'ad kokhavim yaḥtom*), *Who seals up the stars* (ibid.)—his brothers, of whom is written *and eleven stars* (Genesis 37:9).[436]

"Alternatively, *Who commands the sun*—Jacob, when they told him: *Recognize, please* (ibid., 32).

"*And it does not shine* (Job, ibid.)—when *Shekhinah* withdrew from him.[437]

south; both morning and south symbolize *Ḥesed*, the *sefirah* of Abraham. See above, page 41.

431. ***sons of Elohim*... on the left...** Angels of the left side, under the influence of *Gevurah*, known by the divine name *Elohim* and symbolized by the north. Now these angels and their song blend into the forces of *Ḥesed* on the right.

432. **Israel takes up song... three times a day...** Israel's three daily prayers (morning, afternoon, and evening) correspond to the singing of the angels during the three watches of the night. See above, note 428.

433. **holy living being...** *Shekhinah*, who nourishes the angels above and Israel below. See *Zohar* 1:107a.

434. ***Who commands the sun*...** The verse reads: *Who commands the sun, and it does not shine; who seals up the stars.* See above, page 152.

435. **This is Joseph** Symbolizing *Yesod*, who is also represented by the sun. His light was hidden when he was thrown into the pit and then sold into slavery.

436. **his brothers... *eleven stars*** In his dream (Genesis 37:9), Joseph imagined his brothers as stars: *Look, I dreamed another dream, and, look, the sun and the moon and eleven stars were bowing down to me!* Their light was sealed up when they later descended to Egypt.

437. **Jacob... *Recognize, please*... *Shekhinah* withdrew...** Jacob is symbolized by the sun in Joseph's dream (see the preceding note). When Joseph's brothers sent his blood-stained garment to their father, they included a disingenuous message. See the context in Genesis 37:31–32: *They took Joseph's tunic and slaughtered a goat and dipped the tunic in the blood. They sent the ornamented tunic and had it brought to their father, and they said, "We found this. Recognize, please: is it your son's tunic or not?"* Jacob was fooled by his sons' deception because *Shekhinah* had withdrawn from him,

"ובעד כוכבים יחתם (*Uv'ad kokhavim yaḥtom*), *For the stars He seals up* (ibid.)—because of his sons, his radiance was sealed and concealed.[438] The sun darkened and the stars did not shine, because Joseph separated from his father.

"Come and see: From that day, Jacob abstained from conjugal union and remained in mourning until the day when the good news about Joseph was delivered."[439]

YHVH was with Joseph and he became a successful man, and he was in the house of his Egyptian master (Genesis 39:2).

Rabbi Yose opened, "*He will not abandon* חסידיו (*ḥasidav*), *His faithful ones; they are protected forever* (Psalms 37:28).[440] This verse has been established in relation to Abraham: written חסידו (*ḥasido*), *His faithful one*, as has been said.[441]

"Come and see: Wherever the righteous go, the blessed Holy One protects them and never abandons them. David said, *Though I walk through the valley of the shadow of death*... (Psalms 23:4).[442] Wherever the righteous go, *Shekhinah* accompanies them and never abandons them.[443]

"Joseph walked through the valley of the shadow of death and was brought down to Egypt; *Shekhinah* was with him, as is written: *YHVH was with Joseph.*

depriving him of prophetic vision. For many years, he did not discover Joseph's fate. Appropriately, the verse in Job reads: *Who commands the sun, and it does not shine.*

See *Bereshit Rabbah* 91:1 (and Theodor, ad loc.); *Tanḥuma* (Buber), *Miqqets* 6; above, pp. 94 (and n. 63), 119 (and n. 219).

438. **ובעד כוכבים יחתם (*Uv'ad kokhavim yaḥtom*), *For the stars*...** Understanding the word בעד as "for." For, or because of, his sons' action, Jacob's light and vision were sealed.

439. **abstained from conjugal union...** As an expression of his intense mourning over his son. In this sense too, he was *sealed.*

Cf. *Zohar* 1:153b. On the good news about Joseph being alive and well, see Genesis 45:25–28.

440. ***He will not abandon*...** The full verse reads: *For YHVH loves justice; He will not abandon His faithful ones. They are protected forever, while the seed of the wicked will be cut off.*

441. **Abraham... חסידו (*ḥasido*), *His faithful one*...** In this Psalm, according to Rabbi Yose, the word חסידיו (*ḥasidav*), *His faithful ones,* is spelled without the suffixal י (*yod*): חסידו (*ḥasido*), reflecting the singular sense: *His faithful one.* The Masoretic text of Psalms contains no such spelling, but it does appear in *Bereshit Rabbah* 86:3, where the singular sense is applied to Joseph. The same singular spelling in 1 Samuel 2:9 is applied by various midrashic sources to Abraham, Jacob, or Joseph.

See *Tanḥuma* (Buber), *Vayetse* 3; *Midrash Shemu'el* 5:16; *Aggadat Bereshit* 46:3; BT *Yoma* 38b; *Zohar* 1:112b; *Minḥat Shai* on 1 Samuel 2:9 and Psalms 37:28.

442. ***Though I walk through the valley of the shadow of death*...** The verse continues: *I fear no evil, for You are with me; Your rod and Your staff, they comfort me.*

443. **Wherever the righteous go, *Shekhinah* accompanies them...** See *Bereshit Rabbah* 86:6, in the name of Rabbi Shim'on son of Yoḥai. Cf. *Mekhilta, Pisḥa* 14; BT *Megillah* 29a.

Because *Shekhinah* was with him, whatever he did prospered in his hand. For even if he had something in his hand, and his master demanded something of a different kind, it would change in his hand to the kind desired by the will of his master, as is written: *His master saw that YHVH was with him, and all that he did YHVH made succeed in his hand* (Genesis 39:3)—*made succeed in his hand*, precisely! Because *YHVH was with him.*[444]

"Come and see! It is not written *His master knew that YHVH was with him*, but rather *His master saw*, for with his own eyes he saw every day the miracles that the blessed Holy One performed by his hand.[445] So, *YHVH blessed the house of the Egyptian for Joseph's sake* (ibid., 5). The blessed Holy One protects the righteous, and for their sake He protects the wicked; look, the wicked are blessed on account of the righteous! Similarly it is written: *YHVH blessed the house of Obed-edom... because of the ark of God* (2 Samuel 6:11–12).[446]

"Because of the righteous, others are blessed, while they cannot be sustained by their own merits, as has been established.[447] Joseph's master was blessed for his sake, yet he himself could not escape from him and gain his freedom; afterward he was put into prison, as is said: *His feet were bruised with shackles* (Psalms 105:18).[448] Finally the blessed Holy One set him free and installed him as ruler over the whole land of Egypt. So, *He will not abandon* [189b] חסידו (*ḥasido*), *His faithful one.*[449] The blessed Holy One shields the righteous in this world and in the world that is coming, as is written: *Let all who take refuge in You rejoice; let them ever shout for joy...* (ibid. 5:12)."[450]

444. **if he had something in his hand...** Such miracles are described in midrashic literature. See *Tanḥuma, Vayeshev* 8: "What does this mean: *and all that he did YHVH made succeed in his hand*? He would pour spiced wine for his master. He [Potiphar] would say, 'What did you pour for me?' He would reply, 'Spiced wine.' He would say, 'Absinthe wine is what I want!' And it became absinthe wine. 'Plain wine I want.' And it was plain. 'Cooked wine I want.' And it was cooked. Similarly with water, and with every single thing, as is said: *and all that he did YHVH made succeed in his hand.*"

See *Bereshit Rabbah* 86:4; *Tanḥuma* (Buber), *Vayeshev* 16.

445. **by his hand** By Joseph's hand.

446. ***YHVH blessed the house of Obed-edom...*** The two verses are here conflated. When King David recovered the ark of YHVH from the Philistines, he diverted it to the house of Obed-edom the Gittite, where it remained for three months before its arrival in Jerusalem. Rabbi Yose's point is that Obed, though otherwise unremarkable, was blessed because of the presence of the ark brought there by the righteous King David.

447. **Because of the righteous, others are blessed...** See BT *Berakhot* 17b: "The entire world is sustained by their merit, while they are not sustained even by their own merit."

448. ***His feet were bruised with shackles*** The full verse, describing Joseph's ordeal, reads: *His feet were bruised with shackles; his neck entered a collar of iron.* See Genesis 39:20.

449. **So, *He will not abandon* חסידו (*ḥasido*), *His faithful one*** See above, p. 154 and n. 441.

450. ***Let all who take refuge...*** The full verse reads: *Let all who take refuge in You*

It happened after these things that his master's wife raised her eyes to Joseph (Genesis 39:7).[451]

Rabbi Ḥiyya opened, "*Bless YHVH, O His angels, mighty in strength*... (Psalms 103:20).[452] Come and see how carefully one should guard himself against sin, walking the straight path so as not to be lured by that evil impulse, who assails him every single day, as has been said.[453] Since he assails him constantly, one must overpower him, rising above him into a sphere of strength, because one must be mightier than him, joining the realm of *Gevurah*. For when a person overcomes him, he attains the aspect of *Gevurah*, cleaving there, empowered. Since that evil impulse is strong, one must be even stronger.[454]

"Those humans who grapple with him are called *mighty in strength*—like encountering like. These are angels of the blessed Holy One, issuing from the side of rigorous *Gevurah* to overpower him: *mighty in strength*...[455]

"*Bless YHVH, O His angels*—such as Joseph, who was called Righteous and who guarded the holy covenant engraved in him."[456]

rejoice; let them ever shout for joy. Shelter them, so that those who love Your name may exult in You.

451. ***It happened after these things...*** The full verse reads: *It happened after these things that his master's wife raised her eyes to Joseph and said, "Lie with me."*

452. ***Bless YHVH, O His angels...*** The full verse reads: *Bless YHVH, O His angels, mighty in strength, who fulfill His word, hearkening to the voice of His word.*

453. **evil impulse... assails him every single day...** See BT *Qiddushin* 30b: "Rabbi Yitsḥak said, 'A person's impulse renews itself against him every day.'" See above, pages 85–88.

454. **rising above him into a sphere of strength...** The evil impulse derives ultimately from the left side of the sefirotic tree, specifically from *Gevurah* (Strength). In order to overcome the impulse, one must reach this source. Reciprocally, by overcoming the impulse, one attains *Gevurah*.

455. **called *mighty in strength*—like encountering like...** Attaining *Gevurah*, they become truly strong, capable of matching and defeating the impulse. Thereby, they attain the rank of angels.

See M *Avot* 4:1: "Ben Zoma says, '... Who is strong? One who subdues his impulse.'" On human angels, see *Vayiqra Rabbah* 1:1; *Zohar* 1:90a (*ST*).

456. **Joseph... called Righteous...** Joseph guarded the covenant of circumcision by resisting the sexual advances of Potiphar's wife, and he is therefore called "righteous" in rabbinic literature.

See Genesis 39; BT *Yoma* 35b; *Bereshit Rabbah* 93:7; *Pesiqta de-Rav Kahana, nispaḥim,* 460. Cf. *Tanḥuma, Bereshit* 5, and *Pirqei de-Rabbi Eli'ezer* 38, which cite Amos 2:6.

According to the *Zohar*, Joseph's sexual purity enabled him to scale the sefirotic ladder and attain the rung of *Yesod* (Foundation), the divine phallus and site of the covenant. *Yesod* is known as Righteous, based on Proverbs 10:25: וצדיק יסוד עולם (*Ve-tsaddiq yesod olam*). The verse literally means *The righteous one is an everlasting foundation,* but is understood as *The righteous one is the foundation of the world.*

See BT *Ḥagigah* 12b; *Bahir* 71 (102); Azriel of Gerona, *Peirush ha-Aggadot,* 34; *Zohar* 1:59b; above, page 92; Moses de León, *Sefer ha-Rimmon,* 228; idem, *Sheqel ha-Qodesh,* 50 (62).

Rabbi El'azar said, "*It happened after these things*. What is this? As has been established: the place from which the evil impulse attacks, a rung *after the things*.[457] For Joseph provided him an opening for accusal by curling his hair, dressing up, and adorning himself; so the evil impulse was poised to accuse: 'While his father mourns over him, Joseph is adorning himself and curling his hair!' Immediately, the bear was incited and attacked him.[458]

"*It happened after these things*. Come and see: When the blessed Holy One examines the world in order to judge it and finds wicked people there, what is written? *He will shut the heavens...* (Deuteronomy 11:17).[459] For because of human sin, heaven and earth are shut and their laws fail to operate properly.

"Come and see: Those who do not guard this holy covenant cause separation between Israel and their Father in heaven, for it is written: *so that you turn aside and serve other gods [and bow down to them]* (ibid., 16). This is one who bows down to another god, for he betrays the sign of the holy covenant.[460]

"When the holy covenant is guarded properly in the world, the blessed Holy One bestows blessings above, pouring into the world, as is written: *Abundant rain You showered, O God...* (Psalms 68:10).[461] *Abundant rain*—rain of favor,

457. ***after these things*... place from which the evil impulse attacks...** *Shekhinah*, last of the ten *sefirot*, is the realm of divine speech and is known as דברים (*devarim*), "words, things." Outside, behind, or *after* Her lies the realm of the demonic, from where the evil impulse launches its daily attacks. See *Zohar* 1:119b.

458. **Joseph provided him an opening...** The midrashic basis for Joseph's preening lies in the preceding verse (Genesis 39:6): *Joseph was handsome and good-looking*. Whereas in the rabbinic source, God denounces Joseph's behavior, here the accuser is the evil impulse. The "bear" is Potiphar's wife.

See *Bereshit Rabbah* 87:3; *Tanḥuma, Va-yeshev* 8; Rashi on Genesis 39:6; *Zohar* 2:267a (*Heikh*). Cf. *Bereshit Rabbah* 22:6: "Rabbi Ammi said, 'The evil impulse does not walk on the side but in the middle of the street, and when he sees a person painting his eyes, smoothing his hair, swinging his heel, he says, "This one is mine!"'"

459. ***He will shut the heavens*...** The context (Deuteronomy 11:16–17) reads: *Take care, lest your heart be seduced, so that you turn aside and serve other gods and bow down to them. Then the anger of YHVH will flare up against you, and He will shut the heavens so that there will be no rain and the earth will not yield her fruit, and you will perish quickly from off the good land that YHVH is giving you.*

460. ***so that you turn aside*...** For the context, see the preceding note. Those who are sexually promiscuous betray the covenant of circumcision and ruin the relationship between God and Israel. In the *Zohar*, the command *Do not bow down to another god* (Exodus 34:14) is understood to mean "Do not lie down with a foreign woman."

See *Zohar* 1:131b; 2:3b, 61a, 87b, 90a, 243a; 3:13b; *ZḤ* 21a (*MhN*), 78c (*MhN, Rut*); Moses de León, *Sefer ha-Rimmon*, 212–13; idem, *Sheqel ha-Qodesh*, 51 (63). For the social context, see Assis, "Sexual Behavior in Mediaeval Hispano-Jewish Society."

461. ***Abundant rain You showered*...** The full verse reads: *Abundant rain You showered, O God; Your weary heritage, You restored her.*

when the blessed Holy One delights in Assembly of Israel and desires to pour blessings into Her.[462]

"Then, *Your weary heritage, You restored her* (ibid.). *Your heritage*—Israel, heritage of the blessed Holy One, as is written: *Jacob is His allotted heritage* (Deuteronomy 32:9).[463]

"*Weary*—Assembly of Israel, who is weary on earth, thirsting for drink; so She is *weary*.[464] When that rain of favor is provided, then *You restored her.*

"So heaven and earth and all their powers stand on this foundational covenant, as is written: *Were it not for My covenant day and night...* (Jeremiah 33:25).[465] Therefore one should be careful of this, as has been established. So it is written: *Joseph was handsome and good-looking* (Genesis 39:6), and immediately afterward: *His master's wife raised her eyes to Joseph...*"[466]

Though she spoke to Joseph day after day... (Genesis 39:10).[467]

Rabbi El'azar opened, "*To protect you from the woman of evil, from the smooth tongue of an alien* (Proverbs 6:24). Happy are the righteous who know the paths of the blessed Holy One, how to follow them, since they strive for Torah day and night! For whoever strives for Torah day and night inherits two

462. **rain of favor... delights in Assembly of Israel...** Proper sexual behavior on earth stimulates the divine romance above. Blessing then flows from the divine male to *Shekhinah*, known as Assembly of Israel, and from Her to the world.

The phrase "rain of favor" derives from M *Ta'anit* 3:8, where it implies "neither drizzling rain nor torrential rain." On Assembly of Israel, see above, note 237.

463. ***Jacob is His allotted heritage*** The full verse reads: *For YHVH's share is His people, Jacob His allotted heritage.*

464. ***Weary*—Assembly of Israel...** Exiled among Her people, *Shekhinah* is deprived of the nourishing flow from above.

465. **stand on this foundational covenant...** All of existence depends on *Yesod* (Foundation), the divine covenant and cosmic pillar, whose human counterpart is inscribed with the covenant of circumcision.

For the full verse from Jeremiah (as understood here), see BT *Shabbat* 137b: "Were it not for the blood of the covenant [of circumcision], heaven and earth would not endure, as is said: *Were it not for My covenant day and night, I would not have established the laws of heaven and earth.*"

See BT *Ḥagigah* 12b; *Zohar* 1:32a, 56a, 59b, 66b, 89a, 91b, 93b, 96b, 241b; 2:116a; 3:14a; Moses de León, *Sefer ha-Rimmon*, 61.

The phrase "foundational covenant" renders קיומא (*qiyyuma*), whose range of meaning in the *Zohar* includes both "foundation" and "covenant." See Liebes, *Peraqim*, 358, 361.

466. **be careful of this...** Careful and restrained in sexual behavior, since human sexuality mirrors and affects the divine realm. Here, according to Rabbi El'azar, Joseph's preoccupation with his own looks led to his near seduction, as indicated by the sequence of verses: *Joseph was handsome and good-looking. It happened after these things that his master's wife raised her eyes to Joseph and said, "Lie with me."* See above, p. 157 and n. 458.

467. ***Though she spoke to Joseph day after day...*** The full verse reads: *Though she spoke to Joseph day after day, he would not listen to her, to lie beside her, to be with her.*

worlds: the world above and the lower world. [190a] He inherits this world even if he hasn't engaged in her for her own sake; he inherits that supernal world when he engages in her for her own sake.[468]

"Come and see what is written: *Length of days in her right hand; in her left, riches and honor* (ibid. 3:16). *Length of days in her right hand*—whoever walks to the right of Torah finds length of life in the world that is coming, attaining there the glory of Torah: a glorious crown, to be crowned above all—for the crown of Torah is in that world.[469]

"*In her left, riches and honor*—in this world, for even if one hasn't engaged in her for her own sake, he attains in this world riches and honor.

"Now, when Rabbi Ḥiyya came from there, that is, when he went up to the land of Israel, he read Torah until his face shone like the sun.[470] And when all those who were studying Torah stood before him, he would say, 'This one engages in Torah for her own sake; that one does not.'[471] He would pray for the former that he always do so and attain the world that is coming. He would pray for the latter that he come to engage in her for her own sake and attain eternal life.[472]

"One day he saw a student toiling over Torah whose face turned pale. He said, 'This one is certainly conceiving sin!'[473] Facing him, he held him and drew him

468. **inherits two worlds...** One who studies Torah for her own sake gains true life in the eternal world that is coming, but even one who studies for an ulterior motive finds reward in this world.

See *Avot* 6:7; *Sifrei*, Deuteronomy 48; *Bereshit Rabbah* 59:2; BT *Shabbat* 63a; *Zohar* 1:184b–185a. All these sources cite Proverbs 3:16, which follows here. On studying Torah for her own sake, see *Avot* 6:1; BT *Pesaḥim* 50b, *Sukkah* 49b, *Ta'anit* 7a, *Sanhedrin* 99b.

469. **whoever walks to the right of Torah...** Whoever engages in Torah out of pure motives gains eternal life in the world that is coming. The reward for Torah cannot be expected here on earth, only in that realm.

See Rashi on BT *Shabbat* 63a, s.v. *lamasme'ilin bah*. On the crown of Torah, see M *Avot* 4:13; *Kallah* 1:21.

470. **when Rabbi Ḥiyya came from there...** As in the Jerusalem Talmud, "there" refers to Babylonia. Studying Torah in the land of Israel is more enlightening than anywhere else.

On the shining countenance, see Ecclesiastes 8:1 (*A man's wisdom brightens his face*); Exodus 34:29–35; JT *Shabbat* 8:1, 11a; *Pirqei de-Rabbi Eli'ezer* 2; Naḥmanides, *Kitvei Ramban*, 2:305–6; *Zohar* 2:15a; 3:163a.

471. **he would say, 'This one engages...'** Rabbi Ḥiyya could tell by observing their physiognomy.

472. **He would pray for the latter...** As Rav Safra prayed, according to BT *Berakhot* 17a. See *Pesaḥim* 50b, in the name of Rav: "A person should always engage in Torah and *mitsvot* even if not for their own sake, because by doing them not for their own sake, he eventually does them for their own sake."

473. **turned pale...conceiving sin** See BT *Shabbat* 33a: "Dropsy is a sign of sin; ירקון (*yeraqon*), jaundice, is a sign of causeless hatred."

The root ירק (*yrq*) means "to be green, yellow, pale," and here in the *Zohar* yields

with words of Torah until his spirit settled within. From that day on, he resolved not to pursue evil imaginings and to engage in Torah for her own sake."

Rabbi Yose said, "When one sees that evil imaginings are assailing him, he should occupy himself with Torah, and they will disappear."[474]

Rabbi El'azar said, "When that evil side comes to seduce a person, he should drag him to the house of Torah and he will depart.[475]

"Come and see what we have learned: When this evil side stands before the blessed Holy One to accuse the world of evil deeds, the blessed Holy One feels compassion and offers human beings advice on how to save themselves from him, so that he cannot control them or their actions.[476] What is the advice? To engage in Torah, in order to be saved from him. How do we know? Because it is written: *For a mitsvah is a lamp and Torah is light* (Proverbs 6:23).[477] What is written next? *To protect you from the woman of evil, from the smooth tongue of an alien.* This is the impure side, the Other Side, who stands perpetually before the blessed Holy One, bringing accusations of the sins of human beings, and who stands perpetually below, leading humans astray. He constantly stands above, recounting the sins of human beings and accusing them for their deeds, so that they will be delivered into his power, as he did with Job.[478]

"Similarly, he stands over Israel, accusing, recounting the sins in everything they have done. At those times when the blessed Holy One stands over them in

the verb מוריקן (*moriqan*), "turned pale." In *Zohar* 3:193b, Rabbi Shim'on cites a formulation from the Book of the Wisdom of King Solomon: "*Yeraqon* is a sign of sin."

See Jeremiah 30:6; BT *Yevamot* 60b; Rashi and Tosafot, ad loc.; *Beit ha-Midrash,* 2:120.

474. **they will disappear** See *Avot de-Rabbi Natan* A, 20: "Rabbi Ḥananya, prefect of the priests, says, 'Whoever takes to heart the words of Torah is relieved of . . . the imaginings of the evil impulse.'"

Cf. *Sifrei,* Deuteronomy 45; BT *Berakhot* 5a; *Qiddushin* 30b; *Zohar* 3:268a.

475. **drag him to the house of Torah . . .** See the strategy against the evil impulse recommended in BT *Sukkah* 52b: "A scholar from the school of Rabbi Yishma'el taught, 'If this repulsive one attacks you, drag him to the house of study. If he is of stone, he will dissolve; if of iron he will shatter.'"

476. **evil side stands before the blessed Holy One . . .** Here "evil side" designates specifically Satan the Accuser. See BT *Bava Batra* 16a: "Resh Lakish said, 'Satan, the evil impulse, and the Angel of Death are one and the same.'"

477. ***For a mitsvah is a lamp . . .*** The full verse reads: *For a mitsvah is a lamp and Torah is light, and reproofs of discipline are the way to life.*

478. ***woman of evil* . . . Other Side . . .** The *woman of evil* in Proverbs personifies the demonic realm—both Satan above, accusing human beings, and the evil impulse below, seducing them to sin. The following section includes both male and female personifications of evil. See *Zohar* 1:148a–b (*ST*).

On Satan's divine authorization to test Job with suffering, see Job 1:6–12; 2:1–6. See the description of Satan's itinerary in BT *Bava Batra* 16a: "He descends and leads astray, ascends and arouses wrath, obtains authorization and seizes the soul."

judgment, he rises to accuse them and recount their sins.[479] But the blessed Holy One feels compassion for Israel and has advised them how to save themselves from him. How? With a shofar on Rosh Hashanah,[480] and on Yom Kippur with a goat, given to him so that he will disengage from them and occupy himself with that portion of his, as they have established.[481]

"Come and see what is written: *Her feet descend to death* (ibid. 5:5).[482] Of the mystery of faith, what is written? *Her ways are ways of pleasantness, and all her paths are peace* (ibid. 3:17)—ways and paths of Torah—and all is one. This one, *peace,* and this one *death,* entirely opposite each other.[483]

"Happy is the share of Israel who cleave to the blessed Holy One fittingly! He advises them how to escape all other aspects of the world,[484] for they are a holy

479. **stands over them in judgment...** On Rosh Hashanah and Yom Kippur.

480. **shofar on Rosh Hashanah** The shofar (ram's horn) is intended to confound Satan and interfere with his accusations.

See BT *Rosh ha-Shanah* 16a–b; Rashi and Tosafot, ad loc., s.v. *kedei le-arbev; Zohar* 1:114a–b; Moses de León, *Sefer ha-Mishqal,* 119–22.

481. **on Yom Kippur with a goat...** In the original ritual of Yom Kippur (Leviticus 16:7–10), one goat is sacrificed as a sin offering to God, while a scapegoat bearing the sins of Israel is sent off into the wilderness for the demon Azazel. (Similarly in the Babylonian Akitu ritual, a goat—substituted for a human being—is offered to Ereshkigal, goddess of the Abyss.) According to *Pirqei de-Rabbi Eli'ezer* 46, the goat of Yom Kippur is intended to preoccupy Satan: "They gave him a bribe on Yom Kippur so that he would not nullify Israel's sacrifice."

Cf. BT *Yoma* 20a: "On Yom Kippur, Satan has no permission to accuse. How do we know? Rami son of Ḥama said, 'השטן (*Hasatan*), Satan, equals 364 in numerical value—implying that on 364 days he has permission to accuse, while on Yom Kippur he does not.'"

See *Sifra, Shemini* 1:3, 43c; Naḥmanides on Leviticus 16:8 (cf. 9:7); Moses of Burgos, *Ammud ha-Semali,* 158–59; *Zohar* 1:11a, 64a, 65a, 113b–114b, 138b, 145b, 174b, 210b; 2:154b, 184b–185a, 237b, 266b; 3:63a–b (*Piq*), 102a, 202b–203a, 258b; *ZḤ* 87b–c (*MhN, Rut*); Moses de León, *Sefer ha-Rimmon,* 165–67; idem, *Sefer ha-Mishqal,* 124–27; idem, *She'elot u-Tshuvot,* 49; Tishby, *Wisdom of the Zohar,* 3:890–95.

482. ***Her feet descend to death*** The full verse, warning against the seductive *strange woman,* reads: *Her feet descend to death; her steps grasp Sheol.* Here, the strange woman personifies the demonic powers.

483. **Of the mystery of faith... all is one...** *Shekhinah,* culmination of the *sefirot,* is the realm of mystical faith, and is identified with Oral Torah.

The phrase "all is one" refers either to the inherent unity of Torah and *Shekhinah,* or to the intricate network of Torah's pathways, or perhaps to the ultimate unity of opposites: the divine and the demonic. Elsewhere in the *Zohar,* the description *Her feet descend to death* is applied to *Shekhinah.* See *Zohar* 1:35b, 221b; 2:48b; 3:107b. On the relation between *Shekhinah* and the demonic realm, see Scholem, *On the Mystical Shape of the Godhead,* 189–92; Tishby, *Wisdom of the Zohar,* 1:376–79; Patai, *The Hebrew Goddess,* 249, 251–54.

For a range of interpretations, see *Sullam;* Tishby, ibid., 2:520; Mopsik; *MmD.*

484. **all other aspects of the world** The various demonic powers.

people, His possession and share, so He has provided them advice on everything! Happy are they in this world, happy are they in the world that is coming!

"Come and see: When this evil side descends and roams the world and observes the actions of human beings, all of whom pervert their ways in the world, he ascends and accuses them.[485] If the blessed Holy One did not feel compassion for the works of His hands, they would not survive in the world.

"What is written? *Though she spoke to Joseph day after day* (Genesis 39:10).[486] *Though she spoke* [190b]—for he ascends and accuses every single day, declaring before the blessed Holy One many acts of evil, many slanders in order to destroy the inhabitants of the world.[487]

"What is written? *He would not listen to her* (ibid.), because He feels compassion for the world.[488]

"*To lie beside her* (ibid.). What does this mean? To take control, to dominate the world—and dominion does not prevail until he is empowered.[489]

"Alternatively, *to lie beside her*, as is said: *and for a man who lies with an impure woman* (Leviticus 15:33).[490]

"*To be with her* (Genesis, ibid.)—to give her dignity, blessings, and help.[491] For if she has help from above, not even a single being would be left in the

485. **When this evil side descends...** See above, note 478.

486. ***Though she spoke to Joseph day after day*** The full verse reads: *Though she spoke to Joseph day after day, he would not listen to her, to lie beside her, to be with her.* See above, page 158.

487. ***Though she spoke*—for he ascends...** Potiphar's wife symbolizes the demonic accuser, who ascends to testify against humanity before the blessed Holy One, symbolized by Joseph. On the switch in gender (*she spoke*... he ascends), see above, note 478.

488. ***He would not listen to her...*** Joseph's refusal to be seduced represents God's compassionate refusal to be swayed by Satan's indictment of humanity.

489. ***To lie beside her*...To take control...** If demonic power successfully enticed divine power, it could rule the world.

On the empowerment of the demonic realm, see BT *Bava Batra* 16a (quoted above, note 478). On the switch in gender (*beside her*... he is empowered), see above, notes 478, 487.

490. ***to lie beside her... who lies with an impure woman*** By verbal analogy (*to lie... who lies*), Rabbi El'azar links Joseph's seductress with the *impure woman* of Leviticus. In the biblical context, *impure woman* denotes a menstruant; here, the phrase alludes to the demonic female, who lusts for divine potency, imploring the divine male *to lie beside her*. The erotic tone is highlighted by the fact that Joseph symbolizes specifically the *sefirah* of *Yesod*, the divine phallus (above, note 50). Normally, *Yesod* channels all divine energy to *Shekhinah*; but as a result of human sinfulness (such as being seduced by a foreign woman), the demonic female can supplant *Shekhinah*, receive the potency of *Yesod* herself, and tyrannize the world.

See *Zohar* 1:122a–b, 131b; 2:60b–61a; 3:69a (all of which cite Proverbs 30:23: *a slave girl supplanting her mistress*); Idel, "Seridim Nosafim," 47–53.

491. **to give her dignity, blessings, and help** To strengthen the demonic temptress.

world. But since the blessed Holy One has compassion on the world, the world remains in existence."

Rabbi Abba said, "All is one path, but it is the evil impulse who comes seducing human beings, to pervert their ways—to cling to him. Every single day, at all times, he diverts one from the way of truth to thrust him from the way of life and draw him into Hell.[492]

"A virtuous person—what does he do? He guards his ways and paths so as not to cling to him,[493] corresponding to what is written: *Though she spoke to Joseph day after day, he would not listen to her*—to what she says to him every day. For the impure spirit, the evil impulse, seduces a person every day *to lie beside her* in Hell, to be condemned there *to be with her.*[494]

"Come and see: When a person adheres to that side, he is drawn to her and defiles himself with her in this world and defiles himself with her in the world that is coming.[495]

"Come and see: This impure side is repulsive, it is filth, as is said: 'צא (*Tse*), *Out!' you will call to it* (Isaiah 30:22)—actual צואה (*tso'ah*), excrement![496] One who deviates from Torah is punished in it! Those sinners of the world who have no faith in the blessed Holy One are punished in it![497]

492. **All is one path...** Rabbi Abba indicates that his interpretation does not conflict with the one just offered by Rabbi El'azar. He is discussing the evil impulse, operating psychologically within the human being, whereas his colleague focused on the demonic seducer operating above. Yet "all is one path," above and below. See BT *Bava Batra* 16a: "Resh Lakish said, 'Satan, the evil impulse, and the Angel of Death are one and the same.'"

493. **so as not to cling to him** To the evil impluse. The clause can also be rendered: "so that he [the evil impulse] will not cling to him."

494. ***to lie beside her* in Hell...** Playing on the rabbinic formulation: "*To lie beside her*—in this world. *To be with her*—in the world to come, in Hell."

See *Bereshit Rabbah* 87:6; BT *Yoma* 35b, *Sotah* 3b; *Tanḥuma, Vayeshev* 8.

495. **defiles himself with her in the world that is coming** Cf. BT *Sotah* 3b: "Rabbi Shemu'el son of Naḥmani said in the name of Rabbi Yonatan: 'Whoever fufills a single commandment in this world—it ushers him into the world that is coming.... And whoever commits a single transgression in this world—it clasps him and ushers him into the Day of Judgment....' Rabbi El'azar says, 'It is attached to him like a dog; as is said: *He would not listen to her, to lie beside her, to be with her—to lie beside her* in this world; *to be with her* in the world that is coming.'"

496. **repulsive...** The same word describes the evil impulse in BT *Sukkah* 52b: "If this repulsive one attacks you, drag him to the house of study."

On the interpretation of Isaiah 30:22, see JT *Shabbat* 9:1, 11d; *Pesiqta de-Rav Kahana* 13:2.

497. **One who deviates from Torah is punished in it...** See BT *Eruvin* 21b, in the name of Aḥa son of Ulla: "Whoever mocks the words of the Sages is punished in boiling excrement.'"

The "sinners... who have no faith" are the author's Spanish Jewish contemporaries who—influenced, in part, by rationalistic philosophy—strayed from faith and religious observance. See Scholem, *Major Trends*, 201–4; Matt, *Zohar: The Book of Enlightenment*, 22–24.

"What is written? *It happened, on such a day, that he came into the house...* (Genesis 39:11).[498] *It happened, on such a day*—a day when the evil impulse dominates the world and descends to lead humans astray. When? The day that a person begins to turn back in repentance for his sins, or engage in Torah and fulfill the commands of Torah—at that moment, he descends to lead inhabitants of the world astray.[499]

"*He came into the house to do his work* (ibid.)—to engage in Torah and fulfill the commandments of Torah, for that is a person's work in this world.[500] Now, since a person's work in this world is the service of the blessed Holy One, one must be mighty as a lion on every side so that the Other Side will not overpower him and be able to seduce him.[501] What is written? *And there was no man* (ibid.)[502]—no man to stand up against the evil impulse and wage war with him fittingly.

"What are the ways of the evil impulse? As soon as he sees that this is no man—to confront him and wage battle against him—immediately, *she seized him by his garment* (Genesis 39:12),[503] for when the evil impulse takes control of a person, he dresses him up in fancy clothes and curls his hair, as is written: *She seized him by his garment, saying, 'Lie with me!'*—'cling to me!'[504]

"One who is virtuous steels himself against her, wages war against her. What is written? *He left his garment* [*in her hand and fled, escaping outside*] (ibid.)—he should abandon it and steel himself against her, flee from her to escape her, so that she does not dominate him."[505]

498. ***It happened, on such a day...*** The full verse reads: *It happened, on such a day, that he came into the house to do his work, and there was no man of the men of the house there in the house.*

499. **When? The day that a person begins to turn back...** The evil impulse attacks precisely at that moment, to obstruct one's return to God.

500. ***to do his work*—to engage in Torah...** See M *Avot* 2:15–16: "Rabbi Tarfon says, 'The day is short, the work is much, the workers are lazy, the reward is abundant, and the master of the house is insistent.' He used to say, 'You are not obligated to finish the work, yet you are not free to desist from it. If you have studied much Torah, you are given much reward, and your employer can be trusted to pay you the reward of your labor, and know that the granting of reward to the righteous is for the time to come.'"

Cf. *Midrash Avkir*, 24 (cited in *Yalqut Shim'oni*, Genesis 146): "*He came into the house to do his work.* Rabbi Eli'ezer says, 'It was Sabbath..., so what work did he have? Reciting what his father had taught him.'"

501. **mighty as a lion...** See M *Avot* 5:20: "Yehudah son of Teima says, 'Be bold as a leopard, swift as an eagle, fleet as a gazelle, and mighty as a lion, to do the will of your Father in Heaven.'"

502. ***And there was no man*** For the full verse, see above, note 498.

503. ***she seized him by his garment*** The full verse reads: *She seized him by his garment, saying, 'Lie with me!' And he left his garment in her hand and fled, escaping outside.*

504. **evil impulse... dresses him up...** Tempting him to preen himself. See above, p. 157 and n. 458.

505. ***He left his garment...*** One who is

Rabbi Yitsḥak said, "The righteous are destined to see the evil impulse in the shape of a huge mountain. Astounded, they will say, 'How were we able to overturn such a huge, soaring mountain!' The wicked are destined to see the evil impulse as thin as a single hair. Astounded, they will say, 'How could we fail to overcome this thin thread of hair!' These will weep and those will weep. And the blessed Holy One will eliminate him from the world, slaughtering him before their eyes, and he will no longer have dominion over the world. Seeing this, the righteous will rejoice, as is said: *Surely the righteous will praise Your name; the upright will dwell in Your presence* (Psalms 140:14)."[506] [191a]

It happened after these things that the cupbearer of the king of Egypt [and the baker] offended [their master, the king of Egypt] (Genesis 40:1).

Rabbi Yehudah opened, "*Does a lion roar in the forest when it has no prey?...* (Amos 3:4).[507] Come and see how attentive humans should be to the worship of the blessed Holy One, because whoever engages in Torah and in the worship of the blessed Holy One instills awe and fear in everything. For when the blessed Holy One created the world, He fashioned every single creature of the world in its own fitting image, and afterward He created the human being in a supernal image, granting him dominion over them all through this image.[508] For as long as a human exists in the world, all those creatures of the world raise their heads and gaze upon the supernal image of the human being; then they all fear and tremble before him, as is said: *Fear and dread of you shall be upon every living thing of the earth*... (ibid. 9:2).[509]

virtuous does not surrender to the temptation of dressing up and primping.

For the full verse, see above, note 503. In nearly all versions of the *Zohar*, the end of this paragraph reads "so that he does not dominate him." I have translated here according to the Munich MS (M7): "so that she does not dominate him." On the variation in gender, see above, notes 478, 487, 489.

506. **righteous are destined to see...** A paraphrase of a teaching attributed to Rabbi Yehudah in BT *Sukkah* 52a. Psalm 140 (not cited in the Talmudic passage) constitutes a plea for deliverance from evil enemies, who are represented here by the evil impulse.

507. ***Does a lion roar...*** The full verse reads: *Does a lion roar in the forest when it has no prey? Does a young lion let out a cry from its den without having made a capture?* The verse is part of the *haftarah* (prophetic reading) for Torah portion *Va-Yeshev* (Amos 2:6–3:8).

508. **supernal image... dominion...** The human being, created in the image of God, manifests that image physically and is acknowledged by all other beings. In Kabbalah the divine image corresponds to the ten *sefirot*, depicted in human form.

See Genesis 1:26–28; and the description of the human face on the celestial chariot in *Zohar* 1:19a.

509. **creatures... fear and tremble...** See BT *Shabbat* 151b: "Rabbi Shim'on son of El'azar said, '*Fear and dread of you shall be [upon every living thing of the earth...]*. As long as a human is alive, his fear lies upon creatures; once he dies, fear of him ceases.'"

See *Pirqei de-Rabbi Eli'ezer* 11; *Zohar* 1:13b,

These words apply only when they gaze and see in him this image and a soul is within him."[510]

Rabbi El'azar said, "Even if a soul is not within him, the righteous never undergo a change from the original nature of their image.[511] But when a person does not walk in the ways of Torah, this holy image is exchanged and the beasts of the field can then dominate him because this human image has changed for them.[512]

"Come and see: The blessed Holy One transforms events above and below to restore an entity to its place, so that His will manifest in all affairs of the world. Daniel's image did not change when he was thrown into the lions' den and therefore he was saved."[513]

Rabbi Ḥizkiyah said, "If so, look what is written: *My God sent His angel, and he shut the lions' mouths and they did not harm me* (Daniel 6:23)—implying that because an angel shut their mouths, he was not harmed."[514]

He replied, "Because of this he was not harmed, for look, the image of a virtuous human being is an actual angel, who shut the mouths and bound them

38a, 71a, 221b; 2:55a, 125b; 3:107b; *ZḤ* 38c; Moses de León, *Sefer ha-Rimmon,* 309, 337–38; Ginzberg, *Legends,* 5:119–20, n. 113.

The full verse in Genesis reads: *Fear and dread of you shall be upon every living thing of the earth and upon every bird of the skies, in everything with which the earth teems and in all the fish of the sea. Into your hand they are given.*

510. **soul is within him** As long as he is alive or awake, or as long as he is in a state of purity. Alternatively, as long as he has attained the highest level of soul, known as נשמתא (*nishmeta*), corresponding to Hebrew נשמה (*neshamah*), "soul, breath."

For a range of interpretations, see *OY*; Galante; *NO*; *Adderet Eliyyahu,* 148b, 149a; Tishby, *Wisdom of the Zohar,* 2:786; *MmD.*

511. **Even if a soul is not within him...** Even after death or during sleep, the righteous maintain their pristine nature.

512. **holy image is exchanged...** Failure to live virtuously deteriorates a person's divine image, making him vulnerable to the beasts, who are no longer intimidated by him since he has turned beastly. Now the rhetorical question posed by Amos applies: *Does a lion roar in the forest when it has no prey?*

See *Shir ha-Shirim Rabbah* on 3:7: "It was taught: Before a person sins, he inspires awe and fear, and creatures are afraid of him. Once he sins, he is filled with awe and fear, and he is afraid of others." Cf. BT *Shabbat* 151b: "Rami son of Abba said, 'A wild beast has no power over a person until he appears to it as an animal.'"

See *Sifrei,* Deuteronomy 50; *Zohar* 1:71a; Moses de León, *Sefer ha-Rimmon,* 337–38; *Nefesh David.*

513. **transforms events above and below...** He alters the natural order, for example, by removing the divine image from a sinner who no longer merits it, thereby rendering him vulnerable to attack—an attack that constitutes purging and restitution for his sin ("to restore an entity to its place"). Conversely, God preserves the divine image for a saint such as Daniel, thereby enacting a miracle fittingly.

514. **because an angel shut their mouths...** And not because of Daniel's divine image.

to protect him from being harmed![515] So, *My God sent His angel*—the one in whom all images of the world are engraved—and he strengthened my image within me, so they had no power over me, and he shut their mouths. So, *sent His angel*—precisely![516]

"Concerning this angel in whom all images are engraved, it is written: *He will execute judgment upon the nations—filled with bodies* (Psalms 110:6)—He before whom all images of the world have not changed.[517] A person should therefore beware his ways and paths, so as not to sin before his Lord, and to abide in his image—image of אדם (*adam*).[518]

"Come and see: Ezekiel guarded his mouth from forbidden foods, as is written: *Fouled meat has never entered my mouth* (Ezekiel 4:14). He merited being called בן אדם (*ben adam*), son of man.[519] Of Daniel, what is written? *Daniel made up his mind not to defile himself with the king's portion of food or with the wine he drank* (Daniel 1:8). He merited to abide in the image of *adam*, for all entities of the world are in awe of the image of *adam*, who rules over them all and is king over all."[520]

515. **Because of this...** The verse does not contradict the theory of the power of the image because the image itself is an angel.

516. ***His angel*... in whom all images... are engraved...** *Shekhinah* is known as Angel of *YHVH*, conveying the energy of the higher *sefirot* and conducting the world. She is also the source of all life, embracing the primal form of everything that exists.

On *Shekhinah* as angel, see Jacob ben Jacob ha-Kohen, *Peirush Eser Sefirot*, 230; Moses of Burgos, fragment ed. Scholem, *Le-Ḥeqer Qabbalat R. Yitsḥaq ben Ya'aqov ha-Kohen*, 209–10; Naḥmanides on Exodus 3:2; 23:20; *Zohar* 1:61a, 113a, 120b, 159b, 166a, 228b, 230a, 232a; 3:95b, 187a, 270a; Moses de León, *Sefer ha-Rimmon*, 382; idem, *Sheqel ha-Qodesh*, 75–76 (96); Mopsik. Cf. *Mekhilta*, *Shirta* 3; *Pirqei de-Rabbi Eli'ezer* 40; *Shemot Rabbah* 2:5.

On *Shekhinah* as "the image comprising all images," see Ezra of Gerona, *Peirush Shir ha-Shirim*, 537; *Zohar* 1:13a, 19a; *ZḤ* 59a–c (*MhN*); Moses de León, *Shushan Edut*, 353; idem, *Sefer ha-Mishqal*, 138; idem, *She'elot u-Tshuvot*, 58; Scholem, *On the Mystical Shape of the Godhead*, 179; Liebes, *Peraqim*, 50–51; Wolfson, *Through a Speculum That Shines*, 306–17. The phrase derives from Ibn Ezra on Exodus 33:21.

517. ***filled with bodies*...** The full verse reads: *He will execute judgment upon the nations—filled with bodies—smashing heads over the wide earth.* In the biblical context, the phrase *filled with bodies* refers to the heaps of corpses among the nations. Here, it refers to the images of all beings contained and preserved within *Shekhinah*, including those who have been killed by the enemies of Israel. At the end of days, *Shekhinah* will punish the nations who perpetrated these killings.

See *Zohar* 1:39a, 41a. Cf. *Midrash Tehillim* 9:13; *Yalqut Shim'oni*, Numbers 247, Psalms 643, 869; Tishby, *Wisdom of the Zohar*, 2:787.

518. **אדם (*adam*)** "Adam" or "a human being." This image is maintained by living virtuously.

519. **בן אדם (*ben adam*), son of man** In the book of Ezekiel, God often addresses the prophet with this title (e.g., Ezekiel 2:1). Here, Rabbi El'azar's point is that by shunning forbidden food in the Babylonian exile, Ezekiel preserved the purity of the image of *adam*.

520. **He merited to abide in the image of *adam*...** See above, note 508; *Zohar* 2:125b.

Rabbi Yose said, "Because of this, one should beware of his sins and not deviate right or left. Even so, one should examine his sins every single day,[521] for look, when a person rises from bed, two witnesses stand with him and accompany him all day![522] When a person intends to rise, those witnesses say to him as he opens his eyes: *Let your eyes look directly ahead*... (Proverbs 4:25).[523] Once he rises and readies his feet to walk, those witnesses say, *Smoothen the course of your feet*... (ibid., 26).[524] So as a person proceeds each day, he should beware of his sins, every single day.[525] When night comes, he should contemplate and examine everything he did the whole day, so that he will turn back in repentance—reflecting constantly, as is said: *My sin is always before me* (Psalms 51:5).

"Come and see: When Israel were in the Holy Land, no sin haunted their hands, as has been established, because those offerings that they offered every day [191b] atoned for them.[526] Now that Israel are exiled from the Land and there is no one who atones for them, Torah herself atones for them together with worthy deeds, for *Shekhinah* accompanies them in exile—and whoever does not consider the ways of the blessed Holy One causes *Shekhinah* to cringe in the dust, as is said: *He lays her low, lays her low to the ground,* [*casts her to the dust*] (Isaiah 26:5)."[527]

521. **Even so...** Even if a person is vigilant, it is impossible not to sin, so one should examine one's misdeeds daily.

522. **two witnesses...** Two angels, who fulfill the role of witnesses.

See BT *Ta'anit* 11a; *Zohar* 3:175b. Cf. BT *Berakhot* 60b and Rashi, ad loc., s.v. *hitkabbedu*; *Shabbat* 119b; *Zohar* 1:12b, 144b, 165b; 2:106b, 239a; *ZḤ* 47a, 84b (*MhN*). According to Deuteronomy 19:15, testimony by a single witness is invalid.

523. ***Let your eyes look directly ahead...*** The full verse reads: *Let your eyes look directly ahead, your eyelids straight before you.*

524. ***Smoothen the course of your feet...*** The full verse reads: *Smoothen the course of your feet, and all your ways will be sure.*

525. **every single day** Alternatively, the phrase can be read as part of the following sentence.

526. **those offerings... atoned...** See *Pesiqta de-Rav Kahana* 5:17: "Rabbi Yudan said in the name of Rabbi Simon, 'No one spent a night in Jerusalem with sin in his hand. How so? The morning offering atoned for transgressions committed by night, and the twilight offering atoned for transgressions committed by day. Whatever the case, no one lodged in Jerusalem with sin in his hand.'" Here, Rabbi Yose extends this effect to the entire land of Israel.

See *Shir ha-Shirim Rabbah* on 1:9.

527. **Now that Israel are exiled...** Although priests no longer offer sacrifices in the Temple, Israel can still win atonement by studying Torah and living virtuously. See BT *Menaḥot* 110a: "Resh Lakish said, 'Whoever engages in Torah is as though he offered a burnt-offering, a meal-offering, a sin-offering, and a guilt-offering.'"

See BT *Ta'anit* 27b; *Zohar* 1:100a–b (*MhN*); 3:32a, 35a, 80b, 159a, 164a. On the presence of *Shekhinah* in exile, see above, note 154. The verse from Isaiah describes the humbling of Jerusalem, which in the *Zohar* symbolizes the fallen state of *Shekhinah*.

Rabbi Yitsḥak said, "Correspondingly, one who engages in Torah and worthy deeds enables Assembly of Israel to raise Her head in the midst of exile.[528] Happy is the share of those who engage in Torah day and night!

"Come and see: The blessed Holy One spins revolutions in the world so as to raise the head of the righteous.[529] For look! To enable Joseph to raise his head in the world for being found virtuous before Him, He inflamed a master against his servants, as is said: *The cupbearer of the king of Egypt and the baker offended* [*their master, the king of Egypt*] (Genesis 40:1)—all in order to raise the head of Joseph the Righteous![530]

"Come and see: Through a dream he was overturned by his brothers, and through a dream he was raised over his brothers, raised over the whole world.

"*The two of them dreamed a dream* . . . (Genesis 40:5).[531] Come and see: As has been said, all dreams follow the mouth.[532] Now, when Joseph interpreted their dreams, why did he offer one a good interpretation and the other a bad interpretation?[533] Because actually, those dreams concerned Joseph himself,

528. **Assembly of Israel . . .** *Shekhinah*, the divine counterpart of the earthly Assembly of Israel, the aspect of God most intimately connected with them. Virtuous living restores and invigorates Her. See above, note 237.

529. **spins revolutions . . .** גלגל גלגולין (*Gilgel gilgulin*). The expression derives from a medieval philosophical formula: מסבב הסיבות (*mesabbev ha-sibbot*), "revolves the turn of events." In Maimonides' *Guide of the Perplexed* 1:70 (Ibn Tibbon translation), God is described as מסבב הגלגל (*mesabbev ha-galgal*), "revolving the [celestial] sphere."

The sense here may be influenced by the rabbinic wording related to the Joseph story in BT *Shabbat* 10b: "His brothers became jealous of him, ונתגלגל הדבר (*ve-nitgalgel ha-davar*), and the matter rolled on, and our forefathers descended to Egypt." See the identical expression in *Tanḥuma, Vayeshev* 2. Cf. BT *Bava Metsi'a* 40a, 54a; *Seder Eliyyahu Rabbah* 18 (p. 114).

See Radak on Genesis 41:1 and Isaiah 63:9; *Zohar* 1:109a, 110a–b, 158b, 194b, 196a, 199a, 201b; 2:111b; Moses de León, *Shushan Edut*, 354; idem, *Sefer ha-Rimmon*, 351, 354–55; idem, *Mishkan ha-Edut*, 52a; Gersonides on 1 Kings 2:46; Ben Yehuda, *Dictionary*, s.v. *mesibbah, savav, sibbah, sibbuv;* Liebes, *Peraqim*, 299–300, 328–29; Mopsik.

530. **To enable Joseph to raise his head . . .** To bring about Joseph's reward for withstanding sexual temptation, God brought about the incident involving Pharaoh's two servants, recounted in Genesis 40.

See above, note 50; BT *Megillah* 13b.

531. ***The two of them dreamed a dream . . .*** The full verse reads: *The two of them dreamed a dream, each his own dream, in a single night, each with his own dream's meaning—the cupbearer and the baker of the king of Egypt, who were held in the prison.*

532. **all dreams follow the mouth** The true meaning of a dream depends on its interpretation.

See BT *Berakhot* 55b: "Rabbi El'azar said: 'How do we know that all dreams follow the mouth [of the interpreter]? Because it is said: *As he interpreted to us, so it was* (Genesis 41:13).'" The verse cited by Rabbi El'azar is spoken later by Pharaoh's chief cupbearer, describing how accurately Joseph interpreted his dream and that of the chief baker.

See *Zohar* 1:183a, 194b.

533. **why did he offer . . . ?** Since his interpretation actually determined the outcome of the dream, why couldn't he inter-

and since he knew the essential root of the matter, he interpreted their dreams as required; to each one he offered an interpretation, to restore the matter to its place.[534]

"What is written? *Joseph said to them, 'Do not interpretations belong to God? Tell me, please!'* (Genesis 40:8).[535] Why? Because this is how an interpreter of a dream should entrust interpretation to the blessed Holy One, since from there derives fulfillment of all, therein abides interpretation.

"Come and see: As has been said, the rung of dream is below, the sixth rung—since from the place where prophecy dwells until this rung of dream lie six rungs.[536] Interpretation ascends from the rung of dream to another rung. Dream is the rung below and interpretation stands above; interpretation abides in speech, so the matter depends upon speech, as is written: '*Do not interpretations belong to* אלהים (*Elohim*), *God?' To Elohim*, precisely!"[537]

Come and see what is written: *The chief cupbearer recounted his dream to Joseph*... (Genesis 40:9).[538]

Rabbi El'azar opened, "*As they were crossing* [the Jordan], *Elijah said to Elisha, 'Ask what I can do for you* [*before I am taken from you.'*] ... (2 Kings 2:9).[539] Here

pret both dreams favorably? See Sullam; Mopsik.

534. **concerned Joseph himself...** Joseph understood that these dreams foretold events concerning his family and their descendants: the people of Israel. The cupbearer's dream was full of promise, so Joseph interpreted his dream favorably. The baker's dream predicted the destruction of the Temple and Israel's exile, so he received a negative interpretation. Joseph responded appropriately to each dream and dreamer, "to restore the matter to its place."

See below, pages 172–75.

535. ***Joseph said to them...*** The full verse reads: *They said to him, "We dreamed a dream and there is no one to interpret it." Joseph said to them, "Do not interpretations belong to God? Tell me, please!"*

536. **rung of dream ... sixth rung...** Six stages span the phenomena of prophecy and dream: the *sefirot Netsaḥ*, *Hod*, *Yesod*, and *Shekhinah*, and the first two archangels: Michael and Gabriel.

See above, p. 114 and n. 194; and BT *Berakhot* 57b: "A dream is one-sixtieth of prophecy."

537. **interpretation abides in speech...** Within the realm of *Shekhinah*, who conveys the divine word and is known as Speech and Mouth. She also bears the divine name *Elohim*.

See above, p. 115 and n. 198.

538. ***The chief cupbearer...*** The context (Genesis 40:9–10) reads: *The chief cupbearer recounted his dream to Joseph and said to him, "In my dream—here, a vine in front of me, and on the vine three tendrils, and as she was budding, up came her blossom, her clusters ripened into grapes.*

539. ***As they were crossing...*** The context (2 Kings 2:9–10) reads: *As they were crossing, Elijah said to Elisha, "Ask what I can do for you before I am taken from you." Elisha said, "May a double portion of your spirit be upon me." He said, "You have made a difficult request. If you see me being taken from you, it will be so for you; if not, it will not be."*

one should contemplate! This verse is astonishing: *Elijah said to Elisha, 'Ask what I can do for you.'* Now, was this really in his power? It was in the power of the blessed Holy One! Furthermore, Elisha himself knew this as well, so why did he say, *May a double portion of your spirit be upon me* (ibid.)?

"Certainly, however, one who grasps heaven and earth and the entire world—how could this not be within his power?[540] And surely for Elijah and the other righteous, the blessed Holy One performs their will constantly, as is written: *He performs the will of those in awe of Him* (Psalms 145:19).[541] All the more so since that Holy Spirit that rested upon him he could bequeath to one as righteous as Elisha, who was his servant. Look, the blessed Holy One had told him: *And Elisha son of Shaphat of Abel-meholah, anoint as prophet in your stead* (1 Kings 19:16); so Elisha was entitled to be his heir!

"*A double portion of your spirit* (2 Kings, ibid.). What does *double* mean? Would you ever imagine that he requested two for one? How could he ask for something not in [Elijah's] possession? But really, he did not request double the spirit; rather, he asked—concerning the spirit that [Elijah] possessed—that he be able to enact twice as many miracles in the world through that spirit.[542]

"*He said, 'You have made a difficult request. If you see me [being taken from you, it will be so for you; if not, it will not be]'* (ibid., 10). What does this mean: *if you see me*? He was really telling him: 'If you can comprehend the essence of the spirit that I bequeath to you at the moment I am taken from you, it will be so

540. **one who grasps heaven and earth...** A righteous person such as Elijah links the divine and earthly realms. Thereby, he attains the rung of *Yesod* and unites the divine couple, *Tif'eret* and *Shekhinah*, who are symbolized by heaven and earth. Such a human channels the divine flow and is capable of wonders.

In *Ra'aya Meheimna* and *Tiqqunei ha-Zohar*, the phrase "who grasps heaven and earth" is presented as a Targumic rendering of 1 Chronicles 29:11: *for all that is in heaven and on earth.* The standard Targum on the verse reads differently. See *Zohar* 2:116a (*RM*); *TZ*, intro, 9b; 13, 29a; *NO.*

541. ***He performs the will of those in awe of Him*** See *ZḤ* 26c; and BT *Mo'ed Qatan* 16a, where according to Rabbi Abbahu, God says: "I rule the human being. And who rules Me? A righteous person. For I issue a decree and he annuls it."

542. ***A double portion*** **...two for one?...** Did Elisha really ask for twice as much inspiration as Elijah had received? How could Elijah provide what he didn't possess? Rather, Elisha sought the same inspiration but with twice the miraculous potency.

See Moses de León, *She'elot u-Tshuvot*, 71–72; Mopsik. On the number of miracles performed by the two prophets, see *Baraita di-Shloshim u-Shtayim Middot*, 1 (p. 13); *Midrash ha-Gadol*, Genesis, intro, 23; Ginzberg, *Legends*, 6:343–44, n. 2; 347, n. 21.

The word "miracles" renders נמוסין (*nimosin*), "laws," derived from the Greek *nomos* ("custom, law"). In the *Zohar*, *nimosin* occasionally implies (and involves a play on) נסין (*nissin*), "miracles," supernatural enactments that contravene the "laws" of nature. See *Zohar* 2:37b, 52b; 3:76a, 176a, 297b.

for you.' For that entire essence of spirit, contemplated by him as he saw Elijah, would be absorbed fittingly. [192a]

"Come and see: One who contemplates what he learned from his teacher and sees him in that wisdom can be augmented by that spirit abundantly.[543]

"Come and see: In whatever he was doing, Joseph would contemplate through the spirit of wisdom the image of his father.[544] So the matter prospered, and he was augmented by other spirit with radiance more sublime.

"When that wicked one said to him *Here, a vine in front of me*' (Genesis 40:9), Joseph trembled because he did not know what the matter implied.[545] As soon as he said *and on the vine three tendrils* (ibid., 10), his spirit immediately aroused, augmented by radiance, and he gazed upon the image of his father; then his spirit shone and he knew the matter.[546]

"What is written? *And on the vine three tendrils.* Joseph said, 'Look! This is surely tidings of total joy!' Why? Because that vine appeared to him regarding Assembly of Israel, and Joseph was gladdened by this.[547]

"*And on the vine three tendrils*—three supernal rungs emerging from this vine: priests, Levites, and Israel.[548]

543. **One who contemplates...** By reflecting upon the wisdom transmitted by one's teacher and by envisioning him, a person becomes open to a fresh influx of spirit.

See BT *Eruvin* 13b; *Zohar* 2:123b; David ibn Zimra, *She'elot u-Tshuvot*, 3:472; 6:2; *OY*; *KP*; Galante; Scholem; Mopsik. Cf. above, pages 159–60.

544. **Joseph would contemplate... the image of his father** According to a rabbinic tradition, when Potiphar's wife attempted to seduce Joseph, "he saw the image of his father, and his blood cooled." Here, the theme of Joseph envisioning his father is transformed into a contemplative practice.

See *Bereshit Rabbah* 87:7 (in the name of Rav Mattana). Cf. BT *Sotah* 36b; above, note 40.

545. **When that wicked one said...** When the cupbearer began recounting his dream, Joseph did not know the nature of the vine and its significance. The context (40:9–10) reads: *The chief cupbearer recounted his dream to Joseph and said to him, "In my dream—here, a vine in front of me, and on the vine three tendrils, and as she was budding, up came her blossom, her clusters ripened into grapes.*

546. ***three tendrils... image of his father...*** When Joseph heard the cupbearer refer to *three tendrils*, he realized that these symbolized the sefirotic triad of *Ḥesed*, *Gevurah*, and *Tif'eret*, corresponding to the three patriarchs: Abraham, Isaac, and Jacob. Illuminated, he envisioned his father.

See BT *Ḥullin* 92a; *Zohar* 1:238a; 3:189a–b.

547. **vine appeared to him regarding Assembly of Israel...** The vine appearing in the cupbearer's dream alluded to *Shekhinah*, joined with the patriarchal triad of *sefirot*.

On Assembly of Israel as a name of *Shekhinah*, see above, note 237. On Israel as vine (and vineyard), see Isaiah 5:7; 27:2–4; Jeremiah 2:21; Ezekiel 17:1–10; Hosea 10:1; Psalms 80:9; BT *Ḥullin* 92a; *Zohar* 1:238a.

548. **three supernal rungs emerging...** The triad of *sefirot* (*Ḥesed*, *Gevurah*, and *Tif'eret*) gathers in *Shekhinah* and then manifests below in the three divisions of the people of Israel.

"*And as she was budding, up came her blossom* (ibid.), for by virtue of them, Assembly of Israel ascends and is blessed by the supernal King.[549]

"*Her clusters ripened into grapes* (ibid.)—the righteous of the world, who are like grapes fittingly ripened.

"Alternatively, *Her clusters ripened into grapes*—wine preserved in its grapes since the six days of Creation.[550]

"Until here, Joseph was gladdened by his dream; from here on, the dream is his.[551] For some dreams refer to oneself and to others.

"*And I took the grapes* (ibid., 11)[552]—referring to himself.

"We have learned: One who sees grapes in a dream—if white, a good omen for him; if black, no.[553] Why? Because it is a mystery of two particular rungs—black and white: one is good, the other is not.[554] All those grapes depend upon the mystery of faith, so they diverge in wisdom, either toward good or evil—these, in need of compassion; those, compassionate providence.[555]

549. **by virtue of them, Assembly of Israel ascends...** Through the service and worship of the entire people, *Shekhinah* is stimulated to ascend and receive from *Binah* (or *Tif'eret*).

550. **wine preserved in its grapes...** In rabbinic literature, this primordial vintage awaits the righteous in the world that is coming. In the *Zohar*, the wine symbolizes the deepest secrets of Torah awaiting the righteous—but also the rich emanation stored within, or flowing from, *Binah*, who is known as "the world that is coming."

See BT *Berakhot* 34b (in the name of Rabbi Yehoshu'a son of Levi); *Zohar* 1:135b (*MhN*), 238b; 2:147a; 3:4a, 12b, 39b–40a, 93b, 100a (*RM*); *ZḤ* 28a–b; Moses de León, *Sefer ha-Rimmon*, 130.

551. **Until here, Joseph was gladdened...** Until here, the chief cupbearer's dream conveyed a message to Joseph about the *sefirot*, Israel, and the righteous; from here on, the dream pertained only to the cupbearer himself, predicting his return to Pharaoh's court. See *Zohar* 1:189a.

552. ***And I took the grapes*** The full verse reads: *Pharaoh's cup was in my hand, and I took the grapes and squeezed them into Pharaoh's cup and I placed the cup in Pharaoh's palm.*

553. **One who sees grapes in a dream...** A modification of the rabbinic wording (BT *Berakhot* 56b): "One who sees grapes in a dream: if white, whether in season or not, a good sign; if black—in season, good; if not in season, bad." Rabbi El'azar highlights the contrast to introduce his discussion of two polar opposites.

See *Midrash Tehillim* 128:4; *Zohar* 2:144a; *ZḤ* 64c (*ShS*).

554. **two particular rungs—black and white...** Wine symbolizes *Din* (Judgment), which comes in two varieties: harsh and restrained, black and white.

On wine as Judgment, see Azriel of Gerona, *Peirush ha-Aggadot*, 46; Moses de León, *Sefer ha-Rimmon*, 130; Mopsik.

555. **All those grapes depend...** Both varieties of Judgment are contained within, and conveyed by, *Shekhinah*, the mystery of faith. Dark grapes in a dream foretell the chastisement of stern judgment, so one should seek compassion to sweeten the harshness. Light grapes indicate that Judgment has already been softened by compassionate care and tending.

On the phrase "in need of compassion," see *Midrash Tehillim* 128:4.

"Come and see: Adam's wife squeezed grapes for him, bringing death upon him and upon the whole world.[556] Noah approached these grapes and did not guard himself properly. What is written? *He drank of the wine and became drunk, and exposed himself within* אהלה (*oholoh*), *his tent* (ibid. 9:21).[557] The sons of Aaron drank wine of those grapes and brought an offering with that wine and died, as has been said.[558] Therefore it is written: *Their grapes are grapes of poison, bitter clusters for them* (Deuteronomy 32:32), since those grapes caused this.

"This one saw good grapes in that vineyard, wafting pleasant fragrance on perfect rungs fittingly.[559] So Joseph knew the matter, contemplated the root, and interpreted the dream soundly, because he had been fittingly gladdened by that dream. He therefore offered a favorable interpretation, and so it was fulfilled.[560]

"What is written? *The chief baker saw that he had interpreted favorably* [*and he said to Joseph,* "אף אני (*Af ani*), *Me too! In my dream*...] (Genesis 40:16).[561] Come and see: Cursed be the wicked, whose every action is for evil, whose

556. **Adam's wife squeezed grapes for him...** Grapes of harsh judgment, condemning humans to mortality.

See *Bereshit Rabbah* 19:5: "Rabbi Aivu said, 'She squeezed grapes and offered them to him.'" Cf. *Zohar* 1:36a–b; 2:267b.

557. **Noah approached... אהלה (*oholoh*), *his tent*** Noah also succumbed to the intoxicating brew of harsh judgment within the realm of *Shekhinah*.

In the Torah the final letter of the Hebrew word אהלה (*oholoh*), *his tent,* is a ה (*he*), rather than the normal masculine possessive suffix ו (*vav*). The suffix ה (*he*) usually denotes the feminine possessive, *her.* See *Bereshit Rabbah* 36:4: "Rabbi Yehudah son of Rabbi Simon and Rabbi Ḥanan said in the name of Rabbi Shemu'el son of Rav Yitsḥak, '...It is spelled אהלה (*oholah*), *her tent:* inside the tent of his wife.'" In other words, Noah shamed himself in his wife's tent. See Theodor's note, ad loc.

Here similarly, Rabbi El'azar reads the word as *oholah, her tent,* but he takes this to mean the tent of *Shekhinah,* site of Noah's sin. See *Zohar* 1:73a–b, 83a, 140b.

558. **sons of Aaron drank wine...** Aaron's two eldest sons, Nadab and Abihu, were killed when *they offered strange fire in the presence of YHVH* (Leviticus 10:1–2). According to midrashic tradition, they died because they "entered while drunk with wine."

See *Vayiqra Rabbah* 12:1 (in the name of Rabbi Yishma'el); *Zohar* 1:73b; Moses de León, *Sheqel ha-Qodesh,* 36–37 (43–44).

559. **This one saw good grapes...** The chief cupbearer, in his dream, saw the good variety of grapes within the vineyard of *Shekhinah*, their fragrance stimulating Her union above.

On the arousal of *Shekhinah* by the left side, see *Zohar* 1:133a; Moses de León, *Sheqel ha-Qodesh,* 38 (45); Mopsik.

560. **offered a favorable interpretation...** See Genesis 40:12–13, 20–21.

561. ***The chief baker saw...*** The context (Genesis 40:16–17) reads: *The chief baker saw that he had interpreted favorably, and he said to Joseph, "Me too! In my dream—here, three wicker baskets on my head, and in the top basket all kinds of food for Pharaoh, baker's work, and birds were eating them from the basket above my head."*

every word is spoken for evil, for causing evil![562] As soon as he opened his mouth, he opened with אף (*af*), anger. Immediately, Joseph became frightened, realizing that all his words were intended to cause evil, that tidings of evil filled his mouth.[563]

"*Here, three wicker baskets* [*on my head*] (ibid.). Then Joseph knew he had been informed of the destruction of the Temple, with Israel in exile, for they would be exiled from the Holy Land.[564]

"See what is written: *And in the top basket all kinds of food for Pharaoh, baker's work, and birds were eating them* (ibid., 17)—other nations assembling against Israel, killing them, destroying their homes, scattering them to the four corners of the world. All this Joseph envisaged and knew through that dream. Immediately, he rendered an unfavorable interpretation so that it would be fulfilled.

"For come and see: These two rungs seen by one, seen by the other—this one saw [192b] the supernal rung prevailing, the moon shining; that one saw her darken, dominated by the evil serpent.[565] Therefore Joseph pondered that dream and delivered an unfavorable interpretation. So all depends upon interpretation. Surely they saw these two rungs—this one dominant, that one dominant."

Rabbi Yehudah opened, "*A pure heart, O God, create in me; a firm spirit renew within me* (Psalms 51:12).[566] This verse has been established, but *a pure heart* corresponds to what is said: *Grant Your servant a listening heart* (1 Kings 3:9),[567]

562. **wicked, whose every action is for evil...** An extreme paraphrase of a saying attributed to Rabbi Shemu'el son of Naḥman (*Bereshit Rabbah* 89:7): "Cursed be the wicked, who never perform a kindness wholeheartedly!"

563. **he opened with אף (*af*), anger...** The chief baker began by saying, "אף אני (*Af ani*), *Me too!*" The word אף (*af*), though, means not only "too," but also "anger."

See *Bereshit Rabbah* 19:2; 88:6.

564. ***three wicker baskets*... Israel in exile...** See *Bereshit Rabbah* 88:6, where the three baskets represent the empires of Babylon, Persia, and Greece, and the top basket (in the following verse) symbolizes Rome. Cf. *Targum Yerushalmi*, Genesis 40:18.

565. **two rungs seen...** Both dreamers (the cupbearer and the baker) saw two rungs. The cupbearer saw *Shekhinah* (the moon) illumined by emanation from Her partner, "the supernal rung." The baker saw Her dominated by the demonic serpent, unable to receive or reflect the light.

See above, pp. 97–98 and n. 85, p. 100 and n. 102.

566. ***firm spirit*...** Although Joseph is not mentioned in Rabbi Yehudah's discourse, the reference to "spirit" evokes Joseph's inspiration. See above, page 172; and Pharaoh's rhetorical question (Genesis 41:38): *Could we find a man like this, in whom is the spirit of God?*

567. **This verse has been established, but...** Earlier interpretations of the verse (as found in BT *Sukkah* 52a; *Midrash Mishlei* 20:9) do not satisfy Rabbi Yehudah, so he offers a new one. The verse from Kings records Solomon's request from God for wisdom and discernment.

and similarly to: *A good-hearted person has a continuous feast* (Proverbs 15:15).[568] So, *a pure heart*—precisely!

"*A firm spirit renew within me*—*a firm spirit*, precisely! Because from the Other Side derives an impure heart: a spirit misleading inhabitants of the world, an impure spirit called 'spirit of distortion,' as is said: *YHVH has mingled within her a spirit of distortion* (Isaiah 19:14).[569] So, *a firm spirit renew within me.* Why *renew*? This implies renewal of the moon, at the time of her renewal; therefore, *renew.*"[570]

Rabbi El'azar and Rabbi Yose were walking on the way. Rabbi Yose said to Rabbi El'azar, "Now, it's written *A certain spirit came forward and stood before YHVH and said, 'I will entice him!'* ... (1 Kings 22:21), and we have learned: 'This is the spirit of Naboth the Jezreelite.'[571] But once souls ascend and stand above, can they return to this world?[572] And it's an astonishing thing that he said: *I will go out and be a spirit of falsehood* (ibid., 22)!

568. ***A good-hearted person*...** The full verse reads: *All the days of the poor are wretched, but a good-hearted person has a continuous feast.* See *Zohar* 2:197b, 259b, where the phrase *good-hearted* refers to *Shekhinah*. Cf. BT *Bava Batra* 145b.

569. **from the Other Side derives an impure heart...** The demonic force seduces humanity to sin by means of the evil impulse. See BT *Bava Batra* 16a: "Resh Lakish said, 'Satan, the evil impulse, and the Angel of Death are one and the same.'" The verse from Isaiah refers to God's sowing of confusion among the Egyptians.

570. **renewal of the moon...** Renewal of *Shekhinah*, source of the spirit and the means of its cyclical rejuvenation. See above, pages 87, 98.

Shekhinah, also known as *Malkhut* (Kingdom), is often associated with King David, the ideal king and traditionally the author of Psalms, including this particular verse: *A pure heart, O God, create in me; a firm spirit renew within me.*

571. ***A certain spirit*...Naboth...** In 1 Kings 21, King Ahab of Israel requests to purchase or trade for a vineyard owned by Naboth the Jezreelite adjoining the royal palace, but Naboth refuses to yield his inherited land. Ahab's wife, Jezebel, then arranges for Naboth to be executed on false charges, and Ahab takes possession of the vineyard. Consequently, Ahab is punished by God, killed by a stray arrow in a battle against the Arameans (22:34–35). According to the prophet Michaiah, the king decides to go to battle based on the rosy predictions of false prophecy conveyed by *a certain spirit.* The context (22:20–22) reads: *YHVH said, "Who will entice Ahab so that he will go up and fall at Ramoth-gilead?" One said in this way and another said in that way. Then a certain spirit came forward and stood before YHVH and said, "I will entice him!" YHVH said to him, "With what?" He replied, "I will go out and be a spirit of falsehood in the mouth of all his prophets." He said, "You will entice and you will prevail. Go out and do so!"*

In BT *Shabbat* 149b, this spirit is identified as the spirit of Naboth, seeking his revenge. See Radak, 1 Kings 22:20.

572. **But once souls ascend...** After death, a soul does not return to earth unless she needs to be reincarnated in order to fulfill an important *mitsvah* that she left unfulfilled in her previous incarnation. See above, p. 137 and n. 331. For other exceptions to the rule, see *KP*.

"Further, why was Ahab punished for what he did, seeing that this is a law of Torah presented by Samuel to Israel, as is written: *Your best fields and vineyards and olive groves he will seize* (1 Samuel 8:14)? So if Ahab took that vineyard from Naboth, it was legal.[573] Moreover, he offered him another one or silver, but he refused."[574]

He replied, "You have asked well. Come and see! This spirit, reported to be the spirit of Naboth—here one should examine whether the spirit of Naboth could ascend and stand before Him, as is written: *A certain spirit came forward.*[575] If he was righteous, how could he seek falsehood in that world, the world of truth?[576] For if in this world a virtuous person does not seek falsehood, in that world all the more so! And if he wasn't virtuous, how could he have stood in the presence of the blessed Holy One?

"But surely, Naboth was not virtuous enough to stand in His presence; rather, it was another spirit, who dominates the world: the spirit who stands constantly—ascending before the blessed Holy One—the one who misleads inhabitants of the world with his lies.[577] Whoever is accustomed to falsehood strives for it constantly, so he said, *I will go out and be a spirit of falsehood.* Therefore the blessed Holy One said to him, *Go out and do so!* (1 Kings, ibid.)—'Get out of here!' as they have established, for it is written: *A speaker of lies will not endure before My eyes* (Psalms 101:7).[578] So, this is *a spirit of falsehood*, certainly![579]

"Furthermore, regarding the fact that he killed Naboth and seized his vineyard: let him seize it, but why did he kill him? Actually, though, because he killed him unjustly, he was punished. He killed him unjustly and took his vineyard, so it is written: *Have you murdered and also taken possession?* (1 Kings 21:19). For this he was punished.[580]

573. **why was Ahab punished...** Samuel had warned Israel against the excesses of royal authority, and according to the view of Rabbi Yose (BT *Sanhedrin* 20b), "Everything stated in the Portion of the King [1 Samuel 8], the king is permitted to do."

See Tosafot, ad loc., s.v. *melekh muttar.*

574. **he offered him another one or silver...** According to 1 Kings 21:2, King Ahab offered to provide Naboth with a better vineyard in exchange for his or to purchase it from him.

575. ***A certain spirit came forward*** The verse continues: *and stood before YHVH.*

576. **how could he seek falsehood...** How could he volunteer in heaven to spread falsehood? The heavenly realm is called "world of truth" in *Vayiqra Rabbah* 26:7.

577. **another spirit...** The demonic spirit. See BT *Bava Batra* 16a: "[Satan] descends and leads astray, ascends and arouses wrath, obtains authorization and seizes the soul."

578. **as they have established...** See BT *Shabbat* 149b.

579. **this is *a spirit of falsehood*...** The phrase refers to the demonic spirit, not Naboth's spirit.

580. **he killed Naboth...** King Ahab allowed Naboth to be killed. See above, note 571.

"Come and see how many people in the world this spirit of falsehood misleads by lying! He dominates the world on many flanks, through many activities, as we have established. So, King David sought to guard himself from him, to escape impurity, as is written: *A pure heart, O God, create in me; a firm spirit renew within me* (Psalms 51:12)—this is *a firm spirit*, whereas the other is *a spirit of falsehood.* So, two rungs: one holy, one impure."

He opened, saying, "*And YHVH utters His voice before His forces; for vast is His army, mighty those carrying out His word!*... (Joel 2:11).[581] This verse has been established,[582] but *And YHVH* signifies everywhere 'He and His Court.'[583]

"*Utters* קולו (*qolo*), *His voice*—the voice of which is written *a voice of words* (Deuteronomy 4:12).[584] Here is written *voice of words*, and there is written *no man of words* (Exodus 4:10). What does *man of words* mean? As is said: *man of Elohim* (Deuteronomy 33:1).[585]

581. ***And YHVH... carrying out His word!...*** The verse continues: *For great is the day of YHVH, and very terrible. Who can endure it?*

582. **This verse has been established** See *Pesiqta de-Rav Kahana* 24:3; *Tanḥuma, Vayishlaḥ* 2.

583. ***And YHVH...* 'He and His Court'** Wherever the phrase *And YHVH* appears in the Bible, the word *and* amplifies the meaning of *YHVH* to include the divine court. See *Bereshit Rabbah* 51:2: "Rabbi El'azar said, 'Wherever it is said *And YHVH*, this implies: He and His Court.'"

In Kabbalah this "court" symbolizes *Shekhinah*, who derives from the *sefirah* of *Din* (Judgment) and pronounces the divine decree, so the phrase *And YHVH* encompasses "He [*Tif'eret*, known as *YHVH*] and His Court [*Shekhinah*]."

See *Vayiqra Rabbah* 24:2; JT *Berakhot* 9:5, 14b; Rashi on Exodus 12:29; *Zohar* 1:15b, 64b, 105a, 107b, 159b, 198a, 240a; 2:37b, 44b, 227b; 3:149a. The hermeneutical significance of *and* was championed by Rabbi Akiva. See BT *Yevamot* 68b; *Sanhedrin* 51b.

584. ***voice of words*** The Hebrew word קול (*qol*) means both "voice" and "sound." The verse in Deuteronomy reads: *YHVH spoke to you from the midst of the fire. A sound of words you heard but an image you did not see, only sound.*

In Kabbalah the raw "voice" symbolizes *Tif'eret*, while "words" represents *Shekhinah*, who articulates divine speech. See *Zohar* 1:1b, 119b; 3:191a, 193b.

585. ***no man of words... man of Elohim*** When God called upon Moses to confront Pharaoh, the startled shepherd claimed that he was incapable: *No man of words am I... for I am heavy of mouth and heavy of tongue* (Exodus 4:10). From a kabbalistic perspective, Moses was not yet filled with the divine word, not yet intimate with *Shekhinah*. See *Zohar* 1:119b; 2:25b; above, note 457.

Moses's title, איש האלהים (*ish ha-elohim*), *man of God* (Deuteronomy 33:1; Psalms 90:1), is understood midrashically as "husband of God" (able to command Him) and kabbalistically as "husband of *Shekhinah*" (united with Her).

See *Pesiqta de-Rav Kahana, nispaḥim, Vezot Haberakhah*, 443–44, 448 (variants); *Tanḥuma, Vezot Haberakhah* 2 (*Ets Yosef*, ad loc.); *Devarim Rabbah* (Lieberman), on 33:1; *Midrash Tehillim* 90:5; *Zohar* 1:6b, 21b–22a, 148a, 152a–b, 236b; 239a; 2:22b, 235b, 238b, 244b (*Heikh*); Moses de León, *Sefer ha-Rimmon*, 25.

According to rabbinic tradition, after en-

"*Before His forces*—Israel.[586]

"*For vast is His army*—as is said: *Is there any number to His troops?* (Job 25:3). [193a] For the blessed Holy One has countless officials and emissaries, all of them poised to accuse Israel, so He manifests before Israel in order to protect them, so that they cannot be incriminated.

"*Mighty those carrying out His word.* Who is *mighty*? A virtuous person, one who engages in holy Torah day and night.[587]

"Alternatively, *mighty those carrying out His word*—the Accuser appearing before the blessed Holy One, who is strong as iron, hard as flint.

"*Carrying out His word*—obtaining authorization above and seizing the soul below.[588]

"*For great is the day of YHVH, and very terrible. Who can endure it?* (Joel, ibid.). For He rules over all, supreme and mighty over them all, all subject to His dominion.

"Happy are the righteous, in whom the blessed Holy One constantly delights, rendering them worthy of the world that is coming, gladdening them with the joy of the righteous, who are destined to rejoice in the blessed Holy One, as is written: *Let all who take refuge in You rejoice; let them ever shout for joy. Shelter them, so that those who love Your name may exult in You* (Psalms 5:12)."

countering God on Mount Sinai, Moses abstained from sexual contact with his wife and maintained union with *Shekhinah*.

See *Sifrei*, Numbers 99; BT *Shabbat* 87a; *Tanḥuma, Tsav* 13; Maimonides, *Mishneh Torah, Hilkhot Yesodei ha-Torah* 7:6; *Zohar* 1:22a, 152b, 234b; 2:222a; 3:148a, 180a.

586. ***His forces*—Israel** See *Tanḥuma, Vayishlaḥ* 2; cf. *Pesiqta de-Rav Kahana* 24:3.

587. **Who is *mighty*?...** By virtue of a single person constantly engaged in Torah (the divine word), God guards His entire people. Cf. *Tanḥuma, Vayishlaḥ* 2.

588. **obtaining authorization...** See above, note 577.

פרשת מקץ

Parashat Mi-Qets

"AT THE END" (GENESIS 41:1–44:17)

Rabbi Yehudah opened, "*He puts an end to darkness, every extremity he explores* . . . (Job 28:3). This verse has been discussed.[1] *He puts an end to darkness*—End of the Left,[2] who roams the world, roams above, stands before the blessed Holy One, accuses and denounces the world, as has been said.[3]

"*Every* תכלית (*takhlit*), *extremity, he explores*—for look, none of his actions is intended for good, rather always to destroy, to cause כליה (*kelayah*), extermination, in the world.

"*Land of pitch-black darkness* (ibid. 10:21).[4] Come and see: There is a land of the living above,[5] but this is *a land of pitch-black darkness*. What is *a land of pitch-black darkness*? End deriving from the side of darkness, dross of gold, as has been said.[6]

1. ***He puts an end to darkness* . . .** The full verse reads: *He puts an end to darkness, every extremity he explores—rock of pitch-black gloom.* This section of Job (28:3–11) is traditionally understood as referring to God's penetration of the mysteries of nature, though its more likely referent is human mining operations in remote volcanic regions.

See *Bereshit Rabbah* 89:1; *Tanḥuma, Miqqets* 1; *Zohar* 1:62b, 210b; 2:33a–b; *ZḤ* 69c (*ShS*).

2. **End of the Left** The demonic Other Side, deriving from *Gevurah* on the left side of the sefirotic tree. *Gevurah* is *darkness,* and the demonic realm is the *end* of *darkness.*

See *Zohar* 1:54a, 62b, 63a, 75a (*ST*), 152b, 210b; 2:33a–34a, 134a–b, 181b. Cf. *Eikhah Rabbah* 2:6; *Pesiqta de-Rav Kahana* 17:5.

3. **roams the world . . .** See Job 1:7, and the description of Satan's activities in BT *Bava Batra* 16a: "He descends and leads astray, ascends and arouses wrath, obtains authorization and seizes the soul."

4. ***Land of pitch-black darkness*** As mentioned above (note 1), the verse in Job 28 concludes: *rock of pitch-black gloom.* Rabbi Yehudah, however, offers a somewhat different ending from an earlier chapter of Job. The same switch appears in his name in *Zohar* 1:62b.

See Joseph Angelet, *Livnat ha-Sappir,* 60c; Galante; Mopsik.

5. **land of the living . . .** *Shekhinah,* source of life for all worlds.

See *Zohar* 1:65b–66a, 95b, 115a, 124b, 143b; 3:84a; Moses de León, *Sheqel ha-Qodesh,* 62 (77); Gikatilla, *Sha'arei Orah,* 14a.

6. **deriving from . . . darkness, dross of**

"Come and see how deeply human beings should contemplate the service of the blessed Holy One, engaging in Torah day and night in order to discover and ponder His service. For Torah proclaims every day before a person: *Whoever is simple, turn in here!* (Proverbs 9:4). We have already established this matter.[7] When one engages in Torah and cleaves to her, he becomes worthy of grasping the Tree of Life, as is written: *She is a tree of life to those who grasp her* (ibid. 3:18).[8]

"Come and see: When a person grasps the Tree of Life in this world,[9] he grasps it in the world that is coming. For as souls depart this world, correspondingly rungs are arranged for them in the world that is coming.[10]

"Come and see: The Tree of Life embraces many rungs distinct from one another, yet all is one. In the Tree of Life are rungs one above another: branches and leaves, bark, trunk of the tree, roots—and all is the tree. Similarly, whoever engages Torah is enhanced, grasping the Tree of Life. All scions of faith—Israel—grasp the Tree of Life: some joined to the actual tree, to its trunk; some joined to the branches, some to the leaves, some to the roots. Consequently, all of them are joined to the Tree of Life, and those who engage in Torah [193b] are all joined to the trunk of the tree. So, whoever engages in Torah is joined to all, as has been established and explained."[11]

It happened at the end (Genesis 41:1).[12] What is *at the end*?

Rabbi Shim'on said, "A place without remembering, and this is End of the

gold... The demonic realm originates in *Gevurah,* the attribute of *Din* (Judgment), which is symbolized by darkness. *Gevurah* is also pictured as gold, which after the refining process of emanation leaves behind a dross of evil.

On this dross, see *Zohar* 1:48a, 52a, 73a; 2:236a–b; 3:51a, 56a; Moses de León, *Sheqel ha-Qodesh,* 41 (49). Cf. *Zohar* 1:118b, 153a. On the alchemical associations, see Scholem, *Alchemie und Kabbala,* 40–43.

7. **established this matter** See *Zohar* 1:165a, 227a; 2:99a; 3:58a, 80a.

8. **grasping the Tree of Life...** Torah is identified with the Tree of Life, based on this description of wisdom in Proverbs. In Kabbalah both Torah and Tree of Life symbolize *Tif'eret.*

See BT *Berakhot* 32b; *Zohar* 1:152b, 168a, 174b; 3:53b, 260a; Moses de León, *Sefer ha-Rimmon,* 330.

9. **grasps the Tree of Life in this world** By engaging in Torah.

10. **correspondingly rungs are arranged...** Corresponding to how firmly they grasped Torah on earth.

11. **embraces many rungs...** The various aspects of the Tree of Life correspond to various levels of meaning in Torah, such as literal, midrashic, allegorical, and esoteric. One who engages deeply in Torah grasps the trunk and thereby the entire tree, just as in sefirotic terms, *Tif'eret* encompasses the entire divine organism.

See *Zohar* 3:53b, 202a; Moses de León, *Sefer ha-Rimmon,* 327, 366. On Israel and the Tree, see *Bahir* 67 (98).

12. ***It happened at the end*** The context

Left.[13] Why?[14] Because it is written: *But remember me with you when all goes well for you* (ibid. 40:14).[15] Now, was it proper for Joseph the Righteous to say, *But remember me with you?*[16] However, once Joseph contemplated his dream, he said, 'Surely, this is a dream of remembering!' In this he was wrong, for the blessed Holy One encompasses all.[17] So, a place of forgetting confronted him. What is written? *Yet the chief cupbearer did not remember Joseph, he forgot him* (ibid., 23). Since it says *The chief cupbearer did not remember*, why *he forgot him*? Because *he forgot him* implies a place of forgetting, namely, end of the side of darkness.[18]

"*Two years of days* (ibid. 41:1), for a rung returned to a rung of remembering.[19]

(Genesis 41:1–2) reads: *It happened at the end of two years of days that Pharaoh dreamed, and look, he was standing by the Nile, and look, out of the Nile emerged seven cows, of beautiful appearance and fat in flesh, and they grazed in the reeds.*

13. **place without remembering... End of the Left** The demonic side, which culminates in oblivion, caused the cupbearer to forget about Joseph.

In the *Zohar* the word זכירה (*zekhirah*), "remembering," connotes זכר (*zakhar*), "male," specifically the divine male potency, *Yesod*, often symbolized by Joseph. The demonic realm lacks the flow of emanation from *Yesod*, so it is "a place without remembering." Conversely, *Yesod* is described as "a place without forgetting."

See *Zohar* 1:159b–160a; 2:92b. Cf. *Zohar* 1:48a–b (and Vol. 1, pp. 266–67, n. 1233); *OY*; Mopsik. According to the *Zohar*, the wicked in Hell forget their names. See *ZḤ* 49a, 84c (*MhN, Rut*); cf. *Massekhet Ḥibbut ha-Qever*, 2 (*Beit ha-Midrash*, 1:150).

14. **Why?** Why was he forgotten for so long?

15. ***But remember me...*** Joseph's plea to the cupbearer, after having interpreted his dream favorably. The full verse reads: *But remember me with you when all goes well for you, and do me the kindness, please, of mentioning me to Pharaoh and getting me out of this house.*

16. **was it proper...** Why did Joseph the Righteous, linked with *sefirah* of remembering, have to beg a human being in order to be remembered? Didn't he trust in God's faithfulness?

17. **dream of remembering...** Joseph realized that the cupbearer's dream conveyed secrets of unification within the divine realm, channeled through *Yesod*, the *sefirah* of remembering; so he trusted him to remember his dismal situation. However, he should have trusted in God alone.

On the sefirotic significance of the cupbearer's dream, see above, pages 172–74.

18. **place of forgetting... *he forgot him*...** Because of Joseph's lack of faith in the divine power of memory and deliverance, the demonic realm of oblivion interposed, causing the cupbearer to forget Joseph. This "place of forgetting" is implied by the apparently superfluous expression וישכחהו (*va-yishkaḥehu*), *he forgot him*, which Rabbi Shim'on may be reading as וישכיחהו (*va-yashkiḥehu*), *he* [the demonic] *made him forget.*

19. ***Two years of days...*** For the full verse, see above, note 12. The *two years of days* symbolize two of the cosmic days of Creation, *Yesod* and *Shekhinah*, whose reunion overcame the oblivion brought about by *the end*. Once *Shekhinah* returned to *Yesod*—the *sefirah* of remembering—Joseph was remembered below through the episode of Pharaoh's dream.

"*Pharaoh dreamed, and look, he was standing by the Nile* (ibid.)—this was a dream of Joseph, since every river pertains to Joseph the Righteous.[20] This is the mystery of 'One who sees a river in a dream, sees peace, as is written: *Behold, I will extend peace to her like a river* (Isaiah 66:12).'"[21]

"*It happened at the end of two years of days* (Genesis 41:1).

Rabbi Ḥiyya opened, "*By justice a king sustains the land, but a man of exactions ruins it* (Proverbs 29:4). Come and see: When the blessed Holy One created the supernal world, He arranged everything fittingly and issued lights radiating in all directions, and all is one. He created heaven above and earth above, so that all would be arrayed as one, for the benefit of below.[22]

"Come and see: *By justice a king sustains the land.* Who is *a king*? The blessed Holy One.[23] *By justice*—Jacob, sustenance of the land.[24] So, ו (*vav*) is nourished by ה (*he*), ה (*he*) by ו (*vav*), since sustenance derives from *justice*; for look, *justice sustains the land* with all its array and nourishes her![25]

"Alternatively, *a king*—the blessed Holy One. *By justice*—Joseph. *Sustains the land*—as is written: *All the earth came to Egypt, to Joseph, to get provisions*...

20. **every river pertains to Joseph the Righteous** Because his *sefirah, Yesod,* is the river of emanation.

See above, pages 92, 137–38.

21. **One who sees a river...** See BT *Berakhot* 56b: "Rabbi Yehoshu'a son of Levi said, 'One who sees a river in a dream should rise early and say, *Behold, I will extend peace to her like a river*—before another verse occurs to him: *For distress will come like a river* (Isaiah 59:19).'"

Rabbi Shim'on's reformulation of this Talmudic saying highlights "peace," a symbol of *Yesod,* who brings peace by uniting *Tif'eret* with *Shekhinah.* See BT *Shabbat* 152a, where Rabbi Shim'on son of Ḥalafta refers to the phallus as "peacemaker of the home."

See *Vayiqra Rabbah* 18:1; *Zohar* 1:150b, 197b; 3:31a, 115b.

22. **lights radiating...** The various *sefirot,* including *Tif'eret* and *Shekhinah,* who are known as "heaven" and "earth" and whose union generates sustenance for the lower worlds.

23. **Who is *a king*? The blessed Holy One** *Binah.* See *Bereshit Rabbah* 14:7.

24. ***justice*—Jacob...** Both symbolizing *Tif'eret,* who mediates between the polar opposites *Ḥesed* and *Gevurah,* and sustains *Shekhinah* (*the land*).

See *Zohar* 1:153a, 232b, 237a; 3:40b; Moses de León, *Sefer ha-Rimmon,* 29; idem, *Sheqel ha-Qodesh,* 44–45 (54–55); Gikatilla, *Sha'arei Orah,* 66b.

25. **ו (*vav*) is nourished by ה (*he*)...** The four letters of the name יהוה (*YHVH*) symbolize the entire range of the *sefirot.* The י (*yod*) symbolizes the primordial point of *Ḥokhmah,* while its crown symbolizes *Keter* (Crown). The first ה (*he*), often a feminine marker, symbolizes the Divine Mother, *Binah.* The ו (*vav*), whose numerical value is six, symbolizes *Tif'eret* and the five *sefirot* surrounding Him. The second ה (*he*) symbolizes *Shekhinah.*

Here Rabbi Ḥiyya focuses on the second-through-fourth letters: ה ו ה (*he, vav, he*). ו (*Vav*), symbolizing *Tif'eret* (along with His accompanying *sefirot*), is nourished by the

(Genesis 41:57). Because the blessed Holy One delighted in Jacob, He made Joseph ruler over the land."[26]

Rabbi Yose said, "*A king*—Joseph.[27] *By justice*—Jacob. *Sustains the land*—for look, until Jacob arrived in Egypt, there was no sustenance in the land on account of the famine. As soon as Jacob came to Egypt, through his merit the famine disappeared and the land was sustained.[28]

"Alternatively, *By justice a king sustains the land*—King David, of whom is written *David administered justice and equity* (2 Samuel 8:15).[29] He sustained the land, and through his merit it endured afterward.

"*But a man of exactions ruins it*—Rehoboam.[30]

"Come and see: For the sake of the righteous, the blessed Holy One—even though retribution has been decreed against the world, it is withheld for their sake and does not prevail over the world. All the days of King David, [the land] was sustained for his sake; after he died, it was sustained by his merit, as is written: *I will protect this city, delivering it for My sake and for the sake of My servant David* (Isaiah 37:35). Similarly, all the days of Jacob and all the days of Joseph, retribution did not prevail over the world.[31]

"Come and see: *By justice a king sustains the land*—Joseph. *But a man of exactions ruins it*—Pharaoh, for look, because he hardened his heart against the

first ה (*he*), symbolizing *Binah*; the second ה (*he*), symbolizing *Shekhinah*, is nourished by ו (*vav*). The "array" of *Shekhinah* consists of Her retinue of angels.

See Moses de León, *Sheqel ha-Qodesh*, 87–91 (110–16); Gikatilla, *Sha'arei Orah*, 44a.

26. **Alternatively, *a king*...** According to this view, the verse from Proverbs alludes to how God sustained all those suffering from the famine by means of Joseph, who arranged for grain to be stored and distributed equitably.

The verse in Genesis reads: *All the earth came to Egypt, to Joseph, to get provisions, for the famine was severe in all the earth.*

27. ***A king*—Joseph** Appointed by Pharaoh as vizier. See Genesis 41:37–46.

28. **As soon as Jacob came...** Even though there were supposed to be more years of famine, with Jacob's arrival the famine ceased.

See Genesis 45:6; *Tosefta, Sotah* 10:9; *Sifrei*, Deuteronomy 38; *Bereshit Rabbah* 89:9 (and Theodor's note); *Baraita di-Shloshim u-Shtayim Middot*, 10 (p. 21); Rashi on Genesis 47:19; Naḥmanides on Genesis 47:18; *Zohar* 1:249a.

29. ***David administered justice...*** The full verse reads: *David reigned over all Israel, and David administered justice and equity to all his people.*

30. ***man of exactions ruins it*—Rehoboam** Son of Solomon and King of Judah, during whose reign the united monarchy split into two kingdoms. Rabbi Yose is apparently playing on תרומות (*terumot*), *exactions*, and התרוממות (*hitromemut*), "exaltation, boasting," evidenced by Rehoboam's imperious retort to the representatives of Israel: *My father made your yoke heavy, but I will add to your yoke; my father flogged you with whips, but I will flog you with scorpions* (1 Kings 12:14).

On *terumot* and arrogance, see Rashi on Proverbs 29:4.

31. **retribution did not prevail...** Fam-

blessed Holy One, the land of Egypt was destroyed.[32] Previously, by the hand of Joseph, the land was sustained through that dream that he dreamed, as is written: *It happened at the end of two years of days...*"[33]

It happened at the end of two years of days (Genesis 41:1).

Rabbi El'azar opened, "*YHVH lives! Blessed is my Rock! Exalted be the God of my salvation!* (Psalms 18:47)—spelled אלוהי (*elohei*), *the God of*, with a ו (*vav*).[34] This verse calls for contemplation. *YHVH lives*—Living One, Righteous One, Foundation of the World, called Vitality of the Worlds.[35]

"*Blessed is my Rock*—as is written: *Blessed is YHVH, my Rock* (ibid. 144:1), a world presided over by this Righteous One.[36]

"*Exalted be the God of my salvation! Exalted*—upper world.[37]

"אלוהי (*Elohei*), *the God of*, with a ו (*vav*)—heaven, as is said: *The heavens are YHVH's heavens* (ibid. 115:16).[38]

"Come and see: *Blessed is Adonai. Day by day He bears our burden* (ibid. 68:20). *Blessed is* אדני (*Adonai*), spelled א-ד-נ-י (*alef-dalet-nun-yod*).[39] This verse

ine ceased, and the Israelites were not enslaved by the Egyptians. See *Shemot Rabbah* 1:8.

32. ***man of exactions ruins it*—Pharaoh...** His haughty stubbornness doomed Egypt. See above, note 30.

33. **that he dreamed...** That Pharaoh dreamed. See above, note 12.

34. **spelled אלוהי (*elohei*)... with a ו (*vav*)** Unlike the normal biblical spelling: אלהי (*elohei*), with no ו (*vav*), which appears in the parallel verse, 2 Samuel 22:47. In the entire Bible, the full spelling—with a ו (*vav*)—occurs only in this verse from Psalms.

See *Midrash Ḥaserot vi-Yterot*, 217 (*Battei Midrashot*, 2:309); *Minḥat Shai* on both verses.

35. **Living One... Vitality of the Worlds** *Yesod* (Foundation), who channels the vivifying flow of emanation to *Shekhinah* and the worlds below.

His title Righteous One is based on Proverbs 10:25: וצדיק יסוד עולם (*Ve-tsaddiq yesod olam*). The verse literally means *The righteous one is an everlasting foundation*, but it is understood as *The righteous one is the foundation of the world.* See BT *Ḥagigah* 12b; *Bahir* 71 (102); Azriel of Gerona, *Peirush ha-Aggadot*, 34.

On the various senses of the title Vitality of the Worlds, see Daniel 4:31; 12:7; Ben Sira 18:1; *Mekhilta, Pisḥa* 16; *Bereshit Rabbah* 1:5; Schäfer, *Synopse zur Hekhalot-Literatur*, §275; *Bahir* 123 (180) (and Scholem's note, ad loc.); *Zohar* 1:4b, 18a, 132a, 135b, 164a, 167b; 2:245b (*Heikh*); Moses de León, *Sheqel ha-Qodesh*, 55–56 (68); *NZ*.

36. **world presided over by this Righteous One** *Shekhinah* is a rock and a realm blessed by *Yesod*, who stands above Her. See *Zohar* 1:164a.

37. ***Exalted*—upper world** *Binah*, source of the lower seven *sefirot*.

38. **אלוהי (*Elohei*)... with a ו (*vav*)—heaven...** Now Rabbi El'azar explains that this unusual spelling implies *Tif'eret*, who is symbolized by the letter ו (*vav*). See above, notes 25, 34. *Tif'eret*, the core of the *sefirot*, bears the central divine name *YHVH*.

The full verse in Psalm 115 reads: *The heavens are YHVH's heavens, but the earth He has given to human beings.*

39. **אדני (*Adonai*)...** A divine name meaning "My Lord," pertaining to *Shekhinah*.

constitutes a mystery of wisdom. *Day by day—two years of days,* as is written: [194a] *It happened at the end of two years of days.*[40]

"*And look, he was standing by the Nile* (Genesis 41:2)[41]—a mystery, as has been said: this is Joseph, since 'river' implies Joseph the Righteous.[42]

"*And look, out of the Nile emerged seven cows* (ibid.).[43] *And look, out of the Nile*—for look, from this river all those rungs below are blessed, since that flowing, gushing river waters and nourishes all.[44] And Joseph is a river, thanks to which all the land of Egypt is blessed.

"Come and see: By that river, seven rungs are blessed and watered, these being *of beautiful appearance and fat in flesh* (ibid.).[45]

"*They grazed in the reeds* (ibid.)—in companionship, for division is not to be found among them.[46] All of them stand poised to praise, for all seven of these rungs that we have mentioned constitute a mystery, as is written: *and the seven maids chosen for her from the king's palace* (Esther 2:9). So, *seven cows of beautiful appearance.* Correspondingly, it is written: *the seven eunuchs attending the King* (ibid. 1:10)."[47]

186

Rabbi Yitsḥak said, "*The seven good cows* (Genesis 41:26)—rungs higher than others.[48] *And the seven bad cows* (ibid., 27)—other rungs below.[49] These from the side of holiness, those from the side of defilement."

40. ***Day by day...*** Symbolizing *Shekhinah* and *Yesod,* two of the cosmic days of Creation. Their reunion ensured that Joseph would be remembered by means of Pharaoh's dream, which *happened at the end of two years of days,* namely, when these two days consummated their union. See above, note 19.

41. ***And look, he was standing by the Nile*** The context (41:1–2) reads: *It happened at the end of two years of days that Pharaoh dreamed, and look, he was standing by the Nile, and look, out of the Nile emerged seven cows, of beautiful appearance and fat in flesh, and they grazed in the reeds.*

42. **'river' implies Joseph the Righteous** River symbolizes *Yesod,* Joseph's *sefirah.* See above, page 183.

43. ***And look, out of the Nile...*** See above, note 41.

44. **from this river all those rungs...** From *Yesod,* via *Shekhinah,* all rungs below are nourished. The phrase "flowing, gushing river" derives from Daniel 7:10.

45. **seven rungs...** Seven celestial palaces beneath *Shekhinah,* inhabited by angels and visited by souls.

46. ***in the reeds*—in companionship...** Alluding to the midrashic play on words: אחו (*aḥu*), *reeds,* and אחוותא (*aḥvata*), "companionship."

See *Bereshit Rabbah* 89:4; *Tanḥuma* (Buber), *Miqqets* 3; *Leqaḥ Tov,* Genesis 41:2; Naḥmanides, ad loc.

47. ***seven maids... seven eunuchs...*** Seven angels (and their camps) serving and praising *Shekhinah,* and seven others for King *Tif'eret.*

See 3 Enoch 17:1; *Pirqei de-Rabbi Eli'ezer* 4; *Zohar* 2:260b (*Heikh*); *ZḤ* 64a (*ShS*). The second verse reads: ... *the seven eunuchs attending Ahasuerus the King.*

48. **rungs higher than others** The seven celestial palaces.

49. ***seven bad cows...*** This second troop of cows is described in this verse as *lean and* רעות (*ra'ot*), *ugly* (literally, *bad*). Here they symbolize the seven palaces of impurity, depicted in *Zohar* 2:262b–269a (*Heikh*).

The seven ears of grain (ibid., 26).[50] Rabbi Yehudah said, "These first ones are good because they are from the right side, of which is written *that it was good* (ibid. 1:4); those ones are bad, below them.[51] *The seven ears of grain* are from the side of purity, while those are from the side of impurity. All those rungs stand one above the other, facing one another, and all of them Pharaoh saw in his dream."[52]

Rabbi Yeisa said, "Now, would all of these be shown to that wicked one, Pharaoh?"

Rabbi Yehudah replied, "Their semblance he saw, for there are so many rungs upon rungs—facing one another, one above the other—and he saw those rungs below.[53] As we have already learned, a person is shown in his dream what corresponds to his character; this is how he sees, how his souls ascends and extends, every single one according to its rung, fittingly.[54] So Pharaoh saw befittingly, and no more."

It happened at the end (Genesis 41:1).

Rabbi Ḥizkiyah opened, "*For everything there is a season, and a time for every affair under heaven* (Ecclesiastes 3:1). Come and see: For everything that the blessed Holy One formed below, He set a time, a fixed time. He set a time for light and for darkness, setting a time for the light of other nations who now rule the world, and setting a time for the darkness—namely, the exile of Israel under their dominion. The blessed Holy One has set a time for everything, so *for everything there is a season.*[55]

50. ***seven ears of grain*** In the second segment of Pharaoh's dream, he sees seven healthy ears of grain and seven shriveled ones. See Genesis 41:5–7.

51. **right side . . . below them** The healthy bunch symbolizes holy forces emanating from the right side of the *sefirot*, characterized by *Ḥesed* (Loving-kindness) and the primordial light of the first day of Creation, of which Genesis states: *God saw the light, that it was good*. The shriveled bunch symbolizes demonic forces below, deriving from the left side, which is characterized by *Din* (Judgment).

52. **one above the other, facing one another . . .** The holy above the demonic, existing parallel to one another.

53. **Their semblance . . .** Through the demonic rungs below, Pharaoh glimpsed the higher forms.

54. **person is shown . . .** When a person sleeps at night, his soul ascends and attains a vision corresponding to his level of virtue, a vision conveyed in his dream.

See JT *Ma'aser Sheni* 4:6, 55b: "Rabbi Yose said, '. . . A person dreams corresponding to who he is.'" See *Zohar* 1:149a; above, p. 116 and n. 201.

"Extends" renders אשתטחא (*ishtatteḥa*), "spreads itself out," preserved in the more reliable manuscripts (M7, N23, P2, R1, T1, V5) and reflected in several others, but rejected by the editors of the printed editions in favor of לאשתמודעא (*le-ishtemode'a*), "to recognize, know." The original term appears in similar or related contexts in *Zohar* 2:215b; 3:88b.

55. **exile of Israel . . .** See *Qohelet Rabbah* on 3:8, where the various "times" of Ecclesiastes 3 are correlated with Israel's exile and redemption.

"*And a time for every* חפץ (*ḥefets*), *affair*. What is the meaning of *a time for every ḥefets*? A time for everything, for all that desire manifesting below.[56]

"Alternatively, *and a time for every affair*. What is *time*? As is said: *Time to actualize for YHVH* (Psalms 119:126),[57] and similarly: *Let him not come at just any time* (Leviticus 16:2).[58] This is an empowered rung, as has been established; so, *time* is appointed over *every affair under heaven*.[59]

"*It happened at the end of two years of days*—from the side of that end of darkness Pharaoh saw in his dream; from there he knew and the dream was revealed to him."[60]

In the morning his spirit was disturbed (Genesis 41:8).[61] What does this mean: *his spirit was disturbed*?

Rabbi Yose said, "They have already established this. Of Pharaoh is written ותפעם (*va-tippa'em*), *it was disturbed*; of Nebuchadnezzar, ותתפעם (*va-titpa'em*), *it was disturbed* (Daniel 2:1).[62] This they have established, for of Pharaoh is
188
written *va-tippa'em* because he perceived the dream but not the interpretation, whereas Nebuchadnezzar saw the dream as well as the interpretation, but he forgot everything.[63]

56. ***for every ḥefets*... for all that desire...** Playing on the basic meaning of the word חפץ (*ḥefets*)—"delight, desire"—Rabbi Ḥizkiyah suggests that the verse refers to the time arranged for the realization of everything desired by God.

57. ***Time to actualize for YHVH*** The full verse reads: *Time to act for YHVH; they have violated Your Torah*. Here, *time* denotes *Shekhinah*, who conducts the world according to a cosmic schedule, enabling each phenomenon to unfold in its proper time. According to this reading, the verse calls upon the devout to prepare or "actualize" *Shekhinah for YHVH*, that is, for Her union with *Tif'eret*.

See *Sifrei Zuta* 27:1; BT *Berakhot* 54a, 63a; *Midrash Mishlei* 5:16; *Midrash Tehillim* 119:57; *Zohar* 1:116b; 2:155b; 3:127b–128a (*IR*); Gikatilla, *Sha'arei Orah*, 19b; Liebes, *Studies in the Zohar*, 44–45, 47; Idel, *Kabbalah: New Perspectives*, 185; 367, nn. 82, 86; Mopsik.

58. ***Let him not come at just any time*** The verse restricts the entry of the high priest into the Holy of Holies: *Let him not come at just any time into the Sanctuary*. Here, again, *time* alludes to *Shekhinah*: certain times are propitious, ripe for encountering *Shekhinah*; other times are forbidden and dangerous.

See *Zohar* 1:80a (*ST*), 116b; 2:155b; 3:58a–b.

59. **empowered rung...** Appointed to conduct the affairs of the world in a timely fashion.

60. **end of darkness...** The demonic realm. See above, pages 180–81, 187.

61. ***In the morning his spirit was disturbed*** The full verse reads: *In the morning his spirit was disturbed, and he sent and called for all the magicians of Egypt and all her wise men, and Pharaoh recounted to them his dream, but none could interpret them for Pharaoh*.

62. **of Nebuchadnezzar, ותתפעם (*va-titpa'em*), *it was disturbed*** In the biblical description of Nebuchadnezzar's agitated state upon wakening from his dream, the verb appears in the reflexive form with a double letter ת (*tav*), though with the same meaning as the passive form, ותפעם (*va-tippa'em*). Why the different form and spelling?

63. **Pharaoh... perceived... Nebuchadnezzar... forgot...** Pharaoh lacked only

"But come and see: ותפעם רוחו (*Va-tippa'em ruḥo*), *His spirit was disturbed*, corresponding to what is said: לפעמו (*le-fa'amo*), *to impel him* (Judges 13:25), for the spirit would come and go, come and go, not yet settling upon him fittingly. So it is written: *The spirit of YHVH began to impel him*—that was the beginning. Similarly here, his spirit roused within him and left and roused, never settling to comprehend.[64] As for Nebuchadnezzar, ותתפעם רוחו (*Va-titpa'em ruḥo*), *his spirit was disturbed*—aroused by two arousals, leaving and returning, corresponding to what is said: כפעם בפעם (*ke-fa'am be-fa'am*), *as time upon time*, one time this, [194b] one time that, and his spirit remained unsettled. [65]

"*He sent and called for all the magicians of Egypt* (Genesis, ibid.)—the sorcerers; *and all her wise men* (ibid.)—the bird-diviners.[66] All of them gazed to apprehend but could not grasp."

Rabbi Yitsḥak said, "Although it has been said that a person is shown only what accords with his rung, it is different for kings, who are shown supernal entities, different than for other people. Just as a king's rung transcends all others, so what he is shown accords with a rung beyond all others, as is said: *What God is about to do He has shown Pharaoh* (ibid., 28).[67] But to other people,

the interpretation, indicated by the single letter ת (*tav*) in the word ותפעם (*va-tippa'em*), *it was disturbed*; whereas Nebuchadnezzar saw and then forgot both the interpretation and the dream itself, as indicated by the double ת (*tav*) in the word ותתפעם (*va-titpa'em*).

See *Bereshit Rabbah* 89:5 (and Theodor's note); *Tanḥuma, Miqqets* 3; *Tanḥuma* (Buber), *Miqqets* 4; *Midrash Aggadah* and *Sekhel Tov*, Genesis 41:8; Rashi on Daniel 2:1.

64. **לפעמו (*le-fa'amo*), *to impel him*...** Describing the beginning of Samson's career: *The spirit of YHVH began to impel him in the camp of Dan, between Zorah and Eshtaol* (Judges 13:25). Rabbinic and medieval sources link the word *le-fa'amo* with פעם (*pa'am*), "time," and פעמון (*pa'amon*), "bell." Here Rabbi Yose's point is that at first Samson's inspiration was inconstant, coming to him and then leaving, like the back-and-forth motion of the tongue of a bell. Similarly, Pharaoh's comprehension of his dream would come and then vanish.

See BT *Sotah* 9b; JT *Sotah* 1:8, 17b; Rashi and Gersonides on Judges 13:25; *Sekhel Tov*, Genesis 41:8; Vital. Cf. *Zohar* 2:95a; 3:188b.

65. **aroused by two arousals...** The double ת (*tav*) in ותתפעם (*va-titpa'em*), *it was disturbed*, indicates that Nebuchadnezzar was doubly (or quadruply) shocked: by seeing and then forgetting both the dream and its interpretation.

The phrase כפעם בפעם (*ke-fa'am be-fa'am*), *as time upon time*, appears in a prophetic context in Numbers 24:1 and 1 Samuel 3:10, and pertains to Samson in Judges 16:20.

66. **bird-diviners** Who decipher the secret meaning of the chirping of birds and their motion in flight.

On bird divination, see *Vayiqra Rabbah* 32:2 (citing Ecclesiastes 10:20); *Pesiqta de-Rav Kahana* 4:3; *Tanḥuma, Ḥuqqat* 6; *Tanḥuma* (Buber), *Ḥuqqat* 11 (and Buber's note, ad loc.); BT *Gittin* 45a; Rashi on 2 Chronicles 9:4; Radak on 1 Kings 5:10; Naḥmanides on Deuteronomy 18:9; *Zohar* 1:126b–127a, 183b, 217b; 2:6b; 3:204b.

67. **what accords with his rung... different for kings...** On the correlation between one's dream and one's rung, see above, p. 187 and n. 54. On the contrast between common and royal dreams, see *Bereshit Rabbah* 89:4: "*Pharaoh dreamed.* Well,

the blessed Holy One does not reveal what He is doing—except for prophets, devotees, or sages of the generation, as has been established.[68]

"Come and see what is written: *Me he restored to my post and him he hanged* (Genesis 41:13).[69] From here we learn that a dream follows interpretation.[70] *He restored to my post.* Who restored? It was really Joseph! And *him he hanged* by the interpretation that he provided him, so it is written: *As he interpreted for us, so it was* (ibid.)."[71]

Pharaoh sent and called for Joseph, ויריצוהו (*vayritsuhu*), *and they rushed him, from the pit*... (Genesis 41:14).[72]

Rabbi Abba opened, "*YHVH* רוצה (*rotseh*), *delights, in those in awe of Him, those awaiting His faithful love* (Psalms 147:11). How greatly the blessed Holy One delights in the righteous, for they conduct peace and make peace above and make peace below and conduct the bride to her husband.[73] So the blessed Holy One delights in those who are in awe of Him and do His will.

190 "*Those awaiting His faithful love.* Who are these? You must say: those engaging in Torah at night and becoming partners with *Shekhinah*;[74] when morning comes, they await *His faithful love.* As has been established, when a person engages in Torah by night, a thread of love is drawn upon him by day, for it is written: *By day YHVH directs His love, in the night His song is with me* (Psalms 42:9). Why *by day YHVH directs His love*? Because *in the night His song is with*

don't all people dream? But a king's dream pertains to the whole world." Cf. *Zohar* 2:251b (*Heikh*).

The citation from Genesis here conflates 41:25 and 28.

68. **except for prophets...** See above, p. 118 and n. 215.

69. ***Me he restored...*** So the chief cupbearer tells Pharaoh of Joseph's expertise in interpreting dreams. The full verse reads: *As he interpreted for us, so it was: me he restored to my post and him he hanged.*

70. **dream follows interpretation** See above, p. 115 and n. 196 (citing BT *Berakhot* 55b).

71. **Who restored?... Joseph!...** According to the plain sense of the verse, the subject of *he restored* and *he hanged* is Pharaoh, but here Rabbi Yitsḥak teaches that Joseph is the subject: his power of interpretation determined the meaning of the dream and thus caused the cupbearer's restoration and the baker's execution.

See *Targum Yerushalmi,* Ibn Ezra, and Rashbam, ad loc.

72. ***Pharaoh sent...*** The full verse reads: *Pharaoh sent and called for Joseph, and they rushed him from the pit, and he shaved and changed his clothes and came before Pharaoh.*

73. **conduct peace... conduct the bride...** Through their virtuous action and intense study of Torah, they effect the divine union, thereby ensuring harmony above and below.

See BT *Sanhedrin* 99b: "Rabbi Alexandri said, 'Whoever engages in Torah for her own sake [without ulterior motives] brings peace to the Upper Family and the Lower Family [to angels above and to creatures on earth].'"

See Gikatilla, *Sha'arei Orah,* 19b; Galante. On "peace" as *Yesod,* see above, note 21.

74. **those engaging in Torah at night...** See BT *Tamid* 32b: "Rabbi Ḥiyya taught:

me.[75] Therefore it is written: *YHVH delights* את יראיו (*et yere'av*), *those in awe of Him*—not ביראיו (*biyre'av*), *in those in awe of Him*—one delighting in his goodwill for another, pleased to conciliate him. So, *YHVH delights those in awe of Him.*[76]

"Similarly, Joseph was sunk in sadness of spirit, imprisoned there in sadness of heart. As soon as Pharaoh sent for him, what is written? ויריצוהו (*Vayritsuhu*), *And they rushed him*—they mollified him, approaching him with words of joy, words delighting the heart, because he was saddened by the pit.[77]

"Come and see: Into a pit he fell at first, by a pit he was elevated later."[78]

Rabbi Shim'on said, "Until that incident befell Joseph, he was not called Righteous. Once he guarded that sealed covenant, he was called Righteous, with that rung of Holy Covenant crowning him, crowned by him.[79] Whereas previously he was in a pit, he was elevated thereby, crowned with a well of living waters.[80]

'Whoever engages in Torah at night—*Shekhinah* faces him.'"

75. **thread of love is drawn...** See BT *Ḥagigah* 12b: "Resh Lakish said, 'To one who engages in Torah by night, the blessed Holy One extends a thread of love by day, as is said: *By day YHVH directs His love.* Why? Because *in the night His song is with me.*'" *His song* is the song of Torah.

See above, p. 81 and n. 542.

76. ***YHVH delights* את יראיו (*et yere'av*)... not ביראיו (*biyre'av*)...** In this verse the particle את (*et*) marks the direct object יראיו (*yere'av*), *those in awe of Him.* If instead of *et*, the preposition ב (*be*), "in," had appeared, then the meaning could only be *YHVH delights in...*; but the appearance of *et*, marking the direct object, stimulates Rabbi Abba to reimagine the verb רוצה (*rotseh*) not according to the meaning "delights (in)," but rather as transitive—as if it were in the intensive form: מרצה (*meratstseh*), "delights, conciliates, mollifies."

See *Zohar* 2:62b. Cf. Psalms 149:4.

77. **ויריצוהו (*Vayritsuhu*), *And they rushed him*...** Rabbi Abba now interprets this distinct though similar-sounding verb (from the root רוץ [*ruts*], "to run") as if it were based on the root רצה (*rtsh*), "to delight in," but again according to the intensive form: וירצוהו (*va-yeratstsuhu*), "and they mollified him."

78. **Into a pit...by a pit...** Joseph was cast into a pit by his brothers (Genesis 37:18–24), but now from this second pit (Pharaoh's dungeon), he was about to be raised to unimaginable heights.

See *Midrash Tanna'im*, Deuteronomy 26:15: "With that which He strikes, He heals."

79. **Until that incident...** Until Joseph proved his virtue by refusing the advances of Potiphar's wife, he did not attain the title Righteous. This title corresponds to the covenant of circumcision, which is guarded by maintaining sexual purity, and also to *Yesod*, the divine phallus and site of the covenant. See above, p. 156 and n. 456.

The phrase "crowning him, crowned by him" renders אתעטר ביה (*it'attar beih*), which can be understood in either sense. Having demonstrated virtue, Joseph is crowned with the rung of *Yesod*, which itself is crowned (consummated, fully realized) by such righteous human behavior. (For the first sense, "crowning him," see *Zohar* 3:85a.)

80. **elevated thereby, crowned...** Crowned by *Shekhinah*, who Herself is trans-

"*Pharaoh sent* ויקרא את יוסף (*va-yiqra et yosef*), *and he called for Joseph.* The verse should read לקרא ליוסף (*liqro le-yosef*), *to call for Joseph.*[81] However, *and he called for Joseph*—the blessed Holy One, as is written: *Until the time that His word came to pass, the utterance of YHVH refined him* (Psalms 105:19). *Until the time that His word came to pass*—as is written: *He called Joseph.*[82] Here is written *He called Joseph*, and there is written *He called Moses* (Leviticus 1:1).[83]

"*And he shaved and changed his clothes* (Genesis, ibid.)—out of respect for the king, as has been established."[84]

Rabbi El'azar opened, "*Israel came to Egypt, Jacob sojourned in the land of Ham* (Psalms 105:23). Come and see how the blessed Holy One revolves revolutions in the world, fulfills vows and oaths in order to realize the covenant that He decreed.[85] For we have learned: Were it not for the affection and love felt by the blessed Holy One for the patriarchs, Jacob would have descended to Egypt in iron chains.[86] But out of His love for them, He made his son Joseph monarch

192 and ruler over the whole land, and all of those tribes descended in honor, with Jacob as king.

"Come and see what is written: *Israel came to Egypt, Jacob sojourned in the land of Ham.* Since it is written *Israel came to Egypt*, don't we know that *Jacob sojourned in the land of Ham*? Why is this necessary?[87] Rather, *Israel came to*

formed from a pit into a flowing well by the influx of *Yesod*, Joseph's *sefirah*.

See *Zohar* 1:60a–b; 3:266a. For other interpretations, see *OY*; Vital; Galante; *MM*; *MmD*.

81. **should read** לקרא ליוסף **(*liqro le-yosef*), *to call for Joseph*** Obviously, Pharaoh did not personally call him from the dungeon. Cf. Numbers 16:12.

82. ***he called for Joseph*—the blessed Holy One...** The anonymous subject *he* is divine, since Joseph's liberation from prison was initiated from above: he was called by God's *word* (*Shekhinah*). The context of the verse in Psalms describes Joseph's imprisonment, release, and ascent. Joseph's refining is understood as his test of temptation and his harsh imprisonment.

See *Midrash Tehillim* 26:3; Rashi on Psalms 105:19. Cf. *Zohar* 3:55a.

83. ***He called Joseph... He called Moses*** In both cases, the anonymous subject *He* refers to *Shekhinah*. See above, p. 49 and n. 355.

84. ***And he shaved...*** The verse reads: *And he shaved and changed his clothes and came before Pharaoh.* See *Bereshit Rabbah* 89:9; Rashi on this verse.

85. **revolves revolutions...** See above, p. 169 and n. 529. The divine decree referred to here was announced to Abraham (Genesis 15:13–14): *Know well that your seed will be strangers in a land not theirs, and they will be enslaved and afflicted four hundred years. But upon the nation that they serve I will bring judgment, and afterward they will go forth with great substance.*

See *Zohar* 1:184a, 188b, 196a–b.

86. **iron chains** Since the descent to Egypt was an exile. See the preceding note; BT *Shabbat* 89b, in the name of Rabbi Yoḥanan; and Rashi, ad loc.

87. ***land of Ham*... Why is this necessary?** Ham is a poetic name for Egypt, so

Egypt—the blessed Holy One; *Jacob sojourned in the land of Ham*—Jacob, because for the sake of Jacob and his sons, *Shekhinah* came to Egypt.[88] The blessed Holy One revolved revolutions [195a] and first brought down Joseph, by whose virtue Covenant was sustained with him, making him ruler over the whole land."[89]

What is written? *A king sent and released him, a ruler of peoples set him free* (ibid., 20).

Rabbi Shim'on said, "It is written: *YHVH releases the bound* (ibid. 146:7), and here is written: *A king sent and released him.*[90] Why *a ruler of peoples set him free?*[91] Because: *A king sent*—the blessed Holy One; *a ruler of peoples*—the blessed Holy One. *A king sent*—Supernal King *sent and released him.* And whom did He send? The redeeming angel, *ruler of peoples*, ruling over those below. All is the blessed Holy One.[92]

"ויריצהו (*Vayritsuhu*), *And they rushed him* (Genesis 41:14)—missing a ו (*vav*).[93] Who is that? The blessed Holy One, for no one but He imprisons and liberates, as is written: *A man He locks up cannot be freed* (Job 12:14), and: *If He remains silent, who can condemn? If He hides His face, who will take note of him, be it*

the second half of the verse seems redundant.

88. ***Israel*... blessed Holy One... *Shekhinah*...** Here *Israel* refers not to Jacob, but rather to the divine. In the *Zohar*, "blessed Holy One" often refers specifically to *Tif'eret*, whose full name is *Tif'eret Yisra'el* (Beauty of Israel), but it can also allude to other *sefirot* (*Binah* or *Shekhinah*) or to the divine realm in general.

On the role of *Shekhinah* in exile, see BT *Megillah* 29a: "Rabbi Shim'on son of Yoḥai says, 'Come and see how beloved are Israel in the sight of the blessed Holy One! Wherever they went in exile, *Shekhinah* accompanied them. When they were exiled to Egypt, *Shekhinah* was with them.... When they were exiled to Babylon, *Shekhinah* was with them.... And even when they are destined to be redeemed, *Shekhinah* will be with them.'" See *Mekhilta, Pisḥa* 14.

89. **by whose virtue Covenant was sustained...** See above, note 79.

90. ***YHVH releases... A king... released him*** Was it God or Pharaoh (*a king*) who released Joseph?

91. **Why *a ruler of peoples*...** Furthermore, why the apparent redundancy?

92. ***A king sent*—the blessed Holy One** *A king* refers to the divine king (*Tif'eret* or *Binah*). *A ruler of peoples* refers to *Shekhinah*, known also as the redeeming angel. So there is no contradiction between *YHVH* and *king*, and no redundancy of *king* and *ruler of peoples*. All three terms refer to the divine.

On the range of meaning of "blessed Holy One," see above, note 88. On *Shekhinah* as "redeeming angel," see Naḥmanides on Exodus 23:20; *Zohar* 1:61a, 228a–229a, 230a, 232a; 3:95b, 187a, 270a; Moses de León, *Sheqel ha-Qodesh*, 75–76 (96). Cf. *Mekhilta, Shirta* 3; above, p. 167, n. 516. The phrase originates in Genesis 48:16.

93. **ויריצהו (*Vayritsuhu*)... missing a ו (*vav*)** The verse reads: *And they rushed him from the pit* (see above, note 72). However, ויריצהו (*vayritsuhu*), *and they rushed him*, is spelled without a second ו (*vav*), which stimulates Rabbi Shim'on to read the verb in the singular: ויריצהו (*vayritsehu*), "he rushed him." See *Minḥat Shai*, ad loc.

nation or person? (ibid. 34:29). For He encompasses all, and it is written: *He does as He wishes with the host of heaven and the inhabitants of the earth*... (Daniel 4:32).[94] So, *vayritsehu, and He rushed him, from the pit.*

"What does *vayritsehu* mean? As is said: *He entreats God* וירצהו (*va-yirtsehu*), *and He accepts him* (Job 33:26). Similarly *vayritsehu, and He accepted him, from the pit,* and then *he came before Pharaoh* (Genesis, ibid.).[95]

"Alternatively, *vayritsehu,* for He drew upon him a thread of grace to win him favor before Pharaoh.[96] What is written? *God will answer for Pharaoh's* שלום (*shalom*), *well-being* (ibid., 16)—hastening to greet him, opening with *shalom*."[97]

Rabbi Abba said, "Come and see that evil Pharaoh, who said, *I do not know YHVH* (Exodus 5:2).[98] Now, Pharaoh was wiser than all his magicians![99] But surely, he knew the name *Elohim,* for look at what is written: *Could we find a man like this, in whom is the spirit of Elohim* (Genesis, ibid., 38)![100] However, since Moses approached him only with the name *YHVH*—and not with the name *Elohim*—for him this was the hardest of all, because he knew that this name ruled the earth,[101] whereas he did not know the name *YHVH*; so this name proved difficult for him, as is written: *YHVH hardened Pharaoh's heart* (Exodus 9:12), for this word hardened his heart and rendered him stubborn. Therefore Moses did not inform him of the enunciation of any other name, only the name *YHVH,* as has been established."[102]

He opened, saying, "*Who is like YHVH our God, enthroned on high?* (Psalms 113:5)[103]—ascending His throne of glory, not revealing Himself below: when

94. ***He does as He wishes...*** The verse reads: *He does as He wishes with the host of heaven and the inhabitants of the earth. There is no one who can stay His hand or say to Him, "What have You done?"*

95. **Similarly *vayritsehu, and He accepted him...*** Reading the verb now as וירצהו (*va-yirtsehu*), "and He accepted him," from the root רצה (*rtsh*), "to accept," rather than from the root רוץ (*ruts*), "to run."

96. **Alternatively, *vayritsehu...*** Based on a closely related sense of the root רצה (*rtsh*): "to be favorable."

97. ***God will answer...*** The full verse reads: *Joseph answered Pharaoh, saying, "Not I! God will answer for Pharaoh's well-being."* Joseph's respectful tone and his mention of *shalom* help to win him favor. Cf. *Mekhilta, Pisḥa* 13.

98. ***I do not know YHVH*** Pharaoh's response when Moses and Aaron conveyed the divine message *Let My people go.* The full verse reads: *Pharaoh said, "Who is YHVH, that I should heed His voice to let Israel go? I do not know YHVH, nor will I let Israel go."*

99. **Pharaoh was wiser...** So how could he be ignorant of this divine name?

100. ***Could we find a man like this...*** Pharaoh's reaction when Joseph interpreted his dream. On Pharaoh's knowledge of the name *Elohim,* see Judah Halevi, *Kuzari* 4:15; Ibn Ezra (long) on Exodus 6:2; 8:15; 9:28; 18:1; Naḥmanides on Exodus 5:3.

101. **this name ruled the earth** Pharaoh knew that the name *Elohim,* designating *Shekhinah,* ruled the world. See above, p. 188, n. 59; p. 193.

102. ***YHVH hardened*...this word hardened...** This divine name itself hardened Pharaoh's heart, as was intended. See Exodus 10:1–2; *Zohar* 2:52b.

103. ***Who is like YHVH...*** The context

virtuous people are not to be found in the world, He withdraws from them and does not reveal Himself. *Looking far below* (ibid., 6)[104]—when those present in the world are virtuous, the blessed Holy One descends His rungs toward creatures below to watch over the world and benefit them. For when the virtuous are absent from the world, He withdraws and hides His face from them, does not watch over them, since the righteous are the foundation and sustenance of the world, as is written: *The righteous one is the foundation of the world* (Proverbs 10:25).[105]

"So, the blessed Holy One revealed His holy name only to Israel, His allotted share and heritage, whereas the world He apportioned to shield-bearing deputies, as has been said, for it is written: *When the Most High allotted the nations...* (Deuteronomy 32:8), and similarly: *For YHVH's share is His people...* (ibid., 9)."[106]

Rabbi Ḥiyya and Rabbi Yose were walking on the way. Rabbi Yose said to Rabbi Ḥiyya, "I am astonished at what Solomon said! All his words are concealed words, unknown; for look, in Ecclesiastes he envelops concealed words!"[107] 195

He opened, saying, "*All things are wearisome: no one can utter them; the eye is not satisfied with seeing, nor the ear filled with hearing* (Ecclesiastes 1:8). *All things are wearisome.* Now, are all things so wearisome to express that he would say *no one can utter them...*? Why? Because two of them are not under a person's control, while the mouth is, and as hard as these three struggle, they cannot fathom or grasp everything."[108]

(Psalms 113:5–6) reads: *Who is like YHVH our God, enthroned on high, looking far below upon heaven and earth?* See *Zohar* 2:37a.

104. ***Looking far below*** See the preceding note.

105. ***The righteous one is the foundation of the world*** Literally, the verse means *The righteous one is an everlasting foundation,* but it is understood as *The righteous one is the foundation of the world.* See BT *Ḥagigah* 12b; above, note 35.

106. **shield-bearing deputies...** The other seventy nations of the world are ruled by divinely appointed angels or heavenly princes, whereas Israel is ruled directly by God; to His people alone He revealed the name *YHVH*.

The description "shield-bearing" derives from BT *Berakhot* 27b, where it refers to Torah scholars who contend with one another. The verses in Deuteronomy read in full: *When the Most High allotted the nations, when He dispersed humankind, He set the boundaries of peoples according to the number of the Children of Israel. For YHVH's share is His people, Jacob His allotted inheritance.* See above, pp. 70–71 and nn. 476–77.

107. **I am astonished...** Solomon's words in Ecclesiastes seem shocking and even heretical, yet they conceal wisdom.

See *Vayiqra Rabbah* 28:1; *Pesiqta de-Rav Kahana* 8:1; *Qohelet Rabbah* on 1:3; *Zohar* 1:223a; 3:64a, 157a, 177b, 182a, 236a.

108. **two of them are not under a person's control...** The two organs named in the verse (the eye and ear) function involuntarily, unlike the mouth; all three are incapable of perceiving everything.

On the voluntary and involuntary organs, see *Bereshit Rabbah* 67:3.

Rabbi Ḥiyya said, "So it is, for human speech cannot express, nor eyes see, nor ears hear. *And there is nothing new under the sun* (ibid., 9). Come and see: Even creatures and quaestors[109] formed by the blessed Holy One under the sun cannot express all things of the world; the eye is not [195b] empowered to see, nor the ear to hear. Therefore Solomon, who understood the matter, said this.

"Come and see: All events of the world depend on numerous suzerains,[110] yet all inhabitants of the world neither know nor consider the foundation of their existence.[111] Even Solomon, who was wiser than anyone in the world, could not comprehend them."

196 He opened, saying, "*He has made everything right in its time. He has also set the world in their heart*... (ibid. 3:11).[112] Come and see: Happy are those who engage in Torah and know how to contemplate with the spirit of wisdom! *He has made everything right in its time.* Every action performed by the blessed Holy One in the world, each and every one, has a rung appointed over it,[113] whether for good or for evil, some rungs to the right, some to the left. If a person goes to the right, performing an action, there is a rung appointed to that side, offering him assistance; how many assist him! If a person goes to the left and commits his acts, the act he commits is appointed to that side, accusing him, conducting him to that side, leading him astray.[114]

109. **quaestors** קסטורין (*Qastorin*) apparently derives from the Latin *quaestor*, a Roman official or prosecutor, and refers here to superhuman forces.

See JT *Eruvin* 6:2, 23b; *Zohar* 1:19b, 53b, 64b, 177a; 2:58b, 208b; 3:13a, 107a; *Bei'ur ha-Millim ha-Zarot*, 188. In a number of other Zoharic passages, the word apparently derives from the Latin *castrum* (pl. *castra*), "fortress, military camp," and here it could refer to camps of angels. See *Vayiqra Rabbah* 1:11; *Zohar* 1:29a, 30a; *Nefesh David*; Mopsik.

110. **depend on numerous suzerains** See *Bereshit Rabbah* 10:6: "Rabbi Simon said, 'You cannot find a single blade of grass [below (per Oxford MS 147)] that does not have a constellation in the sky, striking it and telling it: "Grow!"'"

See *Zohar* 1:156b. The word קסירין (*qesirin*), rendered here "suzerains," is a Zoharic neologism of uncertain meaning, perhaps deriving from the Latin *Caesar*. Cf. the neologism קפסורא (*qafsora*), above, p. 72, n. 485.

111. **neither know nor consider...** See BT *Ḥagigah* 12b: "Rabbi Yose said, 'Woe to creatures, for they see but do not know what they see; they stand but do not know on what they stand!'"

See *Zohar* 1:99a, 175b, 203b, 224a, 226b; 2:23b, 142a; 3:77a.

112. ***He has made everything*...** The full verse reads: *He has made everything right in its time. He has also set the world in their heart, yet a human cannot discover what God has done from beginning to end.* The word עלם (*olam*) in this verse may mean "world," "eternity," or "enigma."

113. **Every action...** See above, note 110.

114. **If a person goes to the right...** See BT *Shabbat* 104a: "Resh Lakish said, '...If one comes to defile himself, he is provided an opening; if one comes to purify himself, he is assisted.'"

See M *Avot* 4:11: "Rabbi Eli'ezer son of Ya'akov says, 'One who performs a single *mitsvah* acquires one defender; one who

"So, an act performed fittingly by a person is facilitated by the power appointed on the right. This is *in its time—right in its time*, for that action links with *its time* fittingly.[115]

"*He has also set the world in their heart.* The entire world and all its activity depend solely upon the desire of the heart, as it arises in the will of a human being.[116] Happy are the righteous who attract good deeds, benefiting themselves and the whole world! Woe to those who do not know the *time* of that action and do not care about performing their actions in the world according to the remedy needed by the world, aligning the action with its appropriate rung. Why? Because they do not know.

"So, all is given to human will, as is written: *yet a human cannot discover what God has done*... (ibid.).[117] And since those actions are not performed to be aligned fittingly with their rungs—that this act might be integrated in this rung, perfectly arranged—but rather according to human desire, what is written next? *I know that there is nothing good in them but to be happy and do good in their life* (ibid., 12).[118] *I know that there is nothing good in them*—in those actions performed improperly. *But to be happy* with whatever befalls him and to offer thanks to the blessed Holy One *and do good in his life.* For look, if that action brings evil upon him through the rung appointed over it,[119] he should rejoice in this and offer thanks since he brought it upon himself, going unknowingly like a bird into a snare.[120]

"How do we know all this? As is written: *For a human does not know his time. Like fish caught in a cruel net, like birds seized in a snare, so humans are trapped in a time of calamity, when it falls upon them suddenly* (ibid. 9:12). *For a human*

commits a single transgression acquires one accuser.'"

See *Zohar* 1:53b–54a, 99b, 125b, 129b, 169b, 198b, 200a; 2:50a; 3:47a; Ezra of Gerona, *Peirush Shir ha-Shirim*, 528–29; Moses de León, *Sefer ha-Rimmon*, 28; idem, *Sheqel ha-Qodesh*, 14–15 (17–18). Cf. BT *Makkot* 10b: "Rabbah son of Bar Ḥana said in the name of Rabbi Huna (some say, Rabbi Huna said in the name of Rabbi El'azar), 'From the Torah, the Prophets, and the Writings it can be demonstrated that one is led on the path one wishes to take.'"

115. **links with *its time*...** With a heavenly power issuing from *Shekhinah*, who is known as *time*. See above, note 57.

116. **will of a human being** Choosing good or evil.

117. ***yet a human cannot discover*...** Human beings do not realize the power of free will granted to them.

118. ***nothing good in them but*...** The plain sense of the verse is: *nothing better for them* [for human beings] *than to be happy*, etc. However, Rabbi Ḥiyya proceeds to read the verse differently.

119. **rung appointed over it** A rung on the left side.

120. **snare** טסירא (*Tesira*), a Zoharic neologism whose meaning ranges and is translated here according to the context. See above, p. 79 at n. 531, where it apparently

does not know his time. What is *his time*? The time of that action that he performs, as has been said: *He has made everything right in its time.*[121] So they are *like birds seized in a snare.* So, happy are those engaged in Torah, who know its ways and paths, so as to walk the way of truth.

"Come and see: One should never open his mouth for evil, for he does not know who snatches that word, and when he doesn't know, he stumbles.[122] When the righteous open their mouths, all is שלם (*shelam*), peace. Come and see: When Joseph began to speak to Pharaoh, what is written? *God will answer for Pharaoh's* שלום (*shalom*), *well-being* (Genesis 41:16)."

Rabbi Yehudah said, "As has been explained, the blessed Holy One cares for the well-being of royalty, as is said: *He charged them regarding the Children of Israel and regarding Pharaoh king of Egypt* (Exodus 6:13). [196a] This has been established."[123]

Rabbi Ḥiyya said, "Pharaoh wanted to test Joseph, so he changed his dream.[124] But Joseph, knowing the rungs, contemplated the matter and said, 'This is what you saw'—every item accurately, as is written: *Pharaoh said to Joseph, 'After God has made known to you all this . . .'* (Genesis, ibid., 39). אַחֲרֵי (*Aḥarei*), *After*—אַחֲרַי (*Aḥarai*), 'Behind me, you must have been at the moment I was dreaming.' Therefore he said *all this*—'you knew how it was and you knew its meaning.'"[125]

means "specter, spirit" (as in *Zohar* 1:17b, 20b). Cf. 2:29a, 76a, 240a; 3:126a.

121. **time of that action . . .** See above, pp. 196–97 and n. 115.

122. **One should never open his mouth for evil . . .** See BT *Berakhot* 19a, in the name of Rabbi Yose: "One should never open his mouth for Satan," i.e., one should never utter ominous words, thereby providing an opening for Satan and inviting disaster.

See above, page 57; *Zohar* 2:266a; 3:155b.

123. **blessed Holy One cares . . .** The full verse reads: *YHVH spoke to Moses and to Aaron and He charged them regarding the Children of Israel and regarding Pharaoh king of Egypt, to bring out the Children of Israel from the land of Egypt.* According to the Midrash, the inclusion of Pharaoh's title indicates that God commanded Moses and Aaron to respect his royalty.

See *Tanḥuma, Va'era* 2; *Shemot Rabbah* 7:3; *Mekhilta, Pisḥa* 13; *Zohar* 2:26a–b; above, p. 192 and n. 84.

124. **Pharaoh wanted to test Joseph . . .** There are slight differences between the original account of Pharaoh's dream (Genesis 41:1–7) and Pharaoh's recounting of his dream to Joseph (ibid., 17–24). According to *Tanḥuma, Miqqets* 3, these differences reflect Pharaoh's attempt to test Joseph, challenging him not only to interpret the dream but to reconstruct it precisely. See *KP*; Vital; Galante.

125. ***After God has made known to you . . .*** The full verse reads: *Pharaoh said to Joseph, "After God has made known to you all this, there is no one as discerning and wise as you."* Borrowing from the *Tanḥuma*, Rabbi Ḥiyya reads new meaning into Pharaoh's words.

On the detailed meaning of Pharaoh's dream, see above, pages 186–87.

Rabbi Yitsḥak said, "If so, then Joseph told everything—the dream and its interpretation—just like Daniel, who told the dream and its interpretation."[126]

He replied, "Not so. From Pharaoh's wording, Joseph observed that he was speaking about certain rungs, and he saw that he was mistaken. So he said to him, 'This is how it is, because the rungs proceed in order.' Whereas Daniel didn't observe anything from what Nebuchadnezzar said, and yet told him everything: the dream and its interpretation. What is written of Daniel? *Then in a night vision, the mystery was revealed to Daniel* (Daniel 2:19). *In a night vision.* Who is *a night vision*? Gabriel, who is *vision*, vision from vision.[127]

"Come and see what is written: *Behold, the glory of the God of Israel was coming from the east. Its sound was like the sound of mighty waters, and the earth shone with His glory* (Ezekiel 43:2). What is written next? *The vision was like the vision I had seen—like the vision I had seen when I came to destroy the city, and visions like the vision I had seen by the River Kevar—and I fell on my face* (ibid., 3). All these visions total six—visions, vision of vision; there is a visionary mirror reflecting supernal colors, envisioned in that visionary mirror; there is vision within vision, and vision within vision, one above the other, all poised on specific rungs, presiding, called *night vision.* Through them spread all dreams of the world, these resembling those above them.[128]

"So, *then in a night vision, the mystery was revealed to Daniel.* As has been said, it is not written *the mystery* אתגלי (*itgelei*), *was revealed,* but rather *the mystery* גלי (*gali*), *he revealed*—one of these rungs *revealed* that dream to him along with its interpretation. Whereas Joseph, through Pharaoh's words, contemplated the rungs and spoke.[129]

126. **just like Daniel...** Who revealed to Nebuchadnezzar both the content and the meaning of the king's dream. See Daniel 2; above, pages 188–89.

127. **Who is *a night vision*? Gabriel...** In the book of Daniel (8:16; 9:22), Gabriel interprets revelations; in the *Zohar,* he appears as prince of dreams. Here he is characterized as "vision from vision," deriving from *Shekhinah,* who is Herself called "vision." See above, p. 114 and nn. 192, 194.

128. **visions total six...** There are six references to vision in Ezekiel 43:3 (four in the singular and one in the plural, understood here as two). Elsewhere, the *Zohar* describes six visionary stages spanning the phenomena of prophecy and dream: the *sefirot Netsaḥ, Hod, Yesod,* and *Shekhinah,* and the first two archangels—Michael and Gabriel. The language here is itself dreamy and multivalent. For example, the word חיזו (*ḥeizu*) means "vision" but also (in the *Zohar*) "mirror," alluding to the mirror of *Shekhinah,* which reflects the colors of the six *sefirot* above Her (*Ḥesed* through *Yesod*). Beneath *Shekhinah* lie further visionary stages, resembling those within Her mirror and conveying dreams to humanity.

See above, pages 114–15; *Zohar* 2:23a–b.

129. ***revealed to Daniel*...Whereas Joseph...** In Daniel's case, the angel Gabriel revealed the dream and its interpretation; Joseph, however, contemplated on his own. Actually, the Aramaic form in Daniel 2:19—גלי (*gali*)—is passive: *was revealed.*

"Therefore, he appointed him over the entire land of Egypt, because the blessed Holy One gave Joseph what was already his. A mouth that did not kiss sin—it is written: *Upon your mouth all my people shall kiss* (Genesis 41:40). A hand that did not approach sin—it is written: *He put it on Joseph's hand* (ibid., 42). A neck that did not approach sin—it is written: *He placed the gold chain around his neck* (ibid.). A body that did not approach sin—it is written: *They called out before him,* Avrekh (ibid., 43), and similarly: *He had him ride in the chariot of his viceroy* (ibid.). Everything he received was already his own."[130]

What is written? *Joseph went out from Pharaoh's presence and passed through all the land of Egypt* (ibid., 46). Rabbi Ḥizkiyah said, "Why did he pass through all the land of Egypt? In order to take control, for so they proclaimed before him,[131] and in order to gather grain in every single district."[132]

Rabbi El'azar said, "Joseph gathered grain in every district so that it wouldn't rot."[133]

And Rabbi Shim'on said, "Whatever the blessed Holy One does is intended to
200 revolve revolutions to fulfill the covenant of existence.[134] Come and see: When the blessed Holy One created the world, He first provided all its necessities and then brought the human being into the world, so he found his sustenance.[135]

130. **what was already his...** By withstanding the advances of Potiphar's wife, Joseph demonstrated his virtue and earned all the honor and glory now bestowed upon him by Pharaoh, so in a sense these were already his.

See above, note 79; *Bereshit Rabbah* 90:3; *Vayiqra Rabbah* 23:9; *Tanḥuma, Bereshit* 12, *Miqqets* 3; *ZḤ* 60a–b. The context in Genesis (41:40–43) reads: *Pharaoh said to Joseph, "After God has made known to you all this, there is no one as discerning and wise as you. You shall be over my house, and upon your mouth all my people shall kiss. By the throne alone shall I be greater than you." Pharaoh said to Joseph, "See, I have set you over all the land of Egypt." Pharaoh removed his ring from his hand and put it on Joseph's hand and had him clothed in garments of linen and placed the gold chain around his neck. He had him ride in the chariot of his viceroy, and they called out before him,* Avrekh, *setting him over all the land of Egypt.*

The expression *upon your mouth all my people shall kiss* apparently means "by your command (by the directives you issue) all my people shall be guided," or "to your orders all my people shall submit," or "to you all my people shall pay homage." The exclamation אברך (*avrekh*) is of uncertain origin, perhaps deriving from Assyrian *abarakku*, "chief steward."

131. **take control...** See Ibn Ezra on Genesis 41:45; and *Targum Yerushalmi*, ibid., 46.

132. **gather grain...** In line with Joseph's recommendation. See Genesis 41:33–36.

133. **so that it wouldn't rot** According to *Bereshit Rabbah* 90:5, grain stored in the district where it is grown keeps better.

134. **revolve revolutions...covenant of existence** See above, note 85. The word קיים (*qeyam*), "covenant," is rendered here "covenant of existence," since Rabbi Shim'on may be playing on *qeyam* and קיימא (*qayyama*), "existence."

135. **first provided all its necessities...** Before creating the human being on the sixth day.

See *Tosefta, Sanhedrin* 8:9; BT *Sanhedrin* 38a; *Bereshit Rabbah* 8:6; *Zohar* 1:34b.

"Come and see: The blessed Holy One said to Abraham, *Know well that your seed will be strangers . . . and afterward they will go forth with great substance* (Genesis 15:13–14).[136] When Joseph arrived, there was no great substance there, so He revolved revolutions and brought famine upon the world, and the whole world brought silver and gold to Egypt; then the whole land of Egypt was filled with silver and gold.[137] Once all the *great substance* was prepared, He brought Jacob to Egypt. For such are the ways of the blessed Holy One: first He creates the remedy, then He strikes.[138] So first He prepared *great substance* in Egypt, then [196b] He brought them into exile. Thus He revolved revolutions and brought famine upon the world so that the entire world would bring silver and gold to Egypt.

"Come and see: Because of this, Joseph, who was righteous, enabled Israel to acquire wealth—silver and gold—as is said: *He led them out with silver and gold; none among their tribes stumbled* (Psalms 105:37). By the hand of a righteous one, this came upon Israel, all for the purpose of making them worthy of the world that is coming."[139]

He opened, saying, "*Enjoy life with the woman you love all the days of your fleeting life that He has granted you under the sun—all your fleeting days. For that is your share in life and in your toil that you exert under the sun* (Ecclesiastes 9:9). Come and see: This verse abides in supernal mystery, as has been established.[140] *Enjoy life*—life of the world that is coming, for happy is one who attains that fully.[141]

136. ***Know well . . .*** The verses read: *Know well that your seed will be strangers in a land not theirs, and they will be enslaved and afflicted four hundred years. But upon the nation that they serve I will bring judgment, and afterward they will go forth with great substance.*

137. **whole world brought silver and gold . . .** See Genesis 47:14–15.

138. **first He creates the remedy . . .** See BT *Megillah* 13b: "Resh Lakish said, 'The blessed Holy One does not strike Israel unless He creates healing for them beforehand.'"

See *Shir ha-Shirim Rabbah* on 4:5; *Zohar* 1:14a.

139. **Joseph, who was righteous . . .** Joseph the Righteous symbolizes *Yesod,* also known as Righteous. Just as *Yesod* channels the riches of emanation to *Shekhinah* (known as Assembly of Israel), so Joseph conveyed riches to Israel. The purpose of Israel's harsh enslavement was to purge and refine them for the bliss of the hereafter.

See above, note 35; BT *Pesaḥim* 119a.

140. **as has been established** See *Zohar* 3:177b–178a; above, note 107.

141. **life of the world that is coming . . .** עלמא דאתי (*Alma de-atei*), the Aramaic equivalent of the rabbinic Hebrew העולם הבא (*ha-olam ha-ba*), "the world that is coming," is often understood as referring to the hereafter and is usually translated as "the world to come." From another point of view, however, "the world that is coming" already exists, occupying another dimension.

See *Tanḥuma, Vayiqra* 8: "The wise call it *ha-olam ha-ba* not because it does not exist now, but for us today in this world it is still to come." Cf. Maimonides, *Mishneh Torah, Hilkhot Teshuvah* 8:8; and Guttmann, *Philosophies of Judaism,* 37: "'The world to come'

"*With the woman you love*—Assembly of Israel, for love is ascribed to Her, as is said: *I have loved you with eternal love* (Jeremiah 31:3).[142] When? At the time when the right side grasps Her, as is written: *therefore I have extended grace to you* (ibid.).[143]

"*All the days of your fleeting life*—for She is bound to life.[144] She is a world imbued with life, for this world is not, since that life lies *under the sun* and the rays of that sun do not reach here, having disappeared from the world ever since the day the Temple was destroyed, as is written: *The sun darkened*... (Isaiah 13:10).[145] What does this mean? Its radiance withdrew, shining no more, as is said: *The righteous one loses*... (ibid. 57:1).[146]

"*For that is your share in life*—sun with moon; we must together with the moon enter the sun, and sun in moon, not separating them. This is the share of a human being, entering through them the world that is coming.[147]

does not succeed 'this world' in time, but exists from eternity as a reality outside and above time, to which the soul ascends."

In Kabbalah "the world that is coming" often refers to *Binah,* the continuous source of emanation. See *Zohar* 3:290b (*IZ*): "the world that is coming, constantly coming, never ceasing."

Cf. *Bahir* 106 (160); Asher ben David, *Peirush Shelosh Esreh Middot,* in *Kabbalah* 2 (1997): 293; Moses de León, *Sheqel ha-Qodesh,* 26 (30); idem, *Sod Eser Sefirot,* 375; *Zohar* 1:83a, 92a, 141b.

In this passage both senses of the term apply: the *sefirah* of *Binah* and the hereafter.

142. **Assembly of Israel...** *Shekhinah,* the divine *woman.* On Her name Assembly of Israel, see above, pp. 122–23, n. 237.

The verse in Jeremiah reads: *I have loved you with* אהבת עולם (*ahavat olam*), *eternal love; therefore I have extended grace to you.* Here in the *Zohar, ahavat olam* is understood as "love of the world," namely of *Shekhinah,* also known as "world." God loves Israel with the same love with which He loves *Shekhinah.*

The directive in Ecclesiastes, *Enjoy life with the woman you love,* now means: Draw the *life* emanating from *Binah* (the world that is coming) to *the woman, Shekhinah.*

143. **when the right side grasps Her...** When the divine right arm, *Ḥesed* (Grace, Love), grasps *Shekhinah.*

144. **She is bound to life** To the life issuing from *Binah.*

145. **life lies *under the sun*...** Ever since the destruction of the Temple, the vivifying light of emanation remains directly beneath *Tif'eret* (symbolized by the sun) and fails to penetrate below.

The verse in Isaiah reads: *The sun darkened as it rose.* See *Pesiqta de-Rav Kahana,* add. 6; above, page 108. Cf. BT *Berakhot* 59a, in the name of Rav Ḥisda: "Ever since the day that the Temple was destroyed, the sky has not appeared in all its purity."

146. ***The righteous one loses*...** The verse reads literally: *The righteous one perishes, and no one takes it to heart; devout people are taken away, while no one understands that because of evil the righteous one was taken away.* The verb אבד (*avad*), "perishes," is understood here as "loses," meaning that *Yesod,* known as Righteous One, loses the illumination of *Tif'eret* above.

See *Zohar* 1:55b, 180a, 182a; 2:57a–b; 3:16b, 266b. On *Yesod*'s title Righteous One, see above, note 35.

147. ***your share*... sun with moon...** The challenge for humanity is to draw close to *Shekhinah* (the moon) and then stimulate, and participate in, Her union with *Tif'eret* (the sun), thereby attaining the world that is coming. See above, note 141.

"What is written next? *Whatever your hand finds to do, do with your power. For there is no doing or reasoning or knowing or wisdom in Sheol* (Ecclesiastes 9:10).[148] This verse calls for contemplation! *Whatever your hand finds to do*—now, has the strap been untied, allowing one to do whatever he wishes?[149] Rather, it is written: *to do with your power*, namely, one's soul, which is the power by which one demonstrates virtue in this world.[150]

"Alternatively, *with your power*—*the woman* we have mentioned, who is power, empowering a person in this world and in the world that is coming.[151] One should attain Her in this world, so that he will be strengthened by Her in that world. Why? Because once a person departs this world, he has no power to do anything, or to say, 'From now on, I will act.' Surely, *there is no doing or reasoning or knowing or wisdom in Sheol, where you are going*. If one does not acquire merit in this world, he will not do so later in that world. As has been established, 'Whoever has not prepared provisions for the journey from this world will have nothing to eat in that world.'[152] There are certain good deeds one performs in this world that he can partake of here, yet that remain for the world that is coming, providing nourishment.[153]

"Come and see: Joseph attained this world and attained the world that is coming because he desired to unite with *a woman in awe of YHVH*, as is said: *I would be sinning against Elohim!* (Genesis 39:9).[154] Consequently he was worthy of ruling this world and rendered Israel worthy.

148. ***For there is no doing... in Sheol*** The verse concludes: *in Sheol, where you are going*. Sheol is the underworld, the abode of the dead.

149. **has the strap been untied...** Has all restraint been removed? The image derives from the judicial punishment of flogging.

See M *Makkot* 3:12; *Vayiqra Rabbah* 28:1; *Pesiqta de-Rav Kahana* 8:1; *Qohelet Rabbah* on 1:3; *Zohar* 3:177b.

150. ***to do with your power...*** Rabbi Shim'on reads the verse as follows: *Whatever your hand finds to do with your power, do*. A person's *power* is his spiritual potency, the soul. See *Zohar* 3:220a–b.

151. ***the woman* we have mentioned...** *Shekhinah*, who empowers one to act virtuously. See above, p. 202 and n. 142.

152. **Whoever has not prepared...** See BT *Avodah Zarah* 3a, where God describes the consequences in the hereafter of fulfilling (or failing to fulfill) the Torah in this world: "Whoever prepares on the eve of Sabbath can eat on Sabbath. Whoever has not prepared on the eve of Sabbath, how can he eat on Sabbath?"

153. **certain good deeds...** See M *Pe'ah* 1:1: "These are things whose fruit [or: interest] one enjoys in this world while the principal endures for him in the world that is coming: honoring father and mother, acts of loving-kindness, making peace between one person and another; and the study of Torah is equivalent to them all."

154. **desired to unite...** Joseph desired to unite with *Shekhinah*, identified with *a woman in awe of YHVH* (Proverbs 31:30). She is also known as *Elohim*, and when Joseph rejected the advances of Potiphar's wife, he alluded to Her by telling his seductress: *How could I commit this great wickedness? I would be sinning against Elohim!*

"What is written? *Joseph gathered all the silver* (ibid. 47:14).[155] As was fitting, for that flowing, gushing river gathers all; all riches exist therein. This is the mystery written: *God placed them in the expanse of heaven* (ibid. 1:17).[156] All fittingly: surely Joseph had to rule over the kingdom.[157]

"Come and see what is written: *He had him ride in his second chariot*... (ibid. 41:43).[158] Who is *his second chariot*? The blessed Holy One made the righteous one the ruler because by him the world is nourished and needs to be nourished.[159] The blessed Holy One has a higher chariot and a lower chariot. The lower chariot is *his second chariot*, and Joseph the Righteous should be riding *in his second chariot*—the blessed Holy One's. All abides in supernal mystery, corresponding to the pattern above.[160]

"Come and see: *They called out before him, Avrekh* (ibid.). What is *Avrekh*? A link linking sun with moon, and all kneel to this place.[161]

155. ***Joseph gathered***... The full verse reads: *Joseph gathered all the silver to be found in the land of Egypt and in the land of Canaan in return for the provisions they were buying, and Joseph brought the silver to the house of Pharaoh.*

156. **flowing, gushing river**... Joseph symbolizes *Yesod*, who conveys the riches of emanation to *Shekhinah*. See above, page 183. The phrase "flowing, gushing river" derives from Daniel 7:10.

The verse in Genesis reads: *God placed them in the expanse of heaven to shine upon the earth.* There the context is the creation of the sun, moon, and stars; here *expanse of heaven* symbolizes *Yesod*, who is the *expanse* of *Tif'eret* (*heaven*) and contains the sefirotic lights, with which He illumines *Shekhinah*, symbolized by *earth*. See *Zohar* 1:20a, 34a, 162b, 168b; *ZḤ* 14a (*MhN*).

157. **Joseph had to rule**... Appropriately, Joseph ruled over the kingdom of Egypt, since *Yesod* controls and sustains *Shekhinah*, known as *Malkhut* (Kingdom).

158. ***He had him ride***... The full verse reads: *He had him ride in the chariot of his viceroy, and they called out before him Avrekh, setting him over all the land of Egypt.* The plain sense of the phrase במרכבת המשנה אשר לו (*be-mirkevet ha-mishneh asher lo*) is apparently "in the chariot of his viceroy," but here it is understood as "in his second chariot."

See JT *Kil'ayim* 8:2, 31c; Septuagint, *Targum Onqelos*, *Targum Yerushalmi*, and Rashi on Genesis 41:43; *ZḤ* 60b; Sarna, *Genesis*, ad loc.

159. **made the righteous one the ruler**... God arranged for Joseph the Righteous to rule because his *sefirah*, *Yesod* (known as Righteous One), sustains the world through *Shekhinah*.

160. **higher chariot... lower chariot**... The higher chariot consists of the *sefirot Ḥesed*, *Gevurah*, *Tif'eret*, and *Shekhinah*, while its rider is *Binah* and the realms above Her. The lower chariot (*his second chariot*) is *Shekhinah*, ridden by *Yesod*, so it is fitting for Joseph to ride in this chariot—which is God's, not Pharaoh's.

See *Bereshit Rabbah* 47:6: "Resh Lakish said, 'The patriarchs themselves constitute the [divine] chariot.'" In Kabbalah the three patriarchs (Abraham on the right, Isaac on the left, and Jacob between them) symbolize the sefirotic triad of *Ḥesed*, *Gevurah*, and *Tif'eret*, while King David, symbolizing *Shekhinah*, completes the chariot, serving as the fourth leg of the divine throne.

See Azriel of Gerona, *Peirush ha-Aggadot*, 57; *Zohar* 1:60b, 99a, 150a, 154b, 173b, 248b; 2:144a; 3:38a, 99a; Tishby, *Wisdom of the Zohar*, 2:588–89.

161. **What is *Avrekh*?**... As explained above (note 130), the exclamation אברך

"*Setting him* [*over all the land*] (ibid.)—the whole world acknowledges him. [197a] So all abides in supernal mystery.[162]

"Come and see: The blessed Holy One formed a kingdom on earth as a reflection of the Kingdom of Heaven, corresponding perfectly. Whatever manifests on earth exists before in the presence of the blessed Holy One.[163]

"Come and see: The holy Kingdom did not have complete dominion until it was joined with the patriarchs, since the blessed Holy One formed the supernal Kingdom to be illumined by the mystery of the patriarchs.[164] Once Joseph the Righteous went down to Egypt, he drew *Shekhinah* after him, for *Shekhinah* follows only the righteous one. So Joseph was drawn first to Egypt and obtained all the wealth of the world fittingly; then *Shekhinah* descended along with all the tribes.[165] Therefore Joseph, who guarded the covenant, succeeded in being crowned in his site and attained the kingdom above and the kingdom below.[166] So, whoever guards the holy covenant is considered to have fulfilled the entire Torah, since the covenant is equivalent to the entire Torah."[167]

(*avrekh*) is uncertain. Here several Hebrew meanings are suggested. The first, "link," is based on the rabbinic agricultural term הבריך (*hivrikh*), understood here as "to graft, join," although technically it means "to bend" a vine into the ground and cause it to grow independently, based on the root ברך (*berekh*), "knee." See M *Kil'ayim* 7:1; and for the sense "to graft," BT *Yevamot* 63a. (The author may have in mind the similar-sounding verb הרכיב (*hirkiv*), which actually does mean "to graft" and which appears alongside *hivrikh* in a number of rabbinic passages.) The meaning "link" applies to Joseph because he embodies *Yesod*, who links the divine couple *Tif'eret* and *Shekhinah*, symbolized respectively by the sun and moon.

The second meaning, "kneel," is also based on the root ברך (*berekh*), "knee." See Psalms 95:6; Genesis 24:11; Rashi and Ibn Ezra on Genesis 41:43; below, p. 215 and n. 219. Cf. *Sifrei*, Deuteronomy 1.

162. **whole world acknowledges him...** Since through *Shekhinah*, *Yesod* nourishes all. Similarly, Joseph was acknowledged by all those he sustained during the years of famine. This comment is based on another, apparently related meaning of the root ברך (*brkh*), "to bless, praise."

163. **kingdom on earth... Kingdom of Heaven...** See BT *Berakhot* 58a, in the name of Rav Sheshet: "The kingdom on earth resembles the Kingdom of Heaven."

164. **joined with the patriarchs...** *Shekhinah*, known as *Malkhut* (Kingdom), did not reign supreme until She was linked with the three patriarchs (Abraham, Isaac, and Jacob), whose virtue crowned Her and enabled Her to be illumined by the triad of *Ḥesed*, *Gevurah*, and *Tif'eret*.

See *Zohar* 1:79b, 99a, 125a, 246b; 2:31a; above, note 160.

165. ***Shekhinah* follows only the righteous one...** She is drawn to such a human because he symbolizes *Yesod*, who links Her with the triad of *Ḥesed*, *Gevurah*, and *Tif'eret*.

166. **Joseph, who guarded the covenant...** Through his sexual and moral purity, Joseph attained the covenantal rung of *Yesod* and united with *Malkhut* above, simultaneously attaining earthly rule in Egypt.

See above, p. 191 and n. 79; *Zohar* 1:93b, 106b (*MhN*); 2:60b; 3:213b.

167. **covenant is equivalent to the entire Torah** Preserving the covenant of circumcision and maintaining sexual purity are equivalent to the fulfillment of the whole Torah.

See *Tosefta*, *Nedarim* 2:6; BT *Nedarim* 32a; *Maḥazor Vitri*, 624; *Zohar* 2:61a; 3:13b; Wolf-

Jacob saw that there were provisions in Egypt... (Genesis 42:1).[168]

Rabbi Ḥiyya opened, "*Utterance of the word of YHVH concerning Israel. The declaration of YHVH, who stretches out the heavens and lays the foundation of the earth and forms the spirit of a human within him* (Zechariah 12:1). This verse calls for contemplation. משא (*Massa*), *Utterance of, the word of YHVH*—in all those places where Scripture states *massa: massa*—why? Because wherever the expression *massa* refers to judging other nations, it is positive; and wherever *massa* refers to Israel, it is negative. Wherever it refers to judgment upon other nations, it is positive because *massa* means 'burden'—the security of other nations is a burden, as it were, upon the blessed Holy One, and when judgment is decreed against them, that burden that He bears for them is removed. Wherever *massa* refers to judgment upon Israel, it is a burden, as it were, upon the blessed Holy One. So, *massa*—in either case, it is a burden.[169]

206 "*The declaration of YHVH, who stretches out the heavens and lays the foundation of the earth.* What need is there to add *and forms the spirit of a human within him*? Wouldn't we already know that He *forms the spirit of a human*? This indicates, however, a particular rung on which all spirits and souls of the world exist."[170]

Rabbi Shim'on said, "This verse is difficult. If Scripture had said *and forms the spirit of a human*—and no more—that would be fine. But why בקרבו (*be-qirbo*), *within him*?[171] This, however, is a twofold mystery. For look, from that flowing, gushing river all souls issue and soar, gathering into one site, and that rung *forms the spirit of a human be-qirbo, within itself*, precisely, like a woman

son, "Circumcision and the Divine Name," 104–5. The *gimatriyya* (numerical value) of the word ברית (*berit*), "covenant" of circumcision, is equal to 612, the number of all the other commandments in the Torah.

168. ***Jacob saw...*** The context (Genesis 42:1–2) reads: *Jacob saw that there were provisions in Egypt, and Jacob said to his sons, "Why do you keep looking at one another?" He said, "Look, I have heard that there are provisions in Egypt. Go down there, and get us provisions from there that we may live and not die."*

169. **משא (*Massa*), *Utterance...*** The root נשא (*nasa*) means "to carry, lift, raise." The noun משא (*massa*) can mean "burden" (that which is carried), or "utterance, pronouncement" (raising of the voice). Here Rabbi Ḥiyya plays with both meanings. When a prophetic *massa* announces the impending judgment of Israel's enemies, it is positive because God finds it burdensome to tolerate their security and wellbeing. When a *massa* announces the punishment of Israel, it is negative because God finds it burdensome to make His people suffer.

For similar plays on the two meanings of *massa*, see Jeremiah 23:33–38; *Targum Yonatan*, Ezekiel 12:10; *Zohar* 2:130b.

170. **particular rung...** *Shekhinah*, from whom all souls emerge into the world.

171. **why... *within him*?** Obviously, the soul is within the human being. Why does Scripture need to state the obvious?

conceiving from a male, forming the embryo in her womb until all is fashioned perfectly. So, *and forms the spirit of a human within itself*—abiding within until a person is created in the world, when it is given to him.[172]

"Alternatively, *and forms the spirit of a human within him—within him*, literally! How so? When a human being is created and the blessed Holy One endows him with a soul and he emerges into the atmosphere, that spirit within him does not find enough body into which it can expand, so it remains in an ambulatory inside of him.[173] As the person's body expands, that spirit expands, imparting its energy;[174] as the body grows, the spirit transmits its power within him, invigorating him. So, *forms the spirit of a human within him*, literally.

"Now, you might ask: Why *forms*? Because that spirit needs additional power from above, supporting it, so the blessed Holy One *forms the spirit of a human within him*, providing him with assistance.[175]

"Come and see: When that spirit needs assistance, in accordance with the person's state of being and the body's fitness, the spirit is enhanced, augmented by spirit, attaining perfection. This is *forms the spirit of a human within him.*[176]

"Come and see: When Joseph was lost to his father, Jacob lost that supplemental spirit he possessed and *Shekhinah* withdrew from him. Later, what is written? *The spirit of Jacob their father revived* (Genesis 45:27). Now, was he dead until this moment? [197b] Rather, that supplemental spirit had departed from him, was no longer within him, due to the sadness inside of him, and consequently his spirit lost its vitality. So, *the spirit of Jacob revived.*[177]

172. **from that flowing, gushing river...** From *Yesod,* unformed souls flow into *Shekhinah,* who then *forms* the embryos within Herself before delivering them to new human bodies below.

On the "flowing, gushing river," see above, p. 186 and n. 44; p. 204 and n. 156. On the union of the divine couple and the gestation and birth of the soul, see above, p. 107 and n. 147; *Zohar* 2:12a, 219b–220a; 3:174b; Tishby, *Wisdom of the Zohar*, 2:701–2.

173. **does not find enough body...** The potent soul cannot fully express itself in the infant's body.

The word סיטא (*sita*), rendered here "ambulatory," is apparently based on the Aramaic סטו (*setav*), which derives from the Greek *stoia*, "colonnade, portico, covered ambulatory." see above, p. 97, n. 84. This neologism, preserved in the oldest manuscripts (M7, N23, P2, R1, T1, V5) was later replaced by the more recognizable, bland term סטרא (*sitra*), "side."

174. **spirit expands, imparting its energy** A similar formulation appears in Moses de León, *Shushan Edut*, 336.

175. **Why *forms*?...** Why the present tense, implying a continuous process? Once the person matures, it would seem that the soul is finally complete. In a sense, however, the formation of the soul never ends.

176. **in accordance with the person's state...** Befitting his moral and physical purity.

177. **When Joseph was lost...** Jacob's sadness over the disappearance of Joseph repelled *Shekhinah*, thereby depriving him of extra spirit and of prophetic vision. Years

"Here, having not yet been informed, how did he know? Simply because *Jacob saw* (ibid. 42:1)—he saw the whole country going to Egypt and bringing grain. *Jacob saw.*"[178]

Rabbi Yitsḥak said, "Come and see: King David succeeded in joining the patriarchs and inherited a place among them, as is said: *The stone that the builders rejected has become the cornerstone* (Psalms 118:22)."[179]

Rabbi Yeisa and Rabbi Ḥizkiyah were walking from Cappadocia to Lydda,[180] accompanied by a certain Jew lugging a skin of wine.[181] As they were walking, Rabbi Yeisa said to Rabbi Ḥizkiyah, "Open your mouth and utter

later, when Jacob realized that Joseph was still alive, She returned, and Her power of inspiration reanimated the aged patriarch.

See above, p. 94 and n. 63.

178. **how did he know?...** Since Jacob had not yet heard that Joseph was still alive, his prophetic capabilities were still dormant, so how could he know that grain was available in Egypt? How can Scripture state: *Jacob saw that there were provisions in Egypt*? The explanation must be that he simply *saw* what was going on in his vicinity.

See *Targum Yerushalmi, Leqaḥ Tov,* and Radak, ad loc. Cf. *Bereshit Rabbah* 91:1, 6; *Tanḥuma, Miqqets* 4–5; *Tanḥuma* (Buber), *Miqqets* 5, 7.

179. **King David succeeded...** David joined the triad of patriarchs and served as the fourth leg of the divine throne. See above, notes 160, 164; p. 134, n. 311.

Rabbinic tradition applies this verse from Psalms to David, youngest of Jesse's sons, relegated to tending the flock. See 1 Samuel 16:11; BT *Pesaḥim* 119a; *Midrash Shemu'el* 19:7; *Yalqut ha-Makhiri,* Psalms 118:22, par. 28; *Zohar* 1:20b, 72a, 89b (*ST*); below, pp. 509–10, n. 918.

Rabbi Yitsḥak's brief comment is out of place here. Lavi (*KP*) suggests that it belongs above, page 205: "Come and see: The holy Kingdom did not have complete dominion until it was joined with the patriarchs..." David Luria (*Nefesh David*) adds another possible context: below, page 214 at n. 215.

See, however, *Zohar* 2:31a, and the end of the following note.

180. **from Cappadocia to Lydda** The journey from eastern Asia Minor to Palestine recurs frequently in the *Zohar* and usually includes an encounter with some surprising character. See 1:69b, 132a, 138a (*MhN*), 160a, 223a, 243b; 2:31a, 38b, 80b, 86a; 3:35a, 75b, 221b; *ZḤ* 22a (*MhN*).

The itinerary seems to be intentionally fantastic, though perhaps the author(s) imagined that Cappadocia was a Galilean village near Sepphoris, based on the phrase "Cappadocians of Sepphoris" in JT *Shevi'it* 9:5, 39a. According to a dream interpretation in *Bereshit Rabbah* 68:12, Cappadocia is not far at all from Palestine. Cappadocia figures prominently in M *Ketubbot* 13:11 and BT *Ketubbot* 110b, while Cappadocia and Lydda are linked in *Tosefta, Yevamot* 4:5 and BT *Yevamot* 25b.

See Scholem, in *Zion* (*Me'assef*) 1 (1926): 40–46 (and the appended note by S. Klein, 56); idem, *Major Trends,* 169; idem, *Kabbalah,* 222; Tishby, *Wisdom of the Zohar,* 1:63–64.

This story (until p. 210 at n. 189, below) appears in a longer version in *Zohar* 2:31a–b. See *Nefesh David*; Mopsik.

181. **skin of wine** קטפירא דחמרא (*Qatpira de-ḥamra*). *Qatpira* is a Zoharic neologism that embraces several meanings in the *Zohar,* including "waterskin, wineskin."

See Psalms 119:83; *Zohar* 1:33a, 72a; *KP*; *NO*; Liebes, *Peraqim,* 349–50.

one of those sublime words of Torah that you deliver daily before the Holy Lamp!"[182]

He opened, saying, "*Her ways are ways of delightfulness, and all her paths are peace* (Proverbs 3:17). *Her ways are ways of delightfulness*—ways of Torah, for whoever follows the ways of Torah is showered by the blessed Holy One with the delight of *Shekhinah*, never departing from him. *And all her paths are peace*—for all the paths of Torah are entirely peaceful, providing him peace above, peace below, peace in this world, peace in the world that is coming."

The Jew said, "A coin in a flask is found in this verse!"[183]

They said to him, "How do you know?"

He replied, "I heard from my father, so I learned something here in this verse."

He opened, saying, "This verse is twofold and double-faceted: call it *delightfulness* and call it *peace*, call them *ways* and call them *paths*. Who are *ways* and who are *paths*? Who is *delightfulness* and who is *peace*? Well, *Her ways are ways of delightfulness* corresponds to what is written: *Who makes a way through the sea* (Isaiah 43:16).[184] For look, wherever in Torah one reads *way*, it is a way open to all, like a road open to every person. So, *her ways*—ways opened by the patriarchs, who dug in the great sea and entered her; those ways open up on every side, in every direction of the world.[185]

182. **one of those sublime words...** The expression derives from the Talmud and appears often in the *Zohar*. See BT *Berakhot* 8b; *Ta'anit* 20b; *Ḥagigah* 14a; *Zohar* 1:49b, 87a, 96b; 2:31a; 3:148a, 209b, 231a.

The Holy Lamp—בוצינא קדישא (*Botsina Qaddisha*)—is Rabbi Shim'on, hero of the *Zohar*. See *Zohar* 1:3b–4a, 156a, 217a; 2:4a, 31a, 123b; 3:171a; *ZḤ* 85d (*MhN, Rut*).

See 2 Samuel 21:17; *Bereshit Rabbah* 85:4; BT *Ketubbot* 17a, where Rabbi Abbahu is called: בוצינא דנהורא (*Botsina di-Nhora*), "Lamp of Light"; and *Berakhot* 28b, where Rabban Yoḥanan son of Zakkai is called נר ישראל (*Ner Yisra'el*), "Lamp of Israel."

183. **coin in a flask...** The wandering Jew is playing on a folk saying reported by Ulla in BT *Bava Metsi'a* 85b: "A coin in a bottle goes '*qish qish*.'" There, the point is that a scholar in a family of fools is conspicuous; here, the verse clinks with hidden wisdom. Note that the verse being discussed on the road concerns ways and paths.

The Talmudic wording is איסתירא בלגינא קיש קיש קריא (*Isteira bilgina qish qish qarya*), "A *stater* [coin] in a bottle goes '*qish qish*.'" Here the phrase is איסירא בקיסרא (*isira be-qisra*). The word *isira* is obviously a play on *isteira*; *qisra* may echo *qish qish*, though at the same time it apparently implies *legina*, "bottle." Or perhaps, it is a play on כיס (*kis*), "pocket." See *Zohar* 2:99a. Or it may refer to an image of Caesar on the coin.

184. ***Who makes a way through the sea*** The full verse reads: *Who makes a way through the sea, a path through mighty waters.*

185. **ways opened by the patriarchs...** The patriarchs symbolize the *sefirot Ḥesed, Gevurah*, and *Tif'eret*. They channel the flow of emanation into the sea of *Shekhinah*, by whom the entire world is then nourished.

See Numbers 21:18, quoted in *Zohar* 3:150a–b, 286a; and below, p. 274 and n. 87. On the distinction between "way" and "path," see *Zohar* 2:215a; 3:88a.

"This *delightfulness* is the delight issuing from the world that is coming, and from the world that is coming all lamps radiate, lights scattering everywhere.[186] That goodness and radiance of the world that is coming, absorbed by the patriarchs, is called *delightfulness.*

"Alternatively, the world that is coming is called *delightfulness,* and as it arouses, all goodness and joy, all radiance, all freedom of the world arouse.[187] So we have learned: When Sabbath enters, the wicked in Hell all rest, experiencing freedom and tranquility. When Sabbath departs, we should arouse supernal joy upon us so that we may be saved from the punishment of the wicked, who are doomed from that moment on. We should arouse and recite: *May the delightfulness of YHVH our God be upon us* (Psalms 90:17)—supernal delightfulness, joy of all! So, *Her ways are ways of delightfulness.*[188]

"*And all her paths are peace.* Who are *her paths*? Those paths emerging from above, all gathered by a single covenant named *peace,* peace of the home, who conducts them into the great sea when it is agitated, bringing it peace, as is written: *and all her paths are peace.*[189]

"Come and see: Joseph was covenant of peace, and in Egypt he became ruler and governor of the land, though Jacob, having been deserted by *Shekhinah,* did

186. **world that is coming...** *Binah,* from whom radiate the lower *sefirot* ("lamps"). See above, note 141.

187. **world that is coming is called *delightfulness*...** Since *Binah* is the source of joy and liberation, She Herself is called נעם (*no'am*), *delightfulness.*

See Maimonides, *Mishneh Torah, Hilkhot Teshuvah* 8:4; *Zohar* 2:127a.

188. **wicked in Hell all rest...** Even they enjoy the tranquility of Sabbath. The end of Sabbath marks the return of the wicked to the torments of Hell, and at that moment Jews recite the verse from Psalms to ensure that divine *delightfulness* will overwhelm any demonic powers that could threaten them on earth.

See *Bereshit Rabbah* 11:5; *Tanḥuma, Ki Tissa* 33; *Zohar* 1:14b, 17b, 237b; 2:31b, 88b, 150b–151a, 203b, 207a; 3:94b; *ZḤ* 17a–b (*MhN*).

189. **paths emerging from above...** *Sefer Yetsirah,* the foundational text of Kabbalah, opens by describing "thirty-two wondrous paths of wisdom." These paths, originating in *Hokhkmah* (Wisdom), are more subtle than the ways (see above, note 185). They meet in *Yesod,* the covenant of peace, who then conducts them into the sea of *Shekhinah,* calming Her agitation, which is caused by forces of judgment.

Yesod, the divine phallus, also brings peace by uniting *Tif'eret* with *Shekhinah.* See BT *Shabbat* 152a, where Rabbi Shim'on son of Ḥalafta refers to the phallus as "peacemaker of the home." See above, note 21.

The phrase כד איהו בתוקפיה (*kad ihu betuqpeih*), "when it is agitated," can also be rendered "when he is potent," referring not to the sea of *Shekhinah* but to *Yesod.* See BT *Ḥagigah* 15a: "Shemu'el said, 'Any emission of semen that does not shoot forth like an arrow does not fructify.'" See *Zohar* 1:6a; *KP* and *MM* here. The root *tqf* has a wide range of meaning in the *Zohar* and evidence can be found for each interpretation—both of which, in fact, may be intended here.

not know.[190] Nevertheless, he felt crushed having to purchase grain in Egypt: he foresaw calamity upon calamity in his sons' going down to Egypt.[191]

"*Jacob said to his sons, 'Why should you show yourselves?'* (Genesis 42:1). 'Show yourselves only as hungry, like men who are famished.'"[192]

Rabbi Ḥizkiyah said, "Surely a mystery lies here. For whenever trouble befalls the world, a person should not show himself in the street, so as not to be seized for his sins. That is why he said, *Why should you show yourselves?* This has already been explained.[193]

"Alternatively, *Jacob saw that there was* [198a] שבר (*shever*) *in Egypt* (ibid.)—grain, literally; for the blessed Holy One sent famine into the world in order to bring Jacob and his sons down there, and that is why he saw inhabitants of the land bringing grain from there.[194]

"*Jacob saw that there was shever in Egypt.* Come and see: When Isaac died, Jacob and Esau came to divide the inheritance. Esau abandoned his share of the

190. **Joseph was covenant of peace...** He embodied *Yesod* and appropriately ruled below. See above, p. 205 and n. 166.

On Jacob's lack of knowledge, see above, pp. 207–8 and nn. 177–78. The expression "covenant of peace" appears in Ezekiel 34:25; 37:26.

191. **he felt crushed... foresaw calamity...** Jacob *saw*, or sensed, that his sons' descent to Egypt was ominous, perhaps signaling the fulfillment of the divine decree to Abraham (Genesis 15:13): *Know well that your seed will be strangers in a land not theirs, and they will be enslaved and afflicted four hundred years.*

The wandering Jew is playing on the word שבר (*shever*) in Genesis 42:1: *Jacob saw that there was shever in Egypt.* The plain meaning in the verse is "provisions" or grain, but the root *shvr* means "to break," generating the noun *shever*, "despair, anguish, collapse, crushing." The Aramaic cognate תברא (*tevara*)—or, as here, תבירא (*tevira*)—includes the sense of "calamity."

See *Midrash ha-Gadol*, ad loc., p. 721; *Zohar* 1:211b–212a; Kasher, *Torah Shelemah*, ad loc., n. 8.

192. ***Why should you show yourselves?...*** The verse's plain sense is apparently *Why do you keep looking at one another?* See above, note 168. Here, following a midrashic reading, the sense is: "Why should you make yourselves conspicuous by appearing to be fully sated, thereby arousing envy?"

See BT *Ta'anit* 10b; *Bereshit Rabbah* 91:2. Cf. below, p. 275 and n. 90; *Zohar* 3:92b.

193. **whenever trouble befalls the world...** In time of calamity, one should not go outside, exposing himself to destructive forces. See BT *Bava Qamma* 60a–b: "Rabbi Yosef taught: 'What is the meaning of the verse *None of you shall go out the door of his house until morning* (Exodus 12:22)? Once permission has been granted to the Destroyer, he does not distinguish between righteous and wicked.'... Our Rabbis taught: 'A plague in town? Keep your feet indoors.' ... Our Rabbis taught: 'A plague in town? One should not walk in the middle of the road because the Angel of Death walks there, for as soon as permission has been granted him, he strides brazenly.'"

See above, pp. 112–13 and n. 183.

194. **שבר (*shever*) *in Egypt*—grain, literally...** See above, p. 208 and n. 178, note 191.

land, leaving Jacob to endure exile and obtain all.[195] So he saw that תבירא (*tevira*), calamity, awaited him in Egypt—him and his sons—enduring the exile. Therefore, *Jacob said to his sons, 'Why should you show yourselves* in the presence of supernal judgment? Don't let the Accuser loom over you!'[196]

"*He said, "Look, I have heard that there are provisions in Egypt. Go down there"* (ibid., 2). As they have established, רדו (*redu*), *Go down*—for this numerical value, Israel remained in Egypt."[197]

Joseph was the governor over the land... (Genesis 42:6).[198]

Rabbi Yose opened, "*And now my head will be raised above my enemies surrounding me*... (Psalms 27:6).[199] Come and see: When the blessed Holy One delights in a human being, He raises him above all inhabitants of the world, making him head of all, all subdued beneath him. King David was despised by his brothers, rejected by them, but the blessed Holy One raised his head above all inhabitants of the world.[200] His father-in-law came and he fled from him; the blessed Holy One raised him over his kingdom and all bowed before him.[201] Joseph was despised by his brothers; afterward, they all knelt and bowed before him, as is written: *Joseph's brothers came and bowed down to him, their faces to the ground* (Genesis, ibid.).[202]

195. **When Isaac died...** When his two sons came to divide their father's inheritance, Esau abandoned his share of the Holy Land, leaving Jacob to dwell there and to undergo the exile decreed by God to Abraham, but finally to attain immense reward. See above, pp. 69–70 and nn. 469–74.

196. **תבירא (*tevira*), calamity...** See above, p. 211 and nn. 191, 193.

197. ***Go down there*...** The verse reads: *Go down there, and get us provisions from there that we may live and not die.* The *gimatriyya* (numerical value) of the word רדו (*redu*), *go down*, is 210, which according to the Midrash implies that the Israelites would be enslaved in Egypt for that many years.

See *Bereshit Rabbah* 91:2 (in the name of Rabbi Abba bar Kahana); *Tanḥuma, Miqqets* 8; *Tanḥuma* (Buber), *Miqqets* 10. On the chronology, see *Seder Olam Rabbah* 3; *Pirqei de-Rabbi Eli'ezer* 48; Rashi on Genesis 15:13; Sarna, *Genesis*, 116.

198. ***Joseph was the governor*...** The full verse reads: *Joseph was the governor over the land, he was the provider to all the people of the land. And Joseph's brothers came and bowed down to him, their faces to the ground.*

199. ***And now my head*...** The full verse reads: *And now my head will be raised above my enemies surrounding me, and I will offer in His tent sacrifices of jubilation; I will sing and chant to YHVH.*

200. **King David was despised...** Traditionally, David is the author of Psalms, including the psalm discussed here. On David and his older brothers, see Pseudo-Philo 59:4; *Yalqut ha-Makhiri*, Psalms 118, 28; Ginzberg, *Legends*, 4:82; 6:247, n. 13.

201. **father-in-law...** Before becoming king, David married Michal, a daughter of King Saul. On his tempestuous relationship with his father-in-law who sought to kill him and whom he succeeded to the throne, see 1 Samuel 17 – 2 Samuel 1.

202. **Joseph was despised...** See Genesis 37:1–9.

"*And now my head will be raised.* What is ועתה (*ve-attah*), *and now*? Like ואתה (*ve-attah*), *and You*."[203]

Rabbi Yehudah says, "As has been explained, עת (*et*), time—a supernal rung. And who is this *et*? ה (*He*), and it is called עתה (*attah*), *now*.[204] ועתה (*Ve-attah*), *and now*, is He and His court.[205]

"*My head will be raised*—raised in dignity and dominion.

"*Above my enemies surrounding me*—other kings of the earth.[206]

"*And I will offer in His tent* (ibid.)—Jerusalem. *In His tent*—Tent of Meeting.[207]

"*Sacrifices of jubilation* (ibid.)—so that the whole world will hear.

"*I will sing and chant* (ibid.)—from the side of jubilation, since from there issue song and praise.[208]

203. **ועתה (*ve-attah*), *and now*... ואתה (*ve-attah*), *and You*** The pronunciation of the two words is virtually identical, while the only orthographic difference between them is that the first is spelled with an ע (*ayin*) and the second with an א (*alef*). In the *Zohar*, the second-person pronoun אתה (*attah*) sometimes refers to *Shekhinah*, who, being more revealed than the other *sefirot*, can be addressed directly. According to Rabbi Yose, apparently, King David is praying that *Shekhinah*, known as *Malkhut* (Kingdom), will raise his head.

On *Shekhinah* as אתה (*attah*), see *Zohar* 1:15b, 37a, 154b, 158b, 205b; 2:70a (*RR*), 104a, 138b, 140a, 221a, 261a (*Heikh*); 3:199a. For other sefirotic correspondences of אתה (*attah*), see 3:193b, 271a, 290a (*IZ*); Gikatilla, *Sha'arei Orah*, 67b–68b; *OY*.

204. **עת (*et*), time—a supernal rung...** *Shekhinah* is known as "time" since She conducts the world according to a cosmic schedule, enabling each phenomenon to unfold in its proper time. See above, p. 188 at n. 57. She is also symbolized by the letter ה (*he*), the final letter of the divine name יהוה (*YHVH*). Here Rabbi Yehudah understands עתה (*attah*), *now*, as a combination of these two designations of *Shekhinah*.

205. **ועתה (*Ve-attah*), *and now*, is He and His court** Now Rabbi Yehudah is playing on a midrashic reading of the expression ויהוה (*va-YHVH*), *and YHVH*. In rabbinic exegesis, the conjunction ו (*vav*), *and*, amplifies the meaning of the word to which it is attached, and according to Rabbi El'azar (*Bereshit Rabbah* 51:2): "Wherever it is said ויהוה (*va-YHVH*), *and YHVH*, this implies: He and His Court."

In Kabbalah this court symbolizes *Shekhinah*, who derives from the *sefirah* of *Din* (Judgment) and pronounces the divine decree, so the expression *And YHVH* encompasses "He [*Tif'eret*, known as *YHVH*] and His Court [*Shekhinah*]."

Here, similarly but with a twist, the conjunction ו (*vav*), *and*, amplifies the meaning of עתה (*attah*), *now*, which by itself designates *Shekhinah* (see the preceding note). The expression ועתה (*ve-attah*) is understood to mean: "He [*Tif'eret*, implied by the amplifying *vav*] and His Court [*Shekhinah*, called *attah*]."

See above, p. 178, n. 583.

206. **other kings of the earth** Whom David defeated in battle.

207. ***His tent*—Jerusalem... Tent of Meeting** David's son, Solomon, would eventually construct the Temple (*His tent*) in Jerusalem, but in David's lifetime the Ark of the Covenant was housed in a temporary tent (Tent of Meeting), even after David captured it from the Philistines and brought it to Jerusalem.

See 1 Samuel 2:22; 2 Samuel 6:17; 7:6.

208. **side of jubilation...** *Gevurah*, associated with the singing of the Levites. See *Zohar* 1:103b; 3:39a.

"Alternatively, *My head will be raised*—Assembly of Israel.[209]

"*Above my enemies surrounding me*—Esau and all his lieutenants.[210]

"*And I will offer in His tent*—Israel.[211]

"*Sacrifices of jubilation*—as is written: *Sacrifices of God are a broken spirit* (ibid. 51:19), in order to remove judgment from the world.[212]

"*I will sing and chant*—thanking and praising the blessed Holy One incessantly, forever.

"*My head will be raised*—entirely, the good impulse above the evil impulse.

"*Above my enemies surrounding me*—the evil impulse, surrounding a person, his utter enemy.[213]

"*And I will offer in His tent sacrifices of jubilation*—Torah, given from the side of fire, as is said: *From His right hand, a fiery law for them* (Deuteronomy 33:2). By virtue of Torah, one's head is raised and all his enemies shattered before him, as is said: *Those who rose against me You have subdued beneath me* (Psalms 18:40).[214]

"*My head will be raised*—included among the patriarchs; for King David has to join the patriarchs before being exalted, rising above, in a single bond with them.[215]

"*Above my enemies surrounding me*—those on the left side, all masters of judgment intent on destruction. Then sun unites with moon and all becomes one.[216]

209. ***My head*... Assembly of Israel** *Shekhinah,* David's *sefirah,* will be raised. On Her name Assembly of Israel, see above, pp. 122–23, n. 237.

210. **Esau...** In Genesis 36:1, he is identified with Edom, whom (according to 1 Samuel 8:13–14) David defeated. In rabbinic literature Esau represents the Roman Empire, while in medieval Jewish literature he stands for Christianity.

See *Bereshit Rabbah* 75:12.

211. ***I will offer in His tent*—Israel** That is, Israel will bring offerings to God in the Temple.

212. ***Sacrifices of jubilation... broken spirit*...** Here the word תרועה (*teru'ah*), *jubilation,* is associated with the root רעע (*r''*), "to shatter."

213. **evil impulse... enemy** According to BT *Sukkah* 52a, one of the many names of the evil impulse is "enemy."

214. **Torah, given from the side of fire...** Previously (above, at note 208), *jubilation* was linked with *Gevurah.* Now Torah joins this constellation of meaning through the image of fire, another symbol of *Gevurah.*

On *Gevurah* as the origin of Torah, see *Zohar* 3:80b. On the tension and interplay between left (the side of *Gevurah*) and right (*From His right hand*), see *Zohar* 1:243a; 2:81a, 84a–b, 135a, 166b, 206b; 3:176a; Mopsik. On the link between *jubilation* and the "shattering" of one's enemies, see above, note 212. Although the word for Torah here is the Aramaic אורייתא (*oraita*), Rabbi Yehudah is probably playing on תורה (*torah*) and תרועה (*teru'ah*), *jubilation.*

215. **included among the patriarchs...** *Shekhinah,* symbolized by David, will join the triad of *Ḥesed, Gevurah,* and *Tif'eret,* symbolized by the three patriarchs (Abraham, Isaac, and Jacob). See above, notes 160, 164, 179.

216. **sun unites with moon...** *Tif'eret* unites with *Shekhinah.*

"Come and see: *Joseph was the governor over the land* (Genesis 42:6)—sun governing moon, illumining her, nourishing her.[217]

"*He was the provider to all the people of the land* (ibid.). From that flowing, gushing river, all are nourished; from there souls fly to all.[218] So they all bow to that site,[219] for there is nothing in the world that does not depend on the flux of destiny, since from there all goodness flows into the world. As they have established, all depends on flux."[220]

Joseph recognized his brothers, but they did not recognize him (Genesis 42:8).

Rabbi El'azar opened, "*Why should I fear, in days of evil, the iniquity of my heels encompassing me?* (Psalms 49:6).[221] Come and see: There are three who fear without knowing what they fear, as has been established.[222] However, there is one who fears without knowing what he fears, because of sins that he did not recognize as sins, that he did not consider.[223] It is he who fears *days of evil*—those days designated for the [198b] evil one. And who are they? This is the evil impulse, called evil one,[224] who has certain days on which

217. ***Joseph was the governor*...** The full verse reads: *Joseph was the governor over the land, he was the provider to all the people of the land. And Joseph's brothers came and bowed down to him, their faces to the ground.*

Joseph symbolizes *Yesod,* who shares with *Tif'eret* the designation *sun.* Therefore it was fitting for Joseph to govern *the land,* symbolizing *Shekhinah.*

218. **flowing, gushing river...** The river of *Yesod,* conveying souls to the world via *Shekhinah.* See above, p. 186 and n. 44; p. 204 and n. 156; pp. 206–7 and n. 172.

219. **all bow to that site** To *Yesod.* See the end of the verse, above, note 217; p. 205 and n. 161.

220. **flux of destiny...** מזלא (*Mazzala*) means "constellation, planet, planetary influence, zodiacal sign, destiny, fortune, guardian angel." See BT *Mo'ed Qatan* 28a: "Rava said, 'Life, children, and sustenance do not depend on merit but on *mazzala,* destiny.'"

In the *Zohar, mazzala* is associated with the root נזל (*nzl*), "to flow," and often refers to the flow of emanation from *Binah* through *Yesod.* See above, p. 96 and n. 77.

221. ***Why should I fear*...** The plain sense of the verse is probably *Why should I fear, in days of evil, when the iniquity of my persecutors surrounds me,* or: ... *in days of evil, the encompassing iniquity of those who would supplant* [or: *betray*] *me.* The translation presented above reflects the rabbinic understanding of the verse, as will soon become apparent.

222. **three who fear...** See the apparent (though differing) source in BT *Pesaḥim* 111b–112a: "One who eats cress without washing his hands will fear for thirty days. One who lets blood without washing his hands will fear for seven days. One who trims his hair without washing his hands will fear for three days. One who pares his nails without washing his hands will fear for one day without knowing what frightens him."

223. **because of sins...** On the connection between fear and sinfulness, see BT *Berakhot* 60a.

224. **evil impulse, called evil one** See BT *Sukkah* 52a, quoting Genesis 8:21: ... *for the devisings of the human heart are evil from youth.*

he is authorized in the world to lead astray all those who defile their ways, for one who comes to defile himself, they defile.[225] So these are called *days of evil*, and they are assigned to those sins that people trample underfoot.[226]

"Come and see: All those who defile their ways encounter bands of dazzling demons, defiling them.[227] On the path one wishes to take, on precisely that path he is conducted. If a person comes to purify himself, how many are those who assist him![228]

"We have learned that when a person rises in the morning, he should wash his hands from a receptacle of water—a vessel for pouring water—by means of someone who has already washed his hands, as has been established.[229] Come and see: On account of this receptacle, we have established this matter.[230]

"Further, a person should wash the right hand with the left, so that right prevail over left and right be washed by left; this is the purpose of washing. So one who washes his hands should wash right with left, so as not to provide any opening for the evil impulse to dominate, as we have established.[231]

225. **one who comes to defile himself, they defile** See BT *Shabbat* 104a: "Resh Lakish said, '. . . If one comes to defile himself, he is provided an opening; if one comes to purify himself, he is assisted.'" See above, note 114.

226. **sins that people trample underfoot** Seemingly insignificant misdeeds, peccadilloes. According to the rabbinic reading of Psalms 49:6, such "minor" offenses constitute *the iniquity of my heels*, i.e., sins that are often trampled underfoot as being too trivial to justify altering one's course; yet these very sins threaten to eventually *encompass* the careless person on the Day of Judgment.

See BT *Avodah Zarah* 18a (in the name of Rabbi Shim'on son of Lakish); *Tanḥuma, Eqev* 1.

227. **dazzling demons . . .** טהירין (*Tehirin*), from the Aramaic root meaning "brightness, noon." One class of demons is named טהרי (*tiharei*), "noonday demons."

See Psalms 91:6 and Rashi, ad loc; *Targum*, Song of Songs 4:6; *Targum Yerushalmi*, Numbers 6:24, Deuteronomy 32:24; *Zohar* 1:94a, 125a–b, 130b, 200a, 232b (*Tos*); 2:130a–b, 195b, 205a, 207a. The Hebrew root טהר (*thr*), "pure," lends this demonic name a euphemistic tone.

228. **path one wishes to take . . .** See BT *Makkot* 10b: "Rabbah son of Bar Ḥana said in the name of Rabbi Huna (some say, Rabbi Huna said in the name of Rabbi El'azar), 'From the Torah, the Prophets, and the Writings it can be demonstrated that one is led on the path one wishes to take.'"

See *Zohar* 2:47a; 3:50a; above, notes 114, 225.

229. **wash his hands . . .** A perfect example of a seemingly insignificant yet vital act.

See BT *Berakhot* 51a; *Zohar* 1:10b, 53b; 3:186a–b; above, pages 125–26; Moses de León, *Orḥot Ḥayyim*, pars. 10, 12; idem, *Sefer ha-Rimmon*, 56; Ta-Shma, *Ha-Nigleh she-ba-Nistar*, 31, 121, n. 59.

230. **On account of this receptacle . . .** This teaching has been transmitted in order to emphasize the importance of performing the daily ritual in precisely this way.

231. **wash the right hand with the left . . .** The right hand symbolizes *Ḥesed* (Love), whereas the left hand symbolizes *Din* (Judgment). By washing the right hand with the left, one subjugates left to right, making the left serve the right and thereby ensuring that Love will prevail over Judgment and that the evil impulse, deriving from the left, will be thwarted.

In a discussion of ritual washing before

"Come and see: When evil judgment prevails, it does not refrain from tormenting.[232] When the right prevails over other nations to crush them, the blessed Holy One feels compassion for them and does not annihilate them. Therefore, whoever commits those sins that one tramples underfoot is unaware of them and is constantly afraid.[233] King David was always on guard against these sins, and whenever he went to battle he would search for them; so he did not fear to wage war.[234]

"Come and see: There were four kings; what one requested, another did not.[235] David said, *Let me pursue my enemies and overtake them...* (Psalms 18:38).[236] Why? Because he had guarded himself against those sins, providing no opening for his enemies to prevail; so he asked to pursue them continually—rather than they pursuing him, demanding punishment for his sins, so that he fall into their hands.

"Asa was more afraid, even though he scrutinized his sins—but not like King David.[237] He asked to pursue them but not to attack them, and that the blessed Holy One slay them. And so it was, as is written: *Asa and the army with him pursued them as far as Gerar...*, and: *YHVH struck the Cushites before Asa and Judah, and the Cushites fled* (2 Chronicles 14:11–12).[238] But of David, what is written? *David smote them from twilight until the evening of the next day* (1 Samuel 30:17).[239] Whereas Asa was pursuing and the blessed Holy One striking.

eating (*Zohar* 2:154b), Rabbi Ya'akov insists on the opposite procedure: right hand washing the left. See *ZḤ* 86d (*MhN*, *Rut*); Moses de León, *Maskiyyot Kesef*, 9; Joseph Caro, *Beit Yosef*, *Oraḥ Ḥayyim* 4:8–11; idem, *Shulḥan Arukh*, *Oraḥ Ḥayyim* 4:10; Vital; *MM*; Katz, *Halakhah ve-Qabbalah*, 68.

232. **When evil judgment prevails...** See above, note 193.

233. **whoever commits those sins...** Such a person is tormented: fearing without knowing what he fears. See above at note 223, and note 226.

234. **he would search for them...** To make sure that he had not committed such sins—or if he had, to repent for them.

235. **There were four kings...** This opening line and the passage that follows derive from *Eikhah Rabbah*, *Petiḥta* 30; 4:15. Here Rabbi El'azar interlaces the earlier midrash with the theme of sins trampled underfoot.

236. ***Let me pursue...*** David was confident and fearless.

The verse reads: *I will pursue my enemies and overtake them, and not return till they are destroyed.* The wording *Let me pursue* derives from the parallel passage in 2 Samuel 22:38.

237. **Asa...** King of Judah, who did not examine his conduct as meticulously as David.

238. ***Asa and the army...*** The verses read: *YHVH struck the Cushites before Asa and Judah, and the Cushites fled. Asa and the army with him pursued them as far as Gerar, and many of the Cushites fell, beyond recovery, for they were crushed before YHVH and His camp.* Here the order of the two verses is reversed to fit Rabbi El'azar's wording.

239. ***David smote them...*** The full verse reads: *David smote them from twilight until the evening of the next day, and not a man of them escaped, except four hundred young men who mounted camels and fled.*

"Jehoshaphat king of Judah also asked, saying, 'I can neither pursue nor slay; but I will sing and You slay them'—because he did not scrutinize as thoroughly as Asa. The blessed Holy One did so, as is written: *As they began their jubilation and praise, YHVH set ambushes against the men of Ammon, Moab, and Mount Seir who were invading Judah, and they were struck down* (2 Chronicles 20:22).

"Hezekiah king of Judah also said, 'I can neither sing nor pursue nor wage war'—because he feared those sins that we have mentioned. What is written? *That night an angel of YHVH went out and struck down one hundred and eighty-five thousand in the Assyrian camp* (2 Kings 19:35).[240] Hezekiah stayed at home lying in bed, while the blessed Holy One was slaying them.

"Now, if these righteous ones feared those sins, how much more so should other inhabitants of the world! Therefore one should ferret out those sins that we have mentioned, so that those *days of evil,* who are merciless toward him, will not prevail against him.[241]

"Come and see: *Joseph recognized his brothers*—when they fell into his hands.
218 *But they did not recognize him*—when he fell into theirs.[242] He felt compassion for them because he was peace.[243] *But they did not recognize him*—because they, Simeon and Levi, issued from the side of harsh Judgment, so they felt no compassion for him; for all those masters of judgment have no compassion for people falling into their hands.[244]

"Therefore David said, *Why should I fear, in days of evil?* It is not written *did I fear,* but rather *should I fear,* because 'I have nothing to fear [199a] from those *days of evil,*' as we have said.[245]

"And yet, *the iniquity of my heels encompassing me.* Who are *my heels*? Those referred to mysteriously: *His hand gripping Esau's heel* (Genesis 25:26). This is

240. ***That night...*** The full verse reads: *That night an angel of YHVH went out and struck down one hundred and eighty-five thousand in the Assyrian camp. The people arose early in the morning and behold, they were all dead corpses!*

241. **those *days of evil...*** See above at notes 224–26.

242. ***Joseph recognized his brothers...*** When Joseph's brothers came to Egypt seeking grain from him (the Governor), he immediately recognized them; but years earlier, when he fell into their hands, they did not "recognize" him (that is, treat him as a brother), but rather planned to kill him and eventually sold him into slavery.

See Genesis 37; *Bereshit Rabbah* 91:7; Rashi, ad loc.

243. **because he was peace** Joseph symbolizes *Yesod,* known as "peace." See above, note 21.

244. **Simeon and Levi... harsh Judgment...** Genesis does not specify which brothers hatched the plan to get rid of Joseph, but midrashic tradition assigns the role to Simeon and Levi. According to the *Zohar,* this pair of brothers derives from the *sefirah* of *Din* (harsh Judgment).

See above, p. 123 and n. 244.

245. **It is not written *did I fear...*** Scripture does not employ the past tense but the future, because David was confident

the heel, and those are heels constantly observing the sin that a person tramples with his heel.[246]

"Come and see what is written: *Woe unto them who haul iniquity with flimsy cords, and sin as with cart ropes* (Isaiah 5:18). *With flimsy cords*—that he tramples with the heel unconcernedly; but gradually it is reinforced, becoming like *cart ropes*. That sin is reinforced, leading him astray in this world and in the world that is coming.[247]

"Happy are the righteous who know how to guard themselves against their sins! They constantly scrutinize their actions, so that the Accuser will not loom over them in this world or accuse them in the world that is coming. For Torah prepares ways and paths for them to follow, as is written: *Her ways are ways of delight, and all her paths are peace* (Proverbs 3:17)."

Joseph remembered the dreams he had dreamed about them (Genesis 42:9).[248]

Rabbi Ḥiyya opened, "*When your enemy falls, do not be glad; when he stumbles, let your heart not rejoice* (Proverbs 24:17). Come and see: The blessed Holy One formed the human being for His glory, to serve Him constantly, and to engage in Torah day and night, because the blessed Holy One delights constantly in Torah. As soon as He created Adam, He placed Torah before him and taught her to him, so that he would know her ways. How do we know? As is written: *Then He saw her and declared her; He arranged her and explored her*. And then: *He said to Adam, 'See! Awe of YHVH—she is wisdom; to shun evil is understanding'* (Job 28:27–28).[249] Having seen her, he transgressed

that he had not committed any sins that would haunt him in the hereafter.

246. **Who are *my heels*?... *Esau's heel*...** The heel symbolizes the demonic, lowest realm, linked with Esau. The verse in Genesis reads: *Afterward his brother came out, his hand gripping Esau's* עקב (*aqev*), *heel, so he called him* יעקב (*Ya'aqov*), *Jacob*. According to this folk etymology, Jacob's name means "He grips the heel," trying to prevent the prior birth of his twin. Here Rabbi El'azar implies that Jacob grips Esau's heel in order to subdue evil. The *heels* are demonic forces who spy on carefree sinners.

See *Avot de-Rabbi Natan* A, 31, where the heel represents the Angel of Death. See above, p. 216 and n. 226; *Zohar* 1:138a.

247. ***With flimsy cords*...** At first, one may assume that minor offenses are insignificant (*flimsy*, trivial), but before long they begin to dominate.

The word שוא (*shav*), rendered here *flimsy*, means "deception; worthless, trivial, unreliable." See BT *Sukkah* 52a: "Rabbi Assi said, 'The evil impulse at first resembles the thread of a spider but ultimately it resembles cart ropes, as is said: *Woe unto them who haul iniquity with flimsy cords, and sin as with cart ropes*.'" See *Zohar* 1:5a, 57a.

248. ***Joseph remembered*...** The full verse reads: *Joseph remembered the dreams he had dreamed about them, and he said to them, "You are spies! To see the land's nakedness you have come."*

249. ***He said to Adam*...** The plain sense of the word אדם (*adam*) here is

the command of his Lord and was seized for his sin.[250] All those who transgress a single word of Torah are seized for it.

"King Solomon was wiser than all inhabitants of the world; he transgressed a single word of Torah and caused his disenthronement and the splitting of the kingdom from his descendants.[251] How much more so, for one who transgresses the Torah![252]

"Come and see: Why did Joseph—who was granted dominion by the blessed Holy One—spin schemes around his brothers when they fell into his hands? After all, he knew the Torah that his father had taught him! But perish the thought that Joseph spun those schemes to take revenge upon them! Rather, he did all this only to bring his brother Benjamin, for whom he yearned. He did not let his brothers fall, for look at what is written: *Joseph gave orders to fill their bags with grain*... (Genesis, ibid., 25)—all this so they would not fall."[253]

"human being(s)," but Rabbi Ḥiyya understands it as referring to Adam.

According to the Midrash, God intended to reveal the Torah to Adam, but once Adam sinned, He decided to reserve it for his descendants. See *Bereshit Rabbah* 24:5 (and Theodor's note); *Qohelet Rabbah* on 3:11; *ZḤ* 85c (*MhN, Rut*); Moses de León, *Sefer ha-Rimmon*, 353; Mopsik.

250. **seized...** A rabbinic idiom meaning "punished." See *OY*.

251. **transgressed a single word...** By marrying many wives, amassing great wealth, and acquiring many horses, Solomon violated the restrictions on royalty in Deuteronomy 17:16–17, where the key word is ירבה (*yarbeh*), *he shall* [*not*] *get* [*himself*] *many* [wives or horses or excessive silver and gold]. According to 1 Kings 11, Solomon's wives lured him into idolatry, and as a result God decreed that his entire kingdom except for one tribe (Judah) would be torn away from his son, becoming the northern kingdom of Israel. According to midrashic tradition, Solomon himself was supplanted by the demon Ashmedai (or by an angel) and he was forced to wander as a commoner for years.

On Solomon's violation, see JT *Sanhedrin* 2:6, 20c; *Vayiqra Rabbah* 19:2; *Pesiqta de-Rav Kahana* 26:2; *Qohelet Rabbah* on 2:2; *Tanḥuma, Aḥarei Mot* 1; *Tanḥuma* (Buber), *Aḥarei Mot* 2.

On his disenthronement, see the same sources (except for *Vayiqra Rabbah*); BT *Gittin* 68a–b; *Rut Rabbah* 5:6; *Midrash Tehillim* 78:12; *Bemidbar Rabbah* 11:3; *Beit ha-Midrash*, 6:106–7; *Zohar* 1:53b, 250a; *ZḤ* 70b (ShS); Ginzberg, *Legends*, 6:299–300, n. 86.

252. **How much more so...** If Solomon the Wise was punished for violating a single word of Torah, then the careless disregard of Torah by other humans will be punished more severely.

253. **Why did Joseph...** From the account in Genesis (see above, note 248, and the continuation of the narrative through Genesis 44), it seems that Joseph acted vengefully toward his brothers, in violation of the verse quoted by Rabbi Ḥiyya (*When your enemy falls, do not be glad...*), as well as the explicit command in Leviticus 19:18: *You shall not take vengeance, and you shall not harbor a grudge.*

On Joseph's learning Torah from his father, Jacob, see above, p. 164, n. 500. Genesis 42:25 reads: *Joseph gave orders to fill their bags with grain and to return each one's silver to his sack and to give them provisions for the way; and so it was done for them.*

Rabbi Yehudah said, "Once the blessed Holy One created the moon, He would gaze upon Her, as is said: *The eyes of YHVH your God are perpetually upon her* (Deuteronomy 11:12)—watching over Her constantly.[254] And it is written: *Then He saw her and declared her* (Job, ibid.), for by gazing upon Her, the sun is illumined. ויספרה (*Vaysapperah*), *And declared her.* What does *vaysapperah* mean? As is said: *a place whose stones are* ספיר (*sappir*), *sapphire* (ibid., 6).[255]

"*He arranged her* (ibid., 27), for She sits arrayed in twelve dominions,[256] splaying into seventy suzerains.[257] He established Her with seven supernal pillars, to be illumined, to dwell in perfection.[258]

"*And explored her* (ibid.)—gazing upon Her continually, time after time, ceaselessly.

"Then He warned the human being, saying, *See! Awe of YHVH—she is wisdom* (ibid., 28), for She is crowned above creatures below, so that through Her they may revere and know the blessed Holy One.[259]

"*To shun evil is understanding* (ibid.)—purging of refuse so as not to approach it, or approach with it. Then, manifestation of *understanding*: knowing, contemplating, gazing upon the glory of the supernal King."[260]

254. **blessed Holy One created the moon...** That is, emanated *Shekhinah*, symbolized by the moon. She is also symbolized by the land of Israel, which is the subject of the verse in Deuteronomy.

255. **by gazing upon Her...** By gazing upon and illumining *Shekhinah*, Her partner (*Tif'eret*) is Himself illumined. See *Zohar* 1:136a; and *KP*, where Shim'on Lavi describes how the sun is illumined by shining on the earth.

The assonance of *vaysapperah* and *sappir* allows for a new meaning of the verse in Job 28: *Then He saw her and rendered her sapphirine.* See *Zohar* 1:8a; *ZḤ* 45a.

256. **twelve dominions** Twelve camps of angels beneath *Shekhinah*, corresponding to the twelve tribes of Israel.

The word תחומין (*teḥumin*) means "boundaries, limits, dominions." The phrase here recalls the twelve גבולי אלכסון (*gevulei alakhson*), "diagonal borders" (edges of a cube), mentioned in *Sefer Yetsirah* 5:1.

See *Bahir* 64 (95); Ezra of Gerona, *Peirush Shir ha-Shirim*, 511–12; above, pp. 120–21 and n. 227; *Zohar* 2:229b; Liebes, *Torat ha-Yetsirah shel Sefer Yetsirah*, 25; Mopsik.

257. **seventy suzerains** Heavenly princes, or guardian angels, governing the seventy nations of the world. Their existence and power derive from *Shekhinah*.

See above, pp. 70–71 and nn. 476–77; p. 195 and n. 106. On the word "suzerains," see above, note 110. Cf. *Zohar* 2:58b.

258. **seven supernal pillars...** The seven *sefirot* above *Shekhinah*, from *Binah* through *Yesod*.

259. **She is crowned...** *Shekhinah* is crowned and fulfilled by human virtue. She is known as *awe of YHVH* and lower Wisdom; through Her, human beings perceive and encounter higher realms of divinity.

See above, p. 203 and n. 154. On *Shekhinah* as the divine gate, see *Zohar* 1:103b.

260. **purging of refuse...** Eliminating the demonic refuse that is generated by immorality and taints *Shekhinah*. Such purging is a prerequisite for spiritual growth, enabling one to approach the divine realm and gaze upon *Binah* (*understanding*).

The phrase "so as not to approach it, or approach with it" translates the Aramaic

Rabbi Yose rose at night to engage in Torah, and there was a certain Jew there whom he happened to have met in that house.

Rabbi Yose opened, saying, "*Treasures of wickedness do not avail, but righteousness delivers from death* (Proverbs 10:2). *Treasures of wickedness do not avail*—those who do not engage in Torah, and follow worldly affairs, amassing treasures of wickedness.[261] What is written? *Those riches are lost in a bad venture* (Ecclesiastes 5:13), because they are *treasures of wickedness.*

"*But righteousness delivers from death*—those who engage in Torah and know her ways, contemplating. For Torah, Tree of Life, is called *righteousness*, as is written: *It will be righteousness for us if we are careful to observe this entire commandment* (Deuteronomy 6:25).[262]

"Alternatively, *but* צדקה (*tsedaqah*), *righteousness, delivers from death*—*tsedaqah*, charity, literally. It is twofold and double-faceted: call it Torah [199b] and call it charity, and all is one."[263]

That Jew said, "And call it peace!"[264]

Rabbi Yose said, "Certainly so!"

That Jew rose and joined him. He opened, saying, "*One who tills his land will be sated with bread, but one who chases vanities will be sated with poverty* (Proverbs 28:19). This verse is difficult. How could King Solomon, wiser than

דלא למקרב בהדיה (*de-la le-miqrav ba-hadeih*), which conveys either of these senses, or perhaps here both of them. The first sense—"not to approach it [the refuse]"—accords with Zoharic idiom and syntax and with the verse from Job: *to shun evil.* The second —"not to approach [the divine realm] with it [the refuse]"—matches more normal Aramaic and fits the context well. See Moses de León, commentary on the ten *sefirot*, 364a–365a; *OY*; Soncino; *Sullam*; Tishby, *Mishnat ha-Zohar*, 1:245; Tishby, *Wisdom of the Zohar* (tr. Goldstein), 403; Mopsik; *MmD*; Edri, *Sefer ha-Zohar.*

The phrase "contemplating, gazing" renders לאסתכלא (*le-istakkala*), which conveys both of these meanings.

261. **amassing treasures of wickedness** Ill-gotten gains.

262. **Torah...*It will be righteousness*...** That is, if we observe the commandments of Torah, this will be considered as righteousness, merit, virtue. The full verse reads: *It will be righteousness for us if we are careful to observe this entire commandment before YHVH our God, as He has commanded us.*

See *Midrash Mishlei* 11:4; *Seder Eliyyahu Zuta* 1; *Zohar* 1:76b. On Torah as the Tree of Life, see above, note 8. In Kabbalah all three of these words (Torah, Tree of Life, and *righteousness*) symbolize *Tif'eret*.

263. ***tsedaqah*, charity, literally...** The word צדקה (*tsedaqah*) can be understood literally as "charity" or as a metonym for Torah, both alluding to *Tif'eret* and both overcoming death.

264. **call it peace** *Tsedaqah* (charity, righteousness) also implies peace, since it promotes peace in the world. In the sefirotic realm, peace too alludes to *Tif'eret*, who harmonizes the polar opposites *Ḥesed* and *Gevurah*.

See Isaiah 32:17; M *Avot* 2:7; *Vayiqra Rabbah* 34:16; below, at note 318; *Zohar* 3:108b; *ZḤ* 75c–d (*MhN*, *Rut*); Moses de León, *Shushan Edut*, 356–57; idem, *Sefer ha-Rimmon*, 113–14.

all of humanity, say that one should strive to cultivate the land, devoting himself to that and abandoning eternal life?[265] But it is a mystery!"

He opened, saying, "*YHVH Elohim took the human and placed him in the Garden of Eden to till it and tend it* (Genesis 2:15). They have established that this is the mystery of offerings.[266] Come and see: *To till it*—supernal King; *and tend it*—lower King; supernal world and lower world.[267] *To till it*—for the male, in mystery of זכור (*zakhor*), *remember*; ולשמרה (*ul-shomrah*), *and tend it*—in mystery of שמור (*shamor*), *observe*.[268]

"Therefore, *one who tills his land*—Garden of Eden, which needs to be tilled and cultivated, drawing blessings to Her from above.[269] When She is blessed, drawing blessings from above, he too is blessed along with Her.[270]

265. **abandoning eternal life** Abandoning the study and fulfillment of Torah. See BT *Shabbat* 33b.

266. **mystery of offerings** See *Bereshit Rabbah* 16:5: "[*YHVH Elohim took the human and placed him in the Garden of Eden*] *to till it and tend it*—these are the offerings." According to Kabbalah, sacrificial offerings unite *Shekhinah* (*Garden of Eden*) with the *sefirot* above Her.

See *Zohar* 1:57b, 141b; 2:165b; 3:263a.

267. **supernal King... lower King...** *Binah* and *Shekhinah*. See Moses de León, *Sefer ha-Rimmon*, 105–6; *OY*.

Although *Binah* is often pictured as the Divine Mother, She is also known as King and as "world of the male," encompassing all the *sefirot* beneath Her through *Yesod*. Together these constitute a masculine entity that joins *Shekhinah*.

See *Zohar* 1:29a. On "the world of the male," see *Zohar* 1:96a, 147a, 149a, 160b, 200a, 246a–247a, 248b; 2:101a, 105b, 127b, 165b; *ZḤ* 72b (*ShS*); Moses de León, *Shushan Edut*, 343; idem, *Sefer ha-Rimmon*, 23 (and Wolfson's note 6); idem, commentary on the ten *sefirot*, 375b; Scholem, *Le-Ḥeqer Qabbalat R. Yitsḥaq ben Ya'aqov ha-Kohen*, 66–67. Cf. 1:17b, 46b, 163a; 2:4a.

268. **זכור (*zakhor*), *remember*... שמור (*shamor*), *observe*** The first version of the Ten Commandments reads: זכור (*Zakhor*), *Remember, the Sabbath day to keep it holy* (Exodus 20:8). The second version reads: שמור (*Shamor*), *Observe, the Sabbath day to keep it holy* (Deuteronomy 5:12). According to Kabbalah, *zakhor, remember*, suggests זכר (*zakhar*), "male," signifying the male divine potencies, whereas the alternative formulation, *shamor, observe*, signifies the female, *Shekhinah*. Further, *zakhor* implies the positive commandments of Torah (since time-bound positive commandments are generally incumbent only on men), while *shamor* implies the negative commandments (incumbent on women as well).

See *Mekhilta, Baḥodesh* 7; BT *Berakhot* 20b; *Bahir* 124 (182); Ezra of Gerona, *Peirush Shir ha-Shirim*, 496–97; Naḥmanides on Exodus 20:8; Jacob ben Sheshet, *Sefer ha-Emunah ve-ha-Bittaḥon*, 420; *Zohar* 1:5b, 47b, 48b, 164b, 248a; 2:92b, 138a; 3:81b, 224a; Moses de León, *Sefer ha-Rimmon*, 118; idem, *Sefer ha-Mishqal*, 110; Wolfson, introduction to *Sefer ha-Rimmon*, 63–71; Mopsik.

269. ***one who tills his land*—Garden of Eden...** In Proverbs, then, Solomon is advocating that one cultivate the land of *Shekhinah* (the Garden of Eden) by fulfilling the commands of Torah, thereby ensuring a continual flow of emanation to Her.

270. **he too is blessed along with Her** The human being who cultivates *Shekhinah* by observing Torah shares in Her blessings.

"Come and see: The priest who blesses is blessed, as is said: *and I Myself will bless them* (Numbers 6:27).[271] So, *One who tills his land will be sated with bread*—nourishment from above. *But one who chases vanities*—one who clings to the Other Side—*will be sated with poverty*, surely!"[272]

Rabbi Yose said, "Happy are you to have attained this word!"

He opened further with the verse that follows, "*A faithful man will abound in blessings, but one hurrying to get rich will not remain blameless* (Proverbs, ibid., 20).[273] *A faithful man will abound in blessings*—a man possessing faith in the blessed Holy One, like Rav Yeisa Sava, who, although he had food for that day to eat, would not prepare it before asking for nourishment from the Holy King. After praying and asking for nourishment, he would prepare it; he would always say, 'Let us not prepare until it is provided from the house of the King.'[274]

"*But one hurrying to get rich will not remain blameless*—because he refuses to engage in Torah, which is life for this world and life for the world that is coming.[275] Now that it is time to study Torah, let us engage!"

That man opened with the mystery of a dream, saying, "*Joseph remembered the dreams he had dreamed about them* (Genesis 42:9).[276] Now, why did Joseph remind them of those dreams he had dreamed about them?[277] What good did it do him? Actually, he didn't remind them, because Joseph was wise, and it is written: *Every clever person acts intelligently* (Proverbs 13:16).[278] But when he saw them bowing down to him, their faces to the ground,[279] he was reminded of

271. **priest who blesses...** The verse reads: *They shall set My name upon the Children of Israel, and I Myself will bless them.*

See BT *Sotah* 38b (in the name of Rabbi Yehoshu'a son of Levi); *Zohar* 2:67a; Moses de León, *Sefer ha-Rimmon*, 255.

272. **one who clings to the Other Side...** If one violates the Torah and clings to the demonic realm, he interrupts the flow of emanation to *Shekhinah*, impoverishing Her and consequently himself.

273. **He opened further...** The Jew continued to expound.

274. **Rav Yeisa Sava...** See *Zohar* 2:62b.

275. **life for this world...** See above, pp. 126–27 and n. 263.

276. ***Joseph remembered...*** The full verse reads: *Joseph remembered the dreams he had dreamed about them, and he said to them, "You are spies! To see the land's nakedness you have come."*

277. **remind them...** Rabbi Yose's companion assumes rhetorically and momentarily that the clause *Joseph remembered the dreams he had dreamed about them* actually means "Joseph reminded them of the dreams he had dreamed." This reinterpretation involves understanding the verb ויזכור (*va-yizkor*), "he remembered," as ויזכיר (*va-yazkir*), "he reminded," and construing the word להם (*lahem*) as "them" rather than "about them."

278. **Joseph was wise...** And if he had reminded them of his dreams, they would have realized immediately that he was their long-lost brother—the very fact that he wanted to conceal from them. The verse in Proverbs reads: *Every clever person acts intelligently, but a fool displays stupidity.*

279. **bowing down to him...** See Genesis 42:6, quoted above, note 198.

what he had dreamed about them when he was with them, as is written: *Look, my sheaf arose and actually stood up,* [*and look, your sheaves gathered around and bowed down to my sheaf!*] (Genesis 37:7).[280] When he saw them bowing down before him, then *Joseph remembered the dreams,* because he saw them being fulfilled.

"Further, *Joseph remembered the dreams*—he remembered them because there is no forgetfulness in the presence of the blessed Holy One.[281] A person should remember a good dream, so that it will not be forgotten; then it will be fulfilled. For as it is forgotten by a person, so it is forgotten above him.[282]

"Come and see: A dream uninterpreted is like a letter unread.[283] And come and see: If one does not remember, it is as if one does not know. So, whoever forgets a dream and does not know it—it is not poised above him to be fulfilled. Therefore Joseph remembered his dream, so that it would be fulfilled, so that the dream would never be forgotten by him, and he awaited it constantly. *He said to them, 'You are spies!'* (Genesis 42, ibid.).[284] He remembered the dream, but he did not say a word to them except *You are spies!*"

Rabbi Yose opened, "*For a dream comes through a multitude of affairs...* (Ecclesiastes 5:2).[285] As has been established, a dream has numerous bearers and chieftains, rung upon rung, so that some dreams are entirely true and some contain truth and falsehood. But the truly righteous are shown no false material at all, only truth.[286]

"Come and see what is written of Daniel: *Then in a night vision,* [200a] *the mystery was revealed to Daniel* (Daniel 2:19).[287] And similarly: *Daniel saw a*

280. ***Look, my sheaf...*** The full verse reads: *Look, we were binding sheaves in the field, and look, my sheaf arose and actually stood up, and look, your sheaves gathered around and bowed down to my sheaf!*

281. **no forgetfulness...** God never forgets, so He keeps track of whether a person remembers his dreams or not.

See *Tosefta, Yoma* 2:7; JT *Yoma* 3:9, 41b; BT *Berakhot* 32b; *Eikhah Rabbah* 5:1; *Zohar* 2:92b.

282. **forgotten above him** The dreamer's forgetfulness causes his dream to fall into oblivion.

283. **Like a letter unread** Having no effect.

See BT *Berakhot* 55a; above, p. 117 and n. 212; *MM*.

284. ***You are spies*** For the full verse, see above, note 276.

285. ***For a dream comes...*** The full verse reads: *For a dream comes through a multitude of affairs, and a fool's voice through a multitude of words.*

In biblical Hebrew the word ענין (*inyan*) means "affair, business, activity," whereas in rabbinic Hebrew it means "matter, aspect." Here this later sense is applied to the biblical verse. See *OY*; *KP*; Mopsik.

286. **numerous bearers...** Various powers above convey the dream, including demonic forces who smuggle false material into certain dreams. See above, pp. 114–15 and nn. 189, 195.

287. **what is written of Daniel...** See above, p. 199 and n. 127.

dream and visions of his mind upon his bed; then he wrote down the dream (ibid. 7:1). Now, if it contained false material, why was it recorded among the Writings?[288] However, when the souls of the truly righteous ascend, they are joined only by holy words, informed by words of truth, enduring words, never to be uprooted.[289]

"Now, you might say, 'But we have learned that King David never had a good dream, which implies that David saw things that weren't true.'[290] Surely, however, he engaged all his days in shedding blood and waging war, so all his dreams were bad dreams: destruction, devastation, blood, and bloodshed—not a single dream of peace.[291] And you might ask, 'Is a good person shown a bad dream?' Certainly so: all the evils destined to overtake those who transgress the decrees of Torah and the punishments destined to be inflicted upon them in that world. This is why a virtuous person is shown a bad dream, as has been said.[292]

"Come and see: We have learned that a person who has a dream should
226 disclose it in the presence of those who love him,[293] that their will might rise favorably toward him and they might express themselves favorably, will and word becoming completely favorable: will within thought, beginning of all, and word, culmination of all. Consequently, all is consummation of all, and word fittingly in mystery of faith; consequently, perfection in supernal mystery, so all is fulfilled. A person's friends are essential for the fulfillment of that favorable interpretation, and all is fitting. Therefore the blessed Holy One informs a person, each and every one according to his rung, according to his aspect."[294]

288. **Writings** The third and final division of the Hebrew Bible, which includes the book of Daniel.

289. **souls of the truly righteous ascend...** During sleep. See above, p. 116 and n. 201.

290. **King David never had a good dream...** See BT *Berakhot* 55b.

291. **his dreams were bad dreams...** Reflecting his violent experiences, but they were not false.

292. **virtuous person is shown a bad dream...** In order to remind him of what awaits the wicked, so that he will never abandon his virtuous conduct.

See BT *Berakhot* 55b: "Rav Huna said, 'A good man is not shown a good dream, and a bad man is not shown a bad dream.'" Rashi's reading, ad loc., is closer to the *Zohar*'s: "A good person is shown a bad dream; a bad person is shown a good dream." Cf. *Berakhot* 55a.

293. **disclose it in the presence...** See above, p. 116 and n. 206.

294. **that their will might rise favorably...** So that the dreamer's intimate friends will intend and express a favorable interpretation. Human will and thought correspond to the primal *sefirot Keter* and *Ḥokhmah,* Divine will and thought, while human speech corresponds to the culminating *sefirah, Shekhinah,* who expresses will and thought and is known as the Divine word. By willing, thinking, and speaking favorably, a person's friends imitate and stimulate the sefirotic potencies ("mystery of faith") and

That Jew said, "Surely, a dream is intended only for a virtuous person, so that the dream will be suitable.

"Come and see: When a person is asleep in bed, his soul leaves and roams the world above, entering the place that she enters.[295] Numerous bands of dazzling demons traverse the world, and they accost that soul.[296] If she is virtuous, she ascends, seeing what she sees. If not, she adheres to that side,[297] and they convey false information to her or things that will happen in the near future.[298] As he awakens, the soul within him informs him of what she has seen.

"Therefore, a person who is not virtuous is shown a good dream that is not true—all in order to lead him astray from the path of truth, since he has strayed from the path of truth. For whoever comes to purify himself, they purify; whoever comes to defile himself, they defile."[299]

Rabbi Yose said, "Certainly! So it has been said."

They sat until morning arose. When morning arose, Rabbi Yose said, "Surely, Joseph's name is not mentioned among those banners, as is written: *the banner of the camp of Ephraim* (Numbers 2:18)—and not *the banner of the camp of Joseph*—because he exalted himself over his brothers, as has been said."[300]

That Jew said, "Surely I have heard that Joseph is male, whereas all those tribes are in the world of the female. That is why Joseph, who is in the world of the male, was not included with them.[301]

ensure a positive meaning and fulfillment of the dream. God sends dreams to initiate this process.

295. **his soul leaves and roams...** Entering a celestial site befitting his character and behavior. See above, note 289.

296. **dazzling demons...** Thwarting the soul's ascent. See above, note 227.

297. **that side** The Other Side, the demonic realm.

298. **happen in the near future** Demons can only foresee this far.

See Naḥmanides on Leviticus 17:7; *Zohar* 1:83a, 130a; 2:251b (*Heikh*); 3:25a.

299. **person who is not virtuous...** He is deluded with false promises. See above, note 292.

The last sentence is a paraphrase of BT *Shabbat* 104a: "Resh Lakish said, '...If one comes to defile himself, he is provided an opening; if one comes to purify himself, he is assisted.'" See above, p. 196 and n. 114; p. 216 and n. 225.

300. **Joseph's name is not mentioned...** The book of Numbers describes a plan for the marching order of the Israelite forces, each of the tribes constituting a military unit with its own banner. The marching formation is a protective square, meant to ward off potential assaults from all directions, with the Tent of Meeting inside the square. No tribe is named after Joseph, his place being taken by his two sons, Ephraim and Manasseh (see Genesis 48:5–6). Numbers 2:18–19 reads: *The banner of the camp of Ephraim by their divisions to the west...And by him the camp of Manasseh.*

Here Rabbi Yose explains that Joseph was excluded because he lorded himself over his brothers, first by telling them his self-centered dreams (Genesis 37) and then by his haughty behavior toward them in Egypt.

301. **Joseph is male...** Rabbi Yose's companion offers a different explanation as to why Joseph was not included among the tribes. Joseph symbolizes *Yesod,* the divine

"What is written? נחנו (*Naḥnu*), *We, are all of us sons of one man* (Genesis 42:11). The verse should read אנחנו (*anaḥnu*), *we*. Why is the א (*alef*) missing?[302] Because the mystery of Covenant was absent from them, *alef* withdrew from there, for *alef* is male. So, ב (*bet*) is female; *alef*, male. Therefore, *alef* withdrew from here, and they were left female together with *Shekhinah*.[303] Afterward, they said, אנחנו (*Anaḥnu*), *We, are honest* (ibid.)—an *alef* was added. They spoke without knowing what they were speaking; for Joseph was present there, so they completed the word, saying *anaḥnu*. How do we know? As is written: *They said, 'We your servants are twelve brothers'* (ibid., 13)—including Joseph! When he was included in the count, they said *anaḥnu*; when he was not, they said *naḥnu*."[304]

Rabbi Yose said, "All these words we have spoken delight the blessed Holy One, for *Shekhinah* [200b] has not departed from here, as is said: *Then those who revere YHVH spoke with one another; and YHVH listened attentively, and it was written in a book of remembrance in His presence concerning those who revere YHVH and contemplate His name* (Malachi 3:16)."[305]

phallus and culmination of "the world of the male," which includes all the *sefirot* from *Binah* through *Yesod*. The twelve tribes belong to a different realm, adorning *Shekhinah*, world of the female.

See *Zohar* 1:246b; *ZḤ* 46b; Moses de León, commentary on the ten *sefirot*, 366a; Mopsik. On the tribes, see *Zohar* 1:155a, 157b; above, pp. 120–21 and n. 227. On "the world of the male," see above, note 267.

302. **נחנו (*Naḥnu*), *We, are all of us sons*...** The verse records the brothers' response to Joseph's accusation that they are spies: *We are all of us sons of one man; we are honest; your servants have never been spies!* The normal form אנחנו (*anaḥnu*), "we," is spelled here without the initial א (*alef*): נחנו (*naḥnu*).

303. **mystery of Covenant was absent...** Joseph's *sefirah*, *Yesod* (the divine phallus), is symbolized by the covenant of circumcision. His brothers had sold Joseph and been without him for years—and they thought that they still were—so the masculine "mystery of Covenant" was absent from them and they were rendered female, accompanying *Shekhinah*. Consequently, the masculine letter א (*alef*) withdrew, truncating the pronoun אנחנו (*anaḥnu*) to נחנו (*naḥnu*).

On א (*alef*) and ב (*bet*) as respectively male and female, see *Zohar* 1:30a; 2:228a, 234b; *ZḤ* 74c (*ShS*).

304. **spoke without knowing what they were speaking...** They spoke prophetically, including Joseph among them by saying *twelve brothers*.

On the brothers' unintentional prophetic utterance, see *Bereshit Rabbah* 91:7; *Avot de-Rabbi Natan* B, 43.

305. ***Shekhinah* has not departed...** The Divine Presence manifests when two are studying Torah *with one another*.

See M *Avot* 3:2: "Rabbi Ḥananya son of Teradyon says, '...If two are sitting engaged in words of Torah, *Shekhinah* dwells between them, as is said: *Then those who revere YHVH spoke with one another; and YHVH listened attentively, and it was written in a book of remembrance in His presence concerning those who revere YHVH and contemplate His name*.'"

In the Masoretic text of Malachi, the wording is ויכתב ספר זכרון (*va-yikkatev sefer zikkaron*), *and a book of remembrance was written*. However, the Kaufmann manuscript of the Mishnah reads here (and in M *Avot* 3:6): בספר (*be-sefer*), [*and it was written*] *in a book of* [*remembrance*]. This same reading is

He put them under guard for three days (Genesis 42:17).

Rabbi El'azar said, "Why these three days? Because these correspond to the three days of Shechem, as is written: *It happened on the third day, while they were in pain* (ibid. 34:25).[306]

"Come and see: What is written of Joseph? *Do* זאת (*zot*), *this, and live* (ibid. 42:18)—showing that he did not act as they had: making the men of Shechem accept upon themselves *zot*, mystery of covenant, and after they had enacted this covenant, killing them, not one of them surviving. Whereas of him, what is written? *Do zot and live.* Why? Because *I revere God* (ibid.), guarding the covenant.[307] All this tortuosity was solely for the sake of Benjamin.[308]

"*They said, a man to his brother, 'Truly, we are guilty concerning our brother'* (ibid., 21). *They said, a man to his brother*—Simeon and Levi, like previously, as is written: *They said, a man to his brother, 'Here comes that dream-master!'* (ibid. 37:19). Just as there it is Simeon and Levi, so here it is Simeon and Levi.[309]

preserved here in numerous manuscripts (M7, N23, L2, Pr6, Ms4) and in the Mantua edition, whereas later editors corrected the spelling according to the Masoretic text. See *Zohar* 1:243a; *Minḥat Shai*, ad loc.

306. **three days of Shechem...** After Shechem son of Hamor had raped Dinah, daughter of Jacob, her brothers agreed to let Shechem marry her and to permit intermarriage generally with the locals, on condition that all the males undergo circumcision. The residents of the town (also named Shechem) agreed to the pact, but Simeon and Levi violated it. As the full verse reads: *It happened on the third day, while they were in pain, that two of Jacob's sons, Simeon and Levi, Dinah's brothers, each took his sword and came upon the city unsuspected, and they killed every male.* According to Rabbi El'azar, apparently, Joseph imprisoned his brothers for three days as punishment for this act.

307. ***Do* זאת (*zot*), *this, and live*...** The context (42:18–20) reads: *Joseph said to them on the third day, "Do this and live, for I revere God. If you are honest, let one of your brothers be imprisoned in this guardhouse, and the rest of you go and bring provisions for the famine of your households. Then bring your youngest brother to me, that your words may be verified, and you will not die."*

In Kabbalah, זאת (*zot*), *this*, is a name of *Shekhinah*, the Divine Presence. Here She is also referred to as "mystery of covenant," a designation usually applied to Her partner, *Yesod* (the divine phallus and site of the covenant of circumcision). Unlike his brothers, Joseph loyally guarded the covenant, controlling his passions with Potiphar's wife and keeping faith with his long-lost brothers, providing life and not death.

On *Shekhinah* as both *zot* and "mystery of covenant," see *Zohar* 1:93b, 228a. On guarding the covenant, see Deuteronomy 7:9.

308. **All this tortuosity...** Joseph pretended that his brothers were spies and imprisoned one of them in order to make them bring Benjamin down to Egypt. See above at note 253.

309. ***a man to his brother*—Simeon and Levi...** The full verse reads: *They said, a man to his brother, "Truly, we are guilty concerning our brother, for we saw his soul's distress when he pleaded with us and we did not listen. That is why this distress has overtaken us."* The Torah does not specify who spoke to whom, but by relying on verbal analogy,

"Come and see: Who is *a man*, and who is *his brother*? Well, *a man* must be Simeon; here is written *a man*, and there is written *Look, a man of the Children of Israel came* (Numbers 25:6). Just as there from Simeon, so here Simeon.[310] And because he turned back in repentance for this and felt remorse and said to Levi, *Truly, we are guilty*, his zodiacal sign was modeled on Joseph's—a bull, as is written: *His firstling bull—majesty is his!* (Deuteronomy 33:17), and Simeon's sign is a bull.[311] Therefore, *he took Simeon from them* (Genesis 42:24), so that he would not attack along with Levi, for when Simeon and Levi join together they can attack.[312]

"*And he bound him before their eyes* (ibid.). As they have established, *before their eyes* he bound him; after they left he provided him with food and drink.[313] Now, you might say that Joseph's intention was based on the verse *If your enemy is hungry, give him bread to eat; if he is thirsty, give him water to drink* (Proverbs 25:21). But if so, how could Joseph, who was righteous, act like this? Look at what is written: *For you will be heaping burning coals on his head, and* YHVH *will reward you* (ibid., 22)![314] Far be it from Joseph to feel that way! Rather, like a

Rabbi El'azar concludes that it was Simeon and Levi, who according to the Midrash, schemed to kill Joseph; now they finally acknowledged their guilt. See *Sekhel Tov*, Genesis 42:21.

The earlier context (Genesis 37:19–20) reads: *They said, a man to his brother, "Here comes that dream-master! Come now, let's kill him and throw him into one of the pits, and we'll say, 'A vicious beast devoured him.' We'll see what comes of his dreams."* There too Genesis does not specify which brothers hatched the plan, but midrashic tradition assigns the role to Simeon and Levi. See above, p. 123 and n. 244.

310. ***Look, a man...*** The context in Numbers describes a sexual violation. The full verse reads: *Look, a man of the Children of Israel came and brought forth to his kinsmen a Midianite woman before the eyes of Moses and before the eyes of the whole community of the Children of Israel as they were weeping at the entrance to the Tent of Meeting.* The anonymous perpetrator (*a man*) is identified later in the chapter (verse 14) as *Zimri son of Salu, chieftain of a father's house of the Simeonites.* Relying again on verbal analogy, Rabbi El'azar concludes that here in Genesis *a man* implies Simeon.

311. **zodiacal sign was modeled on Joseph's...** Each of the twelve tribes corresponds to one of the twelve signs of the zodiac.

On Simeon and Taurus the bull, see *Midrash Tehillim* 90:3 (and Buber's note 16); *Zohar* 1:173a, 236a. Cf. *Soferim*, add. 1, 1:3; *Yalqut Shim'oni*, Exodus 418.

312. ***he took Simeon...*** The verse reads: *He took Simeon from them and bound him before their eyes.* According to the *Zohar*, both Simeon and Levi derive from the *sefirah* of *Din* (harsh Judgment), so their combined power is threatening. See above, p. 218 and n. 244.

313. ***before their eyes* he bound him...** See *Bereshit Rabbah* 91:8, in the name of Rabbi Yitsḥak.

314. **Now, you might say...** One might imagine that Joseph considered Simeon his enemy and was treating him well only in accordance with the advice in Proverbs, which indicates that such treatment actually ensures the enemy's torment.

man toward his brother he behaved toward him, in brotherhood and in no other manner—and not toward him alone, but toward all his brothers, as is written: *Joseph gave orders to fill their bags with grain*... (Genesis, ibid., 25), behaving toward them in brotherhood."[315]

Rabbi Yose opened, "*Thus says YHVH: If they are* שלמים (*shelemim*), *united, and likewise numerous, they will likewise be shorn and pass away. I have afflicted you; I will afflict you no more* (Nahum 1:12).[316] This verse has been established, for when an entire people live in שלמא (*shelama*), peace, without enemies, the blessed Holy One feels compassion for them and judgment does not prevail against them. Even if they all worship idols—yet live in peace—judgment has no dominion over them, as is written: *Ephraim is joined to images—leave him alone!* (Hosea 4:17).[317]

"*They will likewise be shorn.* Why *they will likewise be shorn*? The verse should read *They will be shorn.* However, this alludes to the beginning of the verse, namely peace; here too, peace. And what is that? Charity, for charity is peace; whoever lavishes charity increases peace above and increases peace below. So, *they will likewise be shorn*—for they shear their money for charity.[318]

"ועבר (*Ve-avar*), *And pass away.* The verse should read ועברו (*ve-averu*), *and* [*they will*] *pass away.* Why *ve-avar*?[319] However, this is wrathful judgment, as is said: *until wrath passes* (Isaiah 26:20)[320]—*and* judgment *pass away* from them.

"Alternatively, *If they are* שלמים (*shelemim*), *complete*—Israel, to whom the blessed Holy One has granted an enduring covenant, to be guarded constantly, through which a human becomes complete on all sides, above and

315. ***Joseph gave orders*...** The full verse reads: *Joseph gave orders to fill their bags with grain and to return each one's silver to his sack and to give them provisions for the way; and so it was done for them.* See above at note 253.

316. ***If they are* שלמים (*shelemim*), *united*...** The prophet predicts the fall of Nineveh, capital of the Assyrian empire, and assures Israel that their afflictions by God have come to an end.

317. **when an entire people live...** God values peace above monotheistic worship. In Hosea, Ephraim refers collectively to the ten tribes of the northern kingdom of Israel, and the plain meaning of the verse is that because they are addicted to idolatry, rebuking them is futile. According to the midrashic reading, *joined* implies harmonious union among the tribes.

See *Sifrei,* Numbers 42; *Bereshit Rabbah* 38:6; *Tanḥuma, Tsav* 7; *Kallah Rabbati* 5:1; *Derekh Erets* 7:37; *Zohar* 1:76b.

318. **charity is peace...** By shearing money for charity, one increases peace on earth and in the divine realm.

See BT *Gittin* 7a; above, note 264.

319. **Why *ve-avar*?** Why the switch from the plural, ונגזו (*ve-nagozzu*), *they will be shorn*, to the singular, ועבר (*ve-avar*), *and he* [or: *it*] *will pass away*?

320. ***until wrath passes*** The full verse reads: *Go, my people, enter your rooms and shut your doors behind you. Hide yourself for the slightness of a moment, until wrath passes.*

below.[321] If one does not guard it, he is defective, totally defective. How do we know? As is written: *Walk in My presence and be* תמים (*tamim*) (Genesis 17:1). What is *tamim*? Complete—for until the covenant is established in him, he is defective.[322] Therefore, *if they are complete*—guarding this commandment to be *complete* and not be defective.

"*And likewise numerous*—increasing [201a] and multiplying with it, for souls issue into the world only through this covenant.[323]

"*They will likewise be shorn*—this refers to *if they are complete*, guarding it constantly. *They will be shorn*—one who is circumcised, accepting this covenant.

"*And pass away.* To what does this refer? That filth of foreskin that was on him before.[324]

"Alternatively, *Thus says YHVH: If they are complete*—sons of Jacob; for as long as they were together with Joseph, they were *complete*, abiding with the covenant. *They will likewise be shorn*—for they went and abandoned Joseph and Simeon. *And pass*—then judgment befell them, as is written: *YHVH will pass to strike Egypt* (Exodus 12:23).[325]

"Come and see: There is severe Judgment and mild Judgment. Severe Judgment is strong; mild Judgment is weak. When this mild Judgment sucks from severe Judgment, it is intensified and becomes potent.[326] When judgment is

321. **enduring covenant...** The covenant of circumcision, which entails sexual morality and purity. By guarding this covenant, one fulfills his social responsibilities and also imitates *Yesod*, mystery of covenant.

322. ***Walk in My presence...*** The full verse reads: *When Abram was ninety-nine years old, YHVH appeared to Abram and said to him, "I am El Shaddai. Walk in My presence and be tamim."* This divine directive is soon followed by the command of circumcision (verses 9–14).

The word תמים (*tamim*) means "blameless, complete, intact, free of blemish, impeccable, perfect." *Targum Onqelos* renders it שלים (*shelim*), "complete, perfect." Paradoxically, circumcision renders a man complete; without it, he is blemished.

See *Bereshit Rabbah* 46:1, 4–5; *Vayiqra Rabbah* 25:6; BT *Nedarim* 31b–32a; *Zohar* 1:59b, 95a–b, 246a; 3:142a (*IR*), 166a; Moses de León, *Sefer ha-Rimmon*, 228, 376 (and Wolfson's note 9); Mopsik.

323. **increasing and multiplying with it...** With the phallus, bearing the sign of the covenant of circumcision, a man fulfills the command of Genesis 1:28: *Be fruitful and multiply.* The phrase "increasing and multiplying" derives from *Targum Onqelos*, ad loc.

Similarly from above, souls issue into the world through the divine phallus, *Yesod*, also known as Covenant. See above, p. 92 and n. 49; p. 138 and n. 333.

324. **filth of foreskin...** The demonic foreskin must be eliminated.

See *Zohar* 1:13a, 18a, 35b, 91b; Moses de León, *Sheqel ha-Qodesh*, 55 (68).

325. **abiding with the covenant...** As long as the brothers were with Joseph, they were with the covenant, since he symbolizes *Yesod*, mystery of covenant. However, when they left to return to Canaan, abandoning Joseph and their imprisoned brother, Simeon, they were cut off from the covenant and vulnerable to judgment. By verbal analogy, Rabbi Yose indicates that *pass* implies judgment.

326. **severe Judgment and mild Judg-**

executed upon Israel, it is enacted by this mild Judgment, not intensified by that severe Judgment. When judgment is executed upon other nations, this mild Judgment is intensified by severe Judgment above, to gain potency, as is written: *YHVH will pass to strike Egypt.* ועבר (*Ve-avar*), *Will pass*—filled with עברה (*evrah*), wrath, and indignation, intensified by severe Judgment. Here too, *ve-avar*.[327]

"Come and see: When ten gather in synagogue and one of them slips out, the blessed Holy One is angry at him.[328]

"Alternatively, *They will likewise be shorn*—evil deeds removed from them;[329] then, *will pass*. What does *will pass* mean?"

Rabbi Shim'on said, "When the soul leaves this world, she undergoes many judgments before entering her site. Afterward, all those souls have to pass through a certain flowing, gushing river of fire, bathing themselves.[330] Who can rise from there, passing through without fear? As is written: *Who may ascend the mountain of YHVH?* The soul of the righteous passes fearlessly and *stands in His holy place* (Psalms 24:3).[331] And one who engages in charity in this world, offering his money for charity *will pass* that place unafraid.[332] A herald proclaims before that soul: *I have afflicted you; I will afflict you no more.* Whoever is worthy to pass through this is exempt from all further judgments.

"Come and see: All this about Joseph with his brothers and all these incidents, why are they necessary?[333] Oh, but Torah is Torah of truth, and all her ways are holy ways, and you cannot find a single word in Torah that does

ment... *Din* (severe Judgment) and *Shekhinah* (mild Judgment). When *Shekhinah* is influenced directly by *Din* without the mollifying force of *Ḥesed*, She too conveys harsh Judgment.

See *Bereshit Rabbah* 35:3; above, p. 91 and n. 47; *Zohar* 1:137a; 3:231b.

327. **Here too, *ve-avar*** Implying not just *will pass*, but "will be filled with *evrah*, 'wrath.'"

328. **When ten gather...** Apparently, the verse from Nahum is here understood: *If they are complete and likewise numerous* (constituting a quorum of ten), all is well and good. But if they are *shorn* (by one of them slipping away), then *ve-avar*: God will be filled with *evrah*, "wrath." Similarly, when the brothers left Joseph and Simeon, they were fewer than ten, so judgment befell them.

See BT *Berakhot* 6b (in the name of Rabbi Yoḥanan); *Zohar* 2:131a–b. In the Talmudic source, God's anger is not directed specifically at the one who is absent.

329. **evil deeds removed...** Through turning back to God and acting virtuously, or through the purging that is described below.

330. **flowing, gushing river of fire...** In which the taint of sin is washed away.

See Daniel 7:10; 3 Enoch 36; BT *Ḥagigah* 13b–14a; Moses of Burgos, *Ammud ha-Semali*, 149; *Zohar* 1:217b, 218b; 2:210a, 211b, 247a (*Heikh*), 254a (*Heikh*); 3:16b (*RM*), 27a, 30a; Moses de León, *Sefer ha-Rimmon*, 373–74; idem, *Sheqel ha-Qodesh*, 60 (74–75); Mopsik.

331. ***Who may ascend...*** The full verse reads: *Who may ascend the mountain of YHVH? Who may stand in His holy place?*

332. **one who engages in charity...** See *Zohar* 2:59a.

333. **why are they necessary?** What moral or spiritual value derives from this extended narrative?

not contain supernal mysteries and ways for human beings to strengthen themselves."[334]

He opened, saying, "*Do not say,* 'אשלמה *(Ashallemah), I will requite, evil!' Wait for YHVH and He will deliver you* (Proverbs 20:22). Come and see: The blessed Holy One formed the human being to embrace Torah and follow paths of truth—toward the right, not toward the left. Since they must go to the right, they should expand love between one another; there should be no hatred between them, so as not to weaken the right, the place to which Israel cleaves.[335]

"Come and see: Accordingly, there exists a good impulse and an evil impulse, and Israel must enable the good impulse to overpower the evil impulse through worthy deeds.[336] If a person strays to the left, then the evil impulse overpowers the good impulse. Through his sins, he completes the one who was defective, for this repulsive one becomes complete only through human sin.[337] Therefore one must be careful that the evil one not be completed by his sins; he should guard himself constantly, for one should complete the good impulse perfectly, constantly—not the evil impulse. So, *Do not say,* 'אשלמה *(Ashallemah), I will complete, evil!' Wait for YHVH and He will deliver you.*

"Alternatively, *Do not say, 'Ashallemah, I will render, evil!'*—as is said: ומשלמי *(umshallemei), those who render, evil for good* (Psalms 38:21). One should not render evil to a person who rendered him good, because look at what is written: *If one returns evil for good, evil will not depart from his house* (Proverbs 17:13)! Even if one has been rendered evil, he should not render evil in return for that evil rendered to him. Rather, *Wait for YHVH and He will deliver you.*[338]

334. **you cannot find a single word...** A frequent theme in the *Zohar.* See above, p. 140 and n. 349.

335. **embrace Torah...** Or, "strengthen themselves with Torah." In the *Zohar* the word לאתתקפא (*le-ittaqqafa*) conveys both senses.

Right symbolizes *Hesed* (Loving-kindness), whereas left symbolizes *Din* (harsh Judgment) and the demonic realm deriving from there. Human acts of love strengthen divine love, whereas hateful action weakens it.

See above at note 114. On Israel's link with love, see *Midrash Tanna'im,* Deuteronomy 13:18; JT *Qiddushin* 4:1, 65b; BT *Yevamot* 79a; Moses de León, *Sheqel ha-Qodesh,* 44 (53).

336. **good impulse and an evil impulse...** Corresponding to right and left. By acting virtuously, one empowers the good impulse, enabling it to triumph.

See BT *Berakhot* 5a, in the name of Rabbi Shim'on son of Lakish: "A person should always incite the good impulse against the evil impulse."

337. **one who was defective...** The defective evil impulse is strengthened and fulfilled through human sin. The description "this repulsive one" originates in BT *Sukkah* 52b: "A scholar from the school of Rabbi Yishma'el taught, 'If this repulsive one attacks you, drag him to the house of study. If he is of stone, he will dissolve; if of iron he will shatter.'"

338. **Even if one has been rendered evil...** See *Bereshit Rabbah* 38:3, in the name of Rabbi Shim'on son of Abba, who understands the verse to mean: *If one returns evil instead of good, evil will not depart from his house.*

"This verse has been established in relation to Joseph the Righteous, who did not want to render evil to his brothers when they fell into his hands. *Wait for YHVH and He will deliver you*— [201b] he waited constantly for the blessed Holy One."[339]

Rabbi Abba opened, "*The designs in a man's mind are deep waters, but a man of understanding draws them out* (ibid. 20:5). *Deep waters*—the blessed Holy One, for He fashioned *designs* and elicited causes, spinning schemes by the hand of Joseph to fulfill that decree of famine upon the world.[340] *But a man of understanding draws them out*—Joseph, who revealed those depths that the blessed Holy One had decreed upon the world.[341]

"Come and see: Not only did Joseph refrain from rendering evil to his brothers; he acted toward them in true kindness. This is always the way of the righteous, by virtue of which the blessed Holy One has compassion upon them in this world and in the world that is coming.

"*The designs in a man's mind are deep waters*—as they have established, this is Judah, when he approached Joseph on behalf of Benjamin. *But a man of understanding draws them out*—Joseph."[342]

Rabbi Abba was sitting at the gateway of the gate of Lydda.[343] He saw a man come and sit in a dugout in a mound of earth;[344] weary from the road, he settled down and fell asleep there. Meanwhile, he saw a snake approaching him; out came a honey badger, oozing an excretion, and killed it.[345] When the man

339. **Joseph ... did not want to render evil ...** Even though they had caused him so much harm. See above, p. 220 and n. 253.

340. **He fashioned *designs* ...** God arranged for Joseph to be in Egypt in order to fulfill His plan of sustaining Joseph's family along with vast numbers of other people during the widespread famine.

See Genesis 50:20; above, pp. 192–93, 201; p. 211 at n. 194.

341. **Joseph, who revealed those depths ...** By interpreting Pharaoh's dreams.

342. **Judah, when he approached Joseph ...** See Genesis 44:18–34. Rabbi Abba may be alluding here to the midrashic view that Judah approached Joseph with the intent of attacking him. Joseph, though, outmaneuvered him by revealing his own true identity.

See *Bereshit Rabbah* 93:6, in the name of Rabbi Yehudah; *OY*. In *Bereshit Rabbah* 93:4, the identical verse from Proverbs is applied to Judah and Joseph, but with the roles reversed: Judah plumbs the depths of Joseph's mind.

343. **gateway of the gate ...** בבא דתרעא (*Bava de-tar'a*), a redundancy found only in the *Zohar*, perhaps signaling a deep inner meaning about to unfold.

See *Zohar* 2:28a; 3:15a; *ZḤ* 12b (*MhN*); Israel Al-Nakawa, *Menorat ha-Ma'or*, 3:68–69; 4:297–98.

344. **dugout ...** A shelter. The word קולטא (*qulta*) is apparently based on the Hebrew מקלט (*miqlat*), "refuge." For a range of interpretations of both this word and the phrase discussed in the following note, see *OY*; Galante; *DE*; *NO*; *Sullam*; Mopsik; *MmD*.

345. **honey badger, oozing an excretion ...**

awoke, he saw that snake lying dead in front of him. He sprang up, just as that dugout collapsed into the depths below.

Rabbi Abba approached him and said, "Tell me what you do, for look, the blessed Holy One has performed these two miracles for you! It wasn't for nothing!"[346]

That man replied, "All my days, no one in the world ever rendered me evil, with whom I didn't reconcile and whom I didn't forgive. Moreover, if I couldn't reconcile with him, I never climbed into bed before forgiving him and all those who hurt me. I never cared all my days about the evil they rendered me. Not only that—from that day on, I exerted myself to act kindly toward them."[347]

Rabbi Abba wept, and said, "This one's deeds excel those of Joseph! As for Joseph, they were surely his brothers, so he was expected to show them compassion. But this one, by what he did, surpassed Joseph. It is fitting that the blessed Holy One perform for him miracle upon miracle."

He opened, saying, "*One who walks in innocence walks securely, but one who*
 perverts his ways will be found out (ibid. 10:9). *One who walks in innocence walks securely*—the person who walks in ways of Torah. *Walks securely*—for no malignities of the world can harm him.[348] *But one who perverts his ways* יודע (*yivvade'a*), *will be found out*—one who strays from the way of truth and seeks to retaliate against his fellow. *Yivvade'a, Will be known.* What does this mean? He 'will be recognized' by all masters of judgment, for that person's image

קסטופא דגורדנא (*Qastopha de-gurdena*), a cryptic, neologistic phrase. *Qastopha* apparently derives from the Aramaic כוספא (*kuspa*), "residue." See above, p. 10, n. 69.

Gurdena represents the Castilian *garduña*, "weasel." One member of the weasel family, the ratel (or honey badger), discourages enemies by emitting from its protruding anal glands a foul secretion with a suffocating odor. It is a tenacious carnivore with knifelike claws, sharp teeth, and tough skin. In addition to its appetite for honey and bee larvae, this badger feeds on insects, rodents, and snakes (including venomous cobras).

For a similar narrative, see *Zohar* 3:111a.

346. **what you do...** The same question is posed to several remarkable characters in the Talmud by rabbis trying to discover the reason for their special powers or status. See BT *Ta'anit* 22a, 24a. The two miracles are: being saved from the snake and being saved from the sudden collapse of the dugout.

347. **All my days...** On the importance of reconciling with others, see BT *Yoma* 87a. On nightly forgiveness, see BT *Megillah* 28a: "Rabbi Neḥunya son of Ha-Kanah was asked by his disciples, 'How have you lived so long?' He replied, 'Never in my life have I gained honor through my fellow's shame, nor has my fellow's curse climbed into bed with me, and I have been generous with my money.'...'Nor has my fellow's curse climbed into bed with me'—as illustrated by Mar Zutra, who when he climbed into bed used to say, 'I forgive all who have hurt me.'"

348. **malignities of the world...** נזקין דעלמא (*Nizqin de-alma*), "injuries of the world." In the *Zohar* the phrase implies "demons, malignant forces." See *Zohar* 1:100a; 3:122a.

never fades from their memory, in order to bring him to the site of avengement.[349] Therefore, *yivvade'a, will be known.*

"Come and see: One who walks in the way of truth is sheltered by the blessed Holy One, so he is not known or recognized by masters of judgment. But *one who perverts his ways will be known* and recognized by them. Happy are those who walk in the way of truth and walk the world securely, having no fear in this world or in the world that is coming."

The men were afraid at being brought to Joseph's house (Genesis 43:18).[350]

Rabbi Yose said, "Woe to people who do not know or contemplate the ways of Torah! Woe to them when the blessed Holy One comes to demand justice for their deeds, and body and soul rise to render account for all their deeds, before soul separates from body.[351] For that day is the Day of Judgment, the day when books are opened and masters of judgment stand, when the serpent is poised to bite, and all one's limbs tremble. Soul separates from body, roaming about, not knowing which way to go or where she is being carried off.[352]

"Woe for that day, a day of wrath and humiliation! Therefore one should incite his impulse every day and bring to mind that day when he will stand in judgment before the King and be embedded beneath the dust to rot away, soul separating [202a] from him.

"We have learned: A person should always incite the good impulse against the evil impulse and follow it sedulously. If it leaves him, fine; if not, he should engage in Torah, for nothing but Torah can break the evil impulse. If it

349. **site of avengement** In Hell, where he will be punished for retaliating against his fellow instead of forgiving him.

350. ***The men were afraid...*** The full verse reads: *The men were afraid at being brought to Joseph's house, and they said, "Because of the silver put back in our bags the first time we've been brought, in order to fall upon us, to attack us, and to take us as slaves along with our donkeys."*

351. **to demand justice...** At the moment of death, even before the soul leaves the body, both stand together in judgment before God.

See *Zohar* 1:65b, 79a, 98a (*MhN*), 130b, 218b, 227a; 2:199b; 3:53a, 126b; Moses de León, *Sefer ha-Rimmon,* 393; and the parable concerning the joint responsibility of body and soul in *Mekhilta de-Rashbi,* Exodus 15:1; *Vayiqra Rabbah* 4:5; BT *Sanhedrin* 91a–b.

352. **Day of Judgment...** Traditionally, the Day of Judgment comes at the end of days, but in the *Zohar* it transpires for each human being on the day he dies. See *Zohar* 1:98a (*MhN*), 218b, 227a; 3:88a. Cf. *Beit ha-Midrash,* 1:151.

On the heavenly books in which all human deeds are recorded, see Isaiah 65:6; Malachi 3:16; Daniel 7:10 (*the books were opened*); M *Avot* 2:1; 3:16.

The serpent is the Angel of Death, poised to kill, separating body and soul. See *Zohar* 1:148a–b (*ST*); 3:126b. Until the body is buried, the soul cannot ascend.

leaves, fine; if not, he should remind himself of the day of death in order to break it.[353]

"Here one should contemplate, for the evil impulse is identical with the Angel of Death.[354] Now, is the Angel of Death broken when confronted by the day of death? He is the slayer of human beings, so by implication this must delight him. That is why he constantly leads people astray, to lure them to this.[355] Surely, however, what has been said—that a person should remind himself of the day of death—certainly so, because this breaks a person's heart. For look, the evil impulse dwells only in a place where bibulous merriment and arrogance prevail; when a broken spirit prevails, it departs and dwells with him no more. Therefore a person should remind himself of the day of death; then the body is broken and that one goes away.[356]

"Come and see: The good impulse seeks joy and the evil impulse seeks joy. The good impulse seeks joy of Torah, and the evil impulse seeks joy of wine, fornication, and arrogance. So a person should tremble constantly because of
238 that momentous day—Day of Judgment, day of reckoning—for one has nothing to protect him except for worthy deeds that he performs in this world in order to protect him in that hour.

"Come and see: *The men were afraid at being brought to Joseph's house.* Now, all of them were powerful and mighty men, yet when a single youth brought them to Joseph's house, they were frightened; how much more so when the blessed Holy One demands justice of a human being![357] Therefore one must be vigilant in this world in order to be fortified in that world, as we have established.

"Come and see: A person should strengthen himself in the blessed Holy One, placing his stronghold in Him. Even though he has sinned, if he turns back in complete repentance, then he is powerful, fortified by the blessed Holy One as if he had never sinned.

353. **incite his impulse...** See BT *Berakhot* 5a, in the name of Rabbi Shim'on son of Lakish: "A person should always incite the good impulse against the evil impulse.... If he conquers it, fine; if not, he should engage in Torah.... If he conquers it, fine; if not, he should remind himself of the day of death."

See above, note 336. On Torah as an antidote for the evil impulse, see BT *Sukkah* 52b, quoted above, note 337.

354. **evil impulse is identical...** See BT *Bava Batra* 16a: "Resh Lakish said, 'Satan, the evil impulse, and the Angel of Death are one and the same.'"

355. **lure them to this** By seducing people to sin, the demonic force leads them to death.

356. **body is broken...** Physical desire abates and the evil impulse departs. See Mopsik.

357. **how much more so when...** How much more terrifying it is when humans of average strength must face the divine Judge. See *Bereshit Rabbah* 93:11.

"Look, the tribes were afraid because they had sinned by kidnapping Joseph; if they had not sinned, they would not have been afraid at all.[358] For a person's sins break his heart, leaving him with no strength at all. How so? The good impulse is broken within him, leaving him powerless to overcome the evil impulse. Of this is written *Who is the man that is fearful and faint of heart?* (Deuteronomy 20:8)—fearful of those sins of his, which break one's heart.[359]

"Come and see for how many generations the blessed Holy One exacted retribution for that sin of the tribes.[360] For nothing vanishes in the presence of the blessed Holy One; it is requited from generation to generation, and judgment abides before Him continuously until it is exacted and judgment assumes its requisite place.

"How do we know? From Hezekiah. He committed the sin of revealing to other nations the mysteries of the blessed Holy One, which must not be revealed. The blessed Holy One sent Isaiah to him, saying, *Behold, days are coming when everything in your palace will be carried off...* (Isaiah 39:6).[361]

"Come and see how much damage that sin inflicted by exposing what had been concealed. As soon as it was exposed, an opening was provided for the other, undesirable realm to dominate it.[362] Thus, blessing dwells only in a con-

358. **would not have been afraid...** On the link between sin and fear, see above, p. 215 and n. 223.

359. ***Who is the man...*** The verse, addressed to potential Israelite soldiers, reads: *Who is the man that is fearful and faint of heart? Let him go and return to his house, that he not melt the heart of his brothers like his own heart.*

Rabbi Yose's interpretation here derives from BT *Sotah* 43a–44a, in the name of Rabbi Yose the Galilean.

360. **retribution for that sin of the tribes** According to rabbinic tradition, the brothers' sin of selling Joseph was finally requited by the martyrdom of ten prominent rabbis at the hand of the Romans during the Hadrianic persecution in the second century.

See *Midrash Mishlei* 1:13, in the name of Rabbi Yehoshu'a son of Levi, and the statement attributed there to Rabbi Avin, according to which ten martyrs in each generation suffer on account of the brothers' misdeed, "and still that sin lingers."

See *Heikhalot Rabbati* 5:5 (*Battei Midrashot*, 1:74); *Elleh Ezkerah* (*Beit ha-Midrash*, 2:64); *Zohar* 1:106a; 2:33a; *ZḤ* 46a, 89c (*MhN, Rut*); 93b (*MhN, Eikhah*).

361. **revealing to other nations...** According to midrashic tradition, when Babylonian envoys came to visit King Hezekiah, he showed them not only his own treasures but also the treasures of the Holy of Holies and the two tablets of the covenant within the ark.

See Isaiah 39:1–2; Targum, 2 Chronicles 32:31; *Seder Eliyyahu Rabbah* 9; *Pirqei de-Rabbi Eli'ezer* 52; *Yalqut Shim'oni*, 2 Kings, 244. Cf. *Shir ha-Shirim Rabbah* on 3:3.

Isaiah 39:6 reads in full: *Behold, days are coming when everything in your palace, and that which your ancestors have stored up until this day, will be carried off to Babylonia; nothing will be left, says YHVH.*

362. **As soon as it was exposed...** By exposing the holiest treasures of the Temple, Hezekiah rendered it vulnerable both to demonic forces above and to the Babylonians on earth.

cealed place, as has been established.[363] Something may be concealed with blessing hovering over it, but once it is revealed, an opening is provided for the other realm to dominate it.

"It is written: *All who honored her despise her, for they have seen her nakedness* (Lamentations 1:8). This has been established,[364] but *all who honored her*—the kingdom of Babylon, since from there a present was sent to Jerusalem, as is written: *At that time, Merodach-baladan son of Baladan, the king of Babylon, sent letters and a gift to Hezekiah* (Isaiah, ibid., 1). And what was written in them? 'Peace to Hezekiah, king of Judah, and peace to the great God, and peace to Jerusalem.' As soon as the letters left his hands, he reconsidered and said, 'I acted improperly by greeting the servant before greeting his master.' He rose from his throne, took three steps, retrieved the letters, and wrote others in their place, as follows: 'Peace to the great God, peace to Jerusalem, and peace to Hezekiah.' This is *all who honored her.*[365] [202b]

"Afterward, *despise her.* Why did they *despise her*? Because *they have seen her nakedness*, shown to them by Hezekiah; otherwise, they would not have subsequently despised her.[366] But since Hezekiah was so virtuous, the event was postponed, not occurring in his lifetime, as is written: *For there will be peace and security in my days* (ibid., 8). Afterward, that sin was requited upon his descendants.[367]

"Similarly the sin of the tribes endured until later, because judgment above could not prevail against them until the time was ripe for retribution. So whoever possesses sins is constantly afraid, as is said: *You will be terrified night and day* (Deuteronomy 28:66). Therefore, *the men were afraid at being brought to Joseph's house...*"

363. **blessing dwells...** See BT *Ta'anit* 8b: "Rabbi Yitsḥak said, 'Blessing is found only in what is hidden from the eye.'" See *Zohar* 1:5a, 64b.

364. **This has been established** See BT *Yoma* 54b: "Resh Lakish said, 'When the heathens entered the Temple, they saw the cherubs [with their bodies] intertwined. They took them out into the open and said, "These Israelites, whose blessing is a blessing and whose curse is a curse, occupy themselves with such things?" Immediately they despised them, as is said: *All who honored her despise her, for they have seen her nakedness.*'"

365. **kingdom of Babylon...** See *Shir ha-Shirim Rabbah* on 3:3; BT *Sanhedrin* 96a; *Tanḥuma, Ki Tissa* 5; *Zohar* 2:174b–175a.

366. ***seen her nakedness...*** Hezekiah had shown them the innermost secrets of the Holy of Holies. Rabbi Yose may be referring to the intimate embrace of the cherubs within the Holy of Holies (see above, note 364). In Kabbalah their embrace symbolizes the union of the divine couple, *Tif'eret* (or *Yesod*) and *Shekhinah*. See *Zohar* 3:296a–b (*IZ*).

367. **sin was requited...** When the Temple was later destroyed by the Babylonians. See Rashi on Isaiah 39:7.

He raised his eyes and saw Benjamin his brother, his mother's son (Genesis 43:29).

Rabbi Ḥiyya opened, "*Hope deferred is sickness of heart, but a desire come true is a tree of life* (Proverbs 13:12). *Hope deferred*—as we have learned: A person should not examine whether his request before God has been fulfilled or not. Why? Because if he does so, numerous masters of judgment come to examine his deeds.[368] This is a mystery, for his examination of that request causes him *sickness of heart.* Who is *sickness of heart*? The one constantly poised to accuse above and below.[369]

"*But a desire* באה (*ba'ah*), *come true, is a tree of life.* We have learned: Whoever wants the blessed Holy One to accept his prayer should engage in Torah, which is a tree of life; then *a desire ba'ah, comes.*[370] Who is *desire*? The rung holding all prayers of the world, conveying them into the presence of the King.[371] Here is written *comes*, and there is written *In the evening she comes . . .* (Esther 2:14); this is *a desire comes*—coming before the supernal King to fulfill the desire of that human being.[372]

368. **A person should not examine . . .** See BT *Berakhot* 54b–55a: "Rabbi Ḥiyya son of Abba said in the name of Rabbi Yoḥanan, 'Whoever prolongs his prayer and speculates on it [or: expects that it will be granted] will eventually suffer heartache, as is said: *Hope deferred* [i.e., prayer prolonged] *is sickness of heart.*' Rabbi Yitsḥak said, 'Three things cause a person's sins to be remembered [on high]: walking under a shaky wall, speculating on [or: expecting the granting of] prayer, and calling on heaven to punish his fellow.'" See Rashi, ad loc.

369. **one constantly poised . . .** Satan. See BT *Bava Batra* 16a: "He descends and leads astray, ascends and arouses wrath, obtains authorization and seizes the soul."

370. **Whoever wants . . .** See BT *Berakhot* 31a; Tosafot, *Berakhot* 5b, s.v. *ella eima.* On Torah as tree of life, see above, p. 181, n. 8. The word באה (*ba'ah*) means "comes,"—and in the verse in Proverbs, "comes true."

371. **rung holding all prayers of the world . . .** *Shekhinah,* who conveys human prayer to *Tif'eret,* the King. She is called *desire* because of the human desires that She transmits above and because by conveying fervent prayer She arouses the desire of Her partner, *Tif'eret*. Cf. BT *Yevamot* 64a, in the name of Rabbi Yitsḥak: "The blessed Holy One desires [or: yearns for] the prayers of the righteous.'"

See Gikatilla, *Sha'arei Orah,* 4b–5a; *OY*; Mopsik. According to rabbinic and mystical sources, an angel gathers all the prayers and fashions them into crowns, which he places on God's head. See above, pp. 13–14 and n. 96.

372. **Here is written *comes* . . .** The verse in Esther reads: *In the evening she comes, in the morning she returns,* describing the continual stream of maidens coming to King Ahasuerus in the contest to be crowned queen. The following verses describe Esther, so this verse too is sometimes applied specifically to her and to the divine feminine whom she symbolizes, *Shekhinah.* Here, by verbal analogy, Rabbi Ḥiyya concludes that in the verse in Proverbs the word *comes* also refers to *Shekhinah,* who approaches King *Tif'eret* with human prayers.

See *Zohar* 1:106a; 3:220b.

"Alternatively, *Hope deferred is sickness of heart, but a desire come true is a tree of life.* Come and see: *Hope deferred*—a place where that word is delivered; another place, undesirable. Delayed there, it is passed from hand to hand and sometimes never arrives. Why? Because it is diffused and delayed among all those empowered to bring it down to the world.[373]

"*But a desire come true is a tree of life*—a *hope* not delayed among those empowered chariots; rather, the blessed Holy One grants it immediately. For when it is delayed among those chariots empowered, numerous masters of judgment are authorized to examine and scrutinize his case before it is granted; but whatever issues from the palace of the King and is bestowed upon a person is granted immediately whether he is deserving or not. This is *but a desire come true is a tree of life.*[374]

"Alternatively, *hope deferred*—Jacob, whose hope for Joseph was delayed for such a long time.[375]

"*But a desire come true is a tree of life*—Benjamin, because from the moment that Joseph demanded to see him until he arrived only a short time elapsed; there was no delay, as is written: *He raised his eyes and saw Benjamin his brother, his mother's son.* What does *his mother's son* mean? His mother's image appeared in him—his image resembled that of Rachel—so it is written: *his mother's son.*"[376]

Rabbi Yose said, "Look, it was written previously *Joseph saw Benjamin with them* (Genesis 43:16), and now is written *He raised his eyes and saw Benjamin*! What is this 'seeing'? Actually, he saw through the Holy Spirit that Benjamin would have a share with them in the land, and that *Shekhinah* would dwell in the share of Benjamin and Judah, for he saw the Temple standing in their share. This is *Joseph saw Benjamin with them*—him he saw with them, whereas Joseph, his brother, he did not see with them in that share. Similarly, *He raised his eyes and saw Benjamin.* What is written next? *Joseph hurried out because his love for his brother kindled and he wanted to weep*... (ibid., 30)."[377]

373. **another place, undesirable...** The realm of harsh judgment. Unworthy prayers can be delayed interminably, passed from one heavenly power to another, never reaching their destination in heaven and never fulfilled on earth.

See Gikatilla, *Sha'arei Orah*, 3b; Galante; Mopsik. Cf. *Zohar* 2:252a–b (*Heikh*).

374. **This is... *a tree of life*** A worthy prayer is granted immediately by the blessed Holy One, who is known as *tree of life.*

375. **Jacob, whose hope...** He had to wait over twenty years from the time that Joseph disappeared until he finally saw him again in Egypt. See above, p. 117, n. 208; *KP.*

376. **His mother's image...** See *Tanḥuma* (Buber), *Miqqets* 13; *Tanḥuma, Miqqets* 10; *Leqaḥ Tov*, Genesis 43:29.

377. **saw through the Holy Spirit...** Joseph foresaw that Benjamin's tribe would inherit a share in the land of Israel *with them*, that is, along with the other tribes.

Rabbi Ḥizkiyah opened, "*Oracle of the Valley of Vision: What has happened to you now, that you have gone, all of you, up on the roofs?* (Isaiah 22:1).[378] Come and see, as has been established: As the Temple was being destroyed, consumed by fire, all the priests scaled [203a] the heights of the Temple, with all the keys in their hands, and exclaimed, 'Until now we have been Your treasurers. From now on, take [what is Yours!]'[379]

"But come and see: *Valley of Vision* is *Shekhinah*, who resided in the Temple and from whom all inhabitants of the world sucked the milk of prophecy. For although all prophets prophesied from another site, from Her they absorbed their prophecy, so She is called *Valley of Vision.*[380] *Vision*, as has been established, for She is a visionary mirror reflecting all supernal colors.[381]

"*What has happened to you now, that you have gone, all of you, up on the roofs?* For when Jerusalem was destroyed, *Shekhinah* ascended and visited all those places where She had previously dwelled, and She wept for Her dwelling and for Israel who were going into exile and for all the righteous and pious who had been there and perished. How do we know? As is written: *A voice is heard on a height—wailing, bitter weeping—Rachel weeping for her children* (Jeremiah 31:15), as has been said.[382]

Specifically, Joseph saw that the Temple in Jerusalem would straddle the territories of both Benjamin and Judah—whereas his own territorial share (actually, that of his sons, Ephraim and Manasseh) would not include the Temple. However, Joseph also saw the eventual destruction of the Temple, which made him weep for Benjamin's fate.

The closing verse reads in full: *Joseph hurried out because his love for his brother kindled and he wanted to weep, and he went into a chamber and wept there.* See *Sifrei*, Deuteronomy 352; *Bereshit Rabbah* 93:12; BT *Yoma* 12a, *Megillah* 16b, *Zevaḥim* 53b–54b; *Avot de-Rabbi Natan* A, 35.

378. ***Oracle of the Valley*...** Isaiah addresses the city of Jerusalem. The context (Isaiah 22:1–2, 4) reads: *Oracle of the Valley of Vision: What has happened to you now, that you have gone, all of you, up on the roofs? Full of commotion, tumultuous city, exuberant town—your slain are not slain by the sword nor the dead of battle* [i.e., they are executed, not dying in war].... *Therefore I say, "Look away from me, let me weep bitterly. Do not insist on comforting me for the devastation of my beloved people."*

379. **priests scaled the heights...** This story appears is various versions in rabbinic sources. See BT *Ta'anit* 29a; *Avot de-Rabbi Natan* A, 4; *Pesiqta Rabbati* 26; *Targum Sheni*, Esther 1:3. Cf. *Vayiqra Rabbah* 19:6; JT *Sheqalim* 6:3, 50a.

380. **although all prophets...** The source of prophecy is the sefirotic pair of *Netsaḥ* and *Hod*, but they convey the visionary flow through the medium of *Shekhinah*.

See above, p. 114 and n. 190. Cf. JT *Sukkah* 5:1, 55a.

381. **visionary mirror...** *Shekhinah* reflects the colors of the higher *sefirot*.

The Aramaic word חיזו (*ḥeizu*) means "vision, appearance," but in the *Zohar* also "mirror." See 1:88b, 91a, 183a; 2:23a, 267a. This added sense may derive from the Hebrew word מראה (*mar'ah*), which means both "vision" and "mirror."

382. ***Shekhinah* ascended...** Bidding farewell to Her dwelling places within and above the Temple, in Jerusalem, and on the

"Then the blessed Holy One asked *Shekhinah*, '*What has happened to you now, that you have gone, all of you, up on the roofs?*' Why *all of you*? *That you have gone up* would have been sufficient; why *all of you*? To include all the other forces and chariots, all of whom wept along with Her over the destruction of the Temple.[383] So, *What has happened to you?*

"She replied before Him, 'My children are in exile and the Temple is burnt, so what is left for Me here?' She began to say, *Full of commotion, tumultuous city, exuberant town... Therefore I say, 'Look away from me, let me weep bitterly...'* (Isaiah, ibid., 2, 4).[384] And we have established that the blessed Holy One said to Her, *Restrain your voice from weeping...* (Jeremiah, ibid., 16).[385]

"Come and see: Ever since the day that the Temple was destroyed, there has never been a day without curses.[386] For when the Temple existed, Israel would perform rituals, bringing offerings and sacrifices, and *Shekhinah* hovered over them in the Temple like a mother over her children. All faces were radiant, so that blessings appeared above and below; there was never a day without blessings and joys. Israel dwelled securely in the land, and the whole world was nourished because of them.[387]

Mount of Olives. See *Eikhah Rabbah, Petiḥta* 25; *Pesiqta de-Rav Kahana* 13:11; *Avot de-Rabbi Natan* A, 34.

In the *Zohar*, Mother Rachel symbolizes the Divine Mother, *Shekhinah*. See *Bereshit Rabbah* 82:10; *Eikhah Rabbah, Petiḥta* 24; *Zohar* 1:134a; above, p. 104 and n. 132; below, p. 287 and n. 162; 2:29b; 3:20b, 187a; *ZḤ* 92a–b (*MhN, Eikhah*); Moses de León, *Sheqel ha-Qodesh*, 66 (83); Mopsik.

The verse in Jeremiah reads: *A voice is heard on a height—wailing, bitter weeping—Rachel weeping for her children, refusing to be comforted for her children, because they are no more.*

383. **Why *all of you*?...** Since, according to Rabbi Ḥizkiyah, this verse is addressed to *Shekhinah*, why this wording: *all of you*? He answers his own question by explaining that *all* refers to the heavenly powers accompanying Her. See *ZḤ* 88a (*MhN, Rut*).

384. ***Full of commotion...*** *Shekhinah* laments the lost glory of Jerusalem. See above, note 378.

385. ***Restrain your voice...*** The preceding verse appears above, at note 382. The context (Jeremiah 31:16–17) reads: *Thus says YHVH: Restrain your voice from weeping, your eyes from tears; for there is reward for your labor, declares YHVH: they will return from the land of the enemy. There is hope for your future, declares YHVH: children will return to their land.*

See *Eikhah Rabbah, Petiḥta* 24.

386. **day without curses** See M *Sotah* 9:12: "Rabban Shim'on son of Gamli'el says in the name of Rabbi Yehoshu'a: 'Ever since the day the Temple was destroyed, not a single day passes without a curse, dew has never descended as blessing, and flavor has been eliminated from fruit.'"

See above, p. 100 and n. 103.

387. **when the Temple existed...** The sacrificial rites stimulated sefirotic union, ensuring blessing for all worlds. See above, pp. 99–100 and n. 101.

On the nourishment of the world through Israel, see BT *Ta'anit* 10a; Naḥmanides on Deuteronomy 11:10 ; *Zohar* 1:108b; 2:152b; 3:209b.

"Now that the Temple is destroyed and *Shekhinah* is with them in exile, no day passes without curses; the world is cursed, and joy cannot be found above or below.[388] But one day the blessed Holy One intends to raise Assembly of Israel from the dust, as has been said,[389] and to delight the world utterly, as is said: *I will bring them to My holy mountain and give them joy in My house of prayer...* (Isaiah 56:7).[390] And it is written: *With weeping they will come, and with consolations I will guide them* (Jeremiah, ibid., 9). As previously is written, *She weeps bitterly in the night* (Lamentations 1:2), so later they will return in weeping, as is written: *With weeping they will come.*"[391]

As morning dawned, the men were sent off, they and their donkeys (Genesis 44:3).

Rabbi El'azar said, "Here one should contemplate. If they went and were sent on their way, why should it be written in the Torah *they and their donkeys*?[392] Because it is written: *to take us as slaves along with our donkeys* (ibid. 43:18). Therefore, *they and their donkeys*, for they and their donkeys did not remain, as they had declared."[393]

He opened, saying, "*Abraham rose early in the morning and saddled his donkey* (ibid. 22:3).[394] That morning of Abraham shone, presiding over them through his merit; so the merit of Abraham arched over them, and they went in peace and were delivered from judgment. For at that moment, judgment loomed over them, threatening retribution, but the merit of that morning of Abraham

388. ***Shekhinah* is with them...** On the exile of *Shekhinah*, see above, note 88; Moses de León, *Sheqel ha-Qodesh*, 73–74 (92–93).

389. **Assembly of Israel...** Referring both to the people Israel and *Shekhinah*. See above, pp. 122–23, n. 237.

390. ***I will bring them...*** In Isaiah this verse is addressed to foreigners who draw close to God and embrace the covenant. The full verse reads: *I will bring them to My holy mountain and give them joy in My house of prayer. Their ascent-offerings and sacrifices will find favor on My altar; for My house will be called a house of prayer for all peoples.*

391. ***She weeps bitterly...*** Israel's weeping over destruction and exile will be countervailed by their tears of joy over deliverance.

See above, p. 59 and n. 417; *Zohar* 2:12b.

392. **why should it be written...** Obviously, their donkeys accompanied them.

393. **Because it is written...** Earlier, the brothers had feared that they would be attacked and enslaved along with their donkeys, so now the Torah specifies that their donkeys went with them, showing that their fear was unfounded.

The full verse in the previous chapter reads: *The men were afraid at being brought to Joseph's house, and they said, "Because of the silver put back in our bags the first time we've been brought, in order to fall upon us, to attack us, and to take us as slaves along with our donkeys."*

394. ***Abraham rose early...*** These references to *morning* and *donkey* link the story of Abraham's binding of Isaac to the account of Joseph's brothers setting out on their return to Canaan.

protected them and they were sent away from judgment, which could not prevail against them at that time."[395]

Rabbi Yehudah opened, "*Like morning's light when the sun rises, morning without clouds; from radiance, from rain—vegetation from earth* (2 Samuel 23:4). *Like morning's light*—light of that morning of Abraham.

"*When the sun rises*—sun of Jacob, as is written: *The sun rose upon him* (Genesis 32:32).[396]

"*Morning without clouds*—for that morning is not so dense, rather *from radiance, from rain. Radiance, from rain*, for it is rain coming from the side of Isaac, sprouting *vegetation from earth*.[397]

"Alternatively, *Like morning's light*—like that radiance of the morning of Abraham. [203b]

"*When the sun rises*—Jacob, whose radiance resembles that morning.[398]

"*Morning without clouds*—because that morning is not dark but shining, for when morning comes, judgment is totally powerless; rather, all shines from the side of Abraham.[399]

"*From radiance, from rain*—side of Joseph the Righteous, who showers upon earth to sprout vegetation and all goodness of the world."[400]

Rabbi Shim'on said, "Come and see: As night enters and spreads her wings over the world, numerous dazzling, demonic guardians stand poised to emerge and rule the world;[401] numerous masters of judgment arouse on several sides

395. **morning of Abraham...** *Ḥesed*, Abraham's *sefirah*, is symbolized by light and morning. The patriarch attained merit by rising early to fulfill God's command to sacrifice his son Isaac. Now this merit protected his great-grandsons from the punishment they deserved for having sold Joseph into slavery. Abraham's *Ḥesed* (Loving-kindness) counteracted *Din* (Judgment).

On Abraham and morning, see above, p. 112 and n. 180; p. 152 and n. 430. According to BT *Berakhot* 26b, Abraham instituted morning prayer. On the brothers' sin, see above, p. 239, n. 360; page 240.

396. **sun of Jacob...** *Tif'eret*, Jacob's *sefirah*, symbolized by the sun.

The full verse in Genesis 32 reads: *The sun rose upon him as he passed Penuel, and he was limping on his hip.*

397. ***Morning without clouds...*** *Ḥesed* is clear, not dense like the thick clouds of *Gevurah*. Yet the potent rain of *Gevurah* (the *sefirah* of Isaac) must mingle with *Ḥesed* to fructify *Shekhinah*, symbolized by *earth*.

Rabbi Yehudah is playing with two related meanings of עב (*av*): "cloud" and "thick, dense." Rain and *gevurah* are linked in the rabbinic expression גבורות גשמים (*gevurot geshamim*), "the power of rain." See M *Berakhot* 5:2; *Ta'anit* 1:1.

398. **radiance resembles that morning** The brilliance of Jacob's *sefirah* (*Tif'eret*) resembles that of Abraham's (*Ḥesed*).

399. **morning is not dark...** The morning light of *Ḥesed* banishes the dense darkness and judgment of *Gevurah*.

400. **Joseph the Righteous...** *Yesod*, who conveys the flow of emanation to *Shekhinah*. See above, p. 92, n. 50.

401. **dazzling, demonic guardians...** Demonic powers.

The phrase גרדיני טהירין (*gardinei tehirin*)

according to their species and reign over the world.[402] As soon as morning arrives and brightens, they all vanish and rule no longer, every single one entering his place, returning to his site.

"*As morning dawned* (ibid. 44:3)—morning of Abraham.[403]

"*The men were sent off* (ibid.)—masters of judgment who ruled at night.

"*They and their donkeys* (ibid.). *They*—those masters of judgment whom we have mentioned.[404] *And their donkeys*—those wardens of law issuing from the side of impure spirit, unholy, who neither rule nor are to be seen once morning arrives. These wardens of law derive from the side of those donkeys.[405]

"For all supernal rungs include both right and left, compassion and judgment, rungs upon rungs: holy on the side of holiness, impure on the side of impurity, all rungs upon rungs, one upon another.[406] Wherever the morning of Abraham arouses in the world, they all pass away, ruling no more, for they cannot endure on the right side, only on the left. The blessed Holy One made day and night, so that each would be conducted fittingly on its side.[407] Happy is the share of Israel in this world and in the world that is coming!"

Rabbi Ḥiyya opened, "*For you, in awe of My name, the sun of justness will rise, with healing in its wings* (Malachi 3:20). One day, the blessed Holy One will illumine for Israel the sun that He has treasured away since the day the world was created—that He concealed from the wicked of the world, as is written: *The light of the wicked is withheld* (Job 38:15). That light was hidden away by the blessed Holy One; for when it first issued, it radiated from one end of the world to the other, but once He contemplated the generation of Enosh, the generation of the Flood, and the generations of the wicked, He concealed that light.[408]

exhibits the *Zohar*'s linguistic creativity. *Gardinei* derives from the Castilian *guardián* (guardian). See Corominas, *Diccionario,* 3:246–48. On *tehirin,* see above, p. 216, n. 227.

402. **on several sides...** On both the holy side and the demonic side.

403. **morning of Abraham** *Ḥesed.* See above, note 395.

404. ***They*—those masters of judgment...** Issuing from the holy side.

405. ***their donkeys*—those wardens...** From the demonic side. These forces are called *their donkeys* because they convey judgment, inflicting punishment below.

On the demonic nature of *donkeys,* see above, p. 8 and n. 54; p. 43 and n. 314. On the wardens of law, see *Zohar* 1:34a; 2:65a, 245b (*Heikh*); 3:43a; Gikatilla, *Sha'arei Orah,* 75a; Mopsik.

406. **both right and left...** Judgment manifests both in the holy realm of the *sefirot* and in the demonic realm. In the *sefirot,* right and left correspond to *Ḥesed* (Lovingkindness, referred to here as *Raḥamim* [Compassion]) and *Din* (Judgment). But "left" also designates the demonic realm in its entirety, which derives from *Din.*

407. **day and night...** Characterized respectively by *Ḥesed* on the right and *Din* on the left.

408. **sun that He has treasured away...** See *Vayiqra Rabbah* 11:7: "Rabbi Yehudah son of Rabbi Simon said, 'With the light created by the blessed Holy One on the first

"When Jacob appeared and wrestled with Esau's empowered prince—who struck him on the thigh, laming him—what is written? *The sun rose upon him* (Genesis 32:32).[409] Which *sun*? The sun that was hidden away, for it encompasses healing—to heal his hip. Through that sun he was healed, as is written: *Jacob arrived* שלם (*shalem*), *in peace* (ibid. 33:18)—*shalem*, complete, in his body, for he was healed.[410]

"So one day, the blessed Holy One will unsheathe that sun and shine it upon Israel, as is written: *For you, in awe of My name, the sun of justness will rise, with healing in its wings.* What is *the sun of justness*? Sun of Jacob, who was healed by it.[411] *With healing in its wings*—since by that sun, they will all be healed. For when Israel will rise from the dust, many of them will be lame and blind; then the blessed Holy One will shine that sun upon them, healing them, as is written: *with healing in its wings*.[412] Then that sun will radiate from one end of the world to the other—healing Israel, consuming other nations.[413] Of Israel, what is

day, one could gaze and see from one end of the universe to the other. When the Holy One foresaw the corruption of the generation of Enosh and the generation of the Flood, He hid it away from them, as is written: *The light of the wicked is withheld* (Job 38:15). Where did He hide it? In the Garden of Eden. *Light is sown for the righteous, joy for the upright in heart* (Psalms 97:11).'"

See *Bereshit Rabbah* 3:6; 41:3; BT *Ḥagigah* 12a; *Shemot Rabbah* 35:1; *Tanḥuma, Shemini,* 9; *Bahir* 97–98 (147); *Zohar* 1:7a, 31b–32a, 45b–46a, 47a, 59a, 131a; 2:127a, 148b–149a, 220a–b; 3:88a, 173b.

Concerning the generation of Enosh, Genesis 4:26 states: *Then for the first time the name YHVH was invoked.* In the Midrash this is taken to mean that Enosh's generation was the first to worship idols and address them by the name *YHVH*.

See *Mekhilta, Baḥodesh* 6; *Bereshit Rabbah* 23:7; *Targum Yerushalmi* and Rashi on Genesis 4:26; Maimonides, *Mishneh Torah, Hilkhot Avodah Zarah* 1:1; Ginzberg, *Legends,* 5:151, n. 54.

409. **wrestled with Esau's empowered prince...** On the night before Jacob was reunited with Esau, *a man wrestled with him until the break of dawn* (Genesis 32:25). According to midrashic tradition, this *man* was actually Samael, identified here as Esau's heavenly prince.

See *Tanḥuma, Vayishlaḥ* 8; *Bereshit Rabbah* 77:3; *Zohar* 1:146a, 166a, 170a, 179b. The closing verse here (Genesis 32:32) reads in full: *The sun rose upon him as he passed Penuel, and he was limping on his hip.*

410. **Through that sun he was healed...** This motif appears in *Midrash Avkir,* 21 (p. 8). Cf. *Bereshit Rabbah* 78:5; *Tanḥuma* (Buber), *Vayishlaḥ* 10.

See BT *Shabbat* 33b: "*Jacob arrived* שלם (*shalem*), *in peace.* Rav said, '*Shalem,* complete, in his body, complete in his wealth, complete in his Torah.'"

Cf. *Bereshit Rabbah* 79:5; *Tanḥuma* (Buber), *Vayishlaḥ* 10–12; above, p. 43 at n. 308. See also *Zohar* 1:21a–b; Mopsik.

411. **Sun of Jacob...** *Tif'eret,* also known as צדקה (*tsedaqah*), "righteousness, justness." See above, note 396.

412. **many of them will be lame...** See *Tanḥuma* (Buber), *Vayiggash* 9; *Bereshit Rabbah* 95:1; BT *Sanhedrin* 91b; *Zohar* 3:91a.

413. **healing Israel, consuming other nations** See *Bereshit Rabbah* 78:5; BT *Avodah Zarah* 3b–4a, both of which cite the preceding verse in Malachi (3:19), describing the burning of the wicked.

written? *Then your light will burst through like the dawn and your healing quickly sprout* (Isaiah 58:8)."[414]

Let us return to earlier words.[415] *To Joseph two sons were born*... (Genesis 41:50).[416]

Rabbi Yitsḥak opened, "*The remnant of Jacob will be in the midst of many peoples* (Micah 5:6).[417] Come and see: Every single day, as light rises, one bird arouses in a tree of the Garden of Eden and calls three times.[418] A scepter is raised erect and a herald proclaims potently: 'You are addressed, commanders of boorish creatures, whoever among you sees and does not see, existing in the world without knowing the foundation of their existence, oblivious to the glory of their Lord.[419] [204a] Torah stands before them, yet they do not engage in her. Better for them to have never been created than to exist without understanding!

414. ***Then your light...*** The full verse reads: *Then your light will burst through like the dawn and your healing quickly sprout. Your vindicator will march before you, the glory of YHVH will be your rear guard.*

415. **Let us return...** The immediately preceding discussion does not relate to Joseph; now the *Zohar* returns to that narrative. Furthermore, the verse that follows (Genesis 41:50) is from an earlier section of the Joseph narrative than the verse most recently discussed (ibid. 44:3).

For similar expressions, see *Zohar* 1:62b, 80b (*ST*); 2:148a; 3:205b; *ZḤ* 65a (*ShS*), 71d (*ShS*).

416. ***To Joseph...*** The full verse reads: *To Joseph two sons were born before the coming of the year of famine, whom Asenath daughter of Potiphera priest of On bore him.*

417. ***The remnant...*** The full verse reads: *The remnant of Jacob will be in the midst of many peoples like dew from YHVH, like showers on grass, which do not wait for a person or linger for human beings.* The connection between this verse and Rabbi Yitsḥak's discourse is unclear. See *KP*, 2:382a; *MmD*.

418. **one bird arouses...** See *Zohar* 2:130b, where three birds call one time each, followed by a herald's proclamation.

419. **You are addressed...** The herald addresses leaders of the generation who fail to perceive the meaning of existence and to guide the unenlightened masses. See Jeremiah 5:21; Daniel 3:4; *Zohar* 1:77a.

The phrase "commanders of boorish creatures" translates the cryptic Aramaic הורמני דבורייני (*hurmanei de-vuryanei*), as preserved in the more reliable manuscripts (M7, N23, R1). *Hurmanei* is the plural of הרמנא (*harmana*), "command, authority." See *Zohar* 1:15a; Vol. 1, p. 107, n. 1. The precise sense of *buryanei* is uncertain, probably intentionally so; the translation here combines two possible senses, both of which may be implied: "creatures" and "boors." The word בריין (*biryan*) means "creatures," as in *Targum Yonatan*, Ezekiel 1:5, and frequently in the *Zohar*. The word בורייא (*burayya*) means "uncultivated, ignorant people, boors," as in *Vayiqra Rabbah* 18:1; cf. M *Avot* 2:5.

On this phrase, see *Zohar* 1:107b (*ST*), 147a (*Tos*); 251a (*Mat, Hash*); *ZḤ* 2a (*Mat*). Cf. 1:232a (*Tos*); 3:15a. For other interpretations based on various readings, see *OY*; Galante; *KP*; Tishby, *Wisdom of the Zohar*, 2:526; Mopsik.

See above, p. 196 and n. 111, quoting BT *Ḥagigah* 12b: "Rabbi Yose said, 'Woe to creatures, for they see but do not know what they see; they stand but do not know on what they stand!'"

Woe to them when days of evil arouse against them and banish them from the world!'

"What are days of evil? If you imagine days of old age, not so! For if one attains children and grandchildren, then days of old age are days of good. What, then, are days of evil? As has been explained, for it is written: *Remember your Creator in the days of your youth, before the days of evil come* (Ecclesiastes 12:1). Those are not days of old age; rather, the mystery of the matter is as follows.[420]

"When the blessed Holy One created the world, He created it with the letters of Torah,[421] and every single letter entered before Him, until they were all established in the letter ב (*bet*).[422] All those alphabets of revolving, permutating letters poised to create the world. As they revolved, and ט ר (*tet, resh*) joined—these two letters as one—ט (*tet*) rose and would not settle. So the blessed Holy One rebuked her, saying, '*Tet, tet*, why do you rise and not settle in your place?'[423]

"She replied, 'Didn't You make me to be the select letter of טוב (*tov*), good? For look, Torah first displays me with כי טוב (*ki tov*), *that it was good* (Genesis 1:4)! How can I settle, joining with an evil letter?'[424]

"He said to her, 'Return to your place, because you need it. For the human being, whom I am about to create by you, will be created embracing both of you—but with you on the right and him on the left.'[425]

420. **not days of old age...** As implied by the verse in Ecclesiastes. See *Vayiqra Rabbah* 18:1; BT *Shabbat* 151b; *Qohelet Rabbah* and Rashi, ad loc.

421. **created it with the letters...** According to *Sefer Yetsirah* 2:2, God created the world by permuting the twenty-two letters of the Hebrew alphabet: "Twenty-two elemental letters. He engraved them, carved them, weighed them, permuted them and transposed them, forming with them everything formed and everything destined to be formed."

See BT *Berakhot* 55a; *Sanhedrin* 65b; Rashi on Job 28:23.

422. **all established in the letter ב (*bet*)** The opening letter of the Torah. See the story in *Zohar* 1:2b–3b; Vol. 1, p. 11, n. 80.

423. **revolving, permutating letters...** See above, note 421, and the description of permutation in *Sefer Yetsirah* 2:4–5: "Twenty-two elemental letters. He set them in a wheel with 231 gates, turning forward and backward.... How did He permute them? א (*Alef*) with them all, all of them with א (*alef*); ב (*bet*) with them all, all of them with ב (*bet*); and so with all the letters, turning round and round, within 231 gates."

The "231 gates" represent the number of two-letter combinations that can be formed from the twenty-two letters, provided that the same letter is not repeated. According to one scheme of permutation, א (*alef*) is paired with ל (*lamed*), ב (*bet*) with מ (*mem*),... ט (*tet*) with ר (*resh*), etc. Here the letter ט (*tet*) refuses to settle next to ר (*resh*).

See *Zohar* 1:33b, 67b; 2:151b–152a, 159a–160b; Galante; *KP*, 1:100c–d; *NO*; Kaplan, *Sefer Yetzirah*, 108–24; *MmD*.

424. **Didn't You make me...** ט (*Tet*) begins and symbolizes טוב (*tov*), "good," and the first time that this letter appears in the Torah is in Genesis 1:4: *God saw the light, that it was* טוב (*tov*), *good*. Consequently, ט (*tet*) refuses to be paired with the letter ר (*resh*), which begins the word רע (*ra*), "evil."

425. **you need it...** Good and evil are both necessary for the creation of the world

"Then she returned and they settled with one another.

"At that moment, the blessed Holy One separated them, creating for each one certain days and years—these to the right, those to the left. These on the right are called 'days of good'; those on the left are called 'days of evil.' Concerning this, Solomon said, *before the days of evil come*, for these encompass a person with the sins he has committed.

"Once the days of good and the days of evil had been created, they returned and settled, so that the human would include them both.[426] So David said, *Why should I fear, in days of evil?* (Psalms 49:6)—*days of evil*, precisely![427]

"The secret is: These are called 'days of famine, years of famine,' while those are called 'days of plenty, years of plenty.' Mystery of the matter: One should not spout the spring of holy covenant in days of famine, in *the year of famine* (Genesis 41:50). Therefore, Joseph, mystery of covenant, sealed his spring in *the year of famine*, not enabling it to proliferate in the world. So should a person act: when *the year of famine* prevails, he should seal the spring of his holy covenant, preventing it from propagating in the world."[428]

Rabbi Shim'on said, "This mystery is a supernal mystery. When that *year of famine* prevails, one should seal his spring, because otherwise he causes a spirit to be drawn from that side to the fetus, enabling that side to proliferate in the world alongside holiness.[429]

"A further mystery, as is written: *At three things the earth trembles:... [a slave becoming a king,... a loathsome woman getting married, and a slave-girl supplanting her mistress]* (Proverbs 30:21–23).[430] So Joseph the Righteous, mystery of

and specifically for the formation of the human being, who includes both good and evil impulses, and must choose one or the other.

426. **they returned...** The letters ט (*tet*) and ר (*resh*) returned.

427. ***Why should I fear...*** The full verse (in its rabbinic and Zoharic sense) reads: *Why should I fear, in days of evil, the iniquity of my heels encompassing me?* On evil days, a person's sins assail him. See above, pp. 215–16 at nn. 221–26.

428. **One should not spout...** In evil days of famine, one should not engage in sexual union—spouting the phallic spring, which is marked by the covenant of circumcision. A person who indulges sexually at such an inauspicious time stimulates the flow of *Yesod* (the divine phallus), thereby nourishing the prevailing force of evil (*the year of famine*) and helping it to proliferate.

See BT *Ta'anit* 11a: "Resh Lakish said, 'A man is forbidden to have sexual intercourse in years of famine, as is said: *To Joseph two sons were born before the coming of the year of famine* (Genesis 41:50).' A Tanna taught: 'Those who are childless may have sexual intercourse in years of famine.'"

See *Bereshit Rabbah* 31:12; JT *Ta'anit* 1:6, 64d; Rashi on Genesis 41:50. For the halakhic discussion, see Tosafot, BT *Ta'anit* 11a, s.v. *asur*; *NZ*; Kasher, *Torah Shelemah*, Genesis 41:50, nn. 127–28. On Joseph as "mystery of covenant," see above, note 303.

429. **spirit to be drawn...** If his wife conceives at such a time, a spirit from the demonic realm ("that side") enters the fetus.

430. ***At three things...*** Human sin empowers the demonic forces, enthroning Sa-

covenant, withdrew and sealed his spring in *the year of famine*, not mingling with it at all, so as not to provide it scope. Of one who opens his spring at that time, it is written: *They betrayed YHVH because they bore alien children* (Hosea 5:7), for these are called *alien children*, literally! *They betrayed YHVH*, precisely![431] So, happy is the share of holy Israel, who do not exchange a holy site for a defiled site.

"Therefore it is written: *To Joseph two sons were born before the coming of the year of famine*, for as soon as *the year of famine* prevailed, he sealed his spring and withdrew his fountain, so as not to give children to the impure side or exchange a site of holiness for a site of defilement. One should wait for the Master of holiness to come and reign, as is said: *I will wait for YHVH, who is hiding His face from the House of Jacob* (Isaiah 8:17).[432]

"Happy are the righteous who know the ways of the blessed Holy One and keep the commandments, rendering themselves worthy, as is written: *For the ways of YHVH are right; [the righteous walk in them, while transgressors stumble in them]* (Hosea 14:10).[433] And similarly: *You, cleaving to YHVH* (Deuteronomy 4:4); and: *Sanctify yourselves and be holy, for I YHVH am holy* (Leviticus 11:44).[434] For the blessed Holy One wants to sanctify Israel [204b] in everything, so that they have nothing to do with the side of defilement.

"Come and see: When this side dominates the world, a person must not be seen in the street, for he can inflict harm and is empowered to destroy. Come

mael, who should remain subservient, and enabling loathsome Lilith to supplant *Shekhinah* and receive the flow of emanation from *Yesod*.

The verses in Proverbs read: *At three things the earth trembles, four it cannot bear: a slave becoming a king, a scoundrel sated with food, a loathsome woman getting married, and a slave-girl supplanting her mistress.* See *Zohar* 1:122a–b, 131b; 2:60b–61a; 3:69a, 266a. Cf. above, p. 162 and n. 490.

431. ***alien children*, literally...** Such children have demonic spirits and belong to the demonic side.

See *Zohar* 1:93a; 2:87b, 90a.

432. **wait for the Master of holiness...** One should wait for God to end the famine and restore holiness; only then is sexual activity encouraged.

The full verse in Isaiah reads: *I will wait for YHVH, who is hiding His face from the House of Jacob, and I will hope in Him.*

433. ***ways of YHVH are right...*** Referring here particularly to the *mitsvah* of procreation. The righteous perform this at the proper time; the wicked cannot control themselves and thereby stumble.

434. ***You, cleaving...*** The full verse reads: *You, cleaving to YHVH your God, are alive every one of you today!* The biblical context involves rejecting idolatry together with its associated sexual sins and attaining intimacy with God. See the preceding verse and Numbers 25.

The verse in Leviticus reads: *For I am YHVH your God: sanctify yourselves and be holy, for I am holy. Do not defile yourselves*, etc. In rabbinic literature this verse is applied to sanctifying sexual relations. See BT *Shevu'ot* 18b; *Bemidbar Rabbah* 9:7; *Zohar* 1:54a.

and see what is written of Jacob: *Jacob said to his sons, 'Why should you show yourselves?'* (Genesis 42:1)—for one should not be seen in his presence.[435]

"Therefore the blessed Holy One cautioned Israel to sanctify themselves, as has been said: *Sanctify yourselves and be holy, for I YHVH am holy.* Who is *I*? The blessed Holy One, holy Kingdom of Heaven.[436] The wicked kingdom is called Other, as is written: *For you shall bow down to no other god* (Exodus 34:14).[437]

"Come and see: *I*—dominion of this world and of the world that is coming, upon whom all depends. Other—Other Side on the side of defilement; his dominion pertains to this world, but he has nothing in the world that is coming.[438] So whoever cleaves to this *I* has a share in this world and in the world that is coming, but whoever cleaves to the Other perishes from this world and has no share in the world that is coming. In this world, he has a share in defilement, for countless shield-bearing guardians are empowered in that wicked kingdom to rule this world.[439]

"Therefore *Aḥer*, the Other, who descended and clung to this rung, was banished from the world that is coming and was not permitted to turn back in repentance; banished from that world, he was called *Aḥer*.[440]

"So one should separate from all sides in order not to be defiled by that side,

435. **not be seen in the street...** In time of calamity, one should not go outside, exposing himself to the destructive force.

The plain sense of the verse in Genesis 42 is apparently *Why do you keep looking at one another?* Here, following a midrashic reading, the sense is: "Why should you make yourselves conspicuous?" See above, pp. 211–12, n. 192, and n. 193 (which quotes BT *Bava Qamma* 60a–b).

436. **Who is *I*?...** *Shekhinah* (Presence), or *Malkhut* (Kingdom), is known as אני (*ani*), *I*, because through Her the Divine reveals itself, declaring "I am."

See *Zohar* 1:6a–b, 65b, 228a; 2:236b; 3:178b; Moses de León, *Sefer ha-Rimmon*, 380 (and Wolfson's notes 8–9). Cf. M *Sukkah* 4:5; BT *Sukkah* 45a, and Rashi and Tosafot, ad loc., s.v. *ani va-ho*; *Zohar* 1:23a (*TZ*); 3:222b (*RM*), 227a (*RM*), 276b (*RM*).

437. **wicked kingdom is called Other...** Representing the demonic realm, known as the Other Side.

In rabbinic literature the "wicked kingdom" refers to the Roman empire, and in the *Zohar* the phrase sometimes refers to the Gentile oppressors of Israel. See *Bereshit Rabbah* 2:4; BT *Berakhot* 61b; *Zohar* 1:171a; 2:8a, 134a–b, 184a, 240a; Moses de León, *Sod Eser Sefirot Belimah*, 384.

438. **nothing in the world that is coming** See *Zohar* 2:223b.

439. **shield-bearing guardians...** Innumerable demonic powers.

On the components of this phrase, תריסין גרדינין (*terisin gardinin*), see above, p. 195, n. 106; pp. 246–47, n. 401.

440. ***Aḥer*, the Other...** The famous second-century rabbinic heretic, Elisha son of Avuyah, who rejected key doctrines of rabbinic Judaism (reward and punishment, and the resurrection of the dead) and apparently accepted a form of Gnosticism. The Talmud avoids his name, referring to him as אחר (*aḥer*), "the other, another," stranger.

See *Tosefta*, *Ḥagigah* 2:3; JT *Ḥagigah* 2:1, 77b–c; BT *Ḥagigah* 14b–15b, *Qiddushin* 39b; *Shir ha-Shirim Rabbah* on 1:4; *Zohar* 2:254b (*Heikh*); Moses de León, *Sefer ha-Mishqal*, 150; Mopsik.

and cleave to *I*, Kingdom of Heaven—accepting upon oneself the yoke of the Kingdom of Heaven, attaining thereby this world and the world that is coming.[441] So this is blessing and that is curse, this is plenty and that is famine—totally opposite one another, as we have established.[442] Therefore during *the year of famine*, a person should not be seen in the marketplace nor open his spring to engender, giving children to the *other god*, as has been said.[443]

"Happy is one who is careful to walk in the path of truth, cleaving constantly to his Lord, as is written: *To Him you shall cleave, and by His name you shall swear* (Deuteronomy 10:20).[444] It is not written *by Him you shall swear*, but rather *by His name you shall swear*. What is the meaning of תשבע (*tishshave'a*), *you shall swear*? As we have established, to cleave to the mystery of faith: שבעה (*shiv'ah*), seven, rungs above, above, transcending all, mystery of consummation of faith; and seven rungs below them—one bond, one cluster, these with those, so all will be one. Therefore it is written: שבעה (*shiv'ah*), *seven, days and seven days*... (1 Kings 8:65), all in a single bond; and so it is written: *by His name tishshave'a, you shall swear*, from above and below.[445]

"Happy is one who succeeds in cleaving to the blessed Holy One fittingly! Happy is he in this world and in the world that is coming. The blessed Holy One opens for him holy treasures when his prayer needs to be received, as is written: *YHVH will open for you His goodly treasure, the heavens* (Deuteronomy 28:12). את השמים (*Et ha-shamayim*), *The heavens*—treasures above and below; *seven days and seven days*, all of them one, as is written: *His goodly treasure*—*His treasure*, singular, of *et ha-shamayim, the heavens*; *seven and seven channels* (Zechariah 4:2), and they are one."[446]

441. **accepting upon oneself...** Acknowledging the one true God.

See M *Berakhot* 2:2; above, p. 115 and n. 199.

442. **totally opposite...** See above, p. 161 and n. 483; *Zohar* 1:162a (*Tos*).

443. **during *the year of famine*...** See above, pages 251–53.

444. ***To Him you shall cleave*...** The full verse reads: *YHVH your God you shall hold in awe, Him you shall serve, and to Him you shall cleave, and by His name you shall swear.*

445. **It is not written *by Him*...** The wording *by Him* would naturally refer to the divine male, whereas *by His name* alludes to *Shekhinah*, who is known as *name* because She reveals the divine identity. The verb תשבע (*tishshave'a*), *you shall swear*, implies שבעה (*shiv'ah*), "seven," referring to a double seven: the seven *sefirot* from Ḥesed through *Shekhinah* and the seven palaces of *Shekhinah*, which should all be unified by the human devotee.

The verse in Kings, describing the celebration of the festival of Sukkot, reads in full: *Solomon observed the Feast at that time, and all Israel with him—a great assemblage from Lebo-hamath to the Wadi of Egypt—before YHVH our God, seven days and seven days: fourteen days in all.*

See above, p. 102 and n. 119; *Zohar* 1:112b; Asher ben David, *Peirush ha-Shevu'ot*, 205–8; Moses de León, *Shushan Edut*, 360–61.

446. **את השמים (*Et ha-shamayim*), *The heavens*...** *The heavens* refers to *Tif'eret*, along with the other *sefirot* from Ḥesed

Rabbi Ḥiyya and Rabbi Yose were walking on the way, when they saw a man coming enwrapped in a wrap of *mitsvah* underneath which weapons were girded.[447]

Rabbi Ḥiyya said, "This man embodies one of two qualities: he is either completely righteous or he is out to deceive inhabitants of the world."[448]

Rabbi Yose replied, "But the eminent saints have said, 'Judge every person favorably.'[449] And we have learned: A person setting out on a journey should prepare himself for three things: for a present, for combat, and for prayer. How do we know? From Jacob, who prepared and girded himself for a present, for combat, and for prayer.[450] Now, this man is walking on the road and, look, he has a wrap of *mitsvah* and he has weapons for combat. Since he has these two, the third there is no need to pursue."[451]

When he approached them, they greeted him; he did not respond. Rabbi Ḥiyya said, "Here is one of those [205a] two that he apparently lacks, for he has not prepared himself with a present, which includes a greeting."[452]

through *Yesod*, all of which flow into *Shekhinah*, who is designated by the particle את (*et*). Consequently, the phrase *et ha-shamayim* alludes to both the totality of seven *sefirot* from *Ḥesed* through *Shekhinah* and to the seven palaces of *Shekhinah*. The singular form of the noun *treasure* reflects the unity of the two heptads, both of which channel the flow of emanation from above to below.

On *Shekhinah* as et, see above, p. 118, n. 217. The verse in Deuteronomy reads: *YHVH will open for you His goodly treasure, the heavens, to provide your land's rain in its season and to bless all your handiwork.* The verse in Zechariah records the prophet's vision of the menorah in the rebuilt Temple; oil from a bowl flowed through seven ducts into each of the seven lamps.

447. **wrap of *mitsvah*...** A *tallit*, a prayer shawl.

448. **one of two qualities...** He is either genuinely pious, or he is trying to deceive people on the road and rob them.

449. **Judge every person favorably** See M *Avot* 1:6, in the name of Yehoshu'a son of Peraḥiah: "Judge every person in the scale-pan of innocence [or: merit]," i.e., incline the balance in that person's favor.

In *Zohar* 2:49b, these same two rabbis (Rabbi Ḥiyya and Rabbi Yose) encounter another stranger; Rabbi Ḥiyya is suspicious, while Rabbi Yose gives the man the benefit of the doubt.

450. **prepare himself for three things...** See *Qohelet Rabbah* on 9:18: "*Wisdom is better than weapons of war* (Ecclesiastes 9:18). This refers to the wisdom of our father Jacob. *Than weapons of war*—of Esau the wicked. Rabbi Levi said, 'Jacob armed them [his sons and shepherds] with weapons underneath and clothed them in white garments on top. He prepared himself for three things: for prayer, for a present [to mollify Esau], and for battle.'" Rabbi Levi then provides appropriate verses for each of these: Genesis 32:12, 19; 33:2–3.

451. **third there is no need to pursue** "We can assume that he also has a present."

452. **one of those two...** Rabbi Yose just concluded that the anonymous Jew has prepared himself for both prayer and combat, and that he presumably possesses the third requirement for a journey: a present. But when the stranger does not respond to their greeting, Rabbi Ḥiyya declares that he actually lacks two things, since a present also

Rabbi Yose replied, "Perhaps he is engaged in prayer or reciting his learning so as not to forget it."[453]

They walked together, and that man did not speak with them. Later, Rabbi Ḥiyya and Rabbi Yose turned aside and engaged in Torah. As soon as the man saw them engaging in Torah, he drew near them and greeted them. He said, "Gentlemen, what did you suspect when you greeted me and I did not respond?"

Rabbi Yose replied, "Perhaps you were praying or reciting your learning."

He said to them, "May the blessed Holy One judge you favorably![454] But I will tell you: One day I was walking on the road, when a man came along and I greeted him. Well, that man was a robber and he attacked me and harmed me; if I hadn't overpowered him, I would have suffered greatly. Since that day, I vowed never to greet anyone except a righteous person, unless I knew him already, since otherwise he might harm me and overwhelm me by force. For it is forbidden to greet a wicked person, as is written: *There is no peace, says YHVH, for the wicked* (Isaiah 48:22).[455] When I saw you greeting me and I didn't respond, I suspected you because I didn't see a *mitsvah* on you.[456] At the same time, I was going over my learning. But now that I see you are virtuous, the way is smoothened for me!"

He opened, saying, "*A psalm of Asaph. Surely God is good to Israel, to the pure of heart* (Psalms 73:1). Come and see: The blessed Holy One formed right and left to conduct the world, one called good and the other called evil. The human being is composed of both of these, embracing all.[457] Other nations are com-

includes a greeting, neither of which this man has offered them.

The playful numerical phrasing has stumped commentators. *Sullam* reads "one of those three that he should possess, he does not," which makes good sense, but the word "three" has no support in the manuscripts, editions, or witnesses that I have examined. For other attempts at explanation, see Galante; *KP*; *MM*; *Nefesh David*; *MmD*.

453. **engaged in prayer...** And does not want to interrupt his prayer or study. On the halakhic issues involved here, see Vital; *KP*; *MmD*.

454. **May the blessed Holy One...** See BT *Shabbat* 127b: "Just as you judged me favorably, so may the Omnipresent judge you favorably."

455. **forbidden to greet...** To give a greeting of peace.

See *Kallah Rabbati* 3:1; *Sefer Ḥasidim*, ed. Margaliot, par. 51; above, pp. 35–36 at n. 250; *Zohar* 2:23b.

456. **I didn't see a *mitsvah*...** He did not see them wearing a *tallit*. Apparently, the two rabbis were wearing a small *tallit* beneath their outer garments.

See *OY*; Vital; *NO*; *NZ*; *MmD*. Cf. *Zohar* 3:186a, where a child refuses to approach Rabbi Yitsḥak and Rabbi Yehudah because they had not recited the *Shema*.

457. **right and left...** Good and evil each play a role in the world: good as a reward for virtuous living, and evil as punishment for sin. These two qualities manifest as the good and evil impulses within the hu-

posed of that evil, which is left; that is their side, for they are uncircumcised of heart and uncircumcised of flesh, thereby defiled.[458] But of Israel, what is written? *Surely God is good to Israel.*

"Now, if you say, 'To all of them,' not so! Rather, to those undefiled by evil, as is written: *to the pure of heart.*[459] For this is good and that is evil: good for Israel alone, and evil for other nations.[460] *Surely good to Israel*—to cleave to it, and thereby Israel cleaves to supernal mystery, mystery of faith, so that all becomes one."[461]

Rabbi Yose said, "Happy are we not to have mistaken you, since the blessed Holy One sent you to us!"[462]

He said further, "Because *God is good to Israel,* they have a share in this world and in the world that is coming, to see eye to eye the splendor of His glory, as is said: *For eye to eye they will see YHVH returning to Zion* (Isaiah 52:8)."

man being, who is challenged to make moral choices.

See *Bahir* 109 (163); above, p. 250 and n. 425.

458. **uncircumcised of heart...** See Ezekiel 44:7.

459. **Now, if you say, 'To all of them,'...** To all Israelites, regardless of their virtue.

See *Vayiqra Rabbah* 17:1; *Eikhah Rabbah* 3:9.

460. **for Israel alone...** The anonymous Jew may be taking the verse to mean: אך (*Akh*), *Only, to Israel is God good.* See Ibn Ezra, ad loc.

461. **cleave to it...** To goodness, and thereby join the divine realm.

462. **blessed Holy One sent you to us** The rabbis now recognize that the stranger has conveyed to them a gift of wisdom.

פרשת ויגש

Parashat Va-Yiggash

"HE APPROACHED" (GENESIS 44:18–47:27)

Rabbi El'azar opened, "*For You are our Father: though Abraham does not know us and Israel does not recognize us, You, YHVH, are our Father; our Redeemer from of old is Your name* (Isaiah 63:16). This verse has been established,[1] but come and see: When the blessed Holy One created the world, every single day performed a fitting act, on each day as required.[2] When the sixth day arrived and the human being was to be created, Torah approached Him, saying, 'This human being whom You [205b] wish to be created is bound to provoke You. If You are not slow to anger, better for him not to be created!'

"The blessed Holy One replied to her, 'Am I called *slow to anger* for no reason?'[3]

"Truly, all was created through Torah and all was perfected through Torah.[4] For before the blessed Holy One created the worlds, all the letters came before Him, every single letter entering in reverse order.[5]

"ת (*Tav*) entered, saying before Him, 'Do You wish to create the world by me?'

1. **verse has been established** See BT *Shabbat* 89b.

2. **every single day performed...** Each day symbolizes one of the cosmic days, the *sefirot* from *Ḥesed* through *Shekhinah*, which emanated one by one above, stimulating creation below.

3. **Torah approached Him...** See *Tanḥuma, Pequdei* 3; *Pirqei de-Rabbi Eli'ezer* 11; *Zohar* 3:35b, 69b.

God is frequently called *slow to anger*; see Exodus 34:6; Numbers 14:18. Cf. Judah's plea in the opening verse of this Torah portion (Genesis 44:18) that Joseph's *anger not flare.*

4. **created through Torah...** According to M *Avot* 3:14, Torah is the "precious instrument by which the world was created." See *Bereshit Rabbah* 1:1, in the name of Rabbi Osha'ya: "Torah says, 'I was the artistic tool of the blessed Holy One.'...The blessed Holy One gazed into Torah and created the world."

See *Zohar* 1:5a, 47a, 134a–b; 2:161a–b; 3:35b; Wolfson, *Philo,* 1:243–45.

5. **all the letters...** See the fuller account in *Zohar* 1:2b–3b; Vol. 1, p. 11, n. 80; above, pages 250–51.

"He replied, 'No, for by you the righteous are destined to die, as is written: והתוית תיו (*Ve-hitvita tav*), *Make a mark, upon the foreheads of the people*... (Ezekiel 9:4); and we have learned that it is written: *Begin with My sanctuary* (ibid., 6)—do not read ממקדשי (*mi-miqdashi*), *with My sanctuary*, but rather ממקודשי (*mi-mequddashai*), *with My sanctified ones*. Therefore, by you the world will not be created.'[6]

"The three letters ש, ק, ר (*shin, qof, resh*) entered, each on its own. The blessed Holy One said to them, 'You are not worthy to create the world, since you are the letters composing שקר (*sheqer*), lie, and a lie is unworthy to stand before Me.' This has been established.

"צ, פ (*Tsadi, peh*) entered, and so all of them until the letter כ (*kaf*). As soon as כ (*kaf*) descended from כתרא (*kitra*), the Crown, the upper and lower worlds trembled, etc.[7] Finally, all was established by the letter ב (*bet*), sign of ברכה (*berakhah*), blessing; thereby the world was formed and created.[8]

"Now, you might say that א (*alef*) is the head of all letters. However, simply because it indicates ארור (*arur*), cursed, the world was not created by it.[9] Even though א (*alef*) is a letter of supernal mystery,[10] in order not to provide an opening for the Other Side, called Cursed, the world was not created by it.[11] Rather, ב (*bet*) appeared, embracing blessing, and by it the world was formed and created.

"Come and see: *For You are our Father* (Isaiah, ibid.)—for by this rung the world was formed and created; by it the human being was created, issuing into the world.[12]

6. **destined to die...** See Ezekiel 9:3–4: *He* [YHVH] *called to the man dressed in linen with the scribe's kit at his waist, and* YHVH *said to him, "Pass through the city, through Jerusalem, and make a mark upon the foreheads of the people who moan and groan over all the abominations being committed in it."* In the old Hebrew script, the ת (*tav*) was shaped like an X, the simplest mark. Its purpose in Ezekiel was to distinguish the righteous from the rest of the population: only those bearing the mark escape death (ibid., 6). However, according to Rabbi Aḥa son of Rabbi Ḥanina, even the marked righteous were killed, since their silence in the face of the wicked implicated them.

See BT *Shabbat* 55a; *Zohar* 1:2b, 68a.

7. **כ (*kaf*) descended...** From the divine Crown, threatening the stability of all the worlds. The word "etc." refers to the full version of this story. See above, note 5.

8. **letter ב (*bet*)...** With which the Torah begins: בראשית (*Be-reshit*), *In the beginning*.

9. **indicates ארור (*arur*), cursed...** See *Bereshit Rabbah* 1:10.

10. **letter of supernal mystery** Symbolizing the entirety of the *sefirot*, or the first *sefirah*.

See *Zohar* 1:21a (Vol. 1, p. 161, n. 430); 3:73a; 193b; *ZḤ* 5c (*SO*); Moses de León, *Sefer ha-Rimmon*, 77 (and Wolfson's note); idem, *Sheqel ha-Qodesh*, 87–89 (111–12); Gikatilla, *Sha'arei Orah*, 103a; Galante; *NO*.

11. **Other Side...** The demonic realm.

12. ***You are our Father...*** In the *Zohar*, the second-person pronoun אתה (*attah*) sometimes refers to *Shekhinah*, who, being

"*Though Abraham does not know us* (ibid.)—for although the world stands upon him, he did not devote himself to us as he did to Ishmael, saying, *If only Ishmael might live in Your presence!* (Genesis 17:18).[13]

"*And Israel does not recognize us* (Isaiah, ibid.)—for all the blessings that he had to provide to his sons, he left to this rung to be conveyed.[14]

"*You, YHVH, are our Father* (ibid.)—for You stand by us constantly, blessing and caring for us like a father watching over his children, providing whatever they need.

"*Our Redeemer from of old is Your name*—for You are the *Redeemer*, called so: *the angel redeeming me* (Genesis 48:16), precisely! *Our Redeemer from of old is Your name—Your name*, precisely![15]

"We have learned: One does not pause between 'redemption' and prayer,[16]

more revealed than the other *sefirot*, can be addressed directly. Although *Shekhinah* is usually depicted as feminine, here She is seen as Father and architect of Creation. This reference to *Shekhinah* is linked with the previous teaching about the letter ב (*bet*) because that letter also symbolizes *Shekhinah*, who is בית (*bayit*), "house" of the world, and source of ברכה (*berakhah*), "blessing."

On *Shekhinah* as *attah*, see above, p. 213, n. 203. Cf. *Zohar* 3:290a (*IZ*). On *Shekhinah* as *bayit*, see *Zohar* 1:29a–b.

13. ***Abraham does not know us...*** In rabbinic literature, Abraham is described as a cosmic pillar and as the person for whose sake the world was created. Furthermore, his *sefirah* is *Ḥesed* (Love), and the reference to *ḥesed* in Psalms 89:3 is interpreted to mean *The world shall be built on* חסד (*ḥesed*), *love*.

On Abraham as cosmic pillar, see *Tanḥuma, Shemot* 19; *Tanḥuma* (Buber), *Shemot* 16 (both in the name of Rabbi Yehoshu'a son of Korḥah); *Shemot Rabbah* 2:6; Maimonides, *Guide of the Perplexed* 3:29; idem, *Mishneh Torah, Hilkhot Avodat Kokhavim* 1:2. See *Bereshit Rabbah* 12:9 (again in the name of Rabbi Yehoshu'a son of Korḥah), according to which the world was created for the sake of Abraham. On the interpretation of Psalms 89:3, see *Mekhilta, Shirta* 9.

The verse in Genesis 17 records Abraham's response after God promises him that Sarah, age ninety, will bear him a son. On Abraham's lack of compassion for Israel, see BT *Shabbat* 89b; *Midrash ha-Gadol*, Genesis 50:21 (citing Genesis 17:18). Cf. *Zohar* 2:32a.

14. ***Israel does not recognize us...*** When Israel (Jacob) offered blessings to his sons (as recounted in Genesis 49), he did not bless them directly but rather through *Shekhinah*.

See *Tanḥuma, Vayḥi* 16; *Tanḥuma* (Buber), *Vayḥi* 17; Ibn Ezra on Genesis 49:1; Rashi on Genesis 49:28; Naḥmanides on Exodus 25:3 and Deuteronomy 33:1; *Zohar* 1:248a–b; Galante; *KP*.

15. ***angel redeeming me... Your name...*** *Shekhinah* is known as "angel." Because She reveals the divine identity, She is also known as the divine name.

On *Shekhinah* as angel, see above, p. 167 and n. 516.

16. **One does not pause...** "Redemption" is the final blessing of the sitting prayer, which concludes: "Blessed are You, *YHVH*, who has redeemed Israel." According to BT *Berakhot* 4b, 9b, there should be no pause between this blessing and the beginning of the *Amidah*, the "standing" prayer—so central that it is known simply as "Prayer." According to Kabbalah, *Shekhinah* is adorned during the sitting prayer in preparation for Her union with *Tif'eret*, which takes place during the *Amidah*.

See *Zohar* 1:132b, 228b; 2:128b, 138b, 156a,

just as one does not pause between phylactery of the hand and phylactery of the head, for it is essential to show that all is one, as has been established."[17]

Rabbi Yitsḥak and Rabbi Yehudah were sitting one night and studying Torah. Rabbi Yitsḥak said to Rabbi Yehudah, "We have learned that when the blessed Holy One created the world, He formed the lower world on the pattern of the upper world, corresponding entirely to one another, and this is His glory above and below."[18]

Rabbi Yehudah said, "Certainly so! And He created the human being above all, as is written: *I made the earth and created humankind upon it* (Isaiah 45:12). *I made the earth*—obviously! 'Why did I make the earth?' Because *I created humankind upon it*, for he sustains the world, so that all will be indivisibly complete."[19]

He opened, saying, "*Thus says God, YHVH, who creates the heavens and stretches them out, who spreads out the earth and what emerges from it*... (ibid. 42:5).[20] This verse has been established,[21] but *Thus says God, YHVH*—the blessed Holy One, above, above, who *creates the heavens and stretches them out*, arraying them constantly, ceaselessly.[22]

"*Who spreads out the earth and what emerges from it*—Holy Land, bundle of life.

"*Who gives* נשמה (*neshamah*), *soul, to the people upon it*—*the earth* is the one who gives *soul*."[23]

200b, 216b; 3:195b; Moses de León, *Sefer ha-Rimmon*, 78–79; idem, *Sheqel ha-Qodesh*, 75–76 (96).

17. **phylactery of the hand . . . of the head . . .** The two *tefillin* (phylacteries) are bound respectively on the left arm (and hand) and on the head. In the *Zohar* these symbolize respectively *Shekhinah* and *Tif'eret*. By not pausing between binding both of them, one demonstrates the union of the divine couple.

See *Zohar* 1:14a, 132b; above, pp. 20–21, nn. 139–140.

18. **lower world on the pattern of the upper . . .** It is a general principle of Kabbalah that the physical universe reflects and manifests the splendor of the sefirotic realm. Through creation, God is glorified.

See *Zohar* 1:38a, 57b–58a, 129a, 145b, 156b, 158b; 2:15b (*MhN*), 20a (*MhN*), 48b, 82b, 144a, 251a (*Heikh*); 3:45b, 65b; Tishby, *Wisdom of the Zohar*, 1:273. Cf. Isaiah 43:7; BT *Yoma* 38a; *Avot* 6:11.

19. **sustains the world . . .** By living virtuously, the human being links the world below with the divine realm, ensuring both unity and sustenance.

20. ***Thus says God . . .*** The full verse reads: *Thus says God, YHVH, who creates the heavens and stretches them out, who spreads out the earth and what emerges from it, who gives breath to the people upon it and spirit to those who walk thereon.*

21. **This verse has been established** See *Bereshit Rabbah* 12:12.

22. **blessed Holy One, above, above . . .** *Binah*, who transcends the lower *sefirot*, emanated *Tif'eret* (known as *heavens*). The present tense of the verb *creates* implies that *Binah*'s creative flow never ceases.

23. ***earth* . . . Holy Land, bundle of life . . .** All of these refer to *Shekhinah*, who is the

Rabbi Yitsḥak said, "All is above, for from there issues soul of life to this *earth*, and *earth* grasps the soul, giving to all; for that flowing, gushing river conveys souls, conducting them into this *earth*, who grasps them, providing to all.[24]

"Come and see: When the blessed Holy One created the human being, He gathered his dust from the four directions of the world and formed his body on the site of the Temple below and emanated upon him a soul of life from the Temple above.[25]

"The soul comprises three aspects and therefore [206a] has three names, corresponding to supernal mystery: *nefesh, ruaḥ, neshamah*. *Nefesh*, as has been established, is lowest of all. *Ruaḥ* is sustenance, presiding over *nefesh*, a higher rung above her, sustaining her completely, fittingly. *Neshamah* is highest sustaining existence of all, prevailing over all, holy rung transcending all.[26]

"These three rungs are included within human beings—in those who attain devotion to their Lord. For at first, one possesses *nefesh*, a holy preparation by which a person is refined.[27] When one begins to purify himself on this rung, he is ready to be crowned with *ruaḥ*, a holy rung hovering over *nefesh*, by which a virtuous person is aroused. Once he is elevated by *nefesh* and *ruaḥ*, initiated into

reservoir of souls, providing them to humans on earth.

On the phrase "bundle of life," see 1 Samuel 25:29; Moses de León, *Sheqel ha-Qodesh*, 61 (75).

24. **All is above . . .** Rabbi Yitsḥak differs with his colleague, insisting that souls emerge from a higher source, *Binah*. They are then conveyed by the river of *Yesod* to *Shekhinah* (*earth*), who distributes them below.

On *Yesod* as the "flowing, gushing river," see above, p. 186 and n. 44; p. 204 and n. 156; pp. 206–7 and n. 172; p. 215 and n. 218; below, at note 132.

25. **gathered his dust . . .** The human being is a microcosm, including aspects of the entire world. Rabbi Yitsḥak is combining two midrashic motifs. See *Pirqei de-Rabbi Eli'ezer* 11: "He began gathering the dust of Adam [see Genesis 2:7] from the four corners of the earth." Cf. *Pirqei de-Rabbi Eli'ezer* 12: "He created him from a pure, holy site. From where did He take him? From the site of the Temple."

Here the four directions (south, north, east, and west) may symbolize the four elements (water, fire, air, and earth) or the four *sefirot Ḥesed, Gevurah, Tif'eret*, and *Shekhinah*. The human body is formed at the site of the Temple in Jerusalem, whereas the soul emanates from *Shekhinah*, the Temple above.

Cf. 2 Enoch 30:13; *Bereshit Rabbah* 14:8 (and Theodor's note); JT *Nazir* 7:2, 56b; BT *Sanhedrin* 38a–b; *Tanḥuma, Pequdei* 3; *Targum Yerushalmi*, Genesis 2:7; *Zohar* 1:34b, 130b; 2:23b, 24b; 3:83a; Moses de León, *Shushan Edut*, 344.

26. **soul comprises three aspects . . .** The three aspects of the soul are נפש (*nefesh*), "soul, life force"; רוח (*ruaḥ*), "spirit"; and נשמה ("breath, soul, soul-breath"). These correspond respectively to three sefirotic rungs: *Shekhinah, Tif'eret*, and *Binah*.

See *Zohar* 1:83a–b; 2:94b; 3:70b. Cf. *Bereshit Rabbah* 14:9. For an extensive discussion of the three aspects of the soul, see Tishby, *Wisdom of the Zohar*, 2:684–722.

27. **at first, one possesses *nefesh* . . .** This first level of soul provides physical vitality and stimulates spiritual growth.

perfection through serving his Lord, then *neshamah* alights upon him—supernal, holy rung prevailing over all—so that he is crowned by that rung. Then he is consummate, perfected on all sides, worthy of the world that is coming; he is beloved of the blessed Holy One, as is said: *Endowing those who love Me with existence* (Proverbs 8:21). Who are *those who love me*? Those who have a holy *neshamah*."[28]

Rabbi Yehudah said, "If so, look at what is written: *All that had the* neshamah *of the spirit of life in its nostrils, of all that was on dry land, died* (Genesis 7:22)!"[29]

He replied, "Certainly so! For there did not remain among them any of those who possessed a holy *neshamah*, such as Jared, Enoch, or all those righteous ones, whose merit could have saved the world from destruction, as is written: *All that had the* neshamah *of the spirit of life in its nostrils, of all that was on dry land, died*—they had already died and departed from the world; none of them remained to protect the world at that time.[30]

"Come and see: All are rungs, one above the other: *nefesh, ruaḥ, neshamah*—rung upon rung. First, *nefesh*, lowest rung, as we have said. Then, *ruaḥ*, hovering over *nefesh*, sustaining her. *Neshamah*, a rung transcending all, as has been established.

"*Nefesh*—*nefesh* of David, poised to receive *nefesh* from that flowing, gushing river.[31] *Ruaḥ*—*ruaḥ* presiding over it, and *nefesh* is sustained only by *ruaḥ*. This is the *ruaḥ* dwelling between fire and water; from here this *nefesh* is nourished.[32]

28. **consummate, perfected on all sides...** A human who attains *neshamah* reflects the fullness of the divine realm.

"The world that is coming" refers to the hereafter but also alludes to *Binah*, "the world that is constantly coming." See above, pp. 201–2, n. 141. In rabbinic literature the verse in Proverbs is applied to heavenly reward. See M *Avot* 5:19; *Uqtsin* 3:12; *Zohar* 1:6a; Vol. 1, p. 36, n. 249; Gikatilla, *Sha'arei Orah*, 93a–b.

29. **If so, look...** The verse in Genesis describes the death of all living beings during the Flood: *all that had* נשמת רוח חיים (*nishmat ruaḥ ḥayyim*), *the breath of the spirit of life,... died.* If the *neshamah* is so lofty and potent, how can the Torah state that the wicked generation of the Flood possessed it?

30. **Certainly so...** Rabbi Yitsḥak answers by explaining that the verse refers not to the wicked masses who perished in the Flood but rather to the righteous few (such as Jared and Enoch) who possessed this highest level of soul and died before the Flood, *on dry land.*

On Jared and Enoch, see Genesis 5:18–24; *Bereshit Rabbah* 25:1 (and Theodor's note); *Midrash Aggadah*, Genesis 5:18, 24. A fuller version of this question and answer appears in *ZḤ* 11d (*MhN*).

31. ***Nefesh*—*nefesh* of David...** The lowest level of soul corresponds to *Shekhinah*, also known as *Malkhut* (Kingdom), and symbolized by King David. She receives the *nefesh* from the river of *Yesod*.

See above at note 24. On the phrase נפש דוד (*nefesh david*), "soul of David," see 1 Samuel 18:1; 2 Samuel 5:8; *Zohar* 1:101a, 240a; 2:27a, 171a; 3:45b, 182a; Moses de León, *Shushan Edut*, 348; idem, *Sefer ha-Rimmon*, 43; idem, *Sheqel ha-Qodesh*, 61 (75).

32. ***Ruaḥ*—*ruaḥ* presiding...** The sec-

"*Ruaḥ* endures through the sustenance of another, higher rung, called *neshamah*, source of *nefesh* and *ruaḥ*. From there *ruaḥ* is nourished, and when *ruaḥ* receives, *nefesh* receives, and all is one. All draw near one another: *nefesh* to *ruaḥ*, *ruaḥ* to *neshamah*, and all is one.[33]

"Come and see: *He approached him* (Genesis 44:18)—world approaching world, to unite with one another, so that all becomes one. Because Judah is king and Joseph is king, they approach one another and unite."[34]

Rabbi Yehudah opened, "*See, the kings assembled; they advanced together* (Psalms 48:5). *See, the kings assembled*—Judah and Joseph, both whom were kings, and they approached one another to dispute.[35] For Judah had pledged himself to his father for Benjamin and was surety for him in this world and in the world that is coming. He therefore approached Joseph to argue with him concerning Benjamin, so that he would not be banned in this world and in the world that is coming, as is said: *I will be his pledge, from my hand you may seek him. If I do not bring him to you and set him before you, I will bear the blame before you for all time* (Genesis 43:9)—in this world and in the world that is coming.[36]

"So, *See, the kings assembled;* עברו (*averu*), *they advanced, together*—they became

ond level of soul corresponds to *Tif'eret,* who harmonizes the polar opposites *Ḥesed* and *Gevurah* (symbolized respectively by water and fire), and sustains *Shekhinah* (the divine *nefesh*).

See Moses de León, *Sefer ha-Rimmon,* 305.

33. **higher rung, called *neshamah*...** The highest level of soul corresponds to *Binah,* the divine mother and source of both *Tif'eret* and *Shekhinah*.

34. ***He approached him*...** The opening verse of this Torah portion reads: *Judah approached him* [Joseph] *and said, "Please, my lord, let your servant speak a word in my lord's hearing and let your wrath not flare against your servant, for you are like Pharaoh."* For Rabbi Yitsḥak, the brothers Judah and Joseph symbolize two divine realms, *Shekhinah* and *Yesod,* whose convergence creates cosmic harmony.

Joseph is described as "king" because he wielded royal authority in Egypt. On Judah as "king" of the tribes, see *Bereshit Rabbah* 84:17; 93:2; above, p. 132 and n. 301. Judah was also the ancestor of the Davidic dynasty. On Judah as a symbol of *Shekhinah,* see above, p. 134 and nn. 311–12. On Joseph as a symbol of *Yesod,* see above, p. 92, n. 50.

35. ***See, the kings*...** The context (Psalms 48:5–7) describes a failed attack on Jerusalem: *See, the kings assembled; they advanced together. As soon as they saw, they were astounded, they were terrified and fled; trembling seized them there, convulsions like a woman in labor.*

Here Rabbi Yehudah draws on *Bereshit Rabbah* 93:2, which applies the verses from Psalms to the encounter between Judah and Joseph, both of whom were kings. See the preceding note.

36. **Judah had pledged...** Judah had promised his father, Jacob, that he would return Benjamin safely—or else be culpable forever.

See *Bereshit Rabbah* 93:10; *Tanḥuma* (Buber), *Vayiggash* 4; *Midrash Aggadah,* Genesis 44:29; Rashi on Genesis 43:9 and 44:32; *NO*; *NZ*.

angry together, angering one another on account of Benjamin.[37] What is written? *As soon as they saw, they were astounded, they were terrified and fled; trembling seized them there* (Psalms, ibid, 6–7)—all who were there, all the other tribes.

"*Convulsions like a woman in labor* (ibid., 7)—because they feared to kill or to be killed, all on account of Benjamin. For Joseph was sold because of Judah, lost to his father; now he had pledged himself for Benjamin and he feared that he would be lost. Therefore, *Judah approached him* (Genesis 44:18).[38] [206b]

"*See, the kings assembled.* Here lies a mystery of faith! For when Will manifests and a cluster is crowned as one, two worlds join as one, meeting as one: this, opening treasures; that, gathering and absorbing. Then, *See, the kings assembled*—two holy worlds, upper world and lower world.[39]

"עברו (*Averu*), *They passed over, together.* Mystery of the matter: When they unite as one, *they passed over together,* for all sins of the world are not passed over and forgiven until they join as one, as is said: ועובר (*ve-over*), *and passing over, transgression* (Micah 7:18). So, *they passed over together*—those sins passed away and were forgiven because then all faces shone and all sins were passed over."[40]

Rabbi Ḥiyya said, "This mystery pertains to the restorative rite of offering. For when a sacrifice is offered, all are provided for, each one fittingly; then all is linked as one, all faces shine, and a single cluster appears. Then *the kings assembled,* meeting as one to forgive all sins and pass over them; then *the kings assembled,* linked as one; *they passed over together,* to illumine all faces, so that all becomes a single will.[41]

"*As soon as they saw, they were astounded.* Do you imagine that this refers to those kings? Rather, to masters of judgment, who delight in executing the

37. **עברו (*averu*), *they advanced,*... became angry...** Drawing still on *Bereshit Rabbah* 93:2, Rabbi Yehudah plays with עבר (*avar*), "to advance, pass," and עברה (*evrah*), "anger."

38. **Joseph was sold because of Judah...** On Judah's advice. See Genesis 37:26–28.

39. **when Will manifests...** When the primal *sefirah, Keter* (known as Will), manifests its compassion, all of the *sefirot* unite. The expression *the kings* refers to two realms: the world of the male (from *Binah* through *Yesod*) and the world of the female (*Shekhinah*), one pouring the rich flow of emanation into the other. See Moses de León, *Sefer ha-Rimmon,* 69; *OY.*

40. **עברו (*Averu*), *They passed over*...** Now Rabbi Yehudah plays on another meaning of the verb עבר (*avar*), which can mean not only "advance, pass" but also "pass over, forgive (sin)." When the male and female *sefirot* unite, the resultant harmony overwhelms and absolves sin. See *Zohar* 3:66a.

41. **restorative rite of offering...** The sacrifices offered in the Temple in Jerusalem stimulated the union of the *sefirot,* ensuring a flow of blessing to all realms and the forgiving of sin.

See *Zohar* 3:4b–5a; Tishby, *Wisdom of the Zohar,* 3:878–95.

judgment assigned to them. Then, when kings met—both of those worlds sharing one will—*as soon as they saw, they were astounded. As soon as they saw* the will of those two worlds, *they were astounded, they were terrified and fled*—for all those masters of judgment are overwhelmed and removed from the world, unable to prevail, their existence and dominion eliminated."[42]

Rabbi El'azar said, "*Judah approached him.* Why Judah? It had to be so, because he was surety, as is said: *For your servant became pledge for the lad to my father* (Genesis 44:32).[43] Mystery of the matter: Judah and Joseph had to converge as one, for Joseph is Righteous, Judah is king; so *Judah approached him,* because their convergence as one engendered many benefits for the world: bringing peace to all the tribes, bringing peace between them, revitalizing Jacob's spirit, as is said: *The spirit of Jacob their father revived* (Genesis 45:27). So this drawing near was essential for all those aspects above and below."[44]

Rabbi Abba opened, "*Beautiful in loftiness, joy of all the earth, Mount Zion,*
266 *summit of the north, city of the great king* (Psalms 48:3). *Beautiful in loftiness*—Joseph the Righteous, of whom is written *Joseph was beautiful in form and beautiful in appearance* (Genesis 39:6).[45]

"*Joy of all the earth*—joy and delight above and below.[46]

"*Mount Zion, summit of the north*—for in his share stood the tabernacle of Shiloh.[47]

"*Mount Zion*—Jerusalem.[48]

42. **Do you imagine...** It is not *the kings* (the male and female *sefirot*) who are astounded and terrified, but rather the harsh powers of judgment. When *the kings* unite, bestowing good will and forgiveness, these powers of judgment flee in terror.

43. **surety...** See above, p. 264 and n. 36.

44. **Joseph is Righteous, Judah is king...** The convergence of the two brothers stimulated the union of *Yesod* (known as Righteous) and *Shekhinah* or *Malkhut* (Kingdom), thereby spreading harmony and peace. See above, p. 264 and n. 34.

45. ***Beautiful in loftiness*—Joseph...** By verbal analogy between the two verses in Psalms and Genesis (*beautiful in loftiness... beautiful in form*), Rabbi Abba indicates that the subject of both is the same, namely, Joseph —or rather, Joseph's *sefirah, Yesod.*

See *Tanḥuma, Vayiggash* 10; *Tanḥuma* (Buber), *Vayiggash* 11; *Zohar* 3:5a.

46. **joy and delight...** Above, *Yesod* consummates divine union, bringing joy to *Shekhinah* (*earth*). Below, Joseph provides sustenance for the famished masses (Genesis 42:6).

According to earlier, rabbinic exegesis, *joy of all the earth* refers to the joyous relief of atonement provided by offering sacrifice in the Temple. See *Vayiqra Rabbah* 1:2; *Shemot Rabbah* 36:1; *Midrash Tehillim* 48:2; *ZḤ* 28d (*MhN*).

47. **tabernacle of Shiloh** Which stood in the northern part of the land of Israel in the territory of Ephraim son of Joseph.

See *Bereshit Rabbah* 93:12; BT *Megillah* 16b.

48. ***Mount Zion*—Jerusalem** This may be simply a separate comment (*MM*). According to *OY*, it implies that just as Jerusalem (site of the Temple) is called Mount

"*Summit of the north*—surely so, above and below![49]

"*City of the great king*—a site arrayed facing *the great king*: supreme King of all, Holy of Holies, source of all radiance, all blessings, all joy.[50] From there all faces shine and the Temple is blessed, and when it is blessed, blessings issue to all the world, for from there the whole world is blessed."[51]

Rabbi Yehudah and Rabbi Yose met in Kefar Ḥanan. While they were sitting at their inn, a certain man arrived, preceded by a loaded donkey, and he entered the house. Meanwhile, Rabbi Yehudah was saying to Rabbi Yose, "Look, we have learned that King David used to doze like a horse, sleeping just a little. So how could he rise at midnight? It was such a short duration, wouldn't he have awoken even before a third of the night?"[52]

He replied, "When evening entered, he would sit with all the princes of his household, discussing words of Torah. Afterward, he slept until midnight, when he awoke and engaged in the worship of his Lord with songs and praise."

At this moment, the man said, [207a] "This matter that you are discussing, is that what it means? There is a mystery here, for King David lives and endures

Zion, so Joseph's share (site of the tabernacle of Shiloh) is called Mount Zion.

49. ***Summit of the north*... above and below** Above, *Yesod* derives passion from *Gevurah*, identified with the north. Below, sacrifices are slaughtered north of the altar (according to rabbinic tradition). Alternatively, below, Shiloh is located in the northern part of the land of Israel.

See above, note 47; Leviticus 1:11; *Pesiqta Rabbati* 41; *Shemot Rabbah* 36:1; *Midrash Tehillim* 48:2.

50. **facing *the great king*...** *Yesod* receives the flow of emanation from *Binah*, known as *the great king* and Holy of Holies.

On *Binah* as *great king*, see *Zohar* 1:151a. On *Binah* as Holy of Holies, see *Zohar* 2:4a, 239b. Cf. below, p. 384, n. 417.

51. **Temple is blessed...** The Temple in Jerusalem symbolizes *Shekhinah*, source of blessing for all.

52. **King David used to doze...** According to tradition, King David awoke each midnight for study and prayer.

See Psalms 119:62: *At midnight I rise to praise You for Your just laws*. See BT *Berakhot* 3b: "Rabbi Osha'ya said in the name of Rabbi Aḥa, 'David said, "Midnight never passed me by in my sleep."' Rabbi Zeira said, 'Till midnight, he used to doze like a horse; from then on, he became mighty as a lion.' Rav Ashi said, 'Till midnight, he engaged in Torah; from then on, in songs and praises.'... But did David know the exact moment of midnight?... David had a sign, for... Rabbi Shim'on the Ḥasid said, 'There was a harp suspended above David's bed. As soon as midnight arrived, a north wind came and blew upon it, and it played by itself. He immediately arose and engaged in Torah until the break of dawn.'"

In the *Zohar* this legendary custom is expanded into a ritual: all kabbalists are expected to rise at midnight and adorn *Shekhinah* with words of Torah and song in preparation for Her union with *Tif'eret*. See Psalms 119:62; above, p. 77 and n. 518.

Here Rabbi Yehudah wonders about King David's nightly schedule. If he dozed like a horse, then he must have woken up well before midnight. See Scholem, "Parashah Ḥadashah," 436–37.

forever and ever![53] King David was vigilant all his days never to taste the taste of death, for sleep is one-sixtieth of death, and because of his domain, which is alive, he would sleep for only sixty breaths. For until sixty breaths less one, one is alive; from then on, a person tastes the taste of death and is dominated by the side of impure spirit.[54]

"This, King David guarded against, so as not to taste the taste of death, not to be ruled by the Other Side.[55] For sixty breaths less one is mystery of life above —until sixty breaths, namely, sixty supernal breaths, which are their mystery, upon which life depends. From here below is mystery of death.[56]

"So King David calculated the night's duration in order to remain alive, to prevent the taste of death from overpowering him. When night divided, David stood poised in his domain, because as midnight arouses along with the holy crown, David must not be bound to another domain, the domain of death.[57] For when night divides and supernal holiness arouses, if a person lies asleep in bed—not rousing to regard the glory of his Lord—then he is bound to the
268 mystery of death, clinging to another domain. Consequently, King David always rose, alive facing alive, and did not lie asleep, tasting the taste of death. So he dozed like a horse for sixty breaths, but not completely."[58]

Rabbi Yehudah and Rabbi Yose came and kissed him. They asked, "What is your name?"

He replied, "Ḥizkiyah."

53. **King David lives...** See the saying attributed to Rabbi Yehudah ha-Nasi in BT *Rosh ha-Shanah* 25a (based on Psalms 89:38): "David, King of Israel, lives and endures." See *Zohar* 1:82b.

In Kabbalah, King David symbolizes *Shekhinah,* the totality of eternal divine life.

54. **King David was vigilant...** According to BT *Berakhot* 57b, "Sleep is one-sixtieth of death." According to BT *Sukkah* 26b (in the name of Abbaye), David's sleep was like that of a horse, which lasts for sixty breaths. That passage discusses daytime sleep, but see the statement of Rabbi Zeira (quoted above, note 52): "Till midnight, he [David] used to doze like a horse."

Here the anonymous guest combines these rabbinic traditions, suggesting that David slept for only sixty (actually, fifty-nine) breaths in order to escape the demonic, fatal aspect of sleep, which is identified with the last of the sixty breaths. See *Nefesh David.*

55. **Other Side** The demonic realm.

56. **sixty supernal breaths...** The sixty breaths of sleep correspond to "their mystery": sixty supernal breaths, angelic powers beneath *Shekhinah,* which convey divine life to the worlds below. The last of these sixty powers borders on the demonic realm and therefore tastes of death.

See Tishby, *Wisdom of the Zohar,* 2:816.

57. **David calculated...** He determined the precise moment of midnight ("when night divided") and exactly how long he should sleep. Rising at midnight, he entered his domain, the realm of *Shekhinah,* who is known as *Malkhut* (Kingdom) and symbolized by the crown. See *OY.*

58. **sixty breaths, but not completely** Only fifty-nine. See above, note 54.

They said, "May your Torah be firm and strong!"[59]

They sat down. Rabbi Yehudah said, "Since you have begun for us, tell us some more of these sublime secrets that you utter!"

He opened, saying, "*YHVH founded the earth by wisdom; He establishes the heavens by understanding* (Proverbs 3:19). When the blessed Holy One created the world, He saw that it could not exist unless He created Torah, because from her issue all laws above and below; through her, upper and lower beings exist, as is written: *YHVH founded the earth by wisdom.* Through Wisdom, He actualized the existence of everything in the world, all issuing from there.[60]

"Alternatively, *YHVH founded the earth by wisdom*: the upper world was created only from Wisdom; the lower world was created only from Wisdom, all emerging from upper Wisdom and from lower Wisdom.[61]

"*He establishes the heavens by understanding.* Why *establishes*? Because He *establishes*, every single day ceaselessly.[62] They were not arranged at one time; rather, every day He arranges them. This corresponds to the mystery that is written: *The heavens are not pure in His eyes* (Job 15:15).[63] Now, would you imagine that this indicates a defect in the heavens? Rather, their significance, because of the intense love and desire that the blessed Holy One feels toward them and His fondness for them. For even though He arrays them every single day, in His eyes they do not seem fittingly arrayed, because of His love for them and His desire to shine upon them constantly, ceaselessly; for the world that is coming radiates scintillating lights every day continually, incessantly, illumining them. So, *they are not pure in His eyes.* It is not written merely *they are not pure*, but rather, *they are not pure in His eyes.* Therefore, *He establishes the heavens by understanding.*[64]

59. **firm and strong** Playing on the name Ḥizkiyah and its root, חזק (*ḥazaq*), "strong."

60. **could not exist . . .** Without the stabilizing influence of the laws of Torah (identified with *wisdom*), the world could not endure.

See *Bereshit Rabbah* 1:4 (quoting this same verse); above, note 4.

61. **upper world . . . lower world . . .** The divine world extending from *Binah* through *Shekhinah* emanated from *Ḥokhmah* (Wisdom), and the physical world below emerged from *Shekhinah*, who is known as "lower Wisdom."

On *Shekhinah* as "lower Wisdom," see *Zohar* 1:141b, 232b; 2:235b; 3:61b, 182b, 289a (*IZ*), 290a (*IZ*), 296a (*IZ*); Moses de León, *Sheqel ha-Qodesh*, 75 (95); idem, *Sod Eser Sefirot Belimah*, 382.

62. **Why *establishes*? . . .** Since the verse begins in the past tense (*YHVH founded*), why does it switch to the present tense: *He establishes*? Because the present tense implies a continuous process of emanation. See above, p. 261 and n. 22.

63. ***The heavens are not pure . . .*** The full verse reads: *Behold, He puts no trust even in His holy ones; the heavens are not pure in His eyes.*

64. **world that is coming . . . *understanding*** *Binah* (Understanding) is also known as "the world that is coming," constantly flow-

"Who are *the heavens*? Mystery of the patriarchs. And mystery of the patriarchs is Jacob, their totality, for Jacob is Glory of the Patriarchs, poised to illuminate the world.[65] Because he ascends into the world that is coming, one beautiful branch issues from him, radiating all lights, all abundance, and anointing oil to illumine earth.[66] Who is this? Joseph the Righteous, who provides abundance to the whole world, from whom the world is nourished.[67] Therefore, whatever the blessed Holy One does in the world is all through supernal mystery, all as it should be."

Meanwhile, Rabbi El'azar arrived. As soon as he saw them, he said, "Surely, *Shekhinah* is here! What are you engaged in?"[68]

They told him [207b] the whole episode. He said, "He has surely spoken well! However, those sixty breaths are really sixty breaths of life, both above and below. From there below are sixty other breaths, all from the side of death, the rung of death above them; they are called *dormita*, wakeless sleep, all tasting of death.[69]

ing and radiating. Through Her, *the heavens* are established.

See above, note 28; pp. 201–2, n. 141.

65. **Who are *the heavens*?...** These symbolize the sefirotic triad of *Ḥesed, Gevurah,* and *Tif'eret,* who are also symbolized respectively by the three patriarchs: Abraham, Isaac, and Jacob. Jacob is the culmination of all three, just as *Tif'eret* harmonizes and completes the polar opposites *Ḥesed* and *Gevurah*.

See *Bereshit Rabbah* 76:1: "Rabbi Pinḥas said in the name of Rabbi Re'uven, '... The chosen of the patriarchs is Jacob, as is said: *For Yah has chosen Jacob for Himself* (Psalms 135:4).'"

See *Zohar* 1:119b, 133a, 144b, 150a, 152a (*ST*), 163b, 171b, 172b, 173b, 180a, 207a; 2:23a.

66. **Because he ascends...** *Tif'eret* returns to His source in *Binah* ("the world that is coming") and then generates a new branch extending toward *Shekhinah* ("earth") and the earth below.

67. **Joseph the Righteous...** The branch issuing from *Tif'eret* is *Yesod,* symbolized by Joseph. Just as Joseph provided grain for the famished masses, so *Yesod* nourishes the whole world.

See *Zohar* 3:270b; above, note 46. On Joseph the Righteous as a symbol of *Yesod,* see above, p. 92, n. 50.

68. **Surely, *Shekhinah* is here...** Because Rabbi El'azar saw all three of them engaged in Torah. See M *Avot* 3:6: "Rabbi Ḥalafta from Kefar Ḥananya says, 'If ten are sitting engaged in Torah, *Shekhinah* dwells among them... even five... even three... even two... even one.'" Note the similarity between Kefar Ḥananya and the site of the encounter here: Kefar Ḥanan, mentioned above, p. 267.

For the sequence "Meanwhile, so-and-so arrived.... He said, 'What are you engaged in?'" see BT *Yevamot* 105b; *Gittin* 31b. Cf. *Zohar* 1:245a; 2:5a.

69. **sixty breaths of life...** Sixty animating powers in the upper worlds and sixty corresponding breaths here below. In addition, beneath the sixty holy breaths above are sixty demonic breaths, presided over by the power of death.

Rabbi El'azar's depiction differs from the one offered by the guest Ḥizkiyah, who described only one set of sixty otherworldly breaths, the last of which is linked with the demonic realm. See above, p. 268 and n. 56.

The word דורמיטא (*dormita*) appears as a variant reading in *Bereshit Rabbah* 17:5 as

"Consequently, King David clung to those sixty breaths of life, and from then on, he did not sleep at all, as is written: *I will not give sleep to my eyes, or slumber to my eyelids* (Psalms 132:4). So, he spoke well, for David the living would rise on the side of life, not on the side of death."[70]

They all sat engaging in Torah, joined as one.

Rabbi El'azar opened, saying, "*O YHVH, God of my salvation, by day I call out, by night before You* (ibid. 88:2). Come and see: King David used to rise at midnight and engage in Torah, in songs and praises, delighting the King and *Matronita*. This is the joy of faith on earth, for this is the praise of faith appearing on earth.[71] Above, countless supernal angels open joyously in song, praising variously in the night from all sides. Correspondingly, on earth below, if someone praises the blessed Holy One at night, He and all those holy angels praising Him listen to the one praising Him on earth. For this praise is consummate, elevating the glory of the blessed Holy One from below, singing the joy of union.[72]

"Come and see: King David said, '*O YHVH, God of my salvation,* [*by day I call out, by night before You*].' *O YHVH, God of my salvation.* When is He *my salvation*? On the day following the night that I offer praise to You—then He is *my salvation* by day.

"Come and see: Whoever praises his Lord by night with praise of Torah is strengthened potently by day on the right side, for a single thread issues from the right and is then drawn upon him, vitalizing him.[73] Of this he said *O YHVH, God of my salvation, by day I call out, by night before You.* Therefore he said, *It is not the dead who praise Yah* (ibid. 115:17). *Not the dead*—because the living must praise the Living, not the dead, as is written: *It is not the dead who praise Yah....*

one type of תרדמה (*tardemah*), "deep sleep." See the apparatus in Theodor's edition; *Yedei Moshe* and *Ḥiddushei ha-Radal*, ad loc.; *Arukh ha-Shalem*, s.v. *marmata*; *Zohar* 3:142b (*IR*); *ZḤ* 23b (*MhN*). Cf. Latin *dormio*, "to sleep"; *dormito*, "to be sleepy."

70. **King David clung to those sixty...** He slept for a full sixty breaths—not just fifty-nine, as Ḥizkiyah had said. Still, Rabbi El'azar concludes that Ḥizkiyah spoke well.

See above, note 54; *KP*; *MM*; *Nefesh David*.

71. **King David used to rise at midnight...** Delighting the divine couple, *Tif'eret* and His *Matronita* (matron), *Shekhinah;* their union is the focus of true faith. See above, p. 267, n. 52.

72. **listen to the one praising...** The praise offered by humans from below brings particular delight to God. See above, p. 81 and n. 541.

73. **Whoever praises... is strengthened...** See BT *Ḥagigah* 12b: "Resh Lakish said, 'To one who engages in Torah by night, the blessed Holy One extends a thread of love by day, as is said: *By day YHVH directs His love.* Why? Because *in the night His song is with me.*'" *His song* is the song of Torah.

Here Rabbi El'azar traces the thread of חסד (*ḥesed*), "love," to the *sefirah* of *Ḥesed* on the right side. See above, p. 81 and n. 542; pp. 190–91 at n. 75.

But we will bless Yah (ibid., 17–18), for we are alive and have no share at all in the side of death.[74] Hezekiah said, *The living, the living—he will praise You* (Isaiah 38:19), for the living approaches the Living.[75] King David is living, and he approaches Life of the Worlds.[76] Whoever approaches Him is alive, as is written: *You, cleaving to YHVH your God, are alive every one of you today!* (Deuteronomy 4:4). And similarly: *Benayahu son of Yehoyada, son of a living man* (2 Samuel 23:20)."[77]

Following him, that Jew opened, saying, "*You shall eat and be satisfied and bless YHVH your God* (ibid. 8:10).[78] Now, don't we bless the blessed Holy One before we eat? Look, we have to hasten in the morning and arrange His praise fittingly, blessing His name before greeting anyone else in the world.[79] And it is written: *You shall not eat over the blood* (Leviticus 19:26)—one is forbidden to eat before blessing his Lord.[80] Yet now it is written: *You shall eat and be satisfied and bless!*[81]

74. **he said... he said...** David, the traditional composer of Psalms, sang these verses. Here, Rabbi El'azar understands *the dead* as referring to those who sleep the night away and taste death, missing the opportunity to praise God at midnight and be vitalized.

75. **Hezekiah...** King Hezekiah of Judah, who uttered these words after recovering from illness. Note that his name is identical with that of the rabbis' study partner, Ḥizkiyah.

76. **King David is living...** David rose at midnight and maintained his link with the realm of divine life. On "Life of the Worlds," see above, p. 185, n. 35.

77. ***Benayahu...*** A loyal follower of King David who attains mythic status in the *Zohar.*

See BT *Berakhot* 18a–b: "Rabbi Ḥiyya said..., 'The righteous are called "living" even in their death, as is said: *Benayahu son of Yehoyada, son of a living man....* Do you mean to say that all other people are sons of dead men? Rather, *son of a living man,* for even in his death he was called *living...*'"

See *Zohar* 1:6a, 132a, 136a, 164a; Gikatilla, *Sha'arei Tsedeq,* 7a.

78. ***You shall eat...*** The full verse reads: *You shall eat and be satisfied and bless YHVH your God for the good land that He has given you.*

Rabbinic tradition cites this verse as the prooftext for the Grace after Meals. See *Tosefta, Berakhot* 6:1; BT *Berakhot* 21a.

79. **before greeting anyone...** See BT *Berakhot* 14a: "Rav said, 'Whoever greets his fellow before praying has, as it were, made him into a cult site...' Samuel said, 'Why have you esteemed this person and not God?'"

See *Zohar* 1:228a, 248a; 2:182a, 226b; 3:190b; *ZḤ* 90d (*MhN, Rut*).

80. ***over the blood...*** The full verse reads: *You shall not eat over the blood. You shall not divine nor interpret omens.* Originally, eating "over the blood" probably referred to a pagan rite of divination, in which a ritual meal was consumed over a pit or receptacle containing blood, perhaps with the idea that spirits of the dead could be conjured up from the blood. Later, rabbinic tradition understood the verse as a prohibition to eat the flesh of the sacrifice before the blood had been offered to God on the altar, or to eat an animal before it was completely dead.

Here, Ḥizkiyah's interpretation follows the midrashic reading presented in the name of Rabbi Eli'ezer son of Ya'akov in BT *Bera-*

"However, this is a blessing of prayer for unification, and that is a blessing for nourishment—demonstrating satisfaction before the rung of faith, as is fitting, and then blessing it fittingly, so that this rung of faith will be saturated, blessed, and filled with joy from supernal life, as is necessary, in order to provide us with sustenance.[82]

"For the nourishment of a human being is as difficult for the blessed Holy One as splitting the Red Sea![83] Why? Because sustenance of the world derives from above, as we have learned: 'Children, life, and sustenance [do not depend on merit but on *mazzala,* flux of destiny].' Therefore it is difficult for Him, since the matter depends on *mazzala,* from which issue sustenance, life, and children; nourishing the world is difficult for Him because it does not come under His dominion until He is blessed.[84]

"Similarly couplings of the world, which are difficult for Him—all because the heavenly curtain performs no function at all, especially regarding these matters existing above in another realm. Therefore He must be blessed.[85]

khot 10b: "What is the meaning of the verse *You shall not eat over the blood*? You shall not eat before you have prayed for your blood [i.e., your life]."

See *Sifra, Qedoshim* 6:1, 90b; *Targum Yerushalmi,* Leviticus 19:26; BT *Sanhedrin* 63a; Rashbam and Ibn Ezra on Leviticus 19:26; Radak on 1 Samuel 14:32; Naḥmanides on Leviticus 19:26; Milgrom, *Leviticus,* 2:1685–86; Alter, *Five Books of Moses,* 629.

81. **Yet now it is written...** Implying that it *is* permitted to eat before praying.

82. **blessing... for unification... for nourishment...** The prayer that must be recited even before eating in the morning stimulates the union of the *sefirot,* whereas the "blessing of nourishment," recited after each meal, focuses on *Shekhinah,* rung of faith. When one blesses Her while satisfied after eating, he ensures that She will be nourished from above and sustain the world below.

The expression ברכתא דמזונא (*birkheta dimzona*), "blessing of food (or of nourishment)," is the *Zohar*'s Aramaic rendering of the Hebrew term ברכת המזון (*birkat ha-mazon*), "the blessing of food," Grace after Meals.

83. **difficult... as splitting the Red Sea** See BT *Pesaḥim* 118b (in the name of Rabbi El'azar son of Azariah); *Bereshit Rabbah* 97:3 (p. 1245) (in the name of Rabbi Yehoshu'a son of Levi); *Zohar* 2:52b, 170a; 3:292b (*IZ*); *ZḤ* 86d (*MhN, Rut*).

84. **Children, life, and sustenance...** מזלא (*Mazzala*) means "constellation, planet, planetary influence, zodiacal sign, destiny, fortune, guardian angel." See BT *Mo'ed Qatan* 28a: "Rava said, 'Life, children, and sustenance do not depend on merit but on *mazzala,* destiny.'"

In the *Zohar, mazzala* is associated with the root נזל (*nzl*), "to flow," and often refers to the flow of emanation from *Binah* through *Yesod.* See above, p. 96 and n. 77; p. 215 at n. 220.

Here "the blessed Holy One" and the divine pronoun "He" refer to *Shekhinah,* who is normally described in feminine terms. Ḥizkiyah's point is that it is difficult for *Shekhinah* to nourish the world because the source of nourishment is *mazzala,* the flux of destiny issuing from a higher divine realm. Until *Shekhinah* is blessed, He (or She) does not control or channel this flow to the world.

85. **couplings of the world...** *Shekhinah* also finds it difficult to arrange matches between human couples. The "heavenly cur-

"Come and see: All couplings of the world are difficult for this rung; because when holy coupling occurs, all [208a] souls issue from this flux above—that flowing, gushing river—and when desire appears from below upward, souls fly forth and are all conveyed, embracing male and female, to this rung. Afterward, it separates them, each and every one to its appropriate place. Later, it is difficult for this rung to unite them as originally, because they unite only according to human behavior, and all depends upon above.[86]

"So, this is as difficult for Him as the splitting of the Red Sea, for the splitting of the sea—opening paths within it—occurs above: as pathways are opened within, it is split open.[87]

"Therefore all depends upon above, and we must bless Him and give Him power from below, so that He will be blessed from above and empowered fittingly. Consequently it is written: *You shall bless* את יהוה (*et YHVH*) (Deuteronomy, ibid.)—*et*, precisely!"[88]

tain" refers here to *Shekhinah*, last of the *sefirot*, who possesses nothing of His (or Her) own and cannot function properly until receiving the flow from above.

On the difficulties of divine matchmaking, see *Bereshit Rabbah* 68:4; *Vayiqra Rabbah* 8:1; *Pesiqta de-Rav Kahana* 2:4; BT *Sotah* 2a; *Zohar* 1:229a; 2:170b. On the "curtain," see BT *Ḥagigah* 12b: "Rabbi Yehudah said, 'There are two רקיעים (*reqi'im*), firmaments [or: heavens]...' Resh Lakish said, 'Seven, namely, *Vilon* (Curtain), *Raqi'a*, *Sheḥaqim*, *Zevul*, *Ma'on*, *Makhon*, *Aravot*. 'Curtain' performs no function at all except entering in the morning and leaving in the evening, and renewing each day the act of creation.'"

See *Zohar* 1:233b; 3:239b; Moses de León, *Shushan Edut* 338; idem, *Sefer ha-Rimmon*, 6, 257; idem, *Sheqel ha-Qodesh*, 12 (15), 50 (61).

86. **when holy coupling occurs...** When *Shekhinah* unites with Her partner, *Tif'eret*, souls issue from the gushing river of *Yesod*. Stimulated by Her passion from below, the stream of souls flows into Her—each one androgynous, not yet differentiated as male or female. Only later does *Shekhinah* separate the soul into male and female halves, each half destined for a male or female body on earth. Although the halves yearn to reunite, it is often difficult for *Shekhinah* to match them up, because finding one's intended partner depends upon virtuous behavior.

See Plato, *Symposium* 189d–191d; *Zohar* 1:85b (Vol. 2, p. 46 and n. 354), 91b–92a; above, p. 107 and n. 147; below, at notes 132–33; 3:43b, 283b, 296a–b (*IZ*); Tishby, *Wisdom of the Zohar*, 3:1355–56. On the original androgynous nature of Adam, see *Bereshit Rabbah* 8:1. On the link between human conduct and finding one's mate, see BT *Sotah* 2a: "When Resh Lakish opened the discussion of the straying wife, he said as follows: 'A man is only coupled with a woman according to his deeds.'" Cf. *Zohar* 1:229a.

87. **splitting of the sea... occurs above...** The Red Sea symbolizes *Shekhinah*, who when opened from above, channels the flow of emanation to the worlds below, conveying nourishment and marital bliss.

See above, p. 209 and n. 185; *Zohar* 2:52b.

88. **we must bless Him... *et*, precisely** We must bless *Shekhinah*, empowering Him (or Her).

See *Zohar* 3:270b–271a (*Piq*); Moses de León, *Sefer ha-Rimmon*, 34, 362 (and Wolfson's notes). On *Shekhinah*'s name את (*et*), see above, p. 118, n. 217.

"Toward this site, one should demonstrate satisfaction and a radiant face.[89] Toward the Other Side, when it prevails in the world, one should demonstrate famishment, for that rung is hungry, so it is fitting to show famishment, not satisfaction, since satisfaction does not prevail in the world.[90] Therefore, *You shall eat and be satisfied and bless* et *YHVH your God.*"

Rabbi El'azar said, "Certainly so, and so it should be!"

Rabbi Yehudah said, "Happy are the righteous, whose convergence brings peace to the world, for they know how to actualize union and they converge to expand peace in the world.[91] Look, until Joseph and Judah approached one another, there was no peace; as soon as they drew near as one, they extended peace in the world—and joy increased above and below! Just as Joseph and Judah approached, all those tribes became as one together with Joseph, and their approach amplified peace in the world, as we have established, for it is written: *Judah approached him* (Genesis 44:18)."[92]

Joseph could not restrain himself before all who stood by him (Genesis 45:1).[93]

Rabbi Ḥiyya opened, "*He distributes freely to the poor; his righteousness endures forever; his horn will be exalted in honor* (Psalms 112:9). Come and see: The blessed Holy One created the world and enthroned the human being as king.[94] From this human diverge various types in the world: some righteous and some wicked, some foolish and some wise. All of them endure in the world, rich and poor, all so that these will become worthy through those: the righteous through the wicked, the wise through the foolish, the rich through the poor, all

89. **demonstrate satisfaction...** In order to stimulate a flow of blessing to *Shekhinah* from above. See above, p. 273 and n. 82.

90. **Toward the Other Side... famishment...** When the demonic realm prevails, depriving the world of nourishment, one should not appear satisfied but rather famished.

See above, p. 211 and n. 192; *Zohar* 3:92b.

91. **convergence brings peace...** Through their virtuous partnership, they unify the divine realm and bring harmony to the world.

See M *Sanhedrin* 8:5: "The assembling of the wicked harms them and harms the world, whereas that of the righteous benefits them and benefits the world."

92. **Joseph and Judah approached...** These two brothers symbolize, respectively, *Yesod* and *Shekhinah*, whose union ensures peace and well-being.

See above, p. 264 and n. 34; p. 266 at n. 44.

93. ***Joseph could not restrain...*** The full verse reads: *Joseph could not restrain himself before all who stood by him, and he cried, "Send everyone away from me!" And no one stood with him when Joseph made himself known to his brothers.*

94. **human being as king** See Genesis 1:28: *God blessed them, and God said to them, "Be fruitful and multiply and fill the earth and conquer it, and have dominion over the fish of the sea and the birds of the heavens and every living creature that crawls upon the earth."* See *ZḤ* 17d (*MhN*).

through one another.[95] The rich become worthy through the poor, for look, thereby one attains eternal life and is joined to the Tree of Life! Furthermore, the charity that he performs endures forever, as is written: *his* צדקה (*tsedaqah*), *charity, endures forever*."[96]

He distributes freely to the poor. Rabbi El'azar said, "When the blessed Holy One created the world, He established it upon a single pillar, named Righteous.[97] This Righteous One is the sustenance of the world, watering and nourishing all, as is written: *A river issues from Eden to water the garden, and from there it divides* [*and becomes four riverheads*] (Genesis 2:10). What does this mean: *it divides*? The garden absorbs all the nourishment and watering of that river, and then that watering is dispersed to the four directions of the world. How many there are waiting to be watered and nourished from there, as is said: *The eyes of all wait for You, and You give them their food at its proper time* (Psalms 145:15)! So, *He distributes freely to the poor*—Righteous One.[98]

"*His righteousness endures forever*—Assembly of Israel, who thereby abides in mystery of peace, in consummate existence.[99]

"*The wicked will see and be vexed* (ibid. 112:10)—the wicked kingdom.[100]

"Come and see: Kingdom of Heaven is the holy house, sustaining all the poor

95. **these will become worthy through those...** The righteous can reform the wicked and lead them to repentance; the wise can enlighten the foolish; the rich can support the poor.

96. **צדקה (*tsedaqah*), *charity*...** The word means both "righteousness" and "charity."

97. **established it upon a single pillar...** See BT *Ḥagigah* 12b, in the name of Rabbi El'azar son of Shammu'a: "[The earth stands] upon a single pillar named Righteous, as is said: וצדיק יסוד עולם (*ve-tsaddiq yesod olam*), *The righteous one is the foundation of the world* (Proverbs 10:25)." The biblical expression is understood in rabbinic and kabbalistic literature according to this mythical interpretation, although it literally means *The righteous one is an everlasting foundation.* In Kabbalah, *Yesod* (Foundation) is known as *Tsaddiq* (Righteous One).

See *Bahir* 71 (102); Azriel of Gerona, *Peirush ha-Aggadot,* 34.

98. ***A river issues...*** *Yesod* conveys the flow of emanation to *Shekhinah* (*the garden*). From Her, heavenly and earthly creatures are nourished.

99. **Assembly of Israel... mystery of peace...** By receiving the flow of emanation, *Shekhinah* (Assembly of Israel) is joined with *Yesod,* known as "ever" and "peace." The people of Israel below share in the peace and abundance.

On *Shekhinah* as Assembly of Israel, see above, pp. 122–23, n. 237. On *Yesod* as "peace," see above, p. 183, n. 21; and as "ever," see *Zohar* 1:50a, 150a; cf. 1:247b; 2:22a. The term צדקה (*tsedaqah*) usually refers to *Tif'eret,* but here it apparently signifies *Shekhinah*. See *OY*; *NO*.

100. ***wicked will see...*** They will be upset and jealous.

This verse immediately follows the one just discussed by Rabbi Ḥiyya and Rabbi El'azar. In rabbinic literature the "wicked kingdom" refers to the Roman empire, and in the *Zohar* the phrase sometimes refers to the Gentile oppressors of Israel. See above, p. 253 and n. 437.

beneath the shadow of Her dwelling.[101] And this Righteous One is called 'charity collector,' graciously nourishing all, as is written: *He distributes freely to the poor.* Consequently, collectors of charity receive a reward equal to all those who give charity.[102]

"Come and see: *Joseph could not restrain himself before all who stood by him*—all those who stand poised to be nourished and watered by him.[103]

"*No one stood with him* [208b] *when Joseph made himself known to his brothers* (Genesis 45:1). אתו (*Itto*), *With him*—Assembly of Israel.[104] *His brothers*—other chariot-powers, of whom is written *For the sake of my brothers and friends* (Psalms 122:8).[105]

"Alternatively, *No one stood with him*—when the blessed Holy One comes to couple with Assembly of Israel.[106]

"*When Joseph made himself known to his brothers*—when the blessed Holy One joins with Israel, for they alone receive, unaccompanied by other nations. For example, *On the eighth day you shall have a convocation* (Numbers 29:35), for at this time the blessed Holy One is alone in a single bond with Israel, of whom is written *For the sake of my brothers and friends*, as we have established."[107]

Rabbi Yeisa explained the verse as referring to the time when the blessed Holy One will raise Assembly of Israel from the dust and will seek Her vengeance

101. **Kingdom of Heaven...** *Shekhinah* is known as *Malkhut* (Kingdom) and is identified with the Temple.

On the phrase "the shadow of Her dwelling," see *Targum Onqelos*, Genesis 19:8.

102. **charity collector...** *Yesod* collects the riches from above and distributes them below, via *Shekhinah*. See Moses de León, *Sefer ha-Rimmon*, 112.

See BT *Bava Batra* 9a, in the context of charity: "Rabbi El'azar said, 'Greater is one who causes [others] to do good than the doer.'" Cf. *Shabbat* 118b.

103. ***Joseph could not restrain...*** Joseph symbolizes *Yesod*. Those waiting to be nourished are apparently the angelic princes representing other nations of the world.

On Joseph as *Yesod*, see above, p. 92, n. 50.

104. **אתו (*Itto*), *With him*—Assembly of Israel** *Yesod*'s partner, *Shekhinah* (Assembly of Israel), is symbolized by the word את (*et*), whose literal meaning here is "with." See above, p. 118, n. 217.

105. **chariot-powers...** Angelic powers accompanying *Shekhinah*.

The verse in Psalms reads: *For the sake of my brothers and friends, I say, "Peace be within you."* It is addressed to Jerusalem, which symbolizes *Shekhinah*.

106. **blessed Holy One comes...** When *Tif'eret* unites with *Shekhinah*, they are fittingly alone. See *Zohar* 3:66b.

107. ***On the eighth day...*** The seven-day festival of *Sukkot* is immediately followed by an additional holy day known as *Shemini Atseret* (Eighth Day of Convocation). During *Sukkot*, Israel offers seventy bullocks, thereby assuring that the seventy heavenly princes and their earthly nations will be sustained. Then on the eighth day, Israel celebrates alone with God.

See *Eikhah Rabbah* 1:23; *Pesiqta de-Rav Kahana* 28:9; BT *Sukkah* 55b; *Zohar* 1:64a–b; 3:104b; Tishby, *Wisdom of the Zohar*, 3:1251–53.

from the other nations.[108] "Of that time is written *From the nations, no one was with Me* (Isaiah 63:3), and here is written *No one stood with him when Joseph made himself known to his brothers*, as is said: *He lifted them and carried them all the days of old* (ibid., 9)."[109]

Joseph could not restrain himself. Rabbi Ḥizkiyah opened, "*A song of ascents. To You I lift my eyes, O You who dwell in heaven* (Psalms 123:1). This verse has been established and explained.[110] But come and see: *To You I lift my eyes*, and it is written: *I lift my eyes to the mountains* (ibid. 121:1). However, this is above; that is below.

"*I lift my eyes to the mountains*—above, to draw blessings down from above, from those supernal mountains, drawing blessings from them to Assembly of Israel, to be blessed thereby.[111]

"*To You I lift my eyes*—hoping and waiting for those blessings that descend there.[112]

"*O You who dwell in heaven*—for all Her strength, power, and sustenance lie *in heaven*, because when Jubilee opens the fountains of all those gates, they are all *in heaven*, and once heaven absorbs all those lights radiating from Jubilee, it nourishes and waters Assembly of Israel by means of a certain Righteous One.[113] When this one arouses toward Her, how many are poised on all sides

108. **raise Assembly of Israel...** *Shekhinah*'s divine partner will redeem Her along with the people of Israel.

109. ***From the nations, no one was with Me...*** No nation or its heavenly prince will stand in God's way.

110. **This verse has been established...** See *Sifrei*, Deuteronomy 346; *Zohar* 1:229a; 3:265b.

111. ***to the mountains*—above...** In this verse, David the Psalmist seeks to draw blessings to *Shekhinah* from the sefirotic triad of *Ḥesed, Gevurah,* and *Tif'eret*, known collectively as *the mountains.*

The triad of *Ḥesed, Gevurah,* and *Tif'eret* is symbolized by the triad of patriarchs (Abraham, Isaac, and Jacob), who are identified with "mountains" in midrashic literature. See *Sifrei*, Deuteronomy 353; *Vayiqra Rabbah* 36:6; *Shir ha-Shirim Rabbah* on 4:6; *Tanḥuma, Ki Tissa* 28; *Shemot Rabbah* 15:4; *Zohar* 1:87a; 2:58b.

112. ***To You I lift my eyes*—hoping...** In this verse, David yearns for the blessings that have reached *Shekhinah*.

113. **for all Her strength...** *Shekhinah*'s strength and sustenance derive from *Tif'eret* (*heaven*), who in turn receives these from *Binah*, known as Jubilee. From *Tif'eret*, the radiant flow proceeds through *Yesod* (Righteous One) to *Shekhinah* (Assembly of Israel).

According to the Bible, every seventh year is a Sabbatical (שמטה [*shemittah*], "release"), during which the land must lie fallow, and at the end of which all debts are remitted (Leviticus 25:1–24; Deuteronomy 15:1–3). In Kabbalah the Sabbatical symbolizes *Shekhinah*, seventh of the lower *sefirot*.

In the biblical cycle, after seven Sabbaticals comes the Jubilee, proclaimed every fifty years, when slaves are released and land reverts to its original owner (Leviticus 25:8–55). In Kabbalah the Jubilee symbolizes *Binah*, who in general is characterized by the number fifty, based on BT *Rosh ha-Shanah* 21b, where Rav and Shemu'el teach: "Fifty

to be watered and blessed from there, as is said: *The young lions roar for prey, seeking their food from God* (ibid. 104:21)![114] Then She ascends into mystery of mysteries fittingly, receiving delights from Her Husband when they are alone, as is said: *No one stood with him*, and similarly: *Send everyone away from me!* (Genesis 45:1).[115] After She receives delights from Her Husband, they are all watered and nourished, as is said: *They water all beasts of the field; wild asses quench their thirst* (Psalms, ibid., 11)."[116]

Rabbi Yose explained the verse in connection with Elijah, as is written: *He cried out to YHVH and said, "O YHVH, have You brought evil even upon the widow with whom I am staying, by causing her son to die?"* (1 Kings 17:20).[117] "Come and see! There were two who uttered words against the One on high: Moses and Elijah. Moses said, *Why* הרעות (*hare'ota*), *have You done evil, to this people?* (Exodus 5:22). Elijah said, הרעות (*Hare'ota*), *Have You brought evil, by causing her son to die?* Both of them spoke the same word.[118]

"Why? It is really a mystery. Moses said, *Why have You done evil?* Why? Because the Other Side was authorized to rule over Israel. *Have you done evil?*—have You authorized the side of evil to rule over them. Elijah said, *Have You brought evil by causing her son to die?*—You authorized the side of evil to seize this one's soul. This is הרעות (*hare'ota*), *You have done/brought evil*; it is all one mystery.

"Come and see: Elijah said *with whom I am staying* because the blessed Holy One had told Elijah, *I have commanded a widow there to sustain you* (1 Kings, ibid., 9).[119] And whoever nourishes and supports someone in need—especially

gates of בינה (*binah*), understanding, were created in the world, all of which were given to Moses except for one, as is said: *You made him little less than God* (Psalms 8:6)." *Binah* is the source of redemption and liberation, specifically the Exodus from Egypt. See *Zohar* 1:21b, 47b–48a; 2:46a, 83b, 85b, 147b, 151a, 153b–154b, 240b; 3:262a.

114. **When this one arouses...** When *Yesod* arouses toward *Shekhinah*, numerous angelic powers await their sustenance.

See *Zohar* 1:244a; 3:191a.

115. **when they are alone...** The biblical references to Joseph's being alone allude to the intimacy of *Yesod* and *Shekhinah*. See above, page 277.

116. **they are all watered...** Following the union of the divine couple, the angels are nourished.

117. **in connection with Elijah...** God had told the prophet to go to Zarephath near Sidon, where a certain widow would provide for him. Elijah performed a miracle there, ensuring that her flour and oil did not run out. Later, the widow's son became mortally ill and stopped breathing, but Elijah revived him. See 1 Kings 17:7–24.

Rabbi Yose does not establish a connection between the story of Elijah and Genesis 45:1 but only alludes to an associative link. See below, note 124.

118. **Moses and Elijah...** Concerning Moses, see BT *Berakhot* 32a, quoting Numbers 11:2. Cf. Numbers 11:11.

119. ***I have commanded a widow...*** The full verse reads: *Rise, go to Zarephath of Sidon, and stay there; I have commanded a widow there to sustain you.*

in days of famine—embraces the Tree of Life, engendering life for himself and his children, as we have established. Now Elijah said, 'Whoever sustains one soul in the world attains life and grasps the Tree of Life; yet now the Tree of Death, the side of evil, reigns over the widow whom You commanded to nourish me!' Therefore, *have You brought evil.*[120]

"Now, you might say that evil is not committed against a human being by the blessed Holy One.[121] Come and see: When a person goes toward the right, the protection of the blessed Holy One constantly accompanies him, and no one else can dominate him; evil is subdued before him and cannot prevail. As soon as the protection of the blessed Holy One is removed from him—because [209a] he clings to evil—then that evil, seeing him unprotected, dominates him and comes to destroy him; then he is authorized and seizes souls.[122]

"Moses said, *Why have You done evil?*—for the other, evil side had been empowered to rule over Israel, who became enslaved to him.[123]

"Alternatively, *Why have You done evil?*—for he saw so many of them die, delivered to the side of evil.

"Come and see: When good—on the right—arouses, all joy, goodness, and blessings appear, and all is secretly silent, as has been established: '"Blessed be the name of His glorious Kingdom forever and ever!"—in a whisper.' A secret, for then is union, fittingly."[124]

120. **Whoever sustains one soul...** See M *Sanhedrin* 4:5 (Kaufmann MS): "Whoever preserves a single soul—Scripture considers him to have preserved an entire world."

The Tree of Life often symbolizes *Tif'eret*. The expression "Tree of Death" derives from *Seder Eliyyahu Rabbah* 5, where the Tree of Knowledge of Good and Evil is called the Tree of Death, because when Adam and Eve ate of its fruit, death ensued. See Genesis 2:17.

The concluding sentence here means "Therefore, Elijah said, [*O YHVH,*] *have You brought evil* [*even upon the widow with whom I am staying, by causing her son to die?*]" See *Pirqei de-Rabbi Eli'ezer* 33, and David Luria, ad loc., n. 6.

121. **evil is not committed...** See *Bereshit Rabbah* 51:3, in the name of Rabbi Ḥanina son of Pazzi: "Nothing evil descends from above."

122. **authorized...** See the description of Satan's activities in BT *Bava Batra* 16a: "He descends and leads astray, ascends and arouses wrath, obtains authorization and seizes the soul."

See above, p. 179 at n. 588.

123. **other, evil side had been empowered...** Moses saw the Egyptian bondage as a manifestation of the power of evil.

124. **Blessed be the name...** This wording constitutes the second line of the *Shema* and is traditionally recited silently or in a whisper. Here this mode of recital is understood as appropriate to the intimacy of sefirotic union, which is the kabbalistic focus of the *Shema*. "Kingdom" refers to *Shekhinah*, known as *Malkhut* (Kingdom), and by contemplating this line, the kabbalist prepares *Shekhinah* for joining Her divine partner.

See BT *Pesaḥim* 56a; *KP*. Here, apparently, Rabbi Yose understands the secret intimacy of the divine couple as related to Genesis 45:1: *And no one stood with him when Joseph made himself known to his brothers.* See above, note 117; Galante; *Nefesh David.*

Rabbi Ḥiyya said, "Now, whatever Elijah decreed, the blessed Holy One fulfilled, as when he decreed that heaven not send down rain or dew.[125] Why, then, did he fear Jezebel, who threatened him: *By this time tomorrow, I will make your life like the life of one of them* (1 Kings 19:2)? He was immediately afraid and fled for his life!"[126]

Rabbi Yose replied, "They have already established that the righteous do not want to trouble their Lord wherever harm is obvious. For example, with Samuel, as is written: '*If Saul hears, he will kill me.*' He replied, '*Take a heifer with you*' (1 Samuel 16:2). For the righteous do not want to trouble their Lord wherever harm is present. Here too, once Elijah saw that harm was present, he did not want to trouble his Lord."[127]

He said to him, "I have heard a word. For look, of Elijah it is not written ויירא (*Va-yira*), *He was frightened, and he fled for his life*, but rather וירא (*Va-yar*), *He saw* (1 Kings, ibid., 3).[128] He saw a sight. And what did he see? He saw that the Angel of Death had been following him for many years, yet he had not been delivered into his hand.[129] Now, וילך לנפשו (*va-yelekh le-nafsho*), *he went to his soul*. What does this mean? He went to the sustenance of soul. Who is that? Tree of Life, to cleave there.[130]

125. **decreed that heaven not send down rain...** See 1 Kings 17:1. Cf. BT *Mo'ed Qatan* 16b: "*The righteous one rules the awe of God* (2 Samuel 23:3).... Rabbi Abbahu said, '...I [God] rule over humanity. Who rules over Me? The righteous one. For I issue a decree and he abolishes it.'"

126. **Jezebel, who threatened him...** Ahab's wife threatened to avenge the deaths of the prophets of Baal, whom Elijah had killed. See 1 Kings 18:40.

127. **righteous do not want to trouble...** In the book of Samuel, God commands the prophet to go and anoint one of Jesse's sons (David) as king. This verse reads: *Samuel said, "How can I go? If Saul hears, he will kill me." YHVH replied, "Take a heifer with you, and say, 'I have come to sacrifice to YHVH.'"* Samuel fears that King Saul will kill him for the subversive act of anointing another as king; the sacrifice serves to disguise Samuel's mission.

Here Rabbi Yose suggests that Samuel did not want to trouble God by making it necessary for Him to miraculously save him from Saul's wrath. God's response obviates the need for a miracle. Similarly, Elijah fled from Jezebel because he did not want to trouble God for a miracle.

See BT *Pesaḥim* 8b; *Ta'anit* 24a; *Qiddushin* 39b; *Midrash Tehillim* 92:8; *Zohar* 1:230a.

128. **it is not written...** The verse reads: וירא (*Va-yar*), *He saw, and he rose and fled for his life.* Instead of וירא (*va-yar*), *he saw*, some biblical manuscripts read ויירא (*va-yira*), *he was frightened.* This alternative reading, which fits the context well, is also reflected in the Septuagint and adopted by most translations. Here, however, Rabbi Ḥiyya highlights the Masoretic reading and offers a corresponding interpretation.

129. **Angel of Death had been following him...** Elijah's extraordinary nature is soon clarified. The image of the frustrated Angel of Death may also allude to the legend that Elijah is identical with Phinehas, who flourished in the days of Moses. See *KP*; below, note 147.

130. **וילך לנפשו (*va-yelekh le-nafsho*), *he went to his soul*...** The clause is usually

"Come and see: Everywhere else it is written את נפשו (*et nafsho*), *his soul*, yet here is written אל נפשו (*el nafsho*), *to his soul*.[131] I have heard this secret from Rabbi Shim'on, who said: All souls of the world issue from that flowing, gushing river, and all of them are gathered by the bundle of life.[132] When Female conceives from Male, they all inhabit desire of both sides through desire of Female for Male. And when desire of Male issues passionately, those souls are of greater vitality, suffused with passionate desire of the Tree of Life. Elijah was vitalized by that passion more than other humans, and therefore it is written: *el nafsho, to his soul*, and not *et nafsho*—since *et nafsho* is Female.[133]

"Now, you might say אל האשה (*El ha-ishshah*), *To the woman, He said* (Genesis 3:16). Well, this is entirety of male and female; when she is within the male, then, *el ha-ishshah, to the woman, He said*. Whereas, את האשה (*et ha-ishshah*), *the woman*—female alone, not including male.[134]

"Similarly, *el nafsho*—Male alone; *et nafsho*—Female alone. Because he was on the side of Male more than all other inhabitants of the world, he endured more

understood to mean *he fled for his life*, but Rabbi Ḥiyya interprets it hyperliterally. The Tree of Life symbolizes *Tif'eret*, who animates and sustains the soul.

131. **Everywhere else...** The expression את נפשו (*et nafsho*), *his soul*, appears numerous times in the Bible, including once regarding Elijah (in the very next verse, 1 Kings 19:4), whereas the expression אל נפשו (*el nafsho*), *to his soul*, occurs only here.

132. **All souls of the world...** Issue from the river of *Yesod* and flow into *Shekhinah*, known as "bundle of life."

On *Yesod* as a river conveying the soul, see above, p. 262 and n. 24. The image of "bundle of life" derives from 1 Samuel 25:29: *The soul of my lord will be bound in the bundle of life*. See *Zohar* 1:65b, 224b; Moses de León, *Sheqel ha-Qodesh*, 60–61 (75).

133. **When Female conceives from Male...** When *Shekhinah* conceives from *Tif'eret* (via *Yesod*), their mutual desire engenders the soul. If the desire of the Male (symbolized by the Tree of Life) dominates, then the soul possesses greater vitality. In Elijah's case, the divine masculine component was especially dominant, as indicated by the unusual expression אל נפשו (*el nafsho*), *to his soul*—apparently because the near-homonym אל (*el*) means "power" (as in Genesis 31:29; Deuteronomy 28:32; Micah 2:1). The more common expression את נפשו (*et nafsho*), *his soul*, alludes to *Shekhinah*, the Female, who is known as את (*et*). See above, p. 118, n. 217.

See *Zohar* 1:85b; 3:296a–b (*IZ*); above, p. 107 and n. 147.

134. **Now, you might say...** If the word אל (*el*) denotes the masculine, then why in Genesis is it written אל האשה (*el ha-ishshah*), *to the woman*? The full verse reads: *To the woman He said, "I will greatly increase your birth pangs, in pain you will bear children. Your desire will be for your man, and he will rule over you."*

Rabbi Ḥiyya replies to his own question by explaining that the wording *el ha-ishshah* implies the incorporation of the female within the male as a single unit. On the other hand, when the Bible is referring to a woman alone it uses the expression את האשה (*et ha-ishshah*), *the woman*, as in Genesis 12:14 or Numbers 5:18–30.

See *OY*. On the motif of the female contained within the male, see Wolfson, *Circle in the Square*, 80–85.

vitally and did not die like all others, for he derived entirely from the Tree of Life, not from dust. So he ascended and did not die according to the way of all the earth, as is written: *Elijah ascended in a whirlwind to heaven* (2 Kings 2:11).[135]

"Come and see what is written: *suddenly a chariot of fire and horses of fire appeared* [*and separated the two of them*] ... (ibid.)—for then body was stripped from spirit, and he ascended, unlike the rest of the earth, and endured as a holy angel, like other holy supernal beings. He carries out missions in the world, as has been established, for miracles performed in the world by the blessed Holy One are performed by him.[136]

"Come and see what is written: *he asked* את נפשו (*et nafsho*), *for his soul* (1 Kings 19:4).[137] At first, וילך לנפשו (*va-yelekh le-nafsho*), *he went to his soul* (ibid., 3), as has been said: for sustenance.[138] But here, *et nafsho*—for death, the tree in which death abides.[139] There, the blessed Holy One appeared to him, as

135. **endured more vitally...** Elijah did not die a normal death—in fact, he did not die at all—because he derived from the masculine realm (*Tif'eret*, Tree of Life) rather than the feminine realm (*Shekhinah*, symbolized by dust).

On *Shekhinah* as dust, see above, p. 28, n. 189. The full verse in Kings reads: *As they were walking along and talking, suddenly a chariot of fire and horses of fire appeared and separated the two of them, and Elijah ascended in a whirlwind to heaven.*

136. **body was stripped from spirit...** Elijah became pure spirit and was transformed into an angel. Rabbi Ḥiyya may be interpreting the phrase *separated the two of them* as referring not to the separation of Elijah from his disciple, Elisha, but rather to the separation of Elijah's spirit from his body.

In Jewish tradition, Elijah became associated with the Messianic age (Malachi 3:23–24), and in rabbinic literature he is described as "still existing" (BT *Bava Batra* 121b) and revealing divine secrets to righteous humans (BT *Bava Metsi'a* 59b). In Kabbalah mystical experiences are known as revelations of Elijah. See Scholem, *On the Kabbalah*, 19–21; below, pp. 308–9 and n. 36; *Zohar* 1:1b; 1:151a; 3:221a, 231a, 241b; *ZḤ* 59d; 62c (*ShS*), 63d (*ShS*), 70d (*ShS*), 73c (*ShS*).

Various sources allude to Elijah's heavenly or angelic status. See *Midrash Tehillim* 8:7: "*The bird of heaven* (Psalms 8:9)—this is Elijah, who flies through the world as a bird." In *Targum*, Ecclesiastes 10:20, and *Ma'yan Ḥokhmah* (*Beit ha-Midrash*, 1:60) Elijah is identified as "Master of Wings."

See BT *Berakhot* 4b; *Pirqei de-Rabbi Eli'ezer* 29, and David Luria, ad loc., nn. 66–67; *Zohar* 1:46b, 151b, 245b; 2:197a–b; 3:68a–b, 88b; *ZḤ* 84c–d (*MhN, Rut*); Moses de León, *She'elot u-Tshuvot*, 60–63, 68–71; and Cordovero's critique of De León in *Pardes Rimmonim* 24:14.

137. ***he asked...*** The full verse reads: *He himself went a day's journey into the wilderness, and came to a solitary broom bush and sat down under it, and asked for his soul to die. He said, "Enough! Now, O YHVH, take my soul, for I am no better than my fathers."*

138. **At first...** See above, note 130.

139. ***et nafsho*—for death...** The word *et* indicates *Shekhinah* (see above, note 133), who is also symbolized by the Tree of Death. Earlier (above, page 280), this tree signifies the realm of evil, but here it symbolizes *Shekhinah*: if She is separated from the other *sefirot* by human sin, the vivifying flow of emanation is cut off and death dominates.

See above, note 120; *Zohar* 1:12b, 35b–36a, 51a–52a, 53b; 3:157a. On the relation between

is said: *Go out and stand on the mountain*... (1 Kings 19:11). What is written? *After the earthquake—fire; YHVH was not in the fire. After the fire—a sound of sheer silence* (ibid., 12): innermost realm, from which all lights radiate.[140]

"What is written? *When Elijah heard, he wrapped his face in his mantle. And behold, a voice addressed him, saying, 'Why are you here, Elijah?' He replied, 'I have been very zealous'* (ibid., 13–14).[141]

"The blessed Holy One said to him, 'How long will you be zealous for Me? You have locked the door so that [209b] death has no dominion over you, and the world cannot endure you along with human beings.'[142]

"He replied, *For the Children of Israel have forsaken Your covenant* (ibid., 14).[143]

"He said, 'By your life, wherever My children fulfill the holy covenant, you will be present there!' As has been said, because of this a chair is prepared for Elijah, who appears there.[144]

Shekhinah and the demonic realm, see Scholem, *On the Mystical Shape of the Godhead*, 189–92; Tishby, *Wisdom of the Zohar*, 1:373–79; Patai, *The Hebrew Goddess*, 249, 251–54.

140. ***sound of sheer silence*: innermost realm...** *Binah*, the hidden and unperceived source of all the lower *sefirot*.

See *Zohar* 1:98b; 2:81b; 3:30b. The context in Kings reads: *He said, "Go out and stand on the mountain before YHVH." And behold, YHVH was passing by, and a great, mighty wind splitting mountains and shattering rocks before YHVH; YHVH was not in the wind. After the wind—an earthquake; YHVH was not in the earthquake. After the earthquake—fire; YHVH was not in the fire. After the fire—a sound of sheer silence.*

141. ***When Elijah heard*...** The verses read: *When Elijah heard, he wrapped his face in his mantle and went out and stood at the entrance of the cave. And behold, a voice addressed him, saying, "Why are you here, Elijah?" He replied, "I have been very zealous for YHVH, God of Hosts, for the Children of Israel have forsaken Your covenant, torn down Your altars, and killed Your prophets by the sword. I alone am left, and they are seeking to take my life."*

142. **locked the door...** Meaning, "You have barred death from attacking you." The idiom derives from BT *Sanhedrin* 113a, where it pertains to Elijah in a different context.

The world "cannot endure" Elijah because of his extreme zeal.

143. ***For the Children of Israel*...** See above, note 141.

144. **By your life...** God commands Elijah to see with his own eyes that Israel has not forsaken the covenant, namely, the covenant of circumcision. At a ritual circumcision, a special chair is placed at the right of the *sandaq* ("godfather") and the *mohel* (circumciser) declares: "This is the chair of Elijah, may his memory be a blessing."

According to *Pirqei de-Rabbi Eli'ezer* 29, when the Israelites neglected the covenant of circumcision, "Elijah, may his memory be a blessing, was passionately zealous and adjured the heavens not to send down dew or rain upon the earth. Jezebel heard and sought to kill him. Elijah immediately prayed before the blessed Holy One. The blessed Holy One said to him, 'Are you better than your ancestors? Jacob fled [from Esau] and escaped.... Moses fled [from Pharaoh] and escaped.... David fled [from Saul] and escaped....' Elijah immediately fled from the land of Israel and escaped [to Horeb].... The blessed Holy One appeared to him and said, '*Why are you here, Elijah?*' He answered, '*I have been very zealous* [*for YHVH, God of Hosts, for the Children of Israel have*

"Come and see the consequences of Elijah's word, as is written: *I will leave in Israel seven thousand—all the knees that have not knelt to Baal*... (ibid., 18).[145] The blessed Holy One said to him, 'From now on, the world cannot endure you along with human beings. *And Elisha son of Shaphat of Abel-meholah, anoint as prophet in your stead* (ibid., 16)—here is another prophet for My children. As for you, ascend to your site!'[146]

"Come and see: Every person who is zealous for the blessed Holy One cannot be dominated by the Angel of Death as can other human beings. Peace endures for him, as they have established, as is written concerning Phinehas: *I hereby grant him My covenant of peace* (Numbers 25:12)."[147]

He fell upon the neck of his brother Benjamin and wept, and Benjamin wept on his neck (Genesis 45:14).

Rabbi Yitsḥak said, "They have established that he wept over the first Temple and over the second Temple."[148]

He opened, saying, "*Your neck is like the Tower of David, built in terraces; a thousand bucklers hang upon it, all the shields of the warriors* (Song of Songs 4:4). What is *the Tower of David*? Literally, *the Tower*

forsaken Your covenant].' The blessed Holy One said, 'You are always zealous! You were zealous in Shittim on account of sexual immorality [Numbers 25; Elijah is identified with Phinehas]..., and here too you are zealous. By your life! Israel will not enact the covenant of circumcision until you see it with your own eyes.' Because of this the sages ordained that a seat of honor be arranged [at every circumcision] for the Angel of the Covenant [Elijah; see Malachi 3:1]."

See *Halakhot Gedolot* (according to *Shibbolei ha-Leqet* 376:6); *Sefer Ḥasidim*, ed. Wistinetzki, par. 585; *Zohar* 1:13a, 93a; 2:190a; *Shulḥan Arukh, Yoreh De'ah* 265:11; Ginzberg, *Legends*, 6:338, n. 103.

145. **consequences of Elijah's word...** Because Elijah zealously accused the Israelites of forsaking the covenant and spurning God, nearly all of them were killed.

The full verse reads: *I will leave in Israel seven thousand—all the knees that have not knelt to Baal and every mouth that has not kissed him.* See the preceding verse, and above, note 141.

146. **here is another prophet...** Whom the world can bear. Elijah, meanwhile, will ascend and be transformed into an angel in heaven. See *Mekhilta, Pisḥa* 1; above, note 136.

147. **Phinehas...** Phinehas zealously defended God's honor by killing an Israelite man and his forbidden Midianite sexual partner. See Numbers 25:1–15.

Phinehas's zeal prefigures that of Elijah, with whom he is identified. See *Targum Yerushalmi*, Exodus 6:18; Numbers 25:12; *Tanḥuma, Pinḥas* 1; *Bemidbar Rabbah* 21:3; *Pirqei de-Rabbi Eli'ezer* 47; *Zohar* 2:190a; 3:214a, 215a (*RM*); *ZḤ* 84c (*MhN, Rut*); Origen on John 6:7; Ginzberg, *Legends*, 6:316–17, n. 3. Cf. Pseudo-Philo 48:1–2.

148. **wept over the first Temple...** The verse in Genesis reads: *He fell upon* צוארי (*tsavverei*), *the neck of, his brother Benjamin and wept.* Technically, the word *tsavverei* is in the plural ("the necks of"), which stimulated a midrashic interpretation referring to the two Temples built in Jerusalem, which lies in the territory of Benjamin. The first Temple was destroyed by the Babylonians

of David, that David built and raised within Jerusalem.[149] However, *like the Tower of David*—Jerusalem above, of whom is written *The name of YHVH is a tower of strength, into which a righteous one runs, secure* (Proverbs 18:10). Who is *secure*? That *tower* is *secure*, because *a righteous one runs* into it.[150]

"*Your neck*—the Temple below, standing exquisitely arrayed like the neck of the body. As the neck is the beauty of the entire body, so is the Temple the beauty of the whole world.[151]

"*Built* לתלפיות (*le-talpiyyot*), *in terraces*—תלא (*tilla*), a mound, toward which all inhabitants of the world gaze. So they have established: *talpiyyot*—תל (*tel*), a mound, toward which all פיות (*piyyot*), mouths, of the world offer praise and prayer.[152]

"*A thousand bucklers hang upon it*—a thousand ornaments arrayed upon it fittingly.[153]

"*All the shields of* הגבורים (*ha-gibborim*), *the warriors*—for all of them proceed from the side of severe Judgment.[154]

"As all of a woman's adornments suspend from her neck, so all adornments of the world suspend from the Temple.[155] This has been established, as is written: *For our neck we are pursued* (Lamentations 5:5)—for the Temple, beautiful neck of the whole world, *we are pursued*.[156]

in 586 B.C.E.; the second, by the Romans in 70 C.E.

See *Bereshit Rabbah* 93:12; BT *Megillah* 16b; above, p. 37 and n. 260.

149. **Literally, *the Tower of David*...** Referring to the Temple in Jerusalem, which David envisioned, though it was actually built by his son Solomon.

See *Shir ha-Shirim Rabbah* on 4:4.

150. **Jerusalem above... *tower of strength*...** *Shekhinah*, symbolized by Jerusalem. She is known as *Malkhut* (Kingdom) and linked with King David. She is also known as *name of YHVH* because She reveals the divine identity. Here, She is pictured as *a tower* inhabited by *Yesod*, who is known as *righteous one*. Their union brings Her security.

See *Zohar* 1:9a, 37b, 96b; 3:164a–b.

151. **arrayed like the neck...** See *Shir ha-Shirim Rabbah* on 4:4.

152. **לתלפיות (*le-talpiyyot*)...** All those who pray should face Jerusalem.

See JT *Berakhot* 4:5, 8c; BT *Berakhot* 30a; *Shir ha-Shirim Rabbah* on 4:4.

153. **thousand ornaments...** *Shekhinah* is the culmination of the ten *sefirot*, whose number cubed equals one thousand.

154. **הגבורים (*ha-gibborim*), *the warriors* ...Judgment** All their shields proceed from the *sefirah* of *Gevurah*, or *Din* (Judgment).

On the custom of hanging shields on the city walls, see Ezekiel 27:11.

155. **woman's adornments suspend...** Similarly, the Temple guarantees rich sustenance for the entire world.

See *Shir ha-Shirim Rabbah* on 4:4.

156. ***For our neck we are pursued*...** "Because of the Temple, our enemies attack."

See *Yalqut Shim'oni*, Song of Songs 988. The full verse reads: *On our neck we are pursued; we strive, we are given no rest.* The opening word, על (*al*), *on*, is understood here according to another of its meanings: "for, on account of."

"*We strive* (ibid.)—to build it, twice. *We are not allowed* (ibid.)—for we were not permitted: it was destroyed and not rebuilt.[157]

"As when the neck is destroyed the whole body is destroyed along with it, so when the Temple was destroyed and darkened the whole world darkened; heaven, earth, and stars did not shine.[158]

"Therefore Joseph wept over this. And after weeping over this, he wept over all those tribes who were exiled when the Temple was destroyed—for they were all immediately exiled and scattered among the nations—as is written: *He kissed all his brothers and wept over them* (Genesis, ibid., 15). *Over them,* precisely!—over everything he wept: over the Temple that was twice destroyed and over his brothers, the ten tribes, who would be driven into exile and scattered among the nations.[159]

"*And after this, his brothers spoke with him* (ibid.). It is not written that they wept—for he alone wept, because Holy Spirit sparkled within him; whereas they did not weep, because Holy Spirit did not hover over them."[160]

והקל (*Ve-ha-qol*), *And the voice, was heard in the house of Pharaoh* (ibid., 16). והקל (*Ve-ha-qol*), *And the voice*—without a ו (*vav*). Why?[161]

Rabbi El'azar said, "This is *Shekhinah,* who was weeping over the destruction of the Temple and the exile of Israel. Here is written *And the voice was heard,* and there is written *A voice is heard in Ramah* (Jeremiah 31:15). Just as there *Shekhinah,* so here *Shekhinah.*"[162]

157. ***We strive...*** The Temple was built and destroyed twice, but after the second destruction it was never again rebuilt. See *KP.*

For the full verse, see the preceding note. The final clause, ולא הונח לנו (*ve-lo hunaḥ lanu*), *we are given no rest,* is understood here according to another meaning of the verb *hunaḥ*: "be allowed."

158. **neck is destroyed...** See *Shir ha-Shirim Rabbah* on 4:4.

See BT *Berakhot* 59a: "Rafram son of Papa said in the name of Rav Ḥisda: 'Ever since the day that the Temple was destroyed, the sky has not appeared in all its purity, as is said: *I clothe the heavens with blackness and I make a sackcloth their covering.*'"

159. ***Over them,* precisely...** Over all that would be destroyed and exiled. Actually, the ten northern tribes were conquered (and many of them exiled) by the Assyrians in 721 B.C.E., many years before the destruction of the first Temple (in 586 B.C.E.).

160. **Holy Spirit sparkled within him...** Only Joseph foresaw the twofold destruction and exile, and therefore he wept.

161. **והקל (*Ve-ha-qol*), *And the voice...*** The full verse reads: *And the voice was heard in the house of Pharaoh, saying, "Joseph's brothers have come!" And it was good in Pharaoh's eyes and in his servants' eyes.* The word קול (*qol*) means "voice, noise, message." In this verse it is often translated as "report, news," but here Rabbi El'azar and Rabbi Abba understand it more literally as "voice." They also emphasize its unusual spelling, קל (*qol*), without the letter ו (*vav*). See *Minḥat Shai,* ad loc.

162. ***A voice is heard in Ramah...*** The full verse reads: *A voice is heard in Ramah—wailing, bitter weeping—Rachel weeping for*

Rabbi Abba opened, "*My soul yearns, even pines for the courts of YHVH; my heart and my flesh shout for joy to the living God* (Psalms 84:3). Come and see: Every human being who offers a prayer before his Lord should preface it with blessings every single day and offer his prayer to his Lord at the proper time.[163] In the morning, grasping the right arm of the blessed Holy One; in the afternoon prayer, grasping the left.[164] A person needs prayer and supplication every single day in order to unite with Him.

"We have established: Whoever offers a prayer before his Lord should not let his voice be heard while praying. Whoever lets his voice be heard while praying —that prayer is not heard.[165] Why? Because [210a] prayer is not an audible voice; that audible voice is not prayer. What is prayer? Another voice, dependent on the audible voice. Who is the audible voice? קול (*Qol*), Voice, with a ו (*vav*). The voice dependent on it is קל (*qol*), voice, without a ו (*vav*), dependent on it.[166]

"Therefore, a person should not let his voice be heard while praying, but rather pray in a whisper—with that inaudible voice. This is the prayer that is always accepted. Your mnemonic is: והקל (*Ve-ha-qol*), *And the voice, was heard*— קל (*qol*), voice, without a ו (*vav*), is heard. This is silent prayer, accepted by the blessed Holy One when it is fashioned fittingly with passion, intention, and harmony—actualizing every day the unity of one's Lord."[167]

her children, refusing to be comforted for her children, for they are no more.

In the *Zohar*, Mother Rachel symbolizes the Divine Mother, *Shekhinah*. See above, pp. 243–44, n. 382. By verbal analogy, Rabbi El'azar indicates that here too in Genesis the *voice* that was *heard* is the voice of *Shekhinah*.

163. **offers a prayer...** The central prayer is the *Amidah*, the "standing" prayer, recited three times daily. This prayer is preceded by various blessings.

164. **right arm... left...** *Ḥesed* and *Gevurah*, pictured respectively as the right and left arms of the divine body, corresponding to the morning light and the waning sun.

165. **not let his voice be heard...** The *Amidah* should be recited silently; otherwise it is not heard and accepted. According to the *Zohar*, during this prayer *Shekhinah* joins with *Tif'eret*, and silence befits their intimate union.

See BT *Berakhot* 24b, 31a; *Seder Eliyyahu Rabbah* 26 (p. 140); *Zohar* 2:202a; *NO* on *Zohar* 1:210a, n. 1; *NZ*, n. 6, and on 210a, n. 2; Margaliot, *Sha'arei Zohar*, on *Berakhot* 24b; Ta-Shma, *Ha-Nigleh she-ba-Nistar*, 60. Cf. above, p. 280 and n. 124.

166. **What is prayer?...** Genuine, silent prayer corresponds to *Shekhinah*, who lacks the full sound and power of the *sefirot* above Her and yearns to be filled by them. She is symbolized by קל (*qol*), "voice," spelled without the letter ו (*vav*)—a letter whose numerical value of six alludes to the central *sefirah*, *Tif'eret*, and the five *sefirot* surrounding Him (*Ḥesed* through *Yesod*). The full spelling—קול (*qol*), with the ו (*vav*)—symbolizes *Tif'eret* (the audible voice), upon which *Shekhinah* (the inaudible voice) is dependent.

167. **pray in a whisper...** Such prayer corresponds to *Shekhinah* (the inaudible voice), and She transmits it above. Not only is it accepted; it stimulates sefirotic union.

By mentioning "passion" and "intention," Rabbi Abba alludes to the verse in Psalms

Rabbi El'azar said, "A silent voice is the sublime voice, from which all voices issue. But קל (*qol*), voice—without a ו (*vav*)—is prayer below, verging on ascending to *vav*, uniting with it.[168]

"Come and see: והקל (*Ve-ha-qol*), *And the voice, was heard*—קל (*qol*), voice, without a *vav*, weeping over the first Temple and over the second Temple.[169] *Was heard*—as is said: *A voice is heard in Ramah* (Jeremiah 31:15). What is *in Ramah*, a height? Upper world, world that is coming. Your mnemonic is: 'from Ramah to Bethel,' *from world to world* (Psalms 106:48).[170] Here, *in Ramah*—upper world, for when it was *heard in Ramah*, what is written? *YHVH God of Hosts summoned on that day to weeping and mourning...* (Isaiah 22:12).[171]

"והקל (*Ve-ha-qol*), *And the voice, was heard*—above, above. Why? Because ו (*vav*) had ascended, withdrawing far away, and then: *Rachel is weeping for her children, refusing to be comforted for her children,* כי איננו (*ki einennu*), *for they are no more* (Jeremiah, ibid.). We have established: *ki einennu, for he is no more*—because Her Husband is not with Her. If Her Husband were present with Her, She would be comforted for them, because then Her children would no longer be in exile! But because *he is no more*, She is not comforted for Her children, because Her children are far removed from Her on account of His not being with Her.[172]

with which he opened: *My soul yearns, even pines for the courts of YHVH; my heart and my flesh shout for joy to the living God.*

See above, note 165. Later editors of the *Zohar* inserted here the description of Hannah's prayer in 1 Samuel 1:13: *Hannah was speaking in her heart, her lips alone moving and her voice not heard.*

168. **silent voice is the sublime voice...** Rabbi El'azar agrees with Rabbi Abba that the unusual spelling of קל (*qol*), "voice," refers to *Shekhinah*, who yearns to unite with Her missing letter ו (*vav*), symbolizing *Tif'eret*. However, he offers a different interpretation of the "silent voice," which refers not to *Shekhinah* but to a higher, secret realm: *Binah*, the silent source of all voices, namely of all seven lower *sefirot*.

See above, p. 284 and n. 140.

169. **weeping over the first Temple...** *Shekhinah* weeps over the destruction and exile. See above, p. 287 and n. 162.

170. **What is *in Ramah*...** The place name *Ramah* means "height" and, according to Rabbi El'azar, alludes to *Binah*, the upper realm known as "world that is coming." In this higher world *Shekhinah*'s weeping voice is heard.

The expression "from Ramah to Bethel" is a variation on Judges 4:5: *between Ramah and Bethel.* Here, *Bethel* symbolizes *Shekhinah*. The phrase *from world to world* is understood to mean from *Binah* to *Shekhinah*. See M *Berakhot* 9:5; *Tosefta, Berakhot* 6:21; *Zohar* 1:34a, 153b, 158b, 248b; 2:22a, 53b, 144a; 3:145b, 285b, 297b.

171. **when it was *heard in Ramah*...** *Shekhinah*'s weeping aroused mourning throughout the upper worlds.

The full verse in Isaiah reads: *YHVH God of Hosts summoned on that day to weeping and mourning, to tonsuring and girding with sackcloth.* See *Eikhah Rabbah* 1:23.

172. **ו (*vav*) had ascended...** This letter symbolizes *Tif'eret* (see above, note 166). The fact that it is missing from the word והקל

"Come and see! *In the house of* פרעה (*par'oh*), *Pharaoh*—your mnemonic above: the house from which all lights and sparks אתפרעו (*itpera'u*), have been exposed, and revealed. All that was concealed, from there was revealed. Thereby the blessed Holy One radiates all lights and all sparks to illumine that voice called קל (*qol*) without a ו (*vav*).[173]

"Come and see: When the blessed Holy One will raise this voice from the dust so that it unites with *vav*, then all those who became lost in time of exile will revel in supernal radiance, as is said: *On that day a great shofar will be blown, and those who were lost in the land of Assyria* [*and those who were scattered in the land of Egypt will come and worship YHVH on the holy mountain in Jerusalem*] (Isaiah 27:13)."[174]

290

And you are commanded, "Do this: take you from the land of Egypt wagons for your little ones and for your wives, and convey your father..." (Genesis 45:19).[175]

Rabbi Ḥiyya opened, "*Rejoice with Jerusalem and be glad for her, all you who love her! Rejoice with her in joy, all you who mourn over her* (Isaiah 66:10). Come and see: When the Temple was destroyed and sins proved decisive and Israel were exiled from the land, the blessed Holy One withdrew above, above—not looking upon the destruction of His Temple or upon His people who had been exiled. Then *Shekhinah* went into exile with them.[176]

(*ve-ha-qol*), *and the voice*, indicates that *Tif'eret* has withdrawn from *Shekhinah*, thereby ruining their union above and consequently causing destruction and exile below. *Shekhinah* (Rachel) then weeps for Her children.

The word איננו (*einennu*) means literally "he is no more." In the verse in Jeremiah it is understood distributively to refer to *her children*, so it can be translated *they are no more*. Rabbi El'azar, however, insists on reading the word hyperliterally: *he is no more*—referring to *Shekhinah*'s husband, *Tif'eret*, who has abandoned Her, thereby condemning their children to exile.

See *Zohar* 2:29b; 3:20b; *ZḤ* 92a–b (*MhN*, *Eikhah*). Cf. 3:74a–75b.

173. ***In the house...*** The verse reads: *And the voice was heard in the house of Pharaoh, saying, "Joseph's brothers have come!"* Here, Rabbi El'azar plays on the Hebrew root פרע (*pr'*), one of whose meanings is "to expose," and he suggests that *the house of Pharaoh* alludes to *Binah*, from whom the upper lights are revealed and radiated to *Shekhinah*.

174. **raise this voice...** Raise *Shekhinah* and reunite Her with *Tif'eret*.

175. ***and convey your father...*** The verse concludes: *and come*. Joseph is directed by Pharaoh to have his brothers bring Jacob to Egypt.

176. **blessed Holy One withdrew...** On the divine withdrawal, see above at note 172; pp. 243–44 and n. 382.

On the exile of *Shekhinah*, see BT *Megillah* 29a: "Rabbi Shim'on son of Yoḥai says, 'Come and see how beloved are Israel in the sight of the blessed Holy One! Wherever they went in exile, *Shekhinah* accompanied them. When they were exiled to Egypt, *Shekhinah* was with them.... When they were exiled to Babylon, *Shekhinah* was with

"Then He descended. He looked upon His house—it was burnt. He gazed at His people—they had gone into exile. He inquired concerning *Matronita*—She had been driven away. Then, *YHVH God of Hosts summoned on that day to weeping and mourning, to tonsuring and girding with sackcloth* (Isaiah 22:12).[177] And of Her too, what is written? *Girded with sackcloth for the husband of her youth* (Joel 1:8), as is said: *for he is no more* (Jeremiah 31:15), because He had withdrawn from Her and there was separation.[178]

"Even all of heaven and earth mourned, as is written: *I clothe the heavens in blackness, and make sackcloth their covering* (Isaiah 50:3). The supernal angels all mourned for Her, as is written: *Behold, the Erelim cried outside; angels of peace weep bitterly* (Isaiah 33:7). Sun and moon mourned and their lights darkened, as is written: *The sun will darken as it rises [and the moon will not shed its light]* (ibid. 13:10).[179] All above and below wept over Her [210b] and mourned. Why? Because the Other Side dominated Her, obtaining dominion over the Holy Land."[180]

He opened, saying, "*You, son of man, thus says Lord YHVH to the land of Israel: End! Comes the end upon the four corners of the earth!* (Ezekiel 7:2). This verse consists of supernal mystery. *To the land of Israel: End!* What does this mean? Is the land of Israel an end? Well, certainly so! As has been said: There is end on the right, end on the left. End on the right, as is written: *at the end of the right* (Daniel 12:13). End on the left, as is written: *He puts an end to darkness* (Job 28:3). This is *end of all flesh* (Genesis 6:13).[181]

them. . . . And even when they are destined to be redeemed, *Shekhinah* will be with them.'"

See *Mekhilta, Pisḥa* 14; Moses de León, *Sheqel ha-Qodesh*, 73–74 (92–93).

177. **Then He descended...** *Matronita* (the matron) is *Shekhinah*.

See *Zohar* 3:75a; cf. *Eikhah Rabbah* 1:23; BT *Berakhot* 3a.

178. ***Girded with sackcloth...*** *Shekhinah* mourns as well.

The full verse reads: *Lament—like a maiden girded with sackcloth for the husband of her youth!* On the expression *for he is no more*, see above, note 172.

179. **heaven and earth mourned...** See *Eikhah Rabbah* 1:23; BT *Berakhot* 59a (quoted above, note 158); above, p. 109 at n. 159.

On the mourning of the angels and the identity of the Erelim, see above, p. 108 and n. 155. On the mourning of the sun and moon, see *Pesiqta de-Rav Kahana*, add. 6; above, p. 108 at n. 157; p. 202 at n. 145.

180. **Other Side dominated Her...** The foreign dominion over the land of Israel was reflected above by the demonic domination of *Shekhinah*.

181. **end on the right, end on the left...** *Shekhinah* is the culmination of emanation, characterized by the grace of *Ḥesed* on the right, whereas the demonic power derives from the dregs of *Gevurah* on the left and is characterized by evil and death.

The verse in Daniel reads: *As for you, go on till the end; you will rest, and arise for your share* לקץ הימין (*le-qets ha-yamin*), *at the end of days.* The word ימין (*yamin*) is an aramaized form of the Hebrew ימים (*yamim*), "days," but here Rabbi Ḥiyya understands it as the Hebrew ימין (*yamin*), "right."

The verse in Job reads: *He puts an end to*

"End of the right—namely, *to the land of Israel: End.*[182]

"*Comes the end*—end of the left.[183]

"End of the right—of the good impulse. End of the left—evil impulse; because when sins proved decisive, the wicked kingdom was empowered and granted dominion, destroying His house and His Temple, as is written: *Thus says Lord YHVH: Evil! A singular evil; see, it is coming!* (Ezekiel, ibid., 5). All is one.[184]

"Therefore, those above and those below mourned because dominion was given to this end of the left. Consequently, since the Holy Kingdom—Kingdom of Heaven—has been overturned and the wicked kingdom has prevailed, one should mourn with Her and be subdued with Her. Then when She stands erect and the world rejoices, he will rejoice with Her, as is written: *Rejoice with her in joy, all you who mourn over her.*[185]

"Come and see! Of Egypt is written *Egypt is a beautiful* עגלה (*eglah*), *heifer* (Jeremiah 46:20). Mystery of this heifer: Israel were under her rule for such a

darkness, every extremity he explores—rock of pitch-black gloom (Job 28:3). Here, *darkness* symbolizes *Gevurah*, whose *end* is the demonic realm.

The verse in Genesis reads: *God said to Noah, "End of all flesh has come before Me, for the earth is filled with violence because of them. Here, I am about to destroy them, with the earth!"* The expression *end of all flesh* alludes to the Angel of Death.

See *Eikhah Rabbah* 2:6; *Pesiqta de-Rav Kahana* 17:5; *Zohar* 1:54a–b, 62b–63a, 75a (*ST*), 152b; above, p. 180 and nn. 1–3; 2:33a–34a, 134a–b, 181b; Moses de León, *Sefer ha-Rimmon*, 75. On *end of all flesh*, see also 1:35b, 58a.

182. **End of the right—namely...** This end is *Shekhinah*, symbolized by the land of Israel.

183. ***Comes the end...*** According to this dire prophecy, the demonic end of the left *comes* to dominate the land of Israel and *Shekhinah*.

184. **good impulse... evil impulse...** The two impulses correspond respectively to the right and left sides. By giving in to the evil impulse and sinning, Israel empowered the demonic forces and their earthly representatives, Israel's enemies, who destroyed the Temple.

The concluding sentence, "All is one," apparently refers to the interdependence of the evil impulse, demonic power, and earthly destruction—or to the identity of "end of the left" and "evil." See BT *Bava Batra* 16a: "Resh Lakish said, 'Satan, the evil impulse, and the Angel of Death are one and the same.'"

On the "wicked kingdom," see above, p. 253 and n. 437.

185. **Holy Kingdom—Kingdom of Heaven...** *Shekhinah*, known as *Malkhut* (Kingdom).

On mourning over Jerusalem and eventually rejoicing with her, see *Tosefta, Ta'anit* 3:14; BT *Ta'anit* 30b. Here, Jerusalem symbolizes *Shekhinah*.

The expression "has been overturned" renders the Aramaic אתכפיא (*itkafya*); "be subdued" renders לאתכפיא (*le-itkafya*). Cf. the opinion of Rabbi Yehudah (in M *Ta'anit* 4:7) that one should practice the custom of כפית המטה (*kefiyyat ha-mittah*), "overturning the bed," on *Tish'ah be-Av* (the ninth of Av) a sign of mourning for the destruction of the Temple.

long time, for so many years; and because Israel were destined to overpower her, they were now provided a hint: עגלות (*agalot*), *wagons/heifers* (Genesis 45:19)."[186]

Rabbi El'azar said, "Joseph hinted to Jacob concerning the *eglah*, heifer, whose neck is to be broken, for during that chapter he was separated from him, as they have established. This heifer is brought because a dead man is discovered and it is not known who killed him. In order to prevent the unwanted spirit from ruling the land, they offer this heifer as a reparation, so that they will not be regarded by him and he will not dominate them.[187]

"Come and see: All inhabitants of the world pass away by the hand of the Angel of Death—except for this one, taken ahead of time by human beings, before the time had arrived for him to be overpowered, with authorization; for he does not overpower a person until he obtains authorization. Therefore, he is justified in dominating that place: just as *it is not known who struck him* (Deuteronomy 21:1), so is he justified in being unknown in order to attack that place. Consequently, *the elders of that town shall take a heifer of the herd...* (Deuteronomy 21:3), so as to eliminate the judgment of that place and ensure that the Accuser will not dominate it and to be saved from him.[188]

186. **Mystery of this heifer...** For several hundred years, Israel were destined to suffer bondage in Egypt—a nation described by Jeremiah as an עגלה (*eglah*), "heifer." As a hint that Israel would eventually overcome the Egyptians (in the Exodus or at the end of days), Jacob's sons were now told: *Take you from the land of Egypt* עגלות (*agalot*), *wagons, for your little ones and for your wives, and convey your father, and come.* Rabbi Ḥiyya is apparently interpreting *agalot* to mean "heifers." See the following note.

187. **Joseph hinted to Jacob...** According to Deuteronomy 21:1–9, if a murder victim is found and the killer cannot be identified, the elders of the nearest town must atone for the murder by killing a heifer (breaking its neck) and making a public declaration. Here, this ritual is understood as a means of assuaging the evil spirit, so that it will not attack the residents in retaliation for the murder.

The Midrash relates that Joseph was studying this section of the Torah with his father immediately before Jacob sent him to his brothers, who sold him into slavery. Now Joseph sent עגלות (*agalot*)—understood midrashically to mean not "wagons" but "heifers"—to convince Jacob that his son is still alive by reminding him of the biblical passage that they were studying together many years earlier: the ritual of the עגלה (*eglah*), "heifer."

See *Bereshit Rabbah* 94:3 (and *Mattenot Kehunnah*, Maharzu, David Luria, and Theodor, ad loc.); 95:3 (and Theodor, ad loc.); *Tanḥuma, Vayiggash* 11; *Tanḥuma* (Buber), *Vayiggash* 12; Rashi on Genesis 45:27; *Leqaḥ Tov*, Genesis 46:28; Kasher, *Torah Shelemah*, Genesis 45:27, n. 91. On assuaging the demonic powers, see above, p. 161 and n. 481.

188. **by the hand of the Angel of Death...** The Angel of Death has been robbed of this victim who was killed prematurely by an unidentified murderer. Consequently, he is justified in attacking suddenly anyone in the vicinity, without his specific target being known. The only way to thwart him is to offer the heifer instead.

The context in Deuteronomy (21:3–4) reads: *It shall be that the town closest to the slain person, the elders of that town shall take*

"Come and see: When Joseph parted from his father, he was sent off without an escort and without food, and what happened, happened. When Jacob said *Joseph is torn to shreds*, he added, *No, I will go down to my son in mourning, to Sheol* (Genesis 37:33, 35)—'for I caused this! Further, I knew that his brothers hated him, yet I sent him!' He dropped a hint."[189]

Rabbi Yehudah said, "But he sent those *agalot* at Pharaoh's declaration, as is written: *Joseph gave them* agalot *according to the declaration of Pharaoh* (ibid. 45:21)."[190]

He replied, "Precision of the word! As is written: *And you* צֻוֵּיתָה (*tsuvveitah*), *are commanded, 'Do this'* (ibid., 19)—*And you* צִוִּיתָה (*tsivvitah*), *commanded it*, precisely! Therefore it is written with a ה (*he*), implying that Joseph demanded them. Consequently, *Joseph gave them* agalot *according to the declaration of Pharaoh*. And Jacob did not firmly believe the matter until he saw them, as is written: *and he saw the* agalot *that Joseph had sent to carry him, and the spirit of Jacob their father revived* (ibid., 27)."[191]

a heifer of the herd that has not been worked, that has not pulled in a yoke, and the elders of that town shall bring the heifer down to a strongly flowing wadi that is not worked and is not sown, and they shall break the neck of the heifer there in the wadi.

See *Zohar* 1:113b–114a; Galante; *KP*. On the "authorization" of the Angel of Death, see BT *Bava Batra* 16a: "He [Satan] descends and leads astray, ascends and arouses wrath, obtains authorization and seizes the soul." (The Angel of Death is identical with Satan; see above, note 184.)

189. **When Joseph parted...** In a sense, Jacob was responsible for Joseph's being sold by his brothers because he sent him off unescorted, knowing that his brothers hated him. Now, years later, Joseph subtly reminded his father of this misconduct by sending him *agalot* (wagons/heifers), thereby alluding to the *eglah* (heifer); see above, note 187. Joseph's hint is based on a rabbinic interpretation of the declaration made by the town elders after killing the heifer: *Our hands did not spill this blood, our eyes did not see* (Deuteronomy 21:7). On this verse, the Mishnah (*Sotah* 9:6) comments: "Would it enter our minds that the elders of a court of justice spill blood? Rather, '[The victim] did not come to us and then depart without food. We did not see him and let him go unescorted.'"

The first verse in Genesis reads: *A vicious beast has devoured him, Joseph is torn to shreds!* The second reads: *He refused to be consoled and he said, "No, I will go down to my son in mourning, to Sheol."*

190. **at Pharaoh's declaration...** If the *agalot* (wagons/heifers) were sent at Pharaoh's command—and not at Joseph's—then Joseph was not offering any hint about the *eglah* (heifer).

191. **Precision of the word!...** The precise spelling of the word צֻוֵּיתָה (*tsuvveitah*) allows for a creative interpretation. If the word meant simply *you are commanded*, the final letter, ה (*he*), would be superfluous. Rather, Rabbi El'azar suggests, the word should be read צִוִּיתָה (*tsivvitah*), *you commanded it*—with the final ה (*he*) constituting the direct object *it*. Thus, it was Joseph who initially commanded that *agalot* be sent, and Pharaoh confirmed this by royal declaration.

Genesis 45:19 reads in full: *And you are commanded, "Do this: take you from the land of Egypt* agalot, *wagons, for your little ones and*

Rabbi Shim'on said, "At first, *the spirit of Jacob revived*; afterward, *Israel said, 'Enough! Joseph my son is still alive'* (ibid., 28). Well, at first, Torah calls him Jacob because they made *Shekhinah* a partner in that ban when Joseph was sold. Now that *Shekhinah* has arisen: *the spirit of Jacob revived*—mystery of *Shekhinah.*[192] Once She is firmly established, a rung above arouses toward Her—rung of Israel. From here we learn that mystery above does not arouse until first there is arousal below. For here, *the spirit of Jacob revived,* [211a] at first; afterward, *Israel said.*[193]

"*God spoke to Israel* במראות (*be-mar'ot*), *in visions of, the night* (Genesis 46:2)—spelled במראת (*be-mar'at*), *in a vision of.*[194] Come and see: *He offered sacrifices to the God of his father Isaac* (ibid., 1), at first, to arouse left in mystery of love. Then, *God spoke to Israel in visions of the night*—במראת (*be-mar'at*), *in*

for your wives, and convey your father, and come.

The context of the final verse (45:26–28) reads: *They told him, saying, "Joseph is still alive! Indeed, he is ruler of all the land of Egypt!" His heart went numb, for he did not believe them. And they spoke to him all the words of Joseph that he had spoken to them, and he saw the* agalot *that Joseph had sent to carry him, and the spirit of Jacob their father revived. Israel said, "Enough! Joseph my son is still alive. Let me go see him before I die."* See Rashi on Genesis 45:27.

192. ***spirit of Jacob... Israel...*** Rabbi Shim'on explains the change of names in these two adjacent verses. After Joseph's brothers sold him into slavery, they swore an oath not to reveal the deed to their father, Jacob, and they included *Shekhinah* in that "ban." Consequently, She withdrew Her revelatory power from the aging patriarch and he remained unaware of Joseph's fate. Only now, when Jacob finally learned that Joseph was still alive, did he regain Her presence and inspiration. The name Jacob refers to the patriarch's lower status, when he was deprived of *his spirit,* that is, of *Shekhinah.* The name Israel connotes his fulfilled status.

See above, p. 94 and n. 63; p. 119 and n. 219. On the names Jacob and Israel, see above, pp. 50–51 and n. 364.

193. **rung above arouses...** Once *Shekhinah* was freed from the ban and reunited with the earthly Jacob (Israel), then Her partner above, *Tif'eret*—whose full name is *Tif'eret Yisra'el* (Beauty of Israel)—was aroused toward Her. This confirms the kabbalistic principle that there can be no arousal above without a stimulus from below.

See *Zohar* 1:35a, 77b, 82b, 86b, 88a, 156b, 164a, 235a, 244a; 2:31b, 265a; 3:40b, 92a, 110b.

194. ***God spoke to Israel...*** The fact that the word במראת (*be-mar'ot*), *in visions of,* is spelled without a ו (*vav*) stimulates Rabbi Shim'on to interpret it as a singular form: *be-mar'at, in a vision of,* alluding to *Shekhinah,* who is known as *mar'ah,* "vision" or "mirror," revealing or reflecting the other *sefirot.*

See *Zohar* 1:149b; above, p. 114 and n. 192. Cf. above, p. 24 and n. 168; p. 199 and n. 127. The context in Genesis (46:2–4) reads: *God spoke to Israel in visions of the night, and He said, "Jacob! Jacob!" And he said, "Here I am." He said, "I am God, God of your father. Fear not to go down to Egypt, for I will make of you a great nation there. I Myself will go down with you to Egypt and I Myself will surely bring you up as well, and Joseph will lay his hand on your eyes."*

a vision of, the night, on this rung that we have mentioned: vision of the night.[195]

"*He said, 'I am God, God of your father'* (ibid., 3). Why?[196] Because so it is with the side of holiness above. For the side of defilement does not mention the name of the blessed Holy One, whereas the entire side of holiness is referred to by His name.

"*I Myself will go down with you to Egypt* (ibid., 4). From here we learn that *Shekhinah* descended with him into exile, and wherever Israel went in exile, *Shekhinah* was exiled with them, as has been established.[197]

"Come and see: How many wagons were there? Six, as is said: *six covered wagons* (Numbers 7:3). Alternatively, there were sixty. All is one mystery.[198]

"At first is written *in the wagons that Joseph had sent* (Genesis 45:27); and afterward, *that Pharaoh had sent* (ibid. 46:5).[199] However, all those sent by Jo-

195. ***God of his father Isaac,* at first...** Jacob sought to bring about the union of the divine couple, so he aroused *Shekhinah*'s partner by offering sacrifices to the *sefirah* of *Gevurah* on the left, symbolized by Isaac. *Gevurah*'s passion impelled the divine male toward *Shekhinah* (*vision of the night*), who conveyed revelation to Jacob below.

196. **Why?** Why does God provide a particular name?

197. ***Shekhinah* descended with him...** See BT *Megillah* 29a: "Rabbi Shim'on son of Yoḥai says, 'Come and see how beloved are Israel in the sight of the blessed Holy One! Wherever they went in exile, *Shekhinah* accompanied them. When they were exiled to Egypt, *Shekhinah* was with them.... When they were exiled to Babylon, *Shekhinah* was with them.... And even when they are destined to be redeemed, *Shekhinah* will be with them.'"

The image of *Shekhinah*'s descent is linked with this verse (Genesis 46:4) in *Mekhilta, Shirta* 3; *Mekhilta de-Rashbi,* Exodus 3:8; 15:2; *Zohar* 2:4b, 85a. Cf. *Mekhilta, Pisḥa* 14; Kasher, *Torah Shelemah*, Genesis 46:4, n. 24; above, p. 290 and n. 176.

198. **How many wagons...** How many wagons were sent to convey Jacob and his family to Egypt? Rabbi Shim'on first suggests six, corresponding to the number of wagons mentioned in the account of the dedication of the Tabernacle in the wilderness when the tribal chieftains brought an offering. This interpretation is based simply on a verbal analogy between the references to *wagons* in both Genesis and Numbers. According to *KP*, Rabbi Shim'on is implying that the wagons used by the chieftains were the very same ones that had earlier transported Jacob.

The number six also alludes to the mystery of six *sefirot* from *Ḥesed* through *Yesod* (who unite with *Shekhinah*) or to six chariots or camps of angels accompanying *Shekhinah*. Since each of these *sefirot* includes ten aspects, the alternative number of wagons (sixty) alludes to the same sefirotic sextet—or to the sixty myriads of chariots or angels who accompanied *Shekhinah* to Egypt, according to *Zohar* 2:4b–5a.

199. ***Joseph had sent... Pharaoh had sent*** Why are they both mentioned?

The first verse (45:27) reads slightly differently (without the word *in*): *And they* [*Joseph's brothers*] *spoke to him* [*Jacob*] *all the words of Joseph that he had spoken to them, and he saw the wagons that Joseph had sent to carry him, and the spirit of Jacob their father revived.* Cf. above, p. 294 and nn. 190–91.

seph were of a fitting number,[200] whereas those additional ones sent by Pharaoh did not partake of this mystery and were not part of the count. Both these and those arrived; therefore, *that Joseph sent* and *that Pharaoh sent.* When Israel will emerge from exile, what is written? *They will bring all your brothers from all the nations as an offering to YHVH—on horses, in chariots and wagons, on mules and camels—to My holy mountain Jerusalem, says YHVH* (Isaiah 66:20)."[201]

Joseph harnessed his chariot and went up to meet Israel his father in Goshen (Genesis 46:29).[202]

Rabbi Yitsḥak opened, "*An image above the heads of the living being: an expanse like awesome ice, spread out above their heads* (Ezekiel 1:22).[203] This verse has been established,[204] but come and see: There is living being above living being, and there is a holy living being standing above the heads of living beings. And there is a supernal living being above other living beings. This living being rules over all of them, for when this being provides and illumines them all, they all move in its wake, providing to one another, ruling one another.[205]

200. **fitting number** As explained in the preceding paragraph.

201. ***They will bring all your brothers... in chariots and wagons...*** At the end of days, the nations of the world will discover the one God and come to worship Him in Jerusalem, bringing with them all the exiled Israelites. The reference to *the wagons that Pharaoh sent* to transport Jacob and his family down to Egypt prefigures these wagons of the future that will restore the Israelites to their land.

The full verse reads: *They will bring all your brothers from all the nations as an offering to YHVH—on horses, in chariots and wagons, on mules and camels—to My holy mountain Jerusalem, says YHVH, just as the Children of Israel bring an offering in a pure vessel to the House of YHVH.*

202. ***Joseph harnessed his chariot...*** The full verse reads: *Joseph harnessed his chariot and went up to meet Israel his father in Goshen, and he appeared before him and fell on his neck, and wept on his neck a long while.*

203. ***An image above the heads...*** From Ezekiel's vision of the divine throne transported through heaven by angelic beings called חיות (*ḥayyot*), "animals, living beings, creatures." In several verses (1:20–22), this noun appears in the singular—חיה (*ḥayyah*)—apparently to emphasize the unity of the ensemble. See Greenberg, *Ezekiel*, 48.

This foundational vision of Jewish mysticism became known as the Account of the Chariot. Here, Rabbi Yitsḥak associates it with Joseph's chariot.

204. **This verse has been established** See BT *Ḥagigah* 13a; *Zohar* 1:21a; 2:211a–b; Moses de León, *Peirush ha-Merkavah*, 70.

205. **living being above living being...** The term חיה (*ḥayyah*), "living being," applies not only to the angelic beings conveying the divine throne but to the *sefirot* above. The "holy living being standing above the heads of living beings" apparently refers to *Shekhinah*, above the *ḥayyot* carrying the throne. The "supernal living being above other living beings" apparently refers to *Binah*, the Divine Mother above the lower *sefirot*, all of whom are illumined and animated by Her.

See Ezra of Gerona, *Peirush Shir ha-Shirim*, 508–9; *Zohar* 1:12b, 16a, 21a, 46b–47a,

"There is a living being above, over those below, over the other living beings below, all of whom are nourished by it. Four directions of the world are inscribed upon it, specific faces on every side, and She rules over four directions. They have established that there are three on this side and three on that side, and similarly in all four directions of the world.[206]

"There is expanse above expanse, and this expanse prevailing over them, to which all of them gaze.[207] What is written? *Below the expanse, their wings are extended toward one another*... (ibid., 23), for all control what has been assigned, and a measured, concatenated mission inheres in them.[208]

"There are nine on every side, in four directions of the world, totaling thirty-six. When they all conjoin, they become one design in the mystery of a single name in perfect union fittingly.[209] And when they are arrayed around the throne, what is written? *Above the expanse over their heads—like the appearance*

242a; 2:48b, 126a, 242a; 3:39b, 46b; *ZḤ* 9b (*MhN*); Moses de León, *Sefer ha-Rimmon*, 51; idem, commentary on the ten *sefirot*, 338b. On the movement of the *ḥayyot*, see Ezekiel 1:12. For a range of interpretations of this passage, see *OY*; Vital; Galante; *KP*; *MmD*.

206. **living being above, over those below...** Referring once again to *Shekhinah*, above the angelic beings conveying the throne. She rules over the entire world in all four directions. The term "faces" derives from Ezekiel's description of the four animal faces on the head of each of the angelic beings: lion, ox, eagle, and human being (1:6, 10). Not just one but three angels appear on each side of the throne, totaling twelve. See *Zohar* 1:149a–b (*ST*).

207. **expanse above expanse...** The term רקיע (*raqi'a*) means "expanse, firmament." In Genesis 1:6–8, the *raqi'a* is the firm vault of heaven dividing the upper waters from the lower waters. In Ezekiel 1:22, it is the platform on which the throne stands.

See BT *Ḥagigah* 12b: "Rabbi Yehudah said, 'There are two רקיעים (*reqi'im*), firmaments...' Resh Lakish said, 'Seven.'" In the *Zohar*, these seven *reqi'im* represent the seven lower *sefirot*, and here the reference could be to *Shekhinah* or *Yesod*; but it may be better not to insist on a specific sefirotic correlate and rather simply to note that the angelic beings gaze at the *raqi'a* above them.

See especially *Zohar* 2:211a, 212a–213a, and also 1:20a, 21a, 32b, 34a, 85b–86a, 162b, 168b; 2:56b, 209a–b; 3:287a; *ZḤ* 14a (*MhN*). Cf. Moses de León, *Peirush ha-Merkavah*, 70.

208. **all control...** Each angel controls what it has been assigned in the world, transmitting the divine will precisely through the entire chain of being.

The phrase "measured, concatenated mission" renders the cryptic Aramaic שליחו דקוסטא דגופטרא (*sheliḥu de-qusta de-guftera*). *Qusta* derives from the Greek *xestes*, a measure about the size of a pint. See *Bereshit Rabbah* 4:5; *Zohar* 1:33a, 83a, 121b, 162a, 164a. *Guftera* is a variation on the Zoharic neologism קופטרא (*quftera*), which connotes "tying, linking." See above, pp. 71–72, n. 483.

209. **nine on every side...** Previously the angels were said to total twelve, three on each side of the throne (see above at note 206). Now it appears that each of these three is actually a triad of angels, so their number totals thirty-six.

See *Bahir* 64 (95); *Zohar* 1:159a–b; Moses de León, *Seder Gan Eden*, in *Beit ha-Midrash*, 3:140; idem, *Peirush ha-Merkavah*, 62. On the divine name formed by the angelic beings, see *Zohar* 1:159a; Moses de León, *Peirush ha-Merkavah*, 67.

of sapphire, image of a throne. And upon the image of a throne, an image like the appearance of a human being upon it, above (ibid., 26). We have established: The image of this precious stone on the throne, standing on four supports, and upon that throne the image of *a human being*—to join with Him as one, to be blessed fittingly. When She is arrayed for the *human being*—all becoming a holy chariot—then all is a single chariot for this *human being*.[210]

"*Joseph harnessed his chariot*—Righteous One.[211]

"*And went up to meet Israel his father in Goshen. To meet Israel*—mystery of *a human being*.[212] *In Goshen*, 'approaching'—single approach, converging as one, in single convergence and union.[213]

"*And he appeared before him* (Genesis, ibid.)—for when the sun is reflected on the moon, it shines, illumining all those below. Similarly, as long as supernal holiness hovered over the Sanctuary below, the Temple shone, abiding in perfection; but when it withdrew and the Temple was destroyed, then, *he wept on his neck a long while* (ibid.), for all wept over the destroyed Temple.[214]

"*For a long while*. What does this mean? The last exile.[215]

"Then, when Jacob saw and contemplated that the array below was completed corresponding to the pattern above, he said, '*I can die now, after seeing your face, for you are still alive!* (ibid., 30)—for you have abided by mystery of holy Covenant, [211b] called Life of the Worlds.' Thus, *for you are still alive!* So at first he said, *Enough! Joseph my son is still alive* (ibid. 45:28)—for he must abide by the mystery of Life, as has been said."[216]

210. **precious stone on the throne...** *Shekhinah* is pictured as both "precious stone" and "throne." Together with the angels around Her, She constitutes the jeweled chariot-throne, arrayed for Her spouse, *Tif'eret*, the *human being*.

211. ***Joseph harnessed his chariot...*** Joseph symbolizes *Yesod* (known as Righteous One) and unites with the chariot, *Shekhinah*.

For the full verse, see above, note 202. On Joseph as *Yesod*, see above, p. 92, n. 50.

212. ***went up to meet Israel...*** Joseph, symbolizing *Yesod*, raises *Shekhinah* and links Her with *Tif'eret*, the *sefirah* of Israel (Jacob). The full name of *Tif'eret* is *Tif'eret Yisra'el* (Beauty of Israel). As indicated above (note 210), *Tif'eret* is the image of the *human being* on the chariot-throne.

213. ***Goshen*, 'approaching'...** Rabbi Yitsḥak associates the Egyptian place name גשן (*goshen*) with the Hebrew word גישה (*gishah*), "approach," alluding here to the mutual approach of *Shekhinah* and *Tif'eret*.

This Torah portion, of course, is called ויגש (*Va-Yiggash*), "He Approached," based on its opening verse (Genesis 44:18): *Judah approached him* [Joseph], etc. Cf. 45:4.

214. **when the sun is reflected on the moon...** When *Tif'eret* is reflected on *Shekhinah*, She shines, illumining all worlds below. Similarly, as long as divine holiness rested upon the Temple in Jerusalem, it shone.

On the divine withdrawal, see above, p. 289 and n. 172; p. 290 and n. 176. On weeping over the destruction, see above, pp. 285, 287, and nn. 148, 159, 162.

215. **last exile...** Which continues to this day.

216. **array below was completed...** *She-*

Come and see what is written: *Jacob blessed Pharaoh* (ibid. 47:10).

Rabbi Yose said, "Although they have established the meaning of Pharaoh in relation to another mystery, that is merely a Scriptural support.[217] But come and see: *To a mare among Pharaoh's chariots, I have compared you, my beloved* (Song of Songs 1:9).

"Come and see: There are chariots on the left in the mystery of the Other Side, and there are chariots on the right in the mystery of holiness above—these facing those; these, compassion, and those, judgment.[218]

"When the blessed Holy One executed judgment upon the Egyptians, every judgment that He inflicted corresponded precisely to those chariots, precisely to that side. Just as that side kills and extracts the soul, so the blessed Holy One acted in the same manner, as is written: *YHVH killed every firstborn* (Exodus 13:15)—and similarly with everything in Egypt, corresponding precisely.[219] Therefore, *I have compared you, my beloved*—exactly like him, killing, as is written: *I am YHVH* (ibid. 12:12), 'I am He, and no other.'[220] And in the time to come, what is written? *Who is this coming from Edom, in crimsoned garments from Bozrah—majestic in His attire, striding in the greatness of His strength? 'It is I, speaking in righteousness, mighty to save'* (Isaiah 63:1).[221]

"Come and see what is written: *Israel settled in the land of Egypt, in the land of Goshen, and they obtained holdings in it, and were fruitful and multiplied greatly*

khinah was fully arrayed and prepared for union with *Tif'eret,* as He was arrayed above for Her. Jacob realized that Joseph had proven his virtue by guarding the covenant of circumcision and refusing the advances of Potiphar's wife. Thereby, Joseph had attained the *sefirah* of *Yesod,* known as Life of the Worlds.

See above, p. 156 and n. 456. On the title Life of the Worlds, see above, p. 185 and n. 35.

The full verse in Genesis 45 reads: *Israel said, "Enough! Joseph my son is still alive. Let me go see him before I die."*

217. **meaning of Pharaoh...** Earlier, Rabbi El'azar had indicated that the phrase *house of Pharaoh* alludes to *Binah*. See above, p. 290 and n. 173. But Rabbi Yose insists that the biblical phrase was quoted simply as a proof-text; essentially, Pharaoh symbolizes the demonic realm.

218. **chariots on the left... on the right...** There exists an entire series of demonic powers conveying harsh judgment, which stands opposite the compassionate powers of the divine realm.

219. **every judgment... corresponded...** God's punishment of the Egyptians in the course of the Ten Plagues corresponded to the demonic powers symbolized by Pharaoh's chariots.

On the demonic seizure of the soul, see BT *Bava Batra* 16a, quoted above, note 188.

220. **Therefore, *I have compared you*...** God acted precisely like Pharaoh's demonic forces—and without the assistance of any other heavenly powers. The declaration "I am He, and no other" derives from the Passover Haggadah, commenting on the divine prediction of the killing of the firstborn in Exodus 12:12.

221. ***Who is this coming from Edom*...** Here too, when God will one day punish Israel's enemies, He will act directly on His own.

(Genesis 47:27). *They obtained holdings in it*—eternal inheritance. *They obtained holdings in it*—because it was destined for them, as has been established."[222]

Rabbi Yitsḥak said, "*And they were fruitful and multiplied greatly*—surely, for no suffering had befallen them and they sustained themselves with worldly delights. So, *they were fruitful and multiplied greatly.*"[223]

222. **eternal inheritance...** According to *Pirqei de-Rabbi Eli'ezer* 26, an earlier Pharaoh had given Goshen to the matriarch Sarah when he married her (see Genesis 12), so it became Israel's inheritance. See David Luria, ad loc., nn. 30–31; and on chapter 39, n. 15.

The book of Joshua (10:41; 11:16; 15:51) mentions the conquest of Goshen, though this refers to the northern Negev. Radak on 11:16 cites a midrash identifying the two Goshens as one and the same.

223. **no suffering had befallen them...** They were not yet enslaved by the Egyptians.

פרשת ויחי

Parashat Va-Yḥi

"HE LIVED" (GENESIS 47:28–50:26)

Rabbi Ḥiyya opened,[1] "*Your people, all of them righteous, will inherit the land forever—sprout of My planting, work of My hands, that I may be glorified* (Isaiah 60:21). Happy are Israel above all other nations, for the blessed Holy One has called them *righteous*, to bequeath to them an eternal heritage in the world that is coming, a world in which they delight, as is written: *Then you will delight upon YHVH* (ibid. 58:14).[2] Why? Because they cleave to the body of the King, as is written: *You, cleaving to YHVH your God, are alive every one of you today!* (Deuteronomy 4:4)."[3]

Rabbi Yitsḥak said, "*Your people, all of them righteous, will inherit the land*

1. **Rabbi Ḥiyya opened** In the standard printed editions of the *Zohar* (based on the Mantua edition), the portion *Va-Yḥi* begins in the middle of 211b. However, the opening pages (211b–216a [middle]) differ in style from the main body of the *Zohar* and appear to be an imitation, as recognized already by the editors of the Mantua edition. They do not appear in nearly all of the early, more reliable manuscripts (C9, N23, P2, V5, V6) nor in most later manuscripts (including L2, Ms4, O16, P4, Pr6). (They do appear in O2, M7, R1, and V16, and partially later in the Cremona edition.) Most traditional commentators (Cordovero, Galante, Lavi) pass over them. I have not included those pages here; rather, I have begun with Rabbi Ḥiyya's exposition on 216a.

See the note of the Mantua editors (included in the standard printed editions, 211b); the note in *OḤ*, 1:210c; Scholem, *Major Trends*, 387, n. 33; idem, *Kabbalah*, 217; *MmD*.

2. ***Your people, all of them righteous...*** This verse from Isaiah appears dozens of times in the *Zohar*. In M *Sanhedrin* 10:1, it is quoted to demonstrate that "all of Israel have a share in the world that is coming."

In the *Zohar*, the "world that is coming" refers not only to the hereafter but also to *Binah*, the ever-flowing source of all, "the world that is coming, constantly coming, never ceasing" (3:290b [*IZ*]). *Binah* is situated above *Tif'eret*, who is known by the name *YHVH*, so She is *upon* [or: *above*] *YHVH*. See above, pp. 201–2, n. 141; below, p. 322 and n. 113; *Zohar* 2:83a.

3. **body of the King...** *Tif'eret*, trunk of the sefirotic body, known as *YHVH*.

See *Zohar* 1:217b, 219a, 223b; 2:82a, 85b–86a, 87a, 123a, 193b; 3:294b (*IZ*).

forever. This verse is a supernal mystery among the reapers of the field.[4] For in the mystery of *aggadah* Rabbi Shim'on taught that the supernal heritage of this *land* is possessed only by one called *righteous*, because the *Matronita* cleaves to him, becoming fragrant, and the righteous one inherits the *Matronita*, surely![5]

"Here too, in His love for Israel, the blessed Holy One said, *Your people are all righteous*, and therefore *they will inherit the land forever*—they are worthy of inheriting the *Matronita*. Why are they called *righteous*, and why do they inherit the *Matronita*? Because they have been circumcised. For we have learned: Whoever is circumcised and enters this heritage and guards this covenant, enters and cleaves to the body of the King and enters this Righteous One. Thereby they are called *righteous*, and so *they will inherit the land forever*.[6]

"What is this land? The verse continues: *sprout of My planting, work of My hands, that I may be glorified. Sprout of My planting*—a branch of those branches planted by the blessed Holy One when He created the world, as is written: *YHVH Elohim planted a garden in Eden, to the east* (Genesis 2:8). This *land* is one of them; therefore, *sprout of My planting, work of My hands, that I may be glorified*.[7]

"Alternatively, *Your people are all righteous*—Jacob and his sons, who went down to Egypt among a stiff-necked people yet remained entirely righteous.[8] Therefore it is written: [216b] *they will inherit the land forever*, since from there they went up to inherit the Holy Land."

4. **reapers of the field** The Companions who harvest the secrets of Torah sprouting in the field of *Shekhinah*.

This designation appears frequently in the *Zohar*. See 1:156a (*ST*); 2:37a, 79b, 85b, 240b, 258a (*Heikh*); 3:106a, 127b (*IR*), 141b (*IR*), 143a (*IR*), 144a (*IR*), 214b, 297a; *ZḤ* 85d (*MhN, Rut*); *OY*; Galante; *DE*; Liebes, *Studies in the Zohar*, 175–76, n. 99. On *Shekhinah* as field, see Vol. 2, p. 206, n. 22.

5. **supernal heritage of this *land*...** The *land* symbolizes *Shekhinah*. She is also the *Matronita*, married to *Yesod*, who is known as *righteous*. A righteous human attains the rung of *Yesod* and thereby stimulates—and participates in—the union with *Shekhinah*, "inheriting" Her.

On *Yesod* as *righteous*, see above, p. 92, n. 50. מטרוניתא (*Matronita*) is an Aramaized form of Latin *matrona*, "matron, married woman, noble lady," and is often applied in the *Zohar* to *Shekhinah*.

6. **Whoever is circumcised...** By fulfilling the covenant of circumcision and maintaining sexual purity, one enters *Shekhinah* ("this heritage") and *Yesod* (the divine phallus, known as Righteous One), thereby cleaving to *Tif'eret* ("body of the King").

See *Zohar* 1:59b, 89a, 95a–b; 3:166a.

7. **branch of those branches...** *Shekhinah* is one of the sprouting branches—one of the seven lower *sefirot*—that were planted, or emanated, by God.

See *Bereshit Rabbah* 15:1; *Bahir* 117 (172); Ezra of Gerona, *Peirush Shir ha-Shirim*, 504; *Zohar* 1:31a, 35a–b, 37a, 45b, 93a; 2:217b; 3:4b, 217b.

8. **went down...remained entirely righteous** On the ethical behavior of the Israelites in Egypt, see *Vayiqra Rabbah* 32:5; *Shir ha-Shirim Rabbah* on 4:12.

Egypt is referred to as stiff-necked apparently by extension from Pharaoh's stubbornness.

Jacob lived in the land of Egypt (Genesis 47:28). Why is this portion closed?[9]

Rabbi Ya'akov said, "Because when Jacob died, the eyes of Israel were closed."[10]

Rabbi Yehudah said, "Because then they descended into exile and were enslaved."[11]

Rabbi Shim'on said, "What is written above? *Israel settled in the land of Egypt, in the land of Goshen, and they obtained holdings in it, and were fruitful and multiplied greatly* (ibid., 27), and it is written: *Jacob lived*—for it is unfitting to separate one from the other. Just as they abided in royal delights, obtaining pleasure and desirables for themselves, so Jacob too abided in royal delights, in pleasure and desirables for himself—one inseparable from the other.[12]

"Here is said of him *he lived* (ibid., 28)—unsaid for all of his days, all filled and fraught with suffering. Of him is written *I had no ease, no quiet, no rest, and turmoil came* (Job 3:26). After he went down to Egypt, it is said of him *he lived* —he saw his son as king; he saw all his sons virtuous and righteous, all living in pleasure and worldly delights, while he dwelled among them like good wine on its lees. Then is said of him *Jacob lived*, with no separation between *they were fruitful and multiplied greatly* and *Jacob lived*, fittingly."[13]

Seventeen years (Genesis, ibid.).[14] Why *seventeen years*?

Rabbi Shim'on said, "All of Jacob's days were filled with suffering, spent in suffering—at first. When Joseph appeared, standing before him, and when

9. ***Jacob lived*... closed** The full verse reads: *Jacob lived in the land of Egypt seventeen years, and Jacob's days, the years of his life, were one hundred and forty-seven years.*

This is the opening verse of Torah portion *Va-Yḥi* (*He lived*). Usually, the opening verse of a new portion is separated from the end of the concluding verse of the previous portion by extra blank space. Here there is no break.

See *Bereshit Rabbah* 96:1; *Tanḥuma* (Buber), *Vayḥi* 1; *Minḥat Shai* on Genesis 47:28.

10. **eyes of Israel were closed** Because they lost their source of wisdom, or because of the impending enslavement.

See Rashi on Genesis 47:28, paraphrasing *Bereshit Rabbah* 96:1.

11. **enslaved** See *Bereshit Rabbah* 96:1.

12. **unfitting to separate...** Rabbi Shim'on offers another reason for the fact that the opening verse of this portion (*Jacob lived*...) is not separated by any extra space from the concluding verse of the previous portion (*Israel settled*), namely, to demonstrate the logical link between the two statements.

See above, p. 301 at n. 223.

13. **Here is said of him *he lived*...** Only now did Jacob enjoy a fulfilled, tranquil life. His earlier suffering included the enmity of Esau, laboring for Laban, the rape of Dinah his daughter, and the disappearance of Joseph.

See *Bereshit Rabbah* 84:3 (quoting the verse from Job); *Aggadat Bereshit* 60:2; *Leqaḥ Tov* and *Midrash ha-Gadol*, Genesis 47:28; above, pages 88–89. Cf. *Zohar* 1:123a.

Wine ages best on its sediment, or lees. For the expression "like wine on its lees," see *Zohar* 2:87a; 3:128b (*IR*), 140b (*IR*), 248a.

14. ***Seventeen years*** The verse reads: *Jacob lived in the land of Egypt seventeen years.* See above, note 9.

Jacob gazed upon Joseph, his soul was fulfilled as if he had seen his mother—for the beauty of Joseph resembled the beauty of Rachel—and he felt like someone who had never undergone suffering.[15]

"When Joseph parted from him, then was fulfilled *I had no ease, no quiet, no rest, and turmoil came*—for this was harder on Jacob than everything he had endured. At the time that Joseph parted from him, what is written? *Joseph, seventeen years old, was tending the flock*... (ibid. 37:2).[16] All of Jacob's days, he had never seen suffering such as this, and he wept every day for those seventeen years of Joseph.

"What was the response? '*Joseph will lay his hand on your eyes* (ibid. 46:4): here are seventeen other years for you—of delights, pleasures, enjoyments, and desirables'—as is written: *Jacob lived in the land of Egypt seventeen years*.... It has been taught: All those years, *Shekhinah*—Glory of the blessed Holy One—was present with him, and therefore they were called 'life.'[17]

"Come and see what is written: *The spirit of Jacob their father revived* (ibid. 45:27). Apparently, his spirit was previously dead! And he was unprepared to receive another spirit, for the spirit above does not dwell in a void."[18]

Rabbi Yose said, "*Shekhinah* dwells only in a place that is complete, not in a place that is deficient, defective, or sad—rather, in a complete place, a place prepared, a place of joy. Consequently, all those years that Joseph was separated from his father and Jacob was sad, *Shekhinah* did not dwell within him."[19]

15. **seen his mother...** Joseph's mother, Rachel, who was Jacob's wife.

On the resemblance between Joseph and Rachel, see *Bereshit Rabbah* 86:6.

16. **When Joseph parted...** When he was kidnapped by his brothers.

The verse reads: *These are the generations of Jacob: Joseph, seventeen years old, was tending the flock with his brothers.*

17. **seventeen other years...** When Joseph was sold into slavery at age seventeen, Jacob—believing that his son had been killed—was overwhelmed by sadness and mourning. Now, many years later, when Jacob was reunited with Joseph in Egypt, God provided him a corresponding number of years of joy and fulfillment.

See *Midrash Aggadah* and *Midrash ha-Gadol*, Genesis 47:28; above, pp. 92–93 and n. 55.

The context in Genesis (46:2–4) reads: *God spoke to Israel in visions of the night, and He said, "Jacob! Jacob!" And he said "Here I am." He said, "I am God, God of your father. Fear not to go down to Egypt, for I will make of you a great nation there. I Myself will go down with you to Egypt and I Myself will surely bring you up as well, and Joseph will lay his hand on your eyes."*

18. ***spirit of Jacob*... previously dead...** Joseph's disappearance had deadened Jacob spiritually, preventing him from acquiring a higher level of soul and being in contact with *Shekhinah*.

See above, p. 94 and n. 63; p. 207 and n. 177. The context in Genesis (45:26–27) reads: *They told him, saying, "Joseph is still alive! Indeed, he is ruler of all the land of Egypt!" His heart went numb, for he did not believe them. And they spoke to him all the words of Joseph that he had spoken to them, and he saw the wagons that Joseph had sent to carry him, and the spirit of Jacob their father revived.*

19. ***Shekhinah* dwells...** See BT *Shabbat*

It has been taught: Rabbi El'azar said in the name of Rabbi Abba, "*Serve YHVH with joy, come before Him with singing* (Psalms 100:2)—for the worship of the blessed Holy One can be only with joy." For Rabbi El'azar said, "*Shekhinah* does not dwell in sadness, as is written: '*Now bring me* מנגן (*menaggen*), *a minstrel.' And then,* כנגן המנגן (*ke-naggen ha-menaggen*), *as the minstrel was playing,* [*the hand of YHVH came upon him*] (2 Kings 3:15). *Menaggen, menaggen*—three times, why? To arouse spirit from consummation of all: consummate spirit."[20]

Rabbi Abba said, "There we learned: From four sides, all derives; therein all roots of those above and below intertwine. And it has been taught: One enters, another emerges; one conceals, another expresses; linked with one another—fathers of all!"[21]

Rabbi Shim'on said, "*Only your fathers did YHVH desire* (Deuteronomy 10:15). It is written: *your fathers*—precisely, three! As indicated by *only*—literally, *only*! From these, all others branch and intertwine, raising the name to be crowned."[22]

306 It has been taught that Rabbi Yose said, "From the day that Rabbi Shim'on emerged from the cave, words were not concealed from the Companions and supernal mysteries were revealed among them as if they had been given at that

30b: "*Shekhinah* abides neither through sadness nor laziness nor frivolity nor levity nor talk nor idle chatter [or: vain pursuits], but only through the joy of *mitsvah*." See above, p. 94 and nn. 62–63.

20. ***Now bring me* מנגן (*menaggen*), *a minstrel*...** When the prophet Elisha sought divine inspiration, he asked for a musician to play in order to induce a state of joy.

The triple appearance of the root נגן (*ngn*), "to play," alludes to the three levels of soul and their corresponding *sefirot*: *Shekhinah*, *Tif'eret*, and *Binah*, who is "consummation of all."

See above, p. 94 and n. 62; pp. 262–64. For various interpretations of the last sentence, see *OY*; Vital; Galante; *KP*.

21. **From four sides...** The four sides, or directions (south, north, east, and west), or elements (water, fire, air, and earth), symbolize respectively *Ḥesed*, *Gevurah*, *Tif'eret*, and *Shekhinah*. All existence derives from this sefirotic quartet. The last, cryptic sentence alludes to their progressive emanation and may mean: *Ḥesed* enters into *Gevurah*, who then conveys the flow to *Tif'eret*, within whom the flow is temporarily concealed, eventually expressed via *Shekhinah*. These four *sefirot* are also symbolized respectively by the three patriarchs (Abraham, Isaac, and Jacob) and King David.

Rabbi Abba's source ("There we learned") is not identified. See *Zohar* 2:23b–24a; 3:262b. Cf. *Zohar* 1:235a; 3:130b (*IR*). For a range of interpretations, see *OY*; Vital; Galante; *KP*; *MM*.

22. ***Only your fathers*...** Rabbi Shim'on insists that *fathers* refers precisely and *only* to the sefirotic triad *Ḥesed*, *Gevurah*, and *Tif'eret* (symbolized by Abraham, Isaac, and Jacob)—not including *Shekhinah* (symbolized by King David). This last *sefirah* (known as the divine name) is subsequently raised, adorned, and united with Her divine spouse.

See BT *Berakhot* 16b; *Zohar* 3:262b.

moment on Mount Sinai.[23] Once he took his final sleep, it is written: *The wellsprings of the deep were dammed up,* [217a] *and the sluices of heaven* (Genesis 8:2), and the Companions would mouth words uncomprehendingly.[24]

"For one day Rabbi Yehudah was sitting at the gate of Tiberias, and he saw two camels shaking loose the ropes on their humps.[25] A load of balsam fell and birds came,[26] but before reaching it, they burst.[27] Afterward, numerous birds came, and people attacked them, throwing stony clods,[28] but they did not burst; they shouted at them, but they did not disperse.

"They heard a voice: 'Crown of crowns in captivity has cast out its Lord.'[29]

23. **Rabbi Shim'on emerged from the cave...** According to rabbinic tradition, Rabbi Shim'on together with his son, Rabbi El'azar, hid from the Roman authorities in a cave for thirteen years.

See *Bereshit Rabbah* 79:6; JT *Shevi'it* 9:1, 38d; BT *Shabbat* 33b, *Sanhedrin* 98a; *Pesiqta de-Rav Kahana* 11:16; *Qohelet Rabbah* on 10:8; *Midrash Tehillim* 17:13; *Zohar* 1:11a–b, 244b; *ZḤ* 59c–60a.

On the comparison between learning Torah and the experience of revelation at Sinai, see *Sifrei,* Deuteronomy 58; *Vayiqra Rabbah* 16:4; *Tanḥuma* (Buber), *Yitro* 7; *Ki Tavo* 3; *Zohar* 1:94b–95a; 2:206a.

24. **Once he took his final sleep...** Just as Jacob's death caused Israel's eyes to close (above, at note 10), so the death of Rabbi Shim'on caused wisdom to disappear.

25. **ropes...** קטפירא (*Qatpira*), a neologism that connotes "tying, linking." As with other Zoharic neologisms, the word also appears in various metathetic spellings, e.g., קפטירא (*qaftira*) and קופטרא (*quftera*). On *quftera* as "rope," see *Vayiqra Rabbah* 4:2 (and Margulies's n. 3, pp. 81–82; Lieberman's note, p. 871); *Qohelet Rabbah* on 6:6; *Tanḥuma, Miqqets* 10; *Tanḥuma* (Buber), *Miqqets* 15 (and Buber's n. 116); *Arukh* and *Arukh ha-Shalem,* s.v. *pi turei*; Rashi on *Berakhot* 8a, s.v. *ke-fiturei*.

The word could also be rendered here "saddlebag," as in *Zohar* 1:72a. See above, pp. 71–72, n. 483; p. 298, n. 208; below, note 75; *Zohar* 2:209a; 3:6b, 62b; *Bei'ur ha-Millim ha-Zarot,* 188, n. 185; Luria, *Va-Ye'esof David,* s.v. *qftr, qaftera*; Liebes, *Peraqim,* 349–54. For various interpretations of the literal and symbolic meaning of this passage, see *OY*; Galante; *KP*; *DE; NZ*; Tishby, *Wisdom of the Zohar,* 1:165–66; *MmD*; and below.

26. **balsam...** Again, קטפירא (*qatpira*), which here is apparently based on קטפא (*qitpa*), "balsamic resin." See the Talmudic expressions קטפא פירא (*qitpa peira*), "resin (is considered as) fruit" (BT *Niddah* 8a–b), and קטפא דפירא (*qitpa de-feira*), "resin of the fruit" (BT *Niddah* 8b); Mopsik. Cf. JT *Yoma* 4:4, 41d.

On the image of camels carrying balsamic resin, see Genesis 37:25, and *Targum Onqelos,* ad loc.

27. **burst** In the preceding paragraph, Rabbi Yose quoted Genesis 8:2, describing the ending of the Flood: *The wellsprings of the deep were dammed up, and the sluices of heaven.* Now, the "bursting" of the birds recalls the "bursting" at the beginning of the Flood: *All the wellsprings of the great deep burst and the sluices of heaven were opened* (Genesis 7:11). Cf. *Zohar* 1:117a.

28. **stony clods** טרטישא (*Tartisha*), based on Hebrew טרש (*teresh*), "stony ground." See *Tosefta, Sotah* 11:16; *Bereshit Rabbah* 23:6; *Vayiqra Rabbah* 36:2; *Zohar* 1:34a.

29. **Crown of crowns in captivity...** A heavenly voice alludes to the meaning of what Rabbi Yehudah has just witnessed. *Shekhinah,* also known as *Atarah* (Crown), is in exile together with Her people; unable to unite with Her Husband, *Tif'eret,* She has in effect cast Him away. The birds symbolize

"While he was sitting there, a man passed by and gazed upon them. He said, 'This one has not fulfilled what is written: *Vultures came down on the carcasses, but Abram drove them off* (ibid. 15:11).'[30]

"Rabbi Yehudah said, 'I tried, but they won't disperse.'

"The man turned his head and said, 'This one has not yet plucked the hair from the head of his Lord nor shaven the *Matronita*.'[31]

"He pursued him for three miles, but he would not tell him.[32] Rabbi Yehudah's mind languished.

"One day he fell asleep under a tree, and in his dream he saw four wings arrayed, and Rabbi Shim'on ascending on them with a Torah scroll. He left behind no book of mysteries or *aggadah*, but took them away with him. They took him up to heaven, and he saw him disappear from sight, revealed no more.

"When he awoke, he said, 'Surely, ever since Rabbi Shim'on took his final sleep, wisdom has departed from the earth. Woe to the generation that has lost this precious stone, joining upper and lower pillars!'[33]

"He came to Rabbi Abba and told him. Rabbi Abba raised his hands to his

evil powers or Israel's enemies who—though at first unsuccessful (see 2 Kings 18–19)—eventually raided the precious treasure (*Shekhinah*, the Temple, or the people of Israel). See below, p. 325 and n. 130.

The word "captivity" renders קיזרין (*qizrin*), which may derive from Castilian *cazar*, "to seize, catch." This reading is preserved or supported by most of the manuscripts, including C9, L2, P2, P4, Pr6, V6, and the Cremona edition. The other readings, which also fit the context but seem to be later constructions, are קטרין (*qitrin*), "knots, bonds" (M7 and R1), and קדרין (*qadrin*), "darkness" (*OY* and the Mantua edition).

30. **not fulfilled what is written...** Whereas Abram drove off the hostile creatures, Rabbi Yehudah ("this one") did not.

According to rabbinic tradition, the *vultures* represent the nations of the world who threaten Israel. See *Bereshit Rabbah* 44:16 (and Theodor's note); *Targum Yerushalmi* and *Targum Yerushalmi* (frag.), Genesis 15:11.

31. **plucked the hair...** Hair symbolizes the power of harsh judgment, which must be removed from the Divine Male ("his Lord") and *Shekhinah* ("the *Matronita*"). Rabbi Yehudah had failed to remove these harsh forces through contemplative prayer.

See Leviticus 13:40–41; *Targum Onqelos*, Leviticus 13:41; *Zohar* 1:241b; 3:48b–49a, 125b–126a, 127b, 131b–132a (*IR*), 140a (*IR*), 295b (*IZ*); Liebes, *Studies in the Zohar*, 119–26. On the term *Matronita*, see above, note 5.

32. **three miles...** Rabbi Yehudah ran after the anonymous man, hoping to learn the meaning of his words.

According to Rav Sheshet (BT *Sotah* 46b), one should escort his teacher a distance of a parasang. A distinguished teacher, however, is to be escorted for three parasangs. (The Persian parasang equals about 3.5 modern miles. The term here in the *Zohar*, מלין [*milin*], "miles," refers to the Roman mile, slightly shorter than the modern mile.)

See *Pesiqta de-Rav Kahana* 18:5; *Bereshit Rabbah* 32:10; *Zohar* 1:51a, 87a, 96b, 150b; 2:14a, 164a, 187a; 3:8b.

33. **precious stone...** Rabbi Shim'on had linked earth and heaven.

See *Zohar* 1:11a. On the unique status of Rabbi Shim'on, see Liebes, *Studies in the Zohar*, 1–74.

head and wept, and said, 'Rabbi Shim'on, the millstones with which fine manna is ground every day, and then gathered, as is written: *The one with the least gathered ten ḥomers* (Numbers 11:32)![34] Now millstones and manna have disappeared; nothing remains of them in the world except what is written: *Take one jar and put in it a full omer of manna and set it before YHVH for safekeeping* (Exodus 16:33)—it is not written *revealed* but rather *for safekeeping*, for concealment. Now who can reveal secrets, and who will know them?"[35]

"He whispered to Rabbi Yehudah, 'Surely that man you saw was Elijah, and he did not wish to reveal secrets, so that you would realize how worthy Rabbi Shim'on was in his days, and so the generation would weep for him.'[36]

"He replied, 'Just weep like Rabbi Yehudah, who weeps over him every day, for he encountered him in the holy assembly of Rabbi Shim'on and the other Companions.'[37]

"He said, 'Alas, that we did not depart on that day along with those three who departed, so that we would not see this generation transmogrified!'[38]

34. **millstones . . . manna . . .** The manna symbolizes wisdom, refined and conveyed by Rabbi Shim'on.

On grinding the manna with millstones, see Numbers 11:8. On manna as the divine word or wisdom, see Deuteronomy 8:3; Wisdom of Solomon 16:26; Philo, *Deterius*, 118; John 6:31–35; *Mekhilta, Vayassa* 5; *Zohar* 2:61b–62a.

The verse quoted here actually refers not to manna but to the quail, which was also miraculously provided in the wilderness. Cf. the account of gathering the manna in Exodus 16:17–18. A *ḥomer* ("donkey-load") is estimated to be 230 liters.

35. ***Take one jar . . .*** The full verse reads: *Moses said to Aaron, "Take one jar and put in it a full omer of manna and set it before YHVH for safekeeping for your generations."*

The word אצנעותא (*atsna'uta*), "concealment," alludes to the esoteric nature of Kabbalah and the *Zohar*, and perhaps specifically to *Sifra di-Tsni'uta* (The Book of Concealment), a short, cryptic section of the *Zohar* whose subject is the mysteries of divine being (2:176b–179a).

See *Targum Onqelos*, ad loc.; Liebes, *Studies in the Zohar*, 200–1, n. 58; Huss, "Hofa'ato shel 'Sefer ha-Zohar,'" 518; Hellner-Eshed, *Ve-Nahar Yotse me-Eden*, 429–32. An *omer* is estimated by biblical scholars to be 2.3 liters.

36. **man you saw was Elijah . . .** Who never actually died and reappears throughout the generations. See above, p. 283, n. 136.

37. **He replied . . .** Rabbi Yehudah replies to Rabbi Abba, speaking of himself in the third person.

The אדרא קדישא (*iddera qaddisha*), "holy threshing floor (or assembly)," refers to the dramatic and profound gathering of Rabbi Shim'on and the Companions described in *Zohar* 3:127b–145a (known as *Idra Rabba*, "The Great *Idra*").

38. **three who departed . . .** Three of the Companions (Rabbi Yose son of Ya'akov, Rabbi Ḥizkiyah, and Rabbi Yeisa) died toward the end of the holy assembly. See *Zohar* 3:144a.

"Transmogrified" renders the Aramaic מתהפך (*mithappakh*) "overturn, turn around, transform oneself." See Deuteronomy 32:20: דור תהפכת (*dor tahpukhot*), *generation of overturning*, i.e., a wayward, perverse, treacherous generation.

"He said to him, 'Rabbi, tell me. It is written: *They shall take gold, indigo, purple, crimson, and linen* (ibid. 28:5), whereas silver is not mentioned, and yet it is written: *gold and silver* (ibid. 25:3).'[39]

"He replied, 'Bronze as well, for silver and bronze were both enumerated, but not here.[40] Well, if the Holy Lamp had not revealed this in its place, I could not reveal it.'[41]

"He opened, saying, '*Mine is the silver and Mine is the gold* (Haggai 2:8), corresponding to what is written: *The heavens are YHVH's heavens* (Psalms 115:16).[42] In various places I have contemplated these holy garments, as is written: *They are holy garments* (Leviticus 16:4); *They shall make holy garments* (Exodus 28:4). What holiness is here? Oh, but we have learned that they manifest holiness in all places, as is written: *They are holy garments; they shall make holy garments*—corresponding to the pattern above. For it has been taught: High priest above, high priest below; garments of glory above, garments of glory below.[43]

"'As for why Scripture does not state *silver and bronze*, these have been reserved for another place, as is written: *All the posts around the court shall be banded in silver,* [*their hooks silver*] *and their sockets bronze* (ibid. 27:17)—for these are vessels to be utilized for the Tabernacle. But here, with these garments of glory, no one may use them except the high priest, whose head is anointed with holy oil, as is written: *You shall make holy garments for Aaron your brother*

39. **They shall take...** This verse describes the types of material to be used in making the garments for the high priest. Rabbi Yehudah asks Rabbi Abba why silver is not included, since several chapters earlier silver is mentioned together with gold in the list of materials to be donated for the Tabernacle. The verse in Exodus 25 reads: *This is the donation that you shall take from them: gold and silver and bronze.* The following verse includes indigo, purple, crimson, and linen.

40. **Bronze, as well...** Before answering the question, Rabbi Abba sharpens it, by noting that bronze could have been included as well, since it too is specified in Exodus 25:3.

41. **if the Holy Lamp...** If Rabbi Shim'on had not already revealed the reason elsewhere, Rabbi Abba would not dare to.

On Rabbi Shim'on's title בוצינא קדישא (*Botsina Qaddisha*), "Holy Lamp," see above, p. 209 and n. 182.

42. **Mine is the silver...** Silver and gold symbolize, respectively, *Ḥesed* and *Gevurah,* both of which are included in—and balanced by—*Tif'eret,* known as both *heavens* and *YHVH*. *Tif'eret* is the antecedent of *Mine,* as indicated by the conclusion of the verse in Haggai: *Mine is the silver and Mine is the gold, declares YHVH of Hosts.*

The full verse in Psalm 115 reads: *The heavens are YHVH's heavens, but the earth He has given to human beings.*

43. **manifest holiness in all places...** The garments worn by the high priest on earth correspond to spiritual garments robing the *sefirah* of *Ḥesed* above, who is known as "high priest." The wording *they are holy garments* refers to the sefirotic garments, which exist (*are*) eternally, whereas *they shall make holy garments* refers to the garments "made" below for the high priest.

See *Zohar* 1:47b, 87a; 2:67b.

for glory and for splendor (ibid. 28:2)—for in these garments of glory, he resembles the pattern above.'"[44]

It has been taught: *The days of Israel drew near to die* (Genesis 47:29).[45] Rabbi Yehudah said, "Woe to the world, for human beings neither see nor hear nor [217b] know that every single day the voice of a herald is heard in 250 worlds!

"It has been taught: A certain world is known above, and as the herald emerges, that world trembles and quivers. Two birds issue, leaving that world—their abode is beneath a tree containing a vision of life and death.[46] One bird goes toward the south and one toward the north; one bird as day lightens and one as day darkens. Each one calls and proclaims what it hears from that herald. Afterward they want to ascend to their site, but their feet slip into the hollow of the abyss, where they are trapped until midnight.[47] At midnight, a herald proclaims, *Like birds seized in a snare, so humans are trapped...* (Ecclesiastes 9:12)."[48]

Rabbi Yehudah said, "When a person's legs are trapped and his days draw near, that day is called 'Day of YHVH,' to return his soul to Him.[49] It has been taught: At that time, the holy crown visits his spirit. Who is that? As is written: *The days of our lives are seventy years* (Psalms 90:10)—seventh crown of all.[50]

44. **reserved for another place...** Since silver and bronze were utilized in the construction of the outer, more public court of the Tabernacle, it would be inappropriate for these two materials to be used for the holy garments intended for the high priest alone.

45. ***The days of Israel...*** The full verse reads: *The days of Israel drew near to die, and he called for his son Joseph and said to him, "If I have found favor in your eyes, place your hand under my thigh and act toward me with steadfast kindness—please do not bury me in Egypt."*

46. **Two birds...** Two angels who dwell in *Shekhinah*. She is known as the Tree of Knowledge of Good and Evil, comprising life and death.

On the angelic birds of *Shekhinah*, see *Zohar* 1:162b–163a, 172a; 2:179a (*SdTs*). Cf. 1:234a (*Tos*).

47. **hollow of the abyss...** The abode of demonic powers.

48. ***Like birds...*** The full verse reads: *For a human does not know his time. Like fish caught in a cruel net, like birds seized in a snare, so humans are trapped in a time of calamity, when it falls upon them suddenly.*

See above, pp. 197–98 at n. 121; *Zohar* 3:52b–53a.

49. **When a person's legs are trapped...** When a person lies on his deathbed and his days draw near to die (see Genesis 47:29, quoted above, at note 45).

In biblical prophetic literature the "Day of YHVH" is the day on which God will eventually reveal Himself to the nations in all His power and destroy Israel's enemies. Here, it refers to the final day of each person's life, when his soul returns to its divine source.

50. **seventh crown of all** *Shekhinah*, last of the seven lower *sefirot* (which begin with *Ḥesed*). The normal span of human life (*seventy years*) corresponds to this sefirotic septet. At the moment of death, *Shekhinah* (the seventh) comes to retrieve the soul.

The verse in Psalms reads: *The days of our*

And if it derives from the side of *Gevurah*, Strength, it is written *or with* גבורות (*gevurot*), *strength, eighty years* (ibid.)—for the crown of *Gevurah* is the eighth.[51] From here on, there is no room to extend, as is written: *Their extension is toil and sorrow* (ibid.). Where there is no foundation, a building cannot endure."[52]

Rabbi Yehudah said, "Happy are the righteous when the blessed Holy One desires to retrieve his spirit, to draw that spirit into Him.[53] For it has been taught: When the blessed Holy One desires to retrieve his spirit, if it is virtuous, then it is written *The spirit will return to God who gave it* (Ecclesiastes 12:7). But if it is not found to be virtuous, woe to that spirit, for it must be cleansed in blazing fire and refined, so that it can be drawn into the body of the King![54] If unrefined, alas, for then that spirit is whirled like a stone in the hollow of a sling, as is written: *The soul of your enemies He will sling from the hollow of a sling* (1 Samuel 25:29).[55]

lives are seventy years, or with strength, eighty years; their pride is toil and sorrow. See *Zohar* 1:124a–b.

51. **from the side of *Gevurah*...** If the person's soul derives from *Binah* (the source and crown of *Gevurah*), then his life span is eighty years, because *Binah* is the eighth *sefirah*, counting upward from *Shekhinah*.

On the link between *Binah* and *Gevurah*, see *Zohar* 3:293a (*IZ*).

52. **no room to extend...** Eighty years exhausts the sefirotic octet. Anyone living longer than this will suffer greatly because he lacks a divine framework and support.

Their extension renders the Hebrew רהבם (*rohbam*), "*their pride*" or "*the best of them*" (see above, note 50). Rabbi Yehudah's interpretation accords with the Septuagint and Vulgate, which reflect the reading רחבם (*roḥbam*), "their extent, span." See *Zohar* 1:124a; *OY*; Galante; *Sullam*; *MmD*.

53. **retrieve his spirit...** "His" may refer to the righteous human or to God. Just as God breathed the spirit into the human, so He now breathes it back into Himself.

See Genesis 2:7: *He blew into his nostrils the breath of life, and the human became a living being.* See Naḥmanides, ad loc.; below, at note 155.

54. **cleansed in blazing fire...** Purging its sinfulness.

Elsewhere, the *Zohar* teaches that all souls require bathing in the River of Fire. See above, p. 233 and n. 330. On "the body of the King," see above, note 3.

55. **whirled like a stone in the hollow of a sling...** See BT *Shabbat* 152a: "Rabbi Eli'ezer said, '... The souls of the wicked are continually muzzled, while one angel stands at one end of the world and another stands at the other end, and they sling their souls [the souls of the wicked] to each other, as is said: *The soul of your enemies He will sling as from the hollow of a sling*.'"

Although some *Zohar* commentators understand this image as referring to reincarnation, that is unlikely here because for the *Zohar*, reincarnation applies only to certain specific sexual transgressions, especially failing to fulfill the *mitsvah* of procreation.

See Radak on the verse in Samuel; Moses de León, *Shushan Edut*, 351–53 (and n. 171, where Scholem cites De León's likely source in Jacob ha-Kohen's *Sefer ha-Orah*); idem, *Sefer ha-Rimmon*, 373 (and n. 6), 399; *Zohar* 1:77b, 128a; 2:59a, 99b, 103a, 142b; 3:25a, 185b–186a, 213b; Liebes, *Peraqim*, 345–47 (who discusses the Zoharic neologism קוספיתא [*quspita*], "hollow of a sling"). In a later book (*Sefer ha-Mishqal*, 67–68) De León rejects this particular stage of the afterlife.

"It has been taught: If that spirit is worthy, countless benefits are treasured away for it in that world, as is written: *No eye has seen, O God, but You, what You will do for one who awaits You* (Isaiah 64:3)."

Rabbi Yose said, "As that person's days draw near, for thirty days a proclamation is made about him in the world, and even the birds of heaven proclaim. If he is virtuous, for thirty days a proclamation is made about him among the righteous in the Garden of Eden.[56]

"It has been taught: During all those thirty days, his soul departs from him every night, ascending and viewing its place in that world. And that person does not know or perceive or control his soul during all those thirty days as previously, as is written: *No one has power over the spirit, to restrain the spirit...* (Ecclesiastes 8:8)."[57]

Rabbi Yehudah said, "From the moment those thirty days begin, a person's *tselem* darkens, and the image visible on the ground is withheld."[58]

Rabbi Yitsḥak was sitting one day at Rabbi Yehudah's door and he was sad. Rabbi Yehudah emerged and found him by his gate, sitting in sadness. He said to him, "How is this day different from others?"[59]

He replied, "I have come to ask you three things. One, when you speak a word of Torah and you mention some of the words that I have said, that you say

56. **proclamation is made...** Announcing his imminent death. For a virtuous human, a proclamation is made among the righteous souls in Paradise, so that they can prepare to welcome the new arrival.

See *Zohar* 1:123b (*MhN*), 218b, 219b.

57. ***No one has power...*** The verse reads: *No one has power over the spirit, to restrain the spirit; there is no power over the day of death.*

58. ***tselem* darkens...** The צלם (*tselem*), "image," is an ethereal body surrounding the physical body—an intermediate power between soul and body. The soul is clothed in the *tselem* before descending to earth, retains it while in the physical body until shortly before death, and then regains it upon ascending.

A person's shadow is the visible "image" (דיוקנא [*deyoqna*]) of this ethereal image. The link between shadow and *tselem* is accentuated by the fact that the Hebrew word for shadow is צל (*tsel*), and actually *tselem* means "shadow" in Psalms 39:7 (quoted below, at note 64). Here Rabbi Yehudah teaches that thirty days before a person's death, his *tselem* fades and his shadow ("image visible on the ground") disappears.

On the *tselem*, see Genesis 1:27; *Zohar* 1:7a, 90b–91a, 131a, 220a, 227a, 233b; 2:11a, 96b, 161b; 3:13b, 43a–b, 61b, 104a–b; Moses de León, *Sefer ha-Rimmon*, 390; Scholem, "Levush ha-Neshamot," 293–95; idem, *Kabbalah*, 158–59; idem, *On the Mystical Shape of the Godhead*, 251–73; Tishby, *Wisdom of the Zohar*, 2:770–73. Cf. Rashi on BT *Ḥagigah* 12b, s.v. *ve-ruhot unshamot*. On the shadow, see also Naḥmanides on Numbers 14:9; Ginzberg, *Legends*, 5:108; Tishby, *Wisdom of the Zohar*, 2:771.

59. **Rabbi Yitsḥak was sitting...** For an analysis of this story, see Wineman, *Mystic Tales of the Zohar*, 73–87. For similar miraculous tales, see *Zohar* 2:61a–b; 3:204b–205a; *ZḤ* 80b–c (*MhN*, *Rut*).

them in my name, mentioning my name.[60] Another, that you render my son, Joseph, worthy through Torah.[61] And another, that you go to my grave all seven days and offer a prayer for me."[62]

He said to him, "How do you know?"[63]

He replied, "Look, my soul departs from me every night and does not enlighten me with a dream as before. Further, when I pray and reach 'who hears prayer,' I look for my *tselem* on the wall and do not see it, so I conclude that since the *tselem* has disappeared and can no longer be seen, the herald has already gone forth and issued the proclamation, as is written: *Only with a tselem does a human walk about* (Psalms 39:7)—as long as a person's *tselem* does not disappear, *a human walks about*, his spirit sustained within him. Once a person's *tselem* passes away and cannot be seen, he passes away from this world."[64]

He said to him, "And from here, as is written: *For our days upon earth are a shadow* (Job 8:9)."[65] He said, "All these things that you ask I will do. But I ask of

you [218a] to select my place in that world next to you, just as we were in this world."[66]

Rabbi Yehudah wept, and said, "Please, let me stay with you through all of these days!"

They went to Rabbi Shim'on and found him engaged in Torah. Rabbi Shim'on raised his eyes and saw Rabbi Yitsḥak, and he saw the Angel of Death running in front of him, dancing.[67] Rabbi Shim'on rose and grasped Rabbi

60. **when you speak a word of Torah...** See BT *Yevamot* 97a, in the name of Rabbi Shim'on son of Yoḥai: "Whenever a tradition is reported in this world in the name of a scholar, his lips move gently in the grave."

Cf. *Avot* 6:6.

61. **render my son, Joseph, worthy through Torah** By teaching him Torah.

62. **go to my grave all seven days...** During the first week of mourning, when the body suffers most intensely from the judgment known as *ḥibbut ha-qever* (beating in the grave). See above, p. 127 and n. 268.

63. **How do you know?** That you are about to die.

64. **when I pray and reach 'who hears prayer'...** The blessing "who hears prayer" in the *Amidah* is the appropriate place to insert individual requests. But at this point in his prayer, Rabbi Yitsḥak noticed that his shadow had disappeared. The shadow is the visible image of the *tselem*, which is an ethereal body. As one's death approaches, both of these disappear. See above, note 58.

The verse in Psalms is usually understood to mean *As a mere* צלם (*tselem*), *shadow* [or: *phantom*], *a human walks about.* See *Zohar* 3:43a–b. On the proclamation announcing imminent death, see above, at note 56.

65. **And from here...** Rabbi Yehudah quotes another verse that indicates the correlation between a person's life span and his shadow.

66. **select my place...** Rabbi Yehudah asks his colleague to reserve an adjoining place for him in Paradise, so that the two of them can maintain their intimate relationship. Cf. *Zohar* 3:287b (*IZ*).

67. **Angel of Death... dancing** In anticipation. On his dancing, see BT *Berakhot* 51a; *Zohar* 3:172b.

Yitsḥak's hand, saying, "I decree: Whoever is accustomed to enter may enter. Whoever is not accustomed to enter may not."

Rabbi Yitsḥak and Rabbi Yehudah entered; the Angel of Death was bound outside. Rabbi Shim'on gazed and saw that the time had not yet arrived, for it had been arranged for the eighth hour of the day.[68] Rabbi Shim'on seated him in front of him and engaged him in Torah.[69]

He said to his son, Rabbi El'azar, "Sit by the door, and whatever you see, do not speak with it! And if it wants to enter, place it under oath not to."[70]

Rabbi Shim'on said to Rabbi Yitsḥak, "Have you seen the image of your father today?" For we have learned: When a person is about to depart the world, his father and relatives are present with him, and he sees and recognizes them. And all those with whom he shared the same rung in that world, they all gather around him and accompany his soul to the place where she will abide.[71]

He replied, "I have not yet seen anyone."

At once Rabbi Shim'on rose and said, "Master of the world! Rabbi Yitsḥak is well known among us: he is one of the 'seven eyes' here.[72] Look, I am holding him! Give him to me!" 315

A voice issued, proclaiming, "Flying spark of his Lord enveloped in the wings of Rabbi Shim'on![73] Behold, he is yours! You shall bring him with you when you enter to occupy your throne."[74]

68. **time had not yet arrived...** For the Angel of Death to seize Rabbi Yitsḥak.

69. **engaged him in Torah** Because the study of Torah renders the Angel of Death powerless.

See BT *Shabbat* 30b; *Eruvin* 26a, and Rashi, ad loc., s.v. *le-hoshiv yeshivah*; *Bava Metsi'a* 86a; *Makkot* 10a; *Zohar* 1:131b. On Torah as the Tree of Life, see Proverbs 3:18; BT *Berakhot* 32b, 61b.

70. **whatever you see...** Because the Angel of Death may assume various forms.

71. **those with whom he shared...** Those souls with whom he preexisted in heaven before his life on earth.

72. **At once Rabbi Shim'on rose...** Having heard from Rabbi Yitsḥak that his father had not yet appeared, Rabbi Shim'on realized that there was still time to save him from the Angel of Death.

The "seven eyes" are the seven cherished Companions (including Rabbi Shim'on himself) who emerged unscathed from the *Idra Rabbah* (Holy Assembly). See *Zohar* 3:144b (*IR*), quoting Zechariah 4:10: *These seven are the eyes of YHVH.*

73. **Flying spark... enveloped...** A conjectural translation of this cryptic Aramaic pronouncement, which apparently refers to the soul of Rabbi Yitsḥak sheltered beneath the wings of Rabbi Shim'on.

"Flying spark" renders טסיסא (*tesisa*), a neologism that probably derives from the root טוס (*tus*), "to fly." See Luria, *Va-Ye'esof David*, s.v. *tifsa*.

"Enveloped" renders קריפא (*qeripha*), apparently based on Rabbinic Hebrew קרפף (*qarpeph*), "enclosure." See M *Eruvin* 2:3; 9:1; *Ma'arikh*, s.v. *tfs*.

For other readings and interpretations, see Galante; *KP*; *DE*; Tishby, *Wisdom of the Zohar*, 1:136.

74. **when you enter to occupy your throne** "When you depart this world and enter Paradise." On their joint departure, see *Zohar* 3:287b (*IZ*).

Rabbi Shim'on said, "Certainly so!"

Meanwhile, Rabbi El'azar saw that the Angel of Death had departed. He said, "Nothing bound to a glowing ember in the presence of Rabbi Shim'on son of Yoḥai!"[75]

Rabbi Shim'on said to his son, Rabbi El'azar, "Come in here and hold Rabbi Yitshak, for I see that he is frightened."

Rabbi El'azar entered and held him, while Rabbi Shim'on turned his face and engaged in Torah.

Rabbi Yitsḥak fell into a slumber and saw his father. He said to him,[76] "Happy is your share in this world and in the world that is coming! For among the leaves of the Tree of Life in the Garden of Eden is planted a tree, great and mighty in two worlds—Rabbi Shim'on son of Yoḥai![77] He embraces you with his branches. Happy is your share, my son!"

He asked him, "Father, what am I there?"[78]

He replied, "For three days they have been decorating your bedchamber.
316 They have designed open windows for you, illumining you from four directions. When I saw your place, I rejoiced and said, 'Happy is your share!'—except that until now your son has not attained the merit of Torah.[79]

"Just now we were about to come to you—twelve righteous companions[80]—but before we set out, a voice aroused through all worlds: 'Who are the beloved companions here? Adorn yourselves for the sake of Rabbi Shim'on! He made a request and it has been granted.'

"Not only this, for seventy places adorned here belong to him, with every single place opening to seventy worlds, and every single world opening to seventy channels, and every single channel opening to seventy supernal crowns, from which paths open to the Ancient One, concealed of all,[81] to behold the

75. **bound to a glowing ember...** A conjectural translation of a cryptic phrase that obviously refers to the Angel of Death.

The Aramaic reads קופטרא דטיפסא (*quftera de-tifsa*). The Zoharic neologism *quftera* usually implies "linking." See above, note 25. *Tifsa* means various things in the *Zohar*, including "glowing ember, burning coal," as in the passage below, at note 818: "like a flame bound to a *tifsa*," which is obviously based on the description of the interconnectedness of the *sefirot* in *Sefer Yetsirah* 1:7: "like a flame bound to a burning coal." Here, Rabbi El'azar may be implying that the flame of the Angel of Death is quenched by Rabbi Shim'on.

See below, note 134; *Zohar* 3:111a; *Bei'ur ha-Millim ha-Zarot*, 178–79; *MmD*. For other interpretations, see Galante; *KP*; *DE*; *Ma'arikh*, s.v. *quftera*; *NO*; Luria, *Va-Ye'esof David*, s.v. *tifsa*; Tishby, *Wisdom of the Zohar*, 1:136; Liebes, *Peraqim*, 353; Mopsik.

76. **He said to him** Rabbi Yitsḥak's father said to him.

77. **in two worlds...** On earth and in heaven.

78. **what am I there?** What is my situation in Paradise?

79. **your son has not attained...** See above, at note 61.

80. **we were about to come to you...** To escort Rabbi Yitsḥak to Paradise.

81. **Ancient One...** *Keter*, the first and primordial *sefirah*. The name derives from

beauty illumining and delighting all, as is written: *to gaze upon the beauty of YHVH, to contemplate in His temple* (Psalms 27:4). What does this mean: *to contemplate in His temple*? Corresponding to what is written: *In all My house he is trusted* (Numbers 12:7)."[82]

He asked him, "Father, how much time has been granted me in that world?"[83]

He replied, "We are not permitted, nor is a human being informed.[84] But at the wedding feast of Rabbi Shim'on, you will arrange his table, as is said: *O daughters of Zion, come out and gaze upon King Solomon, upon the crown with which his mother crowned him on the day of his wedding, on the day of his heart's delight* (Song of Songs 3:11)."[85]

At once Rabbi Yitsḥak awoke, smiling, his face radiant. Rabbi Shim'on noticed and gazed into his face, and said, "You have heard a new word!"[86]

He replied, "Certainly so!" He told him, and prostrated himself before Rabbi Shim'on.[87]

It has been taught: From that day on, [218b] Rabbi Yitsḥak would grasp his son by the hand and teach him Torah, never leaving him.[88] When he went in to Rabbi Shim'on, he would seat his son outside[89] and sit before Rabbi Shim'on and exclaim: *O YHVH, prolong me! Be my guarantor!* (Isaiah 38:14).[90]

the vision of Daniel (7:9): *The Ancient of Days sat,... the hair on His head like clean fleece, His throne—flames of fire.*

82. **to gaze upon the beauty of *YHVH*...** *Binah* is often referred to as *beauty of YHVH*. In the afterlife, Rabbi Shim'on and other righteous souls will gaze upon this divine beauty from their abode within *Shekhinah*, who is known as *temple* and *My house*.

The full verse in Numbers reads: *Not so My servant Moses, in all My house he is trusted.* See 1:76a; 2:5a, 21b.

83. **in that world** Back on earth.

84. **not permitted...** To reveal this.

85. **wedding feast of Rabbi Shim'on...** The death of Rabbi Shim'on is described as a הלולא (*hillula*), "wedding feast," because he then unites with *Shekhinah*. Here Rabbi Yitsḥak's father promises his son that he too will play a role in this celebration.

Elsewhere in the *Zohar*, the verse from Song of Songs alludes to the union of *Shekhinah* (known as Crown) and Her divine partner (*King Solomon*), who is crowned by *Binah* (*his mother*). Here Rabbi Shim'on assumes the role of the royal groom.

On Rabbi Shim'on's *hillula*, see BT *Ketubbot* 62b; *Zohar* 3:144b (*IR*), 291a–b (*IZ*), 296b (*IZ*). On the verse from Song of Songs, see *Sifra, Shemini, millu'im*, 15, 44c; *Pesiqta de-Rav Kahana* 1:3; *Shir ha-Shirim Rabbah* on 3:11; Naḥmanides on Genesis 24:1; *Zohar* 1:29b, 246a, 248b; 2:22a, 84a, 100b; 3:61b.

86. **You have heard a new word** As indicated by Rabbi Yitsḥak's radiant face.

See Ecclesiastes 8:1; JT *Shabbat* 8:1, 11a; *Zohar* 1:94b; 3:162b–163a, 267a–b; *ZḤ* 5d (*MhN*), 20d (*MhN*).

87. **He told him...** Rabbi Yitsḥak disclosed what he had seen and heard in his dream, and then bowed down in thanks to Rabbi Shim'on for saving him from the Angel of Death.

88. **teach him Torah...** See above, at notes 61, 79.

89. **When he went in...** When Rabbi Yitsḥak went in to study profound secrets of Torah with his master, he left his young son outside.

90. ***O YHVH, prolong me!...*** These words were originally spoken by King Hezekiah of Judah, who fell mortally ill but

It has been taught: On that fierce and terrifying day for a human, when his time arrives to depart from the world, four aspects of the world stand in harsh judgment, and judgments arouse from four directions,[91] and four clusters quarrel, and wrangling prevails among them as they seek to separate, each to its own side.[92]

A herald emerges and proclaims in that world, and it is heard in 270 worlds. If he is virtuous, all those worlds rejoice in welcoming him. If not, woe to that human being and to his share![93]

It has been taught: When the herald proclaims, a flame issues from the side of the north and blazes in the River of Fire, diverging in four directions of the world and burning the souls of the wicked.[94] That flame shoots forth, up and down through the world, and reaches the wings of a black rooster, striking its wings, and it crows at the opening between the gates.[95] The first time it cries:

then prayed to God and was healed and granted fifteen additional years of life. The biblical text reads אדני עשקה לי (*Adonai asheqah li*), commonly understood as *O my Lord, I am oppressed!* In Rabbi Yitsḥak's exclamation, אדני (*Adonai*) is replaced by יהוה (*YHVH*) and the verb that follows is expressed in the imperative: עשקה לי (*osheqah li*), which could mean *deliver me* (based on another meaning of the root עשק [*'shq*], "be strong") but here probably means *prolong me* (i.e., "prolong my life," based on the rabbinic sense of this root, "to increase"). Rabbi Yitsḥak addresses the verse both to God (who has prolonged his life) and to Rabbi Shim'on (his guarantor).

On Rabbi Shim'on as Rabbi Yitsḥak's guarantor, see above, at note 74; *Zohar* 3:187b, 287b (*IZ*). In *Zohar* 2:38a, the name *YHVH* is actually applied to Rabbi Shim'on himself. See 3:79b; and *NZ*, n. 3, on 2:38a.

On the verse in Isaiah, see Rashi and Radak, ad loc.; Zevi Hirsch Koidonover, *Qav ha-Yashar*, chap. 19. Cf. *Midrash Tehillim* 119:54; *Leqaḥ Tov*, Genesis 25:21; *Minḥat Shai* on Isaiah 38:14; Galante.

91. **four aspects...** As the moment of death approaches, the sefirotic quartet *Ḥesed, Gevurah, Tif'eret,* and *Shekhinah* (or their angelic counterparts: Michael, Gabriel, Uriel, and Raphael) stand poised for judgment, dominated by *Gevurah,* which is also known as *Din* (Judgment).

92. **four clusters quarrel...** The four elements composing the human body (water, fire, air, and earth) correspond to the sefirotic quartet. As death nears and the body begins to disintegrate, these elements separate, seeking to return to their respective divine sources.

On the phrase "four clusters," see *Zohar* 2:79a.

93. **herald emerges...** Proclaiming the person's imminent death. See above, at notes 56, 64.

The number 270 is the *gimatriyya* of the word רע (*ra*), "evil." This may imply that if the person has succeeded in subduing his evil impulse he transforms evil into good, and these worlds greet him joyously, whereas if he has succumbed to his impulse, then he is punished by the evil in these worlds.

See *KP*; Tishby, *Wisdom of the Zohar*, 2:855. On the link between judgment and the 270 worlds, see *Zohar* 1:128a, 129a, 135b, 139a, 141a (all *IR*).

94. **flame issues...** From the *sefirah* of *Din* (Judgment), symbolized by north.

On the River of Fire, see Daniel 7:10; BT *Ḥagigah* 13b–14a; above, p. 233 and n. 330; p. 312 and n. 54.

95. **black rooster...** The significance of its color is discussed below.

Cf. *Zohar* 1:77b, 92b; 2:196a; 3:23a–b, 171b.

See, a day is coming for YHVH, burning like a furnace... (Malachi 3:19).[96] The second time it cries: *For see, He forms mountains and creates wind, and declares to a human what his conversation was* (Amos 4:13).[97] At that moment, a person sits among his deeds, which testify before him, and he confesses them.[98] The third time, as they are about to extract his soul, the rooster cries: *Who would not fear You, O King of the nations? For it befits You...* (Jeremiah 10:7).

Rabbi Yose said, "A black rooster—what difference does it make?"[99]

Rabbi Yehudah replied, "Everything done on earth by the blessed Holy One alludes to wisdom—although human beings are unaware—as is written: *O YHVH, how abundant are Your works! In wisdom You have made them all* (Psalms 104:24).[100] Because they are made in wisdom, they all allude to wisdom. As for the black rooster, we have learned that judgment abides only in a place of its own kind, and black derives from the side of Judgment. Therefore, precisely at midnight when the north wind stirs, a flame issues and strikes beneath the wings of a rooster, and it crows—especially a black one, more suitable than any other.[101]

"Here too, when the judgment of a human arouses, it begins to crow, and no one realizes except that human taking his final sleep.[102] For we have learned: When a person takes this sleep and judgment looms over him—to leave this world—supernal spirit increases within him, which he never had before. Once

96. ***See, a day is coming...*** The full verse reads: *For see, the day is coming, burning like a furnace. All the arrogant and every evildoer will be straw, and the day that is coming—says YHVH of Hosts—will burn them up, so that it will leave them neither root nor branch.* See Isaiah 13:9; Zechariah 14:1.

97. ***what his conversation was*** מה שחו (*Mah seḥo*), which is often understood as *what His thought is.* Here, based on a midrashic reading, the phrase implies that all of a person's שיחה (*siḥah*), "conversation"—even his small talk with his wife—is recorded in a heavenly book and read back to him when he dies.

See *Vayiqra Rabbah* 26:7; BT *Ḥagigah* 5b.

98. **sits among his deeds...** Whatever deeds he has committed over the course of his lifetime now confront him, and he must acknowledge them.

See *Zohar* 1:65b, 79a, 98a (*MhN*), 130b, 201b, 227a; 3:126b.

99. **what difference does it make?** Why the color black?

100. ***O YHVH...*** The full verse reads: *O YHVH, how abundant are Your works! In wisdom You have made them all; the earth is full of Your creatures.*

101. **black rooster...** Its color symbolizes harsh Judgment on the left side, which is also symbolized by north.

See above, note 94. On the hour of midnight, see the sources cited above, note 95. On the north wind and midnight, see BT *Berakhot* 3b: "Rabbi Shim'on the Ḥasid said, 'There was a harp suspended above [King] David's bed. As soon as midnight arrived, a north wind came and blew upon it, and it played by itself. He immediately arose and engaged in Torah until the break of dawn.'"

102. **when the judgment of a human arouses...** When the moment of death approaches, the black rooster crows.

this dwells upon him and cleaves to him, he sees what he never attained all his days, because that spirit has increased within him. As it does and he sees, he departs from this world, as is written: *You increase their spirit; they perish and return to their dust* (ibid., 29). Similarly, *No human can see Me and live* (Exodus 33:20)—in their lifetime they cannot attain this; in their death they can.[103]

"It has been taught: When a person sees close to him his relatives and friends from that world, and he recognizes them—all engraved in the image they possessed in this world—if that person is virtuous, they all rejoice before him and greet him.[104] But if he is not virtuous, he cannot recognize them, except for the wicked ones who are tormented every day in Hell; they are all gloomy, opening with 'Woe!' and closing with 'Woe!' He raises his eyes and sees them like a flying cinder ascending from fire.[105] He too opens with 'Woe!'

"It has been taught: When a person's soul departs, all his relatives and friends in that world accompany his soul and show it its place of delight and its place of punishment. If he is virtuous, he sees his place and ascends and dwells and delights in the supernal bliss of that world. If he is not virtuous, that soul remains in this world until the body is buried in the earth. Once it is buried, numerous wardens of law seize it until it reaches Dumah and is brought into the abodes of Hell."[106]

103. **supernal spirit increases...** At death, a person receives an added influx of spirit and is enabled to see *Shekhinah*.

See *Sifra, Vayiqra, dibbura dindavah* 2:12, 4a: "Rabbi Dosa says, 'Scripture states: *No human can see Me and live.* In their lifetime they do not see, but in their death they do!'"

See *Pirqei de-Rabbi Eli'ezer* 34; *Zohar* 1:65b, 79a, 98a (*MhN*), 99a (*ST*), 226a, 245a; 3:88a, 147a. In the verse from Psalm 104, the plain meaning of the verb תוסף (*tosef*) is *You take away (their spirit)*, based on the root אסף (*asf*), but here Rabbi Yehudah understands it as *You increase*, based on the root יסף (*ysf*). See Azriel of Gerona, *Peirush ha-Aggadot*, 59; Moses de León, *Sefer ha-Rimmon*, 206, 392–93. Cf. *Zohar* 1:181a.

104. **When a person sees...** The dying person sees each relative and friend in his individual ethereal "image," which prefigured the physical body and survives it after death.

See above, note 58; Moses de León, *Mishkan ha-Edut*, 54b–55a.

105. **flying cinder** טיסא (*Tisa*), apparently derived from the root טוס (*tus*), "to fly."

See *Zohar* 1:16a; 3:229b (*RM*); above, note 73. Other interpretations include "spark" (*OY*, Galante); "flame" (*DE*, *MmD*); "brand, charred piece of wood" (Galante, *KP*, *NO*); "bird" (Tishby, *Wisdom of the Zohar*, 2:837).

106. **wardens of law seize it...** They seize the soul.

"Wardens" renders גרדיני (*gardinei*), which derives from Castilian *guardián*, "guardian." See above, p. 246 and n. 401; p. 247 and n. 405.

Dumah, literally "silence," is a name for the netherworld in the Bible. See Psalms 94:17: *Unless YHVH had been my help, my soul would have nearly dwelt in dumah.* Cf. Psalms 115:17. In rabbinic literature Dumah is the angel in charge of souls of the dead (BT *Berakhot* 18b, *Shabbat* 152b, *Sanhedrin* 94a). In the *Zohar* he retains this role but also oversees Hell. See 1:8a–b, 62b, 94a, 102a, 124a (*MhN*), 130b, 237b.

Rabbi Yehudah said, "All seven days, the soul goes from his house to his grave, and from his grave to his house, mourning over [219a] the body, as is written: *Surely his flesh feels pain for him and his soul mourns for him* (Job 14:22). She goes and sits in the house, sees all of them sad, and mourns.[107]

"It has been taught: After seven days the body becomes what it becomes, and the soul enters her place. She enters the cave of Machpelah, entering wherever she enters, seeing whatever she sees, until reaching the Garden of Eden and encountering the cherubim and the flame of the sword in the lower Garden of Eden. If she is worthy of entering, she enters.[108]

"It has been taught: Four pillars are poised, an image of a body in their hands.[109] She clothes herself in it joyfully and sits in that abode for the time ordained. Then a herald proclaims and a three-colored pillar appears—a pillar called *foundation of Mount Zion*, as is written: *YHVH will create over the whole foundation of Mount Zion and over her assemblies a cloud by day and smoke with a glow of flaming fire* (Isaiah 4:5). She climbs that pillar to the opening of Righteousness, within which are Zion and Jerusalem.[110]

107. **All seven days...** During the first week of mourning. See BT *Shabbat* 152a: "Rav Ḥisda said, 'A person's soul mourns for him all seven [days], as is said: *and his soul mourns for him*.'"

See *Zohar* 1:122b (*MhN*), 3:206a; above, note 62; below, p. 362 and n. 321; Moses de León, *Sefer ha-Rimmon*, 396–97.

108. **cave of Machpelah...** This cave is first mentioned in Genesis 23 when Abraham purchases it as a burial site for Sarah. Eventually all the matriarchs (except for Rachel) and patriarchs were buried there. According to rabbinic tradition, Adam and Eve were buried in this cave as well. Based on this tradition, the *Zohar* teaches that the cave of Machpelah leads to the Garden of Eden. "The lower Garden of Eden" is the one on earth, whereas "the higher Garden of Eden" (mentioned elsewhere) is *Shekhinah*.

On the cherubim and the flame of the sword, see Genesis 3:24: *He drove out the human and placed east of the Garden of Eden the cherubim and the flame of the whirling sword to guard the way to the Tree of Life.* See *Targum Onqelos*, ad loc.

See *Bereshit Rabbah* 58:8; BT *Eruvin* 53a; *Pirqei de-Rabbi Eli'ezer* 20, 36; *Midrash ha-Gadol*, Genesis 23:9; *Zohar* 1:38b (*Heikh*), 57b, 81a (*ST*), 127a–128b, 248b; 2:151b; 3:164a; *ZḤ* 21a (*MhN*), 79d (*MhN, Rut*).

109. **Four pillars...** Apparently, the four archangels: Michael, Gabriel, Uriel, and Raphael. The image that they hold is the garment woven out of a person's good deeds through the course of his lifetime (see *Zohar* 1:224a–b; 2:210a–b). The *Zohar* combines this motif of the garment with the motif of the ethereal body. See above, note 58; Scholem, *On the Mystical Shape of the Godhead*, 264.

110. **three-colored pillar...** The three colors correspond to three *sefirot* above: *Hesed, Gevurah*, and *Tif'eret*, whose colors are respectively white, red, and green. The multicolored pillar joins the earthly Garden of Eden to the celestial Garden of Eden (*Shekhinah*), enabling the soul to ascend.

The "opening of Righteousness" is the opening of *Shekhinah*, known as Righteousness. Zion and Jerusalem symbolize respectively *Yesod* and *Shekhinah*.

See *Zohar* 1:39a–b (*Heikh*); 2:130b, 184b, 210a, 211a; Moses de León, *Seder Gan Eden*,

"If she is worthy of ascending further, happy is her allotted share—cleaving to the body of the King![111] If she is not worthy of ascending further, it is written: *Whoever is left in Zion, who remains in Jerusalem, will be called holy* (ibid., 3).[112] If she is worthy of ascending further, happy is the one who attains the glory of the King, reveling in supernal delight above the place called Heaven, as is written: *Then you will delight* על יהוה (*al YHVH*), *upon YHVH* (ibid. 58:14)—*above YHVH*, precisely! Happy is the share of one who attains this חסד (*ḥesed*), love, as is written: *Your ḥesed, love, is higher than heaven* (Psalms 108:5).[113]

"Now, is it *higher than heaven*? Look at what is written: *Your ḥesed, love, is high unto heaven* (ibid. 57:11)."[114]

Rabbi Yose said, "There is *ḥesed*, and then there is *ḥesed*! Upper *ḥesed*, lower *ḥesed*. Upper *ḥesed* is *higher than heaven*; lower *ḥesed*, as is written: *faithful* חסדי דוד (*ḥasdei david*), *acts of love for David* (Isaiah 55:3). Of these is written *high unto heaven*."[115]

322 It has been taught: Rabbi Yitsḥak said, "It is written: *a joyous mother of children* (Psalms 113:9). The mother is well known; who are *the children*?"[116]

Rabbi Shim'on replied, "We have already learned that the blessed Holy One has two children: one male and one female.[117] The male He gave to Jacob, as is written: *My son, My firstborn is Israel* (Exodus 4:22), and similarly: *Israel, in whom I glory* (Isaiah 49:3).[118] The daughter He gave to Abraham, as is written:

132–35, 139–40. The verse in Isaiah reads: *YHVH will create over the whole site of Mount Zion and over her assemblies a cloud by day and smoke with a glow of flaming fire by night.* The word מכון (*mekhon*), *site of*, is understood here in the *Zohar* as "foundation of."

111. **body of the King** *Tif'eret*, trunk of the sefirotic body. See above, note 3.

112. **If she is not worthy of ascending further...** She is still called *holy*.

113. **above the place called Heaven...** Even higher than *Tif'eret*, who is known as Heaven and *YHVH*. Such a soul delights על יהוה (*al YHVH*), understood here hyperliterally as *above YHVH*—reveling in the radiant flow from *Binah* that is channeled through *Ḥesed*, both of which are situated above *Tif'eret*. See above, note 2.

114. **Now, is it *higher*...** According to another verse in Psalms, it seems that *Ḥesed* is not higher than heaven, but reaches only *unto heaven*. See BT *Pesaḥim* 50b.

115. **Upper *ḥesed*, lower *ḥesed*...** Upper *ḥesed* refers to the *sefirah* of *Ḥesed*, situated above *Tif'eret* (*heaven*). Lower *ḥesed* refers to the sefirotic pair *Netsaḥ* and *Hod*, situated directly below *Tif'eret* and known as חסדי דוד (*ḥasdei david*), *acts of love for David*, because they convey passionate love to *Shekhinah*, who is symbolized by King David.

See *Zohar* 1:8a; 2:169a; 3:16a, 21a; Moses de León, *Sheqel ha-Qodesh*, 48 (59). For a different distinction between types of *ḥesed*, see *Zohar* 2:177b (*SdTs*); 3:133b (*IR*), 140b (*IR*).

116. ***joyous mother*... well known...** The Divine Mother, *Binah*.

The full verse reads: *He settles the barren woman in her home as a joyous mother of children. Hallelujah!* See *Zohar* 1:157b–158a.

117. **blessed Holy One has two children...** *Tif'eret* and *Shekhinah*.

See *Zohar* 3:10b, 290b (*IZ*).

118. **male He gave to Jacob...** *Tif'eret* (whose full name is *Tif'eret Yisra'el* [Beauty

YHVH blessed Abraham בכל (*ba-kol*), *with everything* (Genesis 24:1)—Abraham had a daughter named *ba-kol, with everything*.[119]

"Mother crouches over them, suckling them, and of this is written *Do not take the mother above the children* (Deuteronomy 22:6). And we have learned: One should not increase his sins below, causing Mother to withdraw from the children.[120] It is also written: *She is your mother—do not expose her nakedness* (Leviticus 18:7). Woe to one who exposes Her nakedness![121]

"When inhabitants of the world return, increasing their virtue before the blessed Holy One, and Mother returns to shelter the children, then She is called *Teshuvah*, Returning. What is Returning? Return of the Mother, who returns with sustenance. Then, *a joyous mother of children—mother of children*, truly![122] Therefore, a person should not abstain from being fruitful until he engenders a son and a daughter."[123]

of Israel]) is linked with Jacob, also called Israel.

The full verse in Isaiah reads: *He said to me, "You are My servant, Israel, in whom* אתפאר (*etpa'ar*), *I glory*." This final word alludes to its cognate noun, תפארת (*Tif'eret*).

119. **daughter He gave to Abraham...** *Shekhinah* is the Divine Daughter. Abraham symbolizes *Ḥesed*, which flows into *Shekhinah*.

See BT *Bava Batra* 16b; *Bahir* 52 (78); Naḥmanides on Genesis 24:1.

120. **Mother crouches...** *Binah* shelters and nourishes Her children (namely, *Tif'eret* and *Shekhinah*, along with the other lower *sefirot*).

The verse in Deuteronomy reads: *Do not take the mother* על (*al*), *along with, the children*—i.e., if you come across a bird's nest, you may take the fledglings or eggs but you should leave the mother. In Kabbalah, this mother bird symbolizes *Binah*, who lies beyond comprehension and so cannot be grasped. So, *send off the mother* (Deuteronomy 22:7)—let Her go, put Her out of your mind, do not even try to capture this subtle dimension of divinity. Rather, focus on *the children*, engendered by *Binah*. Here, though, Rabbi Shim'on reads the verse hyperliterally: *Do not take the mother* על (*al*), *above, the children*—through your sins, do not cause Her to withdraw from the lower *sefirot*.

See *Zohar* 2:85b; *OY*. For the usual kabbalistic interpretation, see *Bahir* 74 (104–105); Naḥmanides and Recanati on Deuteronomy 22:6; Todros Abulafia, *Otsar ha-Kavod, Berakhot* 33b; *Ḥullin* 142a; *Zohar* 1:158a; 2:8a, 93a; 3:254a; Moses de León, *Sefer ha-Rimmon*, 338–39.

121. ***do not expose her nakedness...*** Do not shame Her by sinning, thereby causing Her to withdraw.

In Leviticus, the simple sense of the idiom לגלות ערוה (*le-gallot ervah*), "to expose nakedness," is to have sexual relations. The *Zohar* sometimes plays on two meanings of the root גלה (*glh*), "to uncover" and "to go into exile." See *Zohar* 3:15b, 74b–75a. For other interpretations of *Binah*'s nakedness, see *OY*; *KP*.

122. **When inhabitants of the world return...** Turning back to God in repentance. Their sincerity stimulates *Binah* to return and resume the motherly role of sustaining Her children.

123. **not abstain from being fruitful...** One does not fulfill (and become exempt from) the commandment *Be fruitful and multiply* (Genesis 1:28) until he has engendered both a son and a daughter, thereby imitating the Divine Mother.

See M *Yevamot* 6:6; BT *Yevamot* 61b–62a; *Zohar* 3:7a.

It has been taught: Rabbi Yitsḥak said, "It is written: *to gaze upon the beauty of YHVH, to contemplate in His temple* (Psalms 27:4). The desire of the righteous is to see this, and yet you say *above YHVH* (Isaiah 58:14)!"[124]

Rabbi Shim'on replied, "All is one, as implied by what is written: *beauty of YHVH*—proceeding from the Holy Ancient One to this heaven. The desire of the righteous is certainly so: above heaven. So it is written: *above YHVH*. Happy is the share of one who attains! Surely they are few."[125]

We have learned: Rabbi Shim'on said, "It is written: *My mother's children were incensed at me, they made me guardian of the vineyards* (Song of Songs 1:6).[126] *My mother's children*—as is written: *He has cast down earth from heaven* (Lamentations 2:1). For when the blessed Holy One sought to destroy His house below and to exile Israel among the nations, He removed this *earth* from His presence and it remained at a distance, as is written: *His sister stationed herself at a distance* (Exodus 2:4). When this *earth* was distanced from *heaven*, *earth* below was destroyed and Israel were scattered among the nations.[127] The Assembly of

124. ***to gaze...*** The full verse reads: *One thing I ask of YHVH, this is what I seek: that I may dwell in the house of YHVH all the days of my life, to gaze upon the beauty of YHVH, to contemplate in His temple.*

In Kabbalah, this verse is sometimes understood as describing a vision of *Binah* (*beauty of YHVH*) granted to the souls of the righteous from their vantage point within *Shekhinah* (*house of YHVH, His temple*). (Alternatively, *beauty of YHVH* may mean a vision of *Binah* [*beauty*] reflected in *Tif'eret* [*YHVH*], seen from a vantage point within *Shekhinah*.) Rabbi Yitsḥak wonders about the apparent contradiction between this scenario and the verse in Isaiah: *Then you will delight* על יהוה (*al YHVH*), *upon YHVH*, which can be read hyperliterally to mean that the righteous will delight *above YHVH*. This would imply that they revel in a much higher realm—above *Tif'eret* (*YHVH*).

See above, pp. 316–17 and n. 82, p. 322 and n. 113; Galante.

125. **All is one...** Rabbi Shim'on insists that there is no contradiction. The emanation of *Binah* originates from the Holy Ancient One (the primal manifestation of *Ein Sof* through *Keter*) and proceeds to *Tif'eret*, known as "heaven." Thus the righteous experience a flow that issues from a realm "above heaven" and *above YHVH*—that is, higher than *Tif'eret*.

The phrase על שמים (*al shamayim*), "above heaven," apparently alludes to Psalms 108:5: *Your ḥesed, love, is* גדול מעל שמים (*gadol me-al shamayim*), *higher than heaven*. See above, p. 322 and nn. 113, 115.

On the concluding sentence, see the statement attributed to Rabbi Shim'on son of Yoḥai in BT *Sukkah* 45b: "I have seen the sons of the upper world and they are few." According to Rashi, ad loc., "sons of the upper world" refers to those who will encounter *Shekhinah*.

126. ***My mother's children...*** The verse reads: *My mother's children* [or: *sons*] *were incensed at me, they made me guardian of the vineyards; my own vineyard I did not guard.*

127. ***He has cast down earth...*** When God wanted to destroy the Temple because of Israel's sins, He removed *Shekhinah* (symbolized by *earth*), separating Her from *Tif'eret* (*heaven*). This sefirotic divorce caused destruction and exile below.

The verse in Lamentations reads: *He has cast down from heaven to earth the splendor of*

Israel said, 'Who caused this? Who did this to me? *My mother's children were incensed at me* and distanced themselves from me'—*my mother's children*, precisely!"[128]

Rabbi Yose was walking on the way, accompanied by Rabbi Ḥiyya son of Rav. As they were walking, Rabbi Yose said to Rabbi Ḥiyya, "Do you see what I see?"

He replied, "I see a man in the river and a bird on [219b] his head with a rib in its mouth, and it's eating and trampling with its feet. And that man is shouting out loud, but I don't know what he's saying."[129]

He said, "Let's get closer to him and listen."

He replied, "I'm afraid to go any closer."

He said, "Could that be a human being here? Rather, it is a hint of wisdom given to us by the blessed Holy One!"

They approached him, and heard him saying, "Crown, crown, two children cast outside, outside. No rest, no tranquility until the bird is thrown into a cage."[130]

Israel. Here, Rabbi Shim'on interprets the verse to mean *He has cast down earth from heaven...*, or (construing the concluding phrase as the subject): תפארת ישראל (*Tif'eret Yisra'el*), *The splendor of Israel, has cast down earth from heaven*. See *Zohar* 1:238a, 242b; 2:175a; 3:59b.

The verse in Exodus describes Moses' sister, Miriam, waiting by the Nile to see what will happen to her baby brother. In BT *Sotah* 11a, Rabbi Yitsḥak interprets *sister* as referring to *Shekhinah*. See *Zohar* 1:6a; 2:12a; 3:59b.

128. **Assembly of Israel...** The people of Israel realize that their suffering and exile have been caused by the separation of the divine couple, *Tif'eret* and *Shekhinah*, who are *my mother's children*—the offspring of *Binah*, Mother of all. On account of Israel's sins, *Tif'eret* and *Shekhinah* became alienated from one another and distanced themselves from Israel as well.

129. **I see a man in the river...** This description and the account that follows include several features derived from the prophet Daniel's dream vision of the four beasts (chap. 7), which symbolize four kingdoms. The second beast, resembling a bear, had *three ribs* [or: *fangs, tusks*] *in its mouth* (ibid., 5). The fourth beast *devoured and crushed, and trampled the remains with its feet* (ibid., 7). See *KP*.

130. **Crown, crown...** The meaning, apparently, is: Two *sefirot*, two children—namely, *Tif'eret* and *Shekhinah*—have been excluded from the unified realm. Their disharmony will persist until the hostile power devouring Israel is captured.

See above, p. 307 and n. 29. On *Tif'eret* and *Shekhinah* as the two children of *Binah*, see above, pp. 322–23 and nn. 117–19. On the bird as a symbol of a foreign, hostile power, see above, pp. 307–8 and nn. 29–30.

"Cage" is a conjectured rendering of קיסרא (*qisra*), a Zoharic neologism whose meaning is uncertain. See below, at note 825. Cf. above, p. 197 and n. 120, where the similar neologism טסירא (*tesira*) apparently means "snare." This latter sense is adopted here by Galante; *Nefesh David*; *NZ*; *MmD*.

In *Va-Ye'esof David* (s.v. *qisra*), David Luria suggests "fortress," based on the similar Zoharic term קסטירא (*qastira*), derived from Latin *castrum* (pl. *castra*), "fortress, castle." *KP* reads קיטרא (*qitra*), "smoke," which he

Rabbi Yose wept, and said, "This corresponds to what we have learned: *My mother's children were incensed at me, they made me guardian of the vineyards.* Why? Because *my own vineyard I did not guard* (Song of Songs 1:6)."[131] He said, "Surely, exile drags on! So birds of heaven are not eliminated until the dominion of other nations is eliminated from the world.[132] When? Not until the day arrives that the blessed Holy One arouses His judgments upon the world, as is written: *There will be one day—known to YHVH—neither day nor night...* (Zechariah 14:7)."[133]

As they were walking, they heard a voice proclaiming, "Combustion of conjunction arrives with its judgments!" Out shot a flame and consumed that bird.[134] He said, "Exactly as is written: *consigned to consuming fire* (Daniel 7:11)."[135]

Rabbi Yose said, "The blessed Holy One exiles Israel only when faith is lacking among them.[136] When they are deprived of faith, it becomes so totally, as it were, as is written: *Your covenant with death will be annulled* (Isaiah 28:18)."[137]

Rabbi Ḥiyya said, "What is the meaning of *He will swallow up death forever* (ibid. 25:8)?"

He replied, "When the blessed Holy One arouses His right, death will be denied to the world.[138] But this right arouses only when Israel arouse the right

understands as "fire and smoke," alluding to Daniel 7:11, where the fourth beast is *consigned to consuming fire* (quoted below, at note 135). This reading is not supported by the manuscripts, though it is adopted by Scholem. For other possibilities, see Soncino; *Sullam*; Mopsik.

131. ***My mother's children*... Why?...** Israel incurred divine wrath because they failed to guard the covenant in the land of Israel.

See JT *Eruvin* 3:9, 21c; *Shir ha-Shirim Rabbah* on 1:6; *Pesiqta de-Rav Kahana* 14:4.

132. **birds of heaven are not eliminated...** The hostile nations will not be eliminated until their "dominion," their heavenly princes, are eliminated.

See Galante. On the symbolism of birds, see above, note 130.

133. ***There will be one day*...** When God will vanquish Israel's enemies. The full verse reads: *There will be one day—known to YHVH—neither day nor night, and in the evening, there will be light.*

134. **Combustion of conjunction...** A flame of divine judgment consumes the menacing bird.

"Conjunction" renders the Zoharic neologism קופטירא (*qoftira*), which often implies "linking, tying." The phrase here apparently alludes to the description in *Sefer Yetsirah* 1:7: "like a flame bound to a burning coal." See above, notes 25, 75. Cf. Galante.

135. **He said...** Rabbi Yose said. The phrase from Daniel describes the fate of the fourth beast in the vision, symbolizing one of the hostile empires. See above, notes 129–130.

136. **when faith is lacking...** See Rava's statement in BT *Shabbat* 119b: "Jerusalem was destroyed only because people of faith ceased to exist there."

137. **it becomes so totally...** Nothing in the universe remains faithful to God's will—or perhaps, God's faithfulness with His people also deteriorates—and Israel becomes vulnerable to exile and death.

138. **His right...** *Ḥesed,* the right arm of God, which overcomes the powers of harsh judgment, including death.

of the blessed Holy One. What is that? Torah, as is written: *From His right hand, a fiery law for them* (Deuteronomy 33:2).[139] At that time, '*The right hand of* YHVH *performs valiantly.' I will not die but live, and proclaim the deeds of* YHVH (Psalms 118:16–17)."

It has been taught: A virtuous person in whom the blessed Holy One delights—a herald proclaims for thirty days among the righteous in the Garden of Eden, all of whom rejoice and come to adorn the place of that virtuous one until he comes to dwell among them.[140]

If he is wicked, a herald proclaims in Hell concerning him for thirty days, and all the wicked are sad, and all of them open: "Woe! For a new punishment arouses now on account of so-and-so!" Countless wardens of law confront him and accost him with "Woe!"[141] All of them open, saying, *Woe to the wicked! Evil! For what his hands have perpetrated will be requited to him* (Isaiah 3:11). What does this mean: *what his hands have perpetrated*?

Rabbi Yitsḥak said, "To include one who fornicates with his hands, emitting 327
and wasting seed fruitlessly.[142] For we have learned: Whoever emits his seed fruitlessly is called evil and does not see the face of *Shekhinah*, as is written: *You are not a God who delights in wickedness; evil cannot abide with You* (Psalms 5:5), and similarly: *Er, firstborn of Judah, was evil in the eyes of* YHVH (Genesis 38:7). Here too, *Woe to the wicked! Evil!*—woe to that wicked one, who is *evil*, who made himself *evil*. *For what his hands have perpetrated will be requited to him*—to include one who fornicates with his hands, emitting seed fruitlessly; this one is tormented in that world more than all.[143]

"Come and see! For it is written: *Woe to the wicked! Evil!* Since it is written *Woe to the wicked*, why *evil*?[144] But as I have said: He made himself *evil*. And it is

139. **when Israel arouse the right...** When Israel engages in the study of Torah, which derives from God's right hand. See above, p. 214, n. 214.

140. **herald proclaims...** His imminent death. See above, p. 313 and n. 56.

141. **wardens of law...** See above, note 106.

142. **fornicates with his hands...** Masturbates.

On this idiom, see BT *Niddah* 13b ("committing adultery by hand"); *Zohar* 1:100b, 188a; 2:263b (*Heikh*).

143. **Whoever emits his seed fruitlessly...** In the world of the *Zohar*, masturbation is a heinous sin.

See BT *Niddah* 13b; *Zohar* 1:56b–57a, 62a, 69a, 100b, 188a; 2:214b, 263b; 3:90a, 158a; Moses de León, *Shushan Edut*, 353; idem, *Sefer ha-Rimmon*, 230; Tishby, *Wisdom of the Zohar*, 3:1365–66.

Genesis does not specify the nature of Er's sin, but rabbinic tradition maintains that it was the same as that of his younger brother, Onan, who *wasted* [his seed] *on the ground* (Genesis 38:9). See *Targum Yerushalmi*, Genesis 38:7; *Bereshit Rabbah* 85:4 (and Theodor's note); BT *Yevamot* 34b; *Zohar* 1:56b–57a.

144. **why *evil*?** Why the apparent redundancy? A similar question and a different answer appear in BT *Qiddushin* 40a.

written: *Evil cannot abide with You.* All of them ascend, whereas this one does not.[145] Now, you might ask, 'What about other sinners who have killed people?'[146] Come and see: All of them ascend, but he does not. Why? Because they have killed other human beings, whereas he has killed his children—his very own children!—spilling much blood.[147]

"Come and see: Of other sinners of the world is not written *It was evil in the eyes of YHVH*, whereas here is written *What he did was evil in the eyes of YHVH* (ibid., 10). Why? Because *he wasted* [his seed] *on the ground* (ibid., 9)."[148]

We have learned: Rabbi Yehudah said, "There is nothing in the world for which one cannot repent, except for this.[149] There is no sinner who cannot see the face of *Shekhinah*, except for this one, as is written: *Evil cannot abide with You*—at all!"[150]

Rabbi Yitsḥak said, "Happy are the righteous in this world and in the world that is coming! Of them is written *Your people, all of them righteous, will inherit the land forever* (Isaiah 60:21). What does this mean: *will inherit the land forever*?"

Rabbi Yehudah said, "As is written: *I will walk before YHVH in the land of the living* (Psalms 116:9)."[151]

[221b][152] It has been taught: *The days of Israel drew near to die* (Genesis 47:29).[153] Rabbi Ḥiyya said, "It is written: *Jacob lived in the land of Egypt seventeen years*

145. **All of them ascend...** All other sinners ascend from Hell once they have been purged.

146. **What about other sinners...** What about murderers? Is the punishment of a masturbator more severe than theirs?

147. **he has killed his children...** Wasting the seed of his potential children.

See BT *Niddah* 13a: "Rabbi Yitsḥak and Rabbi Ammi said, '[Whoever emits semen fruitlessly] is as though he sheds blood.'"

148. ***What he did was evil...*** Describing the act of Er's brother, Onan.

149. **except for this** This extreme formulation seems to contradict rabbinic teaching on the universal power of repentance.

See JT *Pe'ah* 1:1, 16b; *Zohar* 2:106a; 3:78b; and on the issue here, *Zohar* 1:62a (Vol. 1, pp. 355–56, n. 109); 2:214b. In his Hebrew writings, Moses de León softens the tone. See *Shushan Edut*, 353; *Sefer ha-Rimmon*, 230. Note the critique by *Zohorei Ya'bets* and the wrestling of the commentators: *OY*; Galante; *NZ*; *MmD*.

150. **who cannot see the face of *Shekhinah*...** Upon death (see above, note 103), or after having been purged in Hell (see above, note 145).

151. ***land of the living*** Symbolizing *Shekhinah*. See above, p. 303 and n. 5.

152. **[221b]** The material printed in the standard editions of the *Zohar* (based on the Mantua edition) from the last line of 219b through the middle of 221b pertains to the *Zohar* on Leviticus. See *Zohar* 3:104b–107b. This material does not appear in the portion of *Va-Yḥi* in most of the early, more reliable manuscripts (C9, N23, P2, V6) nor in most later manuscripts (including L2, Ms4, O16, P4, Pr6) nor in the Cremona edition. (It does appear in O2, M7, and R1.) The traditional commentators Cordovero and Lavi omit it here. I intend to translate this material as part of *Zohar* on Leviticus (3:104b–107b). See Galante; Scholem.

153. ***The days of Israel drew near to die*** For the full verse, see above, note 45.

(ibid., 28). There, in his existence: Jacob; here, in his death: Israel, as is written: *The days of Israel drew near to die.*"[154]

Rabbi Yose said, "Certainly so! For it is not written *The day of Israel drew near to die*, but rather *days*. Now, does a person die on several days? In a single hour, a single moment, he dies and departs from the world. However, we have learned as follows: When the blessed Holy One desires to retrieve his spirit, all those days in which a human has existed in this world are convened before Him and reckoned. As they approach Him to be reckoned, the person dies, and the blessed Holy One retrieves his spirit—the breath that He exhaled and blew into him, He retrieves for Himself.[155]

"Happy is the share of the human being whose days draw near the King without shame, without one of those days being thrust out, upon being identified as the date on which a sin was committed![156] Therefore, of the righteous is written 'drawing near,' because their days draw near the King without shame.

"Woe to the wicked, of whom is not written 'drawing near'! How can their days draw near the King, when all their days are fraught with sins of the world? Therefore, they cannot draw near the King nor be reckoned before Him nor be remembered above. Rather, they are spontaneously destroyed, as is written: *The way of the wicked is like darkness; they do not know what makes them stumble* (Proverbs 4:19). [222a]

"Here, *the days of Israel drew near to die*—literally, without shame, in fullness and complete joy. Therefore, *the days of Israel*, for he was more complete than Jacob. Now, you might say, 'But it is written *Jacob was a* תם (*tam*), *simple, man* (Genesis 25:27)—שלים (*shelim*), complete!'[157] Well, he was complete, but not complete on a supernal rung like Israel."[158]

154. **in his existence: Jacob . . . in his death: Israel . . .** Rabbi Ḥiyya wonders why the patriarch's more elevated name (Israel) is linked with his death, whereas his original name (Jacob) is linked with his life.

155. **desires to retrieve his spirit . . .** "His" may refer to the human being or to God. Just as God breathed the spirit into the human, so He now breathes it back into Himself.

See Genesis 2:7: *He blew into his nostrils the breath of life, and the human became a living being.* See Naḥmanides, ad loc.; above, at note 53.

On a person's days drawing near God, see below, at notes 245–260.

156. **thrust out . . .** When a person dies, any day on which he had committed a sin during his lifetime is now forbidden to enter God's presence.

157. ***Jacob was a* תם (*tam*), *simple, man* . . .** The verse reads: *The boys grew up. Esau became a skilled hunter, a man of the field, while Jacob was a* תם (*tam*), *simple, man, dwelling in tents.* The word *tam* means "simple, innocent, plain, mild, quiet, sound, wholesome." *Targum Onqelos,* ad loc., renders it: שלים (*shelim*), "complete, perfect, consummate."

See above, p. 12 and n. 86; *Zohar* 1:146a.

158. **not complete on a supernal rung like Israel** When Jacob earned the name Israel, he attained fully the rung of *Tif'eret Yisra'el* (Beauty of Israel). Then he became truly complete, balancing the polar opposites *Ḥesed* and *Gevurah,* which had been attained respectively by his grandfather and father,

It has been taught: Rabbi Yose said, "When a person's days are convened before the blessed Holy One, the days of a certain virtuous person may convene, but at a distance from the King, whereas the days of another virtuous person may convene near, right next to the King—not distancing themselves at all—entering and approaching the King without shame. Happy is their share, as is written: *The days of Israel drew near to die!*"[159]

He called for his son Joseph (Genesis 47:29).[160]

Rabbi Yitsḥak said, "Are the other tribes not his sons? Rather, as Rabbi Abba has said, he was *his son* more than all of them.[161] For we have learned: When Potiphar's wife urged Joseph, what is written? *He came into the house to do his work, and there was no man of the men of the house* (ibid. 39:11).[162] This verse should read *and there was no man in the house.* Why *of the men of the house*? To include the image of Jacob, which was present there. Therefore, *of the men of the house*—but another man was there. As soon as Joseph raised his eyes and saw his father's image, he returned to his stability and withdrew.[163]

"Come and see what is written: *He refused. He said to his master's wife* (ibid. 39:8).[164] The blessed Holy One said to him, 'You *refused*; by your life, another

Abraham and Isaac. Appropriately, the name Israel appears in the verse describing how his days drew near to God at the moment of his death.

On the names Jacob and Israel, see above, pp. 50–51 and n. 364; p. 295 and n. 192.

159. **certain virtuous person... another virtuous person...** The first is generally virtuous although some of his days contain misdeeds, whereas the second is completely virtuous.

160. ***He called for his son Joseph...*** The full verse reads: *The days of Israel drew near to die, and he called for his son Joseph and said to him, "If I have found favor in your eyes, place your hand under my thigh and act toward me with steadfast kindness—please do not bury me in Egypt."*

161. **Are the other tribes not his sons?...** Why did Jacob call specifically for Joseph?

See *Bereshit Rabbah* 96:5; ibid. (Vatican MS), p. 1237; *Tanḥuma, Vayḥi* 3; *Tanḥuma* (Buber), *Vayḥi* 5.

162. **When Potiphar's wife urged Joseph...** When she tried to seduce him. The full verse reads: *It happened, on such a day, that he came into the house to do his work, and there was no man of the men of the house there in the house.*

163. **To include the image of Jacob...** Joseph was tempted by Potiphar's wife, but then he saw the image of his father and refused her advances, thereby demonstrating that he was Jacob's genuine son.

On the phrase "returned to his stability," see *Bereshit Rabbah* 87:7, in the name of Rabbi Shemu'el: "The bow was stretched [i.e., Joseph's phallus became erect] and then returned [to its flaccid state]."

See *Targum Yerushalmi,* Genesis 49:24; JT *Horayot* 2:4, 46d; *Bereshit Rabbah* 98:20; BT *Sotah* 36b; *Tanḥuma, Vayeshev* 9; *Pirqei de-Rabbi Eli'ezer* 39 (and Luria's note 21); *Zohar* 1:71b, 247a; 3:66b. Rabbi Yitsḥak's midrashic reading of *no man of the men of the house* is quoted in the name of Moses ha-Darshan in *Tosafot* on *Sotah* 36b, s.v. *be-otah sha'ah.*

164. ***He refused...*** The context (Genesis 39:7–9) reads: *It happened after these things that his master's wife raised her eyes to Joseph*

refused will come to bless your sons, who will thereby be blessed'—as is written: *His father refused and said, 'I know, my son, I know'* (ibid. 48:19).[165] Since he said *I know, my son*, why another *I know*? Because he said *I know my son*—'when you confirmed with your body that you are my son, when you saw my image.' Therefore it is written: *I know my son. I know*—about what you said: that this is the firstborn; *he too will become a people, and he too will be great* (ibid.). So here is written *He called for his son Joseph*—*his* genuine *son, Joseph.*[166]

"Alternatively, *He called for his son Joseph*—for they shared a single image: whoever saw Joseph would testify that he was Jacob's son."[167]

Rabbi Yose said, "Entirely so! Furthermore, Joseph nourished him and his sons in his old age; therefore, *his son*—truly, more than all of them.

"*He called for his son Joseph*—why for Joseph and not another one? Because he had the power to take him out of there."[168]

Rabbi Yose said, "Since Jacob knew that his children would be enslaved in exile there in Egypt, why wasn't he buried there, so that his merit would protect them? Why did he want to leave there? Look at what is written: *As a father has compassion for his children* (Psalms 103:13)! Where is the compassion?[169]

and said, "Lie with me." And he refused. He said to his master's wife, "Look, with me here, my master has given no thought to what is in his house, and all that belongs to him he has placed in my hands. There is no one greater in this house than I, and he has withheld nothing from me except you, since you are his wife. So how could I do this great evil, and sin against God?"

165. **another *refused* will come...** As a reward for Joseph's having *refused*, his two sons were blessed by Jacob and, appropriately, the identical word (*refused*) reappears in that context. Joseph wanted his father to give his older son, Manasseh, the blessing of the firstborn, but Jacob *refused*, insisting that this belonged to Joseph's younger son, Ephraim. The full verse reads: *His father refused and said, "I know, my son, I know. He too will become a people, and he too will be great. But his younger brother will be greater than he, and his seed will be a fullness of nations."*

166. **why another *I know*?...** The apparent redundancy is resolved. First, Jacob said *I know my son*, meaning "When you withstood temptation, I knew that you were truly my son." Then he said *I know*, referring to the matter at hand: Joseph's contention that Manasseh was the firstborn. See the preceding note.

167. **shared a single image...** According to rabbinic tradition, Jacob and Joseph were nearly identical. The kabbalistic twist is that their respective *sefirot*, *Tif'eret*, and *Yesod*, constitute a single male entity uniting with *Shekhinah*.

See *Bereshit Rabbah* 84:6, 8; *Tanḥuma, Vayeshev* 2; *Tanḥuma* (Buber), *Vayeshev* 5; Moses de León, *Sheqel ha-Qodesh*, 10 (12–13); above, p. 68 and n. 461; p. 92 and nn. 52–53.

168. **Because he had the power...** Joseph had authority to convey Jacob's corpse back to Canaan for burial.

See *Bereshit Rabbah* 96:5; *Tanḥuma, Vayḥi* 3; *Tanḥuma* (Buber), *Vayḥi* 5.

169. ***As a father has compassion...*** This verse is applied to Jacob in *Bereshit Rabbah* 78:8; *Pesiqta de-Rav Kahana* 19:3.

"But so we have learned: When Jacob was going down to Egypt, he was afraid. He said, 'What if my children are annihilated among the nations? Perhaps the blessed Holy One will remove His *Shekhinah* from me as before!'[170] What is written? *God appeared to Jacob. . . . 'Fear not to go down to Egypt, for I will make of you a great nation there* (Genesis 46:2–3).[171] And as for what you said—perhaps I will remove My *Shekhinah* from your midst—*I Myself will go down with you to Egypt* (ibid., 4).'

"He said further, 'I am afraid that I might be buried there and not attain the companionship of my fathers.' He replied, '*And I Myself will surely bring you up as well* (ibid.). *I will bring you up*—from Egypt. *Surely as well*—to be buried in the grave of your fathers.'[172]

"Therefore he wanted to be removed from Egypt. First, so that they would not turn him into a deity, for he saw that the blessed Holy One would eventually exact retribution from their gods.[173] Additionally, because he saw that *Shekhinah* would dwell among his children in exile.[174] Also, so that his body would be among his fathers, integrated with them, and not reckoned with the wicked of Egypt.[175] For we have learned: The body of Jacob emanated from the beauty of Adam,[176] and the image of Jacob is a supernal, holy image, image of the holy Throne.[177] So he did not want to be buried among the wicked. Mystery of the

170. **remove His *Shekhinah* from me . . .** As happened after Joseph was kidnapped and sold by his brothers. See above, p. 305 and nn. 18–19.

171. ***Fear not . . .*** The context in Genesis (46:2–4) reads: *God spoke to Israel in visions of the night, and He said, "Jacob! Jacob!" And he said "Here I am." He said, "I am God, God of your father. Fear not to go down to Egypt, for I will make of you a great nation there. I Myself will go down with you to Egypt and I Myself will surely bring you up as well, and Joseph will lay his hand on your eyes."*

The clause *God appeared to Jacob* does not appear in this passage but rather in Genesis 35:9.

172. **not attain the companionship of my fathers . . .** See below, at note 307; *Zohar* 2:53a.

173. **not turn him into a deity . . .** See *Bereshit Rabbah* 96:5; *Tanḥuma, Vayḥi* 3; *Tanḥuma* (Buber), *Vayḥi* 5. On God's intent to punish the gods of Egypt, see Exodus 12:12.

174. ***Shekhinah* would dwell among his children . . .** So Jacob did not have to protect them with his merit by being buried there.

On *Shekhinah* accompanying Israel in exile, see above, pp. 290–91, n. 176.

175. **so that his body would be among his fathers . . .** Completing the sefirotic triad of *Ḥesed, Gevurah,* and *Tif'eret,* symbolized respectively by Abraham, Isaac, and Jacob.

176. **body of Jacob emanated from the beauty of Adam** See BT *Bava Batra* 58a: "The beauty of our father Jacob resembled the beauty of Adam."

See *Bava Metsi'a* 84a; *Zohar* 1:35b (where Jacob rectifies the flaw of Adam's sin), 142b, 145b–146a; *ZḤ* 65a (*ShS*).

177. **image of the holy Throne** According to rabbinic tradition, Jacob's image is engraved on the divine Throne.

See *Bereshit Rabbah* 68:12; 82:2; *Eikhah Rabbah* 2:2; *Targum Yerushalmi* and *Targum Yerushalmi* (frag.), Genesis 28:12; BT *Ḥullin*

matter: Among the patriarchs is no separation at all. Therefore it is written: *I will lie down with my fathers* (ibid. 47:30).[178]

"*He called for his son Joseph* (ibid., 29). *His son*—with an identical face.[179] *His son*—because he engendered him with desire of spirit and heart more than all of them.

"Come and see what is written: *Is your taking my husband a small thing?* (ibid. 30:15). Because Jacob's total desire was for Rachel, and therefore, [222b] *He called for his son Joseph.*"[180]

Rabbi Shim'on opened, "*The hidden are for YHVH our God* (Deuteronomy 29:28).[181] How vigilant should a person be about his sins, scrutinizing himself that he not transgress the will of his Lord! For we have learned: Everything that one does in this world is recorded in a book and reckoned before the Holy King.[182] All is revealed before Him, as is written: '*If one hides in secret places, do I not see him?' declares YHVH* (Jeremiah 23:24). If so, how can a person hide himself to sin before his Lord? And we have learned: Even what a person thinks and what arises in his will is all present before the blessed Holy One, not vanishing from Him.[183]

"Come and see: On the night that Leah went in to Jacob and gave him those tokens that Jacob had given to Rachel, it arose in his will that she was Rachel and he joined with her conjugally.[184] That was Jacob's first drop, as is written:

91b (and Rashi, ad loc., s.v. *bidyoqno*); *Alfa Beita de-Rabbi Akiva* B (*Battei Midrashot*, 2:415–16); *Pirqei de-Rabbi Eli'ezer* 35; *Zohar* 1:72a; above, p. 17 at n. 117; Moses de León, commentary on the ten *sefirot*, 338b; Wolfson, *Along the Path*, 1–62.

178. **no separation at all...** The three patriarchs—symbolizing the triad of *Ḥesed, Gevurah,* and *Tif'eret*—must be together.

The full verse reads: "*I will lie down with my fathers, and you will carry me from Egypt and bury me in their burial place.*" *He said, "I will do as you have spoken."*

179. **with an identical face** See above, p. 331 and n. 167.

180. ***Is your taking my husband a small thing?...*** After Rachel asks Leah to give her some of the mandrakes found by Reuben, Leah responds, "*Is your taking my husband a small thing, that you would take my son's mandrakes too?" Rachel replied, "Then he may lie with you tonight in return for your son's mandrakes.*" The line is quoted here to demonstrate that Rachel had captured Jacob's heart; consequently, Jacob felt a special love for Rachel's firstborn son, Joseph.

181. ***The hidden...*** The full verse reads: *The hidden are for YHVH our God; the revealed are for us and for our children forever to observe all the words of this teaching.*

182. **recorded in a book...** On this image, see M *Avot* 2:1; 3:16; below, at note 340; *Zohar* 3:126b. Cf. Isaiah 65:6; Malachi 3:16; Daniel 7:10.

183. **Even what a person thinks...** See 1 Chronicles 28:9; *Bereshit Rabbah* 9:3.

184. **Leah went in to Jacob...** Laban had promised to give Jacob his younger daughter, Rachel, in marriage, but he tricked him by substituting his older daughter, Leah (Genesis 29). According to BT *Megillah* 13b (in the name of Rabbi El'azar), Rachel told Jacob ahead of time that Laban would not let him marry her before marrying her older

my strength and first fruit of my vigor! (Genesis 49:3), and he thought that she was Rachel.[185] The blessed Holy One, who *reveals the deep and hidden, and knows what is in darkness*,[186] raised that desire to its place and the birthright of Reuben was transferred to Joseph. Why? Because Jacob's desire was for Rachel, and she was the intention of the first drop issuing from Jacob. And because that first drop was hers, Reuben's actual birthright was inherited by Joseph, and Rachel inherited what was hers.[187]

"Consequently, mystery of the matter: Reuben did not attain a name like the other tribes, but rather ראובן (*Re'uven*), 'See! A son,' unidentified. This son's name was unknown, so by this name Leah did not call him 'my son'—he was not named ראובני (*Re'uveni*), 'See! My son'—because Leah knew what had happened.[188]

"We have learned: It was revealed before the blessed Holy One that Jacob did not intend to sin thereby before Him and did not desirously imagine another woman at that moment, like other, wicked ones of the world. Consequently, it
334
is written: *And the sons of Jacob were twelve* (ibid. 35:22). For sons of other, wicked ones of the world who commit this act are called by another name—this matter is known among the Companions. Therefore, *He called for his son Joseph —his son* from beginning to end."[189]

sister, Leah, so Jacob gave Rachel certain tokens by which he could ascertain her identity on the wedding night. Rachel, however, not wanting her sister to be embarrassed, gave these tokens to Leah, who then presented them to Jacob, fooling him into thinking that she was Rachel.

185. **Jacob's first drop...** According to rabbinic tradition, Jacob never experienced a nocturnal emission, so Reuben was actually conceived from his father's first drop of semen.

The verse begins Jacob's blessing to his firstborn son, Reuben, and reads: *Reuben, my firstborn you are—my strength and first fruit of my vigor!* See *Bereshit Rabbah* 97 (p. 1204); 99:6; *Targum Yerushalmi*, Genesis 49:3; BT *Yevamot* 76a; *Tanḥuma, Vayḥi* 9; *Tanḥuma* (Buber), *Vayḥi* 11; Rashi on Genesis 49:3; above, p. 65 at n. 446.

186. ***reveals the deep...*** From Daniel 2:22.

187. **raised that desire to its place...** Because Jacob thought that he was sleeping with Rachel, his desire focused on her; consequently God reserved the birthright for Rachel's firstborn son, Joseph—not for Leah's firstborn son, Reuben.

See above, p. 65 and n. 444; *Zohar* 1:17b, 155a–b (*ST*), 235a, 236a. See 1 Chronicles 5:1: *The sons of Reuben, firstborn of Israel—he was the firstborn; but when he defiled his father's bed, his birthright was given to the sons of Joseph.* According to this verse, Reuben lost the birthright because he slept with his father's concubine Bilhah. See Genesis 35:22; 49:4.

188. **Reuben did not attain a name...** Leah named her son ראובן (*Re'uven*), understood here as meaning simply: ראו בן (*Re'u ven*), "See! A son." His lack of a normal name reflects the fact that his father never intended to engender him from Leah but rather from Rachel—a fact that Leah herself recognized by not claiming the son as "hers." See above, p. 65 and n. 448.

189. **Jacob did not intend to sin...** If Jacob had realized that he was having inter-

Rabbi Yose said, "By what did Jacob make Joseph swear, as is written: *Place your hand under my thigh* (ibid. 47:29)?[190] By that sign of the covenant inscribed on his flesh, for this more than anything is essence of the patriarchs, and this covenant is mystery of Joseph."[191]

Rabbi Shim'on said, "Of Abraham and Jacob is written *place your hand under my thigh*—on that place intimating the holy Name and issuing holy, faithful seed to the world.[192] Of Isaac this is not written, for Esau issued from him.[193]

course with Leah and had fantasized about Rachel, this would have been a horrible sin and the child conceived from this union (Reuben) would have been tainted—considered a demonic bastard ("called by another name")—and not included as one of the twelve tribes. Jacob, however, did not sin, so his sons numbered a full dozen, including both the untainted Reuben and Joseph. The latter was Jacob's son from the beginning (when Jacob intended to engender him with Rachel on the night of his first wedding, even though he was sleeping with Leah) to the end (when Joseph proved his virtue in Egypt).

See BT *Nedarim* 20b; *Zohar* 155a (*ST*); above, p. 65 and n. 447; Galante; *KP*; Scholem. The verse in Genesis 35 reads: *Reuben went and lay with Bilhah, his father's concubine, and Israel heard. And the sons of Jacob were twelve.* According to the rabbinic interpretation, Reuben did not actually sleep with Bilhah but only disheveled his father's bed, and this verse demonstrates that Reuben was still considered one of the twelve tribes. See above, p. 60 and nn. 421, 423.

190. ***Place your hand...*** The verse reads: *If I have found favor in your eyes, place your hand under my thigh and act toward me with steadfast kindness—please do not bury me in Egypt.*

191. **sign of the covenant...** The covenant of circumcision, first established with Abraham and cherished by the patriarchs. See Genesis 17; *Bereshit Rabbah* 59:8; *Tanḥuma* (Buber), *Ḥayyei Sarah* 6; *Pirqei de-Rabbi Eli'ezer* 39.

Joseph is linked with the covenant of circumcision because he overcame sexual temptation, refusing the advances of Potiphar's wife. According to the *Zohar*, his sexual purity enabled him to scale the sefirotic ladder and attain the rung of *Yesod*, the divine phallus and site of the covenant. See above, p. 92, n. 50.

192. **Of Abraham and Jacob...** Abraham made his servant swear this same way when he directed him to journey to the patriarchal birthplace in Mesopotamia in order to seek a wife for Isaac. See Genesis 24:2 and the rabbinic references in the preceding note.

In various sources circumcision is linked with the divine name. See *Tanḥuma, Tsav* 14, where the mark of circumcision is identified with the י (*yod*) of שדי (*Shaddai*). A German Hasidic tradition equates the mark with the *yod* of יהוה (*YHVH*).

See *Zohar* 1:2b, 13a, 56a, 60a, 89a, 95a–b; 2:36a, 216b; 3:142a (*IR*), 215b, 220a; Wolfson, "Circumcision and the Divine Name"; idem, *Circle in the Square*, 29–48.

193. **Of Isaac this is not written...** Esau is considered tainted and impure seed of Isaac his father, so when Isaac commanded Jacob not to marry a Canaanite (Genesis 28:1), he could not make him swear by placing his hand *under my thigh*—because Isaac's thigh had proven imperfect.

Commentators offer various explanations as to why Ishmael did not similarly invalidate Abraham's mark of circumcision. These include the view that Ishmael repented (Galante), that he was born before Abraham was given the command of circumcision (*Nefesh David*), and that the descendants of Ishmael themselves practice circumcision (*KP*). In medieval Jewish literature, Esau symbol-

"Further, why here *place your hand under my thigh . . . please do not bury me in Egypt?*[194] Because Jacob said to Joseph, 'Swear to me by this holy sign—which issued holy, faithful seed to the world and was guarded and never defiled—that I will not be buried among those defiled ones who never guarded it,' of whom is written *whose members are members of donkeys . . .* (Ezekiel 23:20).[195]

"Now, you might say, 'Look at Joseph, who guarded it more than anyone! Why was he buried among them?'[196] But we have learned: *It happened that the word of YHVH came to Ezekiel the priest, son of Buzi, in the land of the Chaldeans by the River Kevar . . .* (Ezekiel 1:3). And we have learned: *Shekhinah* dwells only in the land of Israel. So, why is *Shekhinah* here? Only because it is written *by the River Kevar.* And then, *there the hand of YHVH came upon him* (ibid.). Here too, Joseph's coffin was cast into the water. The blessed Holy One said, 'If Joseph departs from here, the exile will remain unfulfilled. Rather, let his burial be in a place that cannot be defiled, and Israel will endure the exile.'"[197]

izes Christianity, and Ishmael represents Islam; here, the *Zohar* may be expressing particular animus toward its dominant foe.

194. **why here . . . *under my thigh* . . .** The reference to the sign of circumcision (*under my thigh*) is appropriate earlier in Genesis (24:2), where Abraham is about to send his servant to find a wife for Isaac. But what relevance does it have here, where Jacob asks Joseph not to bury him in Egypt?

195. **Because Jacob said . . .** Jacob had always guarded his sign of the covenant, never committing sexual misconduct. Now he wanted to be sure that he would not be buried in Egypt—among those who acted otherwise.

The full verse in Ezekiel reads: *She* [Jerusalem] *lusted after their* [Egypt's] *paramours, whose members are members of donkeys and whose emission is the emission of stallions.* The word *members* renders בשר (*basar*), "flesh," here a euphemism for "penis." See Leviticus 15:2; Ezekiel 16:26.

196. **Look at Joseph . . .** He was the paradigm of proper sexual conduct, so why was he later buried among the Egyptians? See Genesis 50:26.

197. **But we have learned . . .** Generally *Shekhinah* manifests only in the land of Israel, a zone of purity. In the case of Ezekiel, an exception was made because the prophet was standing by the river, which purifies. Similarly, according to rabbinic tradition, Joseph's coffin was deposited in the Nile, so he remained invulnerable to the impurity of Egypt and *Shekhinah* could manifest near him, thereby alleviating Israel's suffering in exile. If Joseph had been buried outside of Egypt, *Shekhinah* would have been deprived of Her human base there and Israel could not have endured the exile, which had to be completed ("fulfilled") before the people could be redeemed and brought to the Promised Land. See Genesis 15:13–14.

The verse in Ezekiel concludes: *and there the hand of YHVH came upon him.*

On *Shekhinah* revealing Herself only in the land of Israel, see *Mekhilta, Pisḥa* 1; *Pirqei de-Rabbi Eli'ezer* 10; *Zohar* 1:85a, 121a; 2:170b. On the relation between prophetic revelation and the purity of water, see *Mekhilta, Pisḥa* 1 (citing Ezekiel 1:3; Daniel 8:2; 10:4); *Zohar* 1:85a, 149a–b; 2:82b. On Joseph's coffin being deposited in the Nile, see *Tosefta, Sotah* 4:7; *Mekhilta, Beshallaḥ, Petiḥta*; *Targum Yerushalmi,* Genesis 50:26; BT *Sotah* 13a; *Pesiqta de-Rav Kahana* 11:12; *Tanḥuma, Beshallaḥ* 2; *Shemot Rabbah* 20:19; *Zohar* 2:46a.

For other interpretations of "the exile will remain unfulfilled," see *OY.*

It has been taught: Rabbi Yose said, "Jacob saw that he was perfectly arrayed in the throne along with the patriarchs.[198] He said, 'If I am buried here, how will this body join the patriarchs? Even the cave where I am to be buried is called Double, because everything double is two and one: the cave also is two and one.[199]

"Come and see: The patriarchs were worthy of being buried there along with their spouses, Jacob [223a] along with Leah. Why not Rachel?[200] After all, it is written: *Rachel was* עקרה (*aqarah*), *barren* (Genesis 29:31), for she was עקרא (*iqqara*), essence, of the house.[201] However, Leah proved worthy of him, engendering more—six tribes of holy stock in the world—so she was placed with him for coupling in the cave."[202]

Rabbi Yehudah said, "All her days, Leah would stand in the crossroads and weep for Jacob, having heard that he was righteous, and she prayed for him zealously, corresponding to what is written: *Leah's eyes were weak* (ibid., 17), as we have established—for she rose early and lingered in darkness, seeking on the

198. **perfectly arrayed in the throne...** Abraham had perfected and attained the quality of *Ḥesed;* Isaac, the quality of *Gevurah;* and Jacob, the quality of *Tif'eret*. This sefirotic triad constitutes a throne for the highest level of divinity. See *Bereshit Rabbah* 47:6: "Resh Lakish said, 'The patriarchs themselves constitute the [divine] Chariot.'" (The divine chariot constitutes a moving throne.)

See Azriel of Gerona, *Peirush ha-Aggadot,* 57; *Zohar* 1:60b, 99a, 150a, 154b, 173b, 186a, 223b–224a, 248b; 2:144a; 3:38a, 99a, 146a, 182a, 262b; Moses de León, *Sefer ha-Rimmon,* 239–40.

199. **cave... is called Double...** The cave of Machpelah, burial site of the patriarchs and matriarchs (except for Rachel). See above, note 108. Here the place-name מכפלה (*Makhpelah*) is interpreted according to the root כפל (*kphl*), "double."

See BT *Eruvin* 53a: "*The cave of Machpelah* (Genesis 23:9). Rav and Shemu'el: One says, 'Two chambers, one within the other.' The other says, 'A chamber and an upper chamber.'" See Rashi and Naḥmanides, ad loc.; *Zohar* 1:128b–129a.

"Two and one" apparently refers to two polar opposites harmonized by a third element. As in the sefirotic triad, *Ḥesed* and *Gevurah* are harmonized by *Tif'eret,* so in the cave, Abraham and Isaac were meant to be harmonized by Jacob. The same expression occurs in a similar sefirotic context in *Zohar* 2:46b, 56b. For somewhat different interpretations, see Galante; *KP* (who offers mathematical theory); *NO.*

200. **Why not Rachel?** As mentioned in the preceding note, she was the only matriarch not buried in the cave.

201. ***Rachel was* עקרה (*aqarah*), *barren*...** The word עקרה (*aqarah*), *barren,* is reinterpreted as עקרא (*iqqara*), "essence." If Rachel was essential, why was she not buried in the cave?

See *Bereshit Rabbah* 71:2; *Pesiqta de-Rav Kahana* 20:2; *Tanḥuma* (Buber), *Vayetse* 15; *Bemidbar Rabbah* 14:8; *Zohar* 1:29a–b, 50a, 149b, 154a, 157b, 158b; Moses de León, *She'elot u-Tshuvot,* 44.

202. **engendering more—six tribes...** Leah gave birth to six of the twelve tribes, whereas Rachel gave birth only to Joseph and Benjamin. These six correspond to the six *sefirot* from *Ḥesed* through *Yesod,* of which *Tif'eret* (Jacob's *sefirah*) is the core.

See Moses de León, *She'elot u-Tshuvot,* 44–45.

roads, whereas Rachel never ventured out. Consequently, she deserved to be buried with him, whereas Rachel's grave stands on the crossroads, where she was buried, as is written: *"As for me, when I was returning from Paddan, Rachel died* עלי (*alai*), *upon me* (ibid. 48:7). What is *alai*? *Alai*, precisely: 'on account of me!' *In the land of Canaan on the way* (ibid.)—'on account of me, she died *on the way*, because she never ventured out for me like her sister.' Therefore, Leah, who went out and wept in the crossroads on account of Jacob, was worthy of being buried with him. Rachel, who did not want to go out and seek for him—her grave is on the crossroads.[203]

"Mystery of the matter, as we have already established: this one, revealed; this one, concealed.[204]

"Come and see: That righteous Leah shed many tears to become the share of Jacob and not of that wicked Esau, corresponding to what we have learned: Every person who weeps and sheds tears before the blessed Holy One—even if a punishment has been decreed upon him, it is torn up and cannot prevail against him. How do we know? From Leah. For Leah was destined to become the share of Esau, but through prayer she attained Jacob first and was not given to Esau."[205]

203. **Leah would stand in the crossroads...** According to midrashic tradition, Leah heard that she and Rachel were to be married respectively to Rebecca's two sons Esau and Jacob, and that since she was the elder daughter, her husband would be Esau, Rebecca's elder son. She then went out to the crossroads to inquire from passersby about the character of the two young men. When she heard that Esau was wicked and Jacob virtuous, she begged God to save her from having to marry Esau, weeping so profusely that her eyes became *weak*. Rachel, on the other hand, was quite satisfied with her prospective husband and never ventured out. Consequently, Leah was granted burial in the cave of Machpelah alongside Jacob, whereas Rachel was buried at the crossroads where she died.

See *Bereshit Rabbah* 70:16; 71:2; *Targum Yerushalmi* and *Targum Yerushalmi* (frag.), Genesis 29:17; BT *Bava Batra* 123a; *Tanḥuma, Vayetse* 4; *Tanḥuma* (Buber), *Vayetse* 12, 20; *Zohar* 2:29b.

Rachel died as she was giving birth to Benjamin. See Genesis 35:16–19. The verse quoted here, in which Jacob describes her death, reads in full: *"As for me, when I was returning from Paddan, Rachel died* עלי (*alai*), *upon me, in the land of Canaan on the way, with still a stretch of land to reach Ephrath, and I buried her there on the way to Ephrath" —which is Bethlehem*. The word עלי (*alai*) means literally "upon me, on me," though it apparently connotes "alas, to my sorrow" (see Psalms 42:6–7). Here, drawing on midrashic tradition, Rabbi Yehudah reads it hyperliterally: "upon me, on account of me"—namely, because she never ventured out for me as her sister did. See above, p. 57 and n. 404.

204. **this one, revealed; this one, concealed** Rachel and Leah symbolize respectively *Shekhinah* (the last, revealed *sefirah*) and *Binah* (the more hidden realm). Therefore it is appropriate that Rachel was buried on the road and Leah concealed in the cave.

See *Zohar* 1:152a (*ST*), 153a–154b, 158a–b; 2:29b; Moses de León, *She'elot u-Tshuvot*, 41, 45.

205. **Leah shed many tears...** As a result, her prayer was answered and she "at-

Rabbi Ḥiyya said, "It is written: '*I will lie down with my fathers, and you will carry me from Egypt and bury me in their burial place.' He said, 'I will do as you have spoken'* (ibid. 47:30).[206]

Rabbi Yitsḥak opened, "*What profit does a human have for all the toil at which he toils under the sun?* (Ecclesiastes 1:3). As has been said in various places, we have contemplated the words of King Solomon and they appear to be obscure. But all those words spoken by Solomon are to be read with wisdom.[207]

"Come and see what is written: *The wisdom of Solomon* תרב (*terev*), *increased* (1 Kings 5:10). In the days of King Solomon the moon assumed fullness, corresponding to what is written: *The wisdom of Solomon terev, surpassed, the wisdom of all the children of the East* (ibid.).[208] Who are *the children of the East*? This has already been established;[209] but *the wisdom of the children of the East* is the wisdom they inherited from Abraham, as is written: *Abraham gave all that he had to Isaac* (Genesis 25:5). What is *all that he had*? Supernal wisdom that he knew through the holy name of the blessed Holy One. *All that he had* indicates that this was his, as we have learned: Abraham had a daughter named *ba-kol, with everything*.[210] And it is written: *To the sons of his concubines Abraham gave*

tained Jacob first," marrying him before Rachel did.

See above, note 203. On the power of weeping, see BT *Berakhot* 32b, in the name of Rabbi El'azar: "Since the day the Temple was destroyed, the gates of prayer have been locked.... Yet even though the gates of prayer have been locked, the gates of tears have not."

See *Zohar* 1:132b; 2:12b, 165a, 245b (*Heikh*); *ZḤ* 80a (*MhN, Rut*).

206. ***He said, 'I will do...'*** The subject is Joseph.

207. **words of King Solomon...** Traditionally, Solomon is regarded as the author of Ecclesiastes. Some of his statements there seem shocking or even heretical, yet when read with wisdom, they reveal a deeper meaning.

See *Vayiqra Rabbah* 28:1; *Pesiqta de-Rav Kahana* 8:1; *Qohelet Rabbah* on 1:3; *Zohar* 1:195a; 3:64a, 157a, 177b, 182a, 236a.

208. ***wisdom of Solomon*...moon...** The full verse reads: *The wisdom of Solomon* תרב (*terev*), *surpassed, the wisdom of all the children of the East and all the wisdom of Egypt*. The word *terev* is interpreted here according to its similar meaning, "increased." *The wisdom of Solomon* symbolizes *Shekhinah*, daughter of *Ḥokhmah* (Wisdom). She is also symbolized by the moon.

According to the Midrash, just as the moon does not become full until the fifteenth day of its cycle, so it remained incomplete until the glorious reign of Solomon in the fifteenth generation from Abraham. See *Pesiqta de-Rav Kahana* 5:12 and *Shemot Rabbah* 15:26: "When Solomon appeared, the disk of the moon became full."

Here Rabbi Yitsḥak teaches that in the days of Solomon *Shekhinah* attained fullness. See *Zohar* 1:73b–74a, 150a, 225b, 238a, 243a, 249b; 2:85a; 3:61a, 74b, 181b; *ZḤ* 83b (*MhN, Rut*); Moses de León, *Shushan Edut*, 342.

209. **already been established** *The children of the East* were famous for their knowledge of astrology and divination.

See *Pesiqta de-Rav Kahana* 4:3; *Qohelet Rabbah* on 7:23; *Tanḥuma, Ḥuqqat* 6; Judah ben Barzillai, *Peirush Sefer Yetsirah*, 159; Naḥmanides, introduction to Commentary on the Torah, and on Deuteronomy 18:10; *Zohar* 1:99b, 133b. All these sources cite the verse in Kings.

210. **Abraham had a daughter...** The

gifts (ibid., 6), for he gave them knowledge of lower crowns. He expelled them *to the land of the East* (ibid.), and from there *the children of the East* inherited wisdom, corresponding to what is written: *the wisdom of all the children of the East.*"[211]

Come and see:[212] One day Rabbi Shim'on was going from Cappadocia to Lydda, accompanied by Rabbi Abba and Rabbi Yehudah.[213] Rabbi Abba was weary, running after Rabbi Shim'on, who was riding.[214] Rabbi Abba said, "*They will follow YHVH, roaring like a lion* (Hosea 11:10)."[215]

Rabbi Shim'on dismounted, and said to him, "Surely it is written: *I sat there with YHVH forty days and forty nights* (Deuteronomy 9:9). Surely, wisdom is enduringly erected only when a person is sitting, not walking or standing erect. We have already established why it is written *I sat there*: the word depends on tranquility."[216]

They sat down. Rabbi Abba said, "It is written: *The wisdom of Solomon* terev, *surpassed, the wisdom of all the children of the East and all the wisdom of Egypt.*

daughter symbolizes *Shekhinah*, through whom Abraham attained wisdom. See above, p. 323 and n. 119.

211. ***To the sons of his concubines...*** The full verse reads: *To the sons of his concubines Abraham gave gifts while he was still alive, and he sent them away from his son Isaac eastward, to the land of the East.*

Here these *gifts* are understood as knowledge of "lower crowns," namely, demonic powers, by which they could perform magic. See BT *Sanhedrin* 91a: "*To the sons of his concubines Abraham gave gifts....* What is the meaning of *gifts*? Rabbi Yirmeyah son of Abba said, 'This teaches that he transmitted to them a name of defilement [by which to conjure demons and engage in sorcery].'"

See Judah ben Barzillai, *Peirush Sefer Yetsirah*, 159; *Zohar* 1:100b, 133b.

212. **Come and see** Following this narrative about Rabbi Shim'on, Rabbi Yitsḥak continues discussing the verse from Ecclesiastes. See below, at note 235.

213. **from Cappadocia to Lydda...** On this fantastic itinerary from eastern Asia Minor to Palestine, see above, p. 208 and n. 180.

214. **riding** On a donkey.

215. ***roaring like a lion*** In the biblical context, this phrase refers to God: *He will roar like a lion.* Here, Rabbi Abba may be applying it to humans striving after God, and to himself running after the godlike Rabbi Shim'on. Alternatively, Rabbi Shim'on is both godlike and *like a lion.*

See BT *Berakhot* 6b; *Zohar* 1:160a; 2:38a (where the name YHVH is actually applied to Rabbi Shim'on); 3:79b; *ZḤ* 21d (*MhN*); above, note 90; *MmD.* On Rabbi Shim'on as a lion, see BT *Bava Metsi'a* 84b; *Zohar* 2:15a; 3:60a, 196a.

216. ***I sat there...*** From Moses' description of his stay on Mount Sinai, Rabbi Shim'on concludes that only in sedentary tranquility can wisdom be properly received or conveyed.

See BT *Eruvin* 64b; *Megillah* 21a; *Shemot Rabbah* 47:8. The verse in Deuteronomy reads: ואשב (*Va-eshev*) *I sat* [or: *stayed*], *on the mountain forty days and forty nights.* Here the *Zohar* conflates this verse with Exodus 34:28: *He was there with YHVH forty days and forty nights.*

What is *the wisdom of Solomon*, and what is *the wisdom of all the children of the East*, and what is *the wisdom of Egypt*?"

He replied,[217] "Come and see: In various places they have established that name of the moon. When She is blessed by all, it is written: *terev, she increased*—in the days of King Solomon when She grew and was blessed and assumed fullness.[218]

"We have learned: A thousand mountains sprout vegetation before Her, all constituting a single bite for Her. A thousand rivers swell toward Her, and She swallows them in a single gulp. Her nails clutch in 1,070 directions; [223b] Her hands grasp in 24,000 directions. Nothing escapes Her on this side and nothing escapes Her on that. Thousands upon thousands of shields adhere to Her hair.[219]

"A single youth, extending from one end of the world to the other, emerges from between Her legs with sixty strokes of fire, decked in his colors. This one is empowered over those below in Her four directions.[220] This is the youth who holds 613 supernal keys from the side of Mother, dangling from the flaming sword girded on his loins.[221]

"That youth is called חנוך (*Ḥanokh*), Enoch, son of Jared in those *baraitot*, as is written: חנוך (*Ḥanokh*), *Train, the youth in the way he should go* (Proverbs

217. **He replied** The subject is Rabbi Shim'on.

218. **that name of the moon...** Both "moon" and *wisdom of Solomon* apply to *Shekhinah*. See above, p. 339 and n. 208.

219. **thousand mountains sprout...** This description of the terrifying aspect of *Shekhinah* derives from a depiction of the legendary animal Behemoth.

See Psalms 50:10; Job 40:15–24; *Vayiqra Rabbah* 22:10; BT *Bava Batra* 74b; *Pesiqta de-Rav Kahana* 6:1; *Tanḥuma, Pinḥas* 12; *Pirqei de-Rabbi Eli'ezer* 11; *Zohar* 1:18b; 3:60a–b, 189a, 217a, 240b; Moses de León, *Sefer ha-Rimmon*, 201–2; Ginzberg, *Legends*, 5:49, nn. 141–42; Scholem, *On the Mystical Shape of the Godhead*, 191–92.

On the relation between *Shekhinah* and the demonic, see above, pp. 283–84, n. 139. Hair symbolizes the power of harsh judgment. See above, note 31; *Zohar* 3:60b.

220. **single youth...** Metatron, the chief angel, known as the "youth" (who grows old and is continually rejuvenated) or heavenly servant, and also as "Prince of the World." Here he is described as being born by *Shekhinah*.

See *Tosafot, Yevamot* 16b, s.v. *pasuq zeh;* Tishby, *Wisdom of the Zohar*, 2:626–31; Scholem, *Kabbalah*, 377–81. On *Shekhinah* as mother of Metatron, see *Zohar* 2:66a. On Metatron's cosmic size, see 3 Enoch 9:2.

The image of "sixty strokes of fire" derives from BT *Ḥagigah* 15a, where Metatron is lashed with sixty strokes of fire to demonstrate that he is subservient to God. See *Zohar* 2:51b, 66b–67a.

221. **613 supernal keys...** The number suggests the 613 *mitsvot* of the Torah, whose observance unlocks treasures with the help of Metatron. Mother denotes *Shekhinah*.

See *OY*. On the keys of Metatron, see Schäfer, *Synopse zur Hekhalot-Literatur*, §72; *Zohar* 1:37b, 181b; 3:60a, 171b; *ZḤ* 39d–40a.

The image of "the flaming sword" derives from Genesis 3:24: *He drove out the human and placed east of the Garden of Eden the cherubim and the flame of the whirling sword to guard the way to the Tree of Life*. See *Targum Onqelos*, ad loc.

22:6).[222] Now, if you say 'Mishnah'—in our Mishnah we have established the matter and it has been explained. All have contemplated a single entity.[223] Beneath him beasts of the field find shade.[224]

"Come and see: Just as holy Israel is called Son of His Mother—as is written: *I was son to my father, tender only child in the sight of my mother* (ibid. 4:3), and similarly: *My son, My firstborn is Israel* (Exodus 4:22)—so too below, he is called Youth, as is written: *When Israel was a youth, I loved him* (Hosea 11:1).[225] In various nuances he is called *son of* ירד (*Yered*), *Jared*, as we have established. But come and see! *Son of Yered*, literally, for we have learned: Ten ירידות (*yeridot*), descents, *Shekhinah* made to earth—all established by the Companions.[226]

222. **youth is called חנוך (*Ḥanokh*), Enoch...** According to Genesis 5:24, *Enoch walked with God, and he was no more, for God took him.* In the postbiblical period, the phrase *for God took him* was taken to mean that God transported Enoch through the heavens, a journey recorded in the pseudepigraphical Enoch literature. According to several sources, through his heavenly journey Enoch was transformed into Metatron, the "youth." Here Rabbi Shim'on proves the identification of Enoch with Metatron by citing the phrase from Proverbs: חנוך לנער (*ḥanokh la-na'ar*), *train the youth*, which is understood to mean that *Ḥanokh* (Enoch) was transformed into Metatron, *the youth.*

A ברייתא (*baraita*), literally, "external" (Hebrew plural, ברייתות [*baraitot*]) is a Tannaitic tradition not included in the canonical Mishnah. Here, it refers to extracanonical works such as the pseudepigraphical book of Enoch.

See 3 Enoch 4:1–10; *Targum Yerushalmi*, Genesis 5:24; *Aggadat Bereshit*, intro, 38; *Midrash Aggadah*, Genesis 5:24; *Tosafot, Yevamot* 16b, s.v. *pasuq zeh; Zohar* 1:37b, 56b; 2:179a (*SdTs*); Ginzberg, *Legends*, 5:156–64, nn. 58–61; Margaliot, *Mal'akhei Elyon*, 80–83, 89–90; Scholem, *Kabbalah*, 378–79.

223. **if you say 'Mishnah'...** In other words, if you claim that the identification of Metatron with Enoch is a standard rabbinic tradition ("Mishnah")—and not extracanonical ("in those *baraitot*")—then we have demonstrated this matter in "our Mishnah." This last expression refers to a secret, mystical Mishnah often cited in the *Zohar* and known to its own circle. Here "our Mishnah" probably alludes specifically to *Sifra di-Tsni'uta*, the cryptic portion of the *Zohar* that in some ways serves as an anonymous Mishnah for other parts of the *Zohar*, which can be seen as its "Talmudic" commentary. The identification of Metatron with Enoch appears near the end of *Sifra di-Tsni'uta* (*Zohar* 2:179a).

"All have contemplated a single entity" apparently means that all of these various sources—both canonical and extracanonical (and whether speaking of Enoch or Metatron)—contemplate the same being.

On the expression "our Mishnah," see *Zohar* 1:37b, 55b, 74a, 91b, 93a, 95b, 96a, 224a, 252a (*Hash*); 3:57b, 61b, 78a, 284b, 285a; Galante; Matt, "Matnita di-Lan." "Our Mishnah" is to be distinguished from the *Matnitin* of the *Zohar*, on which see Scholem, *Kabbalah*, 216.

224. **Beneath him beasts of the field...** This description derives from Daniel's vision of a cosmic tree (4:9). Here it refers to angels ("beasts of the field") who find shelter beneath Metatron.

225. **Israel is called Son...** As *Tif'eret*—whose full name is *Tif'eret Yisra'el* (Beauty of Israel)—is the son of *Binah* (the Divine Mother), so Metatron is the Youth, son of *Shekhinah*.

226. ***son of* ירד (*Yered*), *Jared*...** As indicated above (notes 220, 222), Enoch son

"Beneath this one stand numerous beings called חיות ברא (*ḥeivat bara*), beasts of the field—beasts outside, precisely![227] Beneath those beings adheres Her hair, called 'stars of a scepter,' precisely: masters of measure, masters of balance, masters of severity, masters of reaping—all called 'purple hair.'[228] Her hands and feet grip like a ferocious lion seizing its prey; of this is written *It tears apart, with none to deliver* (Micah 5:7).

"Her nails—all those who call attention to the sins of human beings, inscribing and engraving their sins with the intensity of harsh judgment. Of this is written *The sin of Judah is engraved with a stylus of iron,* בצפורן שמיר (*be-tsipporen shamir*), *with the point of a diamond* (Jeremiah 17:1). What is *shamir*? That which engraves and penetrates stone on every side.[229]

"The dirt under Her nails—all those who do not cleave to the body of the King, who suck from the side of defilement, when the moon abides in defect.[230]

"Because King Solomon inherited the moon in fullness, he sought to inherit her in defect, so he strove for the knowledge of spirits and demons to inherit the moon in all her aspects. In the days of King Solomon the moon shone completely, as is written: *The wisdom of Solomon increased—increased*, precisely![231]

of Jared was transformed into Metatron, who was born by *Shekhinah*. Now Rabbi Shim'on interprets *son of* ירד (*Yered*), *Jared*, to mean "son of *Shekhinah*," because the root ירד (*yrd*) means "to descend," and according to rabbinic tradition the Divine Presence descended and manifested ten times on earth.

See *Mekhilta, Baḥodesh* 3; *Sifrei*, Numbers 93; *Bereshit Rabbah* 38:8; *Avot de-Rabbi Natan* A, 34; B, 37; *Pirqei de-Rabbi Eli'ezer* 14.

227. **חיות ברא (*ḥeivat bara*)...** As indicated above (note 224), this expression refers here to angelic beings beneath Metatron. Now Rabbi Shim'on plays on the closely related sense of ברא (*bara*), "outside," to indicate that these angelic beings lie outside of the purely divine realm.

228. **Her hair, called 'stars of a scepter'...** Hair symbolizes harsh judgment (above, note 219). The hair of *Shekhinah* conveys judgment to the world, weighing human actions and lashing out when necessary—striking like a rod or scepter. "Reaping" probably refers to killing.

See *OY*; Galante. The expression כוכביא דשרביטא (*kokhevayya de-sharvita*), "stars of a scepter," derives from the rabbinic term כוכבא דשביט (*kokheva de-shaveit*), "a star that flies," a comet. See BT *Berakhot* 58b; *Zohar* 2:171b; 3:233a.

229. **בצפורן שמיר (*be-tsipporen shamir*)...** The word צפורן (*tsipporen*) means "point" but also "nail" (on the finger or toe). שמיר (*Shamir*) means "diamond" but is also the name of the legendary worm that could cut through hardest stone. According to rabbinic tradition, Solomon employed the *shamir* in building the Temple.

See M *Sotah* 9:12; BT *Sotah* 48b, *Gittin* 68a–b; *Zohar* 1:74a; Ginzberg, *Legends*, 5:53, n. 165.

230. **dirt under Her nails...** Demonic powers, not an integral part of the divine body. When human sin prevails, *Shekhinah* Herself (the moon) becomes vulnerable to hostile forces of defilement, who then threaten the world.

On dirt under the nails, see *Zohar* 2:208b; 3:60b, 70a, 79a–b. On "the body of the King," see above, note 3.

231. **King Solomon inherited the moon...** In the days of Solomon, *Shekhinah* (symbol-

"*By the wisdom of all* בני קדם (*benei qedem*), *the children of the East*—supernal mystery, as is written: *These are the kings who reigned in the land of Edom* (Genesis 36:31). These are called *benei qedem, children of primordial time.*[232]

"Come and see: Even though the moon shone, she did not shine fully until the arrival of Solomon, who was destined for her, as we have established—for accordingly, his mother was בת שבע (*Bat Sheva*), Bathsheba.[233]

"*And by all the wisdom of Egypt*—lower wisdom, called 'the slave girl behind the millstones.'[234] This wisdom of Solomon encompasses all: *wisdom of the children of the East* and *wisdom of Egypt.*"

Rabbi Abba said, "Blessed be the Compassionate One, that I asked you about this, for now I have gained all these words!"

Rabbi Shim'on said, "We have already established these words and they have been discussed."

"Come and see: *What profit does a human have for all the toil at which he toils?* (Ecclesiastes 1:3).[235] You might think that this includes even toiling over Torah,

ized by the moon) attained fullness, yet he sought to discover also Her dark, demonic side. See above, p. 339 and n. 208.

232. ***By the wisdom...*** Rabbi Shim'on reads the verse: *The wisdom of Solomon increased by means of the wisdom of all the children of the East and by all the wisdom of Egypt.* The fullness of *Shekhinah* and of Solomon's wisdom of Her included wisdom of the demonic realm, which is known as *wisdom of all* בני קדם (*benei qedem*), *the children of the East.* The word קדם (*qedem*), *the East,* is understood here as "primordial time," and linked with the verse in Genesis 36:31: *These are the kings who reigned in the land of Edom before any king reigned over the Children of Israel.* According to the *Zohar,* this verse refers to primordial worlds dominated by harsh judgment, which were created and destroyed prior to our world. Later this conception was elaborated by Isaac Luria in his theory of "the breaking of the vessels."

See *Zohar* 3:128a, 135a–b, 142a (all *IR*), 292a–b (*IZ*); *OY*; *KP*; Tishby, *Wisdom of the Zohar,* 1:276–77, 289–90; Liebes, "Ha-Mashiaḥ shel ha-Zohar," 219–21; idem, *Studies in the Zohar,* 134–35. On the primordial worlds that were destroyed, see *Bereshit Rabbah* 9:2; cf. 12:15.

233. **she did not shine fully...** As indicated above, p. 339 and n. 208.

The name בת שבע (*Bat Sheva*), Bathsheba, means literally "Daughter of Seven," and is understood here as alluding to *Shekhinah,* who is daughter of *Binah* (seven *sefirot* above *Shekhinah*) and is filled by the seven *sefirot* from *Binah* through *Yesod.* Solomon, born to Bathsheba, was destined for *Bat Sheva,* "Daughter of Seven."

234. **slave girl behind the millstones** The phrase derives from Exodus 11:5, describing the victims of the last of the ten plagues in Egypt, the killing of the firstborn: *Every firstborn in the land of Egypt will die, from the firstborn of Pharaoh sitting on his throne to the firstborn of the slave girl who is behind the millstones, and every firstborn of the beasts.* In the *Zohar* this phrase refers to the realm of demons, the source of magic and sorcery. See above, p. 71 and n. 479.

235. **Come and see...** Having concluded the narrative about Rabbi Shim'on and Rabbi Abba, the *Zohar* resumes the discussion between Rabbi Yitsḥak and Rabbi

but the verse states *at which he toils under the sun*—toiling over Torah is different, for it is above the sun!"[236]

Rabbi Ḥiyya said, "Even toiling over Torah, if done for people or for one's own fame—of this is written *under the sun*, for it does not ascend."

"Come and see: Rabbi El'azar said, 'Even if a person lives a thousand years, on the day that he departs from the world it seems to him as if he only lived a single day.'

"*I will lie down with my fathers* (Genesis 47:30).[237] Happy is the share of the patriarchs, whom the blessed Holy One made into a supernal, holy chariot, and in whom He delighted, crowning Himself with them, as is written: *Only your fathers did* YHVH *desire* (Deuteronomy 10:15)![238]

"Rabbi El'azar said, [224a] 'Jacob knew that the patriarchs were to be crowned with him—he would be crowned by the patriarchs and they would be crowned with him.[239] Therefore we have learned in *The Engraved Letters:*[240] "ש (*Shin*) —three joints: two joints on this side and that, and one merging them." This is what we have learned: *The central bar in the middle of the boards, running from end to end* (Exodus 26:28). That joint in the middle links this side and that, and of this is written *I will lie down with my fathers*—precisely!'"[241]

Ḥiyya of the verse in Ecclesiastes. See above, pages 339–40.

The full verse reads: *What profit does a human have for all the toil at which he toils under the sun?*

236. **even toiling over Torah...** Torah derives from heaven, so it possesses ultimate worth—unlike things of the world, which lie *under the sun.*

See *Vayiqra Rabbah* 28:1; *Pesiqta de-Rav Kahana* 8:1; *Qohelet Rabbah* on 1:3.

237. ***I will lie down with my fathers...*** The full verse reads: "*I will lie down with my fathers, and you will carry me from Egypt and bury me in their burial place." He said, "I will do as you have spoken.*"

238. **made into a supernal, holy chariot...** See *Bereshit Rabbah* 47:6: "Resh Lakish said, 'The patriarchs themselves constitute the [divine] Chariot.'" According to Kabbalah, Abraham had perfected and attained the quality of *Ḥesed;* Isaac, the quality of *Gevurah;* and Jacob, the quality of *Tif'eret*. This patriarchal sefirotic triad constitutes a chariot-throne for the highest level of divinity.

Here, according to the *Zohar*, Jacob says *I will lie down with my fathers* because he looks forward to completing the chariot together with them.

See above, p. 337 and n. 198. On the verse from Deuteronomy, see above, at note 22.

239. **Jacob knew...** He knew that they would fulfill one another and together constitute the chariot.

240. ***The Engraved Letters...*** One of the many volumes housed in the real or imaginary library of the author(s) of the *Zohar*. A similar title is cited again in *Zohar* 1:33b; 2:139b; 3:175b, 264b, 285a, 286b. Cf. 3:156b, 180b.

See Matt, *Zohar: The Book of Enlightenment*, 25; and the comment by Shim'on Lavi, *KP*, on *Zohar* 1:7a: "All such books mentioned in the *Zohar*... have been lost in the wanderings of exile.... Nothing is left of them except what is mentioned in the *Zohar*." For a catalogue of these books, see Neuhausen, *Sifriyyah shel Ma'lah.*

241. **ש (*Shin*)—three joints...** The three strokes of the letter ש (*shin*) symbolize the

I will lie down with my fathers (Genesis 47:30).[242]

Rabbi Yehudah opened, "*O deaf ones, listen! O blind ones, look and see!* (Isaiah 42:18). *O deaf ones, listen*—human beings who do not listen to the utterance of Torah, who do not open their ears to hear the commands of their Lord. *O blind ones*—who do not examine to discover the basis of their existence.[243] For every single day a herald emerges and proclaims—and no one pays attention![244]

"We have learned: When a human being is created, on the day he issues into the world, all his days arise in their existence. They come flying through the world, descending, alerting the human—day by day, individually. When a day comes to alert him, if a person commits a sin on that day before his Lord, that day ascends in shame, bears witness, and stands alone outside.[245]

"Come and see: After standing alone, it sits until the person repents from what he has done. If he succeeds, that day returns to its place.[246] If he does not, that day descends and joins the outside spirit, then returns to his house, molding itself into the image of that person in order to torment him, dwelling with him in the house.[247]

"Sometimes its stay is for the good, if he proves virtuous. If not, its stay is evil. In either case, those days are counted as lacking, missing from the ones that remain.[248] Woe to the human being who has diminished his days before the

sefirotic triad *Ḥesed, Gevurah,* and *Tif'eret* (symbolized respectively by Abraham, Isaac, and Jacob). The polar opposites *Ḥesed* and *Gevurah,* situated respectively on the right and the left, are harmonized and united by *Tif'eret.*

The verse from Exodus describes the central wooden crossbar of the Tabernacle in the wilderness. Here, Rabbi El'azar applies this description to *Tif'eret,* the central *sefirah,* who spans *Ḥesed* and *Gevurah.*

See *Zohar* 1:1b (spanning *Binah* and *Shekhinah*), 148b (*ST*); 2:51b, 175b; 3:186a–b; Moses de León, *Sefer ha-Rimmon,* 7; idem, *Sheqel ha-Qodesh,* 41–42 (49–51).

242. ***I will lie down...*** For the full verse, see above, note 237.

243. **who do not examine...** See BT *Ḥagigah* 12b: "Rabbi Yose said, 'Woe to creatures, for they see but do not know what they see; they stand but do not know on what they stand!'" See above, p. 196 and n. 111.

244. **every single day...** See *Avot* 6:2, in the name of Rabbi Yehoshu'a son of Levi, "Every single day an echo reverberates from Mount Horeb [Sinai], proclaiming: 'Woe to creatures for the humiliation of Torah!'"

See *Eikhah Rabbah, Petiḥta* 2.

245. **all his days arise...** At the moment of birth, all the days of a person's life emerge above. As each day of one's life unfolds, the celestial day descends, alerting him to live that day virtuously. If he fails to fulfill the day, it returns to heaven in shame.

246. **to its place** Among the other fulfilled days.

247. **outside spirit...** A demonic spirit lurking outside a person's house. The unfulfilled day now joins forces with this spirit and haunts the person.

See *Zohar* 3:123a (*RM*), 265a–b, 266b–267a.

248. **missing from the ones that remain** From the total of fulfilled days. See *Zohar* 3:92a.

Holy King, and has not bequeathed days above—in which to be adorned in that world, in which to approach the Holy King!

"Come and see: When those days draw near the Holy King, if the person departing from the world is virtuous, he ascends and enters those days, which become garments of glory in which his soul is arrayed. Those are days on which he proved himself worthy, not on which he sinned.[249]

"Woe to him who has diminished his days above! For when he is to be clothed in his days, those days that he spoiled by sinning are missing from that garment and he is clothed in defective wear. All the more so if there are many; then that person will have nothing to wear in that world![250] Woe to him! Woe to his soul! For they punish him in Hell—days for each single day, two for one.[251] For when he departs from this world, he finds no days in which to clothe himself and has no garment for cover. Happy are the righteous, whose days are all stored up with the blessed Holy One, woven into garments of glory to be worn in the world that is coming!

"We have learned in the mystery of our Mishnah: Why is it written *They knew they were naked* (Genesis 3:7)? They knew precisely that the garment of glory made from those days had been withdrawn from them and no day remained in which to be clothed, as is written: *Your eyes saw my embryo; in Your book they were all inscribed, days were fashioned—not one of them exists* (Psalms 139:16). *Days were fashioned*—precisely! *Not one of them exists*—for none of them remained in which to be clothed.[252] Until Adam strove to turn back, and

249. **When those days draw near...** When one is about to die, as indicated in Genesis 47:29: *The days of Israel drew near to die....* To enter and experience higher dimensions, the soul is enveloped in a radiant garment. According to this passage, such a garment is woven out of one's virtuous days. Parallels appear in Islamic and Iranian eschatology—and in Mahayana Buddhism, according to which the Buddha enjoys *sambhogakaya* ("a body of bliss"), generated by merit accrued over aeons.

See *Zohar* 1:66a, 82b, 226b, 233b; 2:210a–b, 229b, 247a (*Heikh*); 3:69a, 92a–b, 101a, 174b–175a, 214a; Moses de León, *Sefer ha-Rimmon,* 404; idem, *Sefer ha-Mishqal,* 56; Gruenwald, *Apocalyptic and Merkavah Mysticism,* 61; Scholem, "Levush ha-Neshamot"; idem, *On the Mystical Shape of the Godhead,* 264–65; Nakamura Hajime, in *Encyclopedia of Religion,* ed. Eliade, 2:458.

The *Zohar* combines the motif of the garment with the motif of the *tselem* ("image," ethereal body). See above, notes 58, 109.

Cf. Matthew 22:1–14; *Sifrei,* Deuteronomy 36; *Bereshit Rabbah* 19:6; *Shemot Rabbah* 1:35; *Pirqei de-Rabbi Eli'ezer* 14.

250. **if there are many...** Many faulty days.

251. **days for each single day...** He is punished for two days in retaliation for each day that he ruined.

See *Zohar* 2:130a. For another interpretation, see Galante; Mopsik.

252. **mystery of our Mishnah...** A secret, mystical Mishnah often cited in the *Zohar* and known to its own circle. See above, note 223.

The verse in Genesis describes the knowledge gained by Adam and Eve from eating the forbidden fruit of the Tree of Knowledge of Good and Evil. The full verse reads: *The*

the blessed Holy One accepted him and made him other garments—not from his days—as is written: *YHVH Elohim made coats of skin for Adam and his wife, and He clothed them* (Genesis 3:21).[253]

"Come and see: Of Abraham, who was virtuous, what is written? בא בימים (*Ba ba-yamim*), *Coming into days* (ibid. 24:1). When he departed from this world, he entered his very own days, clothing himself in them. Nothing was lacking from that garment of glory, as is written: *coming into days*.[254]

"Of Job, what is written? *Naked I issued from my mother's womb, and naked will I return there* (Job 1:21), for no garment remained in which to be clothed.[255]

eyes of the two were opened, and they knew they were naked, and they sewed fig leaves and made themselves loincloths. According to one midrashic tradition, Adam and Eve originally possessed a nail-like skin, which was stripped off of them after eating from the Tree of Knowledge. (On their garments of light, see the following note.) Another rabbinic tradition interprets the couple's nakedness as their being stripped of the beauty of the commandment that they had just violated. Here, Rabbi Yehudah links this latter tradition with the image of the garment of days and attributes the combination to "the mystery of our Mishnah." By sinning so gravely on their very first day of existence, Adam and Eve spoiled all of their days that had been *fashioned* (created) above, ruining the possibility of those days being *fashioned* into a garment.

See *Bereshit Rabbah* 19:6; 20:12; *Targum Yerushalmi*, Genesis 3:7; *Pirqei de-Rabbi Eli'ezer* 14; *Bahir* 141 (200); *Zohar* 1:53a; 2:208b. On the verse in Psalms, see *Bereshit Rabbah* 24:2 (and parallels); *Zohar* 1:91a, 99a, 121a (*MhN*), 233b; Moses de León, *Sefer ha-Rimmon*, 389.

253. **Adam strove to turn back...** In repentance.

The verse in Genesis reads כתנות עור (*kotnot or*), *coats of skin*, but a variant reading found in midrashic literature is כתנות אור (*kotnot or*), *coats of light*, suggesting Adam and Eve's original aura or garment of splendor. The simple meaning of *coats of skin* is "coats of animal skin (hides)," but here Rabbi Yehudah apparently implies that as a result of eating the fruit of the Tree of Knowledge, Adam and Eve lost their primordial luster (*coats of light*)—identified with the garment of days—and from then on they were clothed in human *coats of skin*.

See the preceding note; *Bereshit Rabbah* 12:6; 20:12; *Zohar* 1:36b; 2:208b, 229b; 3:261b; Moses de León, *Sefer ha-Rimmon*, 404; Scholem, *Major Trends*, 404, n. 87. For Gnostic parallels, see Origen, *Contra Celsum* 4:40; *Apocryphon of John* 23:31–32; *Hypostasis of the Archons* 90:16; Irenaeus, *Adversus haereses* 1:5:5.

On Adam's repentance, see *Bereshit Rabbah* 22:13; BT *Avodah Zarah* 8a; *Pirqei de-Rabbi Eli'ezer* 20; *Zohar* 1:55b.

254. **Coming into days...** The full verse reads: *Abraham was old,* בא בימים (*ba ba-yamim*), *coming into days, and YHVH had blessed Abraham in everything.* The idiom *ba ba-yamim* is normally understood as "advanced in days, advanced in years," but here Rabbi Yehudah interprets it hyperliterally.

See *Zohar* 1:103a, 126a (*MhN*), 129a–b, 142a; 3:170b.

255. **Naked I issued...** In rabbinic literature Abraham and Job are contrasted. In the *Zohar*, Job is criticized for denying resurrection and daring to question God's justice. Here he complains (or admits) that such sins have stripped him of his garment of days.

See *Bereshit Rabbah* 49:9; BT *Bava Batra* 16a; Maimonides, *Guide of the Perplexed* 3:23; *ZḤ* 75d (*MhN, Rut*); *KP*.

"Come and see: Happy are the righteous, whose days are pure and endure till the world that is coming! When they depart, they all conjoin and are woven into [224b] a garment of glory.[256] In that garment they are privileged to enjoy the delight of the world that is coming. In that garment they are destined to be revived and resurrected. All those who have a garment will rise, as is written: *They will stand like a garment* (ibid. 38:14).[257] Woe to the wicked of the world, whose days are faulty due to their sins! Nothing of them remains with which to be covered when they leave the world.

"Come and see: All the virtuous ones, entitled to wear a glorious garment of their days, are crowned in that world with crowns adorning the patriarchs, from the stream flowing and gushing into the Garden of Eden, as is written: *YHVH will guide you always; He will satisfy your soul* בצחצחות (*be-tsaḥtsaḥot*), *with radiancies.... You will be like a well-watered garden, like a spring*... (Isaiah 58:11).[258] But the wicked of the world, unworthy of wearing a garment of their days—of them is written *He will be like a shrub in the desert, and will not see when goodness comes*... (Jeremiah 17:6)."[259]

Rabbi Yitsḥak said, "Happy is the share of Jacob, who had extreme trust, as is written: *I will lie down with my fathers* (Genesis 47:30)—for he attained being with them, with no one else! He attained being with them, arrayed in his days and in theirs!"[260]

256. **When they depart, they all conjoin...** When the righteous depart this world, their days all conjoin.

257. **All those who have a garment...** Job, who denied resurrection, has no garment. God's answer to him out of the whirlwind reveals that without such a garment one cannot rise from the dead. A person is resurrected according to how he acted in the world and how he is consequently clothed: *like a garment*, according to his garment of days.

See *Zohar* 3:174b–175a, 214a; Galante. Cf. JT *Kil'ayim* 9:3, 32b; *Bereshit Rabbah* 95:1.

258. **crowned in that world...** See BT *Berakhot* 17a: "A pearl in the mouth of Rav: 'In the world that is coming, there is no eating or drinking or procreation or business or jealousy or hatred or competition; rather, the righteous sit with their crowns on their heads, basking in the radiance of *Shekhinah*.'"

Here the "crowns adorning the patriarchs" are their respective *sefirot: Ḥesed, Gevurah,* and *Tif'eret*. The stream is the flow of emanation from *Binah* that fills *Shekhinah*, the celestial Garden of Eden.

The full verse in Isaiah reads: *YHVH will guide you always; He will satisfy* נפשך (*nafshekha*), *your thirst* [or: *soul*] בצחצחות (*be-tsaḥtsaḥot*), *in parched regions, and invigorate your bones. You will be like a well-watered garden, like a spring whose waters do not fail.* Rabbi Yehudah understands the rare word *be-tsaḥtsaḥot* to mean "with radiancies," based on the root צחח (*tsḥḥ*), "to gleam."

See below, at note 268; *Zohar* 1:113b–114a (*MhN*), 141a; 2:97a, 142b, 210b.

259. ***He will be like a shrub...*** The full verse reads: *He will be like a shrub in the desert, and will not see when goodness comes. He will dwell in scorched places in the wilderness—salty land, uninhabited.*

260. ***I will lie down with my fathers...*** Jacob's life was the culmination of the days and lives of the patriarchs Abraham and

Rabbi Yehudah said, "It is written: *He smelled the fragrance of his garments and blessed him* (ibid. 27:27).[261] *His garments*—the verse should read *the garments of Esau,* because they weren't his but rather Esau's, as is written: *Rebekah took the garments of Esau, her elder son* (ibid., 15). It is written: *the garments of Esau,* whereas here *his garments*—Jacob's![262] However, so we have established: *He smelled*—he gazed further and smelled the fragrance of his garments in that world, and then blessed him. Therefore, it is written: *See, the fragrance of my son is like the fragrance of a field* (ibid., 27)—like that field of holy apples.[263] He said, 'Because you attained those garments of glory, *May God give you of the dew of heaven* (ibid., 28).' What does this imply? That field of holy apples drips with dew every day from the place called *heaven,* as is written: *of the dew of heaven.*"[264]

Isaac. When he was close to death, he yearned to be arrayed in his garment of days and in theirs, because his *sefirah* (*Tif'eret*) harmonizes their *sefirot* (*Ḥesed* and *Gevurah*).

See *Sifrei,* Deuteronomy 312; *Bahir* 131 (190); Azriel of Gerona, *Peirush ha-Aggadot,* 30–31; above, p. 337 and n. 198, p. 345 and nn. 237–39.

261. ***He smelled the fragrance...*** The verse, describing Isaac's act of blessing Jacob, reads: *He smelled the fragrance of his garments and blessed him and said, "See, the fragrance of my son is like the fragrance of a field blessed by YHVH."*

262. **the verse should read *the garments of Esau...*** When Jacob approached his blind father Isaac to obtain the blessing of the firstborn, he was not wearing his own garments but rather the garments of his older brother Esau. So why does this verse state *his* [Jacob's] *garments* and not *the garments of Esau*?

The full earlier verse reads: *Rebekah took the precious garments of Esau, her elder son, which were with her in the house, and clothed Jacob, her younger son.*

263. **he gazed further and smelled the fragrance...** Isaac may have been physically blind, but he perceived beyond and smelled the fragrance of Jacob's garment of days, destined for him in the hereafter, so the verse correctly states *He smelled the fragrance of his* [Jacob's] *garments*—not *the garments of Esau.*

On the "field of holy apples," see BT *Ta'anit* 29b, in the name of Rav: "*He said, 'See, the fragrance of my son is like the fragrance of a field blessed by YHVH'*... Like the fragrance of a field of apple trees."

In Kabbalah the apple orchard symbolizes *Shekhinah*. She is filled with apple trees, namely, the sefirotic triad of *Ḥesed, Gevurah,* and *Tif'eret,* who are symbolized by the three patriarchs and whose respective colors all appear in the apple: the white pulp, the red skin, and the green stem.

See Azriel of Gerona, *Peirush ha-Aggadot,* 35–37; *Zohar* 1:36a, 85a–b, 122a, 128b, 139a, 142b, 143b, 249b; 2:60b, 61b; 3:74a, 84a, 133b (*IR*), 135b (*IR*), 286b–287a, 288a (*IZ*); Moses de León, *Shushan Edut,* 365.

Cf. *Bereshit Rabbah* 65:22; and *Tanḥuma, Toledot* 11: "When Jacob entered, he was accompanied by the fragrance of the Garden of Eden." The Garden likewise symbolizes *Shekhinah.*

264. ***May God give you...*** The full verse reads: *May God give you of the dew of heaven and the fat of the earth, abundance of grain and new wine.*

The apple orchard of *Shekhinah* drips with dew emanating from *Tif'eret,* who is known as *heaven.*

Rabbi Yose said, "He blessed him with everything: *of the dew of heaven and the fat of the earth.* Why? Because *he smelled the fragrance of his garments*—really, as we have said.[265]

"We have learned: Fifteen hundred fragrances waft every day from the Garden of Eden, perfuming those garments of glory in that world, adorned by a person's days."

Rabbi Yehudah asked, "How many garments are there?"

Rabbi El'azar replied, "Mountains of the world differ on this, but there are three.[266] One garment: worn by *ruaḥ* in the terrestrial Garden of Eden. One—most precious of all: worn by *neshamah* within the bundle of life, between the folds of the King's purple robe. One, an external garment: existent and non-existent, visible and invisible. This is worn by *nefesh,* and she goes roaming through the world. On Sabbath and every new moon, she bonds with *ruaḥ,* who is in the terrestrial Garden of Eden, standing in the middle of the precious curtain; from him she learns and knows whatever she knows, and she roams and reveals it in the world.[267]

"Come and see! *Nefesh* is bound in two bonds on every new moon and Sabbath: in the bond of *ruaḥ* amid aromas of spices in the terrestrial Garden of Eden, and from there floating and, together with *ruaḥ,* bonding with *neshamah,* who is bound in the bundle of life. She is saturated and nourished by precious lusters on this side and on that, as is written: *YHVH will guide you always; He will satisfy* נפשך (*nafshekha*), *your soul, with* צחצחות (*tsaḥtsaḥot*) (Isaiah 58:11). What are *tsaḥtsaḥot*? One צחותא (*tsaḥuta*), radiancy, when bonding with *ruaḥ* in the lower Garden; *tsaḥuta* within *tsaḥuta* when they bond with *neshamah* above in

265. **blessed him with everything...** According to Rabbi Yose, Isaac's blessing included the riches of *Tif'eret* (*heaven*) and *Shekhinah* (*earth*)—all this because *he smelled the fragrance of his garments,* namely, Jacob's garment of days.

266. **Mountains of the world...** The towering sages.

In midrashic literature the patriarchs are identified as "mountains." See *Sifrei,* Deuteronomy 353; *Vayiqra Rabbah* 36:6; *Shir ha-Shirim Rabbah* on 4:6; *Tanḥuma, Ki Tissa* 28; *Shemot Rabbah* 15:4; *Zohar* 1:87a; 2:58b; above, p. 278 and n. 111.

267. **One garment: worn...** There are three aspects of the soul: נפש (*nefesh*), "soul," life force; רוח (*ruaḥ*), "spirit"; and נשמה ("breath, soul"). Each of these is clothed in its own garment. *Nefesh,* standing outside the Garden of Eden, appropriately wears an "external" garment—partly physical, partly spiritual. *Ruaḥ* resides within the Garden, whereas *neshamah* is within *Shekhinah,* known as "bundle of life." The "curtain" separates the Garden of Eden from higher worlds.

See *Zohar* 2:141b; 3:70b. On the levels of soul, see above, p. 262, n. 26. On the "bundle of life," see 1 Samuel 25:29; Moses de León, *Sheqel ha-Qodesh,* 61 (75). On God's purple robe, see *Midrash Tehillim* 9:13; *Yalqut Shim'oni,* Numbers 247, Psalms 643, 869; *Zohar* 1:39a, 41a; above, p. 167 and n. 517. On the weekly and monthly visits of the soul, see *Zohar* 1:134b (*MhN*); 3:213b.

the bundle of life. That is *with* צח (*tsaḥ*), *radiancy*, one; צחות (*tsaḥot*), *radiancies*—beyond, beyond, in preciousness of *neshamah*. This is צחצחות (*tsaḥtsaḥot*), *radiancies.* Who inherits this? נפשך (*Nafshekha*), *Your soul—your nefesh*, precisely! Happy is the share of the righteous!"[268]

Rabbi Shim'on said, "When I am among those Companions of Babylonia, they gather around me and learn subjects openly, and then insert them beneath an impregnable seal of iron, shut tight on all sides.[269] How often have I described to them the pathways of the garden of the Holy King and the supernal pathways! How often have I taught them all those rungs of the righteous in that world! They are all afraid to utter [225a] words, but rather toil in study stammeringly. So they are called stammerers, like one who stammers with his mouth.[270]

"But I judge them favorably because they are frightened, for holy air and holy spirit have been withdrawn from them and they suck air and spirit of an alien domain.[271] Furthermore, a rainbow appears above them and they are unworthy; but to their benefit, I am present in the world, I am the sign of the world, for in my lifetime the world does not dwell in suffering and is not punished by judgment above.[272] After me there will not arise a generation like this one. The

268. ***He will satisfy*...** The clause in its simple sense means *He will satisfy* נפשך (*nafshekha*), *your thirst,* בצחצחות (*be-tsaḥtsaḥot*), *in parched regions.* Rabbi El'azar, like his colleague Rabbi Yehudah, understands *nafshekha* as meaning "your *nefesh* (soul)"—namely the lowest level of soul—which is sated and delighted *be-tsaḥtsaḥot,* understood as "with radiancies," based on the root צחח (*tsḥḥ*), "to gleam." See above, note 258.

269. **Companions of Babylonia...** Who conceal the secrets that they learn from Rabbi Shim'on, who lives in the land of Israel.

On the relation between Rabbi Shim'on and these Companions, see *Zohar* 1:96b; 3:158a, 259a; Liebes, "Ziqqat ha-Zohar le-Erets Yisra'el," 35–36. Cf. *Zohar* 3:231b. On the phrase גושפנקא דפרזלא (*gushpanqa de-farzela*), "seal of iron," see BT *Berakhot* 6a; *Zohar* 2:129b, 150b.

270. **stammerers...** פסילוסין (*Pesilosin*), from Greek *psellos*, "stammering, faltering in speech."

See *Vayiqra Rabbah* 10:2; *Pesiqta de-Rav Kahana* 16:4; *Qohelet Rabbah* on 1:1; *Devarim Rabbah* (ed. Lieberman), p. 5.

271. **holy air and holy spirit...** Since they live outside the land of Israel, they are uninspired and find it difficult to comprehend the profound secrets of Torah.

See BT *Bava Batra* 158b, in the name of Rabbi Zeira: "The air [or: climate] of the land of Israel makes one wise." On "sucking from an alien domain," see *Zohar* 1:95b; 3:266b. Cf. *Sifra, Behar* 5:4, 109c: "Every Israelite who dwells in the land of Israel accepts upon himself the yoke of the Kingdom of Heaven, and everyone who leaves the land is like an idol worshiper."

272. **rainbow appears above them...** The rainbow is a sign of the divine covenant with the world (see Genesis 9:12–17), but if a fully righteous person is alive, he himself serves as such a sign and the rainbow is unnecessary. The fact that a rainbow appears above the Babylonian Companions indicates their lack of worth, whereas Rabbi Shim'on, who is "the sign of the world," protects his entire generation.

See *Pesiqta de-Rav Kahana* 11:15; *Bereshit Rabbah* 35:2; JT *Berakhot* 9:2, 13d; BT *Ketubbot* 77b; *Zohar* 2:174b; 3:15a, 36a; *ZḤ* 10d

world is destined to lack anyone who can protect it, and all kinds of impudent faces will haunt above and below—above, on account of sins of those below and their impudence.[273]

"Inhabitants of the world will one day cry out, and no one will care about them. They will turn their heads in every direction and turn back without a remedy. But one remedy I have found in the world and no more. In a place where there exist those who toil in Torah, if there exists among them a Torah scroll free of falsification—when they take this out, for its sake upper and lower beings arouse, especially if the Holy Name is written therein properly. We have already learned this matter.[274]

"Woe to the generation among whom the Torah scroll is exiled, yet beings above and below fail to arouse![275] Who will arouse for it when the world is in greater trouble and the Torah scroll must be exiled further because of the world's distress? For when the world suffers and people pray for mercy at the graves, all the dead arouse for them. *Nefesh* hastens to inform *ruaḥ* that the Torah scroll is in exile—exiled because of the world's distress—and the living are coming and pleading for mercy. Then *ruaḥ* informs *neshamah*, and *neshamah* the blessed Holy One. Then the blessed Holy One arouses and has compassion upon the world—all because the Torah scroll was exiled from its place and the living come to pray for mercy at the graves of the dead.[276] Woe to the genera-

(*MhN*); Scholem, "Parashah Ḥadashah," p. 432, n. 29; Liebes, *Studies in the Zohar*, 15.

273. **generation like this one...** On the unique status of Rabbi Shim'on's generation, see *Bereshit Rabbah* 35:2; *Zohar* 2:147a; 3:58a, 79a, 159a, 206a, 236b, 241b, 287a.

274. **Torah scroll free of falsification...** Containing no errors. For its sake, beings arouse and plead for mercy.

See *Zohar* 3:71a–b. On the custom of taking the Torah outside of the synagogue in order to pray for rain, see M *Ta'anit* 2:1; BT *Ta'anit* 15b–16a. On the precise way of writing the name YHVH in the Torah scroll, see *Zohar* 3:11a–b, 65b.

275. **Torah scroll is exiled...** By being removed from the synagogue. See BT *Ta'anit* 16a, where Resh Lakish explains why the Torah is taken outside: "We have gone into exile [by leaving the synagogue with the Torah]; our exile atones for us."

276. **Torah scroll must be exiled further...** And be brought to the cemetery, so that the dead can be aroused to plead for mercy.

This custom combines two elements that appear separately in BT *Ta'anit* 16a: taking the Torah scroll out of the synagogue (in order to pray for rain) and going to the cemetery to arouse the dead to plead. See *Zohar* 3:70b–71b, and *OY*, ad loc.; Nissim Gerondi's criticism of this combined custom in his commentary on *Ta'anit* 16a; *NZ*, here, n. 4.

On the practice of going to the cemetery (with no reference to the Torah scroll), see also *Tosafot, Ta'anit*, s.v. *yotse'in; Zohar* 2:141b; Moses de León, *Mishkan ha-Edut*, 34a, 70a; *Shulḥan Arukh, Oraḥ Ḥayyim* 559:10, 568:10, 579:3, 581:4, 605:1. Cf. Maimonides' critical remark in *Mishneh Torah, Hilkhot Avel* 4:4. In sixteenth-century Safed, prostrating by the graves of revered sages became a kabbalistic custom. On the three levels of soul, see above, note 267.

tion if the Torah scroll must be exiled from place to place—even from synagogue to synagogue—for they lack anything to stimulate caring for them![277]

"This is unknown by all human beings, for when *Shekhinah* was exiled the last time, before withdrawing above, what is written? *If only I were given a wanderers' lodge in the desert* (Jeremiah 9:1). Later, when great distress befalls the world She is present there, and in the exile of the Torah scroll She is there, and all arouse over it, upper and lower beings."[278]

Rabbi Shim'on said, "If they knew these matters, mysteries of wisdom—foundation of the world's existence and why pillars of the world tremble in times of distress[279]—then they would have known the worth of Rav Yeiva Sava when he was present among them.[280] But they did not know his worth! Look, I have found his words linked with the words of King Solomon in the mystery of wisdom, yet they did not know his worth! And now they pursue a word of wisdom, but no one can comprehend it. Even so, some of them are clever at

277. **Woe to the generation...** Because they lack the merit of good deeds, which would stimulate divine providence, the Torah scroll must be exiled to arouse compassion.

The phrase "exiled... from synagogue to synagogue" derives from the same passage in BT *Ta'anit* 16a. See *Zohar* 3:71b.

278. **This is unknown...** People do not understand why the "exile" of the Torah scroll is effective.

"The last time" refers to the destruction of the Second Temple in 70 C.E. According to BT *Rosh ha-Shanah* 31a (in the name of Rabbi Yoḥanan), *Shekhinah* departed from the Temple (and Jerusalem and earth) in ten stages, the final one being from the desert to Her place in heaven. Here, Rabbi Shim'on teaches that *Shekhinah* returns to earth in response to suffering, sharing in the exile of Israel (who are now, as it were, wandering in the desert) and in the exile of the Torah (even in the graveyard, which resembles a desert). Her exile arouses the entire cosmos to plead for mercy.

The full verse in Jeremiah reads: *If only I were given a wanderers' lodge in the desert, that I might abandon My people and leave them! For they all are adulterers, a band of traitors.* See *Eikhah Rabbah* 3:7; *Zohar* 3:71b; Galante; *Sullam.*

On the exile of *Shekhinah* along with Israel, see BT *Megillah* 29a: "Rabbi Shim'on son of Yoḥai says, 'Come and see how beloved are Israel in the sight of the blessed Holy One! Wherever they went in exile, *Shekhinah* accompanied them. When they were exiled to Egypt, *Shekhinah* was with them.... When they were exiled to Babylon, *Shekhinah* was with them.... And even when they are destined to be redeemed, *Shekhinah* will be with them.'" See *Mekhilta, Pisḥa* 14; Moses de León, *Sheqel ha-Qodesh*, 73–74 (92–93).

279. **why pillars of the world tremble...** Because during times of distress the Torah scroll must be exiled and along with it *Shekhinah*.

280. **Rav Yeiva Sava...** Rav Yeiva the Elder, a minor figure in the Babylonian Talmud who assumes a prominent role in the *Zohar*, culminating in *Sava de-Mishpatim* (2:94b–114a), where he appears as a donkey-driver who turns out to be a master of wisdom. The *Zohar* frequently cites *The Book of Rav Yeiva Sava*. (On books such as this, see above, note 240.)

See BT *Pesaḥim* 103b, *Bava Qamma* 49b, *Ḥullin* 86b; *Zohar* 1:47b, 79b, 117b; 2:6a, 60b,

intercalating years and determining new moons, although this was not granted to them or transmitted to them.[281]

"We have learned: For twelve months *nefesh* is bound to the body in the grave and they are judged as one, except for *nefesh* of the righteous, as we have established. She is present in the grave, aware of its suffering and of the suffering of the living, but she does not exert herself for them.[282] After twelve months, she clothes herself in a certain garment and goes roaming through the world.[283] She discovers from *ruaḥ* what she discovers and exerts herself for the suffering of the world, pleading for mercy and telling them about the suffering of the living.[284]

"Who arouses all this? A virtuous person—when there is one—who informs them fittingly; that virtuous one is recognized by them.[285] Come and see: When a virtuous person endures, he is known among the living and among the dead, for every day he is proclaimed among them. When suffering intensifies in the world and he cannot protect the generation, he informs them of the world's suffering.[286] When there is no virtuous person [225b] to be proclaimed among them, when no one can be found to arouse them for the suffering of the world except for the Torah scroll, then upper and lower beings arouse over it.[287] At

206b; 3:7b, 155b, 289a (*IZ*), 290a (*IZ*), 295a (*IZ*).

281. **intercalating years...** In rabbinic times the new moon was determined by observation and the evidence of witnesses. To make up for the discrepancy between twelve lunar months (comprising 354 days) and the solar year (comprising 365 days), seven leap months were intercalated over the course of a nineteen-year cycle. Both the determination of the new moon and (generally) the intercalation of leap months were made only in the land of Israel, not in the Diaspora, so the Babylonian figures to whom Rabbi Shim'on alludes were not permitted to engage in them.

See JT *Sanhedrin* 1:2, 19a; BT *Sanhedrin* 11b; *Tosafot*, ad loc., s.v. *ein me'abberin*.

282. **For twelve months...** See BT *Shabbat* 152b–153a: "For all twelve months [after death], one's body endures and his soul ascends and descends; after twelve months, the body ceases to exist and the soul ascends and never again descends." See *Zohar* 2:199b.

The *nefesh* of a righteous person does not suffer with the body in the grave. The *nefesh* of one who is not righteous "is present in the grave, aware of its [the body's] suffering."

On the judgment of body and soul and their joint responsibility, see the parable in *Mekhilta de-Rashbi*, Exodus 15:1; *Vayiqra Rabbah* 4:5; BT *Sanhedrin* 91a–b; p. 237 and n. 351. On suffering in the grave, see above, p. 127 and n. 268.

283. **certain garment...** The garment woven from her virtuous days on earth. See above, p. 347 and n. 249.

284. **telling them...** Telling the *ruḥot* (spirits).

285. **Who arouses all this?...** Who informs the dead of the suffering of the living and arouses them to plead for them? A virtuous person, by visiting their graves.

286. **he cannot protect the generation...** By his own merit, because human sinfulness is overwhelming.

287. **upper and lower beings arouse...** Heavenly beings and human souls arouse over the exile of the Torah scroll.

that time, all must engage in *teshuvah*;[288] if they do not, masters of judgment arouse against them—even *ruḥot,* spirits, in the Garden of Eden arouse against them."

I will lie down with my fathers (Genesis 47:30)[289]—in body, *nefesh, ruaḥ, neshamah,* in a single chariot, on a supernal rung.[290]

Rabbi Yehudah said, "How utterly stopped up are inhabitants of the world, neither knowing nor hearing nor contemplating matters of the world, and how the blessed Holy One hovers over them compassionately, constantly. No one is aware!

"Three times a day, one spirit enters the cave of Machpelah and wafts upon the graves of the patriarchs; bones heal and stand vitally erect.[291] That spirit draws dew from above—from the head of the King, site of supernal patriarchs—and when that dew arrives from them, the patriarchs below awaken.[292]

"Come and see: That dew descends by certain levels, level after level, reaching the lower Garden of Eden, where it is infused by spices of the Garden.[293] One spirit arouses—composed of two others—rising, drifting among the spices, entering the opening of the cave. Then the patriarchs awaken, they and their spouses, and plead for mercy for their children.[294]

288. ***teshuvah*** "Returning," returning to God, repentance.

289. ***I will lie down...*** For the full verse, see above, note 237.

290. **in body, *nefesh*...** Jacob felt assured that he would join Abraham and Isaac in body and soul.

On these three levels of soul, see above, note 267. On the chariot, see *Bereshit Rabbah* 47:6: "Resh Lakish said, 'The patriarchs themselves constitute the [divine] Chariot.'" See above, p. 337 and n. 198, p. 345 and n. 238.

291. **Three times a day...** The patriarchs are brought back to life in their burial site, the cave of Machpelah. See above, note 108; *Zohar* 3:71a–b.

The "three times" correspond to the three daily prayers, which traditionally were instituted by the patriarchs. See BT *Berakhot* 26b, in the name of Rabbi Yose son of Rabbi Ḥanina. According to BT *Bava Metsi'a* 85b, Elijah revives the patriarchs one by one so that they can pray.

292. **dew from above...** The dew of revival descends from *Ḥokhmah* and *Binah* ("head of the King") to the triad of *Ḥesed, Gevurah,* and *Tif'eret* ("site of supernal patriarchs") and then to the bodies of the patriarchs in the cave.

See *Pirqei de-Rabbi Eli'ezer* 34: "Rabbi Yehudah said, '... In the time to come the blessed Holy One will bring down a dew of revival, reviving the dead.... *For your dew is a dew of lights* (Isaiah 26:19)....' Rabbi Tanḥum said, '... From where does it descend? From the head of the blessed Holy One. In the time to come, He will shake the hair of His head and bring down a dew of revival, reviving the dead, as is said: *I was asleep, but my heart was awake.... For my head is drenched with dew* (Song of Songs 5:2).'"

See BT *Shabbat* 88b; JT *Berakhot* 5:2, 9b; *Zohar* 1:118a (*MhN*), 130b–131a, 232a; 3:128b (*IR*), 135b (*IR*).

293. **lower Garden of Eden...** The earthly Garden of Eden, which according to the *Zohar* is adjacent to the cave of Machpelah. See above, note 108.

294. **One spirit arouses—composed of two others...** The spirit corresponds to

"When the world is in distress because they are asleep on account of the sins of the world, that dew does not flow or appear until a Torah scroll arouses fittingly in the world.[295] Then *nefesh* informs *ruaḥ*, and *ruaḥ neshamah*, and *neshamah* the blessed Holy One. The King then sits on the throne of mercy, and there issues from the supernal Ancient One a flow of crystal dew, reaching the head of the King, and the patriarchs are blessed, and that dew flows to those sleepers, who then all conjoin, and the blessed Holy One has compassion upon the world.[296]

"Come and see: The blessed Holy One does not have compassion upon the world until He has informed the patriarchs, and for their sake the world is blessed."

Rabbi Yose said, "Certainly so! I have found such words in *The Book of King Solomon*—that supernal one called Counsel of Total Wisdom.[297]

"Rav Yeiva similarly revealed what was shown to him:[298] that Rachel has achieved more than all of them by standing at the crossroads whenever the world is in need. Mystery of the matter: Ark, cover, and cherubim in the share of Benjamin, who was born by the road, and *Shekhinah* above all."[299]

Jacob's *sefirah* (*Tif'eret*), which blends the *sefirot* of Abraham and Isaac (*Ḥesed* and *Gevurah*).

295. **because they are asleep...** The patriarchs remain unrevived because of human sin.

On the link between Torah and dew, see *Yalqut Shim'oni*, Deuteronomy 824, Isaiah 431; BT *Ketubbot* 111b, all quoting Isaiah 26:19: *For your dew is a dew of lights.* See above, pp. 353–56 and n. 292.

296. **sits on the throne of mercy...** Leaving His throne of judgment. On this transition, see *Vayiqra Rabbah* 29:4–5; BT *Avodah Zarah* 3b.

The flow of dew proceeds from the Ancient One (the primordial realm of *Keter*) to the head of the King (*Ḥokhmah* and *Binah*) to the "patriarchs"—namely the patriarchal triad of *Ḥesed, Gevurah,* and *Tif'eret*—finally reaching and reviving the sleeping bodies of the interred patriarchs below.

The phrase "crystal dew" renders טלא דבדולחא (*talla divdulḥa*). The Aramaic בדולחא (*bedulḥa*) derives from Hebrew בדולח (*bedolaḥ*), "bdellium," a word that appears only twice in the Bible, once in the context of the geographical setting of the Garden of Eden (Genesis 2:12) and once describing the color of the manna (Numbers 11:7)—which is also linked with dew (ibid., 9; Exodus 16:14). *Bedolaḥ* is apparently an aromatic yellowish transparent resin of trees, though a number of ancient and medieval sources identify it as a precious stone. Rashi on Numbers 11:7 describes it as "crystal," and in medieval Hebrew *bedolaḥ* means "pearl" and "crystal."

See *Bereshit Rabbah* 16:2; *Zohar* 2:136b, 176b (*SdTs*); 3:49a, 128b (*IR*); *ZḤ* 48c.

297. ***The Book of King Solomon...*** This work is quoted frequently in the *Zohar*.

See 1:7b, 13b; 2:67a, 125a, 139a, 172a, 204b; 3:10b, 65b, 70b, 104a, 151b, 164a, 193b; *ZḤ* 12b (*MhN*); *KP*; Scholem; above, notes 240, 280. Naḥmanides several times refers to, and quotes from, an Aramaic version of the Apocryphal *Wisdom of Solomon*. See the introduction to his Commentary on the Torah, 5–6; idem, *Kitvei Ramban*, 1:163, 182.

298. **Rav Yeiva similarly revealed...** See above, p. 354 and n. 280.

299. **Rachel has achieved more...** Rachel, who was buried by the road, achieved

Israel bowed at the head of the bed (Genesis 47:31).[300] Who is *the head of the bed*? *Shekhinah*.[301]

Rabbi Shim'on said, "Heaven forbid! Rather, to what was his he bowed and prostrated himself. Come and see: *Bed* is *Shekhinah*, as is written: *Look, the bed of Solomon!* (Song of Songs 3:7). *The head of the bed* is Foundation of the World, head of the holy bed. *At the head* is Israel, standing על (*al*), *above, the head of the bed.* So Israel bowed to what was his.[302]

"Or, you might say, 'Look, at that time he was not ill, for only afterward is it written *It happened after these things that Joseph was told, "Look, your father is ill"* (Genesis 48:1), but when he bowed he was not ill! And that is why he knew that he had then attained a supernal, holy rung—perfect throne. He therefore bowed to that supernal chariot, consummation of the grand and mighty tree

even more than the patriarchs, constantly comforting the people of Israel and evoking divine compassion for them.

The mystery is that in her death Rachel gave birth to Benjamin, in whose territory the Temple was eventually built. Benjamin completed the full count of twelve tribes, upon whom *Shekhinah* rested; later She dwelt in the Temple, which contained the ark, its cover, and the winged cherubim. Rachel, symbolizing *Shekhinah*, conveyed Her blessings to the people and aroused compassion above.

On Rachel's death and Benjamin's birth, see Genesis 35:16–20. On her role as comforter, see Jeremiah 31:15–17; above, p. 104 and n. 132, p. 243 and n. 382.

On *Shekhinah* and the twelve tribes, see *Zohar* 1:158a, 174a, 240b–241a, 246a–b; 2:229b–230a; Moses de León, *Sefer ha-Rimmon*, 8. On the ark, cover, and cherubim, see Exodus 25:10–22; 1 Kings 6:19, 23–28; 8:6–7; Milgrom, *Leviticus*, 1:1014.

300. ***Israel bowed...*** The full verse reads: *He said, "Swear to me." And he swore to him. And Israel bowed at the head of the bed.*

301. **Who is *the head*...** Jacob was actually bowing to *Shekhinah*, not (as might seem from the context) to Joseph.

See *Bereshit Rabbah* 96 (p. 1241); *Tanḥuma, Vayḥi* 3; *Targum Yerushalmi, Leqaḥ Tov, Midrash Aggadah*, Rashi, and Radak on Genesis 47:31; *Zohar* 1:99b (*ST*); above, p. 36 and n. 253. Cf. BT *Megillah* 16b. According to BT *Shabbat* 12b, *Shekhinah* appears above the head of one who is sick.

302. **to what was his he bowed...** Jacob, who attained the rung of *Tif'eret*, did not bow to *Shekhinah* but rather to his own rung.

Shekhinah is symbolized by the bed, upon which lies King Solomon (symbolizing *Tif'eret*). Directly above *Shekhinah* stands *Yesod* (Foundation), who is thus *the head of the bed*. *Tif'eret* is situated על (*al*), *at* (understood here hyperliterally as *above*), *the head of the bed*, that is, above *Yesod*.

On *Shekhinah* as "bed" and *bed of Solomon*, see *Zohar* 1:37a, 248b; 2:5a, 48b, 51a; 3:60a, 114a, 118b; Moses de León, *Sefer ha-Rimmon*, 370. Cf. BT *Shabbat* 55b, where it is said that Jacob kept a bed in his tent for *Shekhinah*. See Rashi on Genesis 49:4. According to the eleventh-century Catholic reformer Peter Damian, Mary is the golden couch upon which God, tired out by the actions of humanity and the angels, lies down to rest. See Patai, *The Hebrew Goddess*, 280.

On *Yesod* as *head of the bed*, see *Zohar* 2:54b; Moses de León, *Sheqel ha-Qodesh*, 76 (97). In this last source, De León quotes "Jacob bowed and prostrated himself to what was his" as a traditional interpretation of *Israel bowed at the head of the bed.*

named after him. So, *Israel bowed at the head of the bed—at the head of the bed,* precisely! For he had ascended to his site, crowned with the crowns of the Holy King.'"[303]

He said, "Swear to me"... (Genesis 47:31).[304]

Rabbi Ḥiyya opened, "*All this I tested with wisdom. I said, 'I will become wise'—but it is beyond me* (Ecclesiastes 7:23). Look, we have learned: King Solomon inherited the moon in all its aspects; in his days, the moon was in fullness, blessed by all! When he sought to comprehend the laws of Torah, he said, *I said, 'I will become wise'—but it is beyond me.*"[305]

Rabbi Yehudah said, "Jacob said, *I will lie down with my fathers, and you will carry me from Egypt and bury me in their burial place* (Genesis, ibid., 30). There we have learned: One whose soul departs in a foreign domain [226a] and the body is buried in the Holy Land—of him is written *You came and defiled My land...* (Jeremiah 2:7). Now, Jacob's soul departed in a foreign domain, so why did he say, *Bury me in their burial place?*"[306]

Rabbi Yehudah replied, "Jacob is different, for *Shekhinah* is joined with him, cleaving to him, as is written: *I Myself will go down with you to Egypt and I Myself will surely bring you up as well* (Genesis 46:4). '*I Myself will go down with you to Egypt*—to dwell with you in exile. *And I Myself will surely bring you up as well*—so that your soul will couple with Me and your body will be buried in your fathers' graves.' What does this indicate? Even though his soul departed in a foreign domain. Therefore, *I Myself will surely bring you up as well.*[307]

303. **he was not ill...** Jacob was not ill, so he did not bow to *Shekhinah*—who normally appears above the head of one who is sick (see above, note 301.) Rather, upon sensing the presence of divinity, Jacob realized that he had attained his rung: *Tif'eret Yisra'el* (Beauty of Israel). *Tif'eret* serves as the throne, or chariot, for the highest *sefirot* and is also described as the "tree" or Tree of Life.

See Galante; cf. *MM*; *Nefesh David*. For other interpretations, see *OY*; *KP*; *Sullam*; *MmD*.

304. ***He said, "Swear to me"...*** For the full verse, see above, note 300.

305. **King Solomon inherited the moon...** Solomon (traditionally, author of Ecclesiastes) probed *Shekhinah*, who is symbolized by the moon and known as lower Wisdom. In his days, *Shekhinah* attained fullness. See above, p. 339 and n. 208, p. 343 and n. 231.

According to rabbinic tradition, Solomon sought to fathom the precise explanation of the law of the red heifer (Numbers 19) but finally had to admit: *I said, "I will become wise"—but it is beyond me.* See *Pesiqta de-Rav Kahana* 4:3; *Qohelet Rabbah* on 7:23.

306. **One whose soul departs...** How could Jacob, who was soon to die in Egypt, disregard this rabbinic tradition and ask Joseph to bury him in the cave of Machpelah in the Holy Land?

See JT *Kil'ayim* 9:4, 32c; *Bereshit Rabbah* 96 (p. 1240); *Tanḥuma, Vayḥi* 3; *Tanḥuma* (Buber), *Vayḥi* 6; *Zohar* 2:141b; 3:72b.

307. **Rabbi Yehudah replied...** Answer-

"*And Joseph will lay his hand on your eyes* (ibid.)—for he is firstborn of thought; firstborn, for the first drop was his. Because the blessed Holy One knew this hidden secret, he assured him that it would be Joseph, since all love depended on him."[308]

Will lay his hand on your eyes. What does this indicate?

Rabbi Yose said, "Jacob's honor—and to announce that Joseph was really alive and would be present with him at his death."[309]

Rabbi Ḥizkiyah said, "I know something—I am afraid to reveal it. In events of the world wisdom is discovered."

Rabbi Abba came and knocked him, saying, "Utter your word! Arm yourself with your weapon![310] In the days of Rabbi Shim'on, words are revealed!"[311]

He said, "I learned from a lecture of Rav Yeiva Sava on customs of the world:[312] If a person attains a son in this world, he should sprinkle dust upon his eyes when he is buried. This is an honor for him, showing that the world is closed to him and that he inherits the world in his place.[313]

"For within the eye of a human being appears a vision of the world, in all its revolving colors. The white in it is the vast ocean surrounding the world on all sides. Another color is dry land, encircled by water; as dry land stands in the midst of water, so does this color. Another, third color is in the middle; this is Jerusalem, center of the world. The fourth color is vision of the whole eye,

ing his own question, Rabbi Yehudah explains that Jacob's intimacy with *Shekhinah* guaranteed him burial in the Holy Land even though he was to die in a foreign land.

See above, at note 172; *Zohar* 2:53a. On the union of Jacob's soul and *Shekhinah,* see *Zohar* 1:21b–22a.

308. **firstborn of thought...** When Jacob consummated his marriage with Leah, he thought that he was with Rachel, whom he had been promised by Laban. Therefore the title of firstborn was given to Joseph (Rachel's eventual first child), not to Reuben (who issued from Jacob's union with Leah). Similarly, Jacob's first drop of semen was reserved for Joseph's conception. See above, pp. 333–34 and nn. 184–89.

"All love depended on him" refers to Jacob's special love for Joseph. See Genesis 37:3; *Zohar* 3:169a.

309. **Jacob's honor...** It would be an honor to Jacob if his high-ranking son, Joseph, would lay his hands on Jacob's eyes. Further, this divine declaration to Jacob confirmed that Joseph was still alive.

310. **Arm yourself with your weapon...** To engage in the battle of Torah.

For this metaphor, see BT *Shabbat* 63a (Rav Kahana's interpretation of Psalms 45:4); *Shir ha-Shirim Zuta* on 3:8; *Bemidbar Rabbah* 11:3; below, at note 773; *Zohar* 2:110a–b; 3:127b (*IR*), 188a–189b; *ZḤ* 14a (*MhN*).

311. **In the days of Rabbi Shim'on...** On this theme, see *Zohar* 2:86b, 144a; 3:79a, 105b–106a, 159a, 167b, 179b, 236b, 298a; Matt, "New-Ancient Words," p. 184.

312. **Rav Yeiva Sava...** See above, p. 354 and n. 280.

313. **he should sprinkle dust...** When the father dies, his son should honor him by sprinkling dust on his father's eyes at burial, showing that the father's vision of the world and heritage have now been passed on to the next generation. See *Zohar* 3:169a.

called 'pupil of the eye,' in which a visage appears—most glorious vision of all. This is Zion, central point of all, in which a vision of the whole world appears; there dwells *Shekhinah*—beauty of all, vision of all. The eye is inheritance of the world, so this one leaves it and that one acquires it and inherits it."[314]

He said to him, "Well spoken! But this matter is more concealed, and inhabitants of the world do not know or reflect. For at the moment that a person departs from this world, his *nefesh* is close to him,[315] and before she leaves, a person's eyes see what they see, as has been established, for it is written: *For no human can see Me and live* (Exodus 33:20)—in their lifetime they do not see; in their death they do.[316] The eye is open from the vision that he sees, and those standing by him should place a hand upon his eyes and close them because of what we have learned about the mystery of customs of the world. For when the eye remains open from the vision that he sees—glorious!—if he has attained a son, the son is first to place his hand upon his eyes and close them, as is written: *Joseph will lay his hand on your eyes* (Genesis 46:4). For another vision, unholy, is poised to confront him, and the eye that saw now a holy, supernal vision must not gaze upon an alien vision.[317]

"Furthermore, that *nefesh* is close to him in the house, and if the eye remains open and that other vision settles upon his eyes, whatever he looks upon will be cursed.[318] This is dishonorable to the eye, and even more so to his relatives, and

314. **within the eye...** This passage on the cosmic significance of the eye derives from *Derekh Erets Zuta* 9 (*Derekh Erets*, ed. Higger, 7:38), in the name of Samuel the Small: "This world resembles a human eyeball. The white in it [i.e., the sclera] is the ocean, surrounding the whole world. The black in it [i.e., the iris] is the [inhabited] world. The pit in the black [i.e., the pupil] is Jerusalem. The visage in the pit [i.e., the reflection of one's own "face" seen in the pupil of another person's eye] is the Temple, may it be rebuilt speedily in our days and in the days of all Israel. Amen."

See Azriel of Gerona, *Peirush ha-Aggadot*, 60, 95; *Zohar* 2:23b, 222b; 3:169a.

On Jerusalem as center of the world, see *Tanḥuma, Qedoshim* 10: "The land of Israel sits in the center of the world, Jerusalem in the center of the land of Israel, the Temple in the center of Jerusalem, the nave in the center of the Temple, the ark in the center of the nave, and in front of the ark the Stone of Foundation, from which the world was founded."

See BT *Yoma* 54b; *Zohar* 2:157a, 184b, 193a; 3:65b, 161b. On the Stone (or Rock) of Foundation, see Vol. 2, p. 8, n. 53. On the beauty of Zion, see Psalms 48:3.

In Rabbi Ḥizkiyah's version, Zion refers to the site of the Temple, within which dwells *Shekhinah*. She reflects all of the other *sefirot* and includes within Herself images of all being. The concluding sentence indicates that through the eye the son "inherits" the world from his father because of the eye's cosmic symbolism and, more simply, because sight yields perception and knowledge.

315. ***nefesh* is close to him** The lowest level of soul remains close to the body immediately after death.

316. **see what they see...** Attaining a vision of *Shekhinah*. See above, note 103.

317. **another vision, unholy...** A vision of a demonic power, or the Angel of Death.

318. ***nefesh* is close to him...** The *nefesh* lingers with the body, and if the eye of the

even more so to the dead person, for it dishonors him to look upon something he should not and for an alien entity to settle upon his eyes. Afterward, it should be covered with dust.[319] The Companions have already aroused discussion of the judgment of the grave.[320] It is an honor for the eye to be closed to all by the hand of one's son whom he has left behind in the world.

"Come and see: For all seven days, the *nefesh* goes from the house to the grave, from the grave to the house, mourning over him. Three times a day, *nefesh* and body are judged as one, and no one in the world knows or cares to arouse the heart.[321] Afterward, the body is beset, while the *nefesh* goes to be washed [226b] in Hell—and then emerges, roaming the world and visiting the grave, until it wears the garment that it wears.[322]

"After twelve months, all rest. The body subsides in the dust; *nefesh* is bound to *ruaḥ* in the garment that it wears; *ruaḥ* delights in the Garden; *neshamah* ascends to the bundle of delight of all delights. All are bound to one another at certain times.[323]

"Come and see: Woe to those humans who do not contemplate or know or recognize the foundation of their existence, and who are oblivious to fulfilling the *mitsvot* of Torah![324] For we have learned: Certain *mitsvot* of Torah fashion garments of glory above, certain *mitsvot* of Torah fashion garments of glory below, and certain *mitsvot* of Torah fashion garments of glory for this world. A person needs them all, and they are all woven from his actual days, as we have established."[325]

corpse remains open and vulnerable to demonic power, its stare will transmit a curse wherever it is directed—even to the *nefesh*.

319. **covered with dust** At burial, the son should cover his father's eye(s) with dust. See above, at note 313.

320. **judgment of the grave** When judgment and punishment are administered after burial. Covering the eyes alleviates this suffering. See above, p. 127 and n. 268, p. 314 and n. 62.

321. **For all seven days...** For the first full week after death.

See BT *Shabbat* 152a; above, p. 321 and n. 107. On the judgment of body and soul together, see above, p. 355 and n. 282. "To arouse the heart" means to stimulate *teshuvah,* "turning" back to God.

322. ***nefesh* goes to be washed...** Cleansed and purified from sin. On the soul's glorious garment, see above, p. 347 and n. 249.

323. **After twelve months...** See BT *Shabbat* 152b–153a: "For all twelve months [after death], one's body endures and his soul ascends and descends; after twelve months, the body ceases to exist and the soul ascends and never again descends." See above, at notes 282–84.

Ruaḥ delights in the Garden of Eden, whereas *neshamah* ascends to *Shekhinah*. They are reunited on Sabbaths and new moons. See above, p. 351 and n. 267.

324. **Woe to those humans...** See BT *Ḥagigah* 12b: "Rabbi Yose said, 'Woe to creatures, for they see but do not know what they see; they stand but do not know on what they stand!'" See above, p. 196 and n. 111, p. 346 and n. 243.

325. **Certain *mitsvot*...** Various com-

One day Rabbi Yehudah Sava's mind was agitated.[326] He was shown in a dream his image in dazzling light, radiating in four directions. He asked, "What is this?"

He was told, "Your garment for dwelling here." From that day on, he rejoiced.[327]

Rabbi Yehudah said, "Every single day *ruḥot,* spirits, of the righteous sit arrayed in their garments, row after row in the Garden of Eden, praising the blessed Holy One in supernal glory as is written: *Surely the righteous will praise Your name; the upright will dwell in Your presence* (Psalms 140:14)."

Rabbi Abba said, "At first, what is written? *Israel bowed at the head of the bed* (Genesis 47:31), as we have established: Who is *bed*? Assembly of Israel. *Head*—Righteous One. על (*Al*), *Above, the head of the bed*—Holy King to whom all peace belongs, as is written: *Look, the bed of Solomon!* (Song of Songs 3:7). So Jacob bowed to what was his: the one who stands *above the head of the bed,* named Israel. Therefore, *Israel bowed at the head of the bed.*[328]

"Afterward, once Jacob knew that he was consummated on a supreme rung—that his rung was situated on high with the patriarchs and that he alone was perfect harmony—his heart strengthened and rejoiced, invigorated by the sublime favor of the blessed Holy One. Of him, what is written? *Israel drew strength and sat up* על (*al*), *on, the bed* (Genesis 48:2)—*al, above, the bed,* really, for he had been perfected on a higher rung. Happy is his share!"[329]

mandments (or the days on which they are fulfilled) are woven into various garments. Certain *mitsvot* generate garments for *neshamah* who will reside within *Shekhinah;* others generate garments for *ruaḥ* who resides in the Garden of Eden; and still others are fashioned into garments for *nefesh* who roams this world.

According to Vital and *KP*, the three types of *mitsvot* are: intellectual or emotional (such as love and awe of God and silent prayer), verbal (such as spoken prayer, study of Torah, and reconciling people who are quarreling), and physical (numerous ritual and ethical acts). See above, p. 351 and n. 267; *Zohar* 2:210a–b; Galante; *NO*; *MmD.* On the strands of days, see above, note 249.

326. **Rabbi Yehudah Sava...** Rabbi Yehudah the Elder.

327. **his image... Your garment...** To be worn in the Garden of Eden. The *Zohar* combines the motif of the garment with the motif of the *tselem* ("image," ethereal body). See above, notes 58, 109, 249.

328. **Who is *bed*?...** As explained above (p. 358 and nn. 300–302), *bed* symbolizes *Shekhinah* (known as Assembly of Israel); *head of the bed* symbolizes *Yesod* (known as Righteous One); and על (*al*), *at* (understood here hyperliterally as *above*), *the head of the bed* denotes *Tif'eret* (known as King Solomon), standing above *Yesod.* Thus Israel (Jacob) bowed to "what was his," namely to his divine rung, *Tif'eret Yisra'el* (Beauty of Israel).

For a different interpretation, see Galante. On Assembly of Israel as a name of *Shekhinah,* see above, pp. 122–23, n. 237. On Righteous One as a name of *Yesod,* see above, p. 92, n. 50. On the phrase "King to whom all peace belongs," see *Sifra, Shemini, millu'im,* 15, 44c; *Shir ha-Shirim Rabbah* 1:11 (on 1:1); *Zohar* 1:29a, 184a, 248b. Here, "peace" apparently refers to *Yesod.*

329. **Jacob knew...** Jacob knew that he had fully attained the rung of *Tif'eret,* harmo-

We have learned: Rabbi Yehudah said, "In the Mishnah we have established what we have learned: 'At four periods in the year, the world is judged. At Passover, concerning harvest; at the Assembly, concerning fruits of the tree; on Rosh Hashanah all who come into the world pass before Him in single file; and at the Festival they are judged concerning water.'[330] We have already established these words, but this secret I have learned:[331] 'At Passover, concerning harvest'—corresponding to the supernal chariot, mystery of the patriarchs and King David.[332]

"Further, 'At Passover, concerning harvest,' for so it is, really! They have already established why *matstsah* appears on Passover. Look, it is judgment, and 'judgment of *Malkhuta* is judgment'![333] This is the beginning of Israel's entering the share of the blessed Holy One—and ridding themselves of leaven: foreign gods appointed over other nations, called 'alien gods, leaven, evil impulse'—entering *matstsah*, holy share of the blessed Holy One.[334]

nizing the rungs of his fathers, Abraham and Isaac, namely *Ḥesed* and *Gevurah*. Now he was situated על (*al*), *on* (understood hyperliterally as *above*), *the bed* (symbolizing *Shekhinah*).

330. **At four periods...** Quoting M *Rosh ha-Shanah* 1:2. At Passover, as the crops begin to ripen, God determines whether the harvest will be rich or not. At *Shavu'ot* (Festival of Weeks, called here עצרת [*Atseret*], "Assembly"), when fruit begins to ripen, God determines how abundant it will be. On Rosh Hashanah the whole world is judged. At *Sukkot* (Festival of Weeks, called here חג [*Ḥag*], "Festival"), the start of the rainy season, God determines how much rain will fall. On the day following *Sukkot* prayers are offered for rain, and in the Temple during *Sukkot* water was drawn and poured as a libation on the altar.

331. **but this secret...** See *Zohar* 3:97a, *ZḤ* 14b–c (*MhN*); Moses de León, *Sefer ha-Rimmon*, 140–41; *KP*. In his commentary on this mishnah, Maimonides alludes to a secret meaning.

332. **At Passover...supernal chariot...** This entire mishnah alludes to the sefirotic tetrad of *Ḥesed, Gevurah, Tif'eret*, and *Shekhinah*, symbolized respectively by Abraham, Isaac, Jacob, and King David. Together they constitute a chariot or throne for the highest levels of divinity.

See *Bereshit Rabbah* 47:6: "Resh Lakish said, 'The patriarchs themselves constitute the [divine] Chariot.'" On this image, see above, note 198. On King David as the fourth component of the chariot-throne, see Azriel of Gerona, *Peirush ha-Aggadot*, 57; *Zohar* 1:20a, 89b (*ST*), 154b, 248b. On David and the patriarchs, see above, p. 134 and n. 311.

333. **why *matstsah* appears...** *Matstsah* symbolizes *Shekhinah*, who is known as *Malkhuta* (Kingdom) and is characterized by judgment.

See *Zohar* 1:33a, 47b, 157a; 235b, 245b–246a; 2:40a–b, 61b; Moses de León, *Sefer ha-Rimmon*, 112, 133.

Here Rabbi Yehudah is apparently playing on the homonym מצה (*matstsah*), "strife," associated with judgment. See *Zohar* 2:40a; 3:251b; Moses de León, *Sefer ha-Rimmon*, 135.

The saying דינא דמלכותא דינא (*Dina de-malkhuta dina*), "The law [or: judgment] of the kingdom is law," is attributed to Shemu'el in BT *Nedarim* 28a. Here, *Malkhuta* denotes *Shekhinah*, who conveys *dina* (judgment). See *Zohar* 1:92b; 2:117a; 3:11b.

334. **beginning of Israel's entering...** Eating the *matstsah* on Passover symbolizes Israel's entry into *Shekhinah*, the opening of

"Why תבואה (*tevu'ah*), harvest? As is written: תבואתה (*tevu'atoh*), *His harvest* (Jeremiah 2:3)—with a ה (*heh*), as we have established. The world is judged by this one's judgment.[335]

"'At the Assembly, concerning fruits of the tree.' 'Fruits of the tree'? It should read 'fruits of the trees.' Who are 'fruits of the tree'? This must refer to the grand and mighty tree above. 'Fruits of the tree,' as is written: *I am like a flourishing juniper; from Me your fruit appears* (Hosea 14:9).[336]

"'On Rosh Hashanah all who come into the world pass before Him in single file.' Come and see: 'On ראש השנה (*Rosh ha-Shanah*), Head of the Year'—Head of the King. Who is that? Isaac, who is called Head, one head of the King—a place called Year. Therefore, 'all who come into the world pass before Him in single file.' So we have learned: 'On Rosh Hashanah,' for at the head of the year Isaac presides.[337]

the divine realm. On the eve of Passover, the last remnants of leaven are burned, symbolizing the extermination of the evil impulse and alien powers.

See the prayer attributed to Rabbi Tanḥum in JT *Berakhot* 4:2, 7d: "May it be Your will, *YHVH* my God and God of my fathers, that You break and destroy the yoke of the evil impulse from our heart. For You created us to do Your will, and we must do Your will; You desire it and we desire it. So who prevents it? The leaven in the dough."

See BT *Berakhot* 17a and Rashi, ad loc., s.v. *se'or she-ba-issah*; *Mekhilta, Beshallaḥ* 2; *Tanḥuma* (Buber), *Noaḥ* 4; *Zohar* 1:142a–b; 2:40a–41a, 182a, 183a–b; 3:95b. Moses de León, *Sefer ha-Rimmon*, 132 (and Wolfson's note). The phrase "alien gods" derives from Deuteronomy 31:16; Joshua 24:20; Jeremiah 5:19.

335. **תבואתה (*tevu'atoh*), *His harvest*...** The Mishnah's reference to תבואה (*tevu'ah*), "harvest," is linked with the unusual form of the word in Jeremiah: *Israel is holy to YHVH, first fruits of* תבואתה (*tevu'atoh*), *His harvest*. According to Rabbi Yehudah, the final letter, ה (*he*)—normally a feminine pronominal suffix but here masculine—alludes to the Divine Feminine, *Shekhinah*, who is often symbolized by the second ה (*he*) of יהוה (*YHVH*). On Passover She renders judgment. See *Tanḥuma* (Buber), *Bereshit* 10; *Zohar* 1:121b; 3:297a; Moses de León, *Sefer ha-Rimmon*, 89.

336. **It should read 'fruits of the trees'...** Why does the Mishnah employ the singular *tree*? This must allude to the cosmic tree, *Tif'eret*, whose fruit are souls. (The verse from Hosea is understood as being addressed by *Tif'eret* to *Shekhinah*.) On *Shavu'ot* (known as Assembly), these souls are judged. The link between *Tif'eret* and *Shavu'ot* is strengthened by the fact that this festival celebrates the giving of the Torah, a symbol of *Tif'eret*.

On souls as fruit, see *Bahir* 14 (22); Ezra of Gerona, *Peirush Shir ha-Shirim*, 489, 504; *Zohar* 1:15b, 19a, 33a, 59b–60a, 82b, 85b, 90b, 115a–b, 238a, 249a; 2:166b–167a, 223b; Moses de León, *Sefer ha-Mishqal*, 51; idem, *Sheqel ha-Qodesh*, 56 (69). Cf. Ibn Ezra on Psalms 1:3.

337. **Isaac, who is called Head...** Isaac symbolizes *Gevurah*, also known as *Din* (Judgment), which manifests on Rosh Hashanah, the Day of Judgment. Here this *sefirah* is described as one head of *Tif'eret*, who is known as Year. The other head is *Ḥesed*.

According to rabbinic tradition, Sarah conceived Isaac on Rosh Hashanah. The Torah reading for the two days of the holiday describes the conception, birth, and binding

"'And at the Festival they are judged concerning water.' This is the beginning of the Right of the King, so joy of water prevails everywhere when they pour water and draw it, for water is well known. Thus, at these four periods all appear."[338] [227a]

Rabbi Yose said, "Upon contemplating words, all appear in these periods: Abraham, Isaac, and Jacob, and King David. By these the world is judged. In four periods human beings are judged, on the days when one of these appears in the world.[339] And every single day, books are opened and actions are recorded, yet no one notices and no one inclines his ear.[340] Torah admonishes him every day, and a voice exclaims: *'Whoever is simple, turn in here!' she says to one devoid of sense* (Proverbs 9:4); yet no one listens to its voice.[341]

"Come and see: The moment that a person rises in the morning, witnesses stand facing him, admonishing him, but he pays no attention. The *neshamah* admonishes him constantly, every moment—if he listens, fine; if not, books are opened and actions are recorded."[342]

Rabbi Ḥiyya said, "Happy are the righteous, who have no fear of judgment either in this world or in the world that is coming, as is written: *The righteous are as confident as a young lion* (ibid. 28:1), and similarly: *The righteous will inherit the land* (Psalms 37:29)."[343]

of Isaac (Genesis 21–22). See *Bereshit Rabbah* 73:1; *Tanḥuma, Vayera* 17; BT *Rosh ha-Shanah* 10b–11a; *Zohar* 1:37a, 103a; *ZḤ* 27b.

Cf. *Zohar* 3:99a; *ZḤ* 45a. On *Tif'eret* as Year, see *Zohar* 3:152a. On the relation between *Ḥesed* and *Gevurah* and the head, cf. *Zohar* 2:122b. In *OY,* Cordovero presents and explains two alternative readings of this passage.

338. **beginning of the Right...** On *Sukkot* (known as Festival), *Ḥesed,* the right hand of God, manifests. *Ḥesed* is symbolized by water (as is "well known"), and on this holiday water was joyously drawn and poured as a libation on the Temple altar.

See M *Sukkah* 5:1: "Whoever has not seen the joy of the place of water-drawing has never seen joy in his life." See Moses de León, *Sefer ha-Rimmon,* 182–83.

339. **Abraham, Isaac, and Jacob, and King David...** As each of these four manifests in the world (through their respective *sefirot* on each festival), humanity is judged. See above, p. 364 and n. 332.

340. **books are opened...** On this image, see M *Avot* 2:1; 3:16; above, p. 333 and n. 182. On daily judgment, see JT *Rosh ha-Shanah* 1:3, 57a; BT *Rosh ha-Shanah* 16a, in the name of Rabbi Yose.

341. **Torah admonishes...** See above, p. 181 and n. 7.

342. **witnesses stand facing him...** Angels. See BT *Ta'anit* 11a; above, p. 168 and n. 522; *Zohar* 3:23b.

343. ***inherit the land*** In the world that is coming, the righteous will *inherit Shekhinah,* the supernal land.

See M *Sanhedrin* 10:1: "All of Israel have a share in the world that is coming, as is said: *Your people, all of them righteous, will inherit the land forever—sprout of My planting, work of My hands, that I may be glorified* (Isaiah 60:21)." See *Zohar* 1:93a, 153b, 188a, 245b.

Rabbi Ḥizkiyah opened, "*As the sun was about to set, a deep slumber fell upon Abram—and here, terror and great darkness falling upon him* (Genesis 15:12). This verse has been established; but this is the day of strict judgment, when a human being is removed from this world.[344] Come and see: The day on which a human departs from this world is the day of great judgment, when the sun is obscured from the moon, as is written: *before the sun darkens*... (Ecclesiastes 12:2). This is holy *neshamah*, obscured from a person thirty days before he departs from the world—that is the image withheld from him, invisible.[345]

"Why is it withheld from him? Because holy *neshamah* ascends, removed from him. For do not say that when a person is dying and exhausted this *neshamah* is removed; rather, when he is in vigor holy *neshamah* is removed from him, no longer illumining *ruaḥ*, and *ruaḥ* no longer illumines *nefesh*. Then the image is removed from him, illumining him no more. From that day on, all proclaim his fate, even the birds of heaven. Why? Because *neshamah* has already ascended from him and *ruaḥ* no longer illumines *nefesh*; so *nefesh* is weakened, and eating and all bodily desire depart from him and disappear."[346]

Rabbi Yehudah said, "Even every time that a person falls ill and cannot pray, his *neshamah* is removed and ascends; then *ruaḥ* does not illumine *nefesh* until his judgment is rendered. If he is judged favorably, *neshamah* returns to her place, illumining all. This is when the matter still hangs in the balance of judgment. When it does not, *neshamah* precedes all by thirty days and the image is removed from him.[347]

344. **This verse has been established...** In midrashic literature Abraham's terrifying experience is interpreted as an allusion to the nations that will subjugate Israel. Rabbi Ḥizkiyah, however, applies it to the day of death.

See *Mekhilta, Baḥodesh* 9; *Bereshit Rabbah* 44:17; *Vayiqra Rabbah* 13:5. Traditionally, the Day of Judgment comes at the end of days, but in the *Zohar* it transpires for each human being on the day he dies. See above, p. 237 and n. 352.

345. **sun is obscured from the moon...** The sun symbolizes the *neshamah* (highest level of soul), which illumines the body, symbolized by the moon. Thirty days before death, the *neshamah* begins to withdraw from a person. Here the *neshamah* is linked (or identified) with the *tselem* ("image," ethereal body).

On the *tselem* and its disappearance, see above, p. 313 and n. 58. On the withdrawal of the *neshamah*, see above, at note 57. The verse in Ecclesiastes reads: *before the sun and the light and the moon and the stars darken.*

346. ***neshamah... ruaḥ... nefesh...*** On these three levels of soul, see above, p. 262 and n. 26. Once *nefesh* (the lowest level) is weakened, a person loses his appetite for food and pleasure.

On the birds' proclamation, see above, p. 313 and n. 56.

347. **falls ill and cannot pray...** When a person becomes ill and cannot concentrate enough to pray, this indicates that he is being judged in heaven. His *neshamah* temporarily withdraws until judgment has been rendered above. If, however, the person is sentenced to death, then the *neshamah*'s withdrawal signals his impending demise.

"Come and see: When a person is judged above, his *neshamah* is brought up to the court and judgment proceeds according to her utterance. She testifies to everything—testifying to all the person's thoughts but not to his deeds, because these are already recorded a book—and he is judged for everything.[348]

"When a person is judged above, the body feels greater distress than at other times. If he is judged favorably, he is released—and sweat breaks out over his face; afterward *neshamah* returns, illumining all. A person never rises from his sickbed until he is judged above.

"Now, you might say, 'Look, many sinners of the world, many wicked of the world rise and endure in vitality!'[349] However, the blessed Holy One scrutinizes a person's case. Even though now he does not have merit, if He sees that later he will, He judges him favorably. Or sometimes he will engender a son who will be virtuous in the world, so the blessed Holy One judges him favorably. All the acts of the blessed Holy One are for the good and His judgments are for the good, and He considers everything, as is written: *As I live—declares YHVH Elohim—I do not delight in the death of the wicked, but that he turn from his way and live* (Ezekiel 33:11). Consequently, all those wicked of the world who endure in their vitality are being judged favorably by the blessed Holy One.[350]

"Sometimes those illnesses have run their course, as is said: *malignant and faithful illnesses* (Deuteronomy 28:59)—acting faithfully, for once they befall a person [227b] they depart from him after fulfilling their time, whether for the righteous or the wicked. All is done in justice, as we have said."[351]

Israel saw Joseph's sons and he said, "Who are these?" (Genesis 48:8).

Rabbi Yitsḥak said, "This verse is problematical, for it is written *Israel saw*, yet it is written *Israel's eyes had grown heavy with age, he could not see* (ibid., 10)! If *he could not see*, then how can it say *Israel saw*? Because through the Holy Spirit he saw *Joseph's descendants*—namely, Jeroboam and his

348. **She testifies...** The *neshamah* testifies not to his deeds but to his intentions that motivated the deeds. See above, p. 366 and nn. 340, 342.

349. **many sinners...** Why do sinners and the wicked often recover from illness? Shouldn't they die as punishment for their deeds?

350. **scrutinizes a person's case...** The days of the wicked are prolonged if God foresees that they will turn back from sin or engender worthy children.

See BT *Bava Qamma* 38b; *Vayiqra Rabbah* 32:4; *Zohar* 1:56b, 118a (*MhN*), 140a. The quotation here from Ezekiel incorporates wording from 18:23.

351. **illnesses have run their course...** Sometimes illnesses are decreed to last for a certain time, and after "faithfully" fulfilling their role they depart.

In this verse, the simple sense of the word נאמנים (*ne'emanim*) is "enduring, lingering, persistent, constant, relentless, chronic," but Rabbi Yehudah employs the literal meaning:

associates, for Jeroboam fashioned two golden calves and said, *These are your gods, O Israel!* (1 Kings 12:28). So, *Who are these?*—'Who is it that will one day say of idols *These are your gods?*' Therefore, *Israel saw Joseph's sons.*[352]

"From here we learn that the righteous see events afar, and the blessed Holy One adorns them with His crown. Just as the blessed Holy One sees afar, as is written: *God saw all that He had made, and look, it was very good!* (Genesis 1:31) —for the blessed Holy One saw all phenomena before actualizing them, and they all passed before Him[353]—similarly, all generations of the world, from the beginning of the world to its end, presented themselves before Him before coming into the world, as is written: *calling the generations from the beginning* (Isaiah 41:4)—before the world was created. For all souls that descend to the world stand before the blessed Holy One before descending, in the image they assume in this world, and are called by name, as is written: *He calls them each by name* (ibid. 40:26).[354]

"Similarly, the righteous: the blessed Holy One shows them all generations of the world before these come into existence. How do we know? From Adam, who was the first—the blessed Holy One showed him all those generations before they arrived, as is written: *This is the book of the generations of Adam*

"faithful." See BT *Avodah Zarah* 55a (in the name of Rabbi Yoḥanan); *Leqaḥ Tov*, Deuteronomy 28:59.

352. **through the Holy Spirit he saw...** Jacob foresaw Joseph's descendants (literally, *sons*), in particular, King Jeroboam of Israel —descended from Joseph's son Ephraim (1 Kings 11:26)—who lured his subjects to idolatry by building two golden calves. The word *these* in Jacob's rhetorical question (*Who are these?*) refers to the declaration *These are your gods, O Israel!*—as if Jacob were saying, "Who will eventually issue from your son and say *These are your gods, O Israel?*" Actually, the wording in 1 Kings 12:28 is *Here are your gods, O Israel!* The formulation quoted by Rabbi Yitsḥak derives from the account of the Golden Calf in Exodus 32:4.

The phrase "Jeroboam and his associates" derives from rabbinic literature. See *Tosefta, Ta'anit* 3:8; BT *Rosh Hashanah* 17a; cf. Radak on Hosea 10:4. Here, "his associates" may refer to two other Israelites kings: Ahab (descended from Ephraim) and Jehu (descended from Joseph's other son, Manasseh). Ahab encouraged and participated in the idolatrous cult of Baal and Asherah, and Jehu maintained the worship of Jeroboam's golden calves. See 1 Kings 16:31–33; 2 Kings 10:29.

See *Tanḥuma, Vayḥi* 6; *Pesiqta Rabbati* 3; *Aggadat Bereshit* 5:2; Rashi and *Leqaḥ Tov*, Genesis 48:8; Radak on 1 Kings 12:28; below, p. 373 and n. 370. Cf. *Bereshit Rabbah* 84:10; 97 (p. 1243).

353. ***God saw all that He had made...*** He saw not only what emerged at the beginning of Creation but everything that would ever come into existence. See *Zohar* 1:47a.

354. **all generations... all souls...** Before descending to earth, each soul is clothed in an ethereal body resembling the physical body that she will assume on earth. See above, note 58.

On Isaiah 41:4, see *ZḤ* 37b; cf. *Tanḥuma* (Buber), *Bereshit* 30. The object in Isaiah 40:26 is the heavenly bodies—here substituted by the souls garbed in their ethereal bodies.

(Genesis 5:1), and we have learned: He showed him all those generations destined to come into the world.[355] Similarly with Moses, as is written: *YHVH showed him all the land* (Deuteronomy 34:1), for the blessed Holy One showed him all generations of the world and all leaders of the world and all other prophets before they came into the world.[356]

"Here too, *Israel saw Joseph's sons*—seeing afar, and he trembled and said, *Who are these?* This verse perfects two facets, this one and that.[357] So Joseph replied, *They are my sons, whom God has given me here* (Genesis 48:9).[358] How do we know that the blessed Holy One showed him through the Holy Spirit? As is written: *Look, God has also shown me your seed!* (ibid., 11)—*also*, amplifying the meaning to include those issuing from him.[359]

"*He blessed Joseph and said, 'The God before whom my fathers walked . . .'* (ibid., 15).[360] This verse calls for contemplation: *He blessed Joseph*—we do not find here that he blessed Joseph with any blessing but rather his sons! And if it was his sons, the verse should read *he blessed them*. Why *he blessed Joseph*? We do not find here that Joseph was blessed!"[361]

355. ***This is the book*...** See BT *Avodah Zarah* 5a: "Did not Resh Lakish say: 'What is the meaning of the verse *This is the book of the generations of Adam* . . . ? Did Adam possess a book? Rather, this teaches that the blessed Holy One showed Adam every generation with its expounders, every generation with its sages, every generation with its leaders.'"

See *Seder Olam Rabbah* 30; *Bereshit Rabbah* 24:2 (and parallels discussed in Theodor's note); BT *Bava Metsi'a* 85b–86a, *Sanhedrin* 38b; *Zohar* 1:37a–b, 55a–b, 90b; 2:70a; *ZḤ* 16d (*MhN*), 37b; Ginzberg, *Legends*, 5:117–18, n. 110.

356. **Similarly with Moses...** Moses' view of the whole land of Canaan expands here into a vision of all generations of the world.

See *Tanḥuma, Mas'ei* 4; *Tanḥuma* (Buber), *Mas'ei* 3; *Bemidbar Rabbah* 23:5; *Zohar* 3:157a; Moses de León, *Sefer ha-Rimmon*, 352. Cf. *Sifrei*, Deuteronomy 357; *Vayiqra Rabbah* 26:7; *Seder Eliyyahu Zuta* 6; *Midrash ha-Gadol*, Exodus 4:13.

357. **verse perfects two facets...** It refers to Joseph's actual sons, Ephraim and Manasseh, and also alludes to King Jeroboam. See above, pp. 368–69 and n. 352.

358. ***They are my sons*...** Joseph insisted that Manasseh and Ephraim were righteous and should not be judged on the basis of eventual descendants.

See *Pesiqta Rabbati* 3; *Aggadat Bereshit* 5:2; *NO*. Cf. *Bereshit Rabbah* 97 (p. 1243); *Targum Yerushalmi*, Genesis 48:9; *Kallah Rabbati* 3:15; Rashi and *Midrash Aggadah*, Genesis 48:9; *Midrash ha-Gadol*, Genesis 48:9; *Zohar* 1:229a.

359. ***also*, amplifying...** In rabbinic hermeneutics the word גם (*gam*), "also, too," amplifies the literal meaning of a biblical word or phrase. See *Bereshit Rabbah* 1:14; JT *Berakhot* 9:5, 14b.

360. ***He blessed Joseph*...** The context (48:15–16) reads: *He blessed Joseph and said, "The God before whom my fathers walked, Abraham and Isaac, the God who has tended me since I came to be until this day, the angel redeeming me from all evil—may He bless the lads!"*

361. **we do not find...** The mention of Joseph here is strange since the blessing is delivered solely to his sons. The Septuagint

Rabbi Yose said, "את (*Et*), precisely! For it is written: את (*et*) *Joseph.* The blessing was for his sons, and when his sons were blessed he was blessed, for the blessing of a person's sons is his own blessing."[362]

Rabbi El'azar said, "*He blessed* את (et) *Joseph*—*et*, precisely! For he blessed the את (*at*), sign, of the covenant, mystery of covenant. Once he [Joseph] said *They are my sons, whom God has given me here* (ibid., 9), he [Jacob] blessed that place, mystery of covenant guarded by Joseph. Therefore he is called Righteous. את (*At*), sign, of Joseph—mystery of covenant abiding with Joseph.[363]

"*The Elohim before whom my fathers walked. The Elohim*—mystery of covenant, holy covenant. *Before whom my fathers*—*before whom,* precisely! For they are supernal primordial ones *before* this mystery—*Abraham and Isaac,* by whom that place is nourished and suckled.[364]

"*The Elohim who has tended me* (ibid., 15). Since he already said *the Elohim before whom my fathers walked,* why again *the Elohim*?[365] Because this is a supernal mystery. Here he blessed that place through mystery of Living *Elohim,*

reads more logically "He blessed them," which is also reflected in the Syriac translation and the Vulgate. Rashbam and Radak, ad loc., explain that a father is blessed vicariously through his sons being blessed.

Cf. *Sekhel Tov,* Genesis 48:15; *Bemidbar Rabbah* 14:5; Naḥmanides, ad loc.; *Zohar* 3:187b.

362. **את (*Et*), precisely!...** The verse reads *He blessed* את (*et*) *Joseph.* Technically, the word את (*et*) is an accusative particle with no ascertainable independent sense. Yet already in rabbinic times, Naḥum of Gimzo and his disciple Rabbi Akiva taught that the presence of *et* in a biblical verse amplifies the apparent meaning. Here, according to Rabbi Yose, *et* amplifies the object of the blessing to include Joseph's sons along with him.

See the preceding note. On *et,* see BT *Pesaḥim* 22b, *Ḥagigah* 12a; *Zohar* 1:247a; 2:90a, 135b.

363. ***He blessed* את (*et*) *Joseph*... את (*at*), sign...** Rabbi El'azar expands on the hermeneutical principle invoked by Rabbi Yose, insisting that here the word את (*et*) alludes to *Shekhinah,* who comprises the entire alphabet of divine speech, from א (*alef*) to ת (*tav*). Further, the Hebrew את (*et*) implies the Aramaic את (*at*), "sign"—specifically, the sign of the covenant. Usually in the *Zohar* the covenant is associated with *Yesod,* the *sefirah* of Joseph, but here, *Shekhinah* is linked with *Yesod* and shares in the designations "covenant" and "sign."

The interplay between *Yesod* and *Shekhinah* continues: "That place" is *Shekhinah,* "mystery of covenant." Joseph guards this covenant by refusing the sexual advances of Potiphar's wife; he thereby attains the rung of *Yesod,* along with its title (Righteous), and becomes the intimate partner of *Shekhinah.*

See above, p. 92, n. 50. For a different interpretation (taking "sign" and "covenant" as referring to *Yesod,* not *Shekhinah*), see *Nefesh David.* Arguably, the expression *whom God has given me* בזה (*ba-zeh*), *here* (literally, *with this*) refers to *Yesod,* known as *zeh* (this). See below, notes 372, 411. Cf. above, note 358.

364. ***Elohim before whom*...** The divine name *Elohim* can refer to various *sefirot: Binah, Gevurah,* and *Shekhinah.* Here the reference is to *Shekhinah,* mystery of covenant. *My fathers* designates Abraham and Isaac, symbolizing *Ḥesed* and *Gevurah,* who are *before Shekhinah*—preceding Her, poised above Her, and conveying to Her the flow of emanation.

365. **why again *the Elohim*?** Why is this name repeated in the same verse?

source of life, from whom blessings emerge. So he mentioned himself at this point, saying *the Elohim who has tended me*, for all blessings flowing from the source of life are absorbed by Jacob, and once received by him, this place receives blessings. All depends upon the male, so it is written: *He blessed* את (et) *Joseph.*[366]

"Therefore, wherever blessings need to be bestowed, the blessed Holy One should be blessed first, and then others will be blessed. If the blessed Holy One is not blessed first, those blessings are not [228a] fulfilled.

"Now, you might say, 'Look, when Jacob's father blessed him, he didn't bless the blessed Holy One first!'[367] Come and see: When Isaac blessed Jacob, he did not bless him until he first blessed the blessed Holy One, as is written: *He said, 'See, the fragrance of my son is like the fragrance of a field blessed by YHVH'* (Genesis 27:27). Here a blessing is found for the blessed Holy One, as is written: *blessed by YHVH*—blessed with fulfillment of blessings. Afterward, what is written? *May the Elohim give you* (ibid., 28). Once that field was sustained by blessings, he immediately blessed him: *May the Elohim give you*—mystery of that field from which blessings emerge after being sustained by blessings. Similarly, Jacob first blessed the blessed Holy One and afterward blessed his sons.[368]

"Come and see: In the morning one should first offer blessings to the blessed Holy One and afterward to other inhabitants of the world, as we have established, for it is written: *In the morning consuming prey, at evening dividing the spoil* (ibid. 49:27).[369]

366. **blessed that place through mystery of Living *Elohim*...** Jacob blessed *Shekhinah* (known as *Elohim*) by invoking *Binah*, the Divine Mother and source of life, who is also known as *Elohim* (see above, note 364). Jacob symbolizes *Tif'eret* (the Husband), who receives the flow from *Binah* and conveys it to *Shekhinah* (the Wife, "this place," *et*) through the male potency of *Yesod*, symbolized by Joseph.

Instead of דכורא (*dekhora*), "male," several manuscripts read דבורא (*dibbura*), "word," but the first reading seems to fit the context better. See Galante.

367. **when Jacob's father blessed him...** When Isaac blessed Jacob, he did not begin by blessing God but rather as follows: *May God give you of the dew of heaven and the fat of the earth, abundance of grain and new wine* (Genesis 27:28).

368. **Isaac... first blessed the blessed Holy One...** Before Isaac blessed Jacob, he blessed *Shekhinah* (known here as "the blessed Holy One") by referring to *a field blessed by YHVH*. *Shekhinah* is the field that is watered and blessed by *Tif'eret*, who is known as *YHVH*. Once She had been blessed, *Shekhinah* (known also as *Elohim*) conveyed Isaac's blessing to Jacob.

On *Shekhinah* as "field," see above, p. 350 and n. 263.

369. **first offer blessings...** See BT *Berakhot* 14a: "Rav said, 'Whoever greets his fellow before praying has, as it were, made him into a cult site....' Samuel said, 'Why have you esteemed this person and not God?'"

See above, p. 272 and n. 79. The verse reads: *Benjamin, a ravening wolf, in the morning consuming* עד (ad), *prey, at evening*

"Come and see: When Jacob was about to bless those sons of Joseph, through the Holy Spirit he saw that Jeroboam son of Nebat was destined to issue from Ephraim. He opened and said, '*Who are these?*' (ibid. 48:8).[370] What is different about this act of the aspect of idolatry, where it is said *These are your gods, O Israel*? Well, this is a secret—all those aspects of the evil serpent. That serpent is side of impure spirit, and there is one riding upon it; when they couple, they are called *these*—appearing in the world in all their aspects.[371]

"Holy Spirit is called זאת (*zot*), *this*—mystery of covenant, holy mark always present in a person. Similarly, זה (*Zeh*), *This, is my God—I will glorify Him* (Exodus 15:2); *Zeh, This, is YHVH* (Isaiah 25:9).[372] But those are called *these*, so it is written: *These are your gods, O Israel!* Therefore it is written: *Even these will be forgotten, yet I*—mystery of *zot, this*—*will not forget you* (ibid. 49:15).[373] Simi-

dividing the spoil. The word עד (*ad*), variously construed as "prey, booty, enemy," can refer in the *Zohar* to a sefirotic potency, based on the homonym עד (*ad*), "eternity." The end of this verse is read: *In the morning ad consuming* [the flow stimulated by human blessings and offerings]; *at evening dividing the spoil* [among all those below]. See *Zohar* 1:161b–162a, 247b–248a; 2:22a.

370. **through the Holy Spirit he saw...** As indicated above (p. 369 and n. 352), Jacob's question, *Who are these?* alludes to King Jeroboam—descended from Joseph's son, Ephraim—who built two golden calves and declared *These are your gods, O Israel!* (On this wording, see above, note 352.)

371. **What is different... *these*...** What is the significance of the plural *these*? It refers to the demonic couple—Samael and the female serpent upon which he rides—and to the host of powers engendered by them who appear in the world. The demonstrative plural *these* implies both their multiplicity and their being present here in the world. They are also linked with idolatry.

See *Pirqei de-Rabbi Eli'ezer* 13: "Samael... took his band and descended and saw all the creatures created by the blessed Holy One. He determined that the most cunningly evil was the serpent, as is said: *Now, the serpent was slier than any creature of the field that YHVH Elohim had made.* He [the serpent] looked like a camel, and he [Samael] mounted and rode him."

See *Zohar* 1:35b, 64a, 137b, 146a, 148a (*ST*), 153a, 160b, 169b; 2:236b (which includes the passage here until p. 375 at n. 380). On the plural *these*, see JT *Sanhedrin* 10:2, 28b (citing Nehemiah 9:18); *Shemot Rabbah* 42:3; *Zohar* 2:192b. Cf. BT *Sanhedrin* 63a.

372. **זאת (*zot*), *this*... זה (*Zeh*), *This*...** The divine female (*Shekhinah*) and male (*Yesod*) are each called by the singular demonstrative pronoun *this*—in its Hebrew female and male forms, זאת (*zot*) and זה (*zeh*), respectively. *This* implies "constantly present right here." The singular form highlights the unity of divine realm, as opposed to the multiplicity of the demonic forces (*these*).

Shekhinah is also known as Holy Spirit and "mystery of covenant," the latter referring to the mark of circumcision. See above, p. 371 and nn. 363–64.

373. ***Even these will be forgotten...*** The verse reads literally: *Can a woman forget her suckling, or feel no compassion for the child of her womb? Even these* [or: *she*] *may forget, yet I will not forget you.* Rabbi El'azar's interpretation derives from BT *Berakhot* 32b, where the phrase *these may forget* is understood to mean "the sin of the Golden Calf *will be forgotten*." (See *Targum Yonatan* on this verse.) For Rabbi El'azar, *these* alludes both to the sin of idolatry and to the manifold de-

larly, *Over these I weep* (Lamentations 1:16), for that sin caused them so much weeping![374]

"Alternatively, *Over these I weep*. Why? Because this realm was empowered to dominate Israel and destroy the Temple. Therefore it is written: *over these*. Mystery of the word: *over these*—side of defilement, empowered to dominate. *I weep*—Holy Spirit, called *I*.[375]

"Now, you might say, 'Look, it is written: *These are the words of the covenant* (Deuteronomy 28:69)!' Certainly so! For all of them are fulfilled only through *these*, where all curses impend—as we have established, for he is cursed. Therefore Scripture anticipates by saying *these*, which stands poised for one who transgresses *the words of the covenant*.[376]

"*These are the commandments that YHVH commanded* (Leviticus 27:34)! Because a *mitsvah* of Torah is for a person to be purified—not to deviate to this path, to be on guard, to disengage from them.[377]

"Now, you might say, '*These are the offspring of Noah* (Genesis 6:9)!' Certainly so! For look, Ham issued, who is father of Canaan, and it is written: *Cursed be Canaan* (ibid. 9:25)—he is mystery of *these*![378]

"Thus, all this smelted dross of gold, and so it is written: *Who are these?* (ibid. 48:8). When Israel made the calf, they said likewise, *These are your gods, O Israel!*

monic powers, who will eventually be eliminated from the world and *forgotten*.

Shekhinah, the Divine Presence, is also known as *I*, because through Her the Divine reveals itself, declaring "I am." See above, p. 253 and n. 436.

374. ***Over these I weep*...** The sin of the Golden Calf, indicated by *these* (see above, notes 352, 370), caused much weeping. According to rabbinic tradition, all of Israel's subsequent suffering—including the destruction of the Temple and their exile—is partly a retribution for this sin. See BT *Sanhedrin* 102a.

375. **this realm was empowered...** The demonic realm (indicated by *these*) was empowered by Israel's sinning, and therefore *Shekhinah* weeps.

376. ***These are the words of the covenant*...** How can the word *these* imply the demonic powers if this verse links *these* with *the words of the covenant*? The answer is that the fulfillment of the covenant is based on a threat of punishment and a set of curses, associated with the demonic realm. These curses, which are spelled out in the preceding verses (Deuteronomy 28:15–68), derive from the primordial serpent, who was cursed after seducing Eve to sin. See Genesis 3:14: *Because you have done this, cursed are you among all animals and among all beasts of the field. Upon your belly shall you go and dust shall you eat all the days of your life.*

377. ***These are the commandments*...** Similarly, how can the word *these* imply the demonic forces if there is a verse linking *these* with *the commandments*? The answer is that this verse implies a contrast between the two: each *mitsvah* is intended to refine the human being and help him avoid the path of evil.

378. ***These are the offspring of Noah*...** How can the word *these* be associated with a righteous hero such as Noah? Because Noah's son Ham *saw his father's nakedness* (Genesis 9:22), and for this Ham's son Canaan was cursed. On the demonic nature of Canaan, see *Zohar* 1:73a.

(Exodus 32:4). Aaron offered gold, which is its side, and power of fire. All is one—one side—gold and fire: fortifying impure spirit, which always haunts the wilderness. At that moment, it found a place on which to fasten.[379]

"Whereas when Israel stood upon Mount Sinai, they were purified from that primordial slime that he injected into the world—inflicting death upon all—now he prevailed over them as before, defiling them, overpowering them, bringing death upon them and upon the whole world for generations after, as is written: *I said, 'You are gods. . . .' But you will die like Adam* (Psalms 82:6–7).[380]

"So, when Jacob saw Jeroboam son of Nebat making an idol and saying *These are your gods, O Israel,* he trembled and said, *Who are these?*[381] When afterward he wanted to bless them, he blessed *Shekhinah* first and then blessed them and

379. **smelted dross of gold...** Gold symbolizes the *sefirah* of *Gevurah* or *Din* (strict Judgment) on the left side; the dross of gold symbolizes evil, a residue of the refining process of emanation—or that which derives from *Din* when this divine quality is not balanced by *Ḥesed* (Loving-kindness). Jacob's question—*Who are these?*—alludes to this demonic dross, which characterized Jeroboam's golden calves and the calf constructed by Aaron at Mount Sinai. Both gold and fire represent the left side, origin of evil. For the combination of gold and fire in connection with the Golden Calf, see Aaron's explanation to Moses in Exodus 32:24: *I said to them, "Whoever has gold, take it off." And they gave it to me, and I flung it into the fire, and out came this calf.*

"Dross" renders the Zoharic neologism סוספיתא (*suspita*), apparently based on Aramaic כוספא (*kuspa*), "pomace, husk, residue." See *Zohar* 1:30a, 71b, 118b, 179b; 2:24b, 203a, 224b, 236b; *Bei'ur ha-Millim ha-Zarot,* 182; Scholem, *Major Trends,* 389, n. 54; Liebes, *Peraqim,* 336–38.

On the wilderness as the abode of demonic powers, see *Targum Yerushalmi,* Deuteronomy 32:10; Naḥmanides on Leviticus 17:7; *Zohar* 1:14b, 126a, 169b, 178b; 2:60a, 157a, 184a, 236b–237a; 3:63b.

380. **when Israel stood upon Mount Sinai...** At Sinai, the people of Israel were cleansed of the impurity injected into the world by the primordial serpent in the Garden of Eden, and they could have become immortal. (On mortality as the consequence of eating from the Tree of Knowledge, see Genesis 2:17; 3:3, 19.) But when they sinned by worshiping the Golden Calf, the serpent regained his power over them, condemning them to mortality.

See BT *Shabbat* 145b–146a: "Rav Yosef taught: '. . . When the serpent copulated with Eve, he injected her with זוהמא (*zohama*), filth [or: slime, lewdness]. Israel, who stood at Mount Sinai—their slime ceased. Star-worshipers, who did not stand at Mount Sinai—their slime did not cease.'"

See *Targum Yerushalmi,* Genesis 4:1 (variants); *Pirqei de-Rabbi Eli'ezer* 21; *Zohar* 1:36b–37a, 52a, 54a, 122b, 126a–b, 145b; 2:94a, 193b; 3:14b, 97b; Moses de León, *Sefer ha-Rimmon,* 139.

See BT *Avodah Zarah* 5a, in the name of Rabbi Yose: "Israel accepted the Torah only so the Angel of Death would have no dominion over them, as is said: '*I said, "You are gods, children of the Most High, all of you."* Now that you have acted corruptly [by worshiping the Golden Calf], *you will die like* אדם (*adam*), *humans.*'"

See *Mekhilta, Baḥodesh* 9; *Zohar* 1:52b, 63b, 126b, 131b; 2:193b; 3:162a.

381. **when Jacob saw Jeroboam...** See above, p. 369 and n. 352.

their descendants. Having blessed the blessed Holy One first, afterward—from that place that he had first blessed—he blessed them, as is written: *The angel redeeming me from all evil—may He bless the lads!*" (Genesis 48:16).[382]

Rabbi Yehudah opened, "*Hezekiah turned his face to the wall and prayed to YHVH* (2 Kings 20:2). They have already established that one should only pray near the wall and that nothing should interpose between oneself and the wall, as is written: *Hezekiah turned his face to the wall.*[383] Now, what is different about all others who offered prayer, concerning whom it is not written *He turned his face to the wall*? It would have sufficed to say *He prayed to YHVH*, since one who offers prayer focuses his mind fittingly.[384] For look at what is written of Moses: *Moses prayed to YHVH* (Numbers 11:2), and similarly: *Moses cried out to YHVH* (Exodus 8:8)—and it is not written [228b] *he turned his face!*[385] Here, concerning Hezekiah, why *Hezekiah turned* [*his face to the wall*], and then *and prayed to YHVH*?

376 "Well, this is the mystery of the matter: We have learned that at that time Hezekiah was not married—he had no wife by whom to engender children. What is written? *The prophet Isaiah son of Amoz came to him and said, 'Thus says YHVH: Set your house in order, for you are going to die; you will not live'* (2 Kings 20:1). And we have learned: *for you are going to die*—in this world; *you will not live*—in the world that is coming. Why? Because he did not engender children.[386] For whoever does not strive to engender children in this world does not endure in the world that is coming and will have no share in that world; his soul is cast into the world, finding no rest anywhere. This is the punishment prescribed in Torah: ערירים (*ariri*m)—*they will die* (Leviticus 20:20)—and we translate this: childless. *Shekhinah* does not rest upon him.[387]

382. **wanted to bless them...** When Jacob wanted to bless Joseph's two sons, he first blessed *Shekhinah* (referred to here as the blessed Holy One and *angel redeeming me*); She then conveyed blessing to them and their descendants.

See above, p. 372 and n. 368. On *Shekhinah* as angel, see above, p. 167 and n. 516.

383. ***Hezekiah turned his face...*** The preceding verse (2 Kings 20:1) reads: *In those days Hezekiah became deathly ill. The prophet Isaiah son of Amoz came to him and said, "Thus says YHVH: Set your house in order, for you are going to die; you will not live."* The same passage appears in Isaiah 38:1–2.

Rabbi Yehudah refers to a rabbinic tradition in BT *Berakhot* 5b. See *Zohar* 1:11a, 132a; 2:44a, 133a; 3:260a–b.

384. **It would have sufficed to say...** Scripture could have simply said concerning Hezekiah, *He prayed to YHVH*, without mentioning that he *turned his face to the wall.* Such an action is secondary to the essential element of prayer: proper intention.

385. ***Moses cried out to YHVH...*** This clause reappears in Exodus 17:4 and Numbers 12:13, also without mention of *he turned his face* or the like.

386. **Hezekiah was not married...** See BT *Berakhot* 10a, in the name of Rav Hamnuna; *Zohar* 1:66a.

387. **whoever does not strive...** See BT

"Therefore, *Hezekiah turned his face to the wall.* We have learned that he set his mind and turned his attention to marrying a woman, so that *Shekhinah*—secret of wall—would rest upon him.[388] Afterward, *he prayed to YHVH.* From here we learn that whoever carries a sin and wants to pray for mercy should turn his attention and his thoughts to mending himself of that sin; afterward he can offer a prayer, as is said: *Let us search and examine our ways, and let us return to YHVH* (Lamentations 3:40). *Let us search our ways*—first—and afterward *let us return to YHVH.*[389]

"Similarly here, as soon as Hezekiah became aware of his sin, what is written? *Hezekiah turned his face to the wall*—setting his face to mend himself before *Shekhinah,* for regarding this place he had sinned. For all females of the world abide in the mystery of *Shekhinah.* Whoever has a female, She dwells with him; whoever has no female, She does not. So, he mended himself before Her to be restored, and resolved to marry; afterward, *he prayed to YHVH.*[390]

"קיר (*Qir*), *Wall*—Lord of all the earth; this is *Shekhinah,* as is said: *See, ark of the covenant, Lord of all the earth* (Joshua 3:11).[391]

"*Qir,* as is said: מקרקר קיר (*meqarqar qir*) (Isaiah 22:5)—קרקורא דקיר (*qirqura de-qir*), screaming of *qir*; screaming and groaning of *qir,* who is Lord, when the Temple was destroyed, as is said: *Rachel weeping for her children* (Jeremiah 31:15), as we have established.[392]

Bava Batra 116a: "Rabbi Yoḥanan said in the name of Rabbi Shim'on son of Yoḥai, 'Whoever does not leave a son to succeed him incurs the full wrath of the blessed Holy One.'"

See BT *Yevamot* 63b; *Zohar* 1:13a, 48a, 66a, 90a, 115a, 186b; *ZḤ* 89b (*MhN, Rut*).

The rare biblical term ערירים (*aririm*) apparently means "stripped," hence, "stripped of children, childless." The phrase "we translate" refers to *Targum Onqelos* on the verse (see Rashi, ad loc.). In its original context, the final words of the verse describe the punishment for having sexual relations with one's aunt: *childless they will die* (the plural subject *they* referring to both the nephew and his aunt). Rabbi Yehudah rereads the words as an independent formulation: [Those who sin by remaining] *childless—they will die* [both in this world and in the world that is coming]."

Cf. *Vayiqra Rabbah* 20:9; BT *Yevamot* 63b; *Tanḥuma, Aḥarei Mot* 6; *Tanḥuma* (Buber), *Aḥarei Mot* 7; *ZḤ* 59b.

388. ***Shekhinah*—secret of wall...** This association may derive in part from the fact that *Shekhinah* is the last of ten *sefirot* and thereby separates the purely divine realm from all below. Other explanations appear below.

See *Zohar* 2:44a, 133a; 3:260b.

389. **afterward *let us return to YHVH*** Through prayer.

390. **all females of the world...** *Shekhinah* is the feminine archetype, which is embodied and realized in all female creatures.

See *Zohar* 3:124a; Tishby, *Wisdom of the Zohar,* 2:464; 3:1357, 1373, n. 23.

391. **קיר (*Qir*), *Wall*—Lord...** Associating קיר (*qir*) with Greek *kyrios,* "lord." *Shekhinah,* the last *sefirah,* rules as *Lord* over *the earth.* She is also pictured as the *ark* housing *Yesod,* who is symbolized by *the covenant.*

On *Shekhinah* as ark, see *Zohar* 1:2a, 33b, 50b, 59b, 251a; 2:13a, 235b; Moses de León, *Sheqel ha-Qodesh,* 75 (95). For rabbinic knowledge of Greek *kyrios,* see BT *Avodah Zarah* 11b, *Ḥullin* 139b.

392. **מקרקר קיר (*meqarqar qir*)...** Now

"Come and see: What is written in the prayer? *'Please, O YHVH, remember how I have walked in Your presence in truth and wholeheartedly, and have done what is good in Your eyes.' And Hezekiah wept profusely* (2 Kings 20:3).[393] Here he hinted that he had guarded the holy covenant, not defiled it. Here is written *how I have walked in Your presence*, and there is written *Walk in My presence and be complete, and I will grant My covenant between Me and you* (Genesis 17:1–2).[394]

"*In truth and wholeheartedly*—for he concentrated on all these mysteries of faith, to enfold them *in truth*.[395]

"*And have done what is good in Your eyes*—joining 'redemption' and prayer, and the Companions have established that he focused on effecting unification fittingly. Then, *Hezekiah wept profusely*, for no gate can withstand tears. Redemption—*the redeeming angel* (Genesis 48:16), for this is who manifests in every redemption in the world, as we have established."[396]

Rabbi Yehudah adds another association, based on this ambiguous expression in Isaiah, which may mean *shouting a shout*, or *battering down a wall*. He interprets it as "screaming of *qir* (Lord, *Shekhinah*)," who is symbolized by Mother Rachel weeping over the exile of her children.

The verse in Jeremiah reads: *A voice is heard on a height—wailing, bitter weeping—Rachel weeping for her children, refusing to be comforted for her children, because they are no more.* See above, p. 104 and n. 132, p. 243 and n. 382.

393. **in the prayer...** Offered by King Hezekiah. The same prayer appears in Isaiah 38:3.

394. **guarded the holy covenant...** He had guarded the covenant of circumcision by not committing any sexual sin. Rabbi Yehudah proves this by verbal analogy. Just as the idiom of "walking in God's presence" is linked with the covenant of circumcision in the story of Abraham, so here too with Hezekiah.

The context in Genesis (17:1–2) reads: *When Abram was ninety-nine years old YHVH appeared to Abram and said to him, "I am El Shaddai. Walk in My presence and be* תמים (*tamim*), *complete, and I will grant My covenant between Me and you and I will increase you very greatly."* This divine directive is soon followed by the command of circumcision (verses 9–14), which renders a person *tamim*, "unblemished" or "complete." See above, pp. 231–32 and n. 322.

395. ***In truth...*** He concentrated in prayer and included all the mysteries in *Tif'eret*, the central *sefirah*, known as *truth*.

396. **joining 'redemption' and prayer...** "Redemption" is the final blessing of the sitting prayer, which concludes: "Blessed are You, *YHVH*, who has redeemed Israel." According to BT *Berakhot* 4b, 9b, there should be no pause between this blessing and the beginning of the *Amidah*, the "standing" prayer—so central that it is known simply as "prayer." According to BT *Berakhot* 10b (in the name of Rav), when Hezekiah said to God *I have done what is good in Your eyes*, this meant that he had joined "redemption" and prayer.

Here "redemption" symbolizes *Shekhinah*, also known as *the redeeming angel* (see above, p. 376 and n. 382; below, p. 402 and n. 498). She is adorned during the sitting prayer in preparation for Her union with *Tif'eret*, which takes place during the *Amidah*. By joining "redemption" and prayer, Hezekiah succeeded in initiating the union of the divine couple. See above, pp. 260–61 and n. 16.

On the power of tears, see BT *Berakhot*

The angel redeeming me from all evil (Genesis 48:16).[397]

Rabbi El'azar said, "After Jacob blessed and directed from below to above, he then conducted from above to below, as is written: *the Elohim who has tended me since I came to be until this day* (ibid.). Having received, he gave blessings to this place. Once blessings reached this place, he opened, saying, *The angel redeeming me from all evil—may He bless the lads!*"[398]

He opened, saying, "*For the cherubim spread their wings over the place of the ark, and the cherubim shielded the ark and its poles from above* (1 Kings 8:7). Come and see: The cherubim stood miraculously. Three times a day they would spread their wings, shielding the ark below, as is written: פורשים (*poresim*), *spread, their wings*. It is not written פרושי (*perusei*), [*with wings*] *spread*, but rather, *poresim, spread* [*their wings*].[399]

"Come and see: The blessed Holy One fashioned below corresponding to the pattern above. The image of the cherubim resembles children, and they stand beneath this place on the right and the left. These are blessed first with those blessings flowing from above, and from here blessings flow to those below. Therefore it is written: *The angel redeeming me*—absorbing blessings from colors above. Having absorbed, *may He bless the lads*—mystery of cherubim, from whom blessings flow [229a] from those above to those below."[400]

32b, in the name of Rabbi El'azar: "Since the day the Temple was destroyed, the gates of prayer have been locked.... Yet even though the gates of prayer have been locked, the gates of tears have not." See above, p. 338 and n. 205.

397. ***The angel redeeming me...*** The context (48:15–16) reads: *He blessed Joseph and said, "The God before whom my fathers walked, Abraham and Isaac, the God who has tended me since I came to be until this day, the angel redeeming me from all evil—may He bless the lads!"*

398. **After Jacob blessed...** After he contemplatively drew *Shekhinah* toward the higher *sefirot*, he then drew a flow of blessing from *Binah* (known as *Elohim*) to his own rung, *Tif'eret*. Having received from *Binah*, Jacob (or *Tif'eret*) conveyed blessing to *Shekhinah* ("this place"). Finally, Jacob prayed that *Shekhinah (the angel)* transmit blessing to Joseph's sons. See above, pp. 371–72 and nn. 364–66.

399. ***cherubim spread their wings...*** These winged creatures served as a throne for the Divine Presence. The wording פורשים (*poresim*), *spread* [*their wings*], indicates that the cherubim miraculously spread their wings, whereas פרושי (*perusei*), [*with wings*] *spread*, would have indicated that their wings were always spread.

See Exodus 25:17–22; 1 Kings 6:23–28; 8:6–7; Milgrom, *Leviticus*, 1:1014. On the miraculous posture of the cherubim, see BT *Bava Batra* 99a. On the various forms of the root פרש (*prs*), "to spread," see Exodus 25:20; *Zohar* 3:59a; *ZḤ* 43b; Galante; *KP*; *MM*. Cf. *Zohar* 3:67a.

400. **fashioned below corresponding to the pattern above...** The cherubim in the Temple (and earlier in the Tabernacle) were modeled on the heavenly cherubim, who stand beneath *Shekhinah*. Jacob prayed that *Shekhinah* (*the angel redeeming me*) would receive the flow of blessing from the *sefirot* ("colors") above Her and transmit it to the

The angel redeeming me from all evil—may He bless the lads! (Genesis 48:16).

Rabbi Ḥiyya opened, "*House and wealth are inherited from fathers, but an insightful wife is from YHVH* (Proverbs 19:14). *House and wealth are inherited from fathers.* Now, are they really *inherited from fathers?*[401] Rather, the blessed Holy One gives everything to a person, and once He has transmitted a house to someone, and money, he sometimes bequeaths everything to his son, so it is *inherited from fathers.*[402] But, *an insightful wife is from YHVH*—for when a man possesses a wife, he possesses her from the blessed Holy One, because the blessed Holy One transmits her to someone only when this has been proclaimed above. For the blessed Holy One matches couples before they come into the world. When men become worthy, they are given a wife according to their deeds. All is revealed before the blessed Holy One, and according to virtuous deeds He matches couples.[403]

"Sometimes they balanced on scales,[404] but if that man perverts his way, his mate is transferred to another until he rectifies his deeds. When he rectifies his

heavenly childlike cherubim (*the lads*), who would then convey it below, specifically to Joseph's sons.

On the childlike cherubim, see BT *Sukkah* 5b: "What is כרוב (*keruv*), cherub? Rabbi Abbahu said, 'כרביא (*Ke-ravya*), Like a child, for in Babylon they call a child רביא (*ravya*).'" See *Zohar* 1:18b; 3:60b, 217b.

401. **really *inherited from fathers*** Isn't it God who ultimately determines all such matters?

402. **he sometimes bequeaths...** The father sometimes bequeaths these to his son.

403. **proclaimed above... matches couples...** The idea that a couple's union is proclaimed before they are born, and the apparently conflicting idea that their union depends on good deeds, both derive from BT *Sotah* 2a: "Rav Shemu'el son of Rav Yitsḥak said, 'When Resh Lakish began to teach about the *sotah* [unfaithful wife], he would say as follows: A man is paired with a woman only according to his deeds....' Rabbah son of Bar Ḥanah said in the name of Rabbi Yoḥanan, 'It is as difficult to match them as was the splitting of the Red Sea!...' But is that really so? After all, Rav Yehudah said in the name of Rav, 'Forty days before the formation of an embryo, a divine echo issues and proclaims, 'Daughter of so-and-so for so-and-so!...' There is no contradiction. The latter [their proclamation above] refers to the original couple [who are predestined for one another]; the former [that their union depends on good deeds], to a later couple [a second marriage]."

Here Rabbi Ḥiyya combines the two ideas, implying that even though marriages are arranged in heaven, they take place only if and when the prospective husband proves himself worthy through good deeds.

See BT *Mo'ed Qatan* 18b (quoting Proverbs 19:14); *Zohar* 1:85b, 89a; 90b, 91b, 137a; 2:101a.

404. **they balanced on scales...** According to the *Zohar*, when souls issue from *Shekhinah*, they are weighed on a cosmic scale and each pair of male and female souls that balance perfectly become destined for one another.

The conjectural translation "they balanced on scales" renders the phrase סליקו בקליטין (*seliqu biqlitin*), "they went up in *qelitin*." קליטין (*Qelitin*) may be a play on (or a cor-

deeds, or when his time arrives, one man is thrust out in favor of another, and this one comes to obtain what is his. This is the most difficult of all for the blessed Holy One: to thrust out a person in favor of another.[405]

"Therefore, it is the blessed Holy One who gives a man his wife, and from Him couplings come. So, *an insightful wife is from YHVH*. The blessed Holy One provides a person with everything.

"Now, you might say '*An insightful wife*, but not any other.'[406] Come and see: Even though the blessed Holy One prepares goodness to give to a person, if he deviates from the blessed Holy One toward the Other Side, then from that Other Side to which he clings comes one who brings all sorts of accusations and ills. These do not come to him from the blessed Holy One, but rather from that evil side to which he clung through those deeds he committed.[407]

ruption of) טיקלין (*tiqlin*), a Zoharic neologism with a range of meaning including "scales"—deriving from the Aramaic root תקל (*tql*), "to weigh."

On the image of balancing and matching couples before birth, see JT *Beitsah* 5:2, 63a; *Vayiqra Rabbah* 29:8; *Pesiqta de-Rav Kahana* 23:8; *Pirqei de-Rabbi Eli'ezer*, 16; *Bereshit Rabbati*, p. 95; *Zohar* 2:109a, 255a–b (*Heikh*); Liebes, *Peraqim*, 329. All of the traditional sources cited here quote Psalms 62:10: במאזנים לעלות (*be-moznayim la-alot*), *to be weighed on* [literally, to go up in, i.e., be placed on] *scales*. This idiomatic usage of *la-alot*, "to go up," may explain the *Zohar*'s use of the root סלק (*slq*), "to go up."

Cf. *Zohar* 2:246a (*Heikh*); 3:43b; Tishby, *Wisdom of the Zohar*, 3:1355–56. On *qelitin* and *tiqlin*, see *OL*; *Adderet Eliyyahu*; Tishby, *Wisdom of the Zohar*, 3:1386. Cf. Galante; and the Castilian word *quilate*, a unit of weight, derived from Arabic *qirat* ("bean pod," small weight), from Greek *keration* ("carob bean," small weight); hence, English "carat." See Corominas, *Diccionario*, 4:727.

The Zoharic neologism *qelitin* may also be linked to a specific sense of the root קלט (*qlt*), "to absorb (semen), to conceive," alluding here to the conception of the human soul above. See *Bereshit Rabbah* 40(41):6; *Vayiqra Rabbah* 14:5. For other interpretations of *qelitin*, see *KP*; *DE*; *Adderet Eliyyahu*; *Sullam*. Cf. *ZḤ* 39a.

405. **his mate is transferred...** Despite the fact that two souls may be destined for one another, if the prospective husband lives an unworthy life, another man replaces him, marrying his intended partner. Later, if the originally intended husband mends his ways, the replacement is removed from the world so that the predestined couple can finally unite.

The phrase "when his time arrives" apparently refers to a divine decree that, due to the originally intended husband's misdeeds, he must wait a certain amount of time before he can unite with his destined wife.

See BT *Mo'ed Qatan* 18b; *Zohar* 1:73b, 91b; 2:101a, 102a, 109a; 3:78b, 283b–284a.

On the notion that matchmaking proves difficult even for God, see the statement in the name of Rabbi Yoḥanan (quoted above, note 403): "It is as difficult to match them as was the splitting of the Red Sea!" See above, p. 273 and n. 85.

406. **but not any other** It might seem that a wife who is not *insightful* does not derive from God.

407. **if he deviates...** If a man acts sinfully, seduced by demonic forces (the Other Side), then appropriately he marries a bad or nagging wife.

"Therefore, of a wife who is not *insightful,* Solomon exclaimed *I find the woman more bitter than death* (Ecclesiastes 7:26)—for through his sins a man draws this upon himself, through those deeds he has committed.[408] Consequently, when the blessed Holy One delights in a man because of his worthy deeds, He designates for him a woman who is *insightful* and redeems him from the Other Side.

"Concerning this, Jacob said *The angel redeeming me from all evil.* What does *from all evil* mean? 'That a woman from the Other Side was not designated for me and no defect appeared in my offspring, all of whom are righteous and completely perfect'—because he was redeemed *from all evil,* and Jacob did not cling to that Other Side at all.[409]

"Therefore, *The angel redeeming me from all evil—may He bless the lads!* Why did they deserve to be blessed?[410] Because Joseph preserved the sign of holy covenant. That is why Joseph said *They are my sons, whom God has given me* בזה (*ba-zeh*), *with this* (Genesis 48:9)—showing him the mystery of covenant that he had preserved, because of which they deserved to be blessed and he deserved many blessings. To each of them he gave one blessing, and to Joseph many blessings, as implied by what is written: *Your father's blessings... blessings of breasts and womb... may they rest on the head of Joseph* (Genesis 49:25–26)."[411]

408. ***I find the woman...*** The person himself "finds" this kind of wife—without God's direct intervention—bringing her upon himself through his reprehensible conduct.

409. **no defect appeared in my offspring...** According to rabbinic tradition, Jacob celebrated when he realized that all his sons were virtuous. Here their lack of defect is explained by the fact that Jacob's wives did not derive from the demonic sphere.

See *Sifrei,* Deuteronomy 31.

410. **Why did they deserve to be blessed?** Given that the descendants of Joseph's two sons worshiped idols. See above, pp. 368–69 and n. 352.

411. **Joseph preserved the sign of holy covenant... בזה (*ba-zeh*), *with this*...** Joseph preserved the covenant of circumcision by not succumbing to the sexual advances of Potiphar's wife. His sexual purity enabled him to scale the sefirotic ladder and attain the rung of *Yesod,* the divine phallus and site of the covenant. See above, p. 92, n. 50.

The verse spoken by Joseph is usually taken to mean *They are my sons, whom God has given me* בזה (*ba-zeh*), *here* [in Egypt]. However, Rabbi Ḥiyya insists on the literal meaning of *ba-zeh, with this,* referring to *Yesod*—which is known as זה (*zeh*), *this* (see above, note 372)—and to Joseph's sign of circumcision. When Joseph said בזה (*ba-zeh*), *with this,* he showed his father the sign that he had guarded and preserved in purity, thereby guaranteeing the legitimacy and virtue of his two sons. See above, note 358.

The concluding sentence refers to the series of blessings offered by Jacob to his sons. Actually, Judah, the progenitor of the Davidic dynasty, also receives a multiple blessing. The quotation here rearranges the phrasing of the two biblical verses.

Rabbi Yehudah opened, "*To You I lift my eyes, O You who dwell in heaven* (Psalms 123:1). This verse has been established, but come and see![412] A person's prayer, genuinely intended, reaches above to the high depth whence all blessings and all freedom flow, issuing to sustain all.[413] Therefore, an extra י (*yod*), because *yod* never separates from this place, so it is written היושבי (*ha-yoshevi*), *who dwell, in heaven*—held above, in mystery of supernal Wisdom; held below, sitting on the throne of patriarchs, sitting on the throne called *heaven*. So it is written *ha-yoshevi, who dwell, in heaven*.[414]

"From here—when blessings flow from above, from this depth—they are all absorbed by this place called *heaven*. From here they flow down until reaching the Righteous One, sustaining pillar of the world; from here all those forces and camps are blessed, according to their kinds, as we have established.[415]

"Come and see: In seventy-two lights ascends Crown of all camps. Circle of the world in seventy sites, all of them a single circle. Within that circle, a single point, standing in the middle; from that point, the whole circle is nourished.[416]

412. **This verse has been established...** See *Sifrei*, Deuteronomy 346; *Zohar* 1:208b; 3:265b.

413. **high depth...** *Binah*, Divine Mother and source of emanation for the lower *sefirot*.

See *Sefer Yetsirah* 1:5: "... depth of above, depth of below..." See *Zohar* 1:30b; 2:63b; 3:26a, 70a, 265b. On the ascent of prayer to *Binah*, see *Zohar* 2:153b, 202a.

414. **an extra י (*yod*)...** The word היושבי (*ha-yoshevi*), *who dwell*, is spelled with an apparently superfluous י (*yod*) at the end. Rabbi Yehudah insists that this tiny letter symbolizes the primordial point of *Ḥokhmah* (Wisdom), the Divine Father, who is perpetually joined with the Divine Mother, *Binah*. Thus *Binah* is linked above to *Ḥokhmah* and linked below with the sefirotic triad of *Ḥesed, Gevurah,* and *Tif'eret* (symbolized respectively by the three patriarchs) that forms a throne for *Binah*. The core of this lower triad, *Tif'eret*, is known as *heaven*.

On the throne of the patriarchs, see above, note 198.

415. **when blessings flow...** The flow of emanation proceeds from *Binah* ("this depth") to *Tif'eret* (*heaven*), then on to *Yesod*, the cosmic pillar (known as Righteous One), who nourishes (through *Shekhinah*) all the camps of angels and eventually the worlds below.

Yesod is known as Righteous One and cosmic pillar based on Proverbs 10:25: וצדיק יסוד עולם (*Ve-tsaddiq yesod olam*). The verse literally means *The righteous one is an everlasting foundation*, but it is understood as *The righteous one is the foundation of the world.*

See BT *Ḥagigah* 12b; *Bahir* 71 (102); Azriel of Gerona, *Peirush ha-Aggadot*, 34.

416. **In seventy-two lights...** A veiled description of *Shekhinah*, known as *Atarah* (Crown). She is the central point of a cosmic circle, surrounded by seventy angels (or camps of angels), all of whom are nourished by Her. These angels represent (or convey *Shekhinah*'s nourishment to) seventy heavenly princes, who oversee the nations of the world.

On these princes, see above, pp. 70–71 and n. 476. The number seventy-two apparently alludes to the seventy-two names of God, derived from Exodus 14:19–21. See Vol. 1, p. 312, n. 1525. The circle of seventy resembles the half-circle of seventy-one members of the Sanhedrin (seventy and the presiding officer). The number seventy-two apparently

Chamber of the Holy of Holies is the site [229b] of that spirit of all spirits.[417] Here, mystery of all mysteries hidden within; this one is hidden among Her forces, hidden within, within. When this one ascends, all ascend after Her, as is written: *Draw me after you, let us run!* (Song of Songs 1:4)."[418]

Rabbi Ḥizkiyah, Rabbi Yose, and Rabbi Yehudah were walking on the way. Rabbi Yose said, "Let each one of us speak words of Torah!"

Rabbi Yehudah opened, "*Do not remember against us former iniquities; let* [*Your compassion*] *swiftly meet us*... (Psalms 79:8).[419] Come and see: Out of the compassion that the blessed Holy One feels for Israel, who are His share and heritage, no one but He alone examines their case. And when He does so, He is filled with compassion for them, like a father for his children, as is said: *As a father has compassion for his children, so YHVH has compassion for those who revere Him* (ibid. 103:13). When He discovers their sins, He eliminates them one by one, until they have all been removed from His presence. Having done so, no sins remain upon them that could grant the side of Judgment dominion over them.[420]

also alludes to seventy members of the Sanhedrin plus two scribes. See M *Sanhedrin* 4:3; *Pirqei de-Rabbi Eli'ezer,* 24; Naḥmanides, Numbers 11:16; *Zohar* 1:43b (*Heikh*); 2:251a (*Heikh*); 3:236b; Moses de León, *Sefer ha-Rimmon,* 333 (and Wolfson's note); *OY*; Galante; *KP.*

The single, central point symbolizes *Shekhinah,* though *Ḥokhmah* is also described as a single point. See *Zohar* 1:15a, 30b, 46b, 71b; 2:157a, 180a–b, 184b, 231a, 259b (*Heikh*), 260a (*Heikh*), 268a, 3:191a, 250a–b; *ZḤ* 69d–70a (*ShS*); above, note 414; Scholem, *Major Trends,* 391, n. 80. On the Temple as the center of the world, see *Tanḥuma, Qedoshim* 10, quoted above, note 314.

417. **Chamber of the Holy of Holies...** Referring to the highest (or innermost) of the seven heavenly palaces, the abode of *Shekhinah* (and sometimes spoken of as if it were *Shekhinah* Herself).

For various interpretations, see *OY*; Galante; *KP*; *MM*; *MmD.* On the Holy of Holies as the innermost palace and its relationship to *Shekhinah* and *Binah,* see *Zohar* 1:45a; 2:257b, 258b (all *Heikh*); Tishby, *Wisdom of the Zohar,* 2:593–94, 749.

418. **hidden among Her forces...** *Shekhinah* is concealed among Her hosts of angels. When She ascends to unite with *Tif'eret,* they all ascend along with Her. To Her beloved She says, *Draw me after you*; and then to Her angels, *let us run!* This explains the switch in the verse from singular *me* to plural *us.*

See *Zohar* 3:59a; *ZḤ* 65b (*ShS*), 66d–67b (*ShS*), 68b (*ShS*).

419. ***Do not remember...*** The full verse reads: *Do not remember against us former iniquities; let Your compassion swiftly meet us, for we have sunk very low.*

420. **eliminates them one by one...** See BT *Rosh ha-Shanah* 17a: "It was taught in the school of Rabbi Yishma'el: 'He removes [or: pardons] [their sins] one by one, and such is the [divine] attribute [of compassion or loving-kindness].' Rava said, 'The iniquity itself is not erased, for if there is an excess of iniquities He reckons it along with them [and he is considered guilty].'" See Rashi and Asher ben Yeḥiel, ad loc.

"If they come to sin before Him as previously, He reckons against them those sins that He had eliminated. Concerning this is written *Do not remember against us former iniquities; let Your compassion swiftly meet us.* For if compassion does not come upon Israel, they cannot endure in the world—because countless masters of harsh judgment and shield-bearing warriors, countless informers stand poised over Israel up above, and if the blessed Holy One did not first show compassion for Israel before examining their case, they could not endure in the world. So, *let Your compassion swiftly meet us, for* דלונו מאד (*dallonu me'od*), *we are very impoverished*—דלותא (*dalluta*), impoverishment, of good deeds, impoverishment of worthy deeds.[421]

"Come and see: If Israel would accumulate worthy deeds, other nations would not endure in the world; but Israel themselves enable other nations to hold their head high in the world. For if Israel would not sin before the blessed Holy One, other nations would be subdued before them.[422]

"Come and see: As has been said, if Israel had not, by their evil deeds, drawn the Other Side into the Holy Land, other nations would not have gained dominion over the land of Israel and [Israel] would not have been exiled from the land. Therefore it is written: *for we are very impoverished*, lacking suitably worthy deeds; so, *let Your compassion swiftly meet us.*"

Rabbi Yose opened, "*Serve YHVH with joy, come before Him with singing* (Psalms 100:2). Come and see: Every person who wishes to worship the blessed Holy One in the daily ritual of prayer should worship Him morning and evening. In the morning, as light ascends and arousal of the right side arouses in the world, one should bind himself to the right arm of the blessed Holy One and worship Him through the ritual of prayer, for prayer empowers potency above and draws blessings from the high depth to all those worlds, from there drawing blessings below; so those above and those below are blessed through that ritual of prayer.[423]

"One should serve the blessed Holy One in a ritual of prayer *with joy* and *with singing*, enfolding Assembly of Israel between them, and afterward effecting

421. **דלונו מאד (*dallonu me'od*), *we are very impoverished*...** This clause is often understood as *we have sunk very low* (see above, note 419), but Rabbi Yehudah interprets the verb דלונו (*dallonu*) in the related sense: *we are impoverished*. See BT *Rosh ha-Shanah* 17a, where Rava quotes Psalms 116:6, offering a similar interpretation.

422. **If Israel would accumulate...** Israel's virtuous behavior strengthens the power of holiness and vanquishes Israel's enemies. Conversely, Israel's sinful acts empower the demonic realm and the hostile nations of the world. See *Zohar* 2:58a.

423. **In the morning...** The morning and its prayer correspond to *Ḥesed*, the right arm of God and first of the seven sefirotic rays emerging from *Binah*. Devout prayer at this time stimulates a flow of blessing from *Binah*, known as "high depth" (see above, note 413), to all the upper and lower worlds.

unification fittingly, as is written: *Know that YHVH is Elohim* (ibid., 3)—mystery of unification through mystery of worship.[424] Nevertheless, one should worship the blessed Holy One in joy, manifesting joy in his worship.[425] Corresponding to these two—*joy* and *singing*—are two prayers, two daily offerings, corresponding to these two, *joy* and *singing*: *joy* in the morning, *singing* in the evening. Therefore, *The one lamb you shall offer in the morning and the other lamb you shall offer at twilight* (Exodus 29:39).[426]

"This is why the evening prayer is optional, since at that hour She is distributing food to all Her forces, and it is not the appropriate time to be blessed, but rather to provide nourishment. In the daytime She is blessed from these two sides, in the morning and the evening from *joy* and *singing*. At night She dispenses blessings to all fittingly, as is written: *She rises while it is still night and provides food to her household and a portion to her maidens* (Proverbs 31:15)."[427]

Rabbi Ḥizkiyah opened, saying, "*May my prayer be set as incense before You, the lifting of my palms as an evening offering* (Psalms 141:2). Why *an evening offering* and not a morning prayer? [230a] Why is it not written *May my prayer be set in the morning*? Yet so it has been said: *May my prayer be set as incense before You*—incense comes only for joy, as is written: *Oil and incense rejoice the heart* (Proverbs 27:9). Therefore the priest, while kindling lamps, would offer

424. ***with joy* and *with singing*...** *Joy* symbolizes *Ḥesed,* who is also represented by the priest worshiping in the Temple in joy; *singing* symbolizes *Gevurah,* who is also represented by the Levite who sings in the Temple. These two *sefirot,* the divine right and left arms, embrace *Shekhinah* (known as Assembly of Israel) in preparation for Her union with *Tif'eret*. She is called *Elohim,* and *Tif'eret* is called *YHVH*; the verse *Know that YHVH is Elohim* proclaims their merging as one.

On the joy of the priests, see *Zohar* 1:116a; 3:8a–b, 39a; Rashi on BT *Yoma* 14a, s.v. *mi la mitterid;* Ta-Shma, *Ha-Nigleh she-ba-Nistar,* 105, n. 3. On the singing of the Levites, see BT *Arakhin* 11a; *Zohar* 1:116a; 3:8a–b. See Moses de León, *Sefer ha-Rimmon,* 37, 63. On *Shekhinah* as Assembly of Israel, see above, pp. 122–23, n. 237.

425. **Nevertheless...** Even though *joy* and *singing* allude to specific *sefirot,* they still pertain in their literal sense. One should rejoice during prayer.

426. **Corresponding to these two...** *Joy* and *singing,* symbolizing respectively *Ḥesed* and *Gevurah,* correspond to the morning and afternoon prayers, and to the morning and evening sacrifices offered daily in the Temple. Whereas *Ḥesed* prevails in the morning, *Gevurah* (also known as *Din* [Judgment]) dominates toward darkness.

427. **evening prayer is optional...** According to Rabbi Yehoshu'a (BT *Berakhot* 27b), the evening prayer is optional. Here, Rabbi Yose offers a kabbalistic explanation: During the two daytime prayers (morning and afternoon), *Shekhinah* is embraced by *Ḥesed* and *Gevurah* and united with *Tif'eret,* who infuses Her with blessing. Now in the evening, *Shekhinah* distributes nourishment to Her angels and through them to the worlds below, so arousal by prayer is no longer required; She does not need to receive anything further.

See *Zohar* 1:132b–133a; 2:130a, 162a; Moses de León, *Sefer ha-Rimmon,* 50.

incense, as is said: *When he tends the lamps he shall burn it. And when Aaron lights the lamps at twilight he shall burn it* (Exodus 30:7–8). In the morning for joy, as determined by the hour; in the evening to rejoice the left, as it should be—always coming only for joy.[428]

"Come and see: Incense binds bonds, spreading joy from above to below.[429] This eliminates death, accusation, and wrath, which cannot prevail in the world, as is written: *Moses said to Aaron, 'Take the fire-pan and place fire upon it from the altar and put in incense [and carry it quickly to the community and atone for them, for the fury has gone out from before* YHVH, *the plague has begun!]'* Following this is written: *Aaron took as Moses had spoken, and he ran [into the midst of the assembly, and, look, the plague had begun among the people! He put in incense] and atoned for the people.* And it is written: *He stood between the dead and the living, and the plague was halted* (Numbers 17:11–13)—for no evil aspect or accuser can withstand incense. So it is joy of all, nexus of all.[430]

"At the hour of *minḥah,* when Judgment prevails in the world, David concentrated in this prayer, as is written: *May my prayer be set as incense.* This prayer ascends and eliminates the wrath of harsh Judgment dominant now at this time—like that incense that dispels and eliminates all wrath and accusation in the world. Why? Because it is מנחת ערב (*minḥat erev*), *evening offering,* when Judgment hangs over the world.[431]

428. **incense comes only for joy...** In the morning, characterized by *Hesed,* incense appropriately brings joy. In the evening, characterized by *Gevurah,* incense brings joy by tempering the harsh judgment of the left side.

The verses from Exodus, describing the burning of incense on the altar, read: *Aaron shall burn upon it aromatic incense, morning after morning, when he tends the lamps he shall burn it. And when Aaron lights the lamps at twilight he shall burn it, perpetual incense before* YHVH *throughout your generations.* The lighting of the lamps and the incense parallel the *oil and incense* mentioned in Proverbs.

See *Zohar* 3:8a, 11a, 30b, 105a, 149a, 150a, 151b, 177b. The word in the verse in Exodus בהיטיבו (*be-heitivo*), *when he tends,* is understood here as *when he lights.* See Maimonides, *Mishneh Torah, Hilkhot Temidin* 3:12; Ezra of Gerona, *Peirush Shir ha-Shirim,* 485; Azriel of Gerona, *Peirush ha-Aggadot,* 89; Jacob ben Sheshet, *Meshiv Devarim Nekhoḥim,* 166, 194; *Zohar* 1:16b; 3:11a, 150a; Moses de León, *Sefer ha-Rimmon,* 86, 196 (and Wolfson's note); *MM*; *NZ*; Scholem, *Origins of the Kabbalah,* 292.

429. **Incense binds bonds...** Rabbi Ḥizkiyah connects the Hebrew word קטרת (*qetoret*), "incense," with the Aramaic root קטר (*qtr*), "to tie, knot." Incense links the *sefirot,* spreading joy throughout all worlds.

See *Zohar* 2:219a; 3:11a–b, 37b, 58b, 151b, 177b; Moses de León, *Sefer ha-Rimmon,* 86–87.

430. **eliminates death...** Incense neutralizes demonic power.

See *Zohar* 2:218b; 3:151b; Moses de León, *Sefer ha-Rimmon,* 87. According to BT *Shabbat* 89a (in the name of Rabbi Yehoshu'a son of Levi), the Angel of Death himself transmitted the secret of incense to Moses.

431. **At the hour of *minḥah*...** *Minḥah* (literally, "offering") refers to the afternoon prayer. As evening approaches, the power of

"Come and see: When the Temple was destroyed, the hour it was burned was the time of *minḥah*. Of this is written *Woe to us, for the day is fading, shadows of evening spread!* (Jeremiah 6:4). Who are *shadows of evening*? Those accusers in the world and wrathful powers of Judgment lying in wait at that hour.[432] Concerning this we have learned that one should concentrate his mind in the prayer of *minḥah*—in all prayers one should concentrate his mind, but more so in this prayer because Judgment hangs over the world. Therefore, the time of the *minḥah* prayer was instituted by Isaac, as they have established."[433]

While they were walking, they reached a mountain. Rabbi Yose said, "This mountain is frightening! Let's go on and not linger here because the mountain is terrifying!"

Rabbi Yehudah replied, "If there were one [of us], I would say so, for we have learned that whoever walks alone on the way is liable to death.[434] But we are three, and each and every one of us is worthy of being accompanied by *Shekhinah*!"

388 Rabbi Yose said, "But we have learned that a person should not rely on a miracle! How do we know this? From Samuel, as is written: *How can I go? If Saul hears, he will kill me* (1 Samuel 16:2), and Samuel was more worthy than we are."[435]

harsh Judgment strengthens, and this prayer assuages its threatening wrath, like the incense. This is why David linked *minḥah*—and not the morning prayer—with incense.

See *Zohar* 1:95b, 132b; Tishby, *Wisdom of the Zohar*, 3:963. Rabbi Ḥizkiyah is apparently playing with תכון (*tikkon*), *may [my prayer] be set*, and אתכוון (*itkavvan*), "he concentrated" in his prayer.

432. **When the Temple was destroyed...** See BT *Ta'anit* 29a: "On the seventh [of Av] the heathens [the Babylonians] entered the Temple, ate there, and desecrated it throughout the seventh and eighth. Toward dusk on the ninth, they set fire to it, and it continued burning all that day, as is said: *Woe to us, for the day is fading, shadows of evening spread!*"

See *Zohar* 1:132b; 2:21b; 3:75a, 270a. The verse in Jeremiah opens: *Prepare for battle against her! Arise, let us attack at noon!*

433. **one should concentrate...** See BT *Berakhot* 6b, in the name of Rav Huna: "One should always be conscientious about the prayer of *minḥah*, since Elijah was answered only during this prayer."

See above, p. 112 and n. 182; *Zohar* 1:132b; 2:36b; 3:64b; Moses de León, *Sefer ha-Rimmon*, 67, 87.

According to BT *Berakhot* 26b (in the name of Rabbi Yose son of Rabbi Ḥanina), the three daily prayers were instituted by the patriarchs. Isaac, symbolizing *Gevurah*, appropriately instituted the prayer of *minḥah*, when this *sefirah* prevails.

434. **whoever walks alone...** See M *Avot* 3:4 (in the name of Rabbi Ḥanina son of Ḥakhinai): "One who walks on the way alone... is liable to the death penalty."

435. **not rely on a miracle...** In the book of Samuel, God commands the prophet to go and anoint one of Jesse's sons (David) as king. This verse reads: *Samuel said, "How can I go? If Saul hears, he will kill me." YHVH replied, "Take a heifer with you, and say, 'I have come to sacrifice to YHVH.'"* Samuel fears that King Saul will kill him for the subversive act of anointing another as king; the sacrifice serves to disguise Samuel's mission.

Here Rabbi Yose indicates that Samuel did not want to rely on a miracle from God to

He replied, "Even so, he was alone and the danger was obvious, whereas we are three and there is no danger in sight.[436] As for demons, we have learned that they do not appear to three and inflict no harm at all.[437] As for robbers, they are not to be found here, since this mountain is remote from civilization and there are no people here. But there is a fear of prowling wild beasts."

He opened, saying, "*The angel redeeming me from all evil* (Genesis 48:16). This verse calls for contemplation. *Redeeming*—the verse should read *who redeemed*. Why *redeeming*? Because this one is constantly present with human beings, never departing from a virtuous person. Come and see: *The angel redeeming me*—*Shekhinah*, constantly accompanying a person, never departing, as long as he walks the way of truth and observes the *mitsvot* of Torah.[438] Therefore, one should be careful not to go out alone on the way. What is 'alone'? One should be careful to observe the *mitsvot* of Torah, so that *Shekhinah* will not withdraw from him and he be forced to go alone—without coupling of *Shekhinah*.

"Come and see: When a person sets out on his way, he should arrange his prayer before his Lord in order to draw *Shekhinah* upon himself; then he can set out and he will find coupling of *Shekhinah*, to deliver him on the way, to save him whenever necessary.[439] What is written of Jacob? *If Elohim will be with me*—coupling of *Shekhinah*. *And watch over me on this way* (Genesis 28:20)—deliv-

save him from Saul's wrath. God's response obviates the need for a miracle. See above, p. 281 and n. 127. On not relying on miracles, see also BT *Shabbat* 32a, *Pesaḥim* 64b; *Zohar* 1:111b.

436. **he was alone and the danger was obvious...** Samuel's act of anointing David was bound to arouse Saul's anger. See BT *Qiddushin* 39b.

437. **demons... do not appear to three...** See BT *Berakhot* 43b: "To one person, [a demon] shows himself and causes harm; to two, he shows himself but does not cause harm; to three, he does not show himself at all."

438. **verse should read *who redeemed*...** With these words, Jacob was presumably referring to times in the past when God redeemed him, for example, from Esau and Laban. Why, then, is the verb in the present tense? The answer is that *Shekhinah* (*the angel redeeming me*) constantly accompanies one who is virtuous.

On God's having redeemed Jacob in the past, see *Shemot Rabbah* 32:9. On the present tense of the verb, see Rashi on Genesis 48:16. On *Shekhinah* as "angel," see above, p. 167 and n. 516.

439. **When a person sets out...** One who is beginning a journey should pray, including (or specifically) *Tefillat ha-Derekh* ("The Prayer for the Way"). See BT *Berakhot* 29b: "Elijah said to Rav Yehudah the brother of Rabbi Sala the Ḥasid, 'Do not let your anger boil and you will not sin; do not get drunk and you will not sin; and when you set out on the way, consult your Creator and then set out.' What is meant by 'consult your Creator and then set out'? Rabbi Ya'akov said in the name of Rav Ḥisda, 'This is *Tefillat ha-Derekh*.'" By praying, one ensures that *Shekhinah* will join him and protect him throughout his journey.

See BT *Berakhot* 14a, 30a; *Zohar* 1:49b, 58b, 121a (*MhN*), 178a, 240b; 2:130b; Galante; Vol. 1, p. 275, n. 1292.

ering me from everything.[440] Now, Jacob was alone [230b] at that time, yet *Shekhinah* walked before him; all the more so, Companions sharing words of Torah!"[441]

Rabbi Yose said, "What should we do? If we linger here—look, the day is sinking! If we go on—it's a huge mountain and I am frightened by fear of wild beasts!"

Rabbi Yehudah said, "I'm astonished at you, Rabbi Yose!"

He replied, "But we have learned that one should not rely on a miracle—expecting that the blessed Holy One will perform miracles all the time."[442]

He said, "This applies to one who is alone, but as for three—with words of Torah passing between us and *Shekhinah* along with us—we have nothing to fear."[443]

As they were walking, they saw up on the mountain a cliff in which was a cave. Rabbi Yehudah said, "Let's climb up to that cliff, because I see a cave there."

They climbed there and saw the cave. Rabbi Yose said, "I'm scared that this cave might be a lair for beasts, who could attack us here!"

Rabbi Yehudah said to Rabbi Ḥizkiyah, "I see that Rabbi Yose is frightened. You might say this is because he's a sinner—since anyone frightened is a sinner, as is written: *Sinners in Zion are frightened* (Isaiah 33:14).[444] But he is not a sinner! And it is written *The righteous are as confident as a young lion* (Proverbs 28:1)."

Rabbi Yose said, "Because danger is apparent!"[445]

He replied, "If danger is apparent, so it is; but here danger is absent. And once we enter the cave, no harm will enter to torment us."

440. ***If Elohim will be with me...*** Referring to *Shekhinah*, who is called by this divine name.

The context (28:20–21) reads: *Jacob made a vow, saying, "If Elohim will be with me and watch over me on this way that I go and give me bread to eat and clothing to wear, and if I return in peace to my father's house, then YHVH will be to me Elohim.*

441. **all the more so, Companions...** Rabbi Yehudah reassures Rabbi Yose that *Shekhinah* is surely accompanying them because they are engaged in Torah.

See M *Avot* 3:2: "Rabbi Ḥananya son of Teradyon says, '... If two are sitting engaged in words of Torah, *Shekhinah* dwells between them.'" Cf. ibid, 6, specifying three engaged in Torah.

442. **one should not rely on a miracle...** See BT *Megillah* 7b, in the name of Rabbi Zeira: "Miracles do not happen every moment."

See BT *Pesaḥim* 50b, 64b; *Zohar* 1:111b; above, note 435.

443. **three—with words of Torah...** See above, note 441.

444. **anyone frightened is a sinner...** See BT *Berakhot* 60a; above, p. 78 and n. 525 (where Rabbi Yitsḥak is frightened in similar circumstances).

445. **danger is apparent...** Rabbi Yose tries to explain his fear. According to rabbinic tradition, when danger is obvious one should not rely on miracles.

See BT *Pesaḥim* 8b; *Qiddushin* 39b; *Zohar* 1:112b; above, notes 435–36, 442.

They entered the cave. Rabbi Yehudah said, "Let us divide the night into the three watches that it comprises. Each one of us will stand at his post during these three aspects of the night and we will not sleep."[446]

Rabbi Yehudah opened, saying, "משכיל לאיתן (*Maskil le-Eitan*), *A maskil of Ethan, the Ezrahite* (Psalms 89:1).[447] This praise was uttered by Abraham when he devoted himself to the service of the blessed Holy One and acted in love toward the inhabitants of the world, so that all would perceive that the blessed Holy One reigns over earth. He is called איתן (*Eitan*), Strong, because he grasped the blessed Holy One strongly.[448]

"*Of YHVH's love I will sing forever*... (ibid., 2). Now, does one come to sing from the side of love?[449] Well, here left side and right coalesced. That is why the blessed Holy One tested Abraham and examined him. As has been said, Isaac was thirty-seven years old at the time, so why *tested Abraham* (Genesis 22:1)? The verse should read *tested Isaac*! However, *tested Abraham*—so that he would manifest Judgment, merge with Judgment, becoming fittingly complete. So, *Of YHVH's love I will sing forever*.[450]

446. **three watches that it comprises...** According to BT *Berakhot* 3a (in the name of Rabbi Eli'ezer), the night is divided into three watches. Here, Rabbi Yehudah proposes that the three Companions stay awake all night and take turns expounding words of Torah.

447. **משכיל לאיתן (*Maskil le-Eitan*)...** The context (89:1–5) reads: *A maskil of Ethan the Ezrahite. Of YHVH's love I will sing forever; to all generations I will proclaim Your faithfulness with my mouth. I declare, "Forever is love established; in the heavens You set up Your faithfulness." "I have made a covenant with My chosen one, I have sworn to David, My servant. I will establish your seed forever, I will build your throne for all generations." Selah.*

The word משכיל (*maskil*) is a literary or musical term whose precise meaning is unclear. Ethan was a Temple musician.

448. **uttered by Abraham...** In rabbinic literature Abraham is identified with Ethan. See *Vayiqra Rabbah* 9:1; BT *Bava Batra* 15a; *Pesiqta de-Rav Kahana* 4:3; *Zohar* 2:110a.

On Abraham's extreme hospitality and his efforts to spread the awareness of God, see *Bereshit Rabbah* 48:9; 54:6; BT *Sotah* 10a–b; *Avot de-Rabbi Natan* A, 7; *Tanḥuma, Lekh Lekha* 12; *Midrash Tehillim* 37:1; 110:1.

449. **does one come to sing...** Song is associated with the Levites and with *Gevurah* on the left side of the sefirotic tree, not with *Ḥesed* (Love) on the right side.

450. **left side and right coalesced...** Abraham symbolizes *Ḥesed*. To become complete, he was tested by God and commanded to sacrifice Isaac, in order to experience the dimension of *Gevurah*, or *Din* (harsh Judgment). By accepting this divine challenge, Abraham succeeded in integrating left and right, *Gevurah* and *Ḥesed*. Therefore he could utter this verse—*Of YHVH's love I will sing forever*—combining *Ḥesed* (*YHVH's love*) and *Gevurah* (*I will sing*).

See *Bereshit Rabbah* 55:1; *Zohar* 1:103b–104a, 118a–b, 119b (especially), 133b, 140a; 2:257a (*Heikh*). On Isaac's age at the time of his ordeal, see *Seder Olam Rabbah* 1; *Targum Yerushalmi*, Genesis 22:1; *Eikhah Rabbah, Petiḥta* 24; *Tanḥuma, Vayera* 23; *Tanḥuma* (Buber), *Vayera* 42; *Seder Eliyyahu Zuta* 2; *Pirqei de-Rabbi Eli'ezer* 31; Theodor's note on *Bereshit Rabbah* 55:4, 587–88.

See *Zohar* 1:103a: "Isaac was thirty-seven

"Alternatively, *Of YHVH's love I will sing forever*—those acts of love that the blessed Holy One performs for the world.

"*To all generations I will proclaim Your faithfulness with my mouth* (ibid.)—steadfast kindness that He confers upon all.

"*To all generations I will proclaim Your faithfulness*—faith in the blessed Holy One, which Abraham proclaimed throughout the world and evoked in the mouth of all creatures. So, *I will proclaim Your faith with my mouth.*[451]

"The blessed Holy One revealed to Abraham the mystery of faith, and when he knew the mystery of faith he knew that he was the root and sustenance of the world, for the sake of whom the world was created and endures, as is written: *I declare, 'The world is built on love'* (Psalms, ibid., 3).[452]

"Further, *I declare, 'The world is built on love'*—for when the blessed Holy One created the world, He saw that it could not endure, until He extended His right hand over it, and it endured. If He had not extended His right hand over it, it would not have endured, because this world was created by justice.[453]

years old, while Abraham was an old man, so if he [Isaac] had kicked with one foot he [Abraham] could not have withstood him. Yet he honored his father, allowing himself to be bound like a lamb to fulfill his father's will."

See *Zohar* 1:119b: "Here we should contemplate: *Elohim tested Abraham.* The verse should read *tested Isaac,* since Isaac was already thirty-seven years old and his father was no longer responsible for him. If Isaac had said, 'I refuse,' his father would not have been punished. So why is it written *Elohim tested Abraham,* and not *Elohim tested Isaac?*"

451. **faith in the blessed Holy One . . .** See above, at note 448.

452. **mystery of faith . . .** The secret realm of divine life culminating in *Shekhinah*. When Abraham comprehended this mystery, he understood that "he [or: it] was the root," i.e., that his *sefirah, Ḥesed,* was the foundation of existence. *Ḥesed* (Love) is the first of the seven lower *sefirot* issuing from *Binah,* the Divine Mother, and is identified with the first day of Creation. See *Zohar* 1:83b–85b.

The declaration in Psalms—עולם חסד יבנה (*olam ḥesed yibbaneh*)—is usually understood to mean *Forever is love established,* but here Rabbi Yehudah offers a midrashic reading with a kabbalistic twist: *The world is built on love,* namely, on the *sefirah* of *Ḥesed.*

See *Mekhilta, Shirta* 9; *Sifra, Qedoshim* 10:11, 92d; *Avot de-Rabbi Natan* A, 4; *Targum Yerushalmi,* Leviticus 20:17; JT *Yevamot* 11:1, 11d; BT *Sanhedrin* 58b; *Pirqei de-Rabbi Eli'ezer* 21; *Midrash Tehillim* 89:2; *Zohar* 2:166b; 3:77a, 133b (*IR*), 145b, 259b.

453. **it could not endure . . .** God created the world by the quality of justice because otherwise the moral order would disintegrate. However, if human beings were judged strictly, the world would be condemned to destruction, so God tempered justice with compassion. Here compassion is identified with *Ḥesed* (Love), God's right hand, which balances *Din* (Justice, Judgment), the divine left hand.

On justice as the foundation of the world, see M *Avot* 1:18; *Avot de-Rabbi Natan* B, 43; *Bereshit Rabbah* 14:1; *Shemot Rabbah* 30:13; above, p. 93; *Zohar* 2:122a; 3:30b, 32a; Moses de León, *Sefer ha-Rimmon,* 291, 345.

On the balancing of justice and compassion, see *Bereshit Rabbah* 12:15: "The blessed Holy One said, 'If I create the world by the quality of compassion, its sins will abound; by the quality of justice, the world will not endure. Rather, I will create it by both the

"As we have established, בראשית (*Be-reshit*), *In the beginning* (Genesis 1:1). This mystery is one whole, two aspects here. *Be-reshit*—although we have said that *reshit* is beginning from below to above, so too from above to below.[454] And we have said, 'בית ראשית (*beit reshit*), house of beginning'—as we say 'house of the Holy of Holies'—for this is a house for this *reshit, beginning*, a word merging as one.[455]

"By this בית (*beit*), house, this world was created, but it endured only through the right, as is written: *I declare, 'The world is built on love'*—namely, Abraham, as is written: בהבראם (*be-hibbare'am*), *when they were created* (Genesis 2:4). Do not read בהבראם (*be-hibbare'am*), *when they were created*, but rather באברהם (*be-Avraham*), *through Abraham.*[456]

"The first structuring of the world—that light of the first day, inhering within to sustain. Afterward, on the second day, on the left. Through these, the heavens were arrayed, as is written: *by them, You firmly establish the heavens* (Psalms, ibid.).[457]

quality of justice and the quality of compassion. Oh that it may endure!'" See *Bereshit Rabbah* 8:4; above, p. 93; Rashi on Genesis 1:1; *Zohar* 1:58b; 2:113b; 3:38a.

454. **one whole, two aspects...** The word בראשית (*be-reshit*), *in the beginning*, alludes to two "beginnings": the first *sefirah* from below to above (*Shekhinah*) and the first *sefirah* to emanate from above (*Ḥokhmah*). The first letter of בראשית (*be-reshit*)—ב (*bet*)—is a preposition meaning "in, with," but it also signifies the number two. Here Rabbi Yehudah probably intends both the prepositional and numerical senses, but the preposition he has in mind is "with": "With beginning, God created." With *Ḥokhmah*, God created the upper world; with *Shekhinah*, God created the lower world.

See *Zohar* 1:7b, 15a, 29a–b, 50b. On *reshit* (beginning) as *Ḥokhmah* (Wisdom), see *Targum Yerushalmi* (frag.), Genesis 1:1; *Bereshit Rabbah* 1:1; Vol. 1, p. 109, n. 12. On *be-reshit* as "with beginning," see Vol. 1, p. 110, n. 22.

455. **בית ראשית (*beit reshit*)...** Now the first letter of בראשית (*be-reshit*)—ב (*bet*)—is understood as the word בית (*beit*), "house of," alluding to *Binah*, who houses *Ḥokhmah*, known as "beginning."

See *Zohar* 1:15b, 29a, 50b. Alternatively, בית (*beit*), "house of," alludes to *Shekhinah*, who houses *Ḥokhmah*. See *OY*; *KP*. On the "house (or chamber) of the Holy of Holies," see above, note 417.

456. **By this בית (*beit*)...** The world was created by *Binah*, located on the left side, which is characterized by *Din* (Judgment, Justice). But as we have seen, the world could not endure based on justice alone, so left was balanced by right—by *Ḥesed* (Love), the *sefirah* of Abraham. See above, notes 452–53.

The verse in Genesis reads: *These are the generations of heaven and earth* בהבראם (*be-hibbare'am*), *when they were created*. According to Rabbi Yehoshu'a son of Korḥah (*Bereshit Rabbah* 12:9), the word בהבראם (*be-hibbare'am*), *when they were created*, is an anagram of באברהם (*be-Avraham*), "through Abraham," indicating that *heaven and earth* were created for his sake.

See *Zohar* 1:3b, 86b, 91b, 93a, 105b, 128b, 154b, 247a; 2:31a; 3:117a. Alternatively, בית (*beit*), "house of," refers to *Shekhinah*, through whom the world was created. See *OY*; *KP*.

457. **first structuring...** *Ḥesed*, the primordial light of the first day of Creation, sustained the world. The second day symbolizes *Gevurah*, on the left. *By them* (by the

"Alternatively, *by them, You establish the heavens* [and] *Your faithfulness—the heavens* were arrayed by *YHVH's love* (ibid., 2), and the mystery of faith was thereby arrayed, for She is arrayed only by heaven.[458]

"*I have made a covenant with My chosen one* (ibid., 4)—mystery of faith.[459]

"Alternatively, [231a] Righteous One, from whom blessings issue to all those below. All holy living beings are blessed from that flow streaming to those below; so, *I have made a covenant with My chosen one.*[460]

"*I have sworn to David, My servant* (ibid.)—mystery of faith who abides constantly with Righteous One. This is covenantal vitality of the worlds: they will never separate—except in time of exile, when flow of blessings is withheld, mystery of faith is incomplete, and all joys restrained.[461]

"From the moment night enters, joyous minstrels do not enter before the King. Yet although joyous minstrels do not arouse, they stand outside, chanting song.[462] And at midnight, when arousal ascends from below to above, the

synthesis of these two opposite elements), *Tif'eret* (known as *heavens*) came into being.

The verset in Psalms is normally understood to mean *in the heavens You establish* [or: *set up*] *Your faithfulness* (see above, note 447). For the reinterpretation here, see Galante. For other interpretations, see *OY*; *KP*; *Sullam.*

458. ***by them, You establish...*** According to this interpretation, divine love constituted *Tif'eret* (*heavens*), who then conveyed this love to *Shekhinah* ("mystery of faith").

459. ***I have made a covenant...*** Apparently, *Shekhinah* ("mystery of faith") is the *covenant* made with King David, *My chosen one.*

On *Shekhinah* as covenant, see above, note 363. For another interpretation, see Galante.

460. **Righteous One...** According to this alternative interpretation, the covenant is *Yesod,* the divine phallus and site of the covenant of circumcision. He transmits the flow of blessing (via *Shekhinah*) to the celestial beings and all creatures below. Here Rabbi Yehudah may be reading בְּחִירִי (*beḥiri*), *My chosen one,* as בְּחִירַי (*beḥirai*), *My chosen ones,* referring to the celestial beings.

On *Yesod* as Righteous One, see above, p. 92, n. 50.

461. ***I have sworn to David...*** **mystery of faith...** King David symbolizes *Shekhinah* ("mystery of faith"), also known as *Malkhut* (Kingdom). Ideally, *Yesod* is joined with (*sworn to*) Her, and their covenantal union vitalizes and sustains the world; but during Israel's exile this union is interrupted, so the flow from *Yesod* ceases—leaving *Shekhinah* deprived and unable to convey blessing below.

"Covenantal vitality" renders קיומא (*qiyyuma*), whose range of meaning in the *Zohar* includes "existence, sustenance, life, vitality, pillar, covenant." See Galante; Liebes, *Peraqim,* 355–83.

462. **From the moment night enters...** The Companions are spending the night in a cave. Having mentioned exile, Rabbi Yehudah moves to a discussion of night, whose darkness resembles exile. At night, the joyous angels remain outside God's palace.

"Joyous minstrels" renders דחוון (*daḥavan*), attested by several manuscripts (M7, O2, R1) in the first sentence of this paragraph and numerous manuscripts (M7, N23, O2, P2, R1, V5) in the second sentence. The word, whose precise sense is unclear, is borrowed from a description of the agitated state of King Darius in Daniel 6:19: דחון (*daḥavan*) *were not brought before him.* In the biblical con-

blessed Holy One arouses all hosts of heaven to weep, and He kicks the firmament and all tremble above and below.[463]

"He finds no pleasure except when those below arouse in Torah. When they do, the blessed Holy One and all souls of the righteous listen to that voice; then He finds pleasure together with all those souls of the righteous.[464] For ever since the day that the Temple was destroyed below, the blessed Holy One has sworn that He will not enter Jerusalem above until Israel enters Jerusalem below, as is written: *The Holy One is in your midst, and I will not enter the city* (Hosea 11:9). This has been established by the Companions.[465]

"All those singers stand outside, chanting song during the three segments of the night, all offering specific praises.[466] All the host of heaven arouse at night, and Israel by day, and sanctification is not performed above until Israel sanctifies below. Once Israel has sanctified below, all the host of heaven sanctify the Holy Name in unison. Thus, holy Israel is sanctified by those above and those

text, conjectured meanings include "tables, food, songs or musical instruments, entertainment, concubines." Saadia Gaon, in his commentary on the verse, suggests that דחון (*daḥavan*) is simply a metathetic play on חדון (*ḥedvan*), "joys." Here in the *Zohar*, *ḥedvan* appears at the end of the preceding paragraph ("all חדון [*ḥedvan*], joys, restrained"), and later scribes and editors substituted this more common word for the unusual *daḥavan* in both sentences of this paragraph. It seems, though, that the author(s) of the *Zohar* intended to use *daḥavan* in these two sentences, while playing on *ḥedvan*.

See *Tosefta, Kelim, Bava Metsi'a* 5:3; *Zohar* 1:57a; 3:66a; Galante; Ben Yehuda, *Dictionary*, 2:916; Lieberman, *Tosefet Rishonim*, 3:47–48.

463. **at midnight...** God arouses the heavenly hosts to weep over the destruction of the Temple and the exile of Israel. The arousal ascending "from below" may refer to the mourning of humans, angels, or *Shekhinah* Herself.

See BT *Berakhot* 59a; *Zohar* 1:4a–b; 2:9a, 19a–b, 195b–196a; 3:172a–b; *ZḤ* 53b, 88a (*MhN, Rut*); Moses de León, *Seder Gan Eden*, 133; Galante.

464. **those below arouse in Torah...** When humans below rise at midnight to engage in Torah, God listens attentively along with the souls of the righteous in the Garden of Eden. On this midnight ritual, see above, pp. 77–78, n. 518; below, p. 398 and n. 479.

465. **He will not enter Jerusalem...** God participates in Israel's exile, having vowed that He will not enter the heavenly Jerusalem until Israel returns to the earthly Jerusalem. The verse in Hosea is apparently understood to mean that until God (*the Holy One*), or holiness, is present once again in Jerusalem (*in your midst*), He *will not enter* the heavenly Jerusalem (*the city*).

Here "heavenly Jerusalem" symbolizes *Shekhinah*. The blessed Holy One will not be reunited with Her until Israel returns from exile. Until then, His only pleasure consists in hearing Israel study Torah.

See BT *Ta'anit* 5a, and Rashi, ad loc.; *Tanḥuma, Pequdei* 1; *Midrash Tehillim* 122:4; *Zohar* 1:1b; 3:15b, 68b, 147b–148a. Cf. Revelation 21:2; *Targum Yonatan*, Psalms 122:3.

466. **three segments of the night...** The three watches of the night.

See BT *Berakhot* 3a, and Rashi, ad loc., s.v. *i kasavar*; above, at note 446; *Zohar* 1:188b–189a; 2:195b–196a; *ZḤ* 5d–6a (*MhN*); Moses de León, *Sefer ha-Rimmon*, 403; idem, *Sheqel ha-Qodesh*, 70–71 (88–89).

below, for the sanctity of the name of the blessed Holy One ascends only from above and below as one. Therefore, *You shall be holy, for I YHVH your God am holy* (Leviticus 19:2)."[467]

Rabbi Yose opened, saying, "*On what were her pedestals sunk, or who laid her cornerstone?* (Job 38:6).[468] This verse was spoken by the blessed Holy One, for when He created the world He created it solely upon pillars, the seven pillars of the world, as is written: *She has hewn her seven pillars* (Proverbs 9:1). Upon what those pillars stand is unknown, for that is a deep mystery, concealed of all concealed.[469]

"The world was not created until He took a certain stone—a stone called אבן שתיה (*even shetiyyah*), Foundation Stone. The blessed Holy One took it and cast it into the abyss, and it became lodged from above to below; from this the world disseminated. It is the central point of the whole world, and on this point stands the Holy of Holies, as is written: *or who laid her cornerstone?* (Job, ibid.). *Her cornerstone*—as is written: *a tested stone, precious cornerstone* (Isaiah 28:16), and similarly: *It has become the cornerstone* (Psalms 118:22).[470]

467. **sanctification is not performed above...** The angels do not sanctify God's name in heaven until the people of Israel have sanctified it on earth in the *Qedushah* (prayer of "sanctification").

The statement that "Israel is sanctified by those above and those below" apparently refers to heavenly powers and to Israel's own prayers, which stimulate sanctification above.

See BT *Ḥullin* 91b; *Zohar* 1:40a (*Heikh*), 90a (*ST*); 2:164b; 3:66a, 190b; Moses de León, *Sefer ha-Rimmon*, 91.

468. ***On what were her pedestals sunk...*** The context is God's response to Job out of the whirlwind. The subject of the pronoun *her* is the earth.

469. **seven pillars of the world...** The seven lower *sefirot*, emanating (*hewn*) from *Binah*, the Divine Mother. *Binah* and the realms above Her are hidden and unknowable.

See above, p. 133 and n. 302.

470. **Foundation Stone...** According to midrashic tradition, the world was created from this rock, located in the Holy of Holies in the Temple in Jerusalem. Here, the Foundation Stone symbolizes *Shekhinah*, the central point of the cosmos.

See M *Yoma* 5:2; *Tosefta, Yoma* 2:14; BT *Yoma* 54b; JT *Yoma* 5:2, 42c; *Vayiqra Rabbah* 20:4; *Pesiqta de-Rav Kahana* 26:4; *Pirqei de-Rabbi Eli'ezer* 35; *Zohar* 1:71b–72a; Vol. 2, p. 8, n. 53; Moses de León, *Sefer ha-Rimmon*, 333. On *Shekhinah* as the central point, see above, p. 383 and n. 416. The term Holy of Holies sometimes refers to the innermost of the seven heavenly palaces; see above, note 417.

"Disseminated" renders אשתיל (*ishshetil*), "was planted," which is a play on the rabbinic wording (in a number of the sources cited above, with variations): "from which the world הושתת (*hushtat*), was founded." See Moses de León, *Sheqel ha-Qodesh*, 74–75 (95); *Zohar* 1:72a, 78a, 82a; 2:48b, 222a; *ZḤ* 28a (*MhN*); Liebes, *Peraqim*, 372–73.

In the verse in Job, *laid* (*her cornerstone*) renders ירה (*yarah*), literally "cast," suggesting that God cast the stone into the abyss. The phrase in Isaiah, *tested stone* [or: *stone of testing*], symbolizes *Shekhinah*, by whom the righteous are tested. See *Zohar* 1:140b; 2:230a, 249b (*Heikh*); 3:168a; *KP*. Similarly, *Shekhinah* is symbolized by *the cornerstone* in Psalms:

"Come and see: This stone was created from water, fire, and air, crystallizing from them all, becoming a single stone. That stone stands over the abyss; sometimes waters flow from it, filling the abyss. This stone stands as a sign in the middle of the world.[471] This is the stone that Jacob erected and embedded—seedling and sustaining pillar of the world, as is written: *This stone that I set up as a pillar will be a house of Elohim* (Genesis 28:22).

"But did Jacob really set it up now? Surely it existed before the world was created! Rather, Jacob set up a sustaining pillar above and below; so it is written: *that I set up.* What does this mean? As is written: *will be a house of Elohim,* for he set up the abode of above here.[472]

"Come and see this stone that has seven eyes, as is said: *Upon one stone seven eyes* (Zechariah 3:9).[473] Why is it called שתיה (*shetiyyah*)? Because from it the world אשתיל (*ishshetil*), disseminated. שתיה (*Shetiyyah*)—שת יה (*shat Yah*), *Yah* set, for the blessed Holy One set it up as source of blessing for the world, because by it the world is blessed.[474]

"Come and see: As the sun sets, the cherubim standing in this place, dwelling miraculously, beat their wings above and spread them out, and the melody of their wings is heard above. Then those angels who chant song in the beginning of the night begin to play, so that the glory of the blessed Holy One ascends from below to above. What song is conveyed by the melody of the cherubim's wings? *Here, bless YHVH, all you servants of YHVH, who stand by night in the house of YHVH! Lift your hands toward the sanctuary and bless YHVH* (Psalms 134:1–2). Then, an opening for those supernal angels to sing.[475]

"At the second watch, these cherubim [231b] beat their wings above and the sound of their melody is heard, and then those angels standing in the second

The stone that the builders rejected has become the cornerstone. See above, p. 208 and n. 179.

471. **created from water, fire, and air . . .** *Shekhinah* is the culmination of the *sefirot,* in particular, of the triad of *Ḥesed, Gevurah,* and *Tif'eret,* symbolized respectively by water, fire, and air. She is symbolized by the fourth element, earth—or here, stone.

472. **stone that Jacob erected . . .** Although *Shekhinah* preexisted the world, Jacob united Her above with his *sefirah* (*Tif'eret*), thereby completing the upper world, and established Her firmly on earth as *a house of Elohim,* guaranteeing the sustenance of the world below. The divine name *Elohim* can refer to *Shekhinah,* but also to *Binah,* who manifests below through *Shekhinah.*

See *Zohar* 1:72a–b, 151a; 2:229b–230a. "Sustaining pillar" renders קיומא (*qiyyuma*); see above, note 461.

473. **seven eyes . . .** Symbolizing the seven lower *sefirot.*

474. **Why is it called שתיה (*shetiyyah*)? . . .** Rabbi Yose offers two imaginative etymologies. On the first one, see above, note 470.

475. **cherubim standing in this place . . .** The cherubim standing beneath *Shekhinah.* Their melody is followed by the singing of the angels above; so praise of God ascends "from below to above."

See above, p. 379 and nn. 399–400; *Zohar* 3:67a. On their miraculous posture, see BT *Bava Batra* 99a.

watch begin to play. What song is conveyed by the melody of the cherubim's wings at that moment? *Those who trust in YHVH are like Mount Zion, which cannot be shaken, abiding forever* (ibid. 125:1).[476] Then, an opening for those standing in the second watch to play.

"At the third watch, these cherubim beat their wings and chant song. What song is conveyed by the wings of those cherubs? *Hallelujah! Praise, O servants of YHVH, praise the name of YHVH! Blessed be the name of YHVH from now until eternity. From the rising of the sun to its setting, the name of YHVH is praised* (ibid. 113:1–3). Then all those angels standing in the third watch chant song, and all the stars and constellations of heaven open in song, as is said: *When the morning stars sang together, and all the sons of Elohim shouted for joy* (Job 38:7), and similarly: *Praise Him, all stars of light!* (Psalms 148:3)—for they are stars of light empowered to sing as morning approaches. Following them, Israel takes up song below, and the glory of the blessed Holy One ascends from below and from above—Israel below by day, supernal angels above by night—and thus the holy name is perfected on all sides.[477]

"As for this stone that we have mentioned, all those supernal angels above and Israel below grasp this stone, and it ascends to be adorned among the patriarchs by day.[478] At night the blessed Holy One comes to delight with the righteous in the Garden of Eden. Happy are all those who stand at their posts, engaging in Torah at night, for the blessed Holy One and all the righteous in the Garden of Eden listen to the voices of those engaged in Torah, as is written: *You who dwell in the gardens, companions listen for your voice; let me hear!* (Song of Songs 8:13).[479]

"Come and see: This stone is a precious stone, corresponding to what is written: *You shall set in it a setting of stones, four rows of stone* (Exodus 28:17).[480]

476. ***Those who trust in YHVH...*** Even in the dark of night, when powers of Judgment prevail.

477. **Israel takes up song...** Singing the morning prayers.

478. **this stone...** The Foundation Stone, *Shekhinah* (see above, p. 396 and n. 470). She ascends, accompanied by Israel (through their prayers) and the angels, and joins the triad *Ḥesed, Gevurah,* and *Tif'eret,* symbolized by the three patriarchs. *Shekhinah* rules the night; *Tif'eret* rules the day.

479. **delight with the righteous...** God delights each night with the souls of the righteous in the Garden of Eden, and both He and they listen to those who rise at midnight to study Torah.

The verse from Song of Songs is applied to the study of Torah in BT *Shabbat* 63a: "Rabbi Abba said in the name of Rabbi Shim'on son of Lakish, 'When two disciples of the wise listen to one another in *halakhah,* the blessed Holy One listens to their voice, as is said: *You who dwell in the gardens, companions listen for your voice; let me hear!*'"

See above, p. 395 and n. 464; *Zohar* 1:77b, 92a, 178b, 207b; 2:46a; 3:13a, 22a, 213a.

480. **precious stone...** *Shekhinah,* the Foundation Stone, is also known as "precious stone," and She is surrounded by twelve angels, symbolized by the twelve precious stones arranged in four rows in the breastplate of the high priest. Each of those stones was engraved with a name of one of the twelve tribes.

See *Zohar* 1:147b, 149b (*ST*); 2:229b–230a.

These are the rows of precious stone, settings of precious stone, for there is another stone, of which is written *I will remove the heart of stone from your flesh and give you a heart of flesh.* And it is written: *I will put My spirit within you* (Ezekiel 36:26–27). This is *a tested stone, precious cornerstone* (Isaiah 28:16).[481] Of this mystery is written *tablets of stone* (Exodus 31:18), for those tablets were hewn from here and are therefore named after this stone.[482] This is the mystery written: *From there feeds Stone of Israel* (Genesis 49:24). Surely this one is called *Stone of Israel*, as has been said."[483]

Rabbi Ḥizkiyah opened, saying, "*The stones were according to the names of Israel's sons, twelve according to their names, seal engravings, each with its name for the twelve tribes* (Exodus 39:14).[484] *The stones*—precious, supernal stones called *stones of the place*, as is said: *He took of the stones of the place and put them at his head* (Genesis 28:11), as they have established.[485]

"*According to the names of Israel's sons*—as there are twelve tribes below, so too above are twelve tribes, which are twelve precious stones. And it is written: *There tribes ascend, tribes of* Yah, *a testimony to Israel*—Israel, mystery above—all *to praise the name of* YHVH (Psalms 122:4). So, *The stones were according to the names of Israel's sons, twelve according to their names.*[486]

On *Shekhinah* as "precious stone," see *Zohar* 2:184b; 3:152b.

481. **another stone...** The demonic force manifesting within a person as the evil impulse. Countering and eventually overcoming this demonic power is *Shekhinah*, identified with the Holy Spirit and called *tested stone, precious cornerstone* (see above, note 470).

482. ***tablets of stone...*** Describing the tablets Moses received on Mount Sinai: *tablets of stone inscribed by the finger of God.*

According to rabbinic tradition, the *tablets of stone* were made of sapphire. Here, they are said to derive from the precious stone of *Shekhinah*. See *Sifrei*, Numbers 101; *Vayiqra Rabbah* 32:2; *Qohelet Rabbah* on 10:20; *Tanḥuma, Ki Tissa* 29; Galante.

483. ***From there feeds Stone of Israel...*** The verse reads: *From there,* רועה (*ro'eh*), *the Shepherd, Stone of Israel.* But Rabbi Yose interprets *ro'eh*—whose plain sense is a noun—as a participle that means "feeds, grazes," taking the verse to mean that *Shekhinah* (*Stone of Israel*) *feeds* from *Yesod*.

See *Bahir* 133 (193); *Zohar* 1:146b, 246b.

484. ***The stones were according to the names...*** In the breastplate of the high priest. See above, note 480.

485. ***stones of the place...*** The full verse describes Jacob's journeying: *He encountered a certain place and stayed there for the night because the sun had set, and he took of the stones of the place and put them at his head and lay down in that place.* Here, Rabbi Ḥizkiyah identifies these stones with the twelve stones in the high priest's breastplate, which symbolize not only the twelve tribes but also the twelve angels beneath *Shekhinah*.

See above, note 480; *Bereshit Rabbah* 68:11; *Zohar* 1:147b, 149b (*ST*); 2:229b–230a. Rabbi Ḥizkiyah is likely interpreting the word המקום (*ha-maqom*), *the place*, as referring to *Shekhinah*, based on the rabbinic divine name *Ha-Maqom*, "The Place," the Omnipresent.

486. **twelve tribes below, so too above...** Corresponding to the twelve tribes on earth, there are twelve tribes above, namely, twelve angels beneath *Shekhinah* who are known as "twelve precious stones." These heavenly beings testify to "Israel, mystery above," namely to *Tif'eret*, whose full name is *Tif'eret*

"Just as there are twelve hours in the day, so there are twelve hours in the night. Twelve hours in the day, above; twelve hours in the night, below—all corresponding to one another. These twelve hours of the night are divided into three divisions, with countless shield-bearing deputies stationed beneath them, levels upon levels, all empowered by night, receiving food first.[487]

"Then, at midnight, two rows stand on this side and two rows on the other side, and a supernal spirit wafts between them.[488] Then all those trees in the Garden of Eden open in song, and the blessed Holy One enters the Garden, as is written: *Then the trees of the forest will sing for joy before YHVH, for He comes to judge the earth* (1 Chronicles 16:33), corresponding to what is said: *With righteousness He will judge the poor* (Isaiah 11:4), for judgment enters among them, filling the Garden.[489]

"A north wind arouses in the world and joy prevails; that wind blows on those spices and aromas rise above.[490] The righteous are adorned fittingly in their crowns and bask in the radiance of the resplendent speculum. Happy are the righteous who attain that supernal light! The radiance of the resplendent speculum shines in all directions, and every single one of those righteous absorbs his appropriate share, each one glowing according to the deeds he has

Yisra'el (Beauty of Israel). *The name of YHVH* often refers to *Shekhinah*.

See above, p. 119 and n. 221, pp. 120–21 and n. 227; *Zohar* 1:155a, 157b–158a, 240b–241b; 2:229b; 3:78a, 118b; *ZḤ* 26b (*MhN*); Moses de León, *Sheqel ha-Qodesh*, 34 (41); idem, commentary on the ten *sefirot*, 366b.

487. **twelve hours in the day . . . in the night . . .** The hours of the day correspond to *Tif'eret*, the hours of the night to *Shekhinah*. During the three watches of the night, angels serve and sing, while beneath them stand countless forces who receive sustenance from *Shekhinah*.

On the three watches (or divisions) of the night, see above, p. 395 and n. 466.

488. **at midnight, two rows . . .** Midnight falls in the middle of the second four-hour watch of the night. Here two rows of angels correspond to the two hours preceding midnight, and two other rows to the two hours following midnight. (The "rows" of angels are symbolized by the *rows of stone* in Exodus 28:17. See *Targum Onqelos*, ad loc.; above, at note 480.)

489. **trees in the Garden of Eden open in song . . .** Greeting the blessed Holy One, who enters among them in preparation for uniting with *Shekhinah*. Although their union is consummated in the morning, it is already described (or prefigured) here by various names and symbols. *Tif'eret*, the blessed Holy One, is known as משפט (*mishpat*), "judgment," and the one who comes *to judge*. *Shekhinah* is known as the Garden of Eden, *earth*, *righteousness*, and also *poor*—because She has nothing of Her own and is dependent on the flow of blessing from above.

On the trees opening in song, see *Pereq Shirah*, 2:57, 80; JT *Ḥagigah* 2:1, 77a; BT *Ḥagigah* 14b; *Zohar* 1:7a, 77a; 3:22b; Moses de León, *Seder Gan Eden*, 138.

490. **north wind arouses . . .** Symbolizing *Gevurah*, who arouses passion.

On the north wind and midnight, see BT *Berakhot* 3b: "Rabbi Shim'on the Ḥasid said, 'There was a harp suspended above [King] David's bed. As soon as midnight arrived, a north wind came and blew upon it, and it played by itself. He immediately arose and engaged in Torah until the break of dawn.'"

performed in this world.[491] Some of them are ashamed because of the additional radiance received by a companion, [232a] as we have established.[492]

"Divisions of the night. As night begins to enter, numerous wardens of law arouse, roaming the world, and openings are shut. Afterward, various kinds according to their species, as we have established.[493] Then at midnight, the side of the north descends from above to below and grasps the night until two divisions of night have passed. Afterward, the side of the south arouses until morning arrives, and when morning arrives, south and north grasp it. Israel come below, raising Her above with their prayers and supplications until She ascends and is treasured away between them, receiving blessings from the head of all heads, blessed with dew flowing from above. That dew is distributed in many directions, nourishing countless myriads. By that dew, the dead are destined to be revived in the world that is coming, as is written: *Awake and shout for joy, O dwellers in the dust! For Your dew is a dew of lights* (Isaiah 26:19) —dew of those supernal lights shining above."[494]

491. **righteous are adorned...** See BT *Berakhot* 17a: "A pearl in the mouth of Rav: 'In the world that is coming, there is no eating or drinking or procreation or business or jealousy or hatred or competition; rather, the righteous sit with their crowns on their heads, basking in the radiance of *Shekhinah*.'" See above, p. 349 and n. 258.

Here the righteous share in the ecstasy of the divine union, reveling in the radiance that issues from *Tif'eret*, who is called אספקלריא דנהרא (*ispaqlarya de-nahara*), "the resplendent speculum" (literally, "the speculum that shines").

Ispaqlarya derives from Greek *speklon*, "mirror, window-pane," and Latin *speculum*, "mirror." See BT *Yevamot* 49b: "All the prophets gazed through an opaque glass ["an *ispaqlarya* that does not shine"], while Moses our teacher gazed through a translucent glass ["an *ispaqlarya* that shines"]." See *Vayiqra Rabbah* 1:14. Cf. 1 Corinthians 13:12: "For now we see through a glass darkly, but then face-to-face." In the *Zohar*, *Tif'eret* is the *ispaqlarya* that shines, while *Shekhinah* is the *ispaqlarya* that does not shine on its own but rather reflects (or refracts or diffracts) the other *sefirot*. See above, p. 114 and n. 191; below, note 509.

492. **Some of them are ashamed...** See BT *Bava Batra* 75a: "Rabbah said in the name of Rabbi Yoḥanan, '...The blessed Holy One will fashion a canopy for each and every [righteous] person befitting his honor.'...Rabbi Ḥanina said, '...Each one will be scorched by the canopy of his fellow. Alas for such shame! Alas for such humiliation!'"

See *Zohar* 1:39a (*Heikh*), 130a; 2:246b (*Heikh*); Moses de León, *Shushan Edut*, 348; idem, *Sefer ha-Rimmon*, 374.

493. **Divisions of the night...** On the three divisions, see above, p. 395 and n. 466, p. 400 and n. 487. In the first half of the night, characterized by *Din* (Judgment), harsh "wardens of law" roam the world, followed by various other threatening forces.

"Wardens" renders גרדיני (*gardinei*), which derives from Castilian *guardián*, "guardian." See *Zohar* 1:34a, 203b; 2:65a, 245b (*Heikh*); 3:43a; Gikatilla, *Sha'arei Orah*, 75a; above, pp. 246–47, n. 401; Corominas, *Diccionario*, 3:246–48.

"Openings" apparently refers to openings of the Garden of Eden or the heavenly palaces. See above, p. 41, at note 289.

494. **at midnight...** Now the threatening aspect of night begins to change. The north (symbolizing the passion of *Gevurah*) grasps the night (symbolizing *Shekhinah*) un-

While they were sitting, midnight came upon them. Rabbi Yehudah said to Rabbi Yose, "Now the north wind arouses and night is split. Now is the time when the blessed Holy One yearns for the voice of the righteous in this world—those engaging in Torah. Now the blessed Holy One is listening to us right here! Let us not cease words of Torah!"[495]

He opened, saying, "*The angel redeeming me from all evil* (Genesis 48:16).[496] This has been discussed and established, but come and see! It is written: *Here, I am sending an angel before you* (Exodus 23:20).[497] This is the angel who is Redeemer of the world, protection of human beings. This is the one who arranges blessings for the whole world, receiving them first and then providing them in the world. Therefore, *Here, I am sending an angel before you*, and similarly: *I will send an angel before you and I will drive out* (ibid. 33:2).[498]

"This angel is sometimes male and sometimes female. When providing blessings, it is male and called Male—like a male providing blessings for a female, so He provides blessings for the world. And when it stands in judgment over the world, it is called Female—like a female who is pregnant, so She is filled with

til the end of the second watch of the night, two hours after midnight. The final watch of the night is dominated by *Ḥesed* (symbolized by south) as the light of day approaches. At daybreak, *Gevurah* and *Ḥesed* (the divine left and right arms) together grasp *Shekhinah* in preparation for Her union with *Tif'eret*. Then the people of Israel below, through their prayers, raise Her to be embraced fully by these two arms. As *Shekhinah* is united with *Tif'eret*, She receives a flow of dew from *Keter* ("head of all heads") and then conveys it below. This same dew will one day revive the dead.

See *Pirqei de-Rabbi Eli'ezer* 34: "Rabbi Yehudah said, '...In the time to come, the blessed Holy One will bring down a dew of revival, reviving the dead.... *For your dew is a dew of lights....*' Rabbi Tanḥum said, '...From where does it descend? From the head of the blessed Holy One. In the time to come, He will shake the hair of His head and bring down a dew of revival, reviving the dead, as is said: *I was asleep, but my heart was awake.... For my head is drenched with dew* (Song of Songs 5:2).'"

See BT *Shabbat* 88b; JT *Berakhot* 5:2, 9b; *Zohar* 1:118a (*MhN*), 130b–131a; 3:128b (*IR*), 135b (*IR*); above, pages 356–57.

495. **north wind arouses...** See the preceding note and above, p. 400 and n. 490. On God's listening to those engaged in Torah at this hour, see above, p. 395 and n. 464, p. 398 and n. 479.

496. **He opened...** Rabbi Yehudah opens with a verse describing Jacob's blessing of Joseph's sons. The context (48:15–16) reads: *He blessed Joseph and said, "The God before whom my fathers walked, Abraham and Isaac, the God who has tended me since I came to be until this day, the angel redeeming me from all evil—may He bless the lads!"*

497. ***Here, I am sending...*** The full verse reads: *Here, I am sending an angel before you to guard you on the way and to bring you to the place that I have prepared.*

498. **Redeemer of the world...** *Shekhinah*, who receives the flow of blessing from above and transmits it to the world.

On *Shekhinah* as angel, see above, p. 167 and n. 516. On Her role as redeemer, see above, p. 378 and n. 396. The full verse in Exodus 33 reads: *I will send an angel before you and I will drive out the Canaanite, the*

judgment and is then called Female. Thus sometimes it is called Male and sometimes Female, all one mystery.[499]

"Correspondingly, it is written: *flame of the whirling sword* (Genesis 3:24)—there are angels dispatched in the world who transform into various aspects: sometimes female, sometimes male, sometimes in judgment, sometimes in compassion, yet all in one aspect.[500] Similarly, this angel includes numerous aspects, and all colors of the world appear in this place. This is the mystery of *Like the appearance of the bow in the cloud on a rainy day, so was the appearance of the radiance all around—the appearance of the semblance of the glory of YHVH* (Ezekiel 1:28). Just as it includes all those colors, so it conducts the world."[501]

TOSEFTA.[502] Supernal beloved ones, masters of understanding, observe![503] Authorities proficient in blows on a nail, draw near to know![504] Who among you possesses eyes of discernment to perceive?

Amorite, and the Hittite and the Perizzite, the Hivite and the Jebusite.

499. **sometimes male and sometimes female...** Though usually depicted as female, *Shekhinah* also assumes roles that are traditionally male. In Kabbalah the quality of judgment is associated with the female.

Cf. the pun on עברה (*evrah*), "wrath," and עוברה (*ubbarah*), "pregnant," in BT *Berakhot* 29b; *Shir ha-Shirim Rabbah* on 5:6; *Devarim Rabbah* (ed. Lieberman), p. 49; *Tanḥuma, Vayera* 9; Moses de León, *Sefer ha-Rimmon,* 160. Cf. *Sifrei,* Deuteronomy 29; *Tanḥuma* (Buber), *Va'etḥannan,* add. 2.

500. ***flame of the whirling sword...*** The full verse reads: *He drove out the human and placed east of the Garden of Eden the cherubim and the flame of the whirling sword to guard the way to the Tree of Life.*

Here *whirling* is interpreted as "turning" from one aspect into another. See *Bereshit Rabbah* 21:9: "*Whirling*—changing: sometimes male, sometimes female; sometimes spirits, sometimes angels."

See *Zohar* 1:44a, 53b, 165a (*ST*), 237a; 2:264a (*Heikh*); 3:19b, 73b (*Mat*).

501. **all colors of the world...** *Shekhinah* (*glory of YHVH*) is a rainbow including the colors of the various *sefirot* above Her. She conducts the world below by expressing the qualities associated with these colors.

502. **TOSEFTA** "Addendum, Addenda." The *Matnitin* and *Tosefta* of the *Zohar,* strewn throughout the text, consist mostly of anonymous enigmatic revelations addressed to the Companions, urging them to open their hearts to the mysteries. The terseness of these passages recalls the style of the Mishnah. See Scholem, *Kabbalah,* 216; Gottlieb, *Meḥqarim,* 163–214.

The *Matnitin* and *Tosefta* are not formally part of the *Zohar's* running commentary on the Torah and will consequently be translated separately in a subsequent volume. I have included this passage of *Tosefta* here because it appears in this section of the *Zohar* in numerous manuscripts (including M7, N23, O2, P2, R1, V5). The passage apparently concludes with the quotation from Numbers 4, below at note 511.

503. **Supernal beloved ones...** Similar wording appears in *Zohar* 1:147a; 2:68b, 235b (all *Tos*); 3:270b (*Mat*).

504. **Authorities proficient in blows on a nail...** Conceivably, this cryptic phrase alludes to cracking the shells, mentioned below.

סיכתא (*Sikketa*) means "peg, nail." See BT

When it arose in the will of Secret of Secrets to emit three colors blended as one—white, red, and green—three colors as one commingled, trickling into one another.[505]

A spade below was painted, issuing from these colors. By this all colors are refracted—a vision to gaze upon, like the appearance of crystal: as a color penetrates, so it appears outwardly.[506]

These three colors revolve in this—color moving, ascending, descending—interlaced lusters inlaid within Her. Colors revolve, colors blending as one, raising Her above, above—ascending by day, descending by night. A burning lamp visible by night, by day its light concealed—hidden in 248 worlds, all moving because of Her from above to below, within 365 limbs, treasured away below.[507]

Whoever probes [232b] to find Her must break hidden winged shells and open gates.[508] Whoever attains seeing will see through knowing and under-

Eruvin 53a; *Zohar* 2:92a (*RM*). For other interpretations, see *OY*; *KP*; *DE*; Gottlieb, *Meḥqarim*, 213.

505. **When it arose in the will...** When the impulse arose within *Keter* (known as Will) to emanate the *sefirot*. Out of *Keter* emerges the primordial point (*Ḥokhmah*), which expands into the circle or palace of *Binah*, the Divine Mother. She generates three primary *sefirot: Ḥesed, Gevurah*, and *Tif'eret*, symbolized respectively by the colors white, red, and green. Within *Binah*, these three are still one; once they emerge, they still flow into one another.

506. **spade below... appearance of crystal...** *Shekhinah*, who is formed by emanation of the higher colors, is pictured as a spade or shovel, gathering them. She also resembles a crystal, which, though having no color of its own, refracts (or diffracts) light shining upon it.

On בדולחא (*bedulḥa*), "bdellium, crystal," see above, note 296.

507. **three colors revolve in this...** The colors of the sefirotic triad (*Ḥesed, Gevurah*, and *Tif'eret*) revolve within *Shekhinah*, raising Her to unite above by day, escorting Her below to rule by night. Her nighttime brilliance is not recognized by day. (See BT *Ḥullin* 60b: "What good is a lamp at noon?")

In rabbinic and medieval tradition the numbers 248 and 365 correspond to the 248 limbs of the body and 365 sinews (or 365 days of the solar year), as well as to the 248 positive and 365 negative commandments. Here, 248 apparently corresponds to *Tif'eret* (associated with the positive commandments), and 365 corresponds to *Shekhinah* (associated with the negative commandments).

On the 248 limbs (actually joints or bones covered with flesh and sinews), see M *Oholot* 1:8. On the significance of the 248 and 365 commandments, see BT *Makkot* 23b; *Pesiqta de-Rav Kahana* 12:1; El'azar of Worms, *Peirushei Siddur ha-Tefillah la-Roqeaḥ*, 679. For various interpretations of the passage here, see *OY*; *KP*; *DE*; *MmD*.

"Lusters" renders קסטרין (*qasterin*), a Zoharic neologism apparently derived from קסיטרא (*qasitra*) and Greek *kassiteros*, "tin." See *Targum Yerushalmi* and *Targum Yerushalmi* (frag.), Numbers 31:22; *Zohar* 1:125a, 151a, 168a; 2:24b; *Bei'ur ha-Millim ha-Zarot*, 186, 188; Gottlieb, *Meḥqarim*, 213.

508. **Whoever probes...** Whoever seeks to enter the realm of *Shekhinah* must first break through demonic forces blocking Her gates.

standing, like someone seeing from behind a wall—except for Moses, supernal faithful prophet, who saw eye to eye above in a place unknown.[509]

Whoever does not attain is thrust outside. Numerous bands of dazzling demons confront him, looming over him, removing him so that he cannot gaze upon the delight of the King.[510] Woe to the wicked, unworthy of gazing, as is said: *They shall not come in to see...* (Numbers 4:20).[511]

Rabbi Yehudah said, "I was contemplating, and look, through these radiancies souls of the righteous gaze when they cleave to this place! Through this place, they gaze at these colors ascending, merging as one. Happy is one who knows how to blend and unite them all as one, arranging everything where it should be above, above! Then a person is protected in this world and in the world that is coming."[512]

Rabbi Yose opened, saying, "*Mighty king who loves justice, it was You who established equity* (Psalms 99:4). *Mighty king*—blessed Holy One. *Who loves justice*—blessed Holy One.[513]

509. **seeing from behind a wall...** Only mediated vision of divine reality is possible—except for Moses who saw God face-to-face and eye-to-eye, attaining awareness of the highest sefirotic realms.

See Exodus 33:11; Deuteronomy 34:10; BT *Yevamot* 49b: "All the prophets gazed through an opaque glass, while Moses our teacher gazed through a translucent glass."

In the *Zohar* the "opaque glass" symbolizes *Shekhinah*. See above, note 491; *Vayiqra Rabbah* 1:14; Maimonides, Commentary to M *Sanhedrin* 10:1, *ha-yesod ha-shevi'i*; idem, *Shemonah Peraqim*, 7; *Zohar* 2:69a–b, 82a, 130b, 213a; 3:174b; *ZḤ* 39d. Here, the Aramaic word for "wall" is כותלא (*kutla*); elsewhere in the *Zohar*, *Shekhinah* is symbolized by the Hebrew term קיר (*qir*), "wall." See above, p. 377 and nn. 388–91.

510. **dazzling demons...** טהירין (*Tehirin*), from the Aramaic root meaning "brightness, noon." One class of demons is named טהרי (*tiharei*), "noonday demons."

See Psalms 91:6 and Rashi, ad loc; *Targum*, Song of Songs 4:6; *Targum Yerushalmi*, Numbers 6:24, Deuteronomy 32:24; *Zohar* 1:94a, 125a–b, 130b, 198b, 200a, 237b; 2:130a–b, 195b, 205a, 207a. The Hebrew root טהר (*thr*), "pure," lends this demonic name a euphemistic tone.

511. ***They shall not come in...*** The full verse reads: *They shall not come in to see the sanctuary* [or: *sacred objects*] *for even a moment and die.* In its original context, this verse applies to the Kohathites, a Levitical clan who was assigned to carry the sacred objects of the Tabernacle (such as the ark, table, candelabra, and altars) once these had been safely wrapped by the priests. The Kohathites were forbidden even to see the exposed sacred objects within the Tent of Meeting. Here, remarkably, the verse is transferred from the Levites to the wicked, who are deprived of gazing at the divine splendor.

512. **through these radiancies...** The righteous who cleave to *Shekhinah* gaze into the colors of *Ḥesed, Gevurah,* and *Tif'eret,* reflected (or refracted) within Her; then they see these colors ascending toward their respective *sefirot* above, uniting as three-in-one.

513. ***Mighty king*—blessed Holy One...** *Shekhinah* is called *king* because She rules

"*Mighty king*—the potency empowering the blessed Holy One is solely *justice*, for by *justice* He sustains the earth, as is said: *By justice a king sustains the land* (Proverbs 29:4).[514] Therefore, *who loves justice.* Assembly of Israel is empowered only by *justice*, because from there She is nourished and all blessings She receives, She receives from there. So, *Mighty king who loves justice*—all Her desire and love is toward *justice.*[515]

"*It was You who established* מישרים (*meisharim*), *equity*—mystery of two cherubim below, who align the world and render it habitable, as has been said."[516]

Rabbi Ḥizkiyah opened, saying, "הללויה (*Haleluyah*), *Praise Yah! Praise, O servants of YHVH, praise the name of YHVH!* (Psalms 113:1). This verse calls for contemplation. Since it says *haleluyah, praise Yah,* why *praise, O servants of YHVH*, and afterward *praise the name of YHVH*?[517] But so we have learned: One who praises another should praise him according to his honor; according to his honor, so should be his praise. And we have learned: Whoever praises another undeservedly causes his disgrace to be revealed. Therefore, whoever eulogizes a person should do so according to his honor and no more, otherwise out of his praise will emerge his disgrace. Praise should always accord with the person's honor.[518]

over the lower worlds. She shares the designation blessed Holy One with *Tif'eret,* who is known as *justice.*

On the formula "x—blessed Holy One; y—blessed Holy One," see *Vayiqra Rabbah* 30:9 and *Pesiqta de-Rav Kahana* 27:9, though naturally in these rabbinic sources the referent of each "blessed Holy One" is identical, whereas here each refers to a different *sefirah.*

514. **potency empowering the blessed Holy One...** *Justice* (*Tif'eret*) empowers the *mighty king* (*Shekhinah*), enabling this divine monarch to sustain the world. See above, p. 183 and n. 24; below, p. 440 and n. 662.

515. **Assembly of Israel...** *Shekhinah,* who is animated by *Tif'eret* and in love with Him. On Her name Assembly of Israel, see above, pp. 122–23, n. 237.

516. **two cherubim below...** The angelic creatures standing beneath *Shekhinah,* established by Her. By adorning Her and stimulating divine union, they ensure that *Shekhinah* nourishes and conducts the world below, which is now aligned with the world above. The word מישרים (*meisharim*), *equity,* derives from the root ישר (*yshr*), "to be straight."

On the adornment and arousal by the cherubim, see *Zohar* 1:18b, 156a (*ST*); *ZḤ* 86a (*MhN, Rut*).

517. **Since it says *haleluyah, praise Yah*...** Having said that all should praise God, why does the verse go on to specify *servants of YHVH* and then refer to another divine name? This seems repetitious.

See a similar question in *Zohar* 2:96a. Cf. Ibn Ezra on the verse.

518. **One who praises another...** Excessive praise can lead to disgrace or disparagement, either from the speaker himself (who might add "with the exception of this or that bad habit") or from listeners who may be aroused to counter the praise with criticism.

See BT *Arakhin* 16a: "One should never speak in praise of his neighbor, for through praising him he will come to disgrace him." On not exaggerating in a eulogy, see BT *Berakhot* 62a; Naḥmanides, *Torat ha-Adam,* in *Kitvei Ramban,* 2:82.

"Come and see: הללויה (*Haleluyah*), *Praise Yah*. Here is supreme praise of the Lord of all, a place no eye can penetrate to perceive or gaze, hidden of all hidden. Who is that? יה (*Yah*), a name supreme above all. So, הללויה (*haleluyah*), *praise Yah*—praise and name as one, fused as one.[519] Scripture conceals the matter by saying הללו (*halelu*), *praise*, and not specifying who. *Haleluyah*—to whom was this said? Well, just as *Yah* is concealed, so the praise that is offered is concealed, and those who praise—we do not know who they are. So it should be, all concealed in supernal mystery.[520]

"After concealing in supernal mystery, Scripture reveals by saying *Praise, O servants of YHVH, praise the name of YHVH!* For this is a place not as concealed as that supreme one, hidden of all hidden; this is a place called *name*, as is said: [*over*] *which is called the Name, name of YHVH* (2 Samuel 6:2). The first is concealed, unrevealed; this is concealed and revealed, and because it is capable of being revealed, Scripture specifies those who praise this place, saying that they are *servants of YHVH*, worthy of praising this place.[521]

"*Let the name of YHVH be blessed from now until eternity* (Psalms, ibid., 2). What is different here, leading Scripture to say יהי (*yehi*), *let* [*the name of YHVH*] *be*?[522] Well, יהי (*yehi*) is mystery of emanation from that supernal name that is concealed, which we have mentioned—יה (*Yah*)—until mystery of covenant: lower י (*yod*), resembling upper י (*yod*), beginning like end. So, יהי (*yehi*)—mystery of emanation from hidden of all hidden until the last rung. By

519. **Lord of all . . . יה (*Yah*) . . .** This particular divine name refers to *Ḥokhmah* and *Binah*—or to *Keter, Ḥokhmah,* and *Binah*. The crown of the י (*yod*) can allude to *Keter;* the י (*yod*) itself symbolizes the primordial point of *Ḥokhmah;* the ה (*he*), a feminine marker, points to the Divine Mother, *Binah*. The compound word הללויה (*haleluyah*), *praise Yah,* combines the directive *praise* with the name *Yah* seamlessly. See *Minḥat Shai* on the verse.

See BT *Pesaḥim* 117a: "Rabbi Yehoshu'a son of Levi said, 'The book of Psalms was uttered with ten expressions of praise. . . . The greatest of them all is הללויה (*haleluyah*), for it embraces name and praise simultaneously.'" See *Zohar* 1:178b; 2:173b; 3:101a; *Minḥat Shai* on the verse.

520. **Scripture conceals the matter . . .** Befitting the concealed nature of the name יה (*Yah*), the beginning of the verse does not specify the precise nature of the praise to be offered; nor does it reveal the identity of the praisers.

521. **place not as concealed . . .** The continuation of the verse refers to *Shekhinah,* who is known as *the name of YHVH*, because She conveys the identity of *YHVH*. Though She is normally concealed from creatures, compared to the highest *sefirot* She is revealed, so the verse appropriately specifies those who praise Her: *servants of YHVH*.

The verse in Samuel describes the ark, recaptured by King David from the Philistines. Ark too is a symbol of *Shekhinah;* see above, note 391.

522. **What is different here . . . יהי (*yehi*) . . .** Scripture could have used the single word יתברך (*yitbarekh*), "let it be blessed," rather than the two-word expression יהי . . . מבורך (*yehi . . . mevorakh*), "let it be . . . blessed."

this word, the entire act of Creation was fulfilled, as is said: יהי (*Yehi*), *Let there be, an expanse* (Genesis 1:6); *Yehi, Let there be, lights* (ibid., 14); *Yehi, Let there be, light* (ibid., 3).[523] In all those acts above is written *yehi*; in all the acts below, *yehi* is not written, because this mystery—emanation from supernal mystery, concealed of all concealed—is fulfilled only in those supernal entities above and is not mentioned regarding those [233a] lower entities below.[524] By this, the Holy Name is blessed in all. Therefore, יהי שם יהוה מבורך (*Yehi shem YHVH mevorakh*), *Let the name of YHVH be blessed, from now until eternity.*

"*From the rising of the sun to its setting, the name of YHVH is praised* (Psalms, ibid., 3). *From the rising of the sun*—supernal place from which the sun shines, illumining all; site of the supreme concealed head.[525]

"*To its setting*—place of binding, where faith is fittingly bound. From there issue blessings for all; from here, the world is nourished, as has been said. So this place stands poised to be nourished from above and blessed from there, yet all depends upon arousal from below, aroused by those *servants of YHVH* when they bless the Holy Name, as we have said. Therefore, of this one who is revealed is written *Praise, O servants of YHVH, praise the name of YHVH!*"[526]

Meanwhile, morning was glowing. They emerged from the cave, not having

523. **יהי (*yehi*) is mystery of emanation...** This word alludes to the entire stream of emanation, from the primordial point of *Ḥokhmah* (Wisdom), symbolized the first י (*yod*), through *Shekhinah*, known as "mystery of covenant," "central point," and "lower Wisdom," and symbolized here by the second י (*yod*). The potent command, יהי (*yehi*), "Let there be," appears three times in the opening chapter of Genesis, in connection with the creation of the "expanse" (or "firmament, vault of heaven"); the sun, moon, and stars; and the primordial light of the first day.

On *Shekhinah* as "mystery of covenant, see above, note 363. On Her designation as "point," see above, p. 383 and n. 416, p. 396 and n. 470. On י (*yod*) as the mark of the covenant of circumcision, see above, note 192. On *Shekhinah* as "lower Wisdom," see *Zohar* 1:141b, 207a; 2:235b; 3:61b, 182b, 289a (*IZ*), 290a (*IZ*), 296a (*IZ*); Moses de León, *Sheqel ha-Qodesh*, 75 (95); idem, *Sod Eser Sefirot Belimah*, 382. On *yehi*, see *Zohar* 1:16b; 2:177a (*SdTs*).

524. **acts above... acts below...** The sublime word יהי (*yehi*), *Let there be*, appears only in connection with the "supernal entities" *expanse, lights* (sun, moon, and stars), and the primordial *light*. Regarding the other, earthly acts of Creation in the opening chapter of Genesis, this word does not appear.

525. ***rising of the sun*—supernal place...** *Ḥokhmah* (or *Keter*), source of *Tif'eret* (*the sun*), who then illumines all. *Ḥokhmah* (or *Keter*) is pictured as "the supreme concealed head."

The root of the word מזרח (*mizraḥ*), *rising*, means "rise, come forth, shine."

526. **place of binding...** *Shekhinah*, where the entire sefirotic realm (the realm of "faith") is bound together. She draws from above and conveys below. This entire process depends, however, on human devotion and arousal from below.

On the necessity of "arousal from below," see *Zohar* 1:35a, 77b, 82b, 86b, 88a, 156b, 164a–b, 235a, 244a; 2:31b, 265a; 3:40b, 92a–b, 110b, 112b, 145a (*Piq*); Moses de León, *Sefer ha-Rimmon*, 144.

slept that night. They walked on the way, and when they came out of those mountains they sat down and prayed. They reached a village and stayed the whole day. That night they slept until midnight, and at midnight they rose to engage in Torah.[527]

Rabbi Yehudah opened, saying, "*He blessed them on that day, saying, 'By you will Israel bless'* (Genesis 48:20).[528] Why ביום ההוא (*ba-yom ha-hu*), *on that day*? It would have been sufficient to say *He blessed them*.[529] Further, לאמור (*lemor*), *saying*, is spelled with a ו (*vav*). Why this difference?[530]

"Well, it is a mystery! *He blessed them* ביום ההוא (*ba-yom ha-hu*), *by the day of He*—mystery of the rung empowered over blessings above. *Yom ha-hu, The day of He*—a day from the supernal place called הוא (*hu*), *He*. This is *yom ha-hu*, for there is no separation between *day* and *He*. Everywhere, *yom ha-hu* is two rungs —a higher and a lower rung, as one. So, when Jacob wished to bless Joseph's sons, he blessed them with the union of higher world and lower world as one.[531]

"לאמור (*Lemor*), *Saying*, with a ו (*vav*)—because *vav* is included between them.[532] He unified them with union above, as one, so that their blessings would be fulfilled. Afterward, he encompassed all as one: בך (*Bekha*), *By you, will Israel bless, saying*. What is בך (*bekha*)? *Bekha*, surely! Mystery of unification —at first from below to above: *yom ha-hu, the day of He*, from below to above; afterward descending to the middle: לאמור (*lemor*), *saying*, with a ו (*vav*), the middle; then descending below: *bekha, by you*. This is perfectly fitting: from below to above, from above to below.[533]

527. **at midnight they rose...** On this midnight ritual, see above, pp. 77–78, n. 518; p. 395 at n. 464; p. 398 at n. 479.

528. ***He blessed them...*** The full verse reads: *He blessed them on that day, saying, "By you will Israel bless, saying, 'May God make you like Ephraim and Manasseh'"—and he put Ephraim before Manasseh.* Even though Manasseh was Joseph's firstborn, Jacob blessed Ephraim first.

529. **Why ביום ההוא (*ba-yom ha-hu*), *on that day*?...** Isn't this obvious?

530. **לאמור (*lemor*), *saying*...** This word appears 306 times in the Torah; everywhere else it is spelled without a ו (*vav*) as לאמר. See *Minḥat Shai* on the verse.

531. **ביום ההוא (*ba-yom ha-hu*), *by the day of He*...** The phrase is understood to encompass *Shekhinah* and *Binah*. *Shekhinah* is the last of the seven cosmic "days" of Creation, transmitting blessing to the worlds below. She derives from *Binah*, who, being concealed, is referred to indirectly by the third-person pronoun הוא (*hu*), "He." The two of them are linked by *Tif'eret*.

The prefixed preposition ב (*be*) means "on" but also "by, with." The pronoun הוא (*hu*) means "he"; ההוא (*ha-hu*)—with the additional definite article, ה (*ha*)—is a demonstrative pronoun ("that"), but here Rabbi Yehudah insists on the literal meaning, "he." On *hu* as a name of *Binah*, see *Zohar* 1:154b, 156b, 158b; 2:114a, 221b; 3:171a (discussing *yom ha-hu*), 178a–b, 183b.

532. ***vav* is included between them** The letter ו (*vav*), whose numerical value is six, symbolizes *Tif'eret*, the core of the six *sefirot* from *Ḥesed* through *Yesod*. As mentioned in the preceding note, *Tif'eret* links *Binah* with *Shekhinah*.

533. **What is בך (*bekha*)?...** This word, whose numerical value is twenty-two, sym-

"*By you will Israel bless.* Who is *Israel*? Israel the Elder.[534] It is not written יבורך ישראל (*yevorakh yisra'el*), *will Israel be blessed*, but rather יברך ישראל (*yevarekh yisra'el*), *will Israel bless*, for Israel receives blessings from above and then blesses all through this lower rung—precisely, for he says, בך (*Bekha*), *By you, will Israel bless.*[535]

"*May God make you like Ephraim and Manasseh* (ibid.).[536] He put Ephraim first because Ephraim is called Israel.[537] How do we know? From the time when the tribe of Ephraim left before the completion of the enslavement in Egypt; they forced time and broke out of exile, and their enemies attacked and killed them—as is written: *Son of man, these bones are the whole house of Israel* (Ezekiel 37:11), as implied by *are the whole house of Israel.* Therefore he put Ephraim before Manasseh, and Ephraim journeyed on the west side.[538]

bolizes *Shekhinah,* who includes all twenty-two letters of the Hebrew alphabet, the elements of divine speech. Further, the second-person character of this word fits *Shekhinah,* who, being more accessible than *Binah,* can be addressed directly. See above, note 531.

When read in light of Kabbalah, the verse proceeds from below to above (*yom ha-hu* implying *Shekhinah* and *Binah*), then to the middle (*lemor* implying *Tif'eret*), and finally below (*bekha* implying *Shekhinah*).

534. **Israel the Elder** In midrashic literature this title refers to Israel the patriarch (Jacob), as opposed to the people Israel. Here, it designates *Tif'eret,* whose full name is *Tif'eret Yisra'el* (Beauty of Israel).

See *Bereshit Rabbah* 68:11; Moses de León, *Sheqel ha-Qodesh,* 42–43 (51).

535. **It is not written...** If the verb were written in the passive voice (*will be blessed*), then *Israel* would refer to the people Israel, who are to be blessed by the formula *May God make you like Ephraim and Manasseh* (see above, note 528). However, the active voice (*will bless*) suggests that *Israel* refers to *Tif'eret Yisra'el.* He receives the flow of blessing from above and conveys it to those below through *Shekhinah,* known as בך (*bekha*).

See *Zohar* 3:119b.

536. ***May God make you...*** The verse continues: *and he put Ephraim before Manasseh.* See above, note 528.

537. **Ephraim is called Israel** The tribe of Ephraim, descended from Joseph's son, was the main tribe of northern Israel and came to symbolize the entire northern kingdom. In several midrashic sources, Ephraim stands for the whole people of Israel.

See Isaiah 7:17; Jeremiah 31:9, 20; *Vayiqra Rabbah* 2:1; *Aggadat Bereshit* 5:3; *Zohar* 1:85a.

538. **when the tribe of Ephraim left...** According to rabbinic tradition, the Ephraimites miscalculated the divinely decreed length of the Egyptian bondage and made a premature exodus, for which they were punished, nearly all of them being killed by the Philistines. Eventually their dry bones were resurrected by Ezekiel. God's words to the prophet—*these bones are the whole house of Israel*—indicates that Ephraim is called Israel.

Because Ephraim epitomized all of Israel, Jacob favored him over his older brother Manasseh with the blessing of the firstborn. Consequently, in the wilderness of Sinai the tribe of Ephraim journeyed on the west, symbolizing *Shekhinah,* who is known as Assembly of Israel.

On the premature exodus of the Ephraimites, see *Mekhilta, Beshallaḥ, Petiḥta*; *Mekhilta de-Rashbi,* Exodus 13:17; *Targum Yerushalmi,* Exodus 13:17; BT *Sanhedrin* 92b; *Pesiqta de-Rav Kahana* 11:10; *Shir ha-Shirim Rabbah* on 2:7; *Shemot Rabbah* 20:11; *Pirqei*

"Come and see: In blessing Joseph's sons, why did he offer them blessings before blessing his own sons? From here we learn that the love for one's grandchildren is more precious than the love for one's children. That is why he expressed love toward his grandsons before his sons, blessing them first."

He blessed them on that day, saying. Rabbi Yose opened, "*YHVH* זכרנו (*zekharanu*), *is mindful of us; He will bless. He will bless the house of Israel*... (Psalms 115:12). *YHVH*, זכרנו (*zekharenu*), *our males, He will bless*—the men. *He will bless the house of Israel*—the women. For males should be blessed first, and then women; women are blessed only through blessings of the males, because when males are blessed, then women are blessed.[539]

"Or you might say, 'Look at what is written: *He will atone for himself and for his household* (Leviticus 16:6)—he must first atone *for himself* and afterward *for his household*, because she is blessed through him!'[540]

"Come and see: Women are blessed only through men, when the latter are blessed first; from that blessing, they are blessed. But how can we establish *He will bless the house of Israel*? Well, the blessed Holy One provides extra blessings to the male, so that the woman may be blessed through him. Constantly, [233b] the blessed Holy One gives extra blessings to a married male, so that the female may be blessed thereby. As soon as a man is married, he is given two portions: one for him and one for his female. He receives all: his share and the share of his female.[541]

de-Rabbi Eli'ezer 48; Naḥmanides on Exodus 12:42; Ginzberg, *Legends*, 6:2–3, n. 10. The identification of the Ephraimites with those who were resurrected by Ezekiel is found in BT *Sanhedrin* and *Targum Yerushalmi*.

On the significance of Ephraim's position in the journeying in the wilderness, see Numbers 2:18; *Bereshit Rabbah* 97:5; *Zohar* 3:119b. According to Rabbi Abbahu (BT *Bava Batra* 25a), "*Shekhinah* is in the west."

539. **זכרנו (*zekharanu*), *is mindful of us*...** In its plain meaning, this word in Psalms derives from the verb זכר (*zakhar*), "to remember, be mindful." Rabbi Yose rereads it as *zekharenu*, *our males*, based on the noun זכר (*zakhar*), "male." He then takes the phrase *the house of Israel* as referring to the women.

See *Mekhilta*, *Baḥodesh* 2 (where the similar phrase *the house of Jacob* is interpreted as referring to the women); Ibn Ezra and Radak on Psalms 115:12; *Zohar* 3:117b. On the notion that women are blessed through men, see BT *Berakhot* 51b.

540. **Or you might say...** Quoting a different verse to demonstrate the priority of male over female. The context of the verse is Aaron's sin offering. Here Rabbi Yose's point is that first atonement is made for the male (*himself*), and then for the female (*his household*). This interpretation derives from M *Yoma* 1:1, in the name of Rabbi Yehudah: "*He will atone for himself and for his household*—*his household* means 'his wife.'"

541. **how can we establish *He will bless the house of Israel*?...** From here it seems that women (*the house of Israel*) are blessed directly by God, not by men. The solution to this apparent contradiction is that God provides a double blessing to a married man, who then bestows blessing upon his wife.

See BT *Yevamot* 62b: "Rabbi Tanḥum said

"Come and see: *He blessed them on that day, saying*—blessing them and all who would later issue from them.

"לאמור (*Lemor*), *Saying*—with a ו (*vav*). Here, an allusion to the firstborn son: *My son, My firstborn is Israel* (Exodus 4:22); *Ephraim is My firstborn* (Jeremiah 31:8)—therefore, an extra *vav*."[542]

Rabbi Ḥizkiyah opened, "*Your eyes saw my embryo; in Your book they were all inscribed, days were fashioned—not one of them existing* (Psalms 139:16). This verse has been established in various places, but come and see![543] All those souls that have existed since the day the world was created stand in the presence of the blessed Holy One before descending to the world, in exactly the same form in which they later appear in the world. The bodily appearance of a human being existing in this world is the same above.[544]

"When that soul is about to descend into the world, she stands before the blessed Holy One in exactly the same form that she assumes in this world, and He adjures her to observe the *mitsvot* of Torah and not to violate His covenant.[545] How do we know that they stand before Him? As is written: *As YHVH lives, before whom I stood* (1 Kings 17:1)—*I stood*, precisely, as they have established. Therefore, *Your eyes saw my embryo*—before it appeared in the world.[546]

"*In Your book they were all inscribed*—for all those souls, in their forms, are all inscribed in a book.

"*Days were fashioned*—as they have established, *fashioned*, literally![547]

in the name of Rabbi Ḥanilai, 'Any man without a wife is without joy, without blessing, without goodness.'"

542. **לאמור (*Lemor*), *Saying*...** As indicated above (notes 530, 532), the extra ו (*vav*) in this word symbolizes *Tif'eret Yisra'el* (Beauty of Israel), the divine son who conveys blessing to *Shekhinah* and to all below. Ephraim, who is called Israel (above, at note 537), receives the extra blessing of the firstborn.

543. **This verse has been established...** See *Bereshit Rabbah* 24:2 and parallels; *Zohar* 1:121a–b (*MhN*).

544. **All those souls...** All souls destined to enter the world have already existed since Creation. They stand before God, each one clothed in an ethereal body resembling the physical body that she will assume on earth.

The simple sense of the word גלמי (*golmi*) in Psalm 139 is "my embryo" (or "formless mass"). In *Bereshit Rabbah* 24:2, it refers to Adam's original shapeless state. In *Vayiqra Rabbah* 29:1, *golem* describes Adam's body when it still lacked a soul. Here, it designates the soul's ethereal body, prefigured above.

See *Tanḥuma, Pequdei* 3; Rashi on BT *Ḥagigah* 12b, s.v. *ve-ruḥot unshamot*; *Zohar* 1:7a, 90b–91a, 227b; 2:11a, 96b, 161b; 3:43a–b, 61b, 104a–b; Moses de León, *Sefer ha-Rimmon*, 390; above, note 58.

545. **He adjures her...** See BT *Niddah* 30b; *Zohar* 1:76b (*ST*); 2:161b; 3:13b.

546. ***before whom I stood*...** The past tense implies that his (Elijah's) soul stood in God's presence before he was born.

See *Zohar* 3:68b; *ZḤ* 69a (*ShS*). The verse in 1 Kings 17 reads: *As YHVH lives, the God of Israel before whom I stood....* See 2 Kings 5:16.

547. ***Days were fashioned*... literally** From the moment that a person is born,

"*Not one of them*—in this world who can fathom the existence of their Lord fittingly.[548]

"Come and see: When a person proves himself worthy in this world through good deeds, those days of his are blessed above from the place called 'measure of his days.'"[549]

He opened, saying, "*YHVH, let me know my end, what is the measure of my days* (Psalms 39:5). This verse has been established, but come and see![550] *My end*—end of the right, linked with David.[551]

"*What is the measure of my days*—actually empowered over his days."[552]

Rabbi Yehudah said, "I have heard from Rabbi Shim'on that this verse was uttered for those days decreed for him from Adam—namely seventy. As has been said, he had no life at all, but Adam offered David some of his own days—seventy years.[553] This is the mystery of the heavenly curtain, performing no function at all, and the moon not shining on her own at all—illumined by seventy years on all sides, life of David, unspecified. So David sought to know this mystery—why the moon has no life of her own—and to know his essence.[554]

his days are all fashioned in heaven; then gradually the fulfilled days are fashioned into a garment of splendor for the soul. See above, pp. 346–49 and nn. 245–60.

548. ***Not one of them...*** No human can fully comprehend God.

For other interpretations, see *KP*; *Sullam*; *MmD*. Cf. above, p. 347 and n. 252.

549. **place called 'measure of his days'** *Binah*, from whom all days issue: the cosmic days of Creation (the seven lower *sefirot*) and the days of human life.

550. ***YHVH, let me know...*** The full verse reads: *YHVH, let me know my end, what is the measure of my days, that I may know how ephemeral I am.*

See BT *Shabbat* 30a; *Rut Rabbah* 3:2; *Qohelet Rabbah* on 5:10.

551. **end of the right...** *Shekhinah*, who is the culmination of the flow from *Binah*, which begins to manifest on the right through *Ḥesed*. King David (traditionally, the author of Psalms) is intimately linked with *Shekhinah*, who is known as *Malkhut* (Kingdom).

The phrase קץ הימין (*qets ha-yamin*), "the end of the right," derives from Daniel 12:13, where its simple sense is *the end of days*—the word ימין (*yamin*) being an Aramaized form of the Hebrew ימים (*yamim*). Rabbi Ḥizkiyah, however, understands the word ימין (*yamin*) according to its Hebrew sense, "right." See *Zohar* 1:54a, 62b; below, p. 423 and n. 591.

552. ***measure of my days...*** *Binah*. See above, note 549.

553. **days decreed for him from Adam...** According to a midrashic tradition, King David was destined to be lifeless and die at childbirth, but Adam offered him 70 of his own 1000 allotted years, so David lived for 70 years and Adam for 930.

See Genesis 5:5; Jubilees 4:30; *Pirqei de-Rabbi Eli'ezer* 19, and David Luria, ad loc., n. 31; *Midrash Tehillim* 92:10; *Bemidbar Rabbah* 14:12; *Bereshit Rabbati* 5:5; *Yalqut Shim'oni*, Genesis, 41; *Zohar* 1:55a–b, 91b, 140a, 168a, 248b; 2:103b, 235a; *ZḤ* 67d (*ShS*), 81a (*MhN, Rut*); Moses de León, *Sheqel ha-Qodesh*, 68 (85); idem, *Sod Eser Sefirot Belimah*, 383.

554. **heavenly curtain, performing no function...** See BT *Ḥagigah* 12b: "Rabbi Yehudah said, 'There are two רקיעים (*reqi'im*), firmaments [or: heavens]....' Resh Lakish

"*What is the measure of my days*—upper, concealed rung, poised above all those days constituting Her life, a site illumining all.[555]

"*That I may know how* חדל (*ḥadel*), *ephemeral, I am.* What does this mean? David said, 'That I may know why I am *ḥadel,* destitute, of light of my own, deprived of being like all those other supernal ones, all possessing life. And I, why am I destitute, why am I deprived?' This is what David wanted to know—and was not permitted to know.[556]

"Come and see: All supernal blessings are transmitted to this rung, to bless all. Even though She has no light of Her own, all blessings, all joy, all goodness exist in Her and issue from Her; so She is called 'cup of blessing' and simply 'blessing.' Of this is written *Blessing of YHVH, she enriches* (Proverbs 10:22)—*blessing of YHVH,* truly! And similarly: *Filled with blessing of YHVH, possess the west and the south* (Deuteronomy 33:23). So She shares in all the others, filled by them all, partaking of them all.[557] She is blessed by all [234a] those supernal blessings, transmitted to Her to bless. How do we know this? Rabbi Yitsḥak said, 'Jacob blessed Joseph's sons from this place, to which all blessings were

said, 'Seven, namely, *Vilon* (Curtain), *Raqi'a, Sheḥaqim, Zevul, Ma'on, Makhon, Aravot.* Curtain performs no function at all except entering in the morning and leaving in the evening, and renewing each day the act of creation.'"

Here the "heavenly curtain" refers to *Shekhinah,* last of the *sefirot,* who possesses nothing of Her own and cannot function properly until receiving the flow from above. Similarly, She is symbolized by the moon, which possesses no light of her own but simply reflects the light of the sun—symbolizing *Tif'eret,* who conveys to *Shekhinah* the light of all seven lower *sefirot* ("seventy years"). "Life of David, unspecified" alludes to both the earthly life of King David and the divine vitality of *Shekhinah,* symbolized by David's life. In uttering this verse from Psalms, David sought to fathom these intertwined mysteries.

On the "curtain," see *Zohar* 1:207b; 3:239b; Moses de León, *Shushan Edut* 338; idem, *Sefer ha-Rimmon,* 6, 257; idem, *Sheqel ha-Qodesh,* 12 (15), 50 (61). On the moon possessing no light of her own, see Radak on Genesis 1:16; *Zohar* 1:20a, 31a, 124b–125a, 132b, 179b, 181a, 238a, 249b; 2:43a, 142a, 145b, 215a, 218b; 3:113b; Moses de León, *Shushan Edut,* 338; idem, *Sefer ha-Rimmon,* 188, 257; idem, *Sheqel ha-Qodesh,* 68–69 (85–86); idem, *Sod Eser Sefirot Belimah,* 381. Cf. BT *Shabbat* 156a.

555. **upper, concealed rung...** *Binah,* source of the days and life of *Shekhinah.* See above, note 549.

556. **That I may know...** David speaks also for *Shekhinah.* On God's refusal to let him know, see the rabbinic sources cited above, note 550.

557. **All supernal blessings are transmitted to this rung...** To *Shekhinah,* who receives, and partakes of, all the *sefirot* from *Ḥesed* through *Yesod.* "West" refers to *Shekhinah* (see above, end of note 538); "south" refers to *Ḥesed,* through which the emanation from *Binah* begins to flow.

On Her having no light of Her own, see above, note 554. On Her designation as "cup of blessing," see *Zohar* 1:1a, 250a–b; 2:143b, 157b; Moses de León, *Sod Eser Sefirot Belimah,* 383. On the verse in Proverbs, see *Zohar* 1:70b–71a.

transmitted to convey, as is written: *You will be a blessing* (Genesis 12:2)—from now on, blessings are delivered into your hand.'[558]

"Come and see: Similarly we bless and praise this name, and therefore *Hallel*, on the days that it is recited.[559] For Rabbi Ḥiyya said, 'In *Hallel* three rungs are required: pious, righteous, and Israel—so that the glory of the blessed Holy One be exalted above all by these rungs. Pious, righteous, and Israel: pious from the side of the right, righteous from the side of the left, Israel from all those sides—for Israel embraces them all. Thereby the praise of the blessed Holy One ascends consummately. So too, wherever Israel praise the blessed Holy One from below, His glory ascends consummately.'"[560]

[233b] **Tosefta.**[561] Sound of a sphere revolving from below to above; her braided chariots whirling, a sweet sound ascending and descending, drifting through the world. Sound of a shofar drawn out in depths of rungs, turning the sphere.[562]

558. ***You will be a blessing...*** From God's declaration to Abraham. The verse reads: *I will make you a great nation and I will bless you; I will enhance your name and you will be a blessing.* According to Rabbi Yitsḥak, God assured Abraham that he had attained the rung of *Shekhinah*, source of blessing, and that from now on he could provide blessing to all through Her. Jacob drew on this same power to bless Joseph's sons.

See *Bereshit Rabbah* 39:11; *Zohar* 1:78a.

559. **this name...** *Shekhinah*.

The *Hallel* (Praise) consists of Psalms 113–118 and is recited after the morning service on the three Festivals and on Ḥanukkah. An abbreviated version (omitting the first parts of Psalm 115 and Psalm 116) is recited on the last six days of Passover and on Rosh Ḥodesh.

560. **three rungs are required...** The pious (*ḥasidim*) correspond to *Ḥesed* on the right, the righteous to *Gevurah* on the left, and all the rest of Israel to *Tif'eret Yisra'el* who harmonizes the polar opposites. Together, all of these elevate *Shekhinah* ("glory of the blessed Holy One").

See *Midrash Tehillim* 113:3: "*Hallel* must be recited by no fewer than three." See Buber's note, ad loc.

561. **Tosefta** "Addendum, Addenda." The *Matnitin* and *Tosefta* of the *Zohar*, strewn throughout the text, consist mostly of anonymous enigmatic revelations addressed to the Companions, urging them to open their hearts to the mysteries. See above, note 502.

The *Matnitin* and *Tosefta* are not formally part of the *Zohar*'s running commentary on the Torah and will consequently be translated separately in a subsequent volume. I have included this passage of *Tosefta* here because it appears here in numerous manuscripts (including M7, N23, O2, R1, V5).

562. **Sound of a sphere...** Corresponding to the celestial sphere of medieval Ptolemaic astronomy, which moves all the other heavenly spheres. Here this sphere is linked with *Shekhinah* and revolved by various sefirotic potencies.

The "sweet sound" corresponds to the ancient philosophical notion of the music of the spheres. See *Zohar* 1:41b (*Heikh*), 161b (*ST*); 2:196a, 211a; 3:165a, 209a; Moses de León, *Seder Gan Eden*, 132. The shofar often symbolizes *Binah*, and here the image may imply that Her power turns the sphere.

"Braided" renders טורקהא (*turqaha*), apparently deriving from Latin *torqueo*, "to

Around her lie two spades, on the right and on the left, in two colors intermingling—this one white, that one red—both turning the sphere above. When turning to the right, white ascends; when turning to the left, red descends. [234a] The sphere turns constantly, never subsiding.[563]

Two birds ascend chirping, one to the south, one to the north, soaring through the air.[564] The chirping and the sweet sound of the sphere join as one, then *A psalm, a song for the Sabbath day* (Psalms 92:1), and all blessings flow whisperingly in this sweetness through the passionate sound of the shofar.[565]

For those blessings to be received, they descend from above to below and are treasured away as one within the depth of the well—bubbling of the well, its rippling never ceasing until it is filled.[566] The sphere turns; those two spades turn, the one on the right crying out potently: "Radiance of radiancies, ascending and descending! Two thousand worlds, shine! Middle world within them, shine with the radiance of your Lord!"

All those possessing eyes, gaze! Open your eyes! You will attain this brilliance, this delight—those blessings flowing from above. Whoever is worthy—the sphere turns to the right, conveying a flow upon him, and he is ravished by those sparkling supernal blessings. Happy are those who attain them!

When he is not worthy, the sphere turns and that spade on the left turns and descends below, conveying judgment upon this unworthy one. A voice issues: "Woe to those wicked who have proven unworthy!" From that side shoots forth flaming fire, scorching the heads of the wicked of the world. Happy are all those who walk in the path of truth in this world, attaining that supernal brilliance, radiant blessings, as is said: *He will satisfy your soul with radiancies...* (Isaiah 58:11).[567]

twist." See Rashi on Genesis 19:28; cf. *Tosafot, Nedarim* 41b, s.v. *ki ḥizra*. For other readings and interpretations of this word (and for various interpretations of the entire cryptic passage), see *OY*; *KP*; *Sullam*; *MmD*.

563. **two spades...** Resembling *Ḥesed* and *Gevurah*, respectively white on the right and red on the left.

On "spades," cf. above, p. 404 and n. 506. On the constant motion of the sphere, see Maimonides, *Mishneh Torah, Hilkhot Yesodei ha-Torah* 1:5; *Zohar* 2:220b. Cf. *Sefer Yetsirah* 2:4.

564. **Two birds ascend...** Apparently two angels—one ascending toward the south (symbolizing *Ḥesed*) and one toward the north (symbolizing *Gevurah*). See above, p. 311 and n. 46.

565. ***for the Sabbath day...*** The time of fulfillment and union.

566. **blessings... descend...** The flow of emanation descends to *Shekhinah*, source of blessing for the worlds below.

567. **Whoever is worthy...** Human behavior affects the motion of the sphere, generating either rich blessing or harsh judgment.

Cf. *Zohar* 1:109b–110a; 2:95b; Liebes, *Peraqim*, 327–31. The full verse in Isaiah reads: *YHVH will guide you always; He will satisfy* נפשך (*nafshekha*), *your thirst* [or: *soul*] בצחצחות (*be-tsaḥtsaḥot*), *in parched regions,*

Jacob called his sons and said, "Gather round, that I may tell you [what will befall you in days to come]" (Genesis 49:1).

Rabbi Abba opened, "*He has turned to the prayer of the solitary one and has not spurned their prayer* (Psalms 102:18).[568] This verse has been established by the Companions, who raised an objection to it; but it still contains a nuanced facet:[569] *He has turned*—the verse should read *He has listened* or *He has heard*. Why *He has turned*?

"Well, all prayers of the world are considered prayers, but the prayer of an individual enters before the Holy King only with intense effort. Because before that prayer enters to be crowned in its site, the blessed Holy One examines and inspects it, scrutinizing that person's sins and virtue—which He does not do for the prayer of a congregation. For look, a congregational prayer includes many prayers of those who are not virtuous, and yet they all enter the presence of the King without His turning over their sins![570]

and invigorate your bones. You will be like a well-watered garden, like a spring whose waters do not fail. Here, the rare word *be-tsaḥtsaḥot* is understood as "with radiancies," based on the root צחח (*tsḥḥ*), "to gleam." See above, at note 258.

568. ***solitary one...*** ערער (*Ar'ar*), apparently from the root ערר (*'rr*), "to lay bare, strip." The word is often rendered "destitute," but here Rabbi Abba understands it as "lonely one." Cf. ערירי (*ariri*) "stripped," hence "stripped of children, childless."

569. **Companions... raised an objection...** Midrashic sources question the switch from singular (*the solitary* [or: *destitute*] *one*) to plural (*their prayer*). See *Vayiqra Rabbah* 30:3; *Pesiqta de-Rav Kahana* 27:3; *Midrash Tehillim* 102:3.

"Nuanced facet" renders סטר קורדיטא (*setar qurdita*). *Setar* means "side, aspect, facet." *Qurdita* provides a good example of the *Zohar*'s convoluted creativity. The word apparently derives from כרדוט (*kardut*), employed by *Targum Yonatan* to translate the rare biblical term כונים (*kavvanim*), "cakes," in Jeremiah 7:18; 44:19. In other Targumic passages *kardut* means "a sleeved tunic" (based on Greek *cheiridotos*), but in the Jeremiah passages it may represent a corruption of Greek *chondrites*, "made of groats." Ignoring both of these senses, the *Zohar* refashions *kardut* into *qurdita* and employs it in the sense of כונה (*kavvanah*), "intention, meaning, nuance"—as if this underlay Jeremiah's rare term כונים (*kavvanim*).

See *Arukh*, s.v. *kardat, kardut*; *Arukh ha-Shalem*, s.v. *kardat*; Radak on Jeremiah 7:18 (linking *kavvanim* and *kavvanah*, and quoting the Targumic rendering); 44:19; Amos 5:26; *Zohar* 2:174a; 3:144b (*IR*); *Bei'ur ha-Millim ha-Zarot*, 190; *KP*; *DE*; *NO*; Scholem.

570. **all prayers of the world...** Although all prayers offered sincerely are legitimate, congregational prayer ascends more easily, without meticulous inspection.

On the preferability of communal prayer, see BT *Berakhot* 7b–8a, *Ta'anit* 8a; *Zohar* 1:160b, 167b; 2:245b; Gikatilla, *Sha'arei Orah*, 30b–31b.

Prayers accepted above are fashioned into a crown for *Yesod*. See *Shemot Rabbah* 21:4: "When Israel prays, you do not find them all praying as one, but rather each assembly prays on its own, one after the other. When they have all finished, the angel appointed over prayers gathers all the prayers offered in

"So, *He has turned to the prayer of the solitary one*—turning it over and scrutinizing it: with what heart and intention is it offered? Who is the person presenting this prayer, and what are his deeds? Therefore, one should offer his prayer in a congregation. Why? Because *He has not spurned their prayer*—even though they have not all been offered with devotion and heartfelt intention.[571]

"Alternatively, *He has turned to the prayer of the solitary one*—an individual merged with the many. Who is that? Jacob, embraced by two sides.[572] He called his sons and offered a prayer for them. What prayer? A prayer that they would be completely accepted above, a prayer that they would not be annihilated in exile. At the moment that Jacob called them, *Shekhinah* departed from him, as has been established.[573]

"Come and see: The moment that Jacob called his sons, Abraham and Isaac appeared there, with *Shekhinah* above them. *Shekhinah* was rejoicing in Jacob, to join the patriarchs, [234b] to bind their souls as one, becoming a chariot.[574] As Jacob opened, *Gather round, that I may tell you what will befall you* באחרית הימים (*be-aḥarit ha-yamim*), *in the end of days*—*Shekhinah*, who, as it were, was saddened and departed. Afterward, his sons brought Her back through their verbal unification when they opened and said *Hear O Israel! YHVH our God, YHVH is one!* (Deuteronomy 6:4). Immediately, Jacob stabilized Her by opening and saying 'Blessed be the name of His glorious kingdom forever and ever,' and *Shekhinah* settled there in Her place.[575]

all the synagogues and fashions them into crowns, which he places on the head of the blessed Holy One." See above, pp. 13–14 and n. 96.

571. ***He has turned*... turning it over...** See Gikatilla, *Sha'arei Orah*, 30b–31a; David ben Abraham Maimuni (grandson of Maimonides), *Midrash David*, 31–32.

572. **Alternatively, *He has turned*...** Rabbi Abba now reads the verb *turned* in its simple sense but reinterprets *solitary one*.

Jacob symbolizes *Tif'eret*, who combines the qualities of *Ḥesed* (on the right) and *Gevurah* (on the left). See above, pp. 14–15 and n. 100.

573. ***Shekhinah* departed from him...** See BT *Pesaḥim* 56a, in the name of Rabbi Shim'on son of Lakish: "Jacob wished to reveal to his sons the end of days, but *Shekhinah* departed from him."

See *Bereshit Rabbah* 96:1; 96 (pp. 1200–2); 98:2; *Tanḥuma, Vayera* 6; *Tanḥuma* (Buber), *Vayḥi* 1; Naḥmanides on Genesis 49:1; Kasher, *Torah Shelemah*, Genesis 49:1, n. 20.

574. ***Shekhinah* was rejoicing in Jacob...** The patriarchs constitute a chariot for God. From a higher perspective, they symbolize the sefirotic triad of *Ḥesed, Gevurah*, and *Tif'eret*, which, together with *Shekhinah*, constitutes a chariot for the highest *sefirot*.

See *Bereshit Rabbah* 47:6: "Resh Lakish said, 'The patriarchs themselves constitute the [divine] Chariot.'" See above, p. 337 and n. 198, p. 345 and n. 238, p. 364 and n. 332.

575. ***in the end of days—Shekhinah*...** The phrase באחרית הימים (*be-aḥarit ha-yamim*), often translated in this verse "in days to come," means literally "in the end of days." Rabbi Abba applies it to *Shekhinah* (the "last" of the seven cosmic "days" of Creation, the *sefirot* issuing from *Binah*): saddened by Jacob's predictions of exile, *Shekhinah* withdrew.

By reciting the unification of the opening

"*Jacob called.* Why 'calling' here? In order to establish their place, establishing them above and below.[576]

"Come and see: Everywhere calling follows this pattern, as is written: *Moses called* הושע (*Hoshe'a*), *Hosea, son of Nun* יהושע (*Yehoshu'a*), *Joshua* (Numbers 13:16)—to establish his place, to link him as required.[577] Similarly, *He called him Jacob* (Genesis 25:26), and *God of Israel called him God* (ibid. 33:20)—the blessed Holy One established him by this name. Calling comes to establish.[578]

"Now, you might say, '*They shall call to God* (Jonah 3:8); *Out of my distress*

line of the *Shema,* Jacob's sons restored *Shekhinah.* Jacob's response (with what became the second line of the *Shema*) united Her with Her retinue of angels. See BT *Pesaḥim* 56a: "Rabbi Shim'on son of Lakish said, '. . . [Upon his deathbed] Jacob wished to reveal to his sons the end of days, but *Shekhinah* departed from him. He said, "Perhaps, Heaven forbid, there is someone unfit in my bed [i.e., among my children], like Abraham, from whom issued Ishmael, or like my father Isaac, from whom issued Esau." His sons answered him, "*Hear, O Israel!* [i.e., Jacob]. *YHVH is our God, YHVH is one* (Deuteronomy 6:4): just as there is only *one* in your heart, so there is only *one* in ours." At that moment our father Jacob opened and exclaimed, "Blessed be the name of His glorious kingdom forever and ever."'"

See *Sifra, Beḥuqqotai* 8:7, 112c; *Sifrei,* Deuteronomy 31, 312; *Bereshit Rabbah* 96 (pp. 1200–2); 98:3; *Vayiqra Rabbah* 36:2; *Shir ha-Shirim Rabbah* on 4:7; *Targum Yerushalmi,* Genesis 35:22; *Targum Yerushalmi* (frag.), Genesis 49:2; above, note 573; *Zohar* 1:12a, 18b, 148a; 2:134a–b, 139b; 3:264a; Tishby, *Wisdom of the Zohar,* 3:971–74. On *Shekhinah* as *the end of days,* see *Zohar* 2:189b; 3:270a. On the incompatibility of *Shekhinah* and sadness, see BT *Shabbat* 30b: "*Shekhinah* abides neither through sadness nor laziness nor frivolity nor levity nor talk nor idle chatter [or: vain pursuits], but only through the joy of *mitsvah.*" See above, page 305.

576. **Why 'calling'. . .** Jacob declared and established the place of the tribes, both here on earth and above—located beneath *Shekhinah.* See above, p. 51, n. 369.

577. **הושע (*Hoshe'a*). . . יהושע (*Yehoshu'a*). . .** By adding the letter י (*yod*), Moses linked Joshua to *Shekhinah,* who is pictured as the central point and symbolized by this letter.

See *Zohar* 3:158b. On *Shekhinah* as "point" and *yod,* see above, note 523.

578. ***He called him Jacob*. . .** According to midrashic tradition, the subject *he* refers to God. Here, Rabbi Abba indicates that God established Jacob on his divine rung, *Tif'eret.*

See *Bereshit Rabbah* 63:8; *Tanḥuma, Shemot* 4; *Leqaḥ Tov* and *Midrash Aggadah,* Genesis 25:26; Rashi on this verse; *Zohar* 1:60a, 138a, 186b.

The second verse (Genesis 33:20) reads in full (and is usually translated): *There he* [Jacob] *set up an altar* ויקרא לו אל אלהי ישראל (*va-yiqra lo El Elohei Yisra'el*), *and called it God, God of Israel.* According to the simple sense of the verse, Jacob assigns a divine name to the altar, but Rabbi Abba alludes to a radical reinterpretation that turns *God of Israel* into the subject who names Jacob *God*!

See BT *Megillah* 18a, in the name of Rabbi El'azar: "How do we know that the blessed Holy One called Jacob 'God'? Because it says: *The God of Israel called him God.* For if you imagine that Jacob called the altar 'God,' then the verse should read: *Jacob called it* [*God*]. Rather, *He called him,* namely Jacob, *God.* And who called him *God*? *The God of Israel.*"

See *Bereshit Rabbah* 79:8, and Theodor, ad loc.; Rashi, Naḥmanides, Baḥya ben Asher, and Recanati on Genesis 33:20; *Zohar* 1:138a, 150a; 3:86a.

I called to YHVH, and He answered me (ibid. 2:3)!' Certainly so, to establish vitality above! How so? Arranging the praise of one's Lord and all those things that one asks of his Lord provide vitality to his Lord, by showing that all depends upon Him, not upon anywhere else. Look, establishing vitality![579]

"Correspondingly, *Jacob called his sons*—establishing them in full vitality. Similarly, *He called to Moses* (Leviticus 1:1)—established in his vitality."

Rabbi Yitsḥak asked, "Why is the א (*alef*) of ויקרא (*va-yiqra*), *He called*, small?"[580]

He replied, "Moses was established in wholeness but not totally, for he withdrew from his wife. In books of the ancients they say this in praise; as for us, we have learned: One who would ascend should link himself above and below; then he is complete.[581]

"Further, a small א (*alef*)—deriving from a small place, small becoming great in joining above.[582]

"*And he said* (Genesis 49:1).[583] What does this mean? This has been established, as is said: *He said in his heart* (ibid. 17:17)—saying silently.[584]

579. **Now, you might say...** After the prophet Jonah warned of the destruction of Nineveh, the king commanded that his people call out to God and turn back from their evil ways. Later, Jonah called to God in distress. How can these examples of calling to God imply any kind of "establishing"? In response, Rabbi Abba explains that by calling out to God and beseeching Him, a person demonstrates human dependence on divine aid, thereby strengthening God.

On the concept of strengthening and weakening God, see *Sifrei*, Deuteronomy 319; *Vayiqra Rabbah* 23:12; *Eikhah Rabbah* 1:33; *Pesiqta de-Rav Kahana* 25:1; *Zohar* 2:32b, 65b.

580. **א (*alef*) of ויקרא (*va-yiqra*)...** In the Masoretic text this א (*alef*) is written small.

For other references to, and interpretations of, this phenomenon, see *Midrash Otiyyot Qetanot* (*Battei Midrashot*, 2:478); *Zohar* 1:239a; 3:53b; Gikatilla, *Sha'arei Orah*, 14b; Recanati, *Peirush al ha-Torah*, Leviticus 1:1, 56c; *Ba'al ha-Turim* and *Minḥat Shai*, Leviticus 1:1; Kasher, *Torah Shelemah*, Leviticus 1:1, n. 6.

581. **Moses...withdrew from his wife...** According to rabbinic tradition, after encountering God on Mount Sinai, Moses abstained from sexual contact with his wife and maintained union with *Shekhinah*. Although Moses' abstinence can be seen in a positive light, Rabbi Abba insists that one who seeks to join the divine realm should also be linked on earth with a human partner.

The "books of the ancients" is one of the many sources housed in the fantastic library of the author(s) of the *Zohar*. See above, p. 95, n. 69. Here the term may refer to the rabbinic sources that mention Moses' abstinence (especially *Sifrei* and *Tanḥuma*). See *Sifrei*, Numbers 99; BT *Shabbat* 87a; *Tanḥuma, Tsav* 13; Maimonides, *Mishneh Torah, Hilkhot Yesodei ha-Torah* 7:6; *Zohar* 1:21b–22a, 152b; 2:222a; 3:148a, 180a.

582. **deriving from a small place...** The divine call to Moses issued from *Shekhinah*, last and "smallest" of the *sefirot*, who has nothing of Her own but rather reflects the light of the other *sefirot*. Yet when She is united with the upper *sefirot*, She becomes great.

See *Zohar* 1:138a, 239a; 3:53b.

583. ***And he said*** The full verse reads: *Jacob called his sons and he said, "Gather round, that I may tell you what will befall you in days to come."*

584. ***He said in his heart...*** Just as in this verse in Genesis 17 (concerning Abra-

"האספו (He'asefu), *Be gathered* (ibid.). The verse should read אספו (Isefu), *Gather,* as is said: Isefu, *Gather, to Me My devotees* (Psalms 50:5). But here he established them: He'asefu, *Be gathered,* from a site above; *be gathered* into a complete bond, a single unity.[585]

"ואגידה (Ve-aggidah), *That I may tell, you* (ibid.). What is ve-aggidah? Mystery of wisdom."

Rabbi Yose asked Rabbi Shim'on, "This ואגידה (ve-aggidah), *that I may tell,* or ויגד (va-yagged), *he told,* or ויגידו (va-yaggidu), *they told,* and similarly all of them, which we see to be a mystery of wisdom—why does this word contain a mystery of wisdom?"

He replied, "Because it is a word appearing with ג (gimel) ד (dalet) unseparated. Here is a mystery of wisdom appearing consummately in the mystery of letters. So it is when they abide in wisdom; but dalet without gimel is incomplete, and similarly gimel without dalet, for they are interlinked indivisibly, and whoever separates them inflicts death upon himself. This mystery is the sin of Adam.[586]

ham), the verb *said* refers not to speech but to silent intention, so too here with Jacob, whose silent intention is described in the next word: האספו (He'asefu), *Be gathered.*

On the subtle nature of the verb אמר (amar), "to say," see *Zohar* 1:16b; 2:17a, 25b; 3:132b–133a (*IR*), 161a.

585. **The verse should read אספו (*Isefu*), *Gather*...** Apparently, Rabbi Abba's point is that if Jacob were actually ordering some of his sons to gather the others, the verb should be in the imperative: אספו (isefu), *gather.* The passive voice— האספו (he'asefu), *be gathered*—implies that Jacob was focusing contemplatively on the spiritual source of his sons, intending that they be gathered and united above (or from above) in preparation for receiving the flow of blessing.

See *OY*; Galante; *MM*; *Sullam*; *MmD.*

586. **with ג (*gimel*) ד (*dalet*) unseparated...** The word ואגידה (ve-aggidah), *that I may tell,* includes these two letters, which follow one another in the alphabet. (Their apparent separation in this word is resolved below.) The letter ג (gimel) symbolizes Yesod, who גומל (gomel), "deals (graciously)," with Shekhinah—symbolized by ד (dalet) because She is דלה (dallah), "poor," having nothing of Her own. This pair of letters symbolizes the union of the divine couple.

See BT *Shabbat* 104a: "גימ"ל דל"ת–גמול דלים (Gimel dalet: gemol dallim), Deal kindly with the poor." See *Zohar* 1:3a, 244b; 2:181a; Moses de León, *Shushan Edut,* 340; idem, *Sefer ha-Rimmon,* 229.

On the sense of the verb הגיד (higgid) as "revealing" something concealed or mysterious, see Genesis 3:11; 41:25; Judges 14:12, 15–16; 1 Kings 10:3; Daniel 2:2; Job 11:6. On the significance of higgid, see BT *Shabbat* 87a; *Zohar* 1:86b, 249a; 3:50b, 161a, 292b–293a (*IZ*). On haggadah as referring to the allegorical method of interpretation, see *Zohar* 2:99a; *ZḤ* 83a (*MhN, Rut*); Tishby, *Wisdom of the Zohar,* 3:1083–85; Talmage, "Ha-Munnaḥ 'Haggadah,'" 271–73.

Adam should have united the divine couple through contemplation, but instead he separated them, interrupting the flow of emanation and bringing death into the world.

See *Zohar* 1:12b, 35b–36a, 53b, 237a; Vol. 1, p. 298, n. 1438; Scholem, *Major Trends,* 231–32, 236; Tishby, *Wisdom of the Zohar,* 1:373–76.

"Therefore it is a mystery of wisdom. And though sometimes י (*yod*) intervenes between *gimel* and *dalet,* there is no separation—all is a single cluster. Thus the word is certainly so! ואגידה (*Ve-aggidah*), *That I may tell, you*—mystery of wisdom: he sought to reveal the end of all of Israel's history.[587]

"Now, you might say that he did not reveal what he wanted to reveal, and if so, why does Torah record the words of Jacob the perfect—later tainted and unfulfilled? But surely, fulfilled! All that needed to be revealed he revealed and concealed—uttering a word, revealing outwardly, concealing within. A word of Torah is never tainted, and all is concealed within Torah, for Torah is perfection of all, perfection of above and below; in Torah no word or letter is defective. Jacob said everything that he needed to say, but revealing and concealing, not tainting even a single letter of all that he intended."[588]

Rabbi Yehudah and Rabbi Yose were sitting one day in front of the gate of Lydda. Rabbi Yose said to Rabbi Yehudah, "We see that Jacob blessed his sons—
422 we see this from what is written: *He blessed them* (Genesis 49:28). But where is their blessing?"[589]

He replied, "They are all blessings given by him, for example: *Judah, you, will your brothers acclaim* (ibid., 8); *Dan will judge his people* (ibid., 16); *Asher, rich is his bread* (ibid., 20); and so all of them.[590] But as for what he revealed to them,

587. **though sometimes י (*yod*) intervenes...** Even if the ג (*gimel*) and ד (*dalet*) are separated by the letter י (*yod*)—as in the word ואגידה (*ve-aggidah*), *that I may tell*—this does not really constitute a separation, because *yod* symbolizes a unifying divine element. The reference may be to the primordial point of *Ḥokhmah,* or to יסוד (*Yesod*), which begins with *yod.* Note that the sequence *gimel, yod, dalet* spells גיד (*gid*), "nerve, tendon, fiber," but also a euphemism for "phallus," alluding to *Yesod,* the divine phallus. See *TZ* 19, 41a.

The word *ve-aggidah, that I may tell,* indicates that Jacob was uniting the *sefirot* in order to draw on divine wisdom and reveal the Messianic future.

588. **Now, you might say...** Since Jacob's wish to reveal what would happen at *the end of days* was thwarted (see above, notes 573, 575), why does the Torah mention it? This seems to indicate an imperfection in Jacob or in the Torah itself. However, as Rabbi Shim'on explains, Jacob's blessings to his sons revealed what needed to be revealed at the moment while concealing an inner meaning relating to the distant and Messianic future.

On the significance of every element of Torah, see *Zohar* 1:54a, 135a, 145b, 163a, 187a; 2:12a, 55b–56a, 59b, 65b, 98b–99b; 3:79b, 149a, 152a, 174b, 265a; *ZḤ* 6d (*MhN*). Cf. *Sifrei,* Deuteronomy 336; *Midrash Tanna'im,* Deuteronomy 32:47; BT *Menaḥot* 29b; Maimonides, *Guide of the Perplexed* 3:50.

589. **But where is their blessing?** Jacob's words to his sons in Genesis 49 are mostly predictions of the future of the tribes and not normal blessings. Reuben is sharply criticized; Simeon and Levi are more cursed than blessed. Ibn Ezra poses a similar question in his commentary on Genesis 49:1. See below, at note 631.

590. **They are all blessings...** Rabbi Yehudah quotes several of Jacob's explicit blessings and apparently implies that the pa-

he did not reveal what he wanted to reveal to them: the end. As they have established, there is an end on the right and an end on the left. He wanted to reveal the end to them so that they would be protected [235a] and purified from foreskin. What he revealed to them became openly known before they entered the Holy Land, but other matters are unrevealed—concealed within Torah, in that portion of Jacob and in those blessings."[591]

He opened, saying, "*Reuben, my firstborn are you* (ibid., 3).[592] What prompted Jacob to open with Reuben? He should have opened with Judah, who was first of all camps and king.[593] And we see that he did not bless [Reuben], withdrawing blessings from him until Moses came and prayed for him, as is said: *May Reuben live, and not die* (Deuteronomy 33:6).[594]

"But he surely blessed him, reserving that blessing in its site. This can be compared to a man who had a son. When his time came to depart from the world, the king suddenly appeared. He said, 'Here, let all my money remain in the hands of the king, reserved for my son. When the king sees that my son is

triarch's utterances to the other sons represented blessings expressed as predictions or included concealed blessings. Cf. *Bereshit Rabbah* 99:4.

591. **he did not reveal what he wanted...** See above, end of note 587. Rabbi Yehudah now explains the double meaning of "the end." *Shekhinah* is "end on the right"—the culmination of emanation, characterized by the grace of *Ḥesed* on the right. The demonic power is "end on the left"—deriving from the dregs of *Gevurah* on the left, characterized by evil, and identified with the foreskin (which covers and conceals holiness). Jacob sought to reveal all these secrets, but they remained hidden within the words that he uttered. The sons—and later the tribes in the wilderness—understood only Jacob's predictions of what would happen when the Children of Israel entered the promised land, not the Messianic future or the mystery of the two "ends."

On the two "ends," see *Eikhah Rabbah* 2:6; *Pesiqta de-Rav Kahana* 17:5; *Zohar* 1:54a–b, 62b–63a, 75a (*ST*), 152b; above, p. 180 and nn. 1–3, pp. 291–92 and nn. 181–84; above, note 551; 2:33a–34a, 134a–b, 181b; Moses de León, *Sefer ha-Rimmon*, 73–75, 368–71; idem, *Sheqel ha-Qodesh*, 80–81 (102–3). On the demonic nature of the foreskin, see *Zohar* 1:13a, 18a, 35b, 91b, 201a; Moses de León, *Sheqel ha-Qodesh*, 55 (68).

592. ***Reuben, my firstborn...*** The full verse reads: *Reuben, my firstborn are you—my strength and first fruit of my vigor, surpassing in loftiness, surpassing in might.*

593. **Judah, who was first...** The tribe of Judah led the Israelites as they journeyed through the wilderness. See Numbers 10:14.

On Judah as "king" of the tribes, see *Bereshit Rabbah* 84:17; 93:2; above, p. 132 and n. 301; p. 264 at n. 34. Judah was also the ancestor of the Davidic dynasty.

594. **did not bless [Reuben]...** Jacob's words to Reuben (Genesis 49:3–4) do not constitute an actual blessing and include criticism of Reuben's intercourse with Jacob's concubine Bilhah. Many years later, Moses finally blessed Reuben along with his tribe, assuring him life in the world to come.

See Genesis 35:22; *Sifrei*, Deuteronomy 347; BT *Sanhedrin* 92a; *Targum Onqelos*, *Targum Yerushalmi*, and Rashi on Deuteronomy 33:6; above, p. 60 and n. 421; p. 131 and nn. 290–91.

worthy of it, he will give it to him.' Similarly, Jacob said, '*Reuben, my firstborn are you,* beloved of my inner being; but your blessings will be reserved in the hands of the Holy King until He regards you, because—as translated—"you were carried away by your anger."'"[595]

Reuben, my firstborn are you. Rabbi El'azar opened, "*Prophesy to the* רוח *(ruaḥ)! Prophesy, O son of man, and say to the ruaḥ, 'Thus says YHVH: Come from four ruḥot, O ruaḥ, and breathe into these slain, that they may live'* (Ezekiel 37:9).[596] How closed-minded human beings are, not knowing or considering the glory of their Lord! For look, Torah proclaims before them every day, and no one inclines an ear toward her! This verse is difficult. Since it is written *Prophesy to the ruaḥ,* why once again *Prophesy, O son of man, and say to the ruaḥ*?

"Well, from here we learn a mystery of wisdom. Two vitalizations here: one to arouse from below to above, for without arousal from below there is no arousal above; through arousal below, arousal above. *Prophesy to the ruaḥ*—from below to above. *Prophesy, O son of man, and say to the ruaḥ*—from above to below. For even above, through arousal below, that higher one grasps from one higher still. As in this verse: *Thus says Adonai YHVH: Come from four ruḥot, O ruaḥ. From four ruḥot*—south, east, north, and west. *Ruaḥ* comes from the west through the union of these others, as is said: *that nobles of the people delved* (Numbers 21:18). From here issue spirits and souls to inhabitants of the world, to be formed through them.[597]

595. **"you were carried away by your anger"** So *Targum Onqelos* paraphrases Jacob's criticism of Reuben in Genesis 49:4: *unbridled as water.* According to rabbinic tradition, Reuben's anger was aroused because he feared that after Rachel's death her maid Bilhah (who had been his father's concubine) would supplant or rival the position of Leah his mother as Jacob's chief wife. See above, p. 60 and n. 421.

On the preceding parable, cf. below, at note 616.

596. **רוח (*ruaḥ*)...** The word means "breath, wind, spirit." The context is Ezekiel's vision of the dry bones.

597. **Two vitalizations...** Without arousal from humans below, there is no divine arousal above. Further, within the divine realm itself, *Shekhinah* arouses the *sefirot* above Her to draw on even higher sefirotic sources to convey the flow. The apparently redundant command to Ezekiel actually refers to these two processes.

The four *ruḥot* ("winds" or directions)—south, east, north, and west—symbolize, respectively, *Ḥesed, Tif'eret, Gevurah,* and *Shekhinah*. The animating *ruaḥ* issues from *Shekhinah* (west), but only through Her union with the other three *sefirot*. The verse in Numbers reads: *Well, that princes dug, that nobles of the people delved.* Here, it alludes to the *well* of *Shekhinah,* dug by the sefirotic triad *Ḥesed, Gevurah,* and *Tif'eret,* who are symbolized by the patriarchs (*nobles*).

The closing phrase, "to be formed through them," apparently refers to the soul's role in forming a human being. See *OY*; *MmD*.

On the theme of arousal from below, see above, note 526. On the four *ruḥot,* see *Zohar* 1:139a (*MhN*), 175b–176a; 2:13a–b; 3:130b

"*And breathe* (Ezekiel, ibid.)—as is said: *He blew into his nostrils the breath of life* (Genesis 2:7).[598]

"Come and see: Grasping from one side and giving on another, and thus: *All the streams flow into the sea, yet the sea is not full* (Ecclesiastes 1:7). Why is it not full? Because it grasps and gives, brings in and brings forth."[599]

Rabbi El'azar posed a question to Rabbi Shim'on, asking, "Since it is revealed before the blessed Holy One that human beings will die, why does He bring souls down into the world? Why does He need this?"

He replied, "This question has been posed to the rabbis by so many, and they have established it. However, the blessed Holy One bestows souls who descend to this world to make His glory known, and He gathers them afterward.[600] If so, why did they descend? Well, this mystery is as follows."

He opened, saying, "*Drink water from your cistern, flowing water from the midst of your well* (Proverbs 5:15). *Cistern*—a place not flowing on its own. When do these waters flow? When a soul is perfected in this world, when it ascends to that place to which is linked—then complete on all sides, from below and from above.[601]

"When the soul ascends, desire of female arouses toward male, and then water flows from below upward, and the *cistern* becomes a *well* of bubbling water. Then, joining, union, desire, rapture—for by this soul of the righteous that place is perfected, and love and passion arouse above, joining as one."[602]

(*IR*). On the verse in Numbers, see *Zohar* 2:197b; 3:150a, 286a.

598. ***And breathe*...** The verse from Ezekiel reads: *And breathe into these slain, that they may live.* The verse from Genesis describes God's creation of Adam: *He blew into his nostrils the breath of life, and the human became a living being.*

599. **Grasping... and giving...** *Shekhinah* obtains the flow of emanation (and of souls) from above and conveys it below.

600. **to make His glory known...** Through fulfilling His word and living virtuously.

601. ***cistern*... *well*...** *Shekhinah* does not flow on Her own but only when stimulated from below by a virtuous soul, leading to arousal above, as Rabbi Shim'on goes on to explain. Thus *Shekhinah* becomes complete from below (through the soul) and from above.

Given the context of the dialogue between Rabbi El'azar and Rabbi Shim'on, the phrase "ascends to that place..." refers to the soul's return to *Shekhinah* upon death, but it may also allude to the possibility of union during one's life. See *OY*; Tishby, *Wisdom of the Zohar*, 2:748.

On the soul's perfection in this world, see Saadia Gaon, *Emunot ve-De'ot* 6:4; *Zohar* 1:245b; Moses de León, *Sefer ha-Rimmon*, 299; idem, *Sefer ha-Mishqal*, 46–47 (translated in Matt, *Essential Kabbalah*, 148); idem, *Mishkan ha-Edut*, 8a–10a; Tishby, *Wisdom of the Zohar*, 2:752–54.

602. **desire of female arouses...** *Shekhinah* arouses toward Her partner, *Tif'eret*, who responds and unites with Her—all through the stimulation of the human soul.

See *Zohar* 1:60a–b, 244a–b, 245b.

Reuben, my firstborn are you. Certainly so! He was the first drop of Jacob—whose intention was elsewhere, as has been said.[603]

Come and see: Reuben and all the twelve tribes were linked with *Shekhinah*, and when Jacob saw *Shekhinah* above him, he called his twelve sons to join Her.[604]

Come and see: Since the day that the world was created, there has never been a bed as perfect as in the moment that Jacob was about [235b] to depart from the world: Abraham on his right, Isaac on his left, Jacob lying between them, *Shekhinah* in front of him. As soon as Jacob saw this, he called his sons and linked them around *Shekhinah*, arranging them in perfect order. How do we know that he arranged them around *Shekhinah*? As is written: *Be gathered* (Genesis 49:1). Then perfection of all manifested there, with many supernal chariots encompassing them.[605]

They opened, saying, "*Yours, O YHVH, are* גדולה (*gedullah*), *greatness;* גבורה (*gevurah*), *power;* תפארת (*tif'eret*), *beauty;* נצח (*netsaḥ*), *victory;* הוד (*hod*), *splendor*... (1 Chronicles 29:11)."[606] Then sun was gathered to moon, and east drew near to west, as is written: *He gathered his feet into the bed* (Genesis, ibid., 33). The moon was illumined, attaining fullness. Then surely, we have learned, Jacob did not die. When Jacob saw a complete realm—as happened to no one else—he rejoiced and praised the blessed Holy One, and began blessing his sons, each one fittingly.[607]

603. **Reuben, my firstborn... first drop...** The verse reads: *Reuben, my firstborn are you—my strength and first fruit of my vigor.* According to rabbinic tradition, Jacob never experienced a nocturnal emission, so Reuben was actually conceived from his father's first drop of semen. See above, pp. 333–34 and n. 185.

Laban had promised to give Jacob his younger daughter, Rachel, in marriage, but he tricked him by substituting his older daughter, Leah (Genesis 29). Consequently, on his wedding night, Jacob thought that he was sleeping with Rachel, and his desire focused on her. See above, p. 334 and n. 187.

604. **linked with *Shekhinah*...** Arrayed beneath Her. See above, p. 51, n. 369. On Jacob seeing *Shekhinah* above him, see above, at note 574.

605. **there has never been a bed as perfect...** Jacob's bed was perfect in two senses: first, because all of his offspring were worthy (see above, note 575); and second, because he was now facing *Shekhinah* and flanked by the souls of Abraham and Isaac. Those two patriarchs symbolize respectively *Ḥesed* and *Gevurah*, who are integrated and completed by Jacob's *sefirah*, *Tif'eret*. See below, at note 780.

On the meaning of *be gathered*, see above, p. 421 and n. 585.

606. **They opened... *Yours, O YHVH*...** By opening with this verse, Jacob's sons allude to all seven lower *sefirot*. The verse reads: *Yours, O YHVH, are* גדולה (*gedullah*), *greatness;* גבורה (*gevurah*), *power;* תפארת (*tif'eret*), *beauty;* נצח (*netsaḥ*), *victory;* הוד (*hod*), *splendor—yes, all that is in heaven and on earth.* Quoted often in kabbalistic literature, this biblical list of divine qualities designates *Ḥesed* (also called *Gedullah*), *Gevurah, Tif'eret, Netsaḥ, Hod, Yesod* (known as *all*), and *Shekhinah* (symbolized by *earth*), who is joined with *Tif'eret* (*heaven*).

607. **sun was gathered...** Jacob did not really die; rather he rose to his rung, *Tif'eret*,

Rabbi Yose and Rabbi Yeisa were walking on the way. Rabbi Yeisa said, "Surely we have learned that all of Jacob's sons were arrayed perfectly, and blessed, each one fittingly.[608] What, then, can we say of this verse: *From Asher, rich is his bread*... (Genesis 49:20)?"[609]

He replied, "I don't know, because I haven't heard anything about it. But let us go, you and I, to the Holy Lamp!"[610]

They went. When they reached Rabbi Shim'on, they raised the matter and asked a question. He said to them, "Surely, this is a mystery of wisdom!"

He opened, saying, "*Asher dwelled by the shores of the sea and settled by his coves* (Judges 5:17). Why did he dwell there? Because whoever dwells by the seashore enjoys worldly delights. And here, *Asher*—supernal opening of Righteous One, when He is blessed to pour blessings into the world. This opening is perpetually familiar to blessings of the world and is called אשר (*Asher*), Happiness. This is one of those pillars upon which the world rests.[611] And that place called 'bread of poverty' is refined from this place, as is written: *From Asher,*

and united with *Shekhinah*. *Tif'eret* is symbolized by "sun" and "east," *Shekhinah* by "moon," "west," and also "bed" (above, note 302).

The full verse reads: *Jacob finished instructing his sons, and he gathered his feet into the bed, and he expired, and was gathered to his people.* On the idea that "Jacob did not die," see BT *Ta'anit* 5b, in the name of Rabbi Yoḥanan: "Jacob our father did not die..., as is said: *Do not fear, My servant Jacob—declares YHVH—do not be dismayed, O Israel! For I will save you from afar, your seed from the land of their captivity* (Jeremiah 30:10). The verse compares him to his seed; just as his seed is alive, so he too is alive."

See Rashi and Naḥmanides on Genesis 49:23; *Tosafot, Ta'anit*, s.v. *ya'aqov avinu*; *Zohar* 1:248b; 2:48b; Moses de León, *Sefer ha-Rimmon*, 108–9; idem, commentary on the ten *sefirot*, 336b.

608. **Jacob's sons were arrayed perfectly...** Beneath *Shekhinah*. See above, p. 426 and n. 604.

609. ***From Asher, rich is his bread...*** The full verse reads: *From Asher, rich is his bread; he will provide delicacies of a king.* Apparently Rabbi Yeisa is troubled by the present tense of the first part of the verse (*rich is*), which seems inappropriate for a blessing, or by the strange wording *from Asher.*

610. **Holy Lamp** בוצינא קדישא (*Botsina Qaddisha*), the title of Rabbi Shim'on. See above, p. 209 and n. 182; p. 310 and n. 41.

611. ***Asher*—supernal opening...** *Yesod*, the divine phallus, known as Righteous One, through whom the flow of blessing reaches *Shekhinah* and the worlds below. The name Asher derives from אשר (*osher*), "happiness." See Genesis 30:13.

According to a tradition in BT *Ḥagigah* 12b, the world rests on seven pillars. According to Kabbalah, the world is based on the structure of the seven lower *sefirot*, from *Ḥesed* through *Shekhinah*. Their power is concentrated in *Yesod*, whose title, Righteous One, is based on Proverbs 10:25: וצדיק יסוד עולם (*Ve-tsaddiq yesod olam*). The verse literally means *The righteous one is an everlasting foundation*, but is understood as *The righteous one is the foundation of the world.*

See BT *Ḥagigah* 12b; *Bahir* 71 (102); Azriel of Gerona, *Peirush ha-Aggadot*, 34; *Zohar* 1:82a–b; above, p. 133 at n. 302; p. 396 at n. 469; *ZḤ* 76b (*MhN, Rut*); Moses de León, *Sefer ha-Rimmon*, 199.

On the symbolic meanings of Asher, see *Zohar* 1:15a, 47b, 49a, 244b, 245b–246a; 2:97b; 3:65b. On the title Righteous One, see also above, p. 92, n. 50.

rich is his bread—what had been bread of poverty transforms into pastry, because He infuses it with blessings and delights.[612] As proven by the conclusion of the verse: *he will provide delicacies of a king* (Genesis, ibid.). Who is *a king*? Assembly of Israel, nourished by Him with delights of the world. This one gives the *king* all blessings, all joy, all goodness: He provides, and from Him they issue."[613]

They said, "If we have come into the world just to know this, how good for us!"[614]

Reuben was Jacob's firstborn.

Rabbi Ḥiyya said, "He was entitled, but all was taken away from him: the kingship was given to Judah, the birthright to Joseph, the priesthood to Levi, as is written: *Unbridled as water, you will not remain!* (Genesis 49:4)—you will not retain them.[615]

"As for his saying *my strength and first fruit of my vigor* (ibid., 3), here he blessed him and entrusted him to the blessed Holy One. This can be compared to one beloved of a king, whom the king wished to favor. One day his son was passing in the street, and he said to the king, 'That's my son, true beloved of my

612. **bread of poverty...** In Deuteronomy 16:3, *matstsah* (unleavened bread) is called לחם עני (*leḥem oni*), "bread of poverty (or affliction)." In the *Zohar*, "bread of poverty" symbolizes *Shekhinah*, who remains impoverished until She is filled by the rich ingredients of *Yesod*—*from Asher.*

See above, note 333; *Zohar* 1:47b, 245b–246a, 250b. "Pastry" renders לחם פנג (*leḥem pannag*). *Pannag* is a biblical hapax legomenon (Ezekiel 27:17), apparently meaning "meal, ground seeds of grain."

613. **Who is *a king*? Assembly of Israel...** Although *Shekhinah* is usually depicted as feminine, She is also known as *Malkhut* (Kingdom) and is sometimes called King. Nourished by *Yesod* (*Asher*), the *king* rules and sustains the world. "He [*Yesod*] provides, and from Him [*Shekhinah*, the *king*], they issue."

On the name Assembly of Israel, see above, pp. 122–23, n. 237.

614. **If we have come into the world...** Similar exclamations appear in rabbinic literature and often in the *Zohar*. See BT *Berakhot* 16a, 24b; *Shabbat* 41a; *Pesiqta de-Rav Kahana* 1:3; *Shir ha-Shirim Rabbah* on 3:11; *Qohelet Rabbah* on 6:2; *Qohelet Zuta* 5:17; *Zohar* 1:2a, 148b, 164b, 240a; 2:99a, 121b, 122a, 193b; 3:26a.

615. **He was entitled, but...** As Jacob's firstborn, Reuben was entitled to various rights and privileges, but he did not retain any of these. The Davidic dynasty issued from the tribe of Judah, the birthright was transferred to Joseph, and the priesthood was given to Aaron and his descendants (from the tribe of Levi).

The full verse in Genesis reads: *Unbridled as water, you will not remain! For you mounted your father's bed, then you defiled—my couch he mounted!* The verse refers to Reuben's act of intercourse with his father's concubine Bilhah (see Genesis 35:22). According to 1 Chronicles 5:1, by this impulsive act Reuben forfeited the birthright: *The sons of Reuben, firstborn of Israel—he was the firstborn; but when he defiled his father's bed, his birthright was given to the sons of Joseph.* Different explanations of Reuben's displacement are offered below.

soul!' The king heard and understood that he was seeking favor for his son. So, Jacob said, '*Reuben, my firstborn are you, my strength and first fruit of my vigor*'—here entrusting him to the King.[616]

"*Unbridled as water, you will not remain!* Here he predicted what would befall him: that he would not remain in the land but settle outside.[617] Correspondingly, one deputy on the side of the Tabernacle above, appointed under the aegis of Michael—some say, under the aegis of Gabriel. Michael is always head on the side of *Ḥesed,* and Gabriel on the side of *Gevurah. Judah still rules with* אל (*El*), *God* (Hosea 12:1)—side of *Gevurah* and called Court of Justice—and adjacent to him was Reuben. Although kingship belonged to Judah, Reuben was adjacent to him, opposite him."[618]

Rabbi Shim'on said, "The descendants of Reuben are destined to wage two wars in the land.[619]

"Come and see: *My strength*—in the exile of Egypt.[620]

"*And first fruit of my vigor*—for they preceded their brothers in battle.[621]

"*Surpassing in bearing* (Genesis, ibid.)—in the exile of Assyria, for the descendants of Reuben and Gad went into exile there first of all and suffered many torments and tortures, and till now they have not returned.[622]

616. ***my strength*... here he blessed him...** The full verse reads: *Reuben, my firstborn are you—my strength and first fruit of my vigor, surpassing in loftiness, surpassing in might.* This seems to be a description rather than a blessing, but the parable explains how one leads to the other. Cf. the earlier parable, above at note 595.

617. **he would not remain in the land...** According to biblical tradition, the tribe of Reuben (along with Gad and half of Manasseh) settled in the Transjordan, not in Canaan. See Numbers 32; Joshua 18:7; 22.

618. **Correspondingly, one deputy...** Just as Reuben remained "outside" of the land, the angel appointed over his territory was "on the side of" *Shekhinah* (symbolized by the Tabernacle), beneath the archangel Michael.

Michael and Gabriel head the angelic forces on the right and the left respectively, corresponding to *Ḥesed* and *Gevurah*. Reuben is associated with Michael and *Ḥesed,* whereas Judah is associated with Gabriel and *Gevurah*. Judah, progenitor of the Davidic kings, is also linked with *Shekhinah,* who is known as *Malkhut* (Kingdom) and אל (*El*), *God. Shekhinah* derives from *Gevurah,* who is also known as *Din* (Judgment, Justice), so *Shekhinah* is Court of Justice.

The territory of the tribe of Reuben in the Transjordan lay opposite, and adjacent to, the territory of the tribe of Judah. Just as their territories were adjacent, some say that they shared an angel, under the aegis of Gabriel (associated with Judah).

619. **destined to wage two wars...** One when they helped to lead the other tribes in conquering the land of Canaan, and the other in the time of the Messiah.

On the war in Canaan, see Numbers 32:29–32; Deuteronomy 3:18–20; Joshua 1:12–18; 22:1–3. On the Messianic war, see *Zohar* 1:117a.

620. ***My strength*—in the exile of Egypt** Jacob blessed Reuben so that his descendants could endure Egyptian bondage.

621. **preceded their brothers in battle** See above, note 619.

622. ***Surpassing in bearing*...** *Bearing* renders שאת (*se'et*), "loftiness, exaltation, rank," from the root נשא (*ns'*), "to carry,

"*Surpassing in might* (ibid.)—in the time when King Messiah will arouse in the world: they will go forth and wage wars in the world, conquering and over-powering nations. Inhabitants of the world will fear them and tremble before them.[623] [236a] They will plan to seize the kingship but will not retain it, as is written: *Unbridled as water, you will not remain!* Why will they not remain in kingship, even in a single corner of the world? *For you mounted your father's bed* (ibid., 4)—for they are destined to enter and wage war in the Holy Land. *Your father's bed*, precisely—Jerusalem.[624]

"Come and see: The descendants of Reuben have been scattered in exile to the four corners of the world, corresponding to all of Israel, who have been exiled four times to the four corners of the world, as is written: *my strength*—one; *and first fruit of my vigor*—two; *surpassing in bearing*—three; *surpassing in might*—four. Following this pattern, they are destined to wage war in the four corners of the world and to gain dominion, through battle, over all, conquering many nations and ruling over them.[625]

"*Unbridled as water, you will not remain!* Here, an allusion to the first thought that Jacob had concerning that first drop—about Rachel. For if the thought of that drop had been in its place, Reuben would have retained all. However, *unbridled as water, you will not remain! For you mounted your father's bed*—through another thought—*then you defiled*... (ibid.).[626]

lift, bear, suffer." Here Rabbi Shim'on understands the phrase as referring to Reuben's exceptional capacity to "bear" the suffering of exile.

On these tribes' going into exile first, see 1 Chronicles 5:26; *Eikhah Rabbah, Petiḥta* 5; *Qohelet Rabbah* on 9:18; *Tanḥuma, Mas'ei* 13; *Bemidbar Rabbah* 23:14; *Midrash Avkir* (in *Yalqut Shim'oni*, Genesis 157); *Midrash ha-Gadol*, Genesis 35:23; 49:3.

623. **wage wars in the world...** See *Zohar* 1:117a; above at note 619.

624. ***For you mounted your father's bed...*** According to the simple sense of the verse, this accusation refers to Reuben's sexual sin (see above, note 615), but Rabbi Shim'on reinterprets it as referring to the future battles of the Reubenites in the Holy Land when they will attempt to seize the kingship from King Messiah. Jerusalem, seat of the kingdom, is the place where God rests: *Your father's bed.*

625. **exiled four times...** By the kingdoms of Babylon, Persia, Greece, and Rome. Alternatively, the Egyptian bondage is considered an exile (in which case, Babylon and Persia constitute a single exile).

626. **first thought that Jacob had...** According to rabbinic tradition, Jacob never experienced a nocturnal emission, so Reuben was actually conceived from his father's first drop of semen when Jacob consummated his first marriage with Leah. However, Jacob thought that he was sleeping with Rachel, whom he had been promised by Laban, so his desire focused on her, not on Leah, his actual partner. Because "the thought of that drop" was not "in its place" (not directed toward Leah, but rather toward Rachel), the title of firstborn was transferred to Joseph (Rachel's eventual first child). If Jacob had intended to impregnate Leah, then Reuben would have retained all the prerogatives of the firstborn.

See above, pp. 333–34 and nn. 184–89; p. 360 and n. 308; p. 426 and n. 603.

"Alternatively, *Unbridled as water, you will not remain!* For look, when the descendants of Reuben wage war in the world and conquer many nations, they will not remain in kingship! Why? *For you mounted your father's bed*—for they are destined to wage war in the Holy Land, precisely as is written: *for you mounted* משכבי אביך (*mishkevei avikha*), *your father's bed*—Jerusalem.[627] *Mishkevei, beds*—the word should read משכב (*mishkav*), *bed*. However, this pertains to Israel the Elder: *your father's beds*—not *bed*—because two times Jerusalem was built, and a third time in the era of King Messiah; so, *your father's beds*.[628]

"Here, blessing is revealed, and what happened at that time, and what would transpire when Israel enter the land, and what would happen in the time of King Messiah, concerning the action of Reuben."[629]

Simeon and Levi, brothers—weapons of violence their trade (Genesis 49:5).

Rabbi Yitsḥak said, "He joined them to the left side of *Shekhinah*, because he saw acts of harsh Judgment, which the world could not endure."[630]

Rabbi Yose said, "Where is their blessing?"[631]

Rabbi Yitsḥak replied, "Simeon did not deserve it, because [Jacob] saw his many evil deeds.[632] As for Levi, he issued from the side of harsh Judgment, and

627. **wage war in the world...** See above, pp. 429–30 and nn. 619, 623–24.

628. ***Mishkevei, beds*...** The plural refers to the first and second Temples in the past and the third Temple, to be built in the time of the Messiah.

"Israel the Elder" refers to God. See above, note 534.

629. **blessing is revealed...** Jacob's words to Reuben include blessing (see the parable, above at note 616, and the predictions of Messianic victories at note 623), his loss of the privileges of the firstborn ("what happened at that time"), his eventual settling in the Transjordan when Israel entered the Promised Land, and his failed attempt to seize kingship in the time of the Messiah.

630. **joined them to the left side of *Shekhinah*...** When Dinah was raped by Shechem son of Hamor, her brothers Simeon and Levi avenged the outrage by killing Shechem, Hamor, and all the males of the town (Genesis 34). In his final words to these two sons, Jacob criticized their violence. According to Rabbi Yitsḥak, the patriarch realized that they derived from the *sefirah* of *Din* (Judgment), on the left, and so he joined them to left side of *Shekhinah*, who Herself derives from *Din* but conveys a gentler aspect of this quality. Jacob intended that thereby their harshness would be tempered.

See *Zohar* 1:173a, 184a, 244a; 2:6a, 11a.

631. **Where is their blessing?** Jacob's words to these two sons convey harsh criticism, not blessing. See above, p. 422 and n. 589.

632. **Simeon... many evil deeds** Jacob envisioned three evil deeds related to Simeon—not only his violent conduct in avenging the rape of Dinah (above, note 630), but also how he had plotted to kill Joseph, and the sinful act of his descendant Zimri (Numbers 25).

On Simeon and Levi's plotting to kill Joseph, see above, p. 123 and n. 244. On Jacob's foreknowledge of Zimri's sin, see *Pesiqta de-Rav Kahana*, add. 1, p. 442; *Midrash Tehillim* 90:3.

his blessing did not depend on [Jacob]. Even when Moses came, it did not depend on him, but rather on the blessed Holy One, as is written: *Bless, O YHVH, his abundance, and favor the work of his hands* (Deuteronomy 33:11).[633]

"Come and see! It is written: *This sea, vast and broad of reach, gliding creatures there innumerable, living beings small and great* (Psalms 104:25). *This sea, vast*—*Shekhinah*, who stood above Jacob as he was about to depart from the world.

"*And broad of reach*—completely filled with all the world, which is compressed there.[634]

"*Gliding creatures there innumerable*—for countless supernal angels exist there.

"*Living beings small and great*—the twelve tribes, sons of Jacob, existing there consummately. One a lion and one a deer, one a wolf and one a lamb."[635]

Rabbi Yitsḥak said, "Lion, one; lamb, one; one a wolf and one a kid—and similarly all of them, so that there should be *living beings small and great*."[636]

Rabbi Yehudah said, "All of these are fine, but Judah is a lion, Simeon is an ox. This has been established by the Companions, for they were gazing at one another—one on the right and one on the left. This can be compared to an ox who became vicious. People said, 'Let's draw a picture of a lion in its trough, and [the ox] will see it and be afraid of it.' So, Simeon is an ox, Judah is a lion.[637]

633. **As for Levi...** He too issued from the *sefirah* of *Din* (above, note 630) and was not blessed by either Jacob or Moses, but rather directly by God, who assigned him the role of serving in the Tabernacle and the Temple.

634. **completely filled with all the world...** *Shekhinah* contains all of Creation, which issues from Her and is sustained by Her.

635. **twelve tribes...** The twelve tribes are pictured as arraying and completing *Shekhinah*. See above, p. 51, n. 369; p. 426 and n. 604.

Three of the four animals here correspond to those mentioned in Jacob's blessing of the tribes: lion (Judah), deer (Naphtali), wolf (Benjamin). The lamb may allude to the zodiacal sign of the lamb (Aries), which corresponds to Reuben (according to *Massekhet Soferim*, add. 1, 1:3; *Midrash Tehillim* 90:3). According to *Yalqut Shim'oni*, Exodus 418, Judah corresponds to this sign. For other interpretations of the lamb, see *OY*; *Nefesh David*; *Sullam*.

636. **Lion, one; lamb, one...** Instead of deer, Rabbi Yitsḥak includes גדי (*gedi*), "kid," alluding to the tribe of גד (*Gad*), Gad. Apparently he wants to contrast "lion" with "lamb," and the powerful "wolf" with "kid," thereby illustrating the verset: *living beings small and great*.

637. **Simeon is an ox...** Simeon corresponds to the zodiacal sign of Taurus, the ox (or bull).

See *Midrash Tehillim* 90:3 (and Buber's note 16); *Zohar* 1:173a, 200b. Cf. *Massekhet Soferim*, add. 1, 1:3; *Yalqut Shim'oni*, Exodus 418.

The four creatures seen by the prophet Ezekiel (1:10) each had the face of a lion on the right and the face of an ox on the left. Here, right symbolizes *Ḥesed* (Love), and left *Din* (Judgment); thus the violent behavior of Simeon (the ox on the left) will be overcome through the power of Judah (the lion on the right).

The parable appears in two midrashic sources (*Pesiqta de-Rav Kahana*, add. 1, p. 442; *Midrash Tehillim* 90:3), both of which

"Simeon did not attain blessings; rather, Moses appended him to Judah, as is said: *Hear, O YHVH, the voice of Judah* (Deuteronomy 33:7). It is written *Hear, O YHVH*, and it is written *For YHVH has heard that I am despised* (Genesis 29:33)."[638]

Rabbi Yehudah said, "Simeon and Levi were consigned to Moses."[639]

Rabbi Yose said, "Why did their father consign them to Moses? Let us consign this to the supreme Holy Lamp!"[640]

They came and asked Rabbi Shim'on. He said, "How precious are these words!" Clapping his hands in grief, he cried, and said, "Who will discover you, holy faithful one? In your life you transcended all human beings; in your death you vanished, your image concealed. The keys of your Lord have always been delivered into your hands.[641]

"Come and see: Jacob had four wives and engendered sons by them all, [236b] becoming complete through his wives.[642] As he was about to pass away,

employ the word אבוסו (*avuso*), "its trough (or manger, crib)." Here, this is replaced by the Zoharic neologism קופטיה (*qufteih*), perhaps a playful variation of קופסיה (*qufseih*), "its box," which approximates "its trough." See Luria, *Va-Ye'esof David*, s.v. *qifta*; *Nefesh David*; cf. *Zohar* 3:62b.

638. **Simeon did not attain blessings...** Jacob's words to Simeon do not constitute a blessing, and in Moses' blessing of the tribes (Deuteronomy 33) there appears no clear reference to Simeon. However, according to rabbinic tradition, Moses alluded to שמעון (*Shim'on*), Simeon, when he blessed Judah, saying שמע (*Shema*), *Hear, O YHVH, the voice of Judah*. The verb שמע (*shama*), "to hear," is linked with *Shim'on* by Simeon's mother, Leah: *She conceived again and bore a son, and she said, "For YHVH* שמע *(shama), has heard, that I am despised, so He has given me this one too," and she named him* שמעון *(Shim'on), Simeon.*

See *Sifrei*, Deuteronomy 348; *Targum Yerushalmi*, Deuteronomy 33:7; *Pesiqta de-Rav Kahana*, add. 1, p. 442. Simeon's dependence on Judah reflects the fact that his territory was eventually incorporated into Judah's. See Joshua 19:1–9 and Judges 1:3.

639. **consigned...** Jacob did not offer Simeon and Levi a blessing but rather left this act to Moses.

640. **Let us consign this to the supreme Holy Lamp!** "Let us pose this question to Rabbi Shim'on!" See above, note 610. See *KP*, who notes the humorous element.

641. **Who will discover you...** Or, "...uncover you." Rabbi Shim'on addresses Moses, faithful servant of God, who has vanished and ascended to the heights of divinity and whose burial place is unknown.

See Deuteronomy 34:6: *...and no man has known his burial place to this day.* On Moses as the "faithful one," see Numbers 12:7: *Not so My servant Moses, in all My house he is* נאמן *(ne'eman), trusted* [or: *faithful*]. See *Zohar* 1:76a. Moses is referred to as רועה נאמן (*ro'eh ne'eman*), "Faithful Shepherd," in *Mekhilta, Beshallaḥ* 6; *Sifrei Zuta* 27; *Eikhah Rabbah, Petiḥta* 24 (רעיא מהימנא [*ra'aya meheimna*]); *Rut Rabbah, Petiḥta* 5; *Ester Rabbah* 7:13. See *Zohar* 1:106a; 2:8b, 53b; 2:156a, 193b. Cf. *Tanḥuma, Shemot* 7; *ZḤ* 15a (*MhN*). (On the later section of the *Zohar* entitled *Ra'aya Meheimna*, see the Glossary.)

On the rhetorical question "Who will discover [or: uncover] you?" cf. the rabbinic question "Who will uncover the dust from your eyes?" in M *Sotah* 5:2, 5; *Bereshit Rabbah* 21:7; *Vayiqra Rabbah* 25:2. See Galante; *NO*; Scholem.

642. **Jacob had four wives...** Jacob

Shekhinah stood above him. He wanted to bless these two, but in the presence of *Shekhinah* he could not, for he was afraid. He said, 'What should I do? Look, both of them derive from the side of harsh Judgment! If I coerce *Shekhinah*—I cannot, for I have had four wives, by whom I have become complete. Rather, I will consign them to the master of the house, for the house depends upon his will, and he will do as he wishes.'

"So Jacob said, 'I have obtained my share of wives and children in this world, becoming complete. How can I press the *Matronita* further? Rather, I will consign the matter to the master of the *Matronita;* he will act without fear.'[643]

"Come and see what is written: *This is the blessing that Moses* איש האלהים (*ish ha-Elohim*), *the man of God, bestowed* (Deuteronomy 33:1)—master of the house, master of the *Matronita*—as is written: אישה (*ishah*), *her husband, may let it stand or* ishah, *her husband, may annul it* (Numbers 30:14). For look, it is written כלת משה (*kallat Moshe*), *the bride of Moses* (ibid. 7:1)! So Moses blessed whomever he wished and did not fear. Therefore Jacob said, 'I see that these sons of mine are on the side of harsh Judgment. Let the master of the house come, and he will bless them!'

"Surely, *ish ha-Elohim, husband of God*! He did as he wished with the house, as has been established: *her husband may let it stand or her husband may annul it. Her husband may let it stand*—as is written: *Moses said, 'Arise, O YHVH!'* (ibid. 10:35). *Or her husband may annul it*—as is written: *And when it came to rest, he would say, 'Return, O YHVH!'* (ibid., 36). The master of the house surely did as he wished, with no one hindering him—like a man commanding his wife, and she does what he wishes. So even though Jacob grasped the Tree of Life, he was

married Leah and Rachel, as well as their maidservants, Bilhah and Zilpah. With all four wives, he engendered twelve tribes and attained completeness.

See *Zohar* 1:133a–b. On the symbolic significance of the offspring of each of these wives, see *Zohar* 1:154a, 155a, 158a.

643. **He wanted to bless these two...** Jacob wanted to bless Simeon and Levi, but since they derived from harsh Judgment, he hesitated to impose on *Shekhinah* and seek Her blessing for them, because he had maintained relations with all four of his wives—unlike Moses, who had abstained from sexual relations with his wife and devoted himself exclusively to *Shekhinah*. Moses had thereby become the complete master of *Shekhinah* (known as "house" and *Matronita*) and could direct Her to bless whomever he wished.

See *Zohar* 1:21b–22a; 3:187b; above, p. 420 and n. 581; Galante; *KP*; Scholem; Liebes, "Myth vs. Symbol," 213–19. For somewhat different interpretations, see *OY*; *MmD*. In the *Zohar* the phrase "master of the house" is applied to both Jacob and Moses (1:21b, 138b, 152b, 239a; 2:22b, 235b, 238b, 244b [*Heikh*]; 3:163b) as well as to the mystic who masters the secrets of Torah (2:99b). See Numbers 12:7 (quoted above, note 641): *Not so My servant Moses, in all My house he is trusted.*

מטרוניתא (*Matronita*) is an Aramaized form of Latin *matrona*, "matron, married woman, noble lady," often applied in the *Zohar* to *Shekhinah*.

master of the house only below, whereas Moses was above, and therefore he consigned them to the master of the house."[644]

May my soul never enter סודם (sodam), their council! (Genesis 49:6).[645]

Rabbi Abba opened, "סוד (*Sod*), *The secret of, YHVH is for those who fear Him; to them He reveals His covenant* (Psalms 25:14). *The secret of YHVH is for those who fear Him*—supreme mystery of Torah has been given by the blessed Holy One only to those who fear sin. To those who fear sin, the supreme mystery of Torah has been revealed. What is the supreme mystery of Torah? You must say: the holy covenant, called *secret of YHVH*.[646]

644. ***איש האלהים (ish ha-Elohim), the man of God...*** The full verse reads: *This is the blessing that Moses, the man of God, bestowed upon the Children of Israel before his death.* Based on a radical midrashic interpretation of this verse, Rabbi Shim'on understands the word איש (*ish*), "man," according to its related meaning, "husband," as in the verse in Numbers 30, concerning a wife's vow: אישה (*ishah*), *her husband, may let it stand or her husband may annul it.* As a husband (traditionally) has power over his wife, so Moses had power over *Shekhinah* (who is known as *Elohim*).

See *Midrash Tehillim* 90:5, in the name of Rabbi Shim'on son of Lakish: "Why is he [Moses] called איש האלהים (*ish ha-elohim*) (Psalms 90:1)? Just as a husband can, if he wishes, annul his wife's vow, or, if he wishes, let it stand—as is said: אישה (*ishah*), *her husband, may let it stand or her husband may annul it*—so, as it were, Moses said to the blessed Holy One, *Arise, O YHVH! Return, O YHVH!*"

See *Pesiqta de-Rav Kahana*, add. 1, pp. 443–44, 448 (variants); *Tanḥuma, Vezot Haberakhah* 2 (*Ets Yosef*, ad loc.); *Shemot Rabbah* 43:4; *Devarim Rabbah* (ed. Lieberman), p. 129; *Zohar* 1:6b, 21b–22a, 148a, 239a; 2:22b, 235b, 238b; Moses de León, *Sefer ha-Rimmon*, 25 (and Wolfson's notes). The two verses in Numbers 10 read: *As the ark journeyed, Moses would say, "Arise, O YHVH! May Your enemies be scattered, and Your foes flee before You!" And when it came to rest, he would say, "Return, O YHVH, to the myriads of thousands of Israel!"*

Numbers 7:1 reads: *On the day* כלות משה (*kallot Moshe*), *Moses finished, setting up the Tabernacle....* Although in the Masoretic text the word כלות (*kallot*), *finished*, is spelled with a ו (*vav*), it is interpreted midrashically as if it were spelled without the *vav*, so that it can be read כלת (*kallat*), "the bride of [Moses]." Here, this reading is cited as proof that Moses is *husband of Elohim*, married to his bride, *Shekhinah*.

See *Pesiqta de-Rav Kahana* 1; *Tanḥuma, Naso* 20, 26; *Tanḥuma* (Buber), *Vayishlaḥ* 28, *Naso* 28; *Pesiqta Rabbati* 5; *Bemidbar Rabbah* 12:8; Rashi on Numbers 7:1; *Zohar* 2:5b, 140b, 145a, 235a; 3:4b, 148a, 226b (*RM*), 254a (*RM*); *Minḥat Shai* on Numbers 7:1.

Jacob is linked with *Tif'eret*, the Tree of Life, so he too unites with *Shekhinah* and functions as "master of the house," but Moses is the more supreme master. See *Zohar* 1:21b–22a, 152b; 3:187b; and the preceding note.

645. ***May my soul...*** The verse reads: *May my soul never enter their council, may my presence* [or: *glory*] *never join their assembly!* The word סוד (*sod*) means "council, secret."

646. ***secret of YHVH...*** **supreme mystery...** The *secret* is identified here with *Yesod*, the divine phallus and site of the covenant of circumcision. Those who fear sin (especially sexual sin) and guard the

"Simeon and Levi troubled themselves over this secret with the men of Shechem, so that they would circumcise themselves and accept this secret—and Scripture testifies: *deceitfully* (Genesis 34:13). Further, in the incident of Zimri son of Salu, who rendered this *secret of YHVH* unfit. So Jacob said, *May my soul never enter their secret!* What is *my soul*? The soul who enters and unites with the covenant above and is called 'soul, bundle of life.'[647]

"*May my glory never join their assembly!* (Genesis 49, ibid.)—this has been established, as is said: *Korah assembled against them* (Numbers 16:19). *May my glory never join*—Glory of Israel, unspecified.[648]

covenant of circumcision prove themselves worthy of attaining the secret rung of *Yesod*.

See *Tanḥuma, Lekh Lekha* 19: "*The secret of YHVH is for those who fear Him; to them He reveals His covenant.* Which secret did He reveal to *those in awe of Him*? Circumcision, for the blessed Holy One revealed the mystery of circumcision only to Abraham . . . , to whom was said: *For you fear God* (Genesis 22:12)."

See *Tanḥuma* (Buber), *Lekh Lekha* 23–24; *Bereshit Rabbah* 49:2; *Aggadat Bereshit* 16:2; Ezra of Gerona, *Peirush Shir ha-Shirim*, 526; *Zohar* 1:91a–b, 95a; 2:237b; 3:43b (*Piq*); Moses de León, *Shushan Edut*, 339; idem, *Sefer ha-Rimmon*, 226–298.

647. **Simeon and Levi troubled themselves . . .** When their sister, Dinah, was raped by Shechem son of Hamor, Simeon and Levi deceitfully promised Shechem and his father that if all the males of the town would circumcise themselves, the two groups could intermarry and live together peacefully. The residents complied, but while they were recovering from the mass circumcision, Simeon and Levi killed Shechem, Hamor, and all the males. According to Rabbi Abba, this breach of trust violated the covenant of *Yesod*.

Zimri son of Salu was a chieftain of the tribe of Simeon who had sexual relations with a Midianite woman. According to midrashic sources, Jacob foresaw the sin of Zimri and in saying *May my soul never enter their secret*, he was praying that his name not be associated with Zimri; consequently when the Torah identifies Zimri (Numbers 25:14), it refers to his tribe, Simeon, but not to the patriarch.

Here *my soul* symbolizes *Shekhinah* ("bundle of life") who normally joins with *Yesod* (*secret* and "covenant above"), generating souls for the world. Because Simeon and Levi had tainted *Yesod*, Jacob intended that they (and their descendants) would be incapable of uniting the divine couple—or that *Shekhinah* would not bless their sexual activity.

See Genesis 34; Numbers 25; above, p. 431 and nn. 630, 632. On the allusion to Zimri in Jacob's words, see *Bereshit Rabbah* 98:5; 99:7 (and parallels). On "bundle of life," see 1 Samuel 25:29; Moses de León, *Sheqel ha-Qodesh*, 61 (75); above at note 267.

648. ***their assembly . . . Korah assembled . . .*** According to midrashic sources, Jacob foresaw the rebellion of Korah the Levite, and when he said *May my glory never join their assembly*, he was praying that his name not be linked with Korah's "assembling" against Moses and Aaron. Consequently, when the Torah traces Korah's lineage (Numbers 16:1), it stops at Levi and does not implicate the patriarch.

Here, Rabbi Abba indicates that *glory* refers to *Shekhinah*, the Divine Presence. She is the Glory of *Tif'eret*, whose full name is *Tif'eret Yisra'el* (Beauty of Israel). The word "unspecified" indicates that here "Israel" does not refer specifically to the people Is-

"Therefore, their father did not bless them, consigning them to Moses."[649]

Rabbi Ḥiyya said, "From these verses [we learn] that they were not united with one another, and so it had to be. So, this encompasses all. You cannot find a generation in the whole world upon which their judgment does not descend, bringing accusation, and beggars abound, knocking on people's doors. Look, all this!"[650]

Judah, you, will your brothers acclaim (Genesis 49:8).[651]

Rabbi Yeisa opened, "*He made the moon for seasons; the sun knows when to set* (Psalms 104:19). *He made the moon for seasons*—by which to sanctify new moons and new years. The moon never shines except from the sun, and when the sun reigns the moon does not; when the sun is gathered, then the moon reigns, and there is no reckoning by the moon until the sun is gathered.[652]

"The blessed Holy One made both of them to shine, as is written: *God placed them in the expanse of heaven to shine upon the earth* (Genesis 1:17). *And they will be for signs* (ibid., 14)—Sabbaths, as is written: *for it is a sign* (Exodus 31:17). *And for seasons* (Genesis, ibid.)—Holidays. *For days* (ibid.)—new moons. *And years* (ibid.)—new years. So that the nations of the world will reckon by the sun and Israel by the moon.[653]

rael, but rather to the divine Israel: *Tif'eret Yisra'el*.

On the allusion to Korah, see *Bereshit Rabbah* 98:5; 99:7 (and parallels); BT *Sanhedrin* 109b. On the phrase "Israel, unspecified," see *Zohar* 1:32b, 244b; 3:13a, 146a, 266b.

649. **consigning them to Moses** Who blessed the tribes before his death. See Deuteronomy 33; above, pp. 433–35.

650. **From these verses...** Jacob's last words to Simeon and Levi are *I will divide them in Jacob, disperse them in Israel* (Genesis 49:7). According to Rabbi Ḥiyya, the brothers had to be separated because otherwise their harshness would prove unbearable. Even so, the world still suffers from their legacy, as indicated by the persistence of poverty.

On the notion that the two brothers had to be separated, see *Aggadat Bereshit* 83:1; *Leqaḥ Tov*, Genesis 49:7; *Zohar* 2:6a. According to rabbinic sources, most of the poor among Israel are descended from Simeon. As for Levi, his tribe inherited no land and was dependent on tithes. See *Bereshit Rabbah* 98:5; 99:7; *Tanḥuma, Vayḥi* 10; Rashi and Radak on Genesis 49:7. Many manuscripts indicate that some material is missing in this passage after the phrase "from these verses." See Galante.

651. ***Judah, you...*** The full verse reads: *Judah, you, will your brothers acclaim—your hand on your enemies' nape—your father's sons will bow to you.*

652. **when the sun is gathered...** When the sun sets.

See JT *Rosh ha-Shanah* 2:8, 58b; *Bereshit Rabbah* 6:1; *Pesiqta de-Rav Kahana* 5:1.

653. ***And they will be for signs...*** The full verse in Genesis reads: *God said, "Let there be lights in the expanse of heaven to separate the day from the night, and they will be for signs and for seasons, for days and years."* According to Rabbi Yeisa, God intended that Israel would follow a lunar calendar and other nations a solar calendar.

In the verse in Exodus, Sabbath is called a

"This accords with what Rabbi El'azar has said: 'It is written: *You have magnified the nation; for them, You have increased joy* (Isaiah 9:2). *You have magnified the nation*—Israel, of whom is written *Who is a great nation?* (Deuteronomy 4:7).[654] *For them, You have increased joy*—because of them, *You have increased joy*: the moon, whose light increases because of Israel.[655]

"Nations of the world, by the sun; Israel, by the moon. Which of them is more worthy? Surely, the moon [237a] is above, and the sun of the nations of the world is below this moon, and that sun shines from this moon. See the difference between Israel and them! Israel are joined to the moon, linked with the supernal sun, united with the site that illumines the supernal sun, cleaving there, as is written: *You, cleaving to YHVH your God, are alive every one of you today!* (Deuteronomy 4:4)."[656]

Judah, you, will your brothers acclaim.

438 Rabbi Shim'on said, "Kingship endured for Judah. This accords with what we have said: What is the meaning of the verse *This time I will acclaim YHVH* (Genesis 29:35)? Because he is the fourth, *I will acclaim YHVH*—fourth leg of the throne. יהודה (*Yehudah*), Judah—יה"ו (*yod, he, vav*), engraving of the supernal name. How is it consummated? With ד (*dalet*), corresponding to the last ה (*he*) of the holy name: holy name complete in its letters, with the knot binding them. Therefore, *your brothers will acclaim you*, for your kingship fittingly endures, as

sign: *Between Me and the Children of Israel it is a sign forever that in six days YHVH made heaven and earth and on the seventh day He ceased and was refreshed.*

See *Bereshit Rabbah* 6:1, 3; *Pesiqta de-Rav Kahana* 5:1, 14. On the lunar and solar calendars, see *Mekhilta, Pisḥa* 1; *Tosefta, Sukkah* 2:6; BT *Sukkah* 29a; *Zohar* 1:46b, 239a; 3:220b; *ZḤ* 14a–b (*MhN*); Scholem, "Parashah Ḥadashah," pp. 432–33.

654. ***Who is a great nation?*** The full verse reads: *Who is a great nation that has gods so close to it as YHVH our God, in all our calling upon Him?* Since in this verse *nation* refers to Israel, Rabbi El'azar concludes that the same is true for the verse in Isaiah.

655. **moon, whose light increases...** The moon symbolizes *Shekhinah*, who is augmented and fulfilled for Israel's sake—or alternatively, because of Israel's devotion. She is known as *joy*.

On *Shekhinah* as *joy*, see *Zohar* 3:8b, 118a, 212b.

656. **moon is above...** *Shekhinah*, who governs and sustains the world, is above the sun and illumines it. Israel, who are joined to *Shekhinah*, are thereby linked with Her partner, *Tif'eret*, symbolized by the sun. Through *Tif'eret*, they are also united with His source, *Binah*. The verse in Deuteronomy implies that the people of Israel cleave to *Tif'eret* (*YHVH*), *Shekhinah* (*your Elohim, God*), and *Binah*, the source of חיים (*ḥayyim*), "life" (*alive*).

The connection between Rabbi Yeisa's teaching and the verse in Genesis 49 (*Judah, you, will your brothers acclaim*) is that *Judah* symbolizes *Shekhinah* (the moon), who is acclaimed and acknowledged by *your brothers*—namely Israel, who reckon their calendar according to the moon.

is said: *Judah still rules with* אל (*El*), *God, and is faithful with the holy ones* (Hosea 12:1). Who are *the holy ones*? Supernal holy ones, all of whom acclaim him and consider him *faithful*. So he is first of all, king over all."[657]

Rabbi Shim'on opened, "*All glorious, daughter of the king within, her garment brocaded with gold* (Psalms 45:14). This is Assembly of Israel.[658] *Glorious*—for there is 'glory,' one above the other; one male, the other female, called *glorious*. *Daughter of the king*, namely בת שבע (*Bat Sheva*), Bathsheba, 'daughter of seven'; daughter of the voice, for He is 'a great voice.'[659] This supreme King is *within*,

657. **Kingship endured...** Judah was progenitor of the Davidic dynasty, befitting his link with *Shekhinah*, or *Malkhut* (Kingdom). The verse in Genesis records Leah's reaction at the birth of her fourth son: "*This time* אודה (*odeh*), *I will acclaim, YHVH.*" *So she named him* יהודה (*Yehudah*), *Judah*. Rabbi Shim'on explains that Leah was celebrating the fact that Judah stabilized the divine throne. Her first three sons (Reuben, Simeon, and Levi) symbolize respectively the sefirotic triad of *Ḥesed, Gevurah*, and *Tif'eret*, which constitute three legs of the throne; Judah symbolizes *Shekhinah*, fourth leg of the throne, upon which rests *Binah*, symbolized by Leah herself.

Judah's name, יהודה (*Yehudah*), appears to contain the divine name. The first three letters, יהו (*yod, he, vav*) themselves constitute the holy name יהו (*Yaho*). The *yod* symbolizes *Keter* and the primordial point of *Ḥokhmah*; the feminine marker *he* symbolizes the Divine Mother, *Binah*; the *vav* (whose numerical value is six) symbolizes *Tif'eret* together with the five *sefirot* surrounding Him (*Ḥesed* through *Yesod*). The divine name is completed by the next two letters in the name of יהודה (*Yehudah*): ד (*dalet*) and ה (*he*), both of which symbolize *Shekhinah*. The numerical value of *dalet* is four, which may allude to *Shekhinah*'s role as fourth leg of the throne. Further, *dalet* suggests דלה (*dallah*), "poor," which describes *Shekhinah*, who has nothing of Her own, only what She receives from the *sefirot* above Her. When She is fully united with them, this *dalet* transforms into the second *he* of יהוה (*YHVH*). The *dalet* serves as a link, or "knot," joining the letters יהו (*yod, he, vav*) with the second ה (*he*). This image derives from the tradition that the "knot" of the *tefillah shel rosh* (phylactery worn on the head) is in the shape of the letter ד (*dalet*).

In the verse from Hosea, the word אל (*El*), *God*, refers to *Shekhinah* (see above, p. 429 and n. 618). "Supernal holy ones" refers to the angels. Judah is "first of all" in various ways, for example: first to enter the Red Sea (below, note 672), first to set out journeying in the wilderness (above, note 593), and first to attack the Canaanites (below, note 673).

On the divine chariot-throne, see *Bereshit Rabbah* 47:6: "Resh Lakish said, 'The patriarchs themselves constitute the [divine] Chariot.'" See above, p. 337 and n. 198. On the fourth component of the throne (King David—or here, Judah his ancestor), see *Zohar* 1:154b–156a; above, p. 364 and n. 332. On the name יהו (*Yaho*), see *Sefer Yetsirah* 1:13; Scholem, *Origins of the Kabbalah*, 31–33. On the letters of Judah's name, see *Zohar* 2:104a.

658. **Assembly of Israel** *Shekhinah*. See above, pp. 122–23, n. 237.

659. ***Glorious*—for there is 'glory'...** *Tif'eret*, the Divine Male, is known as כבוד (*kavod*), Glory. *Shekhinah*, His female partner, is called כבודה (*kevuddah*), Glorious—with the addition of the feminine marker ה (*he*). She is the daughter of *Binah*, the Divine Mother—who is also known as *king* and "seven," generating and ruling over all seven lower *sefirot*. Thus *Shekhinah* is called *daughter of the king* and *Bat Sheva* (daughter of seven).

Finally, *Binah* is called "a great voice," a

for there is a king who is not as deeply within. And this one is *glorious, daughter of the king.*[660]

"*Her garment brocaded with gold*—for She is clothed and united with supernal *Gevurah*.[661] This one too is king, through whom the earth endures. When? When He unites with Justice, as is said: *By justice a king sustains the land* (Proverbs 29:4). This we call Kingdom of Heaven; Judah united with it, inheriting the kingdom of earth."[662]

Rabbi Yehudah and Rabbi Yitsḥak were walking on the way. Rabbi Yehudah said, "Let us open with words of Torah as we walk."

Rabbi Yitsḥak opened, saying, "*He drove out* את האדם (*et ha-adam*), *the human, and placed east of the Garden of Eden the cherubim and the flame of the whirling sword to guard the way to the Tree of Life* (Genesis 3:24). This verse has been established by the Companions, but ויגרש (*vaygaresh*), *He drove out*—like a man divorcing his wife. את האדם (*Et ha-adam*), et *Adam*, precisely!

"Come and see the mystery of the matter! Adam was caught by his very sin, inflicting death upon himself and upon the whole world, and causing divorce to that tree by which he sinned—divorced by him and divorced by his descendants forever, as is written: *He divorced* et *Adam*—*et*, precisely, as is said: *I saw* את יהוה (*et YHVH*) (Isaiah 6:1). Here too, *et ha-adam, et Adam.*[663]

phrase that describes the divine voice at Mount Sinai (Deuteronomy 5:18); so, *Shekhinah* is known as בת קול (*bat qol*), "echo" (literally, "daughter of a voice"). In rabbinic literature a heavenly *bat qol* conveys divine messages.

660. **supreme King is *within*...** According to the simple sense of the verse in Psalms, the word *within* describes the *daughter of the king*, but Rabbi Shim'on applies it to the *king*. The *king within* is *Binah*, as opposed to *Tif'eret*, who is also a king but not as deeply hidden. Rabbi Shim'on then repeats that *Shekhinah* is *glorious, daughter of the king*.

661. **She is clothed...** *Shekhinah* is influenced by *Gevurah*, which is symbolized by gold. *Gevurah* is harsh Judgment, whereas *Shekhinah* is mild Judgment.

662. **This one too is king...** *Shekhinah* is also called King, ruling over the lower worlds and conveying to them the nourishment that She receives from *Tif'eret*. Rabbi Shim'on interprets the verse in Proverbs to mean: *By* (uniting with *Tif'eret*, known as) *justice, a king* (*Shekhinah*) *sustains the land* (the world). See above, p. 406 and n. 514.

Shekhinah is known as *Malkhut Shamayim* (Kingdom of Heaven), which is understood as Kingdom of *Tif'eret*, who is Himself known as Heaven.

663. **ויגרש (*vaygaresh*), *He drove out*...** Several midrashim interpret the biblical word ויגרש (*vaygaresh*), *He drove out*, in the sense of the rabbinic Hebrew term גירושין (*geirushin*), "divorce." See *Seder Eliyyahu Rabbah* 1: "*He drove out Adam.* This teaches that the blessed Holy One divorced him like a wife."

See *Ziqquqin de-Nura*, ad loc.; *Bereshit Rabbah* 21:8; *Midrash Avkir*, in *Yalqut Shim'oni*, Genesis, 34; and *Midrash ha-Gadol* on this verse: "This teaches that he was divorced like a wife divorced from her husband because of some indecency."

Adam's harmonious and intimate rela-

"*He placed east of the Garden of Eden the cherubim.* This is below—as there are cherubim above, so there are cherubim below. He spread this tree over them.[664]

tionship with God is ruined by sin. Rabbi Yitsḥak adopts this midrashic view but reassigns the roles: it is not God who initiates the divorce but rather Adam! This radical interpretation depends upon the tiny word את (*et*), which is technically an accusative particle with no clear independent sense. Already in rabbinic times, Naḥum of Gimzo and his disciple Rabbi Akiva taught that the presence of *et* in a biblical verse amplifies the apparent meaning. Here, as often in the *Zohar,* את (*et*) becomes a name of *Shekhinah,* who comprises the totality of divine speech, the entire alphabet from א (*alef*) to ת (*tav*).

See BT *Pesaḥim* 22b, *Ḥagigah* 12a; *Zohar* 1:29b, 112a–b, 247a; 2:90a, 135b; and the Christian parallel in Revelation 1:8: "I am *alpha* and *omega.*"

By dividing the biblical sentence—*He drove out* את (*et*) *Adam*—into two units, Rabbi Yitsḥak transforms its meaning. The first unit consists of *He drove out* את (*et*). The second unit identifies the subject of the sentence, which is shockingly not God, but *Adam.* In other words, the sentence now reads: *He drove out* [or: *divorced*] *et* (*Shekhinah*). (And who drove out *et*?) *Adam.* His sin consists in divorcing *Shekhinah.*

In the *Zohar* the exact nature of Adam's sin is a tightly guarded secret; the biblical account is seen as hiding the true meaning. See *ZḤ* 19a (*MhN*), where Rabbi Shim'on recounts a conversation he had with Adam while selecting his future site in Paradise: "Adam . . . was sitting next to me, speaking with me, and he asked that his sin not be revealed to the whole world beyond what the Torah had recounted. It is concealed in that tree in the Garden of Eden." The Tree of Knowledge of Good and Evil symbolizes *Shekhinah.* Through contemplation, Adam should have united Her with *Tif'eret,* the Tree of Life, but instead he worshiped and partook of *Shekhinah* alone, splitting Her off from the other *sefirot* and divorcing Her from Her divine husband. This separation of *Shekhinah* from the Tree of Life interrupted the flow of emanation and brought death into the world.

See *Zohar* 1:12b, 35b–36a, 53b; *ZḤ* 91c (*MhN, Eikhah*); Moses de León, *Sefer ha-Rimmon,* 369; Scholem, *Major Trends,* 231–32, 236; Tishby, *Wisdom of the Zohar,* 1:373–76. On the psychological plane, the sin corresponds to the splitting off of consciousness from the unconscious. See Volume 1, p. 298, n. 1438.

By divorcing *Shekhinah* from *Tif'eret,* Adam also alienated Her from himself. See *Bereshit Rabbah* 19:7: "Rabbi Abba son of Kahana said, 'The essence of *Shekhinah* was in the lower realms. As soon as Adam sinned, it withdrew to the first heaven.'" See Naḥmanides on Genesis 3:8; *Zohar* 1:53a–b; Gikatilla, *Sha'arei Orah,* 15–17.

Adam's descendants, through their own sins, are seen as perpetuating the divorce and exile of *Shekhinah.* (The phrase "divorced by him and divorced by his descendants" can also be rendered "driven out along with him and driven out along with his descendants.") Finally, the verse from Isaiah is cited to show that here too את (*et*) symbolizes *Shekhinah,* who was the focus of the prophet's vision. See *Zohar* 1:18a, 60a, 247a; 2:81b. The Masoretic text reads: *I saw* את אדני (*et Adonai*), *my Lord.*

664. ***cherubim . . . below . . .*** The angelic cherubim below *Shekhinah,* corresponding to "cherubim above," namely the *sefirot Netsaḥ* and *Hod.*

In the verse in Genesis, *He placed* refers of course to God. Here, Rabbi Yitsḥak apparently understands the subject to be Adam, who drove *Shekhinah* (the Tree of Knowledge) out of the Garden, spreading Her over

"*And the flame of the whirling sword*—flashes of fire from that flaming sword.[665]

"*Whirling*—the one sucking from two sides, turning from this side to that.[666]

"Alternatively, *whirling*—those flashes of flame that we mentioned transform: sometimes female, sometimes male, transforming from their point totally.[667]

"All this, *to guard the way to the Tree of Life*. Who is *the way*? As is said: *who makes a way through the sea* (Isaiah 43:16)."[668]

Rabbi Yehudah said, "Fine! Certainly so! For Adam caused that tree by which he sinned to be divorced—and even other inhabitants of the world as well, as is said: *For your crimes your mother was sent away* (ibid. 50:1).[669] But well said! Because this is implied by the source, as is written: *He divorced* et *the human*—for this was the consummation of humanity.[670] From that day the moon was tainted, until Noah arrived and entered the ark. Then came the wicked, and it was tainted until Abraham arrived. It attained the perfection of Jacob and his sons, and Judah came and grasped it, empowering himself with kingship, possessing it as eternal inheritance—he and all his sons after him—as is written:

the cherubim. See *Zohar* 1:53b; *ZḤ* 91c (*MhN, Eikhah*); Galante. The last sentence can also be translated: "This tree spread over them."

665. **flashes of fire from that flaming sword** Harsh powers emanating from *Shekhinah,* who executes the divine judgment of *Gevurah*.

On *Shekhinah* as "sword," see *Zohar* 1:53b, 66b, 240b; 2:26a, 28b, 66a; 3:19b, 30a; Moses de León, *Sefer ha-Rimmon,* 69, 213. "Flashes" renders טפסי (*tifsei*), a Zoharic neologism sometimes associated with fire and occasionally meaning "glowing ember, burning coal." See *Zohar* 3:111a; *Bei'ur ha-Millim ha-Zarot,* 178–79; Luria, *Va-Ye'esof David,* s.v. *tifsa*; above, note 75.

666. **from two sides...** *Shekhinah* draws from right and left, *Ḥesed* and *Din,* conveying both to the world depending on human conduct.

667. ***whirling*... sometimes female, sometimes male...** The flashing powers issuing from *Shekhinah* become either male or female. See the midrashic comment on this word in *Bereshit Rabbah* 21:9: "*Whirling*—changing: sometimes male, sometimes female; sometimes spirits, sometimes angels."

See *Zohar* 1:44a, 53b, 165a (*ST*), 232a; 2:264a (*Heikh*); 3:19b, 73b (*Mat*).

668. **Who is *the way*?...** *Shekhinah* contains—or constitutes—a way leading to *Tif'eret,* the Tree of Life.

See *Zohar* 2:51a. In the *Zohar, a way through the sea* is often interpreted as "a way through *Shekhinah*." See *Zohar* 1:29b, 48b, 197b, 243b; 2:137a, 215a; 3:171b.

669. **even other inhabitants...** By sinning, Adam's descendants repeat the divorce of *Shekhinah*. In the verse in Isaiah, the community of Israel is pictured as *mother,* who was divorced by God because of the people's sins. In Kabbalah, this *mother* is *Shekhinah,* known as Assembly of Israel; She shares Her people's exile.

See *Zohar* 2:189b; 3:115a.

670. ***He divorced et the human*... consummation...** Adam was the perfect human being, so the verse calls him האדם (*ha-adam*), *the human.* As explained above (note 663), the verse is understood to mean: *He divorced* et (*Shekhinah*). (And who did this?) *Ha-adam*.

Judah, you, will your brothers acclaim, for kingship over them is his, as is said: *For Judah prevailed over his brothers* (1 Chronicles 5:2).[671] *Your brothers will acclaim you*—surely, when Israel stood at the sea, for they all acclaimed him, descending after him into the sea.[672]

"*Your hand on your enemies' nape* (Genesis 49:8)—as is said: *Judah shall go up first* (Judges 1:2).[673]

"*Your father's sons will bow to you* (Genesis, ibid.)—totality of all those other tribes, for he said *your father's sons*, not *your mother's sons. Your father's sons*—all those other tribes; for although they were split into two kingdoms, when they went up to Jerusalem they would kneel and bow down to the king in Jerusalem, because the kingship [237b] deriving from holy Kingdom issued from him.[674]

"*They will bow to you*—it is not written *And they will bow*, because this would include other nations. *And they will bow* is written only of the time when King Messiah will come, as is written: *princes, and they will bow* (Isaiah 49:7). Now that he said *they will bow*, this indicates that all of Israel alone will serve the exilarch in Babylon, not other nations.[675]

671. **moon was tainted...** *Shekhinah*, symbolized by the moon, was tainted by Adam's sin. Later, Noah (symbolizing *Yesod*) entered the ark (symbolizing *Shekhinah*), thereby reestablishing unity and removing the taint (see *Zohar* 1:59b). Subsequent human wickedness tainted Her again until Abraham restored Her. Then Jacob together with his sons completed the process, and Judah (and his Davidic descendants) attained kingship from *Shekhinah*, who is known as *Malkhut* (Kingdom).

The verse in Chronicles reads: *For Judah prevailed over his brothers, and a ruler came from him.*

672. **when Israel stood at the sea...** According to the Midrash, at the Red Sea no one wanted to be the first to enter and cross, until finally Nahshon son of Amminadab from the tribe of Judah jumped in.

See *Mekhilta, Beshallaḥ* 5; BT *Sotah* 37a (both in the name of Rabbi Yehudah).

673. ***Your hand...*** The full verse in Genesis reads: *Judah, you, will your brothers acclaim—your hand on your enemies' nape—your father's sons will bow to you.*

The context in Judges (1:1–2) reads: *After the death of Joshua, the Children of Israel asked YHVH, "Who shall go up for us first against the Canaanites, to attack them?" YHVH replied, "Judah shall go up. Behold, I have given the land into his hand."*

674. ***your father's sons*, not *your mother's sons*...** The latter phrase would have referred only to the other sons born to Leah (Judah's mother), namely Reuben, Simeon, Levi, Issachar, and Zebulun. By saying *your father's sons*, Jacob implied all eleven of Judah's brothers, born to Leah, Rachel, Bilhah, and Zilpah.

Although the Israelite kingdom split into two (Judah and Israel), when the various tribes made pilgrimage to Jerusalem they all acknowledged the Davidic king, whose power derived from *Malkhut* (Kingdom), as conveyed by Judah ("from him").

On the wording *your father's sons*, see *Bereshit Rabbah* 98:6; 99:7.

675. **not written *And they will bow*...** According to rabbinic hermeneutics, the apparently superfluous conjunction ו (*ve*), *and*, can in certain cases amplify the meaning of a biblical word. If Jacob had said וישתחוו (*ve-yishtaḥavu*), *and they will bow*, this would

"*A lion's whelp is Judah* (Genesis 49:9). At first a *whelp*, and afterward *a lion*. Mystery of the matter—at first a youth, and afterward a man: *YHVH is a man of war* (Exodus 15:3).[676]

"*From the prey, O my son, you mount* (Genesis, ibid.). What does this mean: *from the prey*? To include the Angel of Death, who stands over his prey, annihilating inhabitants of the world—and no one offers deliverance, as is said: *It tears apart, with none to deliver* (Micah 5:7). From that prey, *Shekhinah* ascends.[677]

"*He crouches* (Genesis, ibid.)—in the exile of Babylonia. *Lies down* (ibid.)—in the exile of Edom.[678]

"*Like a lion* (ibid.)—who is mighty. *Like the king of beasts*—who is mightier. So Israel are mighty, for all inhabitants of the world entice them and oppress them, yet they persist in their laws and customs *like a lion, like the king of beasts*.[679]

"Although it is written *Fallen, not to rise again, is Virgin Israel* (Amos 5:2), She is mighty *like a lion, like the king of beasts* in that falling. Just as a lion falls only to tear apart its prey and overpower—for the lion scents its prey from afar, and

have implied that not only the Israelites would bow, but also others—namely other nations—who were not represented by those whom Jacob was addressing. Now that he said simply ישתחוו (*yishtaḥavu*), *they will bow*, this indicated only the Israelites—though all of them—who would eventually serve the exilarch. The exilarch was the head of Babylonian Jewry, whose hereditary position maintained the continuity of Davidic rule.

The hermeneutical significance of *and* was championed by Rabbi Akiva. See BT *Yevamot* 68b, *Sanhedrin* 51b. The verse in Isaiah reads: *Kings will see and rise; princes, and they will bow down.*

676. ***A lion's whelp...*** Rabbi Yehudah may be alluding to the stages of King David's rule. At first David was simply *a lion's whelp*—the leader of a band of poor and desperate men (1 Samuel 22:2). Afterward he was recognized as king of all Israel, a mature and mighty *lion*.

The mysterious correlate is that at first *Shekhinah* is called נער (*na'ar*), "youth"—manifesting through Metatron, who is called *na'ar*. Afterward, She wages battle against evil forces and is called *man of war*.

On Metatron, see above, note 220. On *Shekhinah* as *man of war*, see *Zohar* 2:56a. The full verse in Genesis reads: *A lion's whelp is Judah; from the prey, O my son, you mount. He crouches, lies down like a lion, like the king of beasts—who will arouse him?*

677. **Angel of Death... *Shekhinah* ascends** *Shekhinah* (symbolized by Judah) separates Herself from the Angel of Death, who is implied by the word *prey*. Alternatively, *Shekhinah* withdraws from the human victim, who thereby becomes vulnerable to the Angel of Death.

For various interpretations, see *OY*; Galante; *KP*; *MM*; *Nefesh David*; *Sullam*; *MmD*.

678. ***He crouches...*** Here, Judah symbolizes the entire people of Israel who endured the exile in Babylonia and the exile initiated by Rome (symbolized by Edom). Edom also stands for medieval Christianity, under which the Jews suffered discrimination and oppression.

679. **entice them...** Referring to the situation in medieval Christian Spain and Europe, where Jews were urged to abandon their faith and convert.

from that moment it falls, not rising until it leaps upon its prey, consuming it—so *Shekhinah* falls only *like a lion, like the king of beasts*, to take revenge on other nations and leap upon them, as is said: *crouching in the greatness of His strength* (Isaiah 63:1).[680]

"*Who will arouse him?* (Genesis, ibid.) He will not rise to take petty revenge on them; rather, *Who will arouse him*. Who is *who*? As is said: *Who will heal you* (Lamentations 2:13). This is the supernal world, having the power to vitalize all. It is written: *From the womb of who emerged the ice* (Job 38:29), as they have established.[681]

"*The scepter will not depart from Judah*... (Genesis 49:10). The Companions have established this, but *until* שילה (*shiloh*), *Shiloh, comes* (ibid.): with a ה (*he*)—because elsewhere with a ו (*vav*)—indicating here the holy name יה (*Yah*). Elsewhere, שלה (*shiloh*)—without a י (*yod*)—whereas here שילה (*shiloh*), with י ה (*yod, he*), mystery of the supernal name by which *Shekhinah* will rise. This is the mystery of *Who*, as we have said."[682]

680. ***Fallen... is Virgin Israel...*** *Shekhinah*, representing the people Israel and known as *Virgin Israel*, only appears to have fallen. Really, She is a like a lion crouching and lying in wait to take revenge upon Her people's oppressors.

The full verse in Isaiah reads: *Who is this coming from Edom, in crimsoned garments from Bozrah—majestic in His attire,* צעה *(tso'eh) in the greatness of His strength? "It is I, speaking in righteousness, mighty to save."* The word צעה (*tso'eh*) is often emended by modern biblical scholars to צעד (*tso'ed*), "marching, striding," but here Rabbi Yehudah apparently understands it as "bending, crouching." Cf. Isaiah 51:14. Bozrah was the ancient capital of Edom.

681. ***Who will arouse him...*** Rabbi Yehudah reads this not as a rhetorical question but as a declarative statement: *Binah*, the Divine Mother known as מי (*mi*), "Who," will arouse *Shekhinah*, stimulating Her to attack Israel's oppressors.

Binah's name *Who* implies that a seeker may inquire about Her, unlike even higher realms, which are so inaccessible that they cannot even be questioned or explored. The mystical name *Who* becomes a focus of meditation, as question turns into quest. See Shim'on Lavi, *KP*, 1:91a: "Concerning everything that cannot be grasped, its question constitutes its answer."

Already in the Midrash, *Who* appears as a divine name designating "the one to whom Israel said at the [Red] Sea, *Who is like You?* (Exodus 15:11)." See *Eikhah Rabbah* (Buber) 2:13; *Eikhah Rabbah* 2:17; *Pesiqta de-Rav Kahana* 16:3, all of which also quote Lamentations 2:13 (*Who will heal you?*), interpreting it not as a question but as a statement.

Elsewhere in the *Zohar*, the verse from Job—*From the womb of whom emerged the ice?*—is interpreted: *From the womb of who* [*Binah*] *emerged Shekhinah*, whose frozen sea is thawed by the warm flowing love of *Ḥesed*. See *Zohar* 1:29b–30a. For a different interpretation, see *OY*. For other Zoharic references to *Binah* as *Who*, see 1:1b, 45b, 85b–86a; 2:126b–127a, 138a, 139b, 226a, 231b; 3:185b.

682. ***The scepter... until* שילה *(shiloh), Shiloh, comes...*** The full verse reads: *The scepter will not depart from Judah, nor the ruler's staff from between his legs, until Shiloh comes, and to him the submission of peoples.* The phrase עד כי יבא שילה (*ad ki yavo shiloh*) is highly enigmatic; the rendering *until Shiloh comes* represents one traditional meaning

He binds to the vine his donkey, to the noble vine his ass's foal. He washes in wine his garment, in the blood of grapes his cloak (Genesis 49:11).

Rabbi Ḥiyya opened, "*YHVH will guard you from all evil; He will guard your soul* (Psalms 121:7). Since it says *YHVH will guard you from all evil*, why *He will guard your soul*?[683] Because *YHVH will guard you from all evil* in this world; *He will guard your soul* in that world.

"Protection in this world—for a person to be protected from numerous evil species of accusers, roaming the world to denounce human beings and cling to them. In that world, what is it? When a person leaves this world, if he is virtuous his soul ascends to be adorned in its place. If not, many ravaging bands of truculent stingers appear to drag him into Hell, delivering him into the hands of Dumah, appointed over Hell. Twelve thousand myriads of deputies are with him, all designated for the souls of the wicked.[684]

"Come and see: There are seven abodes in Hell and seven gates; the soul of the wicked enters. Numerous stinging dazzling demons, gatekeepers—and over them one officer at every single gate. Souls of the wicked are delivered to those officers by Dumah, and as soon as they are delivered into their hands, gates of blazing fire shut. For there are gates behind gates; all those gates are open and closed—outer ones open, inner ones closed.[685]

assigned to it: until the coming of the Messiah, referred to as *Shiloh*.

See *Bereshit Rabbah* 98:8; *Eikhah Rabbah* 1:51; *Targum Onqelos* and *Targum Yerushalmi*, ad loc.; BT *Sanhedrin* 98b; Rashi, ad loc. Sarna (*Genesis*, ad loc.) discusses possible meanings of the term.

Here Rabbi Yehudah focuses on the unique spelling of the word שילה (*shiloh*). The word appears 33 times in the Bible, but only in this verse is it spelled with both a י (*yod*) and a ה (*he*). In all the other cases, it clearly refers to the city Shiloh in the hill country of Ephraim, site of the Tabernacle. In 11 cases the word is spelled שילו (*shilo*) or שלו (*shilo*), ending with a ו (*vav*) instead of a *he*. In the other 21 cases it is spelled שלה (*shiloh*), without the *yod*. The spelling here with both *yod* and *he* suggests the divine name יה (*Yah*), alluding to the union of the Divine Mother *Binah* (symbolized by the feminine marker, *he*) with *Ḥokhmah* (symbolized by the primordial point, *yod*). *Binah* (united with Her spouse, *Ḥokhmah*) will rouse *Shekhinah*.

On the various spellings of the word, see *Eikhah Rabbah* 1:51; *KP*; *Minḥat Shai*, ad loc.

683. **why *He will guard your soul*?** This seems redundant.

684. **truculent stingers . . . Dumah . . .** "Truculent stingers" renders חבילי טריקין (*ḥavilei teriqin*). The first word derives either from the noun חבל (*ḥevel*), "band, group," or from the verbal root חבל (*ḥvl*), "to injure, destroy." The second word derives from the root טרק (*trq*), "to sting, bite." See *Zohar* 1:62a (*Tos*), 130a, 243b–244a; 3:52b, 62b, 154b, 181a, 291b (*IZ*).

Dumah, literally "silence," is a name for the netherworld in the Bible. See Psalms 94:17: *Unless YHVH had been my help, my soul would have nearly dwelt in dumah*. Cf. Psalms 115:17. In rabbinic literature Dumah is the angel in charge of souls of the dead (BT *Berakhot* 18b, *Shabbat* 152b, *Sanhedrin* 94a). In the *Zohar* he retains this role but also oversees Hell. See 1:8a–b, 62b, 94a, 102a, 124a (*MhN*), 130b, 218b.

685. **seven abodes in Hell . . .** On these

"On every single Sabbath all of them open, and the wicked go out, as far as those outer gates, where they meet other souls tarrying there. When Sabbath departs, a herald proclaims at every single gate, *The wicked shall return to Sheol*... (Psalms 9:18).[686]

"Come and see: Souls of the righteous are protected by the blessed Holy One, so as not to be delivered into the hand of Dumah, as is said: *He will guard your soul.* [238a]

"*He binds to the vine his donkey.* What is the *vine*? Assembly of Israel, as is said: *You plucked up a vine from Egypt* (Psalms 80:9). And it is written: *Your wife—like a fruitful vine* (Psalms 128:3)—*your wife* is like this holy vine."[687]

Rabbi Yose said, "Regarding the blessing that we recite—'... who creates the fruit of the vine': 'who creates' corresponds to what is written: *a tree yielding fruit* (Genesis 1:12). 'Fruit of the vine'—*fruit tree* (ibid., 11). *Yielding fruit*—male; *fruit tree*—female. Therefore, 'who creates the fruit of the vine'—male and female as one. Souls of the righteous are 'fruit of the vine,' as we have said. 'Who creates [the fruit of the vine].'"[688]

seven divisions, see BT *Sotah* 10b; *Midrash Tehillim* 11:6; *Zohar* 1:40a (*Heikh*), 62b; 2:150b, 263a–68b (*Heikh*); 3:178a; *ZḤ* 25b (*MhN*); *Massekhet Geihinnom* (*Beit ha-Midrash*, 1:149); Ginzberg, *Legends*, 5:20, n. 56. On the seven gates, see *Pirqei de-Rabbi Eli'ezer* 53; *ZḤ* 25b (*MhN*).

On the phrase "dazzling demons," see above, note 510. The phrase "outer ones open, inner ones closed" may imply that the wicked may enter the gates of Hell, but once inside they cannot leave.

686. **On every single Sabbath...** Even the wicked in Hell are allowed to rest on Sabbath, enjoying a break from their torments.

The phrase "other souls tarrying there" may refer to souls who have completed their term in Hell but have not yet been allowed to ascend to Paradise—or alternatively, to souls condemned to Hell who have not yet been confined there.

On Sabbath in Hell, see *Bereshit Rabbah* 11:5; *Tanḥuma, Ki Tissa* 33; *Zohar* 1:14b, 17b, 197b; 2:31b, 88b, 150b–151a, 203b, 207a; 3:94b; *ZḤ* 17a–b (*MhN*).

687. **What is the *vine*? Assembly of Israel...** The people of Israel are often compared to a vine or a vineyard. Here *vine* symbolizes *Shekhinah*, known as Assembly of Israel, who was redeemed from Egypt along with Her people and transplanted in the Promised Land. She is the divine wife, who resembles the wife described in Psalm 128: *Your wife—like a fruitful vine in the recesses of your house; your children—like olive shoots around your table.*

On Israel as a vine, see Isaiah 5:1–7; 27:2–4; Jeremiah 2:21; Ezekiel 17:1–10; Hosea 10:1; *Targum Onqelos* on Genesis 49:11. On *Shekhinah* as Assembly of Israel, see above, pp. 122–23, n. 237. The full verse in Psalm 80 reads: *You plucked up a vine from Egypt; You drove out nations and planted it.* On this verse, see *Bereshit Rabbah* 88:5; 99:8; *Vayiqra Rabbah* 36:2; BT *Ḥullin* 92a. On woman as vine, see M *Niddah* 9:11.

688. **'who creates the fruit of the vine'...** From the blessing recited over wine: "Blessed are You, *YHVH* our God, King of the world, who creates the fruit of the vine." See M *Berakhot* 6:1.

The context in Genesis (1:11–12) reads: *God said, "Let the earth sprout grass, plants generating seed, fruit trees* [literally, *a fruit tree*] *yielding fruit of each kind, that has its seed within it upon the earth." And so it was. The earth brought forth grass, plants generating seed of each kind, and trees* [literally, *a*

"*He binds to the vine his donkey*—King Messiah, who is destined to rule over all forces of the nations—forces appointed over other nations, the potency by which they are empowered. King Messiah is destined to overwhelm them, for this *vine* dominates all those lower crowns through which the nations have dominion. This one triumphs above; Israel—'noble vine'—conquers and destroys other forces below. Overpowering all of them, King Messiah, as is written: *poor and riding on an ass, on a donkey* (Zechariah 9:9). *Donkey* and *ass*—two crowns through which the nations rule, from the left side, side of impurity.[689]

"As for saying *poor*—now, is King Messiah called *poor*? However, Rabbi Shim'on said as follows: 'Because he has nothing of his own, and we call him King Messiah—holy moon above, who has no light except from the sun.'[690] This King Messiah will have dominion and unite with his site.[691] Then, *See, your king is coming to you* (ibid.)—unidentified. If below, *poor*, for he is in the aspect of the moon. If above, speculum that does not shine, 'bread of poverty.' Yet even so, *riding on an ass, on a donkey*—power of all nations, to be subdued beneath him, and the blessed Holy One will be fortified in His realm.[692]

tree] *yielding fruit that has its seed within it of each kind, and God saw that it was good.* Rabbi Yose interprets the phrase *yielding fruit* as referring to *Yesod,* who impregnates *Shekhinah* with souls; She is *a fruit tree,* bearing the soul-fruit into the world. Similarly, the blessing "who creates the fruit of the vine" encompasses the creativity of the male and the fruitfulness of female.

See *Zohar* 1:18b, 33a. On souls as fruit, see above, note 336.

689. ***He binds to the vine his donkey*— King Messiah...** Now the subject of the verse (Judah) symbolizes the Messiah (descended from Judah through King David). Described as *riding on an ass, on a donkey,* he will subjugate and "bind" the nations along with their heavenly princes (especially the two "lower crowns" called *ass* and *donkey*) through the power of *Shekhinah* (the *vine*). She will triumph above, Israel (Her offshoot) below, and King Messiah will rule over all.

See *Zohar* 3:207a. On the Messianic interpretation of this verse in Genesis, see *Targum Onqelos* and *Targum Yerushalmi,* ad loc.; *Bereshit Rabbah* 98:9; 99:8. On the heavenly princes of the nations, see above, pp. 70–71 and n. 476. On Israel as "noble vine," see Jeremiah 2:21: *I planted you as a noble vine, of entirely faithful seed. How then did you turn before Me into a corrupt, alien vine?* The verse in Zechariah reads: *See, your king is coming to you: righteous and triumphant is he;* עני (*ani*), *humble* [or: *poor*], *and riding on an ass—on a donkey, foal of a she-ass.*

690. **As for saying *poor*...** The Messiah resembles, and is closely linked with, *Shekhinah* (the moon). She is poor, in the sense that She has nothing of Her own, only what She receives from *Tif'eret* (the sun). Similarly, the Messiah receives all of his power from Her.

On *Shekhinah* and the Messiah, see *Zohar* 1:84a; 2:127b; 3:19b; Moses de León, *Shushan Edut,* 343; idem, *Sheqel ha-Qodesh,* 71–72 (90–91).

691. **with his site** With *Shekhinah.*

692. ***your king*... unidentified...** The verse does not specify the king's name because it alludes to both the Messiah below and *Shekhinah* above. She is known as אספקלריא דלא נהרא (*ispaqlarya de-la nahara*), "the speculum (or glass, mirror, lens) that

"*He washes in wine his garment* (Genesis 49:11)—as is said: *Who is this coming from Edom, in crimsoned garments from Bozrah?* (Isaiah 63:1), and similarly: *I have trodden the wine trough alone* (ibid., 3). *He washes in wine*—side of *Gevurah*, harsh Judgment befalling the nations.[693]

"*In the blood of grapes* (Genesis, ibid.)—the tree below, Court of Judgment, called *grapes*. Wine is preserved in *the blood of grapes*, so that he will be clothed in both of them to crush beneath him all other nations and all kings of the world."[694]

Rabbi Yose opened, "*He binds to the vine his donkey*. It is written: *on the vine three tendrils, and as she was budding, up came her blossom*... (Genesis 40:10).[695] Come and see how closed-minded human beings are, not knowing or considering the glory of their Lord, not contemplating words of Torah or knowing their own ways, in which they will be caught, as is said: *The way of the wicked is like darkness; they do not know what makes them stumble* (Proverbs 4:19).

"In ancient times prophecy rested upon humans, so they knew and contemplated supernal glory. When prophecy ceased, they consulted an echo of the voice.[696] Now prophecy has ceased and the echo has ceased, and human beings

does not shine" on its own but rather transmits (reflects, refracts, or diffracts) the other *sefirot*.

See BT *Yevamot* 49b: "All the prophets gazed through a dim glass [literally, an *ispaqlarya* that does not shine], whereas Moses our teacher gazed through a clear glass [literally, an *ispaqlarya* that shines]." Cf. 1 Corinthians 13:12: "For now we see through a glass darkly, but then face-to-face."

See *Vayiqra Rabbah* 1:14; Azriel of Gerona, *Peirush ha-Aggadot*, 33–34; above, p. 114 and n. 191; above, note 491.

On *Shekhinah* as "bread of poverty," see above, pp. 427–28 and n. 612.

693. ***Who is this coming...*** The passage in Isaiah describes God's vengeance against Israel's enemies, specifically Edom. The metaphor of treading the grapes appears also in Joel 4:13. Here in the *Zohar*, *wine* symbolizes *Gevurah*, also known as *Din* (harsh Judgment).

Isaiah 63:1 reads in full: *Who is this coming from Edom, in crimsoned garments from Bozrah—majestic in His attire, striding in the greatness of His strength? "It is I, speaking in righteousness, mighty to save."* Bozrah was the ancient capital of Edom.

694. ***blood of grapes*—the tree below...** *Shekhinah* is symbolized by the Tree of Knowledge of Good and Evil and pictured as the Court of Judgment, deriving from *Din* (Judgment). The *wine* from above is preserved in Her as *blood of grapes*. The Messiah draws on both of these elements—*wine* and *blood of grapes*—in order to defeat the nations of the world.

On *Shekhinah* as *grapes*, see *Zohar* 3:127a. On the image of wine preserved in its grapes, see below, note 706.

695. ***on the vine three tendrils...*** The full verse reads: *The chief cupbearer recounted his dream to Joseph and said to him, "In my dream—here, a vine in front of me, and on the vine three tendrils, and as she was budding, up came her blossom, her clusters ripened into grapes."*

696. **When prophecy ceased...** Traditionally, following the death of the last biblical prophets (Haggai, Zechariah, and Malachi), prophetic inspiration ceased and the divine will was revealed more indirectly,

consult only a dream. Well, a dream is a lower rung outside, for we have learned: 'A dream is one-sixtieth of prophecy.' Why so? Because it comes from the sixth rung below.[697]

"Come and see: A dream is visible to all, since it comes from the left side, descending various rungs, becoming visible even to the wicked, even to nations of the world.[698] For sometimes those evil species snatch a dream and hear it and inform human beings—some of them toy with humans, conveying false information, and sometimes true information that they have heard. Sometimes they are sent to the wicked, telling them lofty matters.[699]

"This wicked one, what is written of him?[700] He saw a true dream, as is written: *on the vine three tendrils* (Genesis 40:10). Who is the *vine*? Assembly of Israel, as is written: *Look down from heaven and see, and attend to this vine!* (Psalms 80:15). *From heaven*—for from this place it was cast, as is said: *He has cast down earth from heaven* (Lamentations 2:1). *And attend to this vine*—the *vine* that is *this*, literally![701]

through a בת קול (*bat qol*), literally "daughter of a voice"—a reverberating sound or echo, a heavenly voice.

See *Tosefta, Sotah* 13:3; JT *Sotah* 9:12, 24b; BT *Yoma* 9b, *Sotah* 48b; *Shir ha-Shirim Rabbah* on 8:10; Lieberman, *Hellenism in Jewish Palestine*, 194–99; above, note 659.

697. **consult only a dream... lower rung outside...** Prophecy derives from the divine realm, specifically from the *sefirot Netsaḥ* and *Hod*. Dreams, on the other hand, derive from a lower source, namely the archangel Gabriel. From the source of prophecy to this angelic prince of dreams there are six stages: the *sefirot Netsaḥ, Hod, Yesod,* and *Shekhinah,* and the first two archangels: Michael and Gabriel. Here, these six stages are correlated with a Talmudic saying (BT *Berakhot* 57b): "A dream is one-sixtieth of prophecy."

See Maimonides, *Guide of the Perplexed* 2:36; *Zohar* 149a (*ST*), 149a–b, 183a, 191b, 196a; 2:247b; Moses de León, *Shushan Edut*, 369; idem, *Sefer ha-Rimmon*, 126. In the book of Daniel (8:16; 9:22), Gabriel interprets revelations. On dreams as a lower form of divine communication, see BT *Ḥagigah* 5b.

698. **from the left side...** From Gabriel, associated with *Gevurah* on the left.

699. **evil species snatch a dream...** Demonic powers convey the dream, sometimes accurately and sometimes not.

According to a tradition in BT *Berakhot* 55b, angels convey prophetic dreams, whereas demons convey false ones. See *Zohar* 1:83a, 130a, 199b–200a; 2:130a, 195b, 264a (*Heikh*); 3:25a, 156b.

700. **This wicked one...** Pharaoh's chief cupbearer, who related his dream to Joseph in prison.

701. **Who is the *vine*?...** The vine symbolizes *Shekhinah*, Assembly of Israel (above, note 687; above, p. 172 and n. 547). She is also known as *earth* and ideally is united with *Tif'eret*, known as *heaven*. However, when Israel's sins abound, *Shekhinah* is separated from *Tif'eret* (*cast down from heaven*), which causes destruction and exile below.

Shekhinah, the Divine Presence, is also known as *this*, which implies "constantly present right here." See above, note 372.

The verse in Lamentations reads: *He has cast down from heaven to earth the splendor of Israel.* Here, Rabbi Yose interprets it to mean *He has cast down earth from heaven.* See above, note 127.

"*Three tendrils*—as is said: *three flocks of sheep lying beside it* (Genesis 29:2).[702]

"*And as she was budding* (ibid. 40:10)—as is said: *The wisdom of Solomon increased* (1 Kings 5:10), for the moon was illumined.[703]

"*Up came her blossom* (Genesis, ibid.)—Jerusalem below.[704]

"Alternatively, *up came her blossom*—above, that rung standing above Her, suckling Her, as is said: [238b] *that has its seed within it upon the earth* (ibid. 1:11).[705]

"*Her clusters ripened into grapes* (ibid. 40:10)—aging preserved wine within.[706]

"See how much that wicked one saw! What is written? *Pharaoh's cup was in*

702. ***Three tendrils . . . three flocks . . .*** Both triads symbolize the sefirotic triad of *Ḥesed, Gevurah,* and *Tif'eret,* who unite with *Shekhinah.*

See *Zohar* 1:151b–152a; above, p. 172 and n. 548. Cf. *Zohar* 1:151b (*ST*), where the *three tendrils* symbolize the triad of *Netsaḥ, Hod,* and *Yesod.*

The full verse reads: *He looked, and here: a well in the field, and there were three flocks of sheep lying beside it, for from that well the flocks were watered. The stone on the mouth of the well was large.*

703. ***The wisdom of Solomon increased . . .*** The full verse reads: *The wisdom of Solomon* תרב (*terev*), *surpassed, the wisdom of all the children of the East and all the wisdom of Egypt.* The word תרב (*terev*), *surpassed,* is interpreted here according to its similar meaning: "increased." *The wisdom of Solomon* symbolizes *Shekhinah,* daughter of *Ḥokhmah* (Wisdom).

Shekhinah is also symbolized by the moon. According to the Midrash, just as the moon does not become full until the fifteenth day of its cycle, so it remained incomplete until the glorious reign of Solomon in the fifteenth generation from Abraham. See *Pesiqta de-Rav Kahana* 5:12 and *Shemot Rabbah* 15:26: "When Solomon appeared, the disk of the moon became full." Here, according to Rabbi Yose, the verse in Kings indicates that during the days of Solomon *Shekhinah* attained fullness—the same fullness that is signified by the image of budding in the cupbearer's dream.

See *Zohar* 1:73b–74a, 150a, 223a–b, 225b, 243a, 249b; 2:85a; 3:61a, 74b, 181b; *ZḤ* 83b (*MhN, Rut*); Moses de León, *Shushan Edut,* 342.

704. ***her blossom*—Jerusalem below** As *Shekhinah* (Jerusalem above) flourishes, Her earthly counterpart (the city of Jerusalem) flourishes too.

On Jerusalem above and below, see above, p. 395 and n. 465.

705. ***her blossom . . .* rung standing above Her . . .** According to this interpretation, *Shekhinah*'s *blossom* refers to *Yesod,* whose *seed* nourishes *Shekhinah* (*the earth*).

The full verse in the opening chapter of Genesis reads: *God said, "Let the earth sprout grass, plants generating seed, fruit trees yielding fruit of each kind, that has its seed within it upon the earth." And so it was.* See *Zohar* 1:33a; above, p. 447 and n. 688.

706. **aging preserved wine within** Within the grape clusters of *Shekhinah,* the rich wine emanating from above matures.

According to BT *Berakhot* 34b (in the name of Rabbi Yehoshu'a son of Levi), in the world that is coming the righteous will enjoy "wine preserved in its grapes since the six days of Creation." In the *Zohar,* this wine symbolizes both the deepest secrets of Torah and also the emanation stored within, or flowing from, *Binah,* who is known as "the world that is coming."

See *Zohar* 1:135b (*MhN*), 192a; 2:147a; 3:4a, 12b, 39b–40a, 93b, 100a (*RM*); *ZḤ* 28a–b; Moses de León, *Sefer ha-Rimmon,* 130.

my hand, and I took the grapes and squeezed them (ibid., 11).[707] Here he saw that *cup of staggering*—suck of the Court of Judgment issuing from those grapes, given to Pharaoh, who drank it as it was, on account of Israel.[708]

"When Joseph heard, he rejoiced, realizing the true element in this dream. Therefore he interpreted the dream for him favorably, because he had provided this for Joseph.[709]

"Come and see: *He binds to the vine his donkey*—for beneath this vine are subdued all those potent forces of other nations; because of this vine their power is overthrown and bound, as has been said."[710]

Rabbi Shim'on said, "There is a vine, and then there is a vine! Supreme, holy vine; *alien vine* (Jeremiah 2:21), 'daughter of an alien god.' Therefore it is written *this vine* (Psalms 80:15), the one called *entirely faithful seed* (Jeremiah, ibid.). *A noble vine* (ibid.)—Israel, issuing from this vine. When Israel sinned, abandoning this *vine*, what is written? *From the vine of Sodom is their vine* (Deuteronomy 32:32). So, there is a vine, and then there is a vine!"[711]

452

Rabbi Yehudah and Rabbi Yitsḥak were walking on the way. Rabbi Yehudah said to Rabbi Yitsḥak, "Let's go through this field because it's a straighter way."

707. **that wicked one...** Pharaoh's cupbearer. The full verse reads: *Pharaoh's cup was in my hand, and I took the grapes and squeezed them into Pharaoh's cup and I placed the cup in Pharaoh's palm.*

708. ***cup of staggering...*** Wine symbolizes the rich flow of emanation, but its dregs within *Shekhinah* yield a bitter drink, identified with *the cup of staggering* mentioned in Isaiah 51:17, 22. The demonic forces suck this liquid from *Shekhinah*, the Court of Judgment. The cupbearer's dream foretold the bitter plagues that a future Pharaoh would bring upon himself and the Egyptians through his oppression of Israel.

See *Zohar* 2:246b–247a (*Heikh*), 264a (*Heikh*). The conclusion of this passage can also be understood as "... given to Pharaoh, who drank it, as happened [during the ten plagues] on account of Israel."

709. **When Joseph heard...** Joseph understood that the cupbearer's dream revealed secrets of the *sefirot* and foretold Pharaoh's fate and Israel's deliverance, so he offered a favorable interpretation. See above, pp. 172–74.

710. **beneath this vine are subdued...** Through the power of *Shekhinah* (the *vine*), the heavenly princes of Israel's enemies (symbolized by *donkey*) will be vanquished and the Messiah will defeat those enemies on earth. See above, p. 448 and n. 689.

711. **There is a vine...** The holy vine is *Shekhinah*; the *alien vine* is the demonic realm, specifically the demonic feminine, identified with "daughter of an alien god."

Shekhinah is also called *this vine* based on Her name *this* (see above, note 701). Israel, who derives from *Shekhinah*, is *a noble vine*, but when they sin they become contaminated by the demonic *vine of Sodom*.

The verse in Jeremiah reads: *I planted you as a noble vine, of entirely faithful seed. How then did you turn before Me into a corrupt, alien vine?* The phrase "daughter of an alien god" derives from Malachi 2:11: *Judah has desecrated the sanctuary of YHVH, which He loves, and has married the daughter of an alien* [or: *a foreign*] *god.* The verse in Deuteronomy reads: *From the vine of Sodom is their vine, from the vineyards of Gomorrah. Their grapes are grapes of poison, bitter clusters they have.*

They went on. As they were walking, Rabbi Yehudah opened, saying, "*She is not afraid of snow for her household, for all her household is clothed in scarlet* (Proverbs 31:21). This verse has been established by our companion Rabbi Ḥizkiyah, who said, 'The punishment of the wicked in Hell lasts for twelve months—half in heat and half in snow.[712] When they enter the fire they say, "This is really Hell!" Then they enter the snow and say, "This is the fierce winter of the blessed Holy One!" They begin by saying "וה (*Vah*), Ah!" but afterward "וי (*Vai*), Woe!" David said, *He lifted me out of a pit of desolation, out of the mud of* היון (*ha-yaven*), *slime* (Psalms 40:3)—out of the place where they say וה (*vah*) and then וי (*vai*).[713]

"'Where are their souls surrendered? In the snow, as is written: *When Shaddai scatters kings, it snows on Black Mountain* (Psalms 68:15).[714] Could it be the same for Israel? The verse teaches: *She is not afraid of snow for her household.* Why? *For all her household is clothed in* שנים (*shanim*), *scarlet.* Do not read שָׁנִים (*shanim*), *scarlet*, but rather שְׁנַיִם (*shenayim*), *two*—such as circumcision and uncovering, tzitzit and tefillin, mezuzah and the lamp of Hanukkah. . . .'[715]

712. *She is not afraid of snow...* The narrative interpretation presented here in the name of Rabbi Ḥizkiyah appears in his name in rabbinic sources.

See *Pesiqta de-Rav Kahana* 10:4; *Tanḥuma, Re'eh* 13; *Tanḥuma* (Buber), *Re'eh* 10; *Midrash Mishlei* 31:21. On the twelve-month punishment in Hell, see M *Eduyyot* 2:10. On the alternation of heat and cold, see JT *Sanhedrin* 10:3, 29b–c; *Tanḥuma* (Buber), *Bereshit*, 25; *Seder Rabbah di-Vreshit*, 28 (*Battei Midrashot*, 1:35); *Zohar* 1:62b, 68b, 107b.

713. **begin by saying "וה (*Vah*), Ah!"...** Having just emerged from the fires of Hell, the wicked are momentarily relieved by the cold; but soon they begin to suffer from its effects and וה (*vah*), "ah," turns into וי (*vai*), "woe." The word היון (*ha-yaven*), *slime*, in Psalm 40 is interpreted as containing both these exclamations, the letter ו (*vav*) combining first with ה (*he*) to spell וה (*vah*), "ah," and then with י (*yod*) to spell וי (*vai*), "woe."

According to BT *Eruvin* 19a (in the name of Rabbi Yehoshu'a son of Levi), both *pit of desolation* and *mud of slime* are names for Hell. See *Midrash Konen* (*Beit ha-Midrash*, 2:30, 35–36); *Seder Rabbah di-Vreshit*, 28 (*Battei Midrashot*, 1:34); *Zohar* 1:185a; 2:263a (*Heikh*).

714. **Where are their souls surrendered?...** *Black Mountain* renders צלמון (*tsalmon*), which derives from the root צלם (*tslm*), "to be dark, black," and refers in this psalm to a mountain shrouded in dark clouds, probably northeast of the Sea of Galilee. In the midrashic sources of this *Zohar* passage (see above, note 712), the verse is understood to mean that the wicked surrender their souls to final darkness in the snows of Hell—apparently playing on *tsalmon* and משלימין (*mashlimin*), "surrender."

On the idiom of "surrendering one's soul," see *Bereshit Rabbah* 100:1; *Midrash Tehillim* 25:2. Several *Zohar* commentators understand משתלמי (*mishtalemei*)—the Aramaic paraphrase of the midrashic משלימין (*mashlimin*)—not as "surrendered" but rather as "completed, perfected," purged and purified in the snows of Hell. See *OY*; Galante; *Adderet Eliyyahu*; *MmD*.

715. **Do not read שָׁנִים (*shanim*), *scarlet*...** The alternate pronunciation—שְׁנַיִם (*shenayim*), *two*—yields a new meaning for the verse: Israel (or *Shekhinah*, Assembly of Israel) does not fear the snows of Hell, because all of Israel fulfill the various double *mitsvot*.

"Uncovering" refers to the second stage of the ritual of circumcision. First the foreskin

"Come and see: *She is not afraid of snow for her household*—Assembly of Israel, all of whose *household is clothed in scarlet*, as we have said, for it is written: *in crimsoned garments* (Isaiah 63:1)—a garment of harsh Judgment to punish other nations. The blessed Holy One will one day dress in red, with a red sword, to exact retribution from the red. A red garment—as is written: *in crimsoned garments from Bozrah*, and similarly: *Why is your clothing red?* (ibid., 2). A red sword—as is written: *YHVH has a sword, full of blood* (ibid. 34:6). To exact retribution from the red—as is written: *For YHVH has a slaughter in Bozrah* (ibid.).[716]

"Further, *for all her household is clothed in scarlet*—for look, She comes from the side of harsh Judgment!"[717]

Rabbi Yitsḥak said, "Certainly so! However, *for all her household is clothed in* שנים (*shanim*), *scarlet*. What is *shanim*? שנים קדמוניות (*Shanim qadmoniyyot*), Primordial years, for She is composed of all of them, suckling from every side, as is said: *All the streams flow into the sea* (Ecclesiastes 1:7)."[718]

is cut and removed, disclosing the mucous membrane, which is then torn down the center and pulled back, revealing the corona. The act of tearing and pulling back the membrane is called פריעה (*peri'ah*), "uncovering" the corona. See M *Shabbat* 19:6: "If one circumcises but does not uncover the circumcision, it is as if he has not circumcised." The *Zohar* often emphasizes the importance of this "uncovering." See the references in Vol. 1, p. 91, n. 688.

Tzitzit (tassels on the corners of a garment) and tefillin (phylacteries) are worn especially during prayer. The lamp of Hanukkah is traditionally placed directly outside the door of the home, opposite the mezuzah. See BT *Shabbat* 22a; *Soferim* 20:3.

716. **Assembly of Israel . . . *clothed in scarlet* . . .** *Shekhinah* (Assembly of Israel) and Her forces will be clothed in the garments of *Din* (harsh Judgment, symbolized by red) in order to punish Israel's enemies. She will thus have no fear of the harsh, demonic snow. See above, p. 449 and nn. 693–94. On Assembly of Israel as a name of *Shekhinah*, see above, pp. 122–23, n. 237.

"The red" refers to Edom (Esau), whose name is linked with אדום (*adom*), "red." In rabbinic literature Edom symbolizes Rome; in medieval Jewish literature it also stands for Christianity, under which the Jews suffered. See Genesis 25:25, 30; *Bereshit Rabbah* 63:12; *Zohar* 1:139b.

Isaiah 63:1, 3 read: *Who is this coming from Edom, in crimsoned garments from Bozrah—majestic in His attire, striding in the greatness of His strength? "It is I, speaking in righteousness, mighty to save." . . . Why is Your clothing red, Your garments like his who treads in a winepress?* Bozrah was the ancient capital of Edom.

Isaiah 34:6 reads: *YHVH has a sword, full of blood, gorged with fat—with the blood of lambs and goats, with the kidney fat of rams. For YHVH has a slaughter in Bozrah, a great butchery in the land of Edom.* On the divine sword, see above, note 665.

717. **She comes from the side of harsh Judgment** *Shekhinah* is fearless because She derives from *Din* (harsh Judgment), symbolized by the color red.

718. **שנים קדמוניות (*Shanim qadmoniyyot*), Primordial years . . .** Alluding to the *sefirot* from *Ḥesed* through *Yesod*, emanating from *Binah* and culminating in *Shekhinah*. The verse from Ecclesiastes similarly alludes to the streaming energy of these *sefirot* emptying into the sea of *Shekhinah*. Filled with their power, She has no fear.

The phrase "primordial years" derives

While they were walking, they encountered a certain child walking with a wineskin and an old man riding.[719] That old man said to the child, "Son, tell me your verse!'[720]

He replied, "My verse is not one! But come down—or let me ride in front of you—and I will speak."[721]

He said to him, "I don't want to. I'm an old man, and you're a boy. Why should I equalize myself with you?"

He replied, "Well, then why did you ask for my verse?"[722]

He said to him, "So that we could proceed on the way."[723]

He replied, "May that old man's breath expire! He's riding and he knows nothing and he says he won't equalize himself with me."[724] He parted from the old man and went his way.

from Malachi 3:4. See *Zohar* 1:7b; 2:105b; 3:138b (*IR*). For a similar pun, see BT *Shabbat* 89b.

719. **they encountered a certain child...** A shorter version of this story appears in *Zohar* 3:300a–b (*Hash*). These same two rabbis encounter another child in the extended narrative entitled *Yanuqa* (The Child) in *Zohar* 3:186a–192a.

"Wineskin" renders קסטרא דחמרא (*qistera de-ḥamra*). Elsewhere in the *Zohar*, *qistera* and its related forms apparently derive from Latin *castrum* (pl. *castra*), "castle, fortress," or from Latin *quaestor*, a Roman official. Here, however, the author may be playing on (or the text may originally have read) קטפירא (*qatpira*), a Zoharic neologism that embraces several meanings including "wineskin, waterskin." See above, p. 208 (and n. 181) and *Zohar* 1:72a, both in similar narrative contexts; Galante; *Nefesh David*; Scholem; Liebes, *Peraqim*, 349–50, 353.

The word construed here as חמרא (*ḥamra*), "wine," could instead be חמרא (*ḥamara*), "donkey." Both meanings fit the narrative as well as the verse discussed above and below (Genesis 49:11): *He binds to the vine his donkey, to the noble vine his ass's foal. He washes in wine his garment, in the blood of grapes his cloak.*

For other attempts to explain this puzzling phrase, see Lonzano, *Sefer ha-Ma'arikh*, s.v. *qstr*; *DE*; *NO*.

720. **tell me your verse** A nearly identical expression appears in rabbinic literature. There too it is addressed to children, whose casual utterances of biblical verses constitute a form of divination.

See BT *Ḥagigah* 15a–b; *Gittin* 56a, 68a; *Ḥullin* 95b; *Ester Rabbah* 7:13; Lieberman, *Hellenism in Jewish Palestine*, 195–96.

721. **My verse is not one...** The child has more than one verse to deliver and expound. Further, before offering any teaching he wants to be on the same level as the old man, and he asks him to either dismount from the donkey and walk alongside him, or let him sit in front of him on the donkey so that they can ride together.

722. **why did you ask for my verse?** If you don't respect me or consider me your equal, then why did you ask me to offer a biblical verse?

723. **So that we could proceed on the way** To pass the time in discussion and thereby ease the journey.

724. **May that old man's breath expire...** A curse appearing often in rabbinic literature, equivalent to "May he drop dead!" The child responds so extremely because of the old man's lack of learning, his casual attitude toward Torah, and his refusal to meet the child on his own level.

For other examples of this curse in the *Zohar*, see 3:105a, 149b, 152a.

As Rabbi Yehudah and Rabbi Yitsḥak approached, he came up to them. When they asked him, he told them what had happened. Rabbi Yehudah said, 'You acted well! Come with us, and we'll sit here and listen to a word from your mouth."

He replied, "I'm weary, because I haven't [239a] eaten today."

They took out some bread and gave it to him. A miracle happened for them and they found a bubbling spring of water under a tree. He drank from it and they drank, and they sat down.

That child opened, saying, "*Of David. Do not compete with evildoers; do not be envious of those who do wrong* (Psalms 37:1). *Of David*—it doesn't say if this a song, it doesn't say if this is a prayer; but in fact *Of David*, unspecified, always implies being spoken by Holy Spirit.[725]

"*Do not* תתחר (*titḥar*), *compete, with evildoers.* What does this mean? The verse should read *Do not join up with evildoers.* However, do not engage in תחרות (*taḥarut*), competition, *with evildoers*, because you do not know the foundation of your being, and you may not be able to prevail against him. Perhaps he is a tree that has never been uprooted, and you will be repulsed by him.[726]

725. ***Of David*... unspecified... Holy Spirit** Usually when the formula לדוד (*le-David*), *Of David*, appears in the title of a psalm, it is linked with a term such as שיר (*shir*), "song," מזמור (*mizmor*), "song," or תפלה (*tefillah*), "prayer." The child indicates that if no such specific term appears, the simple expression *Of David* implies divine inspiration.

Apparently, the child is playing on a rabbinic interpretation in BT *Pesaḥim* 117a: "לדוד מזמור (*Le-David mizmor*), '*To David, a psalm*,' indicates that *Shekhinah* dwelled upon him and then he exclaimed a song. מזמור לדוד (*Mizmor le-David*), '*A psalm, to David*,' indicates that he exclaimed a song and then *Shekhinah* dwelled upon him." (The prefixed preposition ל [*le*] can mean either "of" or "to.")

See *Midrash Tehillim* 24:1, 3; Rashi on Psalms 23:1; Jacob bar Sheshet, *Meshiv Devarim Nekhoḥim*, 92; Todros Abulafia, *Sha'ar ha-Razim*, 48; *Zohar* 1:39b, 67a; 2:50a, 140a, 170a.

726. ***Do not* תתחר (*titḥar*), *compete*...** In this verse the simple sense of the word is "get excited, be vexed, be wrought up," perhaps referring to the ardor of jealousy, as in the parallel continuation of the verse: *do not be envious of those who do wrong* (see the following note). For the sense of "compete," see Jeremiah 12:5; 22:15; Rashi on this verse; and BT *Berakhot* 7b.

Here the child wonders why the verse doesn't read *Do not join up with evildoers*—a more common warning. He explains that in this context the word *titḥar* means "compete, challenge, strive (against)." One should not engage an evildoer because he may prevail, based on the history of his soul. The expressions "foundation of your being (literally, of your self)" and "a tree that has never been uprooted" allude to states of reincarnation. If the evildoer's soul is an original soul, which has never been reincarnated ("uprooted"), then he may overwhelm even a virtuous person whose soul has undergone reincarnation for previous failures and is therefore less vibrant.

See above, p. 137 at n. 331: "Whenever a person is unsuccessful [in engendering new life] in this world, the blessed Holy One up-

"*Do not* תקנא (*teqanne*), *be zealous, against those who do wrong*—do not observe their deeds, so that you will not become zealous against them. For whoever sees their deeds and is not zealous for the blessed Holy One transgresses three negative precepts, as is written: *You shall have no other gods before Me. . . . You shall not bow to them and you shall not worship them, for I, YHVH your God, am a* קנא (*qanna*), *zealous, god* (Exodus 20:3, 5).[727]

"Therefore, one should separate from them and veer away from them. That is why I departed and diverted my route. Now that I have found you, here is a verse for you!"[728]

He opened, saying, "ויקרא (*Va-yiqra*), *He called, to Moses* (Leviticus 1:1). Here, a small א (*alef*). Why? Because this 'calling' was not consummate. How so? It was only in the Tabernacle and in a foreign land, for consummation is found only in the Holy Land.[729]

"Further, here, *Shekhinah*; there, consummation of male and female: אדם (*Adam*), *Adam, Seth, Enosh* (1 Chronicles 1:1). אדם (*Adam*), *Adam*—consummation of male and female. Here, female.[730]

roots him and replants him several times as before." On such "uprooting," see the parable in *Bahir* 135 (195) and in *ZḤ* 89b (*MhN, Rut*). On reincarnation, see *Zohar* 1:131a; 2:75a, 94b–114a passim; 3:7a; *ZḤ* 59a–c; Scholem, *Major Trends*, 242–43; idem, *Kabbalah*, 344–50. On the weakness of a reincarnated soul, see *Zohar* 2:75a; *NO*; Scholem.

727. ***Do not* תקנא (*teqanne*), *be zealous*...** In this verse the word means "get heated, become excited, be incensed" or "be envious" (see the preceding note). The child understands the word as "be zealous (against, on account of)." His point is that one should stay away from wrongdoers because otherwise one will be obligated to zealously oppose them, which could be dangerous. One who witnesses wrongdoing and does not respond zealously violates the prohibitions against fearing anyone other than God (that is, fearing to reprove sinners), and bowing down or worshiping anyone else (that is, being submissive or sycophantic toward sinners). A virtuous person should be zealous, as God is zealous. See *OY*; Galante.

728. **That is why I departed...** With some hyperbole, the child includes the old man in the category of *evildoers*.

729. **ויקרא (*Va-yiqra*)... small א (*alef*)...** In the Masoretic text this א (*alef*) is written small. According to the child, the reduced size of this letter indicates that something was lacking in the "call" to Moses, namely, that it took place in the Tabernacle—a temporary dwelling in the wilderness of Sinai—not in the Temple in Jerusalem.

See above, p. 420 and nn. 580–82. The child appropriately opens with a verse from Leviticus, which in rabbinic times was the first book studied by children. See *Vayiqra Rabbah* 7:3, where Rabbi Issi attributes the following reasoning to God: "Sacrifices are pure and children are pure; let the pure come and engage in the pure."

730. **here, *Shekhinah*; there, consummation...** The small א (*alef*) symbolizes *Shekhinah*, the female Divine Presence alone, who called to Moses. The word אדם (*Adam*) at the beginning of Chronicles is written with a large א (*alef*), which for the child symbolizes the union of the divine male and female in the Temple—a union generating complete prophetic inspiration.

On אדם (*Adam*) as including male and female, see Genesis 1:26–27; 5:2: *Male and female He created them, and He blessed them*

"Further, the conclusion of the verse: *and YHVH spoke to him from the Tent of Meeting, saying* (Leviticus, ibid.). So, a small *alef*.[731]

"Further, a small *alef*. This can be compared to a king sitting upon his throne, wearing a royal crown; he is called Supreme King. When he descends and goes to his servant's house, he is called Small King. So, as long as the blessed Holy One is above, over all, He is called Supreme King. Once His abode descends below, He is King, but not Supreme as before. So, a small *alef*.[732]

"*He called.* We have learned as follows: He invited him to His palace.

"*From the Tent of* מועד (*mo'ed*), *Meeting.* Who is *Tent of Meeting*? The *tent* on which depends the reckoning of מועדי (*mo'adei*), holidays, festivals, and Sabbaths, as is said: *they will be for signs and for* מועדים (*mo'adim*), *seasons* (Genesis 1:14). There abides reckoning. And who is that? The moon, as is said: *A tent not to be packed up, whose pegs will never be pulled out* (Isaiah 33:20).[733]

"*Saying.* What does this mean? To reveal what was concealed within. Everywhere, *saying*—as is said: *YHVH spoke to Moses, saying* (Exodus 6:10)—implies that permission was granted to reveal. Yet all is one, and this is fine, for that word was designated for the moon from the place where Moses stands. *YHVH spoke*—above. *To Moses*—in the middle. *Saying*—last, where it is permitted to reveal.[734]

and named them אדם (*Adam*), *Human, on the day they were created.* See the interpretation of this verse attributed to Rabbi El'azar in BT *Yevamot* 63a: "Any אדם (*adam*), man, who has no wife is not an *adam*." See *Zohar* 1:34b, 47a, 55b; 3:5a.

On the large א (*alef*) of אדם (*Adam*) in Chronicles, see *Zohar* 2:53b; *Minḥat Shai* on the verse.

731. **Further, the conclusion...** The full verse reads: *He called to Moses, and YHVH spoke to him from the Tent of Meeting, saying.* The second half of the verse implies that *Tif'eret* (known as *YHVH*) spoke to Moses through *Shekhinah* (known as *Tent of Meeting*). This corresponds to the symbolism of the small *alef*, which indicates *Shekhinah*.

On *Shekhinah* as *Tent of Meeting*, see below.

732. **king sitting upon his throne...** When God reigns above, He is transcendent. When His presence descends to dwell in the Tabernacle, He is no longer so supreme.

733. ***From the Tent of* מועד (*mo'ed*), *Meeting*...** *Shekhinah* is the *Tent of* מועד (*mo'ed*), *Meeting*, because She is symbolized by the moon—the basis of reckoning the lunar calendar and the cycle of מועדי (*mo'adei*), "holidays." Although Sabbaths are independent of this calendar, they are also linked with *Shekhinah*, who is the basis of all calculation and who symbolizes the Sabbath Bride.

On *Shekhinah* as *Tent of Meeting*, see *Zohar* 1:52b. On reckoning by the moon (*Shekhinah*), see above, p. 437 and nn. 652–53. The full verse in Genesis reads: *God said, "Let there be lights in the expanse of heaven to separate the day from the night, and they will be for signs and for seasons, for days and years."* On *Shekhinah* as the basis of all calculation, see *Zohar* 1:46b; *OY*. On the verse in Isaiah, see *Zohar* 1:52b, 101b; 2:65b, 194a; Moses de León, *Shushan Edut*, 346; idem, *Sefer ha-Rimmon*, 379.

734. ***Saying.* What does this mean?...** *Saying* is the final word of the opening verse of Leviticus: *He called to Moses, and YHVH spoke to him from the Tent of Meeting, saying.*

"Further, *He called to Moses.* What is written above? *They brought the Tabernacle to Moses* (Exodus 39:33). Why to Moses? They have said as follows: Because Moses had seen it on the mountain, where the blessed Holy One showed it to him before his very eyes, as is written: *as He showed you on the mountain* (ibid. 27:8), and similarly: *See, and make it by their pattern which you are shown on the mountain* (ibid. 25:40). Now they brought it to him so that he could see whether it was identical with the Tabernacle that he had seen.[735]

"But why did they bring *the Tabernacle to Moses*? Well, this can be compared to a king who wished to build a palace for the matron. He ordered the craftsmen, 'This chamber here, that chamber there. Here a place for the bed, there a place for relaxing.' When the craftsmen had finished them, they showed the king.

"Similarly, *they brought the Tabernacle to Moses*—master of the house, husband of *Elohim*. When the *Matronita*'s palace was completed, She invited the king there, She invited Her husband to be with Her. So, *He called to Moses.*[736]

"Since Moses was master of the house, what is written? *Moses would take the Tent and pitch it for himself outside the camp* (Exodus 33:7). Moses, master of the house, [239b] acted so—something permitted to no other human.[737]

According to the child, this word implies that *Shekhinah* "said" and revealed what had been hidden in higher sefirotic realms. Although *Shekhinah* has just been identified with *Tent of Meeting*, She is also implied by the following word, *saying*. As the child notes, "Yet all is one."

The verse *YHVH spoke to Moses, saying* appears seventy times in the Torah. Here, this formula alludes to the process of revelation, which issues from a high source, indicated by *YHVH spoke* (apparently, *Ḥokhmah* and/or *Binah*), then passes through *Tif'eret* in the middle (the *sefirah* of *Moses*), and is finally revealed through *Shekhinah*, implied by *saying*.

On *saying* and "revealing," see BT *Yoma* 4b. On *saying* as alluding to *Shekhinah*, see *Zohar* 1:35b, 60a; Vol. 1, p. 343, n. 28.

735. **Why to Moses?...** When the Tabernacle was completed, it was brought to Moses so that he could inspect it and verify that it had been constructed according to the vision shown to him on Mount Sinai.

On Moses' vision of various components of the Tabernacle, see *Sifrei*, Numbers 61; BT *Menaḥot* 29a; *Tanḥuma*, *Shemini* 8; *Beha'alotekha* 6; *Tanḥuma* (Buber), *Shemini* 11; *Beha'alotekha* 11. The full verse in Exodus 27 (describing the ark) reads: *Hollow boarded you shall make it, as He showed you on the mountain, so they shall do.* The verse in Exodus 25 concerns the lamp stand. See Exodus 25:9; Numbers 8:4.

736. **But why did they bring...** The child explains further that Moses was master of the house (*Shekhinah*), husband of *Elohim* (*Shekhinah*), and he had the Tabernacle constructed for Her. When it was completed, he approved it, and then *Shekhinah* Herself invited him to join Her there.

See *Zohar* 2:235a. On the epithets "master of the house" and "husband of *Elohim*," see above, pp. 434–35 and nn. 643–44. On the title *Matronita*, see above, note 643.

737. ***Moses would take the Tent...*** Only Moses possessed such power over *Shekhinah* (*the Tent*).

See *Zohar* 1:52b; 2:194a, 236a; 3:114a.

"*YHVH spoke to him* (Leviticus 1:1)—another, supernal rung. Then as Moses was about to enter, He opened, saying, *When a person among you brings [an offering]* (ibid., 2).[738] Why אדם (*adam*), *a person*, here? When sun and moon joined as one, He opened and said, '*Adam, Human*' as is written: *Sun, moon* עמד (*amad*), *stood still, in her lofty abode* (Habakkuk 3:11)—עמד (*amad*), *it stood still*; not עמדו (*amedu*), *they stood still*.[739]

"*When* [*adam*] *among you brings*—intimating that one who would perform the ritual of sacrifice perfectly must be male and female, as implied by what is written: מכם (*mi-kem*), *among you*, that he be a reflection of you.[740]

"*An offering to YHVH* (Leviticus, ibid.)—bringing all near, to unite as one above and below.[741]

"*Of animals* (ibid.)—showing that *adam, human*, and *animals* are all as one.[742]

"*From herd and from flock* (ibid.)—those who are pure. For since He said *of animals*, one might think this means any of them, whether pure or impure; so He goes on to say *from herd and from flock*.[743]

"*You shall bring your offering* (ibid.). The verse should read *My offering*; why *your offering*? Because first *an offering to YHVH*, and now *your offering*. *An offering to YHVH*—*adam, human*. *Your offering*—*of animals from herd and from flock*. To demonstrate union from below to above and from above to below—from below to above, namely *an offering to YHVH*; from above to below, namely *your offering*.[744]

738. ***YHVH spoke*** **... another, supernal rung ...** Apparently, *Tif'eret*. According to *OY* and Galante, this refers to *Binah* (see above, note 734).

Leviticus 1:1–2 read in full: *He called to Moses, and YHVH spoke to him from the Tent of Meeting, saying, "Speak to the Children of Israel and say to them, 'When a person among you brings an offering to YHVH, of animals from herd and from flock you shall bring your offering.'"*

739. **Why אדם (*adam*), *a person*, here? ...** אדם (*Adam*), "human" (or "person") alludes to the union of male and female (see above, note 730), so this word was appropriate when *Tif'eret* (sun) and *Shekhinah* (moon) united in the Tabernacle.

According to the child, the verse in Habakkuk demonstrates the complete union of sun and moon because the verb describing their miraculous standing still is in the singular. See *Zohar* 1:165a; Moses de León, *Shushan Edut*, 368.

740. ***When*** **[*adam*] ... מכם (*mi-kem*), *among you* ...** The plural form מכם (*mi-kem*), *among you*, suggests that one who brings a sacrifice must be married (two as one), reflecting the image of a complete אדם (*adam*), "human."

See *Zohar* 3:5b.

741. ***An offering to YHVH*—bringing all near ...** In Kabbalah the purpose of the קרבן (*qorban*) is to "bring near" the various divine qualities, especially *Tif'eret* and *Shekhinah*—based on the root קרב (*qrv*), "to draw near." See *Bahir* 78 (109).

742. ***Of animals*** **...** Alluding to the powers beneath *Shekhinah*, who participate in the unification.

743. ***From herd and from flock*—those who are pure ...** Powers corresponding to kosher animals, not impure, demonic powers. Cf. *Zohar* 1:162a–b (*ST*).

744. **The verse should read *My offer-***

"This can be compared to a king sitting on a lofty three-legged dais high above;[745] a throne is arranged on that dais, with the king supreme above all. A person who brings a gift to the king must climb from level to level, ascending from below to above until he reaches the place where the king is seated, high above all; then everyone knows that a gift has been brought up to the king and that the gift belongs to the king. If a gift descends from above to below, then they know that the gift descends from above to the king's beloved below.

"Similarly, at first *adam* ascends his rungs from below to above, and so, *an offering to YHVH. Of animals from herd and from flock*—descending his rungs from above to below, and so, *your offering.* Therefore it is written: *I have eaten my honeycomb with my honey, I have drunk my wine with my milk* (Song of Songs 5:1)—corresponding to *adam* and *an offering to YHVH. Eat, O friends!* (ibid.)—corresponding to *of animals from herd and from flock.* So, *you shall bring your offering.*"[746]

Rabbi Yehudah and Rabbi Yitsḥak came and kissed him on the head. They said, "Blessed is the Compassionate One, that we were privileged to hear this! Blessed is the Compassionate One, that these words were not wasted on that old man!"[747]

They rose and walked on. As they were walking, they saw a vine planted in a garden. That child opened, saying, "*He binds to the vine his donkey, to the noble vine his ass's foal* (Genesis 49:11). This verse is sublime. אסרי (*Oseri*), *He binds*—the verse should read אסר (*oser*), *he binds.* עירה (*Iroh*), *his donkey*—the verse should read עיר (*ayir*), *a donkey.* However, this is a secret for schoolchildren to

ing... Since this is an offering to God. The child explains, however, that first an offering (or "drawing near") is made *to YHVH* from below to above, uniting the male and female divine aspects, as indicated by the word אדם (*adam*), "human" (see above, note 730). Once the divine union has been consummated, the angelic forces (*of animals from herd and from flock*) receive a flow of nourishment, which is then conveyed to humanity; this is *your offering.*

For a different interpretation, see *KP.* See *Zohar* 1:64b, 248a; 2:238b–239a; *NO.*

745. **three-legged dais...** טורסקא (*Turseqa*), a Zoharic neologism apparently based on טרסקל (*terisqel*), "a three-legged table or chair," derived from Greek *triskeles.*

See *Tanḥuma, Naso* 19; BT *Shabbat* 138a; *Arukh ha-Shalem*, s.v. *trsql*; Scholem. For other interpretations, see *OY*; Galante; *Bei'ur ha-Millim ha-Zarot*, 179; *KP*; *DE*; *NO.*

746. **at first, *adam* ascends...** In this paragraph, *adam* apparently refers both to the human worshiper and to the divine union of male and female. The human being offers a gift to God by ascending and stimulating the union of the divine couple; then he receives a gift of blessing (*your offering*) from this union, conveyed by the angelic powers (*of animals from herd and from flock*).

The verse in Song of Songs reads: *I have eaten my honeycomb with my honey, I have drunk my wine with my milk. Eat, O friends! Drink and be drunk, O lovers!* See *Shir ha-Shirim Rabbah* on 5:1; *Zohar* 1:164a, 248a; 3:3b–4a, 241a–242a.

747. **not wasted on that old man** Whom the child had left, determining him to be unworthy. See above, page 455.

be protected from that donkey's arrow, and the holy Name is interwoven there: יה (*Yah*).[748]

"Just as the holy Name is intimated here, so too ולשורקה (*ve-la-soreqah*), *to the noble vine*—the verse should read שורק (*soreq*), *noble vine*, as is said: *I planted you as* שורק (*soreq*), *a noble vine* (Jeremiah 2:21). בני (*Beni*), *foal*—the verse should read בן (*ben*), *foal*, as is said: בן (*ben*), *foal, of a she-ass* (Zechariah 9:9). Why שורקה (*soreqah*), *noble vine*, and why בני (*beni*), *foal*? Well, just as there is a holy Name to overwhelm the donkey, so there is a holy Name to overwhelm another power, namely the ass. For if the holy Name were not intimated here, they would pulverize the world. יה (*Yah*) for this power, and יה (*Yah*) for that power, so that the world will be protected from them, so that humans will be protected from being dominated by them.[749]

"*He binds to the vine*. What is the *vine*? Assembly of Israel. Why is she called *vine*? Well, just as a vine accepts no alien graft, so too Assembly of Israel accepts none but the blessed Holy One. For the sake of Assembly of Israel, all other powers are overwhelmed, and cannot inflict harm and dominate the world.[750]

"Therefore Scripture inserted a holy Name in their midst, on this side and on that side.[751]

748. **אסרי (*Oseri*) . . . should read אסר (*oser*) . . .** The poetic י (*yod*) at the end of אסרי (*oseri*), *he binds*, seems unnecessary, as does the rare use of ה (*he*) to indicate a masculine possessive at the end of עירה (*iroh*), *his donkey*. (Perhaps the text of the *Zohar* originally read "the verse should read עירו (*iro*), *his donkey*"—employing the more common signifier of the masculine possessive.) The child explains, however, that these two letters are essential, spelling out the divine name יה (*Yah*), which protects children from the demonic power symbolized by the donkey.

See Ibn Ezra on this verse; *Zohar* 3:207a; above, p. 448 and n. 689.

749. **ולשורקה (*ve-la-soreqah*) . . . should read שורק (*soreq*) . . .** Similarly (see previous note), the poetic ה (*he*) at the end of ולשורקה (*ve-la-soreqah*) seems superfluous, as does the poetic י (*yod*) at the end of בני (*beni*), *foal*. But here too, these two letters constitute the divine name יה (*Yah*), offering protection against the demonic ass and preventing the alliance of the two threatening powers.

See the sources cited in the preceding note. "Pulverize" renders מטרטשי (*metarteshei*), "crumble," based on מטרשי (*metareshei*), "make brittle," and טרש (*teresh*), "stony ground." See *Zohar* 1:37a; 2:30a. The full verse in Jeremiah reads: *I planted you as a noble vine, of entirely faithful seed. How then did you turn before Me into a corrupt, alien vine?* The full verse in Zechariah reads: *See, your king is coming to you: righteous and triumphant is he; humble* [or: *poor*] *and riding on an ass—on a donkey, foal of a she-ass*.

750. **What is the *vine*? Assembly of Israel . . .** Here, Assembly of Israel refers primarily to the people of Israel, who remain committed solely to God.

On Israel as *vine*, see above, p. 447 and n. 687. On grafting, see JT *Kil'ayim* 1:7, 27b; BT *Sotah* 43b; *Zohar* 1:26a (*TZ*), 115b; 3:125b, 247a (*RM*); *TZ* 15, 30b; 69, 111a; Immanuel Löw, *Die Flora der Juden*, 1:166.

751. **on this side and on that side** On the side of the donkey and of the ass.

"*His ass's foal*—uprooted for the sake of that noble vine, as is said: *I planted you as a noble vine* (Jeremiah 2:21).[752]

"*He has washed in wine his garment* (Genesis 49:11). *He has washed*—the verse should read *he washes.* However, *he has washed* ever since the day that the world was created. And who is that? King Messiah below. *In wine*—left side. *In the blood of grapes* (ibid.)—left side below. King Messiah is destined [240a] to prevail above over all forces of other nations, crushing their power above and below.[753]

"Alternatively, *He has washed in wine his garment*—just as wine manifests joy yet is totally judgment, so too King Messiah will manifest joy to Israel and be total judgment toward other nations.[754]

"It is written: *The spirit of God hovering over the waters* (Genesis 1:2)—spirit of King Messiah. Ever since the day that the world was created, he has been washing his garment in supernal wine.[755]

"See what is written next: *Eyes darker than wine* (ibid. 49:12)—saturating supernal wine, from which Torah drinks. *Teeth whiter than milk* (ibid.)—Torah. *Wine* and *milk*: Written Torah and Oral Torah.[756]

"It is written: *Wine that gladdens the human heart* (Psalms 104:15). Why? Because it derives from a place of joy. Who is that? The continuation of the verse establishes this, as is written: *to make the face shine from oil* (ibid.)—*from oil*, precisely, from the place called *oil.*[757]

752. **uprooted for the sake of that noble vine...** The demonic power was extirpated for the sake of Israel.

753. ***He has washed...*** The present tense *he washes* is more appropriate for a blessing, implying that the wine is (and will be continue to be) as abundant as water. However, the subject is in fact King Messiah, who ever since Creation has been imbued with *Din* (harsh Judgment on the left, symbolized by *wine*) and with *Shekhinah* (mild Judgment, deriving from *Din* and symbolized by *blood of grapes*). Empowered by these sefirotic forces, the Messiah will defeat Israel's enemies—both their heavenly princes and their earthly forces.

See above, p. 448 and n. 689; p. 449 and nn. 693–94. The verse reads: *He has washed in wine his garment, in the blood of grapes his cloak.*

754. **wine manifests joy yet is totally judgment...** Wine brings delight, but its intoxicating power reflects its corresponding sefirah, *Din* (harsh Judgment).

755. ***The spirit of God...*** **spirit of King Messiah...** See the midrash in the name of Shim'on son of Lakish in *Bereshit Rabbah* 2:4 (see Theodor's note); *Vayiqra Rabbah* 14:1.

The full verse reads: *The earth was an empty waste, with darkness over the deep and the spirit of God hovering over the waters.*

756. ***Eyes darker than wine...*** Wine symbolizes *Din* but also the flowing source of *Din, Binah,* who nourishes *Tif'eret,* symbolized by Torah. More specifically, *Tif'eret* is Written Torah, and *Shekhinah* is Oral Torah; the former is particularly influenced by *Ḥesed* (*milk*), the latter by *Din* (*wine*).

On Torah as wine and milk, see BT *Ta'anit* 7a; *Shir ha-Shirim Rabbah* on 1:2; *Devarim Rabbah* 7:3. For various interpretations of this passage, see *OY*; Galante; *Sullam*; Mopsik.

757. ***Wine that gladdens...*** The deep

"Come and see: The beginning of wine is joy—a place from which all joy issues—and its end is judgment. Why? Because its end is the gathering place of all—it is judgment, by which the world is judged. So, beginning is joy and end is judgment. Therefore, *to make the face shine from oil*—from the source of all joy.[758]

"*And bread that sustains the human heart* (ibid.). Who is *bread*? Bread sustaining the world. Now, if you say that sustenance of the world depends upon it alone—not so! For night does not exist without day, and one must not separate them. Whoever separates them separates himself from life, corresponding to what is written: *in order to make you know that not on bread alone does the human live* (Deuteronomy 8:3)—for they should not be separated.[759]

"Now, you might ask, 'How could David say, *And bread that sustains the human heart*, since sustenance of the world does not depend solely upon it?' However, precision of the word: ולחם (*ve-leḥem*), *and bread*—for a ו (*vav*) has been added, as in ויהוה (*va-YHVH*), *And YHVH*, so all is present as one.[760]

"Come and see: One who offers blessing over food should not bless over an empty table: there should be bread on the table and a cup of wine in the right hand. Why? In order to bind left with right, and for bread to be blessed by them, linked with them; for all to become a single cluster, to bless the holy

source of *wine* is *Ḥokhmah*, symbolized by *oil*.

On *Ḥokhmah* as *oil*, see *Zohar* 3:34a, 39a. Cf. BT *Menaḥot* 85b. The full verse in Psalms reads: *Wine that gladdens the human heart—to make the face shine from oil—and bread that sustains the human heart.*

758. **beginning of wine is joy...** At first, wine brings delight, but eventually it intoxicates. These two properties reflect, respectively, its joyous origin in *Ḥokhmah* and *Binah*, and its culmination in *Shekhinah* ("gathering place of all"), who derives from *Din* and is characterized by judgment.

See *Tanḥuma, Shemini* 11; above, note 754.

759. ***And bread that sustains...*** *Bread* symbolizes *Shekhinah*, who nourishes the world; yet She Herself (symbolized by the moon) needs the illumination of Her partner, *Tif'eret* (the sun). The union of the divine couple must be maintained by human virtue in order to ensure sustenance and life.

The full verse reads: *He afflicted you and made you hunger and fed you the manna, which you did not know nor did your fathers know, in order to make you know that not on bread alone does the human live but on everything emanating from YHVH's mouth does the human live.* *YHVH* symbolizes *Tif'eret*, who conveys the flow of emanation to *Shekhinah* (*bread*), enabling Her to sustain the world.

760. **precision of the word: ולחם (*ve-leḥem*), *and bread*...** *Bread* refers to *Shekhinah*; *and bread* refers to *Tif'eret* as well. Similarly, *YHVH* refers to *Tif'eret*; *and YHVH* refers to *Shekhinah* as well.

See *Bereshit Rabbah* 51:2: "Rabbi El'azar said, 'Wherever it is said *And YHVH*, this implies: He and His Court.'" In Kabbalah this court symbolizes *Shekhinah*, who derives from *Din* (Judgment) and pronounces the divine decree, so the phrase *And YHVH* encompasses "He [*Tif'eret*, known as *YHVH*] and His Court [*Shekhinah*]."

See *Vayiqra Rabbah* 24:2; JT *Berakhot* 9:5, 14b; Rashi on Exodus 12:29; *Zohar* 1:15b, 64b, 105a, 107b, 159b, 192b, 198a; 2:37b, 44b, 227b; 3:149a. The hermeneutical significance of *and* was championed by Rabbi Akiva. See BT *Yevamot* 68b, *Sanhedrin* 51b. Cf. *Zohar* 1:246a.

Name fittingly. For *bread* is joined with *wine*, and *wine* with the right; then blessings abide in the world and the table is fittingly complete."[761]

Rabbi Yitsḥak said, "If we happened upon this way just to hear these words, it is enough for us!"[762]

Rabbi Yehudah said, "It would have been better for this child not to know all this, and I fear that because of this he may not survive in the world!"

Rabbi Yitsḥak asked, "Why?"

He replied, "Because he can gaze upon a place where it is forbidden to gaze, and I fear that before he reaches maturity he will look and gaze and be punished."[763]

That child heard and said, "I never fear punishment, because when my father departed from the world he blessed me and prayed for me, and I know that father's merit will protect me."

They asked him, "Who is your father?"

He replied, "Rav Yehudah son of Rav Hamnuna Sava."[764]

761. **should not bless over an empty table...** When reciting the Grace after Meals, there should be some bread on the table. See BT *Sanhedrin* 92a: "Rabbi El'azar said, 'Whoever does not leave bread on his table will never see a sign of blessing.'"

Here bread symbolizes *Shekhinah* and wine symbolizes *Din* (Judgment, on the left). By holding the cup of wine in the right hand (symbolizing *Ḥesed*), one balances the power of *Din*. Then *Shekhinah* (bread) is embraced by both *Ḥesed* and *Din*, the divine right and left arms, and joined with *Tif'eret*.

On leaving bread on the table, see Naḥmanides on Exodus 25:24; *Zohar* 1:88a, 250a; 2:63b, 67a, 87b, 153b, 155a, 157b; 3:34a; Ta-Shma, *Ha-Nigleh she-ba-Nistar*, 28; idem, *Minhag Ashkenaz ha-Qadmon*, 267–70.

On holding the cup of wine in the right hand, see BT *Berakhot* 51a; *Zohar* 1:156a (*ST*), 250a; 2:138b, 143b, 157b; Moses de León, *Sefer ha-Rimmon*, 105.

762. **If we happened upon this way...** On this type of expression, see above, note 614.

763. **he can gaze upon a place...** The child's ability to probe hidden, forbidden realms endangers his own life.

A rabbinic tradition in BT *Ḥagigah* 13a relates that a certain child who expounded the secrets of Ezekiel's vision was consumed by fire, and according to the Talmud his death was due to his young age. Cf. *Zohar* 3:192a; Scholem.

764. **Rav Yehudah son of Rav Hamnuna Sava** The child apparently identifies himself as the grandson of the famous Rav Hamnuna Sava.

Historically, Rav Hamnuna Sava (the Elder) was a mid-third-century Babylonian teacher, but in the *Zohar* he is a contemporary of Rabbi Shim'on bar Yoḥai (who lived in the second century). In the Talmud, Rav Hamnuna occasionally transmits teachings of Rabbi Shim'on (e.g., BT *Ḥullin* 21a, *Temurah* 15a), and several prayers are attributed to him (BT *Berakhot* 11b, 17a, 58a). In the *Zohar* roles are reversed and Rabbi Shim'on cites Rav Hamnuna (e.g., 1:8a–b). Throughout the *Zohar* Hamnuna is greatly revered, and several original ritual acts are attributed to him. See 1:6a, 250a; 2:88a, 124a, 136b; 3:87b, 103b, 145b (*IR*), 188a; Vol. 1, pp. 37–38, n. 257.

In *Zohar* 1:6a–7a, a donkey-driver who seems to be the son of Rav Hamnuna turns out to be Hamnuna himself, reincarnated. A similar phenomenon is described in 3:188a (*Yanuqa*). See 2:107b–108a.

Galante construes this sentence differ-

They lifted him and carried him on their shoulders for three miles. They exclaimed for him, "*Out of the eater came something to eat, out of the strong came something sweet* (Judges 14:14)."[765]

That child said to them, "A word has come into your hands, interpret it!"

They replied, "The blessed Holy One has paved the way for us, you speak!"[766]

He opened, saying, "*Out of the eater came something to eat.* We have a support for this verse: *Out of the eater*—Righteous One, as is written: *A righteous one eats to satisfy his soul* (Proverbs 13:25). *A righteous one eats*, surely, absorbing all. Why? *To satisfy his soul*—to give satisfaction to the one called *his soul*, Soul of David.[767]

"*Came something to eat*—were it not for Righteous One, nourishment would not issue for the world and the world could not endure.

"*Out of the strong came something sweet*—Isaac, who blessed Jacob with *the dew of heaven and the fat of the earth* (Genesis 27:28).[768] Further—though all is

ently: "Rabbi Yehudah replied, 'The son of Rav Hamnuna Sava.'" He interprets this to mean that Rabbi Yehudah is identifying the child's father as the son of Hamnuna. However, all of the manuscripts that I have consulted (along with *OY* and the Cremona edition) read here "Rav Yehudah" and not "Rabbi (or "R.") Yehudah," which is how the *Zohar* consistently refers to the Companion Rabbi Yehudah. (*OL*, though, reads "Rabbi Yehudah.") Mopsik understands the sentence to mean that Rabbi Yehudah is identifying the child as the son of Hamnuna. *Sullam* deletes "Rav Yehudah" (following the Mantua edition) and understands the response as, "[I am] the son of Rav Hamnuna Sava." See *MM*; *MmD.* On the relation between another child and Rabbi Yehudah, see *Zohar* 3:171a.

765. **three miles...** According to Rav Sheshet (BT *Sotah* 46b), one should escort his teacher a distance of a parasang. A distinguished teacher, however, is to be escorted for three parasangs. (The Persian parasang equals about 3.5 miles.)

See *Pesiqta de-Rav Kahana* 18:5; *Bereshit Rabbah* 32:10; *Zohar* 1:51a, 87a, 96b, 150b; 2:14a, 164a, 187a; 3:8b.

The verse exclaimed by the two rabbis is the riddle propounded by Samson to his wedding guests. Here, it alludes to the child's descent from—and resemblance to—Rav Hamnuna Sava.

766. **The blessed Holy One has paved the way...** That is, "Until now, our journey has been blessed by God through our encounter with you. Please, continue and expound the verse!"

767. **We have a support...** The child quotes a verse demonstrating (by verbal analogy) that *the eater* alludes to *Yesod* (known as Righteous One), who absorbs the nourishing flow from above and conveys it to *Shekhinah, his soul. Shekhinah,* known as *Malkhut* (Kingdom), is linked with King David and called Soul of David.

See Moses de León, *Sod Eser Sefirot Belimah*, 381. On *Yesod* as Righteous One, see above, p. 92, n. 50. On the phrase נפש דוד (*nefesh david*), "soul of David," see 1 Samuel 18:1; 2 Samuel 5:8; *Zohar* 1:101a, 206a; 2:27a, 171a; 3:45b, 182a; Moses de León, *Shushan Edut*, 348; idem, *Sefer ha-Rimmon*, 43; idem, *Sheqel ha-Qodesh*, 61 (75).

768. ***Out of the strong*...Isaac...** Isaac symbolizes *Gevurah* (Power), and he bestowed sweet blessings upon Jacob.

The full verse in Genesis reads: *May God give you of the dew of heaven and the fat of the earth, abundance of grain and new wine.*

one—were it not for the power of strict Judgment, honey would not flow. Who is honey? Oral Torah. *Out of the strong*—Written Torah, as is written: *YHVH gives strength to His people* (Psalms 29:11). *Comes something sweet*—Oral Torah, as is written: *sweeter than honey and drippings of the comb* (ibid. 19:11)."[769] [240b]

They walked together for three days until they reached the outskirts of his mother's village.[770] As soon as she saw them, she prepared the house and they stayed there for three more days. Then they blessed them and went on and arranged words before Rabbi Shim'on.

He said, "Surely, he has inherited the heritage of Torah! Were it not for the merit of fathers, he would have been punished from above. But the blessed Holy One enables those who follow Torah to inherit her—they and their descendants forever, as is written: *As for Me, this is My covenant with them, says YHVH: My spirit that is upon you, and My words that I have put in your mouth, will not depart from your mouth nor from the mouth of your children nor from the mouth of your children's children—says YHVH—from now and forever* (Isaiah 59:21)."[771]

Zebulun will dwell by the shore of the sea (Genesis 49:13).[772]

Rabbi Abba opened, "*Gird your sword upon the thigh, O mighty one, your splendor and your majesty* (Psalms 45:4). Now, is this *splendor* and *majesty*: to gird weapons and arm oneself? One who engages in Torah and fights the battle of Torah, arming oneself with her—this is praiseworthy, this is *splendor* and *majesty*. And 467

769. **Further—though all is one...** The child reveals another way in which sweetness emerges from strength, but he notes that the two interpretations are fully integrated. Written Torah (often symbolizing *Tif'eret*) is a manifestation of Divine Power (*Gevurah*), yet this potent revelation generated Oral Torah (often symbolizing *Shekhinah*), which is sweet as honey.

On Torah as *strength*, see *Mekhilta, Shirta* 3; *Sifrei*, Deuteronomy 343. On the sweetness of Torah, see *Shir ha-Shirim Rabbah* on 2:3; *Zohar* 1:85b.

770. **outskirts of... village** טורסא דקירא (*Tursa de-qira*). *Tursa* may derive from the root טרס (*trs*), "to go around." *Qira* may be based on קריה (*qiryah*), "village."

For other interpretations, see Galante; *KP*; *Adderet Eliyyahu*; *DE*; *NO*; Luria, *Va-Ye'esof David*; *Nefesh David*; *Sullam*; Scholem; *MmD*.

771. **inherited the heritage of Torah...** Being descended from Rav Hamnuna Sava, who is apparently his grandfather. Without such noble lineage, the child would have been punished for penetrating secret realms.

See above, p. 465 and nn. 763–64; *Nefesh David*. See BT *Bava Metsi'a* 85a, in the name of Rabbi Yoḥanan: "Whoever is a scholar, and his son a scholar, and his grandson a scholar—Torah will never cease from his seed, as is said: *As for Me, this is My covenant with them, says YHVH: My spirit that is upon you, and My words that I have put in your mouth, will not depart from your mouth nor from the mouth of your children nor from the mouth of your children's children—says YHVH—from now and forever.*

772. ***Zebulun will dwell...*** The full verse reads: *Zebulun will dwell by the shore of the sea, and he by a haven of ships, his flank upon Sidon.*

yet you say, *Gird your sword upon the thigh, O mighty one, your splendor and your majesty*?[773]

"However, the essence of the matter is: The blessed Holy One bestowed a sign of the holy covenant, inscribing it upon men, so that they would preserve it and not mar the insignia of the King. Whoever mars it is confronted by *a sword avenging with vengeance of the covenant* (Leviticus 26:25), wreaking vengeance for the holy covenant inscribed upon him, marred by him.[774]

"Whoever wishes to guard this place should arm himself and prepare himself, and when the evil impulse attacks him, he should set before himself this *sword* that is found *upon the thigh*, to retaliate against one who damages this place. So, *Gird your sword upon the thigh, O mighty one*—he is *mighty*, called *mighty one*; therefore, *your splendor and your majesty*.[775]

"Alternatively, *Gird your sword upon the thigh, O mighty one*—one who sets out on the way should array himself with the prayer of his Lord, arming himself with Righteousness, supernal sword, before he departs, as is said: *Righteousness goes before him, and he sets out on his way* (Psalms 85:14).[776]

"Come and see: Zebulun always went out on paths and roads, waging wars. Before setting out, he armed himself with this supernal sword by prayers and supplications, and then he defeated nations, overpowering them.[777]

"Now, you might say, 'Judah was arrayed with this to wage wars, arrayed with

773. **fights the battle of Torah...** For this metaphor, see BT *Shabbat* 63a (Rav Kahana's interpretation of the verse in Psalms); *Shir ha-Shirim Zuta* on 3:8; *Bemidbar Rabbah* 11:3; above at note 310; *Zohar* 2:110a–b; 3:127b (*IR*), 188a–189b; *ZḤ* 14a (*MhN*).

774. **sign of the holy covenant...** The mark of circumcision. Whoever mars this holy sign by sinning sexually is attacked by *Shekhinah*, pictured as an avenging sword.

On *Shekhinah* as "sword," see above at note 665; *Zohar* 1:53b, 66b; 2:26a, 28b, 66a; 3:19b, 30a; Moses de León, *Sefer ha-Rimmon*, 69, 213.

775. **guard this place...** To guard the covenantal sign (implied by *the thigh*), one should confront the evil impulse with the sword of *Shekhinah*. Such action exhibits true might and majesty.

See M *Avot* 4:1: "Ben Zoma says, '...Who is strong? One who subdues his impulse.'" See *Zohar* 2:61a.

776. **one who sets out on the way...** By praying before a journey, one arms himself with the sword of *Shekhinah* (known as Righteousness).

See BT *Berakhot* 14a, in the name of Rabbi Yitsḥak son of Ishyan: "Whoever prays and then sets out on the way, the blessed Holy One fulfills his desires, as is said: *Righteousness goes before him, and he sets out on his way*.'" In this Talmudic passage, *righteousness* implies justification by prayer, which guarantees a successful journey. Here in the *Zohar*, *Righteousness* refers to *Shekhinah*. By praying, one secures Her accompanying presence.

See BT *Berakhot* 29b–30a; *Zohar* 1:49b–50a, 58b, 76a, 121a (*MhN*), 178a, 230a–b; 2:130b.

777. **Zebulun always went out...** On the military prowess of Zebulun, see Judges 4:6; 5:18; 1 Chronicles 12:34; *Vayiqra Rabbah* 25:2; Ibn Ezra on Deuteronomy 33:18; *Zohar* 3:150a.

this sword. Why Zebulun?' But come and see: These twelve tribes were all the adornment of *Matronita*.[778]

"Solomon spoke of two arrayals of females in the Song of Songs: one of the supernal Beloved, Jubilee; and one of the Bride, Sabbatical. One, arrayal above, and one, arrayal below. So too, the Act of Creation included both of these sites: one, an act above, and one, an act below. Therefore, ב (*bet*), opening of Torah: an act below corresponding to the pattern above; this one making an upper world, this one making a lower world. Similarly, Solomon spoke of two arrayals: one above and one below—one above, a supernal arrayal of the holy Name; one below, a lower arrayal corresponding to the pattern above.[779]

"Come and see: Happy is the share of holy Jacob, attaining this! As has been said, since the day that the world was created, there has never been a bed as perfect as Jacob's bed. At the moment that Jacob was about to depart from the world, he was complete on all sides: Abraham on his right, Isaac on his left, he himself in the middle, *Shekhinah* in front of him. As soon as Jacob saw this, he called his sons and said to them, *Be gathered* (Genesis 49:1), so that above and below would be arrayed.[780]

778. **Judah was arrayed with this...** Judah in particular is associated with *Shekhinah*; yet, all the tribes constitute Her adornment, as clarified below.

On the link between Judah and *Shekhinah*, see above, notes 618, 657. On his military capability, see Judges 1:2. On the title *Matronita*, see above, note 643.

779. **Solomon spoke of two arrayals...** The female descriptions in Song of Songs allude to *Binah* (the Divine Mother, known as Beloved) and *Shekhinah* (the Bride). *Binah* is symbolized by the Jubilee, *Shekhinah* by the Sabbatical.

The Beloved appears in Song of Songs 4:1, 7, and passim; the Bride, in Song of Songs 4:8–12; 5:1. On the distinction between Beloved and Bride, see *Zohar* 3:77b–78a, 290b (*IZ*); cf. 3:4a.

According to the Bible, every seventh year is a Sabbatical (Hebrew, שמטה [*shemittah*], "release"), during which the land must lie fallow and at the end of which all debts are remitted (Leviticus 25:1–24; Deuteronomy 15:1–3). In Kabbalah the Sabbatical symbolizes *Shekhinah*, seventh of the lower *sefirot*.

In the biblical cycle, after seven Sabbaticals comes the Jubilee, proclaimed every fifty years, when slaves are released and land reverts to its original owner (Leviticus 25:8–55). In Kabbalah the Jubilee symbolizes *Binah*, who in general is characterized by the number fifty, based on BT *Rosh ha-Shanah* 21b, where Rav and Shemu'el teach: "Fifty gates of בינה (*binah*), understanding, were created in the world, all of which were given to Moses except for one, as is said: *You made him little less than God* (Psalms 8:6)." *Binah* is the source of redemption and liberation, specifically the Exodus from Egypt. See *Zohar* 1:21b, 47b–48a; 2:46a, 83b, 85b, 147b, 151a, 153b–154b; 3:262a.

The ב (*bet*) of בראשית (*Be-reshit*), *In the beginning*, has a numerical value of two and here alludes to the dual creation: *Binah* emanating the world of the seven lower *sefirot* (completing, or arraying, the holy Name); *Shekhinah* emanating the lower worlds. See *Zohar* 1:29a–b; Moses de León, *Sefer ha-Rimmon*, 192.

780. **Happy is the share...** Jacob helped to complete both arrayals, as explained below.

His bed was perfect in two senses: first, because all of his offspring were worthy (see

"Come and see the mystery of the matter! Two arrayals manifested there: one above and one below, so that all would be fittingly complete. Supernal arrayal—concealed and revealed, for this is arrayal of Jubilee, the one mentioned by Solomon in Song of Songs, as we have said. The head is concealed, for here it is not revealed and should not be. Arms and body are revealed, as is well known. Thighs, concealed and unrevealed. Why? Because prophecy prevails only in the Holy Land. So this array is concealed and revealed.

"The other, lower arrayal is adornment of the Bride, mentioned by Solomon in Song of Songs. This arrayal is more fully revealed; this arrayal is by twelve tribes [241a] beneath Her, embodying Her adornment."[781]

Rabbi Abba opened, saying, "*He made the sea* [*of cast metal*] (1 Kings 7:23), and it is written: *Standing upon twelve oxen: three facing north, three facing west, three facing south, and three facing east, with the sea set upon them above*... (ibid., 25), and it is written: *the twelve oxen underneath the sea* (ibid., 44). *Standing upon twelve oxen*—certainly so! For this sea is arrayed by twelve in two worlds: by twelve above, appointed chariots; by twelve below, twelve tribes.[782]

"When Jacob saw the supernal array and saw *Shekhinah* standing before him, he wanted to complete Her adornment. He called his twelve sons and said to them, *Be gathered* (Genesis 49:1)—'Prepare yourselves to complete Faith.'[783]

above, note 575); and second, because he was now facing *Shekhinah* and flanked by the souls of Abraham and Isaac. Those two patriarchs symbolize respectively *Ḥesed* and *Gevurah*, who are integrated and completed by Jacob's *sefirah*, *Tif'eret*. As he prepared to die, Jacob called his sons to complete the arrayal of *Shekhinah*. See above, page 426.

781. **Two arrayals manifested there...** The supernal one is of *Binah* (Jubilee), who is arrayed by the lower *sefirot*. The highest three *sefirot* (*Keter*, *Ḥokhmah*, and *Binah* Herself) constitute the head and remain hidden. She is more openly arrayed by the divine arms (*Ḥesed* and *Gevurah*, symbolized respectively by Abraham and Isaac) and the trunk of the sefirotic body (*Tif'eret*, symbolized by Jacob). The legs (*Netsaḥ* and *Hod*) are the source of prophecy, so these remain concealed, because prophecy manifests only in the Holy Land, whereas Jacob passed away in Egypt.

The lower arrayal is of *Shekhinah* (the Bride), who is adorned by the twelve tribes.

On the arrayal of *Binah*, see *Zohar* 1:158a; 2:180b; Moses de León, *Shushan Edut*, 331–32; idem, *Sefer ha-Rimmon*, 8 (and Wolfson's note). On *Shekhinah* and the twelve tribes, see *Zohar* 1:158a, 174a, 225b, 231b, 240b–241a, 246a–b; 2:229b–230a; 3:62a, 118b; Moses de León, *Sefer ha-Rimmon*, 8. On prophecy manifesting only in the land of Israel, see above, note 197.

782. ***He made the sea...*** A large bronze reservoir built by Solomon in the Temple, which rested on twelve bronze oxen, three facing outward in each direction. This *sea* symbolizes *Shekhinah*, who is arrayed above by twelve angelic forces and below by the twelve tribes.

On the *sea*, see *Zohar* 1:154a; 2:164b. On the angelic array, see *Zohar* 149a–b (*ST*).

783. ***Be gathered*** **...to complete Faith** To adorn *Shekhinah*, who is the culmination of the *sefirot*, the realm of faith. See above, note 780.

"Come and see: Twelve tribes with four banners in four directions: *three facing north, three facing west, three south, and three east, with the sea set upon them.* Certainly so! Three tribes in each direction, to the four winds of the world: three tribes to the right arm, three tribes to the left arm, three tribes to the right leg, three tribes to the left leg, and the body of *Shekhinah* above them, as is written: *with the sea set upon them.*[784]

"Why three tribes to the arm and three tribes to the leg, and so on? Well, mystery of the matter: There are three joints in the right arm and three joints in the left arm, three joints in the right leg and three joints in the left leg—consequently, twelve joints in four directions, and the body upon them; consequently, thirteen, counting the body, corresponding to the pattern above. How do we know? Because it is written: *All these are the tribes of Israel, twelve, and this* (Genesis 49:28)—for with Her the count is complete, as has been said: *with the sea set upon them above.*[785]

"Seven eyes of *YHVH* are the eyes of the community, seventy members of the Sanhedrin.[786]

"Her hair—as is written: *All those counted for the camp of Judah: one hundred thousand*... (Numbers 2:9); *All those counted for the camp of Reuben*... (ibid., 16); and so with all of them.[787]

784. **Twelve tribes with four banners...** The arrangement of the twelve tribes in the wilderness of Sinai corresponds to *the twelve oxen underneath the sea* and to the various sefirotic limbs. Three tribes correspond to the right arm (*Ḥesed*), three to the left arm (*Gevurah*), three to the right leg (*Netsaḥ*), and three to the left leg (*Hod*). *Shekhinah* rests above them.

785. **three joints in the... arm... three joints in the... leg...** The three tribes in each direction correspond respectively to the three joints in each limb. The joints of the arm are the shoulder, elbow, and wrist; the joints of the leg are the hip, knee, and ankle. See *Zohar* 1:154a; 2:244a–b; 3:142a–b (*IR*).

In addition to the twelve bodily joints, there is the trunk of the body. Similarly, the body of *Shekhinah* rests upon the twelve tribes, comprising together a holy structure of thirteen. The verse in Genesis 49 refers to this configuration by first mentioning the twelve tribes and then adding the word *this*, which alludes to *Shekhinah*—the Divine Presence who is always right here.

The full verse in Genesis reads: *All these are the tribes of Israel, twelve, and this is what their father spoke to them, blessing them; each according to his blessing, he blessed them.* See *Zohar* 1:248a; 3:62a.

786. **Seven eyes of *YHVH*... Sanhedrin** Rabbi Abba continues the description of *Shekhinah*'s arrayal by mentioning the divine eyes, which represent the seventy members of the Sanhedrin, symbolizing seventy angelic powers through which She sees and conducts the world.

See above, note 416. On the seven eyes, see Zechariah 4:10 (quoted below): *These seven are the eyes of YHVH, ranging over the whole earth.* Cf. ibid. 3:9; 4:1–4. The phrase "eyes of the community" derives from Numbers 15:24 and is interpreted in midrashic sources as referring to the Sanhedrin. See *Eikhah Rabbah* (Buber) 2:4; *Shir ha-Shirim Rabbah* on 1:15.

787. **Her hair... *All those counted*...** The hair represents further angelic powers emanating from *Shekhinah*, symbolized by

"Now, you might ask, 'In Egypt, during Jacob's departure from the world, when there was consummation, where was all this?' Well, there were surely seventy souls, and all those engendered by them during seventeen years, who were innumerable, as is written: *The Children of Israel were fruitful and swarmed and multiplied and became* [*exceedingly*] *numerous* (Exodus 1:7), and similarly: *They have become more numerous than the hairs of my head* (Psalms 40:13). Happy is the share of Jacob the perfect, who perfected above and below!"[788]

Rabbi El'azar said, "Certainly so! But how is all this found in the supernal array of Jubilee?"[789]

He replied, "Once a lion has set his feet to enter the vineyard, who dares enter with him?"[790]

Rabbi El'azar opened, saying, "*He is one, and who can turn Him back? Whatever His soul desires, He does* (Job 23:13). This supernal array is entirely one, containing no division like that lower one—for it is written: *from there it divides* (Genesis 2:10). Yet although it contains division, upon contemplating, all ascends to one.[791]

the vast numbers of the tribal census in the wilderness.

788. **In Egypt, during Jacob's departure...** How could Jacob have succeeded in completing the array of *Shekhinah* immediately before he died, when at that time the number of Israelites was just a fraction of the future total of the census? Rabbi Abba answers this hypothetical question by pointing to the seventy souls who came to Egypt (Jacob, his children, and his grandchildren) and to the large number of their descendants born during Jacob's seventeen years in Egypt. The seventy souls correspond to the seventy members of the Sanhedrin and the seventy angelic powers; the large number of descendants correspond to the immense total of the census and the vast array of other angelic powers (symbolized by hair).

On the seventy souls who came to Egypt, see Genesis 46:8–27; Exodus 1:5; Deuteronomy 10:22. On Jacob's seventeen years in Egypt, see Genesis 47:28. On the immense number of descendants born before he died, see *Bereshit Rabbah* 79:1 (and Theodor's note). The full verse in Exodus reads: *The Children of Israel were fruitful and swarmed and multiplied and became exceedingly numerous, and the land was filled with them.* The verse from Psalms is quoted to show that *numerous* refers to hair. (For a different interpretation, see *KP*; *Adderet Eliyyahu.*)

789. **how is all this found in... Jubilee?** Granted, that *Shekhinah* is arrayed by twelve powers, but regarding *Binah* (Jubilee), there seem to be just six *sefirot* between Her and *Shekhinah*.

790. **Once a lion has set...** Since you—the valiant Rabbi El'azar—have already ventured into this matter by posing the question, who but you can respond?

791. ***He is one...*** Literally, *He is in one,* meaning "He is one, unchangeable, fixed, determined." Rabbi El'azar understands the clause as referring to the arrayal of *Binah* by the *sefirot* beneath Her. Their unity contrasts with the realm beneath *Shekhinah,* which is characterized by multiplicity, as alluded to by the verse in Genesis: *A river issues from Eden to water the garden, and from there it divides and becomes four riverheads*—i.e., the river of emanation waters the garden of *Shekhinah* and from there divides into four angelic realms and the worlds below. Yet,

"However, this supernal array of Jubilee rests on twelve, like the lower one. And although it is one, this one completes every side, on this side and on that. Those six supernal sides are twelve, for each one lends to his neighbor and intermingles with him; so there are twelve and the body. All rests on twelve. Who is the body? Jacob. As has been said, head and body exist as one.[792]

"Further, twelve—three joints of the right arm: *Ḥesed, ḥasadim*; three joints in the left arm: *Gevurah, gevurot*; three joints in the right leg: *Netsaḥ, netsaḥim*; three joints in the left leg: *Hod* and *hodot*. Look, twelve, with the body resting upon them![793]

"Further, with thirteen principles by which Torah is interpreted. And all is one, from above to below in union, until that place presiding over division.[794]

"Seven supernal eyes—of which is written *eyes of YHVH*, משוטטים (*meshotetim*), *ranging* (Zechariah 4:10)—are male, for here is the site of the male. *The eyes of YHVH*, משוטטות (*meshotetot*), *ranging* (2 Chronicles 16:9)—in the adornments of *Shekhinah* below, site of the female. Seven supernal eyes, corresponding to the mystery that is written: *Yours, O YHVH,* [241b] *are* גדולה (*gedullah*), *greatness;* גבורה (*gevurah*), *power;* תפארת (*tif'eret*), *beauty;* נצח (*netsaḥ*), *victory;* הוד (*hod*), *splendor—yes, all that is in heaven and on earth* (1 Chronicles 29:11). This one completes every side.[795]

through contemplation, one discovers that this multiplicity is merely apparent.

See Moses de León, *Sefer ha-Rimmon,* 23, 98. On "He" as designating *Binah,* see above, note 531. On the formulation "upon contemplating, all ascends to one," see *Zohar* 3:6b, 108a, 161b, 288a (*IZ*); Moses de León, *Sheqel ha-Qodesh*, 97 (124).

792. **supernal array of Jubilee rests on twelve...** Although there are six *sefirot* between *Binah* and *Shekhinah,* these six actually constitute an array of twelve, because each one extends itself to its partner and, in turn, is enriched by that partner. For example, *Ḥesed* and *Gevurah* augment one another, producing a total of four aspects: *Ḥesed, Ḥesed-Gevurah, Gevurah,* and *Gevurah-Ḥesed.* Similarly, with *Tif'eret* and *Yesod,* and *Netsaḥ* and *Hod,* yielding a total of twelve plus the body. In the *Zohar* this body is identified with Jacob, symbolizing *Tif'eret,* although here the body is unified with the head, *Binah.*

See *Zohar* 1:158a; 3:39a; *ZḤ* 62b; Moses de León, *Shushan Edut,* 331. For various configurations of the twelvefold array, see *OY*; Galante; *KP*; *MmD.*

793. **twelve—three joints...** Another method of calculating twelve is based on the three joints of each limb (see above, note 785). Thus *Ḥesed* (the right arm) comprises three *ḥasadim* (or *Ḥesed* and two *ḥasadim*), and similarly with the three other sefirotic limbs: *Gevurah* (left arm), *Netsaḥ* (right leg), and *Hod* (left leg).

See *Zohar* 3:136b (*IR*), 293a (*IZ*).

794. **thirteen principles...** The total of twelve plus one also corresponds to the thirteen principles of biblical hermeneutics. The unity of this configuration extends until *Shekhinah,* who presides over the lower realms of multiplicity.

On the thirteen hermeneutical principles, see *Sifra* 1:1, 1a; *Zohar* 3:62a, 149a; *ZḤ* 55d. Cf. the thirteen attributes of divine mercy (Exodus 34:6–7; Micah 7:18–20), which are linked with various aspects of the *sefirot.*

795. **Seven supernal eyes... male... female...** The verse in Zechariah reads:

"Further, hair, for it is written: *Who can utter* גבורות (*gevurot*), *the mighty acts of, YHVH?* (Psalms 106:2). As is written: *They have become more numerous than the hairs of my head* (Psalms 40:13). And it is written: חסדי (*Ḥasdei*), *The loving-kindnesses of, YHVH have not ceased*... (Lamentations 3:22).[796] These arrayals are reserved for another place, although more has been said here, and above and below have been put on the scales. King Solomon spoke of them, though we need to interpret. Happy is the share of the righteous, who know the ways of the blessed Holy One! Here, all is revealed to fathomers."[797]

These seven are the eyes of YHVH, משוטטים *(meshotetim), ranging, over the whole earth.* The verse in 2 Chronicles reads: *For the eyes of YHVH* משוטטות *(meshotetot), are ranging, over the whole earth.* Rabbi El'azar applies the masculine form *meshotetim* to the predominantly masculine realm of *sefirot* (from *Ḥesed* through *Shekhinah*) arraying *Binah*, and the feminine form *meshotetot* to the arrayal of *Shekhinah*.

The higher seven eyes correspond to the list of divine qualities in 1 Chronicles, which —read kabbalistically—includes *Ḥesed* (also called *Gedullah*), *Gevurah, Tif'eret, Netsaḥ, Hod, Yesod* (known as *all*), and *Shekhinah* (symbolized by *earth*), who is joined with *Tif'eret* (*heaven*). See above at note 606. The subject of the concluding sentence ("This one completes every side") is apparently *Shekhinah*, who completes the higher array of seven. For other interpretations, see *OY*; Galante; *MM*.

On *meshotetim* and *meshotetot*, see *Zohar* 2:107a; 3:130a (*IR*), 293b (*IZ*).

796. **hair... גבורות (*gevurot*)...** Rabbi El'azar alludes to the link between divine hair and *Din* (harsh Judgment), also known as *Gevurah* (Strength, Might). The verse from Psalms 40 (also quoted above at note 788) indicates how plentiful hair is. The verse from Lamentations indicates that God balances the harsh Judgment of *Gevurah* with *Ḥesed* (Loving-kindness).

On the harshness of hair, see above, p. 308 and n. 31. The full verse in Psalm 106 reads: *Who can utter the mighty acts of YHVH or declare all His praise?* The full verse in Lamentations reads: *The loving-kindnesses of YHVH have not ceased, His compassion is not spent.*

797. **reserved for another place...** Alluding to the detailed discussion of תקונין (*tiqqunin*), "arrayals, restorations," in the *Idra Rabba* (*Zohar* 3:127b–145a) and *Idra Zuta* (3:287b–296b).

The clause "above and below have been put on the scales" refers to the twelvefold arrays of *Binah* (above) and *Shekhinah* (below), balancing one another. These were alluded to by Solomon in Song of Songs (see above, p. 469 and n. 779), but his words require interpretation.

"Fathomers" renders ידעי מדין (*yade'ei middin*), "those who know *middin*," apparently deriving from the root מדד (*mdd*), "to measure." See Judges 5:10: *you who sit on middin*, where the word is variously rendered as "[extended, wide] carpets, blankets" or—based on דין (*din*), "judgment"—"the judgment seat." See BT *Eruvin* 54b: "It was taught at the school of R. Anan: What is the meaning of the verse... *you who sit on middin*?... you who render judgment in absolute truth."

Here the expression apparently refers to kabbalists who know the מדות (*middot*), the divine "qualities" (*sefirot*), or who know שעור קומה (*shi'ur qomah*), "the measure of the [divine] stature." See Schäfer, *Synopse zur Hekhalot-Literatur*, §952: "Whoever knows this שיעור (*shi'ur*), measure, of our Creator..., concealed from creatures, is assured of life in the world that is coming."

See *Zohar* 1:133a; 2:71b, 130b, 161a; *ZḤ* 73b, 74b (*ShS*), 106b (*Tiq*); *Zohorei Ya'bets*.

Rabbi Yehudah said, "Zebulun and Issachar made a stipulation: one would sit and study Torah, while the other went out and engaged in commerce—supporting Issachar, to fulfill what is written: *Her supporters are happy* (Proverbs 3:18). He would sail the seas, and this was his share, for the sea was his inheritance. Therefore Scripture calls him ירך (*yarekh*), thigh, for the thigh's habit is to come and go, as is written: *Rejoice, Zebulun, in your going out* (Deuteronomy 33:18).[798]

"[*Zebulun*] *will dwell by the shore of the sea* (Genesis 49:13)—among those sailors of the sea, to engage in commerce.[799]

"*By the shore of* ימים (*yammim*), *the seas*—although he possessed one sea in his inheritance, he dwelled by two seas."[800]

Rabbi Yose said, "All the other seamen would search for fish in his sea.[801] *And he by a haven of ships* (ibid.)—a place where all the boats are found, engaging in commerce."

His flank (ibid.). Rabbi Ḥizkiyah said, "His flank reached the boundary of Sidon—his territory extending there—and all the traders would come around to that place with their merchandise."[802]

798. **Zebulun and Issachar made a stipulation...** These two tribes made a pact: Zebulun would sail the seas, engaging in commerce, and thereby support Issachar, who devoted himself to studying Torah.

See *Bereshit Rabbah* 72:5; 97 (p. 1220); 98:12; 99:9; *Tanḥuma, Vayḥi* 11.

The verse from Proverbs, describing wisdom, reads in full: *She is a tree of life to those who grasp her,* ותומכיה (*ve-tomekheha*), *and those who take hold of her, are happy.* Rabbi Yehudah understands *tomekheha* as "those who support her," i.e., those who support students of Torah. See *Zohar* 3:53b.

According to Genesis 49:13, *Zebulun will dwell by the shore of the sea, and he by a haven of ships,* וירכתו (*ve-yarkhato*), *and his flank, upon Sidon.* Rabbi Yehudah interprets *yarkhato, his flank,* as referring to ירך (*yarekh*), "thigh." The verse in Deuteronomy reads: *Rejoice, Zebulun, in your going out, and Issachar, in your tents.* On these two tribes, see also 1 Chronicles 12:33–34.

799. **[*Zebulun*] *will dwell*...** The full verse reads: *Zebulun will dwell by the shore of the sea, and he by a haven of ships, and his flank upon Sidon.*

800. **ימים (*yammim*), *the seas*...** The plural noun suggests that Zebulun dwelled by two seas: the Sea of Galilee—on which his territory (supposedly) bordered—and the Mediterranean, where he camped for trade.

On the question of Zebulun's territorial borders and his living by the sea, see *Zohar* 2:48b and *NZ*, ad loc., n. 9; Sarna, *Genesis*, on this verse.

801. **fish...** קרפולין (*Qarpolin*), a neologism referring either to fish or merchandise. Conceivably, *qarpolin* derives from Castilian *capelan*, "capelin" (although this fish inhabits cold, northern waters), or from Castilian *carpa*, "carp" (although this is a freshwater fish)—or perhaps from a synthesis of the two words.

See *Adderet Eliyyahu*; Corominas, *Diccionario*, 1:4, 885. Several commentators understand the term contextually as referring to merchandise. See *DE*; *Sullam*; *MmD*; cf. *KP*; Scholem. Luria (*Va-Ye'esof David*, s.v. *qarpolin*) suggests more fancifully "subterranean springs" through which these sailors reached Zebulun's Mediterranean waters.

802. ***His flank*...** The verse reads: *His flank upon Sidon.* This port city is located

Rabbi Aḥa said, "It is written: *You shall not omit the salt of the covenant of your God from your grain offering. On each of your offerings you shall offer salt* (Leviticus 2:13).[803] Now, why salt? Because it scours and sweetens bitterness, adding flavor. Were it not for salt, the world could not bear the bitterness, as is written: *When your judgments reach the earth, inhabitants of the world learn righteousness* (Isaiah 26:9), and similarly: *Righteousness and justice are the foundation of your throne* (Psalms 89:15). Salt is the covenant by which the world endures, as is written: *Were it not for My covenant day and night,* [*I would not have established the laws of heaven and earth*] (Jeremiah 33:25). Therefore it is called *covenant of your God,* and it is called the Salt Sea—the sea is named after it."[804]

Rabbi Ḥiyya said, "It is written: *For YHVH is righteous, loving righteousness* (Psalms 11:7)—salt in the sea. Whoever separates them inflicts death upon himself; therefore, *you shall not omit the salt of the covenant of your God,* for one cannot proceed without the other."[805]

Rabbi Aḥa said, "The sea is one, yet it is called ימים (*yammim*), *seas* (Genesis

high up in Phoenicia, but the Bible also uses Sidon to refer to Phoenicia in general. According to Rabbi Ḥizkiyah, Zebulun's territory included a strip of land extending up the Phoenician coast. See above, note 800.

803. ***You shall not omit...*** The full verse reads: *Every offering of your grain you shall season with salt. You shall not omit the salt of the covenant of your God from your grain offering. On each of your offerings you shall offer salt.*

804. **Were it not for salt...** Salt symbolizes *Yesod,* the site of the covenant of circumcision. *Yesod* enables the world to endure by sweetening the bitterness of *Shekhinah,* who is influenced by the harsh quality of *Din.* Rabbi Aḥa understands the verse in Isaiah to mean: When the emanation from *Tif'eret*—who is known as משפט (*mishpat*), "justice, judgment"—reaches *Shekhinah* (known as *earth*) via *Yesod,* sweetening Her bitterness, then *inhabitants of the world* can endure Her quality of *righteousness.* Similarly, he understands the verse in Psalms as implying the stabilizing effects of the union of *Shekhinah* (*righteousness*) and *Tif'eret* (*justice*).

See Naḥmanides on Leviticus 2:13; *Zohar* 3:67b, 80b, 198b.

On the verse in Jeremiah, see BT *Shabbat* 137b: "Were it not for the blood of the covenant [of circumcision], heaven and earth would not endure, as is said: *Were it not for My covenant day and night, I would not have established the laws of heaven and earth.*" Here, the point is that all of existence depends on the covenant of *Yesod.*

See BT *Ḥagigah* 12b; *Zohar* 1:32a, 56a, 59b, 66b, 89a, 91b, 93b, 96b, 189b; 2:116a; 3:14a; Moses de León, *Sefer ha-Rimmon,* 61.

The closing sentence indicates that *Yesod* is called *covenant of your God,* and that *Shekhinah*—symbolized by the sea—is also called the Salt Sea (Dead Sea), because of Her intimate connection with *Yesod* (salt).

805. ***For YHVH is righteous...*** *Righteous* signifies *Yesod,* known as Righteous One; *righteousness* signifies *Shekhinah.* The two must remain united, so that the individual and the world will be sustained by the vital flow issuing from the divine couple.

Similarly, salt (symbolizing *Yesod*) must always be offered along with the grain offering (symbolizing *Shekhinah*).

On Righteous One as a name of *Yesod,* see above, p. 92, n. 50.

49:13)! Well, there is a place in the sea that is clear water, and a place that has sweet water, and a place that has bitter water; so we call it *seas*."[806]

Rabbi Abba said, "Every single tribe—each and every one—constitutes one of those joints that unite in the body."[807]

Rabbi Abba was sitting one night, and he rose to study Torah. While he was sitting, Rabbi Yose came and knocked on the door. He said, "A treasure-chest can be found among preeminent dignitaries!"[808]

They sat and engaged in Torah. Meanwhile, the innkeeper's son rose and sat before them. He asked them, "What is the meaning of the verses *Spare the lives of my father and my mother,* [*my brothers and my sisters, and all who belong to them, and save us from death*], and *Give me a true sign* (Joshua 2:12–13)? What was she asking them for?"[809]

Rabbi Abba replied, "You have asked well! But if you have heard anything, speak, my son!"

He said, "A further question! For look, they gave her something she didn't ask for, as is written: *This cord of crimson thread you shall tie in the window*... (ibid., 18)! But this is what I learned: She asked for a sign of life, as is written: *Spare the lives of my father and my mother.* She said that a sign of life is found only in *a true sign*. What is אות אמת (*ot emet*), *a true sign*? את ו (*At vav*), the letter *vav*, which is imbued with life. And this is what I learned: She was asking for the sign of Moses. So why did they give her a *cord of crimson thread*?[810]

806. **called ימים (*yammim*), *seas*...** The plural form alludes to the many aspects of the earthly sea—and also to the aspects of *Shekhinah*, who is influenced by *Ḥesed, Din,* and *Tif'eret*.

See *Zohar* 2:125a; *OY*; Galante; *Adderet Eliyyahu*; *MM*; *MmD*. Cf. *Bereshit Rabbah* 5:8.

807. **Every single tribe...** According to Rabbi Abba, the various aspects of the sea of *Shekhinah* derive from the fact that each tribe is uniquely linked with Her body. On these joints, see above, p. 471 and n. 785.

808. **treasure-chest can be found...** Rabbi Yose apparently expects to find gems of Torah in the possession of Rabbi Abba.

"Treasure-chest" renders סיפטא (*sifta*), "chest." "Preeminent dignitaries" renders טיפסרא קפטילאי (*tifsera qaftila'ei*). *Tifsera* derives from טפסר (*tifsar*), "military (or administrative) official." See Jeremiah 51:27; Nahum 3:17. *Qaftila'ei* apparently derives from Latin *caput*, "head." See Luria, *Va-Ye'esof David*, s.v. *qaftola'ei*.

For various interpretations of this puzzling line, see Galante; *DE*; *NO*; Soncino; *Sullam*; *MmD*.

809. ***Spare the lives...*** The context concerns Rahab, who protected the two spies sent by Joshua to reconnoiter Jericho. In return for her brave act, she asks the spies to save the lives of her family when the city is conquered. The verses read: *Give me a true sign that you will spare the lives of my father and my mother, my brothers and my sisters, and all who belong to them, and save us from death.* The innkeeper's son wonders about the nature of the sign that Rahab was asking for.

810. **they gave her something...** She asked the spies for אות אמת (*ot emet*), *a*

"Well, they said, 'Moses has departed from the world, for the sun is gathered. The time has come for the moon to rule; we should give you the sign of the moon. What is that? *This cord of crimson thread*—as is said: *Your lips are like a crimson thread*... (Song of Songs 4:3). The sign of Joshua will be yours, because now the moon prevails.'"[811]

Rabbi Abba and Rabbi Yose rose [242a] and kissed him. They said, "Surely you are destined to become the head of an academy or a great man in Israel!" And who is that? Rabbi Bun.[812]

He asked them further, "All of Jacob's sons constituted twelve tribes; so why does Zebulun always precede Issachar in the blessings? After all, Issachar engaged in Torah, and Torah takes precedence everywhere; why did Zebulun precede him in blessings? His father gave him precedence; Moses gave him precedence.[813]

"Well, Zebulun attained this privilege because he took bread out of his own mouth and placed it in the mouth of Issachar—that's why he took precedence in blessings.[814] From here we learn that one who sustains masters of Torah receives blessings from above and below. Furthermore, he attains two tables—something attained by no other human being. He attains wealth—being blessed in this world—and he attains a share in the world that is coming, as is written: *Zebulun will dwell by the shore of the sea, and he by a haven of ships* (Genesis 49:13). Since it is written לחוף (*le-ḥof*), *by the shore of, the sea*, why לחוף (*le-ḥof*), *by a haven of, ships*? Because *le-ḥof, by the shore of, the sea:* in this world; *le-ḥof,*

true sign, and they gave her a *cord of crimson thread* to tie in the window as a sign to Joshua's soldiers that they should spare this house. The boy explains that in asking for an אות (*ot*), "sign," Rahab was actually asking for the את (*at*), "letter," ו (*vav*), whose numerical value of six alludes to *Tif'eret* and the five *sefirot* surrounding Him. *Tif'eret* is known as Tree of Life and "truth," and is symbolized by Moses, who attained this rung.

On the letter *vav*, see *Zohar* 1:12b, 33a–b; 2:137a; 3:2a, 176b.

811. **Moses has departed...** Moses (symbolized by the sun) had died, and now Joshua (symbolized by the moon) ruled. The moon also symbolizes *Shekhinah*, who is characterized by *Din* and its color, red or crimson. The verse from Song of Songs describes the Beloved, *Shekhinah*.

On the sun and moon as symbolizing, respectively, Moses and Joshua, see *Sifrei*, Numbers 140; BT *Bava Batra* 75a.

812. **Rabbi Bun** A variation of "Rabbi Avin," the name of various *amora'im* mentioned in the Talmud. This particular form of the name appears often in the Jerusalem Talmud, as well as in several midrashim and *Midrash ha-Ne'lam* (*Rut*).

813. **why does Zebulun always precede Issachar...** Issachar was born before Zebulun, yet here Jacob blesses Zebulun first, as does Moses (Deuteronomy 33:18).

See *Bereshit Rabbah* 97 (p. 1220); 98:12; 99:9; *Vayiqra Rabbah* 25:2; *Tanḥuma, Vayḥi* 11. On Issachar's wisdom and study of Torah, see also 1 Chronicles 12:33; *Sifrei*, Deuteronomy 354; *Bereshit Rabbah* 72:5.

814. **because he took bread...** See *Bereshit Rabbah* 72:5; 98:12; 99:9; *Vayiqra Rabbah* 25:2; above, p. 475 and n. 798.

by a haven of, ships: for the world that is coming—as is said: *There ships sail*... (Psalms 104:26), for there, is the flow of the world that is coming."[815]

He opened, saying, "*I adjure you, O daughters of Jerusalem! If you find my beloved, what will you tell him? That I am faint with love* (Song of Songs 5:8). Now, who is closer to the King than Assembly of Israel? Why, then, does She say, *If you find my beloved, what will you tell him?* However, *daughters of Jerusalem* are the souls of the righteous, who are constantly near the King and inform Him every day of the affairs of the *Matronita*.[816]

"For so I have learned: When a soul descends into the world, Assembly of Israel makes it enter a sworn covenant that it will see the King and tell Him of Her love for Him, so that He will be reconciled with Her.[817] How? Through a person's obligation to unify the holy Name by mouth, heart, and soul, and to bind all—like a flame bound to a burning coal. By effecting that union, he reconciles the King with the *Matronita* and conveys to the King Her love for Him.[818]

"Alternatively, *daughters of Jerusalem*—the twelve tribes. For we have learned: 'Jerusalem stands on twelve mountains.' One who says 'on seven' does not express perfection completely—although all is one, for there are seven and there

815. **attains two tables...** Such generosity will be rewarded both in this world and in the world that is coming.

The boy interprets the verse from Psalms as referring to heavenly powers (*ships*) sailing the sea of *Shekhinah*, who is fed by the flow of *Binah* (known as "the world that is coming").

On the verse from Psalms, see *Zohar* 1:34b; 2:50b. On the sentence "He attains two tables...," see BT *Berakhot* 5b: "Not everyone attains two tables." On *Binah* as "the world that is coming," see above, note 2.

816. **who is closer to the King...** Who is closer to King *Tif'eret* than *Shekhinah* (known as Assembly of Israel)? So why does She need to ask the *daughters of Jerusalem* to convey Her love to Him? The boy explains that *daughters of Jerusalem* refers here to souls of the righteous, who issue from *Shekhinah*, known as *Jerusalem*.

On Assembly of Israel as a name of *Shekhinah*, see above, pp. 122–23, n. 237. On Her title *Matronita*, see above, note 643.

817. **He will be reconciled with Her** Because now, during Israel's exile, *Shekhinah* is separated from *Tif'eret*.

See BT *Megillah* 29a, in the name of Rabbi Shim'on son of Yoḥai: "Wherever [Israel] went in exile, *Shekhinah* accompanied them." See *Mekhilta, Pisḥa* 14; Moses de León, *Sheqel ha-Qodesh*, 73–74 (92–93). On the soul's oath, cf. above, p. 412 and n. 545.

818. **Through a person's obligation...** Through praying the *Shema* with complete devotion, one rekindles the passion of *Tif'eret* for *Shekhinah* and unifies the *sefirot* (the divine Name).

See Moses de León, *Sefer ha-Rimmon*, 98–99. On the significance of the *Shema*, see Tishby, *Wisdom of the Zohar*, 3:971–74. The phrase "like a flame bound to a burning coal" derives from *Sefer Yetsirah* 1:7. Here, "coal" renders טיפסא (*tifsa*), a Zoharic neologism means various things in the *Zohar*, including "glowing ember, burning coal." See *Zohar* 3:111a; *Bei'ur ha-Millim ha-Zarot*, 178–79; Luria, *Va-Ye'esof David*, s.v. *tifsa*; above, note 75.

are four and there are twelve, and all is one. Surely, She stands on twelve mountains: three mountains on this side, and three mountains on that side, and so on four corners. Then She is called חיה (*Ḥayyah*), Living Being, as is said: *She is the ḥayyah, living being, that I saw beneath the God of Israel* (Ezekiel 10:20). And these are called *daughters of Jerusalem*, for She stands upon them, and they offer testimony concerning Assembly of Israel, as is written: *Tribes of Yah, a testimony to Israel, to praise the name of YHVH* (Psalms 122:4)."[819]

Rabbi Abba said, "Happy is the share of Israel, who know the ways of the blessed Holy One! Of them is written *For you are a people holy to YHVH your God* (Deuteronomy 14:2)."[820]

Issachar, a rawboned donkey (Genesis 49:14).[821]

Rabbi El'azar said, "Now, is Issachar called *a donkey*? If it is because he engaged in Torah, we should call him 'horse' or 'lion' or 'leopard.' Why *donkey*? But they say this is because a donkey bears a burden without kicking its master like other animals, and it has no arrogance and doesn't care about lying down in a nicely prepared place. Similarly, Issachar—engaging in Torah—bears the burden of Torah and does not kick the blessed Holy One. He has no arrogance, just like the donkey, and doesn't care about his own honor but rather about the honor of his Master. *Crouching between the sheepfolds* (ibid.)—as we have said, 'On the ground shall you lie, and a life of trouble shall you live.'"[822]

819. ***daughters of Jerusalem*—the twelve tribes...** The twelve tribes correspond to twelve angels beneath *Shekhinah*, who are here identified with twelve mountains upon which Jerusalem stands. Rabbinic literature describes Jerusalem as standing upon seven mountains (see *Tanḥuma, Vayiqra* 8; *Pirqei de-Rabbi Eli'ezer* 10; Moses de León, *Shushan Edut*, 346). Here, these seven apparently correspond to seven angels accompanying *Shekhinah*; see above, p. 186, n. 47.) The number four corresponds to the four archangels: Michael, Gabriel, Uriel, and Raphael. On the relation between four and twelve, see above, pp. 470–71.

In the *Zohar*, *Shekhinah* is identified with the חיה (*ḥayyah*), "living being," seen by Ezekiel. Here, the innkeeper's son understands *the God of Israel* as referring to *Tif'eret*, whose full name is *Tif'eret Yisra'el* (Beauty of Israel). See above, pp. 297–98, n. 205.

The full verse in Psalms reads: *There tribes ascend, tribes of Yah, a testimony to Israel, to praise the name of YHVH*. Here, *Israel* alludes to *Tif'eret*, to whom the angels offer testimony in praise of *the name of YHVH*—that is, in praise of *Shekhinah*, who expresses and "names" divine being. The angels testify that *Shekhinah* is lovesick for Her partner. Cf. *Zohar* 3:118b.

820. ***For you are a people...*** The full verse reads: *For you are a people holy to YHVH your God, and it is you whom YHVH has chosen to be a treasured people to Him of all the peoples on the face of the earth.*

821. ***Issachar...*** The full verse reads: *Issachar, a rawboned donkey, crouching between two saddle-packs* [or: *the sheepfolds*].

822. **is Issachar called *a donkey*?...** Rabbi El'azar wonders why Jacob did not compare Issachar to a more noble animal.

See *Bereshit Rabbah* 99:10; *Tanḥuma, Va-*

He opened, saying, "*YHVH is my light and my salvation—whom should I fear? YHVH is the stronghold of my life—whom shall I dread?* (Psalms 27:1). How precious are the words of Torah! How precious to the blessed Holy One are those who engage in Torah! For whoever engages in Torah has no fear of mishaps of the world; he is protected above and protected below. Furthermore, [242b] he binds all demons of the world and sends them down to the depths of the great abyss.[823]

"Come and see: When night arouses, openings close; dogs and donkeys prevail, roaming through the world, and permission is granted to destroy. All inhabitants of the world sleep in their beds, and souls of the righteous ascend to delight above.[824]

"When the north wind arouses and night is split, holy arousal rouses in the world. Happy is the share of that human being who rises at that moment and engages in Torah! For as soon as he opens with Torah, he casts all those evil species into the hollows of the great abyss and binds the donkey among subterranean marshals in a filthy cage.[825]

yḥi 11. On the arrogance of the horse, see BT *Pesaḥim* 113b; *Pesiqta de-Rav Kahana* 3:3.

The closing quotation derives from *Avot* 6:4: "This is the way of Torah. Bread with salt shall you eat, and water by measure shall you drink, and on the ground shall you sleep, and a life of trouble shall you live—while you toil in Torah. If you do so, *Happy will you be, and it will be well with you* (Psalms 128:2): *Happy will you be* in this world, *and it will be well with you* in the world that is coming."

823. **whoever engages in Torah...** See BT *Berakhot* 5a, *Bava Batra* 7b–8a; *Tanḥuma, Bereshit* 1. "The great abyss" is the domain of all demons.

"Mishaps of" and "demons of" both render פגעי (*pig'ei*), literally, "mishaps of."

824. **When night arouses...** As darkness falls, heavenly openings are closed and the flow of blessing is temporarily interrupted. Demonic forces (symbolized by dogs and donkeys) prevail.

See above, p. 41 at n. 289. See BT *Berakhot* 3a, in the name of Rabbi Eli'ezer: "In the first watch [of the night], a donkey brays; in the second, dogs bark; in the third, a child sucks from its mother's breast, and a woman converses with her husband."

825. **When the north wind arouses...** At midnight, the threatening aspect of night begins to change as *Gevurah* (symbolized by the north wind) arouses divine passion. That is the appropriate moment for humans to rise and engage in Torah.

On the north wind and midnight, see BT *Berakhot* 3b: "Rabbi Shim'on the Ḥasid said, 'There was a harp suspended above [King] David's bed. As soon as midnight arrived, a north wind came and blew upon it, and it played by itself. He immediately arose and engaged in Torah until the break of dawn.'"

On midnight, see above at notes 490–94. On the midnight ritual of Torah study, see above at notes 464, 479; pp. 77–78, n. 518.

"Marshals" renders טפסירי (*tafsirei*), which derives from טפסר (*tifsar*), "military (or administrative) official." See above, note 808. "Cage" is a conjectured rendering of קסרא (*qisra*), a Zoharic neologism whose meaning is uncertain. See Luria, *Va-Ye'esof David*, s.v. *qisra*; above, p. 325 and n. 130. Cf. Vol. 2, p. 260, n. 15. For various interpretations of this phrase, see *OY*; *KP*; *Adderet Eliyyahu*; *DE*; *NO*; *Nefesh David*; *Sullam*; Scholem; *MmD*.

"Therefore Issachar, engaging in Torah, binds the donkey and sends him down from the top of the steps that he had climbed to harm the world, confining him בין המשפתים (*bein ha-mishpetayim*), among the dunghills—amid the filth of the marshals of dust.[826]

"Come and see what is written: *He saw that the resting place was goodly, that the land was pleasant...* (Genesis 49:15). *He saw that the resting place was goodly*—Written Torah. *That the land was pleasant*—Oral Torah. *And he bent his shoulder to bear* (ibid.)—to bear the yoke of Torah, cleaving to her day and night. *Became a toiling serf* (ibid.)—to serve the blessed Holy One and weaken himself through her."[827]

Rabbi Shim'on, Rabbi Yose, and Rabbi Ḥiyya were walking from Upper Galilee to Tiberias. Rabbi Shim'on said, "Let us engage in words of Torah as we go, for whoever knows how to engage in Torah and does not, is liable to the death penalty.[828] Furthermore, he is subjected to the yoke of earth and wretched servitude, as is written of Issachar: ויט (*va-yet*), *he bent, his shoulder to bear* (Genesis 49:15). What is the meaning of *va-yet*? 'He turned aside,' as is written: ויטו (*va-yittu*), *they turned aside, after gain* (1 Samuel 8:3). Whoever turns aside and deviates, abandoning the yoke of Torah, immediately, *he became a toiling serf* (Genesis, ibid.)."[829]

826. **Issachar... binds the donkey...** Issachar's knowledge of Torah enables him to banish and confine the demonic power.

The expression גרם המעלות (*gerem ha-ma'alot*), "the top of the steps," is an unknown architectural term deriving from 2 Kings 9:13. Here, Rabbi El'azar borrows it because of the association with the wording *Issachar,* חמור גרם (*ḥamor garem*), *a rawboned donkey* (Genesis 49:14).

The continuation of the verse in Genesis reads: *crouching between* המשפתים (*ha-mishpetayim*), *two saddle-packs* [or: *the sheepfolds*]. Rabbi El'azar interprets this last word in the sense of אשפות (*ashpot*), "dunghills." See *Sekhel Tov,* Genesis 49:14; *Yalqut Shim'oni,* Numbers 767.

827. ***He saw...*** The full verse reads: *He saw that the resting place was goodly, that the land was pleasant, and he bent his shoulder to bear, became a toiling serf.*

The concluding phrase, "weaken himself through her," refers to the exhaustion of intense study of Torah. See BT *Sanhedrin* 26b. Rabbi El'azar is apparently playing on מס (*mas*), "serf, forced labor," and the root מסס (*mss*), "to melt, become weak."

See *Targum Yerushalmi* and *Targum Yerushalmi* (frag.) on the verse; *Bereshit Rabbah* 98:12; 99:10; *Tanḥuma, Vayḥi* 11.

828. **whoever knows how to engage...** See M *Avot* 3:7 (Kaufmann MS), in the name of Rabbi Ya'akov: "One who is walking on the road and studying, and interrupts his study and says, 'How beautiful is this tree! How beautiful is this ploughed field!'—he is considered as though he were liable to the death penalty." The standard printed editions of the Mishnah attribute this saying to Rabbi Shim'on, who is speaking here in the *Zohar.*

Cf. M *Avot* 3:4, quoted above, note 434.

829. **subjected to the yoke of earth...** See M *Avot* 3:5, in the name of Rabbi Neḥunya son of Ha-Kanah: "Whoever takes upon himself the yoke of Torah is relieved

Rabbi Shim'on opened, saying, "*So I may endow those who love Me with substance and fill their treasuries* (Proverbs 8:21). Happy are inhabitants of the world—those engaging in Torah—for whoever engages in Torah is beloved above and beloved below, and inherits every day the heritage of the world that is coming, as is written: *So I may endow those who love Me with* יש (*yesh*), *substance*. What is *yesh*? The world that is coming, never ceasing. He receives a fine supernal reward attained by no other human. And what is that? *Yesh*. Therefore, the name יששכר (*Yissachar*), Issachar, hints to us that he engaged in Torah: יש שכר (*yesh sakhar*), *yesh* is the reward—this is the reward for those engaging in Torah: *yesh*![830]

"It is written: *As I watched, thrones were cast down, and the Ancient of Days sat* (Daniel 7:9). *As I watched, thrones were cast down*—when the Temple was destroyed, two thrones fell: two above, two below. Two above—because lower was removed from upper, the throne of Jacob was removed from the throne of David, and the throne of David fell, as is written: *He has cast down earth from heaven* (Lamentations 2:1). Two thrones below: Jerusalem and those masters of Torah. Thrones below resemble thrones above—masters of Torah corresponding to the throne of Jacob, Jerusalem corresponding to the throne of David. Therefore it is written: *As I watched, thrones*—and not *a throne*. Many *thrones* fell, all of them falling solely because of the humiliation of Torah.[831]

of the yoke of government and the yoke of דרך ארץ (*derekh erets*), worldly affairs [literally, "the way of the land (or earth)," i.e., the struggle for livelihood]. And whoever breaks off from himself the yoke of Torah is burdened with the yoke of government and the yoke of worldly affairs."

The full verse in Genesis reads: *He saw that the resting place was goodly, that the land was pleasant, and he bent his shoulder to bear, became a toiling serf*. Cf. above at note 827. The verse in Samuel describes the corrupt behavior of Samuel's sons.

830. ***So I may endow...*** According to rabbinic tradition, this verse describes the abundant reward of the righteous in the afterlife. Here, יש (*yesh*), *substance*, signifies *Binah*, who is known as "the world that is coming—constantly coming, never ceasing" (*Zohar* 3:290b [*IZ*]), overflowing with spiritual substance.

Prompted by the Masoretic spelling of יששכר (*Yissachar*), Issachar, with a superfluous letter ש (*sin*), the Midrash understands the name to imply יש שכר (*yesh sakhar*), "there is reward." Here Rabbi Shim'on builds on the midrashic reading: "*yesh* (namely, *Binah*) is the reward." See Genesis 30:18; *Sekhel Tov*, ad loc.; *Tanḥuma*, *Shemot* 3; *Tanḥuma* (Buber), *Shemot* 5. (All three of these midrashic sources quote Jeremiah 31:16.) On Issachar's devotion to Torah, see above, note 813.

On the verse from Proverbs, see M *Avot* 5:19; *Uqtsin* 3:12; BT *Sanhedrin* 100a; *Pesiqta de-Rav Kahana*, *nispaḥim*, *Vezot Haberakhah*, 451; *Zohar* 1:4b, 88a (*ST*), 158a, 206a; 2:166b.

831. ***As I watched...*** The full verse reads: *As I watched, thrones* רמיו (*remiv*), *were cast down, and the Ancient of Days sat—His garment like white snow, the hair of His head like clean fleece, His throne flames of fire, its wheels blazing fire.*

The basic meaning of the word רמיו (*remiv*) is "were thrown, cast down." In this verse its

"Come and see: When the truly virtuous engage in Torah, all those potencies of other nations and all their forces are overturned and no longer rule the world—and *yesh* manifests upon them, raising them above all. But if not, the donkey causes Israel to go into exile, falling into the hands of the nations and being ruled by them. Why all of this? Because *he saw that the resting place was goodly* (Genesis 49:15) and arranged for him, and that he could thereby obtain many benefits and desirables—yet he turned aside so as not to bear the yoke of Torah, and therefore *he became a toiling serf* (ibid.).[832]

"It is written: *The mandrakes give forth fragrance, at our doors all delicacies; new as well as old, [my love, I have stored away for you]* (Song of Songs 7:14). *The mandrakes*—the ones that Reuben found, as is said: *he found* [243a] *mandrakes in the field* (Genesis 30:14).

"*Give forth fragrance*—for Issachar issued from them; were it not for those mandrakes, Issachar would not have come into the world and words of Torah would not have been innovated by him in Israel, as is said: *Of the children of Issachar, those who had understanding* (1 Chronicles 12:33).[833]

sense is "were placed," but Rabbi Shim'on adopts the hyperliteral meaning, "were cast down," and applies it to the time of the Temple's destruction, when thrones fell above and below. Above, *Shekhinah* (lower throne, throne of David, serving as a throne for *Tif'eret*) separated from *Tif'eret* (upper throne, throne of Jacob, serving as a throne for *Binah*). As *Tif'eret* withdrew from *Shekhinah,* She fell; and in a sense, *Tif'eret* also fell, being bereft of *Shekhinah*. The verse in Lamentations reads: *He has cast down from heaven to earth the splendor of Israel.* Here, Rabbi Shim'on interprets it to mean *He has cast down earth* [*Shekhinah*] *from heaven* [*Tif'eret*]. See above, p. 324 and n. 127, page 450.

The thrones below correspond to these two divine thrones. The throne of masters of Torah corresponds with *Tif'eret* (throne of Jacob), who is often associated with Torah. The throne of Jerusalem corresponds with *Shekhinah* (throne of David), symbolized by Jerusalem.

On the link between destruction and the neglect of Torah, see Jeremiah 9:11–12; *Sifrei,* Deuteronomy 41; JT *Ḥagigah* 1:7, 76c; *Eikhah Rabbah, Petiḥta* 2; BT *Bava Metsi'a* 85b; *Pesiqta de-Rav Kahana* 15. On the verse in Daniel as implying earthly and heavenly thrones, see BT *Ḥagigah* 14a.

832. **When the truly virtuous engage...** The power of Torah overcomes all nations (along with their heavenly princes) who dominate Israel, and the virtuous heroes of Torah are blessed by *Binah,* known as *yesh* (above, note 830). If Torah is neglected, then the demonic power symbolized by the donkey (above, notes 689, 710, 826) forces Israel into exile and servitude.

The phrase חמור גרמא (*ḥamor garema*), "the donkey causes," is a play on חמור גרם (*ḥamor garem*), *[Issachar,] a rawboned donkey* (Genesis 49:14). The following verse reads in full: *He saw that the resting place was goodly, that the land was pleasant, and he bent his shoulder to bear, became a toiling serf.* See above, page 482.

On Torah's power to overcome foreign domination, see *Bereshit Rabbah* 65:20; *Eikhah Rabbah, Petiḥta* 2; *Pesiqta de-Rav Kahana* 15:5; *Zohar* 1:151a, 171a.

833. ***mandrakes*—the ones that Reuben found...** The full verse in Genesis reads: *Reuben went out during the wheat harvest and*

"*At our doors all delicacies*—they caused *all delicacies* to be at the doors of synagogues and houses of study.

"*New as well as old*—so many new and ancient aspects of Torah discovered by them to bring Israel close to their Father above, as is written: *to know what Israel should do* (ibid.).[834]

"*My love, I have stored away for you.* From here we learn that whoever engages in Torah fully—knowing how to render words joyous and innovate words fittingly—those words ascend to the throne of the King, and Assembly of Israel opens gates for them and treasures them away. When the blessed Holy One enters to delight with the righteous in the Garden of Eden, She brings them out before Him, and the blessed Holy One contemplates them and rejoices in them. Then the blessed Holy One is crowned with supernal crowns and rejoices in the *Matronita*, as is written: *new as well as old, my love, I have stored away for you.* From that moment on, his words are inscribed in a book, as is written: *and it was written in a book of remembrance in His presence* (Malachi 3:16). Happy is the share of one who engages in Torah fittingly! Happy is he in this world, happy is he in the world that is coming!"[835]

found mandrakes in the field and brought them to Leah his mother. Rachel said to Leah, "Please give me some of your son's mandrakes." Leah proceeds to give Rachel the mandrakes in exchange for being allowed to sleep with Jacob that night—as a result of which she conceives and gives birth to Issachar.

See *Zohar* 1:156a–157a (*ST*), 156b. The verse in Chronicles reads: *Of the children of Issachar, those who had understanding of the times, to know what Israel should do.* On Issachar's devotion to Torah, see above, note 813. "Innovations" of Torah are new interpretations and discoveries.

834. **all delicacies...** Delicious interpretations of Torah. These new dimensions of meaning and discoveries of lost ancient truth inspire Israel to serve God and rekindle their mutual love.

On the "new and ancient" quality of the *Zohar*'s teachings, see Matt, "New-Ancient Words." For the verse in Chronicles, see the preceding note.

835. **whoever engages in Torah fully...** Joyous and original interpretations of Torah ascend to *Shekhinah* (known as "throne of the King" and Assembly of Israel). She treasures them away and then presents them to the blessed Holy One at the hour of midnight, when He enters the celestial Garden of Eden to delight with the souls of the righteous. These human interpretations and innovations stimulate His love for Her.

See *Zohar* 1:4b–5a; 2:127a; *ZḤ* 62c (*ShS*). On rendering words of Torah joyous, see *Vayiqra Rabbah* 16:4. On Assembly of Israel as a name of *Shekhinah*, see above, pp. 122–23, n. 237. On Her title *Matronita*, see above, note 643. On the midnight encounter between God and the souls of the righteous, see above, pp. 77–78, n. 518; p. 398 and n. 479.

The full verse in Malachi reads: *Then those who revere YHVH spoke with one another; and YHVH listened attentively, and a book of remembrance was written in His presence concerning those who revere YHVH and contemplate His name.* Instead of ויכתב ספר זכרון (*va-yikkatev sefer zikkaron*), *and a book of remembrance was written*, most *Zohar* manuscripts (as well as the Mantua edition and *OY*) read here ויכתב בספר זכרון (*va-yikkatev*

"Until here extends the sway of Judah, arm embracing all—power of all sides, three joints of the arm, to overwhelm all."[836]

Dan will judge his people, as one of the tribes of Israel (Genesis 49:16).

Rabbi Ḥiyya said, "This verse should read as follows: *Dan will judge the tribes of Israel*, or *Dan will judge the tribes of Israel as one*. Why *Dan will judge his people*, and then *as one of the tribes of Israel*?

"Well, Dan is the one of whom is written *the rear guard for all the camps* (Numbers 10:25)—for he is the left thigh, moving last.[837]

"Come and see: Once Judah and Reuben journey, the Levites with the ark unfurl a banner, and the banner of Ephraim journeys, on the west—right thigh journeying in concatenate measure.[838]

"Now, you might say, 'Zebulun is the one who comes and goes, and of whom

be-sefer zikkaron), *and it was written in a book of remembrance*. See above, p. 228 and n. 305 (quoting M *Avot* 3:2); *Minḥat Shai* on the verse.

836. **Until here extends...** Rabbi Shim'on has completed interpreting the blessing of Issachar, whose tribe, along with Zebulun, camped under the banner of Judah. See Numbers 2:3–9. Judah symbolizes the left arm, *Gevurah*, comprising three joints: Judah, Issachar, and Zebulun. On the joints, see above, p. 471 and n. 785.

837. **Dan is... *the rear guard*...** The verse, describing the journeying of the tribes in the wilderness, reads: *The banner of the camp of the children of Dan journeyed on, the rear guard for all the camps by their divisions*. Rabbi Ḥiyya apparently reads the phrase in Genesis 49:16 not as כְּאַחַד (*ke-aḥad*), *as one of, the tribes of Israel*, but rather as כְּאֶחָד (*ke-eḥad*), *as one, the tribes of Israel*—that is, by serving as the rear guard, Dan unites the tribes *as one*. Later, Rabbi Ḥiyya offers another interpretation of this word.

Dan symbolizes the left thigh, *Hod*, last of the *sefirot* before *Shekhinah*.

838. **Once Judah and Reuben journey...** According to the plain sense of Numbers 10:11–28, the tribes journeyed through the wilderness in a single column, with Dan serving as the rear guard (see Milgrom, *Numbers*, p. 76). However, according to one rabbinic view, the tribes marched in the same square arrangement in which they camped (see Numbers 2:1–31): Judah (accompanied by Issachar and Zebulun) on the east, Reuben (accompanied by Simeon and Gad) on the south, the Levites carrying the ark in the middle, Ephraim (accompanied by Manasseh and Benjamin) on the west, and Dan (accompanied by Asher and Naphtali) on the north. (It is unclear how in this arrangement Dan could still serve as the rear guard.) Here, Rabbi Ḥiyya adopts this view, with Ephraim symbolizing *Netsaḥ*, the right thigh.

See *Baraita di-Mlekhet ha-Mishkan* 13; JT *Eruvin* 5:1, 22c; Rashi on Numbers 2:17; 10:25.

Ephraim journeys "in concatenate measure," linked with the two tribes under his banner (Manasseh and Benjamin), or in coordination with all the other tribes. The phrase renders בקטפירי קסטא (*be-qatpirei qista*). The noun *qatpira* is a Zoharic neologism that connotes "tying, linking." See *Bei'ur ha-Millim ha-Zarot*, 188; Luria, *Va-Ye'esof David*, s.v. *qftr*, *qaftera*; Liebes, *Peraqim*, 349–54; above, note 25. *Qista* derives from the Greek *xestes*, a measure about the size of a pint. See *Bereshit Rabbah* 4:5; *Zohar* 1:33a, 83a, 121b, 162a, 164a, 211a. See *DE*; *NO*; *MmD*.

is written *Rejoice, Zebulun, in your going out* (Deuteronomy 33:18), and similarly: *his flank* (Genesis 49:13).' Well, surely Judah comprises all!

"Come and see: Kingdom above comprises all, and Judah is lower kingdom. Just as upper Kingdom comprises all, so too, lower kingdom comprises all—body and thigh—to be potently empowered.[839]

"It is written: *From His right hand, a fiery law for them* (Deuteronomy 33:2)—Torah was given from the side of *Gevurah*, and *Gevurah* embraces the right, the body, the thigh, and all. Similarly, the first array: Judah, who is kingdom issuing from the side of *Gevurah*, embracing right, body, and thigh—embracing all, just as Kingdom above comprises all.[840]

"The second array: Reuben, on the side of the south—and south is right. All the power of the right was taken by Judah, because kingship was removed from Reuben—as is written: *Unbridled as water, you will not remain!* (Genesis 49:4)—and Judah took it over, becoming fortified with potency of the right, which was Reuben's. Similarly, of David is written *YHVH declares to my lord, 'Sit at My right hand'* (Psalms 110:1)—for left was embraced by right and fortified with its power, as is written: *The right hand of YHVH performs valiantly* (ibid. 118:16). Judah and Reuben: two arms.[841]

"The third array: Ephraim, right thigh, always journeying before the left. And

839. **Zebulun is the one...** It might be argued that Zebulun should be associated with the thigh, since he is described as *going out* and the expression ירכתו (*yarkhato*), *his flank*, suggests ירך (*yarekh*), "thigh." Rabbi Ḥiyya explains that Zebulun is included under the banner of Judah, progenitor of the Davidic dynasty and symbol of *Malkhut* (Kingdom). Just as *Malkhut* comprises all the sefirotic limbs, so does Judah.

See above, p. 468 and n. 777, p. 475 and n. 798. The full verse in Genesis 49 reads: *Zebulun will dwell by the shore of the sea, and he by a haven of ships, his flank upon Sidon.*

840. ***From His right hand...*** The verse implies that Torah derives both from *Gevurah* on the left (symbolized by fire) and *Ḥesed* on the right. *Gevurah* follows and includes *Ḥesed*, and generates the subsequent sefirotic limbs (including trunk of the body and thigh). In the first triad of tribes, Judah symbolizes both the left arm (*Gevurah*) and *Malkhut* (Kingdom)—who derives from *Gevurah*—and he comprises all.

See above, note 139; p. 214, n. 214. On *Gevurah* as the origin of Torah, see *Zohar* 3:80b. On the tension and interplay between left and right, see *Zohar* 2:81a, 84a–b, 135a, 166b, 206b; 3:176a.

841. **Reuben, on the side of the south...** Reuben symbolizes *Ḥesed* on the south, balancing Judah, who symbolizes *Gevurah* on the north. However, because of Reuben's sin of sleeping with Jacob's concubine Bilhah, the power of the right and the kingship passed to Judah (who marched first). The full verse in Genesis reads: *Unbridled as water, you will not remain! For you mounted your father's bed, then you defiled—my couch he mounted!* See 1 Chronicles 5:1; above, p. 428 and n. 615.

Similarly, King David (descended from Judah) incorporated the power of the right. The verse in Psalm 110 reads: *YHVH declares to my lord, "Sit at My right hand until I make your enemies your footstool."* See *Zohar* 1:50b.

Dan, left thigh, journeying last; so he is *the rear guard for all the camps by their divisions*, going last.[842]

"Judah absorbed the power of two arms, because Reuben—who is right—lost birthright, priesthood, and kingship. Therefore, of Judah is written *His hands strive for him; a help against his foes may You be* (Deuteronomy 33:7).[843]

"Come and see what is written: *The king made a great throne of ivory* (1 Kings 10:18). Solomon's throne was constructed according to the supernal pattern, and all the images above he fashioned here. Therefore it is written: *Solomon sat upon the throne of YHVH as king* (1 Chronicles 29:23)—a word concealed, unspecified. Similarly, *Solomon sat upon the throne of his father David, and his kingdom was firmly established* (1 Kings 2:12), for the moon assumed fullness.[844]

"*Dan will judge his people*—at first. Then, *as one, the tribes of Israel. As one*—as the Unique One of the world. [243b] As happened with Samson, who singlehandedly enacted judgment in the world: judging and executing as one, needing no assistance."[845]

842. **Ephraim, right thigh... Dan, left thigh...** Symbolizing, respectively, *Netsaḥ* and *Hod*, the right and left thighs. See above at note 837.

843. **Reuben... lost birthright...** As Jacob's firstborn, Reuben was entitled to various rights and privileges, but he did not retain any of these. The Davidic dynasty issued from the tribe of Judah, the birthright was transferred to Joseph, and the priesthood was given to Aaron and his descendants (from the tribe of Levi). See above, note 841, and at note 615.

844. **Solomon's throne...** Solomon was descended from Judah, and his royal throne resembled the divine throne, being engraved with the same images. The wording in Chronicles—*as king*—is intentionally vague, alluding not only to King Solomon but also to *Malkhut* (Kingdom), thereby suggesting that Solomon's enthronement resembled the divine enthronement; in this sense, he *sat upon the throne of YHVH*. Similarly, the clause in Kings—*his kingdom was firmly established*—alludes to *Malkhut* (Kingdom), symbolized by the moon, who attained fullness during Solomon's reign.

According to the Midrash, just as the moon does not become full until the fifteenth day of its cycle, so it remained incomplete until the glorious reign of Solomon in the fifteenth generation from Abraham. See *Pesiqta de-Rav Kahana* 5:12 and *Shemot Rabbah* 15:26: "When Solomon appeared, the disk of the moon became full." See *Zohar* 1:73b–74a, 150a, 223a–b, 225b, 238a, 249b; 2:85a; 3:61a, 74b, 181b; *ZḤ* 83b (*MhN, Rut*); Moses de León, *Shushan Edut*, 342.

On Solomon's glorious throne and its resemblance to the divine throne, see *Pesiqta de-Rav Kahana* 1:7; *Ester Rabbah* 1:12; *Targum Sheni*, Esther 1:2; *Bemidbar Rabbah* 12:17; *Beit ha-Midrash*, 2:83–85; 5:34–37; *Zohar* 1:247b; 2:14b, 78a; Ginzberg, *Legends*, 6:296–97, nn. 69–70. On the phrase "king... unspecified," see *Shir ha-Shirim Rabbah* 1:11 (on 1:1); *Zohar* 1:29a–b, 84a; 2:4a, 127b, 164b; *ZḤ* 67a (*ShS*).

845. ***Dan will judge*... Then, *as one*...** Rabbi Ḥiyya had begun by questioning the wording of this verse (above at note 837). Now he explains that first, Dan judged his own tribe; then, he judged all the tribes *as one*—meaning "as God, the Unique One of the world." Just as God judges and executes without need of a court of law, so Samson (descended from Dan) wreaked vengeance independently against the Philistines.

See *Bereshit Rabbah* 98:13; 99:11; *Tanḥuma, Vayḥi* 12; BT *Sotah* 10a.

Dan will judge his people. Rabbi Yitsḥak said, "Dan corresponds to a serpent lurking by ways and paths. Now, you might say that this refers only to Samson; but similarly above: another serpent, *rear guard for all the camps* (Numbers 10:25), lurking by ways and paths behind forces and camps. From here issue those who waylay human beings for sins that they cast behind their backs."[846]

Rabbi Ḥiyya said, "The primordial serpent, before being assuaged with the wine of joy, is *a serpent on the way* (Genesis 49:17).[847]

"Come and see: Just as there is a *way* above, so there is a *way* below, and the sea branches into many paths in every direction. There is one path that comes and expands the sea, breeding various species of evil fish. Just as waters below generate good fish, bad fish, fish of frogs, similarly: various species of evil fish.[848]

"When they slip away from the path of the sea, they appear to be riding on horses. And if this serpent—who gathers all camps—did not lie in wait at the end of paths and scatter them backward, they would obliterate the world.[849]

846. **Dan corresponds to a serpent...** As in Jacob's blessing (Genesis 49:17): *May Dan be a serpent on the way, a viper on the path, that bites a horse's heels—and its rider tumbles backward.* Rabbi Yitsḥak explains that this comparison refers not just to Samson (descended from Dan) but to an essential characteristic of Dan, who is linked with the demonic power known as *serpent.* From this serpent issue evil forces who attack humans by (or after) tempting them to commit what seem to be minor sins that can be disregarded.

I have adopted the reading נחש אחרא (*naḥash aḥara*), "another serpent," preserved in M7, O2, and R1. Here *OY* reads נחש זוטא (*naḥash zuta*), "a small serpent," which is indirectly supported by the apparently corrupt reading נפש זוטא (*nefesh zuta*), "a small soul," preserved in L2, O16, P4, Pr6, and V6. See *OY*; Galante; *KP*; Tishby, *Wisdom of the Zohar*, 2:499; *MmD*.

On the phrase "behind their backs," see *Zohar* 2:71b; 3:23b.

847. **primordial serpent, before being assuaged...** Before his malicious power is tempered by the sweet flow of emanation, which trickles down to the demonic realm.

For the full verse, see the preceding note. For a different interpretation, see *OY*; *MmD*.

848. ***way* above...*way* below...** The *way* above is the channel of emanation from the higher *sefirot* to *Shekhinah*; the *way* below is the channel from *Shekhinah* to the lower worlds. She is symbolized by the sea, and just as the earthly sea nourishes good and bad creatures, so too from *Shekhinah* issue holy and demonic forces.

See *Zohar* 2:30b–31a.

849. **When they slip away...** These evil forces ride into the world and if the serpent did not restrain them, they would wreak total destruction.

For various interpretations, see *OY*; Galante; *Sullam*; *MmD*. The image of "riding on horses" and the phrase "scatter them backward" are apparently based on Genesis 49:17: *May Dan be a serpent on the way, a viper on the path, that bites a horse's heels—and its rider tumbles backward.*

Cf. *Pirqei de-Rabbi Eli'ezer* 13: "Samael... took his band and descended and saw all the creatures created by the blessed Holy One. He determined that the most cunningly evil was the serpent, as is said: *Now the serpent was slier than any creature of the field that YHVH Elohim had made.* He [the serpent] looked like a camel, and he [Samael]

From their side, sorcery issues into the world. Come and see: Of Balaam is written *He did not go, as time after time, to encounter* נחשים (*neḥashim*), *serpentine sorceries* (Numbers 24:1), because they are poised for sorcerers of the world to cast spells.[850]

"See what is written: *May Dan be a serpent on the way* (Genesis 49:17). What is *on the way*? Well, whoever strives after the serpent impairs the Family above. What is that? That supernal *way* emerging from above, as is said: *who makes a way through the sea*... (Isaiah 43:16). Whoever strives after the serpent treads on that supernal *way*—deteriorating it, as it were—for from that *way* worlds are nourished.[851]

"Now, you might ask, 'Why is Dan on this rung?' Well, as is said: *the flame of the whirling sword to guard the way to the Tree of Life* (Genesis 3:24). So too, *that bites a horse's heels*... (ibid. 49:17)—to protect all the camps."[852]

Rabbi El'azar said, "This is an embellishment of the throne. Come and see: On the throne of King Solomon was a vibrating serpent dangling from the scepter above the lions.[853]

mounted and rode him." See above, p. 373 and n. 371.

The phrase "gathers all camps" is based on the biblical wording מאסף כל המחנות (*me'assef kol ha-maḥanot*), "gathering (or the rear guard for) all the camps," from Numbers 10:25 (quoted above): *The banner of the camp of the children of Dan journeyed on, me'assef kol ha-maḥanot, the rear guard for all the camps, by their divisions.* Here, this description is applied to the serpent, who is linked with Dan.

850. **sorcery... נחשים (*neḥashim*), *serpentine sorceries*...** Sorcery derives from the demonic serpent; so Balaam, the master sorcerer, often practiced his art by drawing on the power of snakes.

The biblical term נחש (*naḥash*), "omen, sorcery," is here (plausibly) connected with its near homonym, נחש (*naḥash*), "serpent." See *Zohar* 1:126a.

851. ***serpent on the way*...** Whoever is drawn to the demonic or indulges in sorcery impairs the holy family of forces above: the process (*way*) through which emanation is conveyed to *Shekhinah* (*the sea*) and through Her to the worlds below.

See BT *Sanhedrin* 67b, where Rabbi Yoḥanan employs the method of *notariqon* (according to which letters of one word stand for initial letters of other words): "Why are they called מכשפים (*mekhashshephim*), sorcerers? Because מכחישין פמליא של מעלה (*makhḥishin pamalya shel ma'lah*), they impair the Family above [i.e., the heavenly household, divine agencies]."

See Moses de León, *Sefer ha-Rimmon*, 279. On the verse in Isaiah, see above, note 668.

852. **Why is Dan on this rung?...** Why is one of the holy tribes associated with the demonic serpent? Rabbi Ḥiyya explains that just as fierce powers guard the way to the Tree of Life, so Dan protects the camps of Israel from any enemies—like a serpent *that bites a horse's heels.*

See *KP*; Tishby, *Wisdom of the Zohar*, 2:500. Cf. Galante. The full verse in Genesis 3 reads: *He drove out the human and placed east of the Garden of Eden the cherubim and the flame of the whirling sword to guard the way to the Tree of Life.* For the full text of Genesis 49:17, see above, note 849.

853. **embellishment of the throne...** The serpent was an embellishment of Solo-

"It is written: *The spirit of YHVH began to impel him in the camp of Dan* (Judges 13:25). Come and see: Samson was a Nazirite, detached from the world, and he was intensely empowered. He was a serpent in this world confronting other nations, for he inherited the share of blessings of his ancestor Dan, as is written: *May Dan be a serpent on the way.*"[854]

Rabbi Ḥiyya said, "*Serpent* is well known, but what is שפיפון (*shefifon*), *viper?*"[855]

He replied, "Mystery of cultivating sorcery is *serpent*; similarly, *shefifon, viper.* And that wicked Balaam had knowledge of everything! Come and see what is written: *He went* שפי (*shefi*), *alone* (Numbers 23:3)—sometimes with this, sometimes with that.[856]

"Now, you might say, 'Dan's rung is not here!' Certainly so! But he was appointed over this rung, to be the final aspect—and that is to his honor. There are those appointed by the King over this, and those appointed over that—and it is an honor for all of them: the King's throne is arrayed by all these officials. Beneath them branch out paths and rungs, some for good and some for evil—all of them linked to embellishments of the throne. So, Dan is on the north side. In the hollow of the great abyss, on the north side, ravaging bands of stingers are poised—all clustered warriors to harass the world.[857] Therefore, Jacob

mon's throne, symbolizing the positive aspect of the demonic element, for example, its role in punishing the wicked.

On Solomon's throne, see above, note 844. On the scepter, see *Pesiqta de-Rav Kahana* 1:7; *Bemidbar Rabbah* 12:17. On the serpent, see *Beit ha-Midrash*, 5:35–36. Cf. BT *Shabbat* 150a.

854. ***The spirit of YHVH began...*** The verse describes the inspiration of Samson, who is descended from Dan. Here, Samson is said to have fought against the Philistines with the power of a serpent.

See BT *Sotah* 9b; above, note 845. On Samson as a Nazirite, see Judges 13:5; 16:17; M *Nazir* 1:2; *Tosefta, Nazir* 1:5; JT *Nazir* 1:2, 51a–b; BT *Nedarim* 19b, *Nazir* 4a–b.

855. **what is שפיפון (*shefifon*), *viper?*** Mentioned next in this verse (Genesis 49:17): *May Dan be a serpent on the way,* שפיפון (*shefifon*), *a viper, on the path.*

856. ***He went* שפי (*shefi*), *alone...*** The rare biblical word שפי (*shefi*) is usually understood to mean either "alone" or "bare height." Here, Rabbi El'azar links it with שפיפון (*shefifon*), "viper," and indicates that Balaam alternated between both instruments of sorcery: serpent and viper.

On *shefi* and *shefifon*, see BT *Sotah* 10a; *Leqaḥ Tov* and *Midrash Aggadah*, Numbers 23:3; above, p. 27 at n. 183; *Zohar* 3:194b. On two types of sorcery, cf. above, p. 11, n. 73.

857. **Dan's rung is not here...** How can Dan be linked with the demonic sphere? (See the similar question posed by Rabbi Ḥiyya, above at note 852.) Rabbi El'azar explains that because Dan corresponds to *Hod,* near the bottom of the sefirotic realm, he is appointed over the demonic realm of the serpent below to restrain and counter it. Further, the tribe of Dan camped on the north side of the Tabernacle (see above, note 838), and north symbolizes harsh Judgment, from which evil forces issue.

"Warriors" renders the plural of טפסירא (*tafsira*), which derives from טפסר (*tifsar*), "military (or administrative) official." See Jeremiah 51:27; Nahum 3:17; above, notes

prayed, *Your deliverance I await, O YHVH!* (Genesis 49:18). Concerning all those tribes, he did not say *Your deliverance I await, O YHVH!* Only here, because he saw fierce power: the serpent generating overwhelming judgment."[858]

Rabbi Yose and Rabbi Ḥizkiyah were going to see Rabbi Shim'on in Cappadocia.[859] Rabbi Ḥizkiyah said, "Concerning what has been said: 'A person should always offer the praise of his Lord first, and then utter his prayer'—well, what about someone whose mind is anxious and he wants to pray, but being in distress, he cannot offer the praise of his Lord properly?"[860]

He replied, "Even though he cannot focus his mind and aspiration, why should he diminish the praise of his Lord? Rather, let him offer the praise of his Lord, even though [244a] he cannot concentrate, and then utter his prayer, as is written: *A prayer of David. Hear righteousness, O YHVH; heed my cry, listen to my prayer*... (Psalms 17:1). First, *Hear righteousness, O YHVH*—because that is the offering of praise for his Lord; then, *heed my cry, listen to my prayer.* Of one who is able to offer the praise of his Lord and does not do so, it is written *Even if you make many prayers, I will not listen* (Isaiah 1:15).[861]

"It is written: *The one lamb you shall offer in the morning and the other lamb you shall offer at twilight* (Exodus 29:39). Prayers were ordained to correspond with the continual offerings.[862] Come and see: By arousal below there is simi-

808, 825. For the sense of "warrior," see *Targum Yonatan* and Rashi on Jeremiah 51:27.

858. **Only here, because he saw fierce power...** Jacob saw Dan's uniquely vulnerable position and prayed that he would be delivered—and would then succeed in delivering Israel.

859. **Cappadocia** See above, p. 208, n. 180.

860. **A person should always offer the praise...** See BT *Berakhot* 32a, in the name of Rabbi Simlai: "A person should always offer the praise of the blessed Holy One first, and then pray." According to Rashi (on BT *Avodah Zarah* 7b, s.v. *yesadder adam*), "praise" refers to the first three blessings of the *Amidah*, while "prayer" refers to various requests that follow. Here, Rabbi Ḥizkiyah wonders about someone who feels anxious and cannot concentrate properly on praising God: should such a person skip the praise and immediately express his needs in prayer, or should he offer praise, even though it lacks *kavvanah* ("intention," devotion)?

See *Zohar* 1:169a; 3:260b, 285a; *ZḤ* 91a (*MhN, Rut*); Galante; *KP*. On the halakhic issue, see Maimonides, *Mishneh Torah, Hilkhot Tefillah* 4:15.

861. ***Hear righteousness... heed my cry...*** In this psalm King David established the model for prayer by first praising God's *righteousness*, and only then asking Him to *heed my cry*.

Cf. *Midrash Tehillim* 17:6. The full verse reads: *A prayer of David. Hear righteousness, O YHVH; heed my cry, listen to my prayer—not from deceitful lips.* The verse in Isaiah reads: *Even if you make many prayers, I will not listen; your hands are full of blood.*

862. **Prayers were ordained...** See BT *Berakhot* 26b: "Rabbi Yose son of Rabbi Ḥanina said, 'The prayers were ordained by the patriarchs.' Rabbi Yehoshu'a son of Levi said, 'The prayers were ordained to correspond with [i.e., to replace] the continual [daily] offerings.'" See *Zohar* 1:133a.

larly arousal above, and by arousal above there is also arousal further above, until arousal reaches the place where a lamp needs to be kindled, and it is. By arousal of smoke below, a lamp is kindled above, and when this is kindled, all other lamps are kindled and all worlds are blessed. Thus arousal of the offering is restoration of the world and blessing of all worlds.[863]

"How is this? Smoke begins to ascend; those holy forms appointed over the world are primed to arouse, and arouse in yearning above, as is said: *The young lions roar for prey, seeking their food from God* (Psalms 104:21). These arouse higher rungs above them, until arousal stimulates desire of the King to unite with the *Matronita*.[864] Through yearning below, lower waters flow toward upper waters; for water flows only through arousal of yearning below—then desire cleaves, lower waters flow toward upper waters, worlds are blessed, all lamps are kindled, and above and below are bathed in blessings.[865]

"Come and see: Priests and Levites arouse to join left with right."[866]

Rabbi Ḥizkiyah said, "All is certainly so! But this is what I have heard: Priests

863. **By arousal below...** Devout human prayer and sacrificial offering below arouse higher forces, whose arousal stimulates still higher forces, until finally the lamp of *Shekhinah* is kindled. Likewise, the ascent of the smoke from the sacrifice kindles *Shekhinah,* in turn kindling all the other *sefirot,* stimulating divine union and drawing blessing to all worlds.

Thus, the sacrificial rites perform a cosmic function. This kabbalistic view contrasts sharply with that of Maimonides, who relativized the importance of the sacrifices and tried to explain them away as a concession to the formerly primitive nature of ancient Israel. See Rashi on BT *Ketubbot* 10b, s.v. *mezin*; Maimonides, *Guide of the Perplexed* 3:32; *Bahir* 78 (109); *Zohar* 1:164a–b, 181a–b; Tishby, *Wisdom of the Zohar,* 3:878–90.

On "arousal from below," see *Zohar* 1:35a, 77b, 82b, 86b, 88a, 156b, 164a–b, 233a, 235a; 2:31b, 265a; 3:40b, 92a–b, 110b, 112b, 145a (*Piq*); Moses de León, *Sefer ha-Rimmon,* 144. On the ascending smoke, see *Zohar* 1:45b (*Heikh*), 51a–b, 70a; 2:122b, 141a, 259b (*Heikh*); 3:294a (*IZ*). On the image of smoke kindling the higher lamp, see Ibn Ezra [pseud.], *Sefer ha-Atsamim,* 20; El'azar of Worms, *Ḥokhmat ha-Nefesh,* 15c; *Zohar* 1:70b, 176b–177a, 247b–248a 3:35b; *KP.*

864. **holy forms...** Angels, agents of *Shekhinah* who help to conduct the world and who seek nourishment from above. They arouse higher heavenly forces until the arousal finally reaches King *Tif'eret,* stimulating Him to unite with *Shekhinah.*

See *Zohar* 1:208b; 3:191a. On the angels as "holy forms" appointed over the world, see *Bahir* 67 (98). On *Shekhinah*'s title *Matronita,* see above, note 643.

865. **Through yearning below, lower waters flow...** Through passionate human prayer and angelic yearning, *Shekhinah* is aroused, and waters issue from Her toward *Tif'eret,* who responds with a flow of upper waters.

On the female and male waters, see *Bereshit Rabbah* 13:13; *Tosefta, Ta'anit* 1:4; JT *Berakhot* 9:2, 14a; 1 Enoch 54:8; *Seder Rabbah di-Vreshit,* 10 (*Battei Midrashot,* 1:25); *Pirqei de-Rabbi Eli'ezer* 23; *Zohar* 1:17b, 29b, 32b, 46a, 60b, 62a, 159a, 235a, 244b, 245b; 3:223b.

866. **Priests and Levites arouse...** Priests symbolize *Ḥesed* (Love) on the right, while Levites symbolize *Gevurah* (or *Din*) on the left. The joint participation of priests and Levites in the Temple ritual unites their two corresponding *sefirot,* thereby assuaging the harshness of *Din.*

and Levites—one arouses right and one arouses left, because union of male with female occurs only through left and right, as is said: *His left hand beneath my head, his right hand embracing me* (Song of Songs 2:6). Then male and female unite, desire prevails, worlds are blessed, and above and below are in joy.[867]

"So priests and Levites arouse something below, arousing yearning and love above; for all depends upon right and left. Thus offering is foundation of the world, restoration of the world, joy of above and below."

Rabbi Yose said, "You have surely spoken well, and so it is! I heard this word before, but I forgot it. Yes, I heard this, and all ascends in oneness.

"Now prayer takes the place of sacrificial offering, and one should arrange the praise of his Lord fittingly.[868] If he does not, his prayer is no prayer at all. Come and see: The perfect arrangement of the praise of the blessed Holy One—one who knows how to unify the holy Name fittingly, for thereby above and below arouse and blessings flow to all worlds."[869]

Rabbi Ḥizkiyah said, "The blessed Holy One cast Israel into exile among the nations only so that the other nations would be blessed because of them, for they draw blessings from above to below every day."[870]

They went on. As they were walking, they saw a snake slithering on the road; they turned aside. Another man approached and the snake killed him. Turning their heads, they saw that man dead. They said, "Surely, that snake was perform-

867. **union... occurs only through left and right...** Rabbi Ḥizkiyah agrees that the priests and Levites symbolize respectively *Ḥesed* and *Gevurah,* but he emphasizes the romantic role played by the two sefirotic hands. First, through their singing in the Temple, the Levites stimulate the passion of the left hand, *Gevurah;* then through their sacrificial worship, the priests stimulate the right hand, *Ḥesed,* which embraces *Shekhinah.* She utters the verse from Song of Songs to Her divine lover.

On this verse, see *Zohar* 1:49a–b, 133a, 136a, 151a, 163b, 245a, 250a; 2:30a, 154b, 169b, 238b; 3:26a, 55a; Moses de León, *Sefer ha-Rimmon,* 63.

868. **prayer takes the place of sacrificial offering...** See above, note 862. On "arranging praise," see above, note 860.

869. **perfect arrangement...** This consists in unifying the *sefirot,* symbolized by the letters of the name יהוה (*YHVH*). The י (*yod*) symbolizes the primordial point of *Ḥokhmah,* while its crown symbolizes *Keter* (Crown). The first ה (*he*), often a feminine marker, symbolizes the Divine Mother, *Binah.* The ו (*vav*), whose numerical value is six, symbolizes *Tif'eret* and the five *sefirot* surrounding Him. The second ה (*he*) symbolizes *Shekhinah.*

870. **cast Israel into exile...** Israel's exile constitutes punishment for their sins, but God could have exiled them all to one foreign country or punished them in other ways. Their dispersal among the nations guarantees those nations nourishment and blessing, which are conveyed by Israel's devotion and prayer.

I have adopted the reading אשדי (*ashdei*), "cast [Israel into exile]," (preserved in M7, Ms4, O16, R1, and the Cremona edition) instead of אשרי (*ashrei*), "caused [Israel] to dwell [in exile]" (preserved in L2, V6, *OY,* and the Mantua edition). The orthographic difference, of course, is miniscule: ד (*dalet*) or ר (*resh*).

ing the mission of his Lord. Blessed is the Compassionate One who saved us!"[871]

Rabbi Yose opened, saying, "*Dan will be a serpent on the way* (Genesis 49:17). When was Dan *a serpent*? In the days of Jeroboam, as is written: *and the other he placed in Dan* (1 Kings 12:29). Why was it placed there? *On the way*—on that road, obstructing the *way* by which they went up to Jerusalem, so that they could not reach there. So Dan was *a serpent* to Israel *on the way*—*on the way*, literally! As is said: *The king took counsel*... (ibid., 28).[872]

"*A viper on the path* (Genesis, ibid.)—stinging Israel.[873] All this happened *on the way* and *on the path*—to prevent Israel from going up to Jerusalem to celebrate their festivals, bring sacrifices and ascent offerings, and worship there. [244b]

"Come and see: When blessings arrived in the hands of Moses, to be conveyed to all the tribes, he saw Dan linked to a serpent. He linked him instead to a lion, as is written: *Dan is a lion's whelp, leaping from Bashan* (Deuteronomy 33:22). Why? So that beginning and end of the four banners would be linked with Judah, who is king, as is said: *A lion's whelp is Judah* (Genesis 49:9) he is beginning of the banners. End of the banners is Dan, as is written: *Dan is a lion's whelp*—so that beginning and end would be linked to one place."[874]

Your deliverance I await, O YHVH! (Genesis 49:18).

Rabbi Ḥiyya said, "As is written: *He will begin to deliver Israel from the hand of the Philistines* (Judges 13:5)."[875]

Rabbi Aḥa said, "Why *I await*? Look, by that time Jacob had already departed the world many years before! Why did he say that he was awaiting that deliverance?"[876]

871. **that snake was performing the mission...** It had been sent by God to kill that particular person.

See *Bereshit Rabbah* 10:7; *Vayiqra Rabbah* 22:4.

872. **days of Jeroboam...** Jeroboam, the first king of the northern kingdom of Israel, feared that his subjects might return to the Davidic king Rehoboam in Jerusalem, so he built two golden calves to dissuade them from making pilgrimage. The context (1 Kings 12:28–29) reads: *The king took counsel, and he made two golden calves. He said to* [the people], *"It is too much for you to go up to Jerusalem* [or: *You have gone up to Jerusalem long enough*]. *These are your gods, O Israel, who brought you up from the land of Egypt!" He set up one in Bethel, and the other he placed in Dan.*

Rabbi Yose explains that by providing a place for one of the golden calves, Dan became *a serpent on the way*, obstructing the way to Jerusalem. See *Zohorei Ya'bets*.

On the northern border city of Dan, see Judges 18:29.

873. ***A viper on the path...*** The full verse reads: *Dan will be a serpent on the way, a viper on the path, that bites a horse's heels—and its rider tumbles backward.*

874. **When blessings arrived...** When the time came for Moses to bless the tribes, he linked Dan to a lion instead of a serpent, so that he would be matched with Judah, who had already been linked to a lion by Jacob. Thereby the lead tribe (Judah) and the rear guard (Dan) were coordinated.

875. **As is written: *He will begin*...** According to Rabbi Ḥiyya, Dan's *deliverance*—

He replied, "Surely, mystery of the matter—as is said: *When Moses would raise his hand, Israel prevailed* (Exodus 17:11)—*Israel*, unspecified! Here too: *He will begin to deliver Israel—Israel*, unspecified! Therefore, *Your deliverance I await, O YHVH*—precisely!"[877]

Rabbi Aḥa said, "Certainly so! Well spoken! Happy is the share of the righteous, who know how to engage in Torah, attaining life above through her, as is said: *She is your life and the length of your days* (Deuteronomy 30:20)."[878]

Gad will be raided by raiders, yet he will raid their heel (Genesis 49:19).

Rabbi Yeisa said, "Surely, גד (*Gad*), *Gad*, implies that troops will go forth to wage battle, as indicated by the spelling גד (*Gad*)—always ג (*gimel*), ד (*dalet*)—troops and camps issuing from them. For ג (*gimel*) gives and ד (*dalet*) gathers; consequently, many troops and camps derive from them."[879]

awaited by Jacob—was initiated by Dan's descendant Samson, who began *to deliver* the nation from the Philistines.

See *Leqaḥ Tov*, Genesis 49:18. The verse from Judges was spoken by an angel to Manoah's wife, predicting Samson's birth.

876. **Why *I await?*...** Jacob died soon after giving this blessing, and Samson did not appear until many generations later; so why did Jacob say that he was awaiting that deliverance?

877. ***Israel prevailed—Israel*, unspecified!...** The full verse, describing the battle against Amalek, reads: *When Moses would raise his hand, Israel prevailed; when he would let down his hand, Amalek prevailed.*

Rabbi Ḥiyya explains that the name *Israel* in this verse is unspecified—applying not just to the people of Israel in their battle against Amalek, but also to Moses' *sefirah, Tif'eret,* whose full name is *Tif'eret Yisra'el* (Beauty of Israel), in His battle against the demonic realm (symbolized by Amalek). Similarly, in the verse in Judges—*He will begin to deliver Israel*—the name *Israel* refers not just to the nation but also to the soul of Jacob (known as Israel) and to his *sefirah, Tif'eret Yisra'el*. So, even though Jacob had died long ago, Samson helped *to deliver* him. Finally, the phrase *your deliverance* refers not only to human deliverance (of Dan, the nation, and Jacob) but also to the deliverance of *Tif'eret,* known as *YHVH*.

See *Zohar* 2:65b–66a; Moses de León, *Sefer ha-Rimmon,* 57. According to Rashi on Numbers 20:15, the patriarchs, buried in their graves, feel pain when Israel suffers.

878. ***She is your life*...** Rabbi Aḥa understands *she* as referring to Torah. The verse reads: *He* [or: *that*] *is your life*..., referring either to God or to loving, heeding, and cleaving to Him (mentioned immediately before). The substitution of היא (*hi*), *She,* for הוא (*hu*), *He* (or *that*), in this verse appears elsewhere, e.g., in *Tanḥuma, Yitro* 15, *Ki Tissa* 15, *Shemini* 11; *Avot de-Rabbi Natan* A, 2; *Zohar* 1:92a, 168a.

879. **גד (*Gad*), *Gad*... ג (*gimel*), ד (*dalet*)...** The two letters spelling the name of the tribe of גד (*Gad*), *Gad,* allude to the divine couple. The letter ג (*gimel*) symbolizes *Yesod,* who גומל (*gomel*), "deals (graciously)," with *Shekhinah*—symbolized by ד (*dalet*) because She is דלה (*dallah*), "poor," having nothing of Her own. The union of these two *sefirot* ensures a powerful array of forces, as indicated in Jacob's blessing.

See BT *Shabbat* 104a: "גימ״ל דל״ת–גמול דלים (*Gimel dalet: gemol dallim*), Deal kindly with the poor." See *Zohar* 1:3a, 234b; 2:181a; Moses

"Come and see: The waters of the river flowing and gushing from Eden never cease and it fulfills the poor; so numerous troops and camps are stationed here and nourished. Therefore, גד (*Gad*)—one generating and giving, the other gathering and grasping—and the house is sustained along with all its members."[880]

Rabbi Yitsḥak said, "If Gad had not been one of the sons of the maids, the time would have been ripe for him to attain greater perfection than all, as is written: בא גד (*Ba gad*), *Fortune has come* (Genesis 30:11)—read but not written. בגד (*Begad*)—missing an א (*alef*), for that moment was perfectly propitious but it vanished from him, as is said: *My brothers* בגדו (*bagedu*), *betrayed me, like a desert stream* (Job 6:15); for that flowing, gushing river withdrew at that moment, so it is spelled בגד (*begad*), *betrayal.* Consequently, he never attained the Holy Land, withdrawing from it."[881]

Rabbi Yehudah said, "How do we know that Reuben followed the same pattern? As is written: *Unbridled as water, you will not remain!* (Genesis 49:4), for waters withdrew, flowing no more—and it has already been explained how he was tainted. Neither of them attained the land, but they sent troops and camps to possess the land for Israel.[882]

de León, *Shushan Edut,* 340; idem, *Sefer ha-Rimmon,* 229.

880. **waters of the river...** The ceaseless flow of emanation issuing from *Ḥokhmah* (Eden) and conveyed by *Yesod* nourishes *Shekhinah,* the paradigm of poverty (see the preceding note). Numerous forces assemble at the site of their union, and *Shekhinah* ("the house") is sustained along with all Her angels.

881. **If Gad had not been...** Gad was the firstborn son of Leah's maid, Zilpah. If he had been born to one of Jacob's two wives (Leah or Rachel), he would have attained an extremely high rung—as indicated by the letters of his name, which signify the promise of divine union (see above, note 879), and by Leah's exclamation at his birth: בא גד (*Ba gad*), *Fortune has come.* However, although this exclamation is traditionally read בא גד (*ba gad*), in the Masoretic text it is written as one word and without the א (*alef*): בגד (*begad*)—alluding to the withdrawal of the flow of emanation because of Gad's being born to a maid. The spelling as בגד (*begad*) also suggests "betrayal," based on the root בגד (*bgd*), "to betray," hinting again at the withdrawal of the divine stream, based on the wording of the verse in Job. Thus the divine union was interrupted.

Gad's lower status helps to explain why his tribe (along with Reuben and half of Manasseh) never entered the Promised Land, settling instead in the Transjordan. See Numbers 32; Joshua 18:7; 22.

On the lower status of the sons of the two maids (Bilhah and Zilpah), see *Zohar* 1:154a.

The full verse in Genesis (according to the Masoretic spelling) reads: *Leah said,* "בגד (*Begad*), *What fortune!" And she named him* גד (*Gad*), *Gad.* (The precise meaning of the single word *begad* is enigmatic.)

882. **Reuben followed the same pattern...** He too could have attained greatness, being Jacob's firstborn, but because he slept with his father's concubine (and Rachel's maid) Bilhah, he was deprived of the rich flow of blessing and consequently lost the birthright, the kingship, and the priesthood. See above, note 615.

"Come and see: What was flawed in Gad was perfected in Asher, as is written: *From Asher, rich is his bread, he will provide delicacies of a king* (ibid., 20). Now ג (*gimel*) completes ד (*dalet*)."[883]

Rabbi El'azar and Rabbi Abba escaped the fierce sun by entering a cave at Lydda—for they had been walking on the way. Rabbi Abba said, "Let us wreathe this cave with words of Torah!"[884]

Rabbi El'azar opened, saying, "*Set me as a seal upon your heart, as a seal upon your arm. For love is fierce as death, jealousy cruel as Sheol; its sparks are sparks of fire, a blazing flame* (Song of Songs 8:6). We have already aroused the meaning of this verse, but one night I was standing before my father and I heard a word from him: The desire and yearning of Assembly of Israel for the blessed Holy One is consummated only by souls of the righteous; for they stimulate the flow of lower waters toward the upper, and at that moment—consummation of desire in single cleaving, yielding fruit.[885]

"Come and see: Once they have cleaved to one another and She has received Her desire, She says, *Set me as a seal upon your heart.* Why *as a seal*? Because by its nature, once a seal is affixed to a certain place, even when it is removed it remains in that place irremovably, for its entire impress and image remain there. So, Assembly of Israel says, 'Look, I have cleaved to You! Even if I am

883. **perfected in Asher...** Asher was Zilpah's second son. His name derives from אשר (*osher*), "happiness," and he symbolizes *Yesod*, who unites joyously with *Malkhut* (Kingdom). As Jacob's blessing indicates, Asher (*Yesod*) conveys *delicacies* to the *king* (*Malkhut*). Thereby, ג (*gimel*)—symbolizing *Yesod*—completes ד (*dalet*), symbolizing *Shekhinah*.

See Genesis 30:13; above, note 611.

884. **entering a cave...** According to rabbinic tradition, a cave figured prominently in the lives of Rabbi El'azar and his father, Rabbi Shim'on: the Romans sought to execute Rabbi Shim'on for criticizing the government, so he hid from the authorities in a cave together with his son for thirteen years.

The cave story here extends until the end of Torah portion *Va-Yḥi* and culminates in an interpretation of Jacob's burial in the cave of Machpelah.

See *Bereshit Rabbah* 79:6; JT *Shevi'it* 9:1, 38d; BT *Shabbat* 33b–34a, *Sanhedrin* 98a; *Pesiqta de-Rav Kahana* 11:16; *Qohelet Rabbah* on 10:8; *Midrash Tehillim* 17:13; *Zohar* 1:11a–b, 216b; *ZḤ* 59c–60a.

On a cave near Lydda, see the story in *Pesiqta de-Rav Kahana* 18:5; *Pesiqta Rabbati* 32; *Zohar* 2:42b; 3:55b (*Tos*); *ZḤ* 20d (*MhN*); Scholem, "She'elot be-Viqqoret ha-Zohar," 51–52; *NZ*, n. 1, in *TZ* 1a. On the connection between the cave here and certain Romans, see below at note 990. On the tradition that the *Zohar* was composed in the cave in which Rabbi Shim'on was hiding, see Tishby, *Wisdom of the Zohar*, 1:13; Huss, "Hofa'ato shel 'Sefer ha-Zohar,'" 528.

885. **desire and yearning of Assembly of Israel...** The union of *Shekhinah* and *Tif'eret* is stimulated by souls of the righteous.

See *Zohar* 1:60b; above at notes 600–602. On the lower and upper waters, see above, note 865. On Assembly of Israel as a name of *Shekhinah*, see above, pp. 122–23, n. 237.

removed from You and go [245a] into exile, *set me as a seal*, so that My entire image will remain in You, like a seal, whose entire image remains in the place where it is affixed.'[886]

"*For love is fierce as death*—as fierce as separation of spirit from body. We have learned: When a human is about to depart from the world, and he sees what he sees, the spirit moves through each member of the body, climbing its waves—like crossing the sea without oars, going up and down ineffectively—and it goes to ask leave of every member of the body. There is nothing as fierce as the day of separation of spirit from body. The fierceness of the love of Assembly of Israel for the blessed Holy One is like the fierceness of death at the moment when they must separate—spirit from body.[887]

"*Jealousy cruel as Sheol*. Whoever loves without being linked to jealousy—his love is not love. Once he becomes jealous, love is complete. From here we learn that a man should be jealous of his wife, so that perfect love will be linked with him, for thereby he will not set his eyes upon another woman.[888]

"What does this mean: *Jealousy* קשה (*qashah*), *hard, as Sheol*? Just as it is *hard* in the eyes of the wicked to go down to *Sheol*, so with *jealousy*: it is *hard* in the eyes of one who loves jealously to separate from his beloved.

"Alternatively, *Jealousy hard as Sheol*—just as with Sheol, when a wicked person is brought down there, he is informed of the sins for which he is brought there and it is hard for him, so one who is jealous demands restitution and suspects various actions, and then he is bound in the bond of love.[889]

"*Its sparks are sparks of fire*, שלהבת יה (*shalhevet Yah*), *a flame of Yah*. What is *shalhevet Yah*? A flame blazing, issuing from the shofar, arousing and kindling the flame of love. Who is that? The left, as is written: *His left hand beneath my head* (Song of Songs 2:6). This kindles the flame of love of Assembly of Israel for the blessed Holy One. Consequently, *many waters cannot quench love* (ibid. 8:7), for when the right—which is *waters*—comes, it intensifies the blaze of love and

886. **Why *as a seal*?...** See *Zohar* 2:114a.

887. **When a human is about to depart...** At death, a human being sees *Shekhinah*, which is forbidden during life. The spirit tries to navigate the body's convulsions, asking leave of each organ and limb.

See *Zohar* 3:54b, 126b. On seeing *Shekhinah* at death, see above, p. 320 and n. 103, page 361.

"Its waves" renders גלגלוי (*galgalloi*), literally, "its wheels," but in medieval Spanish poetry and the *Zohar* גלגל (*galgal*), "wheel," is equivalent to גל (*gal*), "wave." See *Zohar* 2:48b–49a, 50b, 56a; Liebes, *Peraqim*, 296.

888. **Whoever loves without...jealousy...** Such love is unimpassioned and incomplete.

See *Zohar* 3:54b. On the obligation to be jealous of one's wife, see *Sifrei*, Numbers 21; BT *Sotah* 3a.

889. **demands restitution and suspects...** A jealous lover demands a full account from his partner. Once everything is resolved, their love resumes.

For other interpretations, see *KP*; Tishby, *Wisdom of the Zohar*, 367; Mopsik.

does not quench the flame of the left, as is said: *his right hand embracing me* (ibid. 2:6). This is: *many waters cannot quench love.* All follows this pattern."[890]

While they were sitting, they heard the voice of Rabbi Shim'on, who was coming on the way along with Rabbi Yitsḥak and Rabbi Yehudah. As he approached the cave, Rabbi El'azar and Rabbi Abba emerged.

Rabbi Shim'on said, "From the walls of the cave, I see that *Shekhinah* is here!"[891]

They sat down. Rabbi Shim'on said, "What are you engaged in?"[892]

Rabbi Abba replied, "In the love of Assembly of Israel for the blessed Holy One, and Rabbi El'azar was explaining this verse: *Set me as a seal upon your heart.*"

He said, "El'azar, you have been contemplating sublime love and the bond of affection!"

Rabbi Shim'on was silent for a while.

He said, "Silence is necessary everywhere—except for silence of Torah. I have one treasure, treasured away, and I do not want it to be lost to you. It is a supernal word; I found it in the Book of Rav Hamnuna Sava.[893]

"Come and see: Everywhere male pursues female and arouses love in her; yet here we find that She arouses love and pursues Him! According to the way of the world, it is unworthy for female to pursue male. But this is a concealed matter, a supernal matter from the King's treasure-house.[894]

890. **שלהבת יה (*shalhevet Yah*)...** In the verse from Song of Songs, this expression is written as a single word, שלהבתיה (*shalhevet-yah*), with יה (*yah*) constituting a suffix denoting intensity; the word apparently means "an intense (or blazing, mighty) flame." Here, Rabbi El'azar construes the expression as two words: שלהבת יה (*shalhevet Yah*), *a flame of Yah*, a divine flame. *Yah* refers specifically to *Binah* (or *Ḥokhmah* and *Binah*). *Binah* is also pictured as a shofar, from which issues the passionate flame of *Gevurah*, the divine left hand, which arouses the love of *Shekhinah* (Assembly of Israel) for *Tif'eret* (blessed Holy One). The opposite, right hand is *Ḥesed*—symbolized by water—which, rather than quenching the passion, fuels and intensifies it.

See *Zohar* 3:54b. The verse from Song of Songs 2 reads in full: n. 867 *His left hand beneath my head, his right hand embracing me.* See above, p. 494 and n. 867. The verse in Song of Songs 8 reads: *Many waters cannot quench love, nor rivers drown it.* The final sentence here ("All follows this pattern") means that the rest of Song of Songs also alludes to the divine romance.

891. ***Shekhinah* is here** She manifests wherever Torah is being studied.

See M *Avot* 3:2: "Rabbi Ḥananya son of Teradyon says, '... If two are sitting engaged in words of Torah, *Shekhinah* dwells between them.'" Cf. below, note 1024.

892. **What are you engaged in?** For the same question in a similar context, see above, p. 270 and n. 68; *Zohar* 2:5a.

893. **Silence is necessary...** On this notion, see BT *Ḥullin* 89a; *Midrash Shemu'el*, 1:1. Cf. BT *Megillah* 18a; *Zohar* 1:2a; *ZḤ* 82c (*MhN*, *Rut*).

On Rav Hamnuna, whose book is quoted frequently in the *Zohar*, see above, note 764. On books such as this, see above, note 240.

894. **male pursues female...** See BT *Qiddushin* 2b.

"Come and see: There are three souls, ascending by certain rungs, and as for their being three, they are four. One: transcendent soul that cannot be grasped. The supreme royal treasurer is unaware of it, let alone the lower one. This is soul of all souls, concealed, eternally unrevealed, unknowable—and all of them depend upon it.[895]

"This envelops itself in a wrapping of crystal radiance within radiancy, and drips pearls, drop by drop, all linking as one, like joints of limbs of one body—one. It enters into them, displaying through them its activity; this and they are one, inseparable. This supernal soul is hidden to all.[896]

"Another soul: female concealing herself within her forces. She is their soul, and out of them a body is woven, [245b] to display activity through them to

895. **One: transcendent soul...** *Ein Sof,* beyond all comprehension, even by the *sefirot* themselves. (Alternatively, the reference is to *Keter,* coeternal with *Ein Sof.*) "Supreme royal treasurer" apparently refers to *Ḥokhmah*; "the lower one," to *Yesod. Ein Sof* is described as the "soul (or essence) of all souls," a description deriving from Solomon ibn Gabirol's *Keter Malkhut* 4:47: "You are alive but not through... soul, for You are soul of soul." All the *sefirot*—and all worlds and beings below—depend upon *Ein Sof.*

See *Zohar* 1:103b; 3:109b (*RM*), 152a; Scholem, *Major Trends,* 110, 375, n. 97.

"Royal treasurer" renders גזברא דרקטיקא (*gizbera de-raqtiqa*). *Gizbera* means "treasurer." *Raqtiqa* may be based on דריקא (*deriqa*), "royal official," (from Iranian *darik,* "courtier"). I have adopted the reading of M7, N23, and O2. For the second word, the Mantua edition and *OY* read דקרטיטאה (*de-qartita'ah*), which could be rendered "of the treasury (or treasure-house)," based on קורטא (*qurta*), which apparently derives from Greek *kouratoreia,* "treasury." According to this reading, the meaning is more specific: *Ḥokhmah* is the treasurer of *Binah* ("the treasury"), while *Yesod* is the treasurer of *Shekhinah* ("the lower [treasury]"). See Galante; *KP*; Luria, *Va-Ye'esof David,* s.v. *qartita*; above, p. 97, n. 84.

896. **envelops itself...** *Ein Sof* envelops itself, as it were, within the primal, crystalline splendor of *Keter* and begins to emanate the nine lower *sefirot,* which form its ethereal body. Alternatively, *Keter* wraps itself within *Ḥokhmah*. Or possibly, "crystal radiance" refers to *Keter,* and "within radiancy" to *Ḥokhmah*. See *OY.*

On the image of enveloping, see *Tanḥuma* (Buber), *Vayaqhel* 7: "Rabbi Shim'on son of Rabbi Yehotsadak asked Rabbi Shemu'el son of Naḥman, 'Since you are a master of Aggadah, tell me how the blessed Holy One created the world.' He replied, 'When the blessed Holy One wished to create the world, He enwrapped himself in light and created the world, as is said: *He wraps in light as in a garment,* and afterward: *He spreads out the heavens like a curtain* (Psalms 104:2).'"

See *Bereshit Rabbah* 3:4 (and Theodor, ad loc.); *Pirqei de-Rabbi Eli'ezer* 3; Ezra of Gerona, *Peirush Shir ha-Shirim,* 493–94; Ezra's letter, ed. Scholem, "Te'udah Ḥadashah," 157–58; Azriel of Gerona, *Peirush ha-Aggadot,* 110–11; *Zohar* 1:2a, 15b, 29a, 90a (*ST*); 2:39b, 164b; Moses de León, *Mishkan ha-Edut,* 5a.

On the crystalline aspect of *Keter,* see above, p. 357 and n. 296. Instead of the reading בדולחא (*bedulḥa*), "bdellium, crystal" (supported by O2, *OY,* and *OL*), many witnesses read כרמלא (*karmela*), "Carmel," perhaps based on the midrashic interpretation in BT *Shabbat* 105a: "כרמל (*Karmel*), Carmel—כר מלא (*kar male*), rounded and full." Cf. Song of Songs 7:6: *Your head upon you is like Carmel.*

the whole world—like the body, which is an instrument for the soul to convey action. These correspond to those hidden joints above.[897]

"Another soul is souls of the righteous below, for souls of the righteous derive from those higher souls—from soul of female and soul of male. Therefore, souls of the righteous transcend all those forces and camps above.[898]

"Now, you might say, 'Look, they are elevated from two aspects! Why do they descend to this world, and why are they removed from it?'[899] This may be compared to a king to whom a son was born. He sent him to a village to be raised until he came of age and could be taught the ways of the royal palace. The king heard that his son had grown up and come of age. What did he do? Out of love for his son, he sent the matron, his mother, for him, and brought him into his palace and rejoiced with him every day.

"Similarly, the blessed Holy One had a son by the *Matronita*. And who is that? The supernal holy soul. He sent him to a village—to this world—so that he would grow up there and be taught the ways of the royal palace. When the King knows that His son has grown up in this village, and that the time has arrived to come to His palace, what does He do? Out of His love, He sends the *Matronita* for him and brings him into His palace. For the soul does not ascend from this world until the *Matronita* comes for it, escorting it into the palace of the King, where it dwells forever.

"Despite all this, it is the way of the world that those villagers cried over the departure of the king's son. One wise man was there; he said to them, 'Why are you crying? Isn't he the son of the king? It is not fitting for him to dwell any longer among you, but rather in his father's palace!' Similarly, Moses, who was wise, saw the villagers crying over this. He said, '*You are children of YHVH your God! Do not gash yourselves*...' (Deuteronomy 14:1).[900]

897. **Another soul: female...** *Shekhinah*, surrounded by Her camps of angels, who weave and constitute Her body. Her angelic limbs correspond to the sefirotic limbs of *Ein Sof* above.

898. **souls of the righteous...** Who issue from the union of *Shekhinah* (soul of the female) and *Tif'eret* (soul of the male). Because these souls emanate directly from the divine couple, they surpass the angels.

With the allusion to *Tif'eret*, Rabbi Shim'on sheds light on the meaning of the cryptic line above: "as for their being three, they are four." The second soul, *Shekhinah*, includes (or is paired with) *Tif'eret*, thereby yielding a total of four souls: *Ein Sof*, *Shekhinah*, *Tif'eret*, and the souls of the righteous.

On the divine couple as parents of the soul, see *Zohar* 2:12a, 94b; 3:7a, 174b. On the righteous surpassing the angels, see BT *Sanhedrin* 92b–93a.

899. **elevated from two aspects...** Since the souls derive from the union of *Tif'eret* and *Shekhinah*, why do they descend to the material world? And if there is some deep purpose in their descent to the world, then why do they depart?

900. **This may be compared to a king...** The soul descends to this world in order to learn how to serve God and to fulfill itself by

"Come and see: If the righteous all knew this, they would rejoice when the day arrives for them to depart from this world. For is it not a supreme honor that the *Matronita* comes for them, to escort them into the royal palace, so that the King will rejoice with them every day? For the blessed Holy One delights only in the souls of the righteous.

"Come and see: Arousal of love of Assembly of Israel for the blessed Holy One is aroused by souls of the righteous below, for they come from the side of the King—from the side of male—and this arousal is from the side of male, and love is aroused. Thus, male arouses affection and love for female, and then female is bound in love toward him. In the same manner, desire of female to stream lower waters toward upper waters comes only through souls of the righteous.[901]

"Happy are the righteous in this world and in the world that is coming, for upon them stand those above and below! Therefore, *The righteous one is foundation of the world* (Proverbs 10:25)—written unspecifically. Mystery of all: *Righteous one* is *foundation of the world* above and *foundation* below, and Assembly of Israel is encompassed by *righteous one* above and below. *Righteous one* from this side and *righteous one* from that side inherit Her, as is written: *The righteous will inherit the land* (Psalms 37:29)—*will inherit the land*, surely![902]

observing the Torah and living virtuously. Once it has attained these goals, it is escorted back to the palace by *Shekhinah*.

This parable appears (with some variation, together with the interpretation of the verse in Deuteronomy) in Moses de León, *Sefer ha-Rimmon*, 299. See the discussion between Rabbi El'azar and Rabbi Shim'on, above at notes 600–602. On the soul's perfection in this world, see Saadia Gaon, *Emunot ve-De'ot* 6:4; Moses de León, *Sefer ha-Mishqal*, 46–47 (translated in Matt, *Essential Kabbalah*, 148); idem, *Mishkan ha-Edut*, 8a–10a; *OY*; Tishby, *Wisdom of the Zohar*, 2:752–54. Cf. *Bahir* 90 (132).

The full verse in Deuteronomy, forbidding certain mourning rites, reads: *You are children of YHVH your God! Do not gash yourselves and do not make a bald spot between your eyes for the dead.* On *Shekhinah*'s title *Matronita*, see above, note 643.

901. **Arousal of love...** Souls of the righteous stimulate the love of *Shekhinah* (Assembly of Israel) for King *Tif'eret* (the blessed Holy One). Rabbi Shim'on indicates that these souls derive essentially from the male divine partner, thereby solving the problem that he posed above (at note 894): why does the female (*Shekhinah*) pursue the male (*Tif'eret*)? As it turns out, this female pursuit depends on the prior arousal of *Shekhinah* by masculine souls. See above, p. 498 and n. 885.

902. ***The righteous one*...—written unspecifically...** Scripture leaves the identity of *the righteous one* intentionally vague, so that the term can apply both to *Yesod* (known as Righteous One) and to a righteous human. Above, *Yesod* (Foundation) is an extension of *Tif'eret* and thus consummates the union with *Shekhinah*; below, the righteous human performs the vital function of stimulating *Shekhinah*. Thus, *Shekhinah* is embraced above and below by *the righteous one*. Both of Her partners inherit (or possess) Her, as indicated by the verse in Psalms, where *the land* symbolizes *Shekhinah*.

On the intimacy between *Shekhinah* and

"Come and see: *Righteous one* inherits this *land* and pours blessings upon Her every day, providing Her with delicacies and delights by the supernal flow that He draws upon Her. We have already established the mystery that is written: מאשר (*Me-asher*), *From Asher, rich is his bread, he will provide delicacies of a king* (Genesis 49:20). Yet even so, another element, as is written: *Daughters saw her* ויאשרוה (*vay'ashsheruha*), *and called her happy* (Song of Songs 6:9). Of this, Leah said 'באשרי (*Be-oshri*), *Happy am I! For daughters* אשרוני (*ishsheruni*), *will call me happy*' (Genesis 30:13), and all is fine![903]

"Come and see: From the world that is coming emanates a flow to this *righteous one*, to provide delicacies and delights to this *land*, who is bread of poverty, transforming it into pastry, as is said: *From Asher, rich is his bread, he will provide delicacies of a king*—surely, as we have established.[904] [246a]

"Come and see: מאשר (*Me-asher*), *From Asher*—a mystery, alluding to the place that everyone מאשרין (*me'ashsherin*), calls happy. Who is that? The world that is coming, whom those above and below call happy and yearn for.[905]

both righteous ones, see *Zohar* 1:66b, 153b. The verse in Proverbs—וצדיק יסוד עולם (*Ve-tsaddiq yesod olam*)—literally means *The righteous one is an everlasting foundation,* but it is understood as *The righteous one is the foundation of the world.* See BT *Ḥagigah* 12b; *Bahir* 71 (102); Azriel of Gerona, *Peirush ha-Aggadot,* 34.

On the verse in Psalms, cf. M *Sanhedrin* 10:1: "All of Israel have a share in the world that is coming, as is said: *Your people, all of them righteous, will inherit the land forever—sprout of My planting, work of My hands, that I may be glorified* (Isaiah 60:21)." See *Zohar* 1:93a, 153b, 188a, 216a, 227a.

903. ***Righteous one*... pours blessings upon Her...** The name of Jacob's son Asher derives from אשר (*osher*), "happiness," and alludes to *Yesod,* who joyously conveys the delights of emanation to *Shekhinah,* known as *Malkhut* (Kingdom). She is the *king* mentioned in Jacob's blessing. See above at notes 609–613.

Yet, from a higher perspective, Asher alludes to *Binah,* the Divine Mother and source of the delightful flow. She is called *happy* by Her daughters, the lower *sefirot* who issue from Her. She is also symbolized by Leah, who, upon the birth of Asher, proclaimed herself *happy.* See *Zohar* 1:158a.

Ultimately, there is no contradiction between these two interpretations of the name Asher ("all is fine"), because *Binah* and *Yesod* simply represent two stages of the river of emanation. On the symbolic meanings of Asher, see *Zohar* 1:15a, 47b, 49a, 235b, 244b; 2:97b; 3:65b.

904. **From the world that is coming...** From *Binah,* "the world that is coming, constantly coming, never ceasing" (3:290b [*IZ*]), richness flows to *Yesod,* who conveys it to *Shekhinah*. Before receiving this influx, *Shekhinah* is impoverished and called לחם עוני (*leḥem oni*), "bread of poverty (or affliction)"—the designation of *matstsah,* according to Deuteronomy 16:3. Once She is enriched by Asher (the continuum of *Binah* and *Yesod*), She is transformed into לחם פנג (*leḥem pannag*), literally, "bread of *pannag,*" rendered here "pastry." *Pannag* is a biblical hapax legomenon (Ezekiel 27:17), apparently meaning "meal, ground seeds of grain."

See *Zohar* 1:47b; above at note 612.

905. **מאשר (*Me-asher*), *From Asher*—a mystery...** Alluding to *Binah,* the joyous source, to whom all yearn to return. See the preceding two notes.

"*Rich is his bread.* From whom? Until here, he did not explain who is the source. Well, there is bread, and then there is bread—just as there is a tree, and then there is a tree! There is a Tree of Life, and there is a tree upon which death depends. There is bread called 'bread of poverty,' and there is bread called 'pastry.' Who is that? לחם ו (*Leḥem vav*), Bread of *vav*, and this is לחמו (*laḥmo*), *his bread.* Of this is written *Look, I am about to rain down for you bread from heaven* (Exodus 16:4)—*from heaven,* surely![906]

"Therefore, *From Asher, rich is* לחמו (*laḥmo*), *his bread*—לחם ו (*leḥem vav*), bread of *vav*—because by Him this tree is nourished, and He crowns it, as is said: *upon the crown with which his mother crowned him* (Song of Songs 3:11). When He gathers, surely *he will provide delicacies of a king*—Assembly of Israel, nourished by Him. He provides to Her, for Righteous One is sign of the holy covenant, nourishing Her constantly—and from here to other rungs below, all corresponding to the pattern above.[907]

"In the Book of Rav Yeiva Sava he said as follows:[908] *From Asher, rich is his*

906. **Well, there is bread...** There are two varieties of bread and two kinds of trees.

The Tree of Life symbolizes *Tif'eret,* while *Shekhinah* is a tree linked with death. This last symbol derives from *Seder Eliyyahu Rabbah* 5, where the Tree of Knowledge of Good and Evil is called the Tree of Death, because when Adam and Eve ate of its fruit, death ensued. See Genesis 2:17. In Kabbalah, *Shekhinah* is identified with the Tree of Knowledge. When She is united with *Tif'eret,* She conveys life to the world; but if She is separated from Him by human sin, the vivifying flow of emanation ceases and death dominates. See *Zohar* 1:12b, 35b–36a, 51a–52a, 53b, 208b–209a; 3:157a.

On the two types of bread, see above, note 904. Here Rabbi Shim'on focuses on the word לחמו (*laḥmo*), *his bread,* which he divides into לחם (*leḥem*), "bread" (or "bread of"), and the letter ו (*vav*), whose numerical value (six) alludes to *Tif'eret* together with the five *sefirot* surrounding Him (*Ḥesed* through *Yesod*). Thus the word לחמו (*laḥmo*) refers to "bread of *Tif'eret*." This is rich bread, pastry, which is conveyed by *Tif'eret* (through *Yesod*) to *Shekhinah,* bread of poverty. The bread of *Tif'eret* is also known as *bread from heaven,* because *Tif'eret* is symbolized by *heaven.*

Cf. above at n. 760. The verse in Exodus describes the manna from heaven, symbolizing the emanation from *Tif'eret.* See *Zohar* 1:157b; 2:40a, 61b, 183a; 3:95b, 292b (*IZ*); Moses de León, *Sefer ha-Rimmon,* 133.

907. **Therefore, *From Asher*...** The verse now implies: From *Binah* (*Asher*), the bread of *Tif'eret* (*vav*) becomes rich. The tree of *Tif'eret* is nourished and crowned by *Binah* ("Him, He"). Once *Tif'eret* gathers the nourishing flow from *Binah,* He provides it to *Shekhinah* through *Yesod* (Righteous One), symbolized by the covenant of circumcision.

On the masculine designation of *Binah,* see above, note 531. The full verse in Song of Songs reads: *O daughters of Zion, come out and gaze upon King Solomon, upon the crown with which his mother crowned him on the day of his wedding, on the day of his heart's delight.* On this verse, see *Sifra, Shemini, millu'im,* 15, 44c; *Pesiqta de-Rav Kahana* 1:3; *Shir ha-Shirim Rabbah* on 3:11; Naḥmanides on Genesis 24:1; above, note 85; *Zohar* 1:29b; 2:22a, 84a, 100b; 3:61b.

908. **Book of Rav Yeiva Sava...** Quoted frequently in the *Zohar.* On Rav Yeiva, see above, note 280. On books such as this, see above, note 240.

bread—bread of Sabbath, which is pastry, double, as is said: *they gathered double bread* (Exodus 16:22). What does *double* mean? Two breads: *bread from heaven* and bread from earth—one, pastry; one, bread of poverty. On Sabbath lower bread is interbraided with higher bread, one blessed through the other; this is *double bread.*[909]

"He said further: *Double bread*—for Sabbath receives from supernal Sabbath, who flows and illumines all; so bread joins with bread, becoming *double.*[910]

"Everywhere mystery of bread is female. Therefore it is written: שמנה (*shemenah*), *rich*, and not שמן (*shamen*). Similarly, *except the bread that he was eating* (Genesis 39:6)—his wife. Now, you might say, '*The bread* אזל (*azal*), *is gone, from our sacks* (1 Samuel 9:7)—and not אזלת (*azelat*)!' Well, we call other food 'bread,' and it is well known which is other food and which is actual bread. Bread from above is always male; lower bread, female. And we have found that sometimes it is written as masculine and sometimes as feminine. All is one entity, whether this or that, and all is fine![911]

"Come and see: Asher is inscribed above and inscribed below in the adorn-

909. **bread of Sabbath...** According to the account in Exodus, when the Israelites went out to gather manna on the eve of Sabbath, they found a double portion. The verse reads: *On the sixth day, they gathered double bread, two* omers *for each one.* Rav Yeiva explains that the Sabbath portion was double because it comprised the bread of *Tif'eret* (pastry) and the bread of *Shekhinah* (bread of poverty). Their union is consummated on Sabbath.

See *OY*; Galante. The phrase "bread from earth" derives from Psalms 104:14.

910. **Sabbath receives from supernal Sabbath...** *Shekhinah* (or *Tif'eret-Yesod*) receives from *Binah,* and this flow produces double bread.

For a range of interpretations, see *OY*; Galante; *KP*; Tishby, *Wisdom of the Zohar*, 3:1235–36. On the various sefirotic associations of Sabbath, see Tishby, *Wisdom of the Zohar*, 3:1223–26.

911. **mystery of bread is female...** Bread normally alludes to the feminine or specifically to *Shekhinah*. Therefore in Jacob's blessing to Asher, bread is described by the feminine form of the adjective "rich": שמנה (*shemenah*)—rather than the masculine form, שמן (*shamen*).

The verse in Genesis reads: *He* [Potiphar] *left all that he had in Joseph's hands, and, with him there, he gave no thought to anything except the bread that he was eating.* According to the Midrash, *the bread that he was eating* refers to Potiphar's wife.

Actually, the noun לחם (*leḥem*) is rarely feminine and normally masculine—as in the verse in Samuel, where the masculine form of the verb appears. Here, this is explained by the fact that *leḥem* also refers to solid food in general, not just bread; from the context, it is usually clear which sense pertains. The more general sense alludes to *Tif'eret*; the more specific one ("actual bread") to *Shekhinah*. However, both constitute a single entity.

See *Tosafot, Menaḥot* 94a, s.v. *shetei haleḥem*. On the sexual interpretation of *the bread that he was eating,* see *Bereshit Rabbah* 70:4; 86:6; *Targum Yerushalmi* on the verse; *Tanḥuma, Shemot* 11; *Shemot Rabbah* 1:32; Rashi, Ibn Ezra, and *Sekhel Tov* on the verse; *Midrash Aggadah*, Numbers 1:13; *ZḤ* 35c–d.

ments of the Bride. The sea rests upon all twelve tribes and is arrayed in them, as is written: *with the sea set upon them above* (1 Kings 7:25). Mystery of the matter: arrayed above, arrayed below on earth. Arrayed above, in certain adornments corresponding to the supernal world. Arrayed below, in these twelve tribes, corresponding to the pattern above. So, *Shekhinah* above, *Shekhinah* below, by virtue of Israel; She is encompassed and arrayed on both sides.[912]

"Asher inheres in the array like the other tribes, and if Moses did not reveal, it would not be known, for it is written: *dipping in oil his foot* (Deuteronomy 33:24)—showing the location of his link, for he draws that anointing oil from above. Therefore it is written: *Blessed among sons is Asher* (ibid.)."[913]

Rabbi Shim'on opened, "*Naphtali, a hind let loose, who brings forth lovely fawns* (Genesis 49:21). As has been said, the upper world is world of the male.[914] Once anything ascends above Assembly of Israel, all is male. How do we know? From עולה (*olah*), an ascent offering. Why is it called *olah*? Because it 'ascends' above the female. Therefore, *an ascent offering,* זכר תמים (*zakhar tamim*), *an unblemished male*... (Leviticus 1:10). Why *tamim, complete*? Would someone intend to offer it piece by piece, leading Scripture to say *tamim*? What, then, is *tamim*? As is said: *Walk in My presence and be* תמים (*tamim*), *complete* (Genesis 17:1). When was he *complete*? The moment he was circumcised; for one becomes male, and is

912. **Asher is inscribed...** Asher symbolizes *Binah* (and *Yesod*) above; he also adorns *Shekhinah* along with the other tribes below.

The sea refers to a large bronze reservoir built by Solomon in the Temple, which rested on twelve bronze oxen. This *sea* symbolizes *Shekhinah,* who is arrayed above by twelve angelic forces and below on earth by the twelve tribes. The phrase "corresponding to the supernal world" refers to an array of twelve sefirotic forces adorning *Binah*.

The context (1 Kings 7:23, 25) reads: *He made the sea of cast metal... standing upon twelve oxen: three facing north, three facing west, three facing south, and three facing east, with the sea set upon them above.* On the *sea,* see *Zohar* 1:154a; above at notes 782–85. On *Shekhinah* and the tribes, see the sources cited above, note 781. On the angelic array, see *Zohar* 149a–b (*ST*). On the array of *Binah,* see above at notes 789–93.

913. **Asher inheres in the array...** Asher is one of the tribes adorning *Shekhinah,* but when Moses blessed him, he revealed Asher's unique status: his link with *Binah* (or with the continuum of *Binah-Yesod*). The phrase *dipping in oil* alludes to the flow of emanation issuing from *Ḥokhmah* to *Binah,* which Asher draws from above.

The verse reads: *Blessed among sons is Asher; may he be favored of his brothers, dipping in oil his foot.*

914. **upper world is world of the male** Although *Binah* is often depicted as Divine Mother, She is also called "world of the male," encompassing the entire configuration of *sefirot* from *Ḥesed* through *Yesod,* who constitute a masculine entity ready to unite with *Shekhinah*.

See *Zohar* 1:96a, 147a–b, 149a, 160b, 248b; 2:127b; *ZḤ* 72b (*ShS*). Cf. 1:5b, 17b, 46b, 163a; 2:4a.

recognized, only by the place called *tamim*. What is that? Sign of the covenant, by which male is distinguished from female, as is said: *a righteous man—he was tamim* (Genesis 6:9). Therefore, *zakhar tamim, an unblemished male*, so that this member will be recognized, and it will not be castrated.[915]

"Now, you might say, 'Look at what is written: נקבה תמימה (*neqevah temimah*), *an unblemished female* (Leviticus 4:32)!' Certainly so! Just as Righteous One is called *tamim*, so Righteousness is called *temimah*, for She absorbs everything from Him. Therefore *olah*, ascending from female to male; from this place upward all is male, and from female [246b] downward all is female, as we have established.[916]

915. **Once anything ascends above Assembly of Israel...** *Shekhinah* (known as Assembly of Israel) is female; above Her begins the masculine realm, "world of the male." Thus, the *olah* (ascent offering)—ascending to the *sefirot* above *Shekhinah*—must be male.

The word תמים (*tamim*) means "blameless, complete, intact, free of blemish, impeccable, perfect." Rabbi Shim'on wonders about the specific sense of this term as applied to the *olah*. Although this sacrifice (like almost all sacrifices) was cut into sections, all the sections were placed on the altar and burnt together, not piece by piece (see Leviticus 1:5–9). So, of course the *olah* had to be "complete"; why would Scripture need to stipulate this? Rather, this offering is *tamim*, "complete," in another sense—the same sense that applies to Abraham. The context in Genesis (17:1–2) reads: *When Abram was ninety-nine years old, YHVH appeared to Abram and said to him, "I am El Shaddai. Walk in My presence and be* תמים (*tamim*), *complete, and I will grant My covenant between Me and you and I will increase you very greatly."* This divine directive is soon followed by the covenantal command of circumcision (verses 9–14). Through this ritual, a man becomes *tamim*, "complete" or "unblemished"; without circumcision, paradoxically, a man is blemished.

The verse in Genesis reads: *Noah was a righteous man, he was tamim, blameless* [or: *perfect, unblemished, wholehearted*] *in his generation.* This verse links *tamim* with *righteous* (which implies *Yesod*, the divine phallus, known as Righteous One), but it also alludes to the tradition that Noah was born circumcised. See *Avot de-Rabbi Natan* A, 2; *Tanḥuma, Noaḥ* 5; *Zohar* 1:58a–b, 59b; 3:165b–166a.

Rabbi Shim'on concludes that in the context of the *olah*, the word *tamim* indicates that the sacrificial animal must be "a complete, unblemished," uncastrated male.

The full verse in Leviticus reads: *If his offering is from the flock—from the sheep or from the goats—for an ascent offering, an unblemished male he shall offer it.* Cf. Leviticus 1:3. On the male quality of the *olah*, see *Zohar* 1:70a; 3:6a; Moses de León, *Sefer ha-Rimmon*, 54. Cf. 2:238b; 3:26a, 107b, where the *olah* symbolizes *Shekhinah* ascending to unite with the male. On the genitals of the *olah*, cf. *Sifra, Vayiqra, dibbura dindavah* 3:8, 5b.

On *tamim* and circumcision, see *Bereshit Rabbah* 46:5; *Vayiqra Rabbah* 25:6; BT *Nedarim* 31b–32a; *Zohar* 1:59b, 95a–b, 200b; 3:142a (*IR*), 166a; Moses de León, *Sefer ha-Rimmon*, 228, 376. On the phallus as distinguishing male from female, see *Zohar* 2:137a. On Assembly of Israel as a name of *Shekhinah*, see above, pp. 122–23, n. 237.

916. **נקבה תמימה (*neqevah temimah*), *an unblemished female*...** This wording (describing a sheep brought as a purification offering) obviously shows that a female can also be described as *unblemished*. Rabbi Shim'on explains that *Shekhinah* (known as

"Now, you might say, 'There is also female above!' However, consummation of the body demonstrates that the whole body is male. Head of the body is female, until descending to consummation; when consummation appears, it renders everything male. But here, head and end are female, for the entire array of the body is female.[917]

"Come and see: There is one supernal mystery in this matter. For we see that Jacob blessed Joseph among his brothers, but when the blessed Holy One designated four banners for *Shekhinah*—for Her to be arrayed by twelve tribes—He withdrew Joseph from them and replaced him with Ephraim. Why was Joseph removed? If you say, 'Because of his sins'—not so, for he was righteous. Rather, mystery of the matter: Joseph was impress of the male, as is written: *A fruitful son is Joseph, a fruitful son by a spring* (Genesis 49:22), and similarly: *From there feeds Stone of Israel* (ibid., 24)—from there this *Stone* is nourished. *Stone* is Assembly of Israel, of whom David said *The stone that the builders rejected has become the cornerstone* (Psalms 118:22). Because Joseph is impress of the male, he is called Joseph the Righteous, for he is surely righteous: *from there feeds Stone of Israel.*

"Since all adornments of *Shekhinah* are female, Joseph was withdrawn from there and Ephraim was appointed in his place, for he is female for Her adornments. Being so, he was designated for the west side, dwelling place of the female; and that impress that is male was withdrawn from Her adornments—for it is world of the female, not world of the male, and all Her adornments must be female. Therefore, Joseph, who is righteous, was withdrawn from Her adornments, and Ephraim was appointed in his place. So, all twelve tribes are adornments of *Shekhinah,* and all must correspond to the pattern above—excluding the rung of Righteous One, who renders all members male and must not be impaired.[918]

Righteousness) receives the quality of being "complete" or "unblemished" from *Yesod* (known as Righteous One). From Him and above, all is male; from *Shekhinah* and below, all is female.

On Righteous One and Righteousness, see *Zohar* 1:49a, 182b.

917. **also female above...** *Binah* is surely female, because She is known as Divine Mother. However, Rabbi Shim'on explains, the female aspect of *Binah* is simply the head, or beginning, of the sefirotic configuration that culminates in *Yesod,* the phallus. This consummation renders the entire body male. *Shekhinah,* on the other hand, is entirely female from beginning to end, encompassing Her own being and the angelic realms beneath Her (pictured as maidens or daughters).

See *Zohar* 1:5b; above, note 914; Moses de León, *Sheqel ha-Qodesh,* 49 (60).

918. **designated four banners for *Shekhinah*...** God commanded the arrangement of the twelve tribes under four banners around the Tent of Meeting (dwelling place of *Shekhinah*). In this array, Joseph's place was taken by the tribes of his two sons (Ephraim and Manasseh), with Ephraim

"*Naphtali, a hind let loose, who delivers beautiful words.* As is said: ומדברך (*u-midbarekh*), *and your speaking, is lovely* (Song of Songs 4:3)—for voice מדבר ליה לדבור (*medabber leih le-dibbur*), conducts speech, and there is no voice without speech. That voice is let loose from a deep place above, sent forth to conduct speech; for there is no voice without speech, and there is no speech without voice—surely, general needing particular, and particular needing general. This voice, issuing from the south and conducting the west, possesses two sides, as is written: *To Naphtali he said:... Possess the west and the south!* (Deuteronomy 33:23). Above, male; below, female. Therefore, *Naphtali, a hind let loose*—female below. Correspondingly, male above, for it is written: הנותן (*ha-noten*), *who delivers, beautiful words*—*ha-noten*, not הנותנת (*ha-notenet*).[919]

carrying the banner on the west. See Numbers 2:18–24.

Rabbi Shim'on asks why Joseph was replaced by Ephraim. After all, Joseph is regarded as completely righteous: having overcome sexual temptation and refused the advances of Potiphar's wife, he scaled the sefirotic ladder and attained the rung of *Yesod* (known as Righteous One and symbolized by the covenantal "impress" of circumcision). See above, p. 92, n. 50.

Jacob's blessing to Joseph confirms his link with the male potency, for he is called *fruitful son.* Genesis 49:24 reads: *From there,* רועה (*ro'eh*), *the Shepherd, Stone of Israel.* But Rabbi Shim'on interprets *ro'eh* as a verb meaning "feeds, grazes," and takes the verse to mean that *Shekhinah* (*Stone of Israel*) *feeds* from Joseph's *sefirah, Yesod*. See *Bahir* 133 (193); *Zohar* 1:146b, 231b.

The "rejection" of *the stone* (mentioned in Psalm 118) alludes to the diminishment of *Shekhinah*'s light. Yet She becomes vital to the functioning of the *sefirot* and is symbolized as the Foundation Stone of the Temple. See *Zohar* 1:20a–b, 72a, 89b (*ST*); above, p. 208 and n. 179; above, note 470. Cf. *Bahir* 131 (190).

Precisely because of Joseph's link with the divine male (*Yesod*), it was inappropriate for him to participate in the female array of *Shekhinah,* constituted by the twelve tribes. If he had, the male potency could have been impaired. Therefore, he was replaced by Ephraim, who camped on the west, the site of *Shekhinah*.

See above, pp. 227–28 and nn. 300–301; *MM.* On the location of *Shekhinah,* see BT *Bava Batra* 25a, in the name of Rabbi Abbahu: "*Shekhinah* is in the west." On Her tribal array, see above, p. 470 and n. 781.

919. ***Naphtali... who delivers beautiful words...*** The phrase אמרי שפר (*imrei shafer*) can be translated variously, including: "lovely fawns" (based on a Semitic word meaning "lamb") or "beautiful words." Here, Rabbi Shim'on adopts the latter choice, linking it with the verse in Song of Songs, which is understood as referring to the lovely speaking of *Shekhinah*. *Tif'eret,* known as "voice," conducts *Shekhinah,* known as "speech." The two are interdependent, both being essential to expressing the divine message and conveying emanation to the world.

The voice of *Tif'eret* issues from *Binah* ("a deep place above"), being "sent forth" (as in the verse in Genesis: *let loose*) to conduct the speech of *Shekhinah*. The primal voice of *Tif'eret,* not yet divided into syllables, is "general"; the articulated speech of *Shekhinah* is "particular." This reference to "general" and "particular" derives from a rabbinic hermeneutical rule concerning "a generalization that requires a specification" and "a specification that requires a generalization."

Tif'eret's voice can also be said to issue from the south, symbolizing *Ḥesed,* the first *sefirah* below *Binah* and through which Her

"Come and see: Thought is beginning of all, and being Thought, it is within, concealed and unknowable. As this Thought expands further, it approaches the place where spirit dwells, and when it reaches that place it is called *Binah*, Understanding, for it is not as concealed as at first, although it is concealed. This spirit expands and generates a voice blended of fire, water, and spirit—namely, north, south, and east. This voice is totality of all others. This voice conducts speech, conveying a word refinedly; for voice is released from the place of spirit and proceeds to conduct a word, issuing true words.[920]

"When you contemplate rungs—it is Thought, is *Binah*, is voice, is speech, all is one. This itself is Thought, beginning of all; there is no division—rather, all is one. And this cluster—genuine Thought—is linked with Nothingness, eternally inseparable. This is: *YHVH is one and His name One* (Zechariah 14:9).[921]

emanation begins to flow. *Tif'eret* proceeds to conduct *Shekhinah*, symbolized by west (see the end of the preceding note). Thus *Tif'eret*, symbolized by Naphtali, is linked above and below: above to the world of the male (*Binah*), below to the female (*Shekhinah*). The female image of *a hind let loose* alludes to *Tif'eret*'s mission to *Shekhinah*. The masculine verb נותן (*noten*), *delivers*—rather than the expected feminine form, נותנת (*notenet*), which would match the feminine noun אילה (*ayyalah*), *hind*—alludes to *Tif'eret*'s link with *Binah*, by whose masculine power He *delivers*.

On the phrase *imrei shafer*, see *Bereshit Rabbah* 98:17; *Midrash Tehillim* 81:4. The verse from Song of Songs reads: *Your lips are like a crimson ribbon, and your speaking is lovely*.

On voice and speech, see *Zohar* 1:36a, 145a–b; 2:3a, 25b; Moses de León, *Shushan Edut*, 335, 368–69; idem, *Sefer ha-Rimmon*, 96. On the hermeneutical rule of "generalization and specification," see *Sifra*, intro, 9, 2b–c. Cf. *Zohar* 1:16b, 47b; 2:161b; 3:264a; Moses de León, *Sefer ha-Rimmon*, 107–8; Vol. 1, p. 122, n. 105.

920. **Thought is beginning...** *Ḥokhmah* (Wisdom), also known as Thought, is the primordial point of emanation, totally concealed. This point expands into the circle of *Binah* (Understanding), which is more comprehensible, though still concealed. *Binah*, also known as "spirit," then expands and generates the voice of *Tif'eret*, who blends *Ḥesed* and *Gevurah*. The triad of *Gevurah*, *Ḥesed*, and *Tif'eret* is symbolized respectively by fire, water, and spirit—also by north, south, and east. The potent voice of *Tif'eret*, comprising all of the sefirotic powers, conducts the speech of *Shekhinah*.

On Divine Thought and the process of emanation, see *Bahir* 134 (194); *Zohar* 1:21a, 65a, 74a; 3:5b–6a. The phrase מלין תריצין (*millin teritsin*), "true words," derives from *Targum Onqelos*, Exodus 23:8; Deuteronomy 16:19.

921. **When you contemplate...** Through contemplation, one discovers that the apparently separate stages of divine emanation are in fact one.

אין (*Ayin*), "Nothingness," refers to the primal *sefirah* of *Keter*, to which *Ḥokhmah* is eternally linked. This paradoxical name alludes to *Keter*'s incomprehensibility and undifferentiation ("no-thingness"). See Matt, "*Ayin*: The Concept of Nothingness."

The full verse in Zechariah reads: *YHVH will be king over all the earth; on that day YHVH will be one and His name One*. Here, *YHVH* probably alludes to the totality of the *sefirot* (see above, note 869), and *His name* to *Shekhinah*. The unity of all these various aspects demonstrates that God's ultimate name is One.

See Moses de León, *Sheqel ha-Qodesh*, 93 (118).

"So, *who delivers beautiful words*—body. Consummation of body, as is written: *A fruitful son is Joseph, a fruitful son by a spring* (Genesis 49:22). Why twice, *a fruitful son*? Well, *a fruitful son* above, *a fruitful son* below. And why is he not *a fruitful son* below among the adornments of the *Matronita*? Because *daughters stride by a rampart* (ibid.)—for *daughters* are required for Her adornments, not sons.[922]

"Come and see: Holy Kingdom did not attain full kingship until She was joined with the patriarchs, and when She joined with them, She was formed into a complete structure by the upper world, [247a] which is world of the male.[923] Upper world is called 'seven years' because all seven years are within it. Your mnemonic is: *He built it seven years* (1 Kings 6:38)—upper world—and it is not written *in seven years*, as is said: *Six days YHVH made, heaven and earth* (Exodus 20:10).[924] Who is *six days*? Abraham, as is written: *These are the generations of heaven and earth* בהבראם (*be-hibbare'am*), *when they were created*— באברהם (*be-Avraham*), through Abraham. Abraham is called *six days*, and

922. ***who delivers beautiful words*—body...** This clause refers to *Tif'eret*, trunk of the sefirotic body, who conveys words to *Shekhinah*. *Yesod*, consummation of the body, is referred to by the phrase *fruitful son*. See above, notes 918–19.

The repetition of the phrase *fruitful son* alludes to *Yesod*'s role above in the divine realm and Joseph's role below on earth. (For other interpretations, see Galante; *KP*; *MM*; *MmD*.) As already explained (note 918), Joseph plays no part in the female adornment of *Shekhinah* because he symbolizes the male.

The full verse relating to Joseph reads: *A fruitful son is Joseph, a fruitful son by a spring; daughters stride by a rampart*. On *Shekhinah*'s title *Matronita*, see above, note 643.

923. **Holy Kingdom did not attain...** *Shekhinah*, known as *Malkhut* (Kingdom), did not attain full dominion until She was united with the sefirotic triad of *Ḥesed*, *Gevurah*, and *Tif'eret* (symbolized by the patriarchs). Thereby, She was completed by the world of the male (above, note 914).

See *Zohar* 1:79b, 99a, 125a; 2:31a.

924. **Upper world is called 'seven years'...** *Binah* is called by this name because She includes within Herself and generates all seven lower *sefirot* from *Ḥesed* through *Shekhinah*.

The plain meaning of the verse from Kings, describing Solomon's building of the Temple, is *He built it in seven years*. However, the Hebrew wording does not include the preposition ב (*be*), "in," and Rabbi Shim'on exploits this lack, suggesting that *Binah* was *built* or fashioned to be *seven years*, that is, to include *seven years*, namely the seven lower *sefirot*. (Rabbi Shim'on is also playing on בינה [*binah*], "understanding," and ויבנהו [*va-yivnehu*], *he built it*.) Similarly, the verse in Exodus, usually understood to mean *In six days YHVH made heaven and earth*, is now read hyperliterally: *Six days YHVH made*, that is, *Binah* (*YHVH*) emanated *six* cosmic *days*, thereby generating *Tif'eret* (*heaven*) and *Shekhinah* (*earth*).

On the verse in Kings, see *Zohar* 1:147b (*ST*); 2:9b, 31a; Moses de León, *Sefer ha-Rimmon*, 8; idem, *Sefer ha-Mishqal*, 72.

On the verse in Exodus, see Exodus 31:17; Ibn Ezra on Genesis 14:4; *Bahir* 55 (82); Naḥmanides on Exodus 20:10; *Zohar* 1:30a; 2:31a, 89b; 3:94b, 103b, 298b; Moses de León, *Sefer ha-Rimmon*, 134; Gikatilla, *Sha'arei Orah*, 81b.

through him—being *six days*—the world was constructed.[925] Similarly, *he built it seven years*, and these are called 'world of the male.' Correspondingly below, seven years—mystery of lower world, comprising seven days; this is the mystery of what is written: *seven days and seven days: fourteen days* (1 Kings 8:65). Now, since Scripture says *seven days and seven days*, don't we know that seven and seven equal fourteen? However, the point is to show that upper world and lower world are *seven days and seven days*—these male and these female. These female—this lower world rests upon them, as is written: *Many daughters have done valiantly, and you transcend them all* (Proverbs 31:29). *Many daughters* עשו חיל (*asu ḥayil*), *have done valiantly*—the twelve tribes, who *asu ḥayil*, generated forces, as is said: *All those counted for the camp of Judah*... (Numbers 2:9), and similarly all of them.[926]

"Now, you might say, 'רבות (*Rabbot*), *Many*? Look, there are only twelve and no more, aside from those forces that they generated! Why *rabbot*?' Well, as is said: *The outcry of Sodom and Gomorrah, how* רבה (*rabbah*)! (Genesis 18:20)—meaning *great*. Similarly, *rabbot, great*—supreme and grand above all. These are called 'great living beings,' and those forces that they generated, camped by them, are called *living beings, small with the great* (Psalms 104:25)—joining as

925. **Who is *six days*? Abraham...** Abraham symbolizes *Ḥesed*, which is the first cosmic day issuing from *Binah* and which includes potentially the other five cosmic days through *Yesod*. Thus through Abraham, the sefirotic realm was constructed.

The verse in Genesis reads: *These are the generations of heaven and earth* בהבראם (*be-hibbare'am*), *when they were created*. According to Rabbi Yehoshu'a son of Korḥah (*Bereshit Rabbah* 12:9), the word בהבראם (*be-hibbare'am*), *when they were created*, is an anagram of באברהם (*be-Avraham*), "through Abraham," indicating that *heaven and earth* were created for his sake.

See *Zohar* 1:3b, 86b, 91b, 93a, 105b, 128b, 154b, 230b; 2:31a, 79a, 220b; 3:117a. Cf. 1:46a.

926. **Correspondingly below, seven years...** Just as the upper world of *Binah* includes all seven lower *sefirot*, so the lower world of *Shekhinah* includes seven palaces housing angels, referred to as "seven years" or "seven days." The upper septet is male; the lower, female—with *Shekhinah* resting upon them.

The verse in Kings, describing the celebration of the festival of Sukkot, reads in full: *Solomon observed the Feast at that time, and all Israel with him—a great assemblage from Lebo-hamath to the Wadi of Egypt—before YHVH our God, seven days and seven days: fourteen days*. The apparently superfluous total—*fourteen days*—indicates the unification of the two septets. See *Zohar* 1:204b.

The verse in Proverbs alludes to *Shekhinah*, who rests above (*transcends*) all the *daughters*—namely twelve prominent angels, symbolized by the twelve tribes. These angels עשו חיל (*asu ḥayil*), *have done valiantly*—they "produced power," or "generated forces," strengthening *Shekhinah*. These numerous lower angelic powers correspond to the vast numbers of the tribal census in the wilderness, as recorded for example in the verse in Numbers: *All those counted for the camp of Judah, one hundred eighty-six thousand and four hundred, by their divisions. They will journey first*. See above, p. 471 and n. 787. On the twelve angels, see *Zohar* 149a–b (*ST*); above, p. 470 and n. 782.

one, so that the *Matronita* will be arrayed in them, so that above and below will rejoice, as is said: *Leviathan whom You formed to play with* (ibid., 26). Therefore, *Great daughters have generated forces, and you transcend them all,* as is said: *Standing upon twelve oxen: three facing north... with the sea set upon them above* (1 Kings 7:25)—corresponding to *and you transcend them all.*[927]

"So, *daughters* צעדה (*tsa'adah*), *stride, by a rampart* (Genesis 49:22). *Tsa'adah, she strides*—the verse should read צעדות (*tsa'adot*), *they stride.* However, that עין (*ayin*), eye, mentioned above. Who is that? Eye of Justice. He stands עלי עין (*alei ayin*), *over the eye* (ibid.), and that *eye* צעדה (*tsa'adah*), *strides,* and walks to obtain *daughters* for Her adornment; thus, for *daughters she strides*—not sons. *Daughters, she strides*—looking for Her adornments—not sons.[928]

"*Bitterly they shot at him* (Genesis 49:23)—gazing at Him in love, as is said:

927. **רבות (*Rabbot*), *Many*?...** How can the verse in Proverbs be referring to many angels (symbolized by the tribes), when there were only twelve angels (and tribes) —not including the vast numbers of secondary forces (and the census)? (See the preceding note.) Rabbi Shim'on answers by explaining that here the word רבות (*rabbot*) means not "many" but "great," as in the verse in Genesis, where the singular רבה (*rabbah*) means "great." There were twelve "great" angels, who generated many forces; both groups are alluded to in the verse from Psalms, which describes the sea of *Shekhinah*: *This sea, vast and broad of reach, gliding creatures there innumerable, living beings—small with the great.* On this verse, see above at notes 634–36.

Shekhinah is arrayed by all the angels joined together. Apparently, Rabbi Shim'on understands לויתן (*Livyatan*), "Leviathan," as an allusion to "joining," based on the root לוה (*lvh*), "to accompany, join." See Moses de León, *Sefer ha-Rimmon,* 204–5. As elsewhere in the *Zohar,* Leviathan may here symbolize *Yesod,* who by joining with *Shekhinah* generates joy. See *Zohar* 2:11b, 48b, 50b; 3:58a, 60a, all of which quote Psalms 104:26 as the proof-text; *MM.*

The *twelve oxen* symbolize the twelve angels (and the twelve tribes), *with the sea* of *Shekhinah set upon them above.* See above, note 912. The phrase דסמיכין עלייהו (*dismikhin alaihu*), "(camped) by them," derives from *Targum Onqelos,* Numbers 2:20, describing the arrangement of the tribes camped around the Tent of Meeting.

928. **the verse should read צעדות (*tsa'adot*), *they stride*...** The singular form of the verb—צעדה (*tsa'adah*), *she strides*—does not match the plural subject, *daughters.* Rabbi Shim'on explains, however, that the subject is not *daughters,* but rather the עין (*ayin*) mentioned immediately before—which should be understood as *an eye,* not *a spring.* The full verse reads: *A fruitful son is Joseph, a fruitful son* עלי עין (*alei ayin*), *over an eye* [according to the plain sense: *by a spring*]; *daughters stride by a rampart.* According to Rabbi Shim'on, this means that *Yesod* (symbolized by *Joseph, a fruitful son*) stands *over an eye*—over *Shekhinah,* who is known as Eye of Justice, namely the providential eye of *Tif'eret* (called Justice). And that *eye* (*Shekhinah*) *strides* to obtain *daughters* (angels or the tribes) for Her adornment. Rabbi Shim'on may also be playing with the final word of the verse—שור (*shur*), *a rampart*—and the verb שור (*shur*), "to look at, gaze on."

On the female, rather than male, adornments of *Shekhinah,* see above, pp. 509, 512 and nn. 918, 922. The name עין משפט (*ein mishpat*), "spring of judgment" (understood here as "eye of justice") derives from Genesis 14:7.

Turn your eyes away from me, for they overwhelm me! (Song of Songs 6:5). So, *the archers harassed him* (Genesis, ibid.).[929]

"*Yet firm remained his bow, agile were his forearms*... (ibid., 24). *Yet firm remained* this bow. What is *his bow*? His mate. *Firm*—She clothed Herself in strength because of him, Her power unabated, for She knew that Joseph would not stray from that rung of his covenantal sign to the right or to the left.[930]

"ויפזו (*Va-yaphozzu*), *Agile were*. What is *va-yaphozzu*? As is said: *more desirable than gold, than much* פז (*paz*), *pure gold* (Psalms 19:11), and similarly: *nor can she be exchanged for objects of* פז (*phaz*), *pure gold* (Job 28:17). His arms were bejeweled with supernal pearl.[931]

"*By the hands of the Champion of Jacob* (Genesis, ibid.)—by those two sides empowering Jacob.[932]

929. ***Bitterly they shot at him...*** The full verse reads: *Bitterly they shot at him, the archers harassed him.* Rabbi Shim'on interprets this to mean that out of bittersweet yearning the *daughters* (angels or tribes) adorning *Shekhinah* shot arrows of love at *Yesod* (symbolized by Joseph), stimulating His love for Her. *Yesod* begged *Shekhinah* not to arouse Him: *Turn your eyes away from me!*

See *Zohar* 3:84a.

930. ***Yet firm remained his bow...*** *Shekhinah*, the partner of Joseph (symbolizing *Yesod*), is pictured as a bow—and also a rainbow, spanning the colors of the various *sefirot*. She remained firm and powerful because Joseph proved his virtue by resisting the sexual advances of Potiphar's wife, thereby attaining the rung of *Yesod*, site of the covenantal sign of circumcision.

On the concept of strengthening and weakening God, see *Sifrei*, Deuteronomy 319; *Vayiqra Rabbah* 23:12; *Eikhah Rabbah* 1:33; *Pesiqta de-Rav Kahana* 25:1; *Zohar* 2:32b, 65b; above at note 579.

The full verse reads: *Yet firm remained his bow, agile were his forearms—by the hands of the Champion of Jacob, from there the Shepherd, Stone of Israel.* Elsewhere, the clause *yet firm remained his bow* is applied to the attempted seduction of Joseph. See *Bereshit Rabbah* 87:7, which glosses in the name of Rabbi Shemu'el, "The bow was stretched [i.e., Joseph's phallus became erect] and then returned [to its prior, flaccid state]," reading ותשב (*va-teshev*), *remained*, as *va-tashov*, "returned (from being firm)."

See JT *Horayot* 2:4, 46d; *Bereshit Rabbah* 98:20; BT *Sotah* 36b; *Targum Yerushalmi*, Genesis 49:24; *Zohar* 1:71b; 3:66b. In the *Zohar*, "bow" can symbolize both *Yesod* and *Shekhinah*. See *Zohar* 1:18a–b, 71b, 72b; 2:66b; 3:215a–b; Wolfson, *Through a Speculum That Shines*, index, s.v. "rainbow." On Joseph's attaining the rug of *Yesod*, see above, p. 92, n. 50.

931. **ויפזו (*Va-yaphozzu*), *Agile were*...** The verse reads: *Yet firm remained his bow, agile were his forearms.* Playing on ויפזו (*va-yaphozzu*), *agile were*, and פז (*paz*), *pure gold*, Rabbi Shim'on indicates that because of Joseph's virtuous conduct, his arms were bejeweled.

See Genesis 41:42; *Targum Onqelos*, Rashi, *Leqaḥ Tov*, *Sekhel Tov*, *Midrash Aggadah*, and *Midrash ha-Gadol*, Genesis 49:24; *Zohar* 1:71b. The full verse in Psalms, traditionally understood as describing words of Torah, reads: *More desirable than gold, than much pure gold; sweeter than honey and drippings of the comb.* The full verse in Job, singing the praise of wisdom, reads: *Gold and glass cannot equal her, nor can she be exchanged for objects of pure gold.*

932. ***By the hands...*** By the two divine arms, *Ḥesed* on the right and *Gevurah* on the

"*From there feeds Stone of Israel* (ibid.)—from there that precious stone we have mentioned is nourished. From those two sides, that precious stone is sustained—namely, north and south—and She is placed between them to be blessed by them, nourished by them, on the rung of Righteous One.[933]

"Come and see! An additional blessing was bestowed upon Joseph, as is written: *From the God of your father, and may He help you; Shaddai, and may He bless you*... (ibid., 25).[934] This verse is problematical. *From the God of your father,* ויעזרך (*ve-ya'zereka*), *and may He help you*—it should read: *The God of your father* יעזרך (*ya'zereka*), *will help you.* ואת שדי (*Ve-et Shaddai*), *Shaddai*—it should read: ואל שדי (*Ve-El Shaddai*), *El Shaddai,* as is written: (*Ve-El Shaddai*), *May El Shaddai, grant you mercy* (ibid. 43:14). *And may He bless you*—the verse should read *will bless you.*[935]

"However, he bequeathed to him above and below. Above, *from the God of your father*—a supernal heritage, a place called *heaven. And may He help you*—not exchanging this place for another, so that His help would come from this place and from no other.[936]

"ואת שדי (*Ve-et Shaddai*), *Shaddai*. What is *ve-et Shaddai*? Well, that is another, lower rung; for we have learned: Everywhere, את יהוה (*et YHVH*) implies *Shekhinah*, as is said: *I saw* את יהוה (*et YHVH*) (Isaiah 6:1)—*et,* amplifying; *ve-et,* merging day with night and night with day, as is said: *ve-et Shaddai,* for from there issue blessings.[937]

left, which empower Jacob and his *sefirah, Tif'eret*.

933. **From there feeds Stone of Israel...** The verse reads: *From there* רועה (*ro'eh*), *the Shepherd, Stone of Israel.* But Rabbi Shim'on interprets *ro'eh* as a verb meaning "feeds, grazes," and takes the verse to mean that *Shekhinah* (*Stone of Israel*) *feeds* from Joseph's *sefirah, Yesod*. This nourishment is conveyed by the two arms: *Ḥesed* and *Gevurah,* symbolized respectively by south and north. These arms embrace *Shekhinah* as She unites with *Yesod*.

See above, note 918.

934. **additional blessing... Joseph...** The name יוסף (*Yosef*), Joseph, derives from the root יסף (*ysf*), "to add." See Genesis 30:24.

The full verse reads: *From the God of your father, and may He help you; Shaddai, and may He bless you—blessings of heaven above, blessings of the deep crouching below, blessings of breasts and womb.*

935. **This verse is problematical...** Why doesn't the verse read simply *The God of your father will help you, and El Shaddai will bless you*?

936. **However, he bequeathed...** The wording *from the God of your father* identifies the source of the blessing that Jacob bequeathed to Joseph, namely Jacob's *sefirah, Tif'eret,* symbolized by *heaven*. (See the full verse, above, note 934.)

The apparently superfluous ו (*vav*), denoting *and* at the beginning of the following clause—ויעזרך (*ve-ya'zereka*) *and may He help you*—is actually vital because it symbolizes *Tif'eret*. (Its numerical value of six alludes to *Tif'eret* together with the five *sefirot* surrounding Him: *Ḥesed* through *Yesod*.) In uttering the *vav*, Jacob was praying that God's help to Joseph would issue from this central *sefirah* and no other.

For various interpretations of "not exchanging this place for another," see *OY*; Galante; *KP*; *MM*; *MmD*.

937. **ואת שדי (*Ve-et Shaddai*)...** The

"Further, why does it not say *ve-El Shaddai,* seeing that this also implies what we have said, as is written: (*Ve-El Shaddai*), *May El Shaddai, grant you mercy* (Genesis 43:14)? Since all is one place, why abandon ל (*lamed*) and inscribe ת (*tav*)?[938]

"Well, it is a mystery! When those paths emerge from above, [247b] heaven inherits totality of Torah, as is written: את השמים (*et ha-shamayim*), *heaven* (ibid. 1:1)—totality of twenty-two letters. From here, they flow forth to Oral Torah, who is called *earth,* as we say: ואת הארץ (*ve-et ha-arets*), *and earth* (ibid.)—totality of twenty-two letters. *Heaven* contains all as one; then moon is crowned in all, dwelling in fullness, blessings flowing from there. So, ואת שדי (*ve-et Shaddai*).[939]

word את (*et*) is technically an accusative particle with no clear independent sense. Already in rabbinic times, Naḥum of Gimzo and his disciple Rabbi Akiva taught that the presence of *et* in a biblical verse amplifies the apparent meaning. Here, as often in the *Zohar,* את (*et*) becomes a name of *Shekhinah,* who comprises the totality of divine speech, the entire alphabet from א (*alef*) to ת (*tav*). Thus the phrase ואת שדי (*ve-et Shaddai*) encompasses *Yesod* (known by the divine name *Shaddai*) together with "another, lower rung," namely *Shekhinah.* Similarly, the expression את יהוה (*et YHVH*) encompasses *Shekhinah* (*et*) and *Tif'eret* (known as *YHVH*).

The word את (*et*) by itself amplifies meaning, but so can the conjunction ו (*ve*), "and" (according to Rabbi Akiva; see BT *Yevamot* 68b, *Sanhedrin* 51b). So, ואת שדי (*ve-et Shaddai*) now implies three *sefirot*: *Yesod* (*Shaddai*), *Shekhinah* (*et*), and *Tif'eret* (symbolized by the letter *vav*; see the preceding note). Day and night symbolize respectively *Tif'eret* and *Shekhinah,* from whose union (through *Yesod*) blessings flow to the worlds below.

On את (*et*), see BT *Pesaḥim* 22b, *Ḥagigah* 12a; *Zohar* 1:29b, 112a–b; 2:90a, 135b; above, note 663; and the Christian parallel in Revelation 1:8: "I am *alpha* and *omega.*" On the verse in Isaiah, see *Zohar* 1:18a, 60a, 237a; 2:81b. The Masoretic text reads: *I saw* את אדני (*et Adonai*), *my Lord.* Cf. above, note 760.

938. **why does it not say *ve-El Shaddai*...** This expression, like *ve-et Shaddai,* implies the union of *Tif'eret* (symbolized by *vav*), *Shekhinah* (known by the divine name *El*), and *Yesod* (*Shaddai*). Why should אל (*El*), "God"—ending in ל (*lamed*)—be replaced by את (*et*), ending in ת (*tav*)? (Rabbi Shim'on's preference for *El* over *et* may stem from the fact that *El Shaddai* is a divine name.)

The word רחמים (*raḥamim*), "mercy (or compassion)" in Genesis 43:14 may be understood as referring to *Tif'eret,* who is known as *Raḥamim.*

939. **When those paths emerge...** The stream of divine emanation is pictured as the totality of speech: the entire alphabet from א (*alef*) to ת (*tav*), summarized in the word את (*et*). This continuum flows to *Tif'eret* (known as *heaven* and Written Torah), proceeding from Him on to *Shekhinah* (known as *earth,* moon, and Oral Torah). The opening verse of the Torah alludes to this process: *In the beginning God created* את השמים (*et ha-shamayim*), *heaven,* ואת הארץ (*ve-et ha-arets*), *and earth.* The final phrase—ואת הארץ (*ve-et ha-arets*), *and earth*—can be understood to mean "From ו (*vav*), symbolizing *Tif'eret,* the entirety of א (*alef*) to ת (*tav*) flows to *earth* (*Shekhinah*)."

This explains why Jacob said ואת שדי (*ve-et Shaddai*) instead of ואל שדי (*Ve-El Shaddai*)—in order to emphasize the whole stream of divine speech.

On this reading of the opening verse in Genesis, see *Zohar* 1:29b, 30b; 2:234b.

"ויברכך (*Viyvarekheka*), *And may He bless you*—so that he would have extra vitality; for wherever an additional ו (*vav*) appears, vitality appears.[940]

"Until here, in general; following, he offered details, as is written: *blessings of heaven*... (Genesis 49:25).[941]

"*The blessings of your father surpass* (ibid., 26)—*surpass*, surely! For Jacob inherited the finest of all—more than the other patriarchs—being totally complete.[942] And he gave all to Joseph. Why? Because this is fitting; for Righteous One absorbs all as one, all blessings abiding in Him. He pours blessings from the head above, and all members of the body enjoy pouring blessings into Him, and then He becomes a river issuing from Eden.[943]

"What is מעדן (*me-eden*), from Eden? Well, when all members dwell in a single bond—in עדונא (*idduna*), delight, of desire—from the head above to below, and out of their delight and desire they all pour into Him, He becomes a river issuing from עדן (*eden*), Delight, literally![944]

"Further, from supernal *Ḥokhmah* flows all—emanating, forming a river, flowing until it reaches this rung, when all bathe in blessings and all is one.[945]

"*As great as* תאות גבעות עולם (*ta'avat giv'ot olam*), *the bounty of eternal hills* (ibid.)—desire of those *giv'ot olam, hills of the world*. Who are they? Two

940. **ויברכך (*Vi-varekheka*), *And*...** The apparently superfluous ו (*vav*), here denoting *and*, lends extra vitality to the blessings, implying the life force of *Tif'eret* (symbolized by *vav*). See above, notes 936–37.

941. **Until here, in general...** Jacob's blessing to Joseph continues in greater detail. The full verse reads: *From the God of your father, and may He help you; Shaddai, and may He bless you—blessings of heaven above, blessings of the deep crouching below, blessings of breasts and womb.*

942. ***The blessings of your father surpass*...** The verse reads: *The blessings of your father surpass the blessings of my ancestors.* Jacob was more "complete" than Abraham and Isaac in several senses. All of his sons maintained perfect faith, unlike Abraham (who engendered Ishmael) and Isaac (who engendered Esau). Further, Jacob symbolizes *Tif'eret,* who harmonizes and completes the polar opposites *Ḥesed* and *Gevurah,* symbolized respectively by Abraham and Isaac.

See above, notes 157–58, 575, 605; Naḥmanides on Genesis 49:24.

943. **all to Joseph...** It is fitting for Joseph to receive all these blessings because he symbolizes *Yesod* (known as Righteous One), who draws emanation from the topmost *sefirot* and into whom each sefirotic limb pours its measure of the blessed flow.

The image of "a river issuing from Eden" derives from Genesis 2:10: *A river issues from Eden to water the garden, and from there it divides and becomes four riverheads.* On the title Righteous One, see above, p. 92, n. 50.

944. **מעדן (*me-eden*), from Eden...** The word *eden* means "delight" and here alludes to the delight of the sefirotic limbs channeling their energy into *Yesod*.

945. **from supernal *Ḥokhmah*...** "Eden" refers to *Ḥokhmah* (Wisdom), primal source of the flow to *Yesod*.

See *Zohar* 2:90a, 123b; 3:290a–b (*IZ*). According to the second-century Greek physician Galen, sperm originates in the brain; this theory was common in medieval literature.

females, one above and one below, each of whom is called *world.* Desire of all members of the body is for those two mothers—desire to suckle from higher Mother, desire to join lower Mother, and desire of all is one. So, all of them *will rest on the head of Joseph* (ibid.)—so that the rung of Righteous One may be blessed, absorbing all fittingly.[946]

"Happy are those who are called righteous! For only one who preserves this rung—this holy sign, sign of covenant—is called righteous. Happy are they in this world and in the world that is coming!"[947]

They emerged from the cave. Rabbi Shim'on said, "Let each one say a word, and we will proceed on the way."[948]

Rabbi El'azar opened with the following verse: "*Benjamin, a ravening wolf, in the morning consuming prey, at evening dividing the spoil* (Genesis 49:27). Why *a wolf*? Because so he is engraved upon the Throne. For all living beings, great and small, are engraved there, as is written: *living beings, small with the great* (Psalms 104:25). And the throne constructed by Solomon was engraved so, corresponding to the supernal pattern.[949]

"Further, זאב יטרף (*ze'ev yitraf*), *a ravening wolf*—for the altar was in his

946. **תאות גבעות עולם (*ta'avat giv'ot olam*)...** In the verse, this difficult phrase may mean *the bounty* [literally, "desire," that which is desired] *of eternal hills.* Here, Rabbi Shim'on follows the literal meaning.

In biblical Hebrew the word עולם (*olam*) means "eternity," but here Rabbi Shim'on adopts its later meaning, "world." The two *hills of the world* are the two females, *Binah* and *Shekhinah,* each one a divine world. The *desire* of all the sefirotic limbs is to suckle from *Binah* (higher Mother) and join with *Shekhinah* (lower Mother). All the limbs convey their flowing desire to *Yesod* the Righteous One (symbolized by Joseph), who links both *hills of the world.*

The full verse reads: *The blessings of your father surpass the blessings of my ancestors, as great as the bounty of eternal hills. May they rest on the head of Joseph, on the brow of the prince among his brothers.*

See *Zohar* 1:50a; 2:22a; 3:203b. On *hills* as mothers, see also *Mekhilta, Amaleq* 1; *Sifrei,* Deuteronomy 353; *Vayiqra Rabbah* 36:6; *Targum Yerushalmi* (frag.), Genesis 49:26; JT *Sanhedrin* 10:1, 27d; BT *Rosh Hashanah* 11a; *Midrash ha-Gadol,* Genesis 49:26; *Zohar* 2:112a–b.

947. **one who preserves this rung...** By avoiding sexual sin, one preserves the sign of the covenant and attains the level of *Yesod,* Righteous One.

See *Zohar* 1:59b; 2:23a.

948. **emerged from the cave...** In which they had been sharing words of Torah. See above at notes 884, 891.

949. **engraved upon the Throne...** The divine Throne, engraved with images of animals, served as the model for Solomon's throne.

See above, note 844; Moses de León, *Sefer ha-Rimmon,* 308. Cf. Ezekiel's depiction (1:10) of the four *ḥayyot* (living beings) carrying the Throne, each of whom had the faces of a human, a lion, an ox, and an eagle.

The full verse in Psalms reads: *This sea, vast and broad of reach, gliding creatures there innumerable, living beings—small with the great.* See above at notes 634–36.

portion, and the altar is a wolf. For if you say that Benjamin is a wolf, not so! Rather, the altar in his portion was a wolf, consuming flesh every day; and Benjamin would feed it since it was in his portion. It was as if he were sustaining and feeding this wolf![950]

"Further, *ze'ev yitraf*—*a wolf will feed.* Whom? These masters of enmity who stand poised above to accuse, all of whom are appeased by the offering and stimulate arousal above.[951]

"*In the morning consuming* עד (*ad*), *prey.* What does this mean? In the morning, as Abraham rouses in the world and a time of favor appears, an offering generates arousal and pleasure, ascending to *ad*—that place of which is written *You will return ad, to, YHVH your God* (Deuteronomy 30:2).[952]

"Further, *in the morning.* Who is *morning*? Abraham, as we have said, for it is written: *Abraham rose early in the morning* (Genesis 22:3)—when favor prevails.[953] At that time, no one else would consume the offering. Who would consume? That place called *ad*, as is said: לעדי עד (*la-adei ad*), forever and ever, and it is a supernal throne, being *la-adei ad,* forever and ever. The time of

950. **altar was in his portion...** According to a rabbinic tradition, the Temple in Jerusalem straddled the territories of Judah and Benjamin, with the altar (or part of the altar) in Benjamin's terrain. The altar is pictured as a wolf, devouring the daily sacrificial offerings. Here, Rabbi El'azar reads the verse: *Benjamin* זאב יטרף (*ze'ev yitraf*), *will feed the wolf*—that is, by providing the altar with sacrifices, or providing a place for the altar to consume sacrifices.

See *Sifrei,* Deuteronomy 352; *Targum Onqelos* and *Targum Yerushalmi,* Genesis 49:27; *Bereshit Rabbah* 97 (p. 1225); 99:1, 3; BT *Yoma* 12a, *Zevaḥim* 53b–54b; *Midrash Aggadah,* Genesis 49:27; above, p. 242 and n. 377. On the altar as "wolf," see also *Tosefta, Sukkah* 4:28 and parallels; *Avot de-Rabbi Natan* A, 1.

951. ***ze'ev yitraf—a wolf will feed...*** Rather than its simple sense as *a ravening wolf,* the phrase now yields a new meaning: the altar will feed the harsh powers of judgment who threaten and accuse the world. Once appeased by their share of the offering, these powers actually promote harmony and union.

On the demonic share of the sacrifices, see above, p. 161, n. 481.

952. ***In the morning consuming* עד (*ad*)...** Morning is a time of *Ḥesed,* symbolized by Abraham. The daily morning sacrifice stimulates the divine powers and ascends. Whereas the plain meaning of עד (*ad*) in this verse is "prey, booty" or "enemy," Rabbi El'azar connects it with the homonym עד (*ad*), "until, to, as far as," or to another homonym meaning "eternity." The sacrifice consumed on the altar ascends to the place called *ad,* which here apparently implies *Tif'eret,* known as *YHVH*. The verse now means: *In the morning* עד (*ad*) *will consume.*

On Abraham and morning, see above, p. 112 and n. 180, p. 152 and n. 430. On morning as a time of favor, see *Mekhilta, Beshallaḥ* 5. On *ad,* see *Zohar* 1:50a, 150a, 161b–162a; 2:22a; above, note 369. For various interpretations of *ad,* see *OY*; *KP*; *Adderet Eliyyahu*; *MM*; *MmD*.

953. **Who is *morning*? Abraham...** Alluding to *Ḥesed*. See the preceding note.

The verse in Genesis describes Abraham's eagerness to fulfill the divine command to sacrifice Isaac.

consuming is in the morning, and this *ad* is above, as is written: *Trust in YHVH* עדי עד (*adei ad*), *forever and ever* (Isaiah 26:4). *In the morning*—corresponding to *offering to YHVH* (Leviticus 1:2), precisely! *Ad will consume*—and no one else.[954]

"Smoke ascends and arousal of love is bound, aroused above, and one stands facing the other. [248a] A lamp kindles and glows through this arousal below. The priest arouses and Levites praise, manifesting joy; then wine is poured in libation, intermingling with water, and wine shines, manifesting joy. Therefore, good wine below, manifesting joy toward other wine. All arouses so that left will be linked with right.[955]

"Bread, namely semolina—*Malkhut*, stimulating arousal; grasped by left and right, joined to the body. Then supernal oil flows, which She gathers in through Righteous One. So, arousal of semolina must be performed with oil, and all will join as one. Then, delight and pleasure of single union—all those crowns gathering delight and pleasure, linking with one another; moon is illumined, joining with sun, all dwelling in single delight.[956]

954. **Who would consume? That place called *ad*...** *Tif'eret* (known as *ad* and *YHVH*) consumes the morning sacrifice, while He Himself serves as a throne for *Binah*. The sacrifice must be offered to *Tif'eret* (*YHVH*), who balances right and left, not to any other power.

The phrase עדי עד (*adei ad*), *forever and ever*, is apparently taken as referring to *Tif'eret* and the *sefirot* surrounding Him extending up to, but not including, *Binah*. See *Zohar* 1:22a.

The expression לעדי עד (*la-adei ad*), "forever and ever," does not appear in the Bible but rather in Heikhalot literature. See Schäfer, *Synopse zur Hekhalot-Literatur*, §§266, 977.

The verse in Leviticus reads: *When a person among you brings an offering to YHVH, of animals from herd and from flock you shall bring your offering.* On the offering being directed exclusively *to YHVH*, see *Sifrei*, Numbers 143; BT *Menaḥot* 110a; Naḥmanides on Leviticus 1:9; *Zohar* 2:108a; 3:5a; *ZḤ* 3d (*MhN*), 18c (*MhN*), 19c (*MhN*); Moses de León, *Sefer ha-Rimmon*, 287.

I have followed mostly the reading of M7, N23, P2, R1, V5. For other interpretations, see *OY*; Galante; *Adderet Eliyyahu*; *MM*; *MmD*.

955. **Smoke ascends...** The entire Temple ritual stimulates the union of the divine couple above. The lamp of *Shekhinah* is kindled. The priest and the Levites symbolize respectively the right and left arms, *Ḥesed* and *Gevurah*, which are also symbolized by water and wine. Wine is offered as a libation on the altar in the Temple ("below") in order to bring about a mingling of *Gevurah* and *Ḥesed* above, thereby assuaging the harshness of the left.

On the ascending smoke of the sacrifice, see above, pp. 492–93 and n. 863.

956. **Bread, namely semolina...** According to Numbers 15:4, the grain offering of סלת (*solet*), "choice flour, semolina," must be mixed with oil. Here, *solet* symbolizes *Shekhinah*, and the offering stimulates the powers above. The left and right arms (*Gevurah* and *Ḥesed*) embrace *Shekhinah*, joining Her to *Tif'eret* (trunk of the body), and a rich flow (stimulated by the oil of the offering) reaches Her through *Yesod*, known as Righteous One. Thereby all the *sefirot* from *Ḥesed*

"Then, *offering to YHVH*—and to no one else. So, *in the morning, ad will consume*—and no one else; *ad* will consume and delight in His bond first. When? *In the morning*, for the holy Name should be blessed first, and then others will be blessed. Therefore, one is forbidden to greet his fellow in the morning before blessing the blessed Holy One; for He must be blessed first, and then others may be blessed. Thus, *in the morning, ad will consume.*[957]

"*At evening dividing the spoil*—for the offering in the evening is brought entirely to the blessed Holy One, arousal ascending there. Once He has been blessed, He links up with all other supernal powers and distributes blessings to them, each one fittingly, and worlds are sweetened, above and below blessed. This corresponds to the mystery that is written: *I have eaten my honeycomb with my honey...*, first; then dispersing to all of them and saying, *Eat, O friends! Drink and be drunk, O lovers!* (Song of Songs 5:1)—pouring out blessings to all, distributing to each one fittingly. So, *at evening dividing the spoil*—for the holy Name is blessed first, and now He disperses blessings to all worlds. For you should not think that an offering is brought to them or to any other power; rather, all is offered to the blessed Holy One, and He pours out blessings, distributing them to all worlds. Therefore, *offering to YHVH*—and to no one else."[958]

Rabbi Shim'on said, "Well spoken! Further, a single arousal of offering, to draw blessings and stimulate arousal so that all worlds will be blessed. First, *offering to YHVH*—and to no one else. Now, *you shall bring your offering* (Leviticus 1:2)—so that all worlds will be linked as one and above and below be blessed."[959]

through *Yesod* ("crowns") link with one another and with *Shekhinah* (moon), as She unites with *Tif'eret* (sun).

See *Zohar* 3:247a–b. On *Shekhinah* as bread, see above, note 911. On *Yesod* as Righteous One, see above, p. 92, n. 50.

957. ***offering to YHVH*—and to no one else...** The sacrifice must be directed to *Tif'eret* (known as *YHVH* and *ad*), not to any other power. He will consume first; then the flow of blessing will be conveyed to *Shekhinah* and through Her to the worlds below. See above, note 954.

See BT *Berakhot* 14a: "Rav said, 'Whoever greets his fellow before praying has, as it were, made him into a cult site....' Shemu'el said, 'Why have you esteemed this person and not God?'"

See above, p. 272 and n. 79, p. 372 and n. 369.

958. ***At evening dividing the spoil...*** Just as the daily morning offering must be directed to *Tif'eret* (*YHVH*), so too with the evening offering. Once He receives it, He conveys blessing to all powers and worlds through *Shekhinah*.

The verse in Song of Songs reads: *I have eaten my honeycomb with my honey, I have drunk my wine with my milk. Eat, O friends! Drink and be drunk, O lovers!* See above, p. 461 and n. 746.

959. **single arousal...** Which includes two stages. First, the offering is directed *to YHVH*; consequently, a flow of blessing descends, making this *your offering*.

See above, p. 460 and n. 744. The verse in

Rabbi Abba opened with the following verse, saying, "*All these are the tribes of Israel, twelve, and this is what their father spoke to them, blessing them; each according to his blessing, he blessed them* (Genesis 49:28). *All these are the tribes of Israel*—the verse should read *These are the tribes of Israel*; why *all these*? To seal their blessing in a place from which all blessings pour forth.[960]

"*Twelve*, surely! Links of adornments of the *Matronita*, to which She is joined, as is written: *twelve and this*.[961]

"*What their father spoke to them*—for in this place dwells speech.[962]

"Further, אשר דבר (*asher dibber*), *what* [*their father*] *spoke*—here a single link, joining from below and from above. From below, with these twelve—*and this:* joining with them. *Asher dibber, what spoke*—linking with two sides: from below and from above.[963] Finally, he linked them to a place above: male and female, as is written: איש אשר כברכתו (*ish asher ke-virkhato*), *a man according to his blessing.* What is *ke-virkhato, according to his blessing*? His mate."[964]

He opened, saying, "*May YHVH bless you from Zion, and may you gaze upon the goodness of Jerusalem* (Psalms 128:5). *May YHVH bless you from Zion*—for from Him issue blessings to water the garden; He contains all blessings and conveys

Leviticus reads: *When a person among you brings an offering to YHVH, of animals from herd and from flock you shall bring your offering.*

960. **why *all these*?...** The word *all* seems superfluous. However, it alludes to *Yesod*, who channels the entire flow of emanation and is thus known as כל (*kol*), *all.* Jacob sought to seal his sons' blessings in this *sefirah*, guaranteeing their fulfillment.

The rabbinic idiom "to seal a blessing" means to conclude a blessing with a summary statement.

961. **Links of adornments... *twelve and this*** The twelve tribes adorn *Shekhinah*. Her connection with them is indicated by the phrase *twelve and this*, which Rabbi Abba temporarily isolates from its context: *All these are the tribes of Israel, twelve, and this is what their father spoke to them.* The word *this* alludes to *Shekhinah*, the Divine Presence who is always right here.

See above, p. 471 and n. 785. On the tribes as the adornment of *Shekhinah*, see above, p. 470 and n. 781. On Her title *Matronita*, see above, note 643.

962. ***spoke to them*... speech** Alluding to *Shekhinah*, who conveys the divine word and is known as Speech.

963. **אשר דבר (*asher dibber*), *what* [*their father*] *spoke*...** *Shekhinah*, the realm of divine speech, is joined from below by the twelve tribes adorning Her, and from above by *Yesod*, who is known as Asher. The relative pronoun אשר (*asher*), "what, that, which," is identified here with its homonym: the tribe אשר (*Asher*), "Asher."

On Asher as *Yesod*, see above, note 611.

964. **he linked them to a place above...** Jacob linked the tribes to the site of the union of the divine couple, indicated by the phrase איש אשר כברכתו (*ish asher ke-virkhato*), *each* [literally: *a man*] *according to his blessing. Ish, a man*, refers to *Tif'eret*; the relative pronoun *asher* indicates *Yesod*, who links *Tif'eret* with *his blessing*—namely His mate, *Shekhinah*.

On mate as "blessing," see BT *Yevamot* 62b: "Rabbi Tanḥum said in the name of Rabbi Ḥanilai, 'Any man without a wife is without joy, without blessing, without goodness.'"

to Her. Then, *may you gaze upon the goodness of Jerusalem*—showing that all blessings derive from male and female. Similarly, *May YHVH bless you and protect you* (Numbers 6:24)—*May YHVH bless you*, from the male; *and protect you*—from the female. *May YHVH bless you*—from זכור (*zakhor*), *remember*. וישמרך (*Ve-yishmerekha*), *And protect you*—from שמור (*shamor*), *observe*. All is one entity, for from both of them issue blessings to the world. So, [248b] אשר כברכתו (*asher ke-virkhato*), *according to his blessing, he blessed them*."[965]

Rabbi Yehudah opened, "*Jacob finished instructing his sons, and he gathered his feet into the bed, and he expired, and was gathered to his people* (Genesis 49:33). *Instructing his sons*—the verse should read *blessing*. However, he instructed them regarding *Shekhinah*, to be linked with Her.[966] Furthermore, he instructed them

965. ***May YHVH bless you...*** *Zion* alludes to *Yesod*, who pours blessing into *Shekhinah*, the garden. She is also known as *Jerusalem*, while He is *goodness*; so the expression *goodness of Jerusalem* refers to the union of male and female.

See *Tanḥuma, Naso* 10: "*May YHVH bless you*—with sons. *And protect you*—with daughters, since daughters require protection." Apparently, Rabbi Abba draws on this midrash while transforming its meaning, changing "with sons" to "from the male (*Tif'eret-Yesod*)," and "with daughters" to "from the female (*Shekhinah*)." *Tif'eret* is also known as *YHVH*.

Then, Rabbi Abba proceeds to associate male and female respectively with the verbs זכר (*zakhar*), "to remember," and שמר (*shamar*), "to observe, protect." He alludes to the appearance of the infinitive form of these verbs in the two versions of the Ten Commandments. The first version reads: זכור (*Zakhor*), *Remember, the Sabbath day to keep it holy* (Exodus 20:8). The second version reads: שמור (*Shamor*), *Observe, the Sabbath day to keep it holy* (Deuteronomy 5:12). According to Kabbalah, *zakhor, remember*, suggests the adjective זכר (*zakhar*), "male," signifying the male divine potencies, whereas the alternative formulation, *shamor, observe*, signifies the female, *Shekhinah*. Further, *zakhor* implies the positive commandments of Torah (since time-bound positive commandments are generally incumbent only on men), while *shamor* implies the negative commandments (incumbent on women as well).

See *Mekhilta, Baḥodesh* 7; BT *Berakhot* 20b; *Bahir* 124 (182); Ezra of Gerona, *Peirush Shir ha-Shirim*, 496–97; Naḥmanides on Exodus 20:8; Jacob ben Sheshet, *Sefer ha-Emunah ve-ha-Bittaḥon*, 420; *Zohar* 1:5b, 47b, 48b, 164b, 199b; 2:92b, 138a; 3:81b, 224a; Moses de León, *Sefer ha-Rimmon*, 118; idem, *Sefer ha-Mishqal*, 110; Wolfson, introduction to *Sefer ha-Rimmon*, 63–71.

966. ***Instructing his sons*—the verse should read *blessing*...** The immediately preceding verses (49:29–32) contain Jacob's "instruction" to his sons concerning his burial. However, *blessing* more accurately describes Jacob's message in the bulk of the chapter (49:3–27). Rabbi Yehudah explains the use of the word לצוות (*le-tsavvot*), "commanding, instructing," as referring to Jacob's command to his sons that they link themselves with *Shekhinah*.

Rabbi Yehudah may be alluding to the word את (*et*)—in the phrase לצוות את (*le-tsavvot et*), *instructing*—as a name of *Shekhinah*. See above, note 937. He may also be playing on לצוות (*le-tsavvot*), *instructing*, and the verb צות (*tsavat*), "to join, group together."

concerning the cave—which is near the Garden of Eden and where Adam is buried.[967]

"Come and see: The town is called Kiriath-arba, City of Four. Why? Because four couples were buried there: Adam and Eve, Abraham and Sarah, Isaac and Rebekah, Jacob and Leah.[968] Look, there is a difficulty here! For we have learned that the patriarchs are the holy chariot, yet a chariot consists of no less than four. And we have learned that the blessed Holy One joined King David with them and they became a complete chariot, as is written: *The stone that the builders rejected has become the cornerstone* (Psalms 118:22)—King David was conjoined to constitute the chariot along with them. If so, David should have been buried among the patriarchs, so that together with him it would be City of Four. Why wasn't he buried with them?[969]

"Well, King David had a place prepared for him fittingly. Who is that? Zion, to join as one. As for Adam, who was buried among the patriarchs, they were buried with him because he was the primordial king, from whom kingship was removed and conferred upon David. With the days of Adam, King David existed in the world; because a thousand years had been ordained for Adam,

967. **cave... near the Garden of Eden...** Jacob wished to be buried in the cave of Machpelah, which Abraham had purchased as a burial site for Sarah (Genesis 23). Eventually all the matriarchs (except for Rachel) and patriarchs were buried there. According to rabbinic tradition, Adam and Eve were buried in this cave as well. Based on this tradition, the *Zohar* teaches that the cave of Machpelah leads to the Garden of Eden.

See *Bereshit Rabbah* 58:4, 8; BT *Eruvin* 53a; *Pirqei de-Rabbi Eli'ezer* 20, 36; *Midrash ha-Gadol*, Genesis 23:9; *Zohar* 1:38b (*Heikh*), 57b, 81a (*ST*), 127a–128b, 219a, 250b; 2:151b; 3:164a; *ZḤ* 21a (*MhN*), 79d (*MhN*, *Rut*).

Here the Companions are situated near a cave. See above at note 948.

968. **Kiriath-arba, City of Four...** An earlier name for Hebron, the city closest to the cave of Machpelah. See Genesis 23:2, 19; and the preceding note.

969. **patriarchs are the holy chariot...** See *Bereshit Rabbah* 47:6: "Resh Lakish said, 'The patriarchs themselves constitute the [divine] Chariot.'" According to Kabbalah, Abraham had perfected and attained the quality of *Ḥesed*; Isaac, the quality of *Gevurah*; and Jacob, the quality of *Tif'eret*. This patriarchal sefirotic triad constitutes a chariot-throne for the highest level of divinity.

The fourth component of the chariot, lending it greater stability, is King David—symbolizing *Shekhinah*, known as *Malkhut* (Kingdom), who completes the triad of *Ḥesed*, *Gevurah*, and *Tif'eret*. So why, wonders Rabbi Yehudah, wasn't David (rather than Adam) buried along with his three predecessors: Abraham, Isaac, and Jacob?

In rabbinic tradition the verse in Psalms is applied to David, youngest of Jesse's sons, relegated to tending the flock. In Kabbalah the "rejection" of *the stone* alludes to the diminishment of *Shekhinah*'s light; yet She becomes a vital component of the sefirotic chariot and is symbolized as the Foundation Stone of the Temple. See above, note 918; p. 208 and n. 179.

On the patriarchs constituting the chariot, see above, note 198. On King David as the fourth component, see above, note 332. On David and the patriarchs, see above, p. 134 and n. 311.

and the days of King David were removed and withdrawn from him—he provided them. Now, how could the patriarchs endure until King David appeared? Rather, he attained his place fittingly, and was therefore not buried alongside the patriarchs.[970]

"Further, the patriarchs abide in the place of male, David in the place of female. The patriarchs' females were buried with them; David was joined and buried in the place of male fittingly.[971]

"*He gathered his feet into the bed*—for he dwelled in the place of life; when he was about to depart from the world, he lowered his feet toward the bed, was gathered in, and departed from the world, as is written: *he expired, and was gathered to his people.*"[972]

He opened, saying, "*My soul yearns, even pines for the courts of YHVH* (Psalms 84:3). This word has been established by the Companions, but come and see! There are higher abodes and lower abodes. In the higher, no one dwells. Who

970. **King David had a place...** Rabbi Yehudah explains that King David, who symbolizes *Malkhut* (Kingdom), was buried appropriately in Zion, which symbolizes *Malkhut*'s partner, *Yesod*. Adam, having been buried in the cave of Machpelah many generations before the patriarchs, took the place of King David, because Adam himself was the primordial king and the source of David's kingship.

According to a midrashic tradition, King David was destined to die at childbirth, but Adam provided him 70 of his own 1000 allotted years, so David lived for 70 years and Adam for 930.

The patriarchs could not possibly have maintained the chariot without a fourth component until the birth of King David. Rather, Adam completed the quartet above and the patriarchs were buried alongside him in the cave. David eventually "attained his place fittingly," being buried in Zion.

On the years of Adam and David, see Genesis 5:5; Jubilees 4:30; *Pirqei de-Rabbi Eli'ezer* 19, and David Luria, ad loc., n. 31; *Midrash Tehillim* 92:10; *Bemidbar Rabbah* 14:12; *Bereshit Rabbati* 5:5; *Yalqut Shim'oni*, Genesis, 41; *Zohar* 1:55a–b, 91b, 140a, 168a, 233b; 2:103b, 235a; *ZḤ* 67d (*ShS*), 81a (*MhN, Rut*); Moses de León, *Sheqel ha-Qodesh*, 68 (85); idem, *Sod Eser Sefirot Belimah*, 383.

971. **patriarchs..., David...** The patriarchs symbolize the triad of *Ḥesed, Gevurah*, and *Tif'eret*—a masculine unit—so they are fittingly buried with their female spouses, the matriarchs. David, on the other hand, symbolizes the divine female, *Shekhinah*; so he is fittingly buried in Zion, symbolizing the male potency, *Yesod*. In both cases, male and female are united.

972. ***He gathered his feet...*** Jacob symbolizes *Tif'eret*, the Tree of Life. As he left the world, he lowered his feet toward *Shekhinah*, symbolized by *the bed*. His departure from this world was, in fact, a reintegration into divine life.

On *Shekhinah* as bed, see *Zohar* 1:37a, 225b; 2:5a, 48b, 51a; 3:60a, 114a, 118b; Moses de León, *Sefer ha-Rimmon*, 370. Cf. BT *Shabbat* 55b, where it is said that Jacob kept a bed in his tent for *Shekhinah*. See Rashi on Genesis 49:4.

According to the eleventh-century Catholic reformer Peter Damian, Mary is the golden couch upon which God, tired out by the actions of humanity and the angels, lies down to rest. See Patai, *The Hebrew Goddess*, 280.

are they? Inner chambers. Outer chambers are called *the courts of YHVH*, for they sustain desire of love for the female.[973]

"Come and see: As the soul ascends, all arouses toward the female, for she joins in total desire, uniting.[974]

"Jacob did not die—for regarding him, death is not mentioned, rather: *he expired, and was gathered to his people.* See what is written: *He gathered his feet into the bed*—for he was gathered to the moon. The sun does not die, but is gathered from the world and goes toward the moon.[975]

"Come and see: When Jacob was gathered, the moon shone and desire of supernal sun aroused toward her; for as the sun ascends, another sun arouses, one cleaving to the other, and the moon shines."[976]

Rabbi Shim'on said, "You have spoken well! But it has been said: Upper (world of the male) links with lower (world of the female), and lower links with upper—all corresponding to one another.[977] It has been said: There are two

973. ***My soul yearns...*** The soul yearns for *the courts of YHVH*, namely the heavenly palaces ("lower abodes," "outer chambers") —not for the *sefirot* ("higher abodes," "inner chambers"), where no one dwells. The palaces encompass *Shekhinah* with love.

The full verse reads: *My soul yearns, even pines for the courts of YHVH; my heart and my flesh shout for joy to the living God.* See *Midrash Tehillim* 25:4; 84:2; *Zohar* 1:94b, 129b–130a; Moses de León, *Sefer ha-Rimmon*, 388–89.

On the inner and outer chambers, see BT *Ḥagigah* 5b, 12b–13a; *Zohar* 2:18a, 257b–258a; 3:15b; Moses de León, *Shushan Edut*, 337; Scholem.

974. **As the soul ascends...** As the soul ascends toward *Shekhinah*, she (the soul) participates in and stimulates divine desire along with the heavenly palaces, preparing *Shekhinah* for Her union with *Tif'eret*.

See above at notes 600–602. For a somewhat different reading, see *Sullam*.

975. **Jacob did not die...** Jacob did not really die; rather, having attained the rung of *Tif'eret* (symbolized by the sun), he united with *Shekhinah* (symbolized by *the bed* and the moon). This accords with the natural cycle of the sun, which, upon setting, does not die but rather continues to shine and illumines the moon.

See BT *Ta'anit* 5b, in the name of Rabbi Yoḥanan: "Jacob our father did not die..., as is said: *Do not fear, My servant Jacob—declares YHVH—do not be dismayed, O Israel! For I will save you from afar, your seed from the land of their captivity* (Jeremiah 30:10). The verse compares him to his seed; just as his seed is alive, so he too is alive."

See Rashi and Naḥmanides on Genesis 49:23; *Tosafot, Ta'anit* 5b, s.v. *ya'aqov avinu*; *Zohar* 1:235b; 2:48b; Moses de León, *Sefer ha-Rimmon*, 108–9; idem, commentary on the ten *sefirot*, 336b.

976. **When Jacob was gathered...** As Jacob (symbolized by the sun) departed this world, *Shekhinah* (the moon) was illumined and *Tif'eret* (Jacob's *sefirah*, "another sun") was stimulated to join Her.

977. **Upper (world of the male) links with lower...** Rabbi Shim'on extends the unification to include a higher realm. *Binah* (together with the *sefirot* beneath Her from *Ḥesed* through *Yesod*) constitutes the world of the male, which joins with *Shekhinah*, world of the female.

On "world of the male," see above, note 914.

worlds, as is said: *from world to world* (Psalms 106:48). And even though both are females, one is arrayed by male and one by female. This one, seven; that one, בת שבע (*Bat sheva*), *Bathsheba, daughter of seven.* This one, mother; that one, mother. This one is called Mother of Solomon; that one is called the same. This one is mother of Solomon, as is written: *O daughters of Zion, come out and gaze upon King Solomon, upon the crown with which his mother crowned him* (Song of Songs 3:11). *Upon King* שלמה (*Shelomo*) *Solomon*—upon the King to whom all שלמא (*shelama*), peace, belongs. That one is mother of Solomon, as is said: *Bathsheba, mother of Solomon* (1 Kings 1:11). And similarly: *The wisdom of Solomon increased* (1 Kings 5:10)—*wisdom of Solomon* is *mother of Solomon.*[978]

"It is written: *Words of King Lemuel, an utterance with which his mother admonished him* (Proverbs 31:1). *Words of King* למואל (*Lemu'el*), *Lemuel*—the sealed secrecy of this verse is unknown. However, *words of King Lemu'el*—words spoken for *El*, God, [249a] who is *King*. And who is He? *El, God, rages every day* (Psalms 7:12)—*El Shaddai*. למואל (*Lemuel*)—as is said: למו (*lemo*), *to, my mouth* (Job 40:4). למואל מלך (*Lemuel melekh*), 'For *El*, King'—who is *Bat sheva*, Daughter of Seven.[979]

978. **There are two worlds...** *Binah* and *Shekhinah*. Although *Binah* is pictured as Divine Mother, She is arrayed as "world of the male" by the masculine *sefirot* emanating from Her. *Shekhinah* is arrayed as female by Her angels.

Binah is known as "seven" because She includes within Herself all seven lower *sefirot* (*Ḥesed* through *Shekhinah*), while *Shekhinah* is Her daughter: בת שבע (*Bat sheva*), literally *daughter of seven*. *Binah* is the "mother of שלמה (*Shelomo*), Solomon," because She is the mother of *Tif'eret*, "the King to whom all שלמא (*shelama*), peace, belongs"—"peace" symbolizing *Yesod*. *Shekhinah* is the mother of Solomon because She is symbolized by Bathsheba, Solomon's actual mother. *Shekhinah* is also the daughter of *Ḥokhmah* (Wisdom) and is known as "lower *Ḥokhmah*" or *wisdom of Solomon*. In the days of Solomon, She *increased*, attaining fullness.

The phrase *from world to world* is understood to mean from *Binah* to *Shekhinah*. See M *Berakhot* 9:5; *Tosefta, Berakhot* 6:21; *Zohar* 1:34a, 153b, 158b, 210a; 2:22a, 53b, 144a; 3:145b, 285b, 297b.

On *Binah* and *Shekhinah* as "two females," see above at notes 779, 946. On the verse in Song of Songs, see above, notes 85, 907. On the phrase "King to whom all peace belongs," see *Sifra, Shemini, millu'im*, 15, 44c; *Shir ha-Shirim Rabbah* 1:11 (on 1:1); *Zohar* 1:29a, 184a, 226b. On the verse from 1 Kings 5, see above, note 208. On this entire paragraph, see Moses de León, *Shushan Edut*, 342–43.

979. ***Words of King Lemuel...*** The word למואל (*Lemu'el*), *Lemuel*, is found in the Bible only in this verse (with an apparent variant vocalization three verses later). Its precise meaning—or even whether it is a name—is uncertain. Rabbi Shim'on interprets it as two words: למו (*lemo*)—a fuller form of the preposition ל (*le*), "to, for"—and אל (*El*), "God." The entire phrase—*words of* למואל מלך (*lemu'el melekh*), *King Lemuel*—now means "words [spoken] for *El* [who is] King," that is, words spoken for the sake of *Shekhinah*, who is known as *Malkhut* (Kingdom), *El*, and *El Shaddai*. Human wickedness arouses Her to rage daily.

The explanation of *lemu'el* apparently de-

"*An utterance with which his mother admonished him*—when She revealed Herself to him in Gibeon in a dream by night.[980]

"Come and see: Jacob was gathered to the moon, generating fruit within her for the world. There is no generation in the world lacking fruit of Jacob, for he stimulated arousal above, as is written: *He gathered his feet into the bed.*[981] Happy is the share of Jacob, for he was perfected above and below, as is written: *Do not fear, My servant Jacob—declares YHVH—for I am with you!* (Jeremiah 46:28). It is not written *for you are with Me*, but rather *for I am with you*, as has been said."[982]

Rabbi Yitsḥak opened with a verse, saying, "*They came as far as* גרן האטד *(Goren ha-Atad), Threshing-floor of the Bramble, which is across the Jordan, and there they held a very great and heavy lamentation.* And it is written: *The Canaanite inhabitants of the land saw the mourning in Goren ha-Atad and they said, 'This is a heavy mourning for Egypt.' Therefore it was named* אבל מצרים *(Avel Mitsrayim), Mourning of Egypt* (Genesis 50:10–11).[983] These verses call for contemplation! Why did they care that they came *as far as Goren ha-Atad*? And why was this mourning named for Egypt? It should have been named *Mourning of Israel*![984]

"Well, they have said as follows: As long as Jacob was in Egypt, the land was blessed for his sake, and the Nile gushed, irrigating the land. Moreover, the

rives from Rashi, who quotes the same proof-text from Job, which reads: *I lay my hand* למו *(lemo), to* [or: *on*], *my mouth.* See Rashi on this verse and on BT *Sanhedrin* 70b, s.v. *lemu'el melekh*. On the verse in Psalms, see *Zohar* 1:8a, 91a; 2:30b.

980. ***his mother admonished him...*** Rabbi Shim'on identifies Solomon's mother with *Shekhinah*. In the king's dream at Gibeon (1 Kings 3:4–14), he was admonished to walk in God's ways. This admonishment was for Solomon's benefit, but also *lemu'el*—*lemo el*, "for *El*," for the sake of *Shekhinah*.

See *Zohar* 1:149b–150a.

981. **generating fruit...** Jacob ascended to *Shekhinah*, stimulating Her union with his *sefirah* (*Tif'eret*), thereby engendering souls as fruit. This "fruit of Jacob" consists of especially potent and virtuous souls, who appear in each generation.

On souls as fruit, see *Bahir* 14 (22); Ezra of Gerona, *Peirush Shir ha-Shirim*, 489, 504; *Zohar* 1:15b, 19a, 33a, 59b–60a, 82b, 85b, 90b, 115a–b, 226b, 238a; 2:166b–167a, 223b; Moses de León, *Sefer ha-Mishqal*, 51; idem, *Sheqel ha-Qodesh*, 56 (69). Cf. Ibn Ezra on Psalms 1:3.

982. ***for I am with you...*** Jacob attained the *sefirah* of *Tif'eret* above, but he was also fulfilled below, as indicated by the wording *for I am with you*—emphasizing that God came to Jacob, not just vice-versa.

See *Zohar* 2:174a; and for other interpretations, 3:199a; *OY*.

983. **אבל מצרים *(Avel Mitsrayim)*, *Mourning of Egypt*** The plain sense of אבל (*avel*) is "watercourse, stream," but it is construed in folk etymology as אבל (*evel*), "mourning."

984. **verses call for contemplation...** Why did they lament precisely at Goren ha-Atad? And why wasn't the place named for Israel's mourning of the patriarch?

famine ceased on account of Jacob. So, the Egyptians engaged in mourning, and it was named for them."[985]

He opened, saying, "*Who* ימלל (*yemallel*), *can utter, the mighty acts of YHVH or declare all His praise?* (Psalms 106:2). This verse has been established. But why *yemallel, utter*? The verse should read ידבר (*yedabber*), *speak.* For if you say that such is the style of Scripture—that verses are worded like that—no, they all come to demonstrate something! *Who* ימלל (*yemallel*), *can utter*—as is said: *you may pluck* מלילות (*melilot*), *ears, with your hand* (Deuteronomy 23:26). *The mighty acts of YHVH*—for they are numerous, all decrees of judgment issuing from there. So, who can remove and eliminate a single decree of those mighty acts performed by the blessed Holy One?[986]

"Further, *Who yemallel, can utter*—all is one: *yedabber,* can speak. For there are ever so many mighty acts, innumerable: so many masters of judgment, so many shield-bearing warriors, so many wardens of law—and no word can express them. How, then, are they all known? By הגדה (*haggadah*), expounding, which contains a mystery of Wisdom. For by utterance, by talking, one cannot express them or know them; but by *haggadah,* expounding, they become known, as is said: *One generation will praise Your deeds to another, and Your mighty acts* יגידו (*yaggidu*), *they will expound* (Psalms 145:4)—by this mystery they are known. But וגבורתך (*ugvuratekha*), *and of Your might*—lower *Gevurah*—*they will speak,* as is written: *ugvuratekha, and of Your might, they will speak* (ibid., 11).[987]

985. **As long as Jacob was in Egypt...** Even though there were supposed to be more years of famine, with Jacob's arrival the famine ceased and the land flourished.

See Genesis 45:6; *Tosefta, Sotah* 10:9; *Sifrei,* Deuteronomy 38; *Bereshit Rabbah* 84:6; 89:9 (and Theodor's note); *Baraita di-Shloshim u-Shtayim Middot,* 10 (p. 21); Rashi on Genesis 47:19; Naḥmanides on Genesis 47:18; *Zohar* 1:180a, 193b.

986. **why *yemallel*, *utter*?...** Why this unusual verb, rather than the more common word ידבר (*yedabber*), "speak"? Scripture does not resort to mere stylistic variation; each word conveys unique and profound meaning.

Rabbi Yitsḥak explains that the word ימלל (*yemallel*), *utter,* is linked with the expression *pluck* מלילות (*melilot*), *ears* (of corn). The verse in Psalms implies that no one can "pluck" or eliminate any of God's גבורות (*gevurot*), *mighty acts*—divine decrees of judgment issuing from *Binah* or *Gevurah*. The plural—*gevurot, mighty acts*—emphasizes how numerous these are.

On the significance of every detail of Torah, see *Zohar* 1:54a, 135a, 145b, 163a, 187a, 234b; 2:12a, 55b–56a, 59b, 65b, 98b–99b; 3:79b, 149a, 152a, 174b, 265a; *ZḤ* 6d (*MhN*). Cf. *Sifrei,* Deuteronomy 336; *Midrash Tanna'im,* Deuteronomy 32:47; BT *Menaḥot* 29b; Maimonides, *Guide of the Perplexed* 3:50.

On the verse in Psalms, see BT *Megillah* 18a; *Midrash Tehillim* 19:2; *Zohar* 1:241b; 2:64a–b, 83a; 3:137b (*IR*), 294a (*IZ*).

987. **Further, *Who yemallel*...*yedabber*...** Alternatively, *yemallel, can utter,* is simply synonymous with *yedabber,* "can speak." The verse indicates that no human can express the innumerable powers of judgment (deriving from *Binah*) that are commissioned to enforce the law and punish the

"*Or declare all His praise* (ibid. 106:2)—for numerous are the rungs known and united in praise: so many forces, so many camps joined with Her, as is said: *Is there any number to His troops?* (Job 25:3). So, who can declare *all His praise?*[988]

"Come and see: The Egyptians were all wise. From the side of *Gevurah* issue many forces and many camps—numerous rungs upon rungs—finally reaching lower rungs; and the Egyptians were sorcerers, expert in these, knowing sealed secrets of the world. They perceived that as long as Jacob existed in the world, no nation could dominate his children; yet they knew that they would enslave Israel for many years. When Jacob died, they rejoiced; and they saw what would eventually happen, until they reached *as far as* גרן האטד (*Goren ha-Atad*), *Threshing-floor of the Bramble*, which is the prevailing decree of judgment—אטד (*atad*) in *gimatriyya* is יד (*yad*), hand, as is said: *Israel saw the great hand that YHVH had wielded against Egypt* (Exodus 14:31). When they reached this place and saw the mighty acts issuing from this *atad, bramble*, then *there they held a lamentation.* Why is it called *atad, bramble*? Just as from a bramble emerge thorns in this direction and in that, so too from a *yad*, hand, emerge fingers in this direction and in that—each finger culminating in numerous mighty acts, numerous judgments, numerous decrees. So, *there they held a very great and heavy lamentation. Therefore it was named Mourning of Egypt*—surely! *This is a heavy mourning for Egypt*—and for no one else!"[989]

wicked. These can only be known by a more profound method: הגדה (*haggadah*), "telling, expounding," which corresponds to *Ḥokhmah* (Wisdom), beyond *Binah*. In the *Zohar* the term *haggadah* can refer to the allegorical interpretation of Scripture, which unlocks secrets of wisdom that cannot be expressed openly.

The plural גבורותיך (*gevurotekha*), *Your mighty acts*, refers to the many powers of *Gevurah* issuing from *Binah*; whereas later in Psalm 145, the singular גבורתך (*gevuratekha*), *Your might*, alludes to *Shekhinah*, who is known as "lower *Gevurah*." She is the realm of divine speech; so here it is appropriately written: וגבורתך (*ugvuratekha*), *and of Your might, they will speak.* The divine power conveyed by *Shekhinah* can be expressed.

On the sense of the verb הגיד (*higgid*) as "revealing" something concealed or mysterious, see Genesis 3:11; 41:25; Judges 14:12, 15–16; 1 Kings 10:3; Daniel 2:2; Job 11:6. On the significance of *higgid*, see BT *Shabbat* 87a; *Zohar* 1:86b, 234b; 3:50b, 161a, 292b–293a (*IZ*). On *haggadah* as the allegorical method of interpretation, see *Zohar* 2:99a; *ZḤ* 83a (*MhN, Rut*); Tishby, *Wisdom of the Zohar*, 3:1083–85; Talmage, "Ha-Munnaḥ 'Haggadah,'" 271–73.

In Psalm 145:4, the plain meaning of יגידו (*yaggidu*) is *they will proclaim.* Verse 11 reads in full: *Of the glory of Your kingdom they will talk, and of Your might they will speak.* On the expression "wardens of law," see above, note 493.

988. ***Or declare all His praise...*** *Praise* alludes to *Shekhinah*. Even though Her *might* can be expressed, the full extent of Her forces is innumerable.

On *Shekhinah* as *praise*, see *Zohar* 1:36a.

989. **The Egyptians were all wise...** They were masters of sorcery and demonic wisdom, which derive from the dregs of *Gevurah* on the left side. Through this wisdom,

Rabbi Shim'on explained the portion and they returned to the cave. He said, "I see that today a house in town will collapse, and two Roman informers will be eliminated. If I am in the town, the house will not collapse." They went back to the cave and sat down.[990]

Rabbi Shim'on opened, saying, "*Cry out, O Daughter of Gallim! Listen, Laishah! Poor Anathoth!* (Isaiah 10:30). [249b] This verse is addressed to Assembly of Israel, who praises the blessed Holy One with a voice of praise; so, *Cry out!* From here we learn: Whoever wishes to praise the blessed Holy One aloud should have a pleasant voice, sweet to the ears that listen. If not, he should not rise to lift his voice.[991]

"Come and see: Of Levites, deriving from this side, is written *From the age of fifty years he shall retire from the legion of service and serve no more* (Numbers

they knew that Egypt was destined to enslave the Israelites, but they also realized that as long as Jacob remained alive, his descendants were invulnerable. Consequently, when Jacob died they rejoiced. However, gazing into the future, *they came as far as Goren ha-Atad*, whose name indicated to them that God would redeem Israel and smite the Egyptians with His *great hand*, because the *gimatriyya* (numerical value) of the word אטד (*atad*), *bramble*, is equivalent to that of יד (*yad*), *hand*—both equaling fourteen. *Atad* and *yad* symbolize the manifold powers of *Shekhinah*, who executes divine judgment. This explains why the Egyptians held a lamentation when they reached Goren ha-Atad and why the place became known as *Mourning of Egypt*.

The verse in Exodus 14 describes the miracle at the Red Sea. On the Egyptians' expertise in sorcery, see Exodus 7:11; *Bereshit Rabbah* 86:5; BT *Qiddushin* 49b, *Menaḥot* 85b; *Tanḥuma, Va'era* 3; *Tanḥuma* (Buber), *Va'era* 12; *Shemot Rabbah* 9:6–7; *Zohar* 1:83a; 2:30b; 3:50b.

990. **Rabbi Shim'on explained...** He continued expounding the last section of Torah portion *Va-Yḥi*, concerning the death of Jacob and his burial in the cave of Machpelah; then they returned to the cave where they had begun their discussion and from which they had proceeded on the way. The reason for their return was that Rabbi Shim'on foresaw that in the nearby town a house would soon collapse, killing two Romans who were informing against local Jews. He knew that if he were present in town, through his merit the house would remain standing; so he decided to remain in the cave, ensuring the informers' death.

On the cave here, see above at notes 884, 891, 948. As mentioned in note 884, rabbinic tradition relates that after Rabbi Shim'on was sentenced to death by the Romans, he and his son hid from the authorities in a cave for thirteen years. According to one account (BT *Shabbat* 33b), his death sentence resulted from an informer reporting Rabbi Shim'on's criticism of the Romans.

991. ***Cry out, O Daughter...*** In this verse, Isaiah calls on the inhabitants of the city of Bat Gallim (literally, *Daughter of Gallim*) to warn the nation (specifically, the residents of Laishah and Anathoth) of the impending Assyrian invasion. Drawing on midrashic interpretation, Rabbi Shim'on applies the verse to Assembly of Israel, which, in Kabbalah, refers to both the people of Israel and their divine counterpart, *Shekhinah*.

See *Eikhah Rabbah, Petiḥta* 1; BT *Sanhedrin* 94b; *Pesiqta de-Rav Kahana* 13:1; *Zohar* 1:63a–b. On Assembly of Israel, see above, pp. 122–23, n. 237.

The teaching about one who "wishes to praise the blessed Holy One aloud" apparently refers to a would-be cantor.

8:25). Why? Because his voice becomes low and is not sweet to the ears like that of his colleagues; so he is removed from *the legion of service*—from the forces above who stand to play for this *service* and to glorify the holy Name fittingly. For we have learned: Forces and camps are all appointed above, corresponding to those below, to praise the holy Name and chant before it. Therefore, *he shall retire from the legion of service.* And because Assembly of Israel praises the blessed Holy One, Scripture states: *Cry out!*[992]

"בת גלים (*Bat gallim*), *Daughter of Gallim*—daughter of the patriarchs.[993]

"Further, *bat gallim, daughter of waves*—the world that is coming is called *gallim, waves*, for all exists within it, intermingled, heaps upon heaps, issuing to all.[994]

"Further, *bat gallim, daughter of springs*—as is said: *a locked* גל (*gal*), *spring* (Song of Songs 4:12). All those *springs* and bubbling fountains issue from the world that is coming, and Assembly of Israel is *daughter of springs.*[995]

"Come and see: This verse is problematical. First is written *cry out*—to sing and lift the voice. Then is written *listen.* So, why *cry out*, if it is written *listen*? Well, *cry out*, to praise and sing to the blessed Holy One. Come and see: If Israel have begun to praise and sing to the blessed Holy One, then is written *listen.* Why? Because Israel are praising the blessed Holy One for Her; so it is written: *listen.*[996]

992. **Levites, deriving from this side...** From the side of *Gevurah*, associated with song. Corresponding to the Levites, who play instruments and sing in the Temple, angels play and sing above to *Shekhinah* (known as "the holy Name").

On the semi-retirement of the Levites, see the following verse in Numbers (8:26); *Sifrei*, Numbers 63; *Sifrei Zuta* 8:26; *Tosefta, Ḥullin* 1:16; BT *Ḥullin* 24a–b; *Bemidbar Rabbah* 6:8–9; Rashi and Naḥmanides on Numbers 8:25; Maimonides, *Mishneh Torah, Hilkhot Kelei ha-Miqdash* 3:8; idem, *Guide of the Perplexed* 3:45; *Zohar* 3:151b; *ZḤ* 82a–b (*MhN, Rut*).

993. **daughter of the patriarchs** Following midrashic tradition, Rabbi Shim'on interprets the word גלים (*gallim*) as alluding to the patriarchs, either because they were גולים (*golim*), "wanderers (as) in exile," or because they enacted *mitsvot* as profusely as גלים (*gallim*), "waves." See the sources cited above, note 991.

Here, Assembly of Israel is pictured as daughter of the patriarchs—implying that *Shekhinah* is daughter of the sefirotic triad *Ḥesed, Gevurah,* and *Tif'eret*, who are symbolized respectively by the three patriarchs.

994. ***bat gallim, daughter of waves...*** *Shekhinah* is the daughter of the Divine Mother, *Binah*, who is known as "the world that is coming." All existence flows from *Binah*, wave after wave.

On *Binah* as "the world that is coming," see above, note 2.

995. ***bat gallim, daughter of springs...*** *Shekhinah* inherits and contains all the flows of emanation issuing from *Binah*.

The full verse in Song of Songs reads: *A locked garden is my sister, bride; a locked spring, a sealed fountain.* See *Shir ha-Shirim Rabbah* on 4:12; *Shemot Rabbah* 20:5; *Zohar* 1:32b, 63a.

996. **This verse is problematical...** Why does the verse say *cry out*, and then *listen*? Rabbi Shim'on explains that the people of Israel (the earthly Assembly of Israel) are told to *cry out*—to praise the blessed Holy One for the sake of *Shekhinah* (the di-

"לישה (*Layshah*), *Laishah*—for She comes from the side of *Gevurah*, as is said: ליש גבור (*Layish gibbor*), *'Lion, mighty,' among beasts* (Proverbs 30:30), and She is לישה גבורה (*layshah gibborah*), 'lioness, mighty'—smashing forces and powers.[997]

"עניה ענתות (*Aniyyah anatot*), *Poor Anathoth.* Why? Because She is a speculum that does not shine—*poor*, literally: the moon has no light of her own, only what is given her by the sun.[998]

"ענתות (*Anatot*), *Anathoth*, is a field, a village, which is inhabited by poor priests who go begging from door to door like Levites. No one cares about them, because all the residents of that village are scorned by the people and their homes are emptier than anyone else's, containing only what is given to them—like the scorned poor. So, the moon has no light of her own, except when the sun unites with her and she shines.[999]

"Come and see the mystery that is written: *To Abiathar the priest, the king said, 'Go to Anathoth, to your fields! For you are a dead man...'* (1 Kings 2:26). Now, is he called *a dead man* simply because Adonijah invited him? Rather, because he came from a poor place, for the moon—who is עניה ענתות (*Aniyyah anatot*), *Poor Anathoth*—cleaved to him.[1000]

vine Assembly of Israel), that is, to stimulate the union of the divine couple. Correspondingly, *Shekhinah* is told to *listen* to their song.

997. **לישה (*Layshah*), *Laishah*...** Rabbi Shim'on links the otherwise unattested place-name לישה (*layshah*), *Laishah*, with the presumed female version of the animal-name ליש (*layish*), "lion." The lion's mightiness alludes to *Gevurah* (Might), from which *Shekhinah* (known as *Layshah*) derives. She displays might in vanquishing demonic powers. See *Zohar* 1:63b.

998. **עניה ענתות (*Aniyyah anatot*), *Poor Anathoth*...** Rabbi Shim'on associates the place-name ענתות (*anatot*), *Anathoth*, with the word עני (*ani*), "poor." *Shekhinah* (symbolized by the moon) is called *Poor Anathoth* because She has nothing of Her own, only what She receives from *Tif'eret* (symbolized by the sun). Similarly, She is known as אספקלריא דלא נהרא (*ispaqlarya de-la nahara*), "the speculum (or glass, mirror, lens) that does not shine" on its own but rather transmits (reflects, refracts, or diffracts) the other *sefirot*. See above, note 692.

The phrase "has no light of her own" derives from a description of the moon by medieval astronomers. See Radak on Genesis 1:16; *Zohar* 1:20a, 31a, 124b–125a, 132b, 179b, 181a, 233b, 238a; 2:43a, 142a, 145b, 215a, 218b; 3:113b; Moses de León, *Shushan Edut*, 338; idem, *Sefer ha-Rimmon*, 113, 188; idem, *Sheqel ha-Qodesh*, 68–69 (85–86); idem, *Sod Eser Sefirot Belimah*, 381. Cf. BT *Shabbat* 156a.

999. **village... inhabited by poor priests...** Anathoth was a town of priests and is described here as populated by poor priests who were entirely dependent on tithes and offerings.

See 1 Samuel 2:36; 1 Kings 2:26–27; *Bereshit Rabbah* 99:7; BT *Ketubbot* 105b; *Tanḥuma, Vayḥi* 10; *Midrash Mishlei* 29:4; *Midrash Aggadah*, Genesis 49:7; above, note 650.

1000. ***Abiathar the priest*...** Abiathar had been a loyal follower of Solomon's father, King David, and was appointed high priest. However, as a result of Abiathar's support for Solomon's rival, Adonijah (another of David's sons), Solomon banished him to Anathoth.

Rabbi Shim'on explains that the phrase *a dead man* alludes to Abiathar's link with

"Now, you might say, *'and because you were afflicted with all my father's afflictions* (ibid.)—that is why he deserved not to be killed.' However, since Abiathar came from a poor place, David deserved him before ascending to royalty, when Saul lay in ambush for him and he acted like a poor man—Abiathar, similarly. But in the time that Solomon ruled, when the moon assumed fullness and possessed the richness of all, Abiathar did not attain it.[1001]

"Surely, Field of Anathoth is mystery of the matter. And when Jeremiah purchased it, this was entirely to take possession of supernal mystery.[1002]

"Come and see: When the moon reigns, She is called Field of Apples; when She is in poverty, Field of Anathoth.[1003] Therefore, praise from below generates

Shekhinah, who is poor, since poverty is compared to death (see BT *Nedarim* 64b). Furthermore, when *Shekhinah* is united with *Tif'eret*, She conveys life to the world; but if She is separated from Him by human sin, the vivifying flow of emanation ceases and death dominates. See above, note 906.

On Abiathar and Adonijah, see 1 Samuel 22–23; 1 Kings 1; 2:26–27; *Zohar* 1:63b. On Adonijah's "invitation," see 1 Kings 1:9, 19. The full verse in 1 Kings 2 reads: *To Abiathar the priest, the king said, "Go to Anathoth, to your fields! For you are a dead man* [i.e., deserving of death]*; but I will not put you to death on this day, because you carried the Ark of the Lord YHVH before my father David and because you were afflicted with all my father's afflictions."*

1001. **Now, you might say...** From Solomon's explanation as found in Kings, he spared Abiathar largely because that priest had shared the hardships of David (Solomon's father) when both of the latter were fugitives from King Saul (1 Samuel 22:20–23). But Rabbi Shim'on insists that on a deeper level, David and Abiathar shared an identification with the poverty of *Shekhinah*. Later, when Solomon ruled, *Shekhinah* (symbolized by the moon) attained fullness, and Abiathar was no longer linked with Her and had to return to his humble home.

See *Zohar* 1:63b. According to the Midrash, just as the moon does not become full until the fifteenth day of its cycle, so it remained incomplete until the glorious reign of Solomon in the fifteenth generation from Abraham. See *Pesiqta de-Rav Kahana* 5:12 and *Shemot Rabbah* 15:26: "When Solomon appeared, the disk of the moon became full." See *Zohar* 1:73b–74a, 150a, 223a–b, 225b, 238a, 243a; 2:85a; 3:61a, 74b, 181b; *ZḤ* 83b (*MhN, Rut*); Moses de León, *Shushan Edut*, 342.

1002. **Field of Anathoth... Jeremiah...** Anathoth alludes to the poverty of *Shekhinah* (above, note 998). The prophet Jeremiah, who lived in Anathoth, was directed by God to purchase his cousin's field there as a symbol of the divine promise to restore Jerusalem, the house of David, and the Levitical priesthood once the impending punishment (the Babylonian conquest) was completed. See Jeremiah 32.

Here, Jeremiah's purchase of the field in Anathoth symbolizes his efforts to redeem *Shekhinah* from impoverishment and impending exile, and restore Her to union with Her Beloved.

1003. **Field of Apples...** In Her state of fullness, *Shekhinah* is an apple orchard—filled by the sefirotic triad of *Ḥesed*, *Gevurah*, and *Tif'eret*, whose respective colors all appear in the apple: the white pulp, the red skin, and the green stem.

This image derives from BT *Ta'anit* 29b, in the name of Rav: "*... like the fragrance of a field blessed by YHVH* (Genesis 27:27).... Like the fragrance of a field of apple trees."

See Azriel of Gerona, *Peirush ha-Aggadot*,

richness and fullness—just as David strove all his days to fashion fullness for Her, playing and singing below. When David departed from the world, he left Her in fullness, and King Solomon obtained Her in fullness, for the moon had emerged from poverty and entered richness. Consequently, the wealth of Solomon prevailed over all the kings of the earth. So, *silver was not considered* [*as anything*] *in the days of Solomon* (2 Chronicles 9:20); rather, all was gold, because gold abounded. Of that time is written *It has dust of gold* (Job 28:6), for the sun gazed upon dust above, and by the gaze of the sun and its potency, dust produced abundant gold.[1004]

"Come and see: From mountains of radiance, upon which beams intensity of the sun, dust [250a] of the earth in the midst of the mountains all produces gold. And were it not for ferocious beasts breeding there, human beings would not be poor, because power of the sun proliferates gold. So in the days of Solomon, *silver was not considered as anything*, for potency of the sun gazed upon dust, proliferating gold. Further, that dust is on the side of gold, and as the sun gazes upon it, it absorbs power and gold increases.[1005] When Solomon contemplated this, he declared in praise, *All comes from the dust*... (Ecclesiastes 3:20). Therefore, Solomon did not need to play like David—just to utter a song that is passion of richness, encompassing all praises of the world, praise of the *Matronita* sitting upon the throne facing the King.[1006]

35–37; *Zohar* 1:36a, 85a–b, 122a, 128b, 139a, 142b, 143b, 224b; 2:60b, 61b; 3:74a, 84a, 133b (*IR*), 135b (*IR*), 286b–287a, 288a (*IZ*); Moses de León, *Shushan Edut*, 365.

1004. **praise from below generates richness...** Human song and praise helps to transform *Shekhinah* from being poor to being fruitful, by stimulating the love of the divine couple. King David accomplished this by playing the harp and chanting psalms, so King Solomon inherited Her in a state of fullness and richness. Consequently, in the days of Solomon, wealth prevailed to such an extent that *silver was not considered as anything*. *Tif'eret* (symbolized by the sun) shone upon *Shekhinah* (symbolized by dust), which yielded abundant gold.

On *Shekhinah* as dust, see *Zohar* 1:49a, 170a; 2:23b–24b; 3:34b; Moses de León, *Shushan Edut*, 344–45; idem, *Sefer ha-Rimmon*, 171; idem, *Sheqel ha-Qodesh*, 57–58, 62, 93–96 (70–71, 77–78, 118–22). On dust yielding gold, see *Zohar* 2:24a, 236b; Moses de León, *Sheqel ha-Qodesh*, 95 (121).

The full verse in Chronicles reads: *All of King Solomon's drinking vessels were gold, and all the vessels of the House of the Forest of Lebanon were pure gold; silver was not considered as anything in the days of Solomon.* See 1 Kings 10:21. The full verse in Job reads: *A place whose stones are sapphire and that has dust of gold.*

1005. **From mountains of radiance...** The intensity of the sun shining upon mountains turns the dust of the earth within those mountains into gold. Further, *Shekhinah* (symbolized by dust) derives from *Gevurah* (symbolized by gold), and when *Tif'eret* (the sun) shines upon *Shekhinah*, Her potential gold is actualized abundantly. See the preceding note.

1006. ***All comes from the dust...*** Solomon realized that his wealth derived from *Shekhinah* (*the dust*), who was joined and

"*The king made silver as common in Jerusalem as stones* (1 Kings 10:27)—for everything was gold, and dust joined with the left on the side of love, as is said: *His left hand beneath my head, his right hand embracing me* (Song of Songs 2:6). And the sun cleaved to it, not withdrawing.[1007]

"Solomon erred in this—seeing the moon approaching the sun; right hand embracing, left hand beneath its head. As they neared one another he said, 'Look! They approach as one. What is the right doing here? For the right is intended only to draw near. Since they are already near one another, why is it needed?' Immediately, *silver was not considered [as anything] in the days of Solomon.*[1008]

"The blessed Holy One said to him, 'You have rejected the right! Upon your life, you will have need of *ḥesed,* kindness, and will not find it!' Immediately, the sun turned from facing the moon, and the moon began to darken, and Solomon went begging from door to door, saying, *I am Koheleth!* (Ecclesiastes 1:12). But no one showed him any kindness. Why? Because he had rejected the right and not considered it, as is written: *Silver was not considered as anything in the days of Solomon.*[1009]

illumined by *Tif'eret* (the sun). Consequently, he did not need to initiate the passion of the divine couple, as his father had done by playing the harp and chanting psalms; rather, he celebrated their union by composing the greatest of all love songs: the Song of Songs.

On the Song of Songs as "the greatest of songs," see *Shir ha-Shirim Rabbah* 1:11 (on 1:1); *Zohar* 2:144a. On *Shekhinah*'s title *Matronita,* see above, note 643. The verse in Ecclesiastes reads: *All comes from the dust, and all returns to the dust.*

1007. **everything was gold...** Symbolizing *Gevurah,* the divine left hand, whose passion toward *Shekhinah* was accompanied by the embrace of *Ḥesed,* the right hand, culminating in the union of *Tif'eret* (the sun) with *Shekhinah*.

See above, note 867. On the verse in Kings, see the parallel in 2 Chronicles 9:27.

1008. **Solomon erred...** Seeing that the divine couple was about to unite, Solomon concluded that there was no longer any need for the right hand (*Ḥesed*) to draw *Shekhinah* near Her spouse. Therefore, he did not value silver (symbolizing *Ḥesed*), and in his days *silver was not considered as anything*—compared with the abundant gold (symbolizing the passion of *Gevurah*).

1009. **sun turned from facing the moon...** The union of the divine couple was interrupted, causing *Shekhinah* to dim and bringing poverty to the world. King Solomon himself was supplanted by the demon Ashmedai, and he was forced to wander as a commoner for years. Because he had not valued silver (symbolizing *Ḥesed*), now he found no *ḥesed* (kindness).

In the opening chapter of Ecclesiastes, the designation קהלת (*qohelet*)—apparently meaning "one who assembles"—serves as an epithet for a king like Solomon. The full verse in Ecclesiastes 1 reads *I, Koheleth, was king over Israel in Jerusalem.* Here, though, it is understood as the deposed king's desperate claim: *I am Koheleth! I was king over Israel in Jerusalem!*

On Solomon's disenthronement, see JT *Sanhedrin* 2:6, 20c; BT *Gittin* 68a–b; *Pesiqta de-Rav Kahana* 26:2; *Rut Rabbah* 5:6; *Qohelet Rabbah* on 2:2; *Tanḥuma, Aḥarei Mot* 1; *Tan-*

"So, whoever augments praise toward the blessed Holy One augments peace above. Therefore, *Listen, Laishah!*[1010]

"It is written: ליש (*Layish*), *The lion,* אובד (*oved*), *perishes, without prey, and the cubs of the lioness are scattered* (Job 4:11). *Layish* is the same as לישה (*Layshah*), *Laishah*, as is said: חק (*ḥoq*), law; חקה (*ḥuqqah*), statute.[1011]

"אובד (*Oved*), *Wanders*—as is written: האובדים (*ha-ovedim*), *those who were lost, will come* (Isaiah 27:13).[1012]

"*Without* טרף (*taref*), *prey*—for She demands from Him to provide, as is said: *She rises while it is still night and provides* טרף (*teref*), *food, to her household* (Proverbs 31:15).[1013]

"*And the cubs of the lioness are scattered*—for when She provides all those forces with *teref*, they all join as one, suckling as one; but when She sits *without taref*, on account of exile, surely *the cubs of the lioness are scattered*—all dispersing in many directions and paths, prowling to execute judgment.[1014] So, when a sacrifice is offered, all are arrayed, drawing near as one, as we have said. Now that a sacrifice is not offered, surely *the cubs of the lioness are scattered.* Consequently, there is no day unfraught with judgment, for above and below do not arouse in sublime consummation, as we have said.[1015]

ḥuma (Buber), *Aḥarei Mot* 2; *Midrash Tehillim* 78:12; *Bemidbar Rabbah* 11:3; *Beit ha-Midrash,* 6:106–7; *Zohar* 1:53b, 199a; *ZḤ* 70b (*ShS*); Ginzberg, *Legends,* 6:299–300, n. 86.

1010. **whoever augments praise...** Human praise stimulates harmony and love between the divine couple. Therefore, Isaiah calls upon *Shekhinah* (known as *Laishah*) to listen to such praise.

On *Laishah*, see above, note 997.

1011. ***Layish* is the same as לישה (*Layshah*), *Laishah*...** Although the verse in Job employs the masculine form, ליש (*layish*), *lion*, Rabbi Shim'on insists that here this is equivalent to a presumed feminine form—לישה (*layshah*), "lioness" or "*Laishah*," designating *Shekhinah*. Similarly, with the masculine and feminine forms חק (*ḥoq*), "law," and חקה (*ḥuqqah*), "statute"—both of which can denote *Shekhinah*.

See *Zohar* 1:63a–b; above, note 997. On *ḥoq* and *ḥuqqah*, see *Zohar* 2:60b; 3:113a.

1012. **אובד (*Oved*), *Wanders*...** According to Rabbi Shim'on, in the verse from Job, this verb means "wanders (in exile), is lost," as in the verse from Isaiah. *Shekhinah wanders* with Her people in exile.

On the exile of *Shekhinah*, see above, note 278. The full verse in Isaiah reads: *On that day a great shofar will be blown, and those who were lost in the land of Assyria and those who were scattered in the land of Egypt will come and worship YHVH on the holy mountain in Jerusalem.*

1013. **She demands from Him...** *Shekhinah* demands from Her divine partner that He provide sustenance for Her angelic household and, through them, for the worlds below. See above at note 427.

1014. ***cubs of the lioness are scattered...*** Deprived of nourishment from *Shekhinah* (who is separated from Her partner on account of exile), the powers beneath Her disperse throughout the world, executing judgment.

1015. **when a sacrifice is offered...** When the Temple stood in Jerusalem, the sacrificial ritual stimulated divine union

"Come and see: Now the prayer of a human being arouses consummation above and below, and by the blessing that one offers to the blessed Holy One, above and below are blessed. Thus by the prayer of Israel, worlds are blessed. Whoever blesses the blessed Holy One will be blessed, and whoever does not bless will not be blessed, as is written: *For those who honor Me I will honor, and those who spurn Me will be disdained* (1 Samuel 2:30).[1016]

"Rav Hamnuna Sava would not give the cup of blessing to anyone else to recite the blessing, but rather took it first in both his hands and blessed. As we have said, one should take it in the right hand and the left. Even though all have aroused the meaning of this—and that is fine—still, the cup of blessing must be as follows. Cup, as is said: *I raise the cup of salvations* (Psalms 116:13)—for into this cup flow blessings from those *salvations* above, and it receives them and gathers them; there, is preserved supernal wine, collected in that cup. We should bless it in the right hand and not in the left, along with the wine collected in this cup, so that they may be blessed as one. And we should bless over the table so that it will not be empty: bread and wine, all as one.[1017]

and blessing flowed to the world. Now that the Temple has been destroyed, no sacrifices can be offered and judgment prevails.

On the cosmic function of the sacrifices, see above, note 863. On the consequences of the destruction of the Temple, see M *Sotah* 9:12: "Rabban Shim'on son of Gamli'el says in the name of Rabbi Yehoshu'a: 'Ever since the day the Temple was destroyed, not a single day passes without a curse, dew has never descended as blessing, and flavor has been eliminated from fruit.'"

See *Zohar* 1:61b, 70b, 177a, 181b, 203a; 3:15b, 74b.

1016. **Now the prayer...** Now that the Temple no longer stands, prayers fulfill the function of the sacrificial ritual, stimulating union above and blessings below. See BT *Berakhot* 26b: "Rabbi Yehoshu'a son of Levi said, 'The prayers were ordained to correspond with [i.e., to replace] the continual [daily] offerings.'" See above at notes 862, 868.

1017. **Rav Hamnuna Sava...** He was eager to fulfill the *mitsvah* himself, with all its deep meaning. As Rabbi Shim'on explains, the cup symbolizes *Shekhinah*, who is filled with the flow from above (*salvations*, supernal wine). Initially, the cup is taken in both hands, symbolizing *Ḥesed* and *Gevurah*, the two divine hands holding *Shekhinah*. However, when the blessing is recited, the cup should be held only in the right hand, thereby assuaging the harshness of the left (symbolized by wine) with the loving-kindness of the right. ("They"—in the clause "they may be blessed as one"—apparently refers to the cup and the wine.) Further, when reciting the Grace after Meals, there should also be some bread on the table, symbolizing *Shekhinah*. The presence of both bread and wine ensures that the table will never lack food.

See BT *Berakhot* 51a: "Ten things have been said concerning the cup of blessing [held during Grace after Meals]:... it should be full;... one takes it with both his hands and places it in the right hand,... one fixes his eyes upon it."

See *Zohar* 1:1a, 156a (*ST*), 240a; 2:138b, 143b, 157b; 3:245a–b (*RM*); Moses de León, *Sefer ha-Rimmon*, 105. According to *KP*, Rav Hamnuna recited the blessing while holding

"Come and see: Cup of blessing—so is Assembly of Israel called. Since She is cup of blessing, we need right and left to hold it, and for that cup to be placed between right [250b] and left, and to be filled with wine—because of wine of Torah issuing from the world that is coming.[1018]

"Come and see: Cup of blessing! Concerning this, supernal matters have been revealed. Here, since we are in the cave, I will speak. Here is revealed the mystery of the holy Chariot. Cup of blessing should be received by right and left, which are north and south, so that cup of blessing may obtain blessings from them. Who is cup of blessing? Bed of Solomon, which should be placed between north and south. And we should set it in the right hand, with the body aligned with it; and one should gaze upon that cup, blessing it with four blessings, for it is written: *The eyes of YHVH your God are perpetually upon her, from the beginning of the year to the end of the year* (Deuteronomy 11:12). Thus within the cup of blessing is found mystery of faith: north and south, east and west—holy Chariot.[1019]

the cup in both hands. See BT *Berakhot* 51a–b; Galante; *Adderet Eliyyahu*; *MM*; Scholem.

On leaving bread on the table, see BT *Sanhedrin* 92a: "Rabbi El'azar said, 'Whoever does not leave bread on his table will never see a sign of blessing.'" See Naḥmanides on Exodus 25:24; *Zohar* 1:88a, 240a; 2:63b, 67a, 87b, 153b, 155a, 157b; 3:34a; Ta-Shma, *Ha-Nigleh she-ba-Nistar,* 28; idem, *Minhag Ashkenaz ha-Qadmon,* 267–70.

On Rav Hamnuna Sava (the Elder), see above, note 764. The full verse in Psalms reads: *I raise the cup of salvations and invoke the name of YHVH*. See BT *Berakhot* 51b; *Zohar* 1:1a; 2:169a; 3:187b, 245a–b (*RM*).

1018. **Cup of blessing...** The cup, symbolizing *Shekhinah* (Assembly of Israel), should be held in two hands, symbolizing *Ḥesed* and *Gevurah*. (See the preceding note.) It should also be filled with wine, symbolizing the richness of Torah issuing from *Binah* (who is known as "the world that is coming").

On *Shekhinah* as "cup of blessing," see *Zohar* 1:1a, 233b; 2:143b, 157b; Moses de León, *Sod Eser Sefirot Belimah,* 383. On cup as a metaphor for wife, see BT *Nedarim* 20b; *Gittin* 90a. On the cup being full, see BT *Berakhot* 51a, quoted in the preceding note. On the wine of Torah, see above, note 756. On Assembly of Israel as a name of *Shekhinah,* see above, pp. 122–23, n. 237. On *Binah* as "the world that is coming," see above, note 2.

1019. **Cup of blessing... supernal matters...** The supernal matters derive from the statement in BT *Berakhot* 51a (quoted above, note 1017): "Ten things have been said concerning the cup of blessing:... it should be full;... one takes it with both his hands and places it in the right hand,... one fixes his eyes upon it."

The Chariot refers to the quartet of *sefirot*: *Ḥesed, Gevurah, Tif'eret,* and *Shekhinah* (see above, note 969)—which are identified respectively with the four directions: south, north, east, and west. *Shekhinah* (the cup of blessing) is held by *Ḥesed* and *Gevurah* (the right and left hands). *Shekhinah* is likewise identified with the bed of Solomon (mentioned in Song of Songs 3:7), whose placement between *Gevurah* (north) and *Ḥesed* (south) accords with the rabbinic tradition that a person's bed should be "placed between north and south," i.e., aligned north and south.

By aligning the body with the cup, one

"The table with bread—so that it will be blessed on all sides, above and below. Above, through the mystery of the cup of blessing, joining King David with the patriarchs. And blessed below—for 'bread of poverty' will be blessed, becoming pastry, and that person's table will be blessed, providing food constantly."[1020]

They all rose and kissed his hands, and said, "Blessed is the Compassionate One, that we entered here and heard these words!"

They emerged from the cave and walked on. When they entered the town, they saw a ring of people who had died from a house collapsing on them. They sat down, and saw that there was mourning for those who had died along with the Romans.[1021]

Rabbi Shim'on opened, saying, "*They came as far as* גרן האטד (*Goren ha-Atad*), *Threshing-floor of the Bramble,* (Genesis 50:10). What is *Goren ha-Atad*? Well, here is an allusion to dominion being eliminated from Egypt. *Goren ha-Atad, Threshing-floor of the Bramble*—appointed authority of the Egyptians being removed in favor of dominion of Israel; for they saw, as is said: *arrayed in robes at the threshing floor* (1 Kings 22:10). So, *there they held a great and heavy lamentation.... Therefore it was named* אבל מצרים (*Avel Mitsrayim*), *Mourning of Egypt* (Genesis, ibid., 10–11)—for surely it was *of Egypt.* Here too, this weeping is not for the Jews, although Jews died there. And these Jews, if they

ensures that *Tif'eret* (trunk of the divine body) will be aligned with *Shekhinah*. By gazing at the cup while reciting the four blessings of Grace after Meals, one stimulates the divine eyes to gaze upon *Shekhinah*.

On *Shekhinah* as "bed" and *bed of Solomon,* see above, notes 302, 972. On the north-south alignment of the bed, see BT *Berakhot* 5b; *Zohar* 3:118b, 119b–120a; Moses de León, *Sefer ha-Rimmon,* 370. The object of the verse in Deuteronomy (*her*) is the land of Israel, symbolizing here *Shekhinah*. See *Zohar* 1:107a, 199a; 2:157b; Moses de León, *Sefer ha-Rimmon,* 105.

1020. **table with bread...** By keeping bread on the table during Grace after Meals, one ensures that *Shekhinah* (symbolized by King David) will be transformed from "bread of poverty" to pastry through Her union with the sefirotic triad of *Ḥesed, Gevurah,* and *Tif'eret* (symbolized by the patriarchs). This divine union not only enriches *Shekhinah* but generates blessing below, providing the earthly table with an endless supply of food.

On David and the patriarchs, see above, p. 525 and n. 969. On "bread of poverty" and pastry, see above, p. 504 and n. 904.

1021. **ring of people who had died...** Rabbi Shim'on had foreseen this event and decided to remain in the cave, because if he had come to town, his merit would have prevented the disaster, which killed two Roman informers. See above, p. 532 and n. 990. Now Rabbi Shim'on and the Companions witness mourning, apparently for a number of Jews who had also died.

"Ring" renders עירטא (*irta*), apparently a playful variation or corruption of עיטרא (*itra*), "crown." For various renderings, see *OY*; Galante; *KP*; *Adderet Eliyyahu*; *DE*; Luria, *Va-Ye'esof David,* s.v. *artena*; Scholem. Cf. *Targum Yerushalmi,* Genesis 50:26.

had been Jews, would not have died; but because they died, the blessed Holy One has pardoned their sins."[1022]

Rabbi Shim'on said, "Come and see: Although Jacob's soul departed in Egypt, she did not depart in an alien domain. Why? As has been said, since the day that the world was created, there has never been a bed as perfect as the bed of Jacob at the moment that he was departing from the world; and his soul was immediately linked to her place, as we have established.[1023]

"When Jacob entered the cave, all aromas of the Garden of Eden permeated it; the cave emitted light, and a single lamp kindled—for it had kindled, but when the patriarchs entered Jacob's presence in Egypt, to be with him, the light of the lamp withdrew. As soon as Jacob entered the cave, the light of the lamp returned to its place, and then the cave was complete with all that was needed.[1024] For all

1022. **What is *Goren ha-Atad*?...** Rabbi Shim'on explains that at Goren ha-Atad the Egyptians did not mourn primarily for Jacob, but rather for what they foresaw: the eventual end of their own domination over Israel. Therefore the place was called *Mourning of Egypt.* The word גרן (*goren*), *threshing-floor,* alludes to power and authority, as indicated by the verse in Kings. See above, p. 529 and nn. 983–84, p. 531 and n. 989.

Similarly here, the mourning in the town is not for the Jews who had died, but rather Romans mourning for the Roman informers and the eventual end of Roman domination. The clause "if they had been Jews" means "if they had been real, virtuous Jews"—not the kind who consort with Romans.

On death as a means of atonement, see M *Yoma* 8:8; *Tosefta, Yoma* 4:6–9; *Mekhilta, Baḥodesh* 7; Urbach, *The Sages,* 1:430–36.

The context in Genesis (50:10–11) reads: *They came as far as Goren ha-Atad, which is across the Jordan, and there they held a very great and heavy lamentation, and he performed mourning rites for his father seven days. The Canaanite inhabitants of the land saw the mourning in Goren ha-Atad and they said, 'This is a heavy mourning for Egypt.' Therefore it was named Abel-mizraim.*

The full verse in Kings reads: *The king of Israel and Jehoshaphat king of Judah were sitting each on his throne, arrayed in robes, at the threshing floor by the entrance of the gate of Samaria; and all the prophets were prophesying before them.* On the connection between *goren* (threshing-floor) and authority, see the description of the Sanhedrin in M *Sanhedrin* 4:3: "The Sanhedrin was arranged like half of a round threshing-floor, so that they could see one another." See BT *Ḥullin* 5a; *Shemot Rabbah* 5:12; Radak on 1 Kings 22:10.

1023. **Jacob's soul departed in Egypt...** Although his soul departed in a foreign land, she (the soul) was not under the sway of demonic forces, which normally dominate outside the land of Israel. This was because Jacob's bed was perfect in two senses: first, because all of his offspring were worthy; and second, because he was now facing *Shekhinah* and flanked by the souls of Abraham and Isaac. Those two patriarchs symbolize respectively *Ḥesed* and *Gevurah,* who are integrated and completed by Jacob's *sefirah, Tif'eret.*

See above, note 575, and at notes 605, 780; *Zohar* 2:141b. On the destiny of Jacob's soul, see *Zohar* 1:22a.

1024. **Jacob entered the cave...** The cave of Machpelah, purchased by Abraham as a family burial site and identified as the entrance to the Garden of Eden. The lamp apparently symbolizes *Shekhinah,* who had previously illumined the cave but left it in

days of the world, the cave has never received another human being, and it never will. Souls of the virtuous pass before them within the cave, so that they will awaken and see the seed they have left in the world and rejoice before the blessed Holy One."[1025]

Rabbi Abba asked, "The embalming of Jacob—what is it?"

He replied, "Go ask a physician! Come and see what is written: *Joseph ordered his servants the physicians to embalm his father, and the physicians embalmed Israel* (Genesis 50:2). Now, would you ever imagine that this embalming was like that of other people? If you say that it was done because of the journey, look at what is written: *Joseph died, a hundred and ten years old, and they embalmed him and he was placed in a coffin in Egypt* (ibid., 26)! They didn't journey with him, for he was buried right there—yet it is written *they embalmed him.*[1026]

"Rather, this is customary for kings: in order to preserve their bodies, they are embalmed with anointing oil—finest of all oils, blended with spices—and they infuse the body with that excellent oil day after day for forty days, as is written: *Forty full days were spent on him, for such is the full time of embalming* (ibid., 3). Once this is completed, the body perdures intact for a long time.[1027]

order to join Jacob on his deathbed, along with Abraham and Isaac. Now that Jacob entered the cave, the lamp was rekindled.

See *Pirqei de-Rabbi Eli'ezer* 36: "[Abraham] ran to fetch a calf [for the three messengers visiting him (Genesis 18:7)], but the calf ran away from him and entered the cave of Machpelah; so he went in after it, and there he found Adam and Eve lying on their beds asleep, with lamps burning above them and a fragrant aroma around them.... Therefore he desired to possess the cave of Machpelah as a burial site." See above, note 967.

On the rekindling of the lamp, see *Bereshit Rabbah* 60:16: "As long as Sarah existed... the lamp would burn in her tent from one Sabbath eve until the next. As soon as she died, it went out. As soon as Rebekah arrived, it returned." See *Zohar* 1:50a, 133a.

On the presence of Abraham, Isaac, and *Shekhinah* at Jacob's deathbed, see the preceding note. On the presence of *Shekhinah* in the cave, see above at note 891.

1025. **cave has never received another...** Jacob was the last person to be buried in the cave of Machpelah. However, when the righteous die, on their way to the Garden of Eden their souls pass before the patriarchs in the cave.

See *Zohar* 1:81a (*ST*). On these souls' encounter with Adam, see *Tanḥuma, Ḥuqqat* 16; *Tanḥuma* (Buber), *Ḥuqqat* 39; *Bemidbar Rabbah* 19:18; *Zohar* 1:57b, 65b, 127a. On Jacob being the last to be buried in the cave of Machpelah, see Naḥmanides on Genesis 49:31 (quoting *Mekhilta de-Rashbi*); *Midrash ha-Gadol* on Genesis 50:25.

1026. **Go ask a physician...** A doctor can explain the physical procedure of embalming, but Rabbi Shim'on offers a deeper meaning behind the embalming of Jacob and Joseph. First, he rejects the notion that Jacob was embalmed simply because of the long journey from Egypt to the cave of Machpelah in Hebron, because this would not explain the embalming of Joseph, who was buried right in Egypt.

1027. ***Forty full days were spent on him...*** On the embalming of Jacob.

For the entire land of Canaan and the land of Egypt decay and decompose the body [251a] in less time than any other land; so in order to preserve the body, they do this. They perform this embalming both internally and externally. Internally, by placing that oil on the navel, through which it enters within, absorbed by the entrails; so it preserves the body within and without for a long time.

"So it was with Jacob—his body preserved—and so it had to be, for he is body of the patriarchs, and he perdured in body and soul.[1028] Similarly with Joseph, modeled on the body, perduring in body and soul. In body, as is written: *they embalmed him.* In soul, as is written: ויישם בארון (*va-yiysem ba-aron*), *he was placed in a coffin*—spelled with two letters י (*yod*). Why? Because Joseph preserved the covenant below and preserved Covenant above. When he departed from the world, he was placed in two caskets: in an ארון (*aron*), *coffin*, below; and in an *aron*, ark, above. Who is the ark above? As is said: *See, ark of the covenant, Lord of all the earth* (Joshua 3:11)—for the ark above is called *ark of the covenant*, because it is inherited only by one who preserves the covenant. Since Joseph preserved the covenant, he was placed in two caskets: ויישם בארון (*va-yiysem ba-aron*), *He was placed in a casket, in Egypt*—certainly so![1029]

1028. **body of the patriarchs...** Jacob attained the rung of *Tif'eret*, the trunk of the body of the *sefirot*, completing the right and left sides (symbolized respectively by Abraham and Isaac). Just as his soul endured, it was fitting for his physical body to be embalmed and preserved. See *Zohar* 2:141b.

1029. **Joseph, modeled on the body...** By withstanding the sexual advances of Potiphar's wife, Joseph proved his virtue and attained the rung of *Yesod*, the divine phallus and symbol of the covenant of circumcision. *Yesod* is an extension of *Tif'eret*, the body; thus Joseph, symbol of *Yesod*, is "modeled on the body." Through controlling his sexuality, he "preserved the covenant below (the sign of circumcision) and preserved Covenant above (*Yesod*)."

Joseph's double act of preservation was rewarded doubly, as indicated by the double י (*yod*) in the word ויישם (*va-yiysem*), *he was placed* (literally, "he placed"). Each *yod* alludes to one meaning of the word ארון (*aron*): "coffin" and "ark." (The rendering "casket" embraces both these senses.) Joseph's embalmed body "was placed in a coffin," while his soul "was placed in an ark"—namely, in *Shekhinah*, who is called *ark of the covenant*, container of *Yesod*.

On the double י (*yod*) in ויישם (*va-yiysem*), see *Sekhel Tov* on the verse; *Zohar* 2:214b; *ZḤ* 43d; Moses de León, *She'elot u-Tshuvot*, 26–27; Galante; *Minḥat Shai* on the verse; *MM*. Cf. Rashbam, Ibn Ezra, Radak, and Ḥizzekuni on the verse; Ibn Ezra on Exodus 30:32 (short and long), Micah 1:7.

On the two caskets, see *Tosefta, Sotah* 4:7; *Mekhilta, Beshallaḥ, Petiḥta*; *Mekhilta de-Rashbi*, Exodus 13:19; JT *Berakhot* 2:3, 4c; BT *Sotah* 13a–b; *Pesiqta de-Rav Kahana* 11:12; *Tanḥuma, Beshallaḥ* 2.

On *Shekhinah* as "ark of the covenant," see *Zohar* 1:2a, 33b, 50b, 59b, 228b; 2:13a, 214b, 235b, 259a–b (*Heikh*); 3:199a; Moses de León, *Sheqel ha-Qodesh*, 75 (95).

"The verse demonstrates another mystery. For although his soul departed in a foreign domain, it joined with *Shekhinah*, as is written: ויישם בארון (*va-yiysem ba-aron*), *he was placed in a casket*—above and below—because he was righteous. For every righteous one inherits this Holy Land, as is written: *Your people, all of them righteous, will inherit the land forever—sprout of My planting, work of My hands, that I may be glorified* (Isaiah 60:21)."[1030]

1030. **although his soul departed...** Even though Joseph died in Egypt, his soul was not vulnerable to demonic forces (which normally dominate outside the land of Israel), because he lived virtuously and preserved the covenant. Joseph the Righteous ascended to the rung of *Yesod* (known as Righteous One) and inherited *Shekhinah*, known as the Holy Land. He serves as a model for human striving: anyone who becomes righteous will attain *Shekhinah*.

See *Zohar* 2:141b; Moses de León, *She'elot u-Tshuvot*, 26–27; above, note 1023. On the verse in Isaiah, see above, note 2. On *Yesod* as Righteous One, see above, p. 92, n. 50.

REFERENCE MATTER

Abbreviations

ABD	David Noel Freedman, ed., *Anchor Bible Dictionary*
add.	addendum
Add.	Additional
Adderet Eliyyahu	Elijah ben Moses Loanz, *Adderet Eliyyahu*
Arukh	Nathan ben Yeḥiel of Rome, *Sefer he-Arukh*
Arukh ha-Shalem	Nathan ben Yeḥiel of Rome, *Arukh ha-Shalem*
Battei Midrashot	Shlomo Aharon Wertheimer, ed., *Battei Midrashot*
B.C.E.	before the Common Era
Beit ha-Midrash	Adolph Jellinek, ed., *Beit ha-Midrash*
BT	Babylonian Talmud
C9	MS Add. 1023, University Library, Cambridge
ca.	*circa,* approximately
C.E.	Common Era
chap.	chapter
ed.	editor (pl. eds.); edition; edited by
DE	*Derekh Emet,* in *Sefer ha-Zohar,* ed. Reuven Margaliot
diss.	dissertation
frag.	fragmentary
Galante	Abraham Galante, in *Or ha-Ḥammah,* ed. Abraham Azulai
Hash	*Hashmatot*
Heikh	*Heikhalot*
intro	introduction
IR	*Idra Rabba*
IZ	*Idra Zuta*
JT	Jerusalem Talmud
KP	Shim'on Lavi, *Ketem Paz*
L2	MS 762, British Library, London
M	Mishnah
M7	MS Hebr. 217, Bayerische Staatsbibliothek, Munich
Ma'arikh	Menaḥem ben Judah de Lonzano, *Sefer ha-Ma'arikh*
Mat	*Matnitin*
MhN	*Midrash ha-Ne'lam*
MM	Shalom Buzaglo, *Miqdash Melekh*
MmD	Daniel Frisch, *Peirush Matoq mi-Devash*
Mopsik	Charles Mopsik, trans. and ed., *Le Zohar*
MS (plural, MSS)	manuscript(s)

Ms4	MS Guenzburg 779, Russian State Library, Moscow
n. (plural, nn.)	note(s)
N23	MS 1761, Jewish Theological Seminary, New York
n.d.	no date
Nefesh David	David Luria, *Nefesh David*
NO	Ḥayyim Joseph David Azulai, *Nitsotsei Orot*
n.p.	no publisher
NZ	Reuven Margaliot, *Nitsotsei Zohar*
O2	MS 1564, Bodleian Library, Oxford
O16	MS 2433, Bodleian Library, Oxford
OḤ	Abraham Azulai, ed., *Or ha-Ḥammah*
OL	Abraham Azulai, *Or ha-Levanah*
OY	Moses Cordovero, *Or Yaqar*
P2	MS héb. 779, Bibliothèque nationale, Paris
P4	MS héb. 781, Bibliothèque nationale, Paris
par.	paragraph
Pereq Shirah	Malachi Beit-Arié, ed., *Pereq Shirah*
Piq	*Piqqudin*
pl.	plural
Pr6	MS Perreau 15/A, Biblioteca Palatina, Parma
QhM	*Qav ha-Middah*
R1	MS 2971, Biblioteca Casanatense, Rome
RM	*Ra'aya Meheimna*
RR	*Raza de-Razin*
Scholem	Gershom Scholem, *Sefer ha-Zohar shel Gershom Scholem*
SdTs	*Sifra di-Tsni'uta*
ShS	*Shir ha-Shirim*
SO	*Sitrei Otiyyot*
Soncino	Harry Sperling et al., trans., *The Zohar* (Soncino Press)
ST	*Sitrei Torah*
Sullam	Yehudah Ashlag, *Sefer ha-Zohar . . . im . . . ha-Sullam*
T1	MS Friedberg 5-015, University of Toronto Library
Tiq	*Tiqqunim* (in *Zohar Ḥadash*)
Tos	*Tosefta*
trans.	translator(s); translated by
TZ	*Tiqqunei ha-Zohar*
V5	MS ebr. 206, Biblioteca Apostolica, Vatican
V6	MS ebr. 207, Biblioteca Apostolica, Vatican
V16	MS Neofiti 23, Biblioteca Apostolica, Vatican
Vital	Ḥayyim Vital, in *Or ha-Ḥammah*, ed. Abraham Azulai
ZḤ	*Zohar Ḥadash*
Zohorei Ya'bets	Jacob Emden, *Zohorei Ya'bets*

Transliteration of Hebrew and Aramaic

א	*alef*	’[1]	ל	*lamed*	*l*
בּ	*bet*	*b*	מ	*mem*	*m*
ב	*vet*	*v*	נ	*nun*	*n*
ג	*gimel*	*g*	ס	*samekh*	*s*
ד	*dalet*	*d*	ע	*ayin*	’[2]
ה	*he*	*h*	פּ	*pe*	*p*
ו	*vav*	*v*	פ	*phe*	*f*[3]
ז	*zayin*	*z*	צ	*tsadi*	*ts*
ח	*ḥet*	*ḥ*	ק	*qof*	*q*
ט	*tet*	*t*	ר	*resh*	*r*
י	*yod*	*y, i*	שׁ	*shin*	*sh*
כּ	*kaf*	*k*	שׂ	*sin*	*s*
כ	*khaf*	*kh*	ת	*tav*	*t*

The English equivalent letter is doubled when a strong *dagesh* in Hebrew or Aramaic characterizes a verbal conjugation or indicates an assimilated letter, e.g., *dibber, yitten.* The English letter is not doubled when preceded by a hyphenated prefix, e.g., *ha-sefer, la-melekh, mi-tokh.*

Proper names that appear in roman type do not follow the above schema. Biblical names are rendered according to the *JPS Hebrew-English Tanakh.* Rabbinic names are rendered according to common convention, e.g., Akiva, Resh Lakish. Medieval names are Anglicized, e.g., Moses de León, Joseph Gikatilla. Authors' names in the Bibliography follow library listings or the *Encyclopaedia Judaica.*

1. *Alef* is not transliterated at the beginning or end of a word nor after a hyphenated prefix. Elsewhere it is transliterated only when accompanied by a vowel, e.g., *Shemu'el.*
2. *Ayin* is not transliterated at the beginning of a word, nor after a hyphenated prefix, nor, unless accompanied by a vowel, at the end of a word.
3. Occasionally transliterated as *ph* to compare or contrast it to the letter *pe.*

Glossary

aggadah "Tale"; the nonlegal contents of the Talmud and Midrash, often based on biblical exegesis. It includes ethical and moral teaching, theological speculation, legends, and folklore.

alef The first letter of the Hebrew alphabet; the beginning of divine and human speech.

Amidah "Standing"; the central prayer, recited three times daily.

amora, pl. ***amora'im*** "Speaker, interpreter"; a teacher living in the three centuries or so following the compilation of the Mishnah (ca. 200 C.E.) and whose opinions are recorded in subsequent rabbinic literature.

Assembly of Israel Hebrew, כנסת ישראל (*Keneset Yisra'el*); in rabbinic literature, a phrase denoting the people of Israel. In the *Zohar,* the phrase can refer to the earthly community of Israel but also (often primarily) to *Shekhinah,* the divine feminine counterpart of the people.

Ayin "Nothingness"; the creative "no-thingness" of God, out of which all being emanates.

Binah "Understanding"; the third *sefirah;* the Divine Mother who gives birth to the seven lower *sefirot.*

blessed Holy One Common rabbinic name for God. In the *Zohar* it often designates *Tif'eret.*

Din "Judgment"; the fifth *sefirah;* the left arm of the divine body, balancing *Ḥesed.* The roots of evil lie here; also called *Gevurah.*

Eikhah The book of Lamentations.

Ein Sof "There is no end"; that which is boundless; the Infinite. The ultimate reality of God beyond all specific qualities of the *sefirot;* the God beyond God.

Elohim "God, gods"; a biblical name for God. In the *Zohar* it has various sefirotic associations: *Binah, Gevurah, Shekhinah.*

Gedullah "Greatness"; the fourth *sefirah;* the outpouring of God's great goodness; also called *Ḥesed.*

Gevurah "Power"; the fifth *sefirah;* also called *Din.*

gimatriyya Derived from the Greek *geometria* ("measuring the earth"); a method of interpretation based on the numerical value of Hebrew letters.

halakhah "Practice, law," from the root הלך (*hlkh*), "to walk": the way that one should follow.

Hashmatot "Omissions"; additions printed at the end of each of the three standard Aramaic volumes of the *Zohar,* drawn from the Cremona edition and *Zohar Ḥadash.*

ḥasid, pl. *ḥasidim* "Pious one," devotee, saint, lover of God.

Heikhalot "Palaces"; descriptions of the heavenly palaces in *Zohar* 1:38a–45b; 2:244b–268b.

Ḥesed "Loving-kindness, love, grace"; the fourth *sefirah;* the right arm of the divine body, balancing *Din;* also called *Gedullah.*

Hod "Splendor"; the eighth *sefirah;* the left leg of the divine body; source of prophecy along with *Netsaḥ.*

Ḥokhmah "Wisdom"; the second *sefirah;* the primordial point of emanation.

Holy Ancient One The most ancient manifestation of *Ein Sof* through *Keter,* Its crown.

idra "Threshing place," assembly.

Idra Rabba "The Great Assembly"; a description of the gathering of Rabbi Shim'on and the Companions at the threshing house, where profound mysteries of divine being are expounded. *Zohar* 3:127b–145a.

Idra Zuta "The Small Assembly"; a description of the last gathering of Rabbi Shim'on and the Companions, the master's final teachings, and his ecstatic death. *Zohar* 3:287b–296b.

Israel Often, the people of Israel.

Kabbalah Hebrew, קבלה (*qabbalah*), "receiving, that which is received, tradition"; originally referring to tradition in general (or to post-Mosaic Scripture), but from the thirteenth century onward, specifically to the esoteric teachings of Judaism.

Keter "Crown"; the first *sefirah;* coeternal with *Ein Sof;* also called *Ratson* ("Will") and *Ayin* ("Nothingness").

Lilith A demoness who harms babies and seduces men; married to Samael.

Malkhut "Kingdom"; the tenth *sefirah,* ruling the lower worlds; also called *Shekhinah.*

Matnitin "Our Mishnah"; short pieces scattered throughout the *Zohar,* most of which appear as utterances of a heavenly voice urging the Companions to arouse themselves and open their hearts to the mysteries. Some of them contain principles of kabbalistic teaching in a condensed form, constituting a kind of mystical Mishnah, expounded in the main section of the *Zohar.*

Matronita Aramaized form of Latin *matrona,* "matron, married woman, noble lady," often applied in the *Zohar* to *Shekhinah,* the wife of *Tif'eret.*

menorah Candelabrum of seven branches; a feature of the wilderness Tabernacle and of the Temple in Jerusalem.

mezuzah "Doorpost"; small parchment on which are inscribed the first two paragraphs of the *Shema.* The parchment is rolled tightly, placed in a small case, and affixed to the doorposts in the home.

midrash, pl. **midrashim** Homiletical or legal interpretation of the Bible.

Midrash ha-Ne'lam "The Concealed Midrash, the Esoteric Midrash"; an early stratum of the *Zohar.* Its language is a mixture of Hebrew and Aramaic. *Midrash ha-Ne'lam* on the Torah pertains to several portions of Genesis, the beginning of Exodus, and several other portions; it is printed partly alongside the main text of the *Zohar* and partly in *Zohar Ḥadash. Midrash ha-Ne'lam* on Song of Songs, Ruth, and Lamentations is printed in *Zohar Ḥadash.* The subject matter of *Midrash ha-Ne'lam* is mostly Creation, the soul, and the world to come; its style is often allegorical.

Mishnah Collection of oral teachings compiled near the beginning of the third century by Rabbi Yehudah ha-Nasi; the earliest codification of Jewish Oral Law; the core of the Talmud.

mitsvah, pl. ***mitsvot*** "Commandment"; one of the 613 commandments of the Torah or one of various rabbinic precepts; religious duty; by extension, good deed.

nefesh "Soul," life force; the basic level of the soul, animating the human being. (The other two levels are *ruaḥ* and *neshamah.*)

neshamah "Breath, soul," soul-breath; the highest level of the soul. (The other two levels are *nefesh* and *ruaḥ.*)

Netsaḥ "Endurance"; the seventh *sefirah;* the right leg of the divine body; source of prophecy along with *Hod.*

Oral Torah The rabbinic interpretation of the Written Torah (the Five Books of Moses); in Kabbalah, a symbol of *Shekhinah.*

Other Side Aramaic, סטרא אחרא (*Sitra Aḥra*); the demonic realm, shadow of the divine.

parashah "Portion"; portion of the Torah read on a particular Sabbath, named after its opening word (or phrase) or a key word (or phrase) in the opening sentence.

Piqqudin "Commandments"; kabbalistic interpretations of the commandments scattered throughout the *Zohar* (to be distinguished from *Ra'aya Meheimna*).

Qav ha-Middah "The Standard of Measure"; a detailed description of the process of divine emanation, delivered by Rabbi Shim'on. *Zohar Ḥadash* 56d–58d.

Ra'aya Meheimna "The Faithful Shepherd"; a separate composition on the kabbalistic meaning of the commandments, printed piecemeal in the *Zohar.* Here Moses, the Faithful Shepherd, appears to Rabbi Shim'on and the Companions, revealing secrets.

Raḥamim "Compassion"; the sixth *sefirah,* harmonizing the polar opposites *Ḥesed* and *Din;* also called *Tif'eret.*

Raza de-Razin "The Secret of Secrets"; a separate section dealing with physiognomy and chiromancy (*Zohar* 2:70a–75a, *Zohar Ḥadash* 35b–37c). A second version is incorporated into the main body of the *Zohar* (2:70a–78a).

Rosh Hashanah The Jewish New Year, celebrated on the first two days of the Hebrew month Tishrei.

ruaḥ "Spirit, wind, breath"; the second level of soul. (The other two levels are *nefesh* and *neshamah.*)

Rut The book of Ruth.

Samael Prince of demons, married to Lilith; identical with Satan.

Sava "The Elder."

Sava de-Mishpatim "The Old Man of [Torah portion] *Mishpatim*"; an account of the Companions' encounter with a donkey-driver who turns out to be a master of wisdom. *Zohar* 2:94b–114a.

Sefer ha-Zohar "The Book of Radiance."

sefirah, pl. ***sefirot*** Literally, "counting," number, numerical entity; in Kabbalah, one of the ten aspects of divine personality, nine of which emanate from *Ein Sof* and the first *sefirah, Keter.* See the diagram on page ix.

Shaddai An obscure divine name, which may originally have meant "[God of] the mountain." In Kabbalah it often denotes *Shekhinah.*

Shekhinah "Presence," divine immanence; the tenth and last *sefirah;* female partner of *Tif'eret;* also called *Malkhut.*

Shema Literally, "hear"; central prayer recited morning and evening, comprising Deuteronomy 6:4–9; 11:13–21; and Numbers 15:37–41. The opening verse is: *Hear O Israel! YHVH our God, YHVH is one!*

Shir ha-Shirim The book of Song of Songs.

Sifra di-Tsni'uta "Book of Concealment"; an anonymous, highly condensed commentary on the beginning of the Torah in short, obscure sentences, divided into five chapters. Its subject is the mysteries of divine being. *Zohar* 2:176b–179a.

Sitrei Otiyyot "Secrets of the Letters"; a discourse by Rabbi Shim'on focusing on the letters of the divine name *YHVH* and how they symbolize the process of emanation. *Zohar Ḥadash* 1b–7b.

Sitrei Torah "Secrets of Torah"; interpretations of certain verses of Genesis, printed in separate columns parallel to the main body of the *Zohar* and in *Zohar Ḥadash.* It includes allegorical explanations of the mysteries of the soul.

Talmud Each of the two compilations of Jewish law, legend, ethics, and theology comprising the Mishnah and its vast commentary (the Gemara) by rabbis of the third through fifth centuries. The Jerusalem Talmud was compiled ca. 400 C.E.; the Babylonian Talmud, about one hundred years later.

tanna, pl. ***tanna'im*** "One who repeats, teacher"; an authority cited in the Mishnah or belonging to the Mishnaic period (first two centuries of the Common Era); an Amoraic scholar whose task was to memorize and recite tannaitic texts.

Targum "Translation"; an Aramaic translation of the Torah or the Bible.

tav The last letter of the Hebrew alphabet.

tefillin "Phylacteries"; two black leather boxes containing passages from the Torah (Exodus 13:1–10, 11–16; Deuteronomy 6:4–9; 11:13–21) written on parchment. They are bound by black leather straps on the left arm and on the head, and are prescribed for men to wear during weekday morning prayer. Each of the biblical passages indicates that the Children of Israel should place a sign upon their hand and a frontlet (or reminder) between their eyes.

Tif'eret "Beauty, glory"; the sixth *sefirah,* harmonizing the polar opposites *Ḥesed* and *Din;* male partner of *Shekhinah;* the torso of the divine body; also called *Raḥamim.*

Tiqqunei ha-Zohar "Embellishments on the *Zohar*"; an independent book whose setting is similar to *Ra'aya Meheimna.* It comprises a commentary on the beginning of Genesis, each *tiqqun* opening with a new interpretation of the word בראשית (*be-reshit*), "in the beginning."

Tiqqunim "Embellishments"; additional material in the genre of *Tiqqunei ha-Zohar,* printed in *Zohar Ḥadash* 93c–122b.

Torah "Instruction, teaching"; the Five Books of Moses (Genesis through Deuteronomy); by extension, the entire corpus of Jewish religious literature.

Tosefta "Addenda"; in rabbinic literature, a collection of precepts parallel to and contemporary with the Mishnah. In the *Zohar,* a collection similar to *Matnitin.*

Tsaddiq "Righteous One"; a name for *Yesod,* the ninth *sefirah.*

world that is coming Hebrew, העולם הבא (*ha-olam ha-ba*); Aramaic, עלמא דאתי (*alma de-atei*); often understood as referring to the hereafter and usually translated as "the world to come." From another perspective, however, "the world that is coming" already exists—occupying another, timeless dimension. In Kabbalah this phrase often refers to *Binah,* the continuous source of emanation, who "is constantly coming, never ceasing."

Written Torah The Five Books of Moses (Genesis through Deuteronomy); in Kabbalah, a symbol of *Tif'eret.*

Yah A contracted biblical form of the divine name *YHVH.*

Yanuqa "The Child"; the story of a wonder child who confounds and amazes the Companions. *Zohar* 3:186a–192a.

Yesod "Foundation"; the ninth *sefirah,* who channels the flow of emanation to *Shekhinah;* the phallus of the divine body; also called *Tsaddiq.*

YHVH The ineffable name of God, deriving from the root הוה (*hvh*), "to be." In the *Zohar* it often symbolizes *Tif'eret.*

Yom Kippur The Day of Atonement, observed on the tenth of the Hebrew month Tishrei.

zohar "Radiance, splendor."

Zohar Ḥadash "New Zohar"; a collection of Zoharic texts not included in the early editions of the *Zohar.* It was first printed in Salonika in 1597. The title is misleading since *Zohar Ḥadash* contains much of *Midrash ha-Ne'lam,* an early stratum of the *Zohar.*

Bibliography

This bibliography includes works cited and utilized by the translator for this volume, except for standard rabbinic texts and most reference works. A more complete bibliography appears in Volume 1.

1. MANUSCRIPTS OF THE *ZOHAR*[1]

Cambridge, University Library. Heb. Add. 1023.
London, British Library. 762.
Moscow, Guenzburg Collection, Russian State Library. 779.
Munich, Bayerische Staatsbibliothek. Cod. Hebr. 217.
New York, Jewish Theological Seminary. 1761.
Oxford, Bodleian Library. 1564, 2433.
Paris, Bibliothèque nationale. Héb. 779, 781.
Parma, Biblioteca Palatina. Perreau 15/A.
Rome, Biblioteca Casanatense. 2971.
Toronto, Friedberg Collection, University of Toronto Library. 5-015.
Vatican, Biblioteca Apostolica. Ebr. 206, 207, 208; Neofiti 23.

2. EDITIONS OF THE *ZOHAR*

Sefer ha-Zohar. Cremona: Vincenzo Conti, 1558.
Sefer ha-Zohar. 3 vols. Mantua: Meir ben Efraim and Jacob ben Naftali, 1558–60.
Sefer ha-Zohar. 3 vols. Vilna: Romm, 1882.
Sefer ha-Zohar. Edited by Reuven Margaliot. 4th ed. 3 vols. Jerusalem: Mossad Harav Kook, 1964.
Tiqqunei ha-Zohar. Edited by Reuven Margaliot. Jerusalem: Mossad Harav Kook, 1948. Reprint, 1978.
Zohar Ḥadash. Edited by Reuven Margaliot. Jerusalem: Mossad Harav Kook, 1953. Reprint, 1978.

1. For a list of eighty-four *Zohar* manuscripts, see Rubin, "Mif'al ha-Zohar," 172–73.

3. TRANSLATIONS OF THE *ZOHAR*

A. Hebrew

Ashlag, Yehudah, trans. and ed., completed by Yehudah Ẓevi Brandwein. *Sefer ha-Zohar... im... ha-Sullam.* 22 vols. Jerusalem: Ḥevrah Lehotsa'at Hazohar, 1945–58.

Bar-Lev, Yechiel, trans. and ed. *Sefer ha-Zohar... im Bei'ur Yedid Nefesh.* 14 vols. Petaḥ Tikvah: n.p., 1992–97.

Edri, Yehudah, trans. and ed. *Sefer ha-Zohar... meturgam bilshon ha-qodesh.* 10 vols. Jerusalem: Yerid Hasefarim, 1998.

Frisch, Daniel, trans. and ed. *Sefer ha-Zohar... Peirush Matoq mi-Devash.* 15 vols. Jerusalem: Mekhon Da'at Yosef, 1993–99.

Lachower, Fischel, and Isaiah Tishby, trans. and eds. *Mishnat ha-Zohar.* Vol. 1. 3d ed. Jerusalem: Mosad Bialik, 1971. An anthology.

Tishby, Isaiah, trans. and ed. *Mishnat ha-Zohar.* Vol. 2. Jerusalem: Mosad Bialik, 1961. An anthology.

B. English

Berg, Michael, ed. *The Zohar by Rabbi Shimon bar Yochai with the Sulam commentary of Rabbi Yehuda Ashlag.* 23 vols. Tel Aviv: Yeshivat Kol Yehudah, 1999–2003. The English translation is based on the Hebrew translation by Yehudah Ashlag.

Lachower, Fischel, and Isaiah Tishby, Hebrew trans. and eds. *The Wisdom of the Zohar: An Anthology of Texts.* Translated by David Goldstein. Vols. 1 and 2. London: Littman Library of Jewish Civilization, 1989.

Matt, Daniel Chanan, trans. and ed. *Zohar: The Book of Enlightenment.* Mahwah, N.J.: Paulist Press, 1983. An anthology.

———, trans. and ed. *Zohar: Annotated and Explained.* Woodstock, Vt.: Skylight Paths, 2002. An anthology.

Scholem, Gershom G., ed., with the special assistance of Sherry Abel. *Zohar: The Book of Splendor—Basic Readings from the Kabbalah.* New York: Schocken, 1949. Reprint, 1971. An anthology.

Sperling, Harry, Maurice Simon, and Paul P. Levertoff, trans. *The Zohar.* 5 vols. London: Soncino Press, 1931–34.

Tishby, Isaiah, Hebrew trans. and ed. *The Wisdom of the Zohar: An Anthology of Texts.* Translated by David Goldstein. Vol. 3. London: Littman Library of Jewish Civilization, 1989.

Wineman, Aryeh, trans. and ed. *Mystic Tales from the Zohar.* Philadelphia: Jewish Publication Society, 1997.

C. French

Mopsik, Charles, trans. and ed. *Le Zohar.* 4 vols. Lagrasse: Verdier, 1981–96.

4. COMMENTARIES ON THE *ZOHAR*

Ashlag, Yehudah, trans. and ed., completed by Yehudah Ẓevi Brandwein. *Sefer ha-Zohar... im... ha-Sullam.* 22 vols. Jerusalem: Ḥevrah Lehotsa'at Hazohar, 1945–58.

Azulai, Abraham, ed. *Or ha-Ḥammah.* 4 vols. Peremyshlyany: Zupnik, Knoller, and Wolf, 1896–98. Reprint, 4 vols. in 3, Bene-Berak: Yahadut, 1973.

———. *Or ha-Levanah.* Peremyshlyany: Zupnik and Knoller, 1899. Reprint, Jerusalem: Sha'arei Ziv, n.d.
Azulai, Ḥayyim Joseph David. "Nitsotsei Orot." In *Sefer ha-Zohar,* edited by Reuven Margaliot. 4th ed. 3 vols. Jerusalem: Mossad Harav Kook, 1964.
Bar-Lev, Yechiel, trans. and ed. *Sefer ha-Zohar... im Bei'ur Yedid Nefesh.* 14 vols. Petaḥ Tikvah: n.p., 1992–97.
Buzaglo, Shalom. *Miqdash Melekh ha-Shalem.* 5 vols. Jerusalem: Benei Yissakhar, 1995–2000.
Cordovero, Moses. *Or Yaqar.* 21 vols. Jerusalem: Achuzat Israel, 1962–95.
"Derekh Emet." In *Sefer ha-Zohar,* edited by Reuven Margaliot. 4th ed. 3 vols. Jerusalem: Mossad Harav Kook, 1964.
Elijah ben Solomon of Vilna. *Yahel Or.* Vilna: Romm, 1882. Reprint, Jerusalem: n.p., 1972.
Emden, Jacob. *Zohorei Ya'bets.* Edited by Abraham Bick. Jerusalem: Mossad Harav Kook, 1975.
Frisch, Daniel, trans. and ed. *Sefer ha-Zohar... Peirush Matoq mi-Devash.* 15 vols. Jerusalem: Mekhon Da'at Yosef, 1993–99.
Galante, Abraham. *Zohorei Ḥammah.* 2 vols. Vol. 1, Munkacs: P. Bleier, 1881. Vol. 2, Peremyshlyany: Zupnik and Knoller, 1882. An abridgment by Abraham Azulai of Galante's unpublished *Yareaḥ Yaqar,* incorporated into Azulai's *Or ha-Ḥammah.*
Horowitz, Ẓevi Hirsch. *Aspaqlaryah ha-Me'irah.* Fürth: Itzik ve-Yatmei Ḥayyim, 1776. Reprint, Jerusalem: Mekhon Sha'arei Ziv, 1983.

Lavi, Shim'on. *Ketem Paz.* 2 vols. Leghorn: Eli'ezer Sedon, 1795. 1 vol. Djerba: Jacob Haddad, 1940. Reprint, 2 vols. Jerusalem: Ahavat Shalom, 1981. The first vol. of the Jerusalem edition is a reprint of the Djerba edition; the second vol. is a reprint of the second vol. of the Leghorn edition.
Loanz, Elijah ben Moses. *Adderet Eliyyahu.* Jerusalem: Mekhon Sha'arei Ziv, 1998.
Luria, David. "Nefesh David." Addendum to *Yahel Or,* by Elijah ben Solomon of Vilna. Vilna: Romm, 1882. Reprint, addendum to *Sefer Kitvei ha-Ga'on R. David Luria (Pirqei de-Rabbi Eli'ezer).* Jerusalem: n.p., 1990.
Margaliot, Reuven. "Nitsotsei Zohar." In *Sefer ha-Zohar,* edited by Reuven Margaliot. 4th ed. 3 vols. Jerusalem: Mossad Harav Kook, 1964.
Scholem, Gershom. *Sefer ha-Zohar shel Gershom Scholem* [*Gershom Scholem's Annotated Zohar*]. 6 vols. Jerusalem: Magnes Press, 1992.
Vital, Ḥayyim. "Haggahot Maharḥu." In *Sefer ha-Zohar,* edited by Reuven Margaliot. 4th ed. 3 vols. Jerusalem: Mossad Harav Kook, 1964.
Zacuto, Moses ben Mordecai. *Peirush ha-Remez la-Zohar ha-Qadosh.* Moshav Bitḥah: Kol Bitḥah, 1998.

5. LEXICONS OF THE *ZOHAR*

Baer, Issachar. *Imrei Binah.* Prague: Moshe Katz, 1611.
Huss, Boaz, ed. "Bei'ur ha-Millim ha-Zarot she-be-Sefer ha-Zohar." *Kabbalah* 1 (1996): 167–204.
Isaiah ben Eli'ezer Ḥayyim. *Yesha Yah.* Venice: Giovanni Vendramin, 1637.
Liebes, Yehuda. *Peraqim be-Millon Sefer ha-Zohar.* Jerusalem: Hebrew University, 1982.
Lonzano, Menaḥem ben Judah de. *Sefer ha-Ma'arikh.* Printed with *Sefer he-Arukh* by Nathan ben Yeḥiel of Rome, edited by Shemuel Schlesinger. Tel Aviv: Yetsu Sifrei Kodesh, n.d.

Luria, David. "Va-Ye'esof David." Addendum to *Qadmut Sefer ha-Zohar* by David Luria, 73–82. Warsaw: Meir Yeḥiel Halter, 1887.
Neuhausen, Simon A. *Nirdefei Zohar.* Baltimore: Neuhausen, 1923.

6. Other Primary Sources

Abulafia, Todros ben Joseph. *Otsar ha-Kavod ha-Shalem.* Warsaw, 1879. Reprint: Jerusalem: Makor, 1970.
_____. *Sha'ar ha-Razim.* Edited by Michal Kushnir-Oron. Jerusalem: Mosad Bialik, 1989.
Alfonso el Sabio. *Cantigas de Santa Maria.* Edited by Walter Mettman. Vigo: Edicións Xerais de Galicia, 1981.
_____. *Las siete partidas.* Translated by Samuel Parsons Scott. Edited by Robert I. Burns. 5 vols. Philadelphia: University of Pennsylvania Press, 2001.
Al-Nakawa, Israel ben Joseph. *Menorat ha-Ma'or.* Edited by Hyman G. Enelow. 4 vols. New York: Bloch Publishing Company, 1929–32.
Alter, Robert, trans. and ed. *The Five Books of Moses.* New York: W. W. Norton, 2004.
Anav, Ẓedekiah ben Abraham. *Shibbolei ha-Leqet ha-Shalem.* Edited by Solomon Buber. Vilna: Romm, 1886.

Angelet, Joseph [David ben Judah he-Ḥasid, pseud.]. *Livnat ha-Sappir.* Jerusalem: Azriel, 1913. Reprint, Jerusalem: Makor, 1971.
Asher ben David, "Peirush ha-Shevu'ot." In *R. Asher ben David: Kol Ketavav ve-Iyyunim be-Qabbalato,* edited by Daniel Abrams, 205–22. Los Angeles: Cherub Press, 1996.
Azriel ben Menaḥem of Gerona. *Peirush ha-Aggadot le-Rabbi Azri'el.* Edited by Isaiah Tishby. 2d ed. Jerusalem: Magnes Press, 1982.
Baḥya ben Asher. *Bei'ur al ha-Torah.* Edited by Chaim D. Chavel. 3 vols. Jerusalem: Mossad Harav Kook, 1971–72.
Bar Ḥiyya, Abraham. *Megillat ha-Megalleh.* Edited by Zev Posnanski and Isaak Guttmann. Berlin: Zvi Hirsch Itzkovski, 1924.
Beit-Arié, Malachi, ed. "Pereq Shirah: Mevo'ot u-Mahadurah Biqqortit." 2 vols. Ph.D. diss., Hebrew University, 1966.
Cordovero, Moses. *Pardes Rimmonim.* Munkacs: Kahana and Fried, 1906. Reprint, Jerusalem: Mordechai Etyah, 1962.
David ben Abraham Maimuni. *Midrash David.* Translated and edited by Ben-Zion Krynfiss. Jerusalem: n.p., 1944.
David ben Judah he-Ḥasid. *The Book of Mirrors: Sefer Mar'ot ha-Ẓove'ot.* Edited by Daniel Chanan Matt. Chico, Calif.: Scholars Press, 1982.
Dionysius Areopagite [pseud.]. *The Divine Names and Mystical Theology.* Translated by John D. Jones. Milwaukee: Marquette University Press, 1980.
El'azar ben Judah of Worms. "Hilkhot ha-Kisse." In *Merkavah Shelemah,* edited by Shlomo Musajoff, 22b–29b. Jerusalem: n.p., 1921.
_____. *Ḥokhmat ha-Nefesh.* Lemberg: A. N. Süs, 1876.
_____. *Peirushei Siddur ha-Tefillah la-Roqeaḥ.* Edited by Moshe Hershler and Yehudah Alter Hershler. 2 vols. Jerusalem: Mekhon Harav Hershler, 1994.
Ezra ben Solomon of Gerona. "Peirush le-Shir ha-Shirim." In *Kitvei Ramban,* edited by Chaim D. Chavel, 2:471–518. Jerusalem: Mossad Harav Kook, 1964.
Fox, Everett, trans. and ed. *The Five Books of Moses.* New York: Schocken, 1995.
Friedlander, Gerald, trans. and ed. *Pirke de Rabbi Eliezer.* London, 1916. Reprint, New York: Sepher-Hermon Press, 1981.

Friedman, Richard Elliott. *Commentary on the Torah with a New English Translation.* San Francisco: HarperSanFrancisco, 2001.
Gerondi, Jonah ben Abraham. *Sha'arei Teshuvah.* Vilna: n.p., 1841.
Gikatilla, Joseph. *Sha'arei Orah.* Warsaw: Orgelbrand, 1883. Reprint, Jerusalem: Mordechai Etyah, 1960.
———. *Sha'arei Tsedeq.* Cracow: Fischer and Deutscher, 1881.
Gregory of Nyssa. *The Life of Moses.* Translated and edited by Abraham J. Malherbe and Everett Ferguson. New York: Paulist Press, 1978.
Halevi, Judah. *Sefer ha-Kuzari.* Translated by Yehuda Even Shmuel. Tel Aviv: Dvir, 1972.
Ibn Ezra, Abraham [pseud.]. *Sefer ha-Atsamim.* Edited by Menasheh Grossberg. London: Eliyahu Zev Rabinovitch, 1901.
Isaac the Blind. "Peirush Sefer Yetsirah." Appendix to Gershom Scholem, *Ha-Qabbalah be-Provans,* edited by Rivka Schatz. Jerusalem: Academon, 1970.
Jacob ben Jacob ha-Kohen. "Peirush Eser Sefirot." In "Qabbalot R. Ya'aqov ve-R. Yitsḥaq benei R. Ya'aqov ha-Kohen," edited by Gershom Scholem. *Madda'ei ha-Yahadut* 2 (1927): 227–30.
Jacob ben Sheshet. "Ha-Emunah ve-ha-Bittaḥon." In *Kitvei Ramban,* edited by Chaim D. Chavel, 2:339–448. Jerusalem: Mossad Harav Kook, 1964.
———. *Meshiv Devarim Nekhoḥim.* Edited by Georges Vajda. Jerusalem: Israel Academy of Sciences and Humanities, 1968.
Jellinek, Adolph, ed. *Beit ha-Midrash.* 3d ed. 6 vols. in 2. Jerusalem: Wahrmann Books, 1967.
JPS Hebrew-English Tanakh. Philadelphia: Jewish Publication Society, 1999.
Judah ben Barzillai. *Peirush Sefer Yetsirah.* Edited by S. J. Halberstam. Berlin: M'kize Nirdamim, 1885.
Judah ben Samuel he-Ḥasid. *Sefer Ḥasidim.* Edited by Reuven Margaliot. Jerusalem: Mossad Harav Kook, 1957.
———. *Sefer Ḥasidim.* Edited by Jehuda Wistinetzki. Berlin: Itzkowski, 1891. Reprint, Jerusalem: Vagshel, 1998.
Kaplan, Aryeh, trans. and ed. *Sefer Yetzirah: The Book of Creation.* York Beach, Maine: Samuel Weiser, 1990.
Kasher, Menaḥem M. *Ḥumash Torah Shelemah.* 2d ed. 12 vols. Jerusalem: Beth Torah Shelemah, 1992.
Matt, Daniel C., trans. and ed. *The Essential Kabbalah: The Heart of Jewish Mysticism.* San Francisco: HarperSanFrancisco, 1995.
Moses ben Shem Tov de León. *The Book of the Pomegranate: Moses de León's Sefer ha-Rimmon.* Edited by Elliot R. Wolfson. Atlanta: Scholars Press, 1988.
———. Commentary on the Ten *Sefirot* (untitled fragment). MS Hebr. 47, Bayerische Staatsbibliothek, Munich.
———. *Mishkan ha-Edut.* MS Or. Quat. 833, Staatsbibliothek, Berlin.
———. "Or Zaru'a." Edited by Alexander Altmann. *Kovez̧ al Yad,* n.s., 9 (1980): 219–93.
———. *Orḥot Ḥayyim (Tsavva'at Rabbi Eli'ezer).* Edited by Gershon Henikh. Warsaw: Meir Halter, 1891. Reprint, Bene-Berak: Agudat Ḥasidei Radzyn, 1990.
———. *Peirush ha-Merkavah.* Edited by Asi-Farber Ginat. Edited for publication by Daniel Abrams. Los Angeles: Cherub Press, 1998.
———. "Seder Gan Eden." In *Beit ha-Midrash,* edited by Adolph Jellinek, 3:131–40, 194–98. Jerusalem: Wahrmann Books, 1967.

———. "Sefer ha-Mishqal: Text and Study." Edited by Jochanan H. A. Wijnhoven. Ph.D. diss., Brandeis University, 1964. Supersedes an earlier edition: *Ha-Nefesh ha-Ḥakhamah.* Basle: Konrad Waldkirch, 1608.

———. "Sefer Maskiyyot Kesef." Edited by Jochanan H. A. Wijnhoven. M.A. diss., Brandeis University, 1961.

———. "She'elot u-Tshuvot be-Inyenei Qabbalah." In *Ḥiqrei Qabbalah u-Shluḥoteha,* edited by Isaiah Tishby, 1:36–75. Jerusalem: Magnes Press, 1982.

———. *Sheqel ha-Qodesh.* Edited by A. W. Greenup. London, 1911. Reprint, Jerusalem: n.p., 1969.

———. *Sheqel ha-Qodesh.* Edited by Charles Mopsik. Los Angeles: Cherub Press, 1996. Cited in the Commentary according to both this edition and, in parentheses, Greenup's edition.

———. "Shushan Edut." Edited by Gershom Scholem. *Kovez̤ al Yad,* n.s., 8 (1976): 325–70.

———. "Sod Eser Sefirot Belimah." Edited by Gershom Scholem. *Kovez̤ al Yad,* n.s., 8 (1976): 371–84.

Moses ben Simeon of Burgos. "Ammud ha-Semali." In *Le-Ḥeqer Qabbalat R. Yitsḥaq ben Ya'aqov ha-Kohen,* edited by Gershom Scholem, 146–64. Jerusalem: Tarbiz, 1934.

Naḥmanides, Moses. *Kitvei Ramban.* Edited by Chaim D. Chavel. 2 vols. Jerusalem: Mossad Harav Kook, 1964.

Orḥot Tsaddiqim. Edited by Gabriel Zloshinski. New York: Feldheim Publishers, 1991.

"Pirqei Rabbi Eli'ezer." Edited by Michael Higger. *Ḥoreb* 8 (1944): 82–119; 9 (1946): 94–166; 10 (1948): 185–294.

Pirqei Rabbi Eli'ezer. Commentary by David Luria; edited by Samuel ben Eli'ezer Luria. Warsaw: Bomberg, 1852. Reprint, New York: Om, 1946.

Recanati, Menaḥem. *Peirush al ha-Torah (Levushei Or Yeqarot).* Lemberg: Karl Budweiser, 1880–81. Reprint, Jerusalem: Mordechai Etyah, 1961.

Rumi, Jalal ad-Din. *The Mathnawi of Jalalu'ddin Rumi.* Translated and edited by Reynold A. Nicholson. 6 vols. London: E. J. W. Gibb Memorial Trust, 1926.

Schäfer, Peter, ed. *Synopse zur Hekhalot-Literatur.* Tübingen: J. C. B. Mohr, 1981.

Scholem, Gerhard, trans. and ed. *Das Buch Bahir.* Leipzig: W. Drugulin, 1923. Reprint, Darmstadt: Wissenschaftliche Buchgesellschaft, 1970.

Sefer ha-Bahir. Edited by Daniel Abrams. Los Angeles: Cherub Press, 1994. Cited in the Commentary according to both this edition and, in parentheses, Margaliot's edition.

Sefer ha-Bahir. Edited by Reuven Margaliot. Jerusalem: Mossad Harav Kook, 1951. Reprint, 1978.

Sefer ha-Temunah. Lemberg: Rahatin, 1892. Reprint, Israel: Books Export Enterprises, n.d.

Sefer ha-Yashar. Edited by Joseph Dan. Jerusalem: Mosad Bialik, 1986.

Sefer Yetsirah. Jerusalem: Lewin-Epstein, 1965.

Sha'arei Teshuvah (Teshuvot ha-Ge'onim). Edited by Wolf Leiter. Pittsburgh: Maimonides Institute, 1946. Reprint, Jerusalem: H. Vagshel, n.d.

Simḥah ben Samuel of Vitry. *Maḥazor Vitri.* Edited by Shim'on Hurwitz. Nüremberg: J. Bulka, 1923.

Wertheimer, Shlomo Aharon, ed. *Battei Midrashot.* 2d ed., revised by Abraham J. Wertheimer. 2 vols. Jerusalem: Ketav Vasepher, 1980.

7. OTHER SECONDARY SOURCES

Abrams, Daniel. "Zohar, Sefer ve-'Sefer ha-Zohar': Le-Toledot ha-Hannaḥot ve-ha-Tsippiyyot shel ha-Mequbbalim ve-ha-Ḥoqerim." *Kabbalah* 12 (2004): 201–32.
Altmann, Alexander. "Li-Sh'elat Ba'aluto shel Sefer Ta'amei ha-Mitsvot ha-Meyuḥas le-R. Yitsḥaq ibn Farḥi." *Kiryat Sefer* 40 (1965): 256–76, 405–12.
Assis, Yom Tov. "Sexual Behavior in Mediaeval Hispano-Jewish Society." In *Jewish History: Essays in Honour of Chimen Abramsky,* edited by Ada Rapoport-Albert and Steven J. Zipperstein, 25–60. London: Peter Halban, 1988.
Baer, Yitzḥak. *A History of the Jews in Christian Spain.* 2 vols. Translated by Louis Schoffman. Philadelphia: Jewish Publication Society, 1978.
Corbin, Henry. *The Man of Light in Iranian Sufism.* Translated by Nancy Pearson. Boulder: Shambhala, 1978.
Corominas, Joan, with the collaboration of José A. Pascual. *Diccionario Crítico Etimológico Castellano e Hispánico.* 6 vols. Madrid: Editorial Gredos, 1980–91.
Dan, Joseph, Esther Liebes, and Shmuel Reem, eds. *The Library of Gershom Scholem on Jewish Mysticism: Catalogue.* 2 vols., especially 1:174–232. Jerusalem: Jewish National and University Library, 1999.
Eliade, Mircea, ed. *The Encyclopedia of Religion.* 16 vols. New York: Macmillan, 1987.
Ginzberg, Louis. *Legends of the Jews.* 7 vols. Translated by Henrietta Szold and Paul Radin. Philadelphia: Jewish Publication Society, 1909–38.
Gottlieb, Efraim. *Meḥqarim be-Sifrut ha-Qabbalah.* Edited by Joseph Hacker. Tel Aviv: Tel Aviv University, 1976.
Green, Arthur. *Keter: The Crown of God in Early Jewish Mysticism.* Princeton: Princeton University Press, 1997.
Greenberg, Moshe. *Ezekiel 1–20.* Anchor Bible, vol. 22. Garden City, N.Y.: Doubleday, 1983.
Gruenwald, Ithamar. *Apocalyptic and Merkavah Mysticism.* Leiden: E. J. Brill, 1980.
Guttmann, Julius. *Philosophies of Judaism.* Translated by David W. Silverman. New York: Schocken, 1973.
Ḥamiẓ, Joseph ben Judah, ed. *Derekh Emet.* Venice, 1658.
Hecker, Joel. *Mystical Bodies, Mystical Meals: Eating and Embodiment in Medieval Kabbalah.* Detroit: Wayne State University Press, 2005.
Hellner-Eshed, Melila. *Ve-Nahar Yotse me-Eden: Al Sefat ha-Ḥavayah ha-Mistit ba-Zohar.* Tel Aviv: Am Oved, 2005.
Heschel, Abraham J. *Torah min ha-Shamayim ba-Aspaqlaryah shel ha-Dorot.* 3 vols. London: Soncino, 1962–65; Jerusalem: Jewish Theological Seminary of America, 1990.
Huss, Boaz. *Al Adnei Faz: Ha-Qabbalah shel R. Shim'on Ibn Lavi.* Jerusalem: Magnes Press, 1990.
———. "Ḥakham Adif mi-Navi: R. Shim'on bar Yoḥai u-Mosheh Rabbenu ba-Zohar." *Kabbalah* 4 (1999): 103–39.
———. "Hofa'ato shel 'Sefer ha-Zohar.'" *Tarbiz* 70 (2001): 507–42.
Idel, Moshe. *Kabbalah: New Perspectives.* New Haven: Yale University Press, 1988.
———. "Olam ha-Mal'akhim bi-Dmut Adam." *Meḥqerei Yerushalayim be-Maḥashevet Yisra'el* 3 (1984): 1–66.
———. "Peirush Eser Sefirot u-Sridim mi-Ketavim shel R. Yosef ha-Ba mi-Shushan ha-Birah." *Alei Sefer* 6–7 (1979): 74–84.
———. "Seridim Nosafim mi-Kitvei R. Yosef ha-Ba mi-Shushan ha-Birah." *Da'at* 21 (1988): 47–55.

Kaddari, Menaḥem Z. *Diqduq ha-Lashon ha-Aramit shel ha-Zohar.* Jerusalem: Kiryath Sepher, 1971.

Katz, Jacob. *Halakhah ve-Qabbalah.* Jerusalem: Magnes Press, 1984.

Keller, John E. "The Miracle of the Divinely Motivated Silkworms: *Cantiga 18* of the *Cantigas de Santa María.*" *Hispanófila* 28 (1984): 1–9.

Levine, Baruch A. *The JPS Torah Commentary: Leviticus.* Philadelphia: Jewish Publication Society, 1989.

Lieberman, Saul. *Hellenism in Jewish Palestine: Studies in the Literary Transmission, Beliefs and Manners of Palestine in the I Century B.C.E.–IV Century C.E.* 2d ed. New York: Jewish Theological Seminary of America, 1962.

———. *Tosefet Rishonim.* 4 vols. Jerusalem: Bamberger et Vahrman, 1937–39.

———. *Tosefta ki-Fshutah: A Comprehensive Commentary on the Tosefta.* 10 vols. New York: Jewish Theological Seminary of America, 1955–88.

Liebes, Yehuda. "Ivrit va-Aramait ki-Lshonot ha-Zohar." *Zikhronot ha-Aqademyah la-Lashon ha-Ivrit* (in press).

———. "Ha-Mashiaḥ shel ha-Zohar: Li-Dmuto ha-Meshiḥit shel R. Shim'on bar Yoḥai." In *Ha-Ra'yon ha-Meshiḥi be-Yisra'el,* edited by Shemuel Reem, 87–236. Jerusalem: Israel Academy of Sciences and Humanities, 1982.

566 ———. "Myth vs. Symbol in the Zohar and in Lurianic Kabbalah." Translated by Eli Lederhandler. In *Essential Papers on Kabbalah,* edited by Lawrence Fine, 212–42. New York: New York University Press, 1995.

———. *Studies in the Zohar.* Translated by Arnold Schwartz, Stephanie Nakache, and Penina Peli. Albany: State University of New York Press, 1993.

———. *Torat ha-Yetsirah shel Sefer Yetsirah.* Tel Aviv: Schocken, 2000.

———. "Ziqqat ha-Zohar le-Erets Yisra'el." In *Tsiyyon ve-Tsiyyonut be-qerev Yehudei Sefarad ve-ha-Mizraḥ,* edited by W. Zeev Harvey et al., 31–44. Jerusalem: Misgav Yerushalayim, 2002.

Löw, Immanuel. *Die Flora der Juden.* 4 vols. in 5. Vienna: R. Löwit, 1924–34. Reprint, 4 vols., Hildesheim: Georg Olms, 1967.

Margaliot, Reuven. *Mal'akhei Elyon.* Jerusalem: Mossad Harav Kook, 1964.

———. "Ha-Rambam ve-ha-Zohar." *Sinai* 32 (1952–53): 263–74; 33 (1953): 9–15, 128–35, 219–24, 349–54; 34 (1953–54): 227–30, 386–95.

———. *Sha'arei Zohar.* Jerusalem: Mossad Harav Kook, 1978.

———. "She'elot be-Viqqoret ha-Zohar mi-tokh Yedi'otav al Erets Yisra'el." *Sinai* 9 (1941): 237–40.

Matt, Daniel C. "*Ayin*: The Concept of Nothingness in Jewish Mysticism." In *Essential Papers on Kabbalah,* edited by Lawrence Fine, 67–108. New York: New York University Press, 1995.

———. "Matnita di-Lan: Tekhniqah shel Ḥiddush be-Sefer ha-Zohar." In *Sefer ha-Zohar ve-Doro (Meḥqerei Yerushalayim be-Maḥashevet Yisra'el* 8 [1989]), edited by Joseph Dan, 123–45. Jerusalem: Hebrew University, 1989.

———. "'New-Ancient Words': The Aura of Secrecy in the *Zohar.*" In *Gershom Scholem's 'Major Trends in Jewish Mysticism': 50 Years After,* edited by Peter Schäfer and Joseph Dan, 181–207. Tübingen: J. C. B. Mohr, 1994.

May, Florence Lewis. *Silk Textiles of Spain: Eighth to Fifteenth Century.* New York: Hispanic Society of America, 1957.

Meroz, Ronit. "'Va-Ani Lo Hayiti Sham?': Quvlanotav shel Rashbi al pi Sippur Zohari Lo Yadu'a." *Tarbiz* 71 (2002): 163–93.

———. *Ha-Peninah, ha-Dag, ve-ha-Matstsah: Ha-Biyyografyah ha-Ruḥanit shel Rashbi, o Mivnehu ha-Qadum shel Sefer ha-Zohar.* Jerusalem: Mosad Bialik, forthcoming.

———. "Zoharic Narratives and Their Adaptations." *Hispania Judaica Bulletin* 3 (2000): 3–63.
Milgrom, Jacob. *The JPS Torah Commentary: Numbers.* Philadelphia: Jewish Publication Society, 1990.
———. *Leviticus.* Anchor Bible, vols. 3–3B. New York: Doubleday, 1991–2000.
Nathan ben Yeḥiel of Rome. *Arukh ha-Shalem.* 9 vols. Edited by Alexander Kohut, with *Tosefot he-Arukh ha-Shalem,* by Samuel Krauss. Vienna, 1878–92, 1937. Reprint, New York: Pardes, 1955.
———. *Sefer he-Arukh.* Edited by Shemuel Schlesinger. Tel Aviv: Yetsu Sifrei Kodesh, n.d.
Neuhausen, Simon A. *Sifriyyah shel Ma'lah.* Berehovo: Samuel Klein, 1937.
Patai, Raphael. *The Hebrew Goddess.* 3d ed. Detroit: Wayne State University Press, 1990.
Peretz, Eliyahu. *Ma'alot ha-Zohar: Mafteaḥ Shemot ha-Sefirot.* Jerusalem: Academon, 1987.
Rubin, Zvia. "Mif'al ha-Zohar: Mattarot ve-Hessegim." In *Asuppat Kiryat Sefer* (*Musaf le-Kherekh* 68), edited by Yehoshua Rosenberg, 167–74. Jerusalem: Jewish National and University Library, 1998.
———. *Ha-Muva'ot mi-Sefer ha-Zohar be-Feirush al ha-Torah le-R. Menaḥem Recanati.* Jerusalem: Academon, 1992.
Sarna, Nahum M. *The JPS Torah Commentary: Exodus.* Philadelphia: Jewish Publication Society, 1991.
———. *The JPS Torah Commentary: Genesis.* Philadelphia: Jewish Publication Society, 1989.
Scholem, Gershom G. *Alchemie und Kabbala.* Frankfurt am Main: Suhrkamp Verlag, 1984.
———. *Kabbalah.* Jerusalem: Keter, 1974.
———. *Le-Ḥeqer Qabbalat R. Yitsḥaq ben Ya'aqov ha-Kohen.* Jerusalem: Tarbiz, 1934.
———. "Le-Ḥeqer Torat ha-Gilgul ba-Qabbalah be-Me'ah ha-Shelosh-Esreh." *Tarbiz* 16 (1945): 135–50.
———. "Levush ha-Neshamot ve-'Ḥaluqa de-Rabbanan.'" *Tarbiz* 24 (1955): 290–306.
———. *Major Trends in Jewish Mysticism.* 3d. ed. New York: Schocken, 1967.
———. *On the Kabbalah and Its Symbolism.* Translated by Ralph Manheim. New York: Schocken, 1969.
———. *On the Mystical Shape of the Godhead: Basic Concepts in the Kabbalah.* Translated by Joachim Neugroschel, edited by Jonathan Chipman. New York: Schocken, 1991.
———. *Origins of the Kabbalah.* Edited by R. J. Zwi Werblowsky, translated by Allan Arkush. Philadelphia: Jewish Publication Society; Princeton: Princeton University Press, 1987.
———. "Parashah Ḥadashah min ha-Midrash ha-Ne'lam she-ba-Zohar." In *Sefer ha-Yovel li-Khvod Levi Ginzberg,* edited by Saul Lieberman, Shalom Spiegel, Solomon Zeitlin, and Alexander Marx, 425–46. New York: American Academy for Jewish Research, 1945.
———. *Ha-Qabbalah be-Provans.* Edited by Rivka Schatz. Jerusalem: Academon, 1970.
———. "Qabbalot R. Ya'aqov ve-R. Yitsḥaq benei R. Ya'aqov ha-Kohen." *Madda'ei ha-Yahadut* 2 (1927): 163–293.
———. "She'elot be-Viqqoret ha-Zohar mi-tokh Yedi'otav al Erets Yisra'el." *Zion* (*Me'assef*) 1 (1926): 40–55.
———. "Te'udah Ḥadashah le-Toledot Reshit ha-Qabbalah." In *Sefer Bialik,* edited by Jacob Fichman, 141–62. Tel Aviv: Amanut, 1934.

Talmage, Frank. "Ha-Munnaḥ 'Haggadah' be-Mashal ha-Ahuvah ba-Heikhal be-Sefer ha-Zohar." *Meḥqerei Yerushalayim be-Maḥashevet Yisra'el* 4 (1985): 271–73.

Ta-Shma, Israel M. *Minhag Ashkenaz ha-Qadmon: Ḥeqer ve-Iyyun.* 2d ed. Jerusalem: Magnes Press, 1994.

———. *Ha-Nigleh she-ba-Nistar.* 2d ed. Tel Aviv: Hakibbutz Hameuchad, 2001.

Tigay, Jeffrey H. *The JPS Torah Commentary: Deuteronomy.* Philadelphia: Jewish Publication Society, 1996.

Tishby, Isaiah. *Ḥiqrei Qabbalah u-Shluḥoteha.* Vol. 1. Jerusalem: Magnes Press, 1982.

Trachtenberg, Joshua. *The Devil and the Jews: The Medieval Conception of the Jews and Its Relation to Modern Antisemitism.* New Haven: Yale University Press, 1943.

———. *Jewish Magic and Superstition: A Study in Folk Religion.* New York: Atheneum, 1974.

Urbach, Ephraim E. *The Sages: Their Concepts and Beliefs.* 2d ed. 2 vols. Translated by Israel Abrahams. Jerusalem: Magnes Press, 1979.

Verman, Mark. *The Books of Contemplation: Medieval Jewish Mystical Sources.* Albany: State University of New York Press, 1992.

Wolfson, Elliot R. *Along the Path: Studies in Kabbalistic Myth, Symbolism, and Hermeneutics.* Albany: State University of New York Press, 1995.

———. *Circle in the Square: Studies in the Use of Gender in Kabbalistic Symbolism.* Albany: State University of New York Press, 1995.

———. "Circumcision and the Divine Name: A Study in the Transmission of Esoteric Doctrine." *Jewish Quarterly Review* 78 (1987): 77–112.

———. *Through a Speculum That Shines: Vision and Imagination in Medieval Jewish Mysticism.* Princeton: Princeton University Press, 1994.

Wolfson, Harry A. *Philo: Foundations of Religious Philosophy in Judaism, Christianity, and Islam.* 2 vols. Cambridge: Harvard University Press, 1947.

Index of Sources

This index includes sources that are quoted (rather than merely cited or alluded to) by either the *Zohar* or the translator. Biblical passages appear mostly in the text of the *Zohar* itself; other listed works appear almost exclusively in the notes.

BIBLICAL LITERATURE

Tanakh (Hebrew Bible)

Genesis

RABBINIC LITERATURE

RABBINIC LITERATURE: MIDRASH

MEDIEVAL JEWISH SOURCES

POSTBIBLICAL CHRISTIAN SOURCES

OTHER

בראשית

בריש הורמנותא דמלכא גליף גלופי בטהירו עלאה בוצינא
דקרדינותא נפיק גו סתים דסתימו מרישא דא״ין סו״ף
קוטרא בגולמא נעיץ בעזקא לא חוור ולא אוכם לא סומק ולא ירוק ולאו גוון כלל כד
מדיד משיח׳ עביד גוונין לאנהר׳ לגו בגו בוציג׳ נפיק חד נביעו דמניה אצטבעו גוונין
לתתא סתים גו סתימין מרזא דא״ין סו״ף בקע ולא בקע אוירא דיליה לא אתיידע
כלל עד דמגו דחיקו דבקיעותיה נהיר נקודה חדא סתימאה עלאה בתר ההוא נקודה
לא אתיידע כלל ובגין כך אקרי ראשית מאמר קדמאה דכלא׃

והמשכילים יזהירו כזהר הרקיע ומצדיקי הרבים ככוכבים לעולם
ועד׃ **זהר** סתימ׳ דסתימין בטש אוירא דילי׳
דמטי ולא מטי בהאי נקודה וכדין אתפשט האי ראשית ועביד ליה
יקרא להיכליה לתושבחתא׃ תמן זרע זרעא לאולדא לתועלתא דעלמא ורזא דא זרע
קדש מצבתה׃ **זהר** דזרע זרע׳ ליקרי׳ כהאי זרע׳ דמשי דארגוון טב דאתחפי
לגו ועביד ליה היכלא דאיהו תושבחתא דיליה ותועלתא דכלא׃
בהאי ראשית ברא ההוא סתימאה דלא אתיידע להיכלא דא׃ היכלא דא אקרי אלהים
ורזא דא בראשי׳ ברא אלהי׳׃ זהר דמניה כלהו מאמרו׳ אתבריאו ברזא דאתפשטותא
דנקודה דזהר סתים דא׃ אי בהאי כתיב ברא לית תווהא דכתיב ויברא אלהים
את האדם בצלמו׃ **זהר** דא בראשית קדמאה דכלא **אהיה** שמא
קדיש׳ גליפ׳ בסטרוי אלהים גליפא בעיטרא אשר
היכלא טמיר וגניז שירותא דרזא דראשי״ת אש״ר רא״ש דנפיק מראשית׃ וכד